1 MONTH OF
FREE
READING

at

www.ForgottenBooks.com

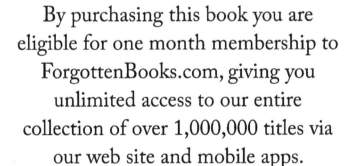

By purchasing this book you are eligible for one month membership to ForgottenBooks.com, giving you unlimited access to our entire collection of over 1,000,000 titles via our web site and mobile apps.

To claim your free month visit:

www.forgottenbooks.com/free165998

ISBN 978-1-5282-8972-6
PIBN 10165998

Forgotten Books is a registered trademark of FB &c Ltd.
Copyright © 2018 FB &c Ltd.
FB &c Ltd, Dalton House, 60 Windsor Avenue, London, SW19 2RR.
Company number 08720141. Registered in England and Wales.

For support please visit www.forgottenbooks.com

PROSE WRITERS OF AMERICA.
1706—1870.

Beny Franklin

THE

' PROSE WRITERS

OF

AMERICA.

WITH

A SURVEY OF THE INTELLECTUAL HISTORY, CONDITION,
AND PROSPECTS OF THE COUNTRY.

BY

RUFUS WILMOT GRISWOLD.

NEW EDITION, REVISED AND ENLARGED.

WITH A SUPPLEMENTARY ESSAY ON THE INTELLECTUAL
PROSPECTS AND CONDITION OF AMERICA,

BY PROF. JOHN H. DILLINGHAM.

PHILADELPHIA:
PORTER & COATES,
822 CHESTNUT STREET.

7572

MEARS & DUSENBERY, STEREOTYPERS.   SHERMAN & CO., P

PREFACE.

THIS volume contains a brief survey of our intellectual history, condition, and prospects, followed by more than seventy biographical and critical notices of authors, chronologically arranged, and illustrated, in most cases, by some fragments or entire short compositions from their works. I have not attempted to describe the merely successful writers, but such as have evinced unusual powers in controlling the national mind, or in forming or illustrating the national character; except in a few instances, in which productions of an artificial and transient popularity are mentioned as indications of dangerous tendencies or influences.

With Dr. Channing, I consider books of every description, whether devoted to the exact sciences, to mental and ethical philosophy, to history and legislation, or to fiction and poetry, as literature; though it is common thus to distinguish none but such as have relation to human nature and human life. As a complete and intelligible reviewal of all our authors, however, would necessarily occupy several volumes like this, and involve discussions of many subjects of little interest to the general reader, I have confined my attention chiefly to the department of belles lettres, only passing its boundaries occasionally to notice some of our most eminent divines, jurists, economists, and other students of particular science, who stand at the same time as representatives of parties and as monuments of our intellectual power and activity.

It seems necessary to a due understanding of an author's mind, that some of the circumstances of his education and general experience should be known to us. To be able to think with him and feel with him, we must live with him; and to do this with contemporaries is sometimes to invade a privacy which is dearer than fame, though a privacy which to some extent is forfeited by the very act of publishing. In the sketches in this volume, I have endeavoured to keep in view the legitimate scope and object of such performances, to be accurate in statement, liberal in principle, and just in criticism; to select and arrange materials with taste, and to form and express opinions with candour.

In discussing the difficulties and dangers in the way of American literature, I have frequently referred to the refusal of our government to protect the copy-

rights of foreigners, in a manner suggested by attentive personal observation of
the influence of the present system. A short time before Mr. Washington Irving
was appointed Minister to Spain, he undertook to dispose of a production of
merit, written by an American who had not yet established a commanding name
in the literary market, but found it impossible to get an offer from any of the
principal publishers. "They even declined to publish it at the author's cost,"
he says, "alleging that it was not worth their while to trouble themselves about
native works, of doubtful success, while they could pick and choose among the
successful works daily poured out by the British press, *for the copyright of
which they had nothing to pay.*" And not only is the American thus in some
degree excluded from the audience of his countrymen, but the publishers, who
have a control over many of the newspapers and other periodicals, exert themselves, in the way of their business, to build up the reputation of the foreigner
whom they rob, and to destroy that of the home author who aspires to a competition with him. This legalized piracy, supported by some sordid and base
arguments, keeps the criminal courts busy ; makes divorce committees in the
legislatures standing instead of special ; every year yields abundant harvests of
profligate sons and daughters ; and inspires a pervading contempt for our plain
republican forms and institutions. Injurious as it is to the foreign author, it is
more so to the American, and it falls with heaviest weight upon the people at
large, whom it deprives of that nationality of feeling which is among the first
and most powerful incentives to every kind of greatness.

Portions of this volume have been prepared hastily. The field surveyed is
extensive, and lingering over pleasant portions of it, I may have given to others
less attention than was necessary for the formation of accurate opinions. I have
in no instance, however, trusted to the reports of others. I have examined for
myself, with more or less care, all the works I have attempted to describe, and
if in any case I have erred in judgment, I believe I have in none failed to write
with entire sincerity.

PHILADELPHIA, May, 1847.

PUBLISHERS' PREFACE.

SINCE the last revision of this work by Dr. Griswold, many authors who were then making their fame have added unfading lustre to their names and to the cause of American Literature; some of whom, such as Irving, Cooper, Paulding, Kennedy, Prescott, Willis, Halleck, have since deceased, while others are enjoying their well-earned laurels. Others, who were at that time neophytes in literature, have produced works which are entitled to an honorable mention in the list of the Prose Writers of America.

To complete the records to the present time of those commenced by Dr. Griswold, and to add accounts of those authors and their works which have since become entitled to a position in this work, has been our aim. We claim no great originality of thought or arrangement, criticism or selection, but simply a clear statement of the facts of each biography and the character of the writings.

The most difficult task has been to make a proper selection from the many names offering for criticism or mention. To give entire satisfaction would be impossible; many will miss their favorite author, others will condemn certain selections made, or think it strange that more space has been allowed to one writer than to another whom they esteem, and perhaps justly, far his superior. To these latter it may be said that we have endeavored to select such passages as would not only give a fair idea of an author's style, but also be of interest to the general reader; and, in some of the most important authors, it was found well-nigh impossible to do so, unless a larger extract was taken than our limited space would permit. While strict attention had to be paid to the limits of this work to keep it within proper bounds, no favoritism has been shown, and no representative of any one particular class or ism has been admitted to the exclusion of others who were entitled to proper mention.

We would also call attention to the additional survey of the progress of American Literature by Prof. Dillingham in a later part of this volume.

THE PUBLISHERS.

PHILADELPHIA, December, 1870.

CONTENTS.

CONTENTS.

CONTENTS.

CONTENTS TO SUPPLEMENT.

THE

INTELLECTUAL HISTORY, CONDITION AND PROSPECTS

OF

THE COUNTRY.

I NEED not dwell upon the necessity of Literature and Art to a people's glory and happiness. History with all her voices joins in one judgment upon this subject. Our legislators indeed choose to consider them of no consequence, and while the states are convulsed by claims from the loom and the furnace for protection, the demands of the parents of freedom, the preservers of arts, the dispensers of civility, are treated with silence. But authors and artists have existed and do exist here in spite of such outlawry; and notwithstanding the obstacles in our condition, and the discouragements of neglect, the Anglo-Saxon race in the United States have done as much in the fields of Investigation, Reflection, Imagination and Taste, in the present century, as any other twelve millions of people—about our average number for this period —in the world.

Doubtless there are obstacles, great obstacles, to the successful cultivation of letters here; but they are not so many nor so important as is generally supposed. The chief difficulty is a want of Patriotism, mainly proceeding from and perpetuated by the absence of a just law of copyright. There is indeed no lack of that spurious love of country which is ever ready to involve us in aimless and disgraceful war; but there is little genuine and lofty national feeling; little clear perception of that which really deserves affection and applause; little intelligent and earnest effort to foster the good we possess or acquire the good we need.

It has been the fate of colonists in all ages to consider the people from among whom they made their exodus both morally and intellectually superior to themselves, and the parent state has had thus a kind of spiritual added to her

political sovereignty.   The American provinces quarreled with England, conquered, and became a separate nation; and we have since had our own Presidents and Congresses; but England has continued to do the thinking of a large
class here—of men who have arrogated to themselves the title of critics—of
our sham sort of men, in all departments.   We have had no confidence in
ourselves; and men who lack self-reliance are rarely successful.   We have not
looked into our own hearts.   We have not inquired of our own necessities.
When we have written, instead of giving a free voice to the spirit within us,
we have endeavoured to write after some foreign model.*   We have been so
fearful of nothing else as of an *Americanism*, in thought or expression.   He
has been deemed greatest who has copied some transatlantic author with most
successful servility.   The noisiest demagogue who affects to despise England
will scarcely open a book which was not written there.   And if one of our countrymen wins some reputation among his fellows it is generally because he has
been first praised abroad.

   The commonly urged barriers to literary advancement supposed to exist in
our form of government, the nature of our institutions, the restless and turbulent movements of our democracy, and the want of a wealthy and privileged
class among us, deserve little consideration.   Tumult and strife, the clashing
of great interests and high excitements, are to be regarded rather as aids than
as obstacles to intellectual progress.   From Athens came the choicest literature and the finest art.   Her philosophers, so calm and profound, her poets,
the dulcet sounds of whose lyres still charm the ears of succeeding ages,
wrote amid continual upturnings and overthrows.   The best authors of Rome
also were senators and soldiers.   Milton, the greatest of the prose writers as
well as the greatest of the poets of England, lived in the Commonwealth, and
participated in all its political and religious controversies.   And what repose
had blind Mæonides, or Camoëns, or Dante, or Tasso?   In the literature of

---

   * The literature of other countries, says M. Sismondi, has been frequently adopted by a young nation
with a sort of fanatical admiration.   The genius of these countries having been so often placed before it,
as the perfect model of all greatness and of all beauty, every spontaneous movement has been repressed in
order to make room for the most servile imitation, and every national attempt to develope an original character has been sacrificed to the reproduction of something conformable to the model which has been
always before its eyes.   Thus the Romans checked themselves in the vigour of their first conceptions to
become emulous copyists of the Greeks; and thus the Arabs placed bounds to their intellectual efforts
that they might rank themselves among the followers of Aristotle.   So the Italians in the sixteenth,
and the French in the seventeenth century, desirous only of imitating the ancients, *did not sufficiently
consult, in their poetical attempts, their own religion, manners, and character.—Literature of the South
of Europe.*

Germany and France, too, the noblest works have been produced amid the shocks of contending elements.

Nor is the absence of a wealthy class, with leisure for such tranquil pursuits, to be much lamented. The privileged classes of all nations have been drones. We have, in the Southern states of this republic, a large class, with ample fortunes, leisure and quiet; but they have done comparatively nothing in the fields of intellectual exertion, except when started into spasmodic activity by conflicts of interest with the North.

To say truth, most of the circumstances usually set down as barriers to æsthetical cultivation here are directly or indirectly advantageous. The real obstacles are generally of a transient kind. Many of them are silently disappearing; and the rest would be soon unknown if we had a more enlightened love of country, and the making of our laws were not so commonly confided to a sort of men whose intellects are too mean or whose principles are too wicked to admit of their seeing or doing what is just and needful in the premises. That property which is most actual, the only property to which a man's right is positive, unquestionable, indefeasible, exclusive—his genius, conferred as by letters patent from the Almighty—is held to be not his, but the public's, and therefore is not brought into use.* The foreign author, by the refusal to recognise his rights, is driven into inveterate enmity to our institutions and interests, and at the same time such advantage is given him in addressing the popular mind as to make opinion here in a large degree dependent on his will.

Nevertheless, much has been accomplished; great advancement has been made against the wind and tide; and at this time the aspects and prospects

---

* All " arguments" against copyright, as universal and perpetual as the life of a book, are but insults to the common sense. Some of them are ingenious, and may be admired on the same principle that the ingenuity of a picklock is admired. The possession of lands is, by privilege, conceded to the individual for the common benefit. The right of an author rests on altogether different grounds. The intangible and inalienable power by which he works, is a direct and special gift to him, to be used in subjection only to the law of God, who mocks at the petty ranks which men establish, by setting the seal of His nobility and conferring His riches upon whom He will. The feudal chief by rapine, or the speculator by cunning, wins an estate, and the law secures him and his heirs in its possession while there are days and nights. An author *creates* a book—which, besides diffusing a general benefit, yields a revenue, as great perhaps as that from the estate which has been acquired by force or fraud, and the law, without alleging any fault, seizes it and bestows it on the mob. The question is commonly discussed as one of expediency. No one has a right so to consider it. But if the argument, even upon this principle, were intelligently and honestly conducted, the result would invariably be in favour of the author. There is among men of sense no actual difference of opinion on this subject. The plunder of the foreign author is sanctioned and enforced under an erroneous impression that something is gained by it, and because an honest law, as it would in a very slight degree increase the prices of new books, might endanger the seat of the member of Congress who should vote for it.

of our affairs are auspicious of scarcely any thing more than of the successful cultivation of National Literature and National Art.

I use the word National because whatever we do well must be done in a national spirit. The tone of a great work is given or received by the people among whom it is produced, and so is national, as an effect or as a cause. While the spirit which animates the best literature of any country must be peculiar to it, its subjects may be chosen from the world. It is absurd to suppose that Indian chiefs or republican soldiers must be the characters of our works of imagination, or that our gloomy forests, or sea-like prairies, or political committee rooms must be their scenes. Paradise Lost and Utopia are as much portions of British literature as Alfred, or London Assurance. It may be regarded as one of the greatest dangers to which our literature is exposed, indeed, that so many are mistaken as to what should distinguish it. Some writers, by no means destitute of abilities, in their anxiety to be national have merely ceased to be natural. Their works may be original, but the men and manners they have drawn have no existence. Least of all do they exist in America. The subjects for the novelist and the poet in our own country are to be preferred because they are striking from their freshness, and because the physical condition of a country, having a powerful influence upon the character of its inhabitants, naturally furnishes the most apposite illustrations of their feelings and habits; but a "national work" may as well be written about the builders of the Pyramids as about the mound builders. In our literature we must regard all men as equal in point of privilege, the church as the whole company of God's acceptable worshippers, the state as a joint stock in which every one holds a share. It must be addressed to the national feelings, vindicate the national principles, support the national honour, be animated by an expansive sympathy with humanity. It must teach that the interests of man are the highest concern of men.

Our forefathers—the men who from Great Britain or the continent settled this new world—were the product of an age prolific in excitements. Their hearts were busy, some with plans of personal ambition, some with great problems for the benefit of humanity. Whatever they found to do, they did, with directness and earnestness. The chief causes of their emigration were religious; the spirit which animated them when here was religious; and their literature—the permanent expression of their character—was a religious literature. Their first works were quaint and curious: many of them were original and profound. It may be that in some cases they gave their flour to the devil, and reserved their bran only for the Lord: but they certainly produced the flour. They were acute, powerful, and independent in argument and conclusion. They commanded the admiration of those who thought with them, and startled the defenders of old and false opinions by their thunders, heard and echoed across the seas. In theology, from the first, our writers were unshackled by foreign models or authorities. They acknowledged no infallible head but God Almighty, and no patristic guides to faith and practice but the holy company of the prophets and apostles.

The history of Newman, whose Concordance of the Bible, made by the light of pine knots in his cottage at Rehoboth, was for more than a century admitted to be the most perfect work of its kind in existence; of the pious and learned Eliot, greatest of all uninspired missionaries, who reduced a barbarous language to order, and laboured year after year to translate into it the scriptures; and of Cotton Mather, the first American Fellow of the Royal Society and one of the greatest scholars of his times, of whose three hundred and eighty-two works one* at least is preserved in the standard religious literature, prove that from the beginning there was in America no deficiency of scholastic learning or literary industry.

Early in the eighteenth century appeared Jonathan Edwards, styled by Dr. Chalmers "the greatest of theologians,"[†] of whom Sir James Mackintosh says, that "in power of subtile argument he was perhaps unmatched, certainly was unsurpassed among men."[‡] "If literary ambition had been the active element of his mind," remarks Taylor, "what higher praise could a scientific writer wish for than that of having by a single and small dissertation reduced a numerous and powerful party in his own and other countries, and from his day to the present time, to the sad necessity of making a blank protest against the argument and influence of his book?"[§] But there are some questions which are always to vex the brains of thinkers. Human pride and ambition will never permit a universal acquiescence in any conclusion. Newton's Principia and the doctrines of Edwards have been attacked with equal earnestness by our living scholars. Dr. Tappan, Mr. Bledsoe, and others, have laboured with ingenuity and candor to establish the self-determining power of the will. The antagonists of Edwards become weary of saying "his reasoning must be sophistical because it overthrows our doctrines."

---

* "Essays to do Good," which, says Franklin, "perhaps gave me a tone of thinking that had an influence on some of the principal future events of my life."—*Memoirs*, p. 16.

† Letter to Dr. Stebbins.　　　　‡ Review of Ethical Philosophy, p. 109.

§ Essay on the Application of Abstract Reasoning to the Christian Doctrines; by the author of The Natural History of Enthusiasm, &c.

Among the contemporaries or immediate successors of Edwards were the eloquent and independent Jonathan Mayhew; Dr. Samuel Johnson, the father of the American Episcopal Church; Dr. Hopkins, whose name is so closely identified with the New England theology of the last century; President Styles, famous for acquirements in almost every department of profane and sacred learning; the younger Edwards; Bellamy, and Dwight, and Emmons, all of whom were men of great abilities and scholarship, whose works have still a powerful influence on opinions.

In the present day no country can boast of a list of theological writers more justly distinguished for learning, logical skill, or literary abilities, than that which includes the names of the Alexanders, Albert Barnes, George Bush, Charles Hodge, John Henry Hopkins, Samuel Farmer Jarvis, Charles P. McIlvaine, Andrews Norton, Edward Robinson, Moses Stuart, Henry Tappan, William R. Williams, James Walker, Leonard Woods, and others whose talents and acquisitions have secured to them a general influence and good reputation.

James Marsh, of Hampden Sidney College in Virginia, and at a later period, of the University of Vermont, deserves particular and honourable mention in every survey of our intellectual advancement and condition. He was a calm, chaste scholar, an earnest and profound thinker, and a powerful and eloquent advocate of the highest principles of religion and philosophy, whose life had that simplicity and grandeur which are constituted by a combination of the rarest and noblest of human virtues. His principal published writings are devoted to those elevated and spiritual principles of philosophy of which Coleridge and Kant were the most celebrated European asserters. Though nearly agreeing with these great men, he was not less original than they, and before the works of the Englishman or the Prussian were known on this continent, by the independent action of his own mind he had formed theories similar to theirs and taught them to his classes.

Many others, dead and living, whose names the present limits do not admit, have been among the foremost teachers of religion and philosophy, and have vindicated by results the relation of civil to intellectual liberty and advancement.

There are few if any kinds of composition requiring a higher order of genius or more profound and varied acquirements than History; and it might be supposed, therefore, that it would be among the last of the fields in which the authors of a new nation would be successful. Yet our literature embraces a fair proportion of historical works of such excellence that any people would refer to them with a proud satisfaction.*

What the estimate of Mr. Prescott would be among ourselves, but for the concurrent judgment of the best European critics that he has no superior if he has an equal among contemporary historians, it might be difficult to tell. His fame, however, is so high, so universal, and so firmly established, and cheap newspapers have made foreign opinions of him so familiar here, that the silliest of those persons who found claims to reputation for taste upon expressions of contempt for what is American, are in the habit of making an exception of his writings from their condemnation. How fortunate for him—if he cares for this home popularity—that his subjects are of such general interest as to have made scholars of all countries the judges of his merit.

Ferdinand and Isabella and The Conquest of Mexico are not only among the finest models of historical composition, but in a very genuine sense they are *national* works, breathing so freely the liberal spirit of our institutions that translators abroad have had to change utterly their tone as well as their language to make them acceptable to the subjects of arbitrary power.

The words of panegyric have been wellnigh exhausted in commentaries upon the Claude-like beauty of Mr. Prescott's descriptions, the just proportion and dramatic interest of his narrative, his skill as a character writer, the expansiveness and completeness of his views, and that careful and intelligent research which enabled him to make his works as valuable for their accuracy as they are attractive by all the graces of style.

Mr. Bancroft has remarkable merits, of a somewhat different nature, and some faults, though not of such sort or magnitude as to prevent his being placed in the very front rank of great historians. He is emphatically an *American*. He thinks, feels, and acts the American. He surveys the train of the ages, and perceives that humanity is *progressive*. In our own polity, our institutions, our universal and safe liberty, he sees the farthest point to which the race has yet attained. He looks hopefully into the future, far as the human eye can see, and his powerful mind kindles with enthusiasm as he finds our country fulfilling her mission, in the subversion of false opinions, the overthrow of tyrannous dynasties, the liberation of mankind. All this is well. But Mr. Bancroft is perhaps too ardent a politician, and too deeply imbued with

* Bancroft, Prescott, and Sparks, have effected so much in historical composition, that no living European historian can take precedence of them, but rather might feel proud and grateful to be admitted as a companion.—*Frederick Von Raumer.*

the principles of his party, to be a calm spectator of the present, or an unprejudiced reviewer of the past. He may serve the spirit of his age, instead
of wrestling with it, and placing himself on an eminence from which to survey
the historical drama of the world. However these things be, his work is
elaborately and strongly, yet elegantly written; it is altogether the most accurate and philosophical account that has been given of the United States;
and parts of it may be reckoned among the most splendid in all historical
literature.

Mr. Sparks is the author of no one extensive and elaborate work which,
perhaps, entitles him to be ranked among the great historians; but his various
and numerous contributions to historical biography and criticism, made accurate by laborious and philosophical research, constitute a claim to the country's
admiration as well as its gratitude.

To Mr. Cooper's admirable Naval History of the United States; the
learned History of the Northmen by Mr. Wheaton; Mr. Irving's classical History of the Life and Voyages of Columbus; Dr. Holmes's Annals; Dr. Belknap's History of New Hampshire, and other histories of individual states
which are admitted to be eminently creditable to their authors, I can here
refer only in this brief manner. It will be conceded that in the department of
History our national literature is not deficient in extent,* in distinctiveness, or in
any of the qualities which should mark this kind of writing.

Our works in Historical Biography are numerous, and many of them are
executed with singular judgment and ability. The lives of Washington by
Marshall and Sparks; Tudor's Life of Otis, Austin's Life of Gerry, Wirt's
Life of Patrick Henry, Wheaton's Life of Pinckney, the Life of the elder
Quincy by his Son, the Life of Franklin by Sparks, the Life of Jefferson by
Tucker, the Life of Hamilton by his Son, Biddle's Life of Sebastian Cabot,
Gibbs's Life of Wolcott, Cooper's Lives of the Naval Commanders of the
United States, many of the lives in Sparks's Library of American Biography,
and others of the same character, will be remembered as productions of per-
manent interest and importance.

The Historical Correspondence of the Revolutionary Age constitutes a very
remarkable portion of American literature, and it equals if it does not surpass
any similar correspondence in any language, not only in the higher qualities of
wisdom and patriotism, which make it chiefly valuable to us, but in literary

---

* More than four hundred large historical works, most of which relate to our own country, have
been written in the United States.

excellence—the graces of expression and felicitous illustration. The letters of George Washington, John Adams, Benjamin Franklin, Thomas Jefferson, John Jay, Gouverneur Morris, Alexander Hamilton, and some of their compatriots, will always possess a peculiar value besides that which they derive from their authorship and the gravity of their subjects.

The Public Speeches of a nation's chief legislators are among the most luminous landmarks of its policy, the most lucid developments of the character and genius of its institutions, and the noblest exhibitions of its intellect. The speeches of many of our greatest orators have not been preserved, and like those of Demades the Athenian, who was deemed by some of the ablest of his contemporaries superior to Demosthenes, they are forgotten. Of the orations of Otis, which were described as "flames of fire," we have but a few meager reports. We are persuaded of the eloquence of Henry only by the history of its effects. The passionate appeals of the elder Adams, which "moved his hearers from their seats," are not in print. But for tradition it would be unknown that Rutledge was one of the greatest of orators. There is in existence scarcely a vestige of the resistless declamation and argument of Pinkney. Some of the speeches of Fisher Ames have come down to us, with their passages of chaste and striking beauty, and they constitute nearly all the recorded eloquence of the time in which he was an actor.

Of the great orators of a later day—Webster, Clay, Calhoun and others—we have the means of forming a more accurate judgment. Their works belong to our Standard Literature. They are thoroughly imbued with the national spirit. They glow with the feelings of the people.

Daniel Webster has written his name in our history. He has graven it indelibly on the rocks of our hills. He has associated it in some way with all that is grand and peculiar about us. Whatever may be the effects of Time upon his reputation as a politician, unless the world return to barbarism it cannot destroy his fame as an author. If I were to compare him to any foreigner it would be to Burke. But he is a greater man than the Irish Colossus. His genius is more various. He is more chaste. His style and argument are not less compact. And his learning is as comprehensive and more profound. The literature of the language has no more splendid rhetoric or faultless logic. Born almost contemporaneously with the nation, he has grown with its growth, strengthened with its strength, and become an impersonation of its character—such an impersonation as we proudly point to when we remember that we also are Americans.

The distinguishing characteristic of the speeches of Henry Clay is an eminent practicalness. They are not imaginative, nor poetical, nor impassioned. They lack the solidity, compactness and inherent force of Webster, and the philosophic generalization of Calhoun; Wright is more plausible and ingenious, Preston is more graceful and fervid, and Choate more brilliant and classically ornate. Yet there is an unaffected earnestness of conviction, a profound heartiness of purpose, a frank and perfect ingenuousness, a manly good sense, exhibited in the works of this great statesman which commend them to the reader's understanding and approval. Although the manner of the orator adds force and significance to the matter, so that his speeches should be heard to be justly estimated, they are found to bear a value in the closet not possessed by the productions of many who have enjoyed the highest eminence in the senate, the forum and the world of letters.

Mr. Calhoun is another author of the highest rank, and his works, though in many respects very different from those of the great orators I have mentioned, are scarcely less peculiar and *national*. It has been too much the habit to consider him only as a politician. His claims as a philosopher have been almost overlooked. No one has more skill as a dialectician. His sententious and close diction, his remarkable power of analysis, his simplicity and dignity —his doctrines, and all the elements of the power with which they are maintained—will secure for his works a permanent place in the world's consideration.

I may here allude to John Quincy Adams as altogether one of the most remarkable men of this century, in whose various and voluminous works there is not only marked nationality, but a wisdom which astonishes by its universality and profoundness; to Edward Everett, as an orator of the most comprehensive learning, elegant taste, and noble spirit; to Hugh S. Legare, as one of the finest of our senatorial rhetoricians; to Tristram Burgess, and many others, whose speeches, when their histories as partisans are forgotten, will be regarded as portions of the classical literature of the country, fit to be ranked among the finest works of their kind produced in the most cultivated ancient or modern nations.

No other of the immortal company by whose genius, virtue and suffering our independence was achieved and our government established, has suffered so much from misrepresentation as Alexander Hamilton, of whom Guizot says justly that "there is not one element of order, strength and durability in our constitution which he did not powerfully contribute to introduce into the scheme and cause to be adopted."* He was the first of our great legislators; and though the world has made some advances since his time in political philosophy, his works are still resorted to by the judicious as a storehouse of the profoundest wisdom. Much of his celebrated Report on Manufactures combats objections to the protective policy, which are no longer urged, and has therefore now only an historical value, but The Federalist will always be a text book among statesmen.†

The writings of Madison, though less important than those of Hamilton, show that he also was a consummate statesman. They are distinguished for an extent and fulness of information, soundness of reasoning, and sagacity, which characterize but few even of the most celebrated works in their department.

The political writings of John Adams, Dickinson, Jefferson, Jay, and others of that age, are likewise remarkable for great and peculiar merits.

A very large proportion of our works in Political Economy relate to the Circulating Medium and Manufactures, and have been occasioned by the movements of parties or the immediate wants of the country. Those on currency and banking by Mr. Gallatin, Mr. Raguet, Mr. Tucker, and some others, with the discussions of this subject by our leading statesmen in the legislative assemblies and through the press, have shown a depth of research and an acuteness of understanding very rarely equalled. Commerce as affecting manufactures has constantly engaged public attention since the days of Hamilton and Madison. Parties have been for or against the *American System*—for free trade or for protection. Jefferson engaged in the controversy, but to suit temporary purposes, and without consistency.‡ Dr. Cooper, when in Pennsylvania, wrote forcibly in favour of protection, and subsequently, when in South Carolina, against it. Mr. Clay has advocated the protective system with consistency and a lucid ability hardly ever surpassed. No man has been more successful in his treatment of the subject in its secondary aspects, though he may have produced little which will survive the changes of the times. Mr. Webster has written ably on both sides of the question, as the circumstances of the country seemed to require; before 1824 for free trade, and

---

* Washington, par M. Guizot. Paris, 1840.

† It ought to be familiar to the statesmen of every nation.—*De Tocqueville.*
It exhibits an extent and precision of information, a profundity of research, and an acuteness of understanding *which would have done honour to the most illustrious statesmen of ancient or modern times.*
—*Edinburgh Review,* No. xxiv.

‡ See his letters to B. Austin in 1816, and a letter written by him on the same subject in 1823.

since for protection. Mr. Calhoun has in both periods been opposed to Mr. Webster, and he is now undoubtedly the ablest economist of his party. The protective policy has also been defended by Mr. Mathew Carey, Mr. Alexander H. Everett, Mr. Lawrence, and Mr. Greeley; and a perfect freedom of trade advocated by Mr. Condy Raguet, Mr. Bryant, Mr. Clement Biddle, Mr. Legget, and Mr. Walker. Many other writers have been more or less prominently engaged in this controversy. Works on Political Economy have also been written by Mr. Cardoza, Professor Dew, Dr. McVickar, Dr. Vethake, Dr. Wayland, Mr. C. Colton, Mr. Middleton, and Mr. Raymond, several of which are text-books in the colleges. Mr. Everett is also the author of a work on New Principles of Population, and Mr. Henry C. Carey has written largely and with ability on Population, the Production of Wealth, and Wages.[†]

Among our writers in Jurisprudence have been many of great ability. Our books of Codes, Statutes, Reports and Essays on Rights, Crimes and Punish-

---

[*] Wayland, Tucker, Dew, etc., agree very well with Ricardo and Malthus. Mr. Carey does not, and he has attempted to show that a proper examination of the facts that are before us prove that their views are unsound. Ricardo teaches that profits fall as wages rise—that the one must fall with the rise of the other—that rent is paid because of a constantly increasing *difficulty* of obtaining food, as population increases, and consequently that the interests of landlord and labourer are always opposed; the one fattening upon the starvation of the other. This whole system is one of discords. Mr. Carey holds, on the contrary, that wages and profits both tend to increase with the growth of capital and the increase of production, but that with the increased productiveness of labour the labourer obtains a constantly increasing proportion, leaving to the capitalist a constantly decreasing proportion, but to both an increased quantity. Thus if at one time the labour of a man produces fifty bushels, of which the landlord takes half, and at another one hundred, of which he takes only one-third, both are improved, although the apparent condition of the landlord is deteriorated from half to one-third.

	50	100
Labourer,—	25	67
Capitalist,—	25—50	33—100

The rent of land is held to be subject to the same law, it being only profit of capital, under another name. With the increased *facility* of obtaining food, as capital is applied to the land, the landlord takes a constantly decreasing proportion, and the labourer has a constantly increasing one. The interests of all therefore are in perfect harmony with each other, and all are benefited by every measure tending to the maintenance of peace and the growth of capital.

Every part of Political Economy is included in the great law, "Do unto your neighbour as you would have your neighbour do unto you." Security of person and property succeed the growth of capital—physical, moral and intellectual improvement are a necessary consequence of such growth, and with every step in his *material* or *moral* advancement man becomes more conscious of the existence of *political* rights, and more able to maintain them. Democracy—self-government—is therefore a necessary consequence of the growth of wealth, and it arises out of the change of proportions, above noted. With every increase in the proportion which capital bears to labour, their relative value changes—labour goes up and capital down—but only so far as *proportions* go—not quantities.

ments, have had a powerful influence on the common and positive laws of Christendom. Bradford and Livingston, with many others, entitled themselves to gratitude by efforts to overthrow the tyranny of Revenge, which until recently has been the first principle in criminal legislation. Their influence has been widely acknowledged in Europe as well as in America. I need but refer to the great Marshall, to Hamilton, "the first of our constitutional lawyers;"* to Parsons, who had no superior in the common law; to Kent, whose decisions are " more signally entitled to respect than those of any English chancellor since the American Revolution, with the single exception, perhaps, of Lord Eldon;"† to the voluminous and able works of Story; or to those of Livingston, Wheaton, Stearns, Duer, Verplanck, Philips, Greenleaf, Binney, and others whose names are associated with these in the memories of the legal profession.

In archæological, oriental and classical learning our scholars may claim an equality with any contemporaries except the Germans. In Biblical Criticism‡ the names of J. A. Alexander, Albert Barnes, George Bush, Charles Hodge, Andrews Norton, Edward Robinson, Moses Stuart,§ James H. Thornwell, and others, are everywhere honourably distinguished. Professors Lewis, Felton, and Woolsey have published editions of Greek classics eminently creditable to themselves and their respective universities, and Dr. Robinson had acquired an enduring fame as a Hellenist before he established a new era in the study of sacred antiquities.‖ Few Americans have written much in the Latin language.¶ The occasions for its use are less frequent than formerly. It is commonly taught however in our schools, and numerous works of unquestionable

---

* 3 Sergeant and Rawle, 194.

† Justice Gibson: 3 Rawle, 139.

‡ Our American neighbours are really *outstripping us in Biblical Literature.—Samuel Lee, Professor of Arabic and Hebrew in the University of Cambridge.*

§ Bloomfield, in his Notes, Critical, Philological and Exegetical upon the New Testament—the most elaborate and popular work of its sort produced in England in the present age—acknowledges that he has made large use of Stuart; and he might say of his last edition that it owes its chief value to Stuart and Robinson.

‖ Professor Ritter, of Berlin, wrote, on reading Dr. Robinson's Researches—"Now just begins a second great era in our knowledge of the Promised Land."

¶ The number of Latin orations before our colleges has been very large. Among the principal other Latin works by natives of the country are the *Pietas et Gratulatio* addressed to George III. by the President and Fellows of Harvard College; Telemachus, in hexameter verse, by the Abbe Veil, of New Orleans; the Life of Washington, by Francis Glass, of Ohio; and a System of Divinity, by Bishop Kendrick, of Pennsylvania.

4   C

merit, among which those of Mr. Leverett and Dr. Anthon may be particularly referred to, have appeared here to facilitate its study.

The philological labours of Dr. Webster are universally known and appreciated. After the devotion of nearly half a century to his Dictionary he saw
it become the most generally approved standard of English orthography.* The
services of the late Dr. John Pickering and others in this department are
likewise honourable to American scholarship.

The Crania Americana of Dr. Morton, a work of immense research, in
which are described the cranial peculiarities of many races which in this
respect were little known, is one of the most important ethnographical works
produced in this age. Mr. Gallatin—on many accounts one of the most
remarkable of men—is perhaps to be longest remembered for his profound
investigations of the languages of the American continent. To the laborious
and ingenious Schoolcraft future ages are to owe the most valuable part of
their knowledge of the habits and intellectual character of the Indian race.
Mr. Catlin, Mr. Hodgson and other American travellers, and our noble company of missionaries, whose heroism puts to shame all that is recorded of the
ages of chivalry, have likewise contributed very largely to our knowledge
of the families of mankind.

The cultivation of purely mechanical and natural science has been carried
much too far in this country, or rather has been made too exclusive and
absorbing. It is not the highest science, for it concerns only that which is
around us—which is altogether outward. Man is greater than the world of
nature in which he lives, and just as clearly must the science of man, the philosophy of his moral and intellectual being, rank far above that of the soulless
creation which was made to minister to his wants. When, therefore, this
lower science so draws to itself the life of any age, as to disparage and shut
out the higher, it works to the well being of that age an injury. Still it is
only thus in comparison with a nobler and more lofty study, that the faintest
reproach should be cast upon that natural science, which in no slight degree
absorbs the intellectual effort of the present generation. Regarded as related
to, and a part of, a complete system of education, with a powerful influence

---

* The American Dictionary of the English Language was published in two quarto volumes in 1828,
after more than thirty years' laborious study by the author. It contained about twelve thousand
words and more than thirty thousand definitions not found in any similar work. Dr. Webster soon
after commenced a new edition, which he completed and published in 1841.

upon the purely æsthetical character of the people, it becomes most important and necessary, and its cultivation even to apparent excess a source of the highest hope.

In Mathematics our first names are Rittenhouse, Bowditch, and Nulty. The great work of Bowditch is his translation of the *Mécanique Céleste* of La Place, which, with his commentary, was published in four very large quarto volumes in the years 1829, 1832, 1834 and 1838. It is more than half an exposition of the original, which was complex and obscure, and a record of new discoveries. It was remarked in the London Quarterly Review, on the appearance of the first volume, that the "idea savoured of the gigantesque," and that even if not completed, the work should be considered "highly creditable to American science, and as the harbinger of future achievements in the loftiest fields of intellectual prowess."

The study of Meteorology has been pursued with more success in the United States than in any other country. At least here the most splendid results have been reached in this important branch of philosophy. The grand discoveries of Franklin* in electricity are of course familiar, but it is not so generally known that some of his observations contain germs of the more recent doctrines of storms. The investigations of this subject by Mr. Redfield and Mr. Espy, and their ingenious theories, have commanded the respect and admiration of scholars ;† and though some of the principles of each are still subjects of controversy, it is everywhere acknowledged that those they have established are of the highest interest and importance. The writings on Meteorology by Dr. Hare and Mr. Loomis, and the theory of Dew by Dr. Wells, are also most honourable to our science.

In Chemistry it is necessary only to refer to the labours of Rumford, Webster, Silliman, Hare and Henry; in Mineralogy, to those of Cleveland, Dana, and Beck; in Geology,‡ to those of Maclure, Hitchcock, Silliman, Mather,

---

* His genius ranks him with the Galileos and the Newtons of the old world.—*Lord Brougham.*

The most rational of philosophers. No individual, perhaps, ever possessed a juster understanding, or was so seldom obstructed in the use of it by indolence, enthusiasm, or authority.—*Lord Jeffrey.*

Antiquity would have raised altars to this mighty genius.—*Mirabeau.*

† See article vi. Edinburgh Review, No. cxxxiii. by Sir David Brewster; Proceedings of British Association, 1840; Report on Mr. Espy's Theory to the French Academy by MM. Arago, Pouillet and Babinet.

‡ The explorations which have been made by authority of the local governments into the Geology and general Natural History of the principal states of the Union are among the proudest achievements of the present day, and I believe are altogether unparalleled in other countries. The published Reports, in nearly one hundred large volumes, are splendid monuments of intelligent enterprise in the cause of science. They will be of incalculable value to students and inquirers for ages to come.

Emmons, Vanuxem, Rogers, Jackson, Troost, Percival, Houghton, and Hall and in Botany to those of Bartram, Barton, Elliott, Bigelow, Gray, Torry, and Darlington. There have been no European Ornithologists during this century to be ranked before or even with Wilson and Audubon.* The works on Entomology by Mr. Say and Mr. Le Conte, on Herpetology by Dr. Holbrook, on Icthyology by Dr. Mitchell, Dr. Holbrook and Dr. Storer, on Mammalogy by Dr. Bachman, and on Conchology by Mr. Lea,† have very great merits, which have been universally acknowledged. The writings of Godman, Hays, and other zoologists have likewise merited and received general applause.

The field of romantic fiction has for a quarter of a century been thronged with labourers. I do not know how large the national stock may be, but I have in my own library more than seven hundred volumes of novels, tales and romances by American writers. Comparatively few of them are of so poor a sort as to be undeserving a place in any general collection of our literature. Altogether they are not below the average of English novels for this present century; and the proportion which is marked by a genuine originality of manner, purpose, and feeling, is much larger than they who have not read them are aware.

Charles Brockden Brown, the pioneer in this department of our literature, was a gentle, unobtrusive enthusiast, whose weak frame was shattered and wrecked by the too powerful pulsations of his heart. He was no misanthrope, but the larger portion of his life, though it was passed in cities, was that of a

---

* Audubon's works are the most splendid monuments which art has erected in honour of Ornithology. —*Cuvier*.

He is the greatest artist in his own walk that ever lived.—*Professor Wilson*.

† Mr. Lea has been much the largest contributor to the Transactions of the American Philosophical Society, having elaborate and important papers upon his favourite science in all the volumes from the third to the tenth. This is a publication of great value and interest, not only on account of the intrinsic excellence of the papers it contains, but because it furnishes an authentic record of the progress of science in America. Voluntary associations of men devoted to scientific investigations, such as the American Philosophical Society, are the only means for extending and rendering vigorous that spirit of research and that intellectual enthusiasm upon which these studies rely for prosperous and beneficent cultivation; for unhappily in the United States such men can look with slight confidence to the local or federal governments for aid or encouragement. The late National Exploring Expedition under Captain Wilkes, and the scientific surveys of the different states, however, are indications that a better spirit is prevailing in the legislatures. The published Transactions of several other societies, and the important Journal of Professor Silliman, and other periodicals, deserve also to be mentioned as repositories of our scientific literature. The papers by Mr. Lea, referred to in the beginning of this note, are the most valuable contributions that have been made to the study of Conchology in this century.

recluse. He lived in an ideal and had little sympathy with the actual world. He had more genius than talent, and more imagination than fancy. It has been said that he outraged the laws of art by gross improbabilities and inconsistencies, but the most incredible of his incidents had parallels in true history, and the metaphysical unity and consistency of his novels are apparent to all readers familiar with psychological phenomena. His works, generally written with great rapidity, are incomplete, and deficient in method. He disregarded rules, and cared little for criticism. But his style was clear and nervous, with little ornament, free of affectations, and indicated a singular sincerity and depth of feeling.

Mr. Paulding's novels are distinguished for considerable descriptive powers, skill in character writing, natural humour, and a strong national feeling, which gives a tone to all his works. The Dutchman's Fireside and Westward Ho! have the fidelity of historical pictures, and they are the best we have of the early settlers of New York and Kentucky.

Timothy Flint is better known by other works than his novels, but Francis Berrian and the Shoshonee Valley are books of merit. Their dramatic interest is not very great, but they are marked by an unstudied *naïveté* and freedom from pretence; they abound in striking and graphic descriptions; and their characters are clearly drawn and well sustained. In every department in which this author wrote at all, he wrote like a scholar, a man of feeling, and a gentleman.

While the author of The Spy receives the applause of Europe;* while the critics of Germany and France debate the claims of Scott to be ranked before him or even with him, his own countrymen deride his pretensions, and Monikin critics affect contempt of him, or make the appearance of his works occasions of puerile personal abuse. I shall not discuss the causes of this feeling, further than by remarking that Mr. Cooper is a man of independence; that he is aware of the dignity of his position; that he thinks for himself in his capacity of citizen; and that he has written above the popular taste, in avoiding the sickly sentimentalism which commends to shop-boys and chamber-maids one half the transatlantic novels of this age. In each of the departments of romantic fiction in which he has written, he has had troops of imitators, and in not one of them an equal. Writing not from books, but from nature, his descriptions, his incidents, his

* The Empire of the sea has been conceded to him by acclamation; in the lonely desert or untrodden prairie, among the savage Indians or scarcely less savage settlers, all equally acknowledge his dominion. " Within this circle none dares walk but he."—*Edinburgh Review*, cxxiii.

c 2

characters, are as fresh as the fields of his triumphs. His Harvey Birch, Leather Stocking, Long Tom Coffin, and other heroes, rise before the mind each in his clearly defined and peculiar lineaments as striking original *creations*, as actual coherent beings. His infinitely varied descriptions of the ocean; his ships, gliding like beings of the air upon its surface; his vast, solitary wildernesses; and indeed all his delineations of nature, are instinct with the breath of poetry. He is both the Horace Vernet and the Claude Lorraine of novelists. And through all his works are sentiments of genuine courtesy and honour, and an unobtrusive and therefore more powerful assertion of natural rights and dignity. I shall not pretend to say how far a good plot is essential to a good novel. Doubtless in a tale, as in a play, the interest, with the vulgar, is dependent in a large degree upon the plot; but the quality of interesting is of secondary importance in both cases. It must be confessed that Mr. Cooper's plots are sometimes of a common-place sort, that they are not always skilfully wrought, and that he has faults of style, and argument, and conclusion. But he is natural, he is original, he is *American*, and he has contributed more than any of his contemporaries to the formation of a really national literature.

The novels of Miss Sedgwick, attempered always by a cheerful philosophy, with portraits drawn with singular fidelity from life, and incidents so natural that the New Englander can scarcely doubt that they are portions of his village's history, are not less American than Mr. Paulding's. They are in many respects very different, but the difference is geographical.

The most voluminous of our novelists, next to Mr. Cooper, is Mr. Simms, and he has many attributes in common with that author. His descriptions are bold and graphic; and his characters have considerable individuality. He is most successful in sketches of rude border life, in bustling, tumultuous action. West, the greatest composer of modern times, seemed content with the demonstration in a few pictures that he was equal even to Corregio as a colourist and anatomist; he gave in too many cases his last touch to works which should have occupied a full decade, in a single year. So Mr. Simms, who is a poet, and has shown himself a master of the intricacies of rhetoric, throws off a volume while he should be engaged on a chapter. Though occasionally correct, animated and powerful, his style is too frequently abrupt, careless, and harsh. The scenes of Mr. Simms are generally in the Southern States, and the society and manners described are very unlike those of the North. One of the most marked of his peculiarities is a sectional feeling which he betrays on almost every occasion. His "true gentlemen," such as they are, are of the country south of Washington; his clowns are direct from Long Island or Connecticut. The aim of a literary class should be to civilize mankind, to soften asperities, to abolish prejudices, to extend the dominion of gentleness. Mr. Simms appears to have thought differently. But with all their faults, of invention, manner and spirit, his works have some striking merits which entitle them to a higher consideration than they have received.

Mr. Hoffman has an eye for natural scenery. By this I do not mean simply a capacity of enjoying it, but a clear perception of its features and a cordial estimate of its peculiarities. With most persons woodland, stream and cloud leave but vague impressions, and in attempting to convey an idea of any prospect or range of country, either with the pen or in conversation, they find their memories or descriptive powers quite inadequate to the task. Mr. Hoffman is admirably organized for the appreciation both of scenery and character. There is a vivacity and actuality in his pictures of rural scenes, which has scarcely been equalled in this country. The heroes and heroines of his fictions have both freshness and individuality, and this is enough to render them not only attractive but natural.

The name of the author of Horse Shoe Robinson, Swallow Barn, Rob of the Bowl, and Quodlibet, is rarely heard by the lovers of good literature without a feeling of regret that politics should have allured from letters one whose genius and accomplishments fit him so well to shine in that field where are won the most enduring as well as the noblest reputations. Mr. Kennedy is more than any other of his contemporaries like Washington Irving. He has much of his graceful expression, quiet humour and cheerful philosophy, with more than he of the constructive faculty. His works abound in the best qualities which should distinguish our American romantic literature, and prove that the will only is necessary for him to secure a place among the great authors of our language.

Calavar and The Infidel were the first novels of Dr. Bird, and there are few American readers who need to be informed of their character or desert; though as their accomplished author has been so long in retirement, the inference is reasonable that their reception was equal neither to their merits nor his expectations. Dr. Bird has great dramatic power, and has shown in several instances considerable ability in the portraiture of character. His historical romances are deserving of that title. His scenes and events from actual life are presented with graphic force and an unusual fidelity. He had the rare merit of understanding his subjects as perfectly as it was possible to do so by the most persevering and intelligent study of all accessible authorities; and in the works I have mentioned has written in an elevated and effective style. In

Calavar, Robin Day, Nick of the Woods, The Hawks of Hawk Hollow, Peter Pilgrim, and Sheppard Lee, he has exhibited a manner as various as his genius, and shown that there is hardly a school of fiction in which he cannot excel.

There are very few works of their sort in the literature of any country comparable to the Zenobia, Probus, and Julian, of William Ware. Mrs. Child's beautiful story of Philothea, in which she has so happily depicted Athenian society in the age of Pericles, is the only American romance of a kind in any degree similar. Mr. Ware's characters are finely discriminated and skilfully executed; and his narratives have a just proportion and completeness. He writes like one perfectly at home amid the ancient grandeur and civilization of his scenes and eras, and in a style of Augustan elegance and purity.

Mr. Osborn's Sixty Years of the Life of Jeremy Levis and Confessions of a Poet are powerfully written and deeply interesting. The latter is more like Mr. Dana's Tom Thornton than any other American novel. It illustrates the metaphysics of passion, and in construction, and in all respects indeed, is superior to his first work, though both inculcate a questionable morality.

I shall have occasion elsewhere to refer to the works in this department by Mr. Allston, Mr. Irving, Mr. Longfellow, Mr. Hall, Mr. Thomas, Mr. Mathews and some other writers.

Since the days of Richardson, when novels were printed sometimes in five quartos and sometimes in ten octavos, their legitimate extent has been in England three duodecimo volumes. The Germans have gone back to the more ancient models, such as were furnished by Boccacio and the authors of the Gesta Romanorum, and many things in our own country have tended to increase the popularity of the tale. Partly in consequence of the demand, perhaps, our productions of this sort have been exceedingly numerous, and without the imprimatur of any foreign publisher they have been read. It has sometimes been amusing, however, to observe the servility of habit and opinion manifested in regard to such of them as have been attributed to foreign writers. In many instances the contents of our magazines, received in silence or with faint praise on their first appearance here, have been copied by British publishers, returned as by British authors, and then sent with extravagant commendations through half the gazettes of the Union.

Admitting, very readily, that it requires more application—more time and toil—to produce a three volume novel, it must not be supposed that the production of the tale is a very easy business. On the contrary, there is scarcely any thing more difficult, or demanding the exercise of finer genius, in the whole domain of prose composition.

Washington Irving is a name of which the country is very reasonably proud. His rich humour, fine sentiment, delicate perception of the beautiful, and taste, are apparent in almost every thing he has written. He has given us but little of a tender or romantic kind indeed, and less perhaps to show the possession of the inventive faculty. The Wife, The Broken Heart, the Widow and her Son, and the Pride of the Village, prove however that he could summon tears from their fountains as easily as he has wakened smiles. I speak of him thus briefly here, because it is not as a writer of such works as are now under observation that he is chiefly distinguished.

Next to Irving, and perhaps before him in point of time, was Richard H. Dana. His stories published originally in *The Idle Man*, are among the most remarkable works of their class in modern literature. Paul Felton is a history of wild passion, in which the characters are portrayed with a master's skill, and there runs through it a strain of lofty and vigorous thought, and a knowledge of human life, which place it in the very first rank of ethical fictions. Edward and Mary, and the Son, are of a more pleasing and touching nature, and are scarcely less deserving of praise.

Nathaniel Hawthorne has published some half a dozen volumes of tales and romantic essays, various in their character, but all marked with his peculiar and happy genius. He is " most musical, most melancholy." He controls his reader as the capricious air does the harp. The handkerchief, raised toward the eye to wipe away the blinding moisture there, is checked at the lips, to suppress a smile, summoned by some touch of delicate and felicitous humour. He has the most unaffected simplicity and sincerity, with the deepest insight into man's nature and the secrets of his action. His style is remarkable for elegance, clearness, and ease, while it is imaginative and metaphysical; and his themes, chosen most frequently from the legends of our colonial age, though occasionally from those of a later period, or from the realm of allegory, are not more national than almost every thing in his fanciful illustrations and quaint and beautiful philosophy. His Twice Told Tales and Mosses from an Old Manse are the perfection of pensive, graceful, humorous writing, quite equal to the finest things of Diedrich Knickerbocker or Geoffrey Crayon, and superior to all else of a similar description in the English language.

The characteristics of Mr. Willis are very striking, and his tales are probably not inferior to any of their kind. His style is felicitous, his fancy warm and exuberant, and he has a ready and sparkling wit. No author has described

5

contemporary society with more vivacity, and in some of its phases perhaps no one has delineated it with more fidelity.

The tales of Mr. Poe are peculiar and impressive. He has a great deal of imagination and fancy, and his mind is in the highest degree analytical. He is deficient in humour, but humour is a quality of a different sort of minds, and its absence were to him slight disadvantage, but for his occasional forgetfulness that he does not possess it. The reader of Mr. Poe's tales is compelled almost at the outset to surrender his mind to his author's control. Unlike that of the greater number of suggestive authors his narrative is most minute, and unlike most who attend so carefully to detail he has nothing superfluous—nothing which does not tend to the production of the desired result. His stories seem to be written *currente calamo*, but if examined will be found to be results of consummate art. No mosaics were ever piled with greater deliberation. In no painting was ever conception developed with more boldness and apparent freedom. Mr. Poe resembles Brockden Brown in his intimacy with mental pathology, but surpasses that author in delineation. No one ever delighted more or was more successful in oppressing the brain with anxiety or startling it with images of horror. George Walker, Anne Radcliffe, or Maria Roche, could alarm with dire chimeras, could lead their characters into difficulties and perils, but they extricated them so clumsily as to destroy every impression of reality. Mr. Poe's scenes all seem to be actual. Taking into view the chief fact, and the characteristics of the *dramatis personæ*, we cannot understand how any of the subordinate incidents in his tales could have failed to happen.

Mrs. Elizabeth Okes Smith is a woman of a most original and poetical mind, who has succeeded, perhaps better than any other person, in appreciating and developing the fitness of aboriginal tradition and mythology for the purposes of romantic fiction.

The tales of Mr. Bryant, Mr. Leggett, Mr. Hoffman, Mr. Simms, Mrs. Child, Mrs. Kirkland, and several others, will be remembered as possessing various and peculiar merits.

I come now to the consideration of the Humorous, the Comic, and the Satirical. It has been so frequently asserted by men of little observation that these qualities are almost or utterly unknown among us, that I should feel some hesitation in speaking of them were the proofs of their existence here less abundant and satisfactory. It is true that we have no Lucian, no Rabelais, no Molière; but the gay, the witty, and the facetious, have nevertheless borne a due proportion to our writers of the graver, profounder, and more imaginative classes.

I am disposed to think that however successful Mr. Irving has been in other departments of literature, he will be longest remembered as a humorist. Of his History of New York, humour is the predominating quality, and it would be difficult to find any thing which possesses it in a higher degree. Mr. Irving's humourous writings are different from nearly all others. The governing attribute of his mind is taste, and he presents nothing to the public before it has been polished with the skill and care of a lapidary. In all his works it would be impossible to find a word that shocks the fastidiously refined by its vulgarity, yet there is in them no lack of freshness or freedom. In his vivacity he is never unguarded, in his gayety he is never unchaste. Humour cannot easily be described. As Barrow so well observes, "It is that we all see and know, but which is properly appreciated only by acquaintance. It is so versatile, so multiform: it appears in so many shapes, so many postures, so many garbs, and is so variously understood by different eyes and judgments, that it would be as easy to paint the face of Proteus as to give a clear and certain idea of it." Yet it may be safely averred that a gentleman had never conception of it which is not illustrated in the works of our author.

Mr. Paulding and Mr. Irving commenced so nearly together that it is difficult to say which had precedence in point of time. The marriage of Paulding's sister to an elder brother of Irving led to the acquaintance of the youthful wits, both of whom had already written some trifles for the gazettes, and it was soon after proposed in a gay conversation that they should establish a periodical, in which to lash and amuse the town. When they next met, each had prepared an introductory paper, and as both had some points too good to be sacrificed they were blended into one, Paulding's serving as the basis. They adopted the title of Salmagundi, and soon after published a small edition of their first number, little thinking of the extraordinary success which awaited it. Upon the completion of two volumes a disagreement with their publisher suddenly caused a suspension of the work, and the sequel to it was written several years afterward while Irving was abroad, exclusively by Paulding. Salmagundi entitles its authors to a very high rank among the comic writers. In this miscellany, The Mirror for Travellers, John Bull and Brother Jonathan, and his other writings, Mr. Paulding has given almost every sort of facetious and satirical composition. He deals more largely than Irving in the whimsical and the burlesque, and he is wanting in the exquisite refinement which lends such a charm to Geoffrey Crayon's humour. The follies of men are often confirmed, rather than cured, by undisguised attacks. Mr. Cooper, by his honest and sensible commentaries upon a class in our American society, gathered the scattered vulgar into a mob. Paulding, who took greater liberties, was perhaps a more efficient reformer, without startling them by an exhibition of their deformities, or attracting their vexed rage to himself. The motley crowds at our watering places, the ridiculous extravagance and ostentation of the suddenly made rich, the ascendency of pocket over brain in the affairs of love, and all the fopperies and follies of our mimic worlds, are described by him in a most diverting manner; while the more serious sins of society are treated with appropriate severity. Besides his occasional coarseness, however, Mr. Paulding has the fault, in common with some others, of *labeling* his characters, gay, sedate, or cynical, as the case may be, in descriptive names, as if doubtful of their possessing sufficient individuality to be otherwise distinguished. If a hero cannot make himself known in his action and conversation he is not worth bringing upon the boards.

Robert C. Sands exhibited considerable humour in both his poems and prose writings. He excelled in burlesque, of which he produced some admirable specimens. Mr. Sands, Mr. Verplanck and Mr. Bryant formed together a " literary confederacy," during the existence of which they wrote the three volumes of The Talisman, except a few pieces by Mr. Halleck, and another friend of theirs. Mr. Villecour and his Neighbours, and Scenes in Washington, in this miscellany, are the joint composition of Sands and Verplanck, and are excellent, except that in a few instances they run into ill-natured caricature. The Peregrinations of Petrus Mudd, in The Talisman, (in which is given a true history of a well-known New Yorker,) and other early writings of Mr. Verplanck, show that that gentleman needed but the impulse to rival the finest wits of the reign of Queen Anne.

John Sanderson, to natural abilities of a high order added a calm, chaste scholarship, an intimate acquaintance with men, a singularly amiable disposition, and a frank and highbred courtesy. In his humour were blended happily the characteristics of Rabelais, Sterne and Lamb. To his appreciation of the comic was added a most delicate perception of the beautiful. He knew society, its selfishness, and its want of honour, but looked upon it less in anger than in sadness. Yet he was no cynic, no Heraclitus. He deemed it wisest to laugh at the follies of mankind. Through all his experience he lost none of his natural urbanity, his freshness of feeling, his earnestness and sincerity. He was not less brilliant in his conversation than in his writings; but he never summoned a shadow to any face, or permitted a weight to lie on any heart.

In the Ollapodiana of Willis Gaylord Clarke are many of the character-istics of Sanderson ; but Clarke lived in a more quiet atmosphere ; or perhaps it were better to say, he had a less independent expression. Born and educated in a rural village, and passing his maturer years in a metropolis, he was fami-liar with almost every váriety of life and manners existing in our own country. His perception of the ludicrous was quick, and his taste rejected all that was coarse or depraving. We find in few works such a pleasing combination of elegant comedy and fine sentiment as in the quaint essays above referred to, and in none, perhaps, a truer index to an author's own habits and feelings.

The Charcoal Sketches, and other humorous writings of Joseph C. Neal, are elaborate, but wanting in the grace and spirit which distinguish many productions of their class. Mr. Neal writes as if he had little or no sympathy with his creations, and as if he were a calm spectator of acts and actors, whimsical or comical,—an observer rather by accident than from desire. It is not always so, however, since in some of his sketches he exhibits not only a happy faculty for the burlesque, and singular skill in depicting cha-racter, but a geniality and heartiness of appreciation which carry the reader's feelings along with his fancy.

I shall but allude here to Judge Breckenridge's Modern Chivalry, Dr. Gil-man's Village Choir, Major McClintock's Yankee Sleigh Ride, Wedding, and other stories, the Jack Downing Letters, (through which runs a very genuine humour of a certain sort,) Mrs. Kirkland's New Home, and other works of a like description written in the northern and eastern states of the Union.

The comic literature of the United States must be looked for chiefly in those parts of the country which have yet furnished little or nothing of a differ-ent sort. There is an originality and riant boldness in some of the productions of the South and West which give abundant promise for the future. And what we have, however coarsely stamped, is of the truest metal. It is necessary only to refer to Judge Longstreet's Georgia Scenes, Thompson's Major Jones's Courtship and Chronicles of Pineville, Mr. Thorpe's Mysteries of the Backwoods and Big Bear of Arkansas, Mr. Hooper's Simon Suggs, Morgan Neville's Mike Fink, and to other characteristic productions of southern and western men, to justify expectations of an original and indigenous literature of this kind from the cotton region and the valley of the Mississippi.

Of humorous and satirical poetry we have no lack of quantity, and there are some good specimens. Trumbull's Progress of Dulness and McFingal, Cliffton's Group and Epistle to Gifford, some of the ballads, etc. of Francis Hopkinson, Fessenden's Terrible Tractoration, and Democracy Unveiled,

D

Verplanck's Bucktail Bards and Dick Shift, Halleck's Fanny, Pierpont's Portrait, Osborne's Vision of Rubeta, The Echo, The Political Greenhouse, and the writings of Sands, Sprague, Holmes, Ward, Benjamin, and others, furnish many passages of humour and caustic wit.

The Essays of a people are among the best indexes to their condition and character. They are often produced by minds transiently released from public affairs, when reflection and speculation employ powers that have been schooled for action. To write just treatises, says Bacon, requireth leisure in the writer and leisure in the reader. The essay is more fit for the nation whose energies and sympathies are lively and diffused. It flourishes most where some degree of cultivation is universal. Like the lecture, it is addressed to those who are familiar with first principles. An era in essay writing was commenced by Steele and Addison, in their periodical papers suggested by the follies of contemporary society. This era closed with the production in America of the Salmagundi of Irving and Paulding, the Old Bachelor of Wirt and his associates, and the Lay Preacher of Dennie. Another era was begun with the Quarterly Reviews,* which, with the magazines, have absorbed so large a proportion of

---

* It is now more than a century since the first American Monthly Magazine was established in Boston, by Jeremy Gridley. It was continued about three years, and was more successful than any work of its sort commenced before the Revolution. The Massachusetts Magazine, to which Drs. Freeman and Howe and Mrs. Morton were contributors, lasted from 1784 to 1795. In 1803 the Anthology Club was formed, to conduct the Monthly Anthology, which had been established by Phineas Adams. Among its members were Professor Ticknor, Alexander H. Everett, William Tudor, Drs. Bigelow and Gardner, and Rev. Messrs. Buckminster, Thatcher and Emerson, (father of Ralph Waldo Emerson.) The Anthology was discontinued in 1811. In 1812 and 1813 four volumes of the General Repertory and Review—the first American quarterly—were issued at Cambridge, under the editorship of Andrews Norton. It was literary and theological, and contained some very able papers. The North American Review was commenced in 1815 by William Tudor. It was transferred in 1817 to Willard Phillips, and in the same year to The North American Club, the most active members of which were Edward T. Channing, Richard H. Dana, and Jared Sparks, then a tutor in Harvard College. In 1819 Edward Everett became editor, and its circulation increased so rapidly that three editions were printed of some of the numbers. Some of Mr. Everett's articles relating to Greece, British travellers in America, and belles lettres, attracted very general attention abroad as well as in the United States. In 1823 the work was placed under the direction of Mr. Sparks, who conducted it until 1830, when it was purchased by Alexander H. Everett, then just returned from his mission to Spain. Mr. Everett surrendered it to Dr. Palfrey, in 1835, and I believe it passed into the hands of its present editor, Mr. Bowen, in 1842. The Christian Examiner, a very able literary and theological review, in 1818 took the place of The Christian Disciple, which had been published six years under the direction of Noah Worcester. The Examiner has contained some of the best essays of Dr. Channing, Dr. Dewey, the Wares, and other eminent Unitarian clergymen. The Christian Review, also quarte:, and devoted both to literature and religion, was established in 1835, and has contained

the best writing of the present age, and the custom of delivering addresses on festival occasions and before societies, which obtains principally in the United States. These last are chiefly historical and moral, are in many instances by

---

articles by Dr. Wayland, Dr. Williams, Dr. Sears, and other leading clergymen of the Baptist churches. The Boston Quarterly Review was commenced in 1837, and its contents have been principally written by its editor, Mr. Brownson. The New England Magazine was established by J. T. Buckingham, the veteran and able editor of the Boston Courier, in 1833, and was discontinued on the close of the sixth volume, principally I believe on account of the death of the editor's son and associate, Mr. Edwin Buckingham. The Dial, a magazine of Literature, Philosophy and Religion, was published from 1841 to 1843 under the direction of Ralph Waldo Emerson.

The New York Magazine and Literary Repository was published from 1787 to 1792. No literary periodical of much merit existed in New York until 1822 and 1823, when The Literary Review was published and Robert C. Sands was among its leading contributors. In the early part of 1824 The Atlantic Magazine was commenced, and Sands became its editor. It was afterwards called The New York Monthly Review, and edited by Sands, and Mr. Bryant, who removed to New York in 1825. The Knickerbocker Magazine was started in December, 1832, by C. F. Hoffman, who in 1833 yielded the editorship to Timothy Flint, who was in turn succeeded in the following year by its present editor, Lewis Gaylord Clark. The Knickerbocker has been one of the most successful and brilliant periodicals of the day. Among its contributors have been Irving, Paulding, Bryant, Longfellow, and nearly all the younger writers of much note in the country. The Democratic Review was commenced in Washington, in 1837, by Mr. O'Sullivan, one of its present editors, and Mr. Langtree, his brother-in-law, since deceased. It was removed to New York in 1841. It has been the most successful magazine of a political character in the United States, and has been conducted with ability, dignity, and good taste. The American Monthly Magazine, which had been published several years under Mr. Herbert, Mr. Hoffman, and Mr. Benjamin, was discontinued in 1838. Arcturus, a Journal of Books and Opinion, was continued about two years by Mr. E. A. Duyckinck and Cornelius Mathews, who wrote its principal contents. The American Review, a Whig Journal, was established by Mr. George H. Colton, in 1844. The American Biblical Repository, devoted to biblical and general literature, theological discussion, the history of theological opinions, etc., was founded in 1831 by Edward Robinson, the distinguished orientalist, who conducted it until 1838. Its present editor is Mr. J. H. Agnew. The New York Review (quarterly) was published from 1837 to 1842, during which time its principal writers were the Rev. Drs. Hawks, Henry and Coggswell, and Messrs. Legare, Henry Reed, and Duyckinck.

In Philadelphia Aitkin's Pennsylvania Magazine was the most popular literary periodical before the Revolution. Thomas Paine and Francis Hopkinson were contributors. It was suspended on the approach of the war. Mathew Carey published the American Museum from 1787 to 1792. In 1805 Charles Brockden Brown began the Literary Magazine and American Register, which he continued five years. In 1809, The Portfolio which had been established eight years before, by Joseph Dennie, was changed from a weekly gazette to a monthly magazine. After the death of Dennie, early in 1812, it was edited for a considerable period by the late celebrated and unfortunate Nicholas Biddle, and in 1816 passed into the hands of Mr. J. E. Hall, who conducted it until it was discontinued in 1821. The Analectic Magazine was established by Moses Thomas in 1813, and I believe was published until 1820. Many of the cleverest men in the country, including Mr. Irving, Mr. Paulding, and Wilson (the ornithologist) wrote for these works, which were more widely and generally read than any periodicals which had been or were then published in this country. They were in royal octavo, each number containing from seventy to one hundred pages, and were embellished with engravings scarcely inferior to the best now produced, from original pictures. In 1827 the American Quarterly Review was established, under the direction of Mr. Robert Walsh, and it was continued ten years. The Lady's Book and Graham's Magazine were in the first place monthly selections of periodical litera-

our most eminent scholars, jurists and statesmen, and constitute a very important part of our literature.

The humour, repose, simplicity and strong sense of Franklin are conspicuous in nearly every thing he wrote. He is among the most national of our authors. The very spirit of New England lives in The Way to Wealth, The Morals of Chess, and The Whistle, as well as in his Letters, so full of prudence and sagacity. His style is elaborate, and in some respects is better than that of any of his contemporaries. It is familiar, condensed, of pure English, and has considerable variety.

The Lay Preacher of Dennie and his articles in the Portfolio seem to me feeble and affected, though occasionally marked by considerable excellence. It was natural to overrate him, as in his time we had very few writers with whom he could be compared. For several years after the death of Brockden Brown I believe he was the only man in the country who made literature a profession.

Mr. Wirt, in the Old Bachelor and The British Spy, wrote in a natural, copious and flowing style, which was occasionally polished into elegance. It was perhaps too full and ornate for a writer, but was admirable for an orator. The story of the Blind Preacher was in his happiest manner, but his disquisitions on eloquence are more carefully composed, and are vigorous and full of just reflections.

Among our historical essayists a distinguished place is held by Mr. Verplanck. Nearly thirty years ago he undertook in various discourses and reviews the eulogy of the excellent men who had most largely contributed to raise or support our national institutions and to form or to elevate our national character. His sketches have in parts the elaboration of cabinet pictures. His colouring and drawing have the fidelity and distinctness of De Leide and

---

ture, but for several years their contents have been original, and their extraordinary sale has enabled their publishers to employ the best writers. Graham's Magazine is embellished with the most costly engravings, and has a circulation of nearly thirty thousand copies. Like their predecessors, The Portfolio and The Analectic, the Philadelphia magazines of the present day owe their principal attractions to New York and New England writers.

The Southern Quarterly Review was established in Charleston in 1828, and suspended in 1833. It was recommenced in 1842, and I believe is now edited by the Rev. Mr. Whittaker. Among its most distinguished writers have been Stephen Elliott, Hugh S. Legare, and W. G. Simms.

The Southern Literary Messenger was founded by Mr. T. W. White, in 1834, and since his death has been under the direction of Mr. B. B. Miner. The best writers of Virginia and some of the other states have contributed to it, and it has been from the beginning a very valuable and interesting work

The New Englander, published at Hartford, Conn., has not been very long established, but it is among the first of our periodicals in character.

Wouvermans. He is the most learned of our writers in the history of Dutch colonization, and occasionally his style is marked by a certain humorous gravity which is inherited by the descendants of the New Netherlanders. All his productions are marked by excellent taste and a most genial spirit.

Robert Walsh was editor of the American Quarterly Review, and a contributor to some similar periodicals abroad. His commentaries on books, the drama, and works of art, exhibited industry and good sense, knowledge and reflection, within a limited range;* but he lacked the earnest sympathy of such critics as Dana, who views books not only as subjects of intellectual observation, but as appealing to man's primal instincts, and whose comments on works of genius are accordingly not merely technical but psychological.

The works of Dr. Channing have had and will continue to exert a powerful and healthful influence. He is original, even when not new or novel, for he gives his own perceptions of truth. His style owes less popularity to its fluency than to its being a just expression of his character: every faculty of his mind and peculiarity of his position being reflected in it. It is marked by feeling, imagination, and moral energy. When he expresses a common idea, it will be found, on examination, that he gives it a new character, by connecting it with the deepest feelings and instincts. His clear perception of man's duties made him particularly insist on many principles which, though universally admitted, do not influence the conduct. His writings are the sincere expressions of an earnest mind. He makes his readers love virtue and truth. He often convicts us of a superficial perception of what we deemed the commonplaces of religion and morality, and makes us feel their depth and great importance.†

Edward Everett is one of our best specimens of culture and scholarship. His style is copious, graceful, and justly modulated. It shows considerable energy and fancy, and great command of language. His brother, Alexander H. Everett, has less tact and taste, but is perhaps equal to him in extent of knowledge and variety of accomplishments. He is the author of more than fifty articles in the North American Review, of which he was a considerable

---

* He wrote a large volume in defence of the moral and intellectual character of the country, in which he presents the claims of many insignificant persons to consideration, but does not once in any way allude to *Jonathan Edwards*, whose simple name was worth all his five hundred pages, for the purpose he had in view. This was perhaps less from ignorance than from prejudice against Edwards's theology and metaphysics.

† Channing is one of those men whose mind is hung upon heaven with golden chords, and whose thoughts vibrate between what is pure below and sublime above.—*Dr. Bowring.*

Dr. Channing, one of those men who are a blessing and an honour to their generation and their country.—*Southey.*

time editor, and has written largely in other periodicals. His favourite subjects are connected with French literature and political history and economy.

Hugh S. Legaré was equal to Edward Everett in classical scholarship, and
superior in the vigour and chasteness of his style. Some of his contributions
to the New York and Southern Quarterly Reviews have scarcely been excelled for
accuracy of investigation and comprehensiveness of views. There was not
however much variety in his subjects or his manner.

The Rev. Dr. Gilman, formerly a frequent contributor to the North American Review, and the author of that graphic and humorous picture of rural manners, the Memoirs of a New England Village Choir, has written forcibly and
with taste upon many subjects connected with philosophy and general literature.

Of contemporary philosophical essayists Ralph Waldo Emerson is the most
distinguished. He is an original and independent thinker, and commands
attention both by the novelty of his views and the graces and peculiarities of
his style. He perceives the evils in society, the falsehoods of popular opinions, the unhappy tendencies of common feelings ; and is free from vulgar cant
and enslaving prejudice. Mr. Emerson is the leader of a considerable party,
which is acquiring strength from the freshness and independence of its literature.

Mr. Orestes A. Brownson is bold and powerful, and I suppose honest, notwithstanding his want of consistency. Conscious of the possession of great
abilities, conscious of the validity of certain claims he has to unattained good
reputation and happiness, he has sought for both through almost every variety
of action and opinion, always thinking himself right, though nearly always, as
he has been doomed to learn, in the wrong. He is an exceedingly voluminous
writer, in religion and politics as well as in metaphysics, and his works, if
collected and chronologically printed, from Charles Elwood down to his last
speech in defence of the Roman religion, would present the most remarkable
and interesting of psychological histories.

Mr. George P. Marsh is one of our most learned essayists, and his writings
are as much distinguished for good sense and acuteness as for scholarship.
They are also marked by a thorough nationality.

C. C. Felton, Greek Professor in Harvard University, is one of the princi
pal writers for the North American Review, and is a discriminating critic. His
style is brilliant and pointed.

The Rev. Dr. Hawks has an easy and copious style, skill in analysis, accu
rate acquaintance with history, caustic wit, and a uniform heartiness of pur
pose, which make him a powerful as well as an attractive character writer.

Francis Bowen, editor of the North American Review, is a clear, forcible, independent thinker, and has much precision and energy of style. His contributions on metaphysical subjects, and on the principles of law and government, are of a very high character. He is a man of large acquirements both in literature and philosophy.

George S. Hillard is one of the most polished writers of New England. His taste is fastidious, and he is a fine rhetorician. He excels in arrangement and condensation, and has an imaginative expression. Of his numerous articles in the North American Review one of the most brilliant is on Prescott's Conquest of Mexico, but I think the happiest of his essays is that on the Mission of the Poet, read before the Phi Beta Kappa Society.

Charles Sumner, though still a young man, is widely known for the extent of his legal knowledge and his general attainments. His style is rapid and energetic, with much fulness of thought and illustration. He has a great deal of enthusiasm and courage, as is shown by his discourse on the True Grandeur of Nations.

Mr. Tuckerman's appreciation of the beautiful seems instinctive, and the style of his criticisms is unaffected, flowing, and graceful. His Thoughts on the Poets contain passages which are the perfection of that sort of writing. He has manly sense, and tenderness without mawkish sentiment, and a just contempt of prudery and hypocrisy. His generous warmth and independence may serve in some degree to counteract in this country the sordid and calculating spirit of the age.

Mr. E. P. Whipple is one of our youngest and most brilliant writers. His papers which have appeared in the reviews and magazines are discriminating and comprehensive, analytical and reflective, and display an extraordinary maturity of judgment.

Respecting Mr. David Hoffman's volumes of pleasant practical morality, Mr. Wilde's ingenious Researches and Considerations concerning Tasso, Mr. Fay's Dreams and Reveries, Mr. Lowell's Essays on the Old Poets, The Analyst of Mr. Jones, and the reviews and other essays on art, literature, philosophy and manners by Dr. Norton, Dr. Bethune, Mr. Hazard, Mr. Parker, Mr. Reed, Mr. Carey, Mr. Hudson, Mr. Simms, Mr. Duyckinck, and many others who have distinguished themselves as essayists and critics, my present limits will not admit any particular commentary.

I shall but allude to our writers of voyages and travels: to the learned, acute and honest Robinson, Stevens, always lively and picturesque, the graphic and reflective Cooper, the discriminating and humorous Sanderson, the animated and genial Headley, and Cheever, Cushing, Dana, Dewey, Mackenzie, Melville, Miss Sedgwick, Willis, and others, whose journals abroad have delighted the readers of both continents; and with the same brevity I must refer to Lewis and Clarke, Long, Flint, and Irving; to the ingenious and laborious Schoolcraft, to Audubon and Catlin, with their enthusiasm, strange adventure and happy delineation, to Stephens and Norman wandering among the vestiges of forgotten nations in the New World, to the intrepid Fremont, and many beside, who have not only added to the literature of the country by their journals, full of novel facts and important observations, or attractive by the graces of style, but have sown seeds for richer harvests in exposing the subjects and materials for the sculptor and painter, the poet and romancer, scattered from the Atlantic to the Pacific and from the Polar to the Carib seas.

I have yet made no particular notice of the contributions to our literature by that sex who until recently were content to be the subjects and the inspiration of the finest creations of genius. Throughout Christendom woman has assumed new offices and achieved new and unlooked-for triumphs. In fifty years she has done more in the domains of intellect than she had done before in five centuries. When Hannah Adams produced her histories she was perhaps not inferior to any historical writer then in America. Miss Sedgwick followed, with her charming pictures of New England Life, Redwood, Clarence, Hope Leslie, the Linwoods, and other novels and tales; Mrs. Child with Hobomok, The Rebels, the classical romance of Philothea, her elegant Biographies, and volumes of Letters; Mrs. Brooks with Zophiel, so full of imagination and passion; Mrs. Hale with Northwood, and Sketches of American Life; Miss Leslie with Mrs. Washington Potts and her other spirited views of society; Miss Beecher with her profound and acute metaphysical and religious writings; Mrs. Gilman with Love's Progress, her graphic Recollections of a Southern Matron, and other works; Mrs. Kirkland with A New Home, Forest Life, and Western Clearings, unequaled as pictures of manners among the pioneers; Miss Fuller with Summer on the Lakes, Woman in the Nineteenth Century, and her brilliant Papers on Literature and Art; Miss Mackintosh with Conquest and Self-conquest, Praise and Principle, and Woman an Enigma; and Mrs. Embury, Mrs. Sigourney, Mrs. Smith, Mrs. Ellet, Mrs. Stephens, Mrs. Worthington, Mrs. Judson,* Mrs. Sedgwick, and

---

* "Fanny Forester."

many others who in various departments of literature have written works honourable to themselves, their sex, the country, and the age.

For a survey of our poetical literature I refer to the eighth edition, recently published, of The Poets and Poetry of America. Not all the specimens in that book are fruits of genius or high cultivation. It was designed to show what had been accomplished in the most difficult field of intellectual exertion in the first half century of our national existence. With much of the highest excellence it includes nothing inferior to some of the contents of the most celebrated anthologies of other countries; and while the whole showed a remarkable diffusion of taste and refinement of feeling, we could point to Mrs. Brooks, Mr. Bryant, Mr. Dana, Mr. Halleck, Mr. Longfellow, and others, as poets of whom any people would be proud.

There is indeed no reason why poetry should not be cultivated here as successfully as in any country. The nature of humanity is the same in all the ages, and man is for ever the theme of the poet's noblest song. Paradise Lost, nor the Inferno, nor Hyperion, nor almost any great poem of any nation is founded on authentic annals. Scriptures are true, and old mythologies survive; the gods of Greece yet live, the sound of the triton's conch is mingling with the roar of waves, and nymphs still stir the forest leaves ; and

> Fable is love's world, his home, his birth-place.
> Delightedly dwells he 'mong fays and talismans
> And spirits; and delightedly believes
> Divinities, being himself divine.
> The intelligible forms of ancient poets,
> The fair humanities of old religion,
> The power, the beauty, and the majesty,
> That had her haunts in dale, or piny mountain,
> Or forest, by slow stream or pebbly spring,
> Or chasms, or watery depths; all these have vanished :
> They live longer in the faith of reason !
> But still the heart doth need a language, still
> Doth the old instinct bring back the old names.

But, were there a necessity of local and special influences, the dim vistas which have been opened to us of ancient civilization on this continent, the shadowy views we have of the strange adventure and heroic achievements of the many-charactered colonists who first invaded its different latitudes, and the long and singular wars by which nation after nation was annihilated, offer boundless fields for the heroic bard ; while our dark old forests, rivers like flowing seas, and lakes which claim fraternity with oceans, valleys, and mountains, and caverns in which whole nations of the Old World might be hidden, and climates and seasons which are our peculiar heritage, are prolific of subjects and illustrations for the poetry of description.

Little has yet been done toward an American drama. Plays, to be successful on the stage, must be "abstracts and brief chronicles of the time." Their living principle must be the spirit of the age and people. Whether the swell and surge of our revolution, which cannot even now be said to have entirely subsided, bear to the present fragments that may be completed and reproduced, or contemporary life be represented in the comedy of manners, or subjects of any other period or description be chosen, the drama must still have its chorusses, not written by the author, but evoked by him from his audiences in appeals to their hearts. The weak and wicked policy of the government respecting copyrights, inducing a deluge of the most worthless foreign literature, and placing under a ban most of those who would give utterance to the true voice of the people, is undermining the foundations of our nationality; but the success of the plays of Bird and Conrad, and the failure of those of Longfellow and Willis, show that there still is patriotism enough among us to prefer works with the American inspiration to those of any degree of artistic merit without it. Besides the authors already mentioned, Mr. Hillhouse, Mr. John Howard Payne, Mr. Epes Sargent, Mr. George H. Calvert, Mr. Cornelius Mathews, Mr. Rufus Dawes, Mr. Lawton Osborne, and Mrs. Mowatt, have written dramatic pieces of literary merit, some of which have been acted with considerable success.

The relation of the plastic arts to poetry is immediate, and the shortest survey of our intellectual history would be incomplete without some reference to the noble works of our painters and sculptors. We may point with pride to Copley, many of whose best pictures grace the collections of his native town; to West, every where reverenced by the greatest critics;* Allston who in the world left

---

* Mr. West produced a series of compositions from sacred and profane history, profoundly studied, and executed with the most facile power, which not only were superior to any former productions of English art, but, far surpassing contemporary merit on the continent, were unequaled at any period below the school of the Caracci.—*Sir Thomas Lawrence.*

In his department Mr. West was the most distinguished artist of the age in which he lived.—*Sir Martin Archer Shee.*

William Beckford, the finest critic of art in our age, exclaims of Mr. West's Lear: "See how his nostril is inflated, like an Arab's in a thunder-storm! I solemnly declare the figure of Lear is as fine

no one worthy to receive his mantle;[*] to Stuart and Inman, equal to the first in portraiture; and to Vanderlyn, Leslie,[†] Sully, Durand, Cole, Wier, Huntington, Leutze, and others, whose places are in the front rank of living painters. With the same feeling we may regard Greenough, whose majestic Washington[‡] sits in grand repose before the capitol; Powers, in whom Thorwaldsen saw the restorer of a glory to the marble it had scarcely known since the days of Praxitiles; and Crawford, Clevenger, and others who promise to make our country a resting place for the eyes of future generations as they travel backward toward Rome and Athens.

Having thus as fully as seemed practicable in such narrow limits exhibited our Intellectual Progress and Condition, attempting to show that considering the facts of our political and social history we have already advanced far beyond the boundaries of reasonable anticipation, we pause on the shore of the dim future to catch the sounds of the voices which are to give expression to the mind of the people, and obtain glimpses of the symbols by which will be shadowed forth their spirit. More than any other nation ours has influenced the character of the last and the present age, but our power has been in acts and institutions, of whose teachings we look for impressive confirmations in our works of taste, imagination and reflection.

Doubtless our literature must continue to be influenced in a large degree by the literatures of other countries. The still increasing facilities of communication between all parts of the world, bringing remotest nations into closer proximity than were formerly cities of the same empire; and the extending and deepening power of the press, which in effect is making of one language all peoples, as they were before the confusion on the plains of Shinar, are rapidly subverting the chief national distinctions, and preparing the way perhaps for the realization of Goethe's idea of a Literature of the World.[§]

---

as the Laocoon, and the tone is as fine as fine can be.....Oh gracious God! he must have been inspired when he painted this—there are drama, expression, drawing, every thing."

The best composer of modern times and equal to Corregio in finish, when he pleased.—*Allston.*

Lawrence, Shee, Beckford, Allston, against the cant of the sciolists.

[*] What Washington was as a statesman, Channing as a moralist, that was Allston as an artist.—*Mrs. Jameson.*

[†] The finest interpreter of the spirit of Shakspeare the world has yet seen.—*Mrs. Jameson.*

[‡] We regard Mr. Greenough's Washington as one of the greatest works of sculpture of modern times.—*Edward Everett.*

[§] I always consult foreign nations, and advise every one to do the same. National literature will do but little. The epoch of a literature of the world is at hand, and every one ought to labour to hasten it.—*Eckermann's Conversations with Goethe.*

But the day of such a consummation is still distant. The New Civilization, of which our fathers were the apostles, is first to be universally diffused. All hereditary distinctions of rank, all differences of political privileges, all restraints upon the freedom of private judgment, are to be broken down. We may adopt, we are adopting, many peculiarities, in manners and opinions, from the various older nations from which our country was settled, and with which we have free and intimate intercourse ; but the recognition of the freedom and dignity of man is to be the vital principle in our literature—its distinctive and diffusive element.

The growth of American Literature cannot be forced by any hotbed process. Except by the acknowledgment of foreign copyrights,* which indeed is needed as much for the protection of morals as for the protection of letters, little can be done for it by any general legislation. Our authors, if admitted to a fair competition with foreigners, will take care of their own interests. But professed

---

* For the information of readers unacquainted with the operation of the present system, it may be necessary to state more particularly than has been done in the text, some of the ways in which it tends to weaken the mind and deprave the heart of the nation. Its literature is the richest boon we receive from the Past, and the literature of the Present, if fairly represented in the republications, would, upon the whole, no doubt, have a most salutary influence. But the denial of copyright to foreigners effectually deprives us of most of the really great works with which the presses of Europe are teeming. while it gives us nearly all they produce that is frivolous and vicious. It costs a great deal of money as well as labour to prepare the market for large works; there must be much advertising, a large distribution of copies, elaborate abstracts in reviews and journals, and many other means to create a demand; and the expenses of these means must be added to those of the mechanical manufacture. Yet now, as has been shown by numerous instances, as soon as a house with enterprise and capital has issued a readable impression of a work, and secured for it such a circulation as promises a fair remuneration, some base fellow is sure to bring out on dingy brown paper and small type a deluge of cheap copies. with which he reaps all the advantages of the first publisher's efforts, and leaves him with his stock unsold, and his investment unreturned. It is true that, notwithstanding these dangers, a few of the more indispensable histories and other fruits of true cultivation are reprinted here : but they are generally issued in the most compact and cheap style, sometimes much abridged, and nearly always without those charts and plates which add so much to the value of many foreign editions. A recognition of the foreign author's right of property would at once remedy this part of the evil entirely.

On the other hand, there is extraordinary activity in the republication of the light and licentious literature of the time. It is sickening to lean over the counters of the shops where cheap books are sold, and survey the trash with which the criminal folly of the government is deluging the country. Every new issue deepens the wide spread depravity, and extends the demand for its successor. As but little capital is required for the business, and the returns are quick, these leprous spots are constantly springing up in the cities; and to gratify the prurient tastes which they create, the literary sewers of Paris and London are dragged for the filthiest stuff which floats or sinks in their turbid waters. The demoralization increases, and the novels of Paul de Kock, disgusting as they are, in the original, (in which a racy style and sparkling wit render them attractive, despite their moral deformity,) are made worse by the addition of gross obscenity by the translator; and from those of Eugene Sue the reflective portions, which serve to neutralize the effects of the narrative, are left out. All private morals, all domestic peace, fly before this withering curse which the Congress persists in sustaining, by its refusal to recognise the rights of the foreign author. For, if the respectable publishers could be protected in their business, they would furnish good editions of good books, that would give a healthy tone to the common sentiment, and drive this profligate literature into oblivion; if the foreign author were protected in his rights, he would be but a competitor of the native author, and would have an inducement to support those liberal principles of society which are here established. thus strengthening them here, and diffusing them in his own country; and if the American were thus admitted to a competition in his own market with the European, our best intellects would be busy with the instruction of the people, which is now in so large a degree surrendered to the supporters of aristocracies.

Within the last year how many fathers, like one in Richmond, (whose testimony at a recent trial in that city attracted to the subject an indignant but momentary attention,) have pointed to these stolen poisons as the prime cause of the demoralization of their daughters,—how many murders, in all parts of the country, have been traced to the same fruitful source of crime and woe! That the literature of a country sinks with its morals, needs hardly to be suggested.

authors alone are not to create a great National Literature ; such a literature is not to be a result of any direct effort for its production. It must be in a large degree but an incidental consequence of energetic and well directed action for the moral and spiritual liberation and elevation of man. To this end, the strong-minded and thoroughly educated, leading the onward march of the race, combating every species of error, in morals and physics, in religion and legis-lation, and never taking a thought whether they are speaking or writing in an American style, or on an American subject, will strike out such sparks from the intellect as will shine like stars into the farthest future ages.

Leaving literature, then, as an object of special public regard, to take care of itself, we must instruct the mind and improve the heart of the people, must develope the great souls that are every day born into the world. The number of colleges need not be increased. It would be better perhaps if half we have were abandoned, and their resources given to the rest. But we need a great university, into which only learned men can enter, where there can be a more thorough literary and scientific culture, where the genius of the Past can be made more familiar, where the genius of the Present can be strengthened and directed : a university that shall have to other schools the relation of a mint to the mines, giving form and authority to the first order of understandings which in them are brought to light. There is no more pernicious error than that the whole people should be instructed alike. There must be a class, the end of whose lives shall be to search after and reveal beauty and truth, a class acting upon the nation, but acted upon both by it and by all nations and all ages. And we need libraries, and learned institutions, and galleries of art. These things are coming rapidly. Their necessity is discerned, and the "vo-luntary principle" in our free states is doing far more than has been elsewhere effected by coercion, to sustain whatever is really calculated in any way to un-fold human nature. Our wise and liberal merchants, manufacturers, farmers, and professional men,—we have no drones,—are beginning to understand that the true doctrine of Progress is comprised in the word Culture. Late events, that have saddened the heart of the intelligent patriot, have brought with them cheering proofs of a conservative element in our society, and the suffering and dishonour which have been caused by the uncultivated and reckless, may be atoned for by the life they will impart to energies that have hitherto been dor-mant. Literature, the condensed and clearly expressed thought of the country, will keep pace with its civilization ; and without any straining after originality, without any tricks of diction, without any aim but to press the truth directly, earnestly and courageously upon the popular heart, under the inspiration of an

7   E

enlightened love of country, and the guidance of a high cultivation, our authors will be sufficiently distinctive and national, in both manner and matter.

There is an absurd notion abroad that we are to create an entirely new literature. Some critics in England, expect us, who write the same language, profess the same religion, and have in our intellectual firmament the same Bacon, Sidney and Locke, the same Spenser, Shakspeare and Milton, to differ more from themselves than they differ from the Greeks and the Romans, or from any of the moderns. This would be harmless, but that many persons in this country, whose thinking is done abroad, are constantly echoing it, and wasting their little productive energy in efforts to comply with the demand. But there never was and never can be an exclusively national literature. All nations are indebted to each other and to preceding ages for the means of advancement; and our own, which from our various origin may be said to be at the confluence of the rivers of time which have swept through every country, can with less justice than any other be looked to for mere novelties in art and fancy. The question between us and other nations is not who shall most completely discard the Past, but who shall make best use of it. The Past belongs not to one people, but to those who best understand it. It cannot be studied too deeply, for unless men know what has been accomplished, they will exhaust themselves in unfolding enigmas that have been solved, or in pursuing *ignes fatui* that have already disappointed a thousand expectations. The Reformation had an extraordinary influence upon the literatures of the world, and some such influence has been exerted by our Revolution and the establishment of our institutions. The intellectual energy of America has been felt far more in Europe, than its own, for the period of our national existence, has been felt here; and with all the enslaving deference to foreign authority and all the imitation of foreign models of which we have had to complain in our inferior authors, there has been no want of the truest nationality in our Franklin, Webster, Channing, Cooper, Prescott, Bancroft, Bryant, Whittier, and others, in almost every department, who have written with an integrity of understanding and feeling.

It has been objected to our society that it is too practical. It has been supposed that this national characteristic forbids the expectation of great achievements in the highest domains of art. But the question *Cui bono?* should always be entertained. Utility is in every thing the truest of principles, though more intelligence and liberality than belong to a low state of civilization are necessary to its just appreciation and application. Whatever contributes to the growth and satisfaction of the mind, whatever has in it any absolute beauty, is beginning to be regarded as not less useful than that which ministers to our physical necessities. All works, even of imagination, must have in them something of genuineness and earnestness. Poets, and novelists, and essayists, when they write, must look not only into their minds but into their hearts. To persons of the sensibility and refinement which are inseparable from high cultivation, all truth is of a practical value, and in the most aerial creations it will be demanded by the first order of critics.

The old sources of intellectual excitement seem to be wellnigh exhausted. Love will still be sung, but in no sweeter strains than those of Petrarch, or Tasso; Courage, such as is celebrated by the old poets and romancers, is happily in disrepute; Religion, as it has commonly appeared in the more elegant forms of literature, has not been of a sort that ennobles man or pleases God; and Ambition, for the most part, has been of a more grovelling kind than may be looked for under the new forms of society. Christian virtue is no longer the observance of senseless pagan forms that have been baptized, but " the love of truth, for its own beauty and sweetness;" and the desire of man is not so much to win titles and power, as the consciousness or the reputation of doing something that shall entitle him to the general respect and gratitude. The materials among us for the externals of literature have been referred to. The elements of its vitality and power, which are most clearly apprehended in this century, though in their nature universal, for many reasons are likely to be most active with us. "Peace on earth and good will to man," is here to be the principle of life and progress, in Letters, as in Religion and Politics.

Considering the present condition of society; that new inventions are constantly releasing immense numbers from a portion of the toil required for the satisfaction of physical necessities, and giving to all more opportunity for intellectual pursuits; that steam and electricity are making of the world a common neighbourhood, knitting its remotest parts together by interchange of fabrics and thoughts; that the press, in the United States alone, scatters every hour more than the contents of the Alexandrian Library, and is increasing in refinement and energy with the expansion of its issues; and that associations for moral and intellectual improvement were never more numerous or efficient,—we cannot doubt that the Progress of Civilization in the coming age will be rapid and universal. This country, which is the centre of the new order of things, is destined to be the scene of the greatest conflicts of opinion. Much as has been done here in literature and art, much as we have surpassed all reasonable expectation in the works of our philosophers, orators, historians and poets, while clearing away the primeval forests, organizing society, and establishing the institutions of scientific and literary culture, we have not yet that distinct image of the feelings of the nation, in a great body of works in all the departments of reflection, imagination, and taste, of which the auspicious commencement of our literature, and our advantageous position with regard to the most important subjects of research and speculation, justify the hope. Schools may be well endowed, and individuals may labour with loving earnestness upon their life poems, but the whole people, by recognising the principle of beauty as a law of life, and cheering with their encouragement its teachers who shall deserve their best approval, and by cherishing a hearty love of our country, and making ceaseless efforts to render it in all respects worthy of affection, must aid in rearing the noble structure of a National Literature that shall fulfil our promise to mankind, and realize the prophecy which nearly a century ago was made of our destiny by one of the wisest of the sons of Europe.

> The Muse, disgusted at an age and clime
>   Barren of every glorious theme,
> In distant lands now waits a better time,
>   Producing subjects worthy fame.
>
> In happy climes, where from the genial sun
>   And virgin earth such scenes ensue,
> The force of art by nature seems outdone,
>   And fancied beauties by the true:
>
> In happy climes, the seat of innocence,
>   Where nature guides and virtue rules;
> Where men shall not impose for truth and sense
>   The pedantry of courts and schools,
>
> There shall be sung another golden age,
>   The rise of empires and of arts,
> The good and great, inspiring epic rage,
>   The wisest heads and noblest hearts.
>
> Not such as Europe breeds in her decay,
>   Such as she bred when fresh and young,
> When heavenly flame did animate her clay,
>   By future poets shall be sung.
>
> Westward the course of empire takes its way;
>   The first four acts already past,
> A fifth shall close the drama with the day—
>   Time's noblest offspring is the last.
>   BERKELEY.

PHILADELPHIA, 1845.

Painted by C.W.Peale.   Engraved by J.B.Gross.

Jonathan Edwards

JONATHAN EDWARDS.

[Born 1703. Died 1758.]

THE first man of the world during the second quarter of the eighteenth century was JONATHAN EDWARDS of Connecticut. As a theologian Robert Hall and Thomas Chalmers admit that he was the greatest who has lived in the Christian ages; and as a metaphysician Dugald Stewart and Sir James Mackintosh agree that he was never surpassed. In Great Britain and on the continent of Europe men disavowed belief in some of his doctrines, but confessed that they had only protests to oppose to them: Edwards had anticipated and refuted all arguments. Adopting some of his principles, others built up for themselves great reputations by perverting them or deducing from them illegitimate conclusions. In whatever light he is regarded he commands our admiration. He was unequalled in intellect and unsurpassed in virtue. Bacon was described as the "wisest and the meanest of mankind;" but Edwards, not inferior to the immortal Chancellor in genius, suffers not even an accusation of any thing unbecoming a gentleman, a philosopher, or a Christian.

Born in a country which was still almost a wilderness; educated in a college which had scarcely a local habitation; settled, a large part of his life, over a church upon the confines of civilization, and the rest of it in the very midst of barbarism, in the humble but honourable occupation of a missionary, he owed nothing to adventitious circumstances. With a fragile body, a fine imagination, and a spirit the most gentle that ever thrilled in the presence of the beautiful, he seemed of all men the least fitted for the great conflict in which he engaged. But He who, giving to Milton the Dorian reed, sent out his seraphim to enrich him with utterance and knowledge, with fire from the same altar purified the lips of Edwards, to teach that "true religion consists in holy affections," the spring of all which is "a love of divine things *for their own beauty and sweetness.*"

The father of Jonathan Edwards was for sixty years the humble pastor of the church in Windsor, on the margin of the Connecticut. He was a man of learning, and of that consistent piety which, in the religious teacher, is the summing up and conclusion of his best argument. Our author was his only son, and he named him "the gift of the Lord." He was carefully instructed from infancy, and at thirteen years of age entered Yale College far advanced in classical and general learning. While a freshman he read Locke on the Human Understanding, with a higher plea sure than the "miser feels when gathering up handfuls of silver and gold from some newly discovered treasure;" and at seventeen he graduated, with great reputation for both knowledge and wisdom. After receiving his first degree, he remained two years in the college, studying divinity, and early in the summer of 1722 was licensed to preach. When only nineteen he accepted an invitation to New York, where his ministry gave abundant satisfaction; but after eight months circumstances induced him to return to his father's house, where the summer of 1723 was devoted to theological studies. He formed warm attachments in New York. "My heart seemed to sink within me," he says, "at leaving the family and city where I had passed so many pleasant days. I went to Wethersfield by water, and as I sailed away I kept sigh of the city as long as I could." But at Saybrook, where he went on shore to spend the Sabbath, he recovered his composure in a "refreshing season, walking alone in the fields."

In the autumn of 1723 Edwards went to New Haven to receive the degree of Master of Arts, and while there was elected a tutor in the college. President Stiles assures us that his "tutorial renown was great and excellent." When he had held the office about two years, he accepted an invitation from the church in Northampton, to become the colleague of his maternal grandfather, a venerable man who for more than half a century had been its pastor. He was installed in February, 1727; and in the following July he was married to

Sarah Pierrepont, a woman of remarkable beauty, as is known both from tradition and from a portrait of her which was painted so late as 1740 for Dr. Erskine of Scotland. Edwards described her before their marriage, when he was himself but twenty years of age. " She has a singular purity in her affections," he says, " and you could not persuade her to do any thing wrong or sinful if you could give her all the world. She is of wonderful gentleness, calmness, and universal benevolence of mind. She will sometimes go about from place to place, singing sweetly ; and seems to be always full of joy and pleasure, and no one knows for what. She loves to be alone, walking in the fields and groves, and seems to have some one invisible always conversing with her." Happy man ! they lived together thirty years, and he was to the end the same enthusiastic admirer. She relieved him from all cares beyond his study, whither every day she carried, in a silver bowl, his simple diet ; and every night, after the other members of their family had retired to rest, they met there to spend an hour in conversation and prayer.

In 1731 Edwards visited Boston, and while there delivered before an association of ministers a sermon, which by their request was published. It was the first of his works which was printed, and it made such an impression that public thanks were offered to the Head of the Church for raising up so great a teacher. Soon afterwards commenced that famous revival of religion upon which the American historians of the last century dwell so frequently. This is not a place for the discussion or even a statement of the questions which at that time occupied more than any other the public mind not only in New England but throughout the settled portions of the country. Edwards was in every thing consistent, and, though earnest, had no sympathy with the miserable fanaticism which has almost always in such periods brought religion into contempt. His Narrative of Surprising Conversions in and about Northampton was published in London from his MS. by the celebrated Dr. Isaac Watts, in 1736.

In the eastern colonies a hundred years ago all the politicians and men of fashion managed to retain a " regular standing " in some religious society ; it was essential to their respectability. The custom had been gradually introduced of making a mere assent to certain opinions the condition of fellowship. About the year 1744 Edwards began to insist upon a return to old usages. The devil had "great speculative knowledge in divinity," more than a " hundred saints of ordinary education," and was very " orthodox in his faith," but he had given " no evidence of saving grace in his heart." More recent events than these in Northampton have shown that, however proper universal suffrage may be in the state, it is far from being expedient in the church. Those who were never there before now thronged the meeting-house to vote against their own disfranchisement ; and after a while the mob succeeded in procuring the dismission of the faithfullest and wisest of pastors. Edwards bore himself heroically through the controversy ; and in 1751 removed to Stockbridge, to preach to the Indians and a small church of Anglo-Americans which had been formed there by an earlier missionary. During his residence in Northampton the famous apostle, David Brainerd, had died in his house, and he had published his Memoirs ; in 1746 he had given to the world his admirable Treatise on Religious Affections ; and he had consented to the publication of some dozen sermons, any one of which contained more thought than the complete works of almost any fashionable preacher of later days.

Soon after his settlement in Stockbridge Edwards announced his intention, in a letter to his friend Erskine, to write a work upon Free Will and Moral Agency, in which he would bring the popular objections to the " Calvinistic divinity " to the test of the strictest reasoning ; "and particularly that great objection in which the modern writers have so much gloried, so long triumphed, with so great a degree of insult toward the most excellent divines, and in effect against the gospel of Christ, *that the Calvinistic notions of God's moral government are contrary to the common sense of mankind.*" It is hardly necessary to speak of the result. The work was written in four months and a half, amid all the cares and labours of his vocation. I never have read or heard that anybody supposed it had been or could be answered.*

---

* Edwards on the Will is a work which never was answered, and which never will be answered.—*Dugald Stewart.*

The subject, since then, has hardly been one of controversy, though it has occasionally been talked about. Some ingenious persons, to attract attention to essays against fatalism, have called them replies to Edwards; but scholars have no need to be informed that Edwards never entertained any such doctrine as that word describes.

In the autumn of 1754 he was seized with a severe fever, from which he did not recover until the following January; and his favourite pursuits were still further interrupted by the war with the French and Indians, during which soldiers were quartered in his house. In the last three years of his residence in Stockbridge, however, he wrote some of his ablest works, among which are the dissertations on God's Last End in the Creation of the World, and on The Nature of True Virtue. The last of these subjects has been a favourite one with ethical writers. Aristotle regarded virtue as *un juste milieu;* Hume says it is whatever is useful or agreeable to ourselves and others; and Paley, who as well as Hume had been a careful reader of Edwards, that it is " the doing good to mankind in obedience to the will of God, and for the sake of everlasting happiness." Edwards held it to be in some sense the same as beauty; in other words, to be every voluntary act of which the ultimate end is the greatest good of the greatest number. The dissertation on the Nature of Virtue is perhaps the most original of his works, and is so conclusive that all others on the subject have since been " considered as objects of curiosity rather than as guides of opinion."*

His Treatise on Original Sin is usually ranked next to that on the Freedom of the Will, for clearness, force and comprehensiveness. It was finished in 1757. Dr. Taylor, of Norwich, had foolishly boasted that his argument on this question could never be answered. The refutation of it by Edwards was so complete that even Taylor was compelled to admit that there could be no rejoinder; his mortification on his ignominious defeat is said to have shortened his days; " the grasp of his antagonist was death."

While Edwards was labouring with his wonted industry at Stockbridge, he received intelligence of the death of his son-in-law, the Rev. Aaron Burr, President of the College of New Jersey;* and in a few days afterward he was advised, in a letter from the Trustees, of his election to the vacant office. In his reply he expressed surprise that gentlemen by whom he was so well known should have thought him worthy of so distinguished an honour. " So far as I myself am able to judge of what talents I have for benefiting my fellow creatures by word," he says, " I think I can write better than I can speak;" and he proceeded to describe several great literary enterprises which he had in view. One was a History of the Work of Redemption, a complete system of divinity on a new plan, in which the events of heaven, earth and hell should be treated in their natural order, and the various parts of dogmatical theology so interwoven as to appear in beautiful contexture and harmony with the whole. This work had already been commenced, but no part of it was prepared for the press. If finished, it probably would have been his masterpiece, and would have raised him in reputation as much higher than he is now, as his completed works entitle him to be ranked above all other theological writers of his age. Another work which he contemplated was a Harmony of the Old and New Testaments.

Edwards determined to submit the question whether he should accept the presidency of the College to some of his most enlightened and pious friends, and upon their advice he left his family in Stockbridge and proceeded to Princeton, where he arrived in January, 1758. A few days afterward he was informed of the death of his father, whose useful life had been lengthened out to nearly ninety years. Several weeks passed before his inauguration, but he preached in the mean time in the college chapel, which his fame caused to be filled on every occasion to its utmost limit. The institution was formally committed to his charge on the sixteenth of February; on the twenty-third of the same month he was inoculated for the small-pox, which then prevailed in the town, and on the twenty-second of March he died of that disease.†

* Among the writers who have been largely indebted to this work was William Godwin, who in his *Political Justice,* as Robert Hall well observes, "with a daring consistence has pursued the principles of Edwards to an extreme from which that most excellent man would have recoiled with horror."

* He was the father of Aaron Burr, afterward Vice President of the United States.
† On Wednesday, the 22d of last month, died of inoculation at Nassau Hall, an eminent servant of God, the

Seeds from Edwards have taken root in strange fields. A single stalk from his philosophy has shed beauty and perfume over wastes of modern speculation. Many, of whose opinions all is dross that is not borrowed from him, have exhibited the poverty of their natural powers in assaults upon his system; and others, incapable of penetrating beyond the shell of his logic, and understanding the beauty of his life and doctrine, have done him much greater injury by professing to be of his school.

The style of Edwards is uncommonly good. It is suitable for his subjects. It has seldom been surpassed in perspicuity and precision. It is deficient in harmony, indeed, and occasionally has other faults of a mechanical sort, but he wrote hastily and printed without revision. Scarcely any of his sermons were intended for the press, and several of his more extended treatises are but rough drafts of what he designed. He appears never to have thought much of the importance of style until a few years before his death, when a copy of Richardson's Sir Charles Grandison falling in his way, he read it with pleasure and discovered the secret of its influence. From this time he attempted to write more gracefully, and the works on the Will and on Original Sin, subsequently finished, show that he improved.

He had a very powerful imagination, and some of his writings are full of the most impressive imagery. In his earlier years he gave free rein to his creative faculty, but afterwards restrained it except when expression of his thought was difficult without its aid. His wit was of the Damascus sort, shining and keen. He delighted in the *reductio ad absurdum*, of which his works probably contain the finest specimens in the English language. He directed his wit against principles, and never against his antagonists.

No assertion in regard to Edwards has been more common than the one that he was not

reverend and pious Mr. Jonathan Edwards, president of the College of New Jersey; a gentleman of distinguished abilities and of a heavenly temper of mind; a most rational, generous, catholic and exemplary Christian, admired by all who knew him for his uncommon candour and disinterested benevolence; a pattern of temperance, meekness, candour and charity; always steady, solemn and serene; a very judicious and instructive preacher, and most excellent divine. And as he lived cheerfully resigned to the will of Heaven, so he died, or rather, as the Scriptures emphatically express it with regard to good men, he fell asleep in Jesus, without the least appearance of pain.—*Boston Gaz., April* 10, 1758.

eloquent. The mountebank declamation of these latter days has so perverted men's judgments that they cannot understand how a preacher who rested one arm upon a high pulpit, with its diminutive and delicately moulded hand holding a small manuscript volume all the while close to his eyes, and with the other made slowly his few and only gestures, could be an orator. But he could keep a congregation that had assembled to hear a morning sermon ignorant of the approach of noon until through the uncurtained windows of the church the setting sun's red rays were shining upon its ceiling. One time when he was discoursing of death and the judgment, people rose up from their seats, with pallor on their faces, to see Christ descend through the parting heavens. Being requested to preach at Enfield, where he was a stranger, and the assembly were so indifferent to religion as to be neglectful of the decency of silence while he prayed, he had not half finished his sermon before the startled sinners, having "already passed through the valley of silence," began to wail and weep so bitterly that he could not go on for their distress. These are triumphs of eloquence* not dreamed of by such as deem themselves masters of the art from reading the foolish recipe ascribed to Demosthenes.

* In the same page of Mr. Gilfillan's Sketches of Modern Literature, in which he declares that Edwards's style "never rises into eloquence," he gives the following anecdote: "He reminded you of Milton's line, 'The ground burns frore, and cold performs the effect of fire.' A signal instance of this is recorded. A large congregation, including many ministers, were assembled to hear a popular preacher, who did not fulfil his appointment. Edwards was selected to fill his place, principally because, being in the habit of reading his discourses, he happened to have a sermon ready in his pocket. He ascended the pulpit accordingly, amid almost audible marks of disappointment from the audience, whom, however, respect for the abilities and character of the preacher prevented from leaving the church. He chose for his text, 'Their foot shall slide in due time,' and began to read in his usual quiet way. At first he had barely their attention; by and by he succeeded in riveting every one of them to his lips; a few sentences more, and they began to rise by twos and threes; a little farther, and tears were flowing; at the close of another, particular deep groans were heard, and one or two went off in fits; and ere he reached the climax of his terrible appeals, the whole audience had risen up in one tumult of grief and consternation. And, amid all this, there stood the calm, imperturbable man, reading on as softly and gently as if he were in his own study. And, in reading the sermon, we do not wonder at the impression it produced upon an audience constituted as that audience must have been. It is a succession of swift thunder-claps, each drowning and deafening the one which preceded it. We read it once to a distinguished *savant*, who, while disapproving of its spirit, was compelled, literally, to shiver under the 'fury of its power.'"—*Sketches of Modern Literature and Eminent Literary Men. London,* 1845.

BENJAMIN FRANKLIN.

[Born 1706. Died 1790.]

FROM the first metaphysician of the age in which he lived we turn to another New Englander, but three years younger than Edwards, whose name, says Lord Brougham, uttering the common judgment of mankind, " in one point of view must be considered as standing higher than any of the others which illustrated the eighteenth century." In statesmanship and philosophy he was equally illustrious, " and his efforts in each," proceeds the noble critic, " were sufficient to have made him greatly famous had he done nothing in the other."

BENJAMIN FRANKLIN was born in Boston on the seventeenth of January, 1706, and was the youngest but two of seventeen children. His parents were poor, but prudent, virtuous, and intelligent. His father had emigrated from England to enjoy religious liberty, and would have educated his youngest son for the ministry, but that his poverty made it necessary to take him from the free grammar school to cut wicks and fill candle moulds in the workshop. This was mortifying to the aspiring boy, and he wished to become a sailor; but his father refused, and at the end of two years apprenticed him to an elder brother who had learned the printing business in London, and returned to set up an office in his native city. His new employment pleased him, and he quickly became familiar with it. He had read Defoe upon Projects, Cotton Mather's Essays to do Good, the Pilgrim's Progress, Plutarch's Lives, and some other books which were owned by his father; and he now stole hours from sleep to study the volumes he was enabled to borrow, each for a single night, from the apprentices of booksellers. Thinking he could write poetry, he composed and printed ballads, which his brother sent him to sell in the streets, and his vanity was flattered by their success; but his father's criticisms discouraged him, and he afterward confined himself to prose writing, in which he constantly and successfully endeavoured to improve. When about sixteen

years of age he abandoned the use of animal food, and agreeing with his brother to support himself with half the money that was paid for his board, managed by cooking his own vegetables to save each week a share of his allowance for the purchase of books. With the increased means and leisure thus acquired he obtained and studied Cocker's Arithmetic, Sturny's and Seller's Navigation, which made him acquainted with geometry, Locke on the Human Understanding, the Art of Thinking by the Port Royalists, and Xenophon's Memorabilia. This sort of education was probably the best for such a mind as Franklin's. It is by no means certain that he would have been so great a philosopher if he had been bred in a university. He is worth contemplating, as he whirls the printer's balls or pulls at the press, silently meditating the questions in logic and mathematics he has studied through the night in his chamber. He perceives that learning is to be his capital for distinction as well as profit, and every principle and combination suggested in his books is revolved in his mind until it is understood, while his hands are so busy with his art.

James Franklin, who had been printer o. the Boston Gazette, the second American newspaper, in 1721, established the fourth one, called the New England Courant, on his own account, and his apprenticed brother carried the copies for subscribers about the city. Anonymously and in a disguised hand he wrote articles for the Courant which were applauded, and by James and his associates attributed in his presence to the cleverest men in Boston. When however the secret was discovered James was displeased, lest the apprentice should become too vain, and from that time treated him with increasing harshness, so that he probably would have broken his indentures had not an unlooked-for circumstance caused them to be surrendered. James was arrested by order of the Assembly and imprisoned on a charge of having published in his paper

8

passages reflecting on the government, the churches, and the college. On being set at liberty he was prohibited from any longer printing the Courant, and after consultation with his friends it was decided to issue it in the name of Benjamin Franklin, whose indentures were therefore cancelled, that they might be shown if any one should be suspicious that the arrangement was but an evasion of the legislative order. Upon their next disagreement, for the new relationship made no difference in the severity of his treatment, he asserted his freedom, and selling his books to obtain money for the expenses of the passage, privately quitted Boston, and in October, 1723, after a fatiguing journey, partly on foot and partly at the oar, reached Philadelphia.

Every one has read in his delightful memoirs—the most natural, ingenuous, and interesting autobiography in our language—of Franklin's arrival in this city ; how with his pockets filled with shirts and stockings, a penny roll under each arm, and eating another, he was seen by Miss Reed, whom he afterward married, walking wearily and awkwardly up Market street, and how he went into a Quaker meeting-house and slept on one of the benches until the people dispersed. "Who would have dreamed," exclaims Brissot de Warville, "that this poor wanderer would become the ornament of the New World, the pride of modern philosophy ?"

After working a short time for the printer Keimer, he attracted the notice of Sir William Keith, governor of the province, who urged him to establish an office on his own account; and he made a journey to Boston, bearing a letter from the governor full of promises of countenance and assurances of success, to ask assistance of his father. But Josiah Franklin thought him too young, and would not help him, though he was proud that his boy had gained so distinguished a friend. "Then," said Sir William, when he heard it, "I myself will set you up, and you shall repay me when you are able ;" and he directed him to be in readiness to go with letters of credit in the next ship to London, that he might in person select the furniture of a printing-house. Franklin accordingly went on board, expecting to find his letters and having for his companion James Ralph, a young Philadelphian, who afterward wrote folio histories, and quarto epics, and,

upon the appearance of his "Night, a poem," was immortalized by Pope in the Dunciad :

Silence, ye wolves, while Ralph to Cynthia howls,
And mak·s *Night* hideous ; answer him, ye owls !

On arriving in London he found that the letters marked to his care had no reference to his business, and that they would have been valueless if of the kind promised, as Keith had no credit for himself. Thus disappointed, he obtained a situation as a compositor, and being employed on an edition of the Religion of Nature, by Wollaston, some of whose reasonings did not appear to him well-founded, he wrote a metaphysical tract in reply, entitled a Dissertation on Liberty and Necessity, Pleasure and Pain, which led to his introduction to Dr. Mandeville, author of the Fable of the Bees, and several other gentlemen, one of whom offered to take him to see the great Newton, who was then alive; but something prevented, and the light of that age set before the new luminary rose above the horizon.

Of Franklin's life in London we have but few glimpses. It is probable that with Ralph he acted some such part as Johnson about the same time did with Savage, though their indulgences could not have been in all respects alike, as Franklin continued to be temperate in his diet. His most expensive amusement was probably the play; but as he attempted to seduce the mistress of his friend, moral principles could not have stood much in the way of his desires. With Ralph's borrowings, and his own habits, though he had constant employment and was a quick workman, he never had money enough to pay his passage to America, and probably would have remained in Europe, had not a Philadelphia shop-keeper, who chanced to be in London, offered to take him home as his clerk. After an absence of nearly two years he reëntered the Delaware, and until the death of his new employer, which occurred a few months afterward, was learning the mysteries of trade ; but that event left him without occupation, and· he returned to Keimer's printing-office, where he remained until he had an opportunity to go into partnership with a young man named Meredith, whose father furnished the necessary capital and offered him half the profits for his attention and skill, and the benefit he expected his son to derive from the connection.

Franklin's ability, industry, and integrity commanded success. Keimer failed and left the country, and his paper was continued and made a source of revenue and influence by Franklin, who soon was able to purchase the interest of his partner, and assume the sole management of the business. Miss Reed, to whom he had been engaged before going to London, and who in consequence of his neglect had suffered herself to be persuaded into a match with an adventurer, who soon afterward was found to have another wife, and compelled to leave the province, was now free again; and by marrying her he "corrected the erratum" of his infidelity. A stationer's shop was opened, which she attended, while he prepared articles for his paper, made contracts, and worked at his trade.

In 1729 Franklin wrote and published an anonymous pamphlet on the Nature and Necessity of a Paper Currency, which in a short time led to the emission of eighty thousand pounds, and much increased his popularity. In 1731 he founded the public library in Philadelphia, and in the following year commenced the publication of Poor Richard's Almanac, celebrated for its maxims of prudence, and which was so well received that in some of the twenty-five years for which it was printed he sold more than ten thousand copies of it. He also founded the American Philosophical Society and the University of Pennsylvania, and was foremost in all enterprises calculated in any way to improve the condition of the people. In 1736 he was chosen clerk of the provincial Assembly; in the following year was made postmaster of Philadelphia; and when the war with France broke out, he published a tract entitled Plain Truth, calling upon the inhabitants of the colony to enrol themselves, to which ten thousand quickly answered with their names. Soon after he was elected a member of the Assembly, and commissioner for making a treaty with the Indians, and in 1753 was appointed postmaster-general for British America, when, the business of his office calling him to New England, Harvard University followed the example of Yale College in presenting him the degree of Master of Arts, in consideration of his improvements in natural philosophy. It was characteristic of our recognitions of genius and learning in Americans, that Yale and Harvard bestowed the Master's degree for the very achievements which soon after led the Oxford, Edinburgh, and St. Andrews universities to declare him a Doctor of Laws.

It was in June, 1752, that Franklin first demonstrated the identity of lightning and electricity, bringing with his hempen lasso the leaping thunderer in perfect docility to acknowledge at his feet the supremacy of man's dominion. While in Boston, six years before, he had seen some imperfect experiments in electricity, which induced him to study the subject, and his investigations had been aided by accounts transmitted by Mr. Peter Collinson, of the Royal Society, to the Philadelphia Library Company. He exhibited ingenuity in experiments, sagacity in deductions, precision in views, and clearness in statements which excited among the learned as much admiration as surprise. As Lord Jeffrey well observes, "the most profound explanations are suggested by him as if they were the most obvious and natural way of accounting for phenomena," and he seems to pride himself so little upon his most splendid discoveries that it is necessary to compare him with others before we can form a just opinion of his merits. The same simplicity, perspicuity, and frankness are shown in the papers respecting all his inventions, discoveries, and observations. His prime aim in every thing was to benefit mankind. Alluding to his contrivance of magical squares, he says, that however wonderful these arithmetical amusements may seem, he cannot value himself upon them, but is rather ashamed to have it known that he had spent any part of his time in an employment that could "not possibly be of any use to himself or others." The construction of fireplaces, improvements in navigation, and other subjects of practical importance were far more interesting to him.

While pursuing his philosophical inquiries, the results of which from 1747 to 1754 were detailed in letters to Mr. Collinson, he was still busy in the public service. At the head of five hundred men he had gone through a laborious campaign in the interior of Pennsylvania, and he had attended and been a principal actor in the congress which assembled at Albany and recommended a union of the colonies under a royal president. It may be regarded as a proof of the excel lence of his plan, which was accepted by the Congress, that it was refused by the assemblies on the ground that it gave too much authority to the crown, and by the ministry because it yielded too much to the representatives of the people. He had been several years the leader of the Assembly of Pennsylvania in a controversy with the governor, who was appointed by the heirs of William Penn and instructed by them to approve no laws for taxing their estates, even for the common defence; and in 1757 he was chosen an agent to represent the province in England, and if unable otherwise to procure redress of grievances, to petition for a change in the charter, so that the chief magistrate might be appointed by the king. His Letters on Electricity had previously been published, in a quarto volume, under the direction of one of his correspondents, and "nothing," says Priestley, "was ever written on the subject more justly applauded. All the world, even kings, flocked to see them, and retired full of admiration." They were verified in Paris before Louis XV. by M. de Loz, in Turin by M. Beccaria, in Russia by Professor Richmann, who was killed by lightning while making one of the experiments, and by not less eminent persons in other parts of Europe. The Royal Society, too, repenting of previous neglect, had elected him a fellow and presented him the Copley medal. As soon as it was known therefore that he was in London, the most distinguished men of that metropolis hastened to pay their respects to him, and the scholars of the continent quickly followed with letters of congratulation. For two months he was confined to his room by illness, but as soon as his health permitted he devoted himself with assiduity to the business of his mission. Early in 1759, to disabuse the popular mind of prejudices which had been created by the partisans of the proprietors, he published a large volume entitled An Historical Review of Pennsylvania, of which he was long supposed to be the author, though it is now certain that he wrote very little of it. It was prepared, under his direction, probably by Ralph, who had now been in England more than thirty years, and was esteemed one of the best political writers in the kingdom. He was finally successful with the ministry, who decided that the landholders should bear a just proportion of the public burdens, and in 1762, having passed five years in Great Britain, he returned to America. While abroad he had written his celebrated pamphlet on the acquisition of Canada and Guadaloupe, distinguished for extraordinary clearness, compactness, and force of reason, and several important papers on scientific subjects; and had added largely to the number of his acquaintances among statesmen and men of letters, particularly Lord Kaimes, David Hume, and Dr. Robertson, with whom he many years kept up an intimate correspondence. Alluding to a visit to his friends in Scotland, made in the summer of 1759, he says that on the whole the time spent among them was "six weeks of the *densest* happiness" he had met with in any part of his life.

Soon after his return, being still colonial postmaster-general, he spent several months in visiting and inspecting the northern and eastern offices. He travelled sixteen hundred miles in a light carriage, driven by himself, with a saddle-horse attached on which his daughter, who accompanied him, occasionally rode. In the different towns he was received with flattering hospitalities by his old friends, and in some of them was detained many days. Upon his return to Philadelphia he entered with characteristic ardor upon public affairs. He was the first citizen of the province, and in every emergency acted with a fearlessness only equalled by his wisdom. The indignant eloquence of his pamphlet on the Paxton insurrection, showed with what feelings he regarded popular violence, and the people might have seen in his stern respect for law the best proof of his fitness for the high duties to which they called him. He perceived, what every man worthy of freedom perceives, that the laws of a state should be as certain of execution as decrees of God, no possible contingency justifying the slightest deviation from them, and proofs of oppressiveness of any kind of unfitness having no proper use but as arguments for modification, or in extremity for revolution.

The controversy between the proprietors and the inhabitants was not yet ended. The administration was inefficient, and every part of the public service embarrassed. In a pamphlet entitled Cool Thoughts on the Present Situation of Affairs, he showed that the evils which all acknowledged to exist were inherent in the nature of the government, and that it was necessary at once to take the chief appointing power from the foreign landholders. A large majority of the people and of the Assembly were of this opinion, and in 1764 Franklin proceeded a second time to England, with a petition for a change of the charter, and to manage the general affairs of the province. But all local controversies were soon forgotten in preparations for a more general and important conflict.

The plan for taxing the colonies had created a profound sensation, and clearsighted men in both countries saw the storm that was approaching. Franklin was appointed agent for Massachusetts, New Jersey, and Georgia, and was looked upon as the representative of the whole American people. In his memorable examination before the House of Commons, in 1766, his simplicity, composure, and firmness, the precision of his language, and the astonishing fulness and impressive character of his information, produced such an effect that the stamp act was repealed. That spirit of obedience, that respect for what is established, as being to us in the place of destiny until reversed by the operation of fit causes, to which allusion has been made, still marked his conduct. It was a part, and one of the best parts, of his nature. He protested, warned, and made argument against the policy of the ministers, as tending to revolution, but was one of the last to revolt. When he saw that that "noble vase," as he styled the British empire, in a letter to Lord Howe, was to be broken, that the civil war which he had laboured with such unwearied earnestness to avert was to come at last with all its dire calamities, he may have faltered a moment, as one who thinks of toil unprofitably spent; but America was to Europe then the country of Franklin, and his wise conduct,—his prudence, moderation, and firmness,—which the rabble on both sides called treason, had its uses, and gained for us a national character, before we had a national existence. The great Lord Chatham did not hesitate, while some in the parliament-house were planning his arrest, to speak of him as t' one who was an honour not to England only, but to human nature;" and the manner in which his grateful countrymen received him, showed that there were few here who did not justly appreciate his character and services.

Immediately after his return he was elected a member of the Congress, then sitting in Philadelphia. Though he seldom addressed that body, he was one of its most efficient members, serving constantly on its important committees. After signing the Declaration of Independence, he was appointed minister plenipotentiary to France, and placing his property at the disposal of Congress, he departed for Paris, where he arrived near the close of December, 1776.

He was not at first formally received by the court, but the French people welcomed him with more than even their characteristic enthusiasm. Portraits of the venerable old man, who joined, it was said, the demeanour of Phocion to the spirit of Socrates, were everywhere to be seen, with Turgot's sublime inscription,

"Eripuit cœlo fulmen, sceptrumque tyrannis;"

busts and prints of him were multiplied and sold in extraordinary numbers; his head was represented on medalions set in snuff-boxes, or worn by both sexes in rings, brooches, and other ornaments; the most eminent persons thronged his house at Passy, and crowds in the streets greeted him with acclamations when he appeared in the city. The aged Voltaire, who, after having received the homage of one generation, reappeared, with a new tragedy, in the midst of anothe , to be crowned with chaplets by posterity, was then in Paris, and when they met, though he had long ceased to speak our language, he made the attempt, and failing, added, " Je n'ai pû résister au desir de parler un moment la langue de Franklin." The philosopher presented his grandson, and asked a blessing: " God and Liberty," said the poet, "is the only one fitting for Franklin's children." The great men met again, says Lord Brougham, at a public sitting of the Academy, and when they took their places, side by side, and shook hands together, a burst of applause involuntarily rose from the whole assembly. After this picture it is needless to detail the story of his negotiations with the court. " His virtues and his renown," observes the historian Lacretelle, " negotiated for him, and before the second year of his mission had expired, no one conceived it possible to refuse fleets and an army to the compatriots of Franklin."

When he had signed the treaty of a !i nce

F

with France, and the definitive treaty of peace with Great Britain, he requested permission to retire from the public service, in which he had now passed more than half a century. But it was still three years before Congress could be induced to appoint his successor. His last official act in Europe was the signing of the treaty with Prussia, containing his philanthropic article against privateering and for the protection of private property in time of war. The emperor of Austria had invited him to visit Vienna, but he was too feeble. The queen's litter was kindly offered him for his journey to Havre, where he arrived in six days after leaving Passy; and on the fourteenth of September, 1785, when he was in the eightieth year of his age, he landed at Philadelphia, on the spot where he had stood sixty-three years before, a poor and friendless youth. Now he was greeted with the acclamations of an admiring people, with the ringing of bells and the discharge of artillery—one of the proudest triumphs in history, won without an act of violence or crime.

For three years he was president of the commonwealth, and in 1787 he sat with Washington and Hamilton in the federal convention which gave his countrymen the freest of constitutions. He had lived long; he had learned that "God governs in the affairs of men," he said, in one of his brief speeches, in which he proposed that the convention in daily prayers should seek His guidance and protection. The last year of his presidency ended in October, 1788, and after that time, though he was often consulted on public affairs, he held no office in the government.

He resided in Philadelphia, with his daughter and grandchildren, in such dignified repose as became a philosopher and sage, until the seventeenth of April, 1790, when he died. " Benjamin and Deborah Franklin, 1790," is the simple and only inscription upon the plain marble under which, with the partner of his youth and middle age, he is sleeping. No column has been raised to him. None is needed.

The news of his death reached Paris, and Mirabeau announced in the General Assembly that " the genius which had freed America and poured a flood of light over Europe, had returned to the bosom of the Divinity." "Every where," to use the language of Rochefoucauld, "he was the object of the regrets, as he had been of the admiration of the friends of liberty."

In all respects Franklin's character was remarkable. The acuteness, solidity and practicalness of his understanding are not more striking than his happy temper. Whether assailed to his face by a brutal Wedderburn, or covertly slandered by an envious and feeble Izard; made the idol of a frivolous court, or greeted with acclamations by an assembly of academicians; he maintained the same unvarying serenity. He would have been more or less than man if insensible of his successes and celebrity, but he was not more humble when trundling paper on a wheelbarrow through the streets, than when standing, the observed of all observers, in the presence of kings; when chronicling the results of everyday experience, than when unfolding the profoundest mysteries of nature; when reconciling the differences of his shop-mates, than when making treaties between belligerent empires.

His moral writings have had a powerful influence upon the character of the American people. They are eminently distinguished for what is called common sense. Their tone is rather below than above that of most similar compositions. His ideal of utility is too humble. His virtue is the doing good to mankind, not for its own sweetness, but that they may do good to us. Yet the sort of persons he addressed, in the essays of " Richard Saunders" and in much of his familiar correspondence, should not be forgotten. Nothing could be better suited to their understandings and conditions.

Franklin's style is in all respects admirable. That of his scientific papers, in simplicity, clearness, precision and condensation is unparalleled. Discarding the symbols of geometry, and indeed all technical language, he succeeded in presenting the most difficult problems and abstruse speculations in the shortest space, and so perspicuously that a child could perfectly understand them. That of his letters and essays is various, but always excellent. It is much better than Addison's, of whom he has absurdly been called a copyist, because he mentions as one of his boyish experiments an attempt to write in the manner of the Spectator. It is more concise and pointed, clear and forcible, and has quite as much wit and humour, ease and elegance. Bowditch might as well be called an imitator of Daboll because he once worked out some of the propositions of that famous arithmetician.

THE WAY TO WEALTH.

COURTEOUS READER, I have heard, that nothing gives an author so great pleasure as to find his works respectfully quoted by others. Judge, then, how much I must have been gratified by an incident I am going to relate to you. I stopped my horse lately, where a great number of people were collected to a auction of merchants' goods. The hour of the sale not being come, they were conversing on the badness of the times; and one of the company called to a plain, clean, old man, with white locks, "Pray, Father Abraham, what think you of the times? Will not these heavy taxes quite ruin the country? How shall we ever be able to pay them? What would you advise us to!" Father Abraham stood up and replied, "If you would have my advice, I will give it you in short; for *A word to the wise is enough*, as Poor Richard says." They joined in desiring him to speak his mind, and gathering round him, he proceeded as follows.

" Friends," said he, "the taxes are indeed very heavy, and, if those laid on by the government were the only ones we had to pay, we might more easily discharge them; but we have many others, and much more grievous to some of us. We are taxed twice as much by our idleness, three times as much by our pride, and four times as much by our folly; and from these taxes the commissioners cannot ease or deliver us, by allowing an abatement. However, let us hearken to good advice, and something may be done for us; *God helps them that help themselves*, as Poor Richard says.

"I. It would be thought a hard government, that should tax its people one-tenth part of their time, to be employed in its service; but idleness taxes many of us much more; sloth, by bringing on diseases, absolutely shortens life. *Sloth, like rust, consumes faster than labour wears; while the used key is always bright*, as Poor Richard says. But *dost thou love life, then do not squander time, for that is the stuff life is made of*, as Poor Richard says. How much more than is necessary do we spend in sleep, forgetting, that *The sleeping fox catches no poultry*, and that *There will be sleeping enough in the grave*, as Poor Richard says.

" *If time be of all things the most precious, wasting time must be*, as Poor Richard says, *the greatest prodigality*; since, as he elsewhere tells us, *Lost time is never found again; and what we call time enough, always proves little enough*. Let us then up and be doing, and doing to the purpose; so by diligence shall we do more with less perplexity. *Sloth makes all things difficult, but industry all easy* · and *He that riseth late must trot all day, and shall scarce overtake his business at night; while Laziness travels so slowly, that Poverty soon overtakes him. Drive thy business, let not that drive thee;* and *Early to bed, and early to rise, makes a man healthy, wealthy, and wise*, as Poor Richard says.

" So what signifies wishing and hoping for better times? We may make these times better, if we bestir ourselves. *Industry need not wish, and he that lives upon hopes will die fasting. There are no gains without pains; then help, hands, for I have no lands;* or, if I have, they are smartly taxed. *He that hath a trade hath an estate; and he that hath a calling, hath an office of profit and honour,* as Poor Richard says; but then the trade must be worked at, and the calling followed, or neither the estate nor the office will enable us to pay our taxes. If we are industrious, we shall never starve; for, *At the working man's house hunger looks in, but dares not enter.* Nor will the bailiff or the constable enter, for *Industry pays debts, while despair increaseth them.* What though you have found no treasure, nor has any rich relation left you a legacy, *Diligence is the mother of good luck, and God gives all things to industry. Then plough deep while sluggards sleep, and you shall have corn to sell and to keep.* Work while it is called to-day, for you know not how much you may be hindered to-morrow. *One to-day is worth two to-morrows,* as Poor Richard says; and further, *Never leave that till to-morrow, which you can do to-day.* If you were a servant, would you not be ashamed that a good master should catch you idle? Are you then your own master? Be ashamed to catch yourself idle, when there is so much to be done for yourself, your family, your country, and your king. Handle your tools without mittens; remember, that *The cat in gloves catches no mice,* as Poor Richard says. It is true there is much to be done, and perhaps you are weak-handed; but stick to it steadily, and you will see great effects; for *Constant dropping wears away stones;* and *By diligence and patience the mouse ate in two the cable;* and *Little strokes fell great oaks.*

" Methinks I hear some of you say, 'Must a man afford himself no leisure?' I will tell thee, my friend, what Poor Richard says: *Employ thy time well, if thou meanest to gain leisure; and, since thou art not sure of a minute, throw not away an hour.* Leisure is time for doing something useful; this leisure the diligent man will obtain; but the lazy man never; for *A life of leisure and a life of laziness are two things. Many, without labour, would live by their wits only, but they break for want of stock;* whereas, industry gives comfort, and plenty, and respect. *Fly pleasures, and they will follow you. The diligent spinner has a large shift;* and now I have a sheep and a cow, everybody bids me good morrow.

" II. But with our industry we must likewise be steady, settled, and careful, and oversee our own affairs, with our own eyes, and not trust too much to others; for, as Poor Richard says,

I never saw an oft-removed tree,
Nor yet an oft-removed family,
That throve so well as those that settled be.

And again, *Three removes are as bad as a fire* and again, *Keep thy shop, and thy shop will keep thee;* and again, *If you would have your business done, go; if not, send.* And again,

He that by the plough would thrive,
Himself must either hold or drive

And again, *The eye of a master will do more work than both his hands;* and again, *Want of care does us more damage than want of knowledge;* and again, *Not to oversee workmen, is to leave them your purse open.* Trusting too much to others' care is the ruin of many; for *In the affairs of this world men are saved, not by faith, but by the want of it;* but a man's own care is profitable; for, *If you would have a faithful servant, and one that you like, serve yourself. A little neglect may breed great mischief; for want of a nail the shoe was lost; for want of a shoe the horse was lost; and for want of a horse the rider was lost, being overtaken and slain by the enemy; all for want of a little care about a horseshoe nail.*

"III. So much for industry, my friends, and attention to one's own business; but to these we must add frugality, if we would make our industry more certainly successful. A man may, if he knows not how to save as he gets, keep his nose all his life to the grindstone, and die not worth a groat at last. *A fat kitchen makes a lean will;* and

Many estates are spent in the getting,
Since women for tea forsook spinning and knitting,
And men for punch forsook hewing and splitting.

If you would be wealthy, think of saving as well as of getting. The Indies have not made Spain rich, because her outgoes are greater than her incomes.

"Away then with your expensive follies, and you will not then have so much cause to complain of hard times, heavy taxes, and chargeable families; for

Women and wine, game and deceit,
Make the wealth small and the want great.

And further, *What maintains one vice would bring up two children.* You may think, perhaps, that a little tea, or a little punch now and then, diet a little more costly, clothes a little finer, and a little entertainment now and then, can be no great matter; but remember, *Many a little makes a mickle.* Beware of little expenses; *A small leak will sink a great ship,* as Poor Richard says; and again, *Who dainties love, shall beggars prove;* and moreover, *Fools make feasts, and wise men eat them.*

"Here you are all got together at this sale of fineries and knick-knacks. You call them *goods;* but, if you do not take care, they will prove *evils* to some of you. You expect they will be sold cheap, and perhaps they may for less than they cost; but, if you have no occasion for them, they must be dear to you. Remember what Poor Richard says: *Buy what thou hast no need of, and ere long thou shalt sell thy necessaries.* And again, *At a great pennyworth pause a while.* He means, that perhaps the cheapness is apparent only, and not real; or the bargain, by straitening thee in thy business, may do thee more harm than good. For in another place he says, *Many have been ruined by buying good pennyworths.* Again, *It is foolish to lay out money in a purchase of repentance;* and yet this folly is practised every day at auctions, for want of minding the Almanac. Many a one, for the sake of finery on the back, have

gone with a hungry belly and half-starved their families. *Silks and satins, scarlet and velvets, put out the kitchen fire,* as Poor Richard says.

"These are not the necessaries of life; they can scarcely be called the conveniences; and yet, only because they look pretty, how many want to have them! By these, and other extravagances, the genteel are reduced to poverty, and forced to borrow of those whom they formerly despised, but who, through industry and frugality, have maintained their standing; in which case it appears plainly, that *A ploughman on his legs is higher than a gentleman on his knees,* as Poor Richard says. Perhaps they have had a small estate left them, which they knew not the getting of; they think, *It is day, and will never be night;* that a little to be spent out of so much is not worth minding; but *Always taking out of the meal-tub, and never putting in, soon comes to the bottom,* as Poor Richard says; and then, *When the well is dry, they know the worth of water.* But this they might have known before, if they had taken his advice. *If you would know the value of money, go and try to borrow some; for he that goes a borrowing goes a sorrowing,* as Poor Richard says; and indeed so does he that lends to such people, when he goes to get it in again. Poor Dick further advises and says,

Fond pride of dress is sure a very curse;
Ere fancy you consult, consult your purse.

And again, *Pride is as loud a beggar as Want, and a great deal more saucy.* When you have bought one fine thing, you must buy ten more, that your appearance may be all of a piece; but Poor Dick says, *It is easier to suppress the first desire, than to satisfy all that follow it.* And it is as truly folly for the poor to ape the rich, as for the frog to swell in order to equal the ox.

Vessels large may venture more,
But little boats should keep near shore.

It is, however, a folly soon punished; for as Poor Richard says, *Pride that dines on vanity, sups on contempt. Pride breakfasted with Plenty, dined with Poverty, and supped with Infamy.* And, after all, of what use is this pride of appearance, for which so much is risked, so much is suffered? It cannot promote health, nor ease pain; it makes no increase of merit in the person; it creates envy; it hastens misfortune.

"But what madness must it be to *run in debt* for these superfluities? We are offered, by the terms of this sale, six months' credit; and that, perhaps, has induced some of us to attend it, because we cannot spare the ready money, and hope now to be fine without it. But, ah! think what you do when you run in debt; you give to another power over your liberty. If you cannot pay at the time, you will be ashamed to see your creditor; you will be in fear when you speak to him; you will make poor, pitiful, sneaking excuses, and, by degrees, come to lose your veracity, and sink into base, downright lying; for *The second vice is lying, the first is running in debt,* as Poor Richard says; and again, to the same purpose, *Lying rides upon Debt's back :* whereas a free-born Englishman ought not to be ashamed nor afraid to see or speak to any man living. But poverty often deprives a man of all spirit and virtue. *It is hard for an empty bag to stand upright.*

" What would you think of that prince, or of that government, who should issue an edict forbidding you to dress like a gentleman or gentlewoman, on pain of imprisonment or servitude ? Would you not say that you were free, have a right to dress as you 'please, and that such an edict would be a breach of your privileges, and such a government tyrannical ? And yet you are about to put yourself under such tyranny, when you run in debt for such dress ! Your creditor has authority, at his pleasure, to deprive you of your liberty, by confining you in jail till you shall be able to pay him. When you have got your bargain, you may, perhaps, think little of payment; but, as Poor Richard says, *Creditors have better memories than debtors ; creditors are a superstitious sect, great observers of set days and times.* The day comes round before you are aware, and the demand is made before you are prepared to satisfy it; or, if you bear your debt in mind, the term, which at first seemed so long, will, as it lessens, appear extremely short. Time will seem to have added wings to his heels as well as his shoulders. *Those have a short Lent, who owe money to be paid at Easter.* At present, perhaps, you may think yourselves in thriving circumstances, and that you can bear a little extravagance without injury; but

For age and want save while you may ;
No morning sun lasts a whole day.

Gain may be temporary and uncertain, but ever, while you live, expense is constant and certain; and *It is easier to build two chimneys, than to keep one in fuel,* as Poor Richard says; so, *Rather go to bed supperless, than rise in debt.*

Get what you can, and what you get hold ;
' Tis the stone that will turn all your lead into gold.

And, when you have got the Philosopher's stone, sure you will no longer complain of bad times, or the difficulty of paying taxes.

" IV. This doctrine, my friends, is reason and wisdom; but, after all, do not depend too much upon your own industry, and frugality, and prudence, though excellent things; for they may all be blasted, without the blessing of Heaven; and, therefore, ask that blessing humbly, and be not uncharitable to those that at present seem to want it, but comfort and help them. Remember, Job suffered, and was afterwards prosperous.

" And now, to conclude, *Experience keeps a dear school, but fools will learn in no other,* as Poor Richard says, and scarce in that; for, it is true, *We may give advice, but we cannot give conduct.* However, remember this, *They that will not be counselled, cannot be helped ;* and further, that, *If you will not hear Reason, she will surely rap your knuckles,* as Poor Richard says."

Thus the old gentleman ended his harangue. The people heard it, and approved the doctrine;

9

and immediately practised the contrary, just as if it had been a common sermon; for the auction opened, and they began to buy extravagantly. I found the good man had thoroughly studied my Almanacs, and digested all I had dropped on these topics during the course of twenty-five years. The frequent mention he made of me must have tired any one else ; but my vanity was wonderfully delighted with it, though I was conscious that not a tenth part of the wisdom was my own, which he ascribed to me, but rather the gleanings that I had made of the sense of all ages and nations. However, I resolved to be the better for the echo of it; and, though I had at first determined to buy stuff for a new coat, I went away resolved to wear my old one a little longer. Reader, if thou wilt do the same, thy profit wilt be as great as mine. I am, as ever, thine to serve thee,

RICHARD SAUNDERS.

————◆————

MORALS OF CHESS.

PLAYING at chess is the most ancient and most universal game known among men ; for its original is beyond the memory of history, and it has, for numberless ages, been the amusement of all the civilized nations of Asia, the Persians, the Indians, and the Chinese. Europe has had it above a thousand years; the Spaniards have spread it over their part of America; and it has lately begun to make its appearance in the United States. It is so interesting in itself, as not to need the view of gain to induce engaging in it; and thence it is seldom played for money. Those, therefore, who have leisure for such diversions, cannot find one that is more innocent; and the following piece, written with a view to correct (among a few young friends) some little improprieties in the practice of it, shows at the same time that it may, in its effects on the mind, be not merely innocent, but advantageous, to the vanquished as well as the victor.

The game of chess is not merely an idle amusement. Several very valuable qualities of the mind, useful in the course of human life, are to be acquired or strengthened by it, so as to become habits, ready on all occasions. For life is a kind of chess, in which we have often points to gain, and competitors or adversaries to contend with, and in which there is a vast variety of good and evil events, that are in some degree the effects of prudence or the want of it. By playing at chess, then, we may learn,

I. *Foresight,* which looks a little into futurity, and considers the consequences that may attend an action; for it is continually occurring to the player, " If I move this piece, what will be the advantage of my new situation ? What use can my adversary make of it to annoy me ? What other moves can I make to support it, and to defend myself from his attacks ?"

II. *Circumspection,* which surveys the whole

F 2

chessboard, or scene of action; the relations of the several pieces and situations, the dangers they are respectively exposed to, the several possibilities of their aiding each other, the probabilities that the adversary may make this or that move, and attack this or the other piece, and what different means can be used to avoid his stroke, or turn its consequences against him.

III. *Caution*, not to make our moves too hastily. This habit is best acquired by observing strictly the laws of the game; such as, " If you touch a piece, you must move it somewhere; if you set it down, you must let it stand;" and it is therefore best that these rules should be observed, as the game thereby becomes more the image of human life, and particularly of war; in which, if you have incautiously put yourself into a bad and dangerous position, you cannot obtain your enemy's leave to withdraw your troops, and place them more securely, but you must abide all the consequences of your rashness.

And, lastly, we learn by chess the habit of *not being discouraged by present appearances in the state of our affairs*, the habit of *hoping for a favourable change*, and that of *persevering in the search of resources*. The game is so full of events, there is such a variety of turns in it, the fortune of it is so subject to sudden vicissitudes, and one so frequently, after long contemplation, discovers the means of extricating one's self from a supposed insurmountable difficulty, that one is encouraged to continue the contest to the last, in hopes of victory by our own skill, or at least of getting a stale mate, by the negligence of our adversary. And whoever considers, what in chess he often sees instances of, that particular pieces of success are apt to produce presumption, and its consequent inattention, by which the losses may be recovered, will learn not to be too much discouraged by the present success of his adversary, nor to despair of final good fortune upon every little check he receives in the pursuit of it.

That we may therefore be induced more frequently to choose this beneficial amusement, in preference to others which are not attended with the same advantages, every circumstance which may increase the pleasures of it should be regarded; and every action or word that is unfair, disrespectful, or that in any way may give uneasiness, should be avoided, as contrary to the immediate intention of both the players, which is to pass the time agreeably.

Therefore, first, if it is agreed to play according to the strict rules, then those rules are to be exactly observed by both parties, and should not be insisted on for one side, while deviated from by the other, for this is not equitable.

Secondly, if it is agreed not to observe the rules exactly, but one party demands indulgences, he should then be as willing to allow them to the other.

Thirdly, no false move should ever be made to extricate yourself out of difficulty, or to gain an advantage. There can be no pleasure in playing with a person once detected in such unfair practice.

Fourthly, if your adversary is long in playing, you ought not to hurry him, or express any uneasiness at his delay. You should not sing, nor whistle, nor look at your watch, nor take up a book to read, nor make a tapping with your feet on the floor, or with your fingers on the table, nor do any thing that may disturb his attention. For all these things displease; and they do not show your skill in playing, but your craftiness or your rudeness.

Fifthly, you ought not to endeavour to amuse and deceive your adversary, by pretending to have made bad moves, and saying, that you have now lost the game, in order to make him secure and careless, and inattentive to your schemes; for this is fraud and deceit, not skill in the game.

Sixthly, you must not, when you have gained a victory, use any triumphing or insulting expression, nor show too much pleasure; but endeavour to console your adversary, and make him less dissatisfied with himself, by every kind of civil expression that may be used with truth, such as, " You understand the game better than I, but you are a little inattentive;" or, " You play too fast;" or, " You had the best of the game, but something happened to divert your thoughts, and that turned it in my favour."

Seventhly, if you are a spectator while others play, observe the most perfect silence. For, if you give advice, you offend both parties, him against whom you give it, because it may cause the loss of his game, him in whose favour you may give it, because, though it be good, and he follows it, he loses the pleasure he might have had, if you had permitted him to think until it had occurred to himself. Even after a move or moves, you must not, by replacing the pieces, show how they might have been placed better; for that displeases, and may occasion disputes and doubts about their true situation. All talking to the players lessens or diverts their attention, and is therefore unpleasing. Nor should you give the least hint to either party, by any kind of noise or motion. If you do, you are unworthy to be a spectator. If you have a mind to exercise or show your judgment, do it in playing your own game, when you have an opportunity, not in criticising, or meddling with, or counselling the play of others.

Lastly, if the game is not to be played rigorously, according to the rules above mentioned, then moderate your desire of victory over your adversary, and be pleased with one over yourself. Snatch not eagerly at every advantage offered by his unskilfulness or inattention; but point out to him kindly, that by such a move he places or leaves a piece in danger and unsupported; that by another he will put his king in a perilous situation, &c. By this generous civility (so opposite to the unfairness above forbidden) you may, indeed, happen to lose the game to your opponent; but you will win, what is better, his esteem, his respect, and his affection, together with the silent approbation and good-will of impartial spectators.

DIALOGUE WITH THE GOUT.

Midnight, 22 October, 1780.

Franklin. Eh! Oh! Eh! What have I done to merit these cruel sufferings?

Gout. Many things; you have ate and drank too freely, and too much indulged those legs of yours in their indolence.

Franklin. Who is it that accuses me?

Gout. It is I, even I, the Gout.

Franklin. What! my enemy in person?

Gout. No, not your enemy.

Franklin. I repeat it—my enemy; for you would not only torment my body to death, but ruin my good name; you reproach me as a glutton and a tippler; now all the world that knows me, will allow that I am neither the one nor the other.

Gout. The world may think as it pleases; it is always very complaisant to itself, and sometimes to its friends; but I very well know that the quantity of meat and drink proper for a man, who takes a reasonable degree of exercise, would be too much for another, who never takes any.

Franklin. I take—Eh! Oh!—as much exercise—Eh!—as I can, Madam Gout. You know my sedentary state, and on that account, it would seem, Madam Gout, as if you might spare me a little, seeing it is not altogether my own fault.

Gout. Not a jot; your rhetoric and your politeness are thrown away; your apology avails nothing. If your situation in life is a sedentary one, your amusements, your recreations, at least, should be active. You ought to walk or ride; or, if the weather prevents that, play at billiards. But let us examine your course of life. While the mornings are long, and you have leisure to go abroad, what do you do? Why, instead of gaining an appetite for breakfast, by salutary exercise, you amuse yourself with books, pamphlets, or newspapers, which commonly are not worth the reading. Yet you eat an inordinate breakfast, four dishes of tea, with cream, and one or two buttered toasts, with slices of hung beef, which I fancy are not things the most easily digested. Immediately afterward you sit down to write at your desk, or converse with persons who apply to you on business. Thus the time passes till one, without any kind of bodily exercise. But all this I could pardon, in regard, as you say, to your sedentary condition. But what is your practice after dinner? Walking in the beautiful gardens of those friends with whom you have dined, would be the choice of men of sense; yours is to be fixed down to chess, where you are found engaged for two or three hours! This is your perpetual recreation, which is the least eligible of any for a sedentary man, because, instead of accelerating the motion of the fluids, the rigid attention it requires helps to retard the circulation and obstruct internal secretions. Wrapt in the speculations of this wretched game, you destroy your constitution. What can be expected from such a course of living, but a body replete with stagnant humors, ready to fall a prey to all kinds of dangerous maladies, if I, the Gout, did not occasionally bring you relief by agitating those humors, and so purifying or dissipating them? If it was in some nook or alley in Paris, deprived of walks, that you played awhile at chess after dinner, this might be excusable; but the same taste prevails with you in Passy, Auteuil, Montmartre, or Sanoy, places where there are the finest gardens and walks, a pure air, beautiful women, and most agreeable and instructive conversation; all of which you might enjoy by frequenting the walks. But these are rejected for this abominable game of chess. Fie, then, Mr. Franklin! But amidst my instructions, I had almost forgot to administer my wholesome corrections; so take that twinge,—and that.

Franklin. Oh! Eh! Oh! Ohhh! As much instruction as you please, Madam Gout, and as many reproaches; but pray, Madam, a truce with your corrections!

Gout. No, sir, no,—I will not abate a particle of what is so much for your good,—therefore—

Franklin. Oh! Ehhh!—It is not fair to say I take no exercise, when I do very often, going out to dine and returning in my carriage.

Gout. That, of all imaginable exercises, is the most slight and insignificant, if you allude to the motion of a carriage suspended on springs. By observing the degree of heat obtained by different kinds of motion, we may form an estimate of the quantity of exercise given by each. Thus, for example, if you turn out to walk in winter with cold feet, in an hour's time you will be in a glow all over; ride on horseback, the same effect will scarcely be perceived by four hours' round trotting; but if you loll in a carriage, such as you have mentioned, you may travel all day, and gladly enter the last inn to warm your feet by a fire. Flatter yourself then no longer, that half an hour's airing in your carriage deserves the name of exercise. Providence has appointed few to roll in carriages, while he has given to all a pair of legs, which are machines infinitely more commodious and serviceable. Be grateful, then, and make a proper use of yours. Would you know how they forward the circulation of your fluids, in the very action of transporting you from place to place; observe when you walk, that all your weight is alternately thrown from one leg to the other; this occasions a great pressure on the vessels of the foot, and repels their contents; when relieved, by the weight being thrown on the other foot, the vessels of the first are allowed to replenish, and, by a return of this weight, this repulsion again succeeds; thus accelerating the circulation of the blood. The heat produced in any given time depends on the degree of this acceleration; the fluids are shaken, the humors attenuated, the secretions facilitated, and all goes well; the cheeks are ruddy, and health is established. Behold your fair friend at Auteuil;* a lady who received from bounteous nature more really useful science than half a dozen such pretenders to philosophy as you have been able to extract from all your books. When

---

* Madame Helvetius.

she honours you with a visit, it is on foot. She walks all hours of the day, and leaves indolence, and its concomitant maladies, to be endured by her horses. In this see at once the preservative of her health and personal charms. But when you go to Auteuil, you must have your carriage, though it is no further from Passy to Auteuil than from Auteuil to Passy.

Franklin. Your reasonings grow very tiresome.

Gout. I stand corrected. I will be silent and continue my office; take that, and that.

Franklin. Oh! Ohh! Talk on, I pray you!

Gout. No, no; I have a good number of twinges for you to-night, and you may be sure of some more to-morrow.

Franklin. What, with such a fever! I shall go distracted. Oh! Eh! Can no one bear it for me?

Gout. Ask that of your horses; they have served you faithfully.

Franklin. How can you so cruelly sport with my torments?

Gout. Sport! I am very serious. I have here a list of offences against your own health distinctly written, and can justify every stroke inflicted on you.

Franklin. Read it then.

Gout. It is too long a detail; but I will briefly mention some particulars.

Franklin. Proceed. I am all attention.

Gout. Do you remember how often you have promised yourself, the following morning, a walk in the grove of Boulogne, in the garden de la Muette, or in your own garden, and have violated your promise, alleging, at one time, it was too cold, at another too warm, too windy, too moist, or what else you pleased; when in truth it was too nothing, but your insuperable love of ease?

Franklin. That I confess may have happened occasionally, probably ten times in a year.

Gout. Your confession is very far short of the truth; the gross amount is one hundred and ninety-nine times.

Franklin. Is it possible?

Gout. So possible, that it is fact; you may rely on the accuracy of my statement. You know Mr. Brillon's gardens, and what fine walks they contain; you know the handsome flight of an hundred steps, which lead from the terrace above to the lawn below. You have been in the practice of visiting this amiable family twice a week, after dinner, and it is a maxim of your own, that " a man may take as much exercise in walking a mile, up and down stairs, as in ten on level ground." What an opportunity was here for you to have had exercise in both these ways! Did you embrace it, and how often?

Franklin. I cannot immediately answer that question.

Gout. I will do it for you; not once.

Franklin. Not once!

Gout. Even so. During the summer you went there at six o'clock. You found the charming lady, with her lovely children and friends, eager to walk with you, and entertain you with their agreeable conversation; and what has been your choice? Why to sit on the terrace, satisfying yourself with the fine prospect, and passing your eye over the beauties of the garden below, without taking one step to descend and walk about in them. On the contrary, you call for tea and the chessboard; and lo! you are occupied in your seat till nine o'clock, and that besides two hours' play after dinner; and then, instead of walking home, which would have bestirred you a little, you step into your carriage. How absurd to suppose that all this carelessness can be reconcilable with health, without my interposition!

Franklin. I am convinced now of the justness of poor Richard's remark. that " Our debts and our sins are always greater than we think for."

Gout. So it is. You philosophers are sages in your maxims, and fools in your conduct.

Franklin. But do you charge among my crimes, that I return in a carriage from Mr. Brillon's?

Gout. Certainly; for, having been seated all the while, you cannot object the fatigue of the day, and cannot want therefore the relief of a carriage.

Franklin. What then would you have me to do with my carriage?

Gout. Burn it if you choose; you would at least get heat out of it once in this way; or, if you dislike that proposal, here's another for you; observe the poor peasants, who work in the vineyards and grounds about the villages of Passy, Auteuil, Chaillot, &c.; you may find every day, among these deserving creatures, four or five old men and women, bent and perhaps crippled by weight of years, and too long and too great labour. After a most fatiguing day, these people have to trudge a mile or two to their smoky huts. Order your coachman to set them down. This is an act that will be good for your soul; and, at the same time, after your visit to the Brillons, if you return on foot, that will be good for your body.

Franklin. Ah! how tiresome you are!

Gout. Well, then, to my office; it should not be forgotten that I am your physician. There.

Franklin. Ohhh! what a devil of a physician!

Gout. How ungrateful you are to say so! Is it not I who, in the character of your physician, have saved you from the palsy, dropsy, and apoplexy? one or other of which would have done for you long ago, but for me.

Franklin. I submit, and thank you for the past, but entreat the discontinuance of your visits for the future; for, in my mind, one had better die than be cured so dolefully. Permit me just to hint, that I have also not been unfriendly to *you.* I never feed physician or quack of any kind, to enter the list against you; if then you do not leave me to my repose, it may be said you are ungrateful too.

Gout. I can scarcely acknowledge that as any objection. As to quacks, I despise them; they may kill you indeed, but cannot injure me. And, as to regular physicians, they are at last convinced, that the gout, in such a subject as you are, is no disease, but a remedy; and wherefore cure a remedy?—but to our business,—there.

Franklin. Oh! Oh!—for Heaven's sake leave me; and I promise faithfully never more to play at chess, but to take exercise daily, and live temperately.

Gout. I know you too well. You promise fair; but, after a few months of good health, you will return to your old habits; your fine promises will be forgotten like the forms of the last year's clouds. Let us then finish the account, and I will go. But I leave you with an assurance of visiting you again at a proper time and place; for my object is your good, and you are sensible now that I am your *real friend.*

TO MADAME HELVETIUS.

WRITTEN AT PASSY.

MORTIFIED at the barbarous resolution pronounced by you so positively yesterday evening, that you would remain single the rest of your life, as a compliment due to the memory of your husband, I retired to my chamber. Throwing myself upon my bed, I dreamt that I was dead, and was transported to the Elysian Fields.

I was asked whether I wished to see any persons in particular; to which I replied, that I wished to see the philosophers. "There are two who live here at hand in this garden; they are good neighbours, and very friendly towards one another." "Who are they?" "Socrates and Helvetius." "I esteem them both highly; but let me see Helvetius first, because I understand a little French, but not a word of Greek." I was conducted to him; he received me with much courtesy, having known me, he said, by character, some time past. He asked me a thousand questions relative to the war, the present state of religion, of liberty, of the government in France. "You do not inquire, then," said I, "after your dear friend, Madame Helvetius; yet she loves you exceedingly; I was in her company not more than an hour ago." "Ah," said he, "you make me recur to my past happiness, which ought to be forgotten in order to be happy here. For many years I could think of nothing but her, though at length I am consoled. I have taken another wife, the most like her that I could find; she is not indeed altogether so handsome, but she has a great fund of wit and good sense; and her whole study is to please me. She is at this moment gone to fetch the best nectar and ambrosia to regale me; stay here awhile and you will see her." "I perceive," said I, "that your former friend is more faithful to you than you are to her; she has had several good offers, but has refused them all. I will confess to you that I loved her extremely; but she was cruel to me, and rejected me peremptorily for your sake." "I pity you sincerely," said he, "for she is an excellent woman, handsome and amiable. But do not the Abbé de la R . . . . and the Abbé M . . . . . visit her?" "Certainly they do; not one of your

friends has dropped her acquaintance." "If you had gained the Abbé M . . . . . with a bribe of good coffee and cream, perhaps you would have succeeded; for he is as deep a reasoner as Duns Scotus or St. Thomas; he arranges and methodizes his arguments in such a manner that they are almost irresistible. Or, if by a fine edition of some old classic, you had gained the Abbé de la R . . . . to speak *against* you, that would have been still better; as I always observed, that when he recommended any thing to her, she had a great inclination to do directly the contrary." As he finished these words the new Madame Helvetius entered with the nectar, and I recognised her immediately as my former American friend, Mrs. Franklin! I reclaimed her, but she answered me coldly; "I was a good wife to you for forty-nine years and four months, nearly half a century; let that content you. I have formed a new connection here, which will last to eternity."

Indignant at this refusal of my Eurydice, I immediately resolved to quit those ungrateful shades, and return to this good world again, to behold the sun and you! Here I am; let us *avenge ourselves!*

AN ARABIAN TALE.

ALBUMAZAR, the good magician, retired in his old age to the top of the lofty mountain Calabut; avoided the society of men, but was visited nightly by genii and spirits of the first rank, who loved him, and amused him with their instructive conversation.

Belubel, the strong, came one evening to see Albumazar; his height was seven leagues, and his wings when spread might overshadow a kingdom. He laid himself gently down between the long ridges of Elluem; the tops of the trees in the valley were his couch; his head rested on Calabut as on a pillow, and his face shone on the tent of Albumazar.

The magician spoke to him with rapturous piety of the wisdom and goodness of the Most High; but expressed his wonder at the existence of evil in the world, which he said he could not account for by all the efforts of his reason.

"Value not thyself, my friend," said Belubel, "on that quality which thou callest reason. If thou knewest its origin and its weakness, it would rather be matter of humiliation."

"Tell me then," said Albumazar, "what I do not know; inform my ignorance, and enlighten my understanding." "Contemplate," said Belubel, "the scale of beings, from an elephant down to an oyster. Thou seest a gradual diminution of faculties and powers, so small in each step that the difference is scarce perceptible. There is no gap, but the gradation is complete. Men in general do not know, but thou knowest, that in ascending from an elephant to the infinitely Great, Good, and Wise, there is also a long gradation of beings, who possess powers and faculties of which thou canst yet have no conception."

THE EPHEMERA;
AN EMBLEM OF HUMAN LIFE.
WRITTEN TO MADAME BRILLON, OF PASSY.

You may remember, my dear friend, that when we lately spent that happy day in the delightful garden and sweet society of the Moulin Joly, I stopped a little in one of our walks, and stayed some time behind the company. We had been shown numberless skeletons of a kind of little fly, called an ephemera, whose successive generations, we were told, were bred and expired within the day. I happened to see a living company of them on a leaf, who appeared to be engaged in conversation. You know I understand all the inferior animal tongues. My too great application to the study of them is the best excuse I can give for the little progress I have made in your charming language. I listened through curiosity to the discourse of these little creatures; but as they, in their national vivacity, spoke three or four together, I could make but little of their conversation. I found, however, by some broken expressions that I heard now and then, they were disputing warmly on the merit of two foreign musicians, the one a *cousin*, the other a *moscheto*; in which dispute they spent their time, seemingly as regardless of the shortness of life as if they had been sure of living a month. Happy people! thought I; you are certainly under a wise, just, and mild government, since you have no public grievances to complain of, nor any subject of contention but the perfections and imperfections of foreign music. I turned my head from them to an old grayheaded one, who was single on another leaf, and talking to himself. Being amused with his soliloquy, I put it down in writing, in hopes it will likewise amuse her to whom I am so much indebted for the most pleasing of all amusements, her delicious company and heavenly harmony.

"It was," said he, "the opinion of learned philosophers of our race, who lived and flourished long before my time, that this vast world, the Moulin Joly, could not itself subsist more than eighteen hours; and I think there was some foundation for that opinion, since, by the apparent motion of the great luminary that gives life to all nature, and which in my time has evidently declined considerably towards the ocean at the end of our earth, it must then finish its course, be extinguished in the waters that surround us, and leave the world in cold and darkness, necessarily producing universal death and destruction. I have lived seven of those hours, a great age, being no less than four hundred and twenty minutes of time. How very few of us continue so long! I have seen generations born, flourish, and expire. My present friends are the children and grandchildren of the friends of my youth, who are now,

alas, no more! And I must soon follow them; for, by the course of nature, though still in health, I cannot expect to live above seven or eight minutes longer. What now avails all my toil and labour, in amassing honey-dew on this leaf, which I cannot live to enjoy! What the political struggles I have been engaged in, for the good of my compatriot inhabitants of this bush, or my philosophical studies for the benefit of our race in general! for, in politics, what can laws do without morals? Our present race of ephemeræ will in a course of minutes become corrupt, like those of other and older bushes, and consequently as wretched. And in philosophy how small our progress! Alas! art is long, and life is short! My friends would comfort me with the idea of a name, they say, I shall leave behind me; and they tell me I have lived long enough to nature and to glory. But what will fame be to an ephemera who no longer exists? And what will become of all history in the eighteenth hour, when the world itself, even the whole Moulin Joly, shall come to its end, and be buried in universal ruin!"

To me, after all my eager pursuits, no solid pleasures now remain, but the reflection of a long life spent in meaning well, the sensible conversation of a few good lady ephemeræ, and now and then a kind smile and a tune from the ever amiable *Brillante*.

APOLOGUE ON WAR.
FROM A LETTER TO THE REV. DR. PRIESTLEY.

In what light we are viewed by superior beings, may be gathered from a piece of late West India news, which possibly has not yet reached you. A young angel of distinction being sent down to this world on some business, for the first time, had an old courier-spirit assigned him as a guide. They arrived over the seas of Martinico, in the middle of the long day of obstinate fight between the fleets of Rodney and De Grasse. When, through the clouds of smoke, he saw the fire of the guns, the decks covered with mangled limbs, and bodies dead or dying; the ships sinking, burning, or blown into the air; and the quantity of pain, misery, and destruction, the crews yet alive were thus with so much eagerness dealing round to one another; he turned angrily to his guide, and said, "You blundering blockhead, you are ignorant of your business; you undertook to conduct me to the earth, and you have brought me into hell!" "No, sir," says the guide, "I have made no mistake; this is really the earth, and these are men. Devils never treat one another in this cruel manner; they have more sense, and more of what men (vainly) call humanity."

THOMAS JEFFERSON.

[Born 1743. Died 1826.]

It was a remarkable exhibition of God's good providence, when the dignity of humanity was to be vindicated anew on these fresh and vast fields which the pious spirit of Columbus had opened to the elder nations, that so many great men stood ready for the apostleship to which they were called. The illustrious person whose name occupies the highest place in our history, had no type in the past, and has had no parallel in the present. The youthful secretary, who in years of turbulent toil shared his midnight conversations, and when Peace smiled upon an exhausted but free people, became the chief architect of that system of government which exists among the noblest monuments of human wisdom, has not received the measure of praise which awaits him, but the rays of his glory brighten as they diverge in the distance of time, and he will yet be regarded as the most gigantic-minded of the statesmen of his century. And that pure and august intelligence, in the alembic of whose mind the treasures of the memory were turned to reason, who seemed while interpreting the laws of man to utter the eternal ordinations of Justice, was worthy, with his friend, to be united, in purpose, principle, and action, to the Great Captain. Washington, Hamilton, and Marshall,—the soldier, the statesman, the jurist—how grateful ought we to be that in the period of our greatest need they were raised up! What hopes of our race are justified by their appearance in these latter days, and in this new world!

But there are others, besides the three who in their respective spheres held such supremacy, to whom we owe the homage of grateful recollection. Franklin, already a sage, approved himself a hero; and the fiery-hearted Adams, the undaunted Henry, the fervid Rutledge, the wise and pure-minded Jay, and at a later time Madison, Bradford, and many more, with powerful mind and peculiar faculties, did ample service to the cause of freedom. And in the second class of our great men, though the receding tide of popular applause may bear him farther toward the sea of undistinguishable men, with bold and peculiar lineaments stands THOMAS JEFFERSON, who as a simple politician, acting for the present, had a more powerful influence than any of his contemporaries or successors.

Thomas Jefferson was born in the county of Albemarle, in Virginia, on the second day of April, 1743. At the age of fourteen, left entirely to himself, with no relative or friend to guide or counsel him, he exhibited a decision and energy of character that secured the esteem of the most respectable persons of his acquaintance. He entered William and Mary College at seventeen, and subsequently studied law under George Wythe. The difficulties with England had already begun, and while a student he was a listener to the celebrated debate on Patrick Henry's resolutions against the Stamp Act. From this period his mind was occupied with public affairs. In 1769 he was chosen to represent his native county in the colonial assembly, and in 1775 took his seat in the old Congress, "where," says John Adams, "though a silent member, he was so prompt, frank, explicit and decisive, upon committees, that he soon seized my heart." He retired from Congress in the autumn of 1776, and was two years engaged in the laborious and important duty of revising and reducing to a single code the statutes of Parliament, the acts of the Virginia Assembly, and parts of the common law. In 1779 he was chosen governor, but resigned the office at the end of two years, and in 1783 was again elected a member of Congress. In 1784 he was appointed Minister to the Court of Paris, where he continued six years, except during brief intervals in which he visited Holland, Piedmont, the southern and western parts of France, and England. In November, 1789, he returned to Virginia, and immediately after was appointed Secretary of State by Washington. He resigned this office in 1793, and was in retirement until 1797, when he was chosen Vice-President of the United States. In 1801 he was elected President, by

71

a majority of one over Mr. Adams, in the House of Representatives, and at the end of eight years he finally quitted public life. The remainder of his days was passed at Monticello, in the care of his estate, in reading and correspondence, and in efforts to promote the prosperity of the University of Virginia, of which he was the founder. He died in the eighty-fourth year of his age, on the fourth of July, 1826, just half a century from the declaration of independence.

Mr. Jefferson's claims to consideration as an author rest chiefly upon his Notes on Virginia, State Papers, and the Autobiography, Correspondence, and Anas, included in the four volumes of his writings, published after his death by Mr. Randolph. The letters which are here printed commence with the year 1775 and continue until a few days before his death. They are addressed to the most distinguished persons of this extraordinary period, so prolific of great men as well as of great events, are upon an infinite variety of subjects, and afford the best view that can be given of his intellectual and moral character. The friendly intercourse between himself and Mr. Adams, which had been suspended in the heats of political controversy, was resumed many years before they died. They forgot the infirmities of age "in the recollection of ancient times;" and perhaps the most interesting portion of this correspondence is that which was addressed to his illustrious associate.

From an early period he had written down all such facts respecting the country as promised to be of use to him in any public or private station, and in 1781, while confined to his chamber by an injury received in falling from his horse, he compiled from his memoranda the Notes on Virginia, to oblige M. de Marbois, of the French legation, who had been instructed by his government to procure information in regard to the natural and political condition of the different states. While in Paris, in 1784, he revised and enlarged the work, and had two hundred copies of it printed for distribution among his friends. One of these, upon the death of the person to whom it had been given, fell into the hands of a bookseller, who employed the Abbé Morellet to translate it, and his version, which was a very poor one, was submitted to Mr. Jefferson for approval. He would gladly have suppressed it, but as this was not practicable he corrected a few of its worst faults, and when, upon its appearance, Stockdale of London applied to him for the original, he consented to the publication of an English edition, though reluctantly, for he feared the effects in Virginia of what he had said in it of slavery. There was no alternative, however, for if he had declined, a retranslation would have been made from the version of Morellet, and he chose to let the world see that his work was not so bad as the abbé had made it appear.

Mr. Jefferson desired that it should be engraved upon his monument that he was the author of the Declaration of Independence, which was reported to the Congress by a committee of which he was a member. A letter on this subject which he wrote to Mr. Adams in 1819 has caused much controversy, and coincidences of expression, which could hardly have been accidental, have been pointed out in the Declaration and documents previously written by other men. The instances are rare in which the committees of public bodies are in any just sense the authors of its reports, which are commonly but embodiments of the spirit of its discussions. While the Congress was in a state of intense excitement, on the seventh of June, 1776, Richard Henry Lee moved that the country be declared independent, and soon after the committee to prepare the declaration was appointed. For twenty days the subject was discussed in fervid and powerful speeches by the ablest men in the assembly : Mr. Jefferson being present all the while, taking notes of the heads of the arguments, and treasuring in his mind every striking expression of fact or opinion. It is reasonable to suppose that no important statement or suggestion is contained in the Declaration which had not been uttered in the debates. Its literary merits are not remarkable, and they were less as it came from the hands of Mr. Jefferson. Mr. Adams and Dr. Franklin suggested some improvements in the committee, and others were made in the House, which struck out or amended the style of several passages.

As a cultivator of elegant literature, under favourable circumstances, Mr. Jefferson would have attained to considerable excellence. His appropriate field perhaps would have been the essay on manners. He was wanting in power, assiduity and integrity for moral speculations, but had the ready penetration and vivacity necessary to a painter of society. His style was flexible, easy, and familiar, and had considerable variety, but was diffuse. He cannot with propriety be said to have been a student, yet he read much, especially in his old age. His reading, however, was one-sided, though discursive, and seldom brought him into contact with the master minds. In his elevation, the air, to his bewildered eyes, was filled with storms of stars, and he mistook the disorder for the perfection of vision. The light which comes from the past to him was darkness. He tells us that " Plato's brain was foggy," and that " a child should be ashamed of his whimsies and peurilities ;" that the sweet singer of Israel, and wisest of kings, gave us but " fumes of disordered imaginations," and that the holy company of the apostles was a " band of dupes and impostors." Christ himself he regarded for his wit, and was kindly incredulous of the " dishonesty" of which he was " reasonably suspected." It was one of his political doctrines that one generation is not bound by the acts of another. Struck with its brevity and point, which would have given it currency, and finally authority, if more plausible, he was ready to publish it with all the circumstance of a new revelation; but Madison saw its absurdity, and persuaded him not to give it to the world. Many of his views, in religion, morals, and politics, were but reflexes of the radicalism of the French revolution, of which he had been a sympathizing spectator.

Mr. Jefferson's hatred of Marshall and Hamilton was deep, constant, and undisguised, and his friendship for Thomas Paine, whose intellect was really almost as mean as his life was scandalous, was to the same degree warm and abiding. He was the associate and patron of several other writers of a similar character. He contracted also an intimacy with Destutt Tracy, whose Commentaries on Montesquieu and Political Economy were translated or edited by him.

A want of steadiness, comprehensiveness, and foresight is apparent in all Mr. Jefferson's controversies and speculations, and we are left in doubt, after the most careful study of his life and works, whether he possessed any inherent greatness, or in any pursuit or condition would have entitled himself to a higher reputation than is awarded to him at the close of the first quarter of a century after his death.

THE HEAD AND THE HEART.

FROM A LETTER TO MRS. COSWAY.

HAVING performed the last sad office of handing you into your carriage, at the pavillon de St. Denis, and seen the wheels get actually into motion, I turned on my heel and walked, more dead than alive, to the opposite door, where my own was awaiting me. M. Danquerville was missing. He was sought for, found, and dragged down stairs. We were crammed into the carriage, like recruits for the Bastile, and not having soul enough to give orders to the coachman, he presumed Paris our destination, and drove off. After a considerable interval, silence was broke, with a ' Je suis vraiment affligé du depart de ces bons gens.' This was a signal for a mutual confession of distress. We began immediately to talk of Mr. and Mrs. Cosway, of their goodness, their talents, their amiability ; and though we spoke of nothing else, we seemed hardly to have entered into the matter, when the coachman announced the rue of St. Denis, and that we were opposite M. Danquerville's. He insisted on descending there, and traversing a short passage to his lodgings. I was carried home. Seated by my fire-side, solitary and sad, the following dialogue took place between my Head and my Heart.

Head. Well, friend, you seem to be in a pretty trim.

Heart. I am indeed the most wretched of all earthly beings. Overwhelmed with grief, every fibre of my frame distended beyond its natural powers to bear, I would willingly meet whatever catastrophe should leave me no more to feel, or to fear.

Head. These are the eternal consequences of your warmth and precipitation. This is one of the scrapes into which you are ever leading us. You confess your follies, indeed; but still you hug and cherish them; and no reformation can be hoped where there is no repentance.

Heart. Oh, my friend ! this is no moment to upbraid my foibles. I am rent into fragments by the force of my grief! If you have any balm, pour it into my wounds; if none, do not harrow them by new torments. Spare me this awful moment! At any other, I will attend with patience to your admonitions.

Head. On the contrary, I never found that the moment of triumph, with you, was the moment of attention to my admonitions. While suffering under your follies, you may perhaps be made sensible of them, but the paroxysm over, you fancy it can never return. Harsh, therefore, as the medicine may be, it is my office to administer it. You will be pleased to remember, that when our friend Trumbull used to be telling us of the merits and talents of these good people, I never ceased whispering to you that we had no occasion for new acquaintances; that the greater their merit and talents, the more dangerous their friendship to our tranquillity, because the regret at parting would be greater.

Heart. Accordingly, sir, this acquaintance was not the consequence of my doings. It was one of your projects, which threw us in the way of it. It was you, remember, and not I, who desired the meeting at Legrand and Motinos. I never trouble myself with domes nor arches. The Halle aux bleds might have rotted down, before I should have gone to see it. But you, forsooth, who are eternally getting us to sleep with your diagrams and crotchets, must go and examine this wonderful piece of architecture; and when you had seen it, oh! it was the most superb thing on earth! What you had seen there was worth all you had yet seen in Paris! I thought so too. But I meant it of the lady and gentleman to whom we had been presented; and not of a parcel of sticks and chips put together in pens. You then, sir, and not I, have been the cause of the present distress.

Head. It would have been happy for you, if my diagrams and crotchets had gotten you to sleep on that day, as you are pleased to say they eternally do. My visit to Legrand and Motinos had public utility for its object. A market is to be built in Richmond. What a commodious plan is that of Legrand and Motinos,; especially, if we put on it the noble dome of the Halle aux bleds. If such a bridge as they showed us can be thrown across the Schuylkill, at Philadelphia, the floating bridges taken up, and the navigation of that river opened, what a copious resource will be added, of wood and provisions, to warm and feed the poor of that city! While I was occupied with these objects, you were dilating with your new acquaintances, and contriving how to prevent a separation from them. Every soul of you had an engagement for the day. Yet all these were to be sacrificed, that you might dine together. Lying messengers were to be despatched into every quarter of the city, with apologies for your breach of engagement. You, particularly, had the effrontery to send word to the Duchess Danville, that on the moment we were setting out to dine with her, despatches came to hand, which required immediate attention. You wanted me to invent a more ingenious excuse; but I knew you were getting into a scrape, and I would have nothing to do with it. Well; after dinner to St. Cloud, from St. Cloud to Ruggieri's, from Ruggieri's to Krumfoltz; and if the day had been as long as a Lapland summer day, you would still have contrived means among you, to have filled it.

Heart. Oh! my dea friend, how you have revived me, oy recalling to mj mind the transactions of that day! How well I remember them all, and that when I came home at night, and looked back to the morning, it seemed to have been a month agone. Go on, then, like a kind comforter, and paint to me the day we went to St. Germains. How beautiful was every object! the Port de Reuilly, the hills along the Seine, the rainbows of the machine of Marley, the terms of St. Germains, the chateaux, the gardens, the statues of Marly, the pavillon of Lucienne. Recollect, too, Madrid Bagatelle, the King's garden, the Des-

sert. How grand the idea excited by the remains of such a column. The spiral staircase, too, was beautiful. Every moment was filled with something agreeable. The wheels of time moved on with a rapidity, of which those of our carriage gave but a faint idea. And yet, in the evening, when one took a retrospect of the day, what a mass of happiness had we travelled over! Retrace all those scenes to me, my good companion, and I will forgive the unkindness with which you were chiding me. The day we went to St. Germains was a little too warm, I think; was it not?

Head. Thou art the most incorrigible of all the beings that ever sinned! I reminded you of the follies of the first day, intending to deduce from thence some useful lessons for you; but instead of listening to them, you kindle at the recollection, you retrace the whole series with a fondness, which shows you want nothing but the opportunity, to act it over again. I often told you, during its course, that you were imprudently engaging your affections, under circumstances that must cost you a great deal of pain; that the persons, indeed, were of the greatest merit, possessing good sense, good humour, honest hearts, honest manners, and eminence in a lovely art; that the lady had, moreover, qualities and accomplishments belonging to her sex, which might form a chapter apart, for her; such as music, modesty, beauty, and that softness of disposition, which is the ornament of her sex and charm of ours: but that all these considerations would increase the pang of separation; that their stay here was to be short; that you rack our whole system when you are parted from those you love, complaining that such a separation is worse than death, inasmuch as this ends our sufferings, whereas that only begins them; and that the separation would, in this instance, be the more severe, as you would probably never see them again.

Heart. But they told me they would come back again, the next year.

Head. But in the mean time, see what you suffer: and their return, too, depends on so many circumstances, that if you had a grain of prudence, you would not count upon it. Upon the whole, it is improbable, and therefore you should abandon the idea of ever seeing them again.

Heart. May heaven abandon me if I do!

Head. Very well. Suppose, then, they come back. They are to stay two months, and when these are expired, what is to follow? Perhaps you flatter yourself they may come to America! *Heart.* God only knows what is to happen. I see nothing impossible in that supposition: and I see things wonderfully contrived sometimes, to make us happy. Where could they find such objects as in America, for the exercise of their enchanting art! especially the lady, who paints landscapes so inimitably. She wants only subjects worthy of immortality, to render her pencil immortal. The Falling Spring, the Cascade of Niagara, the Passage of the Potomac through the Blue Mountains, the Natural Bridge; it is worth r voyage across the Atlantic to see these objects; much more to paint, and make them, and thereby ourselves, known to all ages. And our own dear Monticello; where has nature spread so rich a mantle under the eye? mountains, forests, rocks, rivers. With what majesty do we there ride above the storms! How sublime to look down into the workhouse of nature, to see her clouds, hail, snow, rain, thunder, all fabricated at our feet! and the glorious sun when rising as if out of a distant water, just gilding the tops of the mountains, and giving life to all nature! I hope in God, no circumstance may ever make either seek an asylum from grief! With what sincere sympathy I would open every cell of my composition, to receive the effusion of their woes! I would pour my tears into their wounds; and if a drop of balm could be found on the top of the Cordilleras, or at the remotest sources of the Missouri, I would go thither myself to seek and to bring it. Deeply practised in the school of affliction, the human heart knows no joy which I have not lost, no sorrow of which I have not drank! Fortune can present no grief of unknown form to me! Who, then, can so softly bind up the wound of another, as he who has felt the same wound himself? But Heaven forbid they should ever know a sorrow! Let us turn over another leaf, for this has distracted me.

Head. Well. Let us put this possibility to trial then, on another point. When you consider the • character which is given of our country, by the lying newspapers of London, and their credulous copyers in other countries; when you reflect that all Europe is made to believe we are a lawless banditti, in a state of absolute anarchy, cutting one another's throats, and plundering without distinction, how could you expect that any reasonable creature would venture among us?

Heart. But you. and I know that all this is false: that there is not a country on earth where there is greater tranquillity; where the laws are milder, or better obeyed; where every one is more attentive to his own business, or meddles less with that of others; where strangers are better received, more hospitably treated, and with a more sacred respect.

Head. True, you and I know this, but your friends do not know it.

Heart. But they are sensible people, who think for themselves. They will ask of impartial foreigners, who have been among us, whether they saw or heard on the spot any instance of anarchy. They will judge, too, that a people occupied as we are, in opening rivers, digging navigable canals, making roads, building public schools, establishing academies, erecting busts and statues to our great men, protecting religious freedom, abolishing sanguinary punishments, reforming and improving our laws in general; they will judge, I say, for themselves, whether these are not the occupations of a people at their ease; whether this is not better evidence of our true state, than a London newspaper, hired to lie, and from which no truth can ever be extracted but by reversing every thing it says.

Head. I did not begin this lecture, my friend, with a view to learn from you what America is doing. Let us return, then, to our point. I wish to make you sensible how imprudent it is to place your affections, without reserve, on objects you must so soon lose, and whose loss, when it comes, must cost you such severe pangs. Remember the last night. You knew your friends were to leave Paris to-day. This was enough to throw you into agonies. All night you tossed us from one side of the bed to the other: no sleep, no rest. The poor crippled wrist, too, never left one moment in the same position; now up, now down, now here, now there; was it to be wondered at, if its pains returned? The surgeon then was to be called, and to be rated as an ignoramus, because he could not divine the cause of this extraordinary change. In fine, my friend, you must mend your manners. This is not a world to live at random in, as you do. To avoid those eternal distresses, to which you are for ever exposing us, you must learn to look forward, before you take a step which may interest our peace. Every thing in this world is matter of calculation. Advance then with caution, the balance in your hand. Put into one scale the pleasures which any object may offer; but put fairly into the other, the pains which are to follow, and see which preponderates. The making an acquaintance is not a matter of indifference. When a new one is proposed to you, view it all round. Consider what advantages it presents, and to what inconveniences it may expose you. Do not bite at the bait of pleasure, till you know there is no hook beneath it. The art of life is the art of avoiding pain; and he is the best pilot, who steers clearest of the rocks and shoals with which it is beset. Pleasure is always before us; but misfortune is at our side: while running after that, this arrests us. The most effectual means of being secure against pain, is to retire within ourselves, and to suffice for our own happiness. Those which depend on ourselves, are the only pleasures a wise man will count on; for nothing is ours, which another may deprive us of. Hence the inestimable value of intellectual pleasures. Ever in our power, always leading us to something new, never cloying, we ride serene and sublime above the concerns of this mortal world, contemplating truth and nature, matter and motion, the laws which bind up their existence, and that Eternal Being who made and bound them up by those laws. Let this be our employ. Leave the bustle and tumult of society to those who have not talents to occupy themselves without them. Friendship is but another name for an alliance with the follies and the misfortunes of others. Our own share of miseries is sufficient: why enter then as volunteers into those of another? Is there so little gall poured into our cup, that we must need help to drink that of our neighbour? A friend dies, or leaves us: we feel as if a limb was cut off. He is sick: we must watch over him, and participate of his pains. His fortune is shipwrecked: ours must be laid under contribution. He loses a child, a parent, or a partner: we must mourn the loss as if it were our own.

Heart. And what more sublime delight than to mingle tears with one whom the hand of heaven hath smitten! to watch over the bed of sickness, and to beguile its tedious and its painful moments! to share our bread with one to whom misfortune has left none! This world abounds indeed with misery; to lighten its burden, we must divide it with one another. But let us now try the virtue of your mathematical balance, and as you have put into one scale the burdens of friendship, let me put its comforts into the other. When languishing then under disease, how grateful is the solace of our friends! how are we penetrated with their assiduities and attentions! how much are we supported by their encouragements and kind offices! When heaven has taken from us some object of our love, how sweet is it to have a bosom whereon to recline our heads, and into which we may pour the torrent of our tears! Grief, with such a comfort, is almost a luxury! In a life where we are perpetually exposed to want and accident, yours is a wonderful proposition, to insulate ourselves, to retire from all aid, and to wrap ourselves in the mantle of self-sufficiency! For assuredly, nobody will care for him, who cares for nobody. But friendship is precious, not only in the shade, but in the sunshine of life: and thanks to a benevolent arrangement of things, the greater part of life is sunshine. I will recur for proof to the days we have lately passed. On these, indeed, the sun shone brightly! How gay did the face of nature appear! Hills, valleys, chateaux, gardens, rivers, every object wore its liveliest hue! Whence did they borrow it? From the presence of our charming companion. They were pleasing, because she seemed pleased. Alone, the scene would have been dull and insipid: the participation of it with her gave it relish. Let the gloomy monk, sequestered from the world, seek unsocial pleasures in the bottom of his cell! Let the sublimated philosopher grasp visionary happiness, while pursuing phantoms dressed in the garb of truth! Their supreme wisdom is supreme folly: and they mistake for happiness the mere absence of pain. Had they ever felt the solid pleasure of one generous spasm of the heart, they would exchange for it all the frigid speculations of their lives, which you have been vaunting in such elevated terms. Believe me, then, my friend, that that is a miserable arithmetic which could estimate friendship at nothing, or at less than nothing. Respect for you has induced me to enter into this discussion, and to hear principles uttered which I detest and abjure. Respect for myself now obliges me to recall you the proper limits of your office. When nature assigned us the same habitation, she gave us over it a divided empire. To you, she allotted the field of science; to me, that of morals. When the circle is to be squared, or the orbit of a comet to be traced; when the arch of greatest strength, or the solid of least resistance, is to be investigated, take up the problem; it is yours; nature has given me no cogni-

sance of it. In like manner, in denying to you the feelings of sympathy, of benevolence, of gratitude, of justice, of love, of friendship, she has excluded you from their control. To these she has adapted the mechanism of the heart. Morals were too essential to the happiness of man, to be risked on the uncertain combinations of the head. She laid their foundation, therefore, in sentiment, not in science. That she gave to all, as necessary to all: this to a few only, as sufficing with a few. I know, indeed, that you pretend authority to the sovereign control of our conduct, in all its parts: and a respect for your grave saws and maxims, a desire to do what is right, has sometimes induced me to conform to your counsels. A few facts, however, which I can readily recall to your memory, will suffice to prove to you, that nature has not organized you for our moral direction. When the poor wearied soldier whom we overtook at Chickahomony, with his pack on his back, begged us to let him get up behind our chariot, you began to calculate that the road was full of soldiers, and that if all should be taken up, our horses would fail in their journey. We drove on, therefore. But soon becoming sensible you had made me do wrong, that though we cannot relieve all the distressed, we should relieve as many as we can, I turned about to take up the soldier; but he had entered a by-path, and was no more to be found: and from that moment to this, I could never find him out, to ask his forgiveness. Again, when the poor woman came to ask a charity in Philadelphia, you whispered that she looked like a drunkard, and that half a dollar was enough to give her for the ale-house. Those who want the dispositions to give, easily find reasons why they ought not to give. When I sought her out afterwards, and did what I should have done at first, you know that she employed the money immediately, towards placing her child at school. If our country, when pressed with wrongs at the point of the bayonet, had been governed by its heads instead of its hearts, where should we have been now? Hanging on a gallows as high as Haman's. You began to calculate, and to compare wealth and numbers: we threw up a few pulsations of our blood; we supplied enthusiasm against wealth and numbers; we put our existence to the hazard, when the hazard seemed against us, and we saved our country: justifying, at the same time, the ways of Providence, whose precept is, to do always what is right, and leave the issue to him. In short, my friend, as far as my recollection serves me, I do not know that I ever did a good thing on your suggestion, or a dirty one without it. I do for ever, then, disclaim your interference in my province. Fill paper as you please with triangles and squares: try how many ways you can hang and combine them together. I shall never envy nor control your sublime delights. But leave me to decide, when and where friendships are to be contracted. You say I contract them at random. So you said the woman at Philadelphia was a drunkard. I receive none into my esteem, till I know they are worthy of it. Wealth, title, office, are no recommendations to my friendship. On the contrary, great good qualities are requisite to make amends for their having wealth, title and office. You confess, that in the present case, I could not have made a worthier choice. You only object that I was so soon to lose them. We are not immortal ourselves, my friend; how can we expect our enjoyments to be so? We have no rose without its thorn; no pleasure without alloy. It is the law of our existence; and we must acquiesce. It is the condition annexed to all our pleasures, not by us who receive, but by him who gives them. True, this condition is pressing cruelly on me at this moment. I feel more fit for death than life. But when I look back on the pleasures of which it is the consequence, I am conscious they were worth the price I am paying. Notwithstanding your endeavours, too, to damp my hopes, I comfort myself with expectations of their promised return. Hope is sweeter than despair; and they were too good, to mean to deceive me. ‘In the summer,’ said the gentleman; but ‘in the spring,’ said the lady; and I should love her for ever, were it only for that! Know, then, my friend, that I have taken these good people into my bosom; that I have lodged them in the warmest cell I could find; that I love them, and will continue to love them through life; that if fortune should dispose them on one side the globe, and me on the other, my affections shall pervade its whole mass to reach them. Knowing then my determination, attempt not to disturb it. If you can, at any time, furnish matter for their amusement, it will be the office of a good neighbour to do it. I will, in like manner, seize any occasion which may offer, to do the like good turn for you with Condorcet, Rittenhouse, Madison, La Cretelle, or any other of those worthy sons of science, whom you so justly prize.

I thought this a favourable proposition whereon to rest the issue of the dialogue. So I put an end to it by calling for my night-cap. Methinks, I hear you wish to heaven I had called a little sooner, and so spared you the ennui of such a sermon. I did not interrupt them sooner, because I was in a mood for hearing sermons. You too were the subject: and on such a thesis, I never think the theme long; not even if I am to write it, and that slowly and awkwardly, as now, with the left hand. But that you may not be discouraged from a correspondence which begins so formidably, I will promise you, on my honour, that my future letters shall be of a reasonable length. I will even agree to express but half my esteem for you.

SOCIETY IN FRANCE AND AMERICA.
FROM A LETTER TO MR. BELLINI.

You are, perhaps, curious to know how this new scene has struck a savage of the mountains of America. Not advantageously, I assure you. I find the general fate of humanity here most deplorable. The truth of Voltaire’s observation

offers itself perpetually, that every man here must be either the hammer or the anvil..... While the great mass of the people are thus suffering under physical and moral oppression, I have endeavoured to examine more nearly the condition of the great, to appreciate the true value of the circumstances in their situation, which dazzle the bulk of spectators, and especially, to compare it with that degree of happiness which is enjoyed in America, by every class of people. Intrigues of love occupy the younger, and those of ambition, the elder part of the great. Conjugal love having no existence among them, domestic happiness, of which that is the basis, is utterly unknown. In lieu of this, are substituted pursuits which nourish and invigorate all our bad passions, and which offer only moments of ecstasy, amidst days and months of restlessness and torment. Much, very much inferior, this, to the tranquil, permanent felicity with which domestic society in America blesses most of its inhabitants; leaving them to follow steadily those pursuits which health and reason approve, and rendering truly delicious the intervals of those pursuits.

PASSAGE OF THE POTOMAC THROUGH THE BLUE RIDGE.
FROM THE NOTES ON VIRGINIA.

The passage of the Potomac, through the Blue Ridge, is perhaps one of the most stupendous scenes in nature. You stand on a very high point of land. On your right comes up the Shenandoah, having ranged along the foot of the mountain a hundred miles to seek a vent. On your left approaches the Potomac, seeking a passage also. In the moment of their junction they rush together against the mountain, rend it asunder, and pass off to the sea. The first glance at this scene hurries our senses into the opinion that this earth has been created in time; that the mountains were formed first; that the rivers began to flow afterwards; that, in this place, particularly, they have been dammed up by the Blue Ridge of mountains, and have formed an ocean which filled the whole valley; that, continuing to rise, they have at length broken over at this spot, and have torn the mountain down from its summit to its base. The piles of rock on each hand, but particularly on the Shenandoah, the evident marks of their disruption and avulsion from their beds by the most powerful agents of nature, corroborate the impression. But the distant finishing which Nature has given to the picture is of a different character. It is as placid and delightful as that is wild and tremendous. For, the mountain being cloven asunder, she presents to your eye, through the cleft, a small catch of smooth blue horizon, at an infinite distance in the plain country, inviting you, as it were, from the riot and tumult roaring round, to pass through the beach, and participate of the calm below. Here the eye ultimately composes itself;

G 2

and that way, too, the road happens actually to
lead.   You cross the Potomac above its junction,
pass along its side through the base of the mountain for three miles, its terrible precipices hanging
n fragments over you, and within about twenty
miles reach Fredericktown, and the fine country
round that.   This scene is worth a voyage across
the Atlantic.   Yet here, as in the neighbourhood
of the Natural Bridge, are people who have passed
their lives within half a dozen miles, and have
never been to survey these monuments of a war
between rivers and mountains, which must have
shaken the earth itself to its centre.

PARTY SPIRIT AND GOOD GOVERN-
MENT.

FROM HIS FIRST INAUGURAL ADDRESS.

DURING the contest of opinion through which
we have passed, the animation of discussion and
of exertions has sometimes worn an aspect which
might impose on strangers unused to think freely
and to speak and to write what they think; but,
this being now decided by the voice of the nation,
announced according to the rules of the constitution, all will of course arrange themselves under
the will of the law, and unite in common efforts
for the common good.   All, too, will bear in mind
this sacred principle, that though the will of the
majority is in all cases to prevail, that will, to be
rightful, must be reasonable; that the minority
possess their equal rights, which equal laws must
protect, and to violate which would be oppression.
Let us, then, fellow citizens, unite with one heart
and one mind.   Let us restore to social intercourse
that harmony and affection without which liberty
and even life itself are but dreary things.   And
let us reflect that having banished from our land
that religious intolerance under which mankind so
long bled and suffered, we have yet gained little if we
countenance a political intolerance as despotic, as
wicked, and capable of as bitter and bloody persecutions.   During the throes and convulsions of
the ancient world, during the agonizing spasms of
infuriated man, seeking through blood and slaughter his long lost liberty, it was not wonderful that
the agitation of the billows should reach even this
distant and peaceful shore; that this should be
more felt and feared by some and less by others; that
this should divide opinions as to measures of safety.
But every difference of opinion is not a difference of
principle.   We have called by different names breth-
en of the same principle.   We are all republicans—

we are all federalists.   If there be any among us who
would wish to dissolve this Union or to change
its republican form, let them stand undisturbed as
monuments of the safety with which error of
opinion may be tolerated where reason is left free
to combat it.   I know indeed that some honest
men fear that a republican government cannot be
strong; that this government is not strong enough.
But would the honest patriot, in the full tide of
successful experiment, abandon a government
which has so far kept us free and firm, on the theoretic and visionary fear that this government, the
world's best hope, may by possibility want energy
to preserve itself?   I trust not.   I believe this, on
the contrary, the strongest government on earth.
I believe it the only one where every man, at the
call of the laws, would fly to the standard of the
law, and would meet invasions of the public order
as his own personal concern.   Sometimes it is said
that man cannot be trusted with the government
of himself.   Can he, then, be trusted with the
government of others?   Or have we found angels in the forms of kings to govern him?   Let
history answer this question.

Let us, then, with courage and confidence pursue our own federal and republican principles, our
attachment to our union and representative government.   Kindly separated by nature and a wide
ocean from the exterminating havoc of one quarter of the globe; too high-minded to endure the
degradations of the others; possessing a chosen
country, with room enough for our descendants to
the hundreth and thousandth generation; entertaining a due sense of our equal right to the use
of our own faculties, to the acquisitions of our industry, to honour and confidence from our fellow
citizens, resulting not from birth but from our actions and their sense of them; enlightened by a
benign religion, professed, indeed, and practised
in various forms, yet all of them including honesty,
truth, temperance, gratitude, and the love of man;
acknowledging and adoring an overruling Providence, which by all its dispensations proves that
it delights in the happiness of man here and
his greater happiness hereafter; with all these
blessings, what more is necessary to make us a
happy and prosperous people?   Still one thing
more, fellow citizens,—a wise and frugal government, which shall restrain man from injuring
one another, which shall leave them otherwise free
to regulate their own pursuits of industry and improvement, and shall not take from the mouth of
labour the bread it has earned.   This is the sum
of good government, and this is necessary to close
the circle of our felicities.

JAMES MADISON.

[Born 1751. Died 1836.]

MR. MADISON was born on the sixteenth of March, 1751, in the county of Orange, in Virginia. He was educated at the college of Princeton, in New Jersey, where he received the degree of Bachelor of Arts, from Dr. Witherspoon, in 1771. He appears to have led an inactive life during the early part of the Revolution, or at least to have taken no part in public affairs. In 1776 he was elected to the Virginia Assembly, but was superseded in the following year. The House of Delegates, however, which was more capable of judging of his merits than his constituents had been, chose him to be a member of the Executive Council, in which he continued until transferred to the old Congress, in which he made his first appearance on the twentieth of March, 1780. From this period his name is one of the most prominent in the political history of the country. His writings on the Constitution and other subjects were second only to those of Hamilton in ability and influence ; and his extensive information, sound judgment, skill as a logician, and unvarying courtesy, secured him the highest consideration in the congresses of which he was a member, the National Convention that formed the Constitution, the Virginia Convention to which it was submitted for approval, and the legislature of his state whenever he held a seat in that body. Upon the accession of Mr. Jefferson to the presidency, Mr. Madison was made Secretary of State, and he succeeded Mr. Jefferson as President. At the end of his second term, in 1817, he retired from the public service, and he held no other office except for a short period in 1829, in which he was a member of the Virginia Constitutional Convention. He passed the remainder of his life in dignified retirement at Montpelier, where he died on the twenty-eighth of June, 1836, in the eighty-fifth year of his age.

This great statesman and philosopher was the confidential personal and political friend of Jefferson, but in almost every respect their characters were essentially different. Mr.

Madison's intellect was of a far higher order, and its ascendency over his passions was nearly perfect. His triumphs were those of pure reason. His public and private life were above reproach.

In his correspondence with John Adams Mr. Jefferson had given the first intimation which found its way before the public that Mr. Madison had made a full report of the debates in the Federal Convention. After his death, this manuscript and his reports of debates in the Congress of the Confederation, with a selection from his letters written between 1780 and 1784, were purchased by the government, and in 1840 were published, in three octavo volumes, under the superintendence of Mr. Henry D. Gilpin. They constitute a work of extraordinary value to students in history and political philosophy.

Mr. Madison was the author of a considerable and important portion of the Federalist, written by Mr. Hamilton, Mr. Jay and himself, to secure the adoption of the Constitution, and by his speeches in the Virginia Convention he contributed with equal ability and efficiency to the same object. Upon the appearance of the Proclamation of Neutrality, in 1793, he and Mr. Hamilton were opposed to each other in a debate upon the distribution of the excutive and legislative powers incident to war, and he replied to the Letters of Pacificus, by Mr. Hamilton, in five essays signed Helvidius, in which a degree of asperity scarcely congenial with his nature showed that his more intimate associates had succeeded in lessening his confidence in Mr. Hamilton's attachment to republican principles.

The writings of Mr. Madison would make about fifteen octavo volumes, each of six hundred pages, similar to those already mentioned as published under the authority of the government. They are chiefly on constitutional, political and historical subjects, but among them are some relating to eminent persons, and of a miscellaneous character which will be more generally interesting. His style is clear exact and justly modulated.

VAGUENESS OF PHILOSOPHICAL
DISTINCTIONS.

FROM THE THIRTY-SEVENTH NUMBER OF THE FEDERALIST.

THE faculties of the mind itself have never yet been distinguished and defined, with satisfactory precision, by all the efforts of the most acute and metaphysical philosophers. Sense, perception, judgment, desire, volition, memory, imagination, are found o be separated by such delicate shades and minut. gradations, that their boundaries have eluded the most subtle investigations, and remain a pregnant source of ingenious disquisition and controversy. The boundaries between the great kingdoms of nature, and, still more, between the various provinces and lesser portions into which they are subdivided, afford another illustration of the same important truth. The most sagacious and laborious naturalists have never yet succeeded in tracing with certainty the line which separates the district of vegetable life from the neighbouring region of unorganized matter, or which marks the termination of the former and the commencement of the animal empire. A still greater obscurity lies in the distinctive characters by which the objects in each of these great departments of nature have been arranged and assorted.

When we pass from the works of nature, in which all the delineations are perfectly accurate, and appear to be otherwise only from the imperfection of the eye which surveys them, to the institutions of man, in which the obscurity arises as well from the object itself, as from the organ by which it is contemplated; we must perceive the necessity of moderating still further our expectations and hopes from the efforts of human sagacity. Experience has instructed us, that no skill in the science of government has yet been able to discriminate and define, with sufficient certainty, its three great provinces, the legislative, executive, and judiciary; or even the privileges and powers of the different legislative branches. Questions daily occur in the course of practice, which prove the obscurity which reigns in these subjects, and which puzzle the greatest adepts in political science.

The experience of ages, with the continued and combined labours of the most enlightened legislators and jurists, have been equally unsuccessful in delineating the several objects and limits of different codes of laws and different tribunals of justice. The precise extent of the common law, the statute law, the maritime law, the ecclesiastical law, the law of corporations, and other local laws and customs, remains still to be clearly and finally established in Great Britain, where accuracy in such subjects has been more industriously pursued than in any other part of the world. The jurisdiction of her several courts, general and local, of law, of equity, of admiralty, &c., is not less a source of frequent and intricate discussions, sufficiently denoting the indeterminate limits by which they are respectively circumscribed. All new laws, though penned with the greatest technical skill, and passed on the fullest and most mature deliberation, are considered as more or less obscure and equivocal, until their meaning be liquidated and ascertained by a series of particular discussions and adjudications. Besides the obscurity arising from the complexity of objects, and the imperfection of the human faculties, the medium through which the conceptions of men are conveyed to each other adds a fresh embarrassment. The use of words is to express ideas. Perspicuity therefore requires, not only that the ideas should be distinctly formed, but that they should be expressed by words distinctly and exclusively appropriated to them. But no language is so copious as to supply words and phrases for every complex idea, or so correct as not to include many, equivocally denoting different ideas. Hence it must happen, that however accurately objects may be discriminated in themselves, and however accurately the discrimination may be conceived, the definition of them may be rendered inaccurate, by the inaccuracy of the terms in which it is delivered. And this unavoidable inaccuracy must be greater or less, according to the complexity and novelty of the objects defined. When the Almighty himself condescends to address mankind in their own language, his meaning, luminous as it must be, is rendered dim and doubtful, by the cloudy medium through which it is communicated.

THE RESPONSIBILITY OF OUR COUNTRY TO MANKIND.

FROM AN ADDRESS TO THE PEOPLE OF THE UNITED STATES.

LET it be remembered, that it has ever been the pride and boast of America, that the rights for which she contended were the rights of human nature. By the blessing of the Author of these rights on the means exerted for their defence, they have prevailed over all opposition..... No instance has heretofore occurred, nor can any instance be expected hereafter to occur, in which the unadulterated forms of republican government can pretend to so fair an opportunity of justifying themselves by their fruits. In this view the citizens of the United States are responsible for the greatest trust ever confided to a political society. If justice, good faith, honour, gratitude, and all the other qualities which ennoble the character of a nation, and fulfil the ends of government, be the fruits of our establishments, the cause of Liberty will acquire a dignity and lustre which it has never yet enjoyed; and an example will be set which cannot but have the most favourable influence on the rights of mankind. If, on the other side, our governments should be unfortunately blotted with the reverse of these cardinal and essential virtues, the great cause which we have engaged to vindicate will be dishonoured and betrayed; the last and fairest experiment in favour of the rights of human nature will be turned against them; and their patrons and friends exposed to be insulted and silenced by the votaries of tyranny and usurpation.

TIMOTHY DWIGHT.

[Born 1752. Died 1817.]

HAVING given the personal history of Dr. Dwight in the Poets and Poetry of America, I shall here only present a chronological statement of its principal incidents. His father was a merchant, and his mother was a daughter of the great Jonathan Edwards. They resided in Northampton, Massachusetts, where our author was born on the fourteenth of May, 1752. He was graduated at Yale College in 1769; was chosen a tutor in that institution in 1771, and held the office six years; was licensed to preach in the Congregational church in 1777, and in the same year entered the army as a chaplain; on the death of his father in 1778 resigned his commission and returned to Northampton, where he acted in various capacities until 1782; was installed pastor of the Congregational Church in Greenfield, Connecticut, in 1783; was elected president of Yale College and removed to New Haven in 1795; and died in 1817.

Whether Dr. Dwight has in this country had an equal as a college instructor and president is questionable, but it may be safely said that he has had no superior. The cause of sound learning was in many ways very largely indebted to him. He was also an eloquent and successful preacher, and an accomplished and most agreeable gentleman.

His first literary works were in verse. His Conquest of Canaan, an epic poem, was finished when he was but twenty-two years of age; and he subsequently published several other volumes of poetry, in all of which were passages of considerable beauty, but none of which were of so elevated and sustained a character as to be altogether creditable to a man of his distinguished reputation for talents, scholarship and taste. His fame as an author must therefore rest principally upon his prose writings, and these are of such excellence that no fears need be entertained that it will not be honourable and permanent.

The most important works of Dr. Dwight have been published since his death. Besides his poems, however, he permitted the appearance during his life of many of the discourses which he delivered on public occasions, and he contributed numerous papers to religious periodicals and the memoirs of scientific societies. An anonymous volume entitled Remarks on the Review of Inchiquin's Letters in the Quarterly Review, addressed to the Rt. Hon. George Canning, is likewise attributed to him, though he never publicly acknowledged it.

His Theology Explained and Defended consists of nearly two hundred sermons preached before the classes of Yale College during his presidency. His views as here exhibited are moderately Calvinistic, and are maintained with great ability, dignity and eloquence. Probably no work of the sort in the English language was ever so widely and generally popular.

His Travels in New England and New York are in four octavo volumes. In the college vacations of nearly every year from the commencement of his administration he made excursions in various directions through the northern states, and by personal inquiry and observation collected an extraordinary amount of historical, topographical and statistical information, which will always be interesting and valuable; and no other work presents a view so particular and authentic of American society and manners in the beginning of the present century.

Several works which he left in readiness for the press are still unpublished. The largest and most elaborate of these is on the Character and Writings of St. Paul. Another is called The Friend, and comprises a series of essays commenced during his residence in Greenfield and concluded near the close of his life.

The style of Dr. Dwight is fluent, graceful, picturesque and glowing; but diffuse. The erasure of redundances would render it much more vigorous and attractive. He presented the most abstruse propositions in metaphysics

11

with clearness, and was successful in descriptions of external nature; but hardly a discourse, or essay or letter can be pointed to in all his works the effect of which is not injured by superfluous epithets. Yet for his wisdom, earnestness, and courtesy, greater faults could be easily forgiven and forgotten.

APPROACH OF EVENING ON LAKE GEORGE.

FROM TRAVELS IN NEW ENGLAND AND NEW YORK.

THE whole scenery of this lake is greatly enhanced in beauty and splendour by the progressive change which the traveller, sailing on its bosom, perpetually finds in his position, and by the unceasing variegations of light and shade which attend his progress. The gradual and the sudden openings of scoops and basins, of islands and points, of promontories and summits; the continual change of their forms, and their equally gradual or sudden disappearance; impart to every object a brilliancy, life and motion..... An opening lay before us between the mountains on the West, and those on the East, gilded by the departing sunbeams. The lake, alternately glassy, and gently rippled, of a light and exquisite sapphire, gay and brilliant with the tremulous lustre floating upon its surface, stretched in prospect to a vast distance, through a great variety of larger and smaller apertures. In the chasm formed by the mountains lay a multitude of islands, differing in size, shape and umbrage, and clothed in deeply shaded green. Beyond them, and often partly hidden behind the tall and variously figured trees with which they were tufted, rose a long range of distant mountains, tinged with a deep misty azure, and crowned with an immense succession of lofty pines. Above the mountains, and above each other, were extended in great numbers long streaming clouds, of the happiest forms, and painted with red and orange light in all their diversities of tincture. Between them the sky was illumined with a vivid yellow lustre. The tall trees on the western mountains lifted their heads in the crimson glory, and on this background displayed their diversified forms with a distinctness and beauty never surpassed. On a high and semi-circular summit, the trees, ascending far without limbs, united their crowns above, and thus formed a majestic and extensive arch in the sky, dark, defined, and corresponding with the arch of the summit below. Between this crown and the mountain the vivid orange light, shining through the grove, formed a third arch, equally extended, and striped with black by the stems of the trees.

Directly over the gap which I have mentioned, and through which this combination of beauty was presented to us, the moon, far southward, in her handsomest crescent, sat on the eastern, and the evening star, on the western, side of the opening, at equal distances from the bordering mountains. and, shining from a sky perfectly pure and serene, finished the prospect.

The crimson lustre however soon faded; the mountains lost their gilding, and the clouds, changing their fine glow into a dull, leaden-coloured hue, speedily vanished. The lake, though still brilliant, became misty and dim. The splendour of the moon and of Hesper increased, and trembled on its surface until they both retired behind the western mountains, and just as we reached the shore, left the world to the darkness of night.

SCENE ON THE KAATSKILL MOUNTAINS.

FROM THE SAME.

WE entered the forest on the South; and, after penetrating it about a mile, came to a scene which amply repaid us for our toil. On the rear of the great ridge, stretched out before us two spurs of a vast height. Between them sunk a ravine, several miles in length, and in different places from a thousand to fifteen hundred feet in depth. The mountains on either side were steep, wild and shaggy, covered almost everywhere with a dark forest, the lofty trees of which approached nearer and nearer to each other as the eye wandered toward the bottom. In some places their branches became united; in others, separated by a small distance, they left a line of absolute darkness, resembling in its dimensions a winding rivulet, here somewhat wider, there narrower, and appearing as if it were a solitary by-path to the nether world. All beneath seemed to be midnight, although the day was uncommonly bright and beautiful; and all above a dreary solitude, secluded from the world, and destined never to be wandered over by the feet of man. At the head of this valley stood a precipice; here descending perpendicularly, there overhanging with a stupendous and awful grandeur. Over a bed of stone beside our feet ran a stream, which discharged the waters of the lakes, and from the brow of the precipice rushed in a perpendicular torrent perfectly white and glittering nearly three hundred feet in length. This magnificent current, after dashing upon a shelf, falls over a second precipice of one hundred feet: when it vanishes in the midnight beneath, and rolls over a succession of precipices until it finally escapes from the mountains, and empties its waters into the river Kaaterskill. A cloud of vapour, raised by the dashing of this stream on the successive shelves in its bed, rises above the forests which shroud the bottom of the valley, and winds beautifully away from the sight until it finally vanishes in the bewildered course of this immense chasm. On the bosom of this volume of mist appears to the eye a succession of rainbows, floating slowly and gracefully down the valley, and reluctantly yielding their place to others by which they are continually followed. No contrast can be more perfect than that of these circles of light to the rude scenery by which they are environed; and no object of this nature which I have seen awakens emotions of such grandeur.

THE NOTCH OF THE WHITE MOUNTAINS.

FROM THE SAME.

THE Notch of the White Mountains is a phrase appropriated to a very narrow defile, extending two miles in length between two huge cliffs apparently rent asunder by some vast convulsion of nature. The entrance of the chasm is formed by two rocks standing perpendicularly at the distance of twenty-two feet from each other; one about twenty feet in height, the other about twelve. Half of the space is occupied by the brook mentioned as the head stream of the Saco; the other half by the road. The stream is lost and invisible beneath a mass of fragments partly blown out of the road, and partly thrown down by some great convulsion.

When we entered the Notch we were struck with the wild and solemn appearance of every thing before us. The scale on which all the objects in view were formed was the scale of grandeur only. The rocks, rude and ragged in a manner rarely paralleled, were fashioned and piled by a hand operating only in the boldest and most irregular manner. As we advanced, these appearances increased rapidly. Huge masses of granite, of every abrupt form, and hoary with a moss, which seemed the product of ages, recalling to the mind the *saxum vetustum* of Virgil, speedily rose to a mountainous height. Before us the view widened fast to the south-east. Behind us it closed almost instantaneously, and presented nothing to the eye but an impassable barrier of mountains.

About half a mile from the entrance of the chasm we saw, in full view, the most beautiful cascade, perhaps, in the world. It issued from a mountain on the right, about eight hundred feet above the subjacent valley, and at the distance from us of about two miles. The stream ran over a series of rocks almost perpendicular, with a course so little broken as to preserve the appearance of a uniform current, and yet so far disturbed as to be perfectly white. The sun shone with the clearest splendour, from a station in the heavens the most advantageous to our prospect; and the cascade glittered down the vast steep, like a stream of burnished silver.

At the distance of three quarters of a mile from the entrance, we passed a brook, known in this region by the name of *the flume* · from the strong resemblance to that object exhibited by the channel, which it has worn for a considerable length

in a bed of rocks; the sides being perpendicular to the bottom. This elegant piece of water we determined to examine farther; and, alighting from our horses, walked up the acclivity perhaps a furlong. The stream fell from a height of two hundred and forty or two hundred and fifty feet, over three precipices; the second receding a small distance from the front of the first, and the third from that of the second. Down the first and second it fell in a single current; and down the third in three, which united their streams at the bottom in a fine basin, formed by the hand of nature in the rocks immediately beneath us. It is impossible for a brook of this size to be modelled into more diversified or more delightful forms; or for a cascade to descend over precipices more happily fitted to finish its beauty. The cliffs, together with a level at their foot, furnished a considerable opening, surrounded by the forest. The sunbeams, penetrating through the trees, painted here a great variety of fine images of light, and edged an equally numerous and diversified collection of shadows; both dancing on the waters, and alternately silvering and obscuring their course. Purer water was never seen. Exclusively of its murmurs, the world around us was solemn and silent. Every thing assumed the character of enchantment; and, had I been educated in the Grecian mythology, I should scarcely have been surprised to find an assemblage of Dryads, Naiads and Oreades, sporting on the little plain below our feet. The purity of this water was discernible, not only by its limpid appearance, and its taste, but from several other circumstances. Its course is wholly over hard granite; and the rocks and the stones in its bed and at its side, instead of being covered with adventitious substances, were washed perfectly clean; and, by their neat appearance, added not a little to the beauty of the scenery.

From this spot the mountains speedily began to open with increased majesty; and, in several instances, rose to a perpendicular height little less than a mile. The bosom of both ranges was overspread, in all the inferior regions, by a mixture of evergreens with trees, whose leaves are deciduous. The annual foliage had been already changed by the frost. Of the effects of this change it is, perhaps, impossible for an inhabitant of Great Britain, as I have been assured by several foreigners, to form an adequate conception, without visiting an American forest. When I was a youth, I remarked that Thomson had entirely omitted in his Seasons this fine part of autumnal imagery. Upon inquiring of an English gentleman the probable cause of the omission, he informed me that no such scenery existed in Great Britain. In this country it is often among the most splendid beauties of nature. All the leaves of trees, which are not evergreens, are, by the first severe frost, changed from their verdure toward the perfection of that colour which they are capable of ultimately assuming, through yellow, orange and red, to a pretty deep brown. As the frost affects different trees, and different leaves of the same tree, in very different degrees, a vast multitude of tinctures are commonly found on those of a single tree, and always on those of a grove or forest. These colours also, in all their varieties, are generally full; and, in many instances, are among the most exquisite which are found in the regions of nature. Different sorts of trees are susceptible of different degrees of this beauty. Among them the maple is pre-eminently distinguished by the prodigious varieties, the finished beauty, and the intense lustre of its hues; varying through all the dyes between a rich green and the most perfect crimson, or, more definitely, the red of the prismatic image.

There is, however, a sensible difference in the beauty of this appearance of nature in different parts of the country, even when the forest trees are the same. I have seen no tract where its splendour was so highly finished, as in the region which surrounds Lancaster for a distance of thirty miles. The colours are more varied and more intense; and the numerous evergreens furnish, in their deep hues, the best groundwork of the picture.

I have remarked, that the annual foliage on these mountains had been already changed by the frost. Of course, the darkness of the evergreens was finely illumined by the brilliant yellow of the birch, the beech and the cherry, and the more brilliant orange and crimson of the maple. The effect of this universal diffusion of gay and splendid light was, to render the preponderating deep green more solemn. The mind, encircled by this scenery, irresistibly remembered that the light was the light of decay, autumnal and melancholy. The dark was the gloom of evening, approximating to night. Over the whole, the azure of the sky cast a deep, misty blue; blending, toward the summit, every other hue, and predominating over all.

As the eye ascended these steeps, the light decayed, and gradually ceased. On the inferior summits rose crowns of conical firs and spruces. On the superior eminences, the trees, growing less and less, yielded to the chilling atmosphere, and marked the limit of forest vegetation. Above, the surface was covered with a mass of shrubs, terminating, at a still higher elevation, in a shroud of dark-coloured moss.

As we passed onward through this singular valley, occasional torrents, formed by the rains and dissolving snows at the close of winter, had left behind them, in many places, perpetual monuments of their progress, in perpendicular, narrow and irregular paths of immense length, where they had washed the precipices naked and white, from the summit of the mountain to the base. Wide and deep chasms also met the eye, both on the summits and the sides; and strongly impressed the imagination with the thought, that a hand of immeasurable power had rent asunder the solid rocks, and tumbled them into the subjacent valley. Over all, hoary cliffs, rising with proud supremacy, frowned awfully on the world below, and finished the landscape.

By our side, the Saco was alternately visible and lost, and increased, almost at every step, by the junction of tributary streams. Its course was a perpetual cascade; and with its sprightly murmurs furnished the only contrast to the scenery around us.

THE PLEASURE DERIVED FROM THE BEAUTY OF NATURE.

FROM THEOLOGY EXPLAINED AND DEFENDED.

WERE all the interesting diversities of colour and form to disappear, how unsightly, dull, and wearisome, would be the aspect of the world! The pleasures conveyed to us by the endless varieties with which these sources of beauty are presented to the eye, are so much things of course, and exist so much without intermission, that we scarcely think either of their nature, their number, or the great proportion which they constitute in the whole mass of our enjoyment. But were an inhabitant of this country to be removed from its delightful scenery to the midst of an Arabian desert, a boundless expanse of sand, a waste spread with uniform desolation, enlivened by the murmur of no stream and cheered by the beauty of no verdure, although he might live in a palace and riot in splendour and luxury, he would, I think, find life a dull, wearisome, melancholy round of existence, and amid all his gratifications would sigh for the hills and valleys of his native land, the brooks and rivers, the living lustre of the Spring, and the rich glories of the Autumn. The ever-varying brilliancy and grandeur of the landscape, and the magnificence of the sky, sun, moon, and stars, enter more extensively into the enjoyment of mankind than we, perhaps, ever think, or can possibly apprehend, without frequent and extensive investigation. This beauty and splendour of the objects around us, it is ever to be remembered, are not necessary to their existence, nor to what we commonly intend by their usefulness. It is therefore to be regarded as a source of pleasure gratuitously superinduced upon the general nature of the objects themselves, and in this light, as a testimony of the divine goodness peculiarly affecting.

JOHN MARSHALL.

[Born 1755. Died 1835.]

JOHN MARSHALL, the son of Colonel Thomas Marshall, was born in Germantown, Fauquier county, Virginia, on the twenty-fourth of September, 1755. When twenty-one years of age he was commissioned as a lieutenant in the continental service, and marching with his regiment to the north was appointed captain in the spring of 1777, and in that capacity served in the battles of Brandywine, Germantown, and Monmouth, was at Valley Forge during the winter of 1778, and was one of the covering party at the assault of Stoney Point, in June, 1779. Having returned to his native state at the expiration of the enlistment of the Virginia troops, in 1780 he received a license for the practice of the law, and rapidly rose to distinction in that profession. In 1782 he was chosen a representative to the legislature, and afterward a member of the executive council. In January, 1783, he married Mary Willis Ambler, of York, in Virginia, with whom he lived for fifty years in the tenderest affection. He was a delegate to the convention of Virginia, which met on the second of June, 1788, to take into consideration the new constitution, and in conjunction with his friend Mr. Madison, mainly contributed to its adoption, in opposition to the ardent efforts of Henry, Grayson and Mason. His name first became generally known throughout the nation by his vindication, in the legislature of the state, of the ratification of Jay's treaty by President Washington. No report of that speech remains, but the evidence of its ability survives in the effects which it produced on the legislature and the country. He continued in the practice of the law, having declined successively the offices of Attorney General of the United States and Minister to France, until 1797, when with General Pinckney and Mr. Gerry he was sent on a special mission to the French republic. The manner in which the dignity of the American character was maintained against the corruption of the Directory and its ministers is well known. The letters of the seventeenth of January and third of April, 1798, to Talleyrand the Minister of Foreign

Relations have always been attributed to Marshall, and they rank among the ablest and most effective of diplomatic communications. Mr. Marshall arrived in New York on the seventeenth of June, 1798, and on the nineteenth entered Philadelphia. At the intelligence of his approach the whole city poured out toward Frankford to receive him, and escorted him to his lodgings with all the honours of a triumph. In after years, when he visited Philadelphia, he often spoke of the feelings with which, as he came near the city on that occasion, with some doubts as to the reception which he might meet with in the existing state of parties, he beheld the multitude rushing forth to crowd about him with every demonstration of respect and approbation, as having been the most interesting and gratifying of his life.

On his return to Virginia, at the special request of General Washington,[*] he became a candidate for the House of Representatives, and was elected in the spring of 1799. His greatest effort in Congress was his speech in opposition to the resolutions of Edward Livingston relative to Thomas Nash, alias Jonathan Robbins. Fortunately we possess an accurate report of it, revised by himself. The case was, that Thomas Nash, having committed a murder on board the British frigate Hermione, navigating the high seas under a commission from the British king, had sought an asylum within the United States, and his delivery had been demanded by the British minister under the twenty-seventh article of the treaty of amity between the two nations. Mr. Marshall's argument first established that the crime was within the jurisdiction of Great Britain, on the general principles of public law, and then demonstrated that under the constitution the case was subject to the disposal of the executive, and not the judiciary. He distinguished these departments from one another with an acuteness of discrimination and a force of logic which frustrated the attempt to carry the judiciary out of its orbit,

---

* See notice of Marshall in the Portrait Gallery, written by Judge Story.

and settled the political question, then and for ever. It is said that Mr. Gallatin, whose part it was to reply to Mr. Marshall, at the close of the speech turned to some of his friends and said, " *You* may answer that if you choose; *I* cannot." That argument deserves to rank among the most dignified displays of human intellect. At the close of the session Mr. Marshall was appointed Secretary of War, and soon after Secretary of State. During his continuance in that department our relations with England were in a very interesting condition, and his correspondence with Mr. King exhibits his abilities and spirit in the most dignified point of view. " His despatch of the twentieth of September, 1800," says Mr. Binney, " is a noble specimen of the first order of state papers, and shows the most finished adaptation of parts for the station of an American Secretary of State." On the thirty-first of January, 1801, he was appointed Chief Justice of the United States, in which office he continued until his death. In 1804 he published the Biography of Washington, which for candour, accuracy, and comprehension, will for ever be the most authentic history of the Revolution. He died in Philadelphia on the sixth of July, 1835.

Mr. Marshall's career as Chief Justice extended through a period of more than thirty-four years, which is the longest judicial tenure recorded in history. To one who cannot follow his great judgments, in which, at the same time, the depths of legal wisdom are disclosed and the limits of human reason measured, the language of just eulogy must wear an appearance of extravagance. In his own profession he stands for the reverence of the wise rather than for the enthusiasm of the many. The proportion of the figure was so perfect, that the sense of its vastness was lost. Above the difficulties of common minds, he was in some degree above their sympathy. Saved from popularity, by the very rarity of his qualities, he astonished the most where he was best understood. The questions upon which his judgment was detained, and the considerations by which his decision was at last determined, were such as ordinary understandings, not merely could not resolve, but were often inadequate even to appreciate or apprehend. It was his manner to deal directly with the results of thought and learning, and the length and labour of the processes by which these results were suggested and verified might elude the consciousness of those who had not themselves attempted to perform them. From the position in which he stood of evident superiority to his subject, it was obviously so easy for him to describe its character and define its relations, that we sometimes forgot to wonder by what faculties or what efforts he had attained to that eminence. We were so much accustomed to see his mind move only in the light, that there was a danger of our not observing that the illumination by which it was surrounded was the beam of its own presence, and not the natural atmosphere of the scene.

The true character and measure of Marshall's greatness are missed by those who conceive of him as limited within the sphere of the justices of England, and who describe him merely as the first of lawyers. To have been " the most consummate judge that ever sat in judgment," was the highest possibility of Eldon's merit, but was only a segment of Marshall's fame. It was in a distinct department, of more dignified functions, almost of an opposite kind, that he displayed those abilities that advance his name to the highest renown, and shed around it the glories of a statesman and legislator. The powers of the Supreme Court of the United States are such as were never before confided to a judicial tribunal by any people. As determining, without appeal, its own jurisdiction, and that of the legislature and executive, that court is not merely the highest estate in the country, but it settles and continually moulds the constitution of the government. Of the great work of constructing a nation, but a small part, practically, had been performed when the written document had been signed by the convention : a vicious theory of interpretation might defeat the grandeur and unity of the organization, and a want of comprehension and foresight might fatally perplex the harmony of the combination. The administration of a system of polity is the larger part of its establishment. What the constitution was to be, depended on the principles on which the federal instrument was to be construed, and they were not to be found in the maxims and modes of reasoning by which the law determines upon social contracts between man and man, but were to be sought anew in the elements of political philosophy and the general suggestions of legislative wisdom. To these august duties Judge Marshall brought a greatness of conception that was commensurate with their difficulty; he came to them in the spirit and with the strength of one who would minister to the development of a nation: and it was the essential sagacity of his guiding mind that saved us from illustrating the sarcasms of Mr. Burke about paper constitutions. He saw the futility of attempting to control society by a metaphysical theory; he apprehended the just relation between opinion and life, between the forms of speculation and the force of things. Knowing that we are wise in respect to nature, only as we give back to it faithfully what we have learned from it obediently, he sought to fix the wisdom of the real and to resolve it into principles. He made the nation explain its constitution, and compelled the actual to define the possible. Experience was the dialectic by which he deduced from substantial premises a practical conclusion. The might of reason by which convenience and right were thus moulded into union, was amazing. But while he knew the folly of endeavouring to be wiser than time, his matchless resources of good sense contributed to the orderly development of the inherent elements of the constitution, by a vigour and dexterity as eminent in their kind as they were rare in their combination. The vessel of state was launched by the patriotism of many: the chart of her course was designed chiefly by Hamilton: but when the voyage was begun, the eye that observed, and the head that reckoned, and the hand that compelled the ship to keep her course amid tempests without and threats of mutiny within, were those of the great Chief Justice. Posterity will give him reverence as one of the founders of the nation; and of that group of statesmen who may one day perhaps be regarded as above the nature, as they certainly were beyond the dimensions of men, no figure, save ONE alone, will rise upon the eye in grandeur more towering than that of John Marshall.

The authority of the Supreme Court however is not confined to cases of constitutional law: it embraces the whole range of judicial action, as it is distributed in England, into legal, equitable, and maritime jurisdictions. The equity system of this court was too little developed to enable us to say what Marshall would have been as a chancellor. It is difficult to admit that he would have

been inferior to Lord Eldon: it is impossible to conceive that he could at all have resembled Lord Eldon. But undoubtedly the native region and proper interest of a mind so analytical and so sound, so piercing and so practical, was the Common Law, that vigorous system of manly reason and essential right, that splendid scheme of morality expanded by logic and informed by prudence. Perhaps the highest range of English intelligence is illustrated in the law: yet where in the whole line of that august succession will be found a character which fills the measure of judicial greatness so completely as Chief Justice Marshall? Where in English history is the judge, whose mind was at once so enlarged and so systematic, who so thoroughly had reduced professional science to general reason, in whose disciplined intellect technical learning had so completely passed into native sense? Vast as the reach of the law is, it is not an exaggeration to say that Marshall's understanding was greater, and embraced the forms of legal sagacity within it, as a part of its own spontaneous wisdom. He discriminated with instinctive accuracy between those technicalities which have sprung from the narrowness of inferior minds, and those which are set by the law for the defence of some vital element of justice or reason. The former he brushed away like cobwebs, while he yielded to the latter with a respect which sometimes seemed to those "whose eyes were" not "opened" a species of superstition. In his judicial office the method of Marshall appeared to be, first to bow his understanding reverently to the law, and calmly and patiently to receive its instructions as those of an oracle of which he was the minister; then, to prove these dictates by the most searching processes of reason, and to deliver them to others, not as decrees to be obeyed, but as logical manifestations of moral truth. Undoubtedly he made much use of adjudged cases; but he used them, to give light and certainty to his own judgment, and not for the vindication or support of the law. He would have deemed it a reproach alike to his abilities and his station, if he should have determined upon precedent what could have been demonstrated by reason, or had referred to authority what belonged to principle. With singular capacity, he united systematic reason with a perception of particular equity: too scrupulous a regard for the latter led Lord Eldon in most instances to adjudicate nothing but the case before him; but Marshall remembered that while he owed to the suitors the decision of the case, he owed to society the establishment of the principle. His mind naturally tended, not to suggestion and speculation, but to the determination of opinion and the closing of doubts. On the bench he always recollected that he was not merely a lawyer, and much less a legal essayist; he was conscious of an official duty and an official authority; and considered that questions might be discussed elsewhere, but came to be settled by him. The dignity with which these duties were discharged was not the least admirable part of the display. It was Wisdom on the seat of Power, pronouncing the decrees of Justice.

Political and legal sense are so distinct from one another as almost to be irreconcilable in the same mind. The latter is a mere course of deduction from premises; the other calls into exercise the highest order of perceptive faculties, and that quick felicity of intuition which flashes to its conclusions by a species of mental sympathy rather than by any conscious process of argumentation. The one requires that the susceptibility of the judgment should be kept exquisitely alive to every suggestion of the practical, so as to catch and follow the insensible reasonings of life, rather than to reason itself: the other demands the exclusion of every thing not rigorously exact, and the concentration of the whole consciousness of the mind in kindling implicit truth into formal principles. The wonder, in Judge Marshall's case, was to see these two almost inconsistent faculties, in quality so matchless and in development so magnificent, harmonized and united in his marvellous intelligence. We beheld him pass from one to the other department without confusing their nature, and without perplexing his own understanding. When he approached a question of constitutional jurisprudence, we saw the lawyer expand into the legislator; and in returning to a narrower sphere, pause from the creative glow of statesmanship, and descend from intercourse with the great conceptions and great feelings by which nations are guided and society is advanced, to submit his faculties with docility to the yoke of legal forms, and with impassible calmness to thread the tangled intricacies of forensic technicalities.

There was in this extraordinary man an unusual combination of the capacity of apprehending truth, with the ability to demonstrate and make it palpable to others. They often exist together in unequal degrees. Lord Mansfield's power of luminous explication was so surpassing that one might almost say that he made others perceive what he did not understand himself; but the numerous instances in which his decisions have been directly overthrown by his successors, and the still greater number of cases in which his opinions have been silently departed from, compel a belief that his judgment was not of the truest kind. Lord Eldon's judicial sagacity was a species of inspiration; but he seemed to be unable not only to convince others, but even to certify himself of the correctness of his own greatest and wisest determinations. But Judge Marshall's sense appeared to be at once both instinctive and analytical: his logic extended as far as his perception: he had no propositions in his thoughts which he could not resolve into their axioms. Truth came to him as a revelation, and from him as a demonstration. His mind was more than the faculty of vision; it was a body of light, which irradiated the subject to which it was directed, and rendered it as distinct to every other eye as it was to its own.

The mental integrity of this illustrious man was not the least important element of his greatness. Those qualities of vanity, fondness for display, the love of effect, the solicitation of applause, sensibility to opinions, which are the immoralities of intellect, never attached to that stainless essence of pure reason. He seemed to men to be a passionless intelligence; susceptible to no feeling but the constant love of right; subject to no affection but a polarity toward truth.

—Chief Justice Marshall's History of the Colonies planted by the English on the Continent of North America, from their Settlement to the Commencement of the War which terminated in their Independence, was first printed as an introductory volume to the Life of Washington, but in 1824 was published separately. The Life of Washington, originally in five volumes, in 1832 was republished in two. Both these works had been revised with great care. A volume entitled The Writings of John Marshall upon the Constitution, was published in Boston in 1839, under the direction of Judge Story.

ALEXANDER HAMILTON.

[Born 1757. Died 1804.]

In the summer of 1772 the leeward West India islands were desolated by a hurricane. While its effects were still visible, and men were looking fearfully into the skies, Thomas Hewes's St. Christopher's Gazette was distributed, with an account of the calamity written with such singular ability that when it reached Saint Croix, where it was dated, the governor and chief men of the place set themselves to work to discover its author. It was traced to a youth—in the counting-house of Nicholas Cruger, a merchant there—named ALEXANDER HAMILTON, born some fifteen years before in the island of Nevis; whose father was a decayed Scottish gentleman, and whose mother was of the good Huguenot stock of France. It was a happy day for our young author: a lad who could write in this way should not spend his life in casting up accounts: it was at once determined to send him to New York to complete his education. While on his way, the ship which bore him was on fire, dangerously, but not fatally, and in the month of October, in that year, he landed at Boston.

Francis Barber, afterward a colonel, and a brave man in several battles, was at this time principal of a grammar school in Elizabeth-town, New Jersey: a school of good repute, for Brockholst Livingston and Jonathan Dayton were among his pupils; and hither came the young West Indian to be prepared for college: a handsome youth, erect, graceful, eagle-eyed, and wise in conversation as a man. Before the end of 1773 he had finished his preliminary studies, and with honest Hercules Mulligan, tailor, afterward member of the revolutionary committee, and secret correspondent of the commander-in-chief, he proceeded to Princeton, to inquire of Dr. Wither-spoon if he could enter Nassau Hall with the privilege of passing from class to class as fast as he advanced in scholarship. The president was sorry, but the laws of the institution would not permit. He was more success-ful in New York. In King's College he might sue for a degree whenever he could show the title of sufficient learning. The chrysales of great men were in the college, but there was only one Alexander Hamilton there, and this soon became manifest. In the debating club he controlled every thing by his acuteness and eloquence, and his room-mate was awed, night and morning, by the fervid passion of his prayers. He wrote hymns and burlesqued the royal printer's leaders; he was pious and punctilious; ambitious and gay.

The days of trouble were already come. Macdougal had been imprisoned for his appeal to the betrayed inhabitants of the colony; and the liberty tree, coated with hoops which no garrison axe could cut, had been the rally-ing point for numerous assemblies of the people. All the proceedings were watched by the young collegian, who walked night and morning under the large trees in Batteau street for hours, with a thoughtful face. Every week he read the honest Post Boy, mercenary Hugh Gaines's neutral Mercury, and the unscrupulous "Brussels Gazette" of well-fed James Rivington, printer to the king. On the sixth of July, 1774, the long-remembered great meeting in the fields was held, and as the hot sun was going down, and the multitude was about to separate, a youth of diminutive form and a pale intel-lectual face, ascended the stand, recounted the oppressions of the government, insisted on the duty of resistance, and foretold that the waves of rebellion, sparkling with fire, would wash back to England the wrecks of her wealth and power from the New World. He closed amid breathless silence, and the air was filled with the tumult of wonder and applause. So, at seventeen years of age, Alexander Hamilton commenced his glorious public life.

The Episcopal clergy, all through the country, were opposed to liberty. The king was the head of the church. Doctors Chand-ler, Cooper, Inglis, Seabury, Wilkins, and others, had already written largely in defence of the ministry, and they now redoubled their efforts. With his master, President Myles

Cooper, Hamilton had tried his lance through Holt's paper, and when Seabury and Wilkins attacked the Congress in their Free Thoughts and Congress Canvassed,—distributed by the Tories all through the colonies, and tarred, feathered, and nailed to the pillories by the people—a defence appeared from the student, anonymous, like the pamphlets of the priests, and remarkable for its directness, ingenuity, and spirit. The clerical combatants published A View of the Controversy, and within a month Hamilton produced a rejoinder, in a pamphlet of nearly a hundred pages. It was more able than the first; grasped great principles with a master hand; and by a course of argument equally original and forcible, vindicated the Whigs, while its author seemed to look clearly into the distant future and see our state and policy. The Whigs received these pamphlets as text-books, and they were attributed to the maturest intellects of the party. "How absurd," said Dr. Myles Cooper, "to suppose that they were written by so young a man as Hamilton!" But the truth came out, and the gallant Marinus Willett says, the "Vindicator of Congress," as he was from that time called, "became our oracle."

From this period Hamilton was a "citizen." All his thoughts, all his energies were given to the country. I shall not attempt to trace with particularity his history, except as it is connected with the press. His next publication was Remarks on the Quebec Bill, in two numbers. His style was more highly polished, his views were more statesmanlike and profound. In 1775 he entered a military company, studied tactics, and was engaged in the first act of armed opposition to the ministry.

At the passage of the Raritan, in the memorable retreat through New Jersey, Washington observed with admiration the courage and skill of a youthful artillery officer, and ordered his aid-de-camp, Fitzgerald, to ascertain who he was, and to bring him to head-quarters at the first halt of the army. In the evening of that day the founder of the republic had his first interview with the most illustrious of her statesmen. Hamilton continued in the family of the commander-in-chief until 1781, and from the beginning to the end, to use Washington's own language, was his "principal and most confidential aid."

The embarrassments of the treasury and consequent sufferings of the army led Hamilton to the study of finance, and in 1779, in private and anonymous communications to Robert Morris, he proposed à great financial scheme for the country, in which, rising above all the crude systems of that age, and pointing to a combination of public with private credit as the basis of his plan, he led the way to the establishment of the first American bank. In the following spring, when he was but twenty-three years of age, he wrote his celebrated letter to Mr. Duane on the state of the nation, in which he suggests the national convention to form a constitution, and the mode of recommending it to the people, "in sensible and popular writings," which he afterward pursued in the Federalist.

In December, 1780, he was married to a daughter of General Schuyler, and on the first of March, 1781, he retired from the military family of Washington; with the disinterestedness which characterized all his actions, though without resources, resigning his pay, and retaining his commission only that he might have the power, should there be occasion, still to serve his country in the field. His brilliant conduct at Yorktown closed his military career.

His quick apprehension and solid judgmen enabled him, with almost unprecedented rapidity, to prepare for admission to the bar. He made his first appearance in the courts in 1782, and in the summer of the same year was elected by the legislature of New York to the congress of the confederation. The war at an end, patriotism and enthusiasm seemed to have died. All was apathy and irresolution. The Congress of 1782 was full of weak men and cowards. "The more I see," wrote Hamilton, "the more reason I find for those who love this country to weep over its blindness." His far-reaching sagacity, his solemn regard for justice, and his eloquence soon imparted a new tone to that body. He was always a member and often the chairman of the committees which had in charge the subjects of greatest importance. His reports are evidences of his extraordinary abilities, and of the correctness of the judgment expressed at this period by Washington, that "no one exceeded him in probity and sterling virtue."

At the end of the session he entered with

characteristic ardour upon the duties of his profession, in the city of New York; but his mind was still occupied with extensive schemes for the general benefit, and no man exerted so wide and powerful an influence with his pen. In 1786 he was a member of the New York assembly, and in 1787 was one of the three delegates to the convention for the formation of a federal constitution, which he had proposed in his letter on the state of the nation in 1779. No one will question the justice of the opinion expressed by Guizot respecting his efforts in this celebrated body, when he says, that " there is not one element of order, strength, or durability in the constitution which he did not powerfully contribute to introduce into the scheme and cause to be adopted." With Madison, whose labours in the convention had been of similar importance, and John Jay, one of our purest and ablest statesmen and jurists, upon its adjournment he commenced a series of essays, under the signature of Publius, upon the necessity of the union to the prosperity of the people, the insufficiency of the articles of confederation to maintain it, and the indispensableness of a government organized upon principles and clothed with powers at least equal to those granted in the one proposed. These essays have since been known under the name of The Federalist. They constitute one of the most profound and lucid treatises on politics that has ever been written. Hamilton was the author of nearly three-fourths of them, and admirable for various qualities as are those of his illustrious associates, his are easily distinguished by their superior comprehensiveness, practicalness, originality, and condensed and polished diction. In 1788 he was a member of the New York convention to which the constitution was submitted, and it was owing to his luminous arguments and persuasive eloquence, as it was to Madison's in Virginia, that it was accepted.

Upon the organization of the government, Washington indicated his estimation of the talents and integrity of Hamilton by appointing him secretary of the treasury. This office required the vigorous exercise of all his powers; and his reports of plans for the restoration of public credit, on the protection and encouragement of manufactures, on the necessity and the constitutionality of a national bank, and on the establishment of a mint, would alone have given him the reputation of being one of the most consummate statesmen who have ever lived. The plans which he proposed were adopted by Congress almost without alteration. When he entered upon the duties of his office the government had neither credit nor money, and the resources of the country were unknown; when he retired, at the end of five years, the fiscal condition of no people was better, or more clearly understood. Mr. Gallatin has said that secretaries of the treasury have since enjoyed a sinecure, the genius and labours of Hamilton having created and arranged every thing that was necessary for the perfect and easy discharge of their duties.

While Hamilton was in the treasury the French revolution was at its height, and native demagogues and alien emissaries were busy in efforts to embroil us in foreign war. Hamilton advised the proclamation of neutrality and the mission of Mr. Jay, the two acts which distinguished the external policy of the first administration; and he defended the proclamation under the signatures of No Jacobin and Pacificus, and Jay's treaty under that of Camillus, in essays which at the time had a controlling influence on the public mind, and which are still regarded as among the most profound commentaries which have appeared on the principles of international law and policy to which they had relation.

A false economy in this country has made almost every high office a burden to its possessor. Hamilton's increasing family warned him that his public must in some degree be sacrificed to his private obligations. When he resigned his seat in the cabinet and resumed his profession, his door was thronged with clients, and he seemed on the high road to fortune. The conduct of France meanwhile made every patriot a sentinel, and when her depredations upon our commerce and insults to our ministers left no alternative, under the signature of Titus Manlius, as with a bugle whose familiar sound marshalled to arms, he roused the people to resistance. The recommendations which he made were adopted by Congress, and when the provisional army was organized, Washington accepted the chief command upon condition that his favourite old associate in the field and the council should be his first officer. Upon the death of Washington in 1799, Hamilton became lieutenant-general, and when the army was disbanded he returned to the bar.

The remainder of his life was márked by few incidents, and the melancholy circumstances of its close, at the end of nearly half a century, are still familiar to the people. He was murdered by Aaron Burr, at Weehawken, near the city of New York, on the eleventh of June, 1804. There has been but one other instance of such profound and universal mourning in the United States. Whatever differences of opinion may have divided from him some of his countrymen, there was no one to question that he was a man of extraordinary abilities, virtue, and independence. His assassin, then in the second office of the republic, and the favourite of a powerful party, became a fugitive and a vagabond.

Hamilton was not faultless; but his errors have been greatly exaggerated, and no intelligent man needs be told that Madison was the only one among his distinguished political adversaries whose private character approached his in purity. His public life was without a stain. He was undoubtedly the greatest statesman of the eighteenth century. "He must be classed," says Guizot, "among the men who have best known the vital principles and fundamental conditions of a government worthy of its name and mission." Considering the activity of his life, and that so much of it was passed in the military service, affording but little leisure and opportunity for historical studies, the extent and fulness of his information is astonishing. There was never a statesman whose views were more explicit and comprehensive, and they seem to be results of the closest inductive reasoning from the experience of other nations. But however deliberately formed and firmly founded were his opinions, whenever he discovered that they could not be maintained, he cheerfully acquiesced in the plans which were preferred by his associates, and exerted his abilities to procure their adoption. It is remarkable that a man who on all subjects was so frank and fearless should have been so ill understood. His principles have been systematically perverted and misrepresented, not only without any sort of authority, but in opposition to positive declarations in his writings, speeches, and conversations. He did indeed have fears that the constitution would not ultimately prove to be practicable; that

"if we inclined too much to democracy we should soon shoot into a monarchy;" but no one had more dread of such a result,—no one was more anxious for the greatest freedom to the citizen that was compatible with efficiency in the government. It is an interesting fact, that the most anti-democratic proposition which he made in the federal convention—that for choosing a president and senate to hold their offices during good behaviour—was supported by the democratic states of Pennsylvania and Virginia, and voted for by Mr. Madison. His views on this and other points were essentially modified during the progress of the debates, and he finally voted to limit the presidential term to three years. He however frankly admitted, when questioned, that he had favored the idea of the tenure of good behaviour. "My reasons," he said to General Lewis, "were an exclusion, so far as possible, of the influence of executive patronage in the choice of a chief magistrate, and a desire to avoid the incalculable mischief which must result from the too frequent elections of that officer. You and I, my friend," he continued, "may not live to see the day; but most assuredly it will come, when *every vital interest of the state will be merged in the all-absorbing question of who shall be* NEXT PRESIDENT." The prophecy has become history. It became so earlier than he thought, for both he and his friend saw it fulfilled in the controversy of 1800.

In every page of the works of Hamilton we discover an original, vigorous, and practical understanding, informed with various and profound knowledge. But few of his speeches were reported, and even these very imperfectly; but we have traditions of his eloquence, which represent it as wonderfully winning and persuasive. Indeed it is evident from its known effects that he was a debater of the very first class. He thought clearly and rapidly, had a ready command of language, and addressed himself solely to the reason. He never lost his self-command, and never seemed impatient, but from the braverv of his nature, and his contempt of meanness and servility, he was perhaps sometimes indiscreet. His works were written hastily, but we can discover in them no signs of immaturity or carelessness: on the contrary they are hardly excelled in compactness, clearness, elegance, and purity of language.

THE FATE OF ANDRE.

FROM A LETTER TO COL. LAURENS.

NEVER, perhaps, did any man suffer death with more justice, or deserve it less. The first step he took, after his capture, was to write a letter to General Washington, conceived in terms of dignity without insolence, and apology without meanness. The scope of it, was to vindicate himself from the imputation of having assumed a mean character for treacherous or interested purposes; asserting that he had been involuntarily an impostor, that contrary to his intention, which was to meet a person for intelligence on neutral ground, he had been betrayed within our posts, and forced into the vile condition of an enemy in disguise: soliciting only, that, to whatever rigour policy might devote him, a decency of treatment might be observed, due to a person, who, though unfortunate, had been guilty of nothing dishonourable. His request was granted in its full extent; for, in the whole progress of the affair, he was treated with the most scrupulous delicacy. When brought before the Board of Officers, he met with every mark of indulgence, and was required to answer no interrogatory which could even embarrass his feelings. On his part, while he carefully concealed every thing that might involve others, he frankly confessed all the facts relating to himself; and, upon his confession, without the trouble of examining a witness, the board made their report. The members of it were not more impressed with the candour and firmness, mixed with a becoming sensibility, which he displayed, than he was penetrated with their liberality and politeness. He acknowledged the generosity of the behaviour toward him in every respect, but particularly in this, in the strongest terms of manly gratitude. In a conversation with a gentleman who visited him after his trial, he said he flattered himself he had never been illiberal; but if there were any remains of prejudice in his mind, his present experience must obliterate them.

In one of the visits I made to him, (and I saw him several times during his confinement,) he begged me to be the bearer of a request to the general, for permission to send an open letter to Sir Henry Clinton. "I foresee my fate," said he, "and though I pretend not to play the hero, or to be indifferent about life, yet I am reconciled to whatever may happen, conscious that misfortune, not guilt, has brought it upon me. There is only one thing that disturbs my tranquillity. Sir Henry Clinton has been too good to me; he has been lavish of his kindness. I am bound to him by too many obligations, and love him too well, to bear the thought that he should reproach himself, or that others should reproach him, on the supposition of my having conceived myself obliged, by his instructions, to run the risk I did. I would not, for the world, leave a sting in his mind that should imbitter his future days." He could scarce finish the sentence, bursting into tears in spite of his efforts to suppress them; and with difficulty collected himself enough afterward to add: "I wish to be permitted to assure him, I did not act under this impression, but submitted to a necessity imposed upon me, as contrary to my own inclination as to his orders." His request was readily complied with; and he wrote the letter annexed, with which I dare say you will be as much pleased as I am, both for the diction and sentiment.

When his sentence was announced to him, he remarked, that since it was his lot to die, there was still a choice in the mode, which would make a material difference in his feelings; and he would be happy, if possible, to be indulged with a professional death. He made a second application, by letter, in concise but persuasive terms. It was thought this indulgence, being incompatible with the customs of war, could not be granted; and it was therefore determined, in both cases, to evade an answer, to spare him the sensations which a certain knowledge of the intended mode would inflict.

In going to the place of execution, he bowed familiarly, as he went along, to all those with whom he had been acquainted in his confinement. A smile of complacency expressed the serene fortitude of his mind. Arrived at the fatal spot, he asked, with some emotion, "Must I then die in this manner?" He was told it had been unavoidable. "I am reconciled to my fate," said he, "but not to the mode." Soon, however, recollecting himself, he added: "It will be but a momentary pang;" and, springing upon the cart, performed the last offices to himself, with a composure that excited the admiration and melted the hearts of the beholders. Upon being told the final moment was at hand, and asked if he had any thing to say, he answered, "Nothing, but to request you will witness to the world, that I die like a brave man." Among the extraordinary circumstances that attended him, in the midst of his enemies, he died universally esteemed and universally regretted.

There was something singularly interesting in the character and fortunes of Andre. To an excellent understanding, well improved by education and travel, he united a peculiar elegance of mind and manners, and the advantage of a pleasing person. 'T is said he possessed a pretty taste for the fine arts, and had himself attained some proficiency in poetry, music, and painting. His knowledge appeared without ostentation, and embellished by a diffidence that rarely accompanies so many talents and accomplishments; which left you to suppose more than appeared. His sentiments were elevated, and inspired esteem: they had a softness that conciliated affection. His elocution was handsome; his address easy, polite, and insinuating. By his merit, he had acquired the unlimited confidence of his general, and was making a rapid progress in military rank and reputation. But in the height of his career, flushed with new hopes from the execution of a project, the most beneficial to his party that could be devised, he was at once precipitated from the summit of prosperity, and saw all the expectations of his ambition blasted, and himself ruined.

The character I have given of him is drawn partly from what I saw of him myself, and partly from information. I am aware that a man of real merit is never seen in so favourable a light as through the medium of adversity: the clouds that surround him are shades that set off his good qualities. Misfortune cuts down the little vanities that, in prosperous times, serve as so many spots in his virtues; and gives a tone of humility that makes his worth more amiable. His spectators, who enjoy a happier lot, are less prone to detract from it, through envy, and are more disposed, by compassion, to give him the credit he deserves, and perhaps even to magnify it.

I speak not of Andre's conduct in this affair as a philosopher, but as a man of the world. The authorized maxims and practices of war are the satires of human nature. They countenance almost every species of seduction as well as violence; and the general who can make most traitors in the army of his adversary, is frequently most applauded. On this scale we acquit Andre; while we could not but condemn him, if we were to examine his conduct by the sober rules of philosophy and moral rectitude. It is, however, a blemish on his fame, that he once intended to prostitute a flag: about this, a man of nice honour ought to have had a scruple; but the temptation was great; let his misfortunes cast a veil over his error.

Several letters from Sir Henry Clinton and others were received in the course of the affair, feebly attempting to prove, that Andre came out under the protection of a flag, with a passport from a general officer in actual service; and consequently could not be justly detained. Clinton sent a deputation, composed of Lieutenant-General Robinson, Mr. Elliot, and Mr. William Smith, to represent, as he said, the true state of Major Andre's case. General Greene met Robinson, and had a conversation with him; in which he reiterated the pretence of a flag; urged Andre's release as a personal favour to Sir Henry Clinton; and offered any friend of ours, in their power, in exchange. Nothing could have been more frivolous than the plea which was used. The fact was, that besides the time, manner, object of the interview, change of dress, and other circumstances, there was not a single formality customary with flags; and the passport was not to Major Andre, but to Mr. Anderson. But had there been, on the contrary, all the formalities, it would be an abuse of language to say, that the sanction of a flag for corrupting an officer to betray his trust ought to be respected. So unjustifiable a purpose would not only destroy its validity, but make it an aggravation. Andre, himself, has answered the argument, by ridiculing and exploding the idea, in his examination before the Board of Officers. It was a weakness to urge it.

There was. in truth, no way of saving him. Arnold, or he, must have been the victim: the former was out of our power.

It was by some suspected, Arnold had taken his measures in such a manner, that if the interview had been discovered in the act, it might have been in his power to sacrifice Andre to his own security. This surmise of double treachery made them imagine Clinton might be induced to give up Arnold for Andre; and a gentleman took occasion to suggest this expedient to the latter, as a thing that might be proposed by him. He declined it. The moment he had been capable of so much frailty, I should have ceased to esteem him.

The infamy of Arnold's conduct previous to his desertion, is only equalled by his baseness since. Beside the folly of writing to Sir Henry Clinton, assuring him that Andre had acted under a passport from him, and according to his directions while commanding officer at a post; and that, therefore, he did not doubt, he would be immediately sent in; he had the effrontery to write to General Washington in the same spirit; with the addition of a menace of retaliation, if the sentence should be carried into execution. He has since acted the farce of sending in his resignation. . . .

To his conduct, that of the captors of Andre forms a striking contrast. He tempted them with the offer of his watch, his horse, and any sum of money they should name. They rejected his offers with indignation: and the gold that could seduce a man high in the esteem and confidence of his country, who had the remembrance of past exploits, the motive of present reputation and future glory, to prop his integrity, had no charms for three simple peasants, leaning only on their virtue and an honest sense of their duty. While Arnold is handed down, with execration, to future times, posterity will repeat, with reverence, the names of Van Wart, Paulding, and Williams!

I congratulate you, my friend, on our happy escape from the mischiefs with which this treason was big. It is a new comment on the value of an honest man, and, if it were possible, would endear you to me more than ever.

EFFECTS OF A DISSOLUTION OF THE UNION.

FROM THE FEDERALIST.

Assuming it, therefore, as an established truth, that, in cases of disunion, the several states, or such combinations of them as might happen to be formed out of the wreck of the general confederacy, would be subject to those vicissitudes of peace and war, of friendship and enmity with each other, which have fallen to the lot of all other nations not united under one government, let us enter into a concise detail of some of the consequences that would attend such a situation.

War between the states, in the first periods of their separate existence, would be accompanied with much greater distresses than it commonly is in those countries where regular military establishments have long obtained. The disciplined armies always kept on foot on the continent of Europe, though they bear a malignant aspect to liberty and economy, have, notwithstanding, been productive of the singular advantage of rendering sudden conquests impracticable, and of preventing that rapid desolation which used to mark the progress of war prior to their introduction. The art of fortification has contributed to the same ends. The nations of Europe are encircled with the chains of fortified places, which mutually obstruct invasion. Campaigns are wasted in reducing two or three fortified garrisons, to gain admittance into an enemy's country. Similar impediments occur at every step, to exhaust the strength and delay the progress of an invader. Formerly, an invading army would penetrate into the heart of a neighbouring country almost as soon as intelligence of its approach could be received; but now, a comparatively small force of disciplined troops, acting on the defensive, with the aid of posts, is able to impede, and finally to frustrate, the purposes of one much more considerable. The history of war in that quarter of the globe is no longer a history of nations subdued, and empires overturned; but of towns taken and retaken, of battles that decide nothing, of retreats more beneficial than victories, of much effort and little acquisition.

In this country the scene would be altogether reversed. The jealousy of military establishments would postpone them as long as possible. The want of fortifications, leaving the frontier of one state open to another, would facilitate inroads. The populous states would with little difficulty overrun their less populous neighbours. Conquests would be as easy to be made as difficult to be retained. War, therefore, would be desultory and predatory. Plunder and devastation ever march in the train of irregulars. The calamities of individuals would ever make the principal figure in events, and would characterize our exploits.

This picture is not too highly wrought; though I confess it would not long remain a just one. Safety from external danger is the most powerful director of national conduct. Even the ardent love of liberty will, after a time, give way to its dictates. The violent destruction of life and property incident to war, the continual effort and alarm attendant on a state of continual danger, will compel nations the most attached to liberty to resort for repose and security to institutions which have a tendency to destroy their civil and political rights. To be more safe, they at length become willing to run the risk of being less free. The institutions chiefly alluded to are STANDING ARMIES, and the corresponding appendages of military establishments. Standing armies, it is said, are not provided against in the new constitution; and it is thence inferred that they would exist under it. This inference, from the very form of the proposition, is, at best, problematical and uncertain. But standing armies, it may be replied, must inevitably result from a dissolution of the confederacy. Frequent war and constant apprehension, which require a state of as constant preparation, will infallibly produce them. The weaker states or confederacies would first have recourse to them, to put themselves on an equality with their more potent neighbours. They would endeavour to supply the inferiority of population and resources by a more regular and effective system of defence—by disciplined troops, and by fortifications. They would, at the same time, be obliged to strengthen the executive arm of government; in doing which their constitutions would acquire a progressive direction towards monarchy. It is the nature of war to increase the executive at the expense of the legislative authority. The expedients which have been mentioned would soon give the states, or confederacies, that made use of them, a superiority over their neighbours. Small states, or states of less natural strength, under vigorous governments, and with the assistance of disciplined armies, have often triumphed over large states, or states of greater natural strength, which have been destitute of these advantages. Neither the pride nor the safety of the important states, or confederacies, would permit them long to submit to this mortifying and adventitious superiority. They would quickly resort to means similar to those by which it had been effected, to reinstate themselves in their lost pre-eminence. Thus we should, in a little time, see established in every part of this country the same engines of despotism which have been the scourge of the old world. This, at least, would be the natural course of things; and our reasonings will be likely to be just, in proportion as they are accommodated to this standard. These are not vague inferences, deduced from speculative defects in a constitution, the whole power of which is lodged in the hands of the people, or their representatives and delegates; they are solid conclusions, drawn from the natural and necessary progress of human affairs. . . . .

If we are wise enough to preserve the union, we may for ages enjoy an advantage similar to that of an insulated situation. Europe is at a great distance from us. Her colonies in our vicinity will be likely to continue too much disproportioned in strength to be able to give us any dangerous annoyance. Extensive military establishments cannot, in this position, be necessary to our security. But, if we should be disunited, and the integral parts should either remain separated, or, which is most probable, should be thrown together into two or three confederacies, we should be, in a short course of time, in the predicament of the continental powers of Europe. Our liberties would be a prey to the means of defending ourselves against the ambition and jealousy of each other.

This is an idea not superficial or futile, but solid and weighty. It deserves the most serious and mature consideration of every prudent and honest man of whatever party. If such men will make a firm and solemn pause, and meditate dispassionately on its importance; if they will contemplate it in all its attitudes, and trace it to all its consequences, they will not hesitate to part with trivial objections to a constitution, the rejection of which would, in all probability, put a final period to the union. The airy phantoms that now flit before the distempered imaginations of some of its adversaries, would then quickly give place to more substantial prospects of dangers, real, certain, and extremely formidable.

FISHER AMES.

[Born 1758. Died 1808.]

FISHER AMES was regarded by many of his contemporaries as one of the greatest men who had lived in this country. He was the leader of the federal party in the House of Representatives during the administration of Washington, and was applauded for his eloquence and learning, the solidity of his judgment, and the unsullied purity of his public and private conduct.

He was born in Dedham, Massachusetts, on the ninth of April, 1758; entered Harvard College when twelve years of age; took his degree at sixteen; and in 1781 commenced the practice of the law, having studied his profession in the office of William Tudor.

The ability he had manifested in occasional public speeches, and in various political contributions to the gazettes, in 1788 procured him an election to the Massachusetts convention for ratifying the federal constitution; he was soon after made a member of the state legislature; and the people of Boston chose him to be their first representative in the Congress of the United States.

His most celebrated speech in this body was delivered on the twenty-ninth of April, 1796, in support of the Treaty with Great Britain, which a considerable party was anxious to repudiate, although it had been approved by the executive. He was so feeble, from a severe and protracted illness, when he arose, that it seemed doubtful whether he would be able to do more than enter a protest against the proposed violation of public faith; but as he proceeded he acquired a factitious strength from his enthusiasm, and when he sat down, with an allusion to his "slender and almost broken hold upon life," the effect which had been produced was so great that a postponement of the consideration of the subject was moved on the part of the opposition, lest the House should act under the influence of feelings which would be condemned by their judgment. This and his speech on Mr. Madison's resolutions, are the only ones of which we have reports, though he was not an unfrequent debater.

96

After a service of eight years in Congress, on the retirement of Washington he also quitted public life. He resided on his farm in Dedham, occasionally appearing in th courts, and devoting his leisure to correspondence, and the composition of political essays, which, though published anonymously, had a powerful influence upon public opinion. In 1804 he was elected president of Harvard College, but on account of ill health declined the office. His debility continued gradually to increase until the fourth of July, 1808, when he died.

A selection from the speeches, essays and letters of Mr. Ames, with a memoir by his friend the Rev. Dr. Kirkland, was published in 1809. His reputation has since that time very much decayed, chiefly because the subjects upon which he wrote were of temporary interest or are seen differently in the light o subsequent experience. He regarded the "rabble of great cities as the standing army of ambition." He was fearful of the influence of popular impulses upon public affairs; "the turnpike road of history," he said, "is white with the tombstones of republics" which they have controlled. In France he saw liberty "stripped of its bloody garments to disguise its robbers;" and with intense attention and alarm watched the progress in this country of what were called French opinions. Foreseeing the downfall of the Federal party, he feared that that nation would be engulfed in its ruins. A more hopeful spirit would have made him a happier man, though perhaps not a more useful citizen.

The most striking quality in the writing of Ames is their perfect fearlessness. He disdained to flatter the mob. An ultra-democracy he deemed little better than a hell, and dared to say so. Plain speakers are the salt of a republic. His speeches were deficient in method. They were desultory, full of examples drawn from history, classical allusion, and learned reflection, and every thing helped on his argument and deepened his impression. His letters and essays have the same qualities. His works are perhaps overloaded with imagery, but it is so chaste as to be always pleasing, and its profusion never obscures his meaning. There is great variety in his periods, and his language is always remarkably pure. All his writings are marked in an eminent degree with his individual characteristics.

THE OBLIGATION OF TREATIES.

FROM A SPEECH ON THE BRITISH TREATY.

WILL any man affirm, the American nation is engaged by good faith to the British nation; but that engagement is nothing to this house? Such a man is not to be reasoned with. Such a doctrine is a coat of mail, that would turn the edge of all the weapons of argument, if they were sharper than a sword. Will it be imagined the king of Great Britain and the president are mutually bound by the treaty; but the two nations are free? ....

This, sir, is a cause that would be dishonoured and betrayed, if I contented myself with appealing only to the understanding. It is too cold, and its processes are too slow for the occasion. I desire to thank God, that, since he has given me an intellect so fallible, he has impressed upon me an instinct that is sure. On a question of shame and honour, reasoning is sometimes useless, and worse. I feel the decision in my pulse: if it throws no light upon the brain, it kindles a fire at the heart.

It is not easy to deny, it is impossible to doubt, that a treaty imposes an obligation on the American nation. It would be childish to consider the president and senate obliged, and the nation and house free. What is the obligation? perfect or imperfect? If perfect, the debate is brought to a conclusion. If imperfect, how large a part of our faith is pawned? Is half our honour put at risk, and is that half too cheap to be redeemed? How long has this hair-splitting subdivision of good faith been discovered, and why has it escaped the researches of the writers on the law of nations? Shall we add a new chapter to that law; or insert this doctrine as a supplement to, or more properly a repeal of the ten commandments? ....

On every hypothesis, the conclusion is not to be resisted: we are either to execute this treaty, or break our faith.

To expatiate on the value of public faith may pass with some men for declamation: to such men I have nothing to say. To others I will urge, can any circumstance mark upon a people more turpitude and debasement? Can any thing tend more to make men think themselves mean, or degrade to a lower point their estimation of virtue and their standard of action? It would not merely demoralize mankind; it tends to break all the ligaments of society, to dissolve that mysterious charm which attracts individuals to the nation, and to inspire in its stead a repulsive sense of shame and disgust.

What is patriotism? Is it a narrow affection for the spot where a man was born? Are the very clods where we tread entitled to this ardent preference, because they are greener? No, sir, this is not the character of the virtue, and it soars higher for its object. It is an extended self-love, mingling with all the enjoyments of life, and twisting itself with the minutest filaments of the heart. It is thus we obey the laws of society, because they are the laws of virtue. In their authority we see, not the array of force and terror, but the venerable image of our country's honour. Every good citizen makes that honour his own, and cherishes it not only as precious, but as sacred. He is willing to risk his life in its defence; and is conscious that he gains protection, while he gives it. For what rights of a citizen will be deemed inviolable, when a state renounces the principles that constitute their security? Or, if his life should not be invaded, what would its enjoyments be in a country odious in the eyes of strangers, and dishonoured in his own? Could he look with affection and veneration to such a country as his parent? The sense of having one would die within him; he would blush for his patriotism, if he retained any, and justly, for it would be a vice: he would be a banished man in his native land.

I see no exception to the respect that is paid among nations to the law of good faith. If there are cases in this enlightened period when it is violated, there are none when it is decried. It is the philosophy of politics, the religion of governments. It is observed by barbarians: a whiff of tobacco smoke, or a string of beads, gives not merely binding force, but sanctity to treaties. Even in Algiers, a truce may be bought for money; but, when ratified, even Algiers is too wise or too just to disown and annul its obligation. Thus we see, neither the ignorance of savages, nor the principles of an association for privacy and rapine, permit a nation to despise its engagements. If, sir, there could be a resurrection from the foot of the gallows, if the victims of justice could live again, collect together and form a society, they would, however loath, soon find themselves obliged to make justice, that justice under which they fell, the fundamental law of their state. They would perceive it was their interest to make others respect, and they would therefore soon pay some respect themselves to the obligations of good faith.

It is painful, I hope it is superfluous, to make even the supposition, that America should furnish the occasion of this opprobrium. No, let me not even imagine, that a republican government, sprung, as our own is, from a people enlightened and uncorrupted, a government whose origin is right, and whose daily discipline is duty, can, upon

13

solemn debate, make its option to be faithless; can dare to act what despots dare not avow, what our own example evinces the states of Barbary are unsuspected of. No, let me rather make the supposition, that Great Britain refuses to execute the treaty, after we have done everything to carry it into effect. Is there any language of reproach pungent enough to express your commentary on the fact? What would you say, or, rather, what would you not say? Would you not tell them, wherever an Englishman might travel, shame would stick to him: he would disown his country. You would exclaim, England, proud of your wealth, and arrogant in the possession of power, blush for these distinctions, which become the vehicles of your dishonour. Such a nation might truly say to corruption, thou art my father, and to the worm, thou art my mother and my sister. We should say of such a race of men, their name is a heavier burden than their debt.

I can scarcely persuade myself to believe, that the consideration I have suggested requires the aid of any auxiliary; but, unfortunately, auxiliary arguments are at hand.....

The refusal of the posts—inevitable if we reject the treaty*—is a measure too decisive in its nature to be neutral in its consequences. From great causes we are to look for great effects..... Will the tendency to Indian hostilities be contested by any one? Experience gives the answer. The frontiers were scourged with war, until the negotiation with Great Britain was far advanced; and then the state of hostility ceased. Perhaps the public agents of both nations are innocent of fomenting the Indian war, and perhaps they are not. We ought not, however, to expect that neighbouring nations, highly irritated against each other, will neglect the friendship of the savages. The traders will gain an influence, and will abuse it; and who is ignorant that their passions are easily raised and hardly restrained from violence? Their situation will oblige them to choose between this country and Great Britain, in case the treaty should be rejected: they will not be our friends, and at the same time the friends of our enemies.....

If any, against all these proofs, should maintain, that the peace with the Indians will be stable without the posts, to them I will urge another reply. From arguments calculated to procure conviction, I will appeal directly to the hearts of those who hear me, and ask whether it is not already planted there? I resort especially to the convictions of the Western gentlemen, whether, supposing no posts and no treaty, the settlers will remain in security? Can they take it upon them to say, that an Indian peace, under these circumstances, will prove firm? No, sir, it will not be peace, but a sword; it will be no better than a lure to draw victims within the reach of the tomahawk. On this theme, my emotions are unutterable. If I could find words for them, if my powers bore

---

* By the treaty, certain western posts, necessary to the protection of the frontier, were to be surrendered by the British.—*Editor.*

any proportion to my zeal, I would swell my voice to such a note of remonstrance, it should reach every log house beyond the mountains. I would say to the inhabitants, wake from your false security: your cruel dangers, your more cruel apprehensions are soon to be renewed: the wounds, yet unhealed, are to be torn open again; in the day time, your path through the woods will be ambushed; the darkness of midnight will glitter with the blaze of your dwellings. You are a father—the blood of your sons shall fatten your corn-field: you are a mother—the warhoop shall wake the sleep of the cradle.

On this subject you need not suspect any deception on your feelings: it is a spectacle of horror, which cannot be overdrawn. If you have nature in your hearts, they will speak a language, compared with which all I have said or can say will be poor and frigid.....

Will any one deny, that we are bound, and I would hope to good purpose, by the most solemn sanctions of duty for the vote we give? Are despots alone to be reproached for unfeeling indifference to the tears and blood of their subjects? Are republicans unresponsible? Have the principles, on which you ground the reproach upon cabinets and kings, no practical influence, no binding force? Are they merely themes of idle declamation, introduced to decorate the morality of a newspaper essay, or to furnish pretty topics of harangue from the windows of that state-house? I trust it is neither too presumptuous nor too late to ask: Can you put the dearest interest of society at risk, without guilt, and without remorse?....

There is no mistake in this case: there can be none: experience has already been the prophet of events, and the cries of our future victims have already reached us. The western inhabitants are not a silent and uncomplaining sacrifice. The voice of humanity issues from the shade of the wilderness: it exclaims, that, while one hand is held up to reject this treaty, the other grasps a tomahawk. It summons our imagination to the scenes that will open. It is no great effort of the imagination to conceive that events so near are already begun. I can fancy that I listen to the yells of savage vengeance and the shrieks of torture: already they seem to sigh in the western wind: already they mingle with every echo from the mountains.....

Let me cheer the mind, weary and ready to despond on this prospect, by presenting another which it is yet in our power to realize. Is it possible for a real American to look at the prosperity of this country, without some desire for its continuance, without some respect for the measures which many will say produced, and all will confess have preserved it? Will he not feel some dread, that a change of system will reverse the scene? The well grounded fears of our citizens, in 1794, were removed by the treaty, but are not forgotten. Then they deemed war nearly inevitable, and would not this adjustment have been considered at that day as a happy escape from the calamity? The great interest and the general desire of our people was to enjoy the advantages of neutrality. This instrument, however misrepresented, affords America that inestimable security. The causes of our disputes are either cut up by the roots, or referred to a new negotiation, after the end of the European war. This was gaining every thing, because it confirmed our neutrality, by which our citizens are gaining every thing. This alone would justify the engagements of the government. For, when the fiery vapours of the war lowered in the skirts of our horizon, all our wishes were concentrated in this one, that we might escape the desolation of the storm. This treaty, like a rainbow on the edge of the cloud, marked to our eyes the space where it was raging, and afforded at the same time the sure prognostic of fair weather. If we reject it, the vivid colours will grow pale, it will be a baleful meteor portending tempest and war. . . . .

I rose to speak under impressions that I would have resisted if I could. Those who see me will believe, that the reduced state of my health has unfitted me, almost equally, for much exertion of body or mind. Unprepared for debate by careful reflection in my retirement, or by long attention here, I thought the resolution I had taken, to sit silent, was imposed by necessity, and would cost me no effort to maintain. With a mind thus vacant of ideas, and sinking, as I really am, under a sense of weakness, I imagined the very desire of speaking was extinguished by the persuasion that I had nothing to say. Yet when I come to the moment of deciding the vote, I start back with dread from the edge of the pit into which we are plunging. In my view, even the minutes I have spent in expostulation have their value, because they protract the crisis, and the short period in which alone we may resolve to escape it.

I have thus been led by my feelings to speak more at length than I had intended. Yet I have perhaps as little personal interest in the event as any one here. There is, I believe, no member, who will not think his chance to be a witness of the consequences greater than mine. If, however, the vote should pass to reject, and a spirit would rise, as it will, with the public disorders to make " confusion worse confounded," even I, slender and almost broken as my hold upon life is, may outlive the government and constitution of my country.

INTELLECT IN A DEMOCRACY.
FROM AN ESSAY ON AMERICAN LITERATURE.

INTELLECTUAL superiority is so far from conciliating confidence, that it is the very spirit of a democracy, as in France, to proscribe the aristocracy of talents. To be the favourite of an ignorant multitude, a man must descend to their level; he must desire what they desire, and detest all they do not approve: he must yield to their prejudices, and substitute them for principles. Instead of enlightening their errors, he must adopt them; he must furnish the sophistry that will propagate and defend them.

FREEDOM OF THE PRESS AND LIBERTY.
FROM REVIEW OF THE PRESENT STATE OF THE BRITISH CONSTITUTION.

WE are, heart and soul, friends to the freedom of the press. It is however, the prostituted companion of liberty, and somehow or other, we know not how, its efficient auxiliary. It follows the substance like its shade; but while a man walks erect, he may observe, that his shadow is almost always in the dirt. It corrupts, it deceives, it inflames. It strips virtue of her honours, and lends to faction its wildfire and its poisoned arms, and in the end is its own enemy and the usurper's ally. It would be easy to enlarge on its evils. They are in England, they are here, they are everywhere. It is a precious pest and a necessary mischief, and there would be no liberty without it.

LIBERTY NOT SECURED BY THE DEATH OF TYRANTS.
FROM AN ESSAY ON THE CHARACTER OF BRUTUS.

IT is not by destroying tyrants, that we are to extinguish tyranny: nature is not thus to be exhausted of her power to produce them. The soil of a republic sprouts with the rankest fertility: it has been sown with dragon's teeth. To lessen the hopes of usurping demagogues, we must enlighten, animate, and combine the spirit of freemen; we must fortify and guard the constitutional ramparts about liberty. When its friends become indolent or disheartened, it is no longer of any importance how long-lived are its enemies: they will prove immortal.

GREAT MEN THE GLORY OF THEIR COUNTRY.
FROM A SKETCH OF THE CHARACTER OF ALEXANDER HAMILTON.

THE most substantial glory of a country is in its virtuous great men: its prosperity will depend on its docility to learn from their example. That nation is fated to ignominy and servitude, for which such men have lived in vain. Power may be seized by a nation, that is yet barbarous; and wealth may be enjoyed by one, that it finds, or renders sordid: the one is the gift and the sport of accident, and the other is the sport of power. Both are mutable, and have passed away without leaving behind them any other memorial than ruins that offend taste, and traditions that baffle conjecture. But the glory of Greece is imperishable, or will last as long as learning itself, which is its monument: it strikes an everlasting root, and leaves perennial blossoms on its grave.

JOHN QUINCY ADAMS.

[Born 1767. Died 1848.]

COLONEL JOHN QUINCY, who was born in 1687, and in his long life had shared largely in the civil and military distinctions of the colonies, was dying, on Saturday evening, the eleventh of July, 1767, when word was brought that a great-grandson was born to him in the house of John Adams. In honour of the departed veteran that part of the town of Braintree in which he resided was afterward called Quincy, and the boy was named JOHN QUINCY ADAMS. These two lives have extended over nearly one hundred and sixty years.

A large portion of the youth of Mr. Adams was spent in travel, in the company of his eminent father, and perhaps no statesman ever in all respects more fortunate in the circumstances of his education. In 1778 and the following year he was at school in Paris, and in this period he received the paternal care of Franklin, who was a joint commissioner with his father to the court of Versailles. In 1780 he was placed in the public school of Amsterdam, and subsequently in the University of Leyden. In July, 1781, Francis Dana, —father of our admirable author of that name, and afterward chief justice of Massachusetts,— was appointed minister to Russia; and having accompanied John Adams to Holland, and observed the abilities and accomplishments of his son, then but fourteen years of age, he selected him to be his private secretary. He remained in St. Petersburgh with Mr. Dana until October, 1782, and passed the following winter in travelling through Sweden, Denmark, Hamburg and Bremen, to the Hague, where he rejoined his father, whom he accompanied to Paris, where he was present at the signing of the definitive treaty of peace, and to London, where he listened to the eloquence of Burke, Pitt, Fox, Sheridan, and the other great orators then in Parliament. In his eighteenth year he returned to the United States to complete his education; entered Harvard University, at an advanced standing; and in 1787 received the degree of Bachelor of Arts.

When Mr. George M. Dallas, soon after returning from his mission to Russia, was looking over the manuscript papers of his father, in Philadelphia, he discovered a package so carefully sealed as evidently to have been deemed of some consequence, and opening it discovered that it was the autograph copy of an oration on banking and currency delivered by Mr. Adams on the day of his graduation. It had been listened to by Dr. Belknap, the historian, and Mr. Alexander J. Dallas, who were so pleased with its original and profound views that they addressed a note to the young author requesting a copy for publication. It was the first of his printed writings.

After leaving Cambridge Mr. Adams entered on the study of the law with the celebrated Theophilus Parsons at Newburyport, and on being admitted to the bar removed to Boston, where he was four years engaged in the business of his profession, and in the discussion of various questions of politics through the gazettes. Under the signature of Publicola he replied to the first part of Paine's Rights of Man, and under that of Marcellus, anticipating Washington's proclamation of neutrality, urged the foreign policy which was subsequently adopted by the first administration. In the same period he also published a series of papers vindicating the conduct of the president in regard to Genet, the French minister. Thus commended by his writings, as well as by his known acquaintance with international law and with our foreign relations, he was selected by Washington to be the American minister to the Netherlands; and in the seven years from 1794 to 1801 he was employed in diplomatic services. One of the last official acts of Washington was to appoint him minister to Portugal; but while on his way to Lisbon his destination was changed to Berlin, by his father, who had just succeeded to the presidency, and to whom Washington wrote on the subject that it was his " decided opinion that John Quincy

Adams was the most valuable public character we had abroad," and that there was no doubt in his mind that he would " prove himself to be the ablest of all our diplomatic corps."

During the four years which Mr. Adams passed in Berlin he devoted much attention to the study of the German literature, of which he became an enthusiastic admirer. " At this time," he says,* " Wieland was there the most popular of the German poets, and although there was in his genius neither the originality nor the deep pathos of Goethe, or Klopstock, or Schiller, there was something in the playfulness of his imagination, in the tenderness of his sensibility, in the sunny cheerfulness of his philosophy, and in the harmony of his versification," which delighted him ; and he made a complete translation of his Oberon, which he would have published, but that Mr. Sotheby got the start of him. Wieland read the first canto of Mr. Adams's version, in manuscript, and compared it with Sotheby's, which he thought more poetical, though less accurate.

In the same period he made an excursion into Silesia, and spent several weeks in collecting information respecting the industrial and social state of the country, which he communicated in a series of letters to a younger brother in Philadelphia. These letters were printed in the Port Folio, a weekly miscellany edited by Mr. Dennie,† and subsequently were published in an octavo volume in London. They contain a pleasing view of a people who in condition and character, more than any others in Europe, resemble the inhabitants of New England ; and at that time were particularly interesting on account of the facts they embraced in regard to manufacturing establishments with small capitals.

---

* Letter to Dr. Follen.

† Joseph Dennie was born in Boston in 1768, and graduated at Harvard University in 1790. After being admitted to the bar in Charleston, New Hampshire, he removed to Walpole in that state, where he afterward published The Farmer's Museum. a weekly paper, which his writings, particularly a series of essays entitled the The Lay Preacher, made very popular. He subsequently came to Philadelphia to accept a clerkship offered him by Mr. Pickering, then Secretary of State, and on the dismissal of his patron from the cabinet, in 1801, he established The Port Folio, which he conducted until his death, in 1812. Dennie was a great favourite in society, and his brilliant social qualities gave him a factitious reputation as a man of letters. There is nothing in his writings deserving of preservation.

At the close of his father's administration Mr. Adams returned to the United States, and soon after became a member of the Massachusetts legislature, by which he was elected to the national senate, and he took his seat in that body on the fourth of March, 1803.

In June, 1805, he was chosen professor of rhetoric and oratory in Harvard University, and he accepted the office on condition that he should be allowed to attend to his duties in Congress. He delivered his inaugural discourse on the twelfth of June, 1806, and proceeded with his public lectures weekly in term time, except when his presence was required in the senate, for two years, at the end of which period he resigned to accept the mission to Russia, offered him by President Madison. His lectures had been attended by crowds, from the adjacent country and the neighbouring city of Boston, in addition to his academical hearers, and soon after his resignation were published, in two octavo volumes. They appear to have been treated with undeserved neglect. Certain sins, real or supposed, of the politician, have been visited upon the professor. They are copious in diction and illustration, full of learned allusion and reflection, and point out " the right path of a virtuous and noble education."

From Russia, where his services were in many ways important, Mr. Adams was transferred to Ghent, with Mr. Gallatin, Mr. Clay, and Mr. Bayard, to negotiate a peace between the United States and Great Britain, and upon the conclusion of the labours of the commission, was appointed minister to the court of St. James, where he remained until Mr. Monroe's accession to the presidency, when he was recalled to be secretary of state. In his long, varied and brilliant career as a diplomatist he had perfectly justified the favourable auguries of Washington.

After being eight years at the head of the cabinet, under Mr. Monroe, Mr. Adams was elected President of the United States His administration ended on the third of March, 1829. and he retired to his native town of Quincy, where for a brief period he was without the cares of office. In 1831 however, by the nearly unanimous suffrages of his congressional district, he was elected to the House of Representatives, of which body he continued to be a member until his death.

12

He had been more than half a century in public offices of the greatest dignity and importance, which he filled with honour to himself and advantage to the country. For sixteen years the "old man eloquent" had not been absent a single day from his seat in the national legislature, where his extraordinary experience, various and profound knowledge, and courageous independence, secured for him the highest consideration and influence. Never modifying principles or language to please a man or a party, he invariably maintained what he has deemed the truth, and contended for the perfect freedom of others to do so. Though denounced as a madman and a factionist by every section in its turn, it is hardly doubtful that he was for many years second to no man of the Union in the confidence and veneration of the great body of the people.

The state papers of Mr. Adams are of course very numerous. They are generally distinguished for minuteness, accuracy and extent of information, and comprehensive and statesmanlike views; and some of them, as the report on the history and philosophy of weights and measures, prepared in obedience to a resolution of the senate, in 1817, are exhibitions of great research and learning. His speeches, on nearly all the important questions that have engaged the attention of the government since its formation, would fill many volumes, and are repositories of the richest materials of history and political philosophy.

The largest class of his published writings consists of orations and miscellaneous discourses pronounced before various societies and on anniversary and other occasions, many of which are of great value as historical essays. His eulogy on the life and services of Lafayette is the best memoir of that celebrated person that has been published in this country, and his sketches of Madison and Monroe, in the same form, are the only ones worthy of the subjects. His discourse before the New York Historical Society, on the fiftieth anniversary of the inauguration of Washington, is full of important information and reflection, but is perhaps in some degree unjust in regard to one illustrious person against whom Mr. Adams may be supposed to have inherited prejudices.

He had been all his life a student of Shakspeare. His admiration commenced "ere the

down had darkened on his lip, and continued through five of the seven ages of the drama of life, gaining upon the judgment as it lost to the imagination;" and among his writings is a series of criticisms upon some of his principal characters, in which original and striking views are maintained with great ingenuity.

I have already alluded to his translation of the Oberon of Wieland. In 1832 he published Dermot Mac Morrogh, a Tale of the Twelfth Century, in four cantos, and he has given to the public many shorter poems, chiefly lyrical, which are generally marked by fancy, feeling, and harmonious versification. His hymns have the simplicity, unity and completeness which belong to that sort of compositions, and his satires are neat and pointed. His poetical writings are the unpretending pastimes of a statesman. They would have been much more read and praised if written by a less eminent person.

For more than sixty years Mr. Adams is understood to have kept a diary in which every thing connected with his eventful life is presented with careful minuteness. Such a work will have something of the interest and value of the finest old chronicles. It must be a sort of "autobiography of the country." It has been stated also that he had written a memoir of his father; but I believe he found time to complete only a single volume, of four or five which the plan embraced. John Adams left abundant materials for his later history, but it is doubtful whether any other person will finish as well as the son, the work thus commenced.

The distinguishing characteristics of the writings and speeches of Mr. Adams are an universality of knowledge which they display, and a certain undauntedness, greater as they are more unpopular, with which he maintains his opinions. His taste is not always correct or chaste, and his style and argument are frequently diffuse; but there are in some of his speeches passages of close reasoning and great eloquence, and of fiery denunciation which has carried terror to the hearts of his adversaries.

—These paragraphs were written while Mr. Adams was alive. He died in the capitol, at Washington—in the scene of his chief triumphs—suddenly, on the twenty-third of February, 1848. His writings are soon to be published by his son, Charles Francis Adams.

THE CHARACTER OF DESDEMONA.

FROM ESSAYS ON THE CHARACTERS OF SHAKSPEARE.

THERE are critics who cannot bear to see the virtue and delicacy of Shakspeare's Desdemona called in question; who defend her on the ground that Othello is not an Ethiopian, but a Moor; that he is not black, but only tawny; and they protest against the sable mask of Othello upon the stage, and against the pictures of him in which he is always painted black. They say that prejudices have been taken against Desdemona from the slanders of Iago, from the railings of Roderigo, from the disappointed paternal rancour of Brabantio, and from the desponding concessions of Othello himself.

I have said, that since I entered upon the third of Shakspeare's seven ages, the first and chief capacity in which I have read and studied him is as a *teacher of morals;* and that I had scarcely ever seen a player of his parts who regarded him as a *moralist* at all. I further said, that in my judgment no man could understand him who did study him pre-eminently as a teacher of morals. These critics say they do not incline to put Shakspeare on a level with Æsop! Sure enough *they* do not study Shakspeare as a teacher of morals. To *them,* therefore, Desdemona is a perfect character; and her love for Othello is not unnatural, because he is not a Congo negro but only a sooty Moor, and has royal blood in his veins.

My objections to the character of Desdemona arise not from what Iago, or Roderigo, or Brabantio, or Othello says of her; but from what she herself *does.* She absconds from her father's house, in the dead of night, to marry a blackamoor. She breaks a father's heart, and covers his noble house with shame, to gratify—what! Pure love, like that of Juliet or Miranda? No! unnatural passion; it cannot be named with delicacy. Her admirers now say this is criticism of 1835; that the colour of Othello has nothing to do with the passion of Desdemona. No? Why, if Othello had been white, what ne&d would there have been for her running away with him? She could have made no better match. Her father could have made no reasonable objection to it; and there could have been no tragedy. If the colour of Othello is not as vital to the whole tragedy as the age of Juliet is to her character and destiny, then have I read Shakspeare in vain. The father of Desdemona charges Othello with magic arts in obtaining the affections of his daughter. Why, but because her passion for him is *unnatural;* and why is it unnatural, but because of his colour? In the very first scene, in the dialogue between Roderigo and Iago, before they rouse Brabantio to inform him of his daughter's elopement, Roderigo contemptuously calls Othello "the thick lips." I cannot in decency quote here—but turn to the book, and see in what language Iago announces to her father his daughter's shameful misconduct. The language of Roderigo is more supportable. *He* is a Venetian gentleman, himself a rejected suitor of Desdemona; and who has been forbid-

den by her father access to his house. Roused from his repose at the dead of night by the loud cries of these two men, Brabantio spurns, with indignation and scorn, the insulting and beastly language of Iago; and sharply chides Roderigo, whom he supposes to be hovering about his house in defiance of his prohibitions and in a state of intoxication. He threatens him with punishment. Roderigo replies—

> "*Rod.* Sir, I will answer any thing. But I beseech you,
> If't be your pleasure, and most wise consent,
> (As partly, I find, it is,) that your fair daughter
> At this odd-even and dull watch o' the night,
> Transported—with no worse nor better guard,
> But with a knave of common hire, a gondolier,—
> To the gross clasps of a lascivious Moor,—
> If this be known to you, and your allowance,
> We then have done you bold and saucy wrongs;
> But if you know not this, my manners tell me,
> We have your wrong rebuke. Do not believe,
> That, from the sense of all civility,
> I thus would play and trifle with your reverence:
> Your daughter—if you have not given her leave,—
> I say again, hath made a gross revolt;
> Tying her duty, beauty, wit, and fortunes,
> In an extravagant and wheeling stranger,
> Of here and everywhere; Straight satisfy yourself:
> If she be in your chamber, or your house,
> Let loose on me the Justice of the state
> For thus deluding you."

Struck by this speech as by a clap of thunder, Brabantio calls up his people, remembers a portentous dream, calls for light, goes and searches with his servants, and comes back saying—

> "It is too true an evil : gone she is:
> And what's to come of my despised time,
> Is nought but bitterness."

The father's heart is broken; life is no longer of any value to him; he repeats this sentiment time after time whenever he appears in the scene: and in the last scene of the play, where Desdemona lies dead, her uncle Gratiano says—

> "Poor Desdemona! I am glad thy father's dead,
> Thy match was mortal to him, and pure grief
> Shore his old thread in twain."

Indeed! indeed! I must look at Shakspeare in this as in all his pictures of human life, in the capacity of a teacher of morals. I must believe that in exhibiting a daughter of a Venetian nobleman of the highest rank eloping in the dead of the night to marry a thick-lipped, wool-headed Moor, opening a train of consequences which lead to her own destruction by her husband's hands, and to that of her father by a broken heart, he did not intend to present her as an example of the perfection of female virtue. I must look first at the action, then at the motive, then at the consequences, before I inquire in what light it is received and represented by the other persons of the drama. The first action of Desdemona discards all female delicacy, all filial duty, all sense of ingenuous shame. So I consider it—and so, it is considered by her own father. Her offence is not a mere elopement from her father's house for a clandestine marriage. I hope it requires no unreasonable rigour of morality to consider even *that* as suited to raise a prepossession rather unfavourable to the character of a young woman of refined sensibility and elevated education. But an elopement for a clandestine marriage with a blackamoor!—That is the measure of my estimation of the character of Desdemona from the beginning; and when I have passed my judgment upon it, and find in the play that from the first moment of her father's knowledge of the act it made him loathe his life, and that it finally broke his heart, I am then in time to inquire, what was the deadly venom which inflicted the immedicable wound:—and what is it, but the colour of Othello ?

> "Now, Roderigo,
> Where did'st thou see her ?—Oh, unhappy girl!—
> *With the Moor, say'st thou ?*—Who would be a father ?"

These are the disjointed lamentations of the wretched parent when the first disclosure of his daughter's shame is made known to him. This scene is one of the inimitable pictures of human passion in the hands of Shakspeare, and that half line,

> "With the *Moor* say'st thou ?"

comes from the deepest recesses of the soul. Again, when Brabantio first meets Othello, he breaks out :

> "O, thou foul thief, where hast thou stow'd my daughter ?
> Damn'd as thou art, thou hast enchanted her :
> For I'll refer me to all things of sense,
> If she, in chains of magic were not bound,
> Whether a maid so tender, fair, and happy,
> So opposite to marriage that she shunn'd
> The wealthy *curled* darlings of our nation,
> Would ever have to incur our general mock,
> Run from her guardage *to the sooty bosom*
> Of such a thing as thou ; to fear, not to delight."

Several of the English commentators have puzzled themselves with the inquiry why the epithet "curled" is here applied to the wealthy darlings of the nation; and Dr. Johnson thinks it has no reference to the hair; but it evidently has. The *curled* hair is in antithetic contrast to the sooty bosom, the thick lips, and the woolly head. The contrast of colo   is the very hinge upon which Brabantio founds his charge of magic, counteracting the impulse of nature.

At the close of the same scene (the second of the first act) Brabantio, hearing that the duke is in council upon public business of the State, determines to carry Othello before him for trial upon the charge of magic. "Mine," says he,

> "Mine's not a middle course ; the duke himself
> Or any of my brothers of the state
> Cannot but feel the wrong. as 'twere their own :
> For if such actions may have passage free,
> Bond slaves and Pagans shall our statesmen be."

And Stevens, in his note on this passage, says, "He alludes to the common condition of all blacks who come from their own country, both *slaves* and *pagans:* and uses the word in contempt of Othello and his complexion. If this Moor is now suffered to escape with impunity, it will be such an encouragement to see all the offices of our state filled up by the Pagans and bond-slaves of Africa." Othello himself in his narrative says that he had been taken by the insolent foe and sold to slavery. He *had been* a slave.

Once more—When Desdemona pleads to the Duke and the council for permission to go with Othello to Cyprus, she says,

> "That I did love the Moor, to live with him,
> My downright violence and storm of fortune
> May trumpet to the world: *my heart's subdued,*
> *Even to the very quality of my lord ;*
> I saw Othello's visage in his mind ;
> And to his honours and his valiant parts
> Did I my soul and fortunes consecrate."

In commenting upon this passage, William Henley says, "That *quality* here signifies the Moorish *complexion* of Othello, and not his military profession, (as Malone had supposed,) is obvious from what immediately follows : 'I saw Othello's visage in his mind ;' and also from what the Duke says to Brabantio—

> 'If virtue no delighted beauty lack
> Your son-in-law is far more fair than black.' "

The characters of Othello and Iago in this play are evidently intended as contrasted pictures of human nature, each setting off the other. They are national portraits of man—the ITALIAN and the MOOR. The Italian is *white, crafty* and *cruel ;* a consummate villain ; yet, as often happens in the realities of that description whom we occasionally meet in the intercourse of life, so vain of his own artifices that he betrays himself by boasting of them and their success. Accordingly, in the very first scene he reveals to Roderigo the treachery of his own character :—

> "For when my outward action doth demonstrate
> The native act and figure of my heart
> In compliment extern, 'tis not long after
> But I will wear my heart upon my sleeve
> For daws to peck at ; I am not what I am."

There is a seeming inconsistency in the fact that a double dealer should disclose his own secret, which must necessarily put others upon their guard against him ; but the inconsistency is in human nature, and not in the poet.

The double dealing Italian is a very intelligent man, a keen and penetrating observer, and full of ingenuity to devise and contrive base expedients. His language is coarse, rude, and obscene : his humour is caustic and bitter. Conscious of no honest principle in himself, he believes not in the existence of honesty in others. He is jealous and suspicious ; quick to note every trifle light as air, and to draw from it inferences of evil as confirmed circumstances. In his dealings with the Moor, while he is even harping upon his honesty, he offers to commit any murder from extreme attachment to his person and interests. In all that Iago says of others, and especially of Desdemona, there is a mixture of truth and falsehood, blended together, in which the truth itself serves to accredit the lie ; and such is the ordinary character of malicious slanders. Doctor Johnson speaks of "the soft simplicity," the "innocence," the "artlessness" of Desdemona. Iago speaks of her as a *super-subtle* Venetian ; and when kindling the sparks of jealousy in the soul of Othello, he says,

> "She did deceive her father, marrying you :
> And when she seemed to shake and fear your looks,
> She loved them most."

"And so she did," answers Othello. This charge, then, was true ; and Iago replies :

> "Why, go to, then ;
> She that so young could give out such a seeming
> To seal her father's eyes up, close as oak.—
> He thought 'twas witchcraft."

It was not witchcraft; but surely as little was it simplicity, innocence, artlessness. The effect of this suggestion upon Othello is terrible only because he knows it is true. Brabantio, on parting from him, had just given him the same warning, to which he had not then paid the slightest heed. But soon his suspicions are roused—he tries to repel them; they are fermenting in his brain: he appears vehemently moved and yet unwilling to acknowledge it. Iago, with fiend-like sagacity, seizes upon the paroxysm of emotion, and then comes the following dialogue:—

> " *Iago.* "My lord, I see you are moved.
> *Othello.*　　　　No, not much moved :—
> I do not think but Desdemona's honest.
> *Iago.* Long live she so! and long live you to th nk so!
> *Oth* And yet, how nature erring from itself—
> *Iago.* Ay, there 's the point: As—to be bold with you,—
> Not to affect many proposed matches,
> Of her own clime, complex'on, and degree;
> Whereto, we see, in all things nature tends:
> Foh ! one may smell. in such, a will most rank,
> Foul disproportion, thoughts unnatural."—

The deadly venom of these imputations, working up to phrensy the suspicions of the Moor, consist not in their falsehood but in their truth.

I have said the character of Desdemona was deficient in delicacy. Besides the instances to which I referred in proof of this charge, observe what she says in pleading for the restoration of Cassio to his office, from which he had been cashiered by Othello for beastly drunkenness and a consequent night-brawl, in which he had stabbed Montano—the predecessor of Othello as Governor of Cypress—and nearly killed him: yet in urging Othello to restore Cassio to his office and to favour, Desdemona says—

> "in fa'th, he 's penitent;
> And yet his trespass, in our common reason,
> (Save that. they say, the wars must make examples
> Out of their best,) is not olmost a fault
> To incur a private check."

Now, to palliate the two crimes of Cassio—his drunken fit and his stabbing of Montano—the reader knows that he has been inveigled to the commission of them by the accursed artifices of Iago; but Desdemona knows nothing of this; she has no excuse for Cassio—nothing to plead for him but his penitence. And is this the character for a woman of delicate sentiment to give of such a complicated and heinous offence as that of which Cassio had been guilty, even when pleading for his pardon ? No ! it is not for female delicacy to extenuate the crimes of drunkenness and blood-shed, even when performing the appropriate office of raising the soul-subduing voice of mercy.

Afterwards in the same speech, she says—

> "What! Michael Cassio,
> That came a-wooing with you; and many a time,
> When I have spoke of you dispraisingly,
> Hath ta'en your part; to have so much to do
> To bring him in!"

I will not inquire how far this avowal that she had been in the frequent habit of speaking dispraisingly of Othello at the very time when she was so deeply enamoured with his honours and his valiant parts, was consistent with sincerity. Young ladies must be allowed a little concealment and a

little disguise, even for passions which they have no need to be ashamed. It is the rosy pudency—the irresistible charm of the sex; but the exercise of it in satirical censure upon the very object of their most ardent affections is certainly no indication of innocence, simplicity, or artlessness.

I still retain, then, the opinion—

First. That the passion of Desdemona for Othello is *unnatural*, solely and exclusively because of his colour.

Second. That her elopement *to* him, and secret marriage *with* him, indicate a personal character not only very deficient in delicacy, but totally regardless of filial duty, of female modesty and of ingenuous shame.

Third. That her deficiency in delicacy is discernible in her conduct and discourse throughou the play.

I perceive and acknowledge, indeed, the admirable address with which the part has been contrived to inspire and to warm the breast of the spectator with a deep interest in her fate; and I am well aware that my own comparative insensibility to it is not in unison with the general impression which it produces upon the stage. I shrink from the thought of slandering even a creature of the imagination. When the spectator or reader follows, on the stage or in the closet, the infernal thread of duplicity and of execrable devices with which Iago entangles his victims, it is the purpose of the dramatist to merge all the faults and vices of the sufferers in the overwhelming flood of their calamities, and in the unmingled detestation of the inhuman devil, their betrayer and destroyer. And in all this, I see not only the skill of the artist, but the power of the moral operator, the purifier of the spectator's heart by the agency of *terror* and *pity.*

The characters of Othello and Desdemona, like all the characters of men and women in real life, are of " mingled yarn," with qualities of good and bad—of virtue and vices in proportion differently composed. Iago, with a high order of intellect, is, in moral principle, the very spirit of evil. I have said the moral of the tragedy is, that the intermarriage of black and white blood is a violation of the law of nature. *That* is the lesson to be learned from the play. To exhibit all the natural consequences of their act, the poet is compelled to make the marriage secret. It must commence by an elopement, and by an outrage upon the decorum of social intercourse. He must therefore assume, for the performance of this act, persons of moral character sufficiently frail and imperfect to be capable of performing it, but in other respects endowed with pleasing and estimable qualities. Thus, the Moor is represented as of free, and open and generous nature; as a Christian; as a distinguished military commander in the service of the Republic of Venice; as having rendered important service to the state, and as being in the enjoyment of a splendid reputation as a warrior. The other party to the marriage is a maiden, fair, gentle, and accomplished; born and educated in the proudest rank of Venetian nobility.

14

Othello, setting aside his colour, has every quality to fascinate and charm the female heart. Desdemona, apart from the grossness of her fault in being accessible to such a passion of such an object, is amiable and lovely; among the most attractive of her sex and condition. The faults of their characters are never brought into action excepting as they illustrate the moral principle of the whole story. Othello is not jealous by nature. On the contrary, with a strong natural understanding, and all the vigilance essential to an experienced commander, he is of a disposition so unsuspicious and confiding, that he believes in the *exceeding honesty* of Iago long after he has ample cause to suspect and distrust him. Desdemona, *supersubtle* as she is in the management of her amour with Othello; deeply as she dissembles to deceive her father; and, forward as she is in inviting the courtship of the Moor; discovers neither artifice nor duplicity from the moment that she is Othello's wife. Her innocence, in all her relations with him, is pure and spotless; her kindness for Cassio is mere untainted benevolence; and, though unguarded in her personal deportment toward him, it is far from the slightest soil of culpable impropriety. Guiltless of all conscious reproach in this part of her conduct, she never uses any of the artifices to which she had resorted to accomplish her marriage with Othello. Always feeling that she has given him no cause of suspicion, her endurance of his cruel treatment and brutal abuse of her through all the stages of violence, till he murders her in bed, is always marked with the most affecting sweetness of temper, the most perfect artlessness, and the most endearing resignation. The defects of her character have here no room for development, and the poet carefully keeps them out of sight. Hence it is that the general reader and spectator, with Dr. Johnson, give her unqualified credit for soft simplicity, artlessness, and innocence—forgetful of the qualities of a different and opposite character, stamped upon the transactions by which she effected her marriage with the Moor. The marriage, however, is the source of all her calamities; it is the primitive cause of all the tragic incidents of the play, and of its terrible catastrophe. That the moral lesson to be learned from it is of no practical utility in England, where there are no valiant Moors to steal the affections of fair and high-born dames, may be true; the lesson, however, is not the less, couched under the form of an admirable drama; nor needs it any laborious effort of the imagination to extend the moral precept resulting from the story to a salutary admonition against all ill-assorted, clandestine, and unnatural marriages.

ANCIENT AND MODERN ELOQUENCE.
FROM LECTURES ON RHETORIC AND ORATORY.

WITH the dissolution of Roman liberty, and the decline of Roman taste, the reputation and the excellency of the oratorical art fell alike into decay. Under the despotism of the Cæsars, the end of eloquence was perverted from persuasion to panegyric, and all her faculties were soon palsied by the touch of corruption, or enervated by the impotence of servitude. Then succeeded the midnight of the monkish ages, when with the other liberal arts she slumbered in the profound darkness of the cloister.

At the revival of letters in modern Europe, eloquence, together with her sister muses, awoke, and shook the poppies from her brow. But their torpors still tingled in her veins. In the interval her voice was gone; her favourite languages were extinct; her organs were no longer attuned to harmony, and her hearers could no longer understand her speech. The discordant jargon of feudal anarchy had banished the musical dialects, in which she had always delighted. The theatres of her former triumphs were either deserted, or they were filled with the babblers of sophistry and chicane. She shrunk intuitively from the forum, for the last object she remembered to have seen there was the head of her darling Cicero, planted upon the rostrum. She ascended the tribunals of justice; there she found her child, Persuasion, manacled and pinioned by the letter of the law; there she beheld an image of herself, stammering in barbarous Latin, and staggering under the lumber of a thousand volumes. Her heart fainted within her. She lost all confidence in herself. Together with her irresistible powers, she lost proportionably the consideration of the world, until, instead of comprising the whole system of public education, she found herself excluded from the circle of science, and declared an outlaw from the realms of learning. She was not however doomed to eternal silence. With the progress of freedom and of liberal science, in various parts of modern Europe, she obtained access to mingle in the deliberations of their parliaments. With labour and difficulty she learned their languages, and lent her aid in giving them form and polish. But she has never recovered the grace of her former beauty, nor the energies of her ancient vigour.

THE FATHERS OF NEW ENGLAND.
FROM AN ORATION AT PLYMOUTH.

WORLDLY Fame has been parsimonious of her favour to the memory of those generous champions. Their numbers were small; their stations in life obscure; the object of their enterprise unostentatious; the theatre of their exploits remote: how could they possibly be favourites of worldly Fame?—That common crier, whose existence is only known by the assemblage of multitudes: that pander of wealth and greatness, so eager to haunt the palaces of fortune, and so fastidious to the houseless dignity of virtue: that parasite of pride, ever scornful to meekness, and ever obsequious to insolent power: that heedless trumpeter, whose ears are deaf to modest merit, and whose eyes are blind to bloodless, distant excellence.

CHARLES BROCKDEN BROWN.

[Born 1771. Died 1810.]

CHARLES BROCKDEN BROWN was the first American who chose literature as a profession, and the first to leave enduring monuments of genius in the fields of the imagination. His family were of the Society of Friends. He was born in Philadelphia on the seventeenth of January, 1771. In his youth he was diminutive and feeble, modest and studious. At ten years of age, when some one petulantly called him *boy*, he exclaimed, "What does he mean? does he not know that it is neither age nor size, but sense, that makes the man? I could ask him a hundred questions of which he could not answer one." He studied the humanities with Robert Proud, the historian of Pennsylvania. He was a favourite with his teacher, by whose advice, when close application impaired his health, he went into the country, and in solitary walks received impressions of some of those grand scenes which are described in his works, and habits of abstraction for which he was subsequently distinguished. He quitted school before he was sixteen, and soon after entered upon the study of the law. He joined a society of students, one of whom was the late Dr. Milnor, and in arguments at its meetings exhibited an ability that was deemed the earnest of future triumphs. But the profession became to him every day less attractive, and was finally abandoned. His family remonstrated, but in vain. His dislike to the scenes presented in the courts, and to the tautologies, circuities, artifices, and falsehoods of the law, were invincible. He regarded it as a " tissue of shreds and remnants of a barbarous antiquity, patched by the stupidity of modern workmen into new deformity,"* and would have nothing to do with it.

He was now without any definite aims. He became a prey to melancholy. He sought relief in change of scene, and made excursions through Pennsylvania and the neighbouring states ; but his diary and correspondence show that he found no relief. To one of his friends

---

* " Ormond," chapter ii.

he wrote, "Forget that any latent anguish or corroding sorrow is concealed under that aspect of indifference which has become habitual." He saw an obstacle to the schemes of despair in the sorrow they would occasion to the few who loved him, and for their sakes determined to bear every thing with a heroic calmness.

In 1793 he went to New York. He was warmly attached to Dr. Elihu H. Smith of that city, who had been a student in the Medical College at Philadelphia; and with him and William Johnson, afterward an eminent lawyer, he entered into a domestic partnership, and took a house. His associates introduced him to a literary society called the Friendly Club, among whose members were Dr. Samuel L. Mitchell, Anthony Bleecker, William Dunlap, James Kent, since known as the great chancellor, and others who were afterward distinguished. It was like a new and invigorating atmosphere. The French revolution was then at its heat, and was shaking the institutions of Christendom. Theorists in all countries were busy with schemes for the melioration of the condition of mankind. Brown was affected with the general contagion. He had already been an occasional writer for the periodicals, and had projected epics and romances. He now became a political philosopher, and wrote about Utopias. Near the close of 1797 he published his first work, Alcuin, a Dialogue on the Rights of Women. It is not without ingenuity. In the last few years many women in this country and in Europe, vexed that they could not unsex themselves, have written in the same way. The book was unsuccessful, and the author directed his attention into another department of letters.

I do not know at what time it was written, but it is proper to mention here an unfinished novel, entitled Memoirs of Carwin, the Biloquist, because it contains the early history of one of his most striking characters, the real hero of Wieland, and must be read before that work can be properly appreciated. It should always be printed as an introduction to it.*

Wieland, or the Transformation, the first of the series of brilliant novels by which Brown gained his enduring reputation, was published in 1798. Its appearance marked an era in American literature. It is in all respects a remarkable book. Its plot, characters, and style are original and peculiar. The family of Wieland are of German descent, well-educated, and move in the best society. A tendency to religious fanaticism is hereditary, and the death of the father is mysterious and terrible. The son, an amiable enthusiast, lives with his wife and children in seclusion, near the Schuylkill; near him his sister, to whom he is tenderly attached, and in the neighbourhood Pleyel, his wife's brother. Six years of uninterrupted happiness precede the opening of the drama. A man of middle age, ungainly person, and rustic dress, is now seen frequently wandering in the vicinity. He is accosted by Pleyel, who remembers that they have met in Spain, where he appeared in a different character. His name is Carwin. His knowledge and wit are unbounded, his voice variably musical, and his conversation so attractive that he is with little hesitation received into the society at Mettingen. Soon the nights are made fearful by strange voices, and warnings of danger, or startling by unlooked-for revelations. By Wieland they are referred to a supernatural agency; the others are perplexed; and all seem to be approaching a catastrophe. At length Wieland is summoned in a mysterious manner to testify his submission to the divine will by the sacrifice of his warmest affections, his dearest pleasures; and in obedience to the heavenly messenger destroys his wife and children, and seeks the life of his sister, who escapes by an accident. He is arrested and convicted of murder, but regards the proceedings with heroic calmness, confident that he has but fulfilled the will of God. The key to all this is *ventriloquism*. It is objected by Mr. Prescott and other very able critics, that the explanation is unsatisfactory, and that the character of Carwin is contradictory, unnatural, and devilish.

With deference, I think all who have written upon this point—for no critic has hitherto taken a different view of it—have done so upon a superficial examination of the history, and without a consideration of Wieland's peculiar mind and life. The optical illusions may have been the exaggerations of a heated imagination. Ventriloquism at that time was a faculty not generally known to exist, and it is reasonable to suppose that the actors in this drama had never heard of it. By less powerful means the impostor Matthias produced similar effects.* Alexander Vattemare and others have acquired as perfect a control as is here described over their voices. But notwithstanding the author's opinion, and his own surprise and horror at the catastrophe, Carwin is called a "demon." Driven by a father's brutal severity at an early age from amid the forests into the city, he struggled with "low wants and lofty will" until he attracted the attention of an adventurer, who perceived his genius and trusted by a suitable education to make him an efficient promoter of his plans. After a few years, passed in Europe, he quarrelled with his patron, and returned, poor, friendless, and dispirited. Solitary walks in the vicinity of Philadelphia led to an acquaintance with the Wielands. His principles justified an intrigue with one of their inmates, and though he had forsworn his dangerous art, in an emergency he resorted to it to prevent a discovery which would have been more dangerous to another than himself. Ignorant perhaps of Wieland's superstition, and to test the vaunted courage of his sister, as well as to preserve the secrecy of his amour, he made frequent experiments and found amusement in the wonder and in the discussions they excited. To screen himself from punishment his former patron had accused him before the magistrates of Dublin, and a reward for his apprehension was now offered in the gazettes. He suddenly quitted Mettingen, and on his return learned with undissembled horror the last scenes in the family of Wieland. He was unwise, unfortunate, wicked, but not a "fiend," nor actuated by "diabolical malice." The careful reader of the narrative will perceive that the credulous Wieland already supposed himself in communication with the invisible world, and that on the night when he thought the sacrifice of his family was demanded, the author represents his imagination as heated to

* It is printed in Dunlap's Life and Selections from the works of Brown, vol. ii. p. 200—201.

* Vide Matthias and his Impostures, by William L. Stone.

phrensy by fears respecting his sister. He was in a state to hear voices when no voices sounded, and to see sights invisible to other eyes; Carwin had no direct connection with these last events. It was a terrible but not unparalleled instance of self-delusion. This was evidently the author's meaning. Mr. Prescott curses with Dryden the inventors of fifth acts, by which a tragedy's "pleasing horrors" are unravelled. But Brown had higher objects than to entrance the fancy. He was a careful anatomist of the mind, and, familiar with its wonderful phenomena, had no need of gorgons and chimeras. He would have failed of the end he had in view if he had not shown the causes of his effects; and in considering whether his explanations are sufficient we are not to inquire if we ourselves should have been deceived as Wieland was, but if such an intellect, with such an 'education and experience, and under such circumstances, could have been thus wrecked. I confess that, remembering some of the best authenticated facts in the more recent history of fanaticism and superstition, I can perceive nothing unnatural or improbable in this work, nor do I think that a key to its mysteries renders it in any degree uninteresting.

Brown's second novel is entitled Ormond. The scenes are New York and Philadelphia, and the time near the close of the last century, embracing the period of the yellow fever. The first part of the story is very interesting. The incidents are dramatic and natural, and the characters are drawn with great distinctness. An artist, of taste and cultivation, but moderate powers, finding his professional income insufficient to meet the increasing wants of his family, upon the death of his father embraces the hereditary occupation of pharmacy, and grows rich. A partner, bound to him by every tie of gratitude, robs him and quits the country, leaving him in his old age in blindness and beggary. His daughter, Constantia Dudley, is the heroine, and there are few heroines in American fiction more natural and beautiful. The formal introduction of Ormond is unsuccessful. His character however is soon boldly and clearly exhibited in his action. It is one to be judged differently by different sorts of people. Common morality is very shallow. Common sentiment is sickly. He would be a monster to the vulgar apprehension. Yet he is not without

nobility, nor is his conduct, as presented in the earlier part of the narrative, unnatural or unparalleled in real life. His notions in regard to marriage are peculiar; he keeps a mistress, a woman of education, with whom, as with others, he deals with sincerity and frankness. In the last half of the book the characters are not sustained. Tedious episodes, having no connection with the main story, and new and useless actors are obtruded. In the first part the style is better than in his other works, but in the last part it is feeble. A suspicion arises that, growing weary of his task, he hastily filled out his volumes with fragments of other tales, abandoning any plan he may have entertained for the denouement.

Brown had withdrawn from Philadelphia when the yellow fever approached that city in 1793, but when in 1798 the epidemic threatened to desolate New York, he and his friends determined to continue in their house, which was in a healthy part of the town. Dr. Smith was detained by professional duties; Brown would not go lest his friend should need his personal attention; Smith died, Brown nearly lost his life by his benevolence, and on his partial recovery from a severe illness, accepted an invitation to reside with William Dunlap at Perth Amboy, in New Jersey. Here, while all the horrors of the plague were fresh in his memory, he wrote his third novel, Arthur Mervyn. The hero is the son of an ignorant farmer, whose second marriage with a youthful and vulgar woman drove his only child into the world. His mother had possessed education and refinement above her condition, and Mervyn had received from her and from a stranger who had wandered into the country and died at his father's house, a degree of knowledge unusual among boys of his class in Pennsylvania. On his arrival in the city his services are engaged by Waldeck, an accomplished villain, who keeps a splendid establishment, and transforms the rustic into an elegant young man of the town. Waldeck's character, as a work of art, is the best in the novel, the interest of which arises chiefly from his profligate career, and the ravages of the pestilence, which are described with wonderful fidelity and distinctness. The incidents have little cohesion, the characters are needlessly multiplied, and the careless prolixity of the last volume is redeemed by

K

few such graphic and powerful sketches as in the first enchain the reader's attention.

Arthur Mervyn was followed by Edgar Huntley, the Memoirs of a Somnambulist. The scene is near the forks of the Delaware, in Pennsylvania. A friend of the hero has suddenly disappeared. It is supposed that he is murdered. Huntley, meditating upon his fate, wanders at night by an unfrequented path toward the residence of a friend, and by the moonlight discovers a person digging the ground under a tree; he perceives that he occasionally stops and exhibits intense emotion; his suspicions are aroused, and when the earth is closed up he follows the man through tangled mazes of a forest to a cavern, where he loses sight of him. This man is Clithero, a foreigner employed in the vicinity, who in his sleep has been burying some memorials of an eventful life, which is subsequently detailed to Huntley to avert the impression that Clithero was concerned in his friend's death. In following the sleep-walker on various occasions Huntley is led into extraordinary adventures, and among scenes of gloomy wildness and sublimity, which are described with a freedom, boldness, and occasional minuteness, which are extremely effective. This is the only work in which Brown has introduced Indian characters, and the pictures he has given of savage life are eminently striking. The work exhibits the intensity, and the anatomical knowledge of human passions, for which his previous writings are distinguished, and it has their numerous and various faults, the worst of which perhaps is a want of proportion.

Brown subsequently published Clara Howard, Memoirs of Stephen Calvert, and Jane Talbot. The last is the shortest and least attractive of his fictions.

When he left the retreat of Mr. Dunlap, at Perth Amboy, he returned to Philadelphia, where in 1799 he commenced The Monthly Magazine and American Review. It was discontinued in the following year. In 1804 he married Miss Linn, with whom he had become acquainted in New York. She was the sister of the Rev. Dr. John Blair Linn,* of whom he afterward wrote a memoir. In 1805 he began The Literary Magazine and American Register, which was continued five years,

during which time it was chiefly supported by his own contributions. In 1806 he established The American Register, which appeared in semi-annual volumes until its publication was interrupted by his death. He translated the work on the United States by Volney, with whom he had contracted a friendship during his residence in this country; and he wrote several elaborate political pamphlets, the principal of which were, An Address to the Government of the United States on the Cession of Louisiana to the French, and on the late Breach of Treaty by the Spaniards; The British Treaty; and An Address to the Congress of the United States on the Utility and Justice of Restrictions upon Foreign Commerce, with Reflections upon Foreign Trade in General, and the Future Prospects of America.

The year after his marriage he wrote to Dunlap, " You judge rightly when you think I am situated happily; my present way of life is in every respect to my mind. There is nothing to disturb my felicity but the sense of the uncertainty and instability that clings to every thing human. I cannot be happier than I am. Every change therefore must be for the worse. My business, if I may so call it, is altogether pleasurable. My companion is all that a husband can wish for, and in short, as to my personal situation, *I have nothing to wish but that it may last.*" But it did not last. His constitution, as I have before mentioned, was delicate. His lungs were now affected, and he was compelled to give up active exercise. Confined to his house he pursued with unremitting ardour his favourite studies. His only descendant, my friend William Linn Brown, Esquire, of Philadelphia, has shown me numerous large architectural drawings, executed in his last years with such skill and care, that they seem like engravings; and an elaborate Geography, of which all is written but the book relating to this country. It is in a beautiful round hand, as legible as a printed page. The late John Murray, of London, who once had the MS. in his possession, was of opinion that if it had been finished and published, the great work of Malte-Brun would never have been translated. In 1809 Brown consented to travel, in the hope of benefit from change of scene. By easy stages he visited the states of New Jersey and New York; in November he was confined to his

---

* Author of " Valerian," " The Powers of Genius," etc.

chamber; and on the twenty-second of February, 1810, he died, having just finished the thirty-ninth year of his age.

The distinguishing characteristics of his works I have already noticed. The faults of their construction doubtless were in some degree owing to the great rapidity with which they were written. The author and the printer were engaged at the same time upon nearly every one of them; and he sometimes had three or four under way at once. In all of them are indications that he grew weary before they were finished. His style is not good; in a majority of his works at least it lacks simplicity and directness, and has numerous verbal faults. "Thee," "thou," "thine," are rarely admissible except in addresses to the Deity. Brown was educated a Quaker, and it was no affectation in him therefore to use what this sect calls the "plain language;" but there is

no excuse for "thee" and "thine" in the same sentence with "you" and "yours." He makes "adore" a synonym for "love" or "respect;" "somewhat" for "something," and "ruminate" for "meditate," occur constantly; and the ear is offended by "museful," "deliquiem," or other unusual or pedantic words in almost every page.

If his works were pruned of their redundancies, if their needless episodes were erased, and a judicious proof-reader should make the requisite occasional changes of words, extraordinary merits, which are independent of these blemishes, would secure them a popularity they have never yet possessed.

Brown was a man of unquestionable genius and a true scholar. His works are original, powerful, and peculiar, and with all their faults will continue to be read by educated and thoughtful men.

THE DEFENCE OF WIELAND.
FROM WIELAND.

THEODORE WIELAND, the prisoner at the bar, was now called upon for his defence. He looked around him for some time in silence, and with a mild countenance. At length he spoke:

It is strange; I am known to my judges and my auditors. Who is there present a stranger to the character of Wieland? who knows him not as a husband—as a father—as a friend? yet here am I arraigned as a criminal. I am charged with diabolical malice; I am accused of the murder of my wife and my children!

It is true, they were slain by me; they all perished by my hand. The task of vindication is ignoble. What is it that I am called to vindicate? and before whom?

You know that they are dead, and that they were killed by me. What more would you have? Would you extort from me a statement of my motives? Have you failed to discover them already? You charge me with malice; but your eyes are not shut; your reason is still vigorous; your memory has not forsaken you. You know whom it is that you thus charge. The habits of his life are known to you; his treatment of his wife and his offspring is known to you; the soundness of his integrity and the unchangeableness of his principles are familiar to your apprehension; yet you persist in this charge! you lead me hither manacled as a felon! you deem me worthy of a vile and tormenting death!

Who are they whom I have devoted to death? My wife—the little ones that drew their being from me—that creature who, as she surpassed them in excellence, claimed a larger affection than those whom natural affinities bound to my heart.

Think ye that malice could have urged me to this deed? Hide your audacious fronts from the scrutiny of Heaven. Take refuge in some cavern unvisited by human eyes. Ye may deplore your wickedness or folly, but ye cannot expiate it.

Think not that I speak for your sakes. Hug to your hearts this detestable infatuation. Deem me still a murderer, and drag me to untimely death. I make not an effort to dispel your illusion; I utter not a word to cure you of your sanguinary folly; but there are probably some in this assembly who have come from far. For their sakes, whose distance has disabled them from knowing me, I will tell what I have done, and why. It is needless to say that God is the object of my supreme passion. I have cherished, in his presence, a single and upright heart. I have thirsted for the knowledge of his will. I have burnt with ardour to approve my faith and my obedience. My days have been spent in searching for the revelation of that will; but my days have been mournful, because my search failed. I solicited direction; I turned on every side where glimmerings of light could be discovered. I have not been wholly uninformed; but my knowledge has always stopped short of certainty. Dissatisfaction has insinuated itself into all my thoughts. My purposes have been pure; my wishes indefatigable; but not till lately were these purposes thoroughly accomplished, and these wishes fully gratified.

I thank thee, my Father, for thy bounty! that thou didst not ask a less sacrifice than this! that thou placedst me in a condition to testify my submission to thy will! What have I withheld which it was thy pleasure to exact? Now may I, with dauntless and erect eye, claim my reward, since I have given thee the treasure of my soul!

I was at my own house; it was late in the

evening; my sister had gone to the city, but proposed to return. .... My mind was contemplative and calm; not wholly devoid of apprehension on account of my sister's safety. Recent events, not easily explained, had suggested the existence of some danger; but this danger was without a distinct form in our imagination, and scarcely ruffled our tranquillity.

Time passed, and my sister did not arrive; her house is at some distance from mine, and though her arrangements had been made with a view to residing with us, it was possible that, through forgetfulness, or the occurrence of unforeseen emergencies, she had returned to her own dwelling.

Hence it was conceived proper that I should ascertain the truth by going thither. I went. On my way my mind was full of those ideas which related to my intellectual condition. In the torrent of fervid conceptions, I lost sight of my purpose. Sometimes I stood still; sometimes I wandered from my path, and experienced some difficulty, on recovering from my fit of musing, to regain it. The series of my thoughts is easily traced. At first every vein beat with rapture known only to the man whose parental and conjugal love is without limits, and the cup of whose desires, immense as it is, overflows with gratification. .... The Author of my being was likewise the dispenser of every gift with which that being was embellished. The service to which a benefactor like this was entitled, could not be circumscribed. My social sentiments were indebted to their alliance with devotion for all their value. ....

For a time, my contemplations soared above earth and its inhabitants. I stretched forth my hands; I lifted my eyes, and exclaimed, Oh! that I might be admitted to thy presence! that mine were the supreme delight of knowing thy will, and of performing it! The blissful privilege of direct communication with thee, and of listening to the audible enunciation of thy pleasure! What task would I not undertake, what privation would I not cheerfully endure, to testify my love of thee? Alas! thou hidest thyself from my view; glimpses only of thy excellence and beauty are afforded me. Would that a momentary emanation from thy glory would visit me! that some unambiguous token of thy presence would salute my senses!

In this mood I entered the house of my sister. It was vacant. Scarcely had I regained recollection of the purpose that brought me hither. Thoughts of a different tendency had such absolute possession of my mind, that the relations of time and space were almost obliterated from my understanding. These wanderings, however, were restrained, and I ascended to her chamber. I had no light, and might have known, by external observation, that the house was without any inhabitant. With this, however, I was not satisfied. I entered the room, and the object of my search not appearing, I prepared to return. The darkness required some caution in descending the stair. I stretched my hand to seize the balustrade by which I might regulate my steps.

How shall I describe the lustre which, at that moment, burst upon my vision! I was dazzled. My organs were bereaved of their activity. My eyelids were half-closed, and my hands withdrawn from the balustrade. A nameless fear chilled my veins, and I stood motionless. This irradiation did not retire or lessen. It seemed as if some powerful effulgence covered me like a mantle. I opened my eyes and found all about me luminous and glowing. It was the element of heaven that flowed around. Nothing but a fiery stream was at first visible; but, anon, a shrill voice from behind called upon me to attend. I turned. It is forbidden to describe what I saw; words would be wanting to the task. The lineaments of that being, whose veil was now lifted, and whose visage beamed upon my sight, no hues of pencil or of language can portray. As it spoke, the accents thrilled to my heart.

"Thy prayers are heard. In proof of thy faith, render me thy wife. This is the victim I choose. Call her hither, and here let her fall."

The sound, and visage, and light vanished at once. What demand was this? The blood of Catharine was to be shed. My wife was to perish by my hand. I sought opportunity to attest my virtue: little did I expect that a proof like this would have been demanded. "My wife!" I exclaimed; "O God! substitute some other victim. Make me not the butcher of my wife. My own blood is cheap. This will I pour out before thee with a willing heart; but spare, I beseech thee, this precious life, or commission some other than her husband to perform the bloody deed!" In vain. The conditions were prescribed; the decree had gone forth, and nothing remained but to execute it. I rushed out of the house and across the intermediate fields, and stopped not till I entered my own parlour.

My wife had remained here during my absence, in anxious expectation of my return with tidings of her sister. I had none to communicate. For a time, I was breathless with my speed. This, and the tremors that shook my frame, and the wildness of my looks, alarmed her. She immediately suspected some disaster to her friend, and her own speech was as much overpowered by emotion as mine. She was silent, but her looks manifested impatience to hear what I had to communicate. I spoke, but with so much precipitation as scarcely to be understood; catching her at the same time by the arm, and forcibly pulling her from her seat. "Come along with me; fly; waste not a moment; time will be lost, and the deed will be omitted. Tarry not; question not; but fly with me!"

This deportment added afresh to her alarms. Her eyes pursued mine, and she said, "What is the matter? For God's sake, what is the matter? Where would you have me go?"

My eyes were fixed upon her countenance while she spoke. I thought upon her virtues; I viewed her as the mother of my babes; as my wife; I recalled the purpose for which I thus urged her attendance; my heart faltered, and I saw that I must rouse to this work all my faculties: the danger of the least delay was imminent.

I looked away from her, and again exerting my force, drew her toward the door—"You must go with me—indeed you must."

In her fright she half-resisted my efforts, and again exclaimed, "Good heavens! what is it you mean? Where go? what has happened? have you found Clara?"

"Follow me and you will see," I answered, still urging her reluctant steps forward.

"What phrensy has seized you? Something must needs have happened. Is she sick? Have you found her?"

"Come and see. Follow me, and know for yourself."

Still she expostulated, and besought me to explain. I could not trust myself to answer her; to look at her; but grasping her arm, I drew her after me. She hesitated, rather through confusion of mind than from unwillingness to accompany me. This confusion gradually abated, and she moved forward, but with irresolute footsteps, and continual exclamations of wonder and terror. Her interrogations of "what is the matter?" and "whither are you going?" were ceaseless and vehement. It was the scope of my efforts not to think; to keep up a conflict and uproar in my mind in which all order and distinctness should be lost; to escape from the sensations produced by her voice. I was therefore silent. I strove to abridge this interval by my haste, and to waste all my attention in furious gesticulations. In this state of mind we reached my sister's door. She looked at the windows and saw that all was desolate—"Why come we here? There is nobody here: I will not go in."

Still I was dumb; but opening the door, I drew her in the entry. This was the allotted scene; here she was to fall. I let go her hand, and pressing my palms against my forehead, made one mighty effort to work up my soul to the deed! In vain; it would not be; my courage was appalled; my arms nerveless. I muttered prayers that my strength might be aided. They availed nothing. Horror diffused itself over me. This conviction of my cowardice, my rebellion, fastened upon me, and I stood rigid and cold. From this state I was relieved by my wife's voice, who renewed her supplications to be told why we came hither, and what was the fate of my sister.

What could I answer? My words were broken and inarticulate. Her fears naturally acquired force from the observation of these symptoms; but these fears were misplaced. The only inference she deduced from my conduct was, that some terrible misfortune had befallen Clara. She wrung her hands, and exclaimed in an agony, "O, tell me, where is she? what has become of her? is she sick? dead? is she in her chamber? O let me go thither and know the worst!"

This proposal set my thoughts once more in motion. Perhaps, what my rebellious heart refused to perform here, I might obtain strength enough to execute elsewhere. "Come, then," said I, "let us go."

"I will, but not in the dark. We must first procure a light."

15

"Fly then and procure it; but I charge you, linger not. I will await for your return."

While she was gone, I strode along the entry. The fellness of a gloomy hurricane but faintly resembled the discord that reigned in my mind. To omit this sacrifice must not be; yet my sinews had refused to perform it. No alternative was offered. To rebel against the mandate was impossible; but obedience would render me the executioner of my wife. My will was strong, but my limbs refused their office. She returned with a light; I led the way to the chamber; she looked round her; she lifted the curtain of the bed; she saw nothing. At length, she fixed inquiring eyes upon me. The light now enabled her to discover in my visage what darkness had hitherto concealed. Her cares were transferred from my sister to myself, and she said in a tremulous voice, "Wieland! you are not well; what ails you? Can I do nothing for you?"

That accents and looks so winning should disarm me of my resolution, was to be expected. My thoughts were thrown anew into anarchy. I spread my hand before my eyes that I might not see her, and answered only by groans. She took my other hand between hers, and pressing it to her heart, spoke with that voice which had ever swayed my will, and wafted away sorrow. "My friend! my soul's friend! tell me thy cause of grief. Do I not merit to partake with thee in thy cares? Am I not thy wife?"

This was too much. I broke from her embrace and retired to a corner of the room. In this pause, courage was once more infused into me. I resolved to execute my duty. She followed me, and renewed her passionate entreaties to know the cause of my distress. I raised my head and regarded her with steadfast looks. I muttered something about death, and the injunctions of my duty. At my words she shrunk back, and looked at me with a new expression of anguish. After a pause, she clasped her hands, and exclaimed—"O Wieland! Wieland! God grant that I am mistaken; but surely something is wrong. I see it—it is too plain—thou art undone—lost to me and to thyself." At the same time she gazed on my features with intensest anxiety, in hope that different symptoms would take place. I replied to her with vehemence—"Undone! no; my duty is known, and I thank my God that my cowardice is now vanquished, and I have power to fulfil it. Catharine! I pity the weakness of thy nature; I pity thee, but must not spare. Thy life is claimed from my hands; thou must die!"

Fear was now added to her grief. "What mean you? Why talk you of death? Bethink yourself, Wieland: bethink yourself, and this fit will pass. O, why came I hither? Why did you drag me hither?"

"I brought thee hither to fulfil a divine command. I am appointed thy destroyer, and destroy thee I must." Saying this I seized thy wrists. She shrieked aloud, and endeavoured to free herself from my grasp; but her efforts were vain.

"Surely, surely, Wieland, thou dost not mean

x 2

it. Am I not thy wife? and wouldst thou kill me? Thou wilt not; and yet—I see—thou art Wieland no longer! A fury—resistless and horrible—possesses thee—spare me—spare—help—help—"

Till her breath was stopped she shrieked for mercy. When she could speak no longer, her gestures, her looks appealed to my compassion. My accursed hand was irresolute and tremulous. I meant thy death to be sudden, thy struggles to be brief! Alas! my heart was infirm; my resolves mutable. Thrice I slackened my grasp, and life kept its hold, though in the midst of pangs. Her eyeballs started from their sockets. Grimness, distortion, took place of all that used to bewitch me into transport, and subdue me into reverence. I was commissioned to kill thee, but not to torment thee with the foresight of thy death; not to multiply thy fears, and prolong thy agonies! Haggard, and pale, and lifeless, at length thou ceasedst to contend with thy destiny!

This was a moment of triumph. Thus had I successfully subdued the stubbornness of human passions; the victim which had been demanded was given: the deed was done. I lifted the corpse in my arms and laid it on the bed. I gazed upon it with delight. Such was the elation of my thoughts, that I even broke into laughter. I clapped my hands and exclaimed, "It is done! My sacred duty is fulfilled! To that I have sacrificed, O my God! thy last and best gift, my wife!" For a while I thus soared above frailty. I imagined I had set myself for ever beyond the reach of selfishness; but my imaginations were false. This rapture quickly subsided. I looked again at my wife. My joyous ebullitions vanished, and I asked myself who it was whom I saw? Methought it could not be Catharine. It could not be the woman who had lodged for years in my heart; who had slept, nightly, in my bosom; who had borne in her womb, who had fostered at her breast the beings who called me Father! whom I had watched with delight, and cherished with a fondness ever new and perpetually growing; it could not be the same.....

I will not dwell upon my lapse into desperate and outrageous sorrow. The breath of Heaven that sustained me was withdrawn, and I sunk into *mere man.* I leaped from the floor; I dashed my head against the wall; I uttered screams of horror; I panted after torment and pain. The bickerings of hell, and eternal fire, compared with what I felt, were music and a bed of roses.

I thank my God that this degeneracy was transient, that he deigned once more to raise me aloft. I thought upon what I had done as a sacrifice to duty, and *was calm.* My wife was dead; but I reflected, that though this source of human consolation was closed, yet others were still open. If the transports of a husband were no more, the feelings of a father had still scope for exercise. When remembrance of their mother should excite too keen a pang, I would look upon them and *be comforted.* While I revolved these ideas, new warmth flowed in upon my heart—I was wrong.

These feelings were the growth of selfishness. Of this I was not aware, and to dispel the mist that obscured my perceptions, a new effulgence and a new mandate were necessary.

From these thoughts I was recalled by a ray that was shot into the room. A voice spake like that which I had before heard—"Thou hast done well; but all is not done—the sacrifice is incomplete—thy children must be offered—they must perish with their mother!"——

YELLOW FEVER IN PHILADELPHIA.

FROM ARTHUR MERVYN.

As I drew near the city, the tokens of its calamitous condition became more apparent. Every farm-house was filled with supernumerary tenants; fugitives from home: and haunting the skirts of the road, eager to detain every passenger with inquiries after news. The passengers were numerous; for the tide of emigration was by no means exhausted. Some were on foot, bearing in their countenances tokens of their recent terror, and filled with mournful reflections on the forlornness of their state. Few had secured to themselves an asylum; some were without the means of paying for food or lodging in the coming night; others, who were not thus destitute, knew not where to apply for entertainment, every house being already overstocked with inhabitants, or barring its inhospitable doors at their approach.

Families of weeping mothers and dismayed children, attended with a few pieces of indispensable furniture, were carried in vehicles of every form. The parent or husband had perished; and the price of some movable, or the pittance handed forth by public charity, had been expended to purchase the means of retiring from this theatre of disasters; though uncertain and hopeless of accommodation in the neighbouring districts.

Between these and the fugitives whom curiosity had led to the road, dialogues frequently took place, to which I was suffered to listen. From every mouth the tale of sorrow was repeated with new aggravations. Pictures of their own distress, or of that of their neighbours, were exhibited in all the hues which imagination can annex to pestilence and poverty.....

The sun had nearly set before I reached the precincts of the city. I entered High street after night-fall. Instead of equipages and a throng of passengers, the voice of levity which I had formerly observed, and which the mildness of the season would at other times have produced, I found nothing but a dreary solitude.

The market-place, and each side of this magnificent avenue were illuminated, as before, by lamps; but between the Schuylkill and the heart of the city, I met not more than a dozen figures; and these were ghost-like, wrapt in cloaks, from behind which they cast upon me glances of wonder and suspicion; and, as I approached, changed their course to avoid me. Their clothes were sprinkled with vinegar; and their nostrils defended from contagion by some powerful perfume.

I cast a look upon the houses, which I recollected to have seen brilliant with lights, resounding with lively voices, and thronged with busy faces. Now they were closed, above and below; dark, and without tokens of being inhabited. . . . . I approached a house, the door of which was opened, and before which stood a vehicle, which I presently recognised to be a *hearse*. The driver was seated on it. I stood still to mark his visage, and to observe the course which he proposed to take. Presently a coffin, borne by two men, issued. The driver was a negro, but his companions were white. Their features were marked by indifference to danger or pity. One of them, as he assisted in thrusting the coffin into the cavity provided for it, said, "I'll be damned if I think the poor dog was quite dead. It wasn't the *fever* that ailed him, but the sight of the girl and her mother on the floor. I wonder how they all got into that room. What carried them there?"

The other surlily muttered, "Their legs, to be sure."

"But what should they hug together in one room for?"

"To save us trouble, to be sure."

"And I thank them with all my heart; but damn it, it wasn't right to put him in his coffin before the breath was fairly gone. I thought the last look he gave me told me to stay a few minutes."

"Pshaw! he could not live. The sooner dead the better for him, as well as for us. Did you mark how he eyed us, when we carried away his wife and daughter? I never cried in my life, since I was knee-high, but curse me if I ever felt in better tune for the business than just then. Hey!" continued he, looking up and observing me, standing a few paces distant, and listening to their discourse, "What's wanted? Anybody dead?"

I stayed not to answer or parley, but hurried forward. My joints trembled, and cold drops stood on my forehead. I was ashamed of my own infirmity; and by vigorous efforts of my reason, regained some degree of composure.

INTERVIEW BETWEEN MERVYN AND WELBECK.

FROM ARTHUR MERVYN.

[WELBECK, to avoid his creditors and an arrest for murder, has secretly quitted Philadelphia. Subsequently Mervyn, sick with the yellow fever and fearful of being carried to the hospital, finds his way to the house he had inhabited, in the hope of dying there alone. He is disturbed by the reappearance of Welbeck, whose return had been caused by a suspicion that twenty one-thousand dollar notes are concealed between the leaves of a MS. volume which had belonged to a young foreigner whom he had attended in his last moments, whose property he had seized, and whose sister he had ruined. Mervyn has already discovered this money, and, in the hope of being able to return it to the unfortunate girl, taken pos-

session of it. In the chapter which precedes the following extract, Welbeck relates to Mervyn his adventures since their separation.]

THIS narrative threw new light on the character of Welbeck. If accident had given him possession of this treasure, it was easy to predict on what schemes of luxury and selfishness it would have been expended. The same dependence on the world's erroneous estimation, the same devotion to imposture and thoughtlessness of futurity would have constituted the picture of his future life, as had distinguished the past. This money was another's. To retain it for his own use was criminal. Of this crime he appeared to be as insensible as ever. His own gratification was the supreme law of his actions. To be subjected to the necessity of honest labour, was the heaviest of all evils, and one from which he was willing to escape by the commission of suicide. The volume which he sought was in my possession. It was my duty to restore it to the rightful owner, or, if the legal claimant could not be found, to employ its contents in the promotion of virtue and happiness. To give it to Welbeck was to consecrate it to purposes of selfishness and misery. My right, legally considered, was as valid as his.

But if I intended not to resign it to him, was it proper to disclose the truth? . . . . My understanding had been taught, by recent occurrences, to question the justice, and deny the usefulness of secrecy in any case. My principles were true; my motives were pure; why should I scruple to avow my principles, and vindicate my actions? Welbeck had ceased to be dreaded or revered. That awe which was once created by his superiority of age, refinement of manners, and dignity of garb, had vanished. I was a boy in years, an indigent and uneducated rustic, but I was able to discern the illusions of power and riches, and abjured every claim to esteem that was not founded on integrity. There was no tribunal before which I should falter in asserting the truth, and no species of martyrdom which I would not cheerfully embrace in its cause.

After some pause, I said, "Cannot you conjecture in what way this volume has disappeared?"

"No;" he answered with a sigh. "Why, of all his volumes, this only should have vanished, was an inexplicable enigma."

"Perhaps," said I, "it is less important to know how it was removed, than by whom it is now possessed."

"Unquestionably; and yet unless that knowledge enables me to regain the possession it will be useless."

"Useless then it will be, for the present possessor will never return it to you."

"Indeed," replied he, in a tone of dejection, "your conjecture is most probable. Such a prize is of too much value to be given up."

"What I have said flows not from conjecture, but from knowledge. I know that it will never be restored to you."

At these words, Welbeck looked at me with anxiety and doubt.—"You *know* that it will not!

Have you any knowledge of the book? Can you tell me what has become of it?"

"Yes, after our separation on the river, I returned to this house. I found this volume and secured it. You rightly suspected its contents. The money was there."

Welbeck started as if he had trodden on a mine of gold. His first emotion was rapturous, but was immediately chastised by some degree of doubt. "What has become of it? Have you got it? Is it entire? Have you it with you?"

"It is unimpaired. I have got it, and shall hold it as a sacred trust for the rightful proprietor."

The tone with which this declaration was accompanied, shook the new-born confidence of Welbeck. "The rightful proprietor! true, but I am he. To me only it belongs, and to me you are, doubtless, willing to restore it."

"Mr. Welbeck, it is not my desire to give you perplexity or anguish : to sport with your passions. On the supposition of your death, I deemed it no infraction of justice to take this manuscript. Accident unfolded its contents. I could not hesitate to choose my path. The natural and legal successor of Vincentio Lodi is his sister. To her, therefore, this property belongs, and to her only will I give it."

"Presumptuous boy! And this is your sage decision. I tell you that I am the owner, and to me you shall render it. Who is this girl? childish and ignorant! unable to consult and to act for herself on the most trivial occasion! Am I not, by the appointment of her dying brother, her protector and guardian? Her age produces a legal incapacity of property. Do you imagine that so obvious an expedient, as that of procuring my legal appointment as her guardian, was overlooked by me? If it were neglected, still my title to provide her subsistence and enjoyment is unquestionable. Did I not rescue her from poverty, and prostitution, and infamy? Have I not supplied all her wants with incessant solicitude? Whatever her condition required has been plenteously bestowed. This dwelling and its furniture were hers, as far as a rigid jurisprudence would permit. To prescribe her expenses and govern her family was the province of her guardian. You have heard the tale of my anguish and despair. Whence did they flow, but from the frustration of schemes projected for her benefit, as they were executed with her money and by means which the authority of her guardian fully justified? Why have I encountered this contagious atmosphere, and explored my way, like a thief, to this recess, but with a view to rescue her from poverty and restore to her her own? Your scruples are ridiculous and criminal. I treat them with less severity, because your youth is raw and your conceptions crude. But if, after this proof of the justice of my claim, you hesitate to restore the money, I shall treat you as a robber, who has plundered my cabinet and refused to refund his spoil."

I was acquainted with the rights of guardianship. Welbeck had, in some respects, acted as the friend of this lady. To vest himself with this office was the conduct which her youth and helplessness prescribed to her friend. His title to this money, as her guardian, could not be denied. But how was this statement compatible with former representations? No mention had then been made of guardianship. By thus acting, he would have thwarted all his schemes for winning the esteem of mankind, and fostering the belief which the world entertained of his opulence and independence. I was thrown, by these thoughts, into considerable perplexity. If his statement were true, his claim to this money was established, but I questioned its truth. To intimate my doubts of his veracity would be to provoke outrage. His last insinuation was peculiarly momentous. Suppose him the fraudulent possessor of this money, shall I be justified in taking it away by violence under pretence of restoring it to the genuine proprietor, who, for aught I know, may be dead, or with whom, at least, I may never procure a meeting? But will not my behaviour, on this occasion, be deemed illicit? I entered Welbeck's habitation at midnight, proceeded to his closet, possessed myself of portable property, and retired unobserved. Is not guilt imputable to an action like this? Welbeck waited with impatience for a conclusion to my pause. My perplexity and indecision did not abate, and my silence continued. At length, he repeated his demands with new vehemence. I was compelled to answer. I told him, in few words, that his reasonings had not convinced me of the equity of his claim, and that my determination was unaltered. He had not expected this inflexibility from one in my situation. The folly of opposition, when my feebleness and loneliness were contrasted with his activity and resources, appeared to him monstrous, but his contempt was converted into rage and fear when he reflected that this folly might finally defeat his hopes. He had probably determined to obtain the money, let the purchase cost what it would, but was willing to exhaust pacific expedients before he should resort to force. He might likewise question whether the money was within his reach. I had told him that I had it, but whether it was now about me, was somewhat dubious. Yet, though he used no direct inquiries, he chose to proceed on the supposition of its being at hand. His angry tones were now changed into those of remonstrance and persuasion.

"Your present behaviour, Mervyn, does not justify the expectation I had formed of you. You have been guilty of a base theft. To this you have added the deeper crime of ingratitude. But your infatuation and folly are at least as glaring as your guilt. Do you think I can credit your assertions that you keep this money for another, when I recollect that six weeks have passed since you carried it off? Why have you not sought the owner and restored it to her? If your intentions had been honest, would you have suffered so long a time to elapse without doing this? It is plain that you designed to keep it for your own use. But whether this were your purpose or not, you have no longer power to restore or retain it. You say that you came hither to die. If so, what is to be the fate of the money? In your present situation you cannot gain access to the lady. Some other must inherit this wealth. Next to Signora Lodi, whose right can be put in competition with mine? But if you will not give it to me, on my own account, let it be given in trust for her. Let me be the bearer of it to her own hands. I have already shown you that my claim to it, as her guardian, is legal and incontrovertible; but this claim I waive. I will merely be the executor of your will. I will bind myself to comply with your directions by any oath, however solemn and tremendous, which you shall prescribe."

As long as my own heart acquitted me, these imputations of dishonesty affected me but little. They excited no anger, because they originated in ignorance, and were rendered plausible to Welbeck by such facts as were known to him. It was needless to confute the charge by elaborate and circumstantial details. It was true that my recovery was, in the highest degree, improbable, and that my death would put an end to my power over this money; but had I not determined to secure its useful application in case of my death? This project was obstructed by the presence of Welbeck, but I hoped that his love of life would induce him to fly. He might wrest this volume from me by violence, or he might wait till my death should give him peaceful possession. But these, though probable events, were not certain, and would by no means justify the voluntary surrender. His strength, if employed for this end, could not be resisted; but then it would be a sacrifice, not to choice, but necessity. Promises were easily given, but were surely not to be confided in. Welbeck's own tale, in which it could not be imagined that he had aggravated his defects, attested the frailty of his virtue. To put into his hands a sum like this, in expectation of his delivering it to another, when my death would cover the transaction with impenetrable secrecy, would be indeed a proof of that infatuation which he thought proper to impute to me. These thoughts influenced my resolutions, but they were revolved in silence. To state them was useless. They would not justify my conduct in his eyes. They would only exasperate dispute, and impel him to those acts of violence which I was desirous of preventing. The sooner this controversy should end, and I in any measure be freed from the obstruction of his company, the better.

"Mr. Welbeck," said I, "my regard to your safety compels me to wish that this interview should terminate. At a different time, I should not be unwilling to discuss this matter. Now it will be fruitless. My conscience points out to me too clearly the path I should pursue for me to mistake it. As long as I have power over this money I shall keep it for the use of the unfortunate lady whom I have seen in this house. I shall exert myself to find her, but if that be impossible, I shall appropriate it in a way in which you shall have no participation."

I will not repeat the scene that succeeded between my forbearance and his passions. I listened to the dictates of his rage and his avarice in silence. Astonishment at my inflexibility was blended with his anger. By turns he commented on the guilt and on the folly of my resolutions. Sometimes his emotions would mount into fury, and he would approach me in a menacing attitude, and lift his hand, as if he would exterminate me at a blow. My languid eyes, my cheeks glowing and my temples throbbing with fever, and my total passiveness attracted his attention and arrested his stroke. Compassion would take place of rage, and the belief be revived that remonstrances and arguments would answer his purpose.

This scene lasted I know not how long. Insensibly the passions and reasonings of Welbeck assumed a new form. A grief, mingled with perplexity, overspread his countenance. He ceased to contend or to speak. His regards were withdrawn from me, on whom they had hitherto been fixed; and wandering or vacant, testified a conflict of mind terrible beyond any that my young imagination had ever conceived. For a time, he appeared to be unconscious of my presence. He moved to and fro with unequal steps and with gesticulations that possessed a horrible but indistinct significance. Occasionally he struggled for breath, and his efforts were directed to remove some choking impediment. No test of my fortitude had hitherto occurred equal to this. The suspicion which this deportment suggested was vague and formless. The tempest which I witnessed was the prelude of horror. These were throes which would terminate in the birth of some sanguinary purpose. Did he meditate a bloody sacrifice? Was his own death or was mine to attest the magnitude of his despair, or the impetuosity of his vengeance? Suicide was familiar to his thoughts. He had consented to live but on one condition; that of regaining possession of this money. Should I be justified in driving him, by my obstinate refusal, to this consummation of his crimes? My fear of this catastrophe was groundless. Hitherto he had argued and persuaded, but this method was pursued because it was more eligible than the employment of force, or than procrastination. No. These were tokens that pointed to me. Some unknown instigation was at work within him to tear away his remnant of humanity, and fit him for the office of my murderer. I knew not how the accumulation of guilt could contribute to his gratification or security. His actions had been partially exhibited and vaguely seen. What extenuations or omissions had vitiated his former or recent narrative; how far his actual performances were congenial with the deed which was now to be perpetrated, I knew not. These thoughts lent new rapidity to my blood. I raised my head from the pillow, and watched his deportment with deeper attention. The paroxysm which controlled him at length in some degree subsided. He muttered, "Yes: it must come! My last humiliation must cover me! My last confession must be made!

To die, and leave behind me this train of enormous perils, must not be. O Clemenza! O Mervyn! you have not merited that I should leave you a legacy of persecution and death. Your safety must be purchased at what price my malignant destiny will set upon it. The cord of the executioner, the note of everlasting infamy, is better than to leave you beset by the consequences of my guilt. It must not be!"

Saying this, Welbeck cast fearful glances at the windows and door. He examined every avenue and listened. Thrice he repeated this scrutiny. Having, as it seemed, ascertained that no one lurked within audience, he approached the bed. He put his mouth close to my face. He attempted to speak, but once more examined the apartment with suspicious glances. He drew closer, and at length, in a tone scarcely articulate and suffocated with emotion, he spoke: " Excellent, but fatally obstinate youth! know at least the cause of my importunity; know at least the depth of my infatuation and the enormity of my guilt. The bills— surrender them to me, and save yourself from persecution and disgrace! Save the woman whom you wish to benefit from the blackest imputations; from hazard to her life and her fame; from languishing in dungeons; from expiring on the gallows! The bills—O save me from the bitterness of death! Let the evils to which my miserable life has given birth terminate here and in myself. Surrender them to me, for"—

There he stopped. His utterance was choked by terror. Rapid glances were again darted at the windows and door. The silence was uninterrupted except by far-off sounds, produced by some moving carriage. Once more he summoned resolution and spoke: " Surrender them to me—for— *they are forged.* Formerly I told you that a scheme of forgery had been conceived. Shame would not suffer me to add, that my scheme was carried into execution. The bills were fashioned, but my fears contended against my necessities, and forbade me to attempt to exchange them. The interview with Lodi saved me from the dangerous experiment. I enclosed them in that volume to be used when all other and less hazardous resources should fail. In the agonies of my remorse at the death of Watson, they were forgotten. My wishes pointed to the grave; but the stroke that should deliver me from life was suspended only till I could hasten hither, get possession of these papers and destroy them. When I thought upon the chances that should give them an owner; bring them into circulation; load the innocent with suspicion; and lead them 'to trial and perhaps to death, my sensations were agony; earnestly as I panted for death, it was necessarily deferred till I had gained possession of and destroyed these papers. What now remains? You have found them. Happily they have not been used. Give them therefore to me, that I may crush at once the brood of mischiefs which they could not but generate."

This disclosure was strange. It was accompanied with every token of sincerity. How had I tottered on the brink of destruction! If I had made use of this money, in what a labyrinth of misery might I not have been involved! My innocence could never have been proved. An alliance with Welbeck could not have failed to be inferred. My career would have found an ignominious close; or, if my punishment had been commuted into slavery, would the testimony of my conscience have supported me? I shuddered at the view of the disasters from which I was rescued by the miraculous chance which led me to this house. Welbeck's request was salutary to me and honourable to himself. I could not hesitate a moment in compliance. The notes were enclosed in paper, and deposited in a fold of my clothes. I put my hand upon them. My motion and attention was arrested at the instant, by a noise which arose in the street. Footsteps were heard upon the pavement before the door, and voices, as if busy in discourse. This incident was adapted to infuse the deepest alarm into myself and my companion. The motives of our trepidation were indeed different, and were infinitely more powerful in my case than in his. It portended to me nothing less than the loss of my asylum and condemnation to an hospital. Welbeck hurried to the door to listen to the conversation below. This interval was pregnant with thought. That impulse which led my reflections from Welbeck to my own state, passed away in a moment, and suffered me to meditate anew upon the terms of that confession which had just been made. Horror at the fate which this interview had enabled me to shun, was 'uppermost in my conceptions. I was eager to surrender these fatal bills. I held them for that purpose in my hand, and was impatient for Welbeck's return. He continued at the door; stooping, with his face averted, and eagerly attentive to the conversation in the street.

All the circumstances of my present situation tended to arrest the progress of thought and chain my contemplations to one image; but even now there was room for foresight and deliberation. Welbeck intended to destroy these bills. Perhaps he had not been sincere; or, if his purpose had been honestly disclosed, this purpose might change when the bills were in his possession. His poverty and sanguineness of temper might prompt him to use them. That this conduct was evil and would only multiply his miseries, could not be questioned. Why should I subject his frailty to this temptation? The destruction of these bills was the loudest injunction of duty; was demanded by every sanction which bound me to promote the welfare of mankind. The means of destruction were easy. A lighted candle stood on a table, at the distance of a few yards. Why should I hesitate a moment to annihilate so powerful a cause of error and guilt? A passing instant was sufficient. A momentary lingering might change the circumstances that surrounded me and frustrate my project. My languors were suspended by the urgencies of the occasion. I started from my bed and glided to the table. Seizing the notes with my right hand, I held them in the flame of the candle, and then threw them blazing on the floor. The sudden illumination was perceived by Welbeck. The cause of it appeared to suggest itself as soon. He turned, and marking the paper where it lay, leaped to the spot and extinguished the fire with his foot. His interposition was too late. Only enough of them remained to inform him of the nature of the sacrifice. He now stood with limbs trembling, features aghast, and eyes glaring upon me. For a time he was without speech. The storm was gathering in silence, and at length burst upon me. In a tone menacing and loud, he exclaimed : "Wretch ! What have you done ?"

"I have done justly. These notes were false. You desired to destroy them that they might not betray the innocent. I applauded your purpose, and have saved you from the danger of temptation by destroying them myself."

"Maniac! miscreant! to be fooled by so gross an artifice! The notes were genuine. The tale of their forgery was false, and meant only to wrest them from you. Execrable and perverse idiot! Your deed has sealed my perdition. It has sealed your own. You shall pay for it with your blood. I will slay you by inches. I will stretch you, as you have stretched me, on the rack !"

During this speech, all was phrensy and storm in the features of Welbeck. Nothing less could be expected than that the scene would terminate in some bloody catastrophe. I bitterly regretted the facility with which I had been deceived, and the precipitation of my sacrifice. The act, however, could not be revoked. What remained but to encounter or endure its consequences with unshrinking firmness?

The contest was too unequal. It is possible that the phrensy which actuated Welbeck might have speedily subsided. It is more likely that his passions would have been satiated with nothing but my death. This event was precluded by loud knocks at the street door, and calls by some one on the pavement without, of—Who is within? Is any one within?

"They are coming," said he. "They will treat you as a sick man and a thief. I cannot desire you to suffer worse evil than they will inflict. I leave you to your fate." So saying, he rushed out of the room.

———◆———

SCENE WITH A PANTHER.
FROM EDGAR HUNTLY.

[CLITHERO, the sleep-walker, has become insane, and has fled into one of the wild mountain fastnesses of Norwalk. Edgar Huntly endeavours to discover his retreat.]

I PASSED through the cave. . . . At that moment, torrents of rain poured from above, and stronger blasts thundered amidst these desolate recesses and profound chasms. Instead of lamenting the prevalence of the tempest, I now began to regard it with pleasure. It conferred new forms of sublimity and grandeur on the scene. As I crept with hands and feet along my imperfect bridge, a sudden gust had nearly whirled me into the frightful abyss. To preserve myself, I was obliged to loose my hold of my burden and it fell into the gulf. This incident disconcerted and distressed me. As soon as I had effected my dangerous passage, I screened myself behind a cliff, and gave myself up to reflection. . . . .

While thus occupied, my eyes were fixed upon the opposite steeps. The tops of the trees, waving to and fro, in the wildest commotion, and their trunks, occasionally bending to the blast, which, in these lofty regions, blew with a violence unknown in the tracts below, exhibited an awful spectacle. At length, my attention was attracted by the trunk which lay across the gulf, and which I had converted into a bridge. I perceived that it had already somewhat swerved from its original position, that every blast broke or loosened some of the fibres by which its roots was connected with the opposite bank, and that, if the storm did not speedily abate, there was imminent danger of its being torn from the rock and precipitated into the chasm. Thus my retreat would be cut off, and the evils, from which I was endeavouring to rescue another, would be experienced by myself. . . .

I believed my destiny to hang upon the expedition with which I should recross this gulf. The moments that were spent in these deliberations were critical, and I shuddered to observe that the trunk was held in its place by one or two fibres which were already stretched almost to breaking.

To pass along the trunk, rendered slippery by the wet and unsteadfast by the wind, was eminently dangerous. To maintain my hold in passing, in defiance of the whirlwind, required the most vigorous exertions. For this end it was necessary to discommode myself of my cloak and of the volume. . . . .

Just as · I had disposed of these encumbrances, and had risen from my seat, my attention was again called to the opposite steep, by the most unwelcome object that at this time could possibly present itself. Something was perceived moving among the bushes and rocks, which, for a time, I hoped was no more than a raccoon or opossum, but which presently appeared to be a panther. His gray coat, extended claws, fiery eyes, and a cry which he at that moment uttered, and which, by its resemblance to the human voice, is peculiarly terrific, denoted him to be the most ferocious and untameable of that detested race. The industry of our hunters has nearly banished animals of prey from these precincts. The fastnesses of Norwalk, however, could not but afford refuge to some of them. Of late I had met them so rarely, that my fears were seldom alive, and I trod, without caution, the ruggedest and most solitary haunts. Still, however, I had seldom been unfurnished in my rambles with the means of defence. . . . .

The unfrequency with which I had lately encountered this foe, and the encumbrance of provision made me neglect on this occasion to bring with me my usual arms. The beast that was now before me, when stimulated by hunger, was accustomed to assail whatever could provide him with a banquet of blood. He would set upon the man and the deer with equal and irresistible ferocity. His sagacity was equal to his strength, and he seemed able to discover when his antagonist was armed. . . .

My past experience enabled me to estimate the full extent of my danger. He sat on the brow of the steep, eyeing the bridge, and apparently deliberating whether he should cross it. It was probable that he had scented my footsteps thus far, and should he pass over, his vigilance could scarcely fail of detecting my asylum. . . .

Should he retain his present station, my danger was scarcely lessened. To pass over in the face of a famished tiger was only to rush upon my fate. The falling of the trunk, which had lately been so anxiously deprecated, was now, with no less solicitude, desired. Every new gust I hoped would tear asunder its remaining bands, and, by cutting off all communication between the opposite steeps, place me in security. My hopes, however, were destined to be frustrated. The fibres of the prostrate tree were obstinately tenacious of their hold, and presently the animal scrambled down the rock and proceeded to cross it.

Of all kinds of death, that which now menaced me was the most abhorred. To die by disease, or by the hand of a fellow-creature, was lenient in comparison with being rent to pieces by the fangs of this savage. To perish in this obscure retreat, by means so impervious to the anxious curiosity of my friends, to lose my portion of existence by so untoward and ignoble a destiny, was insupportable. I bitterly deplored my rashness in coming hither unprovided for an encounter like this.

The evil of my present circumstances consisted chiefly in suspense. My death was unavoidable, but my imagination had leisure to torment itself by anticipations. One foot of the savage was slowly and cautiously moved after the other. He struck his claws so deeply into the bark that they were with difficulty withdrawn. At length he leaped upon the ground. We were now separated by an interval of scarcely eight feet. To leave the spot where I crouched was impossible. Behind and beside me the cliff rose perpendicularly, and before me was this grim and terrific visage. I shrunk still closer to the ground and closed my eyes.

From this pause of horror I was aroused by the noise occasioned by a second spring of the animal. He leaped into the pit in which I had so deeply regretted that I had not taken refuge, and disappeared. My rescue was so sudden, and so much beyond my belief or my hope, that I doubted for a moment whether my senses did not deceive me. This opportunity of escape was not to be neglected. I left my place and scrambled over the trunk with a precipitation which had liked to have proved fatal. The tree groaned and shook under me, the wind blew with unexampled violence, and

I had scarcely reached the opposite steep when the roots were severed from the rock, and the whole fell thundering to the bottom of the chasm.

My trepidations were not speedily quieted. I looked back with wonder on my hair-breadth escape, and on that singular concurrence of events which had placed me in so short a period in absolute security. Had the trunk fallen a moment earlier, I should have been imprisoned on the hill or thrown headlong. Had its fall been delayed another moment I should have been pursued; for the beast now issued from his den, and testified his surprise and disappointment by tokens, the sight of which made my blood run cold.

He saw me and hastened to the verge of the chasm. He squatted on his hind-legs and assumed the attitude of one preparing to leap. My consternation was excited afresh by these appearances. It seemed at first as if the rift was too wide for any power of muscles to carry him in safety over; but I knew the unparalleled agility of this animal, and that his experience had made him a better judge of the practicability of this exploit than I was.

Still there was hope that he would relinquish this design as desperate. This hope was quickly at an end. He sprung, and his fore-legs touched the verge of the rock on which I stood. In spite of vehement exertions, however, the surface was too smooth and too hard to allow him to make good his hold. He fell, and a piercing cry, uttered below, showed that nothing had obstructed his descent to the bottom.

INFLUENCE OF FOREIGN LITERATURE.

FROM CLARA HOWARD.

THE ideas annexed to the term peasant are wholly inapplicable to the tillers of ground in America; but our notions are the offspring of the books we read. Our books are almost wholly the productions of Europe, and the prejudices which infect us are derived chiefly from this source. These prejudices may be somewhat rectified by age and by converse with the world, but they flourish in full vigour in youthful minds, reared in seclusion and privacy, and undisciplined by intercourse with various classes of mankind. In me they possessed an unusual degree of strength. My words were selected and defined according to foreign usages, and my notions of dignity were modelled on a scale which the revolution has completely taken away. I could never forget that my condition was that of a peasant, and in spite of reflection, I was the slave of those sentiments of self-contempt and humiliation, which pertain to that condition elsewhere, though chimerical and visionary on the western side of the Atlantic.

WILLIAM WIRT.

[Born 1772. Died 1834.]

WILLIAM WIRT was the youngest son of an emigrant from Switzerland, and was born in Bladensburg, Maryland, on the eighth of November, 1772. His father died while he was an infant, and his mother before he was eight years old. He then became the ward of an uncle, who placed him at a grammar school kept by a Mr. Hunt, in the county of Montgomery, where he remained from 1781 to 1785, in which period he studied the Greek and Latin languages, and indulged in much desultory reading, chiefly of classical authors, of which his teacher had a good collection. During the next year and a half he was a private teacher in the family of Mr. Benjamin Edwards, whose son Ninian, afterward Governor of Illinois, had been his school-mate; and in 1789, on account of impaired health, he went to Augusta, Georgia, where he spent the following winter. On his return to Maryland he commenced the study of the law, and in 1792 he was licensed to practice, and commenced his professional career at Culpepper Court House in Virginia.

He was now twenty-one years of age, with good health, a handsome person, pleasing address, and great fluency in conversation and in debate. From the first he was eminently successful in the courts; and marrying, in 1795, a daughter of Dr. Gilmer, of Charlottesville, and about the same time becoming acquainted and contracting friendships with Mr. Jefferson, Mr. Madison, and other celebrated men, he had before him the promise of a prosperous and happy life.

The death of his wife, however, in 1799, interrupted his pursuits, and for a change of scene he went to Richmond, where he was chosen clerk of the House of Delegates. The respect which he acquired during three terms of service in this body was so great, that upon a new organization of the judiciary, in 1802, when he was but twenty-nine years of age, he was chosen chancellor of the eastern district of the state. He removed to Williamsburgh, but finding the profits of his office less than his probable income as an advocate, and confident of his ability to acquire a higher distinction in a different position, he resigned it at the end of a few months; and having married a daughter of Colonel Gamble, of Richmond, and passed in that city another winter, during which he wrote The British Spy, he selected Norfolk as his place of residence, and there resumed the practice of his profession.

The British Spy was hastily composed, without a thought of its ever attracting attention beyond the circle which was most familiar with the characters described in it, and was published in numbers in the Virginia Argus, in 1803. It purports to be a selection from letters addressed by a young English nobleman, travelling under an assumed name in the United States, to his former guardian, a distinguished member of the House of Commons.

At the end of three years Mr. Wirt returned again to Richmond, where in the winter of 1807 he was retained under the direction of President Jefferson to assist the Attorney-General of the United States in the celebrated prosecution of Aaron Burr for treason. The great Marshall presided, and the first lawyers of the country were engaged for or against the prisoner. The question was argued in a manner worthy of its importance. "A degree of eloquence seldom displayed on any occasion," said the chief justice, "has embellished solidity of argument and depth of research." It is generally admitted that the speech of Mr. Wirt was altogether the most brilliant and effective made during the trial. He was master of all the arts by which the attention is secured and retained. Oratory was his forte as well as his favourite art. Every period, every gesture, every look, was carefully studied. His principal speech occupied four hours, and was faithfully reported, probably by himself. The occasion was fortunate; he exerted his best powers; and made his reputation national. As everybody knows, Burr was acquitted. Luther Martin's remark, that the trial was "much ado about nothing," is now admitted to have been as just as it was happy. There was on the side of the prosecution little opportunity for reasoning, and certainly Mr. Wirt exhibited no great ability in that way; but his speech served his own purposes, and helped to secure the proceeding from immediate contempt.

In 1808 he was elected to represent the city of Richmond in the House of Delegates, and he acquired new distinction by his labours in that body; but though often invited to do so he would never after leave the path of his profession. He wrote, indeed, in support of Mr. Jefferson's administration, and in favour of the nomination of Mr. Madison for the presidency; but except when influenced by private friendship he had as little as possible to do with party politics.

He was now in the height of his popularity, and his office was thronged with suitors; but he still found time for indulgence of his taste for society and literature. His reading was discursive, but the classics, the great historians, and the English dramatists and essayists were his favourites. His memory was exceedingly retentive, and perhaps no one ever surpassed him in readiness and felicity of quotation. Mr. Thomas, the clever author of Clinton Bradshaw, relates a characteristic instance, which occurred, however, at a later period: A Scotch Presbyterian church in Baltimore was divided upon the question of what is called the new school theology, and Mr. Wirt was advocate for the Rev. Mr. Duncan, whom the old school side were endeavouring to eject from the place of pastor. After alluding to the fact that both parties were from Scotland, he described the preacher as being in the condition of the guest of Macbeth, and rebuking the plaintiffs with great effect, said that if they succeeded they would feel like the guilty Thane; for

This *Duncan*
Hath borne his faculties so meek, hath been
So clear in his great office, that his virtues
Will plead like angels, trumpet-tongued, against
The deep damnation of his taking off.

There were in Richmond many persons of congenial tastes, upon whom he frequently urged the custom of authorship, as delightful in itself, and as an honourable and effective means of elevating the national character. The British Spy had been eminently successful; and discussing with some friends, in 1809,

the article on Ashe's Travels in America, which had then just appeared in the Edinburgh Review, he proposed a literary partnership for writing The Old Bachelor. Judge Parker, Beverley Tucker, Dabney Carr, J. W. Mercer, and some others promised assistance, and the publication of that work was soon afterward commenced in the Richmond Enquirer. By far the largest portion of it was written by Mr. Wirt, though several of his friends furnished each one or more essays. In the twelfth number the prime objects in view are stated to be, to diffuse among the people a taste for letters, to make them sensible of the decline of intelligence in the country since the age of the revolution, and to excite a spirit of emulation among the young. Whatever may have been the degeneracy of the Virginians, the contrasts which he describes were nowhere else perceptible; and we can hardly believe, even upon his testimony, that his contemporaries in that state exhibited in so marked a degree " the phenomenon of a young people experiencing the decrepitude of age before they attained maturity." The revolution had called out all our latent energies, and such a crisis at any subsequent period would also have produced what he calls "eruptions of talent." The tone of The Old Bachelor on this subject is uniformly extravagant, and exhibits a curious subserviency to the opinions of the foreign travellers and reviewers which he professes to condemn. Its style is gaudy and feeble.

In 1817 Mr. Wirt published the Life of Patrick Henry, a work for which he had been many years collecting materials, but of which the execution had been delayed by his professional occupations. This is an extraordinary piece of biography, animated and picturesque, and though full of extravagancies, not an unfaithful representation of the celebrated original. It is one of the small class of works for which his genius, or rather his temperament, was best suited. He would have written the life of any other man in the same style, and Henry's was almost the only one which would have borne it. Wirt's whole experience had been a preparation for the portraiture of the great orator, and however hastily it may in the end have been composed, we have no reason to suppose it would have had more unity, completeness, condensation or simplicity, if it had received from him any conceivable amount of labour.

Mr. Wirt was appointed by President Madison in 1816 Attorney for the district of Virginia, and on the election of Mr. Monroe to the presidency, in the following year, he was made Attorney General of the United States. He now removed to Washington, where he resided until 1830, when, at the close of the administration of Mr. Adams, he resigned his office, and took up his residence in Baltimore, where he passed the remainder of his life. He died on the eighteenth of February, 1834, in the sixty-second year of his age.

Mr. Wirt's literary writings, besides those already mentioned, are a Eulogy on the Lives and Characters of Adams and Jefferson; A Discourse before the Societies of Rutgers' College, in 1830; and an Address delivered in Baltimore, in the same year, on the Triumph of Liberty in France.

Mr. Wirt had never the reputation of being a first rate lawyer, but his standing in the Supreme Court, where he was constantly liable to be compared with some of the strongest men of the country, was highly respectable. He had a thorough knowledge of business, felicity in expedients, and great readiness in bringing all his acquisitions into use. He had given much attention to the study of oratory, and in The British Spy, in The Old Bachelor, and in the Life of Henry, had written much on the subject; but in a desultory manner, without apparent design, or consistency, so that no very definite ideas can be gathered of his views respecting it. Yet it is agreed on all hands that he was himself a very ready, pleasing, and effective speaker, inferior perhaps to no one among his contemporaries at the bar in this country.

Of his literary merits I do not think highly.

His abilities were more brilliant than solid. He had a rapid but not skilful command of language, a prolific but not a chaste or correct fancy, and his opinions were generally neither new nor striking.

In his essays he imitated closely the form of the English models in this sort of writing, and both The British Spy and The Old Bachelor contain passages which will bear a favourable comparison perhaps with any thing in the same style written since the time of Johnson; but they are to be regarded altogether as the last productions of an obsolete school, which never could or will be made to flourish in this country.

In private life Mr. Wirt was justly held in the highest estimation. At an early period he had betrayed an unsteadiness of purpose and a feebleness of will from which the worst consequences were apprehended; but " the ship righted," as he remarks in one of his letters, and it sailed gallantly afterward a long voyage, through various seas, to the desired haven. He was in all respects fitted to adorn and charm society. His manners, marked by the kindness which was in his nature, were pleasing and familiar, yet dignified, and his conversation was fluent, eloquent, enlivened by playful and apposite wit, and enriched with the results, always at command, of his extensive and various reading. He wrote verses and composed music with facility, and sung, and performed on various instruments. It is no wonder therefore that he was a favourite of society, and that he is remembered, by those who had the happiness of being personally intimate with him, with an enthusiasm which cannot be felt by those who know him only as a lawyer and man of letters.

~~~~~~~~~~~~~~~~~~~~

THE BLIND PREACHER.

FROM THE BRITISH SPY.

It was one Sunday, as I travelled through the county of Orange, that my eye was caught by a cluster of horses tied near a ruinous, old, wooden house in the forest, not far from the road-side. Having frequently seen such objects before, in travelling through these States, I had no difficulty in understanding that this was a place of religious worship.

Devotion alone should have stopped me, to join in the duties of the congregation; but I must confess, that curiosity to hear the preacher of such a wilderness, was not the least of my motives. On entering, I was struck with his preternatural appearance. He was a tall and very spare old man; his head, which was covered with a white linen cap, his shrivelled hands, and his voice, were all shaking under the influence of a palsy; and a few moments ascertained to me that he was perfectly blind.

The first emotions that touched my breast wer those of mingled pity and veneration. But how soon were all my feelings changed! The lips of Plato were never more worthy of a prognostic swarm of bees, than were the lips of this holy man! It was a day of the administration of the sacrament; and his subject was, of course, the passion of our Saviour. I had heard the subject handled a thousand times: I had thought it exhausted long ago. Little did I suppose that in the wild woods of America, I was to meet with a man whose eloquence would give to this topic a new and more sublime pathos than I had ever before witnessed.

As he descended from the pulpit to distribute the mystic symbols, there was a peculiar, a more than human solemnity in his air and manner, which made my blood run cold, and my whole frame shiver.

He then drew a picture of the sufferings of our Saviour; his trial before Pilate; his ascent up Calvary; his crucifixion; and his death. I knew the whole history; but never until then had I heard the circumstances so selected, so arranged, so coloured! It was all new; and I seemed to have heard it for the first time in my life. His enunciation was so deliberate that his voice trembled on every syllable; and every heart in the assembly trembled in unison. His peculiar phrases had that force of description, that the original scene appeared to be at that moment acting before our eyes. We saw the very faces of the Jews; the staring, frightful distortions of malice and rage. We saw the buffet: my soul kindled with a flame of indignation; and my hands were involuntarily and convulsively clinched.

But when he came to touch on the patience, the forgiving meekness of our Saviour; when he drew, to the life, his blessed eyes streaming in tears to heaven; his voice breathing to God a soft and gentle prayer of pardon on his enemies, "Father, forgive them, for they know not what they do,"—the voice of the preacher, which had all along faltered, grew fainter and fainter, until, his utterance being entirely obstructed by the force of his feelings, he raised his handkerchief to his eyes, and burst into a loud and irrepressible flood of grief. The effect is inconceivable. The whole house resounded with the mingled groans, and sobs, and shrieks of the congregation.

It was some time before the tumult had subsided, so far as to permit him to proceed. Indeed, judging by the usual, but fallacious standard of my own weakness, I began to be very uneasy for the situation of the preacher. For I could not conceive how he would be able to let his audience down from the height to which he had wound them, without impairing the solemnity and dignity of his subject, or perhaps shocking them by the abruptness of the fall. But—no: the descent was as beautiful and sublime as the elevation had been rapid and enthusiastic.

The first sentence, with which he broke the awful silence, was a quotation from Rousseau: "Socrates died like a philosopher, but Jesus Christ, like a God!"

I despair of giving you any idea of the effect produced by this short sentence, unless you could perfectly conceive the whole manner of the man, as well as the peculiar crisis in the discourse. Never before did I completely understand what Demosthenes meant by laying such stress on delivery. You are to bring before you the venerable figure of the preacher; his blindness, constantly recalling to your recollection old Homer, Ossian, and Milton, and associating with his performance the melancholy grandeur of their geniuses; you are to imagine that you hear his slow, solemn, well-accented enunciation, and his voice of affecting, trembling melody; you are to remember the pitch of passion and enthusiasm, to which the congregation were raised; and then the few moments of portentous, deathlike silence, which reigned throughout the house: the preacher removing his white handkerchief from his aged face, (even yet wet from the recent torrent of his tears,) and slowly stretching forth the palsied hand which holds it, begins the sentence, "Socrates died like a philosopher"—then, pausing, raising his other hand, pressing them both, clasped together, with warmth and energy, to his breast, lifting his "sightless balls" to heaven, and pouring his whole soul into his tremulous voice—"but Jesus Christ—like a God!" If he had been indeed and in truth an angel of light, the effect could scarcely have been more divine. Whatever I had been able to conceive of the sublimity of Massillon or the force of Bourdaloue, had fallen far short of the power which I felt from the delivery of this simple sentence.

If this description give you the impression that this incomparable minister had any thing of shallow theatrical trick in his manner, it does him great injustice. I have never seen, in any other orator, such a union of simplicity and majesty. He has not a gesture, an attitude, or an accent, to which he does not seem forced by the sentiment he is expressing. His mind is too serious, too earnest, too solicitous, and, at the same time, too dignified, to stoop to artifice. Although as far removed from ostentation as a man can be, yet it is clear, from the train, the style and substance of his thoughts, that he is not only a very polite scholar, but a man of extensive and profound erudition. I was forcibly struck with a short yet beautiful character, which he drew of your learned and amiable countryman, Sir Robert Boyle: he spoke of him, as if "his noble mind had even before death divested herself of all influence from his frail tabernacle of flesh;" and called him, in his peculiarly emphatic and impressive manner, "a pure intelligence: the link between men and angels."

This man has been before my imagination almost ever since. A thousand times, as I rode along, I dropped the reins of my bridle, stretched forth my hand, and tried to imitate his quotation from Rousseau; a thousand times I abandoned the attempt in despair, and felt persuaded, that his peculiar manner and power arose from an energy of soul, which nature could give, but which no human being could justly copy. As I recall, at this moment, several of his awfully striking attitudes, the chilling tide, with which my blood begins to pour along my arteries, reminds me of the emotions produced by the first sight of Gray's introductory picture of his Bard.

WHO IS BLANNERHASSETT?
FROM A SPEECH ON THE TRIAL OF AARON BURR.

WHO is Blannerhassett? A native of Ireland, a man of letters, who fled from the storms of his own country to find quiet in ours. His history shows that war is not the natural element of his mind. If it had been, he never would have exchanged Ireland for America. So far is an army from furnishing the society natural and proper to Mr. Blannerhassett's character, that on his arrival in America he retired even from the population of the Atlantic States, and sought quiet and solitude in the bosom of our western forests. But he carried with him taste, and science, and wealth; and lo, the desert smiled! Possessing himself of a beautiful island in the Ohio, he rears upon it a palace, and decorates it with every romantic embellishment of fancy. A shrubbery, that Shenstone might have envied, blooms around him. Music, that might have charmed Calypso and her nymphs, is his. An extensive library spreads its treasures before him. A philosophical apparatus offers to him all the secret mysteries of nature. Peace, tranquillity, and innocence shed their mingled delights around him. And to crown the enchantment of the scene, a wife, who is said to be lovely even beyond her sex, and graced with every accomplishment that can render it irresistible, had blessed him with her love and made him the father of several children. The evidence would convince you that this is but a faint picture of the real life. In the midst of all this peace, this innocent simplicity, and this tranquillity, this feast of the mind, this pure banquet of the heart, the destroyer comes; he comes to change this paradise into a hell. Yet the flowers do not wither at his approach. No monitory shuddering through the bosom of their unfortunate possessor warns him of the ruin that is coming upon him. A stranger presents himself. Introduced to their civilities by the high rank which he had lately held in his country, he soon finds his way to their hearts by the dignity and elegance of his demeanour, the light and beauty of his conversation, and the seductive and fascinating power of his address. The conquest was not difficult. Innocence is ever simple and credulous. Conscious of no design itself, it suspects none in others. It wears no guard before its breast. Every door and portal and avenue of the heart is thrown open, and all who choose it enter. Such was the state of Eden when the serpent entered its bowers. The prisoner, in a more engaging form, winding himself into the open and unpractised heart of the unfortunate Blannerhassett, found but little difficulty in changing the native character of that heart and the objects of its affection. By degrees he infuses into it the poison of his own ambition. He breathes into it the fire of his own courage; a daring and desperate thirst for glory; and ardour panting for great enterprises, for all the storm and bustle and hurricane of life. In a short time the whole man is changed, and every object of his former delight is relinquished. No more he enjoys the tranquil

scene; it has become flat and insipid to his taste. His books are abandoned. His retort and crucible are thrown aside. His shrubbery blooms and breathes its fragrance upon the air in vain; he likes it not. His ear no longer drinks the rich melody of music; it longs for the trumpet's clangour and the cannon's roar. Even the prattle of his babes, once so sweet, no longer affects him; and the angel smile of his wife, which hitherto touched his bosom with ecstasy so unspeakable, is now unseen and unfelt. Greater objects have taken possession of his soul. His imagination has been dazzled by visions of diadems, of stars and garters, and titles of nobility. He has been taught to burn with restless emulation at the names of great heroes and conquerors. His enchanted island is destined soon to relapse into a wilderness; and in a few months we find the beautiful and tender partner of his bosom, whom he lately "permitted not the winds of" summer "to visit too roughly," we find her shivering at midnight on the winter banks of the Ohio and mingling her tears with the torrents that froze as they fell. Yet this unfortunate man, thus deluded from his interest and his happiness, thus seduced from the paths of innocence and peace, thus confounded in the toils that were deliberately spread for him, and overwhelmed by the mastering spirit and genius of another—this man, thus ruined and undone, and made to play a subordinate part in this grand drama of guilt and treason, this man is to be called the principal offender, while he by whom he was thus plunged in misery is comparatively innocent, a mere accessory! Is this reason? Is it law? Is it humanity? Sir, neither the human heart nor the human understanding will bear a perversion so monstrous and absurd! so shocking to the soul! so revolting to reason! Let Aaron Burr, then, not shrink from the high destination which he has courted, and having already ruined Blannerhassett in fortune, character, and happiness for ever, let him not attempt to finish the tragedy by thrusting that ill-fated man between himself and punishment.

PATRICK HENRY AGAINST THE PARSONS.
FROM THE LIFE OF PATRICK HENRY.

ABOUT the time of Mr. Henry's coming to the bar, a controversy arose in Virginia, which gradually produced a very strong excitement, and called to it, at length, the attention of the whole state.

This was the famous controversy between the clergy on the one hand, and the legislature of the people of the colony on the other, touching the stipend claimed by the former; and as this was the occasion on which Mr. Henry's genius first broke forth, those who take an interest in his life will not be displeased by a particular account of the nature and grounds of the dispute. It will be borne in mind, that the church of England was at this period the established church of Virginia; and by an act of Assembly, passed so far back as the year 1696, each minister of a parish had been provided with an annual stipend of sixteen thousand pounds of tobacco. This act was re-enacted, with amendments, in 1748, and in this form had received the royal assent. This price of tobacco had long remained stationary at two pence in the pound, or sixteen shillings and eight pence *per* hundred. According to the provisions of the law, the clergy had the right to demand, and were in the practice of receiving, payment to their stipend in the specific tobacco; unless they chose, for convenience, to commute it for money at the market price. In the year 1755, however, the crop of tobacco having fallen short, the legislature passed "an act to enable the inhabitants of this colony to discharge their tobacco debts in money for the present year:" by the provisions of which, "all persons, from whom any tobacco was due, were authorized to pay the same either in tobacco or in money, *af.er the rate of sixteen shillings and eight pence per hundred, at the option of the debtor.*" This act was to continue in force for ten months and no longer, and did not contain the usual clause of suspension, *until it should receive the royal assent.* Whether the scarcity of tobacco was so general and so notorious as to render this act a measure of obvious humanity and necessity, or whether the clergy were satisfied by its generality, since it embraced sheriffs, clerks, attorneys, and all other tobacco creditors, as well as themselves, or whether they acquiesced in it as a temporary expedient, which they supposed not likely to be repeated, it is certain, that no objection was made to the law at that time. They could not, indeed, have helped observing the benefits which the rich planters derived from the act; for they were receiving from fifty to sixty shillings per hundred for their tobacco, while they paid off their debts, due in that article, at the old price of sixteen shillings and eight pence. Nothing, however, was then said in defence either of the royal prerogative or of the rights of the clergy, but the law was permitted to go peaceably through its ten months' operation. The great tobacco planters had not forgotten the fruits of this act, when, in the year 1758, *upon a surmise* that another short crop was likely to occur, the provisions of the act of 1775 were re-enacted, and the new law, like the former, contained no suspending clause. The crop, as had been anticipated, did fall short, and the price of tobacco rose immediately from sixteen and eight pence to fifty shillings per hundred. The clergy now took the alarm, and the act was assailed by an indignant, sarcastic, and vigorous pamphlet, entitled The Two-Penny Act, from the pen of the Rev. John Camm, the rector of York Hampton parish, and the Episcopalian commissary for the colony.[*] He was answered by two pamphlets, written, the

one by Col. Richard Bland, and the other by Col. Landon Carter, in both which the commissary was very roughly handled. He replied, in a still severer pamphlet, under the ludicrous title of The Colonels Dismounted. The Colonels rejoined; and this war of pamphlets, in which, with some sound argument, there was a great deal of what Dryden has called "the horse-play of raillery," was kept up, until the whole colony, which had at first looked on for amusement, kindled seriously in the contest from motives of interest. Such was the excitement produced by the discussion, and at length so strong the current against the clergy, that the printers found it expedient to shut their presses against them in this colony, and Mr. Camm had at last to resort to Maryland for publication. These pamphlets are still extant; and it seems impossible to deny, at this day, that the clergy had much the best of the argument. The king in his council took up the subject, denounced the act of 1758 as a usurpation, and declared it utterly null and void. Thus supported, the clergy resolved to bring the question to a judicial test; and suits were accordingly brought by them, in the various county courts of the colony, to recover their stipends in the specific tobacco. They selected the county of Hanover as the place of the first experiment; and this was made in a suit instituted by the Rev. James Maury, against the collector of that county and his sureties. The record of this suit is now before me. The declaration is founded on the act of 1748, which gives the tobacco; the defendants pleaded specially the act of 1758, which authorizes the commutation into money, at sixteen and eight pence; to this plea the plaintiff demurred; assigning for causes of demurrer, first, that the act of 1758, not having received the royal assent, had not the force of a law; and, secondly, that the king, in council, had declared the act null and void. The case stood for argument on the demurrer to the November term, 1763, and was argued by Mr. Lyons for the plaintiff, and Mr. John Lewis for the defendants; when the court, very much to the credit of their candour and firmness, breasted the popular current by sustaining the demurrer. Thus far, the clergy sailed before the wind, and concluded, with good reason, that their triumph was complete: for the act of 1758 having been declared void by the judgment on the demurrer, that of 1748 was left in full force, and became, in law, the only standard for the finding of the jury. Mr. Lewis was so thoroughly convinced of this, that he retired from the cause; informing his clients that it had been, in effect, decided against them, and that there remained nothing more for him to do. In this desperate situation, they applied to Patrick Henry, and he undertook to argue it for them before a jury, at the ensuing term. Accordingly, on the first day of the following December, he attended the court, and, on his arrival, found in the court-yard such a concourse as would have appalled any other man in his situation. They were not the people of the county merely who were there, but visiters from all the counties, to a considerable distance around. The decision upon the demurrer had produced a violent ferment among the people, and equal exultation on the part of the clergy; who attended the court in a large body, either to look down opposition, or to enjoy the final triumph of this hard-fought contest, which they now considered as perfectly secure. Among many other clergymen, who attended on this occasion, came the Reverend Patrick Henry, who was the plaintiff in another cause of the same nature, then depending in court. When Mr. Henry saw his uncle approach, he walked up to his carriage, accompanied by Col. Meredith, and expressed his regret at seeing him there. "Why so?" inquired the uncle. "Because, sir," said Mr. Henry, "you know that I have never yet spoken in public, and I fear that I shall be too much overawed by your presence, to be able to do my duty to my clients; besides, sir, I shall be obliged to say some *hard things* of the clergy, and I am very unwilling to give pain to your feelings." His uncle reproved him for having engaged in the cause; which Mr. Henry excused, by saying, that the clergy had not thought him worthy of being retained on their side, and he knew of no moral principle by which he was bound to refuse a fee from their adversaries; besides, he confessed, that in this controversy, both his heart and judgment, as well as his professional duty, were on the side of the people : he then requested that his uncle would do him the favour to leave the ground. "Why, Patrick," said the old gentleman, with a good-natured smile, "as to *your* saying hard things of the clergy, I advise you to let that alone: take my word for it, you will do yourself more harm than you will them; and as to my leaving the ground, I fear, my boy, that my presence could neither do you harm nor good in such a cause. However, since you seem to think otherwise, and desire it of me so earnestly, you shall be gratified." Whereupon, he entered his carriage again, and returned home.

Soon after the opening of the court, the cause was called. It stood on a writ of inquiry of damages, no plea having been entered by the defendants since the judgment on the demurrer. The array before Mr. Henry's eyes was now most fearful. On the bench sat more than twenty clergymen, the most learned men in the colony, and the most capable, as well as the severest, critics before whom it was possible for him to have made his *debut*. The courthouse was crowded with an overwhelming multitude, and surrounded with an immense and anxious throng, who, not finding room to enter, were endeavouring to listen without, in the deepest attention. But there was something still more awfully disconcerting than all this; for in the chair of the presiding magistrate sat no other person than his own father. Mr. Lyons opened the cause very briefly : in the way of argument he did nothing more than explain to the jury, that the decision upon the demurrer had put the act of 1758 entirely out of the way, and left the law of 1748 as the only standard of their damages; he then concluded with a highly-wrought eulogium on the benevolence of the clergy. And now

came on the first trial of Patrick Henry's strength. No one had ever heard him speak, and curiosity was on tiptoe. He rose very awkwardly, and faltered much in his exordium. The people hung their heads at so unpromising a commencement; the clergy were observed to exchange sly looks with each other; and his father is described as having almost sunk with confusion from his seat. But these feelings were of short duration, and soon gave place to others, of a very different character. For now were those wonderful faculties which he possessed, for the first time, developed; and now was first witnessed that mysterious and almost supernatural transformation of appearance, which the fire of his own eloquence never failed to work in him. For as his mind rolled along, and began to glow from its own action, all the *exuviæ* of the clown seemed to shed themselves spontaneously. His attitude, by degrees, became erect and lofty. The spirit of his genius awakened all his features. His countenance shone with a nobleness and grandeur which it had never before exhibited. There was a lightning in his eyes which seemed to rive the spectator. His action became graceful, bold, and commanding; and in the tones of his voice, but more especially in his emphasis, there was a peculiar charm, a magic, of which any one who ever heard him will speak as soon as he is named, but of which no one can give any adequate description. They can only say that it struck upon the ear and upon the heart, *in a manner which language cannot tell*. Add to all these, his wonder-working fancy, and the peculiar phraseology in which he clothed its images; for he painted to the heart with a force that almost petrified it. In the language of those who heard him on this occasion, "he made their blood run cold, and their hair to rise on end."

It will not be difficult for any one who ever heard this most extraordinary man, to believe the whole account of this transaction, which is given by his surviving hearers, and from their account the courthouse of Hanover county must have exhibited, on this occasion, a scene as picturesque as has been ever witnessed in real life. They say that the people, whose countenance had fallen as he arose, had heard but a very few sentences before they began to look up; then to look at each other with surprise, as if doubting the evidence of their own senses; then, attracted by some strong gesture, struck by some majestic attitude, fascinated by the spell of his eye, the charm of his emphasis, and the varied and commanding expression of his countenance, they could look away no more. In less than twenty minutes, they might be seen in every part of the house, on every bench, in every window, stooping forward from their stands, in death like silence; their features fixed in amazement and awe; all their senses listening and riveted upon the speaker, as if to catch the last strain of some heavenly visitant. The mockery of the clergy was soon turned into alarm: their triumph into confusion and despair; and at one burst of his rapid and overwhelming invective, they fled from the bench in precipitation and terror. As for the father, such was his surprise, such his amazement, such his rapture, that, forgetting where he was, and the character which he was filling, tears of ecstasy streamed down his cheeks, without the power or inclination to repress them.

The jury seem to have been so completely bewildered, that they lost sight, not only of the act of 1748, but that of 1758, also; for thoughtless even of the admitted right of the plaintiff, they had scarcely left the bar, when they returned with a verdict of *one penny damages.* A motion was made for a new trial; but the court, too, had now lost the equipoise of their judgment, and overruled the motion by a unanimous vote. The verdict and judgment overruling the motion, were followed by redoubled acclamations, from within and from without the house. The people, who had with difficulty kept their hands off their champion, from the moment of closing his harangue, no sooner saw the fate of the cause finally sealed, than they seized him at the bar, and in spite of his own exertions, and the continued cry of " order" from the sheriffs and the court, they bore him out of the courthouse, and raising him on their shoulders, carried him about the yard, in a kind of electioneering triumph.

O! what a scene was this for a father's heart! so sudden; so unlooked for; so delightfully overwhelming! At the time, he was not able to give utterance to any sentiment; but, a few days after, when speaking of it to Mr. Winston, he said, with the most engaging modesty, and with a tremour of voice, which showed how much more he felt than he expressed, " Patrick spoke in this cause near an hour! and in a manner that surprised me! and showed himself well-informed on a subject, of which I did not think he had any knowledge!"

I have tried much to procure a sketch of this celebrated speech. But those of Mr. Henry's hearers who survive, seem to have been bereft of their senses. They can only tell you, in general, that they were taken captive; and so delighted with their captivity, that they followed implicitly whithersoever he led them; that, at his bidding, their tears flowed from pity, and their cheeks flushed with indignation: that when it was over, they felt as if they had just awaked from some ecstatic dream, of which they were unable to recall or connect the particulars. It was such a speech as they believe had never before fallen from the lips of man; and to this day, the old people of that county cannot conceive that a higher compliment can be paid to a speaker, than to say of him, in their own homely phrase:—" *He is almost equal to Patrick, when he plead against the parsons.*"

MONTICELLO.

FROM A EULOGY ON ADAMS AND JEFFERSON.

THE mansion house at Monticello was built and furnished in the days of his prosperity. In its dimensions, its architecture, its arrangements and ornaments, it is such a one as became the character and fortune of the man. It stands upon an elliptic plain, formed by cutting down the apex of a mountain; and, on the west, stretching away to the north and the south, it commands a view of the Blue Ridge for a hundred and fifty miles, and brings under the eye one of the boldest and most beautiful horizons in the world: while on the east, it presents an extent of prospect bounded only by the spherical form of the earth, in which nature seems to sleep in eternal repose, as if to form one of her finest contrasts with the rude and rolling grandeur on the west....

Approaching the house on the east, the visiter instinctively paused, to cast around one thrilling glance at this magnificent panorama: and then passed to the vestibule, where, if he had not been previously informed, he would immediately perceive that he was entering the house of no common man. In the spacious and lofty hall which opens before him, he marks no tawdry and unmeaning ornaments: but before, on the right, on the left, all around, the eye is struck and gratified with objects of science and taste, so classed and arranged as to produce their finest effect. On one side, specimens of sculpture set out, in such order as to exhibit at a *coup d'œil*, the historical progress of that art; from the first rude attempts o the aborigines of our country, up to that exquisi' and finished bust of the great patriot himself, from the masterhand of Caracci. On the other side, the visiter sees displayed a vast collection of specimens of Indian art, their paintings, weapons, ornaments, and manufactures; on another, an array of the fossil productions of our country, mineral and animal; the polished remains of those colossal monsters that once trod our forests, and are no more; and a variegated display of the branching honours of those " monarchs of the waste," that still people the wilds of the American continent.

From this hall he was ushered into a noble saloon, from which the glorious landscape of the west again bursts upon his view; and of which, within, is hung thick around with the finest productions of the pencil—historical paintings of the most striking subjects from all countries, and all ages; the portraits of distinguished men and patriots, both of Europe and America, and medallions and engravings in endless profusion.

While the visiter was yet lost in the contemplation of these treasures of the arts and sciences, he was startled by the approach of a strong and sprightly step, and turning with instinctive reverence to the door of entrance, he was met by the tall, and animated, and stately figure of the patriot himself—his countenance beaming with intelligence and benignity, and his outstretched hand, with its strong and cordial pressure, confirming the courteous welcome of his lips. And then came that charm of manner and conversation that passes all description—so cheerful—so unassuming—so free, and easy, and frank, and kind, and gay—that even the young, and overawed, and embarrassed visiter at once forgot his fears, and felt himself by the side of an old and familiar friend.

JOSIAH QUINCY.

[Born 1772. Died 1864.]

THE late Mr. Justice Story, in dedicating to JOSIAH QUINCY his Miscellaneous Writings, remarks "that few persons have acquired so just a distinction for unspotted integrity, fearless justice, consistent principles, high talents, and extensive literature," and that "still fewer possess the merit of having justified the public confidence by the singleness of heart and purpose with which they have devoted themselves to the best interests of society." Everybody who is acquainted with the venerable statesman and scholar will acknowledge that this praise is deserved.

Josiah Quincy, the third of these names, is of the fifth generation from Edmund Quincy, who came from England with the Rev. John Cotton in 1633; and is the son of Josiah Quincy, the associate of Otis and Warren, whose premature death was one of the severest losses sustained by the country in the beginning of the revolution. "May the spirit of liberty rest upon him," the dying patriot wrote in his will, and left him as a specific legacy the works of Tacitus and Cato, Sydney, Bacon and Locke.

He was graduated at Harvard University in 1790, and in 1804 commenced his public life as a member of the Massachusetts senate. In the same year he was elected to the national House of Representatives, in which he continued until March, 1813, when he declined further service in that body. He however accepted a seat in the legislature of the state, and was a senator from 1813 to 1820, and from the last year to 1822 a member of the lower house, of which he was twice chosen speaker. In 1822 he became judge of the municipal court of Boston, and was mayor of that city from 1823 to 1828, when he declined being again a candidate for the office. From 1829 to 1845 he was president of Harvard University, and was succeeded, upon his resignation, in the last year, by Edward Everett.

Mr. Quincy is an "old federalist," a term which is commonly given as a reproach, and received, where it is merited, as an honour.

The period in which he was in Congress was one of extraordinary interest, when party spirit ran high, and decision, boldness and energy were indispensable qualities for politicians of either side. He was equal to the emergency, and sustained himself on all occasions with manly independence, sound argument, and fervid declamation. One of his most effective speeches was made in the House of Representatives in November, 1808, on a resolution to resist the edicts of Great Britain and France; but this is less celebrated than his speech in 1811 on the bill for the admission of Louisiana. If this bill passes, he said, "the bonds of this Union are virtually dissolved ; the states which compose it are free from their moral obligations, and it will be the right of all and the duty of some to prepare definitely for a separation, *peaceably if we can, forcibly if we must.*" Before such an act, he thought, the bands of the constitution were no more than flax before the fire, or stubble before the whirlwind. The tree has since then become *dry,* yet the Union is not dissolved.

War, right or wrong, always commands the suffrages of the rabble, for to them, as surely as to carrion birds, it furnishes occupation and subsistence. Mr. Quincy rarely referred to himself, but in his speech on the army bill, in 1813, alluding to the charges of vulgar calumny by which the imaginations of most men are affected, he said, "It is not for a man whose ancestors have been planted in this country for almost two centuries .... who is conscious of being rooted in the soil as deeply and as exclusively as the oak which shoots among its rocks .... to hesitate or swerve a hair's breadth from his country's true interests, because of the yelpings, the howlings and the snarlings of that hungry pack which corrupt men keep directly or indirectly in pay, with the view of hunting down every man who dare develope their purposes, a pack composed of some native curs, but for the most part of hounds and spaniels of very recent importation, whose backs are seared with the lash and whose necks are sore with the collars of their former masters." In and out of Congress he was faithful to what he deemed the true interests of the people, and laboured zealously to bring men and measures to the bar of public opinion.

Mr. Quincy has published between thirty and forty speeches, orations, addresses, and miscellaneous tracts; the Life of Josiah Quincy, junior, (his father,) in one octavo volume; the Life of James Grahame, the historian, (in the Massachusetts Historical Collections); and The History of Harvard University, in two large octavo volumes, which appeared in 1840. In the History of Harvard University, the progress of that dis-tinguished seat of learning, which has had so great and beneficent an influence upon the character and condition of this nation, is traced with minuteness and fidelity through the two centuries which had elapsed since its formation. His style is perspicuous and elegant, and the narrative animated, generally well proportioned, and interesting.

He wrote also, The Journals and Life of Maj. Saml. Shaw, Consul at Canton; History of the Boston Atheneum; History of Boston; Life of John Q. Adams; and essays on soiling of Cattle. Since resigning the Presidency of the University, Mr. Quincy lived at his country seat at Quincy, until his death, July 1, 1864.

THE INVASION OF CANADA.
FROM A SPEECH ON THE ARMY BILL.

WHEN I contemplate the character and consequences of this invasion of Canada, when I reflect upon its criminality, and its danger to the peace and liberty of this once happy country, I thank the great Author and source of all virtue, that through his grace, that section of country in which I have the happiness to reside, is in so great a degree free from the iniquity of this transgression. I speak it with pride, the people of that section have done what they could, to vindicate themselves and their children from the burden of this sin. That whole section has risen, almost as one man, for the purpose of driving from power by one great constitutional effort the guilty authors of this war. If they have failed, it has been, not through the want of will or of exertion, but in consequence of the weakness of their political power. When in the usual course of divine providence, who punishes nations as well as individuals, his destroying angel shall, on this account, pass over this country; and sooner or later, pass it will; I may be permitted to hope that over New England his hand will be stayed. Our souls are not steeped in the blood which has been shed in this war. The spirits of the unhappy men who have been sent to an untimely audit have borne to the bar of Divine justice no accusations against us.

AN EMBARGO LIBERTY.
FROM A SPEECH ON FOREIGN RELATIONS.

AN embargo liberty was never cradled in Massachusetts. Our liberty was not so much a mountain, as a sea-nymph. She was free as air. She could swim, or she could run. The ocean was her cradle. Our fathers met her as she came, like the goddess of beauty, from the waves. They caught her as she was sporting on the beach. They courted her whilst she was spreading her nets upon the rocks. But an embargo liberty; a hand-cuffed liberty; a liberty in fetters; a liberty traversing between the four sides of a prison and beating her head against the walls, is none of our offspring. We abjure the monster. Its parent age is all inland.

THE FOUNDERS OF HARVARD COLLEGE.
FROM THE HISTORY OF HARVARD UNIVERSITY.

WHEN we revert to the time and the circumstances in which the foundations of Harvard College were laid, we seem to read not so much the history of real events as the legends of the heroic age and the fictions of romance. The founders of Massachusetts left their native land, and crossed unknown seas to desert wildernesses, bringing with them their household loves and domestic hopes, for the sake of attaining the right to worship God according to the dictates of their own consciences. To place the protection of that right on the basis of sound human learning and faithful intellectual research, they first bade to rise the sanctuaries of religion, and, close by their sacred altars, this temple of science; thus establishing here, in the language of the master genius of their age, " a secure harbour for letters, which, as ships, pass through the vast seas of time, and make ages so distant to participate of the wisdom, the illumination, and inventions the one of the other." What scene more sublime, what more glorious? What can the mind conceive, indicating firmer purpose, wiser forecast, purer intent, bolder daring? They lived not for themselves, but for us, for their posterity! They erected institutions, not for the comfort and pleasure of the passing day, but for the safety, glory, and hope of their own and all future time.

WASHINGTON ALLSTON.

[Born 1779. Died 1843.]

THIS illustrious person, though chiefly distinguished as an artist, entitled himself to an enviable and enduring reputation by various works in literature, which, particularly those executed in his mature years, have much of the character and excellence of his pictures.

Some specimens of his poems, which are chiefly on subjects connected with his other art, may be found in The Poets and Poetry of America, in which volume are also contained more particulars than will here be given of his life.

WASHINGTON ALLSTON was born in Georgetown, South Carolina, on the fifth of November, 1779. His family is respectable, and several members of it have been distinguished in the public service. When he was seven years old he was removed to Newport, Rhode Island, where he continued at school until 1796, when he was transferred to Harvard College. At Newport he became acquainted with Malbone, whose beautiful miniatures were then beginning to attract attention, and was smitten with the love of art, so that meeting him again in Boston, during his freshman year in college, he determined to adopt his profession. Under the casual direction of Malbone he devoted as much time to painting as he could borrow from his other pursuits, until he graduated, when he sold his paternal estate for the purpose of studying in Europe, and sailed for London. West was then president of the Royal Academy, and he received his young countryman very kindly. In a few months he became an exhibitor, and sold one of his pictures. In 1804 he went to Paris, and studied in the Louvre and Luxembourg; and proceeded to Italy, where he remained four years with Coleridge and our own Irving for companions, and Thorwaldsen for a fellow student. At Rome, on account of his fine colouring, they called him the American Titian.

In 1809 Allston returned to Boston, where he remained nearly three years, marrying in this period a sister of Dr. Channing; and in 1811 he went again to England. One of his first works after his arrival was the great picture of The Dead Man Revived by Elijah's Bones, which obtained a prize of two hundred guineas from the British Institution, and is now in the Pennsylvania Academy. While it was in progress he was seized with a dangerous illness, and retired from London to Cliffton, a rural town, where on his recovery he painted portraits of Coleridge, Southey, and some others. When he went back to the city his wife died, suddenly, and "left me," he says in one of his letters, "nothing but my art; and this seemed to me as nothing." His intellect was for a while deranged, but the assiduities of friends, and his own will triumphed, and when his mind had recovered its tone he painted The Mother and Child, now in the collection of Mr. MacMurtrie of Philadelphia; Jacob's Dream, which is owned by the Earl of Egremont; Uriel in the Sun, which was purchased by the Marquis of Stafford; and some other pictures.

In 1818 he came back a second time to Boston, and he resided all the rest of his life near that city. He was married to a sister of Richard H. Dana, a man of kindred genius, and had many warm friends, some of whom could have left him nothing to desire of sympathy or appreciation. Among the pictures which he painted are Rosalie Listening to Music, Ursulina, and The Spanish Maid, which he illustrated with beautiful and exquisitely finished poems; and Miriam Singing her Song of Triumph, Jeremiah Dictating to the Scribe his Prophecy of the Destruction of Jerusalem, Saul and the Witch of Endor, The Angel Liberating Peter from Prison, and Lorenzo and Jessica. In 1814 he had commenced a large picture, Belshazzar's Feast, which it was thought would be his masterpiece; but though he continued to work upon it at times for nearly thirty years, it was never finished. Of his genius as a painter I am not competent to write. As he himself said

131

of Monaldi, doubtless "he differed from his contemporaries no less in kind than degree. If he held any thing in common with others, it was with those of ages past, with the mighty dead of the fifteenth century, from whom he had learned the language of his art; but his thoughts and their turn of expression were his own." I may say with confidence that it is the judgment of the best critics of this age that he left no equal, in his department of art, in the world.

While in London, in 1813, Allston published a small volume entitled The Sylphs of the Seasons and other Poems, and when Mr. Dana projected The Idle Man, in 1820, he wrote for that work his romance of Monaldi. But The Idle Man, for some reason, was discontinued, and Allston's manuscript was laid aside for more than twenty years. It was finally published, in a single volume, in 1841.

The fame of Allston's writings has been so eclipsed by that of his paintings that they are comparatively unknown.* All the specimens that I have seen of his prose indicate a remarkable command of language, great descriptive powers, and rare philosophical as well as imaginative talent. Monaldi is his principal and indeed only acknowledged performance of any length. It is a tale of Italian life written with the vigour and method of a practised romancist. The mind of the true artist appears in several discussions, which are very naturally introduced, on the merits of the old masters; and it is no less evident in the character of the hero, who is a painter, as well as in many very graphic descriptions of scenery. Some of the lights and shades of the landscape are given as they could have been only by one familiar with the practice of art. The style of Monaldi is remarkably concise and unaffected, frequently rising into eloquence and never becoming tame. Its particular merits as a story consist in the masterly analysis of human passion, the lovely unfolding of female character, and the dramatic management of events. There is great metaphysical

truth in the development of love and jealousy, which is its chief purpose. Indeed if Allston had never painted Prophets, these written pictures would have established his fame as an author. The work shows how capable he was of achieving a wide and permanent literary reputation, and forms a most interesting and valuable addition to our romantic fiction.

His other prose writings are chiefly on subjects connected with the arts, and are finished with the same care as his paintings.

Mr. Allston lived in retirement at Cambridgeport, occasionally going into the city, but not often. His health was feeble, for many years, but he was never idle. He spoke to me once of Dunlap's declaration, in his History of the Arts of Design, that he was indolent. "I am famous among my acquaintances," he said, "for industry: I paint every day: and never pass an hour without accomplishing something." At sixty he had as many pictures in contemplation as the most ambitious artist of thirty. An ordinary lifetime would not have sufficed to finish those he had sketched upon canvas. He read much, and delighted all who saw him with his eloquent conversation. Not long before his death I dined with him, and was astonished when a companion intimated that it was after midnight. We had listened six or seven hours without a thought of the lapse of time. His manners were gentle and dignified. His dress was simple and old fashioned: a blue coat with plain bright buttons, a buff vest, and drab pantaloons. His face was thin, and serious, with remarkably expressive eyes; his hair, fine, long and silvery white, fell gracefully upon his shoulders; and his voice was soft, earnest and musical.

The evening of the ninth of June, 1843, he passed cheerfully with his friends. At about eleven o'clock he laid his hands upon the head of a young relative, begged her to live as near perfection as she could, and blessed her fervently. He then retired into his painting room, where he was found a little while afterward, seated before one of his pictures, dead. He was buried by torchlight, in the beautiful cemetery of Mount Auburn, in the presence of a large concourse who had gathered to pay their last tribute to the great genius whose works had added so much to the national glory.

* Any elaborate criticism upon them will soon be superseded by the publication of his life, which is now in course of preparation by his brother in law, Dana. The long and intimate association of the poet with the artist, and his fine insight as a critic, will enable him to analyse Allston's qualifications as an author with skill and authority.

CONSCIENCE AND THE WILL.

FROM MONALDI.

HAVING expressed a wish to see the curiosities of the place, the good prior the next morning offered his services as my *cicerone*. As I followed him to the chapel, he observed, that his convent had little to gratify the taste of an ordinary traveller; " but if you are a connoisseur," he added, " you will find few places better worth visiting. I perceive you think the picture opposite hardly bears me out in this assertion. I agree with you. It is certainly very insipid, and the mass of our collection is little better ; but we have *one* that redeems them all—one picture worth twenty common galleries." As he said this, we stopped before a crucifixion by Lanfranco. Next to his great work at St. Andrea della Valle, it was the best I had seen of that master. Though eccentric and somewhat capricious, it was yet full of powerful expression, and marked by a vigour of execution that made every thing around it look like washed drawings. " Yes," said I, supposing this the picture alluded to, " and I can now agree with you, 't is worth a thousand of the flimsy productions of the last age." "True," answered the prior; " but I did not allude"——— Here he was called out on business of the convent.

After waiting some time for my conductor's return, and finding little worth looking at besides the Lanfranc, I turned to leave the chapel by the way I had entered; but, taking a wrong door, I came into a dark passage, leading, as I supposed, to an inner court. This being my first visit to a convent, a natural curiosity tempted me to proceed, when, instead of a court, I found myself in a large apartment. The light (which descended from above) was so powerful, that for nearly a minute I could distinguish nothing, and I rested on a form attached to the wainscoating. I then put up my hand to shade my eyes, when—the fearful vision is even now before me—I seemed to be standing before an abyss in space, boundless and black. In the midst of this permeable pitch stood a colossal mass of gold, in shape like an altar, and girdled about by a huge serpent, gorgeous and terrible; his body flecked with diamonds, and his head, an enormous carbuncle, floated like a meteor on the air above. Such was the Throne. But no words can describe the gigantic Being that sat thereon—the grace, the majesty, its transcendant form ; and yet I shuddered as I looked, for its superhuman countenance seemed, as it were, to radiate falsehood ; every feature was in contradiction —the eye, the mouth, even to the nostril—whilst the expression of the whole was of that unnatural softness which can only be conceived of malignant blandishment. It was the appalling beauty of the King of Hell. The frightful discord vibrated through my whole frame, and I turned for relief to the figure below ; for at his feet knelt one who appeared to belong to our race of earth. But I had turned from the first, only to witness in this second object its withering fascination. It was a man apparently in the prime of life, but pale and emaci-

ated, as if prematurely wasted by his unholy devotion, yet still devoted—with outstretched hands, and eyes upraised to their idol, fixed with a vehemence that seemed almost to start them from their sockets. The agony of his eye, contrasting with the prostrate, reckless worship of his attitude, but too well told his tale : I beheld the mortal conflict between the conscience and the will—the visible struggle of a soul in the toils of sin. I could look no longer.

As I turned, the prior was standing before me. " Yes," said he, as if replying to my thoughts, " it is indeed terrific. Had you beheld it unmoved, you had been the first that ever did so."

" There is a tremendous reality in the picture that comes home to every man's imagination : even the dullest feel it, as if it had the power of calling up that faculty in minds never before conscious of it."

———◆———

THE TWO STUDENTS.

FROM THE SAME.

AMONG the students of a seminary at Bologna were two friends, more remarkable for their attachment to each other, than for any resemblance in their minds or dispositions. Indeed there was so little else in common between them, that hardly two boys could be found more unlike. The character of Maldura, the eldest, was bold, grasping, and ostentatious ; while that of Monaldi, timid and gentle, seemed to shrink from observation. The one, proud and impatient, was ever labouring for distinction ; the world, palpable, visible, audible, was his idol; he lived only in externals, and could neither act nor feel but for effect; even his secret reveries having an outward direction, as if he could not think without a world to praise, and anxiously referring to the opinion of others; in short, his nightly and his daily dreams had but one subject—the talk and the eye of the crowd. The other silent and meditative, seldom looked out of himself either for applause or enjoyment: if he ever did so, it was only that he might add to, or sympathize in the triumph of another; this done, he retired again, as it were to a world of his own, where thoughts and feelings, filling the place of men and things, could always supply him with occupation and amusement.

Had the ambition of Maldura been less, or his self-knowledge greater, he might have been a benefactor to the world. His talents were of a high order. Perhaps few have ever surpassed him in the power of acquiring ; to this he united perseverance ; and all that was known, however various and opposite, he could master at will. But here his power stopped: beyond the regions of discovered knowledge he could not see, and dared not walk, for to him all beyond was " outer darkness ;" in a word, with all his gifts he wanted that something, whatever it might be, which gives the living principle to thought. But this sole deficiency was the last of which he suspected himself. With that self-delusion so common to young

M

men, of mistaking the praise of what is promising for that of the thing promised, he too rashly confounded the ease with which he carried all the prizes of his school with the rare power of commanding at pleasure the higher honours of the world.

But the honours of a school are for things and purposes far different from those demanded and looked for by the world. Maldura unfortunately did not make the distinction. His various knowledge, though ingeniously brought together, and skilfully set anew, was still the knowledge of other men; it did not come forth as in new birth, from the modifying influence of his own nature. His mind was hence like a thing of many parts, yet wanting a whole—that *realizing* quality which the world must feel before it will reverence. In proportion to its stores such a mind will be valued, and even admired; but it cannot command that inward voice —the only true voice of fame, which speaks not, be it in friend or enemy, till awakened by the presence of a master spirit.

Such were the mind and disposition of Maldura; and from their unfortunate union sprang all the after-evils in his character. As yet, however, he was known to himself and others only as a remarkable boy. His extraordinary attainments placing him above competition, he supposed himself incapable of so mean a passion as envy; indeed the high station from which he could look down on his associates gave a complacency to his mind not unfavourable to the gentler virtues; he was, therefore, often kind, and even generous without an effort. Besides, though he disdained to affect humility, he did not want discretion, and that taught him to bear his honours without arrogance. His claims were consequently admitted by his schoolfellows without a murmur. But there was one amongst them whose praises were marked by such warmth and enthusiasm as no heart not morally sensible could long withstand; this youth was Monaldi. Maldura naturally had strong feelings, and so long as he continued prosperous and happy, their course was honourable. He requited the praises of his companion with his esteem and gratitude, which soon ripened into a friendship so sincere that he believed he could even lay down his life for him.

It was in this way that two natures so opposite became mutually attracted. But the warmth and magnanimity of Monaldi were all that was yet known to the other; for, though not wanting in academic learning, he was by no means distinguished; indeed, so little, that Maldura could not but feel and lament it.

The powers of Monaldi, however, were yet to be called forth. And it was not surprising that to his youthful companions he should have then appeared inefficient, there being a singular kind of passiveness about him easily mistaken for vacancy. But his was like the passiveness of some uncultured spot, lying unnoticed within its nook of rocks, and silently drinking in the light, and the heat, and the showers of heaven, that nourish the seeds of a thousand nameless flowers, destined one day to bloom and to mingle their fragrance with the breath of nature. Yet to common observers the external world seemed to lie only

"Like a load upon his weary eye;"

but to them it appeared so because he delighted to shut it out, and to combine and give another life to the images it had left in his memory; as if he would sleep to the real and be awake only to a world of shadows. But, though his emotions seldom betrayed themselves by any outward signs, there was nothing sluggish in the soul of Monaldi; it was rather their depth and strength that prevented their passage through the feeble medium of words. He regarded nothing in the moral or physical world as tiresome or insignificant; every object had a charm, and its harmony and beauty, its expression and character, all passed into his soul in all their varieties, while his quickening spirit brooded over them as over the elementary forms of a creation of his own. Thus living in the life he gave, his existence was too intense and extended to be conceived by the common mind: hence the neglect and obscurity in which he passed his youth.

But the term of pupilage soon came to an end, and the friends parted—each, as he could, to make his way in the world.

THE POET AND HIS CRITICS.
FROM THE SAME.

THE poem was at length published. Alas, who that knows the heart of an author—of an aspiring one—will need be told what were the feelings of Maldura, when day after day, week after week passed on, and still no tidings of his book. To think it had failed was wormwood to his soul. "No, that was impossible." Still the suspense, the uncertainty of its fate were insupportable. At last, to relieve his distress, he fastened the blame on his unfortunate publisher; though how he was in fault he knew not. Full of this thought, he was just sallying forth to vent his spleen on him, when his servant announced the count Piccini.

"Now," thought Maldura, "I shall hear my fate; and he was not mistaken: for the Count was a kind of talking gazette. The poem was soon introduced, and Piccini rattled on with all he had heard of it: he had lately been piqued by Maldura, and cared not to spare him.

After a few hollow professions of regard, and a careless remark about the pain it gave him to repeat unpleasant things, Piccini proceeded to pour them out one upon another with ruthless volubility. Then, stopping as if to take breath, he continued, "I see you are surprised at all this; but indeed, my friend, I cannot help thinking it principally owing to your not having suppressed your name; for your high reputation, it seems, had raised such extravagant expectations as none but a firstrate genius could satisfy."

"By which," observed Maldura, "I am to conclude that my work has failed?"

"Why, no—not exactly that; it has only not been praised—that is, I mean in the way you might have wished. But do not be depressed; there's no knowing but the tide may yet turn in your favour."

"Then I suppose the book is hardly as yet known?"

"I beg your pardon—quite the contrary. When your friend the Marquis introduced it at his last conversazione, every one present seemed quite *au fait* on it, at least, they all talked as if they had read it."

Maldura bit his lips. "Pray who were the company?" "Oh, all your friends, I assure you: Guattani, Martello, Pessuti, the mathematician, Alfieri, Benuci, the Venetian Castelli, and the old Ferrarese Carnesecchi: these were the principal, but there were twenty others who had each something to say."

Maldura could not but perceive the malice of this enumeration; but he checked his rising choler. "Well," said he, "if I understand you, there was but one opinion respecting my poem with all this company?"

"Oh, by no means. Their opinions were as various as their characters."

"Well, Pessuti—what said he?"

"Why you know he's a mathematician, and should not regard him. But yet, to do him justice, he is a very nice critic, and not unskilled in poetry."

"Go on, sir, I can bear it."

"Why then, it was Pessuti's opinion that the poem had more learning than genius."

"Proceed, sir."

"Martello denied it both; but he, you know, is a disappointed author. Guattani differed but little from Pessuti as to its learning, but contended, that you certainly showed great invention in your fable—which was like nothing that ever did, or could happen. But I fear I annoy you."

"Go on, I beg, sir."

"The next who spoke was old Carnesecchi, who confessed that he had no doubt he should have been delighted with the poem, could he have taken hold of it; but it was so *en regle* and like a hundred others, that it put him in mind of what is called a polished gentleman, who talks and bows, and slips through a great crowd without leaving any impression. Another person, whose name I have forgotten, praised the versification, but objected to the thoughts."

"Because they were absurd?"

"Oh, no, for the opposite reason—because they had all been long ago known to be good. Castelli thought that a bad reason; for his part, he said, he liked them all the better for that—it was like shaking hands with an old acquaintance in every line. Another observed, that at least no critical court could lawfully condemn them, as they could each plead an *alibi*. Not an *alibi*, said a third—but a *double*; so they should be burnt for sorcery. With all my heart, said a fourth—

but not the poor author, for he has certainly satisfied us that he is no conjuror."

"Then Castelli—but, 'faith, I don't know how to proceed."

"You are over delicate, sir. Speak out, I pray you."

"Well, Benuci finished by the most extravagant eulogy I ever heard."

Maldura took breath.

"For he compared your hero to the Apollo Belvedere, your heroine to the Venus de Medicis, and your subordinate characters to the Diana, the Hercules, the Antinous, and twenty other celebrated antiques; declared them all equally well wrought, and beautiful—and like them too, equally cold, hard, and motionless. In short, he maintained that you were the boldest and most original poet he had ever known; for none but a hardy genius, who consulted nobody's taste but his own, would have dared, like you, to draw his animal life from a statue gallery, and his vegetable from a hortus siccus."

Maldura's heart stiffened within him, but his pride controlled him, and he masked his thoughts with something like composure. Yet he dared not trust himself to speak, but stood looking at Piccini, as if waiting for him to go on. "I believe that's all," said the count, carelessly twirling his hat, and raising to take leave.

Maldura roused himself, and, making an effort, said, "No, sir, there is one person whom you have only named—Alfieri; what did he say?"

"Nothing!" Piccini pronounced this word with a graver tone than usual; it was his fiercest bolt, and he knew that a show of feeling would send it home. Then, after pausing a moment, he hurried out of the room.

THE ATHEIST.

FROM THE SAME.

THE sense of guilt will sometimes cow the proudest philosophy. The atheist may speculate, and go on speculating till he is brought up by annihilation; he may then return to life, and reason away the difference between good and evil; he may even go further, and imagine to himself the perpetration of the most atrocious acts: and still he may eat his bread with relish, and sleep soundly in his bed: for his sins wanting, as it were, substance, having no actual solidity to leave their traces in his memory, all future retribution may seem to him a thing with which, in any case, he can have no concern; but let him once turn his theory to practice—let him make crime palpable—in an instant he feels its hot impress on his soul. Then it is, that what may happen beyond the grave becomes no matter of indifference; and, though his *reason* may seem to have proved that death is a final end, then comes the question: what does his reason *know* of death? Then, last of all, the little word *if*, swelling to a fearful size, and standing at the outlet of his theories, like a relentless giant, ready to demolish his conclusions

LOVE MATCHES.

FROM THE SAME.

"MY dear father," said Rosalia, "I would that I could reason on this subject, but—indeed I cannot."

"Strange! You hint not even an objection, and yet— Do you think I overrate him?"

"No; he deserves all you say of him; but yet"—

"You would still reject him?"

Rosalia was silent.

"If you esteem, you may certainly love; nay, it will follow of course."

"Did you *always* think so, sir?"

"Perhaps not. When I was young, I was no doubt fanciful, like others."

"And yet you did not marry till past thirty."

"Well, child?"

"My mother died when I was too young to know her; but I have heard her character so often from yourself and others, that I have it now as fresh before me as if she had never been taken from us. Was she not mild and gentle?"

"As the dew of heaven."

"And her mind?"

"The seat of every grace and virtue."

"And her person too was beautiful?"

"Except yourself, I have never seen a creature so lovely."

"And did she make you a *good* wife?"

Landi turned pale. "Rosalia—my child—why remind me, by these cruel questions, of a loss which the whole world cannot repair?"

"She was then all you wished; and yet I have heard that yours was a *love match*."

"No more," cried Landi, averting his face. "You have conquered."

A SUMMER NOON IN ROME.

FROM THE SAME.

THE air was hot and close, and there was a thin yellow haze over the distance like that which precedes the scirocco, but the nearer objects were clear and distinct, and so bright that the eye could hardly rest on them without quivering, especially on the modern buildings, with their huge sweep of whited walls, and their red tiled roofs, that lay burning in the sun, with the sharp, black shadows, which here and there seemed to indent the dazzling masses, might almost have been fancied the cinder-tracks of his fire. The streets of Rome, at no time very noisy, are for nothing more remarkable than, during the summer months, for their noontide stillness, the meridian heat being frequently so intense as to stop all business, driving every thing within doors with the proverbial exception of dogs and strangers. But even these might scarcely have withstood the present scorching atmosphere. It was now high noon, and the few straggling vine-dressers that were wont to stir in this secluded quarter had already been driven under shelter; not a vestige of life was to be seen, not a bird on the wing, and so deep was the stillness that a litary footfall might have filled the whole air.

AN ITALIAN SUNSET.

FROM THE SAME.

IT was one of those evenings never to be forgotten by a painter—but one too which must come upon him in misery as a gorgeous mockery. The sun was yet up, and resting on the highest peak of a ridge of mountain-shaped clouds, that seemed to make a part of the distance; suddenly he disappeared, and the landscape was overspread with a cold, lurid hue; then, as if molten in a furnace, the fictitious mountains began to glow; in a moment more they tumbled asunder; in another he was seen again, piercing their fragments, and darting his shafts to the remotest east, till, reaching the horizon, he appeared to recall them, and with a parting flash to wrap the whole heavens in flame.

THOUGHTS FROM HIS STUDIO.

[MRS JAMESON, author of the Characteristics of Women, etc., when in this country in 1838, visited the painting room of Allston at Cambridgeport, and found written on the walls many sentences, which, he said, were to serve as "texts for reflection before he began his day's work." A mutual friend was permitted to copy them, and since his death she has published the following in her Memoirs and Essays Illustrative of Art, Literature, and Social Morals.]

THE painter who is content with the praise of the world in respect to what does not satisfy himself, is not an artist, but an artisan; for though his reward be only praise, his pay is that of a mechanic for his time, and not for his art."

He that seeks popularity in art closes the door on his own genius: as he must needs paint for other minds, and not for his own.

Reputation is but a synonym of popularity: dependent on suffrage, to be increased or diminished at the will of the voters. It is the creature, so to speak, of its particular age, or rather of a particular state of society; consequently, dying with that which sustained it. Hence we can scarcely go over a page of history, that we do not, as in a churchyard, tread upon some buried reputation. But fame cannot be voted down, having its immediate foundation in the essential. It is the eternal shadow of excellence, from which it can never be separated, nor is it ever made visible but in the light of an intellect kindred with that of its author. It is that light by which the shadow is projected, that is seen of the multitude, to be wondered at and reverenced, even while so little comprehended as to be often confounded with the substance—the substance being admitted from the shadow, as a matter of faith. It is the economy of Providence to provide such lights: like rising and setting stars, they follow each other through successive ages: and thus the monumental form of Genius stands for ever relieved against its own imperishable glory.

All excellence of every kind is but variety of truth. If we wish, then, for something beyond the true, we wish for that which is false. According to this test how little truth is there in art!

Little indeed! but how much is that little to him who feels it!

Fame does not depend on the *will* of any man, but reputation may be given or taken away: for Fame is the sympathy of kindred intellects, and sympathy is not a subject of *willing:* while Reputation, having its source in the popular voice, is a sentence which may either be uttered or suppressed at pleasure. Reputation being essentially contemporaneous, is always at the mercy of the Envious and the Ignorant. But Fame, whose very birth is *posthumous*, and which is only *known to exist by the echo of its footsteps through congenial minds*, can neither be increased nor diminished by any degree of wilfulness.

What *light* is in the natural world, such is fame in the intellectual: both requiring an *atmosphere* in order to become perceptible. Hence the fame of Michael Angelo is, to some minds, a nonentity; even as the sun itself would be invisible in vacuo.

Fame has no necessary conjunction with praise: it may exist without the breath of a word: it is a *recognition of excellence*, which *must be felt*, but need not be *spoken*. Even the envious must feel it: feel it, and hate it in silence.

I cannot believe, that any man who deserved fame, ever laboured for it: that is, *directly*. For as fame is but the contingent of excellence, it would be like an attempt to project a shadow, before its substance was obtained. Many, however, have so fancied: "I write and paint for fame," has often been repeated: it should have been, "I write, I paint for reputation." All anxiety, therefore, about fame, should be placed to the account of reputation.

A man may be pretty sure that he has not attained *excellence*, when it is not all in all to him. Nay, I may add, that if he looks beyond it, he has not reached it. This is not the less true for being good *Irish*.

An original mind is rarely understood until it has been *reflected* from some half-dozen congenial with it: so averse are men to admitting the *true* in an unusual form: whilst any novelty, however fantastic, however false, is greedily swallowed. Nor is this to be wondered at: for all truth demands a response, and few people care to *think*, yet they must have something to supply the place of thought. Every mind would appear original, if every man had the power of *projecting* his own into the mind of others.

All effort at originality must end either in the quaint or the monstrous. For no man knows himself as an original: he can only believe it on the report of others to whom *he is made known, as he is by the projecting power* before spoken of.

There is an essential meanness in the wish to *get the better* of any one. The only competition worthy of a wise man, is with himself.

Reverence is an ennobling sentiment; it is felt to be degrading only by the vulgar mind, which would escape the sense of its own littleness, by elevating itself into the antagonist to what is above it.

He that has no pleasure in looking up, is not fit to look down; of such minds are the mannerists in art; and in the world, the tyrants of all sorts.

18

The phrenologists are right in putting the organ of self-love in the back part of the head. It being there that a vain man carries his light; the consequence is that every object he approaches becomes obscure by his own shadow.

A witch's skiff cannot more easily sail in the teeth of the wind, than the human *eye* can lie against fact: but the truth will often quiver through *lips* with a lie upon them.

It is a hard matter for a man to lie all *over*, Nature having provided king's evidence in almost every member. The hand will sometimes act as a vane, to show which way the wind blows, when every feature is set the other way: the knees smite together and sound the alarm of fear under a fierce countenance: the legs shake with anger, when all above is calm.

Make no man your idol! For the best man must have faults, and his faults will usually become yours, in addition to your own. This is as true in art, as in morals.

The Devil's heartiest laugh, is at a detracting witticism. Hence the phrase, "devilish good," has sometimes a literal meaning.

There is one thing which no man, however generously disposed, can *give*, but which every one, however poor, is bound to *pay*. This is Praise. He cannot give it, because it is not his own; since what is dependent for its very existence on something in another, can never become to him a *possession;* nor can he justly withhold it, when the presence of merit claims it as a *consequence*. As praise, then, cannot be made a *gift*, so, neither, when not his due, can any man receive it; he may *think* he does, but he receives only *words;* for desert being the essential condition of praise, there can be no reality in the one without the other. This is no fanciful statement: for though praise may be withheld by the ignorant or envious, it cannot be but that, *in the course of time*, an existing merit *will* on *some one* produce its effects; inasmuch as the existence of any cause without its effect is an impossibility. A fearful truth lies at the bottom of this, an *irreversible justice* for the weal or wo of him confirms or violates it.

ON A PICTURE BY CARACCI.
FROM HIS LETTERS.

THE subject was the body of the virgin borne for interment by four apostles. The figures are colossal; the tone dark and of tremendous colour. It seemed, as I looked at it, as if the ground shook at their tread, and the air were darkened by their grief.

SUNRISE AMONG THE ALPS.
FROM THE SAME.

SUCH a sunrise! The giant Alps seemed literally to rise from their purple beds, and putting on their crowns of gold, to send up hallelujahs almost audible!

M 2

JOSEPH STORY.

[Born 1779. Died 1845.]

JOSEPH STORY was a son of Elisha Story, a respectable physician, who had been a surgeon in the revolutionary army. He was born in Marblehead, Massachusetts, on the eighteenth of September, 1779, and at the age of sixteen entered Harvard College, in the class with William Ellery Channing. Immediately after graduating he commenced with Chief Justice Sewall, of his native town, the study of the law, which he afterward pursued with Mr. Justice Putnam, of Salem, where he was admitted to the bar, and began the practice of his profession, in 1801.

In early life he was a democrat, and of course, living in Essex county, in a minority ; but such was his reputation for ability and integrity, that in his twenty-fifth year he was chosen a member of the state house of representatives, to which he was several times re-elected, and in which he was twice made speaker. He became at once the acknowledged leader of his party in the legislature, where he used his power with great magnanimity, on many occasions rising above partisan prejudice and dictation, and so serving the people as to win their nearly unanimous applause.

In 1809 he was elected a member of Congress, to fill a vacancy occasioned by the death of Mr. Crowninshield, but declined a further service than for the remainder of the term, deeming the excitement of political life incompatible with that devotion to his profession which was necessary to the highest success.

The place made vacant on the bench of the Supreme Court of the United States by the death of Judge Cushing, in 1811, was tendered by President Madison to Mr. John Quincy Adams, at that time in Russia, and being declined by him was conferred upon Mr. Story, who was then but thirty-two years of age. So young a man had never before, in England or America, been elevated to so high a judicial position, and much dissatisfaction was occasioned by this appointment ; but every regret and apprehension was soon dissipated by the displays of his extensive and accurate professional learning, excellent judgment, perfect candor, and decided business habits. He remained on the bench until the close of his life, and held no other civil office, except in 1820, when he sat with John Adams, Josiah Quincy, Daniel Webster, and other leading men of Massachusetts, in the convention which revised the constitution of that state.

His judgments in the supreme court of the United States are contained in the Reports of Cranch, Wheaton, Peters and Howard, of which they constitute much more than a just proportion ; and those which he delivered in the courts of the first circuit, embracing the states of Maine, New Hampshire, Massachusetts, and Rhode Island, fill two volumes of Reports by Gallison, five by Mason, three by Sumner, and two by William Story. It is generally admitted that these learned and elaborate performances, on a vast variety of difficult and complicated questions, some of which were entirely new, are not inferior in comprehensiveness, clearness and soundness, to any in the English language.

In 1829 Mr. Nathan Dane, one of the wisest and purest men who have lived in this nation, founded a professorship of law in Harvard College ; and by a condition of the endowment Judge Story became the first occupant of the chair. He had already made acceptable presents to the profession in his Selection of Pleadings, and in his editions of Chitty on Bills of Exchange and Promissory Notes, and Lord Tenterden on the Law of Shipping, to both of which he added many valuable notes. The delivery of courses of lectures, in Dane Hall, upon the law of nature, the laws of nations, maritime and commericial law, equity law, and the constitutional law of the United States, led to the preparation of that series of great works upon which his reputation chiefly rests, and which have made his name familiar in all the high parliaments, judicatures and universities of the world. The first of these was Commentaries

Engraved by G. Parker from a painting by Chester Harding.

JOSEPH STORY L.L.D.

on the Law of Bailments, which appeared in 1832. This was followed in 1833 by Commentaries on the Constitution of the United States, prefaced by a constitutional history of the colonies, and of the states under the confederation. This work, which is of great interest to the student in history as well as to the lawyer, he subsequently abridged, that it might be used as a class book in the schools. In 1834 appeared in three volumes his Commentaries on the Conflict of Laws, in which the opposing laws of different nations are treated with especial reference to marriages, divorces, wills, successions and judgments. It is regarded as the most original and profound of his works, and was the first upon the subject in the English language. In 1836 were published his Commentaries on Equity Jurisprudence, in two volumes, and in 1838 his Commentaries on Equity Pleadings, two works which were equal to his reputation and which were received by the profession with unhesitating approval. He subsequently published Commentaries upon the Laws of Agency, Partnership, Bills of Exchange, and Promissory Notes, but they were composed with less care, and though valuable, might have been written quite as well by a much inferior man.

Although Judge Story must be regarded as a lawyer of the first class, it cannot be said that in this class he was preëminent. Marshall, Hamilton, Parsons, Kent and some others had in various respects merit of precedence, though perhaps not one of these celebrated men could be justly compared with him for extent of acquisitions. Circumstances which will occur to the considerate lawyer gave him an extraordinary reputation abroad, and that enhanced the weight of his authority at home, but it is highly probable that both Marshall and Kent, reasoning from first principles, grounding their judgments upon the nature of things, will have a more solid and permanent renown.

Story was perhaps too sedulous a student of the tone and tendencies of the day, and his want of decidedness and precision often leaves it extremely doubtful what were his own opinions.

His industry was very great. Doubtless his memory was so retentive that a single and hasty reading was quite sufficient to make him familiar with almost any author. Yet when we remember the extent of the literature of his profession, which is probably

twice as great as when Marshall came to the bench, we are struck with the amount of labour necessary to form the most general acquaintance with it. Add to this the number of his works, which are more voluminous* than those of any other lawyer of great eminence, and we cannot understand how he had any leisure for the pursuit of literature or the enjoyment of society. But he was a man of taste, of warm affections, with a wide circle of friends, and of a deep and abiding interest in all the great movements of the people.

During his student life, and soon after he entered upon the practice of the law in Salem, Mr. Story was an occasional writer of verses, and in 1802 he published a didactic poem entitled The Power of Solitude, which was reprinted with several miscellaneous pieces in a duodecimo volume of two hundred and fifty pages in 1804. They have very little merit, of any kind, but their composition may have enabled him to acquire something of that copiousness and harmony for which his prose diction is distinguished.

His principal literary writings are contained in a collection of his discourses, reviews and miscellanies, published in 1835. In this volume are twenty-nine papers, among which are sketches of Samuel Dexter, William Pinkney, Thomas Addis Emmet, John Hooker Ashmun, and Justices Marshall, Trimble, Washington, and Parker; addresses before the Phi Beta Kappa Society of Harvard College, and the Essex Historical Society; his contributions to the North American Review; and various juridical arguments, and political reports, memorials and speeches.

Judge Story's career was undoubtedly the one in which he was fitted to shine most brightly. With vast learning, strong sense, reasoning powers of a high order, and generally correct taste, he would have been eminently respectable in any field of intellectual exertion; but he had too little both of metaphysical power and imagination to make a deep and lasting impression.

He died, after a short illness, at Cambridge, near Boston, on the tenth of September, 1845, having nearly completed the sixty-ninth year of his age.

* His written judgments on his own circuit and his various commentaries occupy twenty-seven volumes, and his judgments in the Supreme Court of the United States form an important part of thirty-four volumes.

INDIAN SUMMER IN NEW ENGLAND.

FROM CENTENNIAL DISCOURSE AT SALEM.

It is now the early advance of autumn. What can be more beautiful or more attractive than this season in New England? The sultry heat of summer has passed away; and a delicious coolness at evening succeeds the genial warmth of the day. The labours of the husbandman approach their natural termination: and he gladdens with the near prospect of his promised reward. The earth swells with the increase of vegetation. The fields wave with their yellow and luxuriant harvests. The trees put forth the darkest foliage, half shading and half revealing their ripened fruits, to tempt the appetite of man, and proclaim the goodness of his Creator. Even in scenes of another sort, where nature reigns alone in her own majesty, there is much to awaken religious enthusiasm. As yet, the forests stand clothed in their dress of undecayed magnificence. The winds, that rustle through their tops, scarcely disturb the silence of the shades below. The mountains and the valleys glow in warm green, of lively russet. The rivulets flow on with a noiseless current, reflecting back the images of many a glossy insect, that dips his wings in their cooling waters. The mornings and evenings are still vocal with the notes of a thousand warblers, which plume their wings for a later flight. Above all, the clear blue sky, the long and sunny calms, the scarcely whispering breezes, the brilliant sunsets, lit up with all the wondrous magnificence of light, and shade, and colour, and slowly settling down into a pure and transparent twilight. These, these are days and scenes, which even the cold cannot behold without emotion; but on which the meditative and pious gaze with profound admiration; for they breathe of holier and happier regions beyond the grave.

PERSECUTION.

FROM THE SAME.

I stand not up here the apologist for persecution, whether it be by Catholic or Protestant, by Puritan or Prelate, by Congregationalist or Covenanter, by Church or State, the monarch or the people. Wherever, and by whomsoever, it is promulgated or supported, under whatever disguises, for whatever purposes, at all times, and under all circumstances, it is a gross violation of the rights of conscience, and utterly inconsistent with the spirit of Christianity. I care not, whether it goes to life, or property, or office, or reputation, or mere private comfort, it is equally an outrage upon religion and the inalienable rights of man. If there is any right, sacred beyond all others, because it imports everlasting consequences, it is the right to worship God according to the dictates of our own consciences. Whoever attempts to narrow it down in any degree, to limit it by the creed of any sect, to bound the exercises of private judgment, or free inquiry, by the standard of his own faith, be he priest or layman, ruler or subject, dishonours, so

far, the profession of Christianity, and wounds it in its vital virtues. The doctrine on which such attempts are founded, goes to the destruction of all free institutions of government. There is not a truth to be gathered from history, more certain, or more momentous, than this, that civil liberty cannot long be separated from religious liberty without danger, and ultimately without destruction to both. Wherever religious liberty exists, it will, first or last, bring in and establish political liberty. Wherever it is suppressed, the Church establishment will, first or last, become the engine of despotism; and overthrow, unless it be itself overthrown, every vestige of political right. How it is possible to imagine, that a religion breathing the spirit of mercy and benevolence, teaching the forgivness of injuries, the exercise of charity, and the return of good for evil; how it is possible, I say, for such a religion to be so perverted as to breathe the spirit of slaughter and persecution, of discord and vengeance, for differences of opinion, is a most unaccountable and extraordinary moral phenomenon. Still more extraordinary, that it should be the doctrine, not of base and wicked men merely, seeking to cover up their own misdeeds; but of good men, seeking the way of salvation with uprightness of heart and purpose. It affords a melancholy proof of the infirmity of human judgment; and teaches a lesson of humility, from which spiritual pride may learn meekness, and spiritual zeal a moderating wisdom.

THE INDIANS.

FROM THE SAME.

There is, in the fate of these unfortunate beings, much to awaken our sympathy, and much to disturb the sobriety of our judgment; much which may be urged to excuse their own atrocities; much in their characters, which betrays us into an involuntary admiration. What can be more melancholy than their history? By a law of their nature, they seem destined to a slow, but sure extinction. Everywhere, at the approach of the white man, they fade away. We hear the rustling of their footsteps, like that of the withered leaves of autumn, and they are gone forever. They pass mournfully by us, and they return no more. Two centuries ago, the smoke of their wigwams and the fires of their councils rose in every valley, from Hudson's Bay to the farthest Florida, from the ocean to the Mississippi and the lakes. The shouts of victory and the war-dance rang through the mountains and the glades. The thick arrows and the deadly tomahawk whistled through the forests; and the hunter's trace and dark encampment startled the wild beasts in their lairs. The warriors stood forth in their glory. The young listened to the songs of other days. The mothers played with their infants, and gazed on the scene with warm hopes of the future. The aged sat down; but they wept not. They should soon be at rest in fairer regions, where the Great Spirit dwelt, in a home prepared for the brave, beyond the western skies. Braver men never lived; truer men never drew the bow. They had courage, and fortitude, and sagacity, and perseverance, beyond most of the human race. They shrank from no dangers, and they feared no hardships. If they had the vices of savage life, they had the virtues also. They were true to their country, their friends, and their homes. If they forgave not injury, neither did they forget kindness. If their vengeance was terrible, their fidelity and generosity were unconquerable also. Their love, like their hate, stopped not on this side of the grave.

But where are they? Where are the villagers, and warriors, and youth; the sachems and the tribes; the hunters and their families? They have perished. They are consumed. The wasting pestilence has not alone done the mighty work. No,—nor famine, nor war. There has been a mightier power, a moral canker, which has eaten into their heart-cores,—a plague, which the touch of the white man communicated—a poison, which betrayed them into a lingering ruin. The winds of the Atlantic fan not a single region, which they may now call their own. Already the last feeble remnants of the race are preparing for their journey beyond the Mississippi. I see them leave their miserable homes, the aged, the helpless, the women, and the warriors, "few and faint, yet fearless still." The ashes are cold on their native hearths. The smoke no longer curls round their lowly cabins. They move on with a slow, unsteady step. The white man is upon their heels, for terror or despatch; but they heed him not. They turn to take a last look of their deserted villages. They cast a last glance upon the graves of their fathers. They shed no tears; they utter no cries; they heave no groans. There is something in their hearts which passes speech. There is something in their looks, not of vengeance or submission; but of hard necessity, which stifles both; which chokes all utterance; which has no aim or method. It is courage absorbed in despair. They linger but for a moment. Their look is onward. They have passed the fatal stream. It shall never be repassed by them,—no, never. Yet there lies not between us and them an impassable gulf. They know and feel that there is for them still one remove farther, not distant, nor unseen. It is to the general burial-ground of their race.

Reason as we may, it is impossible not to read in such a fate much that we know not how to interpret; much of provocation to cruel deeds and deep resentments; much of apology for wrong and perfidy; much of pity mingling with indignation; much of doubt and misgiving as to the past; much of painful recollections; much of dark forebodings.

DESTINY OF THE REPUBLIC.
FROM THE SAME.

WHAT is to be the destiny of this Republic? In proposing this question, I drop all thought of New England. She has bound herself to the fate of the Union. May she be true to it, now, and for ever; true to it, because true to herself, true to her own principles, true to the cause of religion and liberty throughout the world. I speak, then, of our common country, of that blessed mother, that has nursed us in her lap, and led us up to manhood. What is her destiny? Whither does the finger of fate point? Is the career, on which we have entered, to be bright with ages of onward and upward glory? Or is our doom already recorded in the past history of the earth, in the past lessons of the decline and fall of other republics? If we are to flourish with a vigorous growth, it must be, I think, by cherishing principles, institutions, pursuits, and morals, such as planted, and have hitherto supported New England. If we are to fall, may she still possess the melancholy consolation of the Trojan patriot:

"Sat patriæ Priamoque, datum; si Pergama dextrâ
Defendi possent, etiam hâc defensa fuissent."

I would not willingly cloud the pleasures of such a day, even with a transient shade. I would not, that a single care should flit across the polished brow, of hope, if considerations of the highest moment did not demand our thoughts, and give us counsel of our duties. Who, indeed, can look around him upon the attractions of the scene, upon the faces of the happy and the free, the smiles of youthful beauty, the graces of matron virtue, the strong intellect of manhood, and the dignity of age, and hail these as the accompaniments of peace and independence;—who can look around him, and not at the same time feel, that change is written on all the works of man; that the breath of a tyrant, or the fury of a corrupt populace, may destroy, in one hour, what centuries have slowly consolidated? It is the privilege of great minds, that to them "coming events cast their shadows before." We may not possess this privilege; but it is true wisdom, not to blind ourselves to dangers which are in full view; and true prudence, to guard against those, of which experience has already admonished us.

When we reflect on what has been, and is, how is it possible not to feel a profound sense of the responsibleness of this Republic to all future ages? What vast motives press upon us for lofty efforts! What brilliant prospects invite our enthusiasm! What solemn warnings at once demand our vigilance, and moderate our confidence!

THE FIELD OF PEACE.
FROM AN ADDRESS AT THE CEMETERY OF MOUNT AUBURN.

AND what spot can be more appropriate than this, for such a purpose? Nature seems to point it out, with significant energy, as the favourite retirement for the dead. There are around us all the varied features of her beauty and grandeur;— the forest-crowned height; the abrupt acclivity; the sheltered valley; the deep glen; the grassy glade; and the silent grove. Here are the lofty oak, the beach, that "wreaths its old fantastic roots so high," the rustling pine, and the drooping willow;—the tree, that sheds its pale leaves with every autumn, a fit emblem of our own transitory bloom; and the evergreen, with its perennial shoots instructing us, that "the wintry blasts of death kills not the buds of virtue." Here is the thick shrubbery to protect and conceal the new-made grave; and there is the wild flower creeping along the narrow path, and planting its seeds in the upturned earth. All around us there breathes a solemn calm, as if it were in the bosom of a wilderness, broken only by the breeze, as it murmurs through the tops of the forest, or by the notes of the warbler, pouring forth his matin or his evening song.

Ascend but a few steps, and what a change of scenery to surprise and delight us! We seem, as it were, in an instant, to pass from the confines of death, to the bright and balmy regions of life. Below us flows the winding Charles, with its rippling current, like the stream of time hastening to the ocean of eternity. In the distance, the city—at once the object of our admiration and our love—rears its proud eminences, its glittering spires, its lofty towers, its graceful mansions, its curling smoke, its crowded haunts of business and pleasure, which speak to the eye, and yet leave a noiseless loneliness on the ear. Again we turn, and the walls of our venerable University rise before us, with many a recollection of happy days passed there in the interchange of study and friendship, and many a grateful thought of the affluence of its learning, which has adorned and nourished the literature of our country. Again we turn, and the cultivated farm, the neat cottage, the village church, the sparkling lake, the rich valley, and the distant hills, are before us, through opening vistas; and we breathe amidst the fresh and varied labours of man.

There is, therefore, within our reach, every variety of natural and artificial scenery, which is fitted to awaken emotions of the highest and most affecting character. We stand, as it were, upon the borders of two worlds; and, as the mood of our minds may be, we may gather lessons of profound wisdom by contrasting the one with the other, or indulge in dreams of hope and ambition, or solace our hearts by melancholy meditations.

CLASSICAL STUDIES.

FROM A DISCOURSE BEFORE THE PHI BETA KAPPA SOCIETY.

I PASS over all consideration of the written treasures of antiquity, which have survived the wreck of empires and dynasties, of monumental trophies and triumphal arches, of palaces of princes and temples of the gods. I pass over all consideration of those admired compositions, in which wisdom speaks, as with a voice from heaven; of those sublime efforts of poetical genius which still freshen, as they pass from age to age, in undying vigour; of those finished histories which still enlighten and instruct governments in their duty and their destiny; of those matchless orations which roused nations to arms, and chained senates to the chariot-wheels of all-conquering eloquence. These all may now be read in our vernacular tongue. Ay, as one remembers the face of a dead friend by gathering up the broken fragments of his image—as one listens to the tale of a dream twice told—as one catches the roar of the ocean in the ripple of a rivulet—as one sees the blaze of noon in the first glimmer of twilight.....

There is not a single nation from the North to the South of Europe, from the bleak shores of the Baltic to the bright plains of immortal Italy, whose literature is not embedded in the very elements of classical learning. The literature of England is, in an emphatic sense, the production of her scholars; of men who have cultivated letters in her universities, and colleges, and grammar-schools; of men who thought any life too short, chiefly because it left some relic of antiquity unmastered, and any other fame humble, because it faded in the presence of Roman and Grecian genius. He who studies English literature without the lights of classical learning loses half the charms of its sentiments and style, of its force and feelings, of its delicate touches, of its delightful allusions, of its illustrative associations. Who, that reads the poetry of Gray, does not feel that it is the refinement of classical taste which gives such inexpressible vividness and transparency to his diction? Who, that reads the concentrated sense and melodious versification of Dryden and Pope, does not perceive in them the disciples of the old school, whose genius was inflamed by the heroic verse, the terse satire, and the playful wit of antiquity? Who, that meditates over the strains of Milton, does not feel that he drank deep at

> "Siloa's brook, that flow'd
> Fast by the oracle of God"—

that the fires of his magnificent mind were lighted by coals from ancient altars?

It is no exaggeration to declare that he who proposes to abolish classical studies proposes to render, in a great measure, inert and unedifying the mass of English literature for three centuries: to rob us of the glory of the past, and much of the instruction of future ages; to blind us to excellencies which few may hope to equal and none to surpass; to annihilate associations which are interwoven with our best sentiments, and give to distant times and countries a presence and reality as if they were in fact his own.

JAMES KIRKE PAULDING.

[Born 1778. Died 1860.]

It is more than forty years since this veteran author made his first appearance before the public, and at nearly seventy he continued to write with the vivacity, good sense, and strong love of country for which his earliest works were distinguished.

Mr. PAULDING is of Dutch extraction, and was born on the twenty-second of August, 1778, in the town of Pawling, on the Hudson, so named from one of his ancestors. After receiving a liberal education he settled in New York, where except during short intervals he has since resided. Connected with some of the first families of the city, with an income sufficient for his wants, and a love of quiet which forbade his seeking distinction as a lawyer or politician, he would probably have been content with the simple pursuit of ease, had not the follies of the town, and subsequently a conviction of injustice to the country, called into action his powers as a satirist.

The first series of Salmagundi, published in 1807, was the production of Mr. Paulding and Mr. Washington Irving, except the verses and three or four of the concluding essays, which were by Mr. William Irving, a brother-in-law of the former and brother of the latter, who was afterward well known as a representative of the city of New York in Congress. This work had a great deal of freshness; its humour, though unequal, was nearly always gay, and as its satire was general, everybody was pleased. Its success surprised the authors, and was perhaps the determining cause of their subsequent devotion to literature. The publisher found it very profitable, as he paid nothing for the copy; and upon his refusal to make any remuneration for it, the work was suddenly and unexpectedly brought to a close.

In 1813 Mr. Paulding published The Lay of a Scotch Fiddle, a satirical poem, and in the following year The United States and England, in reply to the article on Inchiquin's Letters in the Quarterly Review. The Diverting History of John Bull and Brother Jonathan, the most successful of his satires, appeared in 1816. The allegory is well sustained, and the style has a homely simplicity and vigour that remind us of Swift. A part of this year was passed in Virginia, where he wrote his Letters from the South, which were published in 1817. The humour in them is not of his happiest vein, and the soundness of the views respecting education, paper money, and some other subjects, may be questioned; but the work contains interesting sketches of scenery, manners, and personal character.

In 1818 Mr. Paulding published The Backwoodsman, a poem, and in the next year the second series of Salmagundi, of which he was the sole author. Koningsmarke, or Old Times in the New World, a novel founded on incidents in the history of the Swedish settlements on the Delaware, appeared in 1823; John Bull in America in 1824; and the Merry Tales of the Three Wise Men of Gotham in 1826. The idea that the progress of mankind is more apparent than actual is a favourite one with Mr. Paulding, and modern improvements and discoveries in political economy, and productive labour, law, and philosophy, are in this work ridiculed with considerable ingenuity.

The Book of St. Nicholas, a collection of stories purporting to be translated from the Dutch; The New Pilgrim's Progress, which contains some of the best specimens of his satire, and Tales of the Good Woman by a Doubtful Gentleman, came out in the three following years.

The Dutchman's Fireside was published in 1831. Its success was decided and immediate, and it continues to be regarded as the best of Mr. Paulding's novels. It is a domestic story, of the time of the "old French war." The scenes are among the sources of the Hudson, on the borders of Lake Champlain, and in other parts of the province of New York. The characters are natural, and possess much individuality. From the outset the reader feels as if he had a personal acquaintance with each of them. One of the most cleverly executed is a meddling little old Dutchman, Ariel Vancour, who with the best intentions is continually working mischief: an everyday sort of person, which I do not remember having seen so palpably imbodied by any other author. The hero, Sybrandt Vancour, is educated in almost total seclusion, and finds himself, on the verge of manhood, a scholar, ignorant of the world. He is proud, sensitive, and suspicious: unhappy, and a cause of unhappiness to all about him. His transformation is effected by the famous Sir William Johnson, whom he accompanies on a campaign; and in the end, a self-confident and self-complacent gentleman, he marries a woman whom he had loved all the while, but whom his infirmities had previously rendered as wretched as himself. The work is marked throughout with Mr. Paulding's quaint and peculiar humour, and it is a delightful picture of primitive colonial life, varied with glimpses of the mimic court of the governor, where ladies figure in hoops and brocades, and of the camp in the wilderness, and the strategy of Indian warfare.

In the following year Mr. Paulding published Westward Ho! The moral of this story is, that we are to disregard the *presentiments* of evil, withstand the approaches of fanaticism, and feel confident that the surest means of inducing a gracious interposition of Providence in our favour is to persevere ourselves in all the kind offices of humanity toward the unfortunate. The characters are original and well-drawn. The Virginia planter who squanders his estates in a prodigal hospitality, and with the remnants of a liberal fortune seeks a new home in the untried forests; Zeno and Judith Paddock, a pair of village inquisitors; and Bushfield, an untamed western hunter, are all actual and indigenous beings. Mr. Paulding had already sketched the Kentuckian, with a freer but less skilful hand, in his comedy of Nimrod Wildfire. Whoever wanders in the footsteps of Daniel Boone will still meet with Bushfields, though until he approaches nearer the Rocky Mountains the rough edges of the character may be somewhat softened down; and Dangerfields are not yet strangers in Virginia.

His next work was on slavery in the United States, and this was followed in 1835 by his excellent life of Washington for youth, which is published in Messrs. Harpers' Family Library.

After the close of our second war with Great Britain he resided some time at the seat of government, and 'was subsequently many years navy agent for the port of New York. When President Van Buren formed his cabinet, in the spring of 1837, he was selected to be the head of the Navy Department, and he continued in that office until the close of Mr. Van Buren's administration, in 1841.

Upon retiring from public life, being then more than sixty years of age, he resumed his pen, and some of his magazine papers, written since that time, are equal to any of the productions of his most vigorous days. In 1846 he published The Old Continental, or the Price of Liberty, a novel which he had nearly completed before he entered the cabinet. It has all his peculiarities of manner and spirit.

The various works by Mr. Paulding which I have mentioned make twenty-five volumes, and the stories, essays, and other papers which he has published in the Tales of Glauber Spa, and in periodicals, would increase the number to more than thirty.

Mr. Paulding's writings are distinguished for a decided nationality. He has had no respect for authority unsupported by reason, but on all subjects has thought and judged for himself. He has defended our government and institutions, and has imbodied what is peculiar in our manners and opinions. There is hardly a character in his works who would not in any country be instantly recognised as an American.

He is unequalled in a sort of quaint and whimsical humour, but occasionally falls into the common error of thinking there is humour in epithets, and these are sometimes coarse or vulgar. Humour is a quality of feeling and action, and like any sentiment or habit should be treated in a style which indicates a sympathy with it. He who pauses to invent its dress will usually find his invention exhausted before he attempts its body.

He seems generally to have no regular schemes and premeditated catastrophies. He follows the lead of a free fancy and writes down whatever comes into his mind. He creates his characters, and permits circumstances to guide their conduct.

Mr. Paulding died at Tarrytown, April 4, 1860. His son, W. I. Paulding, published his literary life, April, 1867, and four volumes of his select works were reprinted in New York in 1867-68.

NEW YEAR IN ELSINGBURGH.

FROM KONINGSMARKE.

THE holydays, those wintry blessings which cheer the heart of young and old, and give to the gloomy depths of winter the life and spirit of laughing, jolly spring, were now near at hand. The chopping-knife gave token of goodly minced pies, and the bustle of the kitchen afforded shrewd indications of what was coming by and by. The celebration of the new year, it was well known, came originally from the northern nations of Europe, who still keep up many of the practices, amusements, and enjoyments, known to their ancestors. The Heer Piper valued himself upon being a genuine northern man, and consequently held the winter holydays in special favour and affection. In addition to this hereditary attachment to ancient customs, it was shrewdly suspected that his zeal in celebrating these good old sports was not a little quickened in consequence of his mortal antagonist, William Penn, having hinted, in the course of their controversy, that the practice of keeping holydays savoured not only of popery, but paganism.

Before the Heer consented to sanction the projects of Dominie Kanttwell for abolishing sports and ballads, he stipulated for full liberty, on the part of himself and his people of Elsingburgh, to eat, drink, sing, and frolic as much as they liked, during the winter holydays. In fact, the Dominie made no particular opposition to this suspension of his blue laws, being somewhat addicted to good eating and drinking, whenever the occasion justified; that is to say, whenever such accidents came in his way.

It had long been the custom with Governor Piper, to usher in the new year with a grand supper, to which the Dominie, the members of the council, and certain of the most respectable burghers, were always bidden. This year, he determined to see the old year out and the new one in, as the phrase was, having just heard of a great victory gained by the bulwark of the Protestant religion, the immortal Gustavus Adolphus; which, though it happened nearly four years before, had only now reached the village of Elsingburgh. . . .

Exactly at ten o'clock, the guests sat down to the table, where they ate and drank to the success of the Protestant cause, the glory of the great Gustavus, the downfall of Popery and the Quakers, with equal zeal and patriotism. The instant the clock struck twelve, a round was fired from the fort, and a vast and bottomless bowl, supposed to be the identical one in which the famous wise men of Gotham went to sea, was brought in, filled to the utmost brim with smoking punch. The memory of the departed year and the hopes of the future were then drank in a special bumper, after which the ladies retired, and noise and fun became the order of the night. The Heer told his great story of having surprised and taken a whole picquet-guard, under the great Gustavus; and each of the guests contributed his tale, taking special care, however, not to outdo their host in the mar-

19

vellous, a thing which always puts the governor out of humour.

Counsellor Langfanger talked wonderfully about public improvements; Counsellor Varlett sung, or rather roared, a hundred verses of a song in praise of Rhenish wine; and Othman Pfegel smoked and tippled, till he actually came to a determination of bringing matters to a crisis with the fair Christina the very next day. Such are the wonder-working powers of hot punch! As for the Dominie, he departed about the dawn of day, in such a plight that if it had not been impossible, we should have suspected him of being as it were a little overtaken with the said punch. To one or two persons who chanced to see him, he actually appeared to stagger a little; but such was the stout faith of the good Dominie's parishioners, that neither of these worthy fellows would believe his own eyes sufficiently to state these particulars.

A couple of hours' sleep sufficed to disperse the vapours of punch and pepper-pot; for heads in those days were much harder than now, and the Heer, as well as his roistering companions, rose betimes to give and receive the compliments and good wishes of the season. The morning was still, clear, and frosty. The sun shone with the lustre, though not with the warmth of summer, and his bright beams were reflected with indescribable splendour from the glassy, smooth expanse of ice that spread across, and up and down the broad river, far as the eye could see. The smoke of the village chimneys rose straight into the air, looking like so many inverted pyramids, spreading gradually broader and broader, until they melted away and mixed imperceptibly with ether. Scarce was the sun above the horizon, when the village was alive with rosy boys and girls, dressed in their new suits, and going forth with such warm anticipations of happiness, as time and experience imperceptibly fritter away into languid hopes or strengthening apprehensions. "Happy New Year!" came from every mouth and every heart. Spiced beverages and lusty cakes were given away with liberal open hand; everybody was welcomed to every house; all seemed to forget their little heart-burnings and disputes of yore—all seemed happy, and all were so; and the Dominie, who always wore his coat with four great pockets on new-year's day, came home and emptied them seven times, of loads of new-year cookies.

When the gay groups had finished their rounds in the village, the ice in front was seen all alive with the small fry of Elsingburgh, gambolling and skating, sliding and tumbling, helter skelter, and making the frost-bit ears of winter glad with the sounds of mirth and revelry. . . . All was rout, laughter, and happiness; and that day the icy mirror of the noble Delaware reflected as light hearts as ever beat together in the new world. At twelve o'clock the jolly Heer, according to his immemorial custom, went forth from the edge of the river distributing apples and other dainties, together with handsful of wampum, which, rolling away on the ice in different directions, occasioned innumerable contests and squabbles among the fry,

N

whose disputes, tumbles, and occasional buffetings for the prizes, were inimitably ludicrous upon the slippery element. Among the most obstreperous and mischievous of the crowd was that likely fellow Cupid, who made more noise, and tripped up more heels that day, than any half a dozen of his contemporaries. His voice could be heard above all the rest, especially after the arrival of the Heer, before whom he seemed to think it his duty to exert himself, while his unrestrained, extravagant laugh exhibited that singular hilarity of spirit which distinguishes the deportment of the African slave from the invariable gravity of the free red man of the western world.

All day, and until after the sun had set and the shadows of night succeeded, the sports continued, and the merry sounds rung far and near, occasionally interrupted by those loud noises which sometimes shoot across the ice like a rushing earthquake, and are occasioned by its cracking, as the water rises or falls.

THE QUARREL OF SQUIRE BULL AND HIS SON.

FROM JOHN BULL AND BROTHER JONATHAN.

John Bull was a choleric old fellow, who held a good manor in the middle of a great millpond, and which, by reason of its being quite surrounded by water, was generally called *Bullock Island.* Bull was an ingenious man, an exceedingly good blacksmith, a dexterous cutler, and a notable weaver and pot-baker besides. He also brewed capital porter, ale, and small beer, and was in fact a sort of jack of all trades, and good at each. In addition to these, he was a hearty fellow, an excellent bottle-companion, and passably honest as times go.

But what tarnished all these qualities was a devilish quarrelsome, overbearing disposition, which was always getting him into some scrape or other. The truth is, he never heard of a quarrel going on among his neighbours, but his fingers itched to be in the thickest of them; so that he was hardly ever seen without a broken head, a black eye, or a bloody nose. Such was Squire Bull, as he was commonly called by the country people his neighbours—one of those odd, testy, grumbling, boasting old codgers, that never get credit for what they are, because they are always pretending to be what they are not.

The squire was as tight a hand to deal with in doors as out; sometimes treating his family as if they were not the same flesh and blood, when they happened to differ with him in certain matters. One day he got into a dispute with his youngest son Jonathan, who was familiarly called Brother Jonathan, about whether churches ought to be called churches or meeting-houses; and whether steeples were not an abomination. The squire, either having the worst of the argument, or being naturally impatient of contradiction, (I can't tell which.) fell into a great passion, and swore he would physic such notions out of the boy's noddle.

So he went to some of his *doctors* and got them to draw up a prescription, made up of *thirty-nine different articles,* many of them bitter enough to some palates. This he tried to make Jonathan swallow; and finding he made villanous wry faces, and would not do it, fell upon him and beat him like fury. After this, he made the house so disagreeable to him, that Jonathan, though as hard as a pine knot and as tough as leather, could bear it no longer. Taking his gun and his axe, he put himself in a boat and paddled over the millpond to some new lands to which the squire pretended some sort of claim, intending to settle them, and build a meeting-house without a steeple as soon as he grew rich enough.

When he got over, Jonathan found that the land was quite in a state of nature, covered with wood, and inhabited by nobody but wild beasts. But being a lad of mettle, he took his axe on one shoulder and his gun on the other, marched into the thickest of the wood, and clearing a place, built a log hut. Pursuing his labours, and handling his axe like a notable woodman, he in a few years cleared the land, which he laid out into *thirteen good farms:* and building himself a fine frame house, about half-finished, began to be quite snug and comfortable.

But Squire Bull, who was getting old and stingy, and, besides, was in great want of money, on account of his having lately been made to pay swinging damages for assaulting his neighbours and breaking their heads—the squire, I say, finding Jonathan was getting well to do in the world, began to be very much troubled about his welfare; so he demanded that Jonathan should pay him a good rent for the land which he had cleared and made good for something. He trumped up I know not what claim against him, and under different pretences managed to pocket all Jonathan's honest gains. In fact, the poor lad had not a shilling left for holyday occasions; and had it not been for the filial respect he felt for the old man, he would certainly have refused to submit to such impositions.

But for all this, in a little time, Jonathan grew up to be very large of his age, and became a tall, stout, double-jointed, broad-footed cub of a fellow, awkward in his gait and simple in his appearance; but showing a lively, shrewd look, and having the promise of great strength when he should get his full growth. He was rather an odd-looking chap, in truth, and had many queer ways; but everybody that had seen John Bull saw a great likeness between them, and swore he was John's own boy, and a true chip of the old block. Like the old squire, he was apt to be blustering and saucy, but in the main was a peaceable sort of careless fellow, that would quarrel with nobody if you only let him alone. He used to dress in homespun trousers with a huge bagging seat, which seemed to have nothing in it. This made people say he had no *bottom;* but whoever said so lied, as they found to their cost whenever they put Jonathan in a passion. He always wore a linsey-woolsey coat that did not above half cover his breech, and the sleeves of which were so short that his hand

and wrist came out beyond them, looking like a shoulder of mutton. All which was in consequence of his growing so fast that he outgrew his clothes.

While Jonathan was outgrowing his strength in this way, Bull kept on picking his pockets of every penny he cou'd scrape together; till at last one day when the squire was even more than usually pressing in his demands, which he accompanied with threats, Jonathan started up in a furious passion, and threw the TEA-KETTLE at the old man's head. The choleric Bull was hereupon exceedingly enraged; and after calling the poor lad an undutiful, ungrateful, rebellious rascal, seized him by the collar, and forthwith a furious scuffle ensued. This lasted a long time; for the squire, though in years, was a capital boxer, and of most excellent bottom. At last, however, Jonathan got him under, and before he would let him up, made him sign a paper giving up all claim to the farms, and acknowledging the fee-simple to be in Jonathan for ever.

A NIGHT ADVENTURE DURING THE OLD FRENCH WAR.
FROM THE DUTCHMAN'S FIRESIDE.

"Should you discover the position of the enemy," continued Sir William Johnson to Sybrandt, "you must depend upon your own sagacity, and that of Timothy Weasel for the direction of your subsequent conduct."

"Timothy Weasel! who is he?"

"What! have you never heard of Timothy Weasel, the Varmounter, as he calls himself?"

"Never."

"Well then, I must give you a sketch of his story before I introduce him. He was born in New Hampshire, as he says, and in due time, as is customary in those parts, married, and took possession, by right of discovery I suppose, of a tract of land in what was at that time called the New Hampshire grants. Others followed him, and in the course of a few years a little settlement was formed of real 'cute Yankees, as Timothy calls them, to the amount of sixty or seventy men, women, and children. They were gradually growing in wealth and numbers, when one night, in the dead of winter, they were set upon by a party of Indians from Canada, and every soul of them, except Timothy, either consumed in the flames or massacred in the attempt to escape. I have witnessed in the course of my life many scenes of horror, but nothing like that which he describes, in which his wife and eight children perished. Timothy was left for dead by the savages, who, as is their custom, departed at the dawn, for fear the news of this massacre might rouse some of the neighbouring settlements in time to overtake them before they reached home. When all was silent, Timothy, who, though severely wounded in a dozen places, had, as he says, only been 'playing 'possum,' raised himself up and looked around him. The smoking ruins, mangled limbs, blood-stained snow, and the whole scene, as he describes it with quaint pathos, is enough to make one's blood run cold. He managed to raise himself upright, and, by dint of incredible exertions, to reach a neighbouring settlement, distant about forty miles, where he told his story, and then was put to bed, where he lay some weeks. In the mean time the people of the settlement had gone and buried the remains of his unfortunate family and neighbours. When Timothy got well, he visited the spot, and while viewing the ruins of the houses, and pondering over the graves of all that were dear to him, solemnly devoted the remainder of his life to revenge. He accordingly buried himself in the woods, and built a cabin about twelve miles from hence, in a situation the most favourable to killing the 'kritters,' as he calls the savages. From that time until now he has waged a perpetual war against them, and, according to his own account, sacrificed almost a hecatomb to the manes of his wife and children. His intrepidity is wonderful, and his sagacity in the pursuit of this grand object of his life beyond all belief. I am half a savage myself, but I have heard this man relate stories of his adventures and escapes which make me feel myself, in the language of the red skins, 'a woman' in comparison with this strange compound of cunning and simplicity. It is inconceivable with what avidity he will hunt an Indian; and the keenest sportsman does not feel a hundredth part of the delight in bringing down his game that Timothy does in witnessing the mortal pangs of one of these 'kritters.' It is a horrible propensity: but to lose all in one night, and to wake the next morning and see nothing but the mangled remains of wife, children, all that man holds most dear to his inmost heart, is no trifle. If ever man had motive for revenge, it is Timothy. Such as he is I employ him, and find his services highly useful. He is a compound of the two races, and combines all the qualities essential to the species of warfare in which we are now engaged. I have sent for him, and expect him here every moment."

As Sir William concluded, Sybrandt heard a long dry sort of "H-e-e-m-m," ejaculated just outside of the door. "That's he," exclaimed Sir William; "I know the sound. It is his usual expression of satisfaction at the prospect of being employed against his old enemies the Indians. Come in, Timothy."

Timothy accordingly made his appearance, forgot his bow, and said nothing. Sybrandt eyed his associate with close attention. He was a tall, wind-dried man, with extremely sharp, angular features, and a complexion deeply bronzed by the exposures to which he had been subjected for so many years. His scanty head of hair was of a sort of sunburnt colour; his beard of a month's growth at least, and his eye of sprightly blue never rested a moment in its socket. It glanced from side to side, and up and down, and here and there, with indescribable rapidity, as though in search of some object of interest, or apprehensive of sudden danger. It was a perpetual silent alarum.

"Timothy," said Sir William, "I want to employ you to-night."

"H-e-m-m," answered Timothy.

"Are you at leisure to depart-immediately?"

"What, right off?"

"Ay, in less than no time."

"I guess I am."

"Very well—that means you are certain."

"I'm always sartin of my mark."

"Have you your gun with you?"

"The kritter is just outside the door."

"And plenty of ammunition?"

"Why, what under the sun should I do with a gun and no ammunition?"

"Can you paddle a canoe so that nobody can hear you?"

"Can't I! h-e-e-m-m!"

"And you are all ready?"

"I 'spect so. I knew you didn't want me for nothing, and so got every thing to hand."

"Have you any thing to eat by the way?"

"No; if I only stay out two or three days I sha'n't want any thing."

"But you are to have a companion."

Timothy here manufactured a sort of linsey-woolsey grunt, betokening disapprobation.

"I'd rather go alone."

"But it is necessary you should have a companion; this young gentleman will go with you."

Timothy hereupon subjected Sybrandt to a rigid scrutiny of those busy eyes of his, that seemed to un over him as quick as lightning.

"I'd rather go by myself," said he again.

"That is out of the question, so say no more about it. Are you ready to go now—this minute?"

"Yes."

Sir William then explained the object of the expedition to Timothy much in the same manner he had previously done to Sybrandt.

"But mayn't I shoot one of these tarnil kritters if he comes in my way?" said Timothy, in a tone of great interest.

"No; you are not to fire a gun, nor attempt any hostility whatever, unless it is neck or nothing with you."

"Well, that's what I call hard; but maybe it will please God to put our lives in danger—that's some comfort."

The knight now produced two Indian dresses, which he directed them to put on somewhat against the inclinations of friend Timothy, who observed that if he happened to see his shadow in the water, he should certainly mistake it for one of the tarnil kritters, and shoot himself. Sir William then with his own hand painted the face of Sybrandt so as to resemble that of an Indian—an operation not at all necessary to Timothy; his toilet was already made; his complexion required no embellishment. This done, the night having now set in, Sir William, motioning silence, led the way cautiously to one of the gates of Ticonderoga, which was opened by the sentinel, and they proceeded swiftly and silently to the high bank which hung over the narrow strait in front

of the fort. A little bark canoe lay moored at the foot, into which Sybrandt and Timothy placed themselves flat on the bottom, each with his musket and accoutrements at his side, and a paddle in his hand.

"Now," said Sir William, almost in a whisper, —"now, luck be with you, boys; remember, you are to return before daylight without fail."

"But, Sir William," said Timothy, coaxingly, "now, mayn't I take a pop at one of the tarnal kritters, if I meet 'em?"

"I tell you, No!" replied the other; "unless you wish to be popped out of the world when you come back. Away with you, my boys."

Each seized his paddle; and the light feather of a boat darted away with the swiftness of a bubble in a whirlpool.

"It's plaguy hard," muttered Timothy to himself.

"What?" quoth Sybrandt.

"Why, not to have the privilege of shooting one of these varmints."

"Not another word," whispered Sybrandt; "we may be overheard from the shore."

"Does he think I don't know what's what?" again muttered Timothy, plying his paddle with a celerity and silence that Sybrandt vainly tried to equal.

The night gradually grew dark as pitch. All became of one colour, and the earth and the air were confounded together in utter obscurity, at least to the eyes of Sybrandt Westbrook. Not a breath of wind disturbed the foliage of the trees that hung invisible to all eyes but those of Timothy, who seemed to see best in the dark; not an echo, not a whisper disturbed the dead silence of nature, as they darted along unseen and unseeing, —at least our hero could see nothing but darkness.

"Whisht!" aspirated Timothy, at length, so low that he could scarcely hear himself; and after making a few strokes with his paddle, so as to shoot the boat out of her course, cowered himself down to the bottom. Sybrandt did the same, peering just over the side of the boat, to discover if possible the reason of Timothy's manœuvres. Suddenly he heard, or thought he heard, the measured sound of paddles dipping lightly into the water. A few minutes more and he saw five or six little lights glimmering indistinctly through the obscurity, apparently at a great distance. Timothy raised himself up suddenly, seized his gun and pointed it for a moment at one of the lights; but recollecting the injunction of Sir William, immediately resumed his former position. In a few minutes the sound of the paddles died away, and the lights disappeared.

"What was that?" whispered Sybrandt.

"The Frenchmen are turning the tables on us, I guess," replied the other. "If that boat isn't going a-spying jist like ourselves, I'm quite out in my calculation."

"What! with lights? They must be great fools."

"It was only the fire of their pipes, which the darkness made look like so many candles. . I'm thinking what a fine mark these lights would have bin; and how I could have peppered two or three of them, if Sir William had not bin so plaguy obstinate."

"Peppered them! why, they were half-a-dozen miles off."

"They were within fifty yards—the kritters; I could have broke all their pipes as easy as kiss my hand."

"How do you know they were kritters, as you call the Indians?"

"Why, did you ever hear so many Frenchmen make so little noise?"

This reply was perfectly convincing; and Sybrandt again enjoining silence, they proceeded with the same celerity, and in the same intensity of darkness as before, for more than an hour. This brought them, at the swift rate they were going, a distance of at least twenty miles from the place of their departure.

Turning a sharp angle, at the expiration of the time just specified, Timothy suddenly stopped his paddle as before, and cowered down at the bottom of the canoe. Sybrandt had no occasion to inquire the reason of this action; for, happening to look toward the shore, he could discover at a distance innumerable lights glimmering and flashing amid the obscurity, and rendering the darkness beyond the sphere of their influence still more profound. These lights appeared to extend several miles along what he supposed to be the strait or lake, which occasionally reflected their glancing rays upon its quiet bosom.

"There they are, the kritters," whispered Timothy exultingly; "we've treed 'em at last, I swow. Now, mister, let me ask you one question—will you obey my orders?"

"If I like them," said Sybrandt.

"Ay, like or no like. I must be captain for a little time, at least."

"I have no objection to benefit by your experience."

"Can you play Ingen when you are put to it?"

"I have been among them, and know something of their character and manners."

"Can you talk Ingen?"

"No!"

"Ah! your education has been sadly neglected. But come, there's no time to waste in talking Ingen or English. We must get right in the middle of these kritters. Can you creep on all-fours without waking up a cricket?"

"No!"

"Plague on it! I wonder what Sir William meant by sending you with me. I could have done better by myself. Are you afeared?"

"Try me."

"Well, then, I must make the best of the matter. The kritters are camped out—I see by their fires—by themselves. I can't stop to tell you every thing; but you must keep close to me, do jist as I do, and say nothing; that's all."

"I am likely to play a pretty part, I see."

"Play! you'll find no play here, I guess, mister. Set down close; make no noise; and if you go to sneeze or cough, take right hold of your throat, and let it go downwards."

Sybrandt obeyed his injunctions; and Timothy proceeded toward the lights, which appeared much farther off in the darkness than they really were, handling his paddle with such lightness and dexterity that Sybrandt could not hear the strokes. In this manner they swiftly approached the encampment, until they could distinguish a confused noise of shoutings and hallooings which gradually broke on their ears in discordant violence. Timothy stopped his paddle and listened.

"It is the song of those tarnal kritters, the Utawas. They're in a drunken frolic, as they always are the night before going to battle. I know the kritters, for I've popped off a few, and can talk and sing their songs pretty considerably, I guess. So we'll be among 'em right off. Don't forget what I told you about doing as I do, and holding your tongue."

Cautiously plying his paddle, he now shot in close to the shore whence the sounds of revelry proceeded, and made the land at some little distance, that he might avoid the sentinels, whom they could hear ever and anon challenging each other. They then drew up the light canoe into the bushes, which here closely skirted the waters. "Now leave all behind but yourself, and follow me," whispered Timothy, as he carefully felt whether the muskets were well covered from the damps of the night; and then laid himself down on his face and crawled along under the bushes with the quiet celerity of a snake in the grass.

"Must we leave our guns behind," whispered Sybrandt.

"Yes, according to orders; but it's a plaguy hard case. Yet upon the whole it's best; for if I was to get a fair chance at one of these kritters, I believe in my heart my gun would go off clean of itself. But hush! shut your mouth as close as a powder-horn."

After proceeding some distance, Sybrandt getting well scratched by the briars, and finding infinite difficulty in keeping up with Timothy, the latter stopped short.

"Here the kritters are," said he, in the lowest whisper.

"Where?" replied the other, in the same tone.

"Look right before you."

Sybrandt followed the direction, and beheld a group of five or six Indians seated round a fire, the waning lustre of which cast a fitful light upon their dark countenances, whose savage expression was heightened to ferocity by the stimulant of the debauch in which they were engaged. They sat on the ground swaying to and fro, backward and forward, and from side to side, ever and anon passing round the canteen from one to the other, and sometimes rudely snatching it away when they thought either was drinking more than his share. At intervals they broke out into yelling and discordant songs, filled with extravagant boastings of murders, massacres, burnings, and plunderings, mixed up with threatenings of what they would do to the red-coat long knives on the morrow.

N 2

One of these songs recited the destruction of a village, and bore a striking resemblance to the bloody catastrophe of poor Timothy's wife and children. Sybrandt could not understand it, but he could hear the quick suppressed breathings of his companion, who, when it was done, aspirated, in a tone of smothered vengeance, "If I only had my gun!"

"Stay here a moment," whispered he, as he crept cautiously toward the noisy group, which all at once became perfectly quiet, and remained in the attitude of listening.

"Huh!" muttered one, who appeared by his dress to be the principal.

Timothy replied in a few Indian words, which Sybrandt did not comprehend; and raising himself from the ground, suddenly appeared in the midst of them. A few words were rapidly interchanged; and Timothy then brought forward his companion, whom he presented to the Utawas, who welcomed him and handed the canteen, now almost empty.

"My brother does not talk," said Timothy.

"Is he dumb?" asked the chief of the Utawas.

"No; but he has sworn not to open his mouth till he has struck the body of a long knife."

"Good," said the other; "he is welcome."

After a pause he went on, at the same time eyeing Sybrandt with suspicion; though his faculties were obscured by the fumes of the liquor he still continued to drink, and hand round at short intervals.

"I don't remember the young warrior. Is he of our tribe?"

"He is; but he was stolen by the Mohawks many years ago, and only returned lately."

"How did he escape?"

"He killed two chiefs while they were asleep by the fire, and ran away."

"Good," said the Utawas; and for a few moments sunk into a kind of stupor, from which he suddenly roused himself, and grasping his tomahawk started up, rushed toward Sybrandt, and raising his deadly weapon, stood over him in the attitude of striking. Sybrandt remained perfectly unmoved, waiting the stroke.

"Good," said the Utawas again; "I am satisfied; the Utawas never shuts his eyes at death. He is worthy to be our brother. He shall go with us to battle to-morrow."

"We have just come in time," said Timothy. "Does the white chief march against the red-coats to-morrow?"

"He does."

"Has he men enough to fight them?"

"They are like the leaves on the trees," said the other.

By degrees Timothy drew from the Utawas chief the number of Frenchmen, Indians, and *coureurs de bois*, which composed the army: the time when they were to commence their march; the course they were to take, and the outlines of the plan of attack, in case the British either waited for them in the fort or met them in the field. By the time he had finished his examination, the whole party, with the exception of Timothy, Sybrandt, and the chief, were fast asleep. In a few minutes after, the two former affected to be in the same state, and began to snore lustily. The Utawas chief nodded from side to side; then sunk down like a log and remained insensible to every thing around him, in the sleep of drunkenness.

Timothy lay without motion for awhile, then turned himself over, and rolled about from side to side, managing to strike against each of the party in succession. They remained fast asleep. He then cautiously raised himself, and Sybrandt did the same. In a moment Timothy was down again, and Sybrandt followed his example without knowing why, until he heard some one approach, and distinguished, as they came nigh, two officers, apparently of rank. They halted near the waning fire, and one said to the other in French, in a low tone:

"The beasts are all asleep: it is time to wake them. Our spies are come back, and we must march."

"Not yet," replied the other; "let them sleep an hour longer, and they will wake sober." They then passed on, and when their footsteps were no longer heard, Timothy again raised himself up, motioning our hero to lie still. After ascertaining by certain tests which experience had taught him that the Indians still continued in a profound sleep, he proceeded with wonderful dexterity and silence to shake the priming from each of the guns in succession. After this, he took their powder-horns and emptied them; then seizing up the tomahawk of the Utawas chief, which had dropped from his hand, he stood over him for a moment with an expression of deadly hatred which Sybrandt had never before seen in his or any other countenance. The intense desire of killing one of the kritters, as he called them, struggled a few moments with his obligations to obey the orders of Sir William; but the latter at length triumphed and motioning Sybrandt, they crawled away with the silence and celerity with which they came; launched their light canoe and plied their paddles with might and main. "The morning breeze is springing up," said Timothy, "and it will soon be daylight. We must be tarnal busy."

And busy they were, and swiftly did the light canoe slide over the wave, leaving scarce a wake behind her. As they turned the angle which hid the encampment from their view, Timothy ventured to speak a little above his breath.

"It's lucky for us that the boat we passed coming down has returned, for it's growing light apace. I'm only sorry for one thing."

"What's that?" asked Sybrandt.

"That I let that drunken Utawas alone. If I had only bin out on my own bottom, he'd have bin stun dead in a twinkling, I guess."

"And you, too, I *guess*," said Sybrandt, adopting his peculiar phraseology; "you would have been overtaken and killed."

"Who, I? I must be a poor kritter if I can't dodge half a dozen of these drunken varmints.'

A few hours of sturdy exertion brought them at

length within sight of Ticonderoga, just as the red harbingers of morning striped the pale green of the skies. Star after star disappeared, as Timothy observed, like candles that had been burning all night and gone out of themselves, and as they struck the foot of the high bluff whence they had departed, the rays of the sun just tipped the peaks of the high mountains rising toward the west. Timothy then shook hands with our hero.

"You're a hearty kritter," said he, "and I'll tell Sir William how you looked at that tarnal tomahawk as if it had bin an old pipe-stem."

Without losing a moment, they proceeded to the quarters of Sir William, whom they found waiting for them with extreme anxiety. He extended both hands toward our hero, and eagerly exclaimed—

"What luck, my lads? I have been up all night, waiting your return."

"Then you will be quite likely to sleep sound to-night," quoth master Timothy, unbending the intense rigidity of his leathern countenance. "I am of opinion if a man wants to have a real good night's rest, he's only to set up the night before, and he may calculate upon it with sartinty."

"Hold your tongue, Timothy," said Sir William, good-humouredly, "or else speak to the purpose. Have you been at the enemy's camp?"

"Right in their very bowels," said Timothy.

Sir William proceeded to question, and Sybrandt and Timothy to answer, until he drew from them all the important information of which they had possessed themselves. He then dismissed Timothy with cordial thanks and a purse of yellow boys, which he received with much satisfaction.

"It's not of any great use to me, to be sure," said he as he departed ; "but somehow or other I love to look at the kritters."

"As to you, Sybrandt Westbrook, you have fulfilled the expectations I formed of you on our first acquaintance. You claim a higher reward; for you have acted from higher motives and at least equal courage and resolution. His majesty shall know of this; and in the mean time call yourself Major Westbrook, for such you are from this moment. Now go with me to the commander-in-chief, who must know of what you heard and saw."

DEATH IN THE COUNTRY.
FROM THE SAME.

THERE is to my mind and to my early recollections something exquisitely touching in the tolling of a church-bell amid the silence of the country. It communicates for miles around the message of mortality. The ploughman stops his horses to listen to the solemn tidings ; the housewife remits her domestic occupations, and sits with the needle idle in her fingers, to ponder who it is that is going to the long home ; and even the little thoughtless children, playing and laughing their way from school, are arrested for a moment in their evening gambols by these sounds of melancholy import, and cover their heads when they go to rest.

KENTUCKY HOSPITALITY.
FROM WESTWARD HO!

"You must know, colonel, not long after you went away there came a man riding along here that I calculate had just thrown off his moccasins, with another feller behind him in a laced hat, and for all the world dressed like a militia officer. Well, I hailed him in here, for you know I like to do as you would in your own house; and he came to like a good feller. But the captain, as I took him to be, hung fire and stayed out with the horses. So I went and took hold of him like a snapping-turtle, and says I, 'Captain, one would think you had never been inside of a gentleman's house before.' But he held back like all wrath, and wouldn't take any thing. So says I, 'Stranger, I'm a peaceable man anyhow, but maybe you don't know what it is to insult a feller by sneaking away from his hospitality here in Old Kentuck.' I held on to him all the while, or he'd have gone off like one of these plaguy precussion-locks that have just come into fashion. 'Captain,' says I, 'here's your health, and may you live to be a general.' 'Captain!' says the other, 'he's no captain; he's my servant.' 'What!' says I, 'one white man be a servant to another! make a nigger of himself! come, that's too bad!' and I began to feel a little savage. I asked one if he wasn't ashamed to make a slave of a feller-cretur, and the other if he wasn't ashamed to make a nigger of himself; and they got rather obstropolous. I don't know exactly how it came about, but we got into a fight, and I lick'd them both, but not till they got outside the door, for I wouldn't be uncivil anyhow. Well, what do you think? instead of settling the thing like a gentleman, the feller that had a white man for his nigger, instead of coming out fine, I'll be eternally dern'd if he didn't send a constable after me. Well, I made short work of it, and lick'd him too, anyhow. But I can't stand it here any longer. Poor old Snowball* slipped her bridle the other day, and went out like a flash in the pan ; so I'm my own master again, with nobody to stand in my way at all. I must look out for some place where a man can live independent, where there's no law but gentlemen's law, and no niggers but black ones. I sha'n't see you again, colonel, it's most likely, so good-by all. I expect you'll be after me soon, for I look upon it to be impossible for a man in his senses to live here much longer, to be hoppled like a horse, and not go where he pleases." And away he marched, with a heart as light as a feather, in search of a place where he might live according to his conscience.

* A servant who had died.

TIMOTHY FLINT.

[Born 1780. Died 1840.]

TIMOTHY FLINT was born in Reading, Massachusetts, and was educated at Harvard College, where he graduated when twenty years of age. After devoting two years to the study of theology, he was ordained as minister of the Congregational church in Lunenburg, in the county of Worcester, where he continued until the summer of 1814. In the following year, hoping that travel and the milder airs of the south-west would improve his health, which had been impaired by sedentary habits, he became a missionary for the Valley of the Mississippi. The first winter was passed in Cincinnati, the following spring in making a tour through parts of Ohio, Indiana, and Kentucky, and the summer in St. Louis. In September he arrived at St. Charles, where, occupied in the wide range of his missionary duties, he remained nearly three years. He then descended the Mississippi to Arkansas, but met with disappointments, and after a gloomy summer returned to the counties of Cape Girardeau and St. Genevieve; and in 1821 to his former residence at St. Charles, where, with nearly all the members of his family, he suffered severe and protracted illness. In 1822 he removed to New Orleans; in the following spring to the Florida side of Lake Ponchartrain, where he opened a school; in the autumn back to New Orleans; and in the summer of 1824 to Alexandria, on Red River, where he accepted the charge of a seminary, and continued until, at the end of the year, a broken constitution compelled him to suspend his labours and revisit the northern states.

Soon after his removal to Alexandria, Mr. Flint began to write his Recollections of Ten Years passed in the Valley of the Mississippi, which were published in Boston early in 1826. This was his first work, and its success was decided and immediate. Literature now became his profession. Francis Berrian, or the Mexican Patriot, which was probably commenced before he left the south, appeared in the following summer. It purports to be the autobiography of a New England adventurer, who acted a conspicuous part in the first Mexican revolution, and in the overthrow of Iturbide. The events were too recent and familiar. Three years had not elapsed since the close of the drama, and several of the characters were still before the world. The novelist has not a right to transcend the possible. The condition of Mexico in 1822 presented no barriers to the invention of plots and counterplots as startling, and deeds as chivalrous, as he has described, had not the actors, by name or position, been historical. It seems to be difficult for the writers of romantic fiction to learn when their heroes are sufficiently heroical for necessary purposes. They are generally made to perform works of supererogation. The interest of Francis Berrian would not have been less if the hero had done nothing to startle the credulity of the reader. There is in the details an occasional want of keeping; the letters of Doña Martha are commonplace, and there are some faults of a minor kind. The style however is generally animated and picturesque, and the narrative, in spite of its improbabilities, is interesting.

The Geography and History of the Mississippi Valley was published at Cincinnati, in 1827. It was an original work, composed with great care and labour from original materials, principally collected by the author during his travels. It was subsequently reprinted with a condensed survey of the whole continent. It was at that time the most important contribution which had been made to American geography, and, with the Recollections, it embraces the most graphic and faithful descriptions of the scenery and physical aspect of the western states that has ever yet been written.

Arthur Clenning, a novel, in two volumes, appeared in 1828. The hero leaves the borders of Lake Champlain in his boyhood, and after various adventures is wrecked on an island of the southern ocean. A beautiful girl survives to share his solitude, and after a few years, when they escape to New Holland, is married to him. They reach London, but the lady's father refuses to see her unless she will abandon her husband, which she of course refuses to do, and they come to America and settle on a farm in Illinois. Ultimately the father dies and leaves them his fortune. This, after Robinson Crusoe, was a bold experiment, and it was a failure.

George Mason, the Young Backwoodsman, followed. It is better than Arthur Clenning, but did not increase Mr. Flint's reputation.

The last of his novels was The Shoshonee Valley, published at Cincinnati, in 1830. The principal scene is among the tributaries of the Columbia river. Baptiste Dettier, a reckless and gay Canadian, encounters a Kentucky preacher west of the Mississippi, and they agree to cross the Rocky Mountains in company, one in quest of peltries and adventures, and the other influenced in a large degree by the hope of making converts. Elder Wood is the most original, natural, and successfully sustained character in Mr. Flint's works. He is a man of strong but undisciplined genius, who blends the enthusiasm of the missionary with that of the trapper. "The psalmist," he thought, "had the spirit of a Kentuckian." He had offended the Canadian, by some allusion to his idolatrous worship, and when the articles of agreement were settled, Baptiste complimented him upon his undoubted skill in the hunt, and said, " In a leet time I learn you to trap too, comme un diable! but sare, please take notice, I hab noting to do wit your dem religion!" The minister was as little pleased with this profane allusion to his profession as the other had been with his own description of the Catholic faith, but he said to himself, " I shall be able to bring him also out of the heathenish darkness ;" and thus balancing their disagreements, they set out for the Pacific. They reached the happy Valley of the Shoshonee, to be witnesses of the gradual decay of its patriarchal government and people, from causes connected with the invasion of the whites. The characters, except those which have been mentioned, are not drawn with much skill, and the Indians are hardly distinguishable from the rest. The invention is feeble, and we are conducted to a second catastrophe, apparently for no other reason than that the author was ill satisfied with the first. The tale is nevertheless interesting ; it is distin-

guished for a manly simplicity of style, a vivid freshness of description, and a genuine but unobtrusive religious sentiment.

In 1832 Mr. Flint published, in Boston, Lectures upon Natural History, Geology, Chemistry, The Application of Steam, and Interesting Discoveries in the Arts.

In 1833 he edited several numbers of the Knickerbocker Magazine, which had been established in the beginning of that year by Mr. Charles F. Hoffman, who retired from its management on personal grounds. In the beginning of 1834 the proprietorship of the work was changed, and Mr. Flint's connection with it ceased. He had already published a translation, with original essays on the same subject, from the work of Droz, *sur l'art d'être heureuse*, and in the early part of 1834 he translated Celibacy Vanquished or the Old Bachelor Reclaimed, a novel which gained a considerable though transient popularity.

Mr. Flint now removed to Cincinnati, and became editor of The Western Monthly Magazine, which he conducted with much industry and ability for three years. Besides the volumes which have been mentioned, he wrote several of less importance, and a great number of tales and essays for various periodicals and other works.

During the last year of his life, enfeebled by disease, he wrote but little for the public. He left his Louisiana home early in May, 1840, to visit the place of his nativity, and in the hope that he would derive a benefit from the bracing air of New England. He was at Natchez, on his way, when that city was nearly destroyed by a tornado, and with his son was buried many hours under the ruins. Soon after his arrival in Reading his malady assumed a more malignant character, and he wrote to his wife at Alexandria, that when she received his letter he would no longer be alive. The melancholy news hastened her death. The prediction of his own decease was premature, but he survived only until the eighteenth of August.

Mr. Flint commenced his literary career when forty-five years of age. To its end he was an invalid, but was compelled to write constantly and rapidly, and to print without revision.

His mind was vigorous and imaginative, and enriched with reading and observation.

20

He ad a discriminating judgment, warm affections, and a quick perception of the grand and beautiful. His works are marked by good sense and a genuine Christian philoso-phy. His chief merit is in his descriptions. His landscapes have extraordinary freedom and distinctness, and appear to be copies from nature.

A THUNDER STORM IN MEXICO.
FROM FRANCIS BERRIAN.

THE thunder, which had been rolling at a distance in the mountains, approached nearer. The peals were more frequent, and the echoes more loud and awful. The brassy edges of the clouds rolled together, and sweeping forward, like the smouldering pillars of smoke from some mighty conflagration, were seen looming from the heights and beginning to cover the sun. . . .

The thunder storms of the northern regions seldom give an idea of the assemblage of terrific accompaniments belonging to a severe one in the tropics. A thick mist fills all the distance between the clouds and the earth. A dim and yellowish twilight throws a frightful yellow upon the verdure of the trees.

The storm was tremendous. The commencement was in the stillness of death, and the burst of the winds was as instantaneous as the crash of the thunder. The rain did not descend in drops, or in sheets, but the terrible phenomenon of the bursting of the clouds upon the mountains took place. The roar of the new-formed torrents and cascades pouring down from the mountains, mingled with that of the rain, the thunder, and the winds. The atmosphere was a continued and lurid glare of lightning, which threw a portentous brilliance through the descending waters and the darkness. Many an aged tree, that had remained unscathed for ages, was stript from its summits to its roots by the descending fires. . . .

The sick man, aroused from his sleep, rested his head upon his hand, and his pains seemed to be suspended, while he contemplated the uproar and apparent conflagration of the elements. A blaze of lightning filled the room, and the thunderbolt fell upon a vast cypress, but a few feet from the house. The shock was so violent that each one was thrown from his seat. As we recovered from the blow, we saw how naturally in such moments each one flies to the object in which he has most confidence. The widowed mother sprang to the arms of her son, and Martha at the same moment clung to me. . . . We resumed our seats in a kind of tranquil astonishment, as the storm gradually subsided. The thunder rolled sublimely still, but at a greater distance. The blue of the atmosphere began to show itself at the zenith. The clouds rolled away toward the east, and the sun came forth in his brightness just above the smoking summits of the hills. The scene, that was terrific in the fury of the storm, was now an indescribable mixture of beauty and grandeur. Frequent gleams of the most vivid lightning played on the passing extremities of the clouds. White pillars of mist arose from the earth. The birds welcomed the return of the sun, and the renewed repose of nature, with a thousand mingled songs.

COUNTRY OF THE SEWASSERNA.
FROM THE SHOSHONEE VALLEY.

THE traces of their footsteps and their temporary huts were frequently seen amidst the dark hemlock forests on the Pacific shore. These free rangers of the deserts, as they saw the immense fronts, range behind range, of the ocean surf rolling onward to whiten and burst on the sand at their feet, had their own wild conceptions of the illimitable grandeur, and the mysterious and resistless power of the ever-heaving element. . . .

Their free domain comprised an extent of five hundred leagues. The country of their compact and actual settlement is a vale, than which the earth can show none more beautiful or more secluded, the vale of the Sewasserna. This stream, in which the poets would have placed the crystal caves of the Naiads of the ancient days, comes winding down in a clear, full, strong, and yet equable and gentle tide, from the mountains. Up its pure and ice-formed waters ascend, in their season, countless numbers of the finest salmon; and in its deep and circling eddies play trout, pike, carp, tench, and all the varieties of fish of cold mountain rivers. The Indian, as he glides down the stream, sees the shining rocks at the bottom, covered with tresses of green waving moss, at the depth of twenty feet. This circumstance, along with its transparency, furnishes the etymology of its name, which imports the sea green river. Streaked bass, shiners, gold fishes, and beautiful and undescribed finny tribes, dart from their coverts along the white sand, flit from the shadow of the descending canoe, or turn their green and gold to the light, as they fan as it were with their purple wings, or repose in the sunbeams that find their way through the branches that overhang the banks. . . .

The glossy gray mallard, the beautiful blue winged teal, the green crested widgeon, the little active dipper, the brilliant white diver, the solitary loon raising his lugubrious and ill-omened note in unsocial seclusion, the stately swan sailing in his pride and milky lustre slowly along the stream, the tall sand-hill crane looking at a distance like a miniature camel, the white pelican with his immense pouch in front, innumerable flocks of various species of geese—in short, an unknown variety of water-fowls with their brilliant, variegated, and oiled vestments, their singular languages and cries, were seen gliding among the trees, pattering their broad bills amidst the grasses and weeds on the shores. . . .

It would be useless to think of enumerating the strange and gay birds that sing, play, build, chide, and flutter among the branches of the huge sycamores and peccans. Among the more conspicuous is the splendid purple cardinal, with its glossy and changeable lustre of black crest, the gold-coloured oriole, looking down into its long hanging nest, the flamingo darting up the stream like an arrow of flame, the little peacock of trees, the wakona, or bird of paradise, the parti-coloured jay screaming its harsh notes, the red-winged woodpecker " tapping the hollow tree," the ortolan, in countless flocks, in plumage of the most exquisite softness, deep, shining black—the paroquets with their shrill screams and their splendour of green and gold, numberless humming-birds plunging their needle-shaped bills into the bignonia, grouse, turkies, partridges, in a word an infinite variety of those beautiful and happy tenants of the forest and the prairie, that are formed to sing through their transient but happy day.

The mountains on either side of the valley tower into a countless variety of peaks, cones, and inaccessible elevations, from six to ten thousand feet high. More than half of them are covered with the accumulated snows and ices of centuries, which, glittering in mid air, show in the sunbeams in awful contrast with the black and rugged precipices that arrest the clouds. . . . The rocks, cliffs, and boulders, partly of granite and partly of volcanic character, black and rugged in some places, in others porphyritic, needle or spire-shaped, shoot up into pinnacles, domes, and towers, and in other places lie heaped in huge masses as though shook by earthquakes from the summits where they had originally defied the storms. . . . Yet between these savage and terrific peaks, unvisited except by the screaming eagle, are seen the most secluded and sweet valleys in the world. Here and there appear circular clumps of hemlocks, mountain cedars, silver firs, and above all the glorious Norwegian pines. . . . The breeze that is borne down from the mountains always sighs through these evergreen thickets, playing as it were the deep and incessant voluntary of nature to the Divinity. . . . In numerous little lakes and ponds, where the trout spring up and dart upon the fly and grasshopper, the verdure of the shores is charmingly repainted in contrast with the threatening and savage sublimity of the mountains, whose summits shoot down as deep in the abyss as they stand high in the air. As you turn your eyes from the landscape so faithfully pencilled on the sleeping waters, to see the substance of these shadows, the eye, dazzled with the radiance of the sunbeams playing on the perpetual snows in the regions of mid air, reposes with solace and delight on the deep blue of the sky that is seen between, undimmed except by the occasional passing of the bald eagle or falcon-hawks, sailing slowly from the summit of one mountain to another.

THE MARRIAGE OF BAPTISTE.

FROM THE SAME.

BAPTISTE, always a standing lover and gallant for all the undistinguished Indian girls of the nation, had been observed in earnest dialogue with T'selle'nee, or the *Piony*, the pretty daughter of Mon-son-sah, or the *Spotted Panther*, a proud and fierce Shienne warrior, who doted on this his only child. What injury or insult was offered the belle of round and vermillion rouged cheek, does not appear; but next morning it was the current gossip among the fair of the nation that T'selle'nce had had a "medicine dream." At any rate, she was reported to be in tears, shut up under the customary and severest interdiction of Indian usage. . . . There was a great trouble in the wigwam. The fierce father forced his daughter to confession. The smooth-tongued and voluble Canadian had vague intimations that this affair was likely to bring no good to him. Truth was, as a general lover, he had the reputation of being particularly slippery and unworthy of confidence. Various girls had made calculation upon him for a husband. But Baptiste had a manifest preference for being a general lover, and a specific aversion to matrimony in particular.

Whoever among this people has had a dream of sufficient import to cause the dreamer to wear black paint and to proclaim an interdict, becomes for the time a subject of universal speculation and remark. The general whisper, especially among the women, was, What has Baptiste done? and What has caused the interdict of T'selle'nee?

Mon-son-sah, meanwhile, was not idle. The deepest indignation of his burning spirit was called forth. The frequent amours and infidelities of Baptiste were circulated, and generally not at all to his advantage. An affair of his, touching a Shoshonee girl, was blazoned with many a minute circumstance of wanton cruelty. "What right," they said, "had the proud and babbling pale face to conduct after this fashion toward the red skin girls? They would learn him to repent such courses." The cunning young T'selle'nee, though interdicted, and of course supposed to be unable to see or converse with any one, was in fact at the bottom of all this.

The result of the long-brooded mischief was at length disclosed. Hatch was the envoy of Mon-son-sah to Baptiste Dettier, to make known to him the purposes that were settled in respect to his case. Hatch, Dutch though he was, enjoyed a comfortable broad joke. . . . Baptiste in passing heard him call to him to stop, with a pale face and palpitating heart. He seemed disposed to walk on.

"Will you stop, Mynheer Baptiste?" said the Dutchman, with a visage of mysterious importance: "Perhaps you will find it your interest to hear what I have to say to you."

"Vell, sare," said Baptiste, stopping and squaring himself, "suppose you tell me vat for you stop me from mine promenade. Is it von mighty dem big ting dat you hab to tell me?"

"Oh no, Mynheer Baptiste, it is no great matter. It only conzarns your life."

"Sacre! Monsieur Dutchman," cried Baptiste, shrugging and turning pale, "spose you tink it von mighty dem leet ting to concern my life. Monsieur Dutchman, vat for make you look so dem big? I pray you, sare, speak out vat for you stop me?"

The Dutchman continued to economize the luxury of his joke as long as possible, and proceeded in his customary dialect, and with the most perfect *sang froid*, to ask him if he had ever known such an Indian demoiselle as T'selle'nee?

"Sare, vat for you axe me dat? Tis mine own affair, sare!"

"Well, Baptiste, they say she has had a dream, and that her face is painted as black as a thunder cloud. It is common report that the matter closely concerns you. At any rate, the Spotted Panther is not to be trifled with, and he takes a deep interest in the business. You know the Spotted Panther?"

"Yes, sare, dat garçon is one dem farouche villain."

"Perhaps you like his daughter better?"

"Sacre! no. She is von dem—what you call him in Hinglees?"

"Never mind. She will make you the better wife for that. I have an errand to you from the Spotted Panther."

"You make me frissonne all over my body," said Baptiste, looking deadly pale.

"I have it in charge from the Spotted Panther to ask you, Baptiste, if you are disposed to marry T'selle'nee as soon as she is out of her black paint and her dream? They say she loves you to distraction."

"Sez bien," replied Baptiste, giving his wonted shrug of self-complacency; "so do twentee oder demoiselles of dese dem sauvages. Dut all for vat you stop me?"

"No. I am commissioned only to propose to you the simple question, Do you choose to marry T'selle'nee, or not? and you are to let me report an immediate answer."

"Parbleu! Monsieur Dutchman. Spose I say no?"

"You will hear the consequences, and then I will say him no, if you wish it."

"Vell, sare, vat are de big consequence if I say no? Tis von dem farouche affair, ca!"

"He proposes you one of two alternatives—to marry his daughter, or be roasted alive at a slow fire. It is no great matter, after all. The beautiful T'selle'nee, or a roasting, that's the alternative."

"Tis von dem—what you call him, alternateeve? O mon Dieu! Mon Dieu!" cried Baptiste, crossing himself, and seeming in an agony—"You dem Dutchman have no heart on your body, or you no tell me dat dem word, and half grin your teeth all the time, sacre! You call him leet matter to roast von Christian like a pig, sacre!"

"Why, certainly, you don't think it so great a thing to be roasted? You know, Baptiste, that

an Indian smokes his pipe, and sings songs, and tells stories, and provokes his roasters, and thinks it little more than a comfort to be roasted."

"O ciel!" cried the Canadian, apparently feeling faint at the horror of the idea. "You are von dem hard heart Dutchman, to make sport of dis farouche affair!"

"Still, Baptiste, something must be done. You know the Spotted Panther is not a personage to be trifled with. Have you made up your mind for your answer?"

"Tis von dem sommaire business, ca! O mon Dieu, aidez moi. Oui, oui. I vill marree dis dem crapeau. Spose—how like dem fool you talk!— that it be von leet ting to be roast? Certainment, me no make experimong."

"Very good," answered Hatch, with the same unmoved calmness. "Then we need not discuss the matter of roasting at all. I thought you would prefer the wife. But you will please tell me the very words I am to report to the Spotted Panther."

"O mon Dieu! Tis trop dur, a ting tres miserable. Me love all de demoiselles. Dey all love me. Tis ver.hard affair, to tie me up to von dem crapeau, like un chien in a string."

"Are these the words you wish me to carry back to the Spotted Panther?"

"No, certainment, no. You tell that sauvage gentilhomme, vid my best complimens, that I am trop sensible of de great honneur which his belle fille have don me. Spose his belle fille no say that word to me fuss, den I tell her I offer my love and my devotions and my heart wid von satisfaction infini, and dat I lead her to the altare with great plaisir, sacre!"

Hatch omitted the last word, and reported all the rest with great fidelity. The invincible solemnity of the Dutchman's narrative gave greater zest to the enjoyment of the Indians, who all knew, amidst these forced compliments, what a bitter pill matrimony was to such an indiscriminate gallant.

HEROISM OF THE INDIAN.
FROM THE ART OF BEING HAPPY.

THE timid and effeminate white man shivers and scarcely credits his senses, as he sees the young Indian warrior smoking his pipe, singing his songs, boasting of his victories and uttering his menaces, when enveloped in a slow fire, apparently as unmoved, as reckless, and unconscious of pain as if sitting at his ease in his own cabin. All that has been found necessary by this strange people to procure this heroism, is, that the children from boyhood should be constantly under a discipline, every part and every step of which tends directly to shame and contempt at the least manifestation of cowardice in view of any danger, or of a shrinking consciousness of pain in the endurance of any suffering. The males, so trained, never fail to evidence the fruit of their disciplin. Sentenced to death, they almost invariably scorn to fly from their sentence, when escape is in their power. If in debt, they desire a reprieve, that they may hunt until their debts are paid. They then voluntarily return and surrender themselves to the executioner. Nothing is more common than for a friend to propose to suffer for his friend, a parent for a child, or a child for a parent. When the sufferer receives the blow,· there is an unblenching look which manifests the presence of the same spirit that smokes with apparent unconcern amidst the crackling flames.

A proof that this is the fruit of training and not of native insensibility, as others have thought, and as I formerly thought myself, is, that this contempt of pain and death is considered a desirable trait only in the males. To fly like a woman, like her to laugh, and weep, and groan, are expressions of contempt, which they apply to their enemies with ineffable scorn. The females, almost excluded from witnessing the process of Spartan discipline by which the males acquire their mental hardihood, partake not of the fruits of it, and, with some few exceptions, are shrinking and timid like the children of civilization.

I know that there will not be wanting those who will condemn alike the training and the heroism as harsh, savage, unfeeling, stoical, and unworthy to be admitted as an adjunct to civilization. But no one will offer to deny that the primitive Christian put in conflict with a hungry lion, that Rogers at the Smithfield stake, that the young captive warrior, exulting and chanting his songs while enduring the bitterest agonies that man can inflict, in the serene and sublime triumph of mind over matter, and spirit over the body, is the most imposing spectacle we can witness, the clearest proof we can contemplate, that we have that within us which is not all of clay, nor all mortal; or doubt that these persons endure infinitely less physical pain, in consequence of their heroic self-possession, than they would have suffered had they met their torture in paroxysms of terror, shrinking, and self-abandonment.

THE MISSISSIPPI.
FROM HISTORY AND GEOGRAPHY OF MISSISSIPPI VALLEY.

Below the mouth of Ohio, in the season of inundation, to an observing spectator a very striking spectacle is presented. The river sweeps along, in curves or sections of circles, of an extent of from six to twelve miles, measured from point to point. The sheet of water that is visible between the forests on either side, is not far from the medial width of a mile. On a calm spring morning, and under a bright sun, this, to an eye that takes in its gentle descending, shines like a mass of burnished silver. Its edges are distinctly marked by a magnificent outline of cotton-wood trees, generally of great size, and at this time of the year of the brightest verdure. On the convex, or bar side of the bend, there is generally a vigorous growth of willows, or young cotton-wood trees of such astonishing regularity of appearance, that it always seems to the unpractised spectator a work of art. The water stands among these trees from ten to

fifteen feet in height. Those brilliant birds, the black and red bird of this country, seem to delight to flit among these young groves, that are inundated to half their height. Nature is carrying on her most vigorous efforts of vegetation below. If there be wind or storm, the descending flat and keel boats immediately make for these groves, and plunge fearlessly with all the headway they can command among the trees. Should they be of half the size of the human body, struck fifteen feet from the ground they readily bend, before even a frail boat. You descend the whole distance of a thousand miles to New Orleans, landing at night in fifteen feet water among the trees; but, probably, in no instance within twenty miles of the real shore, which is a bluff. The whole spectacle is that of a vast and magnificent forest emerging from a lake, with its waters, indeed in a thousand places, in descending motion. The experienced savage, or solitary voyager, paddles his canoe through the deep forests, from one bluff to the other. He finds bayous, by which one river communicates with the other. He moves perhaps along the Mississippi forest into the mouth of White river. He ascends that river a few miles, and by the Grand Cut off moves down the forest into the Arkansas. From that river he finds many bayous which communicate readily with Washita and Red river; and from that river, by some one of its hundred bayous, he finds his way into the Atchafalaya and the Teche; and by that stream to the Gulf of Mexico, reaching it more than twenty leagues west of the Mississippi. At that time, this is a river from thirty to an hundred miles wide, all overshadowed with forests, except an interior strip of little more than a mile in width, where the eye reposes on the open expanse of waters, visible between the trees. . . .

No person who descends this river for the first time, receives clear and adequate ideas of its grandeur, and the amount of water which it carries. If it be in the spring, when the river below the mouth of Ohio is generally over its banks, although the sheet of water that is making its way to the gulf is perhaps thirty miles wide, yet finding its way through deep forests and swamps that conceal all from the eye, no expanse of water is seen but the width, that is curved out between the outline of woods on either bank; and it seldom exceeds, and oftener falls short of a mile. But when he sees, in descending the falls of St. Anthony, that it swallows up one river after another, with mouths as wide as itself, without affecting its width at all; when he sees it receiving in succession the mighty Missouri, the broad Ohio, St. Francis, White, Arkansas, and Red rivers, all of them of great depth, length, and volume of water; swallowing up all and retaining a volume, apparently unchanged, he begins to estimate rightly the increasing depths of current that must roll on in its deep channel to the sea. Carried out of the Balize, and sailing with a good breeze for hours, he sees nothing on any side but the white and turbid waters of the Mississippi, long after he is out of sight of land

o

WILLIAM ELLERY CHANNING.

[Born 1780. Died 1842.]

THIS eminent man was born at Newport in Rhode Island on the seventh of April, 1780. His great-grandfather, John Channing, the first of the name who came to America, was a native of Dorsetshire in England; his grandfather, John Channing, was a merchant in Newport; and his father, William Channing, after graduating at Princeton College in 1767, became a lawyer, and was for many years Attorney General of Rhode Island. His mother, to whose piety, gentleness, and faithfulness he bore affectionate and grateful testimony, was a daughter of William Ellery, one of the signers of the Declaration of Independence, and afterward a member of Congress, and Chief Justice of his state. Through her he was descended from Anne Bradstreet, the wife of Governor Bradstreet and daughter of Governor Dudley, who two hundred years ago was styled by one of the most learned and distinguished of the Puritans "the mirror of her age, and glory of her sex."

In 1780 Newport was the residence of two of the most remarkable men who have ever lived in New England, the Reverend Doctor Hopkins, whose writings had so great an influence upon theological opinions in the last century, and the Reverend Doctor Stiles, famous for profound and various learning, and "virtues proportioned to his intellectual acquisitions," who was afterward President of Yale College. They were ministers of the two Congregational churches in the town, and though in many respects very different from each other, and representatives of rival parties, they were both friends of the Attorney General, and often at his house. Doctor Channing states that when a child he regarded Doctor Stiles with more reverence than any other human being, and to the influence of that extraordinary man in the circle in which he was brought up, he attributes a part of the indignation which he felt toward every invasion of human rights. He was also much attached to Doctor Hopkins, whom he used to see riding on horseback through the streets, "in a plaid gown fastened by a girdle round the waist, and with a study cap on his head," appearing like a man who had nothing to do with the world. In a sermon which he preached at Newport, when he was himself an old man, he presented an interesting picture of those peculiar and venerable persons, around whom clung so many recollections of his early life.

Washington Allston, who was but one year his senior, went to Newport in 1787, and contracted an intimacy with him which continued through youth, the strength of manhood, and old age. They roamed together through the picturesque scenery, which still attracts annual crowds of strangers, and "amid this glorious nature" received impressions of the great and beautiful which had an influence in determining their modes of thought and habits of life. Richard H. Dana, a cousin of Channing, and afterward a brother-in-law of Allston, in a few years wandered, an inspired boy, over the same fields, and on the rocky coast listened to the roar and dashing of the waters of that ocean, which he was to describe with such effect in his noble poetry. Allston, Channing, and Dana were thus connected in childhood. In old age they often visited, from their neighbouring homes in Boston, these scenes of their earliest inspiration. Two of them, in the order of their ages, have gone to the world in whose atmosphere they almost seemed to live while here among us.

Channing entered Harvard College when but fourteen years of age. Among his classmates here were the late Judge Story, and Doctor Tuckerman, with whom, until the death of that most amiable man—a period of forty-seven years—he lived as a brother, giving and receiving "thoughts, feelings, reproofs, encouragements, with a faithfulness not often surpassed." He had been through the customary range of study in the Latin and Greek authors before he went to Cambridge, and for a year or two he continued to exhibit a predilection for classical studies, but before the end of his term he became comparatively indifferent to them, and devoted his chief attention to moral philosophy, history, and general literature. His views of life were serious, his plans determined, and his studies were already made to bend in some degree to his prospective pursuits. Yet the highest honours of his class were awarded to him when he graduated, in 1798.

Soon after leaving Cambridge Channing became a private tutor in a family of Virginia, and went to reside in that state. His health hitherto had been remarkably good, but now it failed, and he was to the end of his life an invalid. After his return to Newport he pursued, without any professor or teacher to guide him, his studies in theology. When in the fulness of his years and fame he stood to instruct where in his youth he had been a learner, he reminded his hearers of this period in his life, in a manner equally graphic and beautiful: "I had two noble places of study," he said, "one the edifice now so frequented and useful as a public library, then so deserted that I spent day after day and sometimes week after week amidst its dusty volumes, without interruption from a single visiter;...the other, the beach,...my daily resort, dear to me in the sunshine, still more attractive in the storm. Seldom do I visit it now without thinking of the work, which there, in the sight of that beauty, in the sound of those waves, was carried on in my soul. No spot on earth has helped to form me so much as that beach. There I lifted up my voice in praise amid the tempest. There, softened by beauty, I poured out my thanksgiving and contrite confessions. There, in reverential sympathy with the mighty power around me, I became conscious of power within. There struggling thoughts and emotions broke forth, as if moved to utterance by nature's eloquence of the winds and waves. There began a happiness surpassing all worldly pleasures, all gifts of fortune: the happiness of communing with the works of God." Here is an index to his character. A mild, contemplative enthusiast, with a mind imbued with taste, and stored with the best learning, and an ardent desire that he might be useful, he went into the world, proposing to himself as his mission the elevation of men to his own kindness, serenity, and dignity, and the bringing of them into the same converse with nature and God.

Soon after he began to preach he received and accepted an invitation to become the pastor of the church in Federal street in Boston, and was ordained on the first of June, 1803. The congregation worshipping there was then small, but on this account the situation was preferred to another which was offered to him, for the slenderness and debility of his frame would not allow him to labour much as a parochial minister. His countenance was beautiful, his voice, always tremulous, was variably musical, and his articulation slow and distinct. His manner altogether was natural, persuasive, and earnest. He immediately became popular, and the increase of his society soon rendered necessary the erection of a new and larger place of worship. A visit to Europe much improved his health, and filled his mind and heart with new purposes. He retained his connection with the society until his death, though in 1824 a colleague was associated with him, and in 1840 he was relieved from the obligation of performing any public duties.

Doctor Channing's earliest publications were on controversial theology. His sermon on the Unitarian Belief, preached at the ordination of the Reverend Jared Sparks, in Baltimore, in 1819, is perhaps the most ingenious and polished of his dogmatical essays. It excited an extraordinary degree of attention, and several of the ablest Trinitarian writers in the country replied to it. In 1820 he printed in the Christian Disciple a paper on the same subject, entitled The Moral Argument against Calvinism. But though he continued to feel a deep interest in this and other religious controversies, they could not have been congenial to one who was so sensitively alive to the beautiful; and notwithstanding the reputation he acquired by these writings, he was by no means fitted by his intellectual constitution for a pursuit of which the main element is logic.

He was brought more directly into notice as a literary man by his essay on National Literature, published in 1823, and his Remarks on the Character and Writings of John Milton, which appeared in the Christian Examiner for 1826. This article was written very hastily, and somewhat unwillingly, to oblige a friend who felt an interest in the sale of an edition of Milton's Treatise on Christian Doctrine, then just published in Boston. On reading it in print he concluded not to avow himself its author, which he might well do, for however creditable it would have been to

160 WILLIAM ELLERY CHANNING.

a writer of inferior powers, it was below the level of his own, and had in it very little that was original or distinctive. It was supposed by his more judicious friends, who were not in the secret, to be an imitation of his style, by some clever young man of the university, and one, who has since become eminent as a clergyman, being accused of it, thought it worth while to advise Dr. Channing of his innocence, as he considered the essay a poor one. The surprise of the author at the reputation to which it attained was never concealed. It is but justice to him to state that his own estimate of it was perfectly proper. The Edinburgh reviewer's criticism of it was perhaps just, though it was not fair to judge of the merits of an author by one of his poorest works.

His Remarks on the Life and Character of Napoleon Bonaparte have not been assigned their proper rank among his writings. This article is more able than that on Milton; undoubtedly it was written with care, and contained his deliberately-formed opinions; but much of its celebrity was owing to adventitious circumstances, by which it cannot be sustained. Its merits are in its generalities: it has none as a delineation of the character of that great man, whose name, given to the winds at Toulon, became an undying sound. In the period of his captivity, men held their breath at the stupendous crime, but when he died, one universal hiss from all the quarters of the globe poured upon England, so that every cheek was flushed in the scorching breath of human indignation. An attack upon the victim was a cosmetic for the festering faces of the criminals, all the better for being imported from a nation that was deemed less friendly to Britain than to France. This state of feeling was the secret of the temporary success of Scott's libel on Bonaparte, and it occasioned the republication of Channing's essay in every conceivable form. The republican is a candid judge, it was said, and if his portraiture is correct, it was right to violate every law to rid the world of such a monster. This is Doctor Channing's position: he assumes that Napoleon was resolved to make the earth a slaughter-house, and to crush every will adverse to his own, and denies that against such a person mankind should proceed by written laws and precedents. This is a doctrine which sanctions almost every mob and massacre since the conspiracy against Christ, for

it makes men in all cases the judges of the necessity and justice of their own actions. It is one of the instances in which passion obtained a mastery over his usually serene understanding. He was too sagacious a man not to know that obedience is the first condition of freedom; that it is better for a nation to suffer any thing than to do injustice; that there can be no true liberty where the authority of the law, whether it be right or wrong, while it exists, is not superior to every other possible obligation, contingency, or conviction, except, were such a thing to be looked for, the direct and audible interfering voice of God. The essay is full of misrepresentation and invective, and we are constantly reminded in reading it that the author was labouring to make out a case for which he was sensible that he had inadequate materials.

In 1829 Doctor Channing published in the Christian Examiner his Remarks on the Character and Writings of Fenelon; a paper in which are developed with much ability some of his ethical views, particularly in reference to the dignity of human nature.

There is a perceptible and steady increase of strength and beauty in Doctor Channing's writings, and they are more profound, original, and characteristic, the more he gave himself up to his true mission, which was, not so much to dispute about systems of faith, as to bring acts, customs, and institutions to the standard of Christian morality, and in the spirit of a genuine philanthropy to advocate the cause of peace, gentleness, and righteousness. Of peace he was an early and persevering friend: in 1816 he published his first discourse on the subject; when there was danger of a rupture with France, in 1835, he again raised his voice in remonstrance; and in 1839, when there was a prospect of a conflict with Great Britain, in a lecture before the American Peace Society, he brought out fresh proofs of the insensibility of the mass of the community to the crimes and miseries of war, and the general want of Christian and philanthropic views in regard to this barbarous umpirage of right. He discussed the subject in all its bearings, with a faithfulness, earnestness, and power of illustration, which showed a warm personal sympathy and thorough acquaintance with it; and the extent to which his writings were read and remarked upon proved that they struck a responsive chord in the national heart.

He was also much interested in the plans for the suppression of intemperance, and disclosed the depths of its causes and the essential remedies which it demanded in a discourse which indicates a deep thoughtfulness upon our social relations and necessities, and a true apprehension of the general capacity for a higher range of duties and enjoyments. This was preliminary to, and should be considered with his two noblest productions,— those which bespeak most truly the nature of his ambition, and are likely, from the sagacity and rational views they display, and their rare adaptation to raise the mass of men from the degradation of mind and heart in which they are sunk, to be longest remembered. These are the Address on Self-Culture, delivered in Boston in the fall of 1838 as an introduction to a course of lectures attended chiefly by mechanics, and the Lectures on the Elevation of the Labouring Portion of the Community, delivered before an Apprentices' Library Association in that city in the winter of 1840. They are built upon the principles of the absolute essential equality of all men, and of the dignity of human nature, which makes all assumption of superiority on account of outward privileges a violation of the divine purposes, as well as an infringement of the fundamental law of our social organization. He was far from contending that the mass are competent to form just estimates of the great matters which have relation to their moral and material interests, without previous initiation and discipline; but demanded of society the encouragement to unfold and exercise, and of every individual the development and use, of the highest capacities. He claimed mutual respect, according to virtue, intelligence, and genius, without regard to any factitious distinctions of birth, wealth, or position. But however radical were his views on this subject, he was no leveller in the common acceptation of the term; he would take nothing from the high but their pride, reserve, and contempt, and nothing from the low but their envy, hatred, and jealousy. He would not elevate the labourer above his occupation, but in it; he would dignify the most humble pursuits, that are necessary to human happiness, and persuade their followers that if they had the will and the energy, there was nothing to prevent their elevation to the highest range of cultivation and enjoyment.

Doctor Channing was never a member of any of the anti-slavery societies, and is said to have doubted the wisdom of such associations but he was unhesitating and uncompromising in his opposition to slavery, and his tracts on the Annexation of Texas and the Duties of the Free States, and others of a similar purpose and spirit, with the book on Slavery which he published in 1841, had a more powerful influence on the question than any other writings that have been published in this country. The last public act of his life was an address delivered at Lenox in Massachusetts on the first of August, 1842, in commemoration of Emancipation in the British West Indies.

Doctor Channing's discourses on The Evidences of Revealed Religion, embracing a philosophical and perspicuous statement of the true principles upon which our belief in human testimony is regulated, are the most creditable of his writings of this description. Some of his sermons inculcating the practical duties of religion are of the first order of excellence. He had neither the learning nor the metaphysical power to be a great theologian. In one volume he claims for reason supremacy, and appeals to it as the last umpire; and in another derides the results of the most rigid induction as opposed to his own consciousness. Consciousness was the law of his belief. Logic was resorted to, reluctantly, for its defence: never for its formation. Let no one suppose that this excellence in "practical preaching" is to be lightly esteemed even in comparison with the far higher intellectual force of such men as Edwards. The theory of beauty which Edwards taught, Channing understood and appreciated, and the pure and ardent benevolence which it inculcated he practised. Whether his abstract notions were right or wrong, he really loved virtue "for its own beauty and sweetness," and was eminently successful in implanting a love of it in others. His mind, without being of the first, was of a very high order, his taste was elegant, but not faultless, and he is justly admired for his honesty and heroism. His works will undoubtedly fail to sustain his reputation as a thinker and man of letters.

Dr. Channing passed the last few years of his life in much privacy, at Boston in the winter and at Newport in the summer. He was seized with a typhus fever, while travelling, at Bennington, Vermont, where he died, on the second of October, 1842.

21

o 2

POETRY.

FROM AN ESSAY ON THE WRITINGS OF MILTON.

WE believe that poetry, far from injuring society, is one of the great instruments of its refinement and exaltation. It lifts the mind above ordinary life, gives it a respite from depressing cares, and awakens the consciousness of its affinity with what is pure and noble. In its legitimate and highest efforts, it has the same tendency and aim with Christianity; that is, to spiritualize our nature. True, poetry has been made the instrument of vice, the pander of bad passions; but, when genius thus stoops, it dims its fires and parts with much of its power; and, even when poetry is enslaved to licentiousness or misanthropy, she cannot wholly forget her true vocation. Strains of pure feeling, touches of tenderness, images of innocent happiness, sympathies with suffering virtue, bursts of scorn or indignation at the hollowness of the world, passages true to our moral nature, often escape in an immoral work, and show us how hard it is for a gifted spirit to divorce itself wholly from what is good. Poetry has a natural alliance with our best affections. It delights in the beauty and sublimity of the outward creation and of the soul. It indeed portrays, with terrible energy, the excesses of the passions; but they are passions which show a mighty nature, which are full of power, which command awe, and excite a deep though shuddering sympathy. Its great tendency and purpose is to carry the mind beyond and above the beaten, dusty, weary walks of ordinary life; to lift it into a purer element; and to breathe into it more profound and generous emotion. It reveals to us the loveliness of nature, brings back the freshness of early feeling, revives the relish of simple pleasures, keeps unquenched the enthusiasm which warmed the spring-time of our being, refines youthful love, strengthens our interest in human nature by vivid delineations of its tenderest and loftiest feelings, spreads our sympathies over all classes of society, knits us by new ties with universal being, and, through the brightness of its prophetic visions, helps faith to lay hold on the future life.

We are aware that it is objected to poetry, that it gives wrong views and excites false expectations of life, peoples the mind with shadows and illusions, and builds up imagination on the ruins of wisdom. That there is a wisdom against which poetry wars, the wisdom of the senses, which makes physical comfort and gratification the supreme good, and wealth the chief interest of life, we do not deny; nor do we deem it the least service which poetry renders to mankind, that it redeems them from the thraldom of this earthborn prudence. But, passing over this topic, we would observe, that the complaint against poetry, as abounding in illusion and deception, is in the main groundless. In many poems there is more of truth than in many histories and philosophic theories. The fictions of genius are often the vehicles of the sublimest verities, and its flashes often open new regions of thought, and throw new light on the mysteries of our being. In poetry, when the letter is falsehood, the spirit is often profoundest wisdom. And, if truth thus dwells in the boldest fictions of the poet, much more may it be expected in his delineations of life; for the present life, which is the first stage of the immortal mind, abounds in the materials of poetry, and it is the high office of the bard to detect this divine element among the grosser labours and pleasures of our earthly being. The present. life is not wholly prosaic, precise, tame, and finite. To the gifted eye it abounds in the poetic. The affections which spread beyond ourselves and stretch far into futurity; the workings of mighty passions, which seem to arm the soul with an almost superhuman energy; the innocent and irrepressible joy of infancy; the bloom, and buoyancy, and dazzling hopes of youth; the throbbings of the heart, when it first wakes to love and dreams of a happiness too vast for earth; woman, with her beauty, and grace, and gentleness, and fulness of feeling, and depth of affection, and blushes of purity, and the tones and looks which only a mother's heart can inspire;—these are all poetical. It is not true that the poet paints a life which does not exist. He only extracts and concentrates as it were life's ethereal essence, arrests and condenses its volatile fragrance, brings together its scattered beauties, and prolongs its more refined but evanescent joys. And in this he does well; for it is good to feel that life is not wholly usurped by cares for subsistence and physical gratifications, but admits, in measures which may be indefinitely enlarged, sentiments and delights worthy of a higher being. This power of poetry to refine our views of life and happiness, is more and more needed as society advances. It is needed to withstand the encroachments of heartless and artificial manners, which make civilization so tame and uninteresting. It is needed to counteract the tendency of physical science, which, being now sought, not, as formerly, for intellectual gratification, but for multiplying bodily comforts, requires a new development of imagination, taste, and poetry, to preserve men from sinking into an earthly, material, Epicurean life.

DANCING.

FROM AN ADDRESS ON TEMPERANCE.

DANCING is an amusement which has been discouraged in our country by many of the best people, and not without reason. Dancing is associated in their minds with balls; and this is one of the worst forms of social pleasure. The time consumed in preparation for a ball, the waste of thought upon it, the extravagance of dress, the late hours, the exhaustion of strength, the exposure of health, and the languor of the succeeding day,—these and other evils connected with this amusement are strong reasons for banishing it from the community. But dancing ought not therefore to be proscribed. On the contrary, balls should be discouraged for this among other reasons, that dancing, instead of being a rare pleasure, requiring elaborate preparation, may become an everyday amusement, and may mix with our common intercourse. This exercise is among the most healthful. The body as well as the mind feels its gladdening influence. No amusement seems more to have a foundation in our nature. The animation of youth overflows spontaneously in harmonious movements. The true idea of dancing entitles it to favour. Its end is to realize perfect grace in motion; and who does not know that a sense of the graceful is one of the higher faculties of our nature? It is to be desired, that dancing should become too common among us to be made the object of special preparation as in the ball; that members of the same family, when confined by unfavourable weather, should recur to it for exercise and exhilaration; that branches of the same family should enliven in this way their occasional meetings; that it should fill up an hour in all the assemblages for relaxation, in which the young form a part. It is to be desired that this accomplishment should be extended to the labouring classes of society, not only as an innocent pleasure, but as a means of improving the manners. Why shall not gracefulness be spread through the whole community? From the French nation we learn that a degree of grace and refinement of manners may pervade all classes. The philanthropist and Christian must desire to break down the partition walls between human beings in different conditions; and one means of doing this is, to remove the conscious awkwardness which confinement to laborious occupations is apt to induce. An accomplishment, giving free and graceful movement, though a far weaker bond than intellectual or moral culture, still does something to bring those who partake it, near each other.

THE THEATRE.
FROM THE SAME.

In its present state, the theatre deserves no encouragement. It is an accumulation of immoral influences. It has nourished intemperance and all vice. In saying this, I do not say that the amusement is radically, essentially evil. I can conceive of a theatre which would be the noblest of all amusements, and would take a high rank among the means of refining the taste and elevating the character of a people. The deep woes, the mighty and terrible passions, and the sublime emotions of tragedy, are fitted to thrill us with human sympathies, with profound interest in our nature, with a consciousness of what man can do and dare and suffer, with an awed feeling of the fearful mysteries of life. The soul of the spectator is stirred from its depths; and the lethargy in which so many live is roused, at least for a time, to some intenseness of thought and sensibility. The drama answers a high purpose, when it places us in the presence of the most solemn and striking events of human history, and lays

bare to us the human heart in its most powerful, appalling, glorious workings. But how little does the theatre accomplish its end? How often is it disgraced by monstrous distortions of human nature, and still more disgraced by profaneness, coarseness, indelicacy, low wit, such as no woman, worthy of the name, can hear without a blush, and no man can take pleasure in without self-degradation. Is it possible that a Christian and a refined people can resort to theatres, where exhibitions of dancing are given fit only for brothels, and where the most licentious class in the community throng unconcealed to tempt and destroy? That the theatre should be suffered to exist in its present degradation is a reproach to the community. Were it to fall, a better drama might spring up in its place. In the mean time, is there not an amusement, having an affinity with the drama, which might be usefully introduced among us? I mean Recitation. A work of genius, recited by a man of fine taste, enthusiasm, and powers of elocution, is a very pure and high gratification. Were this art cultivated and encouraged, great numbers, now insensible to the most beautiful compositions, might be waked up to their excellence and power. It is not easy to conceive of a more effectual way of spreading a refined taste through a community. The drama undoubtedly appeals more strongly to the passions than recitation; but the latter brings out the meaning of the author more. Shakspeare, worthily recited, would be better understood than on the stage. Then, in recitation, we escape the weariness of listening to poor performers, who, after all, fill up most of the time at the theatre. Recitation, sufficiently varied, so as to include pieces of chaste wit, as well as of pathos, beauty, and sublimity, is adapted to our present intellectual progress, as much as the drama falls below it. Should this exhibition be introduced among us successfully, the result would be, that the power of recitation would be extensively called forth, and this would be added to our social and domestic pleasures.

RELIGION AND PLEASURE.
FROM THE SAME.

To some, perhaps to many, religion and amusement seem mutually hostile, and he who pleads for the one may fall under suspicion of unfaithfulness to the other. But to fight against our nature is not to serve the cause of piety or sound morals. God, who gave us our nature, who has constituted body and mind incapable of continued effort, who has implanted a strong desire for recreation after labour, who has made us for smiles much more than for tears, who has made laughter the most contagious of all sounds, whose Son hallowed a marriage-feast by his presence and sympathy, who has sent the child fresh from his creating hand to develope its nature by active sports, and who has endowed both young and old with a keen susceptibility of enjoyment from wit and humour,— He who has thus formed us, cannot have intended us for a dull, monotonous life, and cannot frown on pleasures which solace our fatigue and refresh our spirits for coming toils. It is not only possible to reconcile amusement with duty, but to make it the means of more animated exertion, more faithful attachments, more grateful piety. True religion is at once authoritative and benign. It calls us to suffer, to die, rather than to swerve a hair's breadth from what God enjoins as right and good; but it teaches us that it is right and good, in ordinary circumstances, to unite relaxation with toil, to accept God's gifts with cheerfulness, and to lighten the heart, in the intervals of exertion, by social pleasures. A religion giving dark views of God, and infusing superstitious fear of innocent enjoyment, instead of aiding sober habits, will, by making men abject and sad, impair their moral force, and prepare them for intemperance as a refuge from depression or despair.

THE SENSE OF BEAUTY.
FROM SELF-CULTURE.

BEAUTY is an all-pervading presence. It unfolds in the numberless flowers of the spring. It waves in the branches of the trees and the green blades of grass. It haunts the depths of the earth and sea, and gleams out in the hues of the shell and the precious stone. And not only these minute objects, but the ocean, the mountains, the clouds, the heavens, the stars, the rising and setting sun, all overflow with beauty. The universe is its temple; and those men who are alive to it, cannot lift their eyes without feeling themselves encompassed with it on every side. Now this beauty is so precious, the enjoyments it gives are so refined and pure, so congenial with our tenderest and noble feelings, and so akin to worship, that it is painful to think of the multitude of men as living in the midst of it, and living almost as blind to it as if, instead of this fair earth and glorious sky, they were tenants of a dungeon. An infinite joy is lost to the world by the want of culture of this spiritual endowment. Suppose that I were to visit a cottage, and to see its walls lined with the choicest pictures of Raphael, and every spare nook filled with statues of the most exquisite workmanship, and that I were to learn that neither man, woman, nor child ever cast an eye at these miracles of art, how should I feel their privation; how should I want to open their eyes, and to help them to comprehend and feel the loveliness and grandeur which in vain courted their notice! But every husbandman is living in sight of the works of a diviner Artist; and how much would his existence be elevated, could he see the glory which shines forth in their forms, hues, proportions, and moral expression! I have spoken only of the beauty of nature, but how much of this mysterious charm is found in the elegant arts, and especially in literature! The best books have most beauty. The greatest truths are wronged if not linked with beauty, and they win their way most surely and deeply into the soul when arrayed in this their natural and fit attire. Now no man receives the true culture of a man, in whom the sensibility to the beautiful is not cherished; and I know of no condition in life from which it should be excluded. Of all luxuries this is the cheapest and most at hand; and it seems to me to be most important to those conditions, where coarse labour tends to give a grossness to the mind. From the diffusion of the sense of beauty in ancient Greece, and of the taste for music in modern Germany, we learn that the people at large may partake of refined gratifications, which have hitherto been thought to be necessarily restricted to a few.

BOOKS.
FROM THE SAME.

IT is chiefly through books that we enjoy intercourse with superior minds, and these invaluable means of communication are in the reach of all. In the best books great men talk to us, give us their most precious thoughts, and pour their souls into ours. God be thanked for books. They are the voices of the distant and the dead, and make us heirs of the spiritual life of past ages. Books are the true levellers. They give to all, who will faithfully use them, the society, the spiritual presence of the best and greatest of our race. No matter how poor I am. No matter though the prosperous of my own time will not enter my obscure dwelling. If the Sacred Writers will enter and take up their abode under my roof, if Milton will cross my threshold to sing to me of Paradise, and Shakspeare to open to me the worlds of imagination and the workings of the human heart, and Franklin to enrich me with his practical wisdom, I shall not pine for want of intellectual companionship, and I may become a cultivated man though excluded from what is called the best society in the place where I live.

THE BOOK OF BOOKS.
FROM THE MINISTRY FOR THE POOR.

THE poor might enjoy the most important advantages of the rich, had they the moral and religious cultivation consistent with their lot. Books find their way into every house, however mean; and especially that book which contains more nutriment for the intellect, imagination, and heart, than all others; I mean, of course, the Bible. And I am confident that among the poor are those who find in that one book more enjoyment, more awakening truth, more lofty and beautiful imagery, more culture to the whole soul, than thousands of the educated find in their general studies, and vastly more than millions among the rich find in that superficial, transitory literature which consumes all their reading hours.

SPIRITUAL FREEDOM.

FROM A DISCOURSE PREACHED AT THE ANNUAL ELECTION IN 1830.

I MAY be asked what I mean by "inward spiritual freedom?" The common and true answer is, that it is freedom from sin. I apprehend, however, that to many, if not to most, these words are too vague to convey a full and deep sense of the greatness of the blessing. Let me then offer a brief explanation; and the most important remark in illustrating this freedom is, that it is not a negative state, not the mere absence of sin; for such a freedom may be ascribed to inferior animals, or to children before becoming moral agents. Spiritual freedom is the attribute of a mind in which reason and conscience have begun to act, and which is free through its own energy, through fidelity to the truth, through resistance of temptation. I cannot therefore better give my views of spiritual freedom than by saying, that it is moral energy, or force of holy purpose, put forth against the senses, against the passions, against the world, and thus liberating the intellect, conscience, and will, so that they may act with strength and unfold themselves for ever. The essence of spiritual freedom is power. A man liberated from sensual lusts by palsy, would not therefore be inwardly free. He only is free who, through self-conflict and moral resolution, sustained by trust in God, subdues the passions which have debased him, and, escaping the thraldom of low objects, binds himself to pure and lofty ones. That mind alone is free, which, looking to God as the inspirer and rewarder of virtue, adopts his law, written on the heart and in his word, as its supreme rule, and which, in obedience to this, governs itself, reveres itself, exerts faithfully its best powers, and unfolds itself by well doing in whatever sphere God's providence assigns.

It has pleased the all-wise Disposer to encompass us from our birth with difficulty and allurement, to place us in a world where wrong doing is often gainful, and duty rough and perilous, where many voices oppose the dictates of the inward monitor, where the body presses as a weight on the mind, and matter, by its perpetual agency on the senses, becomes a barrier between us and the spiritual world. We are in the midst of influences which menace the intellect and heart, and to be free is to withstand and conquer these.

I call that mind free, which masters the senses, which protects itself against animal appetites, which contemns pleasure and pain in comparison with its own energy, which penetrates beneath the body and recognises its own reality and greatness, which passes life, not in asking what it shall eat or drink, but in hungering, thirsting, and seeking after righteousness.

I call that mind free, which escapes the bondage of matter, which, instead of stopping at the material universe and making it a prison-wall, passes beyond it to its Author, and finds, in the radiant signatures which it everywhere bears of the Infinite Spirit, helps to its own spiritual enlargement.

I call that mind free, which jealously guards its intellectual rights and powers, which calls no man master, which does not content itself with a passive or hereditary faith, which opens itself to light whencesoever it may come, which receives new truth as an angel from heaven, which, while consulting others, inquires still more of the oracle within itself, and uses instruction from abroad, not to supersede, but to quicken and exalt its own energies.

I call that mind free, which sets no bounds to its love, which is not imprisoned in itself or in a sect, which recognises in all human beings the image of God and the rights of his children, which delights in virtue and sympathizes with suffering wherever they are seen, which conquers pride, anger, and sloth, and offers itself up a willing victim to the cause of mankind.

I call that mind free, which is not passively framed by outward circumstances, which is not swept away by the torrents of events, which is not the creature of accidental impulse, but which bends events to its own improvement, and acts from an inward spring, from immutable principles which it has deliberately espoused.

I call that mind free, which protects itself against the usurpations of society, which does not cower to human opinion, which feels itself accountable to a higher tribunal than man's, which respects a higher law than fashion, which respects itself too much to be the slave or tool of the many or the few.

I call that mind free, which, through confidence in God, and in the power of virtue, has cast off all fear but that of wrong doing, which no menace or peril can enthral, which is calm in the midst of tumults, and possesses itself, though all else be lost.

I call that mind free, which resists the bondage of habit, which does not mechanically repeat itself and copy the past, which does not live on its old virtues, which does not enslave itself to precise rules, but which forgets what is behind, listens for new and higher monitions of conscience, and rejoices to pour itself forth in fresh and higher exertions.

I call that mind free, which is jealous of its own freedom, which guards itself from being merged in others, which guards its empire over itself as nobler than the empire of the world.

In fine, I call that mind free, which, conscious of its affinity with God, and confiding in his promises by Jesus Christ, devotes itself faithfully to the unfolding of all its powers, which passes the bounds of time and death, which hopes to advance for ever, and which finds inexhaustible power, both for action and suffering, in the prospect of immortality.

Such is the spiritual freedom which Christ came to give. It consists in moral force, in self-control, in the enlargement of thought and affection, and in the unrestrained action of our best powers. This is the great good of Christianity; nor can we conceive a greater within the gift of God.

FREEDOM.

FROM AN ESSAY ON NATIONAL LITERATURE.

THE question which we most solicitously ask about this country is, what race of men it is likely to produce. We consider its liberty of value only as far as it favours the growth of men. What is liberty? The removal of restraint from human powers. Its benefit is, that it opens new fields for action, and a wider range for the mind. The only freedom worth possessing is that which gives enlargement to a people's energy, intellect, and virtues. The savage makes his boast of freedom. But what is its worth? Free as he is, he continues for ages in the same ignorance, leads the same comfortless life, sees the same untamed wilderness spread around him. He is indeed free from what he calls the yoke of civil institutions. But other and worse chains bind him. The very privation of civil government is in effect a chain; for, by withholding protection from property, it virtually shackles the arm of industry, and forbids exertion for the melioration of his lot. Progress, the growth of power, is the end and boon of liberty; and, without this, a people may have the name, but want the substance and spirit of freedom.

PEACE.

FROM AN ESSAY ON THE WRITINGS OF FENELON.

THERE is a twofold peace. The first is negative. It is relief from disquiet and corroding care. It is repose after conflict and storms. But there is another and a higher peace, to which this is but the prelude, "a peace of God which passeth all understanding," and properly called "the kingdom of heaven within us." This state is any thing but negative. It is the highest and most strenuous action of the soul, but an entirely harmonious action, in which all our powers and affections are blended in a beautiful proportion, and sustain and perfect one another. It is more than silence after storms. It is as the concord of all melodious sounds. Has the reader never known a season when, in the fullest flow of thought and feeling, in the universal action of the soul, an inward calm, profound as midnight silence, yet bright as the still summer noon, full of joy, but unbroken by one throb of tumultuous passion, has been breathed through his spirit, and given him a glimpse and presage of the serenity of a happier world? Of this character is the peace of religion. It is a conscious harmony with God and the creation, an alliance of love with all beings, a sympathy with all that is pure and happy, a surrender of every separate will and interest, a participation of the spirit and life of the universe, an entire concord of purpose with its Infinite Original. This is peace, and the true happiness of man; and we think that human nature has never entirely lost sight of this its great end. It has always sighed for a repose, in which energy of thought and will might be tempered with an all-pervading tranquillity. We seem to discover aspirations after this good, a dim consciousness of it in all ages of the world. We think we see it in those systems of Oriental and Grecian philosophy, which proposed, as the consummation of present virtue, a release from all disquiet, and an intimate union and harmony with the Divine Mind. We even think that we trace this consciousness, this aspiration, in the works of ancient art which time has spared to us, in which the sculptor, aiming to imbody his deepest thoughts of human perfection, has joined with the fulness of life and strength, a repose which breathes into the spectator an admiration as calm as it is exalted. Man, we believe, never wholly loses the sentiment of his true good. There are yearnings, sighings which he does not himself comprehend, which break forth alike in his prosperous and adverse seasons, which betray a deep, indestructible faith in a good that he has not found, and which, in proportion as they grow distinct, rise to God and concentrate the soul in him, as at once its life and rest, the fountain at once of energy and of peace.

DEATH OF A TRUE WIFE.

FROM THE LIFE AND CHARACTER OF DR. TUCKERMAN.

HER reserve and shrinking delicacy threw a veil over her beautiful character. She was little known beyond her home; but there she silently spread around her that soft, pure light, the preciousness of which is never fully understood till it is quenched. Her calm, gentle wisdom, her sweet humility, her sympathy, which, though tender, was too serene to disturb her clear perceptions, fitted her to act instinctively, and without the consciousness of either party, on his more sanguine, ardent mind. She was truly a spirit of good, diffusing a tranquillizing influence too mildly to be thought of, and therefore more sure. The blow which took her from him left a wound which time could not heal. Had his strength been continued so that he could have gone from the house of mourning to the haunts of poverty, he would have escaped, for a good part of the day, the sense of his bereavement. But a few minutes' walk in the street now sent him wearied home. There the loving eye which had so long brightened at his entrance was to shed its mild beam on him no more. There the voice that had daily inquired into his labours, and like another conscience had whispered a sweet approval, was still. There the sympathy which had pressed with tender hand his aching head, and by its nursing care had postponed the hour of exhaustion and disease, was gone. He was not indeed left alone; for filial love and reverence spared no soothing offices; but these, though felt and spoken of as most precious, could not take the place of what had been removed. This great loss produced no burst of grief. It was a still, deep sorrow, the feeling of a mighty void, the last burden which the spirit can cast off. His attachment to life from this moment sensibly declined. In seasons of peculiar sensibility he wished to be gone. He kept near him the likeness of his departed friend, and spoke to me more than once of the solace which he had found in it....He heard her voice from another world, and his anticipations of that world, always strong, became now more vivid and touching

THE PRESENT AGE.

FROM AN ADDRESS DELIVERED IN PHILADELPHIA.

THE grand idea of humanity, of the importance of man as man, is spreading silently, but surely. . . . Even the most abject portions of society are visited by some dreams of a better condition for which they were designed. The grand doctrine, that every human being should have the means of self-culture, of progress in knowledge and virtue, of health, comfort, and happiness, of exercising the powers and affections of a man, this is slowly taking its place as the highest social truth. That the world was made for all, and not for a few; that society is to care for all; that no human being shall perish but through his own fault; that the great end of government is to spread a shield over the rights of all,—these propositions are growing into axioms, and the spirit of them is coming forth in all the departments of life. . . . ⸱

The Present Age! In these brief words what a world of thought is comprehended! what infinite movements! what joys and sorrows! what hope and despair! what faith and doubt! what silent grief and loud lament! what fierce conflicts and subtle schemes of policy! what private and public revolutions! In the period through which many of us have passed what thrones have been shaken! what hearts have bled! what millions have been butchered by their fellow-creatures! what hopes of philanthropy have been blighted! And at the same time what magnificent enterprises have been achieved! what new provinces won to science and art! what rights and liberties secured to nations! It is a privilege to have lived in an age so stirring, so pregnant, so eventful. It is an age never to be forgotten. Its voice of warning and encouragement is never to die. Its impression on history is indelible. Amidst its events, the American Revolution, the first distinct, solemn assertion of the rights of men, and the French Revolution, that volcanic force which shook the earth to its centre, are never to pass from men's minds. Over this age the night will indeed gather more and more as time rolls away; but in that night two forms will appear, Washington and Napoleon, the one a lurid meteor, the other a benign, serene, and undecaying star. Another American name will live in history, your Franklin; and the kite which brought lightning from heaven will be seen sailing in the clouds by remote posterity, when the city where he dwelt may be known only by its ruins. There is, however, something greater in the age than in its greatest men; it is the appearance of a new power in the world, the appearance of the multitude of men on that stage where as yet the few have acted their parts alone. This influence is to endure to the end of time. What more of the present is to survive? Perhaps much, of which we now take no note. The glory of an age is often hidden from itself. Perhaps some word has been spoken in our day which we have not deigned to hear, but which is to grow clearer and louder through all ages. Perhaps some silent thinker among us is at work in his closet whose name is to fill the earth. Perhaps there sleeps in his cradle some reformer who is to move the church and the world, who is to open a new era in history, who is to fire the human soul with new hope and new daring. What else is to survive the age? That which the age has little thought of, but which is living in us all; I mean the Soul, the Immortal Spirit. Of this all ages are the unfoldings, and it is greater than all. We must not feel, in the contemplation of the vast movements of our own and former times, as if we ourselves were nothing. I repeat it, we are greater than all. We are to survive our age, to comprehend it, and to pronounce its sentence. As yet, however, we are encompassed with darkness. The issues of our time how obscure! The future into which it opens who of us can foresee? To the Father of all Ages I commit this future with humble, yet courageous and unfaltering hope.

LITERATURE OF THE PRESENT AGE.

FROM THE DEMANDS OF THE AGE ON THE MINISTRY.

THE character of the age is stamped very strongly on its literary productions. Who, that can compare the present with the past, is not struck with the bold and earnest spirit of the literature of our times. It refuses to waste itself on trifles, or to minister to mere gratification. Almost all that is written has now some bearing on great interests of human nature. Fiction is no longer a mere amusement; but transcendent genius, accommodating itself to the character of the age, has seized upon this province of literature, and turned fiction from a toy into a mighty engine, and, under the light tale, is breathing through the community either its reverence for the old or its thirst for the new, communicates the spirit and lessons of history, unfolds the operations of religious and civil institutions, and defends or assails new theories of education or morals by exhibiting them in life and action. The poetry of the age is equally characteristic. It has a deeper and more impressive tone than comes to us from what has been called the Augustan age of English literature. The regular, elaborate, harmonious strains which delighted a former generation, are now accused, I say not how justly, of playing too much on the surface of nature and of the heart. Men want and demand a more thrilling note, a poetry which pierces beneath the exterior of life to the depths of the soul, and which lays open its mysterious workings, borrowing from the whole outward creation fresh images and correspondences with which to illuminate the secrets of the world within us. So keen is this appetite, that extravagancies of imagination, and gross violations both of taste and moral sentiment, are forgiven when conjoined with what awakens strong emotion; and unhappily the most stirring is the most popular poetry, even though it issue from the desolate soul of a misanthrope and a libertine, and exhale poison and death.

THE DISTINCTION OF RANKS.
FROM ESSAYS ON ELEVATION OF THE LABOURING CLASSES.

It is objected that the distinction of ranks is essential to social order, and that this will be swept away by calling forth energy of thought in all men. This objection, indeed, though exceedingly insisted on in Europe, has nearly died out here; but still enough of it lingers among us to deserve consideration. I reply, then, that it is a libel on social order to suppose that it requires for its support the reduction of the multitude of human beings to ignorance and servility; and that it is a libel on the Creator to suppose that he requires, as the foundation of communities, the systematic depression of the majority of his intelligent offspring. The supposition is too grossly unreasonable, too monstrous to require laboured refutation. I see no need of ranks, either for social order, or for any other purpose. A great variety of pursuits and conditions is indeed to be desired. Men ought to follow their genius, and to put forth their powers in every useful and lawful way. I do not ask for a monotonous world. We are far too monotonous now. The vassalage of fashion, which is a part of rank, prevents continually the free expansion of men's powers. Let us have the greatest diversity of occupations. But this does not imply that there is a need of splitting society into castes or ranks, or that a certain number should arrogate superiority, and stand apart from the rest of men as a separate race. Men may work in different departments of life, and yet recognise their brotherly relation, and honour one another, and hold friendly communion with one another. Undoubtedly, men will prefer as friends and common associates, those with whom they sympathize most. But this is not to form a rank or caste. For example, the intelligent seek out the intelligent; the pious those who reverence God. But suppose the intellectual and the religious to cut themselves off by some broad, visible distinction from the rest of society, to form a clan of their own, to refuse admission into their houses to people of inferior knowledge and virtue, and to diminish as far as possible the occasions of intercourse with them; would not society rise up as one man against this arrogant exclusiveness? And if intelligence and piety may not be the foundations of a caste, on what ground shall they, who have no distinction but wealth, superior costume, richer equipages, finer houses, draw lines around themselves and constitute themselves a higher class? That some should be richer than others is natural, and is necessary, and could only be prevented by gross violations of right. Leave men to the free use of their powers, and some will accumulate more than their neighbours. But to be prosperous is not to be superior, and should form no barrier between men. Wealth ought not to secure to the prosperous the slightest consideration. The only distinctions which should be recognised are those of the soul, of strong principle, of incorruptible integrity, of usefulness, of cultivated intellect, of fidelity in seeking for truth. A man, in proportion as he has these claims, should be honoured and welcomed everywhere. I see not why such a man, however coarsely if neatly dressed, should not be a respected guest in the most splendid mansions, and at the most brilliant meetings. A man is worth infinitely more than the saloons, and the costumes, and the show of the universe. He was made to tread all these beneath his feet. What an insult to humanity is the present deference to dress and upholstery, as if silkworms, and looms, and scissors, and needles could produce something nobler than a man! Every good man should protest against a caste founded on outward prosperity, because it exalts the outward above the inward, the material above the spiritual; because it springs from and cherishes a contemptible pride in superficial and transitory distinctions; because it alienates man from his brother, breaks the tie of common humanity, and breeds jealousy, scorn, and mutual ill-will. Can this be needed to social order?

CHRISTIANITY.
FROM THE EVIDENCES OF REVEALED RELIGION.

Since its introduction, human nature has made great progress, and society experienced great changes; and in this advanced condition of the world, Christianity, instead of losing its application and importance, is found to be more and more congenial and adapted to man's nature and wants. Men have outgrown the other institutions of that period when Christianity appeared, its philosophy, its modes of warfare, its policy, its public and private economy; but Christianity has never shrunk as intellect has opened, but has always kept in advance of men's faculties, and unfolded nobler views in proportion as they have ascended. The highest powers and affections which our nature has developed, find more than adequate objects in this religion. Christianity is indeed peculiarly fitted to the more improved stages of society, to the more delicate sensibilities of refined minds, and especially to that dissatisfaction with the present state, which always grows with the growth of our moral powers and affections. As men advance in civilization, they become susceptible of mental sufferings, to which ruder ages are strangers; and these Christianity is fitted to assuage. Imagination and intellect become more restless; and Christianity brings them tranquillity by the eternal and magnificent truths, the solemn and unbounded prospects which it unfolds. This fitness of our religion to more advanced stages of society than that in which it was introduced, to wants of human nature not then developed, seems to me very striking. The religion bears the marks of having come from a being who perfectly understood the human mind, and had power to provide for its progress. This feature of Christianity is of the nature of prophecy. It was an anticipation of future and distant ages, and, when we consider among whom our religion sprung, where, but in God, can we find an explanation of this peculiarity?

HENRY WHEATON.

[Born 1785. Died 1848.]

THIS eminent scholar and statesman is a native of Providence, Rhode Island. He graduated at Brown University in that city in 1802, and having been admitted to the bar, passed about two years in Europe, principally on the continent, where he acquired that fluency in the use of the French language, and that knowledge of the civil law, which have been so useful to him in his subsequent career. Soon after his return to America he took up his residence in the city of New York, where in the winter of 1812 he became editor of the National Advocate, at the head of which his name appeared the last time on the fifteenth of May, 1815. His experience as a journalist was during the stormy period of the war, when the best talents and soundest discretion were demanded in that responsible profession. The National Advocate was of the first class of journals for ability and decorum, and had much influence on public opinion and action.

It was about this time that Mr. Wheaton became one of the justices of the Marine Court, a tribunal of limited jurisdiction, which of late years has lost much of the consideration which attached to it in former times. It was in presiding here that Jones, Wells, and several of those who subsequently attained to the highest rank at the bar and on the bench of the superior courts of New York, passed some of the early years of their professional life.

In 1815 Mr. Wheaton published A Digest of the Law of Maritime Captures and Prizes, which may be regarded as in some respects the basis of his work on The Elements of International Law; and in 1820 he delivered before the New York Historical Society an address in which we see the germ of his history of this science. In 1824 he pronounced a discourse at the opening of the New York Athenæum, in which he took a rapid survey of what had been accomplished in American literature; and, pointing out the connection between the principles on which the ancient republics were founded and the rapid growth of the arts and sciences to which they gave encouragement—tracing analogies and causes in a manner which indicated deep reflection on the nature, spirit and tendencies of our government—presented an interesting view of the intellectual prospects of the country. In 1825 he published An Account of the Life, Writings and Speeches of William Pinkney, and in 1827 the last volume of his Reports of Cases Argued and Determined in the Supreme Court of the United States, which he had commenced in 1816.

Mr. Wheaton rose rapidly in the public estimation as a man of letters, as a statesman, and as a civilian. In 1819 he received the degree of Doctor of Laws from Harvard College, and in the following year the same distinction was conferred upon him by his own university. In 1821 he held a seat in the convention at Albany for revising the constitution of New York, and he was several years a prominent member of the legislature of that state. He was repeatedly looked to as a justice of the Supreme Court of the United States, and was so especially in the year 1823, on the death of Judge Livingston, when Judge Thompson was appointed to that office. In 1825 he was selected to be one of a commission to revise the laws of New York, but resigned this place in 1826 to accept that of Chargé d'Affaires to the Court of Denmark, then offered to him by President John Quincy Adams.

Before leaving the United States, in addition to his contributions to the daily press, while editor of the Advocate, and the publication of his Treatise on Captures, and his Reports, and Addresses, he had written largely for the North American Review, and edited several foreign law books, adding numerous and valuable notes, adapting them to the use of the legal profession in this country.

Soon after the commencement of his residence at Copenhagen, availing himself of leisure from his diplomatic duties, Mr. Wheaton entered heartily upon historical and literary studies, the first fruit of which was a His-

tory of the Northmen, or Danes and Nor-
mans, from the Earliest Times to the Conquest of England by William of Normandy,
published in London in 1831. As a specimen of historical composition this work has
slight pretensions; but it is interesting as a
series of sketches of the ancient mythology,
chivalry, literature and manners of a remarkable people, of whom little had been written
in the English language. In 1838 he united
with Mr. Crichton of Edinburgh, in writing
a work under the title of Scandinavia, embracing the ancient and modern history of
Denmark, Sweden and Norway, with an account of the geographical features of these
countries, and information respecting the superstitions, customs, and institutions of their
inhabitants; and aided by the materials brought
together for this purpose, and especially by
the Antiquitates Americanæ of Professor Rafn,
he enlarged and very much improved his History of the Northmen, which was then translated into French and published in an octavo
volume of nearly six hundred pages in Paris.*

In 1834 he was transferred by President
Jackson to Prussia, and on the election of Mr.
Van Buren to the presidency was promoted to
the rank of Minister Plenipotentiary at the
court of Berlin.

In 1836 Mr. Wheaton published his most
important work, his Elements of International
Law, which, in a much enlarged form, was reprinted by Messrs. Lea and Blanchard of Philadelphia in 1846. This was the first work
of any importance upon the principles of the
jurisprudence of nations in our language. It
is divided into four parts, which treat respectively of the sources and objects of international law, of the absolute international rights
of states, of the international rights of states in
their pacific relations, and of the international
rights of states in their hostile relations. An
analysis of this treatise is not within the
scope of the present sketch of Mr. Wheaton's
labours. It is founded upon the best preceding works on the subject, particularly the
Précis du Droit des Gens Moderne de l'Europe
and *Cours Diplomatique* of G. F. Martens, and
Klüber's *Droit des Gens Moderne de l'Europe*;

but the author makes large additions, and
infuses into the whole the liberal spirit which
prevails in the institutions and government of
his own country. Connected in its best days
with the highest tribunal of the United States,
the province of which is not only to expound
constitutional and municipal law, but to interpret treaty obligations and the laws of nations,
and subsequently long employed in diplomatic
services, his whole experience seems to have
been a preparation for writing such a work,
and the ability, learning and candour which
characterize the entire performance leave little
or nothing in respect to it to be desired.

Mr. Wheaton's History of the Law of Nations in Europe and America from the Earliest
Times to the Treaty of Washington, appeared
originally in French, at Leipsic, in 1841, under the title of *Histoire du Progrès du Droit
des Gens en Europe depuis la Paix de Westphalie jusqu'au Congrès de Vienne, avec un précis
historique du Droit des Gens Européen avant la
Paix de Westphalie*, in answer to a prize question proposed by the Academy of Moral and
Political Sciences of the Institute of France.
It was much augmented by the author, and
published in the English language in an octavo volume of eight hundred pages in New
York in 1845. The nature of this elaborate
and learned work is sufficiently indicated by
its title. Of its great merits all competent
critics have given the same testimony.*

During the discussion growing out of the
right of *visit* claimed by England on the coast
of Africa, Mr. Wheaton published an Inquiry
into the Validity of the Right of Visitation
and Search. Many of his despatches, particularly those which relate to the negotiations
in Denmark terminating with the treaty of
indemnity for spoliations on our commerce
during the European wars, and the recent discussions at Berlin as to the Zoll Verein treaty,
will be found in the diplomatic papers published by Congress.

Besides the writings of Mr. Wheaton which
have been mentioned, are a series of letters,

---

* *Histoire des Peuples du Nord, ou des Danois et des Nor-
mands, depuis les Temps les plus reculés jusqu'à la Conquête
de l'Angleterre. Par Henri Wheaton. Edition revue et aug-
mentée per l'Auteur, avec Cartes, Inscriptions, et Alphabet
Runiques, etc. Traduit de l'Anglois, par Paul Guillot.*

* That eminent jurist and political economist, Professor Senior, in an article which he wrote for the 156th
number of the Edinburgh Review, on the appearance of
the French version of this work, declares that few men
are better qualified to write the history of the law of
nations than Mr. Wheaton; that whatever may be the
defects of his work, he "has made as much as was to
be made of his materials;" and that it is "an excellent
supplement to his great work on International Law."

upon subjects connected with economy, literature and art, addressed within a few years to the secretary of the National Institution at Washington, and published in the National Intelligencer of that city. They are honourable exhibitions of his taste, research, and erudition.

He is a corresponding member of the Institute of France, and of several other distinguished scientific and literary societies abroad, and is held in the highest respect by the scholars and statesmen of all countries.

On the twenty-second of July, 1846, Mr. Wheaton had his final audience with the King of Prussia, having been recalled by President Polk; and, after a short residence at Paris, he returned to the United States.

—Since these pages were first published, Mr. Wheaton has been added to the company of our illustrious dead. He died suddenly on the eleventh of March, 1848, at Roxbury, near Boston, having taken up his residence there with a view to enter upon the professorship of International Law, in Harvard College, to which he had a short time previously been elected.

SCANDINAVIAN MANNERS.
FROM THE HISTORY OF THE NORTHMEN.

RELIGION had its influence in promoting this spirit of adventurous enterprise. That professed by the people of the north bore the impress of a wild and audacious spirit, such as, according to tradition, marked the character of its founder. Whatever distinction of sects may have existed among the Northern pagans, and however various the objects of their worship, the favourite god of the Vikingar was a Mars and a Moloch. The religion of Odin stimulated the desire of martial renown and the thirst of blood, by promising the joys of Valhall as the reward of those who fell gloriously in battle. His ministering spirits, the Valkyrur, hovered over the bloody field, watched the fortune of battle, and snatching the souls of those who were doomed to fall, bore them away to the blissful presence of the god of war. Those who adhered to the more ancient deities of the North, or rejected indiscriminately all the national objects of religious worship, were animated by a still wilder and more lawless spirit. Some of these chieftains carried their audacity so far as to defy the gods themselves.

Their national freedom, and that proud and independent bearing which always marks the barbarian character, contributed to swell this lofty spirit, which was always fomented by the songs extemporized or recited by the Skalds in praise of martial renown, or the glorious exploits of their ancestors. The kings and other chieftains were surrounded by champions who were devoted to their fortunes, and dependent upon their favour for advancement. These warriors were sometimes seized with a sort of phrensy—a *furor Martis*,—produced by their excited imaginations dwelling upon the images of war and glory,—and perhaps increased by those potations of stimulating liquors, in which the people of the north, like other uncivilized tribes, indulged to great excess. When this madness was upon them, these Orlandos committed the wildest extravagancies, attacked indiscriminately friends and foes, and even waged war against inanimate nature—the rocks and trees. At other times, they defied each other to mortal combat in some lonely and desert isle. The ancient language of the north had a particular term appropriated to distinguish the champions who were subject to this species of martial insanity. They were called *Eersærker*, and the name occurs so frequently in the Sagas, that we must conclude that this disease prevailed generally among the Vikingar, who passed their lives in roving the seas in search of spoil and adventures.

Even the female sex did not escape this widespread contagion of martial fury, and the love of wild and perilous adventure. Women of illustrious birth sometimes became pirates and roved the seas. More frequently, however, they shared the toils and dangers of land-battles. These Amazons were called *Skjöld-meyar*, or virgins of the shield. The romantic Sagas are filled with the most striking traits of their heroic bearing. In the Völsunga-saga we have the romantic tale of Alfhilda, daughter of Sigurdr, king of the Ostrogoths, who was chaste, brave, and fair. She was always veiled from the gaze of vulgar curiosity, and lived in a secluded bower, where she was guarded by two champions of prodigious strength and valour. Sigurdr had proclaimed that whoever aspired to his daughter's hand, must vanquish the two gigantic champions,—his own life to be the forfeit if he failed in the perilous enterprise. Alf, a young sea-king, who had already signalized himself by his heroic exploits, encountered and slew the two champions; but Alfhilda herself was not disposed to surrender tamely. She boldly put to sea with her female companions, all clothed, like herself, in male attire, and completely armed for war. They fell in with a fleet of Vikingar, who having just lost their chieftain, elected the intrepid heroine for his successor. She continued thus to rove the Baltic sea, at the head of this band of pirates, until the wide-spread fame of her exploits came to the ear of Alf, her suitor, who gave chase to her squadron, and pursued it into the Gulf of Finland. The brave Alfhilda gave battle. Alf boarded the bark of the princess, who made a gallant and obstinate resistance, until her helmet being cloven open by one of his champions, disclosed to their astonished view the fair face and lovely locks of his coy mistress, who, being thus vanquished by her magnanimous lover, no longer refuses him the hand he had sought, whilst his gallant champion espouses one of her fair companions.

JOHN CALDWELL CALHOUN.

[Born 1782. D ed 1850.]

JOHN CALDWELL CALHOUN was born in Abbeville, South Carolina, on the eighteenth of March, 1782. His grandfather, who had emigrated from Ireland to Pennsylvania in 1733, was one of the first settlers of that district, and his father, a man of ability and daring energy of character, represented it in the colonial and state legislatures more than thirty years.

In his thirteenth year, Mr. Calhoun was placed at an academy in Georgia, of which Mr. Waddell, a Presbyterian clergyman who had married his sister, was principal. But the death of his father, in 1796, caused an interruption of his studies, which were not resumed until he was nearly nineteen years of age. Having determined to be a planter, he had abandoned all thoughts of a classical education; but an elder brother at this period persuaded him to pursue one of the liberal professions, and he entered so earnestly upon the business of preparation, that within two years from his commencement of the Latin grammar he was received into the junior class of Yale College. It is related that after an animated controversy with the student, which arose during a class recitation from Paley, the eminent head of the college remarked to a friend that "the young man had talents enough to be President of the United States, and would one day attain to that station." The aim of his ambition was shown in the selection of his commencement thesis, which was, "The qualifications necessary to constitute a perfect statesman." He graduated in September, 1804, and immediately began the study of the law, in the well-known school of Litchfield, where he remained nearly two years. He afterward passed several months in the office of the Chancellor De Saussure in Charleston, and was admitted to the bar in Abbeville in 1807. He at once took a high rank in the courts, and in 1809 was elected by a large majority 'o the state legislature, where he so distinguished himself that at the end of his second session he was transferred to the national House of Representatives, in which he made his first appearance in the autumn of 1811.

From this time Mr. Calhoun's history is so closely identified with that of political controversies, of which no intelligible account can be given in the limits which I here prescribe to myself, that I shall do little more than mention the periods during which he has held the various high offices to which he has been called under different administrations.

From his entrance into the House of Representatives until 1817, when he was made Secretary of War, he was the acknowledged leader and most powerful champion of the democratic party in that body, though in this period the supporter of a protective tariff and of a national bank. His services in the War Department during the eight years of Mr. Monroe's administration are universally admitted to have been of vast importance to the country, and the estimation in which they were held at the time is shown in the large majority by which he was chosen Vice President in the celebrated contest of 1824, when there was no choice by the people of President. He was again elected Vice President in 1828, but a rupture occurring between himself and General Jackson, he was thrown into the ranks of the opposition; and South Carolina soon after declaring the tariff law of that year unconstitutional, and threatening forcible resistance of its execution, he resigned the vice presidency to accept a place on the floor of the Senate as the special apologist and vindicator of his state in that memorable crisis of its affairs. His speeches on the Force Bill, on the Federative Principle of the Constitution, and on the Removal of the Deposits, in the sessions of 1833 and 1834, are among the most earnest, able, and characteristic that he has made since his first appearance in Congress. He remained in the Senate until the death of Mr. Secretary Upshur in 1844, when he accepted the place of that gentleman in the Department of State, which he held until the close of Mr. Tyler's administration. For the first time in many years he was without office, but he was soon called from his retirement to resume his place in the Senate, where he appeared immediately after the great southern and western convention at Memphis, of which he was president, near the close of 1845.

A collection of Mr. Calhoun's speeches from 1811 to 1843 was published in New York in 1844. It is incomplete, but perhaps contains every thing he had written in illustration or defence of the principles he held at the time of its appearance. His subsequent speeches and reports, especially his speech on the Oregon question and report on the memorial of the Memphis Convention, are not inferior in terseness and clearness of expression, or in argumentative power, to any of his earlier productions.

The doctrines for the defence of which he is chiefly distinguished are those of free trade and the sovereignty of the individual states. He holds that the union is a league for special purposes between the governments, and not between the people, of the states which "acceded" to the Constitution, and that under certain contingencies each state may decide and act for itself upon the laws of Congress, and, holding them unconstitutional, may oppose its own force to their execution. But "state rights are no more!" he exclaims in his speech on the removal of the deposits: "The bill which vested in the central government the privilege of judging of the extent of its powers, and authorized it to enforce its judgments by the sword, prostrated the states as helpless corporations at its feet." And since the defeat of his party on this question he has generally acted with the one under whose auspices he first came into Congress.

It has been stated that he has devoted his leisure for several years to the composition of a work on the Principles of Government, in which his peculiar views will be more methodically defined and vindicated.

Mr. Calhoun is in many respects one of the most extraordinary men of the nineteenth century, and is undoubtedly one of the few for whom this period will be memorable in after times. His eloquence is altogether unlike that which is supposed to belong to a new country, or to a democracy, which is the eloquence of passion. Its power is from an excessive refinement and compactness of reason, which requires the perfect submission of the mind, and carries it forward with irresistible force; and its glow from the vehement energy and rapidity with which his argument is conducted. In his intellectual constitution

he more than any other statesman resembles Jonathan Edwards. His mind has the same quickness of perception, subtle sharpness of discrimination, and comprehensive grasp. He has the same sincerity of conviction, fervour of tone, and heartiness of purpose. One of the differences between him and Edwards is in the manner of approaching a point of controversy. The great divine who gave to metaphysics so much of the exactness and certainty of mathematics, assailed the central proposition of his antagonist cautiously, and by various trains of reasoning, each of which seemed conclusive, but all of which, starting at different points and ending in the same result, were overwhelming. Mr. Calhoun, on the contrary, fixes his eye at once upon the essential issue, and upon this expends his whole force; and his clear and skilful analysis and rapid generalization are not unworthy of that great master of logic, to whom in perspicuousness of arrangement and in the hard polish of his diction he is frequently superior.

In the Senate Mr. Calhoun's countenance is always serious.

Deep on his front engraven
Deliberation sits and public care.

It has been said that when speaking here he has no action and exhibits no emotion. This may be true, generally, but it is not so always. He was very much excited during the remarkable scene of the declaration of war against Mexico in a preamble to a bill of supplies. I sat near him during one of his speeches on that occasion. He stood erect and motionless at first, but as he proceeded his head turned from side to side, and his eyes glowed, and his words came fast and faster, and when he declared with vehement earnestness of tone that he would sooner stab himself to the heart than vote for that lying clause, he flung the back of his skeletonlike hand upon the desk before him with such energy, that men looked from all parts of the hall as if to see whether it had not been shattered to atoms by the blow. Yet this is not often his manner. He speaks rapidly indeed, but calmly, with the most judicious emphasis, and with perfect distinctness.

—Mr. Calhoun died in Washington on the thirty-first day of March, 1850; in what seemed the most important period of his political life; reverenced for wisdom by his party, and for virtue by all the nation.

P 2

ECONOMY AND HONOUR.

FROM A SPEECH IN REPLY TO JOHN RANDOLPH, IN 1811.

IF taxes should become necessary, I do not hesitate to say the people will pay cheerfully. It is for their government and their cause, and it would be their interest and duty to pay. But it may be, and I believe was said, that the people will not pay taxes, because the rights violated are not worth defending, or that the defence will cost more than the gain. Sir, I here enter my solemn protest against this low and "calculating avarice" entering this hall of legislation. It is only fit for shops and counting-houses, and ought not to disgrace the seat of power by its squalid aspect. Whenever it touches sovereign power, the nation is ruined. It is too short-sighted to defend itself. It is a compromising spirit, always ready to yield a part to save the residue. It is too timid to have in itself the laws of self-preservation. It is never safe but under the shield of honour. There is, sir, one principle necessary to make us a great people—to produce, not the form, but real spirit of union, and that is to protect every citizen in the lawful pursuit of his business. He will then feel that he is backed by the government—that its arm is his arm. He then will rejoice in its increased strength and prosperity. Protection and patriotism are reciprocal. This is the way which has led nations to greatness. Sir, I am not versed in this calculating policy, and will not, therefore, pretend to estimate in dollars and cents the value of national independence. I cannot measure in shillings and pence the misery, the stripes, and the slavery of our impressed seamen; not even the value of our shipping, commercial and agricultural losses, under the orders in council and the British system of blockade. In thus expressing myself, I do not intend to condemn any prudent estimate of the means of a country before it enters on a war. That is wisdom, the other folly.

REBELLION AND REVOLUTION.

FROM A SPEECH ON THE BILL FOR THE ADMISSION OF MICHIGAN INTO THE UNION.

I SHALL resist all encroachments on the Constitution, whether it be the encroachment of this government on the states, or the opposite—the executive on Congress, or Congress on the executive. My creed is to hold both governments, and all the departments of each, to their proper sphere, and to maintain the authority of the laws and the Constitution against all revolutionary movements. I believe the means which our system furnishes to preserve itself are ample, if fairly understood and applied; and I shall resort to them, however corrupt and disordered the times, so long as there is hope of reforming the government. The result is in the hands of the Disposer of events. It is my part to do my duty. Yet, while I thus openly avow myself a conservative, God forbid I should ever deny the glorious right of rebellion and revolution. Should corruption and oppression become intolerable, and cannot otherwise be thrown off—if liberty must perish, or the government be overthrown, I would not hesitate, at the hazard of life, to resort to revolution, and to tear down a corrupt government, that could neither be reformed nor borne by freemen; but I trust in God things will never come to that pass. I trust never to see such fearful times; for fearful indeed they would be if they should ever befall us. It is the last remedy, and not to be thought of till common sense and the voice of mankind would justify the resort.

FORMATION OF THE CONSTITUTION.

FROM A SPEECH ON THE FORCE BILL.

THERE never existed an example before of a free community spreading over such an extent of territory; and the ablest and profoundest thinkers, at the time, believed it to be utterly impracticable that there should be. Yet this difficult problem was solved—successfully solved, by the wise and sagacious men who framed our Constitution. No: it was above unaided human wisdom—above the sagacity of the most enlightened. It was the result of a fortunate combination of circumstances co-operating and leading the way to its formation; directed by that kind Providence which has so often and so signally disposed events in our favour.

THE OLD PARTIES.

FROM THE SAME.

I AVAIL myself of the occasion to avow my high respect for both of the great parties which divided the country in its early history. They were both eminently honest and patriotic, and the preference which each gave to its respective views resulted from a zealous attachment to the public interest. At that early period, before there was any experience as to the operation of the system, it is not surprising that one should believe that the danger was a tendency to anarchy, while the other believed it to be towards despotism, and that these different theoretical views should honestly have a decided influence on their public conduct.

THE DANGER OF SUBSERVIENCY.

FROM A SPEECH ON THE PUBLIC DEPOSITS.

PIRACY, robbery, and violence of every description may, as history proves, be followed by virtue, patriotism, and national greatness; but where is the example to be found of a degenerate, corrupt, and subservient people, who have ever recovered their virtue and patriotism? Their doom has ever been the lowest state of wretchedness and misery: scorned, trodden down, and obliterated for ever from the list of nations. May Heaven grant that such may never be our doom!

DANIEL WEBSTER.

[Born 1782. Died 1852.]

A NOTICE of the great statesman of the south is naturally followed by one of the illustrious New Englander who sat opposite to him in the senate, and who from their first entrance into Congress had been his most powerful and most constant antagonist. Daniel Webster and John Caldwell Calhoun were born in the same year. One was the son of a respectable northern farmer, who emigrated into New Hampshire when it was a wilderness, and served as an officer in the old French war and the Revolution; and the other of a southern planter, of similar circumstances, who was a pioneer in the forests of Carolina, and, with the same rank, fought the Cherokees and the British. The fathers of both, after distinguishing themselves in the field, were called to honourable civil stations, but they continued to be cultivators of the soil, and their sons, after partially acquiring their education, decided to follow their inherited occupations, and passed some three years in the quiet pursuits of agriculture. What changed the purpose of Webster is unknown, but Calhoun was led to study his profession by the just appreciation of an elder brother. When Christopher Gore presented his pupil, young Daniel Webster, for admission to the bar of Boston, he ventured a prediction of his future eminence, which all his present fame has not more than fulfilled ; and Doctor Dwight, about the same time, at the close of a class examination at Yale College, foretold that his southern student, John Caldwell Calhoun, would one day be President of the United States. For a while, they lingered about the northern and southern horizons, and then simultaneously shot up into mid-heaven, with a steady, but different lustre, to fix the gaze, not of their admiring countrymen only, but of mankind. Whatever may now or hereafter be the estimation in which any man or men engaged in our public affairs may be held, Daniel Webster and John Caldwell Calhoun will continue to be regarded as the representatives of the genius and of the leading opinions in political philosophy, held by the northern and southern states of the confederacy in the first half of the nineteenth century.

Mr. Webster was born in Salisbury, a rural town on the headwaters of the Merrimack river, in New Hampshire, in 1782, and after an imperfect preparation, in the common schools, entered Dartmouth College, where he was graduated when about twenty years of age. He soon after turned his attention to the law, but the necessity of exerting himself for his support interrupted and finally induced the abandonment of his studies. The pursuit of business however led him to Boston, and while there into the office of Mr. Gore, who discerned his genius, cultivated his acquaintance, and became his instructor. Here he finished the study of his profession, and was admitted an attorney and counsellor, in 1805. He then opened an office at Boscowen, a small village near his birthplace, but in 1807 removed to Portsmouth, where a larger field was opened to him, and there, in constant competition with the best lawyers of New Hampshire, he rose rapidly until he was acknowledged to be second to no one at the bar in the state.

Among the earliest, perhaps the first of all Mr. Webster's published writings, was an oration " delivered before the Federal gentlemen of Concord and its vicinity" on the fourth of July, 1806. He was then but twenty-four years of age, and the performance is interesting for its subject and its style. He discusses the question whether it be possible to *preserve the Constitution.* He saw thus early the dangers to which it was exposed, and enlisted for life in its defence.

Soon after the declaration of war, in 1812, he was elected a member of the national House of Representatives, in which, during four sessions, he greatly distinguished himself by his eloquence, extensive knowledge, and independent action. Although opposed to the war, he advocated such measures as were essential to the honour and safety of the country, and particularly an increase of the Navy. "Even our party divisions cease at the water's edge," he said : "They are lost in attachment to the national character, where that character is made respectable." We were contending on land for maritime rights. "In time," he continued,

175

"you may be enabled to redress injuries in the places where they are offered, and, if need be to accompany your own flag throughout the world with the protection of your own cannon." But his most important services in this period were rendered to the finances. In 1815 a bill had passed the Senate and was expected to pass the House, for the establishment of a bank, with a capital of fifty millions, nine tenths of which were to consist of depreciated government securities, and it was owing principally to his efforts that it was defeated. In the following year he introduced and secured the adoption of a resolution requiring the payment of revenue in specie or convertible paper. When he retired from Congress, in 1817, his course on these questions had secured to him the reputation of being one of the most practical and sagacious statesmen of the country.

He now removed to Boston, and for five years, except during the period in which he held a seat in the convention for revising the Constitution of Massachusetts, devoted himself exclusively and assiduously to his profession. A few masterly arguments in the Supreme Court confirmed in the general judgment the opinion of his friends, that as a lawyer he had no superior in the United States.

In this time Mr. Webster wrote several articles for the North American Review.* And on the twenty-second of December, 1820, the second centennial anniversary of the landing of the Pilgrims, he delivered at Plymouth his splendid oration on the first settlement of New England; on the seventeenth of June, 1825, fifty years after the battle, his address at the laying of the corner-stone of the Bunker Hill Monument; and on the second of August, 1826, in Faneuil Hall, his Discourse in commemoration of the Lives and Services of Adams and Jefferson.

In December, 1823, Mr. Webster again took his seat in the House of Representatives, and in the following month delivered his celebrated speech in behalf of the Greeks. He remained in the House until 1827, distinguishing himself by his speeches on the Panama mission, the tariff, and internal improvements, and by preparing and securing the passage of the Crimes Act, of 1825.

In 1826 he was elected almost unanimously to represent the city of Boston in the House

* With others, that on the Battle of Bunker Hill, in 1818, and that on the Laws of Debtor and Creditor in 1821.

of Representatives, but before the new Congress assembled a vacancy occurred in the Senate, and the Legislature chose him by acclamation to fill it. He was regularly returned to this body until he resigned the senatorial dignity to become Secretary of State, in 1840.

Near the close of December, 1829, Mr. Foot introduced his celebrated resolutions on the Public Lands. They were the subject of occasional and desultory debate until the nineteenth of January, when General Hayne, of South Carolina, in a vehement speech accused New England of a selfish opposition to the interests of the western states. While he was speaking Mr. Webster entered the Senate, from the Supreme Court, where he had been engaged in an important case, and he would have replied as soon as General Hayne sat down, but that the Senate then adjourned. The next day he delivered one of the most powerful and brilliant speeches that have been heard in modern times. The debate was continued until the twenty-third of January, on both sides with extraordinary ability, but on that of Mr. Webster with a force of logic and splendour of eloquence that had never been equalled in the Senate, that have rarely been equalled in the world. In this famous controversy the doctrine of nullification was first avowed in the Congress, and its triumphant overthrow by Mr. Webster won for him more honourable triumphs than ever rewarded the victories of the field. With its praise the nation "rung from side to side." At the banquet given to him soon after in New York, the great Chancellor of that state said that the discussion had rescued constitutional law from archives and libraries, and placed it "under the eye, and submitted it to the judgment of the American people." In 1838 another attempt was made by an abler champion to enforce the same doctrines in the Senate, but Mr. Webster's victory over Mr. Calhoun was not less decisive than that he had achieved over General Hayne.

In 1839 Mr. Webster visited England, where he was received with the honours due to his genius, acquirements, and illustrious character. When the whig party came into power, in 1841, he was made Secretary of State, and the extraordinary ability which he displayed in negotiating the Treaty of Washington, and in other cases, crowned his name with a new glory. He returned to the Senate

Drawn from life and Engraved by James B Longacre.

DANIEL WEBSTER.

Danl Webster

in 1845, where he remained until 1851. At a magnificent banquet, attended by five hundred gentlemen, which was given to him in Philadelphia on the second of December, 1846, he delivered a speech of nearly four hours, which showed that at sixty-five he retains in perfection his remarkable powers. This is not a place in which it is proper to speak at length of his course in regard to public affairs; but "peace has its victories as well as war," and he is not moved by the spirit of this age or of this nation, who does not look upon a statesman who prevents an appeal to arms as more deserving of applause than a soldier who wins a hundred battles.

Of Daniel Webster as an author, we may speak in every presence with unhesitating freedom. By whatever circumstances educed, his works are "vital in every part." His mind is of the foremost rank, and in that rank will unquestionably always hold a distinguished place. It cannot be doubted that he will be remembered with Franklin, Hamilton, and Marshall, those illustrious countrymen of ours, upon whose intellectual calibre the world has set the seal of its high and final judgment.

Of Mr. Webster's State Papers no collections have been published. For wise apprehension and dialectic skill they are among the finest monuments of his genius. Of his forensic arguments we have but a few meagre outlines, sufficient to justify the measure of his logical endowments which they occasioned, but not sufficient to account for the extraordinary effects which they produced upon the mixed multitude who heard them. A few of his historical addresses and congressional speeches we possess as they came from his hand, with the antique simplicity and strength which are characteristics of the highest order of such productions.

The first volume of his Speeches and Forensic Arguments was published in Boston in 1830, the second in 1838, and a third in 1843: the last ending with his Remarks in the Senate a few days before he resigned his seat to enter the cabinet. Since he went back to the Senate, the most important of his speeches that have been published are one on the Treaty of Washington, and the one delivered in Philadelphia.

His attention has generally been directed to home subjects. He is in every sense American. But in a few of his speeches he has shown a comprehensive and particular familiarity with European history and politics. All his works 23

bear the deeply impressed stamp of nationality: But in his luminous expositions of constitutional law, his discerning examinations of the origin, nature, and influences of our liberty and institutions, his powerful discussions of our policy, and his masterly portraitures of those great men whose fame is one of the choicest inheritances of the nation, are shown most clearly his love of country and the joint action and fusion of his own with the national mind.

He speaks always with a manifest sincerity, and a consciousness of strength. His object is the conviction of the understanding, and he proceeds in effecting it with a simplicity and directness, and a skill in analysis and generalization, which make his advance like that of the sunlight in the track of night. At times the action of the Reason is so intense as to warm into life the Imagination, which follows, with bright-eyed Patriotism, its impetuous and resistless march, to grace and crown its triumph.

Mr. Webster's style is generally plain, sententious, and earnest,—sometimes solemn and imposing,—and at rare intervals brilliant with the play of wit, and keen with sarcasm and invective. The greatest variety to be found in any one of his speeches is in the reply to Hayne, and the most withering resentment and scorn in his merciless arraignment and exposure of Ingersoll and others who assailed the Washington Treaty, and went out of their way to attack its author. He is thoroughly furnished with all solid learning that can be turned to account in the service of the state. He is a classical scholar of the first order, as familiar with the poets as with the historians and publicists, and has a perfect mastery of his native tongue, which has been acquired by a careful study of the Saxon, and the best English literature, particularly the common version of the Bible, and Bacon, Shakspeare, and Milton.

—In June, 1852, the Whig Convention met to nominate a candidate for the Presidency. Mr. Webster failed to get the nomination. On his return to Boston, July 9th, the citizens gave him a grand public reception. He retired to his farm at Marshfield, where he died Sunday, Oct. 24, 1852. His collected works, consisting chiefly of Orations, Speeches, and Essays, with a beautiful and carefully written life by Edward Everett, were published in 1851, in six volumes, 8vo. His life and letters by Geo. T. Curtis, one of his literary executors, in two volumes, 8vo., was published in 1870.

PRIDE OF ANCESTRY.

FROM A DISCOURSE IN COMMEMORATION OF THE FIRST
SETTLEMENT OF NEW ENGLAND.

It is a noble faculty of our nature which enables us to connect our thoughts, our sympathies, and our happiness with what is distant in place or time; and, looking before and after, to hold communion at once with our ancestors and our posterity. Human and mortal although we are, we are nevertheless not mere insulated beings, without relation to the past or the future. Neither the point of time nor the spot of earth in which we physically live, bounds our rational and intellectual enjoyments. We live in the past by a knowledge of its history, and in the future by hope and anticipation. By ascending to an association with our ancestors; by contemplating their example and studying their character; by partaking their sentiments, and imbibing their spirit; by accompanying them in their toils; by sympathizing in their sufferings, and rejoicing in their successes and their triumphs,—we mingle our own existence with theirs, and seem to belong to their age. We become their contemporaries, live the lives which they lived, endure what they endured, and partake in the rewards which they enjoyed. And in like manner, by running along the line of future time; by contemplating the probable fortunes of those who are coming after us; by attempting something which may promote their happiness, and leave some not dishonourable memorial of ourselves for their regard when we shall sleep with the fathers, —we protract our own earthly being, and seem to crowd whatever is future, as well as all that is past, into the narrow compass of our earthly existence. As it is not a vain and false, but an exalted and religious imagination which leads us to raise our thoughts from the orb which, amidst this universe of worlds, the Creator has given us to inhabit, and to send them with something of the feeling which nature prompts, and teaches to be proper among children of the same Eternal Parent, to the contemplation of the myriads of fellow-beings with which his goodness has peopled the infinite of space; so neither is it false or vain to consider ourselves as interested or connected with our whole race through all time; allied to our ancestors; allied to our posterity; closely compacted on all sides with others; ourselves being but links in the great chain of being, which begins with the origin of our race, runs onward through its successive generations, binding together the past, the present, and the future, and terminating at last with the consummation of all things earthly at the throne of God.

There may be, and there often is, indeed, a regard for ancestry, which nourishes only a weak pride; as there is also a care for posterity, which only disguises an habitual avarice, or hides the workings of a low and grovelling vanity. But there is also a moral and philosophical respect for our ancestors, which elevates the character and improves the heart. Next to the sense of religious duty and moral feeling, I hardly know what should bear with stronger obligation on a liberal and enlightened mind, than a consciousness of alliance with excellence which is departed; and a consciousness, too, that in its acts and conduct, and even in its sentiments, it may be actively operating on the happiness of those who come after it. Poetry is found to have few stronger conceptions, by which it would affect or overwhelm the mind, than those in which it presents the moving and speaking image of the departed dead to the senses of the living. This belongs to poetry only because it is congenial to our nature. Poetry is, in this respect, but the handmaid of true philosophy and morality. It deals with us as human beings, naturally reverencing those whose visible connection with this state of being is severed, and who may yet exercise we know not what sympathy with ourselves;—and when it carries us forward, also, and shows us the long-continued result of all the good we do in the prosperity of those who follow us, till it bears us from ourselves, and absorbs us in an intense interest for what shall happen to the generations after us, it speaks only in the language of our nature, and affects us with sentiments which belong to us as human beings.

INFLUENCE OF GREAT ACTIONS.

FROM THE SAME.

Great actions and striking occurrences, having excited a temporary admiration, often pass away and are forgotten, because they leave no lasting results, affecting the prosperity of communities. Such is frequently the fortune of the most brilliant military achievements. Of the ten thousand battles which have been fought; of all the fields fertilized with carnage; of the banners which have been bathed in blood; of the warriors who have hoped that they had risen from the field of conquest to a glory as bright and as durable as the stars, how few that continue long to interest mankind! The victory of yesterday is reversed by the defeat of to-day; the star of military glory, rising like a meteor, like a meteor has fallen; disgrace and disaster hang on the heels of conquest and renown; victor and vanquished presently pass away to oblivion, and the world holds on its course, with the loss only of so many lives and so much treasure.

But if this is frequently, or generally, the fortune of military achievements, it is not always so. There are enterprises, military as well as civil, that sometimes check the current of events, give a new turn to human affairs, and transmit their consequences through ages. We see their importance in their results and call them great, because great things follow. There have been battles which have fixed the fate of nations. These come down to us in history with a solid and permanent influence, not created by a display of glittering armour, the rush of adverse battalions, the sinking and rising of pennons, the flight, the pursuit, and the victory; but by their effect in advancing or retarding human knowledge, in over-throwing or establishing despotism, in extending or destroying human happiness. When the traveller pauses on the plains of Marathon, what are the emotions which strongly agitate his breast; what is that glorious recollection that thrills through his frame, and suffuses his eyes? Not, I imagine, that Grecian skill and Grecian valour were here most signally displayed; but that Greece herself was saved. It is because to this spot, and to the event which has rendered it immortal, he refers all the succeeding glories of the republic. It is because, if that day had gone otherwise, Greece had perished. It is because he perceives that her philosophers and orators, her poets and painters, her sculptors and architects, her government and free institutions point backward to Marathon, and that their future existence seems to have been suspended on the contingency, whether the Persian or Grecian banner should wave victorious in the beams of that day's setting sun. And as his imagination kindles at the retrospect, he is transported back to the interesting moment: he counts the fearful odds of the contending hosts; his interest for the result overwhelms him; he trembles as if it was still uncertain, and seems to doubt whether he may consider Socrates and Plato, Demosthenes, Sophocles, and Phidias, as secure, yet, to himself and to the world.

THE SETTLEMENT OF PLYMOUTH.
FROM THE SAME.

Our fathers came hither to a land from which they were never to return. Hither they had brought, and here they were to fix their hopes, their attachments, and their objects. Some natural tears they shed as they left the pleasant abodes of their fathers, and some emotions they suppressed when the white cliffs of their native country, now seen for the last time, grew dim to their sight. They were acting however upon a resolution not to be changed. With whatever stifled regrets, with whatever occasional hesitation, with whatever appalling apprehensions, which must sometimes arise with force to shake the firmest purpose, they had yet committed themselves to heaven and the elements; and a thousand leagues of water soon interposed to separate them for ever from the region which gave them birth. A new existence awaited them here; and when they saw these shores, rough, cold, barbarous, and barren as then they were, they beheld their country. That mixed and strong feeling, which we call love of country, and which is in general never extinguished in the heart of man, grasped and embraced its proper object here. Whatever constitutes *country*, except the earth and the sun, all the moral causes of affection and attachment which operate upon the heart, they had brought with them to their new abode. Here were now their families and friends, their homes, and their property. Before they reached the shore, they had established the elements of a social system, and at a much earlier period had

settled their forms of religious worship. At the moment of their landing, therefore, they possessed institutions of government, and institutions of religion: and friends and families, and social and religious institutions, established by consent, founded on choice and preference, how nearly do these fill up our whole idea of country!—The morning that beamed on the first night of their repose saw the Pilgrims already established in their country. There were political institutions, and civil liberty, and religious worship. Poetry has fancied nothing in the wanderings of heroes so distinct and characteristic. Here was man indeed unprotected, and unprovided for, on the shore of a rude and fearful wilderness; but it was politic, intelligent, and educated man. Every thing was civilized but the physical world. Institutions containing in substance all that ages had done for human government were established in a forest. Cultivated mind was to act on uncultivated nature; and, more than all, a government and a country were to commence with the very first foundations laid under the divine light of the Christian religion. Happy auspices of a happy futurity! Who would wish that his country's existence had otherwise begun?—Who would desire the power of going back to the ages of fable? Who would wish for an origin obscured in the darkness of antiquity?—Who would wish for other emblazoning of his country's heraldry, or other ornaments of her genealogy, than to be able to say that her first existence was with intelligence; her first breath the inspirations of liberty; her first principle the truth of divine religion?

BUNKER HILL MONUMENT.
FROM AN ADDRESS ON LAYING ITS CORNER-STONE.

We know that the record of illustrious actions is most safely deposited in the universal remembrance of mankind. We know that if we could cause this structure to ascend, not only till it reached the skies, but till it pierced them, its broad surface could still contain but part of that, which, in an age of knowledge, hath already been spread over the earth, and which history charges herself with making known to all future times. We know that no inscription on entablatures less broad than the earth itself, can carry information of the events we commemorate where it has not already gone; and that no structure which shall not outlive the duration of letters and knowledge among men, can prolong the memorial. But our object is, by this edifice, to show our deep sense of the value and importance of the achievements of our ancestors; and by presenting this work of gratitude to the eye, to keep alive similar sentiments, and to foster a similar regard to the principles of the Revolution. Human beings are composed not of reason only, but of imagination also, and sentiment; and that is neither wasted nor misapplied which is appropriated to the purpose of giving right direction to sentiments, and opening proper springs of feeling in the heart.

Let it not be supposed that our object is to perpetuate national hostility, or even to cherish a mere military spirit. It is higher, purer, nobler. We consecrate our work to the spirit of national independence, and we wish that the light of peace may rest upon it for ever. We rear a memorial of our conviction of the unmeasured benefit which has been conferred on our land, and of the happy influences which have been produced, by the same events, on the general interests of mankind. We come as Americans to mark a spot which must be for ever dear to us and our posterity. We wish that whosoever, in all coming time, shall turn his eyes hither, may behold that the place is not undistinguished where the first great battle of the Revolution was fought. We wish that this structure may proclaim the magnitude and importance of that event to every class and every age. We wish that infancy may learn the purpose of its erection from maternal lips, and that weary and withered age may behold it, and be solaced by the recollections which it suggests. We wish that labour may look up here, and be proud in the midst of its toil. We wish that, in those days of disaster which, as they come upon all nations, must be expected to come on us also, desponding patriotism may turn its eyes hither, and be assured that the foundations of our national power still stand strong. We wish that this column, rising toward heaven among the pointed spires of so many temples dedicated to God, may contribute also to produce, in all minds, a pious feeling of dependence and gratitude. We wish, finally that the last object on the sight of him who leaves his native shore, and the first to gladden him who revisits it, may be something which shall remind him of the liberty and glory of his country. Let it rise till it meet the sun in his coming; let the earliest light of morning gild it, and parting day linger and play upon its summit.

TO THE SURVIVORS OF THE BATTLE OF BUNKER HILL.

FROM THE SAME.

VENERABLE men! you have come down to us from a former generation. Heaven has bounteously lengthened out your lives that you might behold this joyous day. You are now where you stood fifty years ago, this very hour, with your brothers and your neighbours, shoulder to shoulder, in the strife of your country. Behold how altered! The same heavens are indeed over your heads; the same ocean rolls at your feet; but all else, how changed! You hear now no roar of hostile cannon, you see no mixed volumes of smoke and flame rising from burning Charlestown. The ground strewed with the dead and the dying; the impetuous charge; the steady and successful repulse; the loud call to repeated assault; the summoning of all that is manly to repeated resistance; a thousand bosoms freely and fearlessly bared in an instant to whatever of terror there may be in war and death;—all these you have witnessed,

but you witness them no more. All is peace. The heights of yonder metropolis, its towers and roofs, which you then saw filled with wives and children and countrymen in distress and terror, and looking with unutterable emotions for the issue of the combat, have presented you to-day with the sight of its whole happy population, come out to welcome and greet you with a universal jubilee. Yonder proud ships, by a felicity of position appropriately lying at the foot of this mount, and seeming fondly to cling around it, are not means of annoyance to you, but your country's own means of distinction and defence. All is peace; and God has granted you this sight of your country's happiness, ere you slumber in the grave for ever. He has allowed you to behold and to partake the reward of your patriotic toils; and he has allowed us, your sons and countrymen, to meet you here, and in the name of the present generation, in the name of your country, in the name of liberty, to thank you!

But, alas! you are not all here! Time and the sword have thinned your ranks. Prescott, Putnam, Stark, Brooks, Read, Pomeroy, Bridge! our eyes seek for you in vain amidst this broken band. You are gathered to your fathers, and live only to your country in her grateful remembrance and your own bright example. But let us not too much grieve that you have met the common fate of men. You lived at least long enough to know that your work had been nobly and successfully accomplished. You lived to see your country's independence established, and to sheathe your swords from war. On the light of liberty you saw arise the light of Peace, like

"another morn,
Risen on mid-noon;"—

and the sky on which you closed your eyes was cloudless.

But—ah!—Him! the first great martyr in this great cause! Him! the premature victim of his own self-devoting heart! Him! the head of our civil councils, and the destined leader of our military bands; whom nothing brought hither but the unquenchable fire of his own spirit; him! cut off by Providence in the hour of overwhelming anxiety and thick gloom; falling ere he saw the star of his country rise; pouring out his generous blood like water before he knew whether it would fertilize a land of freedom or of bondage! how shall I struggle with the emotions that stifle the utterance of his name!—Our poor work may perish; but thine shall endure! This monument may moulder away: the solid ground it rests upon may sink down to a level with the sea; but thy memory shall not fail! Wheresoever among men a heart shall be found that beats to the transports of patriotism and liberty, its aspirations shall be to claim kindred with thy spirit! . . .

Veterans! you are the remnant of many a well-fought field. You bring with you marks of honour from Trenton and Monmouth, from Yorktown, amden, Bennington, and Saratoga. Veterans of half a century! when in your youthful days you put every thing at hazard in your country's cause, good as that cause was, and sanguine as youth is, still your fondest hopes did not stretch onward to an hour like this! At a period to which you could not reasonably have expected to arrive; at a moment of national prosperity, such as you could never have foreseen, you are now met here to enjoy the fellowship of old soldiers, and to receive the overflowings of a universal gratitude.

But your agitated countenances and your heaving breasts inform me that even this is not an unmixed joy. I perceive that a tumult of contending feelings rushes upon you. The images of the dead, as well as the persons of the living, throng to your embraces. The scene overwhelms you, and I turn from it. May the Father of all mercies smile upon your declining years and bless them! And when you shall here have exchanged your embraces; when you shall once more have pressed the hands which have been so often extended to give succour in adversity, or grasped in the exultation of victory; then look abroad into this lovely land, which your young valour defended, and mark the happiness with which it is filled; yea, look abroad into the whole earth and see what a name you have contributed to give to your country, and what a praise you have added to freedom, and then rejoice in the sympathy and gratitude which beam upon your last days from the improved condition of mankind.

LITERARY CHARACTER OF ADAMS AND JEFFERSON.
FROM A EULOGY ON ADAMS AND JEFFERSON.

THE last public labour of Mr. Jefferson naturally suggests the expression of the high praise which is due, both to him and to Mr. Adams, for their uniform and zealous attachment to learning, and to the cause of general knowledge. Of the advantages of learning, indeed, and of literary accomplishments, their own characters were striking recommendations and illustrations. They were scholars, ripe and good scholars; widely acquainted with ancient as well as modern literature, and not altogether uninstructed in the deeper sciences. Their acquirements doubtless were different, and so were the particular objects of their literary pursuits; as their tastes and characters in these respects differed like those of other men. Being also men of busy lives, with great objects requiring action constantly before them, their attainments in letters did not become showy or obtrusive. Yet I would hazard the opinion, that, if we could now ascertain all the causes which gave them eminence and distinction in the midst of the great men with whom they acted, we should find not among the least their early acquisition in literature, the resources which it furnished, the promptitude and facility which it communicated, and the wide field it opened for analogy and illustration; giving them thus, on every subject, a larger view and a broader range, as well for discussion as for the government of their own conduct.

Literature sometimes, and pretensions to it much oftener, disgusts, by appearing to hang loosely on the character, like something foreign or extraneous; not a part, but an ill-adjusted appendage; or by seeming to overload and weigh it down by its unsightly bulk, like the productions of bad taste in architecture, when there is massy and cumbrous ornament without strength or solidity of column. This has exposed learning, and especially classical learning, to reproach. Men have seen that it might exist without mental superiority, without vigour, without good taste, and without utility. But, in such cases, classical learning has only not inspired natural talent; or, at most, it has but made original feebleness of intellect and natural bluntness of perception somewhat more conspicuous. The question, after all, if it be a question, is, whether literature, ancient as well as modern, does not assist a good understanding, improve natural good taste, add polished armour to native strength, and render its possessor not only more capable of deriving private happiness from contemplation and reflection, but more accomplished also for action in the affairs of life, and especially for public action. Those, whose memories we now honour, were learned men; but their learning was kept in its proper place, and made subservient to the uses and objects of life. They were scholars, not common nor superficial; but their scholarship was so in keeping with their character, so blended and inwrought, that careless observers or bad judges, not seeing an ostentatious display of it, might infer that it did not exist; forgetting, or not knowing, that classical learning in men who act in conspicuous public stations, perform duties which exercise the faculty of writing, or address popular, judicial, or deliberative bodies, is often felt where it is little seen, and sometimes felt more effectually because it is not seen at all.

ELOQUENCE.
FROM THE SAME.

WHEN public bodies are to be addressed on momentous occasions, when great interests are at stake, and strong passions excited, nothing is valuable in speech farther than it is connected with high intellectual and moral endowments. Clearness, force, and earnestness are the qualities which produce conviction. True eloquence, indeed, does not consist in speech. It cannot be brought from far. Labour and learning may toil for it, but they will toil in vain. Words and phrases may be marshalled in every way, but they cannot compass it. It must exist in the man, in the subject, and in the occasion. Affected passion, intense expression, the pomp of declamation, all may aspire after it—they cannot reach it. It comes, if it come at all, like the outbreaking of a fountain from the earth, or the bursting forth of volcanic fires with spontaneous, original, native force. The graces taught in the schools, the costly ornaments and studied contrivances of speech, shock and disgust men, when their own lives, and the fate of their wives, their children, and their country hang

Q

on the decision of the hour. Then, words have lost their power, rhetoric is vain, and all elaborate oratory contemptible. Even genius itself then feels rebuked and subdued, as in the presence of higher qualities. Then, patriotism is eloquent; then, self-devotion is eloquent. The clear conception outrunning the deductions of logic, the high purpose, the firm resolve, the dauntless spirit, speaking on the tongue, beaming from the eye, informing every feature, and urging the whole man onward, right onward to his object—this, this is eloquence: or rather it is something greater and higher than all eloquence,—it is action, noble, sublime, godlike action.

PUBLIC OPINION.
FROM A SPEECH ON THE GREEK REVOLUTION.

It may be asked, perhaps, . . . what can *we* do? Are we to go to war? Are we to interfere in the Greek cause, or any other European cause? Are we to endanger our pacific relations?—No, certainly not. What, then, the question recurs, remains for *us?* If we will not endanger our own peace; if we will neither furnish armies nor navies to the cause which we think the just one, what is there within *our* power?

Sir, this reasoning mistakes the age. The time has been, indeed, when fleets, and armies, and subsidies were the principal reliances even in the best cause. But, happily for mankind, there has arrived a great change in this respect. Moral causes come into consideration, in proportion as the progress of knowledge is advanced; and the *public opinion* of the civilized world is rapidly gaining an ascendency over mere brutal force. It is already able to oppose the most formidable obstruction to the progress of injustice and oppression; and, as it grows more intelligent and more intense, it will be more and more formidable. It may be silenced by military power, but it cannot be conquered. It is elastic, irrepressible, and invulnerable to the weapons of ordinary warfare. It is that impassable, unextinguishable enemy of mere violence and arbitrary rule which, like Milton's angels,

"Vital in every part,
Cannot, but by annihilating, die."

Until this be propitiated or satisfied, it is vain for power to talk either of triumphs or of repose. No matter what fields are desolated, what fortresses surrendered, what armies subdued, or what provinces overrun. In the history of the year that has passed by us, and in the instance of unhappy Spain, we have seen the vanity of all triumphs in a cause which violates the general sense of justice of the civilized world. It is nothing that the troops of France have passed from the Pyrenees to Cadiz: it is nothing that an unhappy and prostrate nation has fallen before them; it is nothing that arrests, and confiscation, and execution sweep away the little remnant of national resistance. There is an enemy that still exists to check the glory of these triumphs. It follows the conqueror back to the very scene of his ovations; it calls upon him to take notice that Europe, though silent, is yet indignant; it shows him that the sceptre of his victory is a barren sceptre; that it shall confer neither joy nor honour, but shall moulder to dry ashes in his grasp. In the midst of his exultation it pierces his ear with the cry of injured justice, it denounces against him the indignation of an enlightened and civilized age; it turns to bitterness the cup of his rejoicing, and wounds him with the sting which belongs to the consciousness of having outraged the opinion of mankind.

IMPRISONMENT FOR DEBT.
FROM A SPEECH ON THE BANKRUPT LAW.

We talk much, and talk warmly, of political liberty; and well we may, for it is among the chief of public blessings. But who can enjoy political liberty if he is deprived permanently of personal liberty, and the exercise of his own industry, and his own faculties? To those unfortunate individuals, doomed to the everlasting bondage of debt, what is it that we have free institutions of government? What is it that we have public and popular assemblies? Nay, to them, what is even this Constitution itself, in its actual operation, and as we now administer it,—what is its aspect to them but an aspect of stern, implacable severity?—an aspect of refusal, denial, and frowning rebuke?—nay, more than that, an aspect not only of austerity and rebuke even, but, as they must think it, of plain injustice also; since it will not relieve them, nor suffer others to give them relief. What love can they feel toward the Constitution of their country, which has taken the power of striking off their bonds from their own paternal state governments, and yet, inexorable to all the cries of justice and of mercy, holds it, unexercised, in its own fast and unrelenting clinch? They find themselves bondsmen, because we will not execute the commands of the Constitution—bondsmen to debts they cannot pay, and which all know they cannot pay, and which take away the power of supporting themselves. Other slaves have masters, charged with the duty of support and protection; but their masters neither clothe, nor feed, nor shelter;—they only bind. . . . .

Sir, let us gratify the whole country, for once, with the joyous clang of chains,—joyous because heard falling from the limbs of men. The wisest among those whom I address can desire nothing more beneficial than this measure, or more universally desired; and he who is youngest may not expect to live long enough to see a better opportunity of causing new pleasures and a happiness long untasted to spring up in the hearts of the poor and the humble. How many husbands and fathers are looking with hopes which they cannot suppress, and yet hardly dare to cherish, for the result of this debate! How many wives and mothers will pass sleepless and feverish nights, until they know whether they and their families shall be raised from poverty, despondency, and despair, and restored again to the circles of industrious, independent, and happy life!

REPLY TO A TAUNT OF MR. HAYNE.

FROM A SPEECH ON MR. FOOTE'S RESOLUTION.

It was put as a question for me to answer, and so put as if it were difficult for me to answer, whether I deemed the member from Missouri an overmatch for myself in debate here. It seems to me, sir, that this is extraordinary language, and an extraordinary tone for the discussions of this body.

Matches and over-matches! Those terms are more applicable elsewhere than here, and fitter for other assemblies than this. Sir, the gentleman seems to forget where and what we are. This is a senate: a senate of equals: of men of individual honour and personal character, and of absolute independence. We know no masters; we acknowledge no dictators. This is a hall for mutual consultation and discussion; not an arena for the exhibition of champions. I offer myself, sir, as a match for no man, I throw the challenge of debate at no man's feet. But then, sir, since the honourable member has put the question in a manner that calls for an answer, I will give him an answer; and I tell him that, holding myself to be the humblest of the members here, I yet know nothing in the arm of his friend from Missouri, either alone or when aided by the arm of his friend from South Carolina, that need deter even me from espousing whatever opinions I may choose to espouse, from debating whenever I may choose to debate, or from speaking whatever I may see fit to say on the floor of the Senate. Sir, when uttered as matter of commendation or compliment, I should dissent from nothing which the honourable member might say of his friend. Still less do I put forth any pretensions of my own. But when put to me as a matter of taunt, I throw it back, and say to the gentleman that he could possibly say nothing less likely than such a comparison to wound my pride of personal character. The anger of its tone rescued the remark from intentional irony, which otherwise, probably, would have been its general acceptation. But, sir, if it be imagined that by this mutual quotation and commendation; if it be supposed, that by casting the characters of the drama, assigning to each his part; to one the attack; to another the cry of onset: or, if it be thought that by a loud and empty vaunt of anticipated victory, any laurels are to be won here; if it be imagined, especially, that any or all of these things will shake any purpose of mine, I can tell the honourable member, once for all, that he is greatly mistaken, and that he is dealing with one of whose temper and character he has yet much to learn. Sir, I shall not allow myself, on this occasion, to be betrayed into any loss of temper; but if provoked, as I trust I never shall allow myself to be, into crimination and recrimination, the honourable member may perhaps find that, in that contest, there will be blows to take as well as blows to give; that others can state comparisons as significant, at least, as his own, and that his impunity may, perhaps, demand of him whatever powers of taunt and sarcasm he may possess. I commend him to a prudent husbandry of his resources.

IMPORTANCE OF PRESERVING THE UNION.

FROM THE SAME.

I profess, sir, in my career hitherto to have kept steadily in view the prosperity and honour of the whole country, and the preservation of our federal union. It is to that union we owe our safety at home, and our consideration and dignity abroad. It is to that union that we are chiefly indebted for whatever makes us most proud of our country. That union we reached only by the discipline of our virtues, in the severe school of adversity. It had its origin in the necessities of disordered finance, prostrate commerce, and ruined credit. Under its benign influences, these great interests immediately awoke, as from the dead, and sprang forth with newness of life. Every year of its duration has teemed with fresh proofs of its utility and its blessings; and although our territory has stretched out wider and wider, and our population spread farther and farther, they have not outrun its protection, or its benefits. It has been to us all a copious fountain of national, social, and personal happiness.

I have not allowed myself, sir, to look beyond the union, to see what might lie hidden in the dark recess behind. I have not coolly weighed the chances of preserving liberty, when the bonds that unite us together shall be broken asunder. I have not accustomed myself to hang over the precipice of disunion to see whether, with my short sight, I can fathom the depth of the abyss below; nor could I regard him as a safe counsellor in the affairs of this government, whose thoughts should be mainly bent on considering, not how the union should be best preserved, but how tolerable might be the condition of the people when it shall be broken up and destroyed.

While the union lasts, we have high, exciting, gratifying prospects spread out before us, for us and our children. Beyond that I seek not to penetrate the veil. God grant that, in my day at least, that curtain may not rise. God grant that on my vision never may be opened what lies behind. When my eyes shall be turned to behold, for the last time, the sun in heaven, may I not see him shining on the broken and dishonoured fragments of a once glorious union; on states dissevered, discordant, belligerent; on a land rent with civil feuds, or drenched, it may be, in fraternal blood! Let their last feeble and lingering glance rather behold the gorgeous ensign of the republic, now known and honoured throughout the earth, still full high advanced, its arms and trophies streaming in their original lustre, not a stripe erased or polluted, nor a single star obscured—bearing for its motto no such miserable interrogatory as—What is all this worth? Nor those other words of delusion and folly—liberty first, and union afterward—but everywhere, spread all over in characters of living light, blazing on all its ample folds as they float over the sea and over the land, and in every wind under the whole heavens, that other sentiment dear to every true American heart—liberty and union, now and for ever, one and inseparable!

SOUTH CAROLINA AND MASSACHU-SETTS.
FROM THE SAME.

THE eulogium pronounced on the character of the state of South Carolina by the honourable gentleman, for her revolutionary and other merits, meets my hearty concurrence. I shall not acknowledge that the honourable member goes before me in regard for whatever of distinguished talent, or distinguished character, South Carolina has produced. I claim part of the honour: I partake in the pride of her great names. I claim them for countrymen, one and all. The Laurenses, Rutledges, the Pinckneys, the Sumpters, the Marions —Americans all—whose fame is no more to be hemmed in by state lines, than their talents and patriotism were capable of being circumscribed within the same narrow limits. In their day and generation they served and honoured the country, and the whole country, and their renown is of the treasures of the whole country. Him, whose honoured name the gentleman bears himself—does he suppose me less capable of gratitude for his patriotism, or sympathy for his sufferings, than if his eyes had first opened upon the light in Massachusetts, instead of South Carolina? Sir, does he suppose it in his power to exhibit a Carolina name so bright as to produce envy in my bosom? No, sir,—increased gratification and delight, rather. Sir, I thank God that, if I am gifted with little of the spirit which is said to be able to raise mortals to the skies, I have yet none, as I trust, of that other spirit which would drag angels down.

When I shall be found, sir, in my place here in the Senate, or elsewhere, to sneer at public merit, because it happened to spring up beyond the little limits of my own state and neighbourhood; when I refuse, for any such cause, or for any cause, the homage due to American talent, to elevated patriotism, to sincere devotion to liberty and the country; or if I see an uncommon endowment of heaven—if I see extraordinary capacity and virtue in any son of the south—and if moved by local prejudice, or gangrened by state jealousy, I get up here to abate of a hair from his just character and just fame, may my tongue cleave to the roof of my mouth!

Sir, let me recur to pleasing recollections—let me indulge in refreshing remembrances of the past —let me remind you that in early times no states cherished greater harmony, both of principle and of feeling, than Massachusetts and South Carolina. Would to God that harmony might again return. Shoulder to shoulder they went through the Revolution—hand in hand they stood through the administration of Washington, and felt his own great arm lean on them for support. Unkind feeling, if it exist, alienation and distrust are the growth, unnatural to such soils, of false principles since sown. They are weeds, the seeds of which that same great arm never scattered.

Mr. President, I shall enter on no encomium upon Massachusetts—she needs none. There she is—behold her and judge for yourselves. There

is her history—the world knows it by heart. The past, at least, is secure. There is Boston, and Concord, and Lexington, and Bunker's Hill; and there they will remain for ever. The bones of her sons, fallen in the great struggle for independence, now lie mingled with the soil of every state, from New England to Georgia; and there they will lie for ever. And, sir, where American liberty raised its first voice, and where its youth was nurtured and sustained, there it still lives in the strength of its manhood, and full of its original spirit. If discord and disunion shall wound it—if party strife and blind ambition shall hawk at and tear it: if folly and madness, if uneasiness, under salutary and necessary restraint, shall succeed to separate it from that union, by which alone its existence is made sure, it will stand in the end by the side of that cradle in which its infancy was rocked; it will stretch forth its arm with whatever of vigour it may still retain over the friends who gather round it: and it will fall at last, if fall it must, amidst the proudest monuments of its own glory, and on the very spot of its origin.

DUTY OF THE REPRESENTATIVE.
FROM A SPEECH ON THE PRESIDENT'S PROTEST.

WE have been taught to regard a representative of the people as a sentinel on the watch-tower of liberty. Is he to be blind, though visible danger approaches? Is he to be deaf, though sounds of peril fill the air? Is he to be dumb, while a thousand duties impel him to raise the cry of alarm? Is he not rather to catch the lowest whisper which breathes intention or purpose of encroachment on the public liberties, and to give his voice breath and utterance at the first appearance of danger? Is not his eye to traverse the whole horizon with the keen and eager vision of an unhooded hawk, detecting, through all disguises, every enemy advancing, in any form toward the citadel which he guards? Sir, this watchfulness for public liberty; this duty of foreseeing danger and proclaiming it; this promptitude and boldness in resisting attacks on the Constitution from any quarter; this defence of established landmarks; this fearless resistance of whatever would transcend or remove them, —all belong to the representative character, are interwoven with its very nature.

THE SPIRIT OF LIBERTY.
FROM THE SAME.

THE spirit of liberty is indeed a bold and fearless spirit; but it is also a sharp-sighted spirit; it is a cautious, sagacious, discriminating, far-seeing intelligence; it is jealous of encroachment, jealous of power, jealous of man. It demands checks; it seeks for guards; it insists on securities; it entrenches itself behind strong defences, and fortifies with all possible care against the assaults of ambition and passion.

LIBERTY AND PREROGATIVE.
FROM THE SAME.

THE contest for ages has been to rescue liberty from the grasp of executive power. Whoever has engaged in her sacred cause, from the days of the downfall of those great aristocracies which had stood between the king and the people to the time of our own independence, has struggled for the accomplishment of that single object. On the long list of the champions of human freedom, there is not one name dimmed by the reproach of advocating the extension of executive authority; on the contrary, the uniform and steady purpose of all such champions has been to limit and restrain it. To this end the spirit of liberty, growing more and more enlightened, and more and more vigorous from age to age, has been battering for centuries against the solid butments of the feudal system. To this end, all that could be gained from the imprudence, snatched from the weakness, or wrung from the necessities of crowned heads, has been carefully gathered up, secured, and hoarded as the rich treasures, the very jewels of liberty. To this end, popular and representative right has kept up its warfare against prerogative with various success; sometimes writing the history of a whole age in blood; sometimes witnessing the martyrdom of Sidneys and Russells, often baffled and repulsed, but still gaining, on the whole, and holding what it gained with a grasp which nothing but the complete extinction of its own being could compel it to relinquish. At length the great conquest over executive power, in the leading western states of Europe, has been accomplished. The feudal system, like other stupendous fabrics of past ages, is known only by the rubbish which it has left behind it. Crowned heads have been compelled to submit to the restraints of law, and the PEOPLE, with that intelligence and that spirit which make their voice resistless, have been able to say to prerogative, "Thus far shalt thou come, and no farther." I need hardly say, sir, that, into the full enjoyment of all which Europe has reached only through such slow and painful steps, we sprang at once by the declaration of independence and by the establishment of free representative governments; government borrowing more or less from the models of other free states, but strengthened, secured, improved in their symmetry, and deepened in their foundation by those great men of our own country, whose names will be as familiar to future times as if they were written on the arch of the sky.

INFLUENCE OF WOMAN.
FROM A SPEECH AT RICHMOND.

IT is by the promulgation of sound morals in the community, and more especially by the training and instruction of the young, that woman performs her part toward the preservation of a free government. It is generally admitted that public liberty, the perpetuity of a free constitution, rests on the virtue and intelligence of the community

which enjoys it. How is that virtue to be inspired, and how is that intelligence to be communicated? Bonaparte once asked Madame de Staël in what manner he could most promote the happiness of France. Her reply is full of political wisdom. She said, "Instruct the mothers of the French people." Mothers are, indeed, the affectionate and effective teachers of the human race. The mother begins her process of training with the infant in her arms. It is she who directs, so to speak, its first mental and spiritual pulsations. She conducts it along the impressible years of childhood and youth, and hopes to deliver it to the rough contests and tumultuous scenes of life, armed by those good principles which her child has received from maternal care and love.

If we draw within the circle of our contemplation the mothers of a civilized nation, what do we see? We behold so many artificers working, not on frail and perishable matter, but on the immortal mind, moulding and fashioning beings who are to exist for ever. We applaud the artist whose skill and genius present the mimic man upon the canvas; we admire and celebrate the sculptor who works out that same image in enduring marble; but how insignificant are these achievements, though the highest and the fairest in all the departments of art, in comparison with the great vocation of human mothers! They work, not upon the canvas that shall fail, or the marble that shall crumble into dust, but upon mind, upon spirit, which is to last for ever, and which is to bear, for good or evil, throughout its duration, the impress of a mother's plastic hand.

I have already expressed the opinion, which all allow to be correct, that our security for the duration of the free institutions which bless our country depends upon the habits of virtue and the prevalence of knowledge and of education. Knowledge does not comprise all which is contained in the larger term of education. The feelings are to be disciplined; the passions are to be restrained; true and worthy motives are to be inspired; a profound religious feeling is to be instilled, and pure morality inculcated under all circumstances. All this is comprised in education. Mothers who are faithful to this great duty, will tell their children that neither in political nor in any other concerns of life can man ever withdraw himself from the perpetual obligations of conscience and of duty; that in every act, whether public or private, he incurs a just responsibility; and that in no condition is he warranted in trifling with important rights and obligations. They will impress upon their children the truth, that the exercise of the elective franchise is a social duty, of as solemn a nature as man can be called to perform; that a man may not innocently trifle with his vote; that every free elector is a trustee, as well for others as himself: and that every man and every measure he supports has an important bearing on the interests of others as well as on his own. It is in the inculcation of high and pure morals, such as these, that, in a free republic, woman performs her sacred duty, and fulfils her destiny.

LIBERTY AND THE CONSTITUTION.
FROM A SPEECH DELIVERED IN NEW YORK IN 1837.

UNDER the present Constitution, wisely and conscientiously administered, all are safe, happy, and renowned. The measure of our country's fame may fill all our breasts. It is fame enough for us all to partake in *her* glory, if we will carry her character onward to its true destiny. But if the system is broken, its fragments must fall alike on all. Not only the cause of American liberty, but the great cause of liberty throughout the whole earth depends, in a great measure, on upholding the Constitution and union of these states. If shattered and destroyed, no matter by what cause, the peculiar and cherished idea of United American Liberty will be no more for ever. There may be free states, it is possible, when there shall be separate states. There may be many loose, and feeble, and hostile confederacies, where there is now one great and united confederacy. But the noble idea of United American Liberty, of *our* liberty, such as our fathers established it, will be extinguished for ever. Fragments and severed columns of the edifice may be found remaining; and melancholy and mournful ruins will they be; the august temple itself will be prostrate in the dust. Gentlemen, the citizens of this republic cannot sever their fortunes. A common fate awaits us. In the honour of upholding, or in the disgrace of undermining the Constitution, we shall all necessarily partake. Let us then stand by the Constitution as it is, and by our country as it is, one, united, and entire; let it be a truth engraven on our hearts; let it be borne on the flag under which we rally, in every exigency, that we have ONE COUNTRY, ONE CONSTITUTION, ONE DESTINY.

ARCHITECTS OF RUIN.
FROM A SPEECH ON THE COLLECTION OF DUTIES ON IMPORTS.

IF the friends of nullification should be able to propagate their opinions, and give them practical effect, they would, in my judgment, prove themselves the most skilful "architects of ruin," the most effectual extinguishers of high-raised expectation, the greatest blasters of human hopes, which any age has produced. They would stand up to proclaim, in tones which would pierce the ears of half the human race, that the last great experiment of representative government had failed. They would send forth sounds, at the hearing of which the doctrine of the divine right of kings would feel, even in its grave, a returning sensation of vitality and resuscitation. Millions of eyes, of those who now feed their inherent love of liberty on the success of the American example, would turn away from beholding our dismemberment, and find no place on earth whereon to rest their gratified sight. Amidst the incantations and orgies of nullification, secession, disunion, and revolution, would be celebrated the funeral rites of constitutional and republican liberty.

ILLEGAL INTERFERENCE WITH THE PUBLIC TREASURE.
FROM A SPEECH ON THE PRESIDENT'S PROTEST.

THE Senate regarded this interposition as an encroachment by the Executive on other branches of the government; as an interference with the legislative disposition of the public treasure. It was strongly and forcibly urged, yesterday, by the honourable member from South Carolina, that the true and only mode of preserving any balance of power, in mixed governments, is to keep an exact balance. This is very true, and to this end encroachment must be resisted at the first step. The question is, therefore, whether, upon the true principles of the Constitution, this exercise of power by the President can be justified. Whether the consequences be prejudicial or not, if there be an illegal exercise of power, it is to be resisted in the proper manner. Even if no harm or inconvenience result from transgressing the boundary, the intrusion is not to be suffered to pass unnoticed. Every encroachment, great or small, is important enough to awaken the attention of those who are intrusted with the preservation of a constitutional government. We are not to wait till great public mischiefs come, till the government is overthrown, or liberty itself put in extreme jeopardy. We should not be worthy sons of our fathers, were we so to regard great questions affecting the general freedom. Those fathers accomplished the Revolution on a strict question of principle. The Parliament of Great Britain asserted a right to tax the colonies in all cases whatsoever; and it was precisely on this question that they made the Revolution turn. The amount of taxation was trifling, but the claim itself was inconsistent with liberty; and that was, in their eyes, enough. It was against the recital of an act of Parliament, rather than against any suffering under its enactments, that they took up arms. They went to war against a preamble. They fought seven years against a declaration. They poured out their treasures and their blood like water in a contest in opposition to an assertion which those less sagacious, and not so well schooled in the principles of civil liberty, would have regarded as barren phraseology, or mere parade of words. They saw in the claim of the British Parliament a seminal principle of mischief, the germ of unjust power; they detected it, dragged it forth from underneath its plausible disguises, struck at it; nor did it elude either their steady eye, or their well-directed blow, till they had extirpated and destroyed it to the smallest fibre. On this question of principle, while actual suffering was yet afar off, they raise their flag against a power to which, for purposes of foreign conquest and subjugation, Rome, in the height of her glory, is not to be compared—a power which has dotted over the surface of the whole globe with her possessions and military posts, whose morning drumbeat, following the sun, and keeping company with the hours, circles the earth daily with one continuous and unbroken strain of the martial airs of England.

Painted by F Cruikshank.   Engraved by J.D.Cross

John J. Audubon

JOHN JAMES AUDUBON.

[Born 1780. Died 1851.]

"FORMERLY," said Baron Cuvier, in a report to the Royal Academy of Sciences in Paris, "European naturalists had to make known her own treasures to America; but now her Mitchells, Harlans, and Charles Bonapartes, have repaid with interest the debt which she owed to Europe. The history of the American birds by Wilson already equals' in elegance our most beautiful works in ornithology, and if ever that of Audubon be completed, it will have to be confessed that in magnificence of execution the Old World is surpassed by the New." The work of the "American backwoodsman" thus alluded to has long been completed; the great Cuvier subsequently acknowledged it to be "the most splendid monument which art has erected in honour of ornithology;" and the judgment of mankind has placed the name of our countryman among the first of authors and artists who have illustrated the beautiful branch of natural history to which he has devoted so large a portion of his long and heroic life.

JOHN JAMES AUDUBON was born in Louisiana, May 4th, 1780. He was of French descent, and his parents perceiving early the bent of his genius sent him to Paris to pursue his education. While there he attended schools of natural history and the arts, and in drawing took lessons from the celebrated David. He returned in his eighteenth year, and his father soon after gave him a farm near Philadelphia, where the Perkiomen creek falls into the Schuylkill. Its fine woods offered him numerous subjects for his pencil, and he here commenced that series of drawings which ultimately swelled into the magnificent collection of The Birds of America. Here too he was married, and here was born his eldest son. He engaged in commercial speculations, but was not successful. His love for the fields and flowers, the forests and their winged inhabitants, we readily suppose unfitted him for trade. At the end of ten years he removed to the west. There were then no steamboats on the Ohio, and few villages and no cities on its shores. Reaching that noble river in the warm days of autumn, he purchased a small boat in which with his wife and child and two rowers he leisurely pursued his way down to Henderson in Kentucky, where his family resided several years. He appears at first to have engaged in commerce, for he mentions his meeting with Wilson, of whom till then he had never heard, as having occurred in his counting-room in Louisville in the spring of 1810. His great predecessor was procuring subscriptions for his work. He called on Audubon, explained the nature of his occupations, and requested his patronage. The merchant was surprised and gratified at the sight of his volumes, and had taken a pen to add his name to the list of subscribers, when his partner abruptly said to him in French, "My dear Audubon, what induces you to do so? your own drawings are certainly far better, and you must know as much of the habits of American birds as this gentleman." Wilson probably understood the remark, for he appeared not to be pleased, and inquired whether Audubon had any drawings of birds. A large portfolio was placed upon the table, and all its contents exhibited by the amateur ornithologist. Wilson was surprised; he had supposed he was himself the only person engaged in forming such a collection; and asked if it was intended to publish them. Audubon replied in the negative: he had never thought of presenting the fruits of his labours to the world. Wilson was still more surprised; he lost his cheerfulness; and though before he left Louisville Audubon explored with him the neighbouring woods, loaned him his drawings, and in other ways essayed to promote his interests and happiness, he shook the dust from his feet when he departed, and wrote in his diary that "literature or art had not a friend in the place." Far be it from me to write a word in dispraise of Alexander Wilson. He was a man of genius, enthusiasm, and patient endurance; an honour to the country of his birth, and a glory to that of his adoption; but he evidently could not bear the thought of being excelled. With all his merits he was even then greatly inferior to Audubon, and his heart failed him when he contrasted the performances which had won fame for him with those of the unknown lover of the same mistres , Nature, whom he thus encountered.

Audubon must soon have abandoned or neglected his day-books and ledgers, for in 1811 we find him with his rifle and drawing paper among the bayous of Florida, and in the following years making long and tedious journeys, searching the forests and prairies, the shores of rivers, lakes, gulfs and seas, for the subjects of his immortal work, of the publication of which, however, he had never yet had a thought.

On the fifth of April, 1824, he visited Philadelphia, where the late Dr. Mease, whom he had known on his first arrival in Pennsylvania, presented him to Charles Lucien Bonaparte, who in his turn introduced him to the Lyceum of Natural History. He perceived that he could look for no patronage in this city, and so proceeded to New York, where he was received with a kindness well suited to elevate his depressed spirits, and afterwards ascending the Hudson went westward to the great lakes, and in the wildest solitudes of the pathless forests renewed his labours. He now began to think of visiting Europe; the number of his drawings had greatly increased notwithstanding a misfortune by which two hundred of them, representing nearly a thousand birds, had been destroyed; and he fancied his work under the hands of the engraver. "Happy days and nights of pleasing dreams" followed, as he retired farther from the haunts of men, determined to leave nothing undone which could be accomplished by time or toil. Another year and a half passed by; he returned to his family, then in Louisiana; and having explored the woods of that state, at last sailed for England, where he arrived in 1826. In Liverpool and Manchester his works procured him a generous reception from the most distinguished men of science and letters; and when he proceeded to Edinburgh and exhibited there his four hundred paintings, "the hearts of all warmed toward Audubon," says Professor Wilson, "who were capable of conceiving the difficulties, dangers and sacrifices that must have been encountered, endured and overcome before genius could have embodied these, the glory of its innumerable triumphs."*

"The man himself," at this period writes the same eloquent author in another work, "is just what you would expect from his productions; full of fine enthusiasm and intelligence, most interesting in his looks and manners, a perfect gentleman, and esteemed by all who know him for the simplicity and frankness of his nature."†

His reception encouraged him to proceed immediately with his plans of publication. It was a vast undertaking which it would take probably sixteen years to accomplish, and when his first drawings were delivered to the engraver he had not a single subscriber. His friends pointed out the rashness of the project and urged him to abandon it. "But my heart was nerved," he exclaims, "and my reliance on that Power on whom all must depend brought bright anticipations of success." Leaving his work in the care of his engravers and agents, in the summer of 1828 he visited Paris, and received the homage of the most distinguished men of science in that capital. The ensuing winter was passed in London, and in April, 1829, he returned to America to explore anew the woods of the middle and southern states. Accompanied by his wife he left New Orleans on the eighth of January, 1830, for New York, and on the twenty-fifth of April, just a year from the time of his departure, he was again in the Great Metropolis. Before the close of 1830 he had issued his first volume, containing one hundred plates, representing ninety-nine species of birds, every figure of the size and colours of life. The applause with which it was received was enthusiastic and universal. The kings of England and France had placed their names at the head of his subscription list; he was made a fellow of the Royal Societies of London and Edinburgh; a member of the Natural History Society of Paris, and other celebrated institutions; and Cuvier, Swainson, and indeed the great ornithologists of every country, exhausted the words of panegyric in his praise.

On the first of August, 1831, Audubon arrived once more in New York, and having passed a few days with his friends there and in Philadelphia proceeded to Washington,

* Wilson's Miscellanies. vol. i. p. 118.
† Noctes Ambrosianæ, vol. ii. p. 103.

where the president and other principal officers of the government gave him letters of assistance and protection to be used all along the coasts and inland frontiers where there were collectors of revenue or military or naval forces. He had previously received similar letters from the king's ministers to the authorities of the British colonies.

The ensuing winter and spring were passed in the Floridas and in Charleston; and early in the summer, bending his course northward to keep pace with the birds in their migrations, he arrived in Philadelphia, where he was joined by his family. The cholera was then spreading death and terror through the country, and on reaching Boston he was himself arrested by sickness and detained until the middle of August. "Although I have been happy in forming many valuable friendships in various parts of the world, all dearly cherished by me," he says, "the outpouring of kindness which I experienced in Boston far exceeded all that I have ever met with;"* and he tells us, with characteristic enthusiasm, of his gratitude to the Appletons, Everetts, Quincys, Pickerings, Parkmans, and other eminent gentlemen and scholars of that beautiful and hospitable city.

Proceeding at length upon his mission, he explored the forests of Maine and New Brunswick and the shores of the Bay of Fundy, and chartering a vessel at Eastport, sailed for the gulf of St. Lawrence, the Magdalen Islands and the coast of Labrador. Returning as the cold season approached, he visited Newfoundland and Nova Scotia, and rejoining his family proceeded to Charleston, where he spent the winter, and in the spring, after nearly three years' travel and research, sailed a third time for England.

The second volume of The Birds of America was finished in 1834, and in December of that year he published in Edinburgh the second volume of the Ornithological Biography. Soon after, while he was in London, a nobleman called upon him, with his family, and on examining some of his original drawings, and being told that it would still require eight years to complete the work, subscribed for it, saying, "I may not see it finished, but my children will." The words made a deep impression

on Audubon. "The solemnity of his manner I could not forget for several days," he writes in the introduction to his third volume; "I often thought that neither might I see the work completed, but at length exclaimed, 'My sons may;' and now that another volume, both of my illustrations and of my biographies, is finished, my trust in Providence is augmented, and I cannot but hope that myself and my family together may be permitted to see the completion of my labours." When this was written, ten years had elapsed since the publication of his first plate. In the next three years, among other excursions he made one to the western coast of the Floridas and to Texas, in a vessel placed at his disposal by our government; and at the end of this time appeared the fourth and concluding volume of his engravings, and the fifth of his descriptions. The whole comprised four hundred and thirty-five plates, containing one thousand and sixty-five figures, from the Bird of Washington to the Humming Bird of the size of life, and a great variety of land and marine views, and floral and other productions, of different climates and seasons, all carefully drawn and coloured after nature. Well might the great naturalist felicitate himself upon the completion of his gigantic task. He had spent nearly half a century "amid the tall grass of the far-extended prairies of the west, in the solemn forests of the north, on the heights of the midland mountains, by the shores of the boundless ocean, and on the bosoms of our vast bays, lakes and rivers, searching for things hidden since the creation of this wondrous world from all but the Indian who has roamed in the gorgeous but melancholy wilderness." And speaking from the depth of his heart he says, "Once more surrounded by all the members of my dear family, enjoying the countenance of numerous friends who have never deserted me, and possessing a competent share of all that can render life agreeable, I look up with gratitude to the Supreme Being, and feel that I am happy."

In 1839, having returned for the last time to his native country and established himself with his family near the city of New York, Audubon commenced the publication of The Birds of America in imperial octavo volumes, of which the seventh and last was issued in the summer of 1844. The plates in this edition, reduced from his larger illustrations, were engraved and coloured in the most admirable manner by Mr. Bowen of Philadelphia. They were published with the letter-press in one hundred parts, at one dollar per number, afterwards bound in seven volumes, and now in eight volumes.

Audubon was too sincere a worshipper of nature to be content with inglorious repose, even after having accomplished in action more than was ever dreamed of by any other naturalist; and while the "edition for the people" of his Birds of America was in course of publication, he was busy amid the forests and prairies, the reedy swamps of our southern shores, the cliffs that protect our eastern coasts, by the currents of the Mexican gulf and the tide streams of the Bay of Fundy, with his sons, Victor Gifford and John Woodhouse, making the drawings and writing the biographies of the *Quadrupeds of America*, a work in no respect inferior to that on our birds, which he published in parts, and completed in three volumes in 1849. The plates, on double imperial folio paper, engraved and coloured by Mr. Bowen after the original drawings made from nature by Audubon and his sons, are even more magnificent than those of the Birds of America, which forty years ago delighted and astonished the naturalists of Europe. A smaller edition was afterwards published in 3 vols., imperial 8vo., with the plates much reduced; the only popular work of the kind, except Dr. Goodman's Natural History.

Audubon's highest claim to admiration is founded upon his drawings in natural history, in which he has exhibited an excellence but rarely eclipsed. In all our climates—in the clear atmosphere, by the dashing waters, amid the grand old forests with their peculiar and many-tinted foliage, by him first made known to art—he has represented our feathered tribes, building their nests and fostering their young, poised on the tip of the spray and hovering over the sedgy margin of the lake, flying in the clouds in quest of prey or from pursuit, in love, enraged, indeed in all the varieties of their motion and repose and modes of life, so perfectly, that nearly every bird is represented almost as natural as life.

But he has also indisputable claims to a respectable rank as a man of letters. Some of his written pictures of birds, so graceful, clearly defined, and brilliantly coloured, are scarcely inferior to the productions of his pencil. His powers of general description are also remarkable. The waters seem to dance to his words as to music, and the lights and shades of his landscapes show the practised hand of a master. The evanescent shades of manners, also, upon the extreme frontiers, where the footprints of civilization have hardly crushed the green leaves, have been sketched with graphic fidelity in his journals.

No author has more individuality. The enthusiastic, trustful and loving spirit which breathes through his works distinguishes the man. From the beginning he surrendered himself entirely to his favourite pursuit, and has been intent to learn every thing from the prime teacher, Nature. His style as well as his knowledge is a fruit of his experiences. He had never written for the press until after the age at which most authors have established their reputation; and when he did write his page glowed like the rich wild landscape in the spring, when Nature, then most beautiful, "bathes herself in her own dewy waters." We seem to hear his expressions of wondering admiration, as unknown mountains, valleys and lakes burst upon his view, as the deer at his approach leaps from his ambush into the deeper solitudes, as the startled bird with rushing wings darts from his feet into the sky; or his pious thanksgiving as at the end of a weary day the song of the sparrow or the robin relieves his mind from the heavy melancholy that bears it down.

When the celebrated Buffon had completed the ornithological portion of his great work on natural history, he announced with unhesitating assurance that he had "finished the history of the birds of the world." Twenty centuries had served for the discovery of only eight hundred species, but this number seemed immense, and the short-sighted naturalist declared that the list would admit of "no material augmentation" which embraced hardly a sixteenth of those now known to exist. To this astonishing advance of the science of ornithology no one has contributed more than Audubon, by his magnificent painting and fascinating history.

—Mr. Audubon died in New York, on the twenty-eighth of January, 1851. From papers that he left, an extended account of his life was published in 1869, and will doubtless prove to be one of the most attractive specimens of biography in modern literature.

THE HURRICANE.

FROM ORNITHOLOGICAL BIOGRAPHY.

VARIOUS portions of our country have at different periods suffered severely from the influence of violent storms of wind, some of which have been known to traverse nearly the whole extent of the United States, and to leave such deep impressions in their wake as will not easily be forgotten. Having witnessed one of these awful phenomena, in all its grandeur, I will attempt to describe it. The recollection of that astonishing revolution of the ethereal element even now brings with it so disagreeable a sensation, that I feel as if about to be affected by a sudden stoppage of the circulation of my blood.

I had left the village of Shawaney, situated on the banks of the Ohio, on my return from Henderson, which is also situated on the banks of the same beautiful stream. The weather was pleasant, and I thought not warmer than usual at that season. My horse was jogging quietly along, and my thoughts were, for once at-least in the course of my life, entirely engaged in commercial speculations. I had forded Highland Creek, and was on the eve of entering a tract of bottom land or valley that lay between it and Canoe Creek, when on a sudden I remarked a great difference in the aspect of the heavens. A hazy thickness had overspread the country, and I for some time expected an earthquake, but my horse exhibited no propensity to stop and prepare for such an occurrence. I had nearly arrived at the verge of the valley, when I thought fit to stop near a brook, and dismounted to quench the thirst which had come upon me.

I was leaning on my knees, with my lips about to touch the water, when, from my proximity to the earth, I heard a distant murmuring sound of an extraordinary nature. I drank, however, and as I rose on my feet, looked toward the south-west, where I observed a yellowish, oval spot, the appearance of which was quite new to me. Little time was left to me for consideration, as the next moment a smart breeze began to agitate the taller trees. It increased to an unexpected height, and already the smaller branches and twigs were seen falling in a slanting direction towards the ground. Two minutes had scarcely elapsed, when the whole forest before me was in fearful motion. Here and there, where one tree pressed against another, a creaking noise was produced, similar to that occasioned by the violent gusts which sometimes sweep over the country. Turning instinctively toward the direction from which the wind blew, I saw, to my great astonishment, that the noblest trees of the forest bent their lofty heads for a while, and unable to stand against the blast, were falling into pieces. First, the branches were broken off with a crackling noise; then went the upper part of the massy trunks; and in many places whole trees of gigantic size were falling entire to the ground. So rapid was the progress of the storm, that before I could think of taking measures to insure my safety, the hurricane was passing opposite the place where I

stood. Never can I forget the scene which at that moment presented itself. The tops of the trees were seen moving in the strangest manner, in the central current of the tempest, which carried along with it a mingled mass of twigs and foliage, that completely obscured the view. Some of the largest trees were seen bending and writhing under the gale; others suddenly snapped across; and many, after a momentary resistance, fell uprooted to the earth. The mass of branches, twigs, foliage and dust that moved through the air, was whirled onwards like a cloud of feathers, and on passing, disclosed a wide space filled with fallen trees, naked stumps, and heaps of shapeless ruins, which marked the path of the tempest. This space was about a fourth of a mile in breadth, and to my imagination resembled the dried-up bed of the Mississippi, with its thousands of planters and sawyers, strewed in the sand, and inclined in various degrees. The horrible noise resembled that of the great cataracts of Niagara, and as it howled along in the track of the desolating tempest, produced a feeling in my mind which it is impossible to describe.

The principal force of the hurricane was now over, although millions of twigs and small branches, that had been brought from a great distance, were seen following the blast, as if drawn onwards by some mysterious power. They even floated in the air for some hours after, as if supported by the thick mass of dust that rose high above the ground. The sky had now a greenish lurid hue, and an extremely disagreeable sulphureous odour was diffused in the atmosphere. I waited in amazement, having sustained no material injury, until nature at length resumed her wonted aspect. For some moments, I felt undetermined whether I should return to Morgantown, or attempt to force my way through the wrecks of the tempest. My business, however, being of an urgent nature, I ventured into the path of the storm, and after encountering innumerable difficulties, succeeded in crossing it. I was obliged to lead my horse by the bridle to enable him to leap over the fallen trees, whilst I scrambled over or under them in the best way I could, at times so hemmed in by the broken tops and tangled branches, as almost to become desperate. On arriving at my house, I gave an account of what I had seen, when, to my surprise, I was told that there had been very little wind in the neighbourhood, although in the streets and gardens many branches and twigs had fallen in a manner which excited great surprise.

Many wondrous accounts of the devastating effect of this hurricane were circulated in the country, after its occurrence. Some log houses, we were told, had been overturned, and their inmates destroyed. One person informed me that a wire-sifter had been conveyed by the gust to a distance of many miles. Another had found a cow lodged in the fork of a large half-broken tree. But, as I am disposed to relate only what I have myself seen, I will not lead you into the region of romance, but shall content myself by saying that much damage was done by this awful visitation. The valley is yet a desolate place, overgrown with briars and bushes, thick ly entangled amidst the tops and trunks of the fallen trees, and is the resort of ravenous animals, to which they betake themselves when pursued by man, or after they have committed their depredations on the farms of the surrounding district. I have crossed the path of the storm, at a distance of a hundred miles from the spot where I witnessed its fury, and, again, four hundred miles farther off, in the state of Ohio. Lastly, I observed traces of its ravages on the summits of the mountains connected with the Great Pine Forest of Pennsylvania, three hundred miles beyond the place last mentioned. In all these different parts, it appeared to me not to have exceeded a quarter of a mile in breadth.

DESCENT OF THE OHIO IN 1809.

FROM THE SAME.

It was in the month of October. The autumnal tints already decorated the shores of that queen of rivers, the Ohio. Every tree was hung with long and flowing festoons of different species of vines, many loaded with clustered fruits of varied brilliancy, their rich bronzed carmine mingling beautifully with the yellow foliage, which now predominated over the yet green leaves, reflecting more lively tints from the clear stream than ever landscape painter portrayed or poet imagined.

The days were yet warm. The sun had assumed the rich and glowing hue, which at that season produces the singular phenomenon called there the "Indian Summer." The moon had rather passed the meridian of her grandeur. We glided down the river, meeting no other ripple of the water than that formed by the propulsion of our boat. Leisurely we moved along, gazing all day on the grandeur and beauty of the wild scenery around us.

Now and then, a large cat-fish rose to the surface of the water in pursuit of a shoal of fry, which starting simultaneously from the liquid element, like so many silvery arrows, produced a shower of light, while the pursuer with open jaws seized the stragglers, and, with a splash of his tail, disappeared from our view. Other fishes we heard uttering beneath our bark a rumbling noise, the strange sounds of which we discovered to proceed from the white perch, for on casting our net from the bow we caught several of that species, when the noise ceased for a time.

Nature, in her varied arrangements, seems to have felt a partiality toward this portion of our country. As the traveller ascends or descends the Ohio, he cannot help remarking that alternately, nearly the whole length of the river, the margin, on one side, is bounded by lofty hills and a rolling surface, while on the other, extensive plains of the richest alluvial land are seen as far as the eye can command the view. Islands of varied size and form rise here and there from the bosom of the water, and the winding course of the stream frequently brings you to places, where the idea of being on a river of great length changes to that of floating on a lake of moderate extent. Some of these islands are of considerable size and value; while others, small and insignificant, seem as if intended for contrast, and as serving to enhance the general interest of the scenery. These little islands are frequently overflowed during great *freshets* or floods, and receive at their heads prodigious heaps of drifted timber. We foresaw with great concern the alteration that cultivation would soon produce along those delightful banks.

As night came, sinking in darkness the broader portions of the river, our minds became affected by strong emotions, and wandered far beyond the present moments. The tinkling of bells told us that the cattle which bore them were gently roving from valley to valley in search of food, or returning to their distant homes. The hooting of the Great Owl, or the muffled noise of its wings as it sailed smoothly over the stream, were matters of interest to us; so was the sound of the boatman's horn, as it came winding more and more softly from afar. When daylight returned, many songsters burst forth with echoing notes, more and more mellow to the listening ear. Here and there the lonely cabin of a squatter struck the eye, giving note of commencing civilization. The crossing of the stream by a deer foretold how soon the hills would be covered with snow.

Many sluggish flat-boats we overtook and passed: some laden with produce from the different head-waters of the small rivers that pour their tributary streams into the Ohio; others of less dimensions, crowded with emigrants from distant parts, in search of a new home. Purer pleasures I never felt; nor have you, reader, I ween, unless indeed you have felt the like, and in such company.....

When I think of the times, and call back to my mind the grandeur and beauty of those almost uninhabited shores; when I picture to myself the dense and lofty summits of the forest, that everywhere spread along the hills, and overhung the margins of the stream, unmolested by the axe of the settler; when I know how dearly purchased the safe navigation of that river has been by the blood of many worthy Virginians; when I see that no longer any Aborigines are to be found there, and that the vast herds of elks, deer, and buffaloes which once pastured on these hills and in these valleys, making for themselves great roads to the several salt-springs, have ceased to exist; when I reflect that all this grand portion of our Union, instead of being in a state of nature, is now more or less covered with villages, farms, and towns, where the din of hammers and machinery is constantly heard; that the woods are fast disappearing under the axe by day, and the fire by night; that hundreds of steamboats are gliding to and fro, over the whole length of the majestic river, forcing commerce to take root and to prosper at every spot; when I see the surplus population of Europe coming to assist in the destruction of the forest, and transplanting civilization into its darkest recesses;—when I remember that these extraordinary changes have all taken place in the short period of twenty years, I pause, wonder, and, although I know all to be fact, can scarcely believe its reality.

Whether these changes are for the better or for the worse, I shall not pretend to say; but in whatever way my conclusions may incline, I feel with regret that there are on record no satisfactory accounts of the state of that portion of the country, from the time when our people first settled in it. This has not been because no one in America is able to accomplish such an undertaking. Our Irvings and our Coopers have proved themselves fully competent for the task. It has more proba-bly been because the changes have succeeded each other with such rapidity, as almost to rival the movements of their pen. However, it is not too late yet; and I sincerely hope that either or both of them will ere long furnish the generations to come with those delightful descriptions which they are so well qualified to give, of the original state of a country that has been so rapidly forced to change her form and attire under the influence of increasing population. Yes; I hope to read, ere I close my earthly career, accounts from those de-lightful writers of the progress of civilization in our western country. They will speak of the Clarks, the Croghans, the Boons, and many other men of great and daring enterprise. They will analyze, as it were, into each component part, the country as it once existed, and will render the picture, as it ought to be, immortal.

THE HUMMING BIRD.

FROM THE SAME.

Where is the person, who, on observing this glittering fragment of the rainbow, would not pause, admire, and instantly turn his mind with reverence toward the Almighty Creator, the won-ders of whose hand we at every step discover, and of whose sublime conceptions we everywhere ob-serve the manifestations in his admirable system of creation!—There breathes not such a person; so kindly have we all been blessed with that intui-tive and noble feeling—admiration!

No sooner has the returning sun again intro-duced the vernal season, and caused millions of plants to expand their leaves and blossoms to his genial beams, than the little Humming Bird is seen advancing on fairy wings, carefully visiting every opening flower-cup, and, like a curious florist, re-moving from each the injurious insects that other-wise would ere long cause their beauteous petals to droop and decay. Poised in the air, it is ob-served peeping cautiously, and with sparkling eye, into their innermost recesses, whilst the ethereal motions of its pinions, so rapid and so light, ap-pear to fan and cool the flower, without injuring its fragile texture, and produce a delightful mur-muring sound, well adapted for lulling the insects to repose.....

The prairies, the fields, the orchards and gardens, nay, the deepest shades of the forests, are all visited in their turn, and everywhere the little bird meets with pleasure and with food. Its gorgeous throat in beauty and brilliancy baffles all competition.

Now it glows with a fiery hue, and again it is changed to the deepest velvety black. The upper parts of its delicate body are of resplendent chang-ing green; and it throws itself through the air with a swiftness and vivacity hardly conceivable. It moves from one flower to another like a gleam of light, upwards, downwards, to the right, and to the left. In this manner it searches the extreme northern portions of our country, following with great precaution the advances of the season, and retreats with equal care at the approach of autumn.

THE MOCKING BIRD.

FROM THE SAME.

It is where the Great Magnolia shoots up its majestic trunk, crowned with evergreen leaves, and decorated with a thousand beautiful flowers, that perfume the air around; where the forests and fields are adorned with blossoms of every hue; where the Golden Orange ornaments the gardens and groves; where Bignonias of various kinds in-terlace their climbing stems around the White-flowered Stuartia, and mounting still higher, cover the summits of the lofty trees around, accompanied with innumerable vines, that here and there fes-toon the dense foliage of the magnificent woods, lending to the vernal breeze a slight portion of the perfume of their clustered flowers; where a genial warmth seldom forsakes the atmosphere; where berries and fruits of all descriptions are met with at every step;—in a word, it is where Nature seems to have paused, as she passed over the earth, and opening her stores to have strewed with unsparing hand the diversified seeds from which have sprung all the beautiful and splendid forms which I should in vain attempt to describe, that the Mocking Bird should have fixed its abode, there only that its wondrous song should be heard.

But where is that favoured land?—It is in that great continent to whose distant shores Europe has sent forth her adventurous sons, to wrest for themselves a habitation from the wild inhabitants of the forest, and to convert the neglected soil into fields of exuberant fertility. It is, reader, in Lou-isiana that these bounties of nature are in the greatest perfection. It is there that you should listen to the love-song of the Mocking Bird, as I at this moment do. See how he flies round his mate, with motions as light as those of the butter-fly! His tail is widely expanded, he mounts in the air to a small distance, describes a circle, and, again alighting, approaches his beloved one, his eyes gleaming with delight, for she has already pro-mised to be his and his only. His beautiful wings are gently raised, he bows to his love, and again bouncing upwards, opens his bill, and pours forth his melody, full of exultation at the conquest which he has made.

They are not the soft sounds of the flute or the hautboy that I hear, but the sweeter notes of Na-ture's own music. The mellowness of the song, the varied modulations and gradations, the extent of its compass, the great brilliancy of execution, are

25

R

unrivalled. There is probably no bird in the world that possesses all the musical qualifications of this king of song, who has derived all from Nature's self. Yes, reader, all!

No sooner has he again alighted, and the conjugal contract has been sealed, than, as if his breast was about to be rent with delight, he again pours forth his notes with more softness and richness than before. He now soars higher, glancing around with a vigilant eye, to assure himself that none has witnessed his bliss. When these love scenes are over, he dances through the air, full of animation and delight, and, as if to convince his lovely mate that to enrich her hopes he has much more love in store, he that moment begins anew, and imitates all the notes which nature has imparted to the other songsters of the grove.....

The musical powers of this bird have often been taken notice of by European naturalists, and persons who find pleasure in listening to the song of different birds whilst in confinement or at large. Some of these persons have described the notes of the Nightingale as occasionally fully equal to those of our bird. I have frequently heard both species in confinement, and in the wild state, and without prejudice, have no hesitation in pronouncing the notes of the European Philomel equal to those of a *soubrette* of taste, which, could she study under a MOZART, might perhaps in time become very interesting in her way. But to compare her essays to the finished talent of the Mocking Bird, is, in my opinion, quite absurd.

THE WOOD THRUSH.
FROM THE SAME.

THIS bird is my greatest favourite of the feathered tribes of our woods. To it I owe much. How often has it revived my drooping spirits, when I have listened to its wild notes in the forest, after passing a restless night in my slender shed, so feebly secured against the violence of the storm, as to show me the futility of my best efforts to rekindle my little fire, whose uncertain and vacillating light had gradually died away under the destructive weight of the dense torrents of rain that seemed to involve the heavens and the earth in one mass of fearful murkiness, save when the red streaks of the flashing thunderbolt burst on the dazzled eye, and, glancing along the huge trunk of the stateliest and noblest tree in my immediate neighbourhood, were instantly followed by an uproar of crackling, crashing, and deafening sounds, rolling their volumes in tumultuous eddies far and near, as if to silence the very breathings of the unformed thought! How often, after such a night, when far from my dear home, and deprived of the presence of those nearest to my heart, wearied, hungry, drenched, and so lonely and desolate as almost to question myself why I was thus situated, when I have seen the fruits of my labours on the eve of being destroyed, as the water, collected into a stream, rushed through my little camp, and forced me to stand erect, shivering in a cold fit like that of a severe ague, when I have been obliged to wait with the patience of a martyr for the return of day, silently counting over the years of my youth, doubting perhaps if ever again I should return to my home, and embrace my family!—how often, as the first glimpses of morning gleamed doubtfully amongst the dusky masses of the forest-trees, has there come upon my ear, thrilling along the sensitive cords which connect that organ with the heart, the delightful music of this harbinger of day! —and how fervently, on such occasions, have I blessed the Being who formed the Wood Thrush, and placed it in those solitary forests, as if to console me amidst my privations, to cheer my depressed mind, and to make me feel, as I did, that man never should despair, whatever may be his situation, as he can never be certain that aid and deliverance are not at hand.

The Wood Thrush seldom commits a mistake after such a storm as I have attempted to describe; for no sooner are its sweet notes heard than the heavens gradually clear, the bright refracted light rises in gladdening rays from beneath the distant horizon, the effulgent beams increase in their intensity, and the great orb of day at length bursts on the sight. The gray vapour that floats along the ground is quickly dissipated, the world smiles at the happy change, and the woods are soon heard to echo the joyous thanks of their many songsters. At that moment all fears vanish, giving place to an inspiriting hope. The hunter prepares to leave his camp. He listens to the Wood Thrush, while he thinks of the course which he ought to pursue, and as the bird approaches to peep at him, and learn somewhat his intentions, he raises his mind toward the Supreme Disposer of events. Seldom, indeed, have I heard the song of this Thrush, without feeling all that tranquillity of mind, to which the secluded situation in which it delights is so favourable. The thickest and darkest woods always appear to please it best. The borders of murmuring streamlets, overshadowed by the dense foliage of the lofty trees growing on the gentle declivities, amidst which the sunbeams seldom penetrate, are its favourite resorts. There it is, that the musical powers of this hermit of the woods must be heard, to be fully appreciated and enjoyed.

FLIGHT OF THE GREAT HORNED OWL.
FROM THE SAME.

IT is during the placid serenity of a beautiful summer night, when the current of the waters moves silently along, reflecting from its smooth surface the silver radiance of the moon, and when all else of animated nature seems sunk in repose, that the Great Horned Owl, one of the Nimrods of the feathered tribes of our forests, may be seen sailing along silently yet rapidly, intent on the destruction of the objects destined to form his food. The lone steersman of the descending boat observes the nocturnal hunter, gliding on extended pinions across the river, sailing over one hill and then another, or suddenly sweeping downwards, and again rising in the air like a moving shadow, now distinctly seen, and again mingling with the sombre shades of the surrounding woods, fading into obscurity.

NIAGARA.

FROM THE SAME.

AFTER wandering on some of our great lakes for many months, I bent my course toward the celebrated falls of Niagara, being desirous of taking a sketch of them. This was not my first visit to them, and I hoped it would not be the last.....

Returning as I then was from a tedious journey, and possessing little more than some drawings of rare birds and plants, I reached the tavern at Niagara Falls in such plight as might have deterred many an individual from obtruding himself upon a circle of well-clad and perhaps well-bred society. Months had passed since the last of my linen had been taken from my body, and used to clean that useful companion, my gun. I was in fact covered just like one of the poorer class of Indians, and was rendered even more disagreeable to the eye of civilized man, by not having, like them, plucked my beard, or trimmed my hair in any way. Had HOGARTH been living, there when I arrived, he could not have found a fitter subject for a Ro-BINSON CRUSOE. My beard covered my neck in front, my hair fell much lower at my back, the leather dress which I wore had for months stood in need of repair, a large knife hung at my side, a rusty tin-box containing my drawings and colours, and wrapped up in a worn out blanket that had served me for a bed, was buckled to my shoulders. To every one I must have seemed immersed in the depths of poverty, perhaps of despair. Nevertheless, as I cared little about my appearance during those happy rambles, I pushed into the sitting-room, unstrapped my little burden, and asked how soon breakfast would be ready.

In America no person is ever refused entrance to the inns, at least far from cities. We know too well how many poor creatures are forced to make their way from other countries in search of employment, or to seek uncultivated land, and we are ever ready to let them have what they may call for. No one knew who I was, and the landlord looking at me with an eye of close scrutiny, answered that breakfast would be on the table as soon as the company should come down from their rooms. I approached this important personage, told him of my avocations, and convinced him that he might feel safe as to remuneration. From this moment I was, with him at least, on equal footing with every other person in his house. He talked a good deal of the many artists who had visited the Falls that season, from different parts, and offered to assist me, by giving such accommodations as I might require to finish the drawings I had in contemplation. He left me, and as I looked about the room, I saw several views of the Falls, by which I was so disgusted, that I suddenly came to my better senses. "What!" thought I, "have I come here to mimic nature in her grandest enterprise, and add *my* caricature of one of the wonders of the world to those which I here see? No.—I give up the vain attempt. I will look on these mighty cataracts and imprint them where they alone can be represented, —on my mind!"

THE DEER HUNT.

FROM THE SAME.

WE will suppose that we are now about to follow the *true hunter*, as the Still Hunter is also called, through the interior of the tangled woods, across morasses, ravines, and such places, where the game may prove more or less plentiful, even should none be found there in the first instance. We will allow our hunter all the agility, patience, and care, which his occupation requires, and will march in his rear, as if we were spies, watching all his motions. His dress, you observe, consists of a leather hunting shirt, and a pair of trowsers of the same material. His feet are well moccasined; he wears a belt round his waist; his heavy rifle is resting on his brawny shoulder; on one side hangs his ball-pouch, surmounted by the horn of an ancient buffalo, once the terror of the herd, but now containing a pound of the best gunpowder; his knife is scabbarded in the same strap, and behind is a tomahawk, the handle of which has been thrust through his girdle. He walks with so rapid a step, that probably few men could follow him, unless for a short distance, in their anxiety to witness his ruthless deeds. He stops, looks at the flint of his gun, its priming, and the leather cover of the lock, then glances his eye towards the sky, to judge of the course most likely to lead him to the game.

The heavens are clear, the red glare of the morning sun gleams through the lower branches of the lofty trees, the dew hangs in pearly drops at the top of every leaf. Already has the emerald hue of the foliage been converted into the more glowing tints of our autumnal months. A slight frost appears on the fence-rails of his little cornfield. As he proceeds, he looks to the dead foliage under his feet, in search of the well-known traces of a buck's hoof. Now he bends toward the ground, on which something has attracted his attention. See! he alters his course, increases his speed, and will soon reach the opposite hill. Now, he moves with caution, stops at almost every tree, and peeps forward, as if already within shooting distance of the game. He advances again, but how very slowly! He has reached the declivity, upon which the sun shines in all its glowing splendour; but mark him! he takes the gun from his shoulder, has already thrown aside the leathern cover of the lock, and is wiping the edge of his flint with his tongue. Now he stands like a monumental figure, perhaps measuring the distance that lies between him and the game, which he has in view. His rifle is slowly raised, the report follows, and he runs. Let us run also. Shall I speak to him, and ask him the result of this first essay? Assuredly, for I know him well.

"Pray, friend, what have you killed?" (for to say, "what have you shot at?" might imply the possibility of his having missed, and so might hurt his feelings.) "Nothing but a buck." "And where is it?" "Oh, it has taken a jump or so, but I settled it, and will soon be with it. My ball struck, and must have gone through his heart."

THE LAUREL.

FROM THE SAME.

WHAT a beautiful object, in the delightful season of spring, is our Great Laurel, covered with its tufts of richly, yet delicately, coloured flowers! In imagination I am at this moment rambling along the banks of some murmuring streamlet, overshadowed by the thick foliage of this gorgeous ornament of our mountainous districts. Methinks I see the timid trout eyeing my movements from beneath his rocky covert, while the warblers and other sylvan choristers, equally fond of their wild retreats, are skipping in all the freedom of nature around me. Delightful moments have been to me those when, seated in such a place, with senses all intent, I gazed on the rosy tints of the flowers that seemed to acquire additional colouring from the golden rays of the sun, as he rode proudly over the towering mountains, drawing aside as it were the sable curtain that till now hung over the landscape, and drying up, with the gentleness of a parent toward his cherished offspring, the dewy tears that glittered on each drooping plant.

GUILLEMOTS IN A STORM.

FROM THE SAME.

STAY on the deck of the Ripley by my side this clear and cold morning. See how swiftly scuds our gallant bark, as she cuts her way through the foaming billows, now inclining to the right and again to the left. Far in the east, dark banks of low clouds indicate foul weather to the wary mariner, who watches the approach of a northern storm with anxiety. Suddenly the wind changes; but for this he has prepared; the topsails are snugged to their yards, and the rest are securely reefed. A thick fog obscures all around us. The waters, suddenly checked in their former course, furiously war against those which now strike them in front. The uproar increases, the bark is tossed on every side; now a sweeping wave rushes against the bows, the vessel quivers, while down along her deck violently pour the waters, rolling from side to side, seeking for a place by which they may escape. At this moment all about you are in dismay save the Guillemots. The sea is covered with these intrepid navigators of the deep. Over each tumultuous billow they swim unconcerned on the very spray at the bow of the vessel, and plunging as if with pleasure, up they come next moment at the rudder. Others fly around in large circles, while thousands contend with the breeze, moving directly against it in long lines, toward regions unknown to all, save themselves and some other species of sea birds.

THE LIFE OF A NATURALIST.

FROM THE SAME.

THE adventures and vicissitudes which have fallen to my lot, instead of tending to diminish the fervid enthusiasm of my nature, have imparted a toughness to my bodily constitution, naturally strong, and to my mind, naturally buoyant, an elasticity such as to assure me that though somewhat old, and considerably denuded in the frontal region, I could yet perform on foot a journey of any length, were I sure that I should thereby add materially to our knowledge of the ever interesting creatures which have for so long a time occupied my thoughts by day, and filled my dreams with pleasant images. Nay, reader, had I a new lease of life presented to me, I should choose for it the very occupations in which I have been engaged.

And, reader, the life which I have led has been in some respects a singular one. Think of a person, intent on such pursuits as mine have been, aroused at early dawn from his rude couch on the alder-fringed brook of some northern valley, or in the midst of some yet unexplored forest of the west, or perhaps on the soft and warm sands of the Florida shores, and listening to the pleasing melodies of songsters innumerable saluting the magnificent orb, from whose radiant influence the creatures of many worlds receive life and light. Refreshed and reinvigorated by healthful rest, he starts upon his feet, gathers up his store of curiosities, buckles on his knapsack, shoulders his trusty firelock, says a kind word to his faithful dog, and re-commences his pursuit of zoological knowledge. Now the morning is spent, and a squirrel or a trout afford him a repast. Should the day be warm, he reposes for a time under the shade of some tree. The woodland choristers again burst forth into song, and he starts anew to wander wherever his fancy may direct him, or the objects of his search may lead him in pursuit. When evening approaches, and the birds are seen betaking themselves to the retreats, he looks for some place of safety, erects his shed of green boughs, kindles his fire, prepares his meal, and as the widgeon or blue-winged teal, or perhaps the breast of a turkey or a steak of venison, sends its delicious perfumes abroad, he enters into his parchment-bound journal the remarkable incidents and facts that have occurred in the course of the day. Darkness has now drawn her sable curtain over the scene; his repast is finished, and kneeling on the earth, he raises his soul to Heaven, grateful for the protection that has been granted to him, and the sense of the divine presence in this solitary place. Then wishing a cordial good night to all the dear friends at home, the American woodsman wraps himself up in his blanket, and closing his eyes soon falls into that comfortable sleep which never fails him on such occasions.

ROBERT WALSH.

[Born about 1784. Died 1859.]

Mr. Walsh was of Irish Catholic descent, and was born about the year 1784, in Baltimore, where his father was a merchant. He received a liberal education, and after passing several years in Great Britain, France, and other parts of Europe, for the improvement of his mind, at twenty-six years of age he returned to the United States, selected Philadelphia as his place of residence, was admitted to the bar, and married. The infirmity of partial deafness, or it may be a predominant love of letters, soon induced the abandonment of the profession of law for that of literature. His first essays were in The Port Folio, a monthly miscellany which has been before mentioned in these pages, and which was then in the zenith of its reputation. In December, 1809, he published his first book, under the title of A Letter on the Genius and Dispositions of the French Government, including a View of the Taxation of the French Empire. It is stated in the advertisement that it "was written amid a variety of pursuits in the course of two months," and hastily published, from an impression that it was called for, if at all, at the moment. It secured for him at once a wide popularity. Perhaps nothing from the American press had ever produced a greater sensation. It furnished a subject for the leading article in the next number of the Edinburgh Review : " Here is a stout republican," exclaims the critic, " who praises England and declaims against France, with more zeal and intelligence than any of our own politicians ; who writes better and shows more learning than most of our men of letters ; displays the characteristic keenness of his countrymen, without any of their coarseness, and has all their patriotic prejudices, without their illiberality." Mr. Walsh had made good use of his time while in France, and the fulness of his information respecting that country, and contemporaneous events generally, the boldness and apparent sagacity of his views, and the affluence of his clear and forcible style, naturally won for him the most favourable consideration; but perhaps Mr. Jeffrey might not

have discovered so much literary merit in his Letter, if it had been informed with a more gallican spirit. Mr. Walsh's hatred of France indeed was so strong as even with the British reviewer to cause an instinctive distrust of his accuracy, though it is admitted that the operation of his prejudice was in a great measure corrected by an uprightness of principle and a habit of careful reasoning.

On the first of January, 1811, Mr. Walsh published the initial number of The American Review of History and Politics. This was the first American quarterly, and was too far in advance of the popular taste to be successful. Mr. Walsh himself wrote nearly all the contents of the first and second numbers, among which were two able articles on the life and genius of Alexander Hamilton, and several on his more favourite subject of France and her foreign relations. Altogether the Review was eminently creditable to him, and its discontinuance at the close of the second year of its publication was with good reason lamented by the friends of literature throughout the country.

In 1813 he published his Correspondence with General Harper respecting Russia, and his Essay on the Future State of Europe : works in style and spirit agreeing very closely with his Letter on the French Government. It was about this period, I believe, that he wrote the biographical and critical notices of the British Poets, contained in the part printed under his supervision, of the fifty-volume edition of their works, commenced by Mr. Sanford.

In 1817 he undertook the management of the American Register, a periodical devoted to politics, history, statistics, etc., upon which his labours were arduous and of much temporary importance. Indeed the work is still interesting and valuable, and it proves that the editor must have possessed great industry as well as various intellectual resources.

In 1819 appeared Mr. Walsh's Appeal from the Judgments of Great Britain respecting the United States of America, containing an

Historical Outline of their Merits and Wrongs as Colonies, and Strictures upon the Calumnies of the British Writers. It is an octavo volume of more than five hundred pages, and was the offspring of a more extended and systematic design, "a survey of the institutions and resources of the American republic, and of the real character of the American people;" and was published as an introduction to a work of this nature. The appearance in the Quarterly Review of an article on the United States, in the form of a review of Inchiquin's Letters, distinguished alike for malignity, ignorance, and coarse buffoonery, had somewhat exasperated the feelings of many here who had observed the almost uniform injustice of English writers and orators toward our country. They cared very little for the attacks themselves, which evidently for the most part were by vulgar hirelings, but it was thought with good reason that there must be a pervading and deeply rooted prejudice against us in a community which could make such things profitable to their authors. The Rev. Dr. Dwight, Mr. James K. Paulding, and one or two others, had replied to the Quarterly in volumes marked by trenchant wit as well as by research and solid argument. Mr. Walsh's Appeal was a more extended and comprehensive work of the same sort, and was in the main judiciously and forcibly executed. But his subjection to unworthy prejudices prevented him from making, in an elaborate vindication of our intellectual character which it contained, even the slightest allusion to Jonathan Edwards. One might as well not mention Homer in a history of Greek poetry.

In 1821, Mr. Walsh and Mr. William Fry established in Philadelphia the National Gazette, a small evening newspaper, the editorial control of which was confided to Mr. Walsh. It was at first published but three times a week; but in a short time it was enlarged and issued daily. Under the example of the National Gazette, journalism in this country assumed by degrees some new characteristics. Hitherto the daily press had been chiefly devoted to politics, in the treatment of which the temperance of gentlemanly breeding with the taste of classical training were not often exhibited. Mr. Walsh's system of editing was an innovation. His columns were devoted to literature, science and art, as well as to general intelligence and public affairs. His reviews of books, though lacking the genial sympathy of the best critics, exhibited much knowledge, reflection, and good sense. The same may be said of his notices of the stage. The Gazette rose rapidly in the popular estimation and soon had an unprecedented influence, and its success led in all parts of the country to more attention to matters of taste in the journals.

Since the failure of Mr. Walsh's quarterly, the North American Review had proved a more successful experiment in Boston, and in 1822, resigning the management of the American Magazine of Foreign Literature, he revived the American Quarterly Review, or rather established a new periodical under that title. It was published for ten years, during which time he wrote for it numerous articles, some of which were on subjects requiring very careful and extensive investigations, besides attending assiduously to the National Gazette, writing the valuable papers in American biography in the Encyclopedia Americana, and performing other literary labours.

For fifteen years the prosperity of the National Gazette was unabated; but with changes of times and opinions, and the rise of rival journals with new attractions, it began to lose ground, and in 1837 Mr. Walsh withdrew from it, and quitted the country. Before his departure, he printed two volumes of miscellaneous selections from his manuscripts, newspaper articles, and other ephemera, under the title of Didactics, Social, Literary and Political. He afterwards resided in Paris, where he was the consul of the United States, and the French correspondent of the National Intelligencer, and where he died in 1859.

When Mr. Walsh commenced his career, he was in taste, learning and general information among the first of our writers; and though of all that he has written there is but little that promises to survive him, our literature has undoubtedly been much benefited by his industrious and long continued labours. His reading, in various languages, has been extensive, and his memory is remarkably retentive, as is evident from the copiousness of his quotations and allusions, which are generally applied with much felicity. There is something artificial, a pedantic and stately mannerism, in his style, in which he once seemed to imitate Burke, but which is now a compound of the peculiarities of worse writers, both French and English.

THE GARONNE, THE WYE, AND THE HUDSON.

FROM LETTERS ON FRANCE AND ENGLAND.

No impressions can be more lively, no sensations more rapid and cheerful, than those of a young American, who, leaving his country for the first time, arrives in the river Garonne on a fine day of the month of June, after a sea-voyage of two months accompanied by one unbroken train " of vapours and clouds and storms." Such was exactly my case, and my imagination was never so powerfully affected as by the scenery which I then witnessed, and of which nothing of the same description ever meets the eye of a traveller in this country. Vineyards spread over lofty hills,—chateaux of white stone, built in a style of magnificence, and surrounded by a display of cultivation altogether unknown to us at home,—a multitude of country mansions and of villages delightfully situated either near the edge of the water or along the declivities of the hills; a numerous population of peasantry of an appearance equally novel, and in an attire singularly grotesque; all these present themselves to the view in continuous succession for twenty-one leagues,—the distance from the entrance of the river to the city of Bordeaux. This perspective, so strikingly contrasted with " the sullen and monotonous ocean," appeared at the time sufficient to indemnify me for all the cabin fatigues which I had encountered, and gave me a most delicious foretaste of the satisfactions which I was to derive from the bounties so profusely scattered over this fine region by the hand of nature. I understood then for the first time the force of the exclamation, la belle France, which I had so often heard in the mouth of her sons, and began to form some idea of the nature of that charm which operates upon them like the fascination of magic, after any length of absence, and at any distance of space from their native soil.

We frequently sailed within a hundred feet of the shore, so as to be enabled to converse with the proprietors of the country-seats whom we occasionally observed sitting under the shade of their trees, some of which overhung the banks of the river. The clusters of small islands which we encountered, particularly near the confluence of the Dordogne with the Garonne, and which were covered with the most luxuriant vegetation, heightened the enchantment of the scene.—Nothing is wanting to the Garonne but a translucent wave to supply it with an assemblage of features more smiling, variegated, and picturesque than those which belong, perhaps, to any other river in the world. The waters were turbid at the time we passed up, and I was informed that this was the case during the greater part of the year. I have contemplated since, but with emotions of pleasure not by any means so vivid, the banks of the Hudson in this country, and those of the Wye in England, both so justly celebrated for the magnificence and beauty of the views which they afford. The character of the scenery is indeed totally distinct in these rivers, and, perhaps, the preference which I give to the

first arises from the influence of a particular association of ideas and circumstances. Who is it that has ever experienced the sufferings of a long illness without being, on his convalescence, disposed to repeat with Akenside,

"Fair is nature's aspect
When rural songs and odours wake the morn
To every eye; but how much more to his
Round whom the bed of sickness long diffused
Its melancholy gloom! how doubly fair
When first with fresh-born vigour he inhales
The balmy breeze, and feels the blessed sun
Warm at his bosom, from the springs of life
Chasing oppressive damps and languid pain."

If I could well claim permission to digress so soon from my immediate subject, it would be to talk of the navigation of another stream—the Wye, which I have mentioned above. The English have within their own island much of the finest imagery of nature, embellished by the most perfect labours of art, and by all the luxury of taste. But if I were to be called upon to select any one portion of their scenery upon which I could now dwell, and upon which I have dwelt with most delight, it would be that of the Wye from Ross to Chepstow. For " a picturesque tourist" it is a sort of bonne bouche, an exquisite morceau, with which, moreover, the appetite could scarcely ever be cloyed. The Wye is our Hudson in miniature, but with features of a much softer character, and with Gothic appendages which give to it all the additional and powerful influence over the fancy that belong to " wizard time and antique story." The proportions of nature on the Hudson, for a course of two hundred miles, are of the most gigantic magnificence, and the historical recollections connected with this river are to an American of the most endearing and ennobling kind. The progress of civilization, moreover, as you trace it on its banks so far in the interior of this continent, in the flourishing cities of Hudson, of Athens, and of Albany, swells the mind, and refreshes the spirit of patriotism by the prospect of actual and future improvements almost as stupendous to the imagination as the rocks and mountains in their vicinity are to the eye.

The beauties of the English river are comprised within a space of fifty miles; it winds itself like the Hudson almost into labyrinths, and in a very narrow channel, presents rocks and hills of equal ruggedness, although of dimensions much less colossal. There is, however, about the Wye an indescribable and unrivalled charm; a peculiar " witchery" arising from an admixture of the soft with the savage features of the landscape; and from the Gothic ruins which decorate its banks at intervals; among the rest those of Tintern Abbey, by far the most majestic and imposing of all the decayed edifices of England. In the navigation of this river you can descend from your boat to the banks whenever you please, and you then rarely fail to find the whole poetical assemblage

" Of lofty trees with sacred shades
And perspectives of pleasant glades;
The ruins too of some majestic piece
Boasting the power of ancient Rome or Greece,
Whose statues, friezes, columns, broken lie,
And though defaced, the wonder of the eye."

ENGLAND IN 1808.

FROM A LETTER ON THE FRENCH GOVERNMENT.

WHATEVER may be the representations of those who, with little knowledge of facts, and still less soundness or impartiality of judgment, affect to deplore the condition of England, it is nevertheless true, that there does not exist, and never has existed elsewhere, so beautiful and perfect a model of public and private prosperity,—so magnificent, and at the same time so solid a fabric of social happiness and national grandeur. I pay this just tribute of admiration with the more pleasure, as it is to me in the light of an atonement for the errors and prejudices under which I laboured on this subject, before I enjoyed the advantage of a personal experience. A residence of nearly two years in that country,—during which period I visited and studied almost every part of it,—with no other view or pursuit than that of obtaining correct information, and, I may add, with previous studies well-fitted to promote my object, convinced me that I had been egregiously deceived.

I saw no instances of individual oppression, and scarcely any individual misery but that which belongs, under any circumstances of our being, to the infirmity of all human institutions. I witnessed no symptom of declining trade or of general discontent. On the contrary, I found there every indication of a state engaged in a rapid career of advancement. I found the art and spirit of commercial industry at their acmé—a metropolis opulent and liberal beyond example :—a cheerful peasantry, well fed and commodiously lodged,—an ardent attachment to the constitution in all classes, and a full reliance on the national resources. I found the utmost activity in agricultural and manufacturing labours;—in the construction of works of embellishment and utility ;—in enlarging and beautifying the provincial cities. I heard but few well-founded complaints of the amount, and none concerning the collection of the taxes. The demands of the state create no impediment to consumption or discouragement to industry. I could discover no instance in which they have operated to the serious distress or ruin of individuals. . . .

The agriculture of England is confessedly superior to that of any other part of the world, and the condition of those who are engaged in the cultivation of the soil incontestably preferable to that of the same class in any other section of Europe. An inexhaustible source of admiration and delight is found in the unrivalled beauty, as well as richness and fruitfulness of their husbandry; the effects of which are heightened by the magnificent parks and noble mansions of the opulent proprietors : by picturesque gardens upon the largest scale, and disposed with the most exquisite taste : and by Gothic remains no less admirable in their structure than venerable for their antiquity. The neat cottage, the substantial farm-house, the splendid villa, are constantly rising to the sight, surrounded by the most choice and poetical attributes of the landscape. The painter is there but a mere copyist. A picture of as much neatness, softness, and ele-

gance is exposed to the eye, as can be given to the imagination, by the finest etching, or the most mellowed drawing. The vision is not more delightfully recreated by the rural scenery, than the moral sense is gratified, and the understanding elevated by the institutions of this great country. The first and continued exclamation of an American who contemplates them with an unbiassed judgment is—

Salve magna Parens, frugum saturnia tellus
Magna virum.

It appears something not less than impious to desire the ruin of this people, when you view the height to which they have carried the comforts, the knowledge, and virtue of our species : the extent and number of their foundations of charity ; their skill in the mechanic arts, by the improvement of which alone they have conferred inestimable benefits on mankind; the masculine morality, the lofty sense of independence, the sober and rational piety which are found in all classes; their impartial, decorous, and able administration of a code of laws, than which none more just and perfect has ever been in operation :—their seminaries of education yielding more solid and profitable instruction than any other whatever : their eminence in literature and science—the urbanity and learning of their privileged orders,—their deliberative assemblies, illustrated by so many profound statesmen and brilliant orators. It is worse than ingratitude in us not to sympathize with them in their present struggle, when we recollect that it is from them we derive the principal merit of our own character—the best of our own institutions—the sources of our highest enjoyments—and *the light of freedom itself, which, if they should be destroyed, will not long shed its radiance over this country.*

SLANDER.

FROM DIDACTICS.

IT has been often said that true honour is not *touchy*, but generally indifferent about slander; neither the common sense nor common experience of mankind warrants this theory, supposing *touchy* to mean sensitive. The most pure and delicate, those who have laboured most earnestly to deserve the best reputation—are apt to be tremulously alive to every kind of obloquy and injurious suspicion. Honour may be thoroughly sound and incorruptible, but not *robust* so as to be unaffected by opinion; falsehood alone can annoy it, and does severely in the plurality of cases. There are, indeed, public pursuits and situations, so particularly and constantly liable to obloquy, that the natural susceptibility of true honour is gradually lessened; yet, eminent men of the noblest virtue, public and private, have even perished, in advanced stages, from tenderness, or irritability with regard to their fame. Few are content or able to live down merely "the judgments of ignorance and the inventions of malice." Querulousness, indeed, is never manly, and rarely serviceable; but sensitiveness is common where firm, conscious honour and high moral courage are united.

WASHINGTON IRVING.

[Born 1783. Died 1859.]

THIS charming author, who has delighted the readers of the English language for almost half a century, was born in a house which is still standing,* near the old Dutch church, in William street, in the city of New York, on the third of April, 1783. His father, a respectable merchant, originally from Scotland, died while he was quite young, and his education was superintended by his elder brothers, some of whom† had gained considerable reputation for acquirements and literary taste. In his youth he is said to have been of a meditative and almost melancholy disposition, though at times to have evinced something of that rich and peculiar humour for which he has since been famous; and as his health did not admit of a very close application to business or study, he rambled about the picturesque island of Manhattan, which had then a more distinctive population than now, gathering up those traditions and receiving those impressions which Mr. Seth Handaside's erudite and conscientious lodger has made immortal.

Mr. Irving's first essays in literature were a series of letters under the signature of Jonathan Oldstyle, Gent., published in the Morning Chronicle, of which one of his brothers was editor, in 1802. In consequence of symptoms of pulmonary disease, it was decided in the fol-

* It was pointed out to me not long ago by Dr John W. Francis, to whom I am happy to acknowledge my indebtedness for much information contained in this volume; nor can I forbear to improve the occasion to express the regret I feel, in common with all his friends, that the absorbing duties of professional life debar so enthusiastic and intelligent a lover of literature and science from any but an occasional demonstration of his talents in a field they are so fitted to adorn. Dr. Francis is one of the few whose ardent sympathy with men devoted to these pursuits, and truly national spirit, enable him to recognise what has been and what is likely yet to be accomplished by the genius of our country. [1845.]

† The elder, William, a merchant of high standing, and distinguished for his love of literature, wrote several of the papers in Salmagundi, and was many years a representative of the city of New York, in Congress. The second, Dr. Peter Irving,—the author of the first five chapters of Knickerbocker's History,—after a residence of twenty-five years abroad, returned to his native city in 1837; and the third, the late Judge Irving, a man of large abilities and honorable character, died in New York about the year 1841.

lowing year that he should visit the south of Europe, and embarking in a ship bound for the Mediterranean, he was landed on the southern coast of Sicily, whence he proceeded by way of Palermo and Naples to Rome, and through France to England. His unpublished journal of this tour I have heard described as one of the most interesting of his works.

He returned in 1806, and soon after joined Mr. Paulding, who was a few years his senior, in writing Salmagundi. The sensation produced by this whimsical miscellany is described by the "old inhabitants" as exceeding any thing of the kind ever known in New York. Its amusing ridicule of the ignorance and vulgarity of British tourists, and of all sorts of foreign adventurers and home pretenders, with its occasional dashes of graceful sentiment, captivated the town and decided the fortunes of its authors. Mr. Irving had commenced the study of the law, with the late Judge Josiah Ogden Hoffman, but, with prospects which forbade the expectation of having to rely upon a profession for support, he gave little heed to the masters of the great science. He wrote a few magazine papers, and an elegant sketch of Campbell, which was prefixed to an American edition of Gertrude of Wyoming; and the establishment of the New York Historical Society, with the announcement that one of its members contemplated the preparation from its collections of a history of the early days of the colony, suggesting to him the idea of The History of New York by Diedrich Knickerbocker, he yielded to its inspiration, and produced this finest monument of his genius, the most original and humorous work of the age. By paragraphs in the gazettes the public curiosity respecting it was excited; when it appeared it was bought as a veracious chronicle; and in his character of a descendant of one of the original settlers of Niew Nederlandts the author wore so gravely and naturally the prejudices which such persons might be supposed to inherit, that many read whole chapters before they were undeceived by its inimitable wit and drollery. Some of the real Dutchmen are said to have been little pleased with the burlesque history, and one of them, the learned and excellent Verplanck, in his Discourse before the Historical Society, could not forbear, "though more in sorrow than in anger," to allude to it among instances of national injustice. "It is painful to see a mind," he says, "as admirable for its exquisite perception of the beautiful, as for its quick sense of the ridiculous, wasting the riches of its fancy on an ungrateful theme."

Mr. Irving seems to have thought very little of his success, and for several years after the publication of Knickerbocker's History never to have dreamed of literature as a profession. His only writings for the press in this period, I believe, were the biographies, chiefly of officers in the navy, which he contributed to the Analectic Magazine. His brothers, who were largely and successfully engaged in foreign commerce, admitted him to a partnership, and his attention was principally devoted to trade, until the beginning of the war with Great Britain, when he tendered his services to Governor Tompkins, and was received into his staff as an aid-de-camp. He was frequently employed by the commander in chief on special duties, and was regarded as a very discreet and efficient officer. The peace however put an end to the military life of "Colonel Irving," and in 1815 he went to England, to assist in conducting the business of his firm, in Liverpool. Buoyant with hope, with "enough of the world's geer" for all his wants, he had a prospect of returning home, in a couple of years, with a mind stored with pleasant recollections; but he had hardly landed in England, he tells us in the preface to one of his later works, before a reverse of fortune* cast him down in spirit, and altered the whole tenor of his life. Literature, which had hitherto been his amusement, was now resorted to for "solace and support." It is sad to think our pleasures are a consequence of any man's misfortunes. But whatever were the "baffled plans and deferred hopes" which beguiled him, from year to year, in a path that was too often beset with thorns, we may be sure that he now regrets no more than the world of his admirers those circumstances which made him once more an author

* The house of Irving & Brothers was swept away with many others in the disastrous revulsion after the peace.

The first fruit of Mr. Irving's devotion to letters, after he went to England, was The Sketch Book, which was published in New York and London in 1819 and 1820. It "partakes of the fluctuations of his thoughts and feelings, sometimes treating of scenes before him, sometimes of others purely imaginary, and sometimes wandering back with his recollections to his native country." No book of unconnected tales and essays had ever been so well received, but there was an evident superiority in the fresh and striking passages that related to American scenery, manners, and superstitions, that gave assurance of an inspiring love of home. Nothing in their way can be more beautiful than The Wife, The Broken Heart, and The Pride of the Village; but the vitality of the work was in Rip Van Winkle, and the Legend of Sleepy Hollow. The Sketch Book was followed, in 1822, by Bracebridge Hall, a medley, chiefly descriptive of rural life in England, which he painted with an exactness of detail, a variety of light and shade, and a delicacy of finish, that surprised and delighted his English critics; while its nice apprehension, genial humour, occasional tenderness, and exquisite refinement and melody, made it no less popular in America. About one fourth of the volumes is occupied with legends of the Hudson, by the amiable and unfatiguing historian of the Dutch dynasty, and these were readily recognised as most characteristic of the author's imagination and humour. In 1824 appeared his Tales of a Traveller; and the beautiful novel of Buckthorne, which is among them, and is the last of his writings that have reference to English life, is quite equal to any thing of the same sort that he had published, and has touches of pathos that he has never surpassed. The Money Diggers, a story of New York, sustained his reputation in the field he had first chosen.

While Mr. Irving was at Bordeaux, in the winter after the publication of the Tales of a Traveller, he received a letter from Mr. Alexander H. Everett, then Minister of the United States to Spain, informing him of the researches respecting Columbus by Navarrete, and inviting him to Madrid, to consider the propriety of translating his collection of documents into English. He accepted the invitation, and his residence in the Spanish capital gave a new direction to his literary labours. He soon perceived that the publication of

Navarrete presented not so much a history as the materials for such a work, and with little hesitation soon undertook from this and various other printed and manuscript collections respecting the great navigator, to prepare a work which should be an acceptable gift to his countrymen, and that the world "would not willingly let die." His own reputation, and the friendship of the Americans resident in Spain, secured to him every possible facility, and in 1828 he supplied a desideratum which had existed in the literature of every nation,— a History of the Life and Voyages of Christopher Columbus, that was worthy of its subject. It is not indeed of the first order of historical compositions; it offers no pretensions to philosophical inquiry and generalization; but it is hardly excelled in picturesque description, lively narrative, or scrupulous fidelity. It was greeted with a warm and general approval in America and Europe, and in 1831 was followed by its pendant, the Voyages and Discoveries of the Companions of Columbus, which gave the same unmingled satisfaction.

In his researches connected with the life of the Great Admiral, Mr. Irving had caught glimpses of the romantic grandeur of the Moorish dominion, and of strange adventure in those wars, that ended with the expulsion of the Mohammedans from Spain, in which his hero was sometime an actor; and before the appearance of the work last mentioned, he published his Chronicle of the Conquest of Grenada, in which, under the guise of an imaginary contemporary author, Fray Antonio Agapida, he has presented a view of the knightly emprise and splendid pageantry of the infidel ascendency in Andalusia, which combines the poetical enthusiasm of the old Castilian with the charming simplicity and vivacity of Froissart. In the spring of 1829, after visiting the ruins of the towns and castles, and the wild passes and defiles, which had been the scenes of the most remarkable events in the crusade against the Moors, by a very courteous offer of the king of Spain, he remained several months in the Alhambra, where the Moslem heroes passed the intervals of war in dalliance with their Zaidas and Zalindas, and here wrote the series of tales and sketches which was subsequently published under the name of that enchanted palace.

At length, in 1832, after an absence of seventeen years, Mr. Irving returned to the United States. As he saw the "blue line of his native land" rising like a cloud in that horizon where, so many years before, he had seen it fade away, a doubt whether he would be received as a favourite child or as a stranger, passed like a shadow over his spirit; but it was banished by the enthusiastic greeting which awaited him in the city of his birth,— one of the fairest triumphs that has been accorded to literary merit in this age.

After passing a few weeks in the city of New York, Mr. Irving, for the satisfaction of his curiosity, set out upon a tour through the country, and early in September arrived at St. Louis, where he joined a party consisting of an Indian commissioner of the government, Mr. Latrobe, (the author of Rambles in North America,) and several others, to visit the regions beyond the outposts of civilization in the Far West. He returned in the course of the winter to the Atlantic states, and for some two years seems to have withdrawn his attention from literature, and to have given himself up to the society of the troops of friends who loved him for his amiable and honourable character, and were proud of him for the credit his genius reflected upon his native city and the republic. He purchased the old mansion of the Van Tassels, on the Hudson,—close by the margin of the Tappaan Zee, and in the vicinity of Sleepy Hollow,—"as quiet and sheltered a nook as the heart of man could desire, in which to take refuge from the cares and troubles of the world,"—which he called Wolfert's Roost, and "repaired and renovated with religious care, in the genuine Dutch style, and adorned and illustrated with sundry relics of the glorious days of the New Netherlands." Here he passed his summers; and his winters he spent in New York, in the streets of which Knickerbocker omnibuses rattled by Knickerbocker Halls where Knickerbocker clubs held festivals, and at whose wharves magnificent ships and steamers, coming and going every day, also bore that immortal name,—in pleasing testimony of the universality of his fame, and of the popular apprehension of intellectual merit, and respect for its possessor.

In 1835 Mr. Irving reappeared as an author, in A Tour of the Prairies, in which he gives an account of his wanderings in the Indian country in the autumn of 1832. In description it has the freshness and truth of one of Catlin's sketches, and it charms still more by its agreeable personal narrative. It was fol lowed in the same year by Abbotsford and Newstead Abbey, containing notices of his visits to these places,—sacred to all future ages as the homes of the greatest geniuses of many generations,—and by Legends of the Conquest of Spain, which he had written while a dweller in the Alhambra, but had not before offered to the public.

In 1836 he published Astoria, or Anecdotes of an Enterprise beyond the Rocky Mountains. Many years before, during occasional visits to Canada, he had become acquainted with some of the partners of the great North-West Fur Company, who at that time lived in genial style at Montreal, and at their hospitable boards had met "Sinbads of the Wilderness," whose wanderings and perilous adventures among the Indians had made the lives of trappers and fur traders perfect romance to him; so that afterward, when the friendship of Mr. John Jacob Astor afforded him materials for a history of the enterprise undertaken by that gentleman to establish the fur trade at the mouth of the Columbia river, he engaged in its preparation with enthusiasm, and produced a work admirably fitted to gratify curiosity on the subject.

At the table of Mr. Astor Mr. Irving was accustomed to meet various persons of adventurous character, who had been connected with expeditions to the centre of the continent and to the Pacific, and with them one that "peculiarly took his fancy," Captain Bonneville, of the United States Army, who, engrafting the trapper and hunter on the soldier, had led an enterprise which occupied several years, into the heart of the fur country. From the journal which had been kept by Captain Bonneville, and various other sources, he digested the volumes entitled, The Rocky Mountains, or Scenes, Incidents, and Adventures in the Far West, which appeared in 1837.

The most recent publications of Mr. Irving are a series of sketches of manners, traditions, and travels, which appeared in the Knickerbocker Magazine for 1839 and 1840. They would make some three duodecimo volumes, two of which might appropriately be called A Continuation of the Sketch Book.

In 1841, soon after the whig national administration came into power, Mr. Irving was appointed Minister Plenipotentiary to the court of Spain. In London and Paris, as he passed through those cities, he was warmly greeted by his old friends and associates, and in Madrid, where he resided four years, he renewed his acquaintance with the distinguished Spanish scholars and men of letters whom he had known while writing in that capital his History of Columbus and Conquest of Grenada. On the election of Mr. Polk to the presidency, he was relieved, at his own request, having been absent a year and a half beyond the period contemplated when he accepted the appointment; and in the autumn of 1846 he returned to New York, and retired to "Wolfert's Roost," to spend there the remainder of his days. Although never married, he has for several years had about him a household, the daughters of a brother, who have been to him as his own children, and who bear to him all the love that a father could engage.

It is understood that Mr. Irving finished many years ago an elaborate and important historical work on the Life and Influence of Mohammed, founded on materials that he discovered in the library of the Escurial, which had never been used, and which have since by some accident been destroyed. The piracy against authors, which is sanctioned by the present iniquitous laws regarding copyright, render it unsafe to give to the press any work of great value, and Mr. Irving has retained his manuscript, it is said, in the hope that the government will at length adopt the wiser policy of justice. He at one time contemplated a history of the Conquest of Mexico, a subject that naturally suggested itself to him while writing of the discovery of this continent; but on learning that the eloquent historian of Ferdinand and Isabella was engaged upon such a work he relinquished his design.* And when he was called into the public service,

---

* In the Preface to the "History of Ferdinand and Isabella," I lamented, that, while occupied with that subject, two of its most attractive parts had engaged the attention of the most popular of American authors. Washington Irving. By a singular chance, something like the reverse of this has taken place in the composition of the present history; and I have found myself unconsciously taking up ground which he was preparing to occupy. It was not till I had become master of my rich collection of materials, that I was acquainted with this circumstance; and, had he persevered in this design, I should unhesitatingly have abandoned my own, if not from courtesy, at least from policy: for, though armed with the weapons of Achilles, this could give me no hope of success in a competition with Achilles himself. But no sooner was that distinguished writer informed of the preparations I had made, than, with the gentlemanly spirit which will surprise no one who has the pleasure of his acquaintance, he instantly announced to me his intention of leaving the subject open to me. While I do but justice to Mr. Irving by this statement, I feel the prejudice it does to myself in the unavailing regret I am exciting in the bosom of the reader.—*Preface to Prescott' History of the Conquest of Mexico.*

he was occupied with a Life of Washington, which was to have been illustrated in a costly manner by Mr. Chapman. Whether these works, or any others by him, will be published during his lifetime, is uncertain. It is to be hoped however that he will superintend the republication of his complete writings, including those which he has scattered in half a century through periodicals and other ephemera, so that the country may be advised under his own seal of the true extent of its indebtedness to him.

It has been the custom to speak of Mr. Irving as an author in his sympathies, tastes, and execution, much more English than American, but no such judgment has been formed from an intelligent and candid study of his works. His subjects are as three American and two Spanish to one English; the periods of his residence in America, Spain, and England, in the years of his literary activity, bear to each other about the same proportion; and the productions which have won for him the most reputation, even in Europe, are not only such as had no models in the literatures of the world, but such as could have been written only by one intimately acquainted with the peculiar life and manners by which they were suggested. The History of New York, to the end of the Dutch Dynasty, by Diedrich Knickerbocker, and the various tales and sketches written in the character of that imaginary author, are the foundations of Mr. Irving's fame, and are broad and deep enough always to sustain it. As to the Sketch Book, there is no intimation in many of the most admirable pieces which it contains that they are designed to illustrate English life, and certainly The Wife, and many others, are quite as American as English, to say the least. The truth is, that a certain sort of persons who attempt criticism in Great Britain, seem to regard us as a species of outside barbarians, and demand of us a literature corresponding with our supposed character, and whenever one of our authors produces a book in which is evinced a mastery of our mother tongue, and which has in it unquestionable signs of vitality, they declare it to be thoroughly English; and the key note of cant which they strike is sounded by all those persons at home who are but too happy to impute the public's neglect of themselves to their "uncompromising Americanism." It is not intended in what is here written to as-

sert that Mr. Irving's works are preëminently distinguished for the highest sort of nationality; but merely to deny the justice and reasonableness of a common opinion in respect to his English affinities. It is not in any degree improbable that if Addison, Goldsmith, or Mackenzie had never lived, he would have written exactly as he has written, and upon every subject, except the life of Goldsmith, which has ever occupied his attention.

Mr. Irving has a genuine poetical temperament, and unites to a peculiar sensibility to beauty, in all its manifestations, a quick observation of the follies of society, which has the art of setting in the most comic and whimsical point of view, without ever sacrificing his refinement or delicacy. His humour is bold, original, and indigenous, but never offends the most fastidious by unchasteness or vulgarity. He has a great deal of common sense, and the most perfect candour; and as the true course is usually the middle one, and calls for no special subserviency or acrimony, his tone, which is manly, though gentle, conciliates all, while it shuts him from the sympathies of none. He has a very great variety of scenes and characters, to all of which his manner is adapted with singular skill and felicity. It would scarcely be supposed that the Spanish history, the English essay, and the American legend, were by one author, o. that Fray Antonio Agapida, Geoffrey Crayon, and Diedrich Knickerbocker, had ever even read each other's works.

. His style has the ease and purity and more than the grace and polish of Franklin; without the intensity of Brown, the compactness of Calhoun, or the strength and splendour of Webster,—American authors who preceded him, or were in the strictest sense his contemporaries. His words are selected with the most careful taste, and so arranged as to produce the effect of finished versification. He is not always correct: such unauthorized forms as "*from* thence," and others, occur frequently, and evince more regard for a nice modulation than for perfect grammatical accuracy; but his variously constructed periods, his remarkable elegance, sustained sweetness, and distinct and delicate painting, place him in the very front rank of the masters of our language. It may be said of him, that in whatever he has proposed to himself to do, he has been among the most successful of all authors.

8

The foregoing sketch of Washington Irving and his works was written by Mr. Griswold in 1847, and it only remains for the present editor to give an account of the remaining years of his life to 1859, the time of his decease, and the additional works published by him.

By his engagement with Willis Gaylord Clark, of the Knickerbocker magazine, he furnished for two thousand dollars per annum a monthly article for that periodical, from March 1839, until March 1841. The greater part of these contributions were collected and published under the title of "Wolfert's Roost," in 1855, and had an extraordinary sale. His exquisite sketch of "The Bobolink" in "The Birds of Spring" was at once copied into nearly every paper in the country.

In 1840 he wrote a biography of Goldsmith, for Harper's Family Library, a mere sketch to accompany an edition of Goldsmith's writings, but which he afterwards enlarged into a most delightful biography of that author. In the Spring of 1841 he wrote for Mrs. Davidson a biography of her daughter Margaret, to accompany an edition of her poems, the copyright of which he generously presented to the mother.

In November, 1841, he began the crowning work of his life, the "Life of Washington." which he continued at intervals until its completion. Also about this period he commenced revising his works preparatory to a final publication of an uniform edition, filling in his spare moments from his diplomatic labors in Spain with this duty.

Two years after his return from Spain, he entered into an arrangement with Mr. George P. Putnam for the publication of a new, revised, complete, and uniform edition of all his works. The first volume of which edition, Knickerbocker, was published on the first of September, 1848. The "Sketch Book" followed in Oct., Columbus vol. 1st. in Nov., Bracebridge Hall in Dec. Although forty years since his first work was published, this new edition of his works was received by the public with eagerness, the unprecedented demand increasing with the issue of every new volume, until the books are truly household volumes and to be found in any library of the slightest pretensions to taste or completeness.

From this time, 1850, aged 66, until 1855, he was spending his time in the receipt of attentions of the kindest nature from his attached relatives residing with him at Sunnyside and from numerous aristocratic and literary celebrities from abroad as well as at home; making repeated short trips and visits to friends, and excursions to Washington to examine the archives there for his Life of Washington. His only anxiety at this time mid all his cheerful ease and surroundings, seems to have been his fear that he might not live to accomplish this, his greatest task.

In 1855, the publication of the first volume of the life of Washington soon succeeded the appearance of "Wolfert's Roost." The author, at the age of 72, had just got through correcting the proofs of this volume, when he was thrown from his horse, and severely injured about the head and shoulders, but from which he fortunately recovered in a short time. The first volume met with such great success and cordial reviews from Bancroft, Prescott, and others capable of judging of its merits, as relieved his solicitude, and determined him to complete the work to the death of Washington, the original intention having been to end it with Washington's inauguration as President. Volume 2d appeared in December, 1855, followed by the 3d in July, 1856, the 4th in May, 1857, and the 5th in May, 1859.

During the latter part of 1858, and through 1859, his health was gradually failing. He died from disease of the heart, suddenly, Nov. 28th, and was buried in the churchyard in the vicinity. He did not fear death, but loss of mind, his desire had long been that he might, as he expressed it, "go down with all sail set."

Of the estimation in which he was held during the publication of the revised edition, some idea may be gained when we state that in nine years the sales amounted to 350,000 volumes and he received $80,000, though the Washington was not yet completed; probably quite as many more volumes have been sold to this time.

Those who desire to read in detail the life of this delightful author should get the "Life and Letters, by his nephew, Pierre M. Irving;" one of the most charming biographies ever written, 4 vols. 12 mo., in which Irving is allowed, mainly through his letters, to tell his own story, and thus in reality add so many more volumes to his "works."

PRIMITIVE HABITS IN NEW AMSTERDAM.

FROM THE SAME.

In those happy days a well-regulated family always rose with the dawn, dined at eleven, and went to bed at sun-down. Dinner was invariably a private meal, and the fat old burghers showed incontestable symptoms of disapprobation and uneasiness at being surprised by a visit from a neighbour on such occasions. But though our worthy ancestors were thus singularly averse to giving dinners, yet they kept up the social bands of intimacy by occasional banquetings, called tea-parties. These fashionable parties were generally confined to the higher, classes, or noblesse, that is to say, such as kept their own cows, and drove their own wagons. The company commonly assembled at three o'clock, and went away about six, unless it was in winter time, when the fashionable hours were a little earlier, that the ladies might get home before dark. The tea-table was crowned with a huge earthen dish well stored with slices of fat pork, fried brown, cut up into morsels, and swimming in gravy. The company being seated around the genial board, and each furnished with a fork, evinced their dexterity in lanching at the fattest pieces in this mighty dish—in much the same manner as sailors harpoon porpoises at sea, or our Indians spear salmon in the lakes. Sometimes the table was graced with immense apple-pies, or sauces full of preserved peaches and pears; but it was always sure to boast an enormous dish of balls of sweetened dough, fried in hog's fat, and called doughnuts, or olykoeks—a delicious kind of cake, at present scarce known in this city, excepting in genuine Dutch families.

The tea was served out of a majestic delft tea-pot, ornamented with paintings of fat little Dutch shepherds and shepherdesses tending pigs—with boats sailing in the air, and houses built in the clouds, and sundry other ingenious Dutch fantasies. The beaux distinguished themselves by their adroitness in replenishing this pot from a huge copper tea-kettle, which would have made the pigmy macaronies of these degenerate days sweat merely to look at it. To sweeten the beverage, a lump of sugar was laid beside each cup—and the company alternately nibbled and sipped with great decorum, until an improvement was introduced by a shrewd and economic old lady, which was to suspend a large lump directly over the tea-table by a string from the ceiling, so that it could be swung from mouth to mouth—an ingenious expedient which is still kept up by some families in Albany; but which prevails without exception in Communipaw, Bergen, Flatbush, and all our uncontaminated Dutch villages.

At these primitive tea-parties the utmost propriety and dignity of deportment prevailed. No flirting nor coqueting—no gambling of old ladies, nor hoyden chattering and romping of young ones —no self-satisfied struttings of wealthy gentlemen, with their brains in their pockets—nor amusing conceits and monkey divertisements of smart young gentlemen with no brains at all. On the contrary, the young ladies seated themselves demurely in their rush-bottomed chairs, and knit their own woollen stockings; nor ever opened their lips, excepting to say yaw Mynher, or yah yah Vrouw, to any question that was asked them; behaving in all things like decent, well-educated damsels. As to the gentlemen, each of them tranquilly smoked his pipe, and seemed lost in contemplation of the blue and white tiles with which the fire-places were decorated; wherein sundry passages of scripture were piously portrayed—Tobit and his dog figured to great advantage; Haman swung conspicuously on his gibbet; and Jonah appeared most manfully bouncing out of the whale, like Harlequin through a barrel of fire.

The parties broke up without noise and without confusion. They were carried home by their own carriages, that is to say, by the vehicles Nature had provided them, excepting such of the wealthy as could afford to keep a wagon. The gentlemen gallantly attended their fair ones to their respective abodes, and took leave of them with a hearty smack at the door; which, as it was an established piece of etiquette, done in perfect simplicity and honesty of heart, occasioned no scandal at that time, nor should it at the present—if our great-grandfathers approved of the custom, it would argue a great want of reverence in their descendants to say a word against it.

LADIES OF THE GOLDEN AGE.

FROM THE SAME.

In this dulcet period of my history, even the female sex, those arch innovators upon the tranquillity, the honesty, and gray-beard customs of society, seemed for awhile to conduct themselves with incredible sobriety and comeliness.

Their hair, untortured by the abominations of art, was scrupulously pomatumed back from their foreheads with a candle, and covered with a little cap of quilted calico, which fitted exactly to their heads. Their petticoats of linsey-woolsey were striped with a variety of gorgeous dyes—though I must confess these gallant garments were rather short, scarce reaching below the knee; but then they made up in the number, which generally equalled that of the gentlemen's small clothes; and what is still more praiseworthy, they were all of their own manufacture—of which circumstance, as may well be supposed, they were not a little vain.

These were the honest days in which every woman stayed at home, read the Bible, and wore pockets—ay, and that too of a goodly size, fashioned with patchwork into many curious devices, and ostentatiously worn on the outside. These, in fact, were convenient receptacles where all good housewives carefully stored away such things as they wished to have at hand; by which means they often came to be incredibly crammed—and I remember there was a story current when I was a boy, that the lady of Wouter Van Twiller once had occasion to empty her right pocket in search of a wooden ladle, and the utensil was discovered lying among some rubbish in one corner—but we must not give too much faith to all these stories; the anecdotes of those remote periods being very subject to exaggeration.

Besides these notable pockets, they likewise wore scissors and pincushions suspended from their girdles by red ribands, or, among the more opulent and showy classes, by brass, and even silver chains, indubitable tokens of thrifty housewives and industrious spinsters. I cannot say much in vindication of the shortness of the petticoats; it doubtless was introduced for the purpose of giving the stockings a chance to be seen, which were generally of blue worsted, with magnificent red clocks —or perhaps to display a well-turned ankle, and a neat though serviceable foot, set off by a high-heeled leathern shoe, with a large and splendid silver buckle. Thus we find that the gentle sex in all ages have shown the same disposition to infringe a little upon the laws of decorum, in order to betray a lurking beauty, or gratify an innocent love of finery.

From the sketch here given, it will be seen that our good grandmothers differed considerably in their ideas of a fine figure from their scantily-dressed descendants of the present day. A fine lady, in those times, waddled under more clothes, even on a fair summer's day, than would have clad the whole bevy of a modern ball-room. Nor were they the less admired by the gentlemen in consequence thereof. On the contrary, the greatness of a lover's passion seemed to increase in proportion to the magnitude of its object—and a voluminous damsel, arrayed in a dozen of petticoats, was declared by a Low Dutch sonnetteer of the province to be radiant as a sunflower, and luxuriant as a full-blown cabbage. Certain it is, that in those days the heart of a lover could not contain more than one lady at a time; whereas the heart of a modern gallant has often room enough to accommodate half-a-dozen. The reason of which I conclude to be, that either the hearts of the gentlemen have grown larger, or the persons of the ladies smaller—this, however, is a question for physiologists to determine.

But there was a secret charm in these petticoats, which no doubt entered into the consideration of the prudent gallants. The wardrobe of a lady was in those days her only fortune; and she who had a good stock of petticoats and stockings, was as absolutely an heiress as is a Kamtschatka damsel with a store of bear-skins, or a Lapland belle with a plenty of reindeer. The ladies, therefore, were very anxious to display these powerful attractions to the greatest advantage; and the best rooms in the house, instead of being adorned with caricatures of dame Nature, in water colours and needle-work, were always hung round with abundance of homespun garments, the manufacture and the property of the females—a piece of laudable ostentation that still prevails among the heiresses of our Dutch villages. . . .

Such was the happy reign of Wouter Van Twiller, celebrated in many a long-forgotten song as the real golden age, the rest being nothing but counterfeit copper-washed coin. In that delightful period, a sweet and holy calm reigned over the whole province. The burgomaster smoked his pipe in peace—the substantial solace of his domestic cares, after her daily toils were done, sat soberly at the door with her arms crossed over her apron of snowy white, without being insulted by ribald street-walkers, or vagabond boys—those unlucky urchins, who do so infest our streets, displaying under the roses of youth the thorns and briars of iniquity. Then it was that the lover with ten breeches, and the damsel with petticoats of half a score, indulged in all the innocent endearments of virtuous love, without fear and without reproach; for what had that virtue to fear which was defended by a shield of good linsey-woolseys, equal at least to the seven bull-hides of the invincible Ajax?

Ah! blissful, and never to be forgotten age! when every thing was better than it has ever been since, or ever will be again—when Buttermilk Channel was quite dry at low water—when the shad in the Hudson were all salmon, and when the moon shone with a pure and resplendent whiteness, instead of that melancholy yellow light which is the consequence of her sickening at the abominations she every night witnesses in this degenerate city!

Happy would it have been for New Amsterdam could it always have existed in this state of blissful ignorance and lowly simplicity—but, alas! the days of childhood are too sweet to last! Cities, like men, grow out of them in time, and are doomed alike to grow into the bustle, the cares, and miseries of the world. Let no man congratulate himself when he beholds the child of his bosom or the city of his birth increasing in magnitude and importance—let the history of his own life teach him the dangers of the one, and this excellent little history of Manna-hata convince him of the calamities of the other.

───────♦───────

LAST DAYS OF PETER STUYVESANT

FROM THE SAME.

In process of time, the old governor, like all other children of mortality, began to exhibit tokens of decay. Like an aged oak, which, though it long has braved the fury of the elements, and still retains its gigantic proportions, yet begins to shake and groan with every blast—so was it with the gallant Peter; for though he still bore the port and semblance of what he was in the days of his hardihood and chivalry, yet did age and infirmity begin to sap the vigour of his frame—but his heart, that most unconquerable citadel, still triumphed unsubdued. With matchless avidity would he listen to every article of intelligence concerning the battles between the English and Dutch—still would his pulse beat high whenever he heard of the victories of De Ruyter—and his countenance lower, and his eyebrows knit when fortune turned in favour of the English. At length, as on a certain day he had just smoked his fifth pipe, and was napping after dinner in his arm-chair, conquering the whole British nation in his dreams, he was suddenly aroused by a fearful ringing of bells, rattling of drums, and roaring of cannon, that put all his blood in a ferment. But when he learnt that these rejoicings were in honour of a great victory obtained by the combined English and French fleets over the brave De Ruyter and the younger Von Tromp, it went so much to his heart that he took to his bed, and in less than three days was brought to death's door by a violent cholera morbus! But, even in this extremity, he still displayed the unconquerable spirit of Peter *the Headstrong;* holding out to the last gasp with the most inflexible obstinacy against a whole army of old women, who were bent upon driving the enemy out of his bowels, after a true Dutch mode of defence, by inundating the seat of war with catnip and pennyroyal.

While he thus lay, lingering on the verge of dissolution, news was brought him that the brave De Ruyter had suffered but little loss—had made good his retreat—and meant once more to meet the enemy in battle. The closing eye of the old warrior kindled at the words—he partly raised himself in bed—a flash of martial fire beamed across his visage—he clinched his withered hand, as if he felt within his gripe that sword which waved in triumph before the walls of Fort Christina, and, giving a grim smile of exultation, sunk back upon his pillow and expired.

Thus died Peter Stuyvesant, a valiant soldier—a loyal subject—an upright governor, and an honest Dutchman—who wanted only a few empires to desolate to have been immortalized as a hero !

His funeral obsequies were celebrated with the utmost grandeur and solemnity. The town was perfectly emptied of its inhabitants, who crowded in throngs to pay the last sad honours to their good old governor. All his sterling qualities rushed in full tide upon their recollections, while the memory of his foibles and his faults had expired with him. The ancient burghers contended who should have the privilege of bearing the pall; the populace strove who should walk nearest to the bier—and the melancholy procession was closed by a number of gray-headed negroes, who had wintered and summered in the household of their departed master for the greater part of a century.

With sad and gloomy countenances the multitude gathered around the grave. They dwelt with mournful hearts on the sturdy virtues, the signal services, and the gallant exploits of the brave old worthy. They recalled with secret upbraidings their own factious opposition to his government—and many an ancient burgher, whose phlegmatic features had never been known to relax, nor his eyes to moisten—was now observed to puff a pensive pipe, and the big drop to steal down his cheek—while he muttered with affectionate accent and melancholy shake of the head —" Well den!—Hardkoppig Peter ben gone at last!"

97

THE USES OF HISTORY.
FROM THE SAME.

How vain, how fleeting, how uncertain are all, those gaudy bubbles after which we are panting and toiling in this world of fair delusion! The wealth which the miser has amassed with so many weary days, so many sleepless nights, a spendthrift heir may squander away in joyless prodigality. The noblest monuments which pride has ever reared to perpetuate a name, the hand of time will shortly tumble into ruins—and even the brightest laurels, gained by feats of arms, may wither and be for ever blighted by the chilling neglect of mankind.—" How many illustrious heroes," says the good Boetius, " who were once the pride and glory of the age, hath the silence of historians buried in eternal oblivion !" And this it was that induced the Spartans, when they went to battle, solemnly to sacrifice to the muses, supplicating that their achievements should be worthily recorded. Had not Homer tuned his lofty lyre, observes the elegant Cicero, the valour of Achilles had remained unsung. And such, too, after all the toils and perils he had braved, after all the gallant actions he had achieved, such too had nearly been the fate of the chivalric Peter Stuyvesant, but that I fortunately stepped in and engraved his name on the indelible tablet of history; just as the caitiff Time was silently brushing it away for ever.

The more I reflect, the more am I astonished at the important character of the historian. He is the sovereign censor to decide upon the renown or infamy of his fellow-men—he is the patron of kings and conquerors, on whom it depends whether they shall live in after ages, or be forgotten, as were their ancestors before them. The tyrant may oppress while the object of his tyranny exists, but the historian possesses superior might, for his power extends even beyond the grave. The shades of departed and long-forgotten heroes anxiously bend down from above, while he writes, watching each movement of his pen, whether it shall pass by their names with neglect, or inscribe them on the deathless pages of renown. Even the drop of ink that hangs trembling on his pen, which he may either dash upon the floor or waste in idle scrawlings—that very drop, which to him is not worth the twentieth part of a farthing, may be of incalculable value to some departed worthy—may elevate half a score in one moment to immortality, who would have given worlds, had they possessed them, to insure the glorious meed.

Let not my readers imagine, however, that I am indulging in vain-glorious boastings, or am anxious to blazon forth the importance of my tribe. On the contrary, I shrink when I reflect on the awful responsibility we historians assume—I shudder to think what direful commotions and calamities we occasion in the world—I swear to thee, honest reader, as I am a man, I weep at the very idea Why, let me ask, are so many illustrious men daily tearing themselves away from the embrace of their families—slighting the smiles of beauty

R 2

despising the allurements of fortune, and exposing themselves to the miseries of war?—Why are kings desolating empires and depopulating whole countries! In short, what induces all great men, of all ages and countries, to commit so many victories and misdeeds, and inflict so many miseries upon mankind and on themselves, but the mere hope that some historian will kindly take them into notice, and admit them into a corner of his volume. For, in short, the mighty object of all their toils, their hardships, and privations, is nothing but *immortal fame*—and what is immortal fame?—why, half a page of dirty paper!—Alas! alas! how humiliating the idea—that the renown of so great a man as Peter Stuyvesant should depend upon the pen of so little a man as Diedrich Knickerbocker!

RIP VAN WINKLE.
A POSTHUMOUS WRITING OF DIEDRICH KNICKERBOCKER.
FROM THE SKETCH-BOOK.

WHOEVER has made a voyage up the Hudson must remember the Kaatskill mountains. They are a dismembered branch of the great Appalachian family, and are seen away to the west of the river, swelling up to a noble height, and lording it over the surrounding country. Every change of season, every change of weather, indeed, every hour in the day, produces some change in the magical hues and shapes of these mountains; and they are regarded by all the good wives, far and near, as perfect barometers. When the weather is fair and settled, they are clothed in blue and purple, and print their bold outlines on the clear evening sky; but sometimes, when the rest of the landscape is cloudless, they will gather a hood of gray vapours about their summits, which, in the last rays of the setting sun, will glow and light up like a crown of glory.

At the foot of these fairy mountains, the voyager may have descried the light smoke curling up from a village, whose shingle roofs gleam among the trees, just where the blue tints of the upland melt away into the fresh green of the nearer landscape. It is a little village of great antiquity, having been founded by some of the Dutch colonists in the early times of the province, just about the beginning of the government of the good Peter Stuyvesant, (may he rest in peace!) and there were some of the houses of the original settlers standing within a few years, built of small yellow bricks brought from Holland, having latticed windows and gable fronts, surmounted with weather-cocks.

In that same village, and in one of these very houses, (which, to tell the precise truth, was sadly time-worn and weather-beaten,) there lived many years since, while the country was yet a province of Great Britain, a simple, good-natured fellow, of the name of Rip Van Winkle. He was a descendant of the Van Winkles who figured so gallantly in the chivalrous days of Peter Stuyvesant,

and accompanied him to the siege of Fort Christina. He inherited, however, but little of the martial character of his ancestors. I have observed that he was a simple, good-natured man; he was moreover a kind neighbour, and an obedient hen-pecked husband. Indeed, to the latter circumstance might be owing that meekness of spirit which gained him such universal popularity; for those men are most apt to be obsequious and conciliating abroad, who are under the discipline of shrews at home. Their tempers, doubtless, are rendered pliant and malleable in the fiery furnace of domestic tribulation, and a curtain lecture is worth all the sermons in the world for teaching the virtues of patience and long-suffering. A termagant wife may, therefore, in some respects, be considered a tolerable blessing; and if so, Rip Van Winkle was thrice blessed.

Certain it is, that he was a great favourite among all the good wives of the village, who, as usual with the amiable sex, took his part in all family squabbles, and never failed, whenever they talked those matters over in their evening gossipings, to lay all the blame on Dame Van Winkle. The children of the village, too, would shout with joy whenever he approached. He assisted at their sports, made their playthings, taught them to fly kites and shoot marbles, and told them long stories of ghosts, witches, and Indians. Whenever he went dodging about the village, he was surrounded by a troop of them, hanging on his skirts, clambering on his back, and playing a thousand tricks on him with impunity; and not a dog would bark at him throughout the neighbourhood.

The great error in Rip's composition was an insuperable aversion to all kinds of profitable labour. It could not be from the want of assiduity or perseverance; for he would sit on a wet rock, with a rod as long and heavy as a Tartar's lance, and fish all day without a murmur, even though he should not be encouraged by a single nibble. He would carry a fowling-piece on his shoulder for hours together, trudging through woods and swamps, and up hill and down dale, to shoot a few squirrels or wild pigeons. He would never refuse to assist a neighbour even in the roughest toil, and was a foremost man at all country frolics for husking Indian corn, or building stone fences. The women of the village, too, used to employ him to run their errands, and to do such little odd jobs as their less obliging husbands would not do for them;—in a word, Rip was ready to attend to anybody's business but his own; but as to doing family duty and keeping his farm in order, he found it impossible.

In fact, he declared it was of no use to work on his farm; it was the most pestilent little piece of ground in the whole country; every thing about it went wrong, and would go wrong in spite of him. His fences were continually falling to pieces; his cow would either go astray, or get among the cabbages; weeds were sure to grow quicker in his fields than anywhere else; the rain always made a point of setting in just as he had some out-door work to do; so that though his patrimonial estate had dwindled away under his management, acre by acre, until there was little more left than a mere patch of Indian corn and potatoes, yet it was the worst conditioned farm in the neighbourhood.

His children, too, were as ragged and wild as if they belonged to nobody. His son Rip, an urchin begotten in his own likeness, promised to inherit the habits, with the old clothes of his father. He was generally seen trooping like a colt at his mother's heels, equipped in a pair of his father's castoff galligaskins, which he had much ado to hold up with one hand, as a fine lady does her train in bad weather.

Rip Van Winkle, however, was one of those happy mortals, of foolish, well-oiled dispositions, who take the world easy, eat white bread or brown, whichever can be got with least thought or trouble, and would rather starve on a penny than work for a pound. If left to himself, he would have whistled life away in perfect contentment; but his wife kept continually dinning in his ears about his idleness, his carelessness, and the ruin he was bringing on his family.

Morning, noon, and night her tongue was incessantly going, and every thing he said or did was sure to produce a torrent of household eloquence. Rip had but one way of replying to all lectures of the kind, and that by frequent use had grown into a habit. He shrugged his shoulders, shook his head, cast up his eyes, but said nothing. This, however, always provoked a fresh volley from his wife, so that he was fain to draw off his forces and take to the outside of the house—the only side which, in truth, belongs to a henpecked husband.

Rip's sole domestic adherent was his dog Wolf, who was as much henpecked as his master; for Dame Van Winkle regarded them as companions in idleness, and even looked upon Wolf with an evil eye, as the cause of his master's going so often astray. True it is in all points of spirit befitting an honourable dog, he was as courageous an animal as ever scoured the woods—but what courage can withstand the ever-during and all-besetting terrors of a woman's tongue? The moment Wolf entered the house, his crest fell, his tail drooped to the ground, or curled between his legs; he sneaked about with a gallows air, casting many a sidelong glance at Dame Van Winkle, and at the least flourish of a broomstick or ladle, he would fly to the door with yelping precipitation.

Times grew worse and worse with Rip Van Winkle, as years of matrimony rolled on: a tart temper never mellows with age, and a sharp tongue is the only edge tool that grows keener with constant use. For a long while he used to console himself, when driven from home, by frequenting a kind of perpetual club of the sages, philosophers, and other idle personages of the village, which held its sessions on a bench before a small inn, designated by a rubicund portrait of his majesty, George the Third. Here they used to sit in the shade, of a long lazy summer's day, talking listlessly over village gossip, or telling endless sleepy stories about nothing. But it would have been worth any statesman's money to have heard the profound discussions which sometimes took place, when by chance an old newspaper fell into their hands from some passing traveller. How solemnly they would listen to the contents as drawled out by Derrick Van Bummel, the schoolmaster, a dapper learned little man, who was not to be daunted by the most gigantic word in the dictionary; and how sagely they would deliberate upon public events some months after they had taken place.

The opinions of this junto were completely controlled by Nicholas Vedder, a patriarch of the village and landlord of the inn, at the door of which he took his seat from morning till night, just moving sufficiently to avoid the sun, and keep in the shade of a large tree; so that the neighbours could tell the hour by his movements as accurately as by a sun-dial. It is true he was rarely heard to speak, but smoked his pipe incessantly. His adherents, however, (for every great man had his adherents,) perfectly understood him, and knew how to gather his opinions. When any thing that was read or related displeased him, he was observed to smoke his pipe vehemently, and to send forth short, frequent, and angry puffs; but when pleased, he would inhale the smoke slowly and tranquilly, and emit it in light* and placid clouds, and sometimes taking the pipe from his mouth, and letting the fragrant vapour curl about his nose, would gravely nod his head in token of perfect approbation.

From even this strong hold the unlucky Rip was at length routed by his termagant wife, who would suddenly break in upon the tranquillity of the assemblage, and call the members all to nought; nor was that august personage, Nicholas Vedder himself, sacred from the daring tongue of this terrible virago, who charged him outright with encouraging her husband in habits of idleness.

Poor Rip was at last reduced almost to despair, and his only alternative to escape from the labour of the farm and the clamour of his wife was to take gun in hand and stroll away into the woods. Here he would sometimes seat himself at the foot of a tree, and share the contents of his wallet with Wolf, with whom he sympathized as a fellow-sufferer in persecution. "Poor Wolf," he would say, "thy mistress leads thee a dog's life of it; but never mind, my lad, whilst I live thou shalt never want a friend to stand by thee!" Wolf would wag his tail, look wistfully in his master's face, and if dogs can feel pity, I verily believe he reciprocated the sentiment with all his heart.

In a long ramble of the kind, on a fine autumnal day, Rip had unconsciously scrambled to one of the highest parts of the Kaatskill mountains. He was after his favourite sport of squirrel-shooting, and the still solitudes had echoed and re-echoed with the reports of his gun. Panting and fatigued, he threw himself, late in the afternoon, on a green knoll covered with mountain herbage that crowned the brow of a precipice. From an opening between the trees, he could overlook all the lower country for many a mile of rich woodland. He saw at a distance the lordly Hudson far, far below him, moving on its silent but majestic course, with the reflection of a purple cloud, or the sail of a lagging bark, here and there sleeping on its glassy bosom, and at last losing itself in the blue highlands.

On the other side he looked down into a deep mountain glen, wild, lonely, and shagged, the bottom filled with fragments from the impending cliffs, and scarcely lighted by the reflected rays of the setting sun. For some time Rip lay musing on this scene; evening was gradually advancing; the mountains began to throw their long blue shadows over the valleys; he saw that it would be dark long before he could reach the village; and he heaved a heavy sigh when he thought of encountering the terrors of Dame Van Winkle.

As he was about to descend, he heard a voice from a distance, hallooing, " Rip Van Winkle! Rip Van Winkle!" He looked around, but could see nothing but a crow winging its solitary flight across the mountain. He thought his fancy must have deceived him, and turned again to descend, when he heard the same cry ring through the still evening air: " Rip Van Winkle! Rip Van Winkle!"—at the same time Wolf bristled up his back, and giving a low growl, skulked to his master's side, looking fearfully down into the glen. Rip now felt a vague apprehension stealing over him: he looked anxiously in the same direction, and perceived a strange figure slowly toiling up the rocks, and bending under the weight of something he carried on his back. He was surprised to see any human being in this lonely and unfrequented place, but supposing it to be some one of the neighbourhood in need of his assistance, he hastened down to yield it.

On nearer approach, he was still more surprised at the singularity of the stranger's appearance. He was a short, square-built old fellow, with thick bushy hair and a grizzled beard. His dress was of the antique Dutch fashion—a cloth jerkin strapped round the waist—several pair of breeches, the outer one of ample volume, decorated with rows of buttons down the sides, and bunches at the knees. He bore on his shoulders a stout keg, that seemed full of liquor, and made signs for Rip to approach and assist him with the load. Though rather shy and distrustful of this new acquaintance, Rip complied with his usual alacrity, and mutually relieving each other, they clambered up a narrow gully, apparently the dry bed of a mountain torrent. As they ascended, Rip every now and then heard long rolling peals, like distant thunder, that seemed to issue out of a deep ravine, or rather cleft between lofty rocks, toward which their rugged path conducted. He paused for an instant, but supposing it to be the muttering of one of those transient thunder-showers which often take place in mountain heights, he proceeded. Passing through the ravine, they came to a hollow, like a small amphitheatre, surrounded by perpendicular precipices, over the brinks of which impending trees shot their branches, so that you only caught glimpses of the azure sky and the bright evening cloud. During the whole time, Rip and his companion had laboured on in silence; for

though the former marvelled greatly what could be the object of carrying a keg of liquor up this wild mountain, yet there was something strange and incomprehensible about the unknown, that inspired awe, and checked familiarity.

On entering the amphitheatre, new objects of wonder presented themselves. On a level spot in the centre was a company of odd-looking personages playing at nine-pins. They were dressed in a quaint out-landish fashion: some wore short doublets, others jerkins, with long knives in their belts, and most of them had enormous breeches of similar style with that of the guide's. Their visages, too, were peculiar: one had a large head, broad face, and small piggish eyes; the face of another seemed to consist entirely of nose, and was surmounted by a white sugar-loaf hat, set off with a little red cock's tail. They all had beards of various shapes and colours. There was one who seemed to be the commander. He was a stout old gentleman with a weather-beaten countenance; he wore a laced doublet, broad belt and hanger, high-crowned hat and feather, red stockings, and high-heeled shoes with roses in them. The whole group reminded Rip of the figures in an old Flemish painting in the parlour of Dominie Van Schaick, the village parson, and which had been brought over from Holland at the time of the settlement.

What seemed particularly odd to Rip was, that though these folks were evidently amusing themselves, yet they maintained the gravest faces, the most mysterious silence, and were, withal, the most melancholy party of pleasure he had ever witnessed. Nothing interrupted the stillness of the scene but the noise of the balls, which, whenever they were rolled, echoed along the mountains like rumbling peals of thunder.

As Rip and his companion approached them, they suddenly desisted from their play, and stared at him with such a fixed statue-like gaze, and such strange, uncouth, lack-lustre countenances, that his heart turned within him, and his knees smote together. His companion now emptied the contents of the keg into large flagons, and made signs to him to wait upon the company. He obeyed with fear and trembling; they quaffed the liquor in profound silence, and then returned to their game.

By degrees Rip's awe and apprehension subsided. He even ventured, when no eye was fixed upon him, to taste the beverage, which he found had much of the flavour of excellent Hollands. He was naturally a thirsty soul, and was soon tempted to repeat the draught. One taste provoked another, and he reiterated his visits to the flagon so often, that at length his senses were overpowered, his eyes swam in his head, his head gradually declined, and he fell into a deep sleep.

On waking, he found himself on the green knoll from whence he had first seen the old man of the glen. He rubbed his eyes—it was a bright sunny morning. The birds were hopping and twittering among the bushes, and the eagle was wheeling aloft, and breasting the pure mountain breeze.

"Surely," thought Rip, "I have not slept here all night." He recalled the occurrences before he fell asleep. The strange man with the keg of liquor—the mountain ravine—the wild retreat among the rocks—the wo-begone party at nine-pins—the flagon—"Oh! that wicked flagon!" thought Rip—"what excuse shall I make to Dame Van Winkle!" He looked round for his gun, but in place of the clean, well-oiled fowling-piece, he found an old firelock lying by him, the barrel encrusted with rust, the lock falling off, the stock worm-eaten. He now suspected that the grave roysters of the mountain had put a trick upon him, and having dosed him with liquor, had robbed him of his gun. Wolf too had disappeared, but he might have strayed away after a squirrel or partridge. He whistled after him, and shouted his name, but all in vain; the echoes repeated his whistle and shout, but no dog was to be seen.

He determined to revisit the scene of the last evening's gambol, and if he met with any of the party, to demand his dog and gun. As he rose to walk, he found himself stiff in the joints, and wanting in his usual activity. "These mountain beds do not agree with me," thought Rip, "and if this frolic should lay me up with a fit of the rheumatism, I shall have a blessed time with Dame Van Winkle." With some difficulty he got down into the glen; he found the gully up which he and his companion had ascended the preceding evening; but to his astonishment a mountain stream was now foaming down it, leaping from rock to rock, and filling the glen with babbling murmurs. He, however, made shift to scramble up its sides, working his toilsome way through thickets of birch, sassafras, and witch-hazel; and sometimes tripped up or entangled by the wild grapevines that twisted their coils and tendrils from tree to tree, and spread a kind of network in his path.

At length he reached to where the ravine had opened through the cliffs to the amphitheatre; but no traces of such opening remained. The rocks presented a high impenetrable wall, over which the torrent came tumbling in a sheet of feathery foam, and fell into a broad deep basin, black from the shadows of the surrounding forest. Here, then, poor Rip was brought to a stand. He again called and whistled after his dog: he was only answered by the cawing of a flock of idle crows, sporting high in air about a dry tree that overhung a sunny precipice; and who, secure in their elevation, seemed to look down and scoff at the poor man's perplexities. What was to be done? The morning was passing away, and Rip felt famished for want of his breakfast. He grieved to give up his dog and gun; he dreaded to meet his wife; but it would not do to starve among the mountains. He shook his head, shouldered the rusty fire-lock, and, with a heart full of trouble and anxiety, turned his steps homeward.

As he approached the village he met a number of people, but none whom he knew, which somewhat surprised him, for he had thought himself acquainted with every one in the country round.

Their dress, too, was of a different fashion from that to which he was accustomed. They all stared at him with equal marks of surprise, and whenever they cast eyes upon him, invariably stroked their chins. The constant recurrence of this gesture, induced Rip involuntarily to do the same, when, to his astonishment, he found his beard had grown a foot long!

He had now entered the skirts of the village. A troop of strange children ran at his heels hooting after him, and pointing at his gray beard. The dogs, too, not one of which he recognised for an old acquaintance, barked at him as he passed. The very village was altered: it was larger and more populous. There were rows of houses which he had never seen before, and those which had been his familiar haunts had disappeared. Strange names were over the doors—strange faces at the windows—every thing was strange. His mind now misgave him; he began to doubt whether both he and the world around him were not bewitched. Surely this was his native village, which he had left but a day before. There stood the Kaatskill mountains—there ran the silver Hudson at a distance—there was every hill and dale precisely as it had always been—Rip was sorely perplexed—"That flagon last night," thought he, "has addled my poor head sadly!"

It was with some difficulty that he found the way to his own house, which he approached with silent awe, expecting every moment to hear the shrill voice of Dame Van Winkle. He found the house gone to decay—the roof fallen in, the windows shattered, and the doors off the hinges. A half-starved dog, that looked like Wolf, was skulking about it. Rip called him by name, but the cur snarled, showed his teeth, and passed on. This was an unkind cut indeed.—"My very dog," sighed poor Rip, "has forgotten me!"

He entered the house, which, to tell the truth, Dame Van Winkle had always kept in neat order. It was empty, forlorn, and apparently abandoned. This desolateness overcame all his connubial fears—he called loudly for his wife and children—the lonely chambers rang for a moment with his voice, and then all again was silence.

He now hurried forth and hastened to his old resort, the village inn—but it too was gone. A large rickety wooden building stood in its place, with great gaping windows, some of them broken, and mended with old hats and petticoats, and over the door was painted, "The Union Hotel, by Jonathan Doolittle." Instead of the great tree that used to shelter the quiet little Dutch inn of yore, there now was reared a tall naked pole, with something on the top that looked like a red night-cap, and from it was fluttering a flag, on which was a singular assemblage of stars and stripes—all this was strange and incomprehensible. He recognised on the sign, however, the ruby face of King George, under which he had smoked so many a peaceful pipe, but even this was singularly metamorphosed. The red coat was changed for one of blue and buff, a sword was held in the hand instead of a sceptre, the head was decorated with a cocked hat, and underneath was painted, in large characters, General Washington.

There was, as usual, a crowd of folk about the door, but none that Rip recollected. The very character of the people seemed changed. There was a busy, bustling, disputatious tone about it, instead of the accustomed phlegm and drowsy tranquillity. He looked in vain for the sage Nicholas Vedder, with his broad face, double chin, and fair long pipe, uttering clouds of tobacco smoke, instead of idle speeches, or Van Bummel, the schoolmaster, doling forth the contents of an ancient newspaper. In place of these, a lean bilious-looking fellow, with his pockets full of handbills, was haranguing vehemently about rights of citizens—election—members of Congress—liberty—Bunker's hill—heroes of seventy-six—and other words that were a perfect Babylonish jargon to the bewildered Van Winkle.

The appearance of Rip, with his long grizzled beard, his rusty fowling-piece, his uncouth dress, and the army of women and children that had gathered at his heels, soon attracted the attention of the tavern politicians. They crowded round him, eyeing him from head to foot, with great curiosity. The orator bustled up to him, and, drawing him partly aside, inquired "on which side he voted?" Rip stared in vacant stupidity. Another short but busy little fellow pulled him by the arm, and, rising on tiptoe, inquired in his ear "whether he was Federal or Democrat." Rip was equally at a loss to comprehend the question; when a knowing, self-important old gentleman in a sharp cocked-hat made his way through the crowd, putting them to the right and left with his elbows as he passed, and planting himself before Van Winkle, with one arm a-kimbo, the other resting on his cane, his keen eyes and sharp hat penetrating as it were into his very soul, demanded in an austere tone, "what brought him to the election with a gun on his shoulder, and a mob at his heels, and whether he meant to breed a riot in the village!"

"Alas! gentlemen," cried Rip, somewhat dismayed, "I am a poor quiet man, a native of the place, and a loyal subject of the King, God bless him!"

Here a general shout burst from the bystanders —"a tory! a tory! a spy! a refugee! hustle him! away with him!" It was with great difficulty that the self-important man in the cocked-hat restored order; and having assumed a tenfold austerity of brow, demanded again of the unknown culprit, what he came there for, and whom he was seeking. The poor man humbly assured him that he meant no harm, but merely came there in search of some of his neighbours who used to keep about the tavern.

"Well—who are they?—name them."

Rip bethought himself a moment and inquired, 'Where's Nicholas Vedder?"

There was a silence for a little while, when an old man replied in a thin piping voice, "Nicholas Vedder! why he is dead and gone these eighteen years! There was a wooden tombstone in the church-yard that used to tell all about him, but that's rotten and gone too."

"Where's Brom Dutcher?"

"Oh, he went off to the army in the beginning of the war; some say he was killed at the storming of Stony-Point—others say he was drowned in the squall at the foot of Antony's Nose. I don't know—he never came back again."

"Where's Van Bummel, the schoolmaster?"

"He went off to the wars too, was a great militia-general, and is now in Congress."

Rip's heart died away at hearing of these sad changes in his home and friends, and finding himself thus alone in the world. Every answer puzzled him, too, by treating of such enormous lapses of time, and of matters which he could not understand: war—Congress—Stony-Point!—he had no courage to ask after any more friends, but cried out in despair, "Does nobody here know Rip Van Winkle?"

"Oh, Rip Van Winkle!" exclaimed two or three, "Oh, to be sure! that's Rip Van Winkle yonder, leaning against the tree."

Rip looked and beheld a precise counterpart of himself as he went up to the mountain; apparently as lazy, and certainly as ragged. The poor fellow was now completely confounded. He doubted his own identity, and whether he was himself or another man. In the midst of his bewilderment, the man in the cocked-hat demanded who he was, and what was his name?

"God knows," exclaimed he at his wit's end; "I'm not myself—I'm somebody else—that's me yonder—no—that's somebody else, got into my shoes—I was myself last night, but I fell asleep on the mountain, and they've changed my gun, and every thing's changed, and I'm changed, and I can't tell what's my name, or who I am!"

The bystanders began now to look at each other, nod, wink significantly, and tap their fingers against their foreheads. There was a whisper, also, about securing the gun, and keeping the old fellow from doing mischief; at the very suggestion of which, the self-important man with the cocked-hat retired with some precipitation. At this critical moment a fresh comely woman passed through the throng to get a peep at the gray-bearded man. She had a chubby child in her arms, which, frightened at his looks, began to cry. "Hush, Rip," cried she, "hush, you little fool, the old man won't hurt you." The name of the child, the air of the mother, the tone of her voice, all awakened a train of recollections in his mind. "What is your name, my good woman?" asked he.

"Judith Gardenier."

"And your father's name?"

"Ah, poor man, his name was Rip Van Winkle; it's twenty years since he went away from home with his gun, and never has been heard of since—his dog came home without him; but whether he shot himself, or was carried away by the Indians, nobody can tell. I was then but a little girl."

Rip had but one question more to ask; but he put it with a faltering voice:

"Where's your mother?"

"Oh, she too had died but a short time since:

she broke a blood-vessel in a fit of passion at a New England pedlar."

There was a drop of comfort, at least, in this intelligence. The honest man could contain himself no longer. He caught his daughter and her child in his arms. " I am your father !" cried he —" Young Rip Van Winkle once—old Rip Van Winkle now !—Does nobody know poor Rip Van Winkle ?"

All stood amazed, until an old woman, tottering out from among the crowd, put her hand to her brow, and peering under it in his face for a moment, exclaimed, " Sure enough ! it is Rip Van Winkle—it is himself. Welcome home again, old neighbour—Why, where have you been these twenty long years ?"

Rip's story was soon told, for the whole twenty years had been to him but as one night. The neighbours stared when they heard it; some were seen to wink at each other, and put their tongues in their cheeks; and the self-important man in the cocked hat, who, when the alarm was over, had returned to the field, screwed down the corners of his mouth, and shook his head—upon which there was a general shaking of the head throughout the assemblage.

It was determined, however, to take the opinion of old Peter Vanderdonk, who was seen slowly advancing up the road. He was a descendant of the historian of that name, who wrote one of the earliest accounts of the province. Peter was the most ancient inhabitant of the village, and well versed in all the wonderful events and traditions of the neighbourhood. He recollected Rip at once, and corroborated his story in the most satisfactory manner. He assured the company that it was a fact, handed down from his ancestor the historian, that the Kaatskill mountains had always been haunted by strange beings. That it was affirmed that the great Hendrick Hudson, the first discoverer of the river and country, kept a kind of vigil there every twenty years, with his crew of the Half-moon, being permitted in this way to revisit the scenes of his enterprise, and keep a guardian eye upon the river and the great city called by his name. That his father had once seen them in their old Dutch dresses playing at nine-pins in a hollow of the mountain; and that he himself had heard, one summer afternoon, the sound of their balls like distant peals of thunder.

To make a long story short, the company broke up and returned to the more important concerns of the election. Rip's daughter took him home to live with her; she had a snug, well-furnished house, and a stout cheery farmer for a husband, whom Rip recollected for one of the urchins that used to climb upon his back. As to Rip's son and heir, who was the ditto of himself, seen leaning against the tree, he was employed to work on the farm; but evinced a hereditary disposition to attend to any thing else but his business.

Rip now resumed his old walks and habits; he soon found many of his former cronies, though all rather the worse for the wear and tear of time; and preferred making friends among the rising generation, with whom he soon grew into great favour.

Having nothing to do at home, and being arrived at that happy age when a man can do nothing with impunity, he took his place once more on the bench at the inn door, and was reverenced as one of the patriarchs of the village, and a chronicle of the old times " before the war." It was some time before he could get into the regular track of gossip, or could be made to comprehend the strange events that had taken place during his torpor. How that there had been a revolutionary war—that the country had thrown off the yoke of old England . and that, instead of being a subject of his majesty, George the Third, he was now a free citizen of the United States. Rip in fact was no politician; the changes of states and empires made but little impression on him; but there was one species of despotism under which he had long groaned, and that was—petticoat government. Happily, that was at an end; he had got his neck out of the yoke of matrimony, and could go in and out whenever he pleased without dreading the tyranny of Dame Van Winkle. Whenever her name was mentioned, however, he shook his head, shrugged his shoulders, and cast up his eyes : which might pass either for an expression of resignation to his fate, or joy at his deliverance.

He used to tell his story to every stranger that arrived at Mr. Doolittle's hotel. He was observed at first to vary on some points every time he told it, which was doubtless owing to his having so recently awaked. It at last settled down precisely to the tale I have related, and not a man, woman, or child in the neighbourhood but knew it by heart. Some always pretended to doubt the reality of it, and insisted that Rip had been out of his head, and that this was one point on which he always remained flighty. The old Dutch inhabitants, however, almost universally gave it full credit. Even to this day, they never hear a thunder-storm of a summer afternoon about the Kaatskill, but they say Hendrick Hudson and his crew are at their game of nine-pins; and it is a common wish of all henpecked husbands in the neighbourhood, when life hangs heavy on their hands, that they might have a quieting draught out of Rip Van Winkle's flagon.

THE WIFE.
FROM THE SAME.

I HAVE often had occasion to remark the fortitude with which women sustain the most overwhelming reverses of fortune. Those disasters which break down the spirit of a man and prostrate him in the dust, seem to call forth all the energies of the softer sex, and give such intrepidity and elevation to their character, that at times it approaches to sublimity. Nothing can be more touching than to behold a soft and tender female, who had been all weakness and dependence, and alive to every trivial roughness while treading the prosperous paths of life, suddenly rising in mental force to be the comforter and supporter of her husband under misfortune, and abiding with unshrinking firmness, the bitterest blast of adversity.

As the vine which has long twined its graceful foliage about the oak, and been lifted by it in sunshine, will, when the hardy plant is rifted by the thunderbolt, cling round it with its caressing tendrils and bind up its shattered boughs; so is it beautifully ordered by Providence, that woman, who is the mere dependant and ornament of man in his happier hours, should be his stay and solace wnen smitten with sudden calamity; winding herself into the rugged recesses of his nature, tenderly supporting the drooping head, and binding up the broken heart.

I was once congratulating a friend, who had around him a blooming family, knit together in the strongest affection. "I can wish you no better lot," said he, with enthusiasm, "than to have a wife and children.—If you are prosperous, there they are to share your prosperity; if otherwise, there they are to comfort you." And, indeed, I have observed that a married man falling into misfortune is more apt to retrieve his situation in the world than a single one; partly because he is more stimulated to exertion by the necessities of the helpless and beloved beings who depend upon him for subsistence; but chiefly because his spirits are soothed and relieved by domestic endearments, and his self-respect kept alive by finding that, though all abroad is darkness and humiliation, yet there is still a little world of love at home, of which he is the monarch. Whereas a single man is apt to run to waste and self-neglect; to fancy himself lonely and abandoned, and his heart to fall to ruin like some deserted mansion for want of an inhabitant.

These observations call to mind a little domestic story, of which I was once a witness. My intimate friend, Leslie, had married a beautiful and accomplished girl, who had been brought up in the midst of fashionable life. She had, it is true, no fortune, but that of my friend was ample; and he delighted in the anticipation of indulging her in every elegant pursuit, and administering to those delicate tastes and fancies that spread a kind of witchery about the sex.—"Her life," said he, "shall be like a fairy tale."

The very difference in their characters produced an harmonious combination: he was of a romantic and somewhat serious cast; she was all life and gladness. I have often noticed the mute rapture with which he would gaze upon her in company, of which her sprightly powers made her the delight; and how, in the midst of applause, her eye would still turn to him as if there alone she sought favour and acceptance. When leaning on his arm, her slender form contrasted finely with his tall manly person. The fond confiding air with which she looked up to him seemed to call forth a flush of triumphant pride and cherishing tenderness, as if he doted on his lovely burden for its very helplessness. Never did a couple set forward on the flowery path of early and well-suited marriage with a fairer prospect of felicity.

It was the misfortune of my friend, however, to have embarked his property in large speculations; and he had not been married many months, when, by a succession of sudden disasters, it was swept from him, and he found himself reduced almost to penury. For a time he kept his situation to himself, and went about with a haggard countenance and a breaking heart. His life was but a protracted agony; and what rendered it more insupportable was the keeping up a smile in the presence of his wife; for he could not bring himself to overwhelm her with the news. She saw, however, with the quick eyes of affection, that all was not well with him. She marked his altered looks and stifled sighs, and was not to be deceived by his sickly and vapid attempts at cheerfulness. She tasked all her sprightly powers and tender blandishments to win him back to happiness; but she only drove the arrow deeper into his soul. The more he saw cause to love her, the more torturing was the thought that he was soon to make her wretched. A little while, thought he, and the smile will vanish from the cheek—the song will die away from those lips—the lustre of those eyes will be quenched with sorrow; and the happy heart which now beats lightly in that bosom will be weighed down like mine by the cares and miseries of the world.

At length he came to me one day and related his whole situation in a tone of the deepest despair. When I heard him through I inquired, "Does your wife know all this?"—At the question he burst into an agony of tears. "For God's sake!" cried he, "if you have any pity on me, don't mention my wife; it is the thought of her that drives me almost to madness!"

"And why not?" said I. "She must know it sooner or later: you cannot keep it long from her, and the intelligence may break upon her in a more startling manner than if imparted by yourself; for the accents of those we love soften the harshest tidings. Besides, you are depriving yourself of the comforts of her sympathy; and not merely that, but also endangering the only bond that can keep hearts together—an unreserved community of thought and feeling. She will soon perceive that something is secretly preying upon your mind; and true love will not brook reserve; it feels undervalued and outraged, when even the sorrows of those it loves are concealed from it."

"Oh, but, my friend! to think what a blow I am to give to all her future prospects—how I am to strike her very soul to the earth, by telling her that her husband is a beggar! that she is to forego all the elegancies of life—all the pleasures of society—to shrink with me into indigence and obscurity! To tell her that I have dragged her down from the sphere in which she might have continued to move in constant brightness—the light of every eye—the admiration of every heart! —how can she bear poverty? she has been brought up in all the refinement of opulence. How can she bear neglect? she has been the idol of society. Oh, it will break her heart—it will break her heart!—"

I saw his grief was eloquent, and I let it have its flow; for sorrow relieves itself by words. When his paroxysm had subsided, and he had relapsed into moody silence, I resumed the subject gently, and urged him to break his situation at once to his wife. He shook his head mournfully, but positively.

"But how are you to keep it from her? It is necessary she should know it, that you may take the steps proper to the alteration of your circumstances. You must change your style of living ——nay," observing a pang to pass across his countenance, "don't let that afflict you. I am sure you have never placed your happiness in outward show—you have yet friends, warm friends, who will not think the worse of you for being less splendidly lodged; and surely it does not require a palace to be happy with Mary—"

"I could be happy with her," cried he, convulsively, "in a hovel!—I could go down with her into poverty and the dust!—I could—I could—— God bless her!—God bless her!" cried he, bursting into a transport of grief and tenderness.

"And believe me, my friend," said I, stepping up and grasping him warmly by the hand, "believe me she can be the same with you. Ay, more: it will be a source of pride and triumph to her—it will call forth all the latent energies and fervent sympathies of her nature; for she will rejoice to prove that she loves you for yourself. There is in every true woman's heart a spark of heavenly fire which lies dormant in the broad daylight of prosperity; but which kindles up and beams and blazes in the dark hour of adversity. No man knows what the wife of his bosom is—no man knows what a ministering angel she is—until he has gone with her through the fiery trials of this world."

There was something in the earnestness of my manner and the figurative style of my language that caught the excited imagination of Leslie. I knew the auditor I had to deal with; and following up the impression I had made, I finished by persuading him to go home and unburden his sad heart to his wife.

I must confess, notwithstanding all I had said, I felt some little solicitude for the result. Who can calculate on the fortitude of one whose whole life has been a round of pleasures? Her gay spirits might revolt at the dark downward path of low humility suddenly pointed out before her, and might cling to the sunny regions in which they had hitherto revelled. Besides, ruin in fashionable life is accompanied by so many galling mortifications, to which in other ranks it is a stranger.—In short, I could not meet Leslie the next morning without trepidation. He had made the disclosure.

"And how did she bear it?"

"Like an angel! It seemed rather to be a relief to her mind, for she threw her arms round my neck and asked if this was all that had lately made me unhappy.—But, poor girl," added he, "she cannot realize the change we must undergo. She has no idea of poverty but in the abstract; she has only read of it in poetry, where it is allied to love. She feels as yet no privation; she suffers no loss of accustomed conveniences nor elegancies. When we come practically to experience its sordid cares, its paltry wants, its petty humiliations—then will be the real trial."

"But," said I, "now that you have got over the severest task, that of breaking it to her, the sooner you let the world into the secret the better. The disclosure may be mortifying; but then it is a single misery, and soon over: whereas you otherwise suffer it, in anticipation, every hour in the day. It is not poverty so much as pretence that harasses a ruined man—the struggle between a proud mind and an empty purse—the keeping up a hollow show that must soon come to an end. Have the courage to appear poor, and you disarm poverty of its sharpest sting." On this point I found Leslie perfectly prepared. He had no false pride himself, and as to his wife, she was only anxious to conform to their altered fortunes.

Some days afterward he called upon me in the evening. He had disposed of his dwelling-house, and taken a small cottage in the country, a few miles from town. He had been busied all day in sending out furniture. The new establishment required few articles, and those of the simplest kind. All the splendid furniture of his late residence had been sold, excepting his wife's harp. That, he said, was too closely associated with the idea of herself; it belonged to the little story of their loves: for some of the sweetest moments of their courtship were those when he had leaned over that instrument, and listened to the melting tones of her voice. I could not but smile at this instance of romantic gallantry in a doting husband.

He was now going out to the cottage where his wife had been all day superintending its arrangement. My feelings had become strongly interested in the progress of this family story, and, as it was a fine evening, I offered to accompany him.

He was wearied with the fatigues of the day, and, as we walked out, fell into a fit of gloomy musing.

"Poor Mary!" at length broke with a heavy sigh from his lips.

"And what of her?" asked I: "has any thing happened to her?"

"What," said he, darting an impatient glance, "is it nothing to be reduced to this paltry situation—to be caged in a miserable cottage—to be obliged to toil almost in the menial concerns of her wretched habitation?"

"Has she then repined at the change?"

"Repined! she has been nothing but sweetness and good humour. Indeed, she seems in better spirits than I have ever known her; she has been to me all love, and tenderness, and comfort!"

"Admirable girl!" exclaimed I. "You call yourself poor, my friend; you never were so rich —you never knew the boundless treasure of excellence you possessed in that woman."

"Oh! but, my friend, if this first meeting at the cottage were over, I think I could then be comfortable. But this is her first day of real experience; she has been introduced into an humble

28   T

dwelling—she has been employed all day in arranging its miserable equipments—she has, for the first time, known the fatigues of domestic employment—she has, for the first time, looked round her on a home destitute of every thing elegant,—almost of every thing convenient; and may now be sitting down, exhausted and spiritless, brooding over a prospect of future poverty."

There was a degree of probability in this picture that I could not gainsay, so we walked on in silence.

After turning from the main road up a narrow lane, so thickly shaded with forest trees as to give it a complete air of seclusion, we came in sight of the cottage. It was humble enough in its appearance for the most pastoral poet; and yet it had a pleasing rural look. A wild vine had overrun one end with a profusion of foliage; a few trees threw their branches gracefully over it; and I observed several pots of flowers tastefully disposed about the door and on the grass-plat in front. A small wicket gate opened upon a footpath that wound through some shrubbery at the door. Just as we approached, we heard the sound of music—Leslie grasped my arm; we paused and listened. It was Mary's voice, singing, in a style of the most touching simplicity, a little air of which her husband was peculiarly fond.

I felt Leslie's hand tremble on my arm. He stepped forward to hear more distinctly. His step made a noise on the gravel walk. A bright, beautiful face glanced out at the window and vanished—a light footstep was heard—and Mary came tripping forth to meet us; she was in a pretty rural dress of white; a few wild flowers were twisted in her fine hair; a fresh bloom was on her cheek; her whole countenance beamed with smiles—I had never seen her look so lovely.

"My dear George," cried she, "I am so glad you are come! I have been watching and watching for you; and running down the lane and looking out for you. I've set out a table under a beautiful tree behind the cottage; and I've been gathering some of the most delicious strawberries, for I know you are fond of them—and we have such excellent cream—and we have every thing so sweet and still here—Oh!" said she, putting her arm within his and looking up brightly in his face, " Oh, we shall be so happy!"

Poor Leslie was overcome.—He caught her to his bosom—he folded his arms round her—he kissed her again and again—he could not speak, but the tears gushed into his eyes; and he has often assured me that though the world has since gone prosperously with him, and his life has indeed been a happy one, yet never has he experienced a moment of more exquisite felicity.

THE LOVE OF A MOTHER.
FROM THE SAME.

WHO that has languished, even in advanced life, in sickness and despondency; who that has pined on a weary bed in the neglect and loneliness of a foreign land; but has thought on the mother "that looked on his childhood," that smoothed his pillow and administered to his helplessness? Oh! there is an enduring tenderness in the love of a mother to a son that transcends all other affections of the heart. It is neither to be chilled by selfishness, nor daunted by danger, nor weakened by worthlessness, nor stifled by ingratitude. She will sacrifice every comfort to his convenience; she will surrender every pleasure to his enjoyment; she will glory in his fame, and exult in his prosperity:—and, if misfortune overtake him, he will be the dearer to her from his misfortunes; and if disgrace settle upon his name, she will still love and cherish him in spite of his disgrace; and if all the world beside cast him off, she will be all the world to him.

BROKEN HEARTS.
FROM THE SAME.

IT is a common practice with those who have outlived the susceptibility of early feeling, or have been brought up in the gay heartlessness of dissipated life, to laugh at all love stories, and to treat the tales of romantic passion as mere fictions of novelists and poets. My observations on human nature have induced me to think otherwise. They have convinced me that however the surface of the character may be chilled and frozen by the cares of the world, or cultivated into mere smiles by the arts of society, still there are dormant fires lurking in the depths of the coldest bosom, which, when once enkindled, become impetuous, and are sometimes desolating in their effects. Indeed, I am a true believer in the blind deity, and go to the full extent of his doctrines. Shall I confess it?—I believe in broken hearts, and the possibility of dying of disappointed love. I do not, however, consider it a malady often fatal to my own sex; but I firmly believe that it withers down many a lovely woman into an early grave.

Man is the creature of interest and ambition. His nature leads him forth into the struggle and bustle of the world. Love is but the embellishment of his early life, or a song piped in the intervals of the acts. He seeks for fame, for fortune, for space in the world's thought, and dominion over his fellow-men. But a woman's whole life is a history of the affections. The heart is her world: it is there her ambition strives for empire; it is there her avarice seeks for hidden treasures. She sends forth her sympathies on adventure; she embarks her whole soul in the traffic of affection; and if shipwrecked, her case is hopeless—for it is a bankruptcy of the heart.

To a man the disappointment of love may occasion some bitter pangs: it wounds some feelings of tenderness—it blasts some prospects of felicity; but he is an active being—he may dissipate his thoughts in the whirl of varied occupation, or may plunge into the tide of pleasure; or, if the scene of disappointment be too full of painful associations, he can shift his abode at will, and taking as it were the wings of the morning, can " fly to the uttermost parts of the earth, and be at rest."

But woman's is comparatively a fixed, a secluded, and a meditative life. She is more the companion of her own thoughts and feelings; and if they are turned to ministers of sorrow, where shall she look for consolation? Her lot is to be wooed and won; and if unhappy in her love, her heart is like some fortress that has been captured, and sacked, and abandoned, and left desolate.

How many bright eyes grow dim—how many soft cheeks grow pale—how many lovely forms fade away into the tomb, and none can tell the cause that blighted their loveliness! As the dove will clasp its wings to its side, and cover and conceal the arrow that is preying on its vitals, so it is the nature of woman to hide from the world the pangs of wounded affection. The love of a delicate female is always shy and silent. Even when fortunate, she scarcely breathes it to herself; but when otherwise, she buries it in the recesses of her bosom, and there lets it cower and brood among the ruins of her peace. With her the desire of the heart has failed. The great charm of existence is at an end. She neglects all the cheerful exercises which gladden the spirits, quicken the pulses, and send the tide of life in healthful currents through the veins. Her rest is broken— the sweet refreshment of sleep is poisoned by melancholy dreams—" dry sorrow drinks her blood," until her enfeebled frame sinks under the slightest external injury. Look for her, after a little while, and you will find friendship weeping over her untimely grave, and wondering that one who but lately glowed with all the radiance of health and beauty, should so speedily be brought down to " darkness and the worm." You will be told of some wintry chill, some casual indisposition that laid her low;—but no one knows of the mental malady that previously sapped her strength, and made her so easy a prey to the spoiler.

She is like some tender tree, the pride and beauty of the grove; graceful in its form, bright in its foliage, but with the worm preying at its heart. We find it suddenly withering when it should be most fresh and luxuriant. We see it drooping its branches to the earth, and shedding leaf by leaf; until, wasted and perished away, it falls even in the stillness of the forest; and as we muse over the beautiful ruin, we strive in vain to recollect the blast or thunderbolt that could have smitten it with decay.

HISTORICAL CRITICISM.
FROM THE LIFE AND VOYAGES OF CHRISTOPHER COLUMBUS.

THERE is a certain meddlesome spirit, which, in the garb of learned research, goes prying about the traces of history, casting down its monuments, and marring and mutilating its fairest trophies. Care should be taken to vindicate great names from such pernicious erudition.

COLUMBUS AT BARCELONA.
FROM THE SAME.

THE letter of Columbus to the Spanish monarchs, announcing his discovery, had produced the greatest sensation at court. The event it communicated was considered the most extraordinary of their prosperous reign; and following so close upon the conquest of Granada, was pronounced a signal mark of divine favour for that triumph achieved in the cause of the true faith. The sovereigns themselves were for a time dazzled and bewildered by this sudden and easy acquisition of a new empire, of indefinite extent, and apparently boundless wealth; and their first idea was to secure it beyond the reach of question or competition. Shortly after his arrival in Seville, Columbus received a letter from them, expressing their great delight, and requesting him to repair immediately to court, to concert plans for a second and more extensive expedition. As the summer was already advancing, the time favourable for a voyage, they desired him to make any arrangements at Seville, or elsewhere, that might hasten the expedition, and to inform them by the return of the courier what was necessary to be done on their part. This letter was addressed to him by the title of " Don Christopher Columbus, our admiral of the Ocean sea, and viceroy and governor of the islands discovered in the Indias;" at the same time he was promised still further rewards. Columbus lost no time in complying with the commands of the sovereigns. He sent a memorandum of the ships, men, and munitions that would be requisite; and having made such dispositions at Seville as circumstances permitted, set out on his journey for Barcelona, taking with him the six Indians, and the various curiosities and productions which he had brought from the New World.

The fame of his discovery had resounded throughout the nation, and as his route lay through several of the finest and most populous provinces of Spain, his journey appeared like the progress of a sovereign. Wherever he passed the surrounding country poured forth its inhabitants, who lined the road and thronged the villages. In the large towns, the streets, windows, and balconies were filled with eager spectators, who rent the air with acclamations. His journey was continually impeded by the multitude pressing to gain a sight of him, and of the Indians, who were regarded with as much admiration as if they had been natives of another planet. It was impossible to satisfy the craving curiosity which assailed himself and his attendants, at every stage, with innumerable questions; popular rumour as usual had exaggerated the truth, and had filled the newly-found country with all kinds of wonders.

It was about the middle of April that Columbus arrived at Barcelona, where every preparation had been made to give him a solemn and magnificent reception. The beauty and serenity of the weather in that genial season and favoured climate, contributed to give splendour to this memorable ceremony. As he drew near the place, many of the more youthful courtiers and hidalgos of gallant bearing, together with a vast concourse of the populace, came forth to meet and welcome him. His entrance into this noble city has been compared to one of those triumphs which the Romans were accustomed to decree to conquerors. First were paraded the Indians, painted according to their savage fashion, and decorated with tropical feathers, and with their national ornaments of gold; after these were borne various kinds of live parrots, together with stuffed birds and animals of unknown species, and rare plants supposed to be of precious qualities: while great care was taken to make a conspicuous display of Indian coronets, bracelets, and other decorations of gold, which might give an idea of the wealth of the newly discovered regions. After these followed Columbus, on horseback, surrounded by a brilliant cavalcade of Spanish chivalry. The streets were almost impassable from the countless multitude; the windows and balconies were crowded with the fair; the very roofs were covered with spectators. It seemed as if the public eye could not be sated with gazing on these trophies of an unknown world; or on the remarkable man by whom it had been discovered. There was a sublimity in this event that mingled a solemn feeling with the public joy. It was looked upon as a vast and signal dispensation of providence in reward for the piety of the monarchs; and the majestic and venerable appearance of the discoverer, so different from the youth and buoyancy that are generally expected from roving enterprise, seemed in harmony with the grandeur and dignity of his achievement.

To receive him with suitable pomp and distinction, the sovereigns had ordered their throne to be placed in public, under a rich canopy of brocade of gold, in a vast and splendid saloon. Here the king and queen awaited his arrival, seated in state, with the prince Juan beside them; and attended by the dignitaries of their court, and the principal nobility of Castile, Valentia, Catalonia, and Aragon; all impatient to behold the man who had conferred so incalculable a benefit upon the nation. At length Columbus entered the hall, surrounded by a brilliant crowd of cavaliers, among whom, says Las Casas, he was conspicuous for his stately and commanding person, which, with his countenance rendered venerable by his gray hairs, gave him the august appearance of a senator of Rome. A modest smile lighted up his features, showing that he enjoyed the state and glory in which he came; and certainly nothing could be more deeply moving to a mind inflamed by noble ambition, and conscious of having greatly deserved, than these testimonials of the admiration and gratitude of a nation, or rather of a world. As Columbus approached, the sovereigns rose, as if receiving a person of the highest rank. Bending his knees, he requested to kiss their hands; but there was some hesitation on the part of their majesties to permit this act of vassalage. Raising him in the most gracious manner, they ordered him to seat himself in their presence; a rare honour in this proud and punctilious court.

At the request of their majesties, Columbus now gave an account of the most striking events of his voyage, and a description of the islands which he had discovered. He displayed the specimens he had brought of unknown birds and other animals; of rare plants of medicinal and aromatic virtue; of native gold in dust, in crude masses, or laboured into barbaric ornaments; and above all, the natives of these countries, who were objects of intense and inexhaustible interest; since there is nothing to man so curious as the varieties of his own species. All these he pronounced mere harbingers of greater discoveries he had yet to make, which would add realms of incalculable wealth to the dominions of their majesties and whole nations of proselytes to the true faith.

The words of Columbus were listened to with profound emotion by the sovereigns. When he had finished, they sunk on their knees, and, raising their clasped hands to heaven, their eyes filled with tears of joy and gratitude, they poured forth thanks and praises to God for so great a providence; all present followed their example, a deep and solemn enthusiasm pervaded that splendid assembly, and prevented all common acclamations of triumph. The anthem of *Te Deum laudamus*, chanted by the choir of the royal chapel, with the melodious accompaniments of the instruments, rose up from the midst in a full body of sacred harmony, bearing up as it were the feelings and thoughts of the auditors to heaven, " so that," says the venerable Las Casas, " it seemed as if in that hour they communicated with celestial delights." Such was the solemn and pious manner in which the brilliant court of Spain celebrated this sublime event; offering up a grateful tribute of melody and praise, and giving glory to God for the discovery of another world.

A LETTER
FROM MUSTAPHA RUB-A-DUB KELI KHAN, TO ASEM HACCHEM. PRINCIPAL SLAVE-DRIVER TO HIS HIGHNESS THE BASHAW OF TRIPOLI.
FROM SALMAGUNDI.

SWEET, O Asem! is the memory of distant friends! Like the mellow ray of a departing sun, it falls tenderly yet sadly on the heart. Every hour of absence from my native land rolls heavily by, like the sandy wave of the desert; and the fair shores of my country rise blooming to my imagination, clothed in the soft illusive charms of distance. I sigh, yet no one listens to the sigh of the captive: I shed the bitter tear of recollection, but no one sympathizes in the tear of the turbaned stranger! Think not, however, thou brother of my soul, that I complain of the horrors of my situation; think not that my captivity is attended with the labours, the chains, the scourges, the insults that render slavery with us more dreadful than the pangs of hesitating, lingering death. Light, indeed, are the restraints on the personal freedom of thy kinsman; but who can enter into the afflictions of the mind? who can describe the agonies of the heart? They are mutable as the clouds of the air; they are countless as the waves that divide me from my native country.

I have, of late, my dear Asem, laboured under an inconvenience singularly unfortunate, and am reduced to a dilemma most ridiculously embarrassing. Why should I hide it from the companion of my thoughts, the partner of my sorrows and my joys? Alas! Asem, thy friend Mustapha, the invincible captain of a ketch, is sadly in want of a pair of breeches! Thou wilt doubtless smile, O most grave Mussulman, to hear me indulge in such ardent lamentations about a circumstance so trivial, and a want apparently so easy to be satisfied: but little canst thou know of the mortifications attending my necessities, and the astonishing difficulty of supplying them. Honoured by the smiles and attentions of the beautiful ladies of this city, who have fallen in love with my whiskers and my turban;—courted by the bashaws and the great men, who delight to have me at their feasts; the honour of my company eagerly solicited by every fiddler who gives a concert; think of my chagrin at being obliged to decline the host of invitations that daily overwhelm me, merely for want of a pair of breeches! Oh, Allah! Allah! that thy disciples could come into the world all be-feathered like a bantam, or with a pair of leather breeches like the wild deer of the forest; surely, my friend, it is the destiny of man to be for ever subjected to petty evils, which, however trifling in appearance, prey in silence on this little pittance of enjoyment, and poison these moments of sunshine, which might otherwise be consecrated to happiness.

The want of a garment, thou wilt say, is easily supplied; and thou mayest suppose need only be mentioned to be remedied at once by any tailor of the land. Little canst thou conceive the impediments which stand in the way of my comfort, and still less art thou acquainted with the prodigious great scale on which every thing is transacted in this country. The nation moves most majestically slow and clumsy in the most trivial affairs, like the unwieldy elephant which makes a formidable difficulty of picking up a straw! When I hinted my necessities to the officer who has charge of myself and my companions, I expected to have been forthwith relieved; but he made an amazingly long face —told me that we were prisoners of state—that we must therefore be clothed at the expense of the government; that as no provision has been made by the Congress for an emergency of the kind, it was impossible to furnish me with a pair of breeches until all the sages of the nation had been convened to talk over the matter, and debate upon the expediency of granting my request. Sword of the immortal Khalid, thought I, but this is great!—this is truly sublime! All the sages in an immense logocracy assembled together to talk about my breeches!—Vain mortal that I am! I cannot but own I was somewhat reconciled to the delay which must necessarily attend this method of clothing me, by the consideration that if they made the affair a national act, my "name must of course be imbodied in history," and myself and my breeches flourish to immortality in the annals of this mighty empire!

"But pray, sir," said I, "how does it happen that a matter so insignificant should be erected into an object of such importance as to employ the representative wisdom of the nation? and what is the cause of their talking so much about a trifle?" "Oh," replied the officer, who acts as our slave-driver; "it all proceeds from economy. If the government did not spend ten times as much money in debating whether it was proper to supply you with breeches as the breeches themselves would cost, the people, who govern the bashaw and his divan, would straightway begin to complain of their liberties being infringed—the national finances squandered—not a hostile slang-whanger throughout the logocracy but would burst forth like a barrel of combustion—and ten chances to one but the bashaw and the sages of his divan would all be turned out of office together. My good Mussulman," continued he, "the administration have the good of the people too much at heart to trifle with their pockets; and they would sooner assemble and talk away ten thousand dollars than expend fifty silently out of the treasury—such is the wonderful spirit of economy that pervades every branch of this government." "But," said I, "how is it possible they can spend money in talking: surely words cannot be the current coin of this country?" "Truly," cried he, smiling, "your question is pertinent enough, for words indeed often supply the place of cash among us, and many an honest debt is paid in promises; but the fact is, the grand bashaw and the members of Congress, or grand talkers of the nation, either receive a yearly salary, or are paid by the day."—"By the nine hundred tongues of the great beast in Mahomet's vision, but the murder is out! it is no wonder these honest men talk so much about nothing when they are paid for talking like day-labourers." "You are mistaken," said my driver; "it is nothing but economy."

I remained silent for some minutes, for this inexplicable word economy always discomfits me;—and when I flatter myself I have grasped it, it slips through my fingers like a jack-o'lantern. I have not, nor perhaps ever shall acquire, sufficient of the philosophic policy of this government to draw a proper distinction between an individual and a nation. If a man was to throw away a pound in order to save a beggarly penny, and boast at the same time of his economy, I should think him on a par with the fool in the fable of Alfangi; who, in skinning a flint worth a farthing, spoiled a knife worth fifty times the sum, and thought he had acted wisely. The shrewd fellow would doubtless have valued himself much more highly on his economy could he have known that his example would one day be followed by the bashaw of America, and the sages of his divan.

This economic disposition, my friend, occasion much fighting of the spirit, and innumerable contests of the tongue in this talking assembly Wouldst thou believe it? they were actually employed for a whole week in a most strenuous and eloquent debate about patching up a hole in the wall in the room appropriated to their meetings! A vast profusion of nervous argument and pompous declamation was expended on this occasion.

T 2

Some of the orators, I am told, being rather waggishly inclined, were most stupidly jocular on the occasion; but their waggery gave great offence, and was highly reprobated by the more weighty part of the assembly; who hold all wit and humour in abomination, and thought the business in hand much too solemn and serious to be treated lightly. It was supposed by some that this affair would have occupied a whole winter, as it was a subject upon which several gentlemen spoke who had never been known to open their lips in that place except to say yes and no.—These silent members are by way of distinction denominated orator mums, and are highly valued in this country on account of their great talents for silence;—a qualification extremely rare in a logocracy.

Fortunately for the public tranquillity, in the hottest part of the debate, when two rampant Virginians, brim full of logic and philosophy, were measuring tongues, and syllogistically cudgelling each other out of their unreasonable notions, the president of the divan, a knowing old gentleman, one night slyly sent a mason with a hod of mortar, who in the course of a few minutes closed up the hole, and put a final end to the argument. Thus did this wise old gentleman, by hitting on a most simple expedient, in all probability, save his country as much money as would build a gun-boat, or pay a hireling slang-whanger for a whole volume of words. As it happened, only a few thousand dollars were expended in paying these men, who are denominated, I suppose in derision, legislators.

Another instance of their economy I relate with pleasure, for I really begin to feel a regard for these poor barbarians. They talked away the best parts of a whole winter before they could determine not to expend a few dollars in purchasing a sword to bestow on an illustrious warrior: yes, Asem, on that very hero who frightened all our poor old women and young children at Derne, and fully proved himself a greater man than the mother that bore him.* Thus, my friend, is the whole collective wisdom of this mighty logocracy employed in somniferous debates about the most trivial affairs; as I have sometimes seen a Herculean mountebank exerting all his energies in balancing a straw upon his nose. Their sages behold the minutest object with the microscopic eyes of a pismire; mole-hills swell into mountains, and a grain of mustard-seed will set the whole ant-hill in a hubbub. Whether this indicates a capacious vision, or a diminutive mind, I leave thee to decide; for my part I consider it as another proof of the great scale on which every thing is transacted in this country.

I have before told thee that nothing can be done without consulting the sages of the nation who compose the assembly called the Congress. This prolific body may not improperly be called the "mother of inventions;" and a most fruitful mother it is, let me tell thee, though its children are generally abortions. It has lately laboured with what was deemed the conception of a mighty navy.—All the old women and the good wives that assist the bashaw in his emergencies

hurried to head-quarters to be busy, like midwives, at the delivery. All was anxiety, fidgeting, and consultation; when after a deal of groaning and struggling, instead of formidable first-rates and gallant frigates, out crept a litter of sorry little gunboats. These are most pitiful little vessels, partaking vastly of the character of the grand bashaw, who has the credit of begetting them; being flat shallow vessels that can only sail before the wind; —must always keep in with the land;—are continually foundering or running on shore; and, in short, are only fit for smooth water. Though intended for the defence of the maritime cities, yet the cities are obliged to defend them; and they require as much nursing as so many rickety little bantlings. They are, however, the darling pets of the grand bashaw, being the children of his dotage, and, perhaps from their diminutive size and palpable weakness, are called the "infant navy of America." The art that brought them into existence was almost deified by the majority of the people as a grand stroke of economy. By the beard of Mahomet, but this word is truly inexplicable!

To this economic body therefore was I advised to address my petition, and humbly to pray that the august assembly of sages would, in the plenitude of their wisdom and the magnitude of their powers, munificently bestow on an unfortunate captive a pair of cotton breeches! "Head of the immortal Amrou," cried I, "but this would be presumptuous to a degree:—What! after these worthies have thought proper to leave their country naked and defenceless, and exposed to all the political storms that rattle without, can I expect that they will lend a helping hand to comfort the extremities of a solitary captive?" My exclamation was only answered by a smile, and I was consoled by the assurance that, so far from being neglected, it was every way probable my breeches might occupy a whole session of the divan, and set several of the longest heads together by the ears. Flattering as was the idea of a whole nation being agitated about my breeches, yet I own I was somewhat dismayed at the idea of remaining in *querpo* until all the national graybeards should have made a speech on the occasion, and given their consent to the measure. The embarrassment and distress of mind which I experienced were visible in my countenance, and my guard, who is a man of infinite good nature, immediately suggested, as a more expeditious plan of supplying my wants, a benefit at the theatre. Though profoundly ignorant of his meaning, I agreed to his proposition, the result of which I shall disclose in another letter.

Fare thee well, dear Asem; in thy pious prayers to our great prophet, never forget to solicit thy friend's return; and when thou numberest up the many blessings bestowed on thee by all-bountiful Allah, pour forth thy gratitude that he has cast thy nativity in a land where there is no assembly of legislative chatterers;—no great bashaw, who bestrides a gun-boat for a hobby-horse;—where the word economy is unknown;—and where an unfortunate captive is not obliged to call upon the whole nation to cut him out a pair of breeches.

* General Eaton.

JOSEPH STEVENS BUCKMINSTER.

[Born 1784.   Died 1812.]

I AM inclined to believe that America has produced in the present century more really eloquent preachers than any other country. Although from the foolish and wicked custom which obtains among some sects of admitting uneducated persons to that profession which demands the highest and most patient cultivation, there is in the pulpit doubtless a great deal of ignorance, rant and fanaticism, yet it seems to be the general opinion among foreigners who have visited our churches, and among travelled Americans, that the clergy of no country in Europe can be compared with ours for chaste, impassioned and effective oratory. I write this with a vivid recollection of some of the masterpieces of French and English sermon writing, and of the accounts which have been given of the manner in which they were delivered.

It would appear invidious to allude particularly to any of the living lights of the churches, and I must refer even to Buckminster as the representative of a class rather than as one entitled to be singled out from all others of his time by his preëminent powers and accomplishments.

JOSEPH STEVENS BUCKMINSTER was born on the twenty-sixth of May, 1784, at Portsmouth, in New Hampshire. His ancestors, both by the paternal and the maternal side, for several generations, were clergymen, and some of them were persons of distinguished reputation. He was remarkably precocious, studying the Latin and Greek languages before he was five years of age, and at twelve being ready to enter college. Unwilling however to place him so soon within the influences of a life at Cambridge, his father detained him some time longer at the Exeter Academy, and he was finally admitted to Harvard nearly a year in advance in 1797. His career here was equally honourable to his moral and his intellectual character. President Kirkland's remark of Fisher Ames has been applied to him, that "he did not need the smart of guilt to make him virtuous, nor the regret of folly to make him wise."

He received the degree of Bachelor of Arts in the summer of 1800, and devoted the next four years principally to the study of theology. In January, 1805, he was ordained minister of the Brattle Street Unitarian Society in Boston, and his sermons were listened to, from the first, his biographer assures us, with "delight and wonder." But his labours were soon interrupted by illness, and before the close of the summer renewed attacks of a terrible disorder from which he had been several years a sufferer excited the most painful apprehensions. On the last day of October he wrote in his diary : "Another fit of epilepsy! I pray God that I may be prepared, not so much for death, as for the loss of health, and perhaps of mental faculties. The repetition of these fits must at length reduce me to idiocy. Can I resign myself to the loss of memory, and of that knowledge I may have vainly prided myself upon? O God! enable me to bear this thought, and make it familiar to my mind, that by thy grace I may be willing to endure life as long as thou pleasest to lengthen it It is not enough to be willing to leave the world when God pleases ; we should be willing even to live useless in it, if he, in his holy providence, should send such a calamity upon us. I think I perceive my memory fails me. O God, save me from that hour !"

In the spring of 1806 the increase of his malady induced him to make a voyage to Europe. In May he sailed for Liverpool, and in August, with a friend who had joined him in London, embarked for the continent. He passed rapidly through the chief cities of Holland, ascended the Rhine, and after spending a few weeks in Switzerland, proceeded to Paris, where he remained five months. In February, 1807, he reached London, and having travelled in England, Scotland and Wales, through the spring and summer, returned to Boston early in September. He was received with unabated affection by his congregation, and re-entered earnestly upon the duties of his office. The remaining years of his life were marked by few incidents. The constant calls of professional duty did not prevent him from being a laborious student; he was an active member of the chief literary and charitable societies of the city, and interested in every plan for the elevation of the intellectual, moral and religious character of the people. In 1811 he was appointed the first professor of biblical criticism at Cambridge, and his lectures were looked forward to with the deepest interest by his friends, who knew how much attention he had given to the study of the interpretation of the scriptures, and how very capable he was of communicating the results of the most recent and most profound investigations in this his favourite department of learning; but his brief and brilliant career was suddenly terminated before he commenced the discharge of the duties of his new office; a sudden and violent return of his old malady instantly made a total and irrecoverable wreck of his mind; and after lingering a few days, without a ray of consciousness, he died, on the ninth of June, 1812, having just completed the twenty-eighth year of his age.

The memory of Buckminster is cherished with singular veneration by those who enjoyed his personal intimacy. He became distinguished as a preacher before the sect of which he was an ornament embraced so many gifted persons as at present. With a face remarkable for its pure intellectual expression, and a silvery voice, the tones of which won the devout attention and haunted the memories of all who listened, it is not surprising that in a community where mental power is so highly appreciated as in Boston, the weekly addresses of the youthful divine attracted large and enthusiastic audiences. His manner was artless and impressive, and there was something about the whole man that irresistibly fascinated the taste at the same time that it inspired respect and love. In social life he was remarkable for his urbane spirit, quick intelligence, and refined wit. He was the centre of a rare circle of the good and cultivated, and his death fell upon the hearts of his numerous friends with the solemn pathos of a deep calamity. To the reader of his discourses in whose minds they lack the charm of personal associations, there is perhaps a coldness in their very beauty. Yet few sermons equal them for a happy blending of good sense and graceful imagery.

Truth is enforced with a simple earnestness, and pious thoughts are clothed in language strikingly correct and impressive. One of the most characteristic of these essays is the one on The Advantages of Sickness. It was composed after a dangerous illness of several weeks. On the Sabbath morning when Buckminster was to reappear before the anxious congregation, at an early hour, before rising, he called for the necessary materials, and wrote the entire sermon in bed, after having meditated the subject during the night. The bell had ceased tolling when his diminutive figure was seen gliding up the aisle of the church, thronged with expectant faces. He ascended the pulpit stairs with feeble steps, and went through the preparatory exercises in a suppressed voice. Still weak from long confinement, as he leaned upon the desk and gave out his theme, every ear hung upon the cherished accents. The effect of his address is said to have been affecting in the highest degree. As it proceeded, he kindled into that calm and earnest ardour for which he was remarkable, and vindicated the benignity and the wisdom of the heavenly Father who had so recently afflicted him, in a strain so exalted and sincere that to this day all who heard him dwell with enthusiasm upon the scene.

It is said that the printed remains of Buckminster afford but an inadequate idea of his great mental resources and classical taste. His learned and distinguished friend Mr. Andrews Norton, in an eloquent eulogy written soon after his death, says that in his opinion he was far beyond all rivalship the most eminent literary man of all those of whom the country retained only the memory. Pulpit oratory has advanced in this country since his day, but to readers of cultivation whose sense of beauty is keen and elevated, of whatever denomination, there is a moral dignity and subdued gracefulness of feeling and style in his sermons which render them models in this department of literature.

Mr. Buckminster was succeeded as minister of the Brattle Street society by Edward Everett, of whose life and genius some account will be given in another part of this volume; and William Ellery Channing was chosen in his place as lecturer on biblical criticism in the university.

FAITH TO THE AFFLICTED.

FROM SERMONS.

Would you know the value of this principle of faith to the bereaved? Go, and follow a corpse to the grave. See the body deposited there, and hear the earth thrown in upon all that remains of your friend. Return now, if you will, and brood over the lesson which your senses have given you, and derive from it what consolation you can. You have learned nothing but an unconsoling fact. No voice of comfort issues from the tomb. All is still there, and blank, and lifeless, and has been so for ages. You see nothing but bodies dissolving and successively mingling with the clods which cover them, the grass growing over the spot, and the trees waving in sullen majesty over this region of eternal silence. And what is there more? Nothing.—Come, Faith, and people these deserts! Come, and reanimate these regions of forgetfulness! Mothers! take again your children to your arms, for they are living. Sons! your aged parents are coming forth in the vigour of regenerated years. Friends! behold, your dearest connections are waiting to embrace you. The tombs are burst. Generations long since in slumbers are awakening. They are coming from the east and the west, from the north and from the south, to constitute the community of the blessed.

But it is not in the loss of friends alone, that faith furnishes consolations which are inestimable. With a man of faith not an affliction is lost, not a change is unimproved. He studies even his own history with pleasure, and finds it full of instruction. The dark passages of his life are illuminated with hope; and he sees, that although he has passed through many dreary defiles, yet they have opened at last into brighter regions of existence. He recalls, with a species of wondering gratitude, periods of his life, when all its events seemed to conspire against him. Hemmed in by straitened circumstances, wearied with repeated blows of unexpected misfortunes, and exhausted with the painful anticipation of more, he recollects ·years, when the ordinary love of life could not have retained him in the world. Many a time he might have wished to lay down his being in disgust, had not something more than the senses provide us with, kept up the elasticity of his mind. He yet lives, and has found that light is sown for the righteous, and gladness for the upright in heart. The man of faith discovers some gracious purpose in every combination of circumstances. Wherever he finds himself, he knows that he has a destination—he has, therefore, a duty. Every event has, in his eye, a tendency and an aim. Nothing is accidental, nothing without purpose, nothing unattended with benevolent consequences. Every thing on earth is probationary, nothing ultimate. He is poor—perhaps his plans have been defeated —he finds it difficult to provide for the exigencies of life—sickness is permitted to invade the quiet of his household—long confinement imprisons his activity, and cuts short the exertions on which so many depend—something apparently unlucky

mars his best plans—new failures and embarrassments among his friends present themselves, and throw additional obstruction in his way—the world look on and say all these things are against him. Some wait coolly for the hour when he shall sink, under the complicated embarrassments of his cruel fortune. Others, of a kinder spirit, regard him. with compassion, and wonder how he can sustain such a variety of wo. A few there are, a very few, I fear, who can understand something of the serenity of his mind, and comprehend something of the nature of his fortitude. There are those, whose sympathetic piety can read and interpret the characters of resignation on his brow. There are those, in fine, who have felt the influence of faith.

In this influence there is nothing mysterious, nothing romantic, nothing of which the highest reason may be ashamed. It shows the Christian his God, in all the mild majesty of his parental character. It shows you God, disposing in still and benevolent wisdom the events of every individual's life, pressing the pious spirit with the weight of calamity to increase the elasticity of the mind, producing characters of unexpected worth by unexpected misfortune, invigorating certain virtues by peculiar probations, thus breaking the fetters which bind us to temporal things, and

> "From seeming evil still educing good.
> And better thence again, and better still,
> In infinite progression."

When the sun of the believer's hopes, according to common calculations, is set, to the eye of faith it is still visible. When much of the rest of the world is in darkness, the high ground of faith is illuminated with the brightness of religious consolation.

Come now, and follow me to the bed of the dying believer. Would you see in what peace a Christian can die? Watch the last gleams of thought which stream from his dying eyes. Do you see any thing like apprehension? The world, it is true, begins to shut in. The shadows of evening collect around his senses. A dark mist thickens, and rests upon the objects which have hitherto engaged his observation. The countenances of his friends become more and more indistinct. The sweet expressions of love and friendship are no longer intelligible. His ear wakes no more at the well-known voice of his children, and the soothing accents of tender affection die away unheard, upon his decaying senses. To him the spectacle of human life is drawing to its close, and the curtain is descending, which shuts out this earth, its actors, and its scenes. He is no longer interested in all that is done under the sun. O! that I could now open to you the recesses of his soul; that I could reveal to you the light, which darts into the chambers of his understanding. He approaches that world which he has so long seen in faith. The imagination now collects its diminished strength, and the eye of faith opens wide. Friends! do not stand, thus fixed in sorrow, around this bed o. death. Why are you so still and silent? Fear not to move—you cannot disturb the last visions which enchant this holy spirit. Your lamenta-

29

tions break not in upon the songs of seraphs, which inwrap his hearing in ecstasy. Crowd, if you choose, around his couch—he heeds you not —already he sees the spirits of the just advancing together to receive a kindred soul. Press him not with importunities; urge him not with alleviations. Think you he wants now these tones of mortal voices—these material, these gross consolations? No! He is going to add another to the myriads of the just, that are every moment crowding into the portals of heaven! He is entering on a nobler life. He leaves you—he leaves *you*, weeping children of mortality, to grope about a little longer among the miseries and sensualities of a worldly life. Already he cries to you from the regions of bliss. Will you not join him there? Will you not taste the sublime joys of faith? There are your predecessors in virtue; there, too, are places left for your contemporaries. There are seats for you in the assembly of the just made perfect, in the innumerable company of angels, where is Jesus, the mediator of the new covenant, and God, the judge of all.

TRUE SOURCES OF HAPPINESS.
FROM THE SAME.

WE are very much in the habit of keeping ourselves in ignorance of the real sources of our happiness. The unexpected events of life, and, much more, those on which we calculate, are far from being those which constitute its real enjoyment. Even events of public good-fortune, which call forth the most frequent and audible acknowledgments, are, really, not those which contribute most to our personal well-being; and much less do we depend, for our most valuable happiness, on what we call fortunate occurrences, or upon the multiplication of our public amusements, or the excitement, the novelty, the ecstasy, which we make so essential to our pleasures, and for which we are always looking out with impatience. It is not the number of the great, dazzling, affecting, and much talked of pleasures, which makes up the better part of our substantial happiness; but it is the delicate, unseen, quiet, and ordinary comforts of social and domestic life, for the loss of which, all that the world has dignified with the name of pleasure would not compensate us. Let any man inquire, for a single day, what it is which has employed and satisfied him, and which really makes him love life, and he will find that the sources of his happiness lie within a very narrow compass. He will find that he depends almost entirely on the agreeable circumstances which God has made to lie all around him, and which fill no place in the record of public events. Indeed, we may say of human happiness what Paul quotes for a more sacred purpose, " It is not hidden from thee; neither is it far off; it is not in heaven, that thou shouldst say, Who shall go up for us, and bring it unto us? neither is it beyond the sea, that thou shouldst say, Who shall go over the sea for us, and bring it unto us? but is very nigh unto thee in thy mouth, and in thy heart."

CICERO AND ATTICUS.
FROM AN ORATION BEFORE THE PHI BETA KAPPA SOCIETY.

THE history of letters does not, at this moment, suggest to me a more fortunate parallel between the effects of active and of inactive learning, than in the well-known characters of Cicero and Atticus. Let me hold them up to your observation, not because Cicero was faultless, or Atticus always to blame, but because, like you, they were the citizens of a republic. They lived in an age of learning and of dangers, and acted upon opposite principles, when Rome was to be saved, if saved at all, by the virtuous energy of her most accomplished minds.

If we look now for Atticus, we find him in the quiet of his library, surrounded with books; while Cicero was passing through the regular course of public honours and services, where all the treasures of his mind were at the command of his country. If we follow them, we find Atticus pleasantly wandering among the ruins of Athens, purchasing up statues and antiques; while Cicero was at home, blasting the projects of Catiline, and, at the head of the senate, like the tutelary spirit of his country, as the storm was gathering, secretly watching the doubtful movements of Cæsar. If we look to the period of the civil wars, we find Atticus always reputed, indeed, to belong to the party of the friends of liberty, yet originally dear to Sylla, and intimate with Clodius, recommending himself to Cæsar by his neutrality, courted by Antony, and connected with Octavius, poorly concealing the Epicureanism of his principles under the ornaments of literature and the splendour of his benefactions; till at last this inoffensive and polished friend of successive usurpers hastens out of life to escape from the pains of a lingering disease. Turn now to Cicero, the only great man at whom Cæsar always trembled, the only great man whom falling Rome did not fear. Do you tell me that his hand once offered incense to the dictator? Remember it was the gift of gratitude only, and not of servility; for the same hand launched its indignation against the infamous Antony, whose power was more to be dreaded, and whose revenge pursued him till this father of his country gave his head to the executioner without a struggle, for he knew that Rome was no longer to be saved. If, my friends, you would feel what learning, and genius, and virtue, should aspire to in a day of peril and depravity, when you are tired of the factions of the city, the battles of Cæsar, the crimes of the triumvirate, and the splendid court of Augustus, do not go and repose in the easy chair of Atticus, but refresh your virtues and your spirits with the contemplation of Cicero.

GULIAN C. VERPLANCK.

[Born 1781. Died 1870.]

In the veins of GULIAN CROMMELIN VER-PLANCK mingles the best blood of the Holland-er, the Huguenot, and the Puritan. Without knowing the exact proportions, we may sup pose he was half Dutch, a third French, and a sixth Yankee: which is perhaps as good a composition for a man as has yet been disco-vered. After alluding to his descent from the stock of Grotius and De Witt, in his Address at Amherst College, he remarks, " I cannot but remember also that I have New England blood in my veins, that many of my happiest youth-ful days were passed in her villages, and that my best education was bestowed by the more than parental care of one of the wisest and most excellent of her sons.* Imitating there-fore the language in which an ancient scholar expressed his attachment for all that partook of the common Gaelic descent, I too can say that *Nil Nov-Anglicum à me alienum puto.*†

On completing his academical education at Columbia College, in his native city of New York, Mr. Verplanck studied the law, and soon after his admission to the bar he went abroad, and passed several years in travelling or resid-ing in Great Britain and central Europe. On his return he became interested in politics, and in 1814 was a candidate of the " Malcontents"‡ in New York for the Assembly, from which it may be inferred that he was from the begin-ning distinguished for that independence which has marked his more recent public life. When the " Bucktails" and " Clintonians" were the prominent factions, he amused himself occa-sionally with writing satires, and his State Triumvirate, a Political Tale, published in 1819, and other works of a similar description, of which he was the principal or only author, are among the happiest specimens of this sort of composition that the country has furnished.

Mr. Verplanck acquired at an early age an extraordinary and well-merited reputation for scholarship and taste; but he published nothing under his own name until 1818, when he de-

livered an address before the New York His-torical Society, which was printed and soon passed through several editions. The task which he assigned himself in this performance was the grateful one of commemorating " some of those virtuous and enlightened men of Eu-rope, who, long ago, looking with a prophetic eye toward the destinies of this new world, and regarding it as the chosen refuge of freedom and truth, were moved by a holy ambition to become the ministers of the most High, in be-stowing upon it the blessings of religion, morals, letters, and liberty." After a brief re-view of the progress of Spanish discovery and conquest on this continent, and the scenes of avarice and cruelty with which they were at-tended, he relieves the gloomy exhibition by in-troducing a portrait of the young ecclesiastic Las Casas, whom he vindicates with generous warmth from the accusation of having, in mis-taken philanthropy, originated the plan of ne-gro slavery. Among his other subjects are Roger Williams, the legislator for whom was reserved the glory of setting the first example of a practical system of religious freedom; William Penn, General Oglethorpe, Bishop Berkeley, Thomas Hollis, and Louis the Six-teenth. The whole discourse is a group of ad-mirable historical portraits, with New Eng-land Puritanism, in shadow except where re-lieved by the name of the founder of Rhode Island, for a background, and glowing sketches of the Dutch colonists of New Amsterdam and the Huguenot settlers of Carolina and New York, in front.

In 1820 we find that Mr. Verplanck was a prominent member of the New York legisla-ture, in which, as chairman of the appropriate committee, he had the especial charge of the interests of education. He must have with-drawn his attention from politics soon after, however, as he accepted the professorship of the Evidences of Christianity in the Theolo gical Seminary of the Protestant Episcopal Church, in New York, and for some time oc-cupied himself with his new duties, and cor-responding studies. In 1824 he published,

---

* William Samuel Johnson, of Connecticut.
† Alluding to a passage in George Buchanan.
‡ See The Evening Post for that year.

227

in one octavo volume, his Essays on the Nature and Uses of the Various Evidences of Revealed Religion, in which he treats largely and in the most perspicuous and philosophical manner of " the highest, noblest and most universal of all evidence, that which results from the majesty and excellence of principle," so much neglected and indeed contemned by many who have discussed very learnedly and ably the critical and historical testimony. The work is written with simplicity and elegance, and admirable temper. It is one of the very few books on this subject which are not by professed theologians and metaphysicians, and distinguished for a hue and tone of the closet and desk which render them by no means agreeable to readers of other classes ; and there is not another work in our language, perhaps, which is calculated to be more useful in confirming the convictions of intelligent and honest inquirers, of the truth of Christianity. In 1825 appeared Mr. Verplanck's Essay on the Doctrine of Contracts, being an Inquiry how Contracts are affected in Law and Morals by Concealment, Error, or Inadequate Price. The great object of the work is, to examine the propriety and justice of the maxim which the common law applies to sales, and most other contracts, " *Caveat emptor*,"—let the buyer beware,—with reference to those principles of expediency and justice which should be the foundation of all law; and the discussion is conducted with great learning, ability, and impartiality.

About this time Mr. Verplanck and three of his friends, of as many different professions, formed an association of a somewhat remarkable character, under the name of the Literary Confederacy. The number was limited to four, and they bound themselves to an intimate fellowship, and to endeavour by all proper means to advance their mutual and individual interests, and proposed to unite from time to time in literary publications. In the first year of its existence the Confederacy (of which Mr. Bryant, and the late Mr. Sands, were members) contributed largely to the literary and critical magazines, and the daily journals, but in 1827, under the name and character of an imaginary author, Francis Herbert, Esquire, they published The Talisman, a decorated miscellany of prose and verse, of which a second and a third volume followed in 1829 and 1830. Of this work Mr. Verplanck composed nearly

one half. His papers are distinguished for a quiet, genial and peculiar humour, and several of them bear witness of a lingering fondness for New York as it was before its social aspects had been changed or obliterated by the commercial class and spirit.

For eight years from 1825 Mr. Verplanck was a member of Congress for the city of New York. He did not very often take a part in the debates, but his high reputation secured for him the most flattering attention when he addressed the House, and several elaborate and very able reports which he made on subjects of general interest commanded the respectful consideration of statesmen throughout the country. He particularly distinguished himself during the session of 1831–32 by his agency in procuring the passage of an act which gave much additional security to copyrights, and more than doubled the term of legal protection to them ; and upon the adjournment of Congress, a public dinner was given to him by the authors and artists of New York, at which he made the speech published in his collected Discourses, on the legislation of the United States upon the subject of literary property. Since the close of his last term in Congress he had been several years a member of the New York Senate, which until the adoption of the Constitution of 1846 was also the highest court of judicature in the state.

In 1833 Mr. Verplanck published in one volume his Discourses and Addresses on Subjects of American History, Art, and Literature, and A Discourse on the Right Moral Influence and Use of Liberal Studies ; and in 1834, Discourses on the Connexion of Morals and Learning, and their Influence upon Each Other.

The last and most important of Mr. Verplanck's literary labours, in which he has well sustained his reputation as a literary and historical critic, is his splendid edition of Shakspeare, of which the publication was commenced in 1844 and completed in December, 1846. The plates were destroyed in the great fire at Harper's building in 1851. It was in some sort, a comprehensive commentary, embracing the varying opinions of all the most eminent critics upon doubtful readings and the points of literary history involved, with elaborate, acute and appreciatory introductions and notes by Mr. Verplanck himself, and pictorial illustrations executed under the direction of his friend Mr. R. W. Wier.

MAJOR EGERTON.

FROM THE TALISMAN.

THE critic's first and last injunction to the author and the artist is, to " copy nature." For my own part, I never more than half believed in this standing stock rule of common-place criticism. Nature, and beautiful nature too, may be so very natural, that, if too accurately copied, it will seem unnatural. This assertion has a most paradoxical sound, I confess, and is quite worthy of a Kantian metaphysician. Still it is the fact. That which is true is not always probable. Who has not observed, in natural scenery, a brilliancy of colour, or some singular effect of form or light, which, if faithfully transferred to the canvas, would be pronounced at once, by ninety-nine out of a hundred, to be an extravagant and fantastical *cappricio* of the art. So, too, in real life—occurrences happen every day before our eyes, which if related in a novel, or interwoven in a drama, would be branded by the whole critical brotherhood as too far out of probability to be tolerated, even in professed fiction.

For myself, though I have been bandied a good deal about the globe, I have encountered no marvellous vicissitudes of fortune. Yet, if I were to tell nakedly, and without explanation, many of the incidents of my life, they would hardly gain credence. For instance, I have at different periods dined familiarly with five European kings, played chess with an empress, given alms to an archbishop and had my soup cooked by a duke. This is very astounding, and the reader is doubtless already either penetrated with respect for my high rank, or else sets me down in his heart for an impudent liar. Yet upon a little consideration, he may satisfy himself that within the last thirty years, a plain American citizen might, without any marvel, have relieved the wants or received the services of a French temporal or spiritual peer, have dined at *tables d'hôte* and on broad steam-boats, with Lewis of Holland, Joseph of Spain, Jerome of Westphalia, and Gustavus of Sweden ; and have been beaten, at Washington, at the royal game of chess, by a Mexican ex-empress. The fifth, in my catalogue of royal acquaintance, is his present majesty of the Netherlands, who, when a poor prince of Germany, was a very conversable, pleasant Dutchman. I might add, that I have received lessons in mathematics from another prince, who though not exactly the next in succession, now looks proudly towards the first throne on the European continent.

There is one extraordinary chain of incidents in my life, which I have often been tempted (when seized with a fit of authorship) to make the foundation of a Gil Blas or Anastasius novel. But I have always been deterred from executing it, by the conviction, that though I should task my fancy solely for the minor incidents, and add no decorations but the necessary colouring of sentiment, character and description, the very skeleton and ground-work of the whole, though strictly true, would still be so outrageously improbable, as to shock even the easy credulity of the novel-reader.

My readers may perhaps anticipate that after this deprecatory prologue, I am about to unfold a tale of love and arms, or else of wild adventure, of which I am myself to be the prince Arthur, the Amadis or the Rinaldo—or at least the Gil Blas or Tom Jones. No, I am not the hero of it. Right gladly would I transform myself into a hero, at the expense of any danger or hardships, (so that all were now well over,) if I could thus be enabled to make bright eyes weep over my sorrows, and lovely forms bend entranced over the page that speaks of me.

Such, alas! is not my good fortune. But to my story, which, I begin to fear, will scarcely equal the expectations this introduction may raise.

It was longer ago than I commonly care to tell without special necessity, that, having finished my professional studies, I spent my first fashionable winter in New York. The gay and polite society of the city, which every day's necessity is now dividing up into smaller and more independent circles, was then one very large one, wherein whoever was introduced, circulated freely throughout the whole. I of course went everywhere ; and everywhere did I meet with MAJOR EGERTON. He was a young British officer, of high connections. Not one of your Lord Mortimers or Marquises de Crillon, who have so often taken in our title-loving republicans of fashion ; but a real officer of the —— regiment, a major at the age of twenty-six, and the nephew of a distinguished English general ; in proof of which he had brought the best letters to the "best good men," in our chief cities. He was quite the fashion, and he deserved to be so. Most people thought him handsome : tall and well-made, and young and accomplished he certainly was ; of easy and graceful manners, ready and bold address, and fluent rattling conversation. He danced to the admiration of the ladies ; and that at a time when our belles were accustomed to the incredible performances of so many Parisian partners, was no mean feat for an Englishman. He was overflowing with anecdotes of the great and the gay of London ; and listening dinner tables and drawing-rooms hung upon his lips, while he discoursed about the Duchess of Devonshire, Lord Dudley and Ward, the Duke of Norfolk, Lady Louisa Mildmay, Mrs. Siddons, Lord Nelson, Kemble, and the Countess of Derby.

Still, I know not why, I liked not the man. There was something singularly disagreeable in the tone, or rather the croak, of his voice. His ready and polite laugh never came from the heart —and his smile, when by a sudden draw of the lip he showed his white teeth, contrasting with his black brow and sallow cheek, had a covert ferocity in it which almost made me shudder.

One evening, at the theatre—it was when Fennel and Cooper were contending for the palm in Othello and Iago—we were crowded together in a corner of the stage-box.

" Mr. Herbert," said he suddenly to me, " you do not seem to know that you and I are quite old acquaintances."

U

"I don't understand you, Major——"

"Some six or seven years ago you, then a lad, accompanied your father to the west on his mission as a commissioner to make an Indian treaty."

"Yes."

"Did you remember among the Tuscaroras the Black Wild Cat, a youth of white blood, the adopted son of Good Peter, the great Indian orator? I mean the one who, after giving you a lesson on the bow and arrow, surprised a reverend divine of your party by reading in his Greek testament, and then mortified him by correcting his pronunciation of Latin, which, like other American scholars, he pronounced in a way intolerable to the ears of one who has had longs and shorts flogged into him at an English school."

"Certainly, I remember him; and it is a mystery which has often puzzled me ever since."

"Then you have now the solution of it. I am the Black Wild Cat."

"You—how!"

"After leaving Harrow I accompanied my uncle to Canada. There a boyish frolic induced me to join an Indian party, who were returning home from Montreal. Good Peter (a great man by the way, very like our Erskine) took a fancy to me, and I spent my time pleasantly enough. It is certainly a delicious life that of savages, as we call them. But my uncle coaxed me back. I am not sure that I was not a fool for accepting his offer, but I could not resist the temptation of the red coat and an epaulette. The old man has pushed me on as fast as money and interest could promote me. The rest I can do for myself; and if Pitt will leave off his little expeditions to pick up colonies, and give us a fair chance on the continent, the major at six and twenty will be a general, and a peer at thirty."

Here the rising of the curtain interrupted us. Business called me to Albany the next day, and before my return Major Egerton had sailed for England.

I did not, however, forget him; and I often related, as one of the odd vicissitudes of life, the contrast between the young Black Wild Cat, as I first saw him in a Tuscarora wigwam, and the elegant major, glittering in scarlet and gold, when I met him again in the British Consul's ball-room.

A year or two after this I went to England, and not long after my arrival spent a week at Bath. All who are at all learned in English dramatic history, know that the Bath company is commonly good, the Bath audience fashionable and critical, and that there, many of the stars of the theatrical firmament have first risen. Whilst I was there, a first appearance was announced. Mr. Monfort, of whom report spoke favourably, was to make his debut as Romeo. I went with the crowd to see it. Romeo entered, and thunders of applause welcomed the handsome and graceful lover.

Could I believe my eyes? Can this be Major Egerton? Yes—he smiles—that wicked and heartless smile cannot be mistaken; and his voice—that tuneless grating voice.—It is he. What can it

mean? Is it a joke or a frolic, or some strange caprice of fortune?

That grating voice which betrayed him to me ruined him with the house. It had sudden and most ludicrous breaks from a high hoarse croak, down at once into a shrill squeak; so that in spite of grace and figure, and a tolerable conception of his author, he was fairly laughed down. I did my best to sustain him, but I was almost alone in the good-natured attempt.

Two days after, turning short round the transept of the Abbey church, I came full upon Major Egerton, who was standing alone, with a listless and melancholy air.

"Major," said I—then correcting myself—"Mr. Monfort"—with an offer of my hand. He met me boldly—"Herbert," said he, "I see you know my misfortunes." "Not at all—I saw you in Romeo, but wherefore you were Romeo I could not guess."

"Sheer necessity—a run of ill luck and other misfortunes to which young soldiers are exposed, threw me out of favour with my uncle the old general, and into the King's Bench. At last I sold my commission, and resolved on a new profession. I had trusted to succeed on the stage; I knew that this husky throat of mine made the attempt hazardous, yet Gifford and his brother wags had laughed at "the hoarse croak of Kemble's foggy throat," and if art and taste had overcome his defects, why might not mine also? But it is all over now."

"Then you do not mean to pursue the profession?" "No—the manager talks of twelve and sixpence a week, and ordered me to study Bardolph for Cooke's Falstaff on Monday. I must seek my fortune elsewhere. If nothing better offers, I'll to my old trade, and enlist as a soldier. In the meanwhile lend me a guinea for old acquaintance sake.

I did so, and saw no more of him at Bath. I soon after left England for the continent. At Dover, before the quarters of some general officer, I saw the ci-devant Major Egerton on duty as a sentinel—a private soldier. I did not speak to him, nor did he seem to observe me; but I was sure of my man.

The studies and the amusements of Paris, during the winter, and the excitement of travel for the rest of the year, soon put my unlucky major out of my head; except that now and then when I fell into a narrative mood, I would tell his story to some of my young countrymen, generally ending it with a Johnsonian morality; "that nothing could supply the want of prudence, and that continued irregularity will make knowledge useless, wit ridiculous, and talent contemptible."

In those days it was not easy to get a comfortable passage from France to the United States, so that I was obliged to return home by the way of England. I therefore crossed from Holland to Harwich. Not far from the road up to London was the country-seat of a wealthy gentleman, who had married a pretty American cousin of mine. I gladly seized the opportunity of paying Sophia a visit, and as willingly accepted her husband's invitation to spend a day or two with them. The next day was Sunday.

"You will go with us to church," said Sophia; "your passion for gothic churches and old monuments will be gratified there. We have an old carved pulpit, said to be without its match in England."

"Yes, cousin, but what shall we find in the pulpit to-day?"

"Oh, our rector I suppose. He is not quite such a preacher as your Dr. Mason, yet they say he is very agreeable in society; though I know little about him, for my husband holds him in perfect detestation."

So we went to the village church. As I followed Sophia up the aisle, the "Dearly beloved brethren," grated on my ear in that voice which I can never forget. I looked up in amazement. In the reading desk, duly attired in surplice and band, stood Major Egerton!

I could not allow my cousin to enter the pew, without asking her, in a hurried whisper: "Who is the clergyman?" "Mr. Egerton, the rector," she replied, as coldly as if there was nothing strange in the matter. I was lost in wonder, and stood during the whole service leaning over the high oak pew, gazing at the rector in all the fidgetty impatience of curiosity. He rattled through the service, psalms, lessons, litany and all, in little more than half an hour, and then preached a sermon of twelve minutes, which I believe was a paper of the Rambler, with a scriptural text substituted for the classical motto. To do Egerton justice, there was nothing of levity or affectation in his manner; but it was as rapid, cold, and mechanical as possible.

As soon as it was over, without thinking of my friends, or any one else, I bustled through the retiring congregation, and met the rector alone at the foot of his pulpit stairs. He had observed me before, and now greeted me with a laugh. "So," said he, "Herbert, you see circumstances have altered with me since you saw me at Dover, a poor private in the 49th."

"They have indeed, but what does it mean?"

"Nothing more than that a rich and noble cousin was ashamed of having a relation and a godson who bore his name, and had borne a commission in his Majesty's service, now known to be a private of foot. He paid my debts, took me out of the ranks, and was about to ship me off for Sierra Leone, as clerk of the courts there, when this living, which is his gift, became vacant. I had Greek and Latin enough left out of my old Harrow stock for any ordinary parson; and the living is not bad. So having no particular fancy to spend my days 'all among the Hottentots a capering on shore,' I begged the living, and got myself japanned."

"Japanned!" said I.

"Yes, got my red coat dyed black, you know. The Bishop of London was squeamish about me, though I don't see why; but his Lordship of —— had no such silly scruples, and I have been these two months rector of Buffington cum Norton."

My fair cousin and her worthy husband were waiting for me at the church door, and our conversation ended abruptly with some common-place offers of civility. When I rejoined my friends, the suspicious looks which my host cast at me, showed that my apparent intimacy with his new rector was not at all calculated to raise me in his estimation. I had to explain, by relating my former New York acquaintance with the ex-major; and then by way of repelling all suspicions of too close intimacy, on our way home took occasion to vent my indignation at the system of church and state, which could tolerate such abuses of the ecclesiastical establishment. At last I grew eloquent and declamatory, and finished by quoting Cowper:

"From such apostles, oh ye mitred heads,
Preserve the church! and lay not careless hands
On skulls that cannot teach and will not learn."

The John Bullism of my good host was roused. He could not bear that a foreigner should censure any institution of his country, whatever he might think of it himself. He too became eloquent; and thus we lost sight of the rector in the dust of an argument which lasted till evening.

On Monday I went up to London, and soon after returned home.

On my second visit to Europe some years after, I became very intimate with a party of young Cantabs, some of them rich, and all of them well educated, who were suffering under that uneasiness at home, and desire of locomotion abroad, which infects idle Englishmen of all ages; a malady of which, by the way, we have inherited a full share with our English blood. Shut out from the common tour of Europe by the domination of Napoleon, my Cambridge friends had planned a grand tour to Russia, Greece, Turkey, Egypt, and thence perhaps to Persia and India. I was easily persuaded to be of the party.

This, of course, is not the place to relate my travels, nor, indeed, is it necessary that I should ever do it. My companions have long ago anticipated me in sundry well printed London quartos, with splendid engravings; wherein I have the honour to be perpetuated by the burin of Heath and other great artists, now, perched half way up a pyramid, then jolting on the bare back of a hard-trotting camel, and sometimes sitting cross-legged on the floor between two well-bearded Turks, at a Pasha's dinner table, eating roast lamb and rice with my fingers. Meanwhile, in the letter press I go down to posterity as the author's "intelligent friend," his "amusing friend," and even his "enterprising friend." Thus, upon the whole, without the risk or trouble of authorship, I have gained a very cheap and agreeable literary immortality, except, however, that when any disaster occurs in the tour, I am somehow made to bear a much larger portion of it than I can recollect to have ever actually fallen to my share. On all such occasions I am made to figure as "our unfortunate friend."

It was not till we had again turned our faces towards civilized Europe, after having traversed in all directions the frozen North and the gorgeous

East, and gazed on many a "forest and field and flood, temple and tower," renowned in song or in story, that we reached the land of Egypt.

We had consumed a full year in our tour more than we had calculated on, and were all of us in a feverish anxiety to return home. We therefore, *una voce*, gave up the thoughts of penetrating to the sources of the Nile, and of eating live beef-steaks with Bruce's Abyssinian friends.

But the Pyramids and the Sphinx, and the other wonders of antiquity thereunto appurtenant, we could not return without seeing, though they must be seen in haste. And we did see them.

It was after having seen all the sights, and explored the great Pyramid in the usual way within, and clambered to its top without, whilst my fatigued companions were resting in the shade with our guard, that I, who am proof against any fatigue of this sort, and a little vain too of being so, strolled forward towards the Sphinx, which, as everybody knows, rears its ugly colossal head out the sand at some distance in front of what is called the second Pyramid. I was standing near it, making a sketch, after my fashion, of the relative position of the four great Pyramids, when I was startled by the sudden appearance of a gay troop of Mameluke horse, whose approach had been hidden from my sight by the ruins of the small pyramid on my left, and who now suddenly darted by me in gallant style. To my surprise, the leader of the troop, who, from the dazzling splendour of his equipments, seemed to be a chief of rank, in passing looked me full in the face, and then rapidly wheeling twice round me, sprang from his horse. In the meanwhile, his party, to whom he gave some brief command, went on at a slow walk, and halted in the shade of a neighbouring ruin.

The stranger stood silently before me, tall and stately, in that gorgeous amplitude and splendour of dress which Eastern warriors love. His wide scarlet trowsers marked him as a Mameluke. A rich cashmere shawl, such as an English Duchess might have envied, was fancifully wreathed, turban-like, round his helm, and fell over his shoulders. This, as well as his clasped and silver-mounted pistols and jewel-hilted dagger in his belt, and his crooked cimeter in its crimson velvet sheath, with gold bosses and hilt, marked the rank and wealth of the wearer. So too did his slender-limbed, small-headed, bright-eyed iron-gray Arabian, with black legs, mane, and tail, and sprinkled all over with little stars of white, who had a moment before passed me with the swiftness of an arrow's flight, and who now stood behind his master, with the reins loose on his neck, gentle and docile as a spaniel.

Supposing that this might be some Turk whom I had known at Alexandria or Cairo, I looked him full in the face, but could not recollect having seen him before. He appeared young, except that his coal-black whiskers and beard were here and there grizzled by a grayish hair. The scar of a deep sabre cut across the forehead and left cheek, showed him no holiday soldier. There was nothing in his manner to excite alarm, and besides, my friends, with a very strong guard of horse, were within hearing.

After mutually gazing on each other for some moments, the customary *salaam* of oriental salutation was on my lips, when I was startled by his grasping my hand with a genuine English shake, and calling me by name, in a well-known voice. Then, too, the thickly mustachioed upper lip drew back, and showed me the well-remembered tiger-like smile.

"Egerton—can it be?—Major—" said I.

"No—Hussein—Hussein Al Rus.".

"Then this is not the Reverend Rector of—" I proceeded, perplexed and confused, though certain as to my man.

"Yes—but that was six long years ago. An awkward circumstance occurred which made it expedient for me to leave England; as I had no fancy to gain posthumous renown, like Dr. Dodd, by preaching my own funeral sermon and being hung in my canonicals."

"But how is it that you are in Egypt; and that, it seems, in honour and affluence?"

"Yes. It goes well enough with me here. Accident brought me to Egypt. The Pasha wanted men who knew European tactics, and I found a place in his service. Another accident, of which I bear the mark, (passing his hand across his forehead,) placed me about his person. *Au reste*, I made my own way, and have a very pretty command, which I would not care to exchange for any regiment in his Majesty's service."

"But the language?"

"Oh—I have a great facility in catching languages by the ear. I believe I owe it to my Tuscarora education. *Apropos*—How is Good Peter? Is the old man alive?" I was about to tell him what I knew about Good Peter, when he again interrupted me. "But for yourself—what are *you* doing here? Have you money-making Yankees caught the English folly of digging up mummies, measuring pyramids, and buying stone coffins?—sarcophagi of Alexander and Ptolemy, as the fools call them."

"As respects myself," I answered, "it seems so."

"Then I may serve you. You once did me a favour, perhaps I can repay it now."

"I have no favours to ask, but that of your company, and the information you can give me. I am with an English party, under the protection of the British consulate at Cairo, and have no projects independent of my friends."

"Ah!—is it so?—then you need nothing from me. John Bull is in power here just now, and is your best protector. I am sorry that the company you are in may prevent my seeing much of you. But we'll meet somewhere again. Good by," said he, leaping on his Arabian. In a few minutes he was at the head of his troop, and in a few more, out of sight.

"Fare thee well," muttered I to myself, following him with my eyes till he was out of their reach, "better thus than as I saw thee last—better a Mohammedan renegado than a profligate priest."

But why Hussein? Zimri should be your name. You are the very Zimri of Dryden's glorious satire."

"In the first rank of these did Zimri stand;
A man so various as he seemed to be,
Not one, but all mankind's epitome."

Thus musing and quoting I rejoined my friends; whom, by the way, I did not let into the whole history of the Mameluke, as he had reposed some degree of confidence in me. I satisfied them with some general account of meeting a Turk whom I had seen before in England.

We returned to Cairo, and soon left Egypt. Six months after I landed once more in New York. Years rolled on, all pregnant with great events to the world, and with smaller ones of equal interest to myself. I did not talk any more about Egerton; for his transformations had now become so multiplied, that they began to sound too like a traveller's story to be told by as modest a man as I am. Besides there was then no need of telling any old stories; for those were the glorious and stirring days of Napoleon, when

"Events of wonder swelled each gale,
And each day brought a varying tale."

Meantime my natural instinct for travel—for it is certainly an instinct—Dr. Gall, himself, once pointed me out in his own lecture-room as wholly deficient in the organ of *inhabitiveness*, and equally conspicuous for my capacity for *localities*. This instinct, though long restrained, was as ardent as ever; and when my old friend Commodore —— invited me to accompany him in his Mediterranean cruise, to try a new seventy-four, and parade our naval force before Turks and Christians, I could not refuse him.

Once more then I gazed on the towers and minarets of Constantinople. Once more that fair scene—but all that is in Dr. Clarke and the other travellers, and I hate telling thrice-told tales.

Whilst at Constantinople, or rather in its suburbs, with a party of American officers, after having satisfied our curiosity, as far as we could, on the shore of European Turkey, my friends were anxious to take a look at the Asiatic coast, where the true Turk was to be seen in more unadulterated purity. So, among other excursions we went to Scutari. It is an old Turkish town, full of mosques, and monasteries of Dervishes; and the great lion of the place is the exhibition of the *Mehveleveh*, or dancing Dervishes, one of the very few religious ceremonies of the Mohammedans which an infidel is allowed to witness.

It is a strange thing that there is so little variety among men in this large world. Nature is inexhaustible in her changes, but man is always alike. Here are we all, east, west, north, and south, and have been these two thousand years, telling and hearing the same stories, laughing at the same jokes, and playing the fool all over in the same dull way. That the business of life, and its science and its passions, should be uniform, is a matter of course. People must, of necessity, till their fields and learn their mathematics, must make money, make war, make shoes, and make love, pretty much as the rest of the world do. But

their fancies and their follies, one would think, might be dissimilar, irregular, wild, capricious, and original. Nevertheless the nonsense of the world smacks everywhere of wearisome sameness; and wherever the traveller roams, the only real variety he finds in man is that of coat, gown, cloak, or pelisse—hat, cap, helm, or turban—the sitting cross-legged or on a chair—the eating dinner with a fork or the fingers.

This nonsense of the dancing and howling Dervishes at Scutari, is very much the same nonsense that many of my readers must have seen at Lebanon and Niskayuna among our Shakers. It is a kind of dancing by way of religious exercises, at first heavy, and then becoming more and more violent. The chief difference is, that the Turks, when once excited, have more violence in whirling round and round on their tip-toes, with shouting and howling, than I have ever seen in our placid and well-fed Shaker monks. The Turks have, besides, the music of flutes and tambour, and the psalter of patriarchal days, which they accompany with a maniac guttural howling of *Ullah-hoo, Ullah-hoo.* Those who pretend to special sanctity, add some slight of hand tricks, such as seeming to drive daggers into their flesh, and taking hot irons into their mouths.

Altogether it is a very tedious and very disgusting spectacle.

The emir or abbot of the Mohammedan monastery was old and feeble, and the chief duty of leading the dance and setting the howl, devolved upon a kind of aid-de-camp, to whom great respect was evidently paid. He had the ordering of the whole ceremony, and the arranging of spectators, and was in fact, as one of my naval companions called him, the Beau Nash of the Dervishes' ball-room.

He was a stout dirty Turk, with bushy gray locks and beard, dressed in the old costume of his fraternity; his brow overshadowed by the cap which they wear instead of the graceful turban of the east, and his cheek swelled up with that tumour and scar, which is left by the peculiar distemper of some Syrian cities, and is called, in Turkey, the Aleppo tumour. I remarked too, that his eyes, before he was excited by the dance, had that dreamy vacancy, and his skin that ghastly pale glossiness, which indicate the habitual opium-taker.

This fellow eyed our party frequently and closely, and, as I thought, seemed to meditate some plan for laying us under special contribution.

When the dance was over, and the rabble, who formed the mass of the congregation, had gone off, our guide proceeded to show us the monastery, which I thought curious only because it differed less than I had expected from the convents of Europe. Just as we were going off, an underling howler pulled me by the coat, and pointed to a cell with many gesticulations, and some words which I could not understand. Our guide told me that I was specially honoured, for I was invited to converse separately with the Dervish Yussuf the Wise, a most holy man, and, as he said, commonly called the Wise, because he was thought to be out of his senses.

30   u 2

I entered, and found my dirty, dancing, howling, swelled-faced, gray-bearded Beau Nash of the morning's service, stretched on a carpet, evidently overcome with fatigue, and solacing himself with a little box of *Mash-Allah*, a kind of opium lozenges. Scarcely were we alone, than he rose with an air of dignity, and startled me by addressing me in English.

"Time has laid his hand gently upon you, Francis Herbert. You are stouter—and I see gray hairs straggling through your brown curls—otherwise you are unchanged since I left you in America twenty-five years ago. I am old. I am old before my time. Prisons and battles and the plague have borne me down. But the hand of God is with me. He is great, Mohammed is his prophet. Mohammed Resoul Allah!"

"What—Egerton!—Hussein!—when—how—why left you Egypt?"

"It was so written in the eternal councils of him who fashions all things to his will. It was fore-ordained—even as all things are fore-ordained—that I should escape from the tyrant and become a prophet, and a holy one. In that predestination is thy fate mysteriously linked to mine."

His eye kindled, his form dilated, and he burst into the horrible howl of his order—*Ullah-hoo*.

Was this fanaticism? Was this lunacy? Was it the temporary intoxication of opium; or was this wretched man masking under wild enthusiasm some deep plot of ambition or fraud?

I know not. I was glad to leave the cell. I left it wondering, sorrowing, disgusted, and have never since seen him.

Yet frequently in crowds, or in the hurry of commercial cities, I have met faces that seemed familiar to me, though I knew them not, and I have often fancied some of them to be his.

Sometimes, too, I dream of this fearful Proteus, and meet him in new shapes.

It was but last week that I supped in company with an intelligent English officer, who had accompanied Lord Amherst in his mission to Pekin, and went to bed with my head full of China and its customs. I dreamt that our government had sent out Dr. Mitchell as ambassador to the Celestial Empire, and that I accompanied my learned friend. The moment we arrived at Canton, a fat old mandarin, with a blue button in his cap, and a gilt dragon on his breast, came on board our frigate, flourished his hands twenty times, and thumped his forehead as often on the deck, and then jumping up, burst into a laugh, and asked me if I did not recollect the Black Wild Cat, alias the Reverend Major, Rector, Romeo, Bardolph, Hussein, Yussuf Egerton.

———

THE UNIVERSITY OF OXFORD.
FROM AN ADDRESS ON THE FINE ARTS.

I WELL remember the vivid impressions produced upon my own mind several years ago, when I first saw the University of Oxford. The quiet grandeur and the pomp of literary ease which are there displayed, did not wholly disarm that dislike; I could not help feeling towards an establishment, which, possessing so much learning and so much real talent, had for the last century, in its public and academic capacity, done so very little for the improvement of education, and had so long been the sanctuary of unworthy prejudices, and the solid barrier against liberal principles. But when I beheld her halls and chapels, filled with the monuments, and statues, and pictures, of the illustrious men who had been educated in her several colleges; when I saw the walls covered with the portraits of those great scholars and eloquent divines, whose doctrines are taught, or whose works are daily consulted by the clergy of all sects throughout our republic—of the statesmen, and judges, whose opinions and decisions are every day cited as authorities at our bar and in our legislative bodies—of the poets and orators, whose works form the study of our youth and the amusement of our leisure,—I could not but confess that the young man who lived and studied in such a presence must be dull and brutal indeed, if he was not sometimes roused into aspirations after excellence, if the countenances of the great men who looked down upon him did not sometimes fill his soul with generous thoughts and high contemplations.

———

THE FUTURE.
FROM THE SAME.

FOREIGN criticism has contemptuously told us, that the national pride of Americans rests more upon the anticipation of the future, than on the recollections of the past. Allowing for a little malicious exaggeration, this is not far from the truth. It is so. It ought to be so. Why should it not be so?

Our national existence has been quite long enough, and its events sufficiently various, to prove the value and permanence of our civil and political establishments, to dissipate the doubts of their friends, and to disappoint the hopes of their enemies. Our past history is to us the pledge, the earnest, the type of the greater future. We may read in it the fortunes of our descendants, and with an assured confidence look forward to a long and continued advance in all that can make a people great.

If this is a theme full of proud thoughts, it is also one that should penetrate us with a deep and solemn sense of duty. Our humblest honest efforts to perpetuate the liberties, or animate the patriotism of this people, to purify their morals, or to excite their genius, will be felt long after us, in a widening and more widening sphere, until they reach a distant posterity, to whom our very names may be unknown.

Every swelling wave of our doubling and still doubling population, as it rolls from the Atlantic coast, inland, onward toward the Pacific, must bear upon its bosom the influence of the taste, learning, morals, freedom of this generation.

AMERICAN HISTORY.
FROM DISCOURSE BEFORE THE NEW YORK HISTORICAL SOCIETY.

THE study of the history of most other nations fills the mind with sentiments not unlike those which the American traveller feels on entering the venerable and lofty cathedral of some proud old city of Europe. Its solemn grandeur, its vastness, its obscurity, strike awe to his heart. From the richly painted windows, filled with sacred emblems and strange antique forms, a dim religious light falls around. A thousand recollections of romance and poetry, and legendary story, come thronging in upon him. He is surrounded by the tombs of the mighty dead, rich with the labours of ancient art, and emblazoned with the pomp of heraldry.

What names does he read upon them? Those of princes and nobles who are now remembered only for their vices; and of sovereigns, at whose death no tears were shed, and whose memories lived not an hour in the affections of their people. There, too, he sees other names, long familiar to him for their guilty or ambiguous fame. There rest, the blood-stained soldier of fortune—the orator, who was ever the ready apologist of tyranny—great scholars, who were the pensioned flatterers of power—and poets, who profaned the high gift of genius, to pamper the vices of a corrupted court.

Our own history, on the contrary, like that poetical temple of fame, reared by the imagination of Chaucer, and decorated by the taste of Pope, is almost exclusively dedicated to the memory of the truly great. Or rather, like the Pantheon of Rome, it stands in calm and severe beauty amid the ruins of ancient magnificence and "the toys of modern state." Within, no idle ornament encumbers its bold simplicity. The pure light of heaven enters from above and sheds an equal and serene radiance around. As the eye wanders about its extent, it beholds the unadorned monuments of brave and good men who have bled or toiled for their country, or it rests on votive tablets inscribed with the names of the best benefactors of mankind.

> Hic manus, ob patriam pugnando. volnera passi,
> Quique sacerdotes casti, dum vita manebat,
> Quique pii vates, et Phoebo digna locuti,
> Inventas aut vitam excoluere per artes,
> Quique sui memores, alios fecere merendo.*

Doubtless, this is a subject upon which we may be justly proud. But there is another consideration, which, if it did not naturally arise of itself, would be pressed upon us by the taunts of European criticism.

What has this nation done to repay the world for the benefits we have received from others? We have been repeatedly told, and sometimes, too, in a tone of affected impartiality, that the highest praise which can fairly be given to the American mind, is that of possessing an enlightened selfishness; that if the philosophy and talents of this country, with all their effects, were for ever swept into oblivion, the loss would be felt only by ourselves; and that if to the accuracy of this general charge, the labours of Franklin present an illustrious, it is still but a solitary, exception.

The answer may be given, confidently and triumphantly. Without abandoning the fame of our eminent men, whom Europe has been slow and reluctant to honour, we would reply, that the intellectual power of this people has exerted itself in conformity to the general system of our institutions and manners; and therefore, that, for the proof of its existence and the measure of its force, we must look not so much to the works of prominent individuals, as to the great aggregate results; and if Europe has hitherto been wilfully blind to the value of our example and the exploits of our sagacity, courage, invention, and freedom, the blame must rest with her, and not with America.

Is it nothing for the universal good of mankind to have carried into successful operation a system of self-government, uniting personal liberty, freedom of opinion, and equality of rights, with national power and dignity; such as had before existed only in the Utopian dreams of philosophers? Is it nothing, in moral science, to have anticipated in sober reality, numerous plans of reform in civil and criminal jurisprudence, which are, but now, received as plausible theories by the politicians and economists of Europe? Is it nothing to have been able to call forth on every emergency, either in war or peace, a body of talents always equal to the difficulty? Is it nothing to have, in less than a half century, exceedingly improved the sciences of political economy, of law, and of medicine, with all their auxiliary branches; to have enriched human knowledge by the accumulation of a great mass of useful facts and observations, and to have augmented the power and the comforts of civilized man, by miracles of mechanical invention? Is it nothing to have given the world examples of disinterested patriotism, of political wisdom, of public virtue; of learning, eloquence, and valour, never exerted save for some praiseworthy end? It is sufficient to have briefly suggested these considerations; every mind would anticipate me in filling up the details.

No—Land of Liberty! thy children have no cause to blush for thee. What though the arts have reared few monuments among us, and scarce a trace of the Muse's footstep is found in the paths of our forests, or along the banks of our rivers; yet our soil has been consecrated by the blood of heroes, and by great and holy deeds of peace. Its wide extent has become one vast temple and hallowed asylum, sanctified by the prayers and blessings of the persecuted of every sect, and the wretched of all nations.

Land of Refuge—Land of Benedictions! Those prayers still arise, and they still are heard: "May peace be within thy walls, and plenteousness within thy palaces!" "May there be no decay, no leading into captivity, and no complaining in thy streets!" "May truth flourish out of the earth, and righteousness look down from Heaven."

---

* Patriots are here, in Freedom's battles slain,
Priests, whose long lives were closed without a stain,
Bards worthy him who breathed the poet's mind,
Founders of arts that dignify mankind,
And lovers of our race, whose labours gave
Their names a memory that defies the grave.
VIRGIL—From the MS. of Bryant.

ANDREWS NORTON.

[Born 1786. Died 1852.]

Mr. NORTON was born in Hingham, a rural town near Boston, and was educated at Cambridge, where he received the degree of Bachelor of Arts in 1804. He subsequently studied divinity, but never became a settled clergyman. He was for a time tutor in Bowdoin College, and in 1811 was appointed tutor and librarian in Harvard University, in which he succeeded William Ellery Channing as lecturer on biblical criticism, in 1813, and upon the new organization of the theological department, in 1819, was made the first Dexter Professor of Sacred Literature, which office he held until compelled by ill health to resign it in 1830. During all this period Mr. Norton was a close student, and besides the ordinary advantages of American scholars he had the intimate friendship of many learned men, and the constant use of the best library on the continent. His attainments were not merely scholastic. The cultivation of his taste and understanding was as remarkable as the compass of his classical studies. There were few subjects of metaphysics with which he was not familiar, and he could turn from the driest disquisition to discuss with equal discrimination the last new poem or romance.

Although while connected with the university Mr. Norton wrote many articles for the literary and theological journals, and in the same period published several tracts, and in every thing displayed exact and comprehensive learning, and a style singularly clear, compact, and beautiful, yet his reputation as a man of letters and as a theologian rests chiefly upon his Evidences of the Genuineness of the Gospels, to which he has devoted nearly half of his life, a longer time than has been given to the composition of any other work in American literature. The first volume appeared in 1837, eight years after its commencement, and the second and third in 1844. In these are comprised the historical proofs that the gospels were actually written by the persons wnose names they bear, and in a fourth volume he proposes to discuss the internal evidence of the same fact.

Although the subject of this work has been so fruitful of discussion for many centuries, Mr. Norton's treatment of it is eminently original both in positions and in scope and manner of argument. The edifice of Christian evidence he has entirely reconstructed. His object appears to be not so much to combat infidels, popularly so called, as a class of nominally Christian critics, most common in Germany, who as if intent upon astonishing the world with the independence of their faith, proclaim it while endeavouring to batter down all the foundations upon which that of others is founded. They admit that Matthew, Mark, and Luke were in some sense the authors of the books which are attributed to them, but deny that these books are their original, independent, and uncorrupted compositions; and while less doubtful of the genuineness of the gospel of John, are not prepared to admit that it is beyond controversy. Mr. Norton on the contrary maintains the real Christian doctrine respecting the authorship of the gospels, and that they contain true narratives of our Saviour's life and ministry; and does this with such copiousness of learning, particularly in Greek philosophy and patristic literature; soundness of judgment as to the value of different kinds of testimony, and closeness and clearness of reasoning, that his work may undoubtedly be ranked with Clarke's, Butler's, Lardner's, or any other of the great defences of the Christian religion.

Mr. Norton has some opinions not held by the mass of Christian scholars, but whatever may be thought of them, he must be respected for the deliberation with which they were formed and are published. They are contained in his dissertation on the Old Testament, in the remarks prefatory to which he observes, that it seems to him "a weighty offence against society to advance and maintain opinions on any important subject connected with religion without carefully weighing them, and without feeling assured, as far as may be, that we shall find no reason to change our belief." The views to which reference has been made were therefore not given to the public until more than ten years after that part of his work in which they are embraced was originally written. They have relation to the books of the Old Testament, for the genuineness, authenticity, and moral and religious teachings of which he does not consider Christianity responsible, any more than it is for what is related in the ecclesiastical histories of Eusebius, Sozomen, and Theodoret. He contends that if this proposition is true, it goes far to remove difficulties which have embarrassed Christians in all ages, as the most popular and effective ob-

jections of unbelievers have been directed not against Christianity, but against the Jewish writings in the divine origin of which its truth has been held to be involved.

Mr. Norton's style is chaste, compact, and nervous. He expresses his meaning in as few and plain words as possible. This is the best evidence of true scholarship and refinement of taste.

Besides his theological works and criticisms and other contributions to periodicals, he has published a few poems of singular merit, of which specimens are included in The Poets and Poetry of America. Died 1853.

THE RELIGION OF SENTIMENT.
FROM THOUGHTS ON TRUE AND FALSE RELIGION

WHEN the religion publicly taught is of such a character that reason turns away from it, and refuses to acknowledge its authority, it can have but a weak hold on the minds of the more intelligent, and exercise but little influence upon their habitual affections and daily conduct. But there is a spurious sort of religion of the imagination and of temporary sentiment, which sometimes supplies the place of the religion of the understanding. Some of the infidel writers of Germany are willing to admire Christianity as a beautiful fable. There is such desolation and heartlessness in utter skepticism, that we are ready to turn from it even to a shadowy, unsubstantial image of the truth. The resemblance may indeed be preferred to the reality; for if it has far less of joy and hope, it is also far less solemn and awful and authoritative. Where real living religion does not exercise its permanent, unremitting influence, we may often find in its stead a poetical, theatrical, mystical religion, which may furnish themes for the expression of fine sentiment and the indulgence of transient emotion; which delights to talk about sacrifices, but forgets duties, and has nothing to do with the unnoticed patience of obscure suffering, the unpraised self-denials of humble goodness, the strong and silent feelings of habitual piety; or indeed with any virtues but what are splendid and popular, and fit for exhibition. It is such a religion which the authoress of Delphine has celebrated with her passionate and enthusiastic eloquence. It is this religion which the writer of the Philosophical Dictionary, not mention any work more infamous, could introduce into his tragedies; and it is for such a religion that Moore and Byron may compose sacred songs. Nobody, I trust, will so far misunderstand me, as to suppose it my intention to deny that the sentiments expressed by such writers are sometimes very beautiful and correct. I only mean that there is a religion, not of the understanding and not of the heart, which terminates in the expression of fine sentiments.

REFORMERS.
FROM THE SAME.

IT is delightful to remember that there have been men, who, in the cause of truth and virtue, have made no compromises for their own advantage or safety; who have recognised " the hardest duty as the highest;" who, conscious of the possession of great talents, have relinquished all the praise that was within their grasp, all the applause which they might have so liberally received, if they had not thrown themselves in opposition to the errors and vices of their fellow-men, and have been content to take obloquy and insult instead; who have approached to lay on the altar of God " their last infirmity." They, without doubt, have felt that deep conviction of having acted right, which supported the martyred philosopher of Athens, when he asked, " What disgrace is it to me if others are unable to judge of me, or to treat me as they ought?" There is something very solemn and sublime in the feeling produced by considering how differently these men have been estimated by their contemporaries, from the manner in which they are regarded by God. We perceive the appeal which lies from the ignorance, the folly, and the iniquity of man, to the throne of Eternal Justice. A storm of calumny and reviling has too often pursued them through life, and continued, when they could no longer feel it, to beat upon their graves. But it is no matter. They had gone where all who have suffered, and all who have triumphed in the same noble cause, receive their reward; but where the wreath of the martyr is more glorious than that of the conqueror.

THE LESSONS OF DEATH.
FROM A PAPER ON BUCKMINSTER.

IT will be in vain for us to stand by the open grave of departed worth if no earthly passion grows cool, and no holy purpose gains strength.

We are liable in this world to continual delusion; to a most extravagant over-estimate of the value of its objects. With respect to many of our cares and pursuits, the sentiment expressed in the words of David must have borne with all its truth and force upon the mind of every considerate man in some moments, at least, of serious reflection: *Surely every one walketh in a vain show; surely they are disquieted in vain.* The events of the next month, or the next year, often assume in our eyes a most disproportionate importance, and almost exclude from our view all the other infinite variety of concerns and changes which are to follow in the course of an immortal existence. The whole happiness of our being seems sometimes to be at stake upon the success of a plan, which,. when we have grown but a little older, we may regard with indifference. These are subjects on which reason too commonly speaks to us in vain. But there is one lesson which God sometimes gives us, that brings the truth home to our hearts. There is an admonition which addresses itself directly to our feelings, and before which they bow in humility and tears. We can hardly watch the gradual decay of a man eminent for virtue and talents, and hearing him uttering, with a voice that will soon be heard no more, the last expressions of piety and holy hope, without feeling that the delusions of life are losing their power over our minds. Its true purposes begin to appear to us in their proper distinctness. We are accompanying one who is about to take his leave of present objects; to whom the things of this life, merely, are no longer of any interest or value. The eye, which is still turned to us in kindness, will in a few days be closed for ever. The hand by which ours is still pressed will be motionless. The affections, which are still warm and vivid—they will not perish; but we shall know nothing of their exercise. We shall be cut off from all expressions and return of sympathy. He whom we love is taking leave of us for an undefined period of absence. We are placed with him on the verge between this world and the eternity into which he is entering; we look before us, and the objects of the latter rise to view in all their vast and solemn magnificence.

There is, I well know, an anguish which may preclude this calmness of reflection and hope. Our resolution may be prostrated to the earth; for he, on whom we are accustomed to rely for strength and support, has been taken away. We return to the world, and there is bitterness in all it presents us; for every thing bears impressed upon it a remembrance of what we have lost. It has one, and but one, miserable consolation to offer:

"That anguish will be wearied down, I know,
What pang is permanent with man? From th' highest,
As from the vilest thing of every day,
He learns to wean himself. For the strong hours
Conquer him."

It is a consolation, which, offered in this naked and offensive form, we instinctively reject. Our recollections and our sorrows, blended as they are together, are far too dear to be parted with upon such terms. But God giveth not as the world giveth. There is a peace which comes from him, and brings healing to the heart. His religion would not have us forget, but cherish our affections for the dead; for it makes known to us that

these affections shall be immortal. It gradually takes away the bitterness of our recollections, and changes them into glorious hopes; for it teaches us to regard the friend, who is with us no longer, not as one whom we have lost on earth, but as one whom we shall meet as an angel in heaven.

EXAMPLES OF THE DEAD.
FROM THE SAME.

THE relations between man and man cease not with life. The dead leave behind them their memory, their example, and the effects of their actions. Their influence still abides with us. Their names and characters dwell in our thoughts and hearts. We live and commune with them in their writings. We enjoy the benefit of their labours. Our institutions have been founded by them. We are surrounded by the works of the dead. Our knowledge and our arts are the fruit of their toil. Our minds have been formed by their instructions. We are most intimately connected with them by a thousand dependencies. Those whom we have loved in life are still objects of our deepest and holiest affections. Their power over us remains. They are with us in our solitary walks; and their voices speak to our hearts in the silence of midnight. Their image is impressed upon our dearest recollections and our most sacred hopes. They form an essential part of our treasure laid up in heaven. For, above all, we are separated from them but for a little time. We are soon to be united with them. If we follow in the path of those we have loved, we too shall soon join the innumerable company of the spirits of just men made perfect. Our affections and our hopes are not buried in the dust, to which we commit the poor remains of mortality. The blessed retain their remembrance and their love for us in heaven; and we will cherish our remembrance and our love for them while on earth.

Creatures of imitation and sympathy as we are, we look around us for support and countenance even in our virtues. We recur for them, most securely, to the examples of the dead. There is a degree of insecurity and uncertainty about living worth. The stamp has not yet been put upon it, which precludes all change, and seals it up as a just object of admiration for future times. There is no service which a man of commanding intellect can render his fellow-creatures better than that of leaving behind him an unspotted example. If he do not confer upon them this benefit; if he leave a character dark with vices in the sight of God, but dazzling with shining qualities in the view of men; it may be that all his other services had better have been forborne, and he had passed inactive and unnoticed through life. It is a dictate of wisdom, therefore, as well as feeling, when a man, eminent for his virtues and talents, has been taken away, to collect the riches of his goodness and add them to the treasury of human improvement. The true Christian *liveth not for himself, and dieth not for himself*; and it is thus, in one respect, that he dieth not for himself.

JOHN SANDERSON.

[Born 1783. Died 1844.]

JOHN SANDERSON, the son of a farmer in moderate circumstances, who had served in the army through the Revolution, was born near Carlisle in Pennsylvania, in 1783. There were few schools in the interior, and he had to ride between seven and eight miles every morning for three years to recite lessons to a clergyman, in the valley of the Juniata, who by teaching the ancient languages added something to a small income derived from his congregation. In 1806 he went to Philadelphia and commenced the study of the law, but at the end of two years, finding it necessary to have recourse to employments more immediately productive, he accepted the situation of assistant teacher in the Clermont Seminary, then under the charge of Mr. John T. Carré, whose daughter he subsequently married, and with whom he was many years associated as partner. In this period he was a frequent contributor to Dennie's Port Folio, and an occasional one to the Aurora newspaper. His favourite studies were the Greek, Roman and French literatures, and his chief amusement music. His violin, on which he had learned to play at a very early age, was a cherished companion to the end of his life.

In 1820 Mr. Sanderson wrote the first and second of the eight volumes of the Lives of the Signers of the Declaration of Independence, a work composed from original materials and therefore of considerable historical value, which retains its place among the popular collections of biographies. The soundness of his scholarship and his love of learning led him on several occasions to undertake the defence of classical studies, and to combat that empiricism in teaching, which has been so successfully practised in different periods in most of our cities. He put down by a pamphlet a plan which had grown into favour for a college from which Greek and Latin were to be excluded, and by a series of essays in a newspaper drove from the country one of the most notorious of those pretenders who are constantly offering in a certain number of lessons to impart a knowledge of sciences or arts of which they themselves have learned scarcely more than the names. In 1833 he wrote the letters which appeared under the signature of *Robertjeot*, against the system of instruction proposed for the school founded by Stephen Girard, in which a classical culture is insisted upon with his usual earnestness and good judgment.

His health now began to fail, and he reluctantly gave up his school. He enjoyed in an eminent degree the respect and confidence of his pupils, in whom he felt a parental interest, and his success showed that the public entertained a just sense of his professional character, abilities and services.

In the hope of deriving advantage from foreign travel, he sailed for Havre on the first of June, 1835, and on the fourth of the following month arrived in Paris. His *bon hommie*, general information, and scholarship here made him a favourite alike with wits and men of learning; the time passed pleasantly, his health improved, and he became much attached to the city and its society, which he described to his friends at home in the series of letters afterward published under the title of The American in Paris. At the end of a year he went to London, but the Great Metropolis did not please him, and in the autumn of 1836 he returned to the United States, and soon after resumed the occupation of a teacher in the Philadelphia High School, in which he was appointed Professor of the Greek and Latin languages.

In 1839 he gave to the public The American in Paris, in two volumes, which were soon after, on the recommendation of Mr. Theodore Hook, republished in London, and in 1843 in Paris, in a French version by Jules Janin, from which a retranslation appeared in the same year in London and New York. He also commenced the preparation of a work to be called The American in London, parts of which were printed in the Knickerbocker Magazine, for which, and the Lady's Book, he wrote from time to time various sketches of travel and descriptive and humorous essays.

I became acquainted with him in 1841, and few except the members of his own family saw more of him during the remainder of his life. For some time he resided in a house nearly opposite to mine, and frequently in the pleasant mornings and evenings we walked together, or if the weather was unpropitious, discussed the merits of men, books and opinions, by the fireside. His hair ... white with age, but his eyes reflected his heart, and had the glow of youth. Though he continued to be a sufferer from ill health, he lost none of his amiable cheerfulness, or warm sympathy with all about him. His manners were quiet and simple, his conversation various, and enriched with learning and wide observation, and his trenchant wit and sportive humour unfailing sources of delight to all who could appreciate their keenness and delicacy. No one could fail to perceive that while he was sensitively alive to the ludicrous, and sketched follies quaintly, forcibly and effectively, the kindness of nature, which gave a tone to his familiar intercourse with the world, prevented his ever summoning a shadow to any face or permitting a weight to lie on any heart. Indeed an incident connected with our first meeting so well illustrates his social character that it will serve better than any thing else I can write to make the reader acquainted with him. For some reason I retired at an early hour from a party given by a common friend, at which he was present and had satirized with a freedom unusual to him a person in public life with whom, he heard in the course of the evening, I was personally intimate. His gayety was at an end, and after the middle of the night, while a storm was raging, he called to express his regrets; he "could not sleep with any such annoying recollection." His observations had been so good natured and ingenius that even the subject of them could not have been offended, and it happened afterward that he and Sanderson regarded each other with great respect and kindness.

No man was ever more fond of his children. He was particularly attached to a daughter, who superintended his house; for his wife, whose memory he fondly cherished, was dead, and he should "sleep well beside her!"—he rose suddenly, with averted face, from my table, one day, as he said these words, and soon, from the window by the street, I saw him entering his own door. I understood that silent language, and when we met again, a few hours after, it was felt that no explanation was needed. The last time I saw him we took tea together at the house of an eminent lawyer, and it has been often mentioned since, that on that occasion he playfully exacted from me, and made our host and his family witnesses of it, a promise to be the recorder of his virtues after his death. I am able to fulfil the readily given pledge but imperfectly. I can only hope to renew in the minds of some who knew him the remembrance of his admirable qualities. He died very suddenly in the following week, on the fifth of April, 1844, in consequence of a slight cold which I believe he received that very night.

In the beginning of his book on Paris, on which principally rests his reputation as a writer, he says that he will be a Boswell to that city. The work is certainly unsurpassed in its way, a very mirror of that home of the gay, the brilliant and profound, of all in life or art that attracts the man of genius, learning, or taste. It displays excellent humour, accuracy of observation, and skill in character writing; and occasionally a compass of knowledge, a judicious philanthropy, and a soundness of judgment, for which those who had little knowledge of him would not have been likely to give him credit. His essays, entitled The French and English Kitchen, and miscellaneous magazine papers, are not less admirable in their way; and the anonymous satires, in which at an earlier period he assailed popular absurdities and abuses, show how well he could have kept fools and knaves in a restraining terror, had not his good nature, and delicate taste and perception, led him to the study of the beautiful.

'When hearts, whose truth was proven,
    Like thine, are laid in earth,
There should a wreath be woven
    To tell the world their worth.

"And I, who woke each morrow
    To clasp thy hand in mine,
Who shared thy joy and sorrow,
    Whose weal and wo were thine,—

"It should be mine to braid it
    Around thy faded brow;
But I've in vain essay'd it.
    And feel I cannot now."*

* Lines on the Death of Joseph Rodman Drake, by Halleck.

TAGLIONI.

FROM THE AMERICAN IN PARIS.

THERE was a flutter through the house, the music announcing some great event, and at length amidst a burst of acclamations, Mademoiselle Taglioni stood upon the margin of the scene. She seemed to have alighted there from some other sphere.

I expected to be little pleased with this lady, I had heard such frequent praises of her accomplishments, but was disappointed. Her exceeding beauty surpasses the most excessive eulogy. Her dance is the whole rhetoric of pantomime; its movements, pauses and attitudes in their purest Attic simplicity, chastity and urbanity. She has a power over the feelings which you will be unwilling to concede to her art. She will make your heart beat with joy: she will make you weep by the sole eloquence of her limbs. What inimitable grace! In all she attempts you will love her, and best in that which she attempts last. If she stands still, you will wish her a statue that she may stand still always; or if she moves, you will wish her a wave of the sea that she may do nothing but that—"move still, still so, and own no other function." To me she appeared last night to have filled up entirely the illusion of the play—to have shuffled off this gross and clumsy humanity, and to belong to some more airy and spiritual world.

But my companion, who is a professor, and a little ecclesiastical, and bred in that most undancing country, New England, was scandalized at the whole performance. He is of the old school, and has ancient notions of the stage, and does not approve this modern way of "holding the mirror up to nature." He was displeased especially at the scantiness of the lady's wardrobe. I was born ferther south and could better bear it.

The art of dressing has been carried often by the ladies to a blamable excess of quantity; so much so, that a great wit said in his day, woman was "the least part of herself." Taglioni's sins, it is true, do not lie on this side of the category; she produced last evening nothing but herself— Mademoiselle Taglioni in the abstract. Ovid would not have complained of her. Her lower limbs wore a light silk, imitating nature with undistinguishable nicety, and her bosom a thin gauze which just relieved the eye, as you have seen a fine fleecy cloud play upon the dazzling sun. But there is no gentleman out of New England who would not have grieved to see her spoilt by villanous mantuamakers. She did not, moreover, exceed what the courtesy of nations has permitted, and what is necessary to the proper exhibition of her art. . . .

Dancing, you know, is a characteristic amusement of the French, and you may suppose they have accommodations to gratify their taste to its fullest extent. There are elegant rotundas for dancing in nearly all the public gardens, as at "Tivoli," "Waxhal d' Eté," and the "Chaumière de Mont Parnasse." Besides there are "Guinguettes" at every Barrière; and in the "Village Fetes," which endure the whole summer, dancing is the chief amusement and public ball-rooms are

31

distributed through every quarter of Paris, suited to every one's rank and fortune. The best society of Paris go to the balls of Ranelah, Auteuil and St. Cloud. The theatres, too, are converted into ball-rooms, especially for the masquerades, from the beginning to the end of the Carnival.

I hired a cabriolet and driver the other night, and went with a lady from New Orleans, to see the most famous of the "Guinguettes." Here all the little world seemed to me completely and reasonably happy; behaving with all the decency, and dancing with almost the grace of high life. We visited half a dozen, paying only ten sous at each for admission. I must not tell you it was Sunday night; it is so difficult to keep Sunday all alone, and without any one to help you; the clergy find a great deal of trouble to keep it themselves here, there is so little encouragement. On Sunday only these places are seen to advantage. I am very far from approving of dancing on this day, if one can help it; but I have no doubt that in a city like Paris, the dancers are more taken from the tavern and gin shops than from the churches. I do not approve, either, of the absolute denunciation this elegant amusement incurs from many of our religious classes in America. If human virtues are put up at too high a price no one will bid for them. Not a word is said against dancing in the Old or New Testament, and a great deal in favour. Miriam danced, you know how prettily; and David danced "before the Lord with all his might;" to be sure the manner of his dancing was not quite so commendable according to the fashion of our climates. If you will accept classical authority I will give you pedantry *pardessus la tête*. The Greeks ascribed to dancing a celestial origin, and they admitted it even amongst the accomplishments and amusements of their divinities. The Graces are represented almost always in the attitude of dancing; and Apollo, the most amiable of the gods, and the god of wisdom too, is called by Pindar the "dancer." Indeed, I could show you, if I pleased, that Jupiter himself sometimes took part in a cotillon, and on one occasion danced a gavot.

Μεσοισιν δ' ωρχειτο πατηρ ανδρωντε θεωντε.

There it is proved to you from an ancient Greek poet. I could show you, too, that Epaminondas, amongst his rare qualities, is praised by Cornelius Nepos for his skill in dancing; and that Themistocles, in an evening party at Athens, passed for a clown for refusing to take a share in a dance. But it is so foppish to quote Greek and to be talking to women about the ancients. Don't you that dancing is not a natural inclination, or I will set all the savages on you of the Rocky Mountains; and I don't know how many of the dumb animals —especially the bears, who, even on the South Sea Islands, where they could not have any relations with the Académie Royale de Musique, always express their extreme joy, Captain Cook says, by this agreeable agitation of limbs. And if you won't believe all this, I will take you to see a Negro holiday on the Mississippi.

X

DINING IN PARIS.

FROM THE FRENCH AND ENGLISH KITCHEN.

THE English are before all nations in bull-dogs; perhaps also in morals; but for the art of dressing themselves and their dinners the first honours are due by general acknowledgement to the French. The French are therefore entitled to our first and most serious consideration.

The Revolution having broken up the French clerical nobility, cookery was brought out from the cloisters, and made to breathe the free and ventilated air of common life, and talents no longer engrossed by the few were forced into the service of the community. A taste was spread abroad, and a proper sense of gastronomy impressed upon the public mind. Eating-houses, or *restaurans* and *cafés*, multiplied, and skill was brought out by competition to the highest degree of cultivation and development. The number of such houses now in Paris alone, exceeds six thousand. But the shortest way to give value to a profession is to bestow honour and reward upon those who administer its duties, and to this policy, nowhere so well understood as in Paris, the French kitchen chiefly owes its celebrity. I begin therefore with a brief notice of some of its most distinguished artists.

I must premise, however, that in fine arts generally, and eating in particular, America lags behind the civilization of Europe, a deficiency the more to be deplored that ingenious foreigners who visit us do not fail to infer from it a low state of morals and intellect. How, indeed, entertain a favourable opinion of a nation which gives us bad dinners! I must observe, too, that women are the natural pioneers in this and other matters of taste, and that their special province is to take care their country be not justly at least subjected to these injurious imputations. Men, it is true, are accounted the best cooks, and the kitchen, like the grammar, prefers the masculine to the feminine gender; but this argues no incapacity in the sex, as I shall show hereafter, but a mere physical inferiority. The best culinary critics and natural legislators in this department are indisputably women. And farther, it is scarcely possible to impress the world with an idea of one's gentility without a studied knowledge of this science, its very language having become a part of the vocabulary of polite conversation. All over Europe it is ranked with the liberal sciences, and has its apparatus, its technology like the rest. Indeed, a very sensible French writer, president of the court of Cassation, has declared gastronomy to be of greater use and dignity than astronomy; "for," says he, "we have stars enough, and we can never have enough of dishes." Nor is it to be looked at as a mere accomplishment to him or her who visits Paris, but a dire necessity. How often, alas, have I seen a poor countryman seated in despair at a French table, scratching his head over its crabbed catalogue of hard names, as a wrecked voyager who looks from his plank upon the desolate sea for some signs of safety—upon its fifty soups, its *consommé ; puré a la julienne;* its *casserole, grenouilles, poulets en blanquettes, &c.* Nothing can he see, for the life

of him, in all this, but castor oil, green owls, and chickens in blankets.

Some writers do indeed pretend that republicanism is of a gross nature, and opposed to any high degree of polish in this and the other arts. But it is sheer assertion without a shadow of evidence. Surely, the Roman who dined at Lucullus's, with Tully and Pompeius Magnus, in the "Hall of Apollo;" and surely the Athenian, who passed his morning at an oration of Pericles in the senate, who strolled after dinner with Phidias to the Pantheon, who went to the new piece of Sophocles at night, and to complete his day supped with Aspasia, was not greatly to be pitied or contemned by the most flagrant *gourmands* of Crockford's or Tortoni's. These are but foreign and monarchical prejudices, which will wear away under the slow but sure influence of time and the ladies. Indeed, if I am not greatly mistaken, there is a revolution in eating silently going on in this country at this very time. Many persons in our large cities begin already to show taste in culinary inquiries, and a proper appreciation of the dignity of the subject; and, in some instances, a degree of the enthusiasm which always accompanies and intimates genius, and which leaves the question about capacity for the higher attainments indisputable. I know a lady of this city—a Quaker lady—who never speaks of terrapins without placing her hand upon her heart. I shall now proceed, without any apology for selecting the "Lady's Book" as a proper medium, to offer some remarks upon this interesting subject.

The classical school has at its head the name of Beauvilliers, of the Rue Richelieu, No. 20. He was in great vogue at the end of the imperial government, and in 1814-15, shared with Very the favour of " our friends the enemy," as he used to call the allies. He left a standard work, in one vol. 8vo, on the *Art de Cuisine*, and closed his illustrious career the same year as Napoleon, and his monument rivals those of the heroes of Wagram and Rivoli, at Pere la Chaise. He died, too, of a good old age, in the course of nature; while the tap of the drum was thy death larum, Prince of Moscow.

At the head of the romantic school, and ahead at no moderate distance, is Jean de Carême, whose works are in the hands of every one, and whose name is identified with the great personages of his age. His descent is from the famous Chief of Leo X., and is called Jean de Carême, (Jack of Lent,) in honour of a *soupe maigre* he invented for his holiness during the abstemious season. He began his studies with a regular course of roasting, under celebrated professors, served his time to sauces under Richaut, of the House of the Prince de Condé, and finished his studies with Robert the elder, author of " *Elégance Moderne*," a person remarkable not only for his great invention, but for a bad memory, as you may see in his epitaph—

Qui dès l'age le plus tendre,
Inventa la soupe Robert ;
Mais jamais il ne peut apprendre
Ni son Credo ni son Pater.

After refusing nearly all the sovereigns of Europe, he was prevailed upon to become chief to George

IV. at 1600 guineas per annum. But at Carlton House, he was before the age, and quit after a few months, indignant at wasting his time upon a nation so imperfectly able to appreciate his services. On his return he accepted an appointment from the Baron Rothschild, and remained with "the Jew," dining the best men of a glorious age, and acquiring new laurels till the close of life, with the conscious pride of having consecrated his entire mind to the advantage and honour of his native country.—Drop a tear, gentle reader, if thou hast ever tasted a *soupe maigre à la Pape Pie-sept*, or *Potage à la Rothschild*—a tear upon the memory of Jack of Lent!

Very, of the Palais Royal, also is of this school, and belongs to the *haute cuisine*. He feasted the allied sovereigns, and has a monument at *Pere la Chaise*, on which you will read this simple inscription,

"His life was devoted to the useful arts."

This is a name also to be revered wherever eating is held in proper veneration—a veritable and authentic artist, seeking fame by no diplomatic trick, no *ruse de cuisine*, but honestly and instinctively obeying the impulses of his splendid abilities. He employed his mornings and heat of imagination in composing—pouring out a vast number of dishes, as Virgil used to do verses of the Æneid, and giving his afternoons, when fancy was cool and judgment predominated, to revisal, correction, and experiment. A person came in once of a morning inconsiderately to consult him, and addressing the waiter, "*Pas visible, Monsieur*," replied the garçon, with an air significative of his sense of the impropriety, "*Il compose;*"—and the gentleman with an apologetic bow retired.

I omit many others of nearly equal dignity, for want of space. There is one, however, of the old school, who like Homer or Hesiod, announced from afar the future glory of his country, whom I cannot pass altogether in silence—*Vatel*. While in Paris, I went out to Chantilly—the Utica of the gourmands —not, as you may conceive, to see the races, or the stables of the great Condé, that cost thirty millions, or his *magnifique maison de Plaisance*, which opened its folding doors to a thousand guests of a night, but ... I stood in the very spot in which the illustrious Martyr fell upon his sword—the very spot in which he screamed in glorious agony— "*Quoi le marais n'arrive pas encore!*" and died. Poor fellow! scarce had they drawn the fatal knife from his throat when the codfish arrived. I would give more of this tragical history, but it is told in its beautiful details by Madame de Sevigné, to whom the reader is respectfully referred ... I must hasten to other branches of my subject.

Houses of established notoriety in Paris are quite numerous, beginning, most of them, upon the fame of a single dish, and many new ones are struggling into notice by some specific excellence. So ingenious persons often practise one of the virtues, and thereby get up a reputation for all the others. For ices you go to Tortoni's, of course; for a *vol-au-vent*, to the Provincial Brothers; for a delicious *salmi*, to the Café de Paris; to Very's for *truffles*, and to the Rocher Cancale for *turbots, frogs,* and its exquisite wines. The great repute of this house (the Rocher) was originally founded upon oysters. It first overcame the prejudice against those months which are undistinguished by the letter *r*, serving its oysters equally delicious in all the months of the year. It gave a dinner in 1819, which was the topic of general conversation for one month— about two weeks more than is given in Paris to a revolution. The bill is published for the eye of the curious in the *Almanach des Gourmands*. Frogs having been made to talk by Æsop, and looking so very like little babies, when swimming in their ponds, many dilettanti, especially ladies, feel an aversion to eating them; and the French, being the first of the moderns to introduce them generally upon the table, have infixed thereby a stigma indelibly upon the French name, their *buctrachonymical* designation being now as significative as the "John Bull" of a neighbouring kingdom. An Englishman being compelled lately to go to Paris on business, and holding frogs in abhorrence, especially French frogs, carried his provisions with him. I take the occasion to state that this was an idle apprehension, and that Paris not only has other provisions now, but that this quadruped is even less common, perhaps, in the French than the English kitchen. But, indeed, to the refined and ingenious it is in good esteem, always—especially to professors, doctors, *savans*, and diplomatists, the classes most addicted to gourmandize in all countries. These do not forget that the same immortal bard who sang of heroes and the gods, sang also of bulfrogs.

The French being naturally a more social people than the English, and being less wealthy, and having less comfortable homes, frequent more public-houses; so that these establishments are, of course, made to excel in decoration and convenience as well as science. Indeed, cookery at home, and many other things at home, will always want the stimulus necessary to a very high state of improvement. No one of the arts has attained eminence ever, unless fostered by rivalship and public patronage, and brought under the popular inspection. Much is said about the undomesticated way of the French living; but certain it is that the social qualities have gained more than the domestic have lost, and it is certain that the wealthy and fashionable French are after all less erratic in their habits and less discontented with their homes than the domestic and comfortable English. Comfort! comfort! nothing but comfort! To escape they wander everywhere upon the broad sea and land, and reside among the Loo-koos, Creeks, and Negroes —everywhere disgusted. Where—into what uncivilized nook of earth can you go without finding even their women?

"If to the west you roam,
There some blue's 'at home'
    Among the blacks of Carolina.
Or fly you to the east, you see
Some Mrs. Hopkins at her tea
    And toast, upon the walls of China."

The very genteel Parisians do not encumber their houses with kitchens at all, and that ugly hebdomadal event, a washday, is totally unknown in the Parisian domestic economy. The families dine out in a family group, or by appointment with friends, or the dinner is served in their apartments—a duty which is assigned to an individual you meet everywhere in a white nightcap and apron, and whom they call a *traiteur*. Not a fellow to be quartered and his head set up on the Temple Bar, but a loyal subject, very welcome in the best houses, and dignified as the *entrepreneur general* of diplomatic dinners.

What a gay and animated picture the Parisian restaurant with its spacious mirrors, and marble tables gracefully distributed, with its pretty woman at the comptoir, erected for her often at the expense of many thousand francs, and with its linen of the winnowed snow, the whole displayed at night under a blaze of glittering chandeliers, and alive with its joyous and various company ! The custom of dining the best bred ladies in these public saloons gives them an air of elegance, decency and vivacity it is in vain to hope for under any direction where there is a public separation of the sexes, as in England and America.

Cooking, like the drama, will conform with public opinion, and bad eaters and bad judges of a play are alike the ruin of good houses, and the reputation of the artists. Wo to the gastronomy of a people whose public taste is gross and uncultivated. In those countries where men dine with cynical voracity in fifteen minutes, why talk of it?—*dine*, as Careme eloquently and indignantly expresses it, as if they had craws for the comminution of their food after its deglutition.

I remember about five hundred dyspeptics who used to group themselves about the Red Sulphur, (which they preferred of all the Virginia Springs for the abundance of its table;) how they used to saunter about in little squads, or huddle altogether at the source of the little ruby and sulphurous fountain, and discourse the live-long day of gastric juices, peristaltic motions, kneading of stomachs, virtues of aliments and remedies, inquiring diligently into the cause that might be assigned for the almost epidemic prevalence of this disease; some blaming the stars, some hot rolls, others the cacochymical qualities of our American climate, and a few threatened to leave the country. Two Virginia members believed it was the exciting nature of our institutions, and they sat about upon stumps, (these gentlemen having a great affinity for stumps,) pale, abdominous, and wan, and nearly disgusted with republicanism; and there was an Irish gentleman, who had a strong suspicion he might have been changed at nurse, for he was a healthy baby.

These things are better managed in China. Chewing is done, they say, at a large Chinese ordinary, by a kind of isochronical movement, regulated by music. They have a leader, as at our concerts, and up go the jaws upon sharp F, and down upon G flat. I wish our "Conscript Fathers" at Washington, if it would not interfere too much with the liberty of the subject, would take this matter under consideration, and if, themselves, they would chew and digest a little more their dinners

and speeches, I beg leave to intimate, it would be not only a personal comfort, but an economy of the money and reputation of the republic. The destiny of a nation, says a sensible French writer, may depend upon the digestion of the first minister. Who knows, then, but the distress that has fallen, without any assignable cause, like a blight upon our prosperity ; that the contentious ill-humours of our two houses; their sparrings, duellings, floggings, removal of deposits, expungings, vetoings, and disruption of cabinets, may not be chiefly owing to an imperfect mastication by the two honourable bodies, the president, secretaries, and others intrusted with the mismanagement of the country. Legislation on such subjects is not without respectable precedent. The emperor Domitian had it brought regularly before *his* senate what sauce he should employ upon a turbot. It was put to vote in committee of the whole, and the decree (as related by Tacitus, and translated by the *Almanach des Gourmands*)was a *sauce piquante.*

The entire force of appetite is concentrated in Paris, upon two meals, and an infinite variety of dishes is sought to give enjoyment to these two meals. To dine on a single dish the French call an "atrocity." The precept of the *gourmand* is to economize appetite and prolong pleasure, and therefore intermediate refreshments of all kinds are strictly forbidden. Cake-shops are patronized by foreigners only. Madame Felix—alas, how difficult to resist her seducing little pies !—sells 15,000 daily ! If you offer to touch one in company with a Frenchwoman, she insists on your not impairing the integrity of your appetite for the regular meals ; and she only remarks, " *C'est pour les Anglais*." While the allies stayed in Paris, Madame Sullot sold from her room, twelve feet square, of her incomparable *petits patés* 12,000 per day. The Englishman will have his breakfast, will have his lunch, his dinner and supper, and thus anticipating hunger has no meal at all of enjoyment. So, also, is he morose and peevish, snuffing with suspicious nose the flavour of his wine, and approaching his dishes with a degustatory fastidiousness, not unlike that town mouse so well described by Lafontaine. In the cafés you see him alone at his table, spooning his soup, and encouraging appetite by preliminary excitements, or with newspaper, eating and perusing, apparently seeing no one, with an air that intimates the very great honour he does the French nation by dining at all. Moreover, they do not in Paris, as in London, under pretext of giving an appetite, cozen you out of your dinner by oysters. A Frenchman, on a visit to England, once tried this experiment ; but, after eating three dozen, he declared he did not feel in the least more hungry than when he began.

The rules of eating of the French table are as accurately defined as axioms of geometry—but these rules I defer to another occasion.

The French Breakfast.—It is not your ghost of a breakfast, tea and toast and the newspaper, to guests eating in their sleep. It is late; it is at eleven; above all it is with appetite sharp from early exercise ; it is the ornamental butter of gold 'n a fine frost-work, as if winter herself had woven it, spicy as Epping or Goshen, and the little loaf and heaving omelet, the agreeable ragout, the fruit and fragrant Burgundy, spread as by the fair hand of Ceres herself upon the snowy linen, bordered blue or red, to enhance its immaculate whiteness. And for those who love better Araby and the Indies, coffee poured from the strainer, fresh and aromatic, into the gilded porcelain, with rich cream, or of a strength to be diluted with more than half milk, poured out exactly at the point of ebullition;—but the Chambertin or Burgundy to refined tastes is better. Coffee, pure, and at its side the little glass of Cognac or Maraschino, worth a pilgrimage to Mocha, is the glorious appendix of the dinner.

The French Dinner.—Atmosphere from 13 to 16 degrees, Reaumur. Dining-room simple, with only mirrors and a few agreeable pictures by Teniers. A light soup introduces this meal, by all means without bread, followed by a gentle glass of claret. A rich and heavy soup, where any thing else is to be served, is a total misconception of a dinner. Then follow, with a nice regard to succession and analogy, fish, poultry, roasts, with the entremets, and finally game. A delicate eater may begin with a *paté* of larks or other *petit plat*, and overleap the fish, which deadens somewhat the sense of delicious aromas ; and the dessert is spared always by the very prudent of both sexes. The monstrous desserts are superseded by a better taste. Instead of the Louvre or St. Peter's, of such dimensions as required sometimes the ceiling to be removed, you have now for the robust olfactories a little Gruer cheese—or for the softer sex, perhaps, an ice, a *creme soufflé*, and you may offer a Dutch lady an accompaniment to her coffee, a little Cupid just starting from sugar candy into life. Each service must have the air of abundance. Any apprehension of deficiency, or the being obliged to refuse out of politeness, would check the appetite and natural impulses of the guests. All that you admit upon your plate is to be eaten ; in your glass to be drunk ; you intimate otherwise the badness of the fare, and insult your host ; besides, to have the eyes larger than the appetite is proverbially vulgar. No solos are allowed, or " long yarn," as it is styled, and lions are in bad taste. Also, there is no rush of waiters; servants at the slightest hint anticipate your wants, and a tender conversation is never interrupted by the untimely interposition or removal of a dish; observing always that a sentence, though two-thirds gone, should it even be a declaration, is to be suspended at the entrance of a *dinde aux truffes*. No one at table descants on the excellence of a dish or the wine. There is no surprise at what one is used to daily. In conversation gentlemen are to be without pretension, and ladies, if possible, without coquetry, and the mind, by all means, left to its natural impulses. No one is pressed—all is " fortuitous elegance and unstudied grace ;" this is one of Johnson's definitions of happiness. In the first course the guest is required to be polite merely; he is expected to be gallant in the second, and at the dessert he may

be affectionate ; but after the champagne ... (no rules of propriety are laid down in any of the books.)

In the drawing-room is merry conversation and music, if excellent, tea of a rich flavour, or punch of the best. Together at eleven—in bed at midnight.

The English and French hare with truffles, is a delicacy well worth our canvas-backs. The Roman ladies believed the food of hares improved beauty. Martial, in an epigram, tells of a woman so ugly in his time, as to set hares at defiance. I do not know if the modern hare inherits this beautifying quality, and few of my female acquaintances have any interest in the inquiry. Many sensible people, however, believe there is such efficacy in nourishment, and it is worth consideration. Achilles, they remind us, was fed on lion's marrow, and Madame Grisi, I have heard said, was nourished in her tender years upon nightingales' tongues, a diet much to be recommended to others of the quire, some of whom seem to have been brought up upon bulfrogs.

It is a matter of much interest to those who would dine out to have their sense of eating, as far as possible, refined. By rich persons, who entertain, bad eaters are held in a kind of horror, and shunned as much as tuneless ears by musicians. To serve an exquisite dish to a face that expresses no rapture—it is Timotheus' song to the Scythian, who preferred the neighing of a horse. And well-bred gourmands are known to have applied often certain diagnostics by which to detect indifferent or refined eaters. When a dish of indisputable excellence is served, it is expected the very aspect of it will excite in a well-organized person all the powers of taste, and any one who, under such circumstances, shows no flashes of desire, no radiant ecstasy of countenance, is noted down at once as unworthy, and left out in subsequent invitations.

The learned author of the *Physiognomie du Gout*, has given three sets of dishes, (I beg leave to translate for your edification,) which he calls *eprouvettes gastronomiques*, or tests of good eaters, suited to three several conditions of fortune—for you are not to suppose a person born in the *Rue Coquenard*, though equally endowed, should have the same acumen as one bred *au premier* in the *Rue Rivoli*, or the vicinity of the *Palais Royal.* Here they are :

FIRST CLASS.

Revenue 5000 francs. (*Mediocrity*)
A large veal steak, larded, and done in its own gravy.
A farmyard turkey, stuffed with chestnuts, from Lyons.
Tame-pigeons, fattened, and larded with a slice of bacon, done nicely.
Eggs *à la neige*
A dish of sour-kraut, garnished with sausages, and crowned with bacon from Strasbourg.
Expressions.—Pest ! that looks well : we must do it honour.

SECOND CLASS.

Revenue 15,000 francs (*Easy circumstances.*)
Chine of beef *cœur rosé, piqué* done in its own gravy.
Haunch of venison, chopped-pickle-sauce.
A boiled turbot.
Leg of mutton. *presalé à la Provençale.*
A turkey with truffles.
Early sweet peas.
Expressions.—Mami ! a delicious spectacle.—This is indeed a *regale.*

x 2

THIRD CLASS.

Revenue 30,000 francs. (*Affluence.*)

A piece of poultry, 7 lbs., stuffed with truffles of Perigord till it becomes a spheroid.

An enormous pie of Strasbourg, in form of a bastion.

A large carp from the Rhine, *à la Chambord* richly decorated.

Quails with truffles, *à la Mosle*, laid on pieces of buttered toast, and sweet basil.

A rich pike, piqué, stuffed and soaked in cream of lobsters, *secundum artem.*

A pheasant *à son point, piqué en troufet*, resting on a roast. done holy-alliance-fashion

One hundred asparagus, 5 or 6 lines in diameter, in season, *sauce à l'osmagôme.*

Two dozen ortolans. *à la Provençale*, as described in the secretaire, and cuisinier.

A pyramid of *maringues*, with vanilla and rose. (This last for women only, and men of feminine and delicate habits)

Expressions.—Ah, milord! An admirable man is your cook! Such dishes are found on your table only.

The last of these bills, our learned author thinks a decisive test of cultivated taste and natural endowments. "I was lately," says he, "at a dinner of gourmands of this third category, and had a fair chance of verifying the effects. After a first course an enormous *roc-vierge de Burbezieux, truffé à tout rompre, et un Gibraltar de foie gras de Strasbourg*, was brought in.... In the whole assembly this apparition produced a marked effect, but difficult to be described. Something like the silent laugh described by Cooper. In fact conversation ceased among all the guests. Their hearts were too full! The attentions of all were soon turned to the skill of the carvers, and when the plates of distribution were passed round, I saw succeed each other, in every countenance, the fire of desire, the ecstasy of joy, the perfect repose of beatitude!"

Persons are rarely subject to these violent emotions, if not bred in Paris, and to many they might appear exaggerated, but let them look into history. I will cite a few authentic anecdotes in illustration of this part of the subject; and I will show, too, that these gastronomic emotions and elegant dinners do not appertain exclusively to the French, and are marks of a high civilization in all countries.

Fontenelle, dining a friend one day, and his politeness getting the better of his reason, yielded reluctantly to his desire of having the asparagus dressed with butter instead of oil, and went slowly towards the head of the stairs to give orders to this effect. During the absence his friend had fallen down in apoplexy, which observing at his return, he hastened back to the stairs : " Cook! cook! cook!" he cried out in a subdued voice, " you can dress them with oil!" and he afforded them to his deceased friend the due offices of humanity.

Judge Savarin, hunting one day with Jefferson, near Paris, caught a couple of hares, and they returned home with their game late in the evening. To lighten the way, the American ambassador related to the judge various anecdotes of Washington; and was encouraged to continue for two or three miles by the close attention and meditative air of his companion. But at length the judge awaking up and breaking through his long silence, said, with the decision of one who has made up his mind, " Yes! I will cook them with truffles," Jefferson being about half through the battle of the Cowpens.

Among the Latins and Greeks a great many interesting examples are recorded of the same kind. *Cratinus* seeing his wine spilt, one day, died of grief; he had survived the loss of his wife. His fate is recorded in Aristophanes. *Apicius* sailed to Africa to pass his life there, hearing that the oysters were better than in his native country; but finding them worse, sailed back again. An epicurean is mentioned by Athenæus, who, having eaten a sturgeon at a meal—all but the head—fell into indigestion, and was given up by the doctors—says he, " Well! if I must die, I'll thank you to bring me in the rest of the fish." Apicius, as it is well known, spent two millions of dollars upon his table, and when he had but a *fippenny-bit* left, blew out his brains.

Some very creditable instances have been found even in England. Pope, the actor, one day received the invitation of a lord : " Dear Pope, if you can dine on a roast, come at six; we have nothing else." He came and acted accordingly. At the conclusion, however, a truffled hare of most appetizing flavour was brought in. Astonishment and dismay succeeded in Pope's countenance, as he looked at it, scarce believing his eyes. He took up his knife, tried, but could not ... At length, after several vain efforts, pushing his plate aside and putting down his knife, he said. tears starting in his eyes, " From an old friend, I did not expect this!"

Of Lady Morgan's France, one of the prettiest pages by far, is her description of a dinner at Rothschild's villa, near Paris, served up by the celebrated Carême, at which she was present. A few sentences of which will show that the fair authoress would have run no risk from M. Gerardin's " *Gastronomical eprouvettes*," and furnish proof, if proof be wanting in a matter of such notoriety, that ladies have talents for eating, when rightly cultivated, quite equal to the other sex.

" With less genius," says her ladyship, " than went to the composition of this dinner, men have written epic poems; and if crowns were distributed to cooks as to actors, the wreath of Pesta and Sontag (divine as they are) was never more fairly won than the laurel that should have graced the brow of Carême for this specimen of the intellectual perfection of his art—the standard and gauge of modern civilization. Cruelty, violence, barbarism were the characteristics of men who fed upon the tough fibres of half-fed oxen. Humanity, knowledge, refinement, of the generation, whose tastes and temper are regulated by the science of such philosophers as Carême, and such Amphytrions as Rothschild."

Of the dinner, she says, " It was in season; it was up to the time—in the spirit of the age. There was no *perruque* in its composition, no trace of the 'wisdom of our ancestors,' in a single dish; no high-spiced sauces, no *sauce blanche :* no flavour of cayenne and alspice, no tincture of catsup, and walnut pickles; no visible agency of those vulgar elements of cookery of the good old times. Fire and water distillations of the most delicate viands exhaled in silver dews, with chemical precision,

'On tepid clouds of rising steam,

formed the *fond* of all. Every meat presented its natural aroma; every vegetable its shade of verdure; *margonnese* was fried in ice, (as Ninon said of Sevigne's heart,) and the tempered chill of the *plobian*, which held the place of the eternal *fondus* and *souffiets* of an Englishman's table, anticipated the shock, and broke it of the exaggerated avalanche," &c. &c.

It is scarcely fair to quote farther of a work so accessible to all, or I would give you also her description of the dining-room, so romantically standing apart from the house, in the shade of oranges; of the elegant pavilion of green marble, refreshed by fountains that shot into the air through scintillating streams. Of the table itself, covered with its beautiful and picturesque dessert, emitting no odour that was not in perfect conformity with the freshness of the scene, and fervour of the season.— " No burnished gold reflected the glowing sunset, nor brilliant silver dazzled the eye; porcelain, beyond the price of all precious metals by its beauty and its fragility; every plate a picture, consorted with the general character of sumptuous simplicity, which reigned over the whole, and showed how well the master of the feast had consulted the genius of the place in all."

Lady Morgan solicited and obtained permission to see and converse with the illustrious chéf, who in the evening entered the circle of the saloon, where a feeling and interesting interview ensued. (See her own account of it.) Such honours are every day lavished upon heroes, and surely he who teaches to nourish men is well worth him who teaches to kill them.

Lord Byron has expressed his dislike of " eating women." But his lordship had an infinity of little capricious dislikes. Monsieur Savarin, of much better taste in such matters, describes his " pretty gourman le under arms," as one of the most interesting of objects. From the stimulus of eating, she has greater brilliancy of eyes and grace of conversation; the vermilion of her lips is of a deeper dye, and she is improved in all the attributes of her beauty, and in all respects better recommended to our sympathies, as the honey-bee that sips the golden flower is better liked for its appetites. Nothing that is natural can be justly called an imperfection, and I would respectfully suggest in reply to his fastidious lordship that the first temptation of mankind was eating, and that it began with the fair sex.

———◆———

LONDON OMNIBUSES.

FROM THE AMERICAN IN LONDON.

———

IF first impressions are so very potent, I shall hate London abominably. I have come in by the East End, which is enough for ill humour of itself, and I am lodged in Threadneedle-street, with the instinct of the owl, who finds out a sickly cave to mope and be melancholy in. A single ray of sun has not fallen upon the island since I set foot on it, four days ago. I left in Paris an agreeable circle of friends, bright suns, and the lilacs of the Tuileries in bloom, and am here, doing penance in a back room of " Little Britain," where Boreas shakes blue devils from his dripping wings. . . . .

The crowd upon the street, of vehicles crammed to suffocation, and the dense mass of pedestrians, with the addition of umbrellas, on a wet day, is indeed a spectacle. As I stood wrapped up in a stupid astonishment, and looking on, I met an adventure, which made me a ridiculous part of the exhibition. I saw a person at some distance, a little above the others, who, with a most affable smile of recognition, beckoned me toward him. Supposing it a friend, of whom I had just now so much need, who had observed me, I made haste to obey. He had mounted on the rear of an omnibus, the better to draw my attention. Close by, in a similar situation, was another, who, as I approached, disputed with him the honour of my acquaintance. " This vay, sir !" said the one; " This vay, sir !" said the other, both with great animation. I now thought they were warning me of some imminent danger, but not knowing in what direction, I stood still, paying them my respects alternately; a kind of Scotch reel, setting now to this lady, now to that; till at length I made up my mind in favour of one, without giving preference to either, as happens often in love, or a president's election, and stepped in, aided by the civility of the gentleman, who slammed the door upon my heels. In a French omnibus, you get in, to be sure, with impediments, sitting about on the women's laps; but they take it in good part, and assist your movements, and you even sometimes get into little conversations : " I hope I have not hurt you, Ma'am !" " *Au contraire, Monsieur ;*" and the whole affair is agreeable enough. But only think of running the gauntlet between two rows of Englishmen's faces ! " Take care, sir !"—" Hal-loo !" It is a cold bath at the Yellow Springs ! But I had no sooner reached the back seat, than I recollected, with great presence of mind, that I had not the slightest intention of riding, and that I must absolutely, and in spite of the general displeasure, get out. However, I found that one always leaves a crowded vehicle with general consent, and I passed out without any other obstacle than from the conductor (classically " cad") insisting on sixpence, his fee for having outwitted me, which I willingly paid, and again set foot on the pavement. I observed, by the faces of my fellow passengers, that they understood the joke, and enjoyed it at my expense; but swearing a little French, in getting out, put the scandal upon the French nation, and spared brother Jonathan's blushes. The mistake was natural enough, since neither in France nor America do they solicit passengers in this senseless manner.

RICHARD H. DANA.

[Born 1787.]

It is a disgrace to the literary character of this nation that so little is known of the works of RICHARD HENRY DANA, who as a poet and as a novelist is worthy to be ranked with any living writer in the English language. For himself he can afford to "bide his time," but it is a loss as well as a dishonour to the people that The Buccaneer and Paul Felton and his other productions are not more read. In the preface to the only and very imperfect edition of his prose works that has been published he says, "To be liked of those whose hearts and minds I esteem would be unspeakable comfort to me, and would open sympathies with them in my nature, which lie deep in the immortal part of me, and which, therefore, though beginning in time, will doubtless live on in eternity." To such he commends himself, and by such, so far as he is known, he is appreciated; but for more than ten years, owing to our system of literary piracy, which by giving all foreign works to American publishers without copy-money shuts out the native author from competition, there has not been a set of his poems, tales, or essays in the market, and the great mass even of intelligent readers know nothing about them.

Mr. Dana comes of good blood. His grandfather, Richard Dana, was an eminent lawyer in Massachusetts and an active whig before the Revolution, and his father, Francis Dana, was minister to Russia, member of Congress, and of the convention in Massachusetts for the adoption of the Federal Constitution, and afterward chief justice of the Commonwealth. His mother's father, William Ellery, of Rhode Island, was a signer of the Declaration of Independence, and through him he is descended from the early governors, Bradstreet and Dudley.

Mr. Dana was born at Cambridge, near Boston, on the fifteenth of November, 1787. When nine or ten years of age he went to Newport, Rhode Island, where he remained until within a year or two of entering Harvard College, in which he was a student three years. In time he became a member of the bar, but feeble health and great constitutional sensitiveness soon convinced him that the practice of the law would never do for him, as much as he had been interested in the study of it. Yet one would almost have supposed he should have "taken naturally" to the profession, seeing that his father and grandfather were of it, and his mother's father and grandfather also. However, he was long enough at the bar to prevent the double line that had come down to him being broken, and his two sons, (the eldest of whom, Richard H. Dana, Jr., is well known in the literary world by his admirable work entitled Two Years before the Mast,) are now among the most successful counsellors and advocates of Boston.

Mr. Dana was of the glorious old federal party, of which Washington, Hamilton, Marshall, Jay, Ames, and so many other great men had been ornaments; and his first public production was a politico-literary oration, pronounced on the fourth of July, 1814. From this time he wrote little, perhaps nothing, for the press, until 1817, when he contributed his first article to the North American Review. It was a brilliant and justly severe criticism of the poetry of Moore.* Not long after, he became a member of the North American Club, and when his relative, Edward T. Channing, now a Harvard professor, was made editor of the Review, he took some part in the management of it, according to an agreement between them, and continued to do so until Channing entered the college, in 1820, when his connection with the work entirely ceased. Among the articles which he wrote for it was one on Hazlitt's Lectures on the British Poets, which excited much attention at the time. The Pope and Queen Anne school was then triumphant, and the dicta of Jeffrey were law. Dana praised Wordsworth and Coleridge, and saw much to admire in Byron; he thought poetry was something more than a recreation; that it was something superinduced upon the realities of life; he believed the ideal and the spiritual might be as real as the visible and the tangible;

thought there were truths beyond the understanding and the senses, and not to be reached by ratiocination; and indeed broached many paradoxes not to be tolerated by the literary men of Boston and Cambridge then, but which now the same community has taken up and carried to an extent at that time unthought of.

Soon after his withdrawal from the North American Club, Mr. Dana began The Idle Man, of which the first volume appeared in 1821. In the following year came out what was intended for the first number of the second volume, but receiving information from his publisher that he was writing himself into debt, he stopped. In The Idle Man was first printed Tom Thornton, his other stories, and several essays, with poems by Bryant, and a few pieces by a third hand. Allston wrote for it Monaldi, which would have formed part of the second volume had the work been continued.

Bryant had also contributed to the North American Review while Dana was connected with it, (among other things Thanatopsis, the finest poem ever produced by a youth of eighteen,) and in 1825, when he was editor of the New York Review, Dana in turn became a writer for that miscellany, in which he published his first poem, The Dying Raven.

Discouraged by the failure of The Idle Man, Dana did not make another attempt for himself until 1827, when he gave to the public a small volume entitled The Buccaneer and other Poems, which was well received, the popular taste having in the five years which had elapsed since the publication of The Idle Man been considerably improved; but as his publishers failed soon after it was printed, he was not made any richer by it. In 1833 he published his Poems and Prose Writings, including The Buccaneer, and other pieces embraced in his previous volume, with some new poems, and The Idle Man except the few papers written for it by his friends. For this he received from his bookseller about enough to make up for the loss he had originally sustained by the last mentioned volume.

Here I must again refer to the atrocious system of robbery of foreign authors, which, like every other sort of crime, however imperceptibly, brings sure punishment to the criminals. The printer to whom the privilege of snatching the bread from the mouth of the European author was secured by act of Congress, was not going to pay copy money to an American. Had The Idle Man succeeded, as it would have done if not undersold, and thus Mr. Dana encouraged to go on, he would have been a voluminous writer, a benefactor and a glory to the nation. As it is, indeed, what man that is a man does not feel that he has done more for the substantial advantage and honour of his country than the greatest of our heroes, so called, who have lived in this generation.

Since 1833 Mr. Dana has published nothing except two or three articles in the Literary and Theological Review, and the Spirit of the Pilgrims, and a few poems, which appeared in a magazine of which the writer of this was editor; but in the winters of 1839 and 1840 he delivered a series of ten lectures upon Shakspeare, in the cities of Boston, New York, and Philadelphia, which were listened to with extreme interest and satisfaction by assemblies composed of the very best portions of the people of those cities.

Of Mr. Dana's poems I shall here say but little. The Buccaneer must undoubtedly be considered one of the first productions of this age, and his other pieces are such as any poet might be proud to have written. But they are not likely to be very popular; they have none of the mawkish sentiment which introduces so many worthless volumes to the drawing-room; nor are they of so thin a texture and so easily to be understood, as to commend themselves to shop-boys and chambermaids. Whether in verse or prose Mr. Dana addresses himself to men, and in a style that is a praise of his audience.

Of his novels, Tom Thornton was the first, and perhaps it has been most generally read. The hero, a youth of reckless independence and vehemence of character, unrestrained by principle, but not without traits of generosity and nobleness, leaves a home in which the too fond indulgence of a weak mother and the injudicious severity of a passionate father had nearly blighted what in him was good, and caused what was evil to grow with an unnatural luxuriance. An old school-fellow whom he finds in the city, under a specious show of friendship assists him with money, introduces him to votaries of pleasure, and for selfish purposes leads him from one difficulty into another until he is utterly ruined. Discovering at length his treachery Thornton murders him, and the death of his father and mother, hastened by his own wickedness, occurring soon after, "remorse, defeated pride, prosperity subverted," drive him to madness, and he dies. The story is one of extraordinary interest, but this is a quality of secondary importance. The grossness and vulgar sufferings of vice, which, as he remarks in his essay on the poetry of Moore, are generally kept very much out of sight in such compositions, he has painted with startling fidelity and effect.

Edward and Mary is a tale of quiet domestic life, in which love is exhibited as a sentiment; and The Son, which is little more than a record of the feelings of a young man of a thoughtful, dreamy mind, on the death of his mother, is of a similar character. They appropriately follow the powerful and terrible exhibitions of passion in Tom Thornton and Paul Felton.

This last is altogether the most striking and impressive of his novels. The hero is a moody man, delighting in self-torture, who becomes the slave of the phantoms of his imagination, and is driven to acts of which, a little time before, the prophecy would have filled him with horror. I shall not attempt an outline of the story. Indeed it is so rapid in action, so sudden in its revelations of passion, in all respects so closely woven, as to seem itself but a skilful abstract of a longer tale.

It used to be the custom with tricksters in literature to startle with the pasteboard horrors of old castles, and caverns, and shadowy woods, and all the machinery of the melodrama. The time for this sort of stuff has gone by. Among the multitudes of readers there are scarce any to be satisfied with it. And it is not an object with the true artist to produce such an effect, though sometimes the blood congeals and the hair stands on end as he lifts the curtain from the soul in its conflict with sin.

The strength of Mr. Dana lies very much in the union of sentiment with imagination, or perhaps in an ascendency of sentiment over his other faculties. It is this which makes every character of his so actual, as if he entered into each with his own conscience, and in himself suffered the victories over the will, and the remorse which follows them. There are beautiful touches of fancy in his tales, but as in his poems, the fancy is inferior and subject to the imagination.

He has a solemn sense of the grandeur and beauty of nature, and his descriptions, sometimes by a single sentence, have remarkable vividness and truth. His observations on society are particular and profound, and he brings his characters before us with singular facility and distinctness, and invests them, to our view, with the dignity and destiny of immortal beings.

Of Mr. Dana's essays that on Kean's acting is one of the best, though his unpublished dramatic lectures are commonly thought to excel any thing in this way that he has printed. These are preëminently distinguished for the ability they exhibit in the analysis of the nicest shades as well as of the boldest traits of character. Another that was printed in the Idle Man, is entitled Musings, and seems to reflect more fully and exactly his own mind than any other single piece he has written. It is an exhibition of the thoughts and feelings of a man of genius, the appearance which outward objects take from the assimilating influence of his own spirit, his sources of enjoyments, and the trials he must endure from those who cannot understand or appreciate the workings of his mind. Among his contributions to the Spirit of the Pilgrims is an excellent essay on a man's keeping a diary, and another on religious controversy.

His mind is earnest, serious, and benevolent, delicately susceptible of impressions of beauty, and apt to dwell upon the ideal and spiritual. Its characteristics pervade his style, which is pure English, and has a certain antique energy about it, and an occasional simple but deep pathos which is sure to awaken a kindred feeling in the mind of the reader.

—Since this notice was written, the reproach with which it opens has been removed by the republication, in a suitable manner, of all Mr. Dana's works that had been printed before 1850. We still have to look for the appearance of his admirable lectures, the fruits of his profoundest studies and reflections, and perhaps the perfectest flowering of his genius and taste.

Mr. Dana resides in Boston, for the most part, during the winters, and, in the summers, a few miles from the city, in a cottage by the sea; regarded always, by as many as know him, with admiration and the most reverent affection.

KEAN'S ACTING.

[What a sad reflection upon our nature it is, that an amusement so intellectual in its character, as seeing a play is, and capable of being made to administer so much to our moral state, should be so tainted with impurity—that the theatre should be a place where congregate the most licentious appetites and passions, and from which is breathed out so foul an atmosphere. Such as it *is*. I am now done with it. I would sooner forego the intellectual pleasure I might receive from another Kean, (were there ever to be another Kean,) than by yielding to it, give countenance to vice, by going where infecting and open corruption sits, side by side, with the seemly.]

I HAD scarcely thought of the theatre for several years, when Kean arrived in this country; and it was more from curiosity than from any other motive, that I went to see, for the first time, the great actor of the age. I was soon lost to the recollection of being in a theatre, or looking upon a grand display of the "mimic art." The simplicity, earnestness, and sincerity of his acting made me forgetful of the fiction, and bore me away with the power of reality and truth. If this be acting, said I, as I returned home, I may as well make the theatre my school, and henceforward study nature at second hand.

How can I describe one who is nearly as versatile and almost as full of beauties as nature itself—who grows upon us the more we are acquainted with him, and makes us sensible that the first time we saw him in any part, however much he may have moved us, we had but a vague and poor apprehension of the many excellencies of his acting. We cease to consider it as a mere amusement: It is a great intellectual feast; and he who goes to it with a disposition and capacity to relish it, will receive from it more nourishment than he would be likely to in many other ways in four-fold the time. Our faculties are opened and enlivened by it; our reflections and recollections are of an elevated kind; and the very voice which is sounding in our ears long after we have left him, creates an inward harmony which is for our good.

Kean, in truth, stands very much in that relation to other players whom we have seen, that Shakspeare does to other dramatists. One player is called classical; another makes fine points here, and another there. Kean makes more fine points than all of them together; but in him these are only little prominencies, showing their bright heads above a beautifully undulated surface. A constant change is going on in him, partaking of the nature of the varying scenes he is passing through, and the many thoughts and feelings which are shifting within him.

In a clear autumnal day, we may see here and there a deep white cloud shining with metallic brightness against a blue sky, and now and then a dark pine swinging its top in the wind with the melancholy sound of the sea; but who can note the shifting and untiring play of the leaves of the wood and their passing hues, when each one seems a living thing full of delight, and vain of its gaudy attire? A sound, too, of universal harmony is in our ears, and a wide-spread beauty before our eyes, which we cannot define; yet a joy is in our hearts. Our delight increases in these, day after day, the

longer we give ourselves to them, till at last we become as it were a part of the existence without us. So it is with natural characters. They grow upon us imperceptibly till we become fast bound up in them, we scarce know when or how. So it will fare with the actor who is deeply filled with nature, and is perpetually throwing off her beautiful *evanescences.* Instead of becoming tired of him, as we do, after a time, of others, he will go on, giving something which will be new to the observing mind; and will keep the feelings alive, because their action will be natural. I have no doubt that, excepting those who go to a play as children look into a show-box to admire and exclaim at distorted figures, and raw, unharmonious colours, there is no man of a moderately warm temperament, and with a tolerable share of insight into human nature, who would not find his interest in Kean increasing with a study of him. It is very possible that the excitement would in some degree lessen, but there would be a quieter delight, instead of it, stealing upon him as he became familiar with the character of his acting.

The versatility in his playing is striking. He seems not the same being, taking upon him at one time the character of Richard, at another that of Hamlet; but the two characters appear before you as distinct individuals, who had never known nor heard of each other. So completely does he become the character he is to represent, that we have sometimes thought it a reason why he was not universally better liked here in Richard; and that because the player did not make *himself* a little more visible, he must needs bear a share of our hate toward the cruel king. And this may the more be the case, as his construction of the character, whether right or wrong, creates in us an unmixed dislike of Richard, till the anguish of his mind makes him the object of pity; from which moment to the close, Kean is allowed to play the part better than any one has before him.

In his highest wrought passion, when every limb and muscle are alive and quivering, and his gestures hurried and violent, nothing appears ranted or over-acted; because he makes us feel that, with all this, there is something still within him vainly struggling for utterance. The very breaking and harshness of his voice in these parts, though upon the whole it were better otherwise, help to this impression upon us, and make up in a good degree to the defect.

Though he is on the very verge of truth in his passionate parts, he does not pass into extravagance; but runs along the dizzy edge of the roaring and beating sea, with feet as sure as we walk our parlours. We feel that he is safe, for some preternatural spirit upholds him as it hurries him onward; and while all is uptorn and tossing in the whirl of the passions, we see that there is a power and order over the whole.

A man has feelings sometimes which can only be breathed out; there is no utterance for them in words. I had hardly written this when the terrible and indistinct, "Ha!" with which Kean makes Lear hail Cornwall and Regan, as they enter, in the fourth scene of the second act, came to my mind. That cry seemed at the time to take me up and sweep me along in its wild swell. No description in the world could give a tolerably clear notion of it; it must be formed, as well as it may be, from what has just been said of its effect.

Kean's playing is frequently giving instances of various, inarticulate sounds—the throttled struggle of rage, and the choking of grief—the broken laugh of extreme suffering, when the mind is ready to deliver itself over to an insane joy—the utterance of over-full love, which cannot, and would not speak in express words—and that of bewildering grief, which blanks all the faculties of man.

No other player whom I have heard has attempted these, except now and then; and should any one have made the trial in the various ways in which Kean gives them, no doubt he would have failed. Kean thrills us with them as if they were wrung from him in his agony. They have no appearance of study or artifice. The truth is, that the labour of a mind in his genius constitutes its existence and delight. It is not like the toil of ordinary men at their task-work. What shows effort in them, comes from him with the freedom and force of nature.

Some object to the frequent use of such sounds; and to others they are quite shocking. But those who permit themselves to consider that there are really violent passions in man's nature, and that they utter themselves a little differently from our ordinary feelings, understand and feel their language, as they speak to us in Kean. Probably no actor ever conceived passion with the intenseness and life that he does. It seems to enter into him and possess him, as evil spirits possessed men of old. It is curious to observe how some who have sat very contentedly year after year, and called the face-making which they have seen expression, and the stage-stride dignity, and the noisy declamation, and all the rhodomontade of acting, energy and passion, complain that Kean is apt to be extravagant; when in truth he seems to be little more than a simple personation of the feeling or passion to be expressed at the time.

It has been so common a saying, that Lear is the most difficult of all characters to personate, that we had taken it for granted no man could play it so as to satisfy us. Perhaps it is the hardest to represent. Yet the part which has generally been supposed the most difficult, the insanity of Lear, is scarcely more so than the choleric old king. Inefficient rage is almost always ridiculous; and an old man, with a broken down body and a mind falling in pieces from the violence of its uncontrolled passions, is in constant danger of exciting along with our pity a feeling of contempt. It is a chance matter to which we are moved. And this it is which makes the opening of Lear so difficult.

We may as well notice here the objection which some make to the abrupt violence with which Kean begins in Lear. If this is a fault, it is Shakspeare, and not Kean, who is to blame. For we have no doubt that he has conceived it according to his author. Perhaps, however, the mistake lies in this case, where it does in most others—with those who put themselves into the seat of judgment to pass upon greater men.

In most instances, Shakspeare has given us the gradual growth of a passion with such little accompaniments as agree with it, and go to make up the whole man. In Lear, his object being to represent the beginning and course of insanity, he has properly enough gone but a little back of it, and introduced to us an old man of good feelings, but one who had lived without any true principle of conduct, and whose ungoverned passions had grown strong with age, and were ready, upon any disappointment, to make shipwreck of an intellect always weak. To bring this about, he begins with an abruptness rather unusual; and the old king rushes in before us with all his passions at their height, and tearing him like fiends.

Kean gives this as soon as a fit occasion offers itself. Had he put more of melancholy and depression, and less of rage into the character, we should have been very much puzzled at his so suddenly going mad. It would have required the change to have been slower; and, besides, his insanity must have been of another kind. It must have been monotonous and complaining, instead of continually varying; at one time full of grief, at another playful, and then wild as the winds that roared about him, and fiery and sharp as the lightning that shot by him. The truth with which he conceived this was not finer than his execution of it. Not for an instant, in his utmost violence, did he suffer the imbecility of the old man's anger to touch upon the ludicrous: when nothing but the most just conception and feeling of character could have saved him from it.

It has been said that Lear was a study for any one who would make himself acquainted with the workings of an insane mind. There is no doubt of it. Nor is it less true, that the acting of Kean was a complete imbodying of these workings. His eye, when his senses are first forsaking him, giving a questioning look at what he saw, as if all before him was undergoing a strange and bewildering change which confused his brain—the wandering, lost motions of his hands, which seemed feeling for something familiar to them, on which they might take hold and be assured of a safe reality—the under monotone of his voice, as if he was questioning his own being, and all which surrounded him—the continuous, but slight oscillating motion of the body—all these expressed with fearful truth the dreamy state of a mind fast unsettling, and making vain and weak efforts to find its way back to its wonted reason. There was a childish, feeble gladness in the eye, and a half piteous smile about the mouth at times, which one could scarce look upon without shedding tears. As the derangement increased upon him, his eye lost its notice of what surrounded him, wandering over every thing as if he saw it not, and fastening upon the creatures of his crazed brain. The helpless and delighted fondness with which he clings to Edgar, an insane brother, is another instance of the just ness of Kean's conceptions. Nor does he lose the air of insanity even in the fine moralizing parts, and where he inveighs against the corruptions of the world: There is a madness even in his reason.

The violent and immediate changes of the passions in Lear, so difficult to manage without offending us, are given by Kean with a spirit and with a fitness to nature which we had hardly imagined possible. These are equally well done both before and after he loses his reason. The most difficult scene, in this respect, is the last interview between Lear and his daughters, Goneril and Regan—(and how wonderfully does Kean carry it through!)—the scene which ends with the horrid shout and cry with which he runs out mad from their presence, as if his very brain had taken fire.

The last scene which we are allowed to have of Shakspeare's Lear, for the simply pathetic, was played by Kean with unmatched power. We sink down helpless under the oppressive grief. It lies like a dead weight upon our bosoms. We are denied even the relief of tears; and are thankful for the startling shudder that seizes us when he kneels to his daughter in the deploring weakness of his crazed grief.

It is lamentable that Kean should not be allowed to show his unequalled powers in the last scene of Lear, as Shakspeare has written it; and that this mighty work of genius should be profaned by the miserable, mawkish sort of by-play of Edgar's and Cordelia's loves: Nothing can surpass the impertinence of the man who made the change, but the folly of those who sanctioned it.

When I began, I had no other intention than that of giving a few general impressions made upon me by Kean's acting; but, falling accidentally upon his Lear, I have been led into more particulars than I was aware of. It is only to take these as some of the instances of his powers in Lear, and then to think of him as not inferior in his other characters, and a slight notion may be formed of the effect of Kean's playing upon those who understand and like him. Neither this, nor all I could say, would reach his great and various powers.

Kean is never behind his author; but stands forward the living representative of the character he has drawn. When he is not playing in Shakspeare, he fills up where his author is wanting, and when in Shakspeare, he gives not only what is set down, but whatever the situation and circumstances attendant upon the being he personates would naturally call forth. He seems, at the time, to have possessed himself of Shakspeare's imagination, and to have given it body and form. Read any scene of Shakspeare—for instance, the last of Lear that is played, and see how few words are there set down, and then remember how Kean fills it out with varied and multiplied expressions and circumstances, and the truth of this remark will be obvious at once. There are few men, I believe, let them have studied the plays of Shakspeare ever so attentively, who can see Kean in them without confessing that he has helped them

almost as much to a true conception of the author, as their own labours had done for them.

It is not easy to say in what character Kean plays best. He so fits himself to each in turn, that if the effect he produces at one time is less than at another, it is because of some inferiority in stage-effect in the character. Othello is probably the greatest character for stage-effect; and Kean has an uninterrupted power over us in playing it. When he commands, we are awed; when his face is all sensitive with love, and love thrills in his soft tones, all that our imaginations had pictured to us is realized. His jealousy, his hate, his fixed purposes, are terrific and deadly; and the groans wrung from him in his grief have the pathos and anguish of Esau's when he stood before his old blind father, and sent up "an exceeding bitter cry."

Again, in Richard, how does he hurry forward to his object, sweeping away all between him and it! The world and its affairs are nothing to him till he gains his end. He is all life, and action, and haste—he fills every part of the stage, and seems to do all that is done.

I have before said that his voice is harsh and breaking in his high tones, in his rage, but that this defect is of little consequence in such places. Nor is it well suited to the more declamatory parts. This again is scarce worth considering; for how very little is there of mere declamation in good English plays! But it is one of the finest voices in the world for all the passions and feelings which can be uttered in the middle and lower tones. In Lear—

"If you have poison for me, I will drink it."

And again,

"You do me wrong to take me o' the grave.
Thou art a soul in bliss."

Why should I cite passages? Can any man open upon the scene in which these are contained, without Kean's piteous looks and tones being present to him? And does not the mere remembrance of them, as he reads, bring tears into his eyes? Yet, once more, in Othello—

"Had it pleased heaven
To try me with affliction," &c.

In the passage beginning with—

"O now for ever
Farewell the tranquil mind,"—

there was "a mysterious confluence of sounds" passing off into infinite distance, and every thought and feeling within him seemed travelling with them.

How very graceful he is in Othello. It is not a practised, educated grace, but the "unbought grace" of his genius uttering itself in its beauty and grandeur in each movement of the outward man. When he says to Iago so touchingly, "Leave me, leave me, Iago," and turning from him, walks to the back of the stage, raising his hands, and bringing them down upon his head with clasped fingers, and stands thus with his back to us, there is a grace and imposing grandeur in his figure which we gaze on with admiration.

Talking of these things in Kean is something like reading the "Beauties of Shakspeare;" for he

Y

is as good in his subordinate as in his great parts. But he must be content to share with other men of genius, and think himself fortunate if one in a hundred sees his lesser beauties, and marks the truth and delicacy of his under playing. For instance; when he has no share in the action going on, he is not busy in putting himself into attitudes to draw attention, but stands or sits in a simple posture, like one with an engaged mind. His countenance is in a state of ordinary repose, with only a slight, general expression of the character of his thoughts; for this is all the face shows when the mind is taken up in silence with its own reflections. It does not assume marked or violent expressions, as in soliloquy. When a man gives utterance to his thoughts, though alone, the charmed rest of the body is broken; he speaks in his gestures too, and the countenance is put into a sympathizing action.

I was first struck with this in his Hamlet; for the deep and quiet interest so marked in Hamlet, made the justness of Kean's playing, in this respect, the more obvious.

Since then, I have observed him attentively, and have found the same true acting in his other characters.

This right conception of situation and its general effect, seems to require almost as much genius as his conceptions of his characters. He deserves praise for it; for there is so much of the subtilty of nature in it, if I may so speak, that while a very few are able from his help to put themselves into the situation, and admire the justness of his acting in it, the rest, both those who like him upon the whole, as well as those who profess to see little that is good in him, will be very apt to let it pass by them without observing it.

Like most men, however, Kean receives a partial reward, at least, for his sacrifice of the praise of the many to what he thinks the truth. For when he passes from the state of natural repose, even into that of gentle motion and ordinary discourse, he is at once filled with a spirit and life which he makes every one feel who is not armour proof against him. This helps to the sparkling brightness and warmth of his playing; the grand secret of which, like that of colours in a picture, lies in a just contrast. We can all speculate concerning the general rules upon this; but when the man of genius gives us their results, how few are there who can trace them out with an observant eye, or look with a full pleasure upon the grand whole. Perhaps this very beauty in Kean has helped to an opinion, which, no doubt, is sometimes true, that he is too sharp and abrupt. For I well remember, while once looking at a picture in which the shadow of a mountain fell in strong outline upon a stream, I overheard some quite sensible people expressing their wonder that the artist should have made the water of two colours, seeing it was all one and the same thing.

Instances of Kean's keeping of situations were very striking in the opening of the trial scene in the Iron Chest, and in Hamlet when the father's ghost tells the story of his death.

The determined composure to which he is bent up in the first, must be present with every one who saw him. And, though from my immediate purpose, shall I pass by the startling and appalling change, when madness seized upon his brain with the deadly swiftness and power of a fanged monster? Wonderfully as this last part was played, we cannot well imagine how much the previous calm and the suddenness of the unlooked for change from it added to the terror of the scene.— The temple stood fixed on its foundations; the earthquake shook it, and it was a heap.—Is this one of Kean's violent contrasts?

While Kean listened in Hamlet to the father's story, the entire man was absorbed in deep attention, mingled with a tempered awe. His posture was quite simple, with a slight inclination forward. The spirit was the spirit of his father whom he had loved and reverenced, and who was to that moment ever present in his thoughts. The first superstitious terror at meeting him had passed off. The account of his father's appearance given him by Horatio and the watch, and his having followed him some distance, had in a degree familiarized him to the sight, and he stood before us in the stillness of one who was to hear, then or never, what was to be told, but without that eager reaching forward which other players give, and which would be right, perhaps, in any character but that of Hamlet, who always connects with the present the past and what is to come, and mingles reflection with his immediate feelings, however deep.

As an instance of Kean's familiar, and, if I may be allowed the term, domestic acting, the first scene in the fourth act of his Sir Giles Overreach may be taken. His manner at meeting Lovell, and through the conversation with him, the way in which he turns his chair and leans upon it, were all as easy and natural as they could have been in real life had Sir Giles been actually existing, and engaged at that moment in conversation in Lovell's room.

It is in these things, scarcely less than in the more prominent parts of his playing, that Kean shows himself the great actor. He must always make a deep impression; but to suppose the world at large capable of a right estimate of his various powers, would be forming a judgment against every-day proof. The gradual manner in which the character of his playing has opened upon me, satisfies me that in acting, as in every thing else, however great may be the first effect of genius upon us, we come slowly, and through study, to a perception of its minute beauties and fine characteristics; and that, after all, the greater part of men seldom get beyond the first vague and general impression.

As there must needs go a *modicum* of fault-finding along with commendation, it may be proper to remark, that Kean plays his hands too much at times, and moves about the dress over his breast and neck too frequently in his hurried and impatient passages,—that he does not always adhere with sufficient accuracy to the received readings of Shakspeare, and that the effect would be greater upon the whole, were he to be more sparing of sudden changes from violent voice and gesticulation to a low conversation tone and subdued manner.

His frequent use of these in Sir Giles Overreach is with great effect, for Sir Giles is playing his part; so, too, in Lear, for Lear's passions are gusty and shifting; but, in the main, it is a kind of playing too marked and striking to bear frequent repetition, and had better sometimes be spared, where, considered alone, it might be properly enough used for the sake of bringing it in at some other place with greater effect.

It is well to speak of these defects, for though the little faults of genius, in themselves considered, but slightly affect those who can enter into its true character, yet such persons are made impatient at the thought that an opportunity is given those to carp who know not how to commend.

Though I have taken up a good deal of room, I must end without speaking of many things which occur to me. Some will be of the opinion that I have already said enough. Thinking of Kean as I do, I could not honestly have said less; for I hold it to be a low and wicked thing to keep back from merit of any kind its due,—and, with Steele, that "there is something wonderful in the narrowness of those minds which can be pleased, and be barren of bounty to those who please them."

Although the self-important, out of self-concern, give praise sparingly, and the mean measure theirs by their likings or dislikings of a man, and the good even are often slow to allow the talents of the faulty their due, lest they bring the evil into repute, yet it is the wiser as well as the honester course, not to take away from an excellence because it neighbours upon a fault, nor to disparage another with a view to our own name, nor to rest our character for discernment upon the promptings of an unkind heart. Where God has not feared to bestow great powers, we may not fear giving them their due; nor need we be parsimonious of commendation, as if there were but a certain quantity for distribution, and our liberality would be to our loss; nor should we hold it safe to detract from another's merit, as if we could always keep the world blind; lest we live to see him whom we disparaged praised, and whom we hated loved.

Whatever be his failings, give every man a full and ready commendation for that in which he excels; it will do good to our own hearts, while it cheers his. Nor will it bring our judgment into question with the discerning; for strong enthusiasm for what is great does not argue such an unhappy want of discrimination, as that measured and cold approval which is bestowed alike upon men of mediocrity, and upon those of gifted minds.

CHILDREN.
FROM DOMESTIC LIFE.

"Heaven lies about us in our infancy," says Wordsworth. And who of us that is not too good to be conscious of his own vices, who has not felt rebuked and humbled under the clear and open countenance of a child?—who that has not felt his impurities foul upon him in the presence of a sinless child? These feelings make the best lesson that can be taught a man; and tell him in a way, which all else he has read or heard never could, how paltry is all the show of intellect compared with a pure and good heart. He that will humble himself and go to a child for instruction, will come away a wiser man.

If children can make us wiser, they surely can make us better. There is no one more to be envied than a goodnatured man watching the workings of children's minds, or overlooking their play. Their eagerness, curious about every thing, making out by a quick imagination what they see bu a part of—their fanciful combinations and magic inventions, creating out of ordinary circumstances and the common things which surround them, strange events and little ideal worlds, and these all working in mystery to form matured thought, is study enough for the most acute minds, and should teach us, also, not too officiously to regulate what we so little understand. The still musing and deep abstraction in which they sometimes sit, affect us as a playful mockery of older heads. These little philosophers have no foolish system, with all its pride and jargon, confusing their brains. Theirs is the natural movement of the soul, intense with new life and busy after truth, working to some purpose, though without a noise.

When children are lying about seemingly idle and dull, we, who have become case-hardened by time and satiety, forget that they are all sensation, that their outstretched bodies are drinking in from the common sun and air, that every sound is taken note of by the ear, that every floating shadow and passing form come and touch at the sleepy eye, and that the little circumstances and the material world about them make their best school, and will be the instructors and formers of their characters for life.

And it is delightful to look on and see how busily the whole acts, with its countless parts fitted to each other, and moving in harmony. There are none of us who have stolen softly behind a child when labouring in a sunny corner digging a lilliputian well, or fencing in a six-inch barn-yard, and listened to his soliloquies and his dialogues with some imaginary being, without our hearts being touched by it. Nor have we observed the flush which crossed his face when finding himself betrayed, without seeing in it the delicacy and propriety of the after man.

A man may have many vices upon him, and have walked long in a bad course, yet if he has a love of children, and can take pleasure in their talk and play, there is something still left in him to act upon—something which can love simplicity and truth. I have seen one in whom some low vice had become a habit, make himself the plaything of a set of riotous children with as much delight in his countenance as if nothing but goodness had ever been expressed in it; and have felt as much of kindness and sympathy toward him as I have of revolting toward another who has gone through life with all due propriety, with a cold and supercilious bearing toward children, which makes them shrinking and still. I have known one like the latter attempt, with uncouth condescension, to court an open-hearted child who would draw back with an instinctive aversion; and I have felt as if there were a curse upon him. Better to be driven out from among men than to be disliked of children.

THE MURDER.

FROM PAUL FELTON.

PAUL drew near the house and watched till the last light was put out.—" The innocent and guilty both sleep, all but Paul! Not even the grave will be a resting-place for me! They hunt and drive me to the deed; and when 'tis done, will snatch the abhorred soul to fires and tortures. Why should I rest more? The bosom I slept sweetly on—blissful dreams stealing over me—the bosom that to my delighted soul seemed all fond and faithful—why, what harboured in it? Lust and deceit, and sly, plotting thoughts, showing love where they most loathed. They stung me,— ay, in my sleep, crept out upon me and stung me, —poisoned my very soul—hot, burning poisons! —Peace, peace, your promptings, Ye that put me to this deed,—drive me not mad! Am I not about it?"

He walked up cautiously to the door, and taking a key from his pocket unlocked it and went in. There was now a suspense of all feeling in him. He entered the parlour. His wife's shawl was hanging on the back of a chair; books in which he had read to her were lying on the table, and her work-table near it open. His eye passed over them, but there was no emotion. He left the room and ascended the stairs with a slow, soft step, stealing through his own house cautiously as a thief. He unlocked the door of his dressing-room, and passed on without noticing any part of it. His hand shook as he partly opened his wife's chamber-door. He listened—all was still. He cast his eye round, then entered and shut the door after him. He walked up by the side of her bed without turning his eyes toward it, and seated himself down upon it by her. Then it was he dared to look on her, as she lay in all her beauty, wrapt in a sleep so gentle he could not hear her breathing. She looked as if an angel talked with her in her dreams. Her dark, glossy hair had fallen over her bright fair neck and bosom, and the moonlight, striking through it, pencilled it in beautiful thready shadows on her.

Paul sat for awhile with folded arms, looking down on her. His eye moved not, and in his dark face was the unchanging hardness of stone. His mind appeared elsewhere. There was no longer feeling in him. He seemed waiting the order of some stern power. The command at last came. He laid his hand upon her heart and felt its regular beat; then drew the knife from his bosom.

Once more he laid his hand upon her heart; then put the point there. He pressed his eyes close with one hand, and the knife sunk to the handle. There was a convulsive start and a groan. He looked on her. A slight flutter passed over her frame, and her filmy eyes opened on him once; but he looked as senseless as the body that lay before him. The moon shone fully on the corpse, and on him that sat by it; and the silent night went on. By and by, up came the sun in the hot flushed sky, and sent his rays over them. Paul moved not, nor heeded the change. There was no noise nor motion—there were they two together, like two of the dead.

At last Esther's attendant, entering suddenly, saw the gloomy figure of Paul before her. She ran out with a cry of terror, and in a moment the room was filled with servants. The old man came in trembling and weak; no tear was wrung from him, nor a groan. He bowed his head as saying, It is done.

The alarm was given, and Frank, with the neighbours, went up to the chamber. Though the room was nearly full, not a sound was heard. The stillness seemed to spread from Paul and the dead over them all. Frank and some others came near him and stood before him; but he continued looking on his wife, as he sat with his crossed hands resting on his thigh; while the one which had done the murder still held the bloody knife.

No one moved. At last they looked at each other, and one of them took Paul by the wrist. He turned his slow, heavy eye on them, as if asking who they were, and what they wanted. They instinctively shrunk back, letting go their hold, and his arm fell like a dead man's.

There was a movement near the door; and presently Abel stood directly before Paul, his hands drawn between his knees, his body distorted and writhing as with pain. . . . There was a gleam and glitter, and something of a laugh and anguish, too, in his crazed eye, as it flitted back and forth from Esther to Paul. At last Paul glanced upon him. At the sight of Abel he gave a shuddering start that shook the room. He looked once more on his wife; his hair rose up, and his eyes became wild.—" Esther!" he gasped out, tossing up his arms as he threw himself forward. He struck the bed and fell to the floor. Abel looked and saw his face black with the rush of blood to the head; then giving a leap at which he nearly touched the ceiling, with a deafening shriek that wrung through the house, darted out of the chamber, and, at a spring, reached the outer door.

They felt of Paul.—Life had left him.

Frank took the father from the room. Preparations were hastily made; and about the close of the day Esther's body, followed by a few neighbours and friends, was carried to the grave. The grave-yard was not far from the foot of the stony ridge. As they drew near it, the sun was just going down, and the sky clear, and of a bright warm glow. Presently a figure was seen running and darting in crossing movements along the top of the ridge, leaping from point to point more like a creature of the air than of the earth, for it hardly seemed to touch on any thing. It was mad Abel. So swift and shooting were his motions, and so quickly did he leap and dance to and fro, that it appeared to the dazzled eye as if there were hundreds holding their hellish revels in the air; and now and then a wild laugh reached the mourners, that seemed to come out from the still sky. When it was night, the men who had made Paul's grave a little without the consecrated ground came to the house, and taking up the body moved off toward the place in which they were to lay it.—No bell tolled for the departed; no one followed to mourn over him, as he was laid in the ground away from man, or to hear the earth fall on his coffin—that sound which makes us feel as if our living bodies, too, were crumbling into dust.

It had been a chilly night; and while the frost was yet heavy on the grass, some of the neighbours went to wonder and moralize over Paul's grave. There appeared something singular upon it. They ventured timidly on, and found lying across it poor Abel. He was apparently dead; and some of the boldest took hold of him. He opened his eyes a little and uttered a faint, weak cry. They dropped their hold; his limbs quivered and stretched out rigid—then relaxed. His breath came once, broken and quick—it was his last.

LOVE.

FROM EDWARD AND MARY.

To love deeply and to believe our love returned, and yet to be sensible that we should not make our love known, is one of the hardest trials a man can undergo. It asks the more of us, because the passion is the most secret in our natures. All sympathy is distasteful except that of one being, and that, in such a case, we must deny ourselves. In our sorrow at the loss of friends, if we shun direct and proffered consolations, we love the assuagings which another's pity administers to us in the gentle tones, mild manners, kind looks, and nameless little notices which happen in the numberless affairs of daily life. But the man that loves is unhappy, starts at a soothing voice as if he were betrayed; eyes turned in affectionate regard upon him, seem to search his heart; his way is not in the path of other men, and his suffering must be borne unseen and alone.

This severance from the world, this desertion of intercourse with man, gives a bitterness to grief greater than any evil life shares in, and yet here we drink it of ourselves; we make our own solitude, root up the flowers in it, and watch them as they wither; we lay it bare of beauty and make it empty of life, and then feel as if others had spoiled us and left us to perish. Relief from troubles may be found in society and employment: but unprosperous love goes everywhere with a man; his thoughts are for ever upon it; it is in him and around him like the air, breaking his night-rest, and causing him to hide himself from

the morning light. The music of the open sky sings a dirge over his joys, and the strong trees of the forest droop over the grave of all he held dear.

Thwarted love is more romantic than even that which is blessed; the imagination grows forgetive, and the mind idles, in its melancholy, among fantastic shapes; all it hears or sees is turned to its own uses, taking new forms and new relations, and multiplying without end; and it wanders off amongst its own creations, which crowd thicker round it the farther it goes, till it loses sight of the world and becomes bewildered in the many and uneven paths that itself had trodden out.

IDEAL CHARACTER OF A TRUE LIFE.

FROM MUSINGS.

To the man of fine feeling and deep and delicate and creative thought, there is nothing in nature which appears only as so much substance and form, nor any connections in life which do not reach beyond their immediate and obvious purposes. Our attachments to each other are not felt by him merely as habits of the mind given to it by the customs of life; nor does he hold them to be only as the goods of this world, and the loss of them as merely turning him forth an outcast from the social state; but they are a part of his joyous being, and to have them torn from him, is taking from his very nature.

Life, indeed, with him, in all its connections and concerns, has an ideal and spiritual character, which, while it loses nothing of the definiteness of reality, is for ever suggesting thoughts, taking new relations, and peopling and giving action to the imagination. All that the eye falls upon and all that touches the heart, run off into airy distance, and the regions into which the sight stretches are alive and bright and beautiful with countless shapings and fair hues of the gladdened fancy. From kind acts and gentle words and fond looks there spring hosts many and glorious as Milton's angels; and heavenly deeds are done, and unearthly voices heard, and forms and faces, graceful and lovely as Uriel's, are seen in the noonday sun. What would only have given pleasure for the time to another, or, at most, be now and then called up in his memory, in the man of feeling and imagination, lays by its particular and short-lived and irregular nature, and puts on the garments of spiritual beings, and takes the everlasting nature of the soul. The ordinary acts which spring from the good will of social life, take up their dwelling within him and mingle with his sentiment, forming a little society in his mind, going on in harmony with its generous enterprises, its friendly labours, and tasteful pursuits. They undergo a change, becoming a portion of him, making a part of his secret joy and melancholy, and wandering at large among his far-off thoughts. All that his mind falls in with, it sweeps along in its deep and swift and continuous flow, and bears onward with the multitude that fills its shoreless and living sea.

RICHARD HENRY WILDE.

[Born 1789. Died 1847.]

THE youth of Mr. Wilde was passed in Baltimore, where his father, who had emigrated from Dublin near the close of the American revolution, was engaged in commerce, until his death, which occurred in 1801. By the mismanagement of a partner in Dublin he had lost nearly all his property, and his widow with her children, in 1803, removed to Augusta, Georgia, where under various disadvantages our author acquired a gentlemanly education, and laid the basis of his high professional reputation.

Unable, in consequence of the reduced circumstances of his family, to pay the customary fees for instruction, but determined nevertheless to study the law, he secretly borrowed a few elementary books from his friends, and while attending to business in his mother's store, tasked himself every day to read fifty pages and write five pages of notes; and to overcome a natural diffidence, increased by a slight impediment in his speech, he became a member of a dramatic society and frequently appeared as an actor, from which his older acquaintances, ignorant of his designs, argued badly of his future life. He bore their injustice in silence, and at the end of a year and a half, pale, emaciated, feeble, and with a consumptive cough, sought a distant court to be examined, that, if rejected, the news of his defeat might not reach his mother. Upon his arrival, he found he had been wrongly informed, and that the judges had no power to admit him. He met a friend there, however, who was going to the Greene Superior Court, and, on being invited by him to do so, determined to proceed immediately to that place. It was the March term for 1809, Judge Early presiding; and the young applicant, totally unknown to every one, save the friend who accompanied him, was at intervals, during three days, subjected to a most rigorous examination. Judge Early was well known for his strictness, and the circumstances of a youth leaving his own circuit excited his suspicion; but every question was answered to the satisfaction and even admiration of the examining committee, and he declared that " the young man could not have left his circuit because he was unprepared." His friend certified to the correctness of his moral character, and he was admitted without a dissenting voice, and returned in triumph to Augusta. He was at this time under twenty years of age.

His health improved, but at the same time the small profits from his profession ceased, for the courts of law were closed by an act of the legislature on account of the general distress of the country. Though clearly impairing the obligation of contracts, and therefore unconstitutional, this statute, familiarly called the Alleviating Law, was a great favourite with the debtor class, then a large majority of the people of Georgia, and was continued with various modifications for several years, with certain exceptions, such as criminal process against absconding debtors, &c. At this time in that part of the country the principles of constitutional law were little understood. Even the right of the judiciary to declare a law unconstitutional was vehemently denied by many of the most distinguished politicians. The contrary doctrine was fiercely denounced on all sides as a dangerous usurpation. War had added its calamities. Many of the militia were in the field, and the necessity of protecting their property from the gripe of avaricious creditors was added to all the other pleas of overruling necessity. Unawed by popular clamour, convinced of the injustice, impolicy and unconstitutionality of the law, and urged by some clients to make the point at whatever personal hazard, Mr. Wilde brought up the question at two different circuits, argued it before the courts, and printed his argument for the public at his own expense. Though unnecessarily diffuse, and embracing numerous authorities from the laws of nature and nations, which a court under such circumstances could not adopt as rules of decision, this argument embraces the constitutional grounds since recognised by the highest tribunal of the Union, and illustrates on principles of natural justice the iniquity and impolicy of legislative interference with private contracts. The judges held the cases under advisement, and in the mean time the act expired. The legislature renewed it, but Judge Early was now governor, and that able and upright lawyer interposed his veto on constitutional grounds. The judges also assembled and declared the law unconstitutional. Both were violently denounced, but the storm was in part allayed by the news of peace. The judges of Georgia are elected every third year, and, at the next election, those at this time in office were all but one turned out. Mr. Wilde's argument, however, won him reputation as a lawyer, and he lost less of the esteem and respect of his fellow citizens by his fearless discharge of professional duty than his best friends had predicted. He was shortly afterward elected Attorney-General of the state.

While receiving these honours his life was embittered by the loss of his younger brother, James Wilde, an officer of the army of the United States who had served in the first campaign against the Florida Indians, and for whom, during their familiar correspondence, a poem had been projected, in honour of his and his companion's exploits. This was the origin of the song, since so well known, entitled The Lament of the Captive.* James Wilde, from the moment of obtaining his commission, had shared with his brother the expense of maintaining their mother and sisters, by whom he was tenderly loved. He was shot through the heart in a duel, but a few days before he had promised his family a visit. The manner and suddenness of his death overcame his mother's fortitude. She lingered some months, but never recovered from the shock.

In 1815, when but a fortnight over the age required by law, Mr. Wilde was chosen a member of the national House of Representatives, but at the next election being defeated, with all but one of his colleagues, he returned to the bar, at which he remained, except during a short service in the same body in 1825, until 1828, when he again became a representative, and so continued until 1835. In Congress he

seldom spoke, and scarcely ever without having thoroughly reflected on his subject: rarely addressed himself to passion or party prejudice, or argued ad captandum. When called upon by the necessity of the case to reply to personal attacks, his retorts were good humoured, though often pungent enough to be well remembered by his antagonists. He cultivated none of the arts of conciliation, and was therefore rather respected than popular.* He was never a warm partisan, because, as he himself said, he had "found no party which did not require of its followers what no honest man should, and no gentleman would do." His speeches on the relative advantages and disadvantages of a Small Note Currency, on the Tariff, and on the Removal of the Deposits by General Jackson, bear witness to his industry and sagacity as a politician, and his honesty can hardly be questioned, even upon his own caustic rule, since he " gained nothing by it."†

Having seceded from a majority of Congress on occasion of the Force Bill, which he thought a measure calculated to produce civil war, and voted upon other questions with the opposition to President Jackson's administration, at the election of 1834 he was left out of the Georgia delegation. This afforded him an opportunity he had long desired of going abroad, and in June, 1835, he sailed for Europe. He spent two years in travelling through England, France, Belgium, Switzerland and Italy, and remained three years more in Florence, where he occupied himself entirely with literature.

The principal fruit of his studies nere that has been given to the public is his Conjectures and Researches concerning the Love, Madness, and Imprisonment of Torquato Tasso, which was published in two volumes, in New York, in 1842. This is a work of extraordinary merit, and of great interest to all lovers of literary history. The subject, it need hardly be stated, had long been involved in mystery; but few facts had been established; and no two persons seemed to agree as to the conclusions to be drawn from the little that could be ascertained. Mr. Wilde collected his mate-

* This beautiful song, commencing, "My life is like the summer rose," is printed in The Poets and Poetry of America, eighth edition, p. 108. The statement of Captain Basil Hall that it was written in Germany, of others that it was by an Irish poet, and of a third party that it was from the Greek of Alcæus, gave rise to an amusing controversy, in which, I scarcely need state, its originality and Mr Wilde's authorship of it were established.

* The standing of Mr. Wilde in the House is indicated by the following vote for Speaker in 1834.—Wilde, 64; Polk,(now President of the United States,) 42; Sutherland, 34; Bell, 30; others, 32. Finally Mr. Bell was chosen.
† Speech on the Force Bill.

rials with a patient industry only surpassed by the clear and luminous manner in which he lays the whole evidence before the reader, and by the ingenuity with which he makes his deductions. The whole investigation indeed is conducted with the care and skill of a practised lawyer. The title of the work is perfectly descriptive of its contents ; for starting with no theory, assuming nothing, nor seeking to establish any preconceived opinion, Mr. Wilde has been content to bring together all the facts bearing on the points at issue, to indicate very ably all the deductions that may be made from them, and there to leave the reader, fairly in possession of the case, to judge for himself, and form his own opinion. This plan is original and proves the writer's honesty and candour, but most persons would have been better satisfied if he had indicated clearly what he wished to prove, and gone on, step by step, to prove it. By a close comparison of Tasso's writings, especially his sonnets and *canzone*, and a searching cross-examination of their hidden meanings, he convinces us that Tasso was really in love with Leonora of Este, and that she was the person to whom he addressed his amatory poems ; that this princess granted to him all that virtue should have denied, and that he wrote private pieces of poetry proclaiming the fact, which were stolen by a traitorous friend ; that fearing his amour had been revealed to the duke Alphonso, he fled to Sorrento, but his passion for the princess overcoming his fears, returned to Ferrara, where the duke, having been made acquainted with all the circumstances, instead of putting the parties to death and thus blazoning the dishonour of his house, attempted to throw discredit upon the whole affair by compelling Tasso to feign madness and lead a dissolute life ; that the poet for a time complied with these conditions, but at length escaped to Turin, whence, urged by his extreme passion, he returned, with permission, professing himself cured of his malady, and was ultimately, upon his bursting out into some public paroxysm of rage at the treatment he received from the court, thrown into prison and there detained seven weary years. This is a very meagre outline of what seems to be perfectly established in Mr. Wilde's masterly examination of Tasso's mysterious history. The work contains numerous admirable trans-

lations from the Italian, and the style of it throughout is chaste and classical.

Upon the completion of this work Mr. Wilde began the translation of specimens of Italian lyric poetry, and the composition of biographical and critical sketches of their authors. Embarrassed with the contradictions in accounts of Dante, he obtained from the Grand Duke of Tuscany permission to examine the secret archives of Florence, for the period in which he lived, and with indefatigable ardour devoted himself to this difficult labour many months, in which he succeeded in discovering many interesting facts, obscurely known, or altogether forgotten, even by the people of Italy. Having learned incidentally one day, in conversation with an artist, that an authentic portrait of this great poet, from the pencil of Giotto, probably still existed in the *Bargello*, (anciently both the prison and the palace of the republic,) on a wall, which by some strange neglect or inadvertence had been covered with whitewash, he set on foot a project for its discovery and restoration, which, after several months, was crowned with complete success. This discovery of a veritable portrait of Dante, in the prime of his days, says Washington Irving, " produced throughout Italy some such sensation as in England would follow the sudden discovery of a perfectly well authenticated likeness of Shakspeare, with a difference in intensity, proportioned to the superior sensitiveness of the Italians." It is understood that Mr. Wilde afterwards finished his life of Dante, but it has not yet been offered to the public. His printed writings on subjects connected with Italian literature, besides the work on Tasso, are an elaborate notice of Petrarch, in the form of a review of Campbell's worthless biography of that poet, and a Letter to Mr. Paulding on Count Alberto's pretended mss. of Tasso. His miscellanies, in several magazines, mostly written during moments of relaxation while he was a member of Congress, or engaged in the business of his profession, are elegant and scholarly, and make us regret that his whole attention was not given to letters.

Soon after his return from Europe, Mr. Wilde resumed the practice of the law, and become a professor of law in the University of Louisiana, in New Orleans, where he died suddenly, on the tenth of September, 1847.

STARS IN THE XIVᴛʜ CONGRESS.

FROM A SPEECH ON THE TARIFF.

I HAVE neither time, nor strength, nor ability, to speak of the legislators of that day as they deserve; nor is this the fit occasion. Yet the coldest or most careless nature cannot recur to such associates, without some touch of generous feeling.....

Pre-eminent—yet not more proudly than humbly pre-eminent—among them, was a gentleman from South Carolina, now no more; the purest, the calmest, the most philosophical of our country's modern statesmen. One no less remarkable for gentleness of manners, and kindness of heart, than for that passionless, unclouded intellect, which rendered him deserving of the praise, if ever man deserved it, of merely standing by, and letting reason argue for him. The true patriot, incapable of all selfish ambition, who shunned office and distinction, yet served his country faithfully, because he loved her. He, I mean, who consecrated, by his example, the noble precept, so entirely his own, that the first station in the republic was neither to be sought after nor declined—a sentiment so just and so happily expressed, that it continues to be repeated, because it cannot be improved.

There was, also, a gentleman from Maryland, whose ashes now slumber in our cemetery. It is not long since I stood by his tomb, and recalled him, as he was then, in all the pride and power of his genius. Among the first of his countrymen and contemporaries as a jurist and statesman, first as an orator, he was, if not truly eloquent, the prince of rhetoricians. Nor did the soundness of his logic suffer any thing by a comparison with the richness and classical purity of the language in which he copiously poured forth those figurative illustrations of his argument, which enforced while they adorned it. But let others pronounce his eulogy. I must not. I feel as if his mighty spirit still haunted the scene of its triumphs, and, when I dared to wrong them, indignantly rebuked me.

These names have become historical. There were others of whom it is more difficult to speak, because yet within the reach of praise or envy. For one who was, or aspired to be, a politician, it would be prudent, perhaps wise, to avoid all mention of these men. Their acts, their words, their thoughts, their very looks, have become subjects of party controversy. But he whose ambition is of a higher or lower order, has no need of such reserve. Talent is of no party exclusively; nor is justice.

Among them, but not of them, in the fearful and solitary sublimity of genius, stood a gentleman from Virginia, whom it was superfluous to designate. Whose speeches were universally read? Whose satire was universally feared? Upon whose accents did this habitually listless and unlistening house hang, so frequently, with wrapt attention? Whose fame was identified with that body for so long a period? Who was a more dexterous debater, a riper scholar, better versed in the politics of our own country, or deeper read in the history of others? Above all, who was more thoroughly imbued with the idiom of the English language—

more completely master of its strength, and beauty, and delicacy, or more capable of breathing thoughts of flame in words of magic, and tones of silver?

There was, also, a son of South Carolina, still in the republic, then, undoubtedly, the most influential member of this House. With a genius eminently metaphysical, he applied to politics his habits of analysis, abstraction, and condensation, and thus gave to the problems of government something of that grandeur which the higher mathematics have borrowed from astronomy. The wings of his mind were rapid, but capricious, and there were times when the light which flashed from them as they passed glanced like a mirror in the sun, only to dazzle the beholder. Engrossed with his subject—careless of his words—his loftiest flights of eloquence were sometimes followed by colloquial or provincial barbarisms. But, though often incorrect, he was always fascinating. Language with him was merely the scaffolding of thought—employed to raise a dome, which, like Angelo's, he suspended in the heavens.

It is equally impossible to forget, or to omit, a gentleman from Kentucky, whom party has since made the fruitful topic of unmeasured panegyric and detraction. Of sanguine temperament, and impetuous character, his declamation was impassioned, his retorts acrimonious. Deficient in refinement rather than in strength, his style was less elegant and correct than animated and impressive. But it swept away our feelings with it like a mountain torrent, and the force of the stream left you little leisure to remark upon its clearness. His estimate of human nature was, probably, not very high. It may be that his past associations had not tended to exalt it. Unhappily, it is, perhaps, more likely to have been lowered than raised by his subsequent experience. Yet then, and even since, except when that imprudence, so natural to genius, prevailed over his better judgment, he had generally the good sense, or good taste, to adopt a lofty tone of sentiment, whether he spoke of measures or of men, of friend or adversary. On many occasions he was noble and captivating. One I can never forget. It was the fine burst of indignant eloquence with which he replied to the taunting question, " What have we gained by the war?"

Nor may I pass over in silence a representative from New Hampshire, who has almost obliterated all memory of that distinction, by the superior fame he has attained as a senator from Massachusetts. Though then but in the bud of his political life, and hardly conscious, perhaps, of his own extraordinary powers, he gave promise of the greatness he has achieved. The same vigour of thought; the same force of expression; the short sentences; the calm, cold, collected manner; the air of solemn dignity; the deep, sepulchral, unimpassioned voice; all have been developed only, not changed, even to the intense bitterness of his frigid irony. The piercing coldness of his sarcasms was indeed peculiar to him; they seemed to be emanations from the spirit of the icy ocean. Nothing could be at once so novel and so powerful; it was frozen mercury becoming as caustic as red hot iron.

PETRARCH AND LAURA.

FROM REVIEW OF CAMPBELL'S LIFE OF PETRARCH.

OF all the women who have been deified by their poetic adorers, Laura seems to us one of the least interesting. Why, then, did Petrarch love her? If we consult our own experience and observation, we shall not ask that question, nor its converse— why did she not love him? Love is commonly the result of accident or caprice, rarely of any intellectual merit. The hope to win it by celebrity, though frequently indulged, is among the vainest of illusions, and Laura may have smiled at such a folly without being unusually stupid or insensible. The greater part of her sex, like the greater part of ours, have no just conception or ardent love of glory. In general they hold immortality as cheap as the mother of mankind or the widow of Napoleon.

There have been remarkable and splendid examples to the contrary, it is true, but fortunately or unfortunately for us, and for themselves, the mass remains unchanged. Many have indeed been inseparably associated with undying names, often undeservedly, sometimes in their own despite; but most, being of the earth, earthy, would have lost that privilege, had not the weakness of vanity or tenderness preserved the memorials of their triumph, and thus rescued them from merited oblivion. Nina, who would be called nothing but the Nina of Dante, is the exception, not the rule. Even she, perhaps, was thought very naughty in her lifetime, and if she sacrificed temporary good repute to long ages of celebrity, had nearly made the sacrifice in vain, since, though a poetess herself, she was so little of a critic as to choose Dante da Maiano, an indifferent versifier. Far be it from us to malign the fairer part of creation, to whom every rhymer is a born bondsman; but, in truth and prose, the condition of woman excludes her for the most part from these lofty aspirations. Shut up within the narrow circle of petty vanities, household cares, frivolous amusements, devotional exercises, and trivial occupations, she rarely feels inclined to look beyond it, and if she does, is visited with the anger of all her sisterhood. There is little reason to believe that Laura burst the spell, or was in any wise exempted from the common destiny, except by the fortune of a more illustrious lover. Her long continued system of alternate encouragement and repulse, so delicately managed and adroitly blended, as always to keep alive his hopes, yet always disappoint them, may not deserve to be stigmatized as the refinement of heartless coquetry, but certainly excludes the idea of warm and sincere attachment. The very ascendency she acquired over him, by her constant self-possession and invariable calmness, indicates the action of a more phlegmatic, on a more impassioned nature. For the rest, discretion, sweetness, good sense, religious faith, and serenity, make up the sum of an amiable and tranquil disposition, as feminine as you please, and as remote as possible from all our early romantic conceptions......

Could the veil of ages be withdrawn, she might be found either frail or cold, and, whichever the alternative, must lose a portion of her worshippers. Now, on the contrary, those who are not satisfied with either part of this dilemma have still open to their faith the further supposition, that Laura, tenderly loving Petrarch, concealed or governed her affection for one-and-twenty years, never driving him to despair by her rigour, nor betraying the secret of her weakness. But whether she was enamoured and virtuous, or only coquetish, prudent or indifferent, it must not be inferred she took no pleasure in her lover's praises. Who is offended by a delicate and well-turned compliment?—or what woman, however insensible to the beauties of poetry, ever failed to admire a sonnet to her own eye-brow? Love is not kindled by rhyme, but self-love is fed by it, nor should we without reflection condemn Laura for not valuing more highly, or making a more grateful return for the offering. We behold in Petrarch the restorer of learning, the creator of a new poetry, the beautifier of a language which is all melody. She saw in him only a persevering sonneteer, who annoyed her with complaints, or soothed her by flattery. To us he appears with the glory of five centuries. Could he have laid it all at her feet, possibly she might have yielded. With the confidence of genius he often promised her immortality. But how could she believe him? Did he always believe himself? So far from it, he at one time set little value on his love verses, building his hopes of fame upon his Latin poems.

The lady whose apotheosis has been made by the love and poetry of Petrarch, there is every reason to believe, was any thing but happy. His devotion, which alone has embalmed her memory, we may readily suppose, brought upon her both envy and censure. The propriety of her conduct is said indeed to have been such as to defy the gossips of Avignon. The offence of being beautiful and idolized, however, is rarely expiated even by an abandonment of the heart's affections. Our contemporaries ever judge us harshly. The living rarely get credit for their real worth. Nay, they are often hated for the very virtues by which they eclipse others, while, in the eyes of posterity, every fault and almost every crime is absolved by greatness. Laura, we may believe, if she really loved Petrarch, sacrificed her attachment to duty or to reputation, though she was unable or unwilling to forego the incense offered to her charms. The sacrifice was in vain, save to her own conscience, for Ugo, her husband, was harsh and jealous, and so little attached to her memory that he married shortly after her death; while her daughter, Ogiera, so far forgot the maternal example, even in her mother's lifetime, that the honour of the family obliged them to shut her up in a convent. Thus the celebrity of Laura arises from a homage which it was weakness, perhaps worse, to allow, while her virtues were inadequate to insure her domestic happiness, and most certainly alone would never have preserved her from oblivion. So strange are the caprices of fame and fortune, so uncertain and inconsequent the judgments of mankind.

J. Fenimore Cooper

JAMES FENIMORE COOPER.

[Born 1789. Died 1851.]

WILLIAM COOPER, the emigrant ancestor of JAMES FENIMORE COOPER, arrived in this country in 1679, and settled at Burlington, New Jersey. He immediately took an active part in public affairs, and his name appears in the list of members of the Colonial Legislature for 1681. In 1687, or subsequent to the establishment of Penn at Philadelphia, he obtained a grant of land opposite the new city, extending several miles along the margin of the Delaware and the tributary stream which has since borne the name of Cooper's Creek. The branch of the family to which the novelist belongs removed more than a century since into Pennsylvania, in which state his father was born. He married early, and while a young man established himself at a hamlet in Burlington county, New Jersey, which continues to be known by his name, and afterward in the city of Burlington. Having become possessed of extensive tracts of land on the border of Otsego Lake, in central New York, he began the settlement of his estate there in the autumn of 1785, and in the following spring erected the first house in Cooperstown. From this time until 1790 Judge Cooper resided alternately at Cooperstown and Burlington, keeping up an establishment at both places. James Fenimore Cooper was born at Burlington on the fifteenth of September, 1789, and in the succeeding year was carried to the new home of his family, of which he is now proprietor.

Judge Cooper being a member of the Congress, which then held its sessions in Philadelphia, his family remained much of the time at Burlington, where our author, when but six years of age, commenced under a private tutor of some eminence his classical education. In 1800 he became an inmate of the family of Rev. Thomas Ellison, Rector of St. Peter's, in Albany, who had fitted for the university three of his elder brothers, and on the death of that accomplished teacher was sent to New Haven, where he completed his preparatory studies. He entered Yale College at the beginning of the second term for 1802. Among his classmates were the Hon. John A. Collier, Judge Cushman, and the late Mr. Justice Sutherland of New York, Judge Bissel of Connecticut, Colonel James Gadsden of Florida, and several others who afterward became eminent in various professions. The Hon. John C. Calhoun was at the time a resident graduate, and Judge Jay of Bedford, who had been his room-mate at Albany, entered the class below him. The late James A. Hillhouse originally entered the same class with Mr. Cooper; there was very little difference in their ages, both having been born in the same month, and both being much too young to be thrown into the arena of college life. Hillhouse was judiciously withdrawn for this reason until the succeeding year, leaving Cooper the youngest student in the college; he, however, maintained a respectable position, and in the ancient languages particularly had no superior in his class.

In 1805 he quitted the college, and obtaining a midshipman's warrant, entered the navy. His frank, generous and daring nature made him a favourite, and admirably fitted him for the service, in which he would unquestionably have obtained the highest honours had he not finally made choice of the ease and quiet of the life of a private gentleman. After six years afloat—six years not unprofitably passed, since they gave him that knowledge of maritime affairs which enabled him subsequently, almost without an effort, to place himself at the head of all the writers who in any period have attempted the description of the sea— he resigned his office, and on the first day of January, 1811, was married to Miss De Lancey, a sister of the present Bishop of the Diocese of Western New York, and a descendant of one of the oldest and most influential families in America.

Before removing to Cooperstown he resided a short time in Westchester, near New York, and here he commenced his career as an author. His first book was Precaution. It was undertaken under circumstances purely accidental, and published under great disadvan-

263

tages. Its success was moderate, though far from contemptible. It is a ludicrous evidence of the value of critical opinion in this country, that Precaution was thought to discover so much knowledge of *English* society, as to raise a question whether its alleged author could have written it. More reputation for this sort of knowledge accrued to Mr. Cooper from Precaution than from his subsequent real work on England. It was republished in London, and passed for an English novel.

The Spy followed. No one will dispute the success of The Spy. It was almost immediately republished in all parts of Europe. The novelty of an American book of this character probably contributed to give it circulation. It is worthy of remark that all our own leading periodicals looked coldly upon it; though the country did not. The North American Review—ever unwilling to do justice to Mr. Cooper—had a very ill-natured notice of it, professing to place the New England Tale far above it. In spite of such shallow criticism, however, the book was universally popular. It was decidedly the best historical romance then written by an American; not without faults, indeed, but with a fair plot, clearly and strongly drawn characters, and exhibiting great boldness and originality of conception. Its success was perhaps decisive of Mr. Cooper's career, and it gave an extraordinary impulse to literature in the country. More than any thing that had before occurred, it roused the people from their feeling of intellectual dependence.

In 1823 appeared The Pioneers. This book, it seems to me, has always had a reputation partly factitious. It is the poorest of the Leather Stocking tales, nor was its success either marked or spontaneous. Still, it was very well received, though it was thought to be a proof that the author was written out. With this book commenced the absurdity of saying Mr. Cooper introduced family traits and family history into his novels.

The Pilot succeeded. The success of The Pilot was at first a little doubtful in this country; but England gave it a reputation which it still maintains. It is due to Boston to say that its popularity in the United States was first manifested there. I say *due* to Boston, not from considerations of merit in the book, but because, for some reason, praise for Mr. Cooper, from New England, has been so rare.

America has no original literature, it is said. Where can the model of The Pilot be found? I know of nothing which could have suggested it but the following fact, which was related to me in a conversation with Mr. Cooper. The Pirate had been published a short time before. Talking with the late Charles Wilkes, of New York—a man of taste and judgment—our author heard extolled the universal knowledge of Scott, and the sea portions of The Pirate cited as a proof. He laughed at the idea, as most seamen would, and the discussion ended by his promising to write a sea story which could be read by landsmen, while seamen should feel its truth. The Pilot was the fruit of that conversation. It is one of the most remarkable novels of the time, and everywhere obtained instant and high applause.

Lionel Lincoln followed. This was a second attempt to imbody history in an American work of fiction. It failed, and perhaps justly; yet it contains one of the nicest delineations of character in Mr. Cooper's works. I know of no instance in which the distinction between a maniac and an idiot is so admirably drawn; the setting was bad, however, and the picture was not examined.

In 1826 came The Last of the Mohicans. This book succeeded from the first, and all over Christendom. It has strong parts and weak parts, but it was purely original, and originality always occupies the ground. In this respect it is like The Pilot.

After the publication of The Last of the Mohicans, Mr. Cooper went to Europe, where his reputation was already well established as one of the greatest writers of romantic fiction which our age, more prolific in men of genius than any other, had produced. The first of his works after he left his native country was The Prairie. Its success was decided and immediate. By the French and English critics it was deemed the best of his stories of Indian life. It has one leading fault, however, that of introducing any character superior to the family of the squatter. Of this fault Mr. Cooper was himself aware before he finished the work; but as he wrote and printed simultaneously, it was not easy to correct it. In this book, notwithstanding, Natty Bumpo is quite up to his mark, and is surpassed only in The Pathfinder. The reputation of The Prairie, like that of The Pioneers, is in a large degree owing to the opinions of the reviews;

it is always a fault in a book that appeals to human sympathies, that it fails with the multitude. In what relates to taste, the multitude is of no great authority ; but in all that is connected with feeling, they are the highest; and for this simple reason, that as man becomes sophisticated he deviates from nature, the only true source of all our sympathies. Our feelings are doubtless improved by refinement, and vice versa ; but their roots are struck in the human heart, and what fails to touch the heart, in these particulars, fails, while that which does touch it, succeeds. The perfection of this sort of writing is that which pleases equally the head and the heart.

The Red Rover followed The Prairie. Its success surpassed that of any of its predecessors. It was written and printed in Paris, and all in a few months. Its merits and its reception prove the accuracy of those gentlemen who allege that "Mr. Cooper never wrote a successful book after he left the United States." It is certainly a stronger work than The Pilot, though not without considerable faults.

The Wept of Wish-ton-Wish was the next novel. The author I believe regards this and Lionel Lincoln as the poorest of his works. It met with no great success.

The Water Witch succeeded, but is inferior to any of the other nautical tales.

Of all Americans who ever visited Europe, Mr. Cooper contributed most to our country's good reputation. His high character made him everywhere welcome ; there was no circle, however aristocratic or distinguished, in which, if he appeared in it, he was not observed of all observers ; and he had the somewhat singular merit of *never forgetting that he was an American.* Halleck, in his admirable poem of Red Jacket, says well of him—

COOPER, whose name is with his country's woven,
First in her fields, her pioneer of mind,
A wanderer now in other lands, has proven
His love for the young land he left behind.

After having been in Europe about two years he published his Notions of the Americans, in which he "endeavoured to repel some of the hostile opinions of the other hemisphere, and to turn the tables on those who at that time most derided and calumniated us." It contained some unimportant errors, from having been written at a distance from necessary documentary materials, but was altogether as just as it was eloquent in vindication of our institutions, manners, and history. It shows

34

how warm was his patriotism, how fondly, while receiving from strangers an homage withheld from him at home, he remembered the scenes of his first trials and triumphs, and how ready he was to sacrifice personal popularity and profit in defence of his country.

He was not only the first to defend and to praise America, but the first to whom appeals were made for information in regard to her by statesmen who felt an interest in our destiny. Following the revolution of the Three Days, in Paris, a fierce controversy took place between the absolutists, the republicans, and the constitutionalists. Among the subjects introduced in the Chambers was the comparative cheapness of our system of government; the absolutists asserting that the people of the United States paid more direct and indirect taxes than the French. Lafayette appealed to Mr. Cooper, who entered the arena, and though, from his peculiar position, at a heavy pecuniary loss, and the danger of incurring yet greater misfortunes, by a masterly *exposé* silenced at once the popular falsehoods. So in all places, circumstances, and times, he was the "*American* in Europe," as jealous of his country's reputation as his own.

Immediately after he published The Bravo, the success of which was very great : probably equal to that of The Red Rover. It is one of the best, if not the very best of the works Mr. Cooper had then written. Although he selected a foreign scene on this occasion, no one of his works is more American in its essential character. It was designed not only to extend the democratical principle abroad, but to confirm his countrymen in the opinion that nations "cannot be governed by an irresponsible minority without involving a train of nearly intolerable abuses." It gave aristocracy some hits, which aristocracy gave back again. The best notice which appeared of it was in the famous Paris gazette entitled *Figaro*, before Figaro was bought out by the French government. The change from the biting wit which characterized this periodical, to the grave sentiment of such an article, was really touching, and added an indescribable grace to the remarks.

The Heidenmaur followed. It is impossible for one to understand this book who has not some acquaintance with the scenes and habits described. It was not very successful. The Headsman of Berne did much better.

Z

It is inferior to The Bravo, though not so clashing to aristocracy. It met with very respectable success. It was the last of Mr. Cooper's novels written in Europe, and for some years the last of a political character.

The first work which Mr. Cooper published after his return to the United States was A Letter to his Countrymen. They had yielded him but a hesitating applause until his praise came back from Europe, and when the tone of foreign criticism was changed, by acts and opinions of his which should have banded the whole American press for his defence, he was assailed here in articles which either echoed the tone, or were actual translations of attacks upon him by foreigners. The custom peculiar to this country of " quoting the opinions of foreign nations by way of helping to make up its own estimate of the degree of merit which belongs to its public men," is treated in this letter with caustic and just severity, and shown to be " destructive of those sentiments of self-respect and of that manliness and independence of thought, that are necessary to render a people great or a nation respectable." The controlling influence of foreign ideas over our literature, fashions, and even politics, are illustrated by the manner in which he was himself treated, and by what he considers the English doctrines which have been broached in the speeches of many of our statesmen. It is a frank and honest book, which was unnecessary as a vindication of Mr. Cooper, but was called for by the existence of the abuse against which it was chiefly directed, though it seems to have had little effect upon it. Of the political opinions it contains I have no more to say than that I do not believe in their correctness.

It was followed by The Monikins, a political satire, which was a failure.

The next publications of Mr. Cooper were his Gleanings in Europe. Sketches of Switzerland, first and second series, each in two volumes, appeared in 1836, and none of his works contain more striking and vivid descriptions of nature, or more agreeable views of character and manners. It was followed by similar works on France, Italy, and England. All of these were well received, notwithstanding an independence of tone which is rarely popular, and some absurdities, as, for example, the imputations upon the American Federalists, in the Sketches of Switzerland. The

book on England excited most attention, and was reviewed in that country with as much asperity as if its own travellers were not proverbially the most shameless libellers that ever abused the hospitality of nations. Altogether the ten volumes which compose this series may be set down as the most intelligent and philosophical books of travels which have been written by our countrymen.

The American Democrat, or Hints on the Social and Civil Relations of the United States of America, was published in 1835. The design is stated to be, " to make a commencement toward a more just discrimination between truth and prejudice." It is essentially a good book on the virtues and vices of American character.

For a considerable time Mr. Cooper had entertained an intention of writing the History of the Navy of the United States, and his early experience, his studies, his associations, and above all the peculiar felicity of his style when treating of nautical affairs, warranted the expectation that his work would be a solid and brilliant contribution to our historical literature. It appeared in two octavo volumes in 1839, and reached a second edition in 1840, and a third in 1846.* The public had no reason to be disappointed; great diligence had been used in the collection of materials; every subject connected with the origin and growth of our national marine had been carefully investigated, and the result was presented in the most authentic and attractive form. Yet a warm controversy soon arose respecting Mr. Cooper's account of the battle of Lake Erie, and in pamphlets, reviews, and newspapers, attempts were made to show that he had done injustice to the American commander in that action. The multitude rarely undertake particular investigations; and the attacks upon Mr. Cooper, conducted with a virulence for which it would be difficult to find any cause in the History, assuming the form of vindications of a brave and popular deceased officer, produced an impression so deep and so general that he was compelled to defend the obnoxious passages, which he did triumphantly in a small volume entitled The

---

* The first and second editions appeared in Philadelphia, and the third in Cooperstown. It was reprinted in 1839 in London, Paris, and Brussels, and an abridgment of it, by the author, has recently been largely introduced into our common schools.

Battle of Lake Erie, or Answers to Messrs. Burgess, Duer, and Mackenzie, published in 1843, and in the notes to the last edition of his Naval History. Those who read the whole controversy will perceive that Mr. Cooper was guided by the authorities most entitled to the consideration of an historian, and that in his answers he has demonstrated the correctness of his statements and opinions; and they will perhaps be astonished that he in the first place gave so little cause for dissatisfaction on the part of the friends of Commodore Perry. Besides the Naval History and the essays to which it gave rise, Mr. Cooper has published, in two volumes, the Lives of American Naval Officers, a work of the highest merit in its department, every life being written with conciseness yet fulness, and with great care in regard to facts; and in the Democratic Review has published an unanswerable reply to the attacks upon the American marine by James and other British historians.

The first novel published by Mr. Cooper after his return to the United States was Homeward Bound. The two generic characters of the book, however truly they may represent individuals, have no resemblance to classes. There may be Captain Trucks, and there certainly are Steadfast Dodges, but the officers of the American merchant service are in no manner or degree inferior to Europeans of the same pursuits and grade; and with all the abuses of the freedom of the press here, our newspapers are not worse than those of Great Britain in the qualities for which Mr. Cooper arraigns them. The opinions expressed of New York society in Home as Found are identical with those in Notions of the Americans, a work almost as much abused for its praise of this country as was Home as Found for its censure, and most men of refinement and large observation seem disposed to admit their correctness. This is no doubt the cause of the feeling it excited, for a *nation* never gets in a passion at misrepresentation. It is a miserable country that cannot look down a falsehood, even from a native.

The next novel was The Pathfinder. It is a common opinion that this work deserves success more than any Mr. Cooper has written. I have heard Mr. Cooper say that in his own judgment the claim lay between The Pathfinder and The Deerslayer, but for my-

self I confess a preference for the sea novels. Leather Stocking appears to more advantage in The Pathfinder than in any other book, and in Deerslayer next. In The Pathfinder we have him presented in the character of a lover, and brought in contact with such characters as he associates with in no other stages of his varied history, though they are hardly less favourites with the author. The scene of the novel being the great fresh water seas of the interior, sailors, Indians, and hunters are so grouped together, that every kind of novelwriting in which he has been most successful is combined in one complete fiction, one striking exhibition of his best powers. Had it been written by some unknown author, probably the country would have hailed him as much superior to Mr. Cooper.

Mercedes of Castile, a Romance of the Days of Columbus, came next. It may be set down as a failure. The necessity of following facts that had become familiar, and which had so lately possessed the novelty of fiction, was too much for any writer.

The Deerslayer was written after Mercedes and The Pathfinder, and was very successful. Hetty Hunter is perhaps the best female character Mr. Cooper has drawn, though her sister is generally preferred.

The Two Admirals followed The Deerslayer. This book in some respects stands at the head of the nautical tales. Its fault is dealing with too important events to be thrown so deep into fiction; but this is a fault that may be pardoned in a romance. Mr. Cooper has written nothing in description, whether of sea or land, that surpasses either of the battle scenes of this work; especially that part of the first where the French ship is captured. The Two Admirals appeared at an unfortunate time, but it was nevertheless successful.

Wing-and-Wing, or Le Feu Follet, was published in 1842. The interest depends chiefly upon the manœuvres by which a French privateer escapes capture by an English frigate. Some of its scenes are among Mr. Cooper's best, but altogether is inferior to several of his nautical novels.

Wyandotte, or the Hutted Knoll, in its general features resembles The Pathfinder and the Deerslayer. The female characters are admirable, and but for the opinion, believed by some, from its frequent repetition, that Mr. Cooper is incapable of depicting a woman,

Maud Meredith would be regarded as among the very first class of such portraitures.

Next came the Autobiography of a Pocket Handkerchief, in one volume. It is a story of fashionable life in New York, in some respects peculiar among Mr. Cooper's works, and was decidedly successful. It appeared originally in a monthly magazine, and was the first of his novels printed in this manner. Ned Myers, in one volume, which followed in the same year, is a genuine biography, though it was commonly regarded as a fiction.

In the beginning of 1844 Mr. Cooper published Ashore and Afloat, and a few months afterward Miles Wallingford, a sequel to that tale. They have the remarkable minuteness yet boldness of description, and dramatic skill of narration, which render the impressions he produces so deep and lasting. They were as widely read as any of his recent productions.

The extraordinary state of things which for several years has disgraced a part of the state of New York, where, with unblushing effrontery, the tenants of several large proprietors have refused to pay rents, and claimed, without a shadow of right, to be absolute possessors of the soil, gave just occasion of alarm to the intelligent friends of our institutions; and this alarm increased, when it was observed that the ruffianism of the "anti-renters," as they are styled, was looked upon by many persons of respectable social positions with undisguised approval. Mr. Cooper addressed himself to the exposure and correction of the evil, in a series of novels, purporting to be edited from the manuscripts of a family named Littlepage; and in the preface to the first of these, entitled Satanstoe, a Tale of the Colony, published in 1845, announces his intention of treating it with the utmost freedom, and declares his opinion, that "the existence of true liberty among us, the perpetuity of our institutions, and the safety of public morals, are all dependent on putting down, wholly, absolutely, and unqualifiedly, the false and dishonest theories and statements that have been advanced in connection with this subject." Satanstoe presents a vivid picture of the early condition of colonial New York. The time is from 1737 to the close of the memorable campaign in which the British were so signally defeated at Ticonderoga. Chainbearer, the second of the series, tracing the family history through the Revolution, also appeared in

1845, and the last, The Red Skins, a story of the present day, in 1846. "This book," says the author in his preface, "closes the series of the Littlepage manuscripts, which have been given to the world as containing a fair account of the comparative sacrifices of time, money, and labour made respectively by the landlord and the tenants on a New York estate, together with the manner in which usages and opinions are changing among us, and the causes of these changes." These books, in which the most important practical truths are stated, illustrated and enforced, in a manner equally familiar and powerful, were received by the educated and right-minded with a degree of favour that showed the soundness of the common mind beyond the crime infected districts, and their influence will add to the evidences of the value of the novel as a means of upholding principles in art, literature, morals, and politics.

In 1847 appeared "The Crater; or, Vulcan's Peak," a story of the shores of the Pacific; followed in 1848, by "Oak Openings; or, the Bee Hunter," and "Jack Tier; or, the Florida Reef," a tale of the sea, similar to the Waterwitch. The last of the long series of sea novels, "The Sea Lions; or, the Lost Sealers," a tale of the Antarctic Ocean, was published in 1849. And the last of all his novels, "The Ways of the Hour," exhibiting the evils of the trial by jury, was issued in 1850. His ever active mind was preparing an historical work on "The Towns of Manhattan," and shaping the outline of a sixth Leather-stocking tale, when his apparently robust frame succumbed to dropsy, Sept. 14, 1851, in his 62d year.

It used to be the custom of the North American Review to speak of his works as "translated into French," as if this were giving the highest existing evidence of their popularity, while there was not a language in Europe into which they did not all, after the publication of The Red Rover, appear almost as soon as they were printed in London. He has been the chosen companion of the prince and the peasant, on the borders of the Volga, the Danube, and the Guadelquiver; by the Indus and the Ganges, the Paraguay and the Amazon; where the name even of Washington was never spoken, and our country is known only as the home of Cooper. The world has living no other writer whose fame is so universal.

Mr. Cooper has the faculty of giving to his pictures an astonishing reality. They are not mere transcripts of nature, though as such they would possess extraordinary merit, but actual creations, imbodying the very spirit of intelligent and genial experience and observation. His Indians, notwithstanding all that has been written to the contrary, are no more inferior in fidelity than they are in poetical interest to those of his most successful imitators or rivals. His hunters and trappers have the same vividness and freshness, and in the whole realm of fiction there is nothing more actual, harmonious, and sustained. They evince not only the first order of inventive power, but a profoundly philosophical study of the influences of situation upon human character. He treads the deck with the conscious pride of home and dominion: the aspects of the sea and sky, the terrors of the tornado, the excitement of the chase, the tumult of battle, fire, and wreck, are presented by him with a freedom and breadth of outline, a glow and strength of colouring and contrast, and a distinctness and truth of general and particular conception, that place him far in advance of all the other artists who have attempted with pen or pencil to paint the ocean. The same vigorous originality is stamped upon his nautical characters. The sailors of Smollett are as different in every respect as those of Eugene Sue and Marryatt are inferior. He goes on board his ship with his own creations, disdaining all society and assistance but that with which he is thus surrounded. Long Tom Coffin, Tom Tiller, Trysail, Bob Yarn, the boisterous Nightingale, the mutinous Nighthead, the fierce but honest Boltrope, and others who crowd upon our memories, as familiar as if we had ourselves been afloat with them, attest the triumph of this self-reliance. And when, as if to rebuke the charge of envy that he owed his successes to the novelty of his scenes and persons, he entered upon fields which for centuries had been illustrated by the first geniuses of Europe, his abounding power and inspiration were vindicated by that series of political novels ending with The Bravo, which have the same supremacy in their class that is held by The Pilot and The Red Rover among stories of the sea.

It has been urged that his leading characters are essentially alike, having no difference but that which results from situation. But this opinion will not bear investigation. It evidently arose from the habit of clothing his heroes alike with an intense individuality, which under all circumstances sustains the sympathy they at first awaken, without the aid of those accessories to which artists of less power are compelled to resort. Very few authors have added more than one original and striking character to the world of imagination; none has added more than Cooper; and his are all as distinct and actual as the personages that stalk before us on the stage of history.

To be American, without falling into Americanism, is the true task that is set before the native artist in literature, the accomplishment of which awaits the reward of the best approval in these times, and the promise of an enduring name. Some of our authors, fascinated very excusably with the faultless models of another age, have declined this condition, and have given us Spectators and Tatlers with false dates, and developed a style of composition of which the very merits imply an anachronism in the proportion of excellence. Others have understood the result to be attained better than the means of arriving at it. They have not considered the difference between those peculiarities in our society, manners, tempers, and tastes, which are genuine and characteristic, and those which are merely defects and errors upon the English system; they have acquired the force and gayety of liberty, but not the dignity of independence, and are only provincial, when they hoped to be national. Mr. Cooper has been more happy than any other writer in reconciling these repugnant qualities, and displaying the features, character, and tone of a great national style in letters, which, original and unimitative, is yet in harmony with the ancient models.

A public meeting was held in New York, Feb. 24, 1852, to honor his memory, and raise funds for a monument. Daniel Webster presided, and made his last address to a New York assemblage, and Wm. C. Bryant read a discourse. Otsego Hall, his residence, was destroyed by fire in 1853

z 2

THE PRAIRIE ON FIRE.

FROM THE PRAIRIE. ,

THE sleep of the fugitives lasted for several hours. The trapper was the first to shake off its influence, as he had been the last to court its refreshment. Rising, just as the gray light of day began to brighten that portion of the studded vault which rested on the eastern margin of the plain, he summoned his companions from their warm lairs, and pointed out the necessity of their being once more on the alert. . . .

"See, Middleton!" exclaimed Inez, in a sudden burst of youthful pleasure, that caused her for a moment to forget her situation. "How lovely is that sky; surely it contains a promise of happier times!"

"It is glorious!" returned her husband. "Glorious and heavenly is that streak of vivid red, and here is a still brighter crimson—rarely have I seen a richer rising of the sun."

"Rising of the sun!" slowly repeated the old man, lifting his tall person from its seat, with a deliberate and abstracted air, while he kept his eye riveted on the changing, and certainly beautiful tints that were garnishing the vault of heaven. "Rising of the sun! I like not such risings of the sun. Ah's me! the imps have circumvented us with a vengeance. The prairie is on fire!"

"God in heaven protect us!" cried Middleton, catching Inez to his bosom under the instant impression of the imminence of their danger. "There is no time to lose, old man; each instant is a day; let us fly."

"Whither?" demanded the trapper, motioning him with calmness and dignity, to arrest his steps. "In this wilderness of grass and reeds, you are like a vessel in the broad lakes without a compass. A single step on the wrong course might prove the destruction of us all. It is seldom danger is so pressing that there is not time enough for reason to do its work, young officer; therefore, let us await its biddings."

"For my own part," said Paul Hover, looking about him with no unequivocal expression of concern, "I acknowledge, that should this dry bed of weeds get fairly in a flame, a bee would have to make a flight higher than common to prevent his wings from scorching. Therefore, old trapper, I agree with the captain, and say mount and run."

"Ye are wrong—ye are wrong—man is not a beast to follow the gift of instinct, and to snuff up his knowledge by a taint in the air, or a rumbling in the sound; but he must see and reason, and then conclude. So follow me a little to the left, where there is a rise in the ground, whence we may make our reconnoitrings."

The old man waved his hand with authority, and led the way without further parlance to the spot he had indicated, followed by the whole of his alarmed companions. An eye less practised than that of the trapper might have failed in discovering the gentle elevation to which he alluded, and which looked on the surface of the meadow like a growth a little taller than common. When they reached the place, however, the stinted grass itself announced the absence of that moisture which had fed the rank weeds of most of the plain, and furnished a clue to the evidence by which he had judged of the formation of the ground hidden beneath. Here a few minutes were lost in breaking down the tops of the surrounding herbage, which, notwithstanding the advantage of their position, rose even above the heads of Middleton and Paul, and in obtaining a look-out that might command a view of the surrounding sea of fire. . .

The examination which his companions so instantly and so intently made, rather served to assure them of their desperate situation than to appease their fears. Huge columns of smoke were rolling up from the plain, and thickening in gloomy masses around the horizon. The red glow which gleamed upon their enormous folds, now lighting their volumes with the glare of the conflagration, now flashed to another point, as the flame beneath glided ahead, leaving all behind enveloped in awful darkness, and proclaiming louder than words the character of the imminent and rapidly approaching danger.

"This is terrible!" exclaimed Middleton, folding the trembling Inez to his heart. "At such a time as this, and in such a manner!"

"The gates of heaven are open to all who truly believe," murmured the pious devotee in his bosom.

"This resignation is maddening! But we are men, and will make a struggle for our lives! How now, my brave and spirited friend, shall we yet mount and push across the flames, or shall we stand here and see those we most love perish in this frightful manner without an effort?"

"I am for a swarming time, and a flight before the hive is too hot to hold us," said the bee-hunter, to whom it will be at once seen that the half-distracted Middleton addressed himself. "Come, old trapper, you must acknowledge this is but a slow way of getting out of danger. If we tarry here much longer, it will be in the fashion that the bees lie around the straw after the hive has been smoked for its honey. You may hear the fire begin to roar already, and I know by experience, that when the flame once gets fairly into the prairie grass, it is no sloth that can outrun it."

"Think you," returned the old man, pointing scornfully at the mazes of the dry and matted grass which environed them, "that mortal feet can outstrip the speed of fire on such a path?"

"What say you, friend doctor," cried the bewildered Paul, turning to the naturalist, with that sort of helplessness with which the strong are often apt to seek aid of the weak, when human power is baffled by the hand of a mightier being, "what say you; have you no advice to give away, in a case of life and death?"

The naturalist stood, tablets in hands, looking at the awful spectacle with as much composure as though the conflagration had been lighted in order to solve the difficulties of some scientific problem. Aroused by the question of his companion, he turned to his equally calm though differently occupied associate the trapper, demanding, with the most provoking insensibility to the urgent nature of their situation—"Venerable hunter, you have often witnessed similar prismatic experiments—"

He was rudely interrupted by Paul, who struck the tablets from his hands with a violence that betrayed the utter intellectual confusion which had overset the equanimity of his mind. Before time was allowed for remonstrance, the old man, who had continued during the whole scene like one much at a loss how to proceed, though also like one who was rather perplexed than alarmed, suddenly assumed a decided air, as if he no longer doubted on the course it was most advisable to pursue.

"It is time to be doing," he said, interrupting the controversy that was about to ensue between the naturalist and the bee-hunter; "it is time to leave off books and moanings, and to be doing."

"You have come to your recollections too late, miserable old man," cried Middleton; "the flames are within a quarter of a mile of us, and the wind is bringing them down in this quarter with dreadful rapidity."

"Anan! the flames! I care but little for the flames. If I only knew how to circumvent the cunning of the Tetons, as I know how to cheat the fire of its prey, there would be nothing needed but thanks to the Lord for our deliverance. Do you call this a fire? If you had seen what I have witnessed in the eastern hills, when mighty mountains were like the furnace of a smith, you would have known what it was to fear the flames, and to be thankful that you were spared! Come, lads, come; 'tis time to be doing now, and to cease talking; for yonder curling flame is truly coming on like a trotting moose. Put hands upon this short and withered grass where we stand, and lay bare the 'arth."

"Would you think to deprive the fire of its victims in this childish manner?" exclaimed Middleton.

A faint but solemn smile passed over the features of the old man as he answered—"Your gran'ther would have said, that when the enemy was nigh, a soldier could do no better than to obey."

The captain felt the reproof and instantly began to imitate the industry of Paul, who was tearing the decayed herbage from the ground in a sort of desperate compliance with the trapper's direction. Even Ellen lent her hands to the labour, nor was it long before Inez was seen similarly employed, though none amongst them knew why or wherefore. When life is thought to be the reward of labour, men are wont to be industrious. A very few moments sufficed to lay bare a spot of some twenty feet in diameter. Into one edge of this little area the trapper brought the females, directing Middleton and Paul to cover their light and inflammable dresses with the blankets of the party. So soon as this precaution was observed, the old man approached the opposite margin of the grass, which still environed them in a tall and dangerous circle, and selecting a handful of the driest of the herbage, he placed it over the pan of his rifle. The light combustible kindled at the flash. Then

he placed the little flame into a bed of the standing fog, and withdrawing from the spot to the centre of the ring, he patiently awaited the result.

The subtle element seized with avidity upon its new fuel, and in a moment forked flames were gliding among the grass, as the tongues of ruminating animals are seen rolling among their food apparently in quest of its sweetest portions.

"Now," said the old man, holding up a finger and laughing in his peculiarly silent manner, "you shall see fire fight fire! Ah's me! many is the time I have burnt a smootly path from wanton laziness to pick my way across a tangled bottom."

"But is this not fatal?" cried the amazed Middleton; "are you not bringing the enemy nigher to us instead of avoiding it?"

"Do you scorch so easily?—your gran'ther had a tougher skin. But we shall live to see; we shall all live to see."

. The experience of the trapper was in the right. As the fire gained strength and heat it began to spread on three sides, dying of itself on the fourth for want of aliment. As it increased, and the sullen roaring announced its power, it cleared every thing before it, leaving the black and smoking soil far more naked than if the scythe had swept the place. The situation of the fugitives would have still been hazardous had not the area enlarged as the flame encircled them. But by advancing to the spot where the trapper had kindled the grass, they avoided the heat, and in a very few moments the flames began to recede in every quarter, leaving them enveloped in a cloud of smoke, but perfectly safe from the torrent of fire that was still furiously rolling onward.

The spectators regarded the simple expedient of the trapper with that species of wonder with which the courtiers of Ferdinand are said to have viewed the manner in which Columbus made his egg to stand on its end, though with feelings that were filled with gratitude instead of envy.

"Most wonderful!" said Middleton, when he saw the complete success of the means by which they had been rescued from a danger that he had conceived to be unavoidable. "The thought was a gift from heaven, and the hand that executed it should be immortal."

"Old trapper," cried Paul, thrusting his fingers through his shaggy locks, "I have lined many a loaded bee into his hole, and know something of the nature of the woods, but this is robbing a hornet of his sting without touching the insect!"

"It will do—it will do," returned the old man, who after the first moment of his success seemed to think no more of the exploit... "Let the flames do their work for a short half hour and then we will mount. That time is needed to cool the meadow, for these unshod beasts are tender on the hoof as a barefooted girl."

The veteran, on whose experience they all so implicitly relied for protection, employed himself in reconnoitring objects in the distance, through the openings which the air occasionally made in the immense bodies of smoke, that by this time lay in enormous piles on every part of the plain

THE ARIEL AMONG THE SHOALS.
FROM THE PILOT.

THE extraordinary activity of Griffith, which communicated itself with promptitude to the whole crew, was produced by a sudden alteration in the weather. In place of the well-defined streak along the horizon, that has been already described, an immense body of misty light appeared to be moving in with rapidity from the ocean, while a distinct but distant roaring announced the sure approach of the tempest that had so long troubled the waters. Even Griffith, while thundering his orders through the trumpet, and urging the men by his cries to expedition, would pause for instants to cast anxious glances in the direction of the coming storm, and the faces of the sailors who lay on the yards were turned instinctively toward the the same quarter of the heavens, while they knotted the reef-points, or passed the gaskets that were to confine the unruly canvas to the prescribed limits.

The pilot alone, in that confused and busy throng, where voice rose above voice and cry echoed cry in quick succession, appeared as if he held no interest in the important stake. With his eyes steadily fixèd on the approaching mist, and his arms folded together in composure, he stood calmly awaiting the result.

The ship had fallen off with her broadside to the sea, and was become unmanageable, and the sails were already brought into the folds necessary to her security, when the quick and heavy fluttering of canvas was thrown across the water with all the gloomy and chilling sensations that such sounds produce, where darkness and danger unite to appal the seaman.

"The schooner has it!" cried Griffith; "Barnstable has held on, like himself, to the last moment—God send that the squall leave him cloth enough to keep him from the shore!"

"His sails are easily handled," the commander observed, "and she must be over the principal danger. We are falling off before it, Mr. Gray; shall we try a cast of the lead?"

The pilot turned from his contemplative posture and moved slowly across the deck before he returned any reply to this question—like a man who not only felt that every thing depended on himself, but that he was equal to the emergency.

"'Tis unnecessary," he at length said; "'twould be certain destruction to be taken aback, and it is difficult to say, within several points, how the wind may strike us."

"'Tis difficult no longer," cried Griffith; "for here it comes, and in right earnest!"

The rushing sounds of the wind were now, indeed, heard at hand, and the words were hardly passed the lips of the young lieutenant before the vessel bowed down heavily to one side, and then, as she began to move through the water, rose again majestically to her upright position, as if saluting, like a courteous champion, the powerful antagonist with which she was about to contend. Not another minute elapsed before the ship was throwing the waters aside with a lively progress, and, obedient to her helm, was brought as near to the desired course as the direction of the wind would allow. The hurry and bustle on the yards gradually subsided, and the men slowly descended to the deck, all straining their eyes to pierce the gloom in which they were enveloped, and some shaking their heads in melancholy doubt, afraid to express the apprehensions they really entertained. All on board anxiously waited for the fury of the gale; for there were none so ignorant or inexperienced in that gallant frigate, as not to know that they as yet only felt the infant efforts of the winds. Each moment, however, it increased in power, though so gradual was the alteration, that the relieved mariners began to believe that all their gloomy forebodings were not to be realized. During this short interval of uncertainty, no other sounds were heard than the whistling of the breeze, as it passed quickly through the mass of rigging that belonged to the vessel, and the dashing of the spray that began to fly from her bows like the foam of a cataract.

"It blows fresh," cried Griffith, who was the first to speak in that moment of doubt and anxiety; "but it is no more than a cap-full of wind after all. Give us elbow-room and the right canvas, Mr. Pilot, and I'll handle the ship like a gentleman's yacht in this breeze."

"Will she stay, think ye, under this sail?" said the low voice of the stranger.

"She will do all that man in reason can ask of wood and iron," returned the lieutenant; "but the vessel don't float the ocean that will tack under double-reefed topsails alone against a heavy sea. Help her with the courses, pilot, and you'll see her come round like a dancing-master."

"Let us feel the strength of the gale first," returned the man who was called Mr. Gray, moving from the side of Griffith to the weather gang-way of the vessel, where he stood in silence, looking ahead of the ship with an air of singular coolness and abstraction.

All the lanterns had been extinguished on the deck of the frigate, when her anchor was secured, and as the first mist of the gale had passed over, it was succeeded by a faint light that was a good deal aided by the glittering foam of the waters, which now broke in white curls around the vessel in every direction. The land could be faintly discerned, rising like a heavy bank of black fog above the margin of the waters, and was only distinguishable from the heavens by its deeper gloom and obscurity. The last rope was coiled and deposited in its proper place by the seamen, and for several minutes the stillness of death pervaded the crowded decks. It was evident to every one that their ship was dashing at a prodigious rate through the waves; and, as she was approaching, with such velocity, the quarter of the bay where the shoals and dangers were known to be situated, nothing but the habits of the most exact discipline could suppress the uneasiness of the officers and men within their own bosoms. At length the voice of Captain Munson was heard calling to the pilot.

"Shall I send a hand into the chains, Mr. Gray," he said, " and try our water?" . . .

" Tack your ship, sir, tack your ship; I would see how she works before we reach the point where she *must* behave well, or we perish."

Griffith gazed after him in wonder, while the pilot slowly paced the quarter-deck, and then, rousing from his trance, gave forth the cheering order that called each man to his station to perform the desired evolution. The confident assurances which the young officer had given to the pilot respecting the qualities of his vessel, and his own ability to manage her, were fully realized by the result. The helm was no sooner put a-lee, than the huge ship bore up gallantly against the wind, and, dashing directly through the waves, threw the foam high into the air as she looked boldly into the very eye of the wind, and then, yielding gracefully to its power, she fell off on the other tack with her head pointed from those dangerous shoals that she had so recently approached with such terrifying velocity. The heavy yards swung round as if they had been vanes to indicate the currents of the air, and in a few moments the frigate again moved with stately progress through the water, leaving the rocks and shoals behind her on one side of the bay, but advancing toward those that offered equal danger on the other.

During this time, the sea was becoming more agitated, and the violence of the wind was gradually increasing. The latter no longer whistled amid the cordage of the vessel, but it seemed to howl surlily as it passed the complicated machinery that the frigate obtruded in its path. An endless succession of white surges rose above the heavy billows, and the very air was glittering with the light that was disengaged from the ocean. The ship yielded each moment more and more before the storm, and, in less than half an hour from the time that she had lifted her anchor, she was driven along with tremendous fury by the full power of a gale of wind. Still, the hardy and experienced mariners who directed her movements, held her to the course that was necessary to their preservation, and still Griffith gave forth, when directed by their unknown pilot, those orders that turned her in the narrow channel where safety was alone to be found.

So far the performance of his duty appeared easy to the stranger, and he gave the required directions in those still, calm tones that formed so remarkable a contrast to the responsibility of his situation. But when the land was becoming dim, in distance as well as darkness, and the agitated sea was only to be discovered as it swept by them in foam, he broke in upon the monotonous roaring of the tempest with the sounds of his voice, seeming to shake off his apathy and rouse himself to the occasion.

" Now is the time to watch her closely, Mr. Griffith," he cried; " here we get the true tide and the real danger. Place the best quarter-master of your ship in those chains, and let an officer stand by him and see that he gives us the right water."

35

" I will take that office on myself," said the captain; " pass a light into the weather main-chains."

" Stand by your braces!" exclaimed the pilot with startling quickness. " Heave away that lead!"

These preparations taught the crew to expect the crisis, and every officer and man stood in fearful silence at his assigned station awaiting the issue of the trial. Even the quarter-master at the cun gave out his orders to the men at the wheel in deeper and hoarser tones than usual, as if anxious not to disturb the quiet and order of the vessel.

While this deep expectation pervaded the frigate, the piercing cry of the leadsman, as he called, " By the mark seven!" rose above the tempest, crossed over the decks, and appeared to pass away to leeward, borne on the blast like the warnings of some water-spirit.

" 'Tis well," returned the pilot, calmly; " try it again."

The short pause was succeeded by another cry, " and a half-five!"

" She shoals! she shoals!" exclaimed Griffith; " keep her a good full."

" Ay! you must hold the vessel in command, now," said the pilot, with those cool tones that are most appalling in critical moments, because they seem to denote most preparation and care.

The third call of " By the deep four!" was followed by a prompt direction from the stranger to tack.

Griffith seemed to emulate the coolness of the pilot, in issuing the necessary orders to execute this manœuvre.

The vessel rose slowly from the inclined position into which she had been forced by the tempest, and the sails were shaking violently, as if to release themselves from their confinement while the ship stemmed the billows, when the well-known voice of the sailing-master was heard shouting from the forecastle—" Breakers! breakers, dead ahead!"

This appalling sound seemed yet to be lingering about the ship, when a second voice cried—" Breakers on our lee-bow!"

" We are in a bight of the shoals, Mr. Gray," said the commander. " She loses her way; perhaps an anchor might hold her."

" Clear away that best-bower!" shouted Griffith through his trumpet.

" Hold on!" cried the pilot, in a voice that reached the very hearts of all who heard him; " hold on every thing."

The young man turned fiercely to the daring stranger who thus defied the discipline of his vessel, and at once demanded—" Who is it that dares to countermand my orders?—is it not enough that you run the ship into danger, but you must interfere to keep her there? If another word—"

" Peace, Mr. Griffith," interrupted the captain, bending from the rigging, his gray locks blowing about in the wind, and adding a look of wildness to the haggard care that he exhibited by the light of his lantern; " yield the trumpet to Mr. Gray; he alone can save us."

Griffith threw his speaking trumpet on the deck,

and, as he walked proudly away, muttered in bitterness of feeling—"Then all is lost, indeed, and,
among the rest, the foolish hopes with which I
visited this coast."

There was, however, no time for reply; the
ship had been rapidly running into the wind, and,
as the efforts of the crew were paralyzed by the
contradictory orders they had heard, she gradually
lost her way, and in a few seconds all her sails
were taken aback.

Before the crew understood their situation the
pilot had applied the trumpet to his mouth, and,
in a voice that rose above the tempest, he thundered forth his orders. Each command was given
distinctly, and with a precision that showed him
to be master of his profession. The helm was
kept fast, the head yards swung up heavily against
the wind, and the vessel was soon whirling round
on her heel with a retrograde movement.

Griffith was too much of a seaman not to perceive that the pilot had seized, with a perception
almost intuitive, the only method that promised to
extricate the vessel from her situation. He was
young, impetuous, and proud; but he was also
generous. Forgetting his resentment and his mortification, he rushed forward among the men, and,
by his presence and example, added certainty to
the experiment. The ship fell off slowly before
the gale, and bowed her yards nearly to the water,
as she felt the blast pouring its fury on her broadside, while the surly waves beat violently against
her stern, as if in reproach at departing from her
usual manner of moving.

The voice of the pilot, however, was still heard,
steady and calm, and yet so clear and high as to
reach every ear; and the obedient seamen whirled
the yards at his bidding in despite of the tempest,
as if they handled the toys of their childhood.
When the ship had fallen off dead before the wind,
her head sails were shaken, her after-yards trimmed,
and her helm shifted before she had time to run
upon the danger that had threatened, as well to
leeward as to windward. The beautiful fabric,
obedient to her government, threw her bows up
gracefully toward the wind again, and, as her sails
were trimmed, moved out from amongst the dangerous shoals in which she had been embayed, as
steadily and swiftly as she had approached them.

A moment of breathless astonishment succeeded
the accomplishment of this nice manœuvre, but
there was no time for the usual expressions of surprise. The stranger still held the trumpet, and
continued to lift his voice amid the howlings of
the blast, whenever prudence or skill directed any
change in the management of the ship. For an
hour longer, there was a fearful struggle for their
preservation, the channel becoming at each step
more complicated, and the shoals thickening around
the mariners on every side. The lead was cast
rapidly, and the quick eye of the pilot seemed to
pierce the darkness with a keenness of vision that
exceeded human power. It was apparent to all
in the vessel, that they were under the guidance
of one who understood the navigation thoroughly,
and their exertions kept pace with their reviving

confidence. Again and again the frigate appeared
to be rushing blindly on shoals, where the sea was
covered with foam, and where destruction would
have been as sudden as it was certain, when the
clear voice of the stranger was heard warning them
of the danger, and inciting them to their duty.
The vessel implicitly yielded to his government, and during those anxious moments, when
she was dashing the waters aside, throwing the
spray over her enormous yards, each ear would
listen eagerly for those sounds that had obtained
a command over the crew, that can only be acquired, under such circumstances, by great steadiness and consummate skill. The ship was recovering from the inaction of changing her course
in one of those critical tacks that she had made so
often, when the pilot for the first time addressed
the commander of the frigate, who still continued
to superintend the all-important duty of the leadsman.

"Now is the pinch," he said; "and if the ship
behaves well, we are safe—but if otherwise, all we
have yet done will be useless."

The veteran seaman whom he addressed left the
chains at this portentous notice, and, calling to
his first lieutenant, required of the stranger an ex
planation of his warning.

"See you yon light on the southern headland?"
returned the pilot; "you may know it from the
star near it by its sinking, at times, in the ocean.
Now observe the hummock, a little north of it,
looking like a shadow in the horizon—'tis a hill
far inland. If we keep that light open from the
hill, we shall do well—but if not, we surely go to
pieces."

"Let us tack again!" exclaimed the lieutenant.

The pilot shook his head, as he replied—"There
is no more tacking or box-hauling to be done to-
night. We have barely room to pass out of the
shoals on this course, and if we can weather the
'Devil's Grip,' we clear their outermost point—
but if not, as I said before, there is but an alternative."

"If we had beaten out the way we entered,"
exclaimed Griffith, "we should have done well."

"Say, also, if the tide would have let us do so,"
returned the pilot calmly. "Gentlemen, we must
be prompt; we have but a mile to go, and the
ship appears to fly. That topsail is not enough
to keep her up to the wind; we want both jib and
mainsail."

"'Tis a perilous thing to loosen canvas in such
a tempest!" observed the doubtful captain.

"It must be done," returned the collected stranger; "we perish without—see! the light already
touches the edge of the hummock; the sea casts us
to leeward!"

"It shall be done!" cried Griffith, seizing the
trumpet from the hand of the pilot.

The orders of the lieutenant were executed almost as soon as issued, and, every thing being
ready, the enormous folds of the mainsail were
trusted loose to the blast. There was an instant
when the result was doubtful; the tremendous
threshing of the heavy sails seeming to bid defiance

to all restraint, shaking the ship to her centre; but art and strength prevailed, and gradually the canvas was distended, and, bellying as it filled, was drawn down to its usual place by the power of a hundred men. The vessel yielded to this immense addition of force, and bowed before it like a reed bending to a breeze. But the success of the measure was announced by a joyful cry from the stranger that seemed to burst from his inmost soul.

"She feels it! she springs her luff! observe," he said, "the light opens from the hummock already; if she will only bear her canvas, we shall go clear!"

A report like that of a cannon interrupted his exclamation, and something resembling a white cloud was seen drifting before the wind from the head of the ship, till it was driven into the gloom far to leeward.

"'Tis the jib blown from the bolt-ropes," said the commander of the frigate. "This is no time to spread light duck—but the mainsail may stand it yet."

"The sail would laugh at a tornado," returned the lieutenant; "but that mast springs like a piece of steel."

"Silence all!" cried the pilot. "Now, gentlemen, we shall soon know our fate. Let her luff—luff you can!"

This warning effectually closed all discourse, and the hardy mariners, knowing that they had already done all in the power of man to insure their safety, stood in breathless anxiety awaiting the result. At a short distance ahead of them, the whole ocean was white with foam, and the waves, instead of rolling on in regular succession, appeared to be tossing about in mad gambols. A single streak of dark billows, not half a cable's length in width, could be discerned running into this chaos of water; but it was soon lost to the eye amid the confusion of the disturbed element. Along this narrow path the vessel moved more heavily than before, being brought so near the wind as to keep her sails touching. The pilot silently proceeded to the wheel, and with his own hands he undertook the steerage of the ship. No noise proceeded from the frigate to interrupt the horrid tumult of the ocean, and she entered the channel among the breakers with the silence of a desperate calmness. Twenty times, as the foam rolled away to leeward, the crew were on the eve of uttering their joy, as they supposed the vessel past the danger; but breaker after breaker would still rise before them, following each other into the general mass to check their exultation. Occasionally the fluttering of the sails would be heard; and when the looks of the startled seamen were turned to the wheel, they beheld the stranger grasping its spokes, with his quick eye glancing from the water to the canvas. At length the ship reached a point where she appeared to be rushing directly into the jaws of destruction, when suddenly her course was changed, and her head receded rapidly from the wind. At the same instant the voice of the pilot was heard shouting—"Square away the yards!—in mainsail!"

A general burst from the crew echoed, "Square away the yards!" and quick as thought the frigate was seen gliding along the channel before the wind. The eye had hardly time to dwell on the foam, which seemed like clouds driving in the heavens, and directly the gallant vessel issued from her perils, and rose and fell on the heavy waves of the open sea.

THE REGATTA AT VENICE.

FROM THE BRAVO.

VENICE, from her peculiar formation and the vast number of her watermen, had long been celebrated for this species of amusement. Families were known and celebrated in her traditions for dexterous skill with the oar, as they were known in Rome for feats of a far less useful and of a more barbarous nature. It was usual to select from these races of watermen the most vigorous and skilful; and, after invoking the aid of patron-saints, and arousing their pride and recollections by songs that recounted the feats of their ancestors, to start them for the goal with every incitement that pride and the love of victory could awaken.

Most of these ancient usages were still observed. As soon as the Bucentaur was in its station, some thirty or forty gondoliers were brought forth, clad in their gayest habiliments and surrounded and supported by crowds of anxious friends and relatives. The intended competitors were expected to sustain the long-established reputations of their several names, and they were admonished of the disgrace of defeat. They were cheered by the men, and stimulated by the smiles and tears of the other sex. The rewards were recalled to their minds; they were fortified by prayers to the saints; and then they were dismissed amid the cries and the wishes of the multitude to seek their allotted places beneath the stern of the galley of state.

The city of Venice is divided into two nearly equal parts by a channel much broader than that of the ordinary passages of the town. This dividing artery, from its superior size and depth, and its greater importance, is called the grand canal. Its course is not unlike that of an undulating line, which greatly increases its length. As it is much used by the larger boats of the bay—being in fact a sort of secondary port—and its width is so considerable, it has throughout the whole distance but one bridge—the celebrated Rialto. The regatta was to be held on this canal, which offered the requisites of length and space, and which, as it was lined with most of the palaces of the principal senators, afforded all the facilities necessary for viewing the struggle.

In passing from one end of this long course to the other, the men destined for the race were not permitted to make any exertion. Their eyes roamed over the gorgeous hangings, which, as is still wont throughout Italy on all days of festa, floated from every window, and on groups of females in rich attire, brilliant with the peculiar charms of the famed Venetian beauty that clustered in the balconies. Those who were domestics rose and answered to the encouraging signals thrown from above, as they passed the palaces of their masters; while those who were watermen of the public endeavoured to gather hope among the sympathizing faces of the multitude.

At length every formality had been duly observed, and the competitors assumed their places. The gondolas were much larger than those commonly used, and each was manned by three watermen in the centre, directed by a fourth, who, standing on the little deck in the stern, steered while he aided to impel the boat. There were light, low staffs in the bows, with flags that bore the distinguishing colours of several noble families of the republic, or which had such other simple devices as had been suggested by the fancies of those to whom they belonged. A few flourishes of the oars, resembling the preparatory movements which the master of fence makes ere he begins to push and parry, were given; a whirling of the boats, like the prancing of curbed racers, succeeded; and then at the report of a gun, the whole darted away as if the gondolas were impelled by volition. The start was followed by a shout which passed swiftly along the canal, and an eager agitation of heads that went from balcony to balcony, till the sympathetic movement was communicated to the grave load under which the Bucentaur laboured.

For a few minutes the difference in force and skill was not very obvious. Each gondola glided along the element, apparently with that ease with which a light-winged swallow skims the lake, and with no visible advantage to any one of the ten. Then, as more art in him who steered, or greater powers of endurance in those who rowed, or some of the latent properties of the boat itself came into service, the cluster of little barks which had come off like a closely-united flock of birds taking flight together in alarm, began to open till they formed a long and vacillating line in the centre of the passage. The whole train shot beneath the bridge, so near each other as to render it still doubtful which was to conquer, and the exciting strife came more in view of the principal personages of the city.

But here those radical qualities, which insure success in efforts of this nature, manifested themselves. The weaker began to yield, the train to lengthen, and hopes and fears to increase, until those in the front presented the exhilarating spectacle of success, while others offered the still more noble sight of men struggling without hope. Gradually the distances between the boats increased, while that between them and the goal grew rapidly less, until three of those in advance came in, like glancing arrows, beneath the bridge of the Bucentaur, with scarce a length between them. The prize was won, the conquerors were rewarded, and the artillery gave forth the usual signals of rejoicing. Music answered to the roar of cannon and the peals of bells, while sympathy with success, that predominant and so often dangerous principle of our nature, drew shouts even from the disappointed.

The clamour ceased, and a herald proclaimed aloud the commencement of a new and a different struggle. The last, and what might be termed the national race, had been limited, by an ancient usage, to the known and recognised gondoliers of Venice. The prize had been awarded by the state, and the whole affair had somewhat of an official and political character. It was now announced, however, that a race was to be run in which the reward was open to all competitors, without questioning as to their origin, or as to their ordinary occupations. An oar of gold, to which was attached a chain of the same precious metal, was exhibited as the boone of the doge to him who showed most dexterity and strength in this new struggle; while a similar ornament of silver was to be the portion of him who showed the second-best dexterity and bottom. A mimic boat of less precious metal was the third prize. The gondolas were to be the usual light vehicles of the canals, and as the object was to display the peculiar skill of that city of islands, but one oarsman was allowed to each, on whom would necessarily fall the whole duty of guiding while he impelled his little bark. Any of those who had been engaged in the previous trial were admitted to this; and all desirous of taking part in the new struggle were commanded to come beneath the stern of the Bucentaur, within a prescribed number of minutes, that note might be had of their wishes. As notice of this arrangement had been previously given, the interval between the two races was not long.

The first who came out of the crowd of boats which environed the vacant place that had been left for the competitors, was a gondolier of the public landing, well known for his skill with the oar, and his song on the canal.

"How art thou called, and in whose name dost thou put thy chance?" demanded the herald of this aquatic course.

"All know me for Bartolomeo, one who lives between the Piazzetta and the Lido, and, like a loyal Venetian, I trust in San Teodoro."

"Thou art well protected; take thy place and await thy fortune."

The conscious waterman swept the water with a back stroke of his blade, and the light gondola whirled away into the centre of the vacant spot like a swan giving a sudden glance aside.

"And who art thou?" demanded the official of the next that came.

"Enrico, a gondolier of Fusina. I come to try my oar with the braggarts of the canals."

"In whom is thy trust?"

"Sant' Antonio di Padua."

"Thou wilt need his aid, though we commend thy spirit. Enter and take place."—"And who art thou?" he continued, to another, when the second had imitated the easy skill of the first.

"I am called Gino of Calabria, a gondolier in private service."

"What noble retaineth thee?"

"The illustrious and most excellent Don Camillo Monforte, Duca and Lord of Sant' Agata in Napoli, and of right a senator in Venice."

"Thou shouldst have come of Padua, friend, by thy knowledge of the laws! Dost thou trust in him thou servest for the victory?"

There was a movement among the senators at the answer of Gino; and the half-terrified varlet thought he perceived frowns gathering on more than one brow. He looked around in quest of him whose greatness he had vaunted, as if he sought succour.

"Wilt thou name thy support in this great trial of force?" resumed the herald.

"My master," uttered the terrified Gino, "St. Januarius, and St. Mark."

"Thou art well defended. Should the two latter fail thee, thou mayest surely count on the first!"

"Signor Monforte has an illustrious name, and he is welcome to our Venetian sports," observed the doge, slightly bending his head toward the young Calabrian noble, who stood at no great distance in a gondola of state, regarding the scene with a deeply-interested countenance. This cautious interruption of the pleasantries of the official was acknowledged by a low reverence, and the matter proceeded.

"Take thy station, Gino of Calabria, and a happy fortune be thine," said the latter; then turning to another, he asked in surprise—"Why art thou here?"

"I come to try my gondola's swiftness."

"Thou art old and unequal to this struggle; husband thy strength for daily toil. An ill-advised ambition hath put thee on this useless trial."

The new aspirant had forced a common fisherman's gondola, of no bad shape and of sufficient lightness, but which bore about it all the vulgar signs of its daily uses, beneath the gallery of the Bucentaur. He received the rebuke meekly, and was about to turn his boat aside, though with a sorrowing and mortified eye, when a sign from the doge arrested his arm.

"Question him, as of wont," said the prince.

"How art thou named?" continued the reluctant official, who, like all of subordinate condition, had far more jealousy of the dignity of the sports he directed than his superior.

"I am known as Antonio, a fisherman of the Lagunes."

"Thou art old!"

"Signore, none know it better than I. It is sixty summers since I first threw net or line into the water."

"Nor art thou clad as befitteth one who cometh before the state of Venice in a regatta."

"I am here in the best that I have. Let them who would do the nobles greater honour come in better."

"Thy limbs are uncovered—thy bosom bare—thy sinews feeble—go to; thou art ill advised to interrupt the pleasures of the nobles by this levity."

Again Antonio would have shrunk from the ten thousand eyes that shone upon him, when the calm voice of the doge once more came to his aid.

"The struggle is open to all," said the sovereign; "still I would advise the poor and aged man to take counsel; give him silver, for want urges him to this hopeless trial."

"Thou hearest; alms are offered thee; but give place to those who are stronger and more seemly for the sport."

"I will obey, as is the duty of one born and accustomed to poverty. They said the race was open to all, and I crave the pardon of the nobles, since I meant to do them no dishonour."

"Justice in the palace, and justice on the canals," hastily observed the prince. "If he will continue, it is right. It is the pride of St. Mark that his balances are held with an even hand."

A murmur of applause succeeded the specious sentiment, for the powerful rarely affect the noble attribute of justice, however limited may be its exercise, without their words finding an echo in the tongues of the selfish.

"Thou hearest—his highness, who is the voice of a mighty state, says thou mayest remain;—though thou art still advised to withdraw."

"I will then see what virtue is left in this naked arm," returned Antonio, casting a mournful glance, and one that was not entirely free from the latent vanity of man, at his meagre and threadbare attire. "The limb hath its scars, but the infidels may have spared enough for the little I ask."

"In whom is thy faith?"

"Blessed St. Anthony, of the Miraculous Draught."

"Take thy place!—Ha! here cometh one unwilling to be known! How now! who appears with so false a face?"

"Call me, Mask."

"So neat and just a leg and arm need not have hid their fellow countenance. Is it your highness's pleasure that one disguised should be entered for the sports?"

"Doubt it not. A mask is sacred in Venice. It is the glory of our excellent and wise laws, that he who seeketh to dwell within the privacy of his own thoughts, and to keep aloof from curiosity by shadowing his features, rangeth our streets and canals, as if he dwelt in the security of his own abode. Such are the high privileges of liberty, and such it is to be a citizen of a generous, a magnanimous, and a free state!"

A thousand bowed in approbation of the sentiment, and a rumor passed from mouth to mouth that a young noble was about to try his strength in the regatta, in compliment to some wayward beauty.

"Such is justice!" exclaimed the herald in a loud voice, admiration apparently overcoming respect in the ardour of the moment. "Happy is he that is born in Venice, and envied are the people in whose councils wisdom and mercy preside, like lovely and benignant sisters! On whom dost thou rely?"

"Mine own arm."

"Ha! This is impious! None so presuming may enter into these privileged sports."

The hurried exclamation of the herald was accompanied by a general stir, such as denotes sudden and strong emotion in a multitude.

2 A

"The children of the republic are protected by an even hand," observed the venerable prince. "It formeth our just pride, and blessed St. Mark forbid that aught resembling vain-glory should be uttered! but it is truly our boast that we know no difference between our subjects of the islands, or those of the Dalmatian coast; between Padua or Candia; Corfu or St. Giorgio. Still it is not permitted for any to refuse the intervention of the saints."

"Name thy patron, or quit the place," continued the observant herald, anew.

The stranger paused, as if he looked into his mind, and then he answered—

"San Giovanni of the Wilderness."

"Thou namest one of blessed memory!"

"I name him who may have pity on me in this living desert."

"The temper of thy soul is best known to thyself, but this reverend rank of patricians, yonder brilliant show of beauty, and that goodly multitude may claim another name.—Take thy place."

While the herald proceeded to take the names of three or four more applicants, all gondoliers in private service, a murmur ran through the spectators, which proved how much their interest and curiosity had been awakened by the replies and appearance of the two last competitors. In the mean time, the young nobles who entertained those who came last, began to move among the throng of boats with the intention of making such manifestations of their gallant desires and personal devotion as suited the customs and opinions of the age. The list was now proclaimed to be full, and the gondolas were towed off, as before, toward the starting point, leaving the place beneath the stern of the Bucentaur vacant. The scene that followed consequently passed directly before the eyes of those grave men, who charged themselves with most of the private interests, as well as with the public concerns of Venice. . . . .

It has been seen that the gondolas which were to contend in the race, had been towed toward the place of starting, in order that the men might enter on the struggle with undiminished vigour. In this precaution, even the humble and half-clad fisherman had not been neglected, but his boat, like the others, was attached to the larger barges to which this duty had been assigned. Still, as he passed along the canal, before the crowded balconies and groaning vessels which lined its sides, there arose that scornful and deriding laugh, which seems ever to grow more strong and bold as misfortune weighs most heavily on its subject.

The old man was not unconscious of the remarks of which he was the subject; and, as it is rare indeed that our sensibilities do not survive our better fortunes, even he was so far conscious of a fall as not to be callous to contempt thus openly expressed. He looked wistfully on every side of him, and seemed to search in every eye he encountered some portion of the sympathy which his meek and humble feelings still craved. But even the men of his caste and profession threw jibes upon his ear; and, though of all the competitors perhaps the one whose motive most hallowed his ambition, he was held to be the only proper subject of mirth. For the solution of this revolting trait of human character, we are not to look to Venice and her institutions, since it is known that none are so arrogant on occasions as the ridden, and that the abject and insolent spirits are usually tenants of the same bosom.

The movement of the boats brought those of the masked waterman and the subject of these taunts side by side.

"Thou art not the favourite in this strife," observed the former, when a fresh burst of jibes were showered on the head of his unresisting associate. "Thou hast not been sufficiently heedful of thy attire; for this is a town of luxury, and he who would meet applause must appear on the canals in the guise of one less borne upon by fortune."

"I know them! I know them!" returned the fisherman; "they are led away by their pride, and they think ill of one who cannot share in their vanities. But, friend unknown, I have brought with me a face which, old though it be, and wrinkled, and worn by the weather like the stones of the sea-shore, is uncovered to the eye and without shame."

"There may be reasons which thou knowest not why I wear a mask. But if my face be hid, the limbs are bare, and thou seest there is no lack of sinews to make good that which I have undertaken. Thou shouldst have thought better of the matter ere thou puttest thyself in the way of so much mortification. Defeat will not cause the people to treat thee more tenderly."

"If my sinews are old and stiffened, Signor Mask, they are long used to toil. As to shame, if it is a shame to be below the rest of mankind in fortune, it will not now come for the first time. A heavy sorrow hath befallen me, and this race may lighten the burden of grief. I shall not pretend that I hear this laughter, and all these scornful speeches as one listens to the evening breeze on the Lagunes—for a man is still a man, though he lives with the humblest, and eats of the coarsest. But let it pass; Sant' Antonio will give me heart to bear it."

"Thou hast a stout mind, fisherman; and I would gladly pray my patron to grant thee a stronger arm, but that I have much need of this victory myself. Wilt thou be content with the second prize, if, by any manner of skill, I might aid thee in thy efforts?—for, I suppose, the metal of the third is as little to thy taste as it is to my own."

"Nay, I count not on gold or silver."

"Can the honour of such a struggle awaken the pride of one like thee?"

The old man looked earnestly at his companion; but he shook his head without answer. Fresh merriment at his expense, caused him to bend his face toward the scoffers; and he perceived they were just then passing a numerous group of his fellows of the Lagunes, who seemed to feel that his unjustifiable ambition reflected, in some degree, on the honour of their whole body.

" How now, old Antonio !" shouted the boldest of the band—" is it not enough that thou hast won the honours of the net, but thou wouldst have a golden oar at thy neck ?"

" We shall yet see him of the senate !" cried a second.

" He standeth in need of the horned bonnet for his naked head," continued a third. " We shall see the brave Admiral Antonio sailing in the Bucentaur with the nobles of the land !"

Their sallies were succeeded by coarse laughter. Even the fair in the balconies were not uninfluenced by these constant jibes, and the apparent discrepancy between the condition and the means of so unusual a pretender to the honours of the regatta. The purpose of the old man wavered ; but he seemed goaded by some inward incentive that still enabled him to maintain his ground. His companion closely watched the varying expression of a countenance that was far too little trained in deception to conceal the feelings within ; and, as they approached the place of starting, he again spoke.

" Thou mayest yet withdraw," he said ;—" why should one of thy years make the little time he has to stay bitter, by bearing the ridicule of his associates for the rest of his life ?"

" St. Anthony did a greater wonder when he caused the fishes to come upon the waters to hear his preaching, and I will not show a cowardly heart at a moment when there is most need of resolution."

The masked waterman crossed himself devoutly ; and, relinquishing all further design to persuade the other to abandon the fruitless contest, he gave all his thoughts to his own interest in the coming struggle.

The narrowness of most of the canals of Venice, with the innumerable angles and the constant passing, have given rise to a fashion of construction and of rowing that are so peculiar to that city and its immediate dependencies, as to require some explanation. The reader has doubtless already understood that a gondola is a long, narrow, and light boat, adapted to the uses of the place, and distinct from the wherries of all other towns. The distance between the dwellings, on most of the canals, is so small, that the width of the latter does not admit of the use of oars on both sides at the same time. The necessity of constantly turning aside to give room for others, and the frequency of the bridges and the corners, have suggested the expediency of placing the face of the waterman in the direction in which the boat is steering, and of course of keeping him on his feet. As every gondola, when fully equipped, has its pavilion in the centre, the height of the latter renders it necessary to place him who steers on such an elevation, as will enable him to overlook it. From these several causes, a one-oared boat in Venice is propelled by a gondolier who stands on a little angular deck in its stern, formed like the low roof of a house ; and the stroke of the oar is given by a push instead of a pull, as is common elsewhere. This habit of rowing erect, however, which is usually done by

a forward, instead of a backward, movement of the body is not unfrequent in all the ports of the Mediterranean, though in no other is there a boat which resembles the gondola in all its properties or uses. The upright position of the gondolier requires that the pivot on which the oar rests should have a corresponding elevation ; and there is, consequently, a species of bumkin raised from the side of the boat to the desired height, and which, being formed of a crooked and very irregular knee of wood, has two or three row-locks, one above the other, to suit the stature of different individuals, or to give a broader or narrower sweep of the blade as the movement shall require. As there is frequent occasion to cast the oar from one of these row-locks to the other, and not unfrequently to change its side, it rests in a very open bed ; and the instrument is kept in its place by great dexterity alone, and by a perfect knowledge of the means of accommodating the force and the rapidity of the effort to the forward movement of the boat and the resistance of the water. All these difficulties united render skill in a gondolier one of the most delicate branches of a waterman's art, as it is clear that muscular strength alone, though of great aid, can avail but little in such a practice.

The great canal of Venice, following its windings, being more than a league in length, the distance in the present race was reduced nearly half by causing the boats to start from the Rialto. At this point, then, the gondolas were all assembled, attended by those who were to place them. As the whole of the population, which before had been extended along the entire course of the water, was now crowded between the bridge and the Bucentaur, the long and graceful avenue resembled a vista of human heads. It was an imposing sight to look along that bright and living lane, and the hearts of each competitor beat high, as hope, or pride, or apprehension became the feeling of the moment.

" Gino of Calabria," cried the marshal who placed the gondolas, " thy station is on the right. Take it, and St. Januarius speed thee !"

The servitor of Don Camillo assumed his oar, and the boat glided gracefully into its berth.

" Thou comest next, Enrico of Fusina. Call stoutly on thy Paduan patron, and husband thy strength ; for none of the main have ever yet borne away a prize in Venice."

He then summoned in succession those whose names have not been mentioned, and placed them, side by side, in the centre of the canal.

" Here is place for thee, Signore," continued the officer, inclining his head to the unknown gondolier ; for he had imbibed the general impression that the face of some young patrician was concealed beneath the mask to humour the fancy of some capricious fair.—" Chance hath given thee the extreme left."

" Thou hast forgotten to call the fisherman," observed the masker, as he drove his own gondola into its station.

" Does the hoary fool persist in exposing his vanity and his rags to the best of Venice ?"

"I can take place in the rear," meekly observed Antonio. "There may be those in the line it doth not become one like me to crowd; and a few strokes of the oar, more or less, can differ but little in so long a strife."

"Thou hadst better push modesty to discretion, and remain."

"If it be your pleasure, Signore, I would rather see what St. Anthony may do for an old fisherman, who has prayed to him, night and morning, these sixty years?"

"It is thy right; and as thou seemest content with it, keep the place thou hast in the rear. It is only occupying it a little earlier than thou wouldst otherwise. Now, recall the rules of the games, hardy gondoliers, and make thy last appeal to thy patrons. There is to be no crossing or other foul expedients; naught except ready oars and nimble wrists. He who varies needlessly from his line until he leadeth, shall be recalled by name; and whoever is guilty of any act to spoil the sports, or otherwise to offend the patricians, shall be both checked and punished. Be ready for the signal."

The assistant, who was in a strongly manned boat, fell back a little, while runners, similarly equipped, went ahead to prepare the curious from the water. These preparations were scarcely made, when a signal floated on the nearest dome. It was repeated on the campanile, and a gun was fired at the arsenal. A deep but suppressed murmur arose in the throng, which was as quickly succeeded by suspense.

Each gondolier had suffered the bows of his boat to incline slightly toward the left shore of the canal, as the jockey is seen at the starting-post to turn his courser aside, in order to repress its ardour, or divert its attention. But the first long and broad sweep of the oar brought them all in a line again, and away they glided in a body.

For the first few minutes there was no difference in speed, nor any sign by which the instructed might detect the probable evidence of defeat or success. The whole ten which formed the front line skimmed the water with an equal velocity, beak to beak, as if some secret attraction held each in its place, while the humble, though equally light bark of the fisherman steadily kept its position in the rear.

The boats were soon held in command. The oars got their justest poise and widest sweep, and the wrists of the men accustomed to their play. The line began to waver. It undulated, the glittering prow of one protruding beyond the others; and then it changed its form. Enrico of Fusina shot ahead, and, privileged by success, he insensibly sheered more into the centre of the canal, avoiding by the change the eddies, and the other obstructions of the shore. This manœuvre, which, in the language of the course, would have been called "taking the track," had the additional advantage of throwing upon those who followed some trifling impediment from the back-water. The sturdy and practised Bartolomeo of the Lido, as his companions usually called him, came next,

occupying the space on his leader's quarter, where he suffered least from the reaction caused by the stroke of his oar. The gondolier of Don Camillo, also, soon shot out of the crowd, and was seen plying his arms vigorously still farther to the right, and a little in the rear of Bartolomeo. Then came, in the centre of the canal, and near as might be in the rear of the triumphant waterman of the main, a dense body, with little order and varying positions, compelling each other to give way, and otherwise increasing the difficulties of their struggle. More to the left, and so near to the palaces as barely to allow room for the sweep of his oar, was the masked competitor, whose progress seemed retarded by some unseen cause, for he gradually fell behind all the others, until several boats' lengths of open water lay between him and even the group of his nameless opponents. Still he applied his arms steadily, and with sufficient skill. As the interest of mystery had been excited in his favour, a rumour passed up the canal that the young cavalier had been little favoured by fortune in the choice of a boat. Others, who reflected more deeply on causes, whispered of the folly of one of his habits, taking the risk of mortification by a competition with men whose daily labour had hardened their sinews, and whose practice enabled them to judge closely of every chance of the race. But when the eyes of the multitude turned from the cluster of passing boats to the solitary barge of the fisherman, who came singly on the rear, admiration was again turned to derision.

Antonio had cast aside the cap he wore of wont and the few straggling hairs that were left streamed about his hollow temples, leaving the whole of his swarthy features exposed to view. More than once, as the gondola came on, his eyes turned aside reproachfully, as if he keenly felt the stings of so many unlicensed tongues applied to feelings which, though blunted by his habits and condition, were far from extinguished. Laugh rose above laugh, however, and taunt succeeded taunt more bitterly, as the boats came among the gorgeous palaces which lined the canal nearer to the goal. It was not that the owners of these lordly piles indulged in the unfeeling triumph, but their dependants, constantly subject themselves to the degrading influence of a superior presence, let loose the long-pent torrents of their arrogance on the head of the first unresisting subject which offered.

Antonio bore all these jibes manfully, if not in tranquillity, and always without retort, until he again approached the spot occupied by his companions of the Lagunes. Here his eye sunk under the reproaches, and his oar faltered. The taunts and denunciations increased as he lost ground, and there was a moment when the rebuked and humbled spirit of the old man seemed about to relinquish the contest. But dashing a hand across his brow, as if to clear a sight which had become dimmed and confused, he continued to ply the oar, and happily he was soon past the point most trying to his resolution. From this moment the cries against the fisherman diminished, and as the Bucentaur, though still distant, was now in sight, interest in the issue of the race absorbed all other feelings.

Enrico still kept the lead; but the judges of the gondoliers still began to detect signs of exhaustion in his faltering stroke. The waterman of the Lido pressed him hard, and the Calabrian was drawing more into a line with them both. At this moment, too, the masked competitor exhibited a force and skill that none had expected to see in one of his supposed rank. His body was thrown more upon the effort of the oar, and as his leg was stretched behind to aid the stroke, it discovered a volume of muscle, and an excellence of proportion that excited murmurs of applause. The consequence was soon apparent. His gondola glided past the crowd in the centre of the canal, and by a change that was nearly insensible, he became the fourth in the race. The shouts which rewarded his success had scarcely parted from the multitude, ere their admiration was called to a new and an entirely unexpected aspect in the struggle.

Left to his own exertions, and less annoyed by that derision and contempt which often defeat even more generous exertions, Antonio had drawn nearer to the crowd of nameless competitors. Though undistinguished in this narrative, there were seen, in that group of gondoliers, faces well known on the canals of Venice, as belonging to watermen, in whose dexterity and force the city took pride. Either favoured by his isolated position, or availing himself of the embarrassment these men gave to each other, the despised fisherman was seen a little on their left, coming up abreast with a stroke and velocity that promised farther success. The expectation was quickly realized. He passed them all amid a dead and wondering silence, and took his station as fifth in the struggle.

From this moment all interest in those who formed the vulgar mass was lost. Every eye was turned toward the front, where the strife increased at each stroke of the oar, and where the issue began to assume a new and doubtful character. The exertions of the waterman of Fusina were seemingly redoubled, though his boat went no faster. The gondola of Bartolomeo shot past him; it was followed by those of Gino and the masked gondolier, while not a cry betrayed the breathless interest of the multitude. But when the boat of Antonio also swept ahead, there arose such a hum of voices as escapes a throng, when a sudden and violent change of feeling is produced in their wayward sentiments. Enrico was frantic with the disgrace. He urged every power of his frame to avert the dishonour with the desperate energy of an Italian, and then he cast himself into the bottom of the gondola, tearing his hair and weeping in agony. His example was followed by those in the rear, though with more governed feelings, for they shot aside among the boats which lined the canal, and were lost to view.

From this open and unexpected abandonment of the struggle, the spectators got the surest evidence of its desperate character. But as a man has little sympathy for the unfortunate, when his feelings are excited by competition, the defeated

were quickly forgotten. The name of Bartolomeo was borne high upon the winds by a thousand voices, and his fellows of the Piazzetta and the Lido called upon him aloud to die for the honour of their craft. Well did the sturdy gondolier answer to their wishes, for palace after palace was left behind, and no further change was made in the relative positions of the boats. But, like his predecessors, the leader redoubled his efforts with a diminished effect, and Venice had the mortification of seeing a stranger leading one of the most brilliant of her regattas. Bartolomeo no sooner lost place, than Gino, the masker, and the despised Antonio in turn shot by, leaving him who had so lately been first in the race, the last. He did not, however, relinquish the strife, but continued to struggle with the energy of one who merited a better fortune.

When this unexpected and entirely new character was given to the contest, there still remained a broad sheet of water between the advancing gondolas and the goal. Gino led, and with many favourable symptoms of his being able to maintain his advantage. He was encouraged by the shouts of the multitude, who now forgot his Calabrian origin in his success, while many of the servingmen of his master cheered him on by name. All would not do. The masked waterman, for the first time, threw the grandeur of his skill and force into the oar. The ashen instrument bent to the power of an arm, whose strength appeared to increase at will, and the movements of his body became rapid as the leaps of the greyhound. The pliant gondola obeyed, and amid a shout which passed from the Piazzetta to the Rialto, it glided ahead.

If success gives force and increases the physical and moral energies, there is a fearful and certain reaction in defeat. The follower of Don Camillo was no exception to the general law, and when the masked competitor passed him, the boat of Antonio followed as if it were impelled by the same strokes. The distance between the two leading gondolas even now seemed to lessen, and there was a moment of breathless interest, when all there expected to see the fisherman, in despite of his years and boat, shooting past his rival.

But expectation was deceived. He of the mask, notwithstanding his previous efforts, seemed to sport with the toil, so ready was the sweep of his oar, so sure its stroke, and so vigorous the arm by which it was impelled. Nor was Antonio an antagonist to despise. If there was less of the grace of a practised gondolier of the canals in his attitudes, than in those of his companions, there was no relaxation in the force of his sinews. They sustained him to the last with that enduring power which had been begotten by threescore years of unremitting labour, and while his still athletic form was exerted to the utmost, there appeared no failing of its energies.

A few moments sent the leading gondolas several lengths ahead of their nearest followers. The dark beak of the fisherman's boat hung upon the quarter of the more showy bark of his antagonist,

36
2 A 2

but it could do no more. The port was open before them, and they glanced by church, palace, barge, mystick, and felucca, without the slightest inequality in their relative speed. The masked waterman glanced a look behind, as if to calculate his advantage, and then bending again to his pliant oar, he spoke loud enough to be heard only by him who pressed so hard upon his track.

"Thou hast deceived me, fisherman!" he said; "there is more of manhood in thee, yet, than I had thought."

"If there is manhood in my arms, there is childishness and sorrow at the heart;" was the reply.

"Dost thou so prize a golden bauble? Thou art second; be content with thy lot."

"It will not do; I must be foremost, or I have wearied my old limbs in vain!"

This brief dialogue was uttered with an ease that showed how far use had accustomed both to powerful bodily efforts, and with a firmness of tones that few could have equalled in a moment of so great physical effort. The masker was silent, but his purpose seemed to waver. Twenty strokes of his powerful oar-blade and the goal was attained: but his sinews were not so much extended, and that limb, which had shown so fine a development of muscle, was less swollen and rigid. The gondola of old Antonio glided abeam.

"Push thy soul into the blade," muttered he of the mask, "or thou wilt yet be beaten!"

The fisherman threw every effort of his body on the coming effort, and he gained a fathom. Another stroke caused the boat to quiver to its centre, and the water curled from its bows like the ripple of a rapid. Then the gondola darted between the two goal-barges, and the little flags that marked the point of victory fell into the water. The action was scarce noted, ere the glittering beak of the masker shot past the eyes of the judges, who doubted for an instant on whom success had fallen. Gino was not long behind, and after him came Bartolomeo, fourth and last, in the best-contested race which had ever been seen on the waters of Venice.

When the flags fell, men held their breaths in suspense. Few knew the victor, so close had been the struggle. But a flourish of the trumpets soon commanded attention, and then a herald proclaimed that—

"Antonio, a fisherman of the Lagunes, favoured by his holy patron of the Miraculous Draught, had borne away the prize of gold—while a waterman, who wore his face concealed, but who hath trusted to the care of the blessed San Giovanni of the Wilderness, is worthy of the silver prize, and that the third had fallen to the fortunes of Gino of Calabria, a servitor of the illustrious Don Camillo Monforte, Duca di Sant' Agata, and lord of many Neapolitan Seignories."

When this formal announcement was made, there succeeded a silence like that of the tomb. Then there arose a general shout among the living mass, which bore on high the name of Antonio, as if they celebrated the success of some conqueror. All feeling of contempt was lost in the influence of his triumph. The fishermen of the Lagunes, who so lately had loaded their aged companion with contumely, shouted for his glory with a zeal that manifested the violence of the transition from mortification to pride, and, as has ever been and ever will be the meed of success, he who was thought least likely to obtain it was most greeted with praise and adulation, when it was found that the end had disappointed expectation. Ten thousand voices were lifted in proclaiming his skill and victory, and young and old, the fair, the gay, the noble, the winner of sequins and he who lost, struggled alike to catch a glimpse of the humble old man, who had so unexpectedly wrought this change of sentiment in the feelings of a multitude.

Antonio bore his triumph meekly. When his gondola had reached the goal, he checked its course, and, without discovering any of the usual signs of exhaustion, he remained standing, though the deep heaving of his broad and tawny chest proved that his powers had been taxed to their utmost. He smiled as the shouts arose on his ear, for praise is grateful even to the meek; still he seemed oppressed with an emotion of a character deeper than pride. Age had somewhat dimmed his eye, but it was now full of hope. His features worked, and a single burning drop fell on each rugged cheek. The fisherman then breathed more freely.

Like his successful antagonist, the waterman of the mask betrayed none of the debility which usually succeeds great bodily exertion. His knees were motionless, his hands still grasped the oar firmly, and he too kept his feet with a steadiness that showed the physical perfection of his frame. On the other hand, both Gino and Bartolomeo sunk in their respective boats, as they gained the goal in succession; and so exhausted was each of these renowned gondoliers, that several moments elapsed before either had breath for speech. It was during this momentary pause that the multitude proclaimed its sympathy with the victor by their longest and loudest shouts. The noise had scarcely died away, however, before a herald summoned Antonio of the Lagunes, the masked waterman of the Blessed St. John of the Wilderness, and Gino the Calabrian, to the presence of the doge, whose princely hand was to bestow the promised prizes of the regatta.

VENICE AT NIGHT.
FROM THE SAME.

THE moon was at the height. Its rays fell in a flood on the swelling domes and massive roofs of Venice, while the margin of the town was brilliantly defined by the glittering bay. The natural and gorgeous setting was more than worthy of that picture of human magnificence; for at that moment, rich as was the queen of the Adriatic in her works of art, the grandeur of her public monuments, the number and splendour of her palaces, and most else that the ingenuity and ambition of man could attempt, she was but secondary in the glories of the hour.

Above was the firmament gemmed with worlds, and sublime in immensity. Beneath lay the broad expanse of the Adriatic, endless to the eye, tranquil as the vault it reflected, and luminous with its borrowed light. Here and there a low island, reclaimed from the sea by the patient toil of a thousand years, dotted the Lagunes, burdened by the group of some conventual dwellings, or picturesque with the modest roofs of a hamlet of the fishermen. Neither oar, nor song, nor laugh, nor flap of sail, nor jest of mariner disturbed the stillness. All in the near view was clothed in midnight loveliness, and all in the distance bespoke the solemnity of nature at peace. The city and the Lagunes, the gulf and the dreamy Alps, the interminable plain of Lombardy, and the blue void of heaven lay alike in a common and grand repose.

RAISING THE WIND.
FROM THE CHAINBEARER.

"JAAP"—I asked of my companion, as we drew near to the hamlet where I intended to pass the night, and the comforts of a warm supper on a sharp frosty evening began to haunt my imagination—"Jaap, how much money may you have about you?"

"I, Masser Mordaunt!—Golly! but dat a berry droll question, sah!"

"I ask, because my own stock is reduced to just one York shilling, which goes by the name of only a ninepence in this part of the world."

"Dat berry little, to tell 'e trut', sah, for two gentleum, and two large, hungry hosses. Berry little, indeed, sah! I wish he war' more."

"Yet, I have not a copper more. I gave one thousand two hundred dollars for the dinner and baiting and oats, at noon."

"Yes, sah—but, dat conternental, sah, I supposes—no great t'ing, a'ter all."

"It's a great thing in sound, Jaap, but not much when it comes to the teeth, as you perceive. Nevertheless, we must eat and drink, and our nags must eat too—I suppose *they* may *drink*, without paying."

"Yes, sah—dat true 'nough, yah—yah—yah" —how easily that negro laughed!—"But 'e cider wonnerful good in dis part of 'e country, young masser; just needer sweet nor sour—den he strong as 'e jackass."

"Well, Jaap, how are we to get any of this good cider, of which you speak?"

"You t'ink, sah, dis part of 'e country been talk to much lately 'bout Patty Rism and 'e country, sah?"

"I am afraid Patty has been overdone here, as well as in most other counties."

I may observe here, that Jaap always imagined the beautiful creature he had heard so much extolled, and commended for her comeliness and virtue, was a certain young woman of this name, with whom all Congress was unaccountably in love at the same time.

"Well, den, sah, dere no hope, but our wits. Let me be masser to-night, and you mind ole Jaap, if he want good supper. Jest ride ahead, Masser Mordaunt, and give he order like General Littlepage son, and leave it all to ole Jaap."

As there was not much to choose, I did ride on, and soon ceased to hear the hoofs of the negro's horse at my heels. I reached the inn an hour ere Jaap appeared, and was actually seated at a capital supper before he rode up, as one belonging only to himself. Jaap had taken off the Littlepage emblems, and had altogether a most independent air. His horse was stabled alongside of mine, and I soon found that he himself was at work on the remnants of my supper, as they retreated toward the kitchen.

A traveller of my appearance was accommodated with the best parlour, as a matter of course; and, having appeased my appetite, I sat down to read some documents that were connected with the duty I was on. No one could have imagined that I had only a York shilling, which is a Pennsylvania "levy," or a Connecticut "ninepence," in my purse; for my air was that of one who could pay for all he wanted; the certainty that, in the long run, my host could not be a loser, giving me a proper degree of confidence. I had just got through with the documents, and was thinking how I should employ the hour or two that remained until it would be time to go to bed, when I heard Jaap tuning his fiddle in the bar-room. Like most negroes, the fellow had an ear for music, and had been indulged in his taste, until he played as well as half the country fiddlers that were to be met.

The sound of a fiddle in a small hamlet, of a cool October evening, was certain of its result. In half an hour, the smiling landlady came to invite me to join the company, with the grateful information I should not want for a partner, the prettiest girl in the place having come in late, and being still unprovided for. On entering the bar-room, I was received with plenty of awkward bows and curtsies, but with much simple and well-meaning hospitality. Jaap's own salutations were very elaborate, and altogether of a character to prevent the suspicion of our ever having met before.

The dancing continued for more than two hours with spirit, when the time admonished the village maidens of the necessity of retiring. Seeing an indication of the approaching separation, Jaap held out his hat to me, in a respectful manner, when I magnificently dropped my shilling into it, in a way to attract attention, and passed it round among the males of the party. One other gave a shilling, two clubbed and actually produced a quarter, several threw in sixpences, or fourpence-halfpennies, and coppers made up the balance. By way of climax, the landlady, who was goodlooking and loved dancing, publicly announced that the fiddler and his horse should go scot free, until he left the place. By these ingenious means of Jaap's, I found in my purse next morning seven-and-sixpence in silver, in addition to my own shilling, besides copper enough to keep a negro in cider for a week.

I have often laughed over Jaap's management, though I would not permit him to repeat it.

ALEXANDER H. EVERETT.

[Born 1790. Died 1847.]

RICHARD EVERETT, the first American ancestor of ALEXANDER HILL EVERETT, was one of the earliest settlers of Dedham, in Massachusetts, his name appearing in the public records of that town for the year 1630. His grandfather, Ebenezer Everett, was a respectable farmer, and his father, Oliver Everett, was apprenticed to a carpenter, but on coming of age, prepared himself for college, and having obtained a degree at Cambridge, and completed his theological studies, was ordained minister of the New South Church, in Boston, in 1782. At the end of ten years, in which he had acquired much reputation for talents, declining health compelled him to relinquish his position, and he removed to Dorchester, where he was engaged in the cultivation of a small farm and in the discharge of the duties of a Justice of the Common Pleas, until his death, in 1802.

Alexander H. Everett was born in Boston on the nineteenth of March, 1790. He was prepared for college in the free school of Dorchester, and entered Harvard in the thirteenth year of his age. Though the youngest of his class, he graduated with the highest honours, in 1806, and at the end of a year, passed as assistant teacher in the Phillips Exeter Academy, commenced the study of the law in the office of John Quincy Adams, in Boston. In this city he became a member of the club formed about that time by several gentlemen of taste an leisure to conduct The Monthly Anthology, in which miscellany appeared his first essays in literature. In 1809 he accompanied Mr. Adams on his mission to Russia, and after studying in St. Petersburgh for two years the modern languages, public law, political economy, and history, proceeded to London, where he remained about a year, except during a short visit to Paris, in 1812. Upon the declaration of war he returned to the United States, was admitted to the bar, and opened an office in Boston; but devoting more attention to literature and politics than to his profession, had probably few clients, and so accepted without much hesitation the office of Secretary of Legation to the Netherlands. Having remained a year or two in this situation he returned home, but on the retirement of Mr. Eustis from that mission, in 1818, he was appointed to succeed him as chargé d'affaires, and continued to occupy this post until 1824.

A portion of his leisure during this period was employed in the composition of Europe, or a General Survey of the Political Situation of the Principal Powers, with Conjectures on their Future Prospects, published in London and Boston in 1821. This work was translated into German, French and Spanish, and the German version was edited by Professor Jacobi, of the University of Halle. In the following year he published in the same cities New Ideas on Population, with Remarks on the Theories of Godwin and Malthus. This work is able and ingenious, and though in most respects original, is not so much a proposition of novelties on the subject as a defence of the old and common opinion against the modern and infidel notion of Mr. Malthus and his followers that an increase of population, except in some peculiar cases, is a public misfortune, which it is the business of wise legislators to check. Lord Brougham declared in the House of Commons that he could see no error in the argument of Malthus, but that he was so disgusted with his conclusions that he would vote a civic crown to any one who would prove his theory to be untrue. Many volumes were written on the subject by able men, but none of them met the difficulty. Mr. Everett's plan is to give men liberty, to permit them everywhere to enjoy the fruits of their labour, which, being more productive in proportion to the density of the population, because more skilfully applied, would, through the distributing processes of trade, invariably furnish a supply of the means of subsistence equal to the demand. He regards the progress of population as a principle of abundance rather than as one of scarcity. He has since discussed the same subject in a correspondence with Professor George Tucker, of the University of Virginia, which was published in 1845.

During his residence in the Netherlands Mr. Everett also wrote many articles for the North American Review,* which at this time was edited by his brother Edward, and in the zenith of its popularity.

In 1824 he returned to the United States, on leave of absence, and in the spring of the following year was appointed by President Adams minister to Spain. At this time the Spanish mission was one of much interest and importance, on account of the state of our relations with that court, partly growing out of our recognition of the independence of the Spanish American states, and Mr. Everett's judicious and arduous labours not only gave abundant satisfaction to his countrymen, but were productive of much advantage to the new nations. In the midst of his official duties he found leisure for literary pursuits, and besides many elaborate articles in the North American Review,† wrote his work entitled America, or a General Survey of the Political Situation of the Several Powers of the Western Continent, with Conjectures on their Future Prospects. The greater part of it is devoted to the consideration of the position of our own country in the general political system, of our condition, and of our prospective situation and influence on the fortunes of the world; and he dwells with enthusiasm on his anticipations of the continued progress and final success of the cause of civilization and humanity throughout this whole continent. It was much read at home, in Great Britain, and in central and southern Europe, where it was republished in three or four languages. Its style is very good, though by no means deserving of the praises lavished upon it by a friendly critic in the North American Review, soon after its appearance. Mr. Everett also served the cause of letters while in Spain by inviting Mr. Irving to Madrid and

procuring for him access to the public archives from which he drew many of the materials for his Life of Columbus and other works on Spanish subjects, and by aiding Mr. Prescott, Mr. Longfellow and other Americans in their literary pursuits.

He returned to the United States in the autumn of 1829, and determining to devote himself chiefly to literature, became soon after proprietor and editor of the North American Review, which he conducted for about five years. His papers* during this period were on a considerable variety of subjects, and were generally indicative of erudition and a wide range of information; but they lacked the condensation, point and vivacity essential in writings for such periodicals, and I believe the Review gained little in reputation or influence while he was thus connected with it.

From 1830 to 1835 he was a senator or representative in the legislature of Massachusetts; in 1831 a delegate from that state in the convention at Baltimore which nominated Mr. Clay for the presidency, and author of the address in which this body urged the election of its candidate; and in 1833 a leading member of the Tariff Convention in the city of New York, and as chairman of one of its committees prepared the memorial which it addressed to Congress as a reply to one written by Mr. Gallatin for the Free Trade Convention held in Philadelphia. After the close of the first term of President Jackson's administration he acted with the democratic party, advocated its policy in various writings and public speeches, and on several occasions was among its unsuccessful candidates for elective offices.

His attention was never long diverted, however, from literary studies, and in addition to his political addresses he delivered many orations† before societies of scholars and

* His principal contributions are on the following subjects:—French Dramatic Literature; Louis Bonaparte; Private Life of Voltaire; Literature of the Eighteenth Century; Dialogue on Representative Government, between Dr. Franklin and President Montesquieu; Bernardin de St. Pierre; Madame de Staël; J. J. Rousseau; Mirabeau; Schiller; Chinese Grammar; Cicero on Government; Memoirs of Madame Campan; Degerando's History of Philosophy; Lord Byron.

† He wrote, while in Spain, articles under the following titles:—M'Culloch's Political Economy; Authorship of Gil Blas; Baron de Staël's Letters on England; Paraguay; The Art of Being Happy; Politics of Europe; Chinese Manners; Irving's Columbus; Definitions in Political Economy by Malthus; Cousin's Intellectual Philosophy; Canova.

* The most important ones are on the following subjects: British Opinions on the Protecting System; Politics of Europe; Tone of British Criticism; Stewart's Moral Philosophy; The American System; Life of Henry Clay; Life and Writings of Sir James Mackintosh; Irving's Alhambra; Nullification; The Union and the States; Hamilton's Men and Manners in America; Early Literature of Modern Europe; Early Literature of France; Progress and Limits of Social improvement; Origin and Character of the Old Parties; Character of Jefferson; Dr. Channing; Thomas Carlyle.

† His published orations are on The Progress and Limits of the Improvement of Society; The French Revolution; The Constitution of the United States; State

philanthropists, and wrote largely for the Boston Quarterly Review, the Democratic Review, and other periodicals.*

In the winter of 1840 he resided in the Island of Cuba, as a confidential agent of the government, and while there was appointed President of Jefferson College in Louisiana. He accepted this office and entered upon the discharge of its duties in June, 1841, but ill health did not permit him long to retain it, and he returned to New England.

In 1845 he published, under the title of Critical and Miscellaneous Essays to which are added a Few Poems, a selection from his con-

tributions to the reviews and other periodicals. A second volume appeared in 1847.

Soon after the return of Mr. Caleb Cushing from his mission to China, Mr. Everett was appointed to succeed him as Minister Plenipotentiary to that empire, and he sailed for Canton in a national ship on the fourth of July, 1845. Arriving at Rio de Janeiro he was detained by illness, and despairing of recovery he returned to the United States; but in the summer of 1846 his health was sufficiently restored for him to proceed again upon the voyage, and he succeeded in reaching Canton, but died there on the 28th of June, 1847.

BOOK MAKING.
FROM AN ARTICLE ON MADAME DE SÉVIGNÉ.

It is remarkable that many of the best books of all sorts have been written by persons who, at the time of writing them, had no intention of becoming authors. Indeed, with a slight inclination to systemize and exaggerate, one might be almost tempted to maintain the position,—however paradoxical it may at first blush appear,—that no good book can be written in any other way; that the only literature of any value is that which grows indirectly out of the real action of society, intended directly to effect some other purpose; and that when a man sits down doggedly in his study, and says to himself, "I mean to write a good book," it is certain, from the necessity of the case, that the result will be a bad one.

To illustrate this by a few examples: Shakspeare, the Greek Dramatists, Lope and Calderon, Corneille, Racine, and Molière,—in short, all the dramatic poets of much celebrity, prepared their works for actual representation, at times when the drama was the favourite amusement. Their plays, when collected, make excellent books. At a later

of Polite Literature in England and the United States; Moral Character of the Literature of the last and present century; Literary Character of the Scriptures; Progress of Moral Science; Discovery of America by the Northmen; German Literature; Battle of New Orleans; Battle of Bunker Hill. This list, I believe, is incomplete.

* In the Quarterly Review he wrote chiefly or altogether on the Currency. In the Democratic Review his principal articles are entitled The Spectre Bridegroom, from Bürger; The Water King, a Legend of the Norse; The Grecian Gossips, imitated from Theocritus; The Worth of Woman, from Schiller; Enigma; The Framers of the Constitution (two articles); Mrs. Sigourney; Sketch of Harro Harring, The Texas Question; The Re-annexation of Texas; Contemporary Spanish Poetry; Greenough's Statue of Washington; The Young American; The Malthusian Theory discussed in Letters to Professor George Tucker; The Portress, a Ballad; The Funeral of Goethe, from Harro Harring.

period, when the drama had in a great measure gone out of fashion, Lord Byron, a man not inferior, perhaps, in poetical genius to any of the persons just mentioned, undertakes, without any view to the stage, to write a book of the same kind. What is the result? Something which, as Ninon de l'Enclos said of the young Marquis de Sévigné, has very much the character of fricasseed snow. Homer, again, or the Homerites, a troop of wandering minstrels, composed, probably without putting them to paper, certain songs and ballads, which they sung at the tables of the warriors and princes of their time. Some centuries afterwards, Pisistratus made them up into a book, which became the bible of Greece. Voltaire, whose genius was perhaps equal to that of any of the Homerites, attempted, in cold blood, to make just such a book; and here, again, the product called the Henriade is no book, but another lump of fricasseed snow. What are all your pretended histories? Fables, jest books, satires, apologies, any thing but what they profess to be. Bring together the correspondence of a distinguished public character, a Washington, a Wellington, and then, for the first time, you have a real history. Even in so small a matter as a common letter to a friend, if you write one for the sake of writing it, in order to produce a good letter as such, you will probably fail. Who ever read one of Pliny's precious specimens of affectation and formality, without wishing that he had perished in the same eruption of Vesuvius that destroyed his uncle? On the contrary, let one who has any thing to say to another at a distance, commit his thoughts to paper merely for the purpose of communicating them, and he will not only effect his immediate object, but, however humble may be his literary pretensions, will commonly write something that may be read with pleasure by an indifferent third person. In short, experience seems to show that every book, prepared with a view to mere book-making, is necessarily a sort of counterfeit, bearing the same relation to a real book which the juggling of the Egyptian magicians did to the miracles of Moses.

CLAIMS OF LITERATURE UPON AMERICANS.

FROM ORATIONS AND ADDRESSES.

INDEPENDENCE and liberty, the great political objects of all communities, have been secured to us by our glorious ancestors. In these respects, we are only required to *preserve* and transmit unimpaired to our posterity the inheritance which our fathers bequeathed to us. To the present, and to the following generations, is left the easier task of enriching, with arts and letters, the proud fabric of our national glory. Our Sparta is indeed a noble one. Let us then do our best for it.

Let me not, however, be understood to intimate, that the pursuits of literature or the finer arts of life, have been, at any period of our history, foreign to the people of this country. The founders of the colonies, the Winthrops, the Smiths, the Raleighs, the Penns, the Oglethorpes, were among the most accomplished scholars and elegant writers, as well as the loftiest and purest spirits of their time. Their successors have constantly sustained, in this respect, the high standard established by the founders. Education and Religion,—the two great cares of intellectual and civilized men,—were always with them the foremost objects of attention. The principal statesmen of the Revolution were persons of high literary cultivation; their public documents were declared, by Lord Chatham, to be equal to the finest specimens of Greek and Roman wisdom. In every generation, our country has contributed its full proportion of eminent writers. Need I mention names in proof of this? Recollect your Edwards, erecting, in this remote region, the standard of Orthodoxy, for enlightened Protestant Europe. Recollect your Franklin, instructing the philosophers of the elder world in the deepest mysteries of science; her statesmen in political economy, her writers in the forms of language. In the present generation, your Irvings, your Coopers, your Bryants, with their distinguished contemporaries, form, perhaps, the brightest constellation that remains in the literary hemisphere, since the greater lights to which I have pointed your attention already were eclipsed; while the loftier heights of mathematical, moral and political science are occupied with not inferior distinction, by your Bowditches, your Adamses, your Channings, your Waylands and your Websters.

In this respect, then, our fathers did their part; our friends of the present generation are doing theirs, and doing it well. But thus far the relative position of England and the United States has been such that our proportional contribution to the common literature was naturally a small one. England, by her great superiority in wealth and population, was of course the head-quarters of science and learning. All this is rapidly changing. You are already touching the point when your wealth and population will equal those of England. The superior rapidity of your progress will, at no distant period, give you the ascendency. It will then belong to your position to take the lead in arts and letters, as in policy, and to give the tone to the literature of the language. Let it be your care and study not to show yourselves unequal to this high calling,—to vindicate the honour of the new world in this generous and friendly competition with the old. You will perhaps be told that literary pursuits will disqualify you for the active business of life. Heed not the idle assertion. Reject it as a mere imagination, inconsistent with principle, unsupported by experience. Point out to those who make it, the illustrious characters who have reaped in every age the highest honours of studious and active exertion. Show them Demosthenes, forging by the light of the midnight lamp those thunderbolts of eloquence, which

" Shook the arsenal and fulmined over Greece—
To Macedon and Artaxerxes' throne."

Ask then if Cicero would have been hailed with rapture as the father of his country, if he had not been its pride and pattern in philosophy and letters. Inquire whether Cæsar, or Frederick, or Bonaparte, or Wellington, or Washington, fought the worse because they knew how to write their own commentaries. Remind them of Franklin, tearing at the same time the lightning from heaven, and the sceptre from the hands of the oppressor. Do they say to you that study will lead you to skepticism? Recall to their memory the venerable names of Bacon, Milton, Newton and Locke. Would they persuade you that devotion to learning will withdraw your steps from the paths of pleasure? Tell them they are mistaken. Tell them that the only true pleasures are those which result from the diligent exercise of all the faculties of body, and mind, and heart, in pursuit of noble ends by noble means. Repeat to them the ancient apologue of the youthful Hercules, in the pride of strength and beauty, giving up his generous soul to the worship of virtue. Tell them your choice is also made. Tell them, with the illustrious Roman orator, you would rather be in the wrong with Plato, than in the right with Epicurus. Tell them that a mother in Sparta would have rather seen her son brought home from battle a corpse upon his shield, than dishonoured by its loss. Tell them that your mother is America, your battle the warfare of life, your shield the breast-plate of Religion.

GREENOUGH'S STATUE OF WASHINGTON.

GREENOUGH'S great work has surpassed my expectations, high as they were. It is truly sublime. The statue is of colossal grandeur; about twice the size of life. The hero is represented in a sitting posture. A loose drapery covers the lower part of the figure, and is carried up over the right arm, which is extended, with the elbow bent and the forefinger of the hand pointed upward. The left arm is stretched out a little above the thigh: and the hand holds a Roman sword reversed.

The design of the artist was, of course, to indicate the ascendency of the civic and humane over the military virtues, which distinguished the whole career of Washington, and which forms the great glory of his character. It was not intended to bring before the eye the precise circumstance under which he resigned his commission as commander-in-chief. This would have required a standing posture and a modern military costume ; and, without an accompanying group of members of Congress, would have been an incomplete work. The sword reversed, and the finger pointed upward, indicate the moral sentiment, of which the resignation of his commission, as commander-in-chief, was the strongest evidence, without the details, which were inconsistent with the general plan.

The face is that of Stuart's portrait, modified so as to exhibit the highest point of manly vigour and maturity. Though not corresponding exactly with any of the existing portraits, it is one of the aspects which the countenance of Washington must necessarily have worn in the course of his progress through life, and is obviously the proper one for the purpose. In expression, the countenance is admirably adjusted to the character of the subject and the intention of the work. It is stamped with dignity, and radiant with benevolence and moral beauty.

The execution is finished to the extreme point of perfection, as well in the accessories as in the statue itself. The seat is a massy arm-chair of antique form and large dimensions, the sides of which are covered with exquisitely wrought bas-reliefs. The subject of one is the infant Hercules strangling the serpent in his cradle : that of the other, Apollo guiding the four steeds that draw the chariot of the sun. The back of the chair is of open work. At the left corner is placed a small statue of Columbus, holding in his hand a sphere, which he is examining with fixed attention : at the right corner is a similar small statue of an Indian chief. The effect of these comparatively diminutive images is to heighten by contrast the impression of grandeur, which is made by the principal figure.....

I make no pretensions to connoisseurship in the art of sculpture, and judge of the merit of the work merely by the impression which it makes upon my own mind ; but I can say for myself, that after seeing the most celebrated specimens of ancient and modern sculpture to be found in Europe, including the Laocoon and the Apollo Belvedere, with the finest productions of Canova, Thorwaldsen, Sergell and Chantry, I consider the Washington of Greenough as superior to any of them, and as the master-piece of the art. The hint seems to have been taken from the Olympian Jupiter of Phidias, who said himself that he had caught the inspiration under which he conceived the plan of that great glory of ancient sculpture, from a passage in the Iliad. In this way the noble work of Greenough connects itself by the legitimate filiation of kindred genius, transmitting its magnetic impulses through the long lines of intervening centuries with the poetry of Homer. The vast dimensions of the Jupiter of Phidias may have made it to the eye a more imposing and majestic monument; but if the voluntary submission of transcendant power to the moral law of duty be, as it certainly is, a more sublime spectacle than any positive exercise of the same power over inferior natures, then the subject of the American sculptor is more truly divine than that of his illustrious prototype in Greece. When Jupiter shakes Olympus with his nod, the imagination is affected by a grand display of energy, but the heart remains untouched. When Washington, with an empire in his grasp, resigns his sword to the President of Congress, admiration of his great intellectual power is mingled with the deepest emotions of delightful sympathy.

THE DURABILITY OF REPUTATION.

FROM MISCELLANIES.

The age of Louis XIV. is universally considered as one of the brightest periods in the history of civilization. What gave it this splendid preëminence ? Louis XIV. himself, although he possessed great qualities and eclipsed the glory of most of his predecessors, now comes in for a very moderate share of the attention we bestow on the time in which he lived. His generals, Condé, Turenne, Luxemburg, and the rest,—unquestionably men of distinguished talent,—were yet in no way superior to the thunderbolts of war that have wasted mankind from age to age, and are now forgotten. His ministers, Fouquet, Colbert, Louvois, have left no marked traces in history. The celebrated beauties that charmed all eyes at the court festivals have long since mouldered into dust. Yet we still cling with the deepest interest to the memory of the age of Louis XIV., because it was the age of Pascal and Corneille, of Racine, Molière, and La Fontaine, of Bossuet, Fenelon, Bourdaloue, Massillon, La Bruyère, La Rochefoucalt, and Madame de Sévigné. The time will probably come, in the progress of civilization, when the military and civic glories of this period will be still more lightly, because more correctly, estimated than they are now : when the King, who could make war upon Holland, because he was offended by the device of a bourgomaster's seal, and the general who burnt the Palatinate in cold blood, will be looked upon,—with all their refinement and merit of a certain kind,—as belonging essentially to the same class of semi-barbarians with the Tamerlanes and Attilas, the Rolands and the Red Jackets : when the Fouquets and Colberts will be considered as possessing a moral value very little higher than that of the squirrels and snakes, which they not inappropriately assumed as their emblems. But the maxims of La Rochefoucault will never lose their point, nor the poetry of Racine its charm. The graceful eloquence of Fenelon will flow for ever through the pages of Telemachus, and the latest posterity will listen with as much or even greater pleasure than their contemporaries to the discourses of Bossuet and Massillon. The masterly productions of these great men and their illustrious contemporaries will perpetuate to the 'last syllable of recorded time' the celebrity which they originally conferred upon the period when they lived, and crown with a light of perennial and unfading glory the age of Louis XIV.

JAMES HALL.

[Born 1793. Died 1868.]

JAMES HALL, a son of John Hall, formerly marshal for the District of Pennsylvania, was born in Philadelphia in 1793. Intending to educate him for the mercantile profession, his father placed him at an early age in a counting-house; but the business was not congenial to his tastes, and he soon quitted it to enter upon the study of the law, in which he was engaged on the breaking out of the war in 1812. He now joined the Washington Grays, a corps composed from the most respectable young men of the city, under Captain Condy Raguet, and marched to Camp Dupont, where he received a commission as lieutenant in the army of the United States. Transferred to the company of Captain Biddle, he proceeded to Canada, and distinguished himself in the battles of Chippewa, Lundy's Lane, and Niagara; and being despatched on a private mission to the enemy by General Brown, was detained, and finally compelled to find his way home by the St. Lawrence and Quebec. At the close of the war, disliking the inactivity and monotony of a military life in time of peace, he resumed the study of the law under Mr. James Ross, of Pittsburgh, who had long been intimately acquainted with his family, and on being admitted to the bar, resigned his commission and removed to Shawneetown, in Illinois.

Mr. Hall had already shown a decided predilection for literature and had written many spirited or graceful trifles for the gazettes, and he now became wedded to the occupation of an author by establishing a weekly newspaper and The Illinois Monthly Magazine, both of which were conducted by him several years with much industry and ability.

Descending the Ohio river on the way to his new home, in an ark, as a kind of boat on the western waters is called, he commenced a series of letters for publication in the Port Folio* at Philadelphia, which were subsequently rewritten, and printed in London under the title of Letters from the West. They form an interesting account of the natural and social condition of the western states as they were twenty years ago.*

Besides editing and publishing his newspaper and magazine, Mr. Hall practised successfully as a counsellor. He rose steadily in the estimation of the people; was appointed district attorney, and subsequently one of the justices of the Circuit Court; and on the reorganization of the judiciary was elected treasurer of the state. His new duties rendering it necessary for him to reside in the capital, he disposed of his property at Shawneetown and removed to Vandalia, where he remained until he lost his office by the accession to power of an opposing political party, when he went to Cincinnati, to practise his profession and continue his literary pursuits.

His first publication in Cincinnati was The Western Souvenir for 1829. Among the articles written for it by himself was a graceful poem entitled Wedded Love's First Home,† and several tales and sketches, and it contained pieces by Timothy Flint, Morgan Neville, and other authors, which were quite equal in their way to the best contents of the more elegant annuals published in the eastern cities. In 1832 he gave to the public his Legends of the West, of which a second edition was issued in the following year, and about the same time The Soldier's Bride and Other Tales. In 1833 he commenced The Western Monthly Magazine, a literary miscellany which was continued three years, and made attractive chiefly by his own various and numerous contributions. He also published in Philadelphia in 1833 The Harpe's Head, a Legend of Kentucky, in 1834 Tales of the Border, and in 1835 Statistics of the West, which in 1838 was reprinted, much enlarged, under the title of Notes on the Western States.

---

*Then edited by his brother, Mr. John E. Hall, who was also editor of the American Law Journal, and other works on jurisprudence.

*Letters from The West, containing Sketches of Scenery, Manners and Customs, and Anecdotes connected with the First Settlements of the western sections of the United States: By the Hon. Judge Hall. 1 vol. 8vo, pp. 386. London, Henry Colburn, 1828.
† See Poets and Poetry of America, 8th ed. page 538.

The splendidly illustrated work in three folio volumes entitled A History of the Indian Tribes of North America, with Biographical Sketches and Anecdotes of the Principal Chiefs, by Mr. Hall and Mr. T. L. McKenny, a large part of whose life had been passed in the service of the government as Indian agent, was begun about the year 1836, and finished in 1844. It contains one hundred and twenty portraits, engraved and coloured by Mr. Bowen, from original pictures by Mr. McKenny, and the literary part of it, which is understood to have been written chiefly by Mr. Hall, has much of the freshness and spirit, and to the common reader all of the interest, of the sketches by Audubon, or Wilson.

In 1845 Mr. Hall published in Wiley and Putnam's Library of American books The Wilderness and the War Path, a collection of tales illustrative of western life and manners, most of which had appeared in his earlier vo-

lumes. A new edition of his works, in four vols. revised by himself, was published about 1856. Judge Hall died in Cincinnati, in July, 1868.

Mr. Hall's writings are pervaded by a gentlemanly tone and spirit, and have touches of humour and reflective sentiment. The subjects of some of his happiest sketches are the early French settlers of Illinois. The manners and customs which have prevailed in this state he has depicted with much fidelity, though he has been less successful than some others in representing the frontier Indian, to whose character he seems to have given little attention. The descriptions of western scenery scattered through his works are generally graphic and truthful.

His Sketches of the West and Notes on the Western States are valuable for the information they contain, and will be likely to live longer than any of his other writings.

PETE FEATHERTON.
FROM THE WILDERNESS AND THE WAR PATH.

EVERY country has its superstitions, and will continue to have them, so long as men are blessed with lively imaginations, and while any portion of mankind remain ignorant of the causes of natural phenomena. That which cannot be reconciled with experience will always be attributed to supernatural influence; and those who know little, will imagine much more to exist than has ever been witnessed by their own senses. I am not displeased with this state of things, for the journey of life would be dull indeed, if those who travel it were confined for ever to the beaten highway, worn smooth by the sober feet of experience. To turnpikes, for our beasts of burden, I have no objection; but I cannot consent to the erection of railways for the mind, even though the architect be " wisdom, whose ways are pleasant, and whose paths are peace." It is sometimes agreeable to stray off into the wilderness which fancy creates, to recline in fairy bowers, and to listen to the murmurs of imaginary fountains. When the beaten road becomes tiresome, there are many sunny spots where the pilgrim may loiter with advantage —many shady paths, whose labyrinths may be traced with delight. The mountain and the vale, on whose scenery we gaze enchanted, derive new charms, when their deep caverns and gloomy recesses are peopled with imaginary beings.

But above all, the enlivening influence of fancy is felt when it illumines our firesides, giving to the wings of time, when they grow heavy, a brighter plumage, and a more sprightly motion. There are seasons when the spark of life within us seems to burn with less than its wonted vigour; the

blood crawls heavily through the veins; the contagious chillness seizes on our companions, and the sluggish hours roll painfully along. Something more than a common impulse is then required to awaken the indolent mind, and give a new tone to the flagging spirits. If necromancy draws her magic circle, we cheerfully enter the ring; if folly shakes her cap and bells, we are amused; a witch becomes an interesting personage, and we are even agreeably surprised by the companionable qualities of a ghost.

We, who live on the frontier, have little acquaintance with imaginary beings. These gentry never emigrate; they seem to have strong local attachments, which not even the charms of a new country can overcome. A few witches, indeed, were imported into New England by the Puritans; but were so badly used, that the whole race seems to have been disgusted with new settlements. With them the spirit of adventure expired, and the weird women of the present day wisely cling to the soil of the old countries. That we have but few ghosts will not be deemed a matter of surprise by those who have observed how miserably destitute we are of accommodations for such inhabitants. We have no baronial castles, nor ruined mansions;—no turrets crowned with ivy, nor ancient abbeys crumbling into decay; and it would be a paltry spirit who would be content to wander in the forest by silent rivers and solitary swamps.

It is even imputed to us as a reproach by enlightened foreigners, that our land is altogether populated with the living descendants of Adam— creatures with thews and sinews, who eat when they are hungry, laugh when they are tickled, and die when they are done living. The creatures of romance, say they, exist not in our territory. A witch, a ghost, or a brownie perishes in America, as a serpent is said to die the instant it touches the uncongenial soil of Ireland. This is true only in part. If we have no ghosts, we are not without miracles. Wonders have happened in these United States. Mysteries have occurred in the Valley of the Mississippi. Supernatural events have transpired on the borders of "the beautiful stream;" and in order to rescue my country from undeserved reproach, I shall proceed to narrate an authentic history which I received from the lips of the party principally concerned.

A clear morning had succeeded a stormy night in December; the snow laid ankle-deep upon the ground, and glittered on the boughs, while the bracing air and the cheerful sunbeams invigorated the animal creation, and called forth the tenants of the forest from their warm lairs and hidden lurking-places.

The inmates of a small cabin on the margin of the Ohio were commencing with the sun the business of the day. A stout, raw-boned forester plied his keen axe, and, lugging log after log, erected a pile on the ample hearth, sufficiently large to have rendered the last honours to the stateliest ox. A female was paying her morning visit to the cow-yard, where a numerous herd of cattle claimed her attention. The plentiful breakfast followed; corn-bread, milk, and venison covered the oaken board, while a tin coffee-pot of ample dimensions supplied the beverage which is seldom wanting at the morning repast of the substantial American farmer.

The breakfast over, Mr. Featherton reached down a long rifle from the ra'ters and commenced certain preparations, fraught with danger to the brute inhabitants of the forest. The lock was carefully examined, the screws tightened, the pan wiped, the flint renewed, and the springs oiled; and the keen eye of the backwoodsman glittered with an ominous lustre, as its glance rested on the destructive engine. His blue-eyed partner, leaning fondly on her husband's shoulder, essayed those coaxing and captivating blandishments, which every young wife so well understands, to detain her husband from the contemplated sport. Every pretext was urged with affectionate pertinacity which female ingenuity could supply;—the wind whistled bleakly over the hills, the snow lay deep in the valleys, the deer would surely not venture abroad in such bitter cold weather, the adventurous hunter might get his toes frost-bitten, and her own hours would be sadly lonesome in his absence. He smiled in silence at the arguments of his bride, for such she was, and continued his preparations with the cool, but good-natured determination of one who is not to be turned from his purpose.

He was indeed a person with whom such arguments, except the last, would not be very likely to prevail. Mr. Peter Featherton, or as he was familiarly called by all who knew him, Pete Featherton, was a bold, rattling Kentuckian of twenty-five, who possessed the characteristic peculiarities of his countrymen—good and evil—in a striking degree. His red hair and sanguine complexion announced an ardent temperament; his tall form and bony limbs indicated an active frame inured to hardships; his piercing eye and high cheek-bones evinced the keenness and resolution of his mind. He was adventurous, frank, and social—boastful, credulous, illiterate, and at times wonderfully addicted to the marvellous. His imagination was a warm and fruitful soil, in which "tall oaks from little acorns grew," and his vocabulary was overstocked with superlatives. He loved his wife—no mistake about that—but next to her his affections entwined themselves about his gun, and expanded over his horse; he was true to his friends, never missed an election day, turned his back upon a frolic, nor affected to dislike a social glass.

He believed that the best qualities of all countries were combined in Kentucky; and had the most whimsical manner of expressing his national attachments. He was firmly convinced that the battle of the Thames was the most sanguinary conflict of the age—"a raal reg'lar skrimmage,"—and extolled Colonel Dick Johnson as a "severe old colt." He would admit freely that Napoleon was a great genius—Metternich, Castlereagh "and them fellows" knew "a thing or two," but then they "were no part of a priming to Henry Clay."

When entirely "at himself"—to use his own language—that is to say, when duly sober, Pete was friendly and rational, courteous, and considerate, and a better tempered fellow never shouldered a rifle. But he was a social man, who was liable to be "overtaken," and let him get a glass too much, and there was no end to his extravagance. Then it was that his genius bloomed and brought forth strange boasts and strong oaths, his loyalty to old Kentuck waxed warm, and his faith in his horse, his gun, and his own manhood grew into idolatry. Always bold and self-satisfied, and habitually energetic in the expression of his predilections, he now became invested with the agreeable properties of the snapping-turtle, the alligator, and the steamboat, and gifted with the most affable and affectionate spirit of autobiography. It was now that he would dwell upon his own bodily powers and prowess with the enthusiasm of a devotee, and as the climax of this rhetorical display, would slap his hands together, spring perpendicularly into the air, and after uttering a yell worthy of the stoutest Winnebago, swear that he was "the best man in the country," and "could whip his weight in wild cats," "no two ways about it" —he was "not afraid of no man, no way you could fix it;" and finally, after many other extravagancies, he would urge, with no gentle asseveration, his ability to "ride through a crab-apple orchard on a streak of lightning."

In addition to all this, which one would think was enough for any reasonable man, Pete would sometimes brag that he had the best gun, the prettiest wife, the best-looking sister, and the fastest nag in all Kentuck; and that no man dare say to the contrary. It is but justice to remark, that there was more truth in this last boast than is usually found on such occasions, and that Pete had good reason to be proud of his horse, his gun, and his lady-love.

These, however, were the happy moments which are few and far between; they were the brilliant inspirations playing like the lightning in an overheated atmosphere,—gleaming over the turbid stream of existence, as the meteor flashes through the gloom of the night. When the fit was off, Pete was a quiet, good-natured, listless soul, as one would see on a summer's day—strolling about with a grave aspect, a drawling, and a deliberate gait, a stoop of the shoulders, and a kind of general relaxation of the whole outward and inward man—in a state of entire freedom from restraint, reflection, and want, and without any impulse strong enough to call forth his latent manhood—as the panther, with whom he often compared himself, when his appetite for food is sated, sleeps calmly in his lair, or wanders harmlessly through his native thickets.

Our hero was a farmer, or as the very appropriate phrase is, "made a *crap*" on his own hand—for besides making a crop he performed but few of the labours of the husbandman. While planting his corn, tending it, and gathering in the harvest, he worked with a good will; but these, thanks to a prolific soil and a free country, were all his toils, and they occupied not half of the year, the remainder of which was spent in the more manly and gentlemanly employments of hunting, attending elections, and officiating at horse-races. He was a rare hand at a "shucking," a house raising, or a log rolling; merry and strong, he worked like a young giant, and it was worth while to hear the gladsome tones of his clear voice, and the inspiring sound of his loud laugh; while the way he handled the axe, the beauty and keenness of the implement, the weight and precision of the blows, and the gracefulness of the action, were such as are not seen except in the wilderness, where chopping is an accomplishment as well as the most useful of labours.

It will readily be perceived that our hunter was not one who could be turned from his purpose by the prospect of danger or fatigue; and a few minutes sufficed to complete his preparations. His feet were cased in moccasins, and his legs in wrappers of dressed deerskin; and he was soon accoutred with a powder-horn, quaintly carved all over with curious devices,—an ample pouch with flints, patches, balls, and other "fixens"—and a hunter's knife,—and throwing "Brown's Bess," for so he called his rifle, over his shoulder, he sallied forth.

But in passing a store hard by, which supplied the country with gunpowder, whisky, and other necessaries, as well as with the luxuries of tea, sugar, coffee, calico, calomel, and chandlery, he was hailed by one of the neighbours, who invited him to "light off and take something." Pete said he had "no occasion," but "rather than be nice," he dismounted and joined a festive circle, among whom the cup was circulating freely. Here he was soon challenged to swap rifles, and being one of those who could not "stand a banter," he bantered back again without the least intention of parting with his favourite weapon. Making offers

like a skilful diplomatist, which he knew would not be accepted, and feigning great eagerness to accede to any reasonable proposition, while inwardly resolved to reject all, he magnified the perfections of Brown Bess.

"She can do any thing but talk," said he. "If she had legs she could hunt by herself. It is a pleasure to *tote* her—I naterally believe there is not a rifle south of Green river that can throw a ball so far, or so true. I can put a bullet in that tree, down the road, a mile off."

"You can't do it, Pete—I'll bet a treat for the whole company."

"No"—said the hunter. "I could do it—but I don't want to strain my gun."

These discussions consumed much time and much whisky—for the rule on such occasions is, that he who rejects an offer to trade must treat the company, and thus every point in the negotiation costs a pint of spirits.

At length, bidding adieu to his companions, Pete struck into the forest—it was getting late, and he "must look about pretty peart," he said, to get a venison before night. Lightly crushing the snow beneath his active feet, he beat up the coverts and traversed all the accustomed haunts of the deer. He mounted every hill and descended into every valley—not a thicket escaped the penetrating glance of his practised eye. Fruitless labour! not a deer was to be seen. Pete marvelled at this unusual circumstance, as the deer were very abundant in this neighbourhood, and no one knew better where to look for them than himself.

But what surprised him still more, was, that the woods were less familiar to him than formerly. He knew them "like a book." He thought he was acquainted with every tree within ten miles of his cabin; but now, although he certainly had not wandered so far, some of the objects around him seemed strange, while others again were faintly recognised; and there was, altogether, a singular confusion in the character of the scenery, which was partly familiar and partly new; or rather, in which many of the component parts were separately well known, but were so mixed up and changed in relation to each other, as to baffle even the knowledge of an expert woodsman.

The more he looked, the more he was bewildered. Had such a thing been possible, he would have thought himself a lost man. He came to a stream which had heretofore rolled to the west, but now its course pointed to the east; and the shadows of the tall trees, which, according to Pete's experience and philosophy, ought at noon to fall toward the north, all pointed to the south. He looked at his right and his left hands, somewhat puzzled to know which was which; then scratched his head—but scratching the head, though a good thing in its way, will not always get a man out of a scrape. He cast his eye upon his own shadow, which had never deceived him—when lo! a still more extraordinary phenomenon presented itself. It was travelling round him like the shade on a dial—only a great deal faster, as it veered round to all the points of the compass in the course of a single minute. Mr. Peter Featherton was "in a bad fix."

It was very evident, too, from the dryness of the snow and the brittleness of the twigs which snapped off as he brushed his way through the thickets, that the weather was intensely cold; yet the perspiration was rolling in large drops from his brow. He stopped at a clear spring, and thrusting his hands into the cold water, attempted to carry a portion to his lips; but the element recoiled and hissed, as if his hands and lips had been composed of red hot iron. Pete felt quite puzzled when he reflected on all these contradictions in the aspect of nature; and began to consider what act of wickedness he had been guilty of which could have rendered him so hateful, that the deer fled at his approach, the streams turned back, and the shadows fell the wrong way, or danced round their centre.

He began to grow alarmed, and would have liked to turn back, but was ashamed to betray such weakness, even to himself; and being naturally bold, he resolutely kept on his way. At last, to his great joy, he espied the tracks of deer imprinted on the snow: they were fresh signs—and, dashing upon the trail with the alacrity of a well-trained hound, he pursued in hopes of soon overtaking the game. Presently he discovered the tracks of a man who had struck the same trail in advance of him, and supposing it to be one of his neighbours, he quickened his pace, as well to gain a companion, which in the present state of his feelings he so much needed, as to share the spoil with his fellow-hunter. Indeed, in his present situation and condition of mind, Pete thought he would be willing to give half of what he was worth for the sight of a human face.

"I don't like the signs, no how," said he, casting a rapid glance around him; and then throwing his eyes downward at his own shadow, which had ceased its rotatory motion, and was now swinging backward and forward like a pendulum—"I don't like the signs, no way they can be fixed."

"You are not scared, are you, Pete?" he continued, smiling at the oddity of such a question.

"Oh no, bless your heart, Mr. Featherton, I'm not scared—I'm not of that breed of dogs—there's no back out in me—but then I must say—to speak sentimentally—that I feel sort o' jubus—I do so. But I'll soon see whether other people's shadows act the fool like mine."

Upon further observation, there appeared to be something peculiar in the human tracks before him, which were evidently made by a pair of feet which were not fellows—or were odd fellows—for one of them was larger than the other. As there was no person in the settlement who was thus deformed, Pete began to doubt whether it might not be the devil, who in borrowing shoes to conceal his cloven hoofs might have got those that did not match. He stopped and scratched his head, as many a learned philosopher has done, when placed between the horns of a dilemma less perplexing than that which now vexed the spirit of our hunter. It was said long ago, that there is a tide in the

affairs of men; and although our good friend Pete had never seen this sentiment in black and white, yet it is one of those truths which are written in the heart of every reasonable being, and was only copied by the poet from the great book of nature, a source from which he was a great borrower. It readily occurred to Pete on this occasion; and as he had enjoyed through life an uninterrupted tide of success, he reflected whether the stream of fortune might not have changed its course like the brooks he had crossed, whose waters, for some sinister reason, seemed to be crawling up-hill.

He stopped, drew out his handkerchief, and wiped the perspiration from his brow. "This thing of being scared," said he, "makes a man feel mighty queer—the way it brings the sweat out is curious!" And again it occurred to him, that it was incumbent on him to see the end of the adventure, as otherwise he would show a want of that courage which he had been taught to consider as the chief of the cardinal virtues.

"I can't back out," said he, "I never was raised to it, no how; and if the devil's a mind to hunt in this range, he shan't have all the game."

Then falling into the sentimental vein, as one naturally does from the heroic: "Here's this hankercher that my Polly hemmed for me, and marked the two first letters of my name on it—P. for Pete and F. Featherton—would she do the like of that for a coward? Could I ever look in her pretty face again if I was mean enough to be scared? No—I'll go ahead—let what will come."

He soon overtook the person in advance of him, who, as he had suspected, was a perfect stranger. He had halted and was quietly seated on a log, gazing at the sun, when our hunter approached and saluted him with the usual hearty, "How are you, stranger?" The person addressed made no reply, but continued to gaze at the sun, as if totally unconscious that any other individual was present. He was a small, thin old man, with a gray beard of about a month's growth, and a long sallow melancholy visage, while a tarnished suit of snuff-coloured clothes, cut after the quaint fashion of some religious sect, hung loosely about his shrivelled person.

Our bold backwoodsman, somewhat awed, now coughed, threw the butt end of his gun heavily upon the frozen ground, and, still failing to elicit any attention, quietly seated himself on the other end of the log occupied by the stranger. Both remained silent for some minutes—Pete with open mouth and glaring eyeballs, observing his companion with mute astonishment, and the latter looking at the sun.

"It's a warm day, this," said Pete, at length, passing his hand across his brow as he spoke, and sweeping off the heavy drops of perspiration that hung there. But receiving no answer, he began to get nettled. He thought himself not civilly treated. His native assurance, which had been damped by the mysterious deportment of the person who sat before him, revived. "One man's as good as another"—thought he; and screwing up his courage to the sticking point, he arose, ap-

2 B 2

proached the silent man, and slapping him on the back, exclaimed—

"Well, stranger! don't the sun look mighty droll away out there in the north?"

As the heavy hand fell on his shoulder, the stranger slowly turned his face toward Pete, who recoiled several paces,—then rising without paying the abashed hunter any further attention, he began to pursue the trail of the deer. Pete prepared to follow, when the other, turning upon him with a stern glance, inquired:

"Who are you tracking?"

"Not you," replied the hunter, whose alarm had subsided when the enemy began to retreat; and whose pride, piqued by the abruptness with which he had been treated, enabled him to assume his usual boldness of manner.

"Why do you follow this trail, then?"

"I trail deer."

"You must not pursue them further, they are mine!"

The sound of the stranger's voice broke the spell which had hung over Peter's natural impudence, and he now shouted—

"Your deer! that's droll too! who ever heard of a man claiming the deer in the woods!"

"Provoke me not,—I tell you they are mine."

"Well, now—you're a comical chap! Why stranger,—the deer are wild! They're jist nateral to the woods here, the same as the timber. You might as well say the wolves and the painters are yours, and all the rest of the wild varments."

"The tracks you behold here are those of wild deer, undoubtedly—but they are mine. I routed them from their bed, and am driving them home."

"Home—where is your home?" inquired Pete, at the same time casting an inquisitive glance at the stranger's feet.

To this home question no reply was given, and Pete, fancying that he had got the best of the altercation, pushed his advantage,—adding sneeringly—

"Couldn't you take a pack or two of wolves along? We can spare you a small gang. It is mighty wolfy about here."

"If you follow any further it is at your peril," said the stranger.

"You don't reckon I'm to be skeered, do you? If you do, you are barking up the wrong tree. There's no back out in none of my breed, no how. You mustn't come over them words agin, stranger."

"I repeat ——"

"You had best not repeat—I allow no man to do that to me"—interrupted the irritated woodsman. "You must not imitate the like of that. I'm Virginy born, and Kentucky raised, and drot my skin, if I take the like of that from any man—no, sir!"

"Desist, rash man, from altercation—I despise your threats!"

"The same to you, sir!

"I tell you what, stranger!" continued Pete, endeavouring to imitate the coolness of the other, "as to the vally of a deer or two—I don't vally them to the tantamount of this here cud of tobacco; but I'm not to be backed out of my tracks. So keep off, stranger—don't come fooling about me. I might hurt you. I feel mighty wolfy about the head and shoulders. Keep off, I say, or you might run agin a snag."

With this the hunter "squared himself, and sot his triggers," fully determined either to hunt the disputed game, or be vanquished in combat. To his surprise, the stranger, without appearing to notice his preparations, advanced and blew with his breath upon his rifle.

"Your gun is charmed!" said he. "From this day forward you will kill no deer."

So saying, that mysterious old man, with the most provoking coolness, resumed his way; while Pete remained bewildered; and fancied that he smelt brimstone.

Pete Featherton remained a moment or two lost in confusion. He then thought he would pursue the stranger, and punish him as well for his threats as for the insult intended to his gun; but a little reflection induced him to change his decision. The confident manner in which that singular being had spoken, together with a kind of vague assurance in his own mind that the spell had really taken effect, so unmanned and stupified him, that he quietly "took the back track" and strode homeward. He had not gone far, when he saw a fine buck half-concealed among the hazel bushes which beset his path; and resolved to know at once how matters stood between Brown Bess and the pretended conjurer, he took a deliberate aim, fired,—and away bounded the buck unharmed!

With a heavy heart our mortified forester re entered his own dwelling and replaced his degraded weapon in its accustomed berth under the rafters.

"You have been long gone," said his wife, "but where is the venison you promised me?"

Pete was constrained to confess that he had shot nothing.

"That is strange!" said the lady, "I never knew you fail before."

Pete framed twenty excuses. He had felt unwell—his gun was out of fix—it was a bad day for hunting—the moon was not in the right place —and there were no deer stirring.

Had not Pete been a very young husband, he would have known that the vigilant eye of a wife is not to be deceived by feigned apologies. Female curiosity never sleeps; and the love of a devoted wife is the most sincere and the most absorbing of human passions. Pretty Mrs. Featherton saw at a glance that something had happened to her helpmate, more than he was willing to confess; and being quite as tenacious as himself, in her reluctance against being "backed out of her tracks," she determined to bring her inferior moiety to auricular confession, and advanced firmly to her object, until Pete was compelled to own, "That he believed Brown Bess was, somehow—sort o'— charmed."

"Now, Mr. Featherton!" remonstrated his sprightly bride, leaning fondly on his shoulder and parting the long red locks on his forehead— "are you not ashamed to tell me such a tale as that? Charmed indeed! Ah, well, I know how it is. You have been down at the store shooting for half pints!"

"No, indeed—" replied the husband emphatically, "I wish I may be kissed to death if I've pulled a trigger for a drop of liquor this day."

Ah, Peter—what a sad evasion was that! Surely the adversary when he blew his breath—sadly sulphureous of smell—upon thy favourite gun, breathed into thee the spirit of lying, of which he is the father. Mrs. Featherton saw farther into a millstone than he was aware of—but she kept her own counsel.

"I believe you, Peter,—you did not *shoot* for it —but do now—that's a dear good soul!—tell me where you have been, and what has happened? You are not well—or something is wrong—for never did Pete Featherton and Brown Bess fail to get a venison any day in the year."

Soothed by this well-timed compliment, and not unwilling to have the aid of counsel in this trying emergency, and to apply to his excited spirit the balm of conjugal sympathy, Pete narrated minutely to his wife all the particulars of his meeting with the mysterious stranger. The lady was all attention; but was as much wonder-struck as Pete himself. She had heard of spells being cast upon guns, and so had Peter—often—but then neither of them had ever known such a case in their own experience; and although she had recipes for pickling fruit, and preserving life, and preventing various maladies, she knew of no remedy which would remove the spell from a rifle. As she could give no sage advice, she prescribed sage tea, bathing the feet, and going to bed, and Pete submitted passively to all this—not perceiving, however, how it could possibly affect his gun.

When Pete awoke the next morning, the events which we have described appeared to him as a dream; indeed, he had been dreaming of them all night, and it was somewhat difficult to unravel the tangled thread of recollection, so as to separate the realities of the day from the illusions of the pillow. But resolving to know the truth, he seized his gun and hastened to the woods. Alas! every experiment produced the same vexatious result. The gun was charmed! "No two ways about that!" It was too true to make a joke of; and the hunter stalked harmlessly through the forest.

Day after day he went forth, and returned with no better success. The very deer became sensible of his inoffensiveness, and would raise their heads and gaze mildly at him as he passed; or throw back their antlers and bound carelessly across his path. Day after day and week after week passed without bringing any change; and Pete began to feel very ridiculously. A harmless man—a fellow with a gun that could not shoot! he could imagine no situation more miserable than his own. To walk through the woods, to see the game, to come within gun-shot of it, and yet to be unable to kill a deer, seemed to be the height of human wretchedness. He felt as if he was "the meanest kind of a white man." There was a littleness, an insignificance attached to the idea of not being

able to kill a deer, which, to Pete's mind, was downright disgrace. More than once he was tempted to throw the gun into the river; but the excellence of the weapon, and the recollection of former exploits restrained him; and he continued to stroll through the woods, firing now and then at a fat buck, under the hope that the charm would expire some time or other by its own limitation; but the fat bucks continued to treat him with a familiarity amounting to contempt, and to frisk fearlessly in his path.

At length Pete bethought him of a celebrated Indian doctor, who lived at no great distance. We do not care to say much of doctors, as they are a touchy race—and shall therefore touch upon this one briefly. An Indian doctor is not necessarily a descendant of the Aborigines. The title, it is true, originates from the confidence which many of our countrymen repose in the medical skill of the Indian tribes. But to make an Indian doctor a red skin is by no means indispensable. To have been taught by a savage, to have seen one, or, at all events, to have heard of one, is all that is necessary to enable any individual to practise this lucrative and popular branch of the healing art. Neither is any great proficiency in literature requisite; it is important only to be expert in spelling. Your Indian doctor is one who practises without a diploma—the only degree he exhibits is a high degree of confidence. He neither nauseates the stomach with odious drugs, nor mars the fair proportions of nature with the sanguinary lancet. He believes in the sympathy which is supposed to exist between the body and the mind, which, like the two arms of a syphon, always preserve a corresponding relation to each other; and the difference between him and the regular physician—called in the vernacular of the frontier the marcury doctor—is that they operate at different points of the same figure—the one practising on the immaterial spirit, while the other grapples with the bones and muscles. I cannot determine which is right; but must award to the Indian doctor at least this advantage, that his art is the most widely beneficial; for while your doctor of medicine restores a lost appetite, his rival can, in addition, recover a strayed or stolen horse. If the former can bring back the faded lustre to a fair maiden's cheeks, the latter can remove the spell from a churn or a rifle. The dyspeptic and the dropsical may hie to the disciples of Rush and Wistar, but the crossed-in-love and lack-adaysical find a charm in the practitioner who professes to follow nature.

To a sage of this order did Pete disclose his misfortune, and apply for relief. The doctor examined the gun and looked wise; and having measured the calibre of the bore with a solemnity which was as imposing as it was unquestionably proper on so serious an occasion, directed the applicant to come again.

At the appointed time, the hunter returned and received from the wise man two balls, one of pink, the other of a silver hue. The doctor instructed him to load his piece with one of these bullets, which he pointed out, and proceed through the woods to a certain secluded hollow, at the head of which was a spring. Here he would see a white fawn, at which he was to shoot. It would be wounded, but would escape, and he was to pursue its trail until he found a buck, which he was to kill with the other ball. If he accomplished all this accurately, the charm would be broken; but success would depend upon his having faith, keeping up his courage, and firing with precision.

Pete, who was well acquainted with all the localities, carefully pursued the route which had been indicated, treading lightly along, sometimes elated with the prospect of speedily breaking the spell, and restoring his beloved gun to usefulness and respectability—sometimes doubting the skill of the doctor—admiring the occult knowledge of men who could charm and uncharm deadly weapons—and ashamed alternatively of his doubts and his belief. At length he reached the lonely glen; and his heart bounded with delight as he beheld the white fawn quietly grazing by the fountain. The ground was open, and he was unable to get within his usual distance before the fawn raised her delicate head, looked timidly around, and snuffed the breeze, as if conscious of the approach of danger. Pete trembled with excitement—his heart palpitated. It was a long shot and a bad chance—but he could not advance a step further without danger of starting the game—and Brown Bess could carry a ball farther than that with fatal effect.

"Luck's a lord," said he, as he drew the gun up to his face, took a deliberate aim and pulled the trigger. The fawn bounded aloft at the report, and then darted away through the brush, while the hunter hastened to examine the signs. To his great joy he found the blood profusely scattered; and now flushed with the confidence of success, he stoutly rammed down the other ball, and pursued the trail of the wounded fawn. Long did he trace the crimson drops upon the snow without beholding the promised victim. Hill after hill he climbed, vale after vale he passed—searching every thicket with penetrating eyes; and he was about to renounce the chase, the wizard, and the gun, when lo!—directly in his path stood a noble buck, with numerous antlers branching over his fine head!

"Aha! my jolly fellow! I've found you at last!" exclaimed the delighted hunter, "you are the very chap I've been looking after. Your blood shall wipe off the disgrace from my charming Bess, that never hung fire, burned priming, nor missed the mark in her born days till that vile abominable varment blowed his brimstone breath on her! Here goes—"

He shot the buck. The spell was broken—Brown Bess was restored to favour, and Pete Featherton never again wanted venison.

⸺✦⸺

THE PRAIRIES.
FROM THE SAME.

The smaller prairies, or those in which the plain and woodland alternate frequently, are the most beautiful. The points of woodland which make into them like so many capes or promontories, and the groves which are interspersed like islands, are in these lesser prairies always sufficiently near to be clearly defined to the eye, and to give the scene an interesting variety. We see plains, varying from a few hundred acres to several miles in extent, not perfectly level, but gently rolling and undulating, like the swelling of the ocean when nearly calm. The graceful curve of the surface is seldom broken, except when here and there the eye rests upon one of those huge mounds, which are so pleasing to the poet and so perplexing to the antiquarian. The whole is overspread with grass and flowers, constituting a rich and varied carpet, in which a ground of lively green is ornamented with a profusion of the gaudiest hues, and fringed with a rich border of forest and thicket. Deep recesses in the edge of the timber resemble the bays and inlets of a lake; while occasionally a long vista, opening far back into the forest, invites the eye to roam off and refresh itself with the calm beauty of a distant perspective.

The traveller, as he rides along over these smaller prairies, finds his eye continually attracted to the edges of the forest, and his imagination employed in tracing the beautiful outline, and in finding out resemblances between these wild scenes and the most tastefully embellished productions of art. The fairest pleasure-grounds, the noblest parks of European noblemen and princes, where millions have been expended to captivate the senses with Elysian scenes, are but mimic representations, on a reduced scale, of the beauties which are here spread by nature; for here are clumps and lawns, groves and avenues, the tangled thicket, and the solitary tree, the lengthened vista, and the secluded nook, and all the varieties of scenic attraction, but on a plan so extensive as to offer a wide scope and an endless succession of changes to the eye.

There is an air of refinement here that wins the heart,—even here, where no human residence is seen, where no foot of man intrudes, and where not an axe has ever trespassed on the beautiful domain. It is a wilderness shorn of every savage association, a desert that "blossoms as the rose." So different is the feeling awakened from any thing inspired by mountain or woodland scenery, that the instant the traveller emerges from the forest into the prairie, he feels no longer solitary. The consciousness that he is travelling alone, and in a wilderness, escapes him; and he indulges in the same pleasing sensations which are enjoyed by one who, having lost his way, and wandered bewildered among the labyrinths of a savage mountain, suddenly descends into rich and highly cultivated plains, and sees around him the delightful indications of taste and comfort. The gay landscape charms him. He is encompassed by the refreshing sweetness and graceful beauty of the rural scene; and recognises at every step some well-remembered spot, or some ideal paradise in which the fancy had loved to wander, enlarged and beautified, and as it were retouched by nature's hand. The clusters of trees so fancifully arranged, the forest outline so gracefully curved, seem to have been disposed by the hand of taste for the enjoyment of intelligent beings; and so complete is the illusion, that it is difficult to dispel the belief that each avenue leads to a village, and each grove conceals a splendid mansion.

Widely different was the prospect exhibited by the more northern and central districts of the state. Vast in extent, the distant forest was either beyond the reach of the eye, or was barely discernible in the shapeless outline of blue faintly impressed on the horizon. As the smaller prairies resembled a series of larger and lesser lakes, so these boundless plains remind one of the ocean waste. Here and there a solitary tree, torn by the wind, stood alone like a dismantled mast in the ocean. As I followed my guide through this lonely region, my sensations were similar to those of the voyager when his bark is launched upon the sea. Alone, in a wide waste, with my faithful pilot only, I was dependent on him for support, guidance, and protection. With little to diversify the path, and nothing to please the eye but the carpet of verdure, which began to pall upon the sense, a feeling of dreariness crept over me—a desolation of the spirit, such as one feels when crossed in love, or when very drowsy on a hot afternoon after a full dinner. But these are feelings which, like the sea-sickness of the young mariner, are soon dispelled. I began to find a pleasure in gazing over this immense, unbroken waste, in watching the horizon under the vague hope of meeting a traveller, and in following the deer with my eyes as they galloped off—their agile forms growing smaller and smaller as they receded, until they shrunk into nothing. Sometimes I descried a dark spot at an immense distance, and pointed it out to my companion with a joy like that of the seaman who discovers a sail in the distant speck which floats on the ocean. When such an object happened to be in the direction of our path, I watched it with interest as it rose and enlarged upon the vision—supposing it at one moment to be a solitary horseman, and wondering what manner of man he would turn out to be—at another supposing it might be a wild animal, or a wagon, or a pedestrian; until, after it had seemed to approach for hours, I found it to be a tree.

PIERRE BLONDO'S FIRST SIGHT OF A PRAIRIE ON FIRE.
FROM THE SAME.

THE shades of night had begun to close, when they again ascended one of those elevations which swells so gradually that the traveller scarcely remarks them until he reaches the summit and beholds, from a commanding eminence, a boundless landscape spread before him. The veil of night, without concealing the scene, rendered it indistinct; the undulations of the surface were no longer perceptible; and the prairie seemed a perfect plain. One phenomenon astonished and perplexed him: before him the prairie was lighted up with a dim but supernatural brilliancy, like that of a distant fire, while behind was the blackness of darkness. An air of solitude reigned over that wild plain, and not a sound relieved the desolation of the scene. A chill crept over him as he gazed around, and not an object met his eye but that dark maid, who stood in mute patience by his side as waiting his pleasure; but on whose features, as displayed by the uncertain light that glimmered on them, a smile of triumph seemed to play. He looked again, and the horizon gleamed brighter and brighter, until a fiery redness rose above its dark outline, while heavy, slow-moving masses of cloud curled upward above it. It was evidently the intense reflection and the voluminous smoke of a vast fire. In another moment the blaze itself appeared, first shooting up at one spot, and then at another, and advancing until the whole line of horizon was clothed with flames that rolled around, and curled, and dashed upward like the angry waves of a burning ocean. The simple Frenchman had never heard of the fires that sweep over our wide prairies in the autumn, nor did it enter into his head that a natural cause could produce an effect so terrific. The whole western horizon was clad in fire, and, as far as the eye could see, to the right and left, was one vast conflagration, having the appearance of angry billows of a fiery liquid dashing against each other, and foaming, and throwing flakes of burning spray into the air. There was a roaring sound like that caused by the conflict of waves. A more terrific sight could scarcely be conceived; nor was it singular that an unpractised eye should behold in that scene a wide scene of flame, lashed into fury by some internal commotion.

Pierre could gaze no longer. A sudden horror thrilled his soul. His worse fears were realized in the tremendous landscape. He saw before him the lake of fire prepared for the devil and his angels. The existence of such a place of punishment he had never doubted; but, heretofore, it had been a mere dogma of faith, while now it appeared before him in its terrible reality. He thought he could plainly distinguish gigantic black forms dancing in the flames, throwing up their long mis-shapen arms, and writhing their bodies into fantastic shapes. Uttering a piercing shriek, he turned and fled with the swiftness of an arrow. Fear gave new vigour to the muscles which had before been relaxed with fatigue, and his feet, so lately heavy, now touched the ground with the light and springy tread of the antelope. Yet, to himself, his steps seemed to linger as if his heels were lead.

38

HENRY ROWE SCHOOLCRAFT.

[Born 1793. Died 1864.]

MR. SCHOOLCRAFT was of English descent by the paternal side, his great-grandfather having come from England during the wars of Queen Anne, and settled in what is now Schoharie county in New York, where in old age he taught the first English school in that part of the country, from which circumstance his name was not unnaturally changed by the usage of the people from Calcraft to Schoolcraft. Our author recently attempted in his own person to revive the old family name, but soon abandoned it, and concluded to retain that which was begotten upon his native soil, and by which he has long been so honourably distinguished. He is a son of Colonel Lawrence Schoolcraft, who joined the revolutionary army at seventeen years of age and participated in the movements under Montgomery and Schuyler, and the memorable defence of Fort Stanwix under Gansevoort. He was born in Guilderland, near Albany, on the twenty-eighth of March, 1793. In a secluded part of the country where there were few advantages for education and scarce any persons who thought of literature, he had an ardent love of knowledge, and sat at home with his books and pencils while his equals in age were at cock-fights and horse-races, for which Guilderland was then famous. He is still remembered by some of the octogenarians of the village as the "learned boy." At thirteen he drew subjects in natural history, and landscapes, which attracted the attention of the late Lieutenant-Governor Van Rensselaer, then a frequent visiter of his father, through whose agency he came near being apprenticed to one Ames, the only portrait painter at that time in Albany; but as it was demanded that he should commence with house painting the plan was finally abandoned. At fourteen he began to contribute pieces in prose and verse to the newspapers, and for several years after he pursued without aid the study of natural history, English literature, Hebrew, German, and French, and the philosophy of language.

Mr. Schoolcraft's first work was an elaborate treatise, but partly known to the public,
298

entitled Vitreology, which was published in 1817. The design of it was to exhibit the application of chemistry to the arts in the fusion of siliceous and alkaline substances in the production of enamels, glass, etc. He had had opportunities of experimenting largely and freely by his position as conductor for a series of years of the extensive works of the Ontario Company at Geneva in New York, the Vermont Company at Middlebury and Salisbury in Vermont, and the foundery of crystal glass at Keene, in New Hampshire. In 1818 and the following year, he made a geological survey of Missouri and Arkansas to the spurs of the Rocky Mountains, and in the fall of 1819 published in New York his View of the Lead Mines of Missouri, which is said by Professor Silliman to have been "the only elaborate and detailed account of a mining district in the United States" which had then appeared. It attracted much attention and procured for the author the friendship of many eminent men. In the same year he printed Transallegania, a poetical *jeu d'esprit* of which mineralogy is the subject, and which preceded some clever English attempts in the same vein. It was republished in London by Sir Richard Phillips in the next year.

Early in 1820 he published a Journal of a Tour in the Interior of Missouri and Arkansas, extending from Potosi toward the Rocky Mountains. His writings having attracted the notice of the government, he was commissioned by Mr. Calhoun, then Secretary of War, to visit the copper region of Lake Superior, and to accompany General Cass in his expedition to the head waters of the Mississippi. His Narrative Journal of this tour was published in 1821, and was eminently successful, an edition of twelve hundred copies being sold in a few weeks. In the same year he was appointed secretary to the commission for treating with the Indian tribes at Chicago, and on the conclusion of his labours published his sixth work, entitled Travels in the Central Portions of the Mississippi Valley, in which he described the country between the regions of which he had given an account in his previous works. His reputation was now widely and firmly established as an explorer, and as a man of science and letters. From this time his attention was devoted principally to the Red Race, though he still cultivated natural history, and wrote occasionally for the reviews and magazines.

In 1822 he was appointed by President Monroe agent for Indian Affairs, to reside at St. Mary's, at the foot of Lake Superior. In the years 1825, 1826 and 1827 he attended the important convocations of the north-west tribes at Prairie du Chien, Pont du Lac, and Buttes des Morts. In 1831 he was sent on a special embassy, accompanied by troops, to conciliate the Sioux and Odjibwas, and bring the existing war between them to a close. In 1832 he proceeded in the same capacity to the tribes near the head waters of the Mississippi, and availed himself of the opportunity to trace that river, in small canoes, from the point where Pike stopped in 1807 and Cass in 1820, to its true source in Itasca Lake, upon which he entered on the thirteenth of July, the one hundred and forty-ninth anniversary of the discovery of the mouth of the river by La Salle. His account of this tour was published in New York in 1834, under the title of An Expedition to Itasca Lake, and attracted much attention in all parts of the country.

From 1827 to 1831 Mr. Schoolcraft was a member of the legislative council of Michigan. In 1828 he organized the Michigan Historical Society, in which he was elected president on the removal of General Cass to Washington, in 1831. In the fall of the same year he set on foot the Algic Society at Detroit, before which he delivered a course of lectures on the grammatical construction of the Indian languages,* and at its first anniversary a poem on The Indian Character. Guided by patriotism and good taste, he took a successful stand in the west against the absurd nomenclature which has elsewhere made such confusion in geography by repeating over and over the names of European places and characters, giving us Romes, Berlins and Londons, in the wilderness, and Hannibals, Scipios, Homers, and Hectors, wherever there was sufficient learning to make its possessors ridicu-

* Two of these lectures were published in 1834, translated into French by the late Mr Du Ponceau, and subsequently read before the National Institute of France.

lous. He submitted to the legislature of the territory a system of county and township names based upon the Indian vocabularies with which he was familiar, and happily secured its general adoption.

At Sault Ste. Marie Mr. Schoolcraft became acquainted with Mr. John Johnston, a gentleman from the north of Ireland, who had long resided there, and in the person of his eldest daughter married a descendant of the hereditary chief of Lake Superior, or Lake Algoma, as it is known to the Indians. She had been educated in Europe, and was an accomplished and highly interesting woman. After a residence there of eleven years he removed to Michilimackinac and assumed the joint-agency of the two districts. In 1836 he was appointed by President Jackson a commissioner to treat with the north-west tribes for their lands in the region of the upper lakes, and succeeded in effecting a cession to the United States of some sixteen millions of acres. In the same year he was appointed acting Superintendent of Indian Affairs for the Northern Department, and in 1839 principal disbursing agent for the same district.

In the last mentioned year he published two volumes of Algic Researches, comprising Indian Tales and Legends, and soon after, having passed more than twenty years as a traveller or resident on the frontiers, he removed to the city of New York, intending to prepare for the press the great mass of his original papers which had accumulated in this long period. In 1841 he issued proposals for an Indian Cyclopedia, geographical, historical, philological, etc., of which only one number was printed, no publisher appearing willing to undertake so costly and extensive a work of such a description. In 1842 he visited England, France, Germany, Prussia, and Holland. During his absence his wife died, at Dundee, in Canada West, where she was visiting her sister. Soon after his return he made another journey to the west to examine some of the great mounds, respecting which he has since communicated a paper to the Royal Geographical Society of Denmark, of which he was many years ago elected an honorary member, and soon after published a collection of his poetical writings, under the title of Alhalla, or the Lord of Talladega, a Tale of the Creek War, with some Miscellanies, chiefly of early date. In 1844 he commenced in numbers the publication of Oneota, or the Red Race in America, their History, Traditions, Customs, Poetry, Picture Writing, etc., in Extracts from Notes, Journals, and other Unpublished Writings, of which one octavo volume has been completed. In 1845 he delivered an address before a society known as the "Was-ah Ho-de-no-sonne, or New Confederacy of the Iroquois," and published Observations on the Grave Creek Mound in Western Virginia, in the Transactions of the American Ethnological Society; and early in the following year presented in the form of a Report to the legislature of his native state, his Notes on the Iroquois, or Contributions to the Statistics, Aboriginal History, and General Ethnology of Western New York. His latest essay was an Address delivered at the anniversary meeting of the New York Historical Society, on the first Tuesday of December, 1846.

Mr. Schoolcraft's ethnological writings are among the most important contributions that have been made to the literature of this country. His long and intimate connection with the Indian tribes, and the knowledge possessed by his wife and her family of the people from whom they were descended by the maternal side, with his power of examining their character from the European point of view, have enabled him to give us more authentic and valuable information respecting their manners, customs, and physical traits, and more insight into their moral and intellectual constitution, than can be derived, perhaps, from all other authors. His works abound in materials for the future artist and man of letters, and will on this account continue to be read when the greater portion of the popular literature of the day is forgotten. With the forests which they inhabited, the red race have disappeared with astonishing rapidity; until recently they have rarely been the subjects of intelligent study; and it began to be regretted, as they were seen fading from our sight, that there was so little written respecting them that had any pretensions to fidelity. I would not be understood to undervalue the productions of Eliot, Loskiel, Heckewelder, Brainerd, and other early missionaries, but they were restricted in design, and it is not to be denied that confidence in their representations has been much impaired, less perhaps from doubts of their integrity than of their ability and of the advantages of the points

of view from which they made their observations. The works on Indian philology by Roger Williams and the younger Edwards are more valuable than any others of the seventeenth and eighteenth centuries, but it now appears that these authors knew very little of the philosophy of the American language. Du Ponceau's knowledge was still more superficial, and excepting Mr. Gallatin and the late Mr. Pickering, who made use of the imperfect data furnished by others, I believe no one besides Mr. Schoolcraft has recently produced any thing on the subject worthy of consideration. Something has been done by General Cass, and Mr. McKenny and Mr. Catlin have undoubtedly accomplished much in this department of ethnography; but allowing all that can reasonably be claimed for these artist-travellers, Mr. Schoolcraft must still be regarded as the standard and chief authority respecting the Algic tribes.

The influence which the original and peculiar myths and historical traditions of the Indians is to have on our imaginative literature, has been recently more than ever exhibited in the works of our authors. The tendency of the public taste to avail itself of the American mythology as a basis for the exhibition of "new lines of fictitious creations" has been remarked by Mr. Schoolcraft himself in Oneota, and he refers to the tales of Mrs. Oakes Smith, and to the Wild Scenes in the Forest and the Prairie, and the Vigil of Faith, by Mr. Charles F. Hoffman, as works in which this tendency is most distinctly perceptible. In the writings of W. H. C. Hosmer, the legends of Mr. Whittier, and some of the poems of Mr. Longfellow, and Mr. Lowell, we see manifestations of the same disposition.

In 1847, Mr. Schoolcraft married Miss Howard, of South Carolina, and resided in Washington, till his death, Dec. 10, 1864. The results of his busy life are best shown in the 41 distinct works, and numerous essays, that he wrote, edited, or published, for list of which, see Allibone's Dicty., II., 1951. His most important work, "On the Indian Tribes of the U. S.", was published by Congress, 1851–57, in 6 vols., 4to., fully illustrated. A mass of facts useful to the future historian, but an ill-digested compilation, of little interest to the general reader. A cheaper edition, comprising a portion of this work was published in 3 vols.

SCENERY OF LAKE SUPERIOR.
FROM ONEOTA.

Few portions of America can vie in scenic attractions with this interior sea. Its size alone gives it all the elements of grandeur, but these have been heightened by the mountain masses which nature has piled along its shores. In some places these masses consist of vast walls of coarse gray or drab sandstone, placed horizontally until they have attained many hundred feet in height above the water. The action of such an immense liquid area, forced against these crumbling walls by tempests, has caused wide and deep arches to be worn into the solid structure at their base, into which the billows rush with a noise resembling low pealing thunder. By this means, large areas of the impending mass are at length undermined and precipitated into the lake, leaving the split and rent parts from which they have separated standing like huge misshapen turrets and battlements. Such is the varied coast called the Pictured Rocks.

At other points of the coast volcanic forces have operated, lifting up these level strata into positions nearly vertical, and leaving them to stand like the leaves of an open book. At the same time, the volcanic rocks sent up from below have risen in high mountain piles. Such is the condition of things at the Porcupine Mountains.

The basin and bed of this lake act as a vast geological mortar, in which the masses of broken and fallen stones are whirled about and ground down till all the softer ones, such as the sandstones, are brought into the state of pure yellow sand. This sand is driven ashore by the waves, where it is shoved up in long wreaths till dried by the sun. The winds now take it up and spread it inland, or pile it immediately along the coast, where it presents itself in mountain masses. Such are the great Sand Dunes of the Grande Sables.

There are yet other theatres of action for this sublime mass of inland waters, where it has manifested perhaps still more strongly, if not so strikingly, its abrasive powers. The whole force of the lake, under the impulse of a north-west tempest, is directed against prominent portions of the shore, which consist of the black and hard volcanic rocks. Solid as these are, the waves have found an entrance in veins of spar or minerals of softer structure, and have thus been led inland, and torn up large fields of amygdaloid and other rock, or left portions of them standing in rugged knobs or promontories. Such are the east and west coasts of the great peninsula of Keweena, which has recently become the theatre of mining operations.

When the visiter to these remote and boundless waters come to see this wide and varied scene of complicated attractions, he is absorbed in wonder and astonishment. The eye, once introduced to this panorama of waters, is never done looking and admiring. Scene after scene, cliff after cliff, island after island, and vista after vista, are presented. One day's scenes are but the prelude to another, and when weeks and months have been spent in picturesque rambles along its shores, the traveller has only to ascend some of its streams and go inland to find falls and cascades, and cataracts of the most magnificent character. Go where he will, there is something to attract him. Beneath his feet the pebbles are agates. The water is of the most crystalline purity. The sky is filled at sunset with the most gorgeous piles of clouds. The air itself is of the purest and most inspiriting kind. To visit such a scene is to draw health from its purest fountains, and to revel in intellectual delights.

SHINGEBISS.
FROM THE SAME.
[From the Odjibwa-Algonquin.]

There was once a Shingebiss,* living alone in a solitary lodge on the shores of the deep bay of a lake, in the coldest winter weather. The ice had formed on the water, and he had but four logs of wood to keep his fire. Each of these would, however, burn a month; and, as there were but four cold winter months, they were sufficient to carry him through till spring.

Shingebiss was hardy and fearless, and cared for no one. He would go out during the coldest day and seek for places where flags and rushes grew through the ice, and plucking them up with his bill, would dive through the openings in quest of fish. In this way he found plenty of food, while others were starving; and he went home daily to his lodge, dragging strings of fish after him on the ice.

Kabebonicca† observed him, and felt a little piqued at his perseverance and good luck in defiance of the severest blasts of wind he could send from the North-West. "Why! this is a wonderful man," said he; "he does not mind the cold, and appears as happy and contented as if it were the month of June. I will try whether he cannot be mastered." He poured forth ten-fold colder blasts and drifts of snow, so that it was next to impossible to live in the open air. Still the fire of Shingebiss did not go out; he wore but a single strip of leather around his body, and he was seen in the worst weather searching the shores for rushes and carrying home fish.

"I shall go and visit him," said Kabebonicca one day, as he saw Shingebiss dragging along a quantity of fish; and accordingly that very night he went to the door of his lodge. Meantime Shingebiss had cooked his fish and finished his meal, and was lying, partly on his side, before the fire, singing his songs. After Kabebonicca had come to the door and stood listening there, he sang as follows:

Ka be bon oc ca Nee′ ɹ. .n ec we-ya !
Ka be bon oc ca Neej in in ec we-ya!

The number of words in this song are few and simple, but they are made up from compounds

----

* The name of a kind of duck.
† A personification of the North-West.

9 Ω

which carry the whole of their original meanings, and are rather suggestive of the ideas floating in the mind than actual expressions of those ideas. Literally he sings:

Spirit of the North-West! you are but my fellow-man.

By being broken into syllables to correspond with a simple chant, and by the power of intonation and repetition, with a chorus, these words are expanded into melodious utterance, if we may be allowed the term, and may be thus rendered·

> Windy god, I know your plan,
> You are but my fellow-man;
> Blow you may your coldest breeze,
> Shingebiss you cannot freeze;
> Sweep the strongest wind you can,
> Shingebiss is still your man.
> Heigh! for life—and ho! for bliss;
> Who so free as Shingebiss?

The hunter knew that Kabebonicca was at his door, for he felt his cold and strong breath; but he kept on singing his songs, and affected utter indifference. At length Kabebonicca entered, and took his seat on the opposite side of the lodge; but Shingebiss did not regard or notice him. He got up as if nobody were present, and, taking his poker, pushed the log, which made his fire burn brighter, repeating as he sat down again:

You are but my fellow-man.

Very soon the tears began to flow down Kabebonicca's cheeks, which increased so fast that presently he said to himself, "I cannot stand this—I must go out." He did so, and left Shingebiss to his songs; but resolved to freeze up all the flag orifices and make the ice thick, so that he could not get any more fish. Still Shingebiss, by dint of great diligence, found means to pull up new roots and dive under for fish. At last Kabebonicca was compelled to give up the contest. "He must be aided by some Monedo," said he; "I can neither freeze him, nor starve him; he is a very singular being. I will let him alone."

THE IROQUOIS.

FROM AN ADDRESS BEFORE THE WAS-AH HO-DE-NO-SON-NE.

LOOKING around over the wide forests and translucent lakes of New York, we have beheld the footprints of the lordly Iroquois, crowned by the feathers of the eagle, bearing in his hand the bow and arrows, and scorning by the keen glances of his black eye, and the loftiness of his tread, the very earth that bore him up. History and tradition speak of the story of this ancient race.—They paint him as a man of war—of endurance—of indomitable courage—of capacity to endure tortures without complaint—of a heroic and noble independence. They tell us that these precincts, now waving with yellow corn, and smiling with villages, and glittering with spires, were once vocal with their war songs, and resounded with the chorusses of their corn feasts. We descry, as we plough the plain, the well-chipped darts which pointed their arrows, and the elongated pestles that crushed their maze. We exhume from their obliterated and simple graves the pipe of steatite, in which they smoked, and offered incense to these deities, and the fragments of the culinary vases, around which the lodge circle gathered to their forest meal. Mounds and trenches and ditches speak of the movement of tribe against tribe, and dimly shadow forth the overthrow of nations. There are no plated columns of marble—no tablets of inscribed stone—no gates of rust-coated brass. But the man himself survives in his generation. He is a walking statue before us. His looks and his gestures and his language remain. And he is himself an attractive monument to be studied. Shall we neglect him and his antiquarian vestiges, to run after foreign sources of intellectual study? Shall we toil amid the ruins of Thebes and Palmyra, while we have before us the monumental enigma of an unknown race? Shall philosophical ardour expend itself in searching after the buried sites of Nineveh, and Babylon, and Troy, while we have not attempted, with decent research, to collect, arrange, and determine the leading data of our aboriginal history and antiquities? . . .

No branch of the human family is an object unworthy of high philosophic inquiry. Their food, their language, their arts, their physical peculiarities, and their mental traits are each topics of deep interest, and susceptible of being converted into evidences of high importance. Mistaken our Red Men clearly were, in their theories and opinions on many points. They were wretched theologists and poor casuists. But not more so, in three-fourths of their dogmas, than the disciples of Zoroaster, or Confucius. They were polytheists from their very position. And yet, there is a general idea, that under every form they acknowledged but one divine intelligence under the name of the Great Spirit.

They paid their sacrifices to the imaginary and fantastic gods of the air, the woods and water, as Greece and Rome had done, and done as blindly, before them. But they were a vigorous, hardy, and brave off-shoot of the original race of man. They were full of humanities. They had many qualities to command admiration. They were wise in council, they were eloquent in the defence of their rights. They were kind and humane to the weak, bewildered, and friendless. Their lodge-board was ever ready for the wayfarer. They were constant to a proverb in their *professed* friendships. They never forgot a kind act. Nor can it be recorded, to their dispraise, that they were a terror to their enemies. Their character was formed on the military principle, and to acquire distinction in this line, they roved over half the continent. . . .

But all their efforts would have ended in disappointment had it not been for that principle of confederation, which, at an early day, pervaded their councils and converted them into a phalanx, which no other tribe could successfully penetrate or resist. It is this trait by which they are most distinguished from the other hunter nations of North America; and it is to their rigid adherence to the verbal compact, which bound them together as tribes and clans, that they owe their present celebrity, and owed their former power.

ORVILLE DEWEY.

[Born 1793.]

THE REVEREND ORVILLE DEWEY, D.D., was born in Sheffield, Berkshire county, Massachusetts, in the year 1794, and after graduating in 1814 at Williams College, studied theology in the seminary at Andover. His views respecting the doctrine of the Trinity had from the first been unsettled, and at the end of a year from his first entrance into the ministry he joined the Unitarians. When Dr. Channing, soon after, went to Europe, Mr. Dewey took his place; and that he was able for a long time to give perfect satisfaction to a society accustomed to the sermons of Channing is evidence that he had great merits as a preacher.

He was subsequently pastor of a church in New Bedford, for about ten years, at the end of which period ill health made necessary his temporary retirement from the pulpit, and he passed two years in foreign travel. Soon after his return he became pastor of the church of the Messiah in New York, with which he has since retained his connection, except during a second visit to Europe in 1841 and 1842.

In 1835 he published Discourses on Various Subjects, selected from those he had preached to his congregation at New Bedford, and containing some of his finest religious essays.

This volume was followed in the spring of 1836 with The Old World and the New, being a Journal of Observations and Reflections made on a Visit to Europe in 1833 and 1834: a very interesting work, with descriptive passages quite equal to any in the books of Slidell Mackenzie, Caleb Cushing, or the later American travellers in the same countries, and others betraying a profound sympathy with humanity, and containing just reflections on the social, political and religious condition of the people, under various institutions, which place it in the first class of speculative diaries.

In 1838 he published Moral Views of Commerce, Society and Politics, in Twelve Discourses, on the moral laws of trade, the uses of labour and passion for a fortune, the moral limits of accumulation, the natural and artificial relations of society, the moral evil to which American society is exposed, the place which education and religion must have in the improvement of society, and on associations, social ambition, war, political morality, and the blessings of freedom: subjects out of the usual range of pulpit discussion, (which still has too little to do with the great mass of human actions and interests,) but none the less worthy on this account of being treated by a Christian minister. This is one of the best practical books on the dangers and duties of the Christian freeman that has been written. The interesting questions which it embraces are discussed with calmness, candor, and generally sound judgment. Customs and opinions are subjected to the test of Christian morality, and whatever will not bear this, however sanctioned by observance or authority, is with vigor and manly frankness pointed out and condemned. In 1841 he gave to the public his fourth work, under the title of Discourses on Human Life; and in 1846 a fifth, embracing Discourses and Reviews on Questions relating to Controversial Theology and Practical Religion. In addition to these volumes he has published many single sermons, eulogies and other tracts, some of which are among his best and most useful performances.

Dr. Dewey is one of the most popular pulpit orators this country has produced. He is admired by those who are capable of appreciating the philosophy of morals, without reference to his peculiar theological belief. His reasoning is generally comprehensive, and his illustrations often poetical. There is a happy mixture of ease and finish in his style, and he is remarkable for interesting the hearer in themes which would be trite if treated with less earnestness. Perhaps the pathos of his rhetoric is its most effective characteristic. In speaking of the wants, sufferings and destinies of humanity, there is frequently a touching eloquence in his appeals which strikes a responsive chord in every sensitive and thoughtful heart.

An edition of his works has recently been published in England, and another, enlarged, was published in 1847, in New York, in 3 vols.

THE DANGER OF RICHES.
FROM MORAL VIEWS OF SOCIETY, ETC.

Ah! the rust of riches!—not that portion of them which is kept bright in good and holy uses—"and the consuming fire" of the passions which wealth engenders! No rich man—I lay it down as an axiom of all experience—no rich man is safe, who is not a benevolent man. No rich man is safe, but in the imitation of that benevolent God, who is the possessor and dispenser of all the riches of the universe. What else mean the miseries of a selfish, luxurious and fashionable life everywhere? What mean the sighs that come up from the purlieus, and couches, and most secret haunts of all splendid and self-indulgent opulence? Do not tell me that other men are sufferers too. Say not that the poor, and destitute and forlorn, are miserable also. Ah! just heaven! thou hast in thy mysterious wisdom appointed to them a lot hard, full hard, to bear. Poor houseless wretches! who "eat the bitter bread of penury, and drink the baleful cup of misery;" the winter's winds blow keenly through your "looped and windowed raggedness;" your children wander about unshod, unclothed and untended; I wonder not that ye sigh. But why should those who are surrounded with every thing that heart can wish, or imagination conceive—the very crumbs that fall from whose table of prosperity might feed hundreds—why should they sigh amidst their profusion and splendour? *They have broken the bond that should connect power with usefulness, and opulence with mercy.* That is the reason. They have taken up their treasures, and wandered away into a forbidden world of their own, far from the sympathies of suffering humanity; and the heavy night-dews are descending upon their splendid revels; and the all-gladdening light of heavenly beneficence is exchanged for the sickly glare of selfish enjoyment; and happiness, the blessed angel that hovers over generous deeds and heroic virtues, has fled away from that world of false gaiety and fashionable exclusion.

FREEDOM OF OPINION.
FROM THE SAME.

Observe, in how many relations, political, religious and social, a man is liable to find bondage instead of freedom. If he wants office, he must attach himself to a party, and then his eyes must be sealed in blindness, and his lips in silence, toward all the faults of his party. He *may* have his eyes open, and he may see much to condemn, but he must *say* nothing. If he edits a newspaper, his choice is often between bondage and beggary. That may actually be the choice, though he does not know it. He may be so completely a slave, that he does not feel the chain. His passions may be so enlisted in the cause of his party, as to blind his discrimination, and destroy all comprehension and capability of independence. So it may be with the religious partisan. He knows, perhaps, that there are errors in his adopted creed, faults in his sect, fanaticism and extravagance in some of its

measures. See if you get him to speak of them. See if you can get him to breathe a whisper of doubt. No, he is always believing. He has a convenient phrase that covers up all difficulties in his creed. He believes it "for *substance* of doctrine." Or if he is a layman, perhaps he does not believe it at all. What then is his conclusion? Why, he has friends who do believe it; and he does not wish to offend them. And so he goes on, listening to what he does not believe; outwardly acquiescing, inwardly remonstrating; the slave of fear or fashion, never daring, not once in his life daring, to speak out openly the thought that is in him. Nay, he sees men suffering under the weight of public reprobation, for the open espousal of the very opinions *he* holds, and he has never the generosity or manliness to say, "*I* think so too." Nay, more; by the course he pursues, he is made to cast his stone, or he holds it in his hand, at least, and lets another arm apply the force necessary to cast it, at the very men who are suffering a sort of martyrdom *for his own faith!*

I am not now advocating any particular opinions. I am only advocating a manly freedom in the expression of those opinions which a man does entertain. And if those opinions are unpopular, I hold that, in this country, there is so much the more need of an open and independent expression of them. Look at the case most seriously, I beseech you. What is ever to correct the faults of society, if nobody lifts his voice against them; if every body goes on openly doing what everybody privately complains of; if all shrink behind the faint-hearted apology, that it would be over-bold in them to attempt any reform? What is to rebuke political time-serving, religious fanaticism, or social folly, if no one has the independence to protest against them? Look at it in a larger view. What barrier is there against the universal despotism of public opinion in this country, but individual freedom? Who is to stand up against it here, but the possessor of that lofty independence? There is no king, no sultan, no noble, no privileged class; nobody else to stand against it. If you yield this point, if you are for ever making compromises, if all men do this, if the entire policy of private life here, is to escape opposition and reproach, every thing will be swept beneath the popular wave. There will be no individuality, no hardihood, no high and stern resolve, no self-subsistence, no fearless dignity, no glorious manhood of mind, left among us. The holy heritage of our fathers' virtues will be trodden under foot, by their unworthy children. *They* feared not to stand up against kings and nobles, and parliament and people. Better did they account it, that their lonely bark should sweep the wide sea in freedom—happier were they, when their sail swelled to the storm of winter, than to be slaves in palaces of ease. Sweeter to their ear was the music of the gale, that shrieked in their broken cordage, than the voice at home that said, "submit, and you shall have rest." And when they reached this wild shore, and built their altar, and knelt upon the frozen snow and the flinty rock to worship, they built that altar to freedom, to individual freedom, to freedom of conscience and opinion ; and their noble prayer was, that their children might be thus free. Let their sons remember the prayer of their extremity, and the great bequest which their magnanimity has left us. Let them beware how they become entangled again in the yoke of bondage. Let the ministers at God's altar, let the guardians of the press, let all sober and thinking men, speak the thought that is in them. It is better to speak honest *error*, than to suppress conscious truth. Smothered error is more dangerous than that which flames and burns out. But do I speak of danger ? I know of but one thing safe in the universe, and that is truth. And I know of but one way to truth for an individual mind, and that is, unfettered thought. And I know but one path for the multitude to truth, and that is, thought, freely expressed. Make of truth itself an altar of slavery, and guard it about with a mysterious shrine ; bind thought as a victim upon it ; and let the passions of the prejudiced multitude minister fuel ; and you sacrifice upon that accursed altar, the hopes of the world !

FREEDOM AND PATRIOTISM.

FROM THE SAME.

God has stamped upon our very humanity this impress of freedom. It is the unchartered prerogative of human nature. A soul ceases to be a soul, in proportion as it ceases to be free. Strip it of this, and you strip it of one of its essential and characteristic attributes. It is this that draws the footsteps of the wild Indian to his wide and boundless desert-paths, and makes him prefer them to the gay saloons and soft carpets of sumptuous palaces. It is this that makes it so difficult to bring him within the pale of artificial civilization. Our roving tribes are perishing—a sad and solemn sacrifice upon the altar of their wild freedom. They come among us, and look with childish wonder upon the perfection of our arts, and the splendour of our habitations : they submit with ennui and weariness, for a few days, to our burdensome forms and restraints ; and then turn their faces to their forest homes, and resolve to push those homes onward till they sink in the Pacific waves, rather than not be free.

It is thus that every people is attached to its country, just in proportion as it is free. No matter if that country be in the rocky fastnesses of Switzerland, amidst the snows of Tartary, or on the most barren and lonely Island-shore ; no matter if that country be so poor as to force away its children to other and richer lands, for employment and sustenance ; yet when the songs of those free homes chance to fall upon the exile's ear, no soft and ravishing airs that wait upon the timid feastings of Asiatic opulence ever thrilled the heart with such mingled rapture and agony as those simple tones. Sad mementoes might they be of poverty and want and toil ; yet it was enough that they were mementoes of happy freedom. And more than once has it been necessary to forbid by

39

military orders, in the armies of the Swiss mercenaries, the singing of their native songs.

And such an attachment, do I believe, is found in our own people, to their native country. It is the country of the free ; and that single consideration compensates for the want of many advantages which other countries possess over us. And glad am I, that it opens wide its hospitable gates, to many a noble but persecuted citizen, from the dungeons of Austria and Italy, and the imprisoning castles and citadels of Poland. Here may they find rest, as they surely find sympathy, though it is saddened with many bitter remembrances !

Yes, let me be free ; let me go and come at my own will ; let me do business and make journeys, without a vexatious police or insolent soldiery to watch my steps ; let me think, and do, and speak, what I please, subject to no limit but that which is set by the common weal ; subject to no law but that which conscience binds upon me ; and I will bless my country, and love its most rugged rocks and its most barren soil.

I have seen my countrymen, and have been with them a fellow-wanderer, in other lands ; and little did I see or feel to warrant the apprehension, sometimes expressed, that foreign travel would weaken our patriotic attachments. One sigh for home— home, arose from all hearts. And why, from palaces and courts—why, from galleries of the arts, where the marble softens into life, and painting sheds an almost living presence of beauty around it—why, from the mountain's awful brow, and the lovely valleys and lakes touched with the sunset hues of old romance—why, from those venerable and touching ruins to which our very heart grows—why, from all these scenes, were they looking beyond the swellings of the Atlantic wave, to a dearer and holier spot of earth—their own, own country. Doubtless, it was, in part, because it is their country ? But it was also, as every one's experience will testify, because they knew that *there* was no oppression, no pitiful exaction of petty tyranny ; because that *there*, they knew, was no accredited and irresistible religious domination ; because that *there*, they knew, they should not meet the odious soldier at every corner, nor swarms of imploring beggars, the victims of misrule ; that *there*, no curse causeless did fall, and no blight, worse than plague and pestilence, did descend amidst the pure dews of heaven ; because, in fine, that *there*, they knew, was liberty—upon all the green hills, and amidst all the peaceful valleys— liberty, the wall of fire around the humblest home ; the crown of glory, studded with her ever-blazing stars upon the proudest mansion !

My friends, upon our own homes that blessing rests, that guardian care and glorious crown ; and when we return to those homes, and so long as we dwell in them—so long as no oppressor's foot invades their thresholds, let us bless them, and hallow them as the homes of freedom ! Let us make them, too, the homes of a nobler freedom—of freedom from vice, from evil, from passion—from every corrupting bondage of the soul.

2 c 2

MORAL DANGER OF BUSINESS.
FROM THE SAME.

I ASK, if there is not good ground for the admonitions on this point, of every moral and holy teacher of every age? What means, if there is not, that eternal disingenuity of trade, that is ever putting on fair appearances and false pretences—of "the buyer that says, it is naught, it is naught, but when he is gone his way, then boasteth"—of the seller, who is always exhibiting the best samples, not fair but false samples, of what he has to sell; of the seller, I say, who, to use the language of another, "if he is tying up a bundle of quills, will place several in the centre, of not half the value of the rest, and thus sends forth a hundred liars, with a fair outside, to proclaim as many falsehoods to the world?" These practices, alas! have fallen into the regular course of the business of many. All men expect them; and therefore, you may say, that nobody is deceived. But deception is intended: else why are these things done? What if nobody is deceived? The seller himself is corrupted. He may stand acquitted of dishonesty in the moral code of worldly traffic; no man may charge him with dishonesty; and yet to himself he is a dishonest man. Did I say that nobody is deceived? Nay, but somebody is deceived. This man, the seller, is grossly, wofully deceived. He thinks to make a little profit by his contrivances; and he is selling, by pennyworths, the very integrity of his soul. Yes, the prettiest shop where these things are done, may be to the spiritual vision, a place of more than tragic interest. It is the stage on which the great action of life is performed. There stands a man, who in the sharp collisions of daily traffic, might have polished his mind to the bright and beautiful image of truth, who might have put on the noble brow of candor, and cherished the very soul of uprightness. I have known such a man. I have looked into his humble shop. I have seen the mean and soiled articles with which he is dealing. And yet the process of things going on there, was as beautiful as if it had been done in heaven! But now, what is this man—the man who always turns up to you the better side of every thing he sells—the man of unceasing contrivances and expedients, his life long, to make things appear better than they are? Be he the greatest merchant or the poorest huckster, he is a mean, a knavish—and were I not awed by the thoughts of his immortality, I should say—a contemptible creature; whom nobody that knows him can trust, whom nobody can reverence. Not one thing in the dusty repository of things, great or small, which he deals with, is so vile as he. What *is* this *thing* then, which is done, or may be done, in the house of traffic? I tell you, though you may have thought not so of it—I tell you that *there*, even *there*, a soul may be lost!—that that very structure, built for the gain of earth, may be the gate of hell! Say not that this fearful appellation should be applied to worse places than that. A man may as certainly corrupt all the integrity and virtue of his soul in a warehouse or a shop, as in a gambling-house or a brothel.

THE PEOPLE NOT ALWAYS RIGHT.
FROM THE SAME.

I MAINTAIN, that our democratic principle is not that the people are always right. It is this rather; that although the people may sometimes be wrong, yet that they are not so likely to be wrong and to do wrong as irresponsible, hereditary magistrates and legislators; that it is safer to trust the many with the keeping of their own interests, than it is to trust the few to keep those interests for them. The people are *not* always right; they are often wrong. They must be so, from the very magnitude, difficulty and complication of the questions that are submitted to them. I am amazed, that thinking men, conversant with these questions, should address such gross flattery and monstrous absurdity to the people, as to be constantly telling them, that *they* will put all these questions right at the ballot-box. And I am no less amazed, that a sensible people should suffer such folly to be spoken to them. Is it possible that the people believe it? Is it possible that the majority itself of any people can be so infatuated as to hold, that in virtue of its being a majority, it is always right? Alas! for truth, if it is to depend on votes! *Has* the majority always been right in religion or in philosophy? But the science of politics involves questions no less intricate and difficult. And on these questions, there are grave and solemn decisions to be made by the people; great state problems are submitted to them; such, for instance, as concerning internal improvements, the tariff, the currency, banking, and the nicest points of construction; which cost even the wisest men much study; and what the people require for the solution of these questions, is *not* rash haste, boastful confidence, furious anger and mad strife, but sobriety, calmness, modesty—qualities, indeed, that would go far to abate the violence of our parties, and to hush the brawls of our elections. I do not deny, that questions of deep national concern may justly awaken great zeal and earnestness; but I do deny, that the public mind should be bolstered up with the pride of supposing itself to possess any complete, much less, any suddenly acquired knowledge of them. I am willing to take my fellow-citizens for my governors, with all their errors; I prefer their will, legally signified, to any other government; but to say or imply, that they do not err and often err, is a doctrine alike preposterous in general theory, and pernicious in its effects upon themselves.

JARED SPARKS.

[Born about 1794.   Died 1866.]

THE former Professor of History in Harvard University is a native of Connecticut. He graduated at Cambridge in 1815, and was subsequently for some time one of the tutors there. Having completed his theological studies, and entered the ministry, he was ordained over the first Unitarian Church in Baltimore on the fifth of May, 1819, on which occasion Dr. Channing delivered his celebrated sermon on Unitarian Christianity.

For several years Mr. Sparks wrote largely upon subjects of theological and ecclesiastical controversy, and published, with other works, in 1820, Letters on the Ministry, Ritual and Doctrines of the Protestant Episcopal Church, and in 1823, An Inquiry into the Comparative Moral Tendency of Trinitarian and Unitarian Doctrines, in a series of Letters to Samuel Miller, D. D. of Princeton. From 1823 to 1830 he conducted The North American Review, and in 1828 he commenced that noble series of volumes illustrative of American history to which he has nearly ever since devoted himself, and which have for ever associated his own with the names of the most illustrious of our countrymen.

The first of his historical works was The Life of John Ledyard, the American Navigator and Traveller, in one octavo volume, composed chiefly from manuscripts in possession of Ledyard's family. The second was The Diplomatic Correspondence of the American Revolution, in twelve volumes, published from 1829 to 1831, by order of Congress, under the direction of the President of the United States. The third was The Life of Gouverneur Morris, in three volumes, issued in 1832. The curious details contained in the diary of Morris respecting the Revolution in France, where he was our minister during the Reign of Terror, and the vivacity and point of his correspondence with the most celebrated persons of his age, render this work one of the most interesting in our historical literature. Mr. Sparks exhibited in the selection and arrangement of his materials discriminating judgment and integrity; and the favour with which it was received encouraged him to proceed in the preparation of his Life and Writings of Washington, which was published in twelve octavo volumes, between the years 1833 and 1840. He had access not only to the manuscripts of Washington but to every thing that could illustrate his subject in the archives of the United States, England and France, and produced a work in all respects as nearly perfect as possible. The memoir by Mr. Sparks, which occupies the first volume, with a selection of the most important of the letters, was translated into French and published in Paris, in six volumes, by Guizot, who added an original essay on Washington's character; and the whole work was translated into German and published at Leipsic by Von Raumer.

In 1835 he commenced the publication of his admirable edition of the Complete Works of Franklin, with a memoir, of which the tenth and last volume appeared in 1840. The autobiography of Franklin is continued by Mr. Sparks to his death, the numerous questions respecting the authorship of writings attributed to him are satisfactorily decided, and elucidatory notes added wherever they are necessary. It was a labour of difficulty, owing to the carelessness of Franklin respecting his literary reputation, and on other accounts, and it was executed with a diligence and discretion which left nothing to be desired.

The Library of American Biography was commenced by Mr. Sparks in 1835, and the first series of ten volumes was completed in 1839. In this he wrote the lives of Ethan Allen, Benedict Arnold, and Father Marquette. The second series of ten volumes, for which he wrote the lives of Pulaski, La Salle, Ribault, and Charles Lee, was begun in 1843 and finished in 1846. These twenty volumes, in the preparation of which he was aided by the Everetts, Prescott, Wheaton, Charles F. Hoffman, Henry Reed, George Hillard, and other distinguished men of letters, is second in interest and value to no series of original works ever printed in this country.

There is little danger of estimating the labours of Mr. Sparks too highly. He at an early age entered with enthusiasm on his favourite pursuit, and has devoted to it the best years of his life. His researches have been prosecuted with untiring diligence, and with such success that almost every question within their scope, which was open at their commencement, has through them been definitively settled. We feel sure that the documentary evidence he brings to bear on any point is as full and satisfactory as can be had ; and his mere opinion, observes one of our most acute and well informed critics,* is entitled to great weight, when not supported by direct proof. His negative testimony, when he says nothing can be found to support an allegation, is nearly conclusive, for we are confident the assertion is not lightly made, and may fairly presume that what has escaped his researches does not exist.

The great merits of Mr. Sparks are reverence for truth, soundness of judgment in regard to evidence, and exhausting fulness of detail and illustration. His defect as a historian seems to be a certain timidity, an unwillingness to disturb old prejudices, which occasionally has prevented his removing masks behind which he himself has seen. A little more boldness, a determination to give the whole truth as well as nothing but the truth, would have proved as advantageous for the present and more so for the future.

The style of Mr. Sparks is clear and exact, but it has little variety or vivacity. He lacks skill in grouping, but compensates for this by the accuracy of his drawing, and the studied propriety of his costume. It is less probable that he will be a popular historian than that he will be an enduring and in many cases an ultimate authority.

Mr. Sparks was appointed in 1839, Professor of History in Harvard, and in 1849 succeeded Mr. Everett as president, but resigned in 1853, on account of ill health. In 1854, appeared the Correspondence of the American Revolution, 4 vols., 8vo. He visited Europe in 1858 to obtain materials to assist him in his preparation of a History of the Revolution, which he did not live to complete or publish, as he died at Cambridge, March 14, 1866.

AMERICAN HISTORY.

In many respects the history of North America differs from that of every other country, and in this difference it possesses an interest peculiar to itself, especially for those whose lot has been cast here, and who look back with a generous pride to the deeds of ancestors, by whom a nation's existence has been created, and a nation's glory adorned. We shall speak of this history, as divided into two periods, the Colonial, and the Revolutionary.

When we talk of the history of our country, we are not to be understood as alluding to any particular book, or to the labours of any man, or number of men, in treating this subject. If we have a few compilations of merit, embracing detached portions and limited periods, there is yet wanting a work, the writer of which shall undertake the task of plodding his way through all the materials, printed and in manuscript, and digesting them into a united, continuous, lucid, and philosophical whole, bearing the shape, and containing the substance of genuine history. No tempting encouragement, it is true, has been held out to such an enterprise. The absorbing present, in the midst of our stirring politics, and jarring party excitements, and bustling activity, has almost obliterated the past, or at least has left little leisure for pursuing the footsteps of the pilgrims, and the devious

* Mr. William B. Reed. In the North American Review, and in various tracts, he has discussed several historical and social questions with signal ability.

fortunes of our ancestors. The public taste has run in other directions, and no man of genius and industry has been found so courageous in his resolves, or prodigal of his labour, as to waste his life in digging into mines for treasures, which would cost him much, and avail him little. But symptoms of a change are beginning to appear, which it may be hoped will ere long be realized.

And when the time shall come for illustrating this subject, it will be discovered, that there are rich stores of knowledge among the hidden and forgotten records of our colonial history ; that the men of those days thought, and acted, and suffered with a wisdom, a fortitude, and an endurance, which would add lustre to any age ; and that they have transmitted an inheritance as honourable in the mode of its acquisition as it is dear to its present possessors. Notwithstanding the comparatively disconnected incidents in the history of this period, and the separate communities and governments to which it extends, it has nevertheless a *unity* and a consistency of parts, as well as copiousness of events, which make it a theme for the most gifted historian, and a study for every one who would enlarge his knowledge and profit by high example.

Unlike any other people, who have attained the rank of a nation, we may here trace our country's growth to the very elements of its origin, and consult the testimonies of reality, instead of the blind oracles of fable, and the legends of a dubious tradition. Besides a love of adventure, and an enthusiasm that surmounted every difficulty, the character of its founders was marked by a hardy enterprise and sturdiness of purpose, which carried them onward through perils and sufferings, that would have appalled weaker minds and less resolute hearts. This is the first great feature of resemblance in all the early settlers, whether they came to the north or to the south, and it merits notice from the influence it could not fail to exercise on their future acts and character, both domestic and political. The timid, the wavering, the feeble-minded, the sons of indolence and ease, were not among those who left the comforts of home, braved the tempests of the ocean, and sought danger on the shores of an unknown and inhospitable world. Incited by various motives they might have been; by a fondness for adventure, curiosity, gain, or a dread of oppression; yet none but the bold, energetic, determined, persevering, would yield to these motives or any other.

Akin to these characteristics, and indeed a concomitant with them, was a spirit of freedom, and a restlessness under constraint. The New England settlers, we know, came away on this ground alone, goaded to a sense of their invaded rights by the thorns of religious intolerance. But whatever motives may have operated, the prominent fact remains the same, and in this we may see throughout the colonies a uniform basis of that vigour of character, and indomitable love of liberty, which appeared ever afterwards, in one guise or another, whenever occasions called them out.

Hence it was, also, that the different colonies, although under dissimilar modes of government, some more and some less dependent on the crown, preserved a close resemblance in the spirit of their internal regulations, that spirit, or those principles, which entered deeply into the opinions of the people, and upon which their habits were formed.

Beginning everywhere in small bodies, elections implied almost a universal suffrage, and every individual became acquainted with his rights, and accustomed to use the power they gave him. Increase of numbers made no change in this respect. Charters were given and taken away, laws were annulled, and the King's judges decided against the colonial pretensions. The liberties of the mass were thus abridged, and the powers of legislation curtailed, but the people still went on, voting for their representatives and their municipal officers, and practising all the elementary acts of independent government; and the legislatures had new opportunities of asserting their rights before the world, studying them more deeply, watching over them more cautiously, and in this way gaining strength to their cause, through the agency of the very means that were employed to depress or destroy it. The primary elections were never reached by these oppressive measures of the supreme power, and, as they were founded on principles of close analogy in all the colonies, conformable to the circumstances of their origin, they were not only the guardian of the liberties of each, from its first foundation, but they became at last the cementing force, which bound them together, when a great and united effort was necessary.

Another element of unity in the colonial period was the fact of the colonists springing from the same stock; for although Holland, Germany and Sweden contributed a few settlers, yet the mass was of English origin, inheriting the free spirit that had been at work from the era of Runny Mead downwards, in building up the best parts of the British Constitution, and framing laws to protect them. The Sidneys, and Miltons, and Lockes of England were teachers in America as well as in their native land, and more effectual, because their instructions fell in a readier soil, and sprang up with a livelier and bolder growth. The books of England were the fountains of knowledge in America, from which all parts drew equally, imbibing common habitudes of thought and opinion, and an intellectual uniformity. Our fathers soon saw, that the basis of virtue, the security of civil order and freedom, must be laid in the intelligence of the people. Schools were established and means provided, not everywhere with a zeal so ardent, and a forethought so judicious, as among the descendants of the pilgrims, but yet in all places according to their situation, and the tendency of controlling causes.

The colonial wars form another combining principle in the unity of that period, and furnish materials for vivid delineations of character and animated narrative. The English and French colonies were always doomed to espouse the quarrels and participate in the broils of their rival heads in Europe, who continued to nourish a root of bitterness, that left but few intervals of peace, and fewer still of harmonious feeling. When the fire of discord was kindled into open hostility, its flame soon reached America, and roused all hearts to the conflict. Louisburg and Nova Scotia, Lake George and Braddock's field, Oswego and Niagara, have witnessed the bravery of our ancestors, and the blood they expended, fighting the battles as well of transatlantic ambition as of self-defence.

But there was a great moral cause at work in this train of events. By these trials, costly and severe as they were, the colonists were learning the extent of their physical resources, acting as one people, gaining the experience and nerving the sinews, that were at a future day to serve them in a mightier contest. Much blood was shed, but it was the price of future glory to their country, many a fair flower was cut off in the freshness of its bloom, many a sturdy oak was felled in the majesty of its strength, yet posterity will not forget the maxim of the Roman law, that they, who fall for their country, live in the immortality of their fame.

Next come the Indian wars, which commenced with the first landing of the pilgrim wanderers, and ceased not till the proud sons of the forest had melted away like an evening cloud, or disappeared in the remote solitudes of their own wildernesses. The wars of the Indians, their character and manners, their social and political condition, are original, having no prototype in any former time or race of men. They mingle in all the incidents of our colonial history, and stamp upon it an impression novel and peculiar.

With a strength of character and a reach of intellect, unknown in any other race of absolute savages, the Indian united many traits, some of them honourable and some degrading to humanity, which made him formidable in his enmity, faithless in his friendship, and at all times a dangerous neighbour: cruel, implacable, treacherous, yet not without a few of the better qualities of the heart and the head; a being of contrasts, violent in his passions, hasty in his anger, fixed in his revenge, yet cool in counsel, seldom betraying his plighted honour, hospitable, sometimes generous. A few names have stood out among them, which, with the culture of civilization, might have been shining stars on the lists of recorded fame. Philip, Pondiac, Sassacus, if the genius of another Homer were to embalm their memory, might rival the Hectors and Agamemnons of heroic renown, scarcely less savage, not less sagacious or brave.

Indian eloquence, if it did not flow with the richness of Nestor's wisdom, or burn with Achilles' fire, spoke in the deep strong tones of nature, and resounded from the chords of truth. The answer of the Iroquois chief to the French, who wished to purchase his lands, and push him farther into the wilderness, Voltaire has pronounced superior to any sayings of the great men commemorated by Plutarch. "We were born on this spot; our fathers were buried here. Shall we say to the bones of our fathers, arise, and go with us into a strange land?"

But more has been said of their figurative language, than seems to be justified by modern experience. Writers of fiction have distorted the Indian character, and given us anything but originals. Their fancy has produced sentimental Indians, a kind of beings that never existed in reality; and Indians clothing their ideas in the gorgeous imagery of external nature, which they had neither the refinement to conceive, nor words to express. In truth, when we have lighted the pipe of concord, kindled or extinguished a council fire, buried the bloody hatchet, sat down under the tree of peace with its spreading branches, and brightened the chain of friendship, we have nearly exhausted their flowers of rhetoric. But the imagery prompted by internal emotion, and not by the visible world, the eloquence of condensed thought and pointed expression, the eloquence of a diction extremely limited in its forms, but nervous and direct, the eloquence of truth unadorned and of justice undisguised, these are often found in Indian speeches, and constitute their chief characteristic.

It should, moreover, be said for the Indians, that, like the Carthaginians, their history has been written by their enemies. The tales of their wrongs and their achievements may have been told by the warrior-chiefs to stimulate the courage, and perpetuate the revenge of their children, but they were traces in the sand; they perished in a day, and their memory is gone.

Such are the outlines of our colonial history, which constitute its unity, and make it a topic worthy to be illustrated by the labours of industry and talent. The details, if less imposing, are copious and varied. The progress of society developing itself in new modes, at first in isolated communities scattered along the sea-coast, and then gradually approximating each other, extending to the interior, subduing the forests with a magic almost rivalling the lyre of Orpheus, and encountering everywhere the ferocity of uncivilized man; the plans of social government necessarily suggested by such a state of things, and their operations in the advancing stages of improvement and change; the fantastic codes of laws, and corresponding habitudes, that sprang from the reveries of our Puritan fathers; the admirable systems which followed them, conceived by men tutored only in the school of freedom and necessity, exceeding in political wisdom and security of rights the boasted schemes of ancient lawgivers; the wild and disorganizing frenzies of religious fanaticism; the misguided severities of religious intolerance; the strange aberrations of the human mind, and abuses of power, in abetting the criminal folly of witchcraft; the struggles, that were ever going on, between the Governors and the Assemblies, the former urging the demands of prerogative, the latter maintaining the claims of liberty; the sources of growing wealth; the influence of knowledge widely diffused, of religion unshackled by the trammels of power; the manners and habits of the people at different times and in different places, taking their hue from such a combination of causes; these, and a thousand other features deeply interesting and full of variety, belong to the portraiture of colonial history, giving symmetry to its parts, and completeness to the whole.

The Revolutionary period, like the Colonial, has hitherto been but imperfectly elucidated, and perhaps for the same reason. The voluminous materials, printed and unprinted, widely scattered in this country and in Europe, some obvious and well known, many unexplored, have been formidable obstacles to the execution of such an undertaking. No Rymers have yet appeared among us, who were willing to spend a life in gathering up and embodying these memorials; and, till public encouragement shall prompt and aid such a design, till the national representatives shall have leisure to pause for a moment from their weighty cares in adjusting the wheels of state, and emulate the munificent patriotism of other governments, by adopting measures to collect and preserve the perishing records of the wisdom and valour of their fathers; till this shall be done, the historian of the Revolution must labour under disadvantages, which his zeal will hardly stimulate him to encounter, nor his genius enable him to surmount.

The subject itself is one of the best that ever employed the pen of the writer, whether considered in the object at stake, the series of acts by which it was accomplished, or its consequences. It properly includes a compass of twenty years, extending from the close of the French war in America to the general peace at Paris. The best history in existence, though left unfinished, that of the Peloponnesian war, by Thucydides, embraces exactly the same space of time, and is not dissimilar in the details of its events. The revolutionary period, thus defined, is rounded with epic exactness, having a beginning, a middle, and an end; a time for causes to operate, for the stir of action, and for the final results.

The machinery in motion is on the broadest scale of grandeur. We see the new world, young in age, but resolute in youth, lifting up the arm of defiance against the haughtiest power of the old; fleets and armies, on one side, crossing the ocean in daring attitude and confiding strength; on the other, men rallying round the banner of union, and fighting on their natal soil for freedom, rights, existence; the long struggle and successful issue; hope confirmed, justice triumphant. The passions are likewise here at work, in all the changing scenes of politics and war, in the deliberations of the senate, the popular mind, and the martial excitements of the field. We have eloquence and deep thought in counsel, alertness and bravery in action, self-sacrifice, fortitude, and patient suffering of hardships through toil and danger to the last. If we search for the habiliments of dignity with which to clothe a historical subject, or the looser drapery of ornament with which to embellish a narrative, where shall we find them thronging more thickly, or in happier contrasts, than during this period?

The causes of the revolution, so fertile a theme of speculation, are less definite than have been imagined. The whole series of colonial events was a continued and accumulating cause. The spirit was kindled in England; it went with Robinson's congregation to Holland; it landed with them at Plymouth; it was the basis of the first constitution of these sage and self-taught legislators; it never left them nor their descendants. It extended to the other colonies, where it met with a kindred impulse, was nourished in every breast, and became rooted in the feelings of the whole people.

The revolution was a change of forms, but not of substance; the breaking of a tie, but not the creation of a principle; the establishment of an independent nation, but not the origin of its intrinsic political capacities. The foundations of society, although unsettled for the moment, were not essentially disturbed; its pillars were shaken, but never overthrown. The convulsions of war subsided, and the people found themselves, in their local relations and customs, their immediate privileges and enjoyments, just where they had been at the beginning. The new forms transferred the supreme authority from the King and Parliament of Great Britain to the hands of the people. This was a gain, but not a renovation; a security against future encroachments, but not an exemption from any old duty, nor an imposition of any new one, farther than that of being at the trouble to govern themselves.

Hence the latent cause of what has been called a revolution was the fact, that the political spirit and habits in America had waxed into a shape so different from those in England, that it was no longer convenient to regulate them by the same forms. In other words, the people had grown to be kings, and chose to exercise their sovereign prerogatives in their own way. Time alone would have effected the end, probably without so violent an explosion, had it not been hastened by particular events, which may be denominated the proximate causes.

These took their rise at the close of the French war, twelve years before the actual contest began. Relieved from future apprehensions of the French power on the frontiers, the colonists now had leisure to think of themselves, of their political affairs, their numbers, their united strength. At this juncture, the most inauspicious possible for the object in view, the precious device of taxing the colonies was resorted to by the British ministry, which, indeed, had been for some time a secret scheme in the cabinet, and had been recommended by the same sagacious governor of Virginia, who found the people in such a republican way of acting, that he could not manage them to his purpose.

The fruit of this policy was the Stamp Act, which has been considered a primary cause; and it was so, in the same sense that a torch is the cause of a conflagration, kindling the flame, but not creating the combustible materials. Effects then became causes, and the triumphant opposition to this tax was the case of its being renewed on tea and other articles, not so much, it was avowed, for the amount of revenue it would yield, as to vindicate the principle, that Parliament had a right to tax the colonies. The people resisted the act, and destroyed the tea, to show that they likewise had a principle, for which they felt an equal concern.

By these experiments on their patience, and these struggles to oppose them, their confidence was increased, as the tree gains strength at its root, by the repeated blasts of the tempests against its branches. From this time a mixture of causes was at work; the pride of power, the disgrace of defeat, the arrogance of office, on the one hand; a sense of wrong, indignant feeling, an enthusiasm for liberty on the other. These were secondary, having slight connection with the first springs of the Revolution, or the pervading force by which it was kept up, although important filaments in the network of history.

The acts of the Revolution derive dignity and interest from the character of the actors, and the nature and magnitude of the events. It has been remarked, that in all great political revolutions, men have arisen, possessed of extraordinary endowments, adequate to the exigency of the time. It is true enough, that such revolutions, or any remarkable and continued exertions of human power, must be brought to pass by corresponding qualities in the agents; but whether the occasion makes the men, or men the occasion, may not always be ascertained with exactness. In either case, however, no period has been adorned with examples more illustrious, or more perfectly adapted to the high destiny awaiting them, than that of the American Revolution.

Statesmen were at hand, who, if not skilled in the art of governing empires, were thoroughly imbued with the principles of just government, intimately acquainted with the history of former ages, and, above all, with the condition, sentiments, feelings of their countrymen. If there were no Richelieus nor Mazarines, no Cecils nor Chathams, in America, there were men, who, like Themistocles, knew how to raise a small state to glory and greatness.

The eloquence and the internal counsels of the Old Congress were never recorded; we know them only in their results; but that assembly, with no other power than that conferred by the suffrage of the people, with no other influence than that of their public virtue and talents, and without precedent to guide their deliberations, unsupported even by the arm of law or of ancient usages—that assembly levied troops, imposed taxes, and for years not only retained the confidence and upheld the civil existence of a distracted country, but carried through a perilous war under its most aggravating burdens of sacrifice and suffering. Can we imagine a situation, in which were required higher moral courage, more intelligence and talent, a deeper insight into human nature and the principles of social and political organizations, or, indeed, any of those qualities which constitute greatness of character in a statesman? See, likewise, that work of wonder, the Confederation, a union of independent states, constructed in the very heart of a desolating war, but with a beauty and strength, imperfect as it was, of which the ancient leagues of the Amphictyons, the Achæans, the Lycians, and the modern confederacies of Germany, Holland, Switzerland, afford neither exemplar nor parallel.

In their foreign affairs these same statesmen showed no less sagacity and skill, taking their stand boldly in the rank of nations, maintaining it there, competing with the tactics of practised diplomacy, and extorting from the powers of the old world not only the homage of respect, but the proffers of friendship.

The military events of the Revolution, which necessarily occupy so much of its history, are not less honourable to the actors, nor less fruitful in the evidences they afford of large design and ability of character. But these we need not recount. They live in the memory of all; we have heard them from the lips of those who saw and suffered; they are inscribed on imperishable monuments; the very hills and plains around us tell of achievements which can never die; and the day will come, when the traveller, who has gazed and pondered at Marathon and Waterloo, will linger on the mount where Prescott fought and Warren fell, and say— Here is the field where man has struggled in his most daring conflict; here is the field where liberty poured out her noblest blood, and won her brightest and most enduring laurels.

Happy was it for America, happy for the world, that a great name, a guardian genius, presided over her destinies in war, combining more than the virtues of the Roman Fabius and the Theban Epaminondas, and compared with whom, the conquerors of the world, the Alexanders and Cæsars, are but pageants crimsoned with blood and decked with the trophies of slaughter, objects equally of the wonder and the execration of mankind. The

hero of America was the conqueror only of his country's foes, and the hearts of his countrymen. To the one he was a terror, and in the other he gained an ascendency, supreme, unrivalled, the tribute of admiring gratitude, the reward of a nation's love.

The American armies, compared with the embattled legions of the old world, were small in numbers, but the soul of a whole people centred in the bosom of these more than Spartan bands, and vibrated quickly and keenly with every incident that befell them, whether in their feats of valour, or the acuteness of their sufferings. The country itself was one wide battle-field, in which not merely the life-blood, but the dearest interests, the sustaining hopes, of every individual, were at stake. It was not a war of pride and ambition between monarchs, in which an island or a province might be the award of success; it was a contest for personal liberty and civil rights, coming down in its principles to the very sanctuary of home and the fireside, and determining for every man the measure of responsibility he should hold over his own condition, possessions, and happiness. The spectacle was grand and new, and may well be cited as the most glowing page in the annals of progressive man.

The instructive lesson of history, teaching by example, can nowhere be studied with more profit, or with a better promise, than in this revolutionary period of America; and especially by us, who sit under the tree our fathers have planted, enjoy its shade, and are nourished by its fruits. But little is our merit, or gain, that we applaud their deeds, unless we emulate their virtues. Love of country was in them an absorbing principle, an undivided feeling; not of a fragment, a section, but of the whole country. Union was the arch on which they raised the strong tower of a nation's independence. Let the arm be palsied, that would loosen one stone in the basis of this fair structure, or mar its beauty; the tongue mute, that would dishonour their names, by calculating the value of that which they deemed without price.

They have left us an example already inscribed in the world's memory; an example portentous to the aims of tyranny in every land; an example that will console in all ages the drooping aspirations of oppressed humanity. They have left us a written charter as a legacy, and as a guide to our course. But every day convinces us, that a written charter may become powerless. Ignorance may misinterpret it; ambition may assail and faction destroy its vital parts; and aspiring knavery may at last sing its requiem on the tomb of departed liberty. It is the spirit which lives; in this are our safety and our hope; the spirit of our fathers; and while this dwells deeply in our remembrance, and its flame is cherished, ever burning, ever pure, on the altar of our hearts; while it incites us to think as they have thought, and do as they have done, the honour and the praise will be ours, to have preserved unimpaired the rich inheritance, which they so nobly achieved.

JOHN NEAL.

[Born 1793.]

JOHN NEAL was born in Portland, October 25th, 1793. His parents were Quakers, but his father died while he was an infant, and his mother, though she put him in drab, could by no means instil into him the peaceable notions of which that colour is the sign, as appeared when he disturbed the silence of a meeting in which there had been no moving of a better spirit, by knocking down a young broad-rim who had insulted him. This was when he was about ten years of age. It was a bad beginning for a disciple of George Fox; and he was probably " turned out of meeting" at once, for he has been combating something or other ever since. At school he is said to have been most remarkable for his ingenious and daring evasions of the master's authority; he did not "take much to the learning of books;" but in a dry goods shop, in which he was placed at twelve, he did better, and soon became master of the eloquence, arts, and mysteries of bargaining. He continued to be a salesman or accountant five or six years, in Portland and Portsmouth, and was then a teacher of penmanship and drawing in the principal eastern villages, and at twenty went to Boston, and soon after to New York, in which cities he was a clerk, shopkeeper, and speculator in general, until, having acquired considerable money, he proceeded to Baltimore, where he commenced more extensive operations, with John Pierpont, who had been educated for the bar, and in consequence of ill-health had given up his profession for the more active one of a merchant. They established a wholesale store in Charleston, and two of the same kind in Baltimore, where they also had a shop for retailing. They did a great business, until their failure, which occurred in a reasonable time; and then Pierpont studied divinity and wrote the Airs of Palestine, and Neal studied law, and wrote such books and did such other things as will be hereinafter mentioned.

At the time of the bursting of his commercial bubbles, Mr. Neal was but twenty-three years of age. He had not saved a cent, and

was out of business. He had energy and a genius for any thing or every thing, and he must do something, or starve. After a short deliberation he determined, as has been intimated, to be a lawyer, but the rules of court, whatever might be his knowledge, required the devotion of years to the study of the books; and how was he to live meanwhile? He would turn author! he had scarcely any education, was ignorant even of the first principles of English grammar, and had never written a line for the press except his advertisements; but nevertheless he determined to be a scholar and critic, and do what no other person was then able to do in this country, gain a living by literature.

He made his first appearance as an author in a review of the works of Byron, in The Portico. It gained him much reputation, and he was immediately engaged as a regular contributor to that then popular magazine. Within a month or two he became editor of the Baltimore Telegraph, for which he wrote largely every day upon whatever was attracting attention. In 1817 he published his first book, Keep Cool, a Novel, written in Hot Weather, which he himself has described characteristically as " a foolish, fiery thing, with a good deal of nature and originality, and much more nonsense and flummery in it." About the same time he prepared an index to Niles' Weekly Register, which made over two hundred and fifty very closely printed imperial octavo pages, and is spoken of by Mr. Niles as "probably the most laborious work of the kind that ever appeared in any country." In 1818 he published The Battle of Niagara, Goldau the Maniac Harper, and Other Poems, by "Jehu O'Cataract,"* and Otho, a Tragedy, and in the following year he assisted Dr. Watkins in writing the History of the American Revolution, which is com-

---

* This name was given to him by the members of a club of which he was then a member, and was characteristic of his impetuous and stormful temperament. In the second edition of his poems, in which they were much improved, he substituted John Neal for it, on the title-page.

monly ascribed to Paul Allen. He had succeeded in supporting himself very handsomely
by these literary labours, and was now admitted to the bar, and with flattering prospects
entered upon the practice of his profession.

In 1822 appeared his second novel, Logan,
a sort of rhapsody, in two thick volumes,
which was followed in the spring of 1823 by
Seventy-Six, a work which showed more dramatic method, and was more popular than
either of its predecessors. Within two or
three months after, he published Randolph,
which he informs us was written in thirty-six
days, with an interval of about a week between the two volumes, in which he wrote
nothing. A sensation was made by the notices which it contained of the most prominent
statesmen, orators, authors, artists, and other
public characters of the time, who were criti-
cised in it with unhesitating freedom, in a style
peculiarly his own, and often with great keenness and discrimination. A sketch of William
Pinkney, in which that eminent lawyer had
full justice done to his abilities and acquisitions, gave offence to his son, Edward Coate
Pinkney, then a midshipman in the navy, and
afterward distinguished as a very graceful and
elegant poet. Young Pinkney was a sort of
sentimental Quixote, so sudden in quarrel as
to be avoided as much as possible by his peace
loving acquaintances, but so skilful in finding
causes of feud, that the most careful of them
would not at any time have been surprised by
his challenge. Mr. Neal denied that he could
be held accountable for the contents of an anonymous and unacknowledged publication, and as
he had been for several months writing against
the custom of duelling, would probably for the
sake of consistency have refused under any
circumstances to fight. On receiving his answer Pinkney posted him as a " craven," and
for a week afterward walked two hours every
day before his office, that he might have ample
opportunities of taking satisfaction on his person. But our author, whose courage, or rashness even, appears not to have been doubted,
was preparing a different revenge, and soon
printed the correspondence, gave a fac simile
of the " posting," and turned the whole affair
into ridicule, in a postscript to his next new
novel. This was Errata or the Works of Will
Adams, completing eight stout volumes in a
single year, in addition to his essays in the
periodicals, and his labours in the courts,
which are said to have been quite sufficient
to have kept on the rack the mind of a common lawyer.

Logan and Seventy-Six had been much
praised, though less than his later novels,
and had been republished, and favourably noticed by some of the reviewers in London.
He began to think of a wider field of action,
and had dreams of a European reputation.
"I talked the matter over with a friend," he
says in a letter printed in the London Magazine, " and we agreed that if I could only get
to London, I should cut a figure in the literary world. He went so far, indeed, as to
say that I never should return to America, for
my value would be known here, and after it
was known would the people of this country
ever think of parting with such a prize? I
got up from the table—I went to the fire—I
stood leaning my forehead on the mantel-piece.
' By the Lord, Harry, then,' said I, ' I will go.'
' Go—go where?' said he, starting up; for
he had hardly thought me serious before, and
my eagerness terrified him—' go where?' ' To
England,' said I. It was done. I made all
my arrangements before the sunset on that
very day; and before three weeks were over,
I had closed my affairs, got my letters ready,
transferred my clients to a successor and a
friend, put a young lawyer into my office,
borrowed cash enough, added to the little I
had, to pay my passage and support me for a
few months here, and set sail for England,
satisfied that, happen what would, if people
gave any thing for books here, they would
not be able to starve me, since I could live
upon air, and write faster than any man that
ever yet lived."

Mr. Neal arrived in Liverpool in January,
1824. He soon became a contributor to various periodicals, for which he wrote, chiefly
under the guise of an Englishman, numerous
articles to correct erroneous opinions which
prevailed in regard to the social and political
condition of the United States. He made his
first appearance in Blackwood's Magazine, in
Sketches of the Five American Presidents
and the Five Candidates for the Presidency,
which was followed by numerous other papers in the various gazettes, magazines, and
reviews, and by a novel in three volumes entitled Brother Jonathan.

Jeremy Bentham heard of him through
some of his disciples, who had met him at a

club, and invited him to dinner. The philosopher was pleased with his original character, and soon after at his request Mr. Neal removed to his house, in Queen's Square, which was his home until the conclusion of his residence in London. "There," he says in the biography prefixed to the translation of the Principles of Legislation from the French of Dumont, "I had a glorious library at my elbow, a fine large comfortable study, warmed by a steam-engine, exercise under ground, society, and retirement, all within my reach. In fact there I spent the happiest, and I believe the most useful days that I passed at that period of my life." He left London early in 1827 for Paris, and, after travelling a short time in France, returned to the United States.

He now established a weekly miscellany under the title of The Yankee, at Portland, and soon after removed to Boston, for the purpose of continuing it in that city. At the end of a year, I believe, it was united with the New England Galaxy, and Mr. Neal then went back to Portland.

In 1828 he published Rachel Dyer, a story of the days of Cotton Mather; in 1830 Authorship, a Tale, by a New Englander over the Sea; in 1831 The Down Easters; and more recently Ruth Elder, the last and in some respects the best of his novels. His tales, essays, and other writings for periodicals would fill many volumes.

Of Mr. Neal's poems, I may repeat what I have remarked elsewhere.* They have the unquestionable stamp of genius. He possesses imagination in a degree of sensibility and energy hardly surpassed in this age. The elements of poetry are poured forth in his verses with a prodigality and power altogether astonishing. But he is deficient in the constructive faculty. He has no just sense of proportion. No one with so rich and abundant materials had ever less skill in using them. Instead of bringing the fancy to adorn the structures of the imagination, he reverses the poetical law, giving to the imagination the secondary office, so that the points illustrated are quite forgotten in the accumulation and splendour of the imagery. The "Battle of Niagara," with its rapid and slow, gay and solemn movement, falls on the ear as if it were composed to martial music. It is marred,

* See Poets and Poetry of America, eighth edition, page 169.

however, by his customary faults. The isthmus which bounds the beautiful is as narrow as that upon the borders of the sublime, and he crosses both without hesitation. Passages in it would be magnificent but for lines or single words which, if the reader were not confident that he had before him the author's own edition, he would think had been thrown in by some burlesquing enemy.

Of his novels it may be said that they contain many interesting and some striking and brilliant passages—filling enough, for books of their sort, but rarely any plot to serve for warp. They are original, written from the impulses of the author's heart, and pervaded by the peculiarities of his character; but most of them were produced rapidly and carelessly, and are without unity, aim, or continuous interest. The best of them would be much improved by a judicious distribution of points, and the erasure of tasteless extravagancies.

Dean Swift, in the preface to the Tale of a Tub, assures us that where sentences are unfinished, "there is some design in it;" but all Mr. Neal's letter-writers, whatever their character, condition, or sex, and most of his colloquists, fall into this habit, whenever they get upon stilts, and are unable to reach a period.

He finds fault, with good reason, with those who have attempted to delineate New England character; but though he has avoided some common defects he can scarcely be said to have succeeded better than his contemporaries. His sketches are caricatures, but have so much of nature as to be easily enough recognised.

It is common to speak of Mr. Neal as an *American* author par excellence; but his claims to such distinction, like those of many others, are chiefly of a negative character.

We rise from the perusal of his works with a feeling of regret at the waste of talents, which might, under a just direction and steady application, have gained enduring honour for their possessor and his country.

Mr. Neal continues to reside in Portland. His youth was passed in tumult and adventure, and he waits the approach of age in independence and ease, a model in his relations as a man and as a citizen.

He published, in 1869, Wandering Recollections of a Somewhat Busy Life. A rambling autobiography, detailing his many experiences, literary and otherwise.

A SURPRISE.

FROM LOGAN.

ONE day, while the middle colonies were agitated to distraction by the increasing inroads and massacres of the warlike and exasperated Indians; when every thing had been attempted that human wisdom could suggest to conciliate them; and just at the time when the existence of a formidable and threatening confederacy between all the most powerful tribes in America was becoming every day more and more probable; when every hour was bringing to light and concentrating the scattered proof that something tremendous was in contemplation—inscrutable and inevitable; some unimaginable but overwhelming evil maturing in the portentous tranquillity of many nations who from being hereditary and mortal foes were now holding their midnight councils in the deepest and most unfathomable recesses of the country—in the lone cavern, on the high mountain top, by the shores of the cold lake; while all was consternation and dismay from uncertainty concerning the manner and time of the mysterious calamity that seemed thickening about them; when council after council had been summoned and dismissed by the white settlers without coming to any satisfactory determination; while the uninterrupted and useless expenditure of warlike stores, at all times dangerous to the whites, had been unwisely augmented in the hope of buying the forbearance of the Indians, till the blindest and weakest were shuddering at the consequences of their pusillanimity and shortsightedness; while the savages grew every day more familiar with the timidity and disorder of the whites; carefully evading all interrogations and baffling all conjecture by their sullen, shrewd, and obstinate silence; and nothing seemed left to the scattered and trembling colonists but to muster themselves, every man of them capable of wielding a tomahawk, for a war of extermination—to concentrate their power, leave their firesides undefended for a time, and hunt their wily and terrible enemy back to his most secret hiding-places—— just at this time—it was midnight—another council board had just been dismissed—there stood, without being announced, without preparation, before the governor of the colony, in his very presence chamber too, a man of gigantic stature, in the garb of an Indian.

The governor was leaning his face upon his hands. His thin gray locks were blowing about his fingers, in the strong night wind, from an open window that looked toward the town. That he was in some profound and agitating inquiry with himself, could be seen by the movement of the swollen veins upon his forehead, distended and throbbing visibly under the pressure of his aged fingers. . . . It would have made the heart of such a being as Michael Angelo himself swell to study the head of the old man: the capacity and amplitude of the brow; the scattered and beautiful white, thin locks of threaded silver; the trembling hands; the occasional movement of a troubled expression, almost articulate, over the established serenity of the forehead: all so venerable, placid, and awful, as in the confirmed discipline and habit of many years, and all yielding now to the convulsive encroachment of emotion. . . .

The stranger contemplated the picture in silence. He was greatly wrought upon by the aged presence, and felt perhaps somewhat as the profaning Gaul did when he saw what he took to be the GODS of ROME—her old men sitting immovably in their chairs.

The governor at length, like one who is determined, resolved, and impatient for action, lifted his head, smote the table heavily with his arm, and was rising from his seat——why that pause?—he gasps for breath—can it be—can the proportions, the mere outline of humanity so disturb a man, an aged man, familiar for half a century with danger and death?

He fell back upon his chair and locked his hands upon his heart, as if —for it grew audible in its hollow palpitations—as if to stifle its irregularity for ever, if he could, even though he were suffocated in the effort, rather than betray the unmanly infirmity—a disobedient pulse. He gazed steadily upon the being before him, but with an expression of doubt and horror, like that with which the prophet dwelt upon the sheeted Samuel, as doubting the evidence of his own eyes, yet daring not to withdraw them, though the cold icy sweat started from the very ends of his fingers lest something yet more terrible might appear.

The Indian stood before him like an apparition. His attitude was not entirely natural, nor perhaps entirely unstudied. He stood motionless and appalling; the bleak, barren, and iron aspect of a man, from head to foot strong and sinewed with desperation, and hardened in the blood and sweat of calamity and trial. He stood, with somewhat of high and princely carriage, like the fighting gladiator, but more erect and less threatening, more prepared and collected. Indeed it was the gladiator still—but the gladiator in defence rather than attack.

The governor was brave, but who would not have quaked at such a moment? To awake, no matter how, when the faculties, or the body and limbs are asleep, in a dim light, alone, helpless, and to find a man at your side, an Indian!—it would shake the nerves, ay, and the constitution too, of the bravest man that ever buckled a sword upon his thigh.

"Great God!" articulated he at last, in the voice of one suffocating and gasping—"Great God! what art thou? speak!"

No answer was returned—no motion of head or hand.

The governor's terror increased, but it was evidently of a different kind now, the first shock of surprise having passed—"Speak!" he added in a tone of command—"speak! how were you admitted? and for what?"

A scornful writhing of the lip; a sullen, deadly smile, as in derision, when the bitterness of the heart rises and is tasted, was the prelude to his answer. The Indian was agitated—but the agitation passed off like the vibration of molten iron when it trembles for the last time before it becomes solid for ever. Then he smiled. . . .

" Hell and furies! who are you? what are you? whence are you? what your purpose?" . . .

The Indian slowly unwrapped his blanket, and then *as* slowly, in barbarous dalliance with the terrors of the palsied old man, extended a bayonet toward him recking with blood.

The governor was silent. It was a fearful moment. His paroxysm appeared to abate at his will now—and by his manner it would appear that some master-thought had suddenly risen in its dominion, and bound hand and foot all the rebellious and warring passions of his nature. Did he hope for succour? or did he look, by gaining time, to some indefinite advantage by negotiation? It would be difficult to tell. But however it might be, his deportment became more worthy of him, more lofty, collected, imposing, and determined. . . . In desperate emergencies our souls grow calm, and a power is given to them to gaze, as dying men will sometimes, upon the shoreless void before them with preternatural composure. Here was an enemy, and one, of all enemies the most terrible, dripping with recent slaughter, and so situated that he could not escape but by dipping his hands anew in blood.

The governor dared not to call out, and dreaded, as the signal of his own death, the sound of any approaching footstep. To get there, where he was, the Indian must have come, willing and prepared for, and expecting certain death; of what avail then the whole force of the government household? . . .

There was a sword near the governor; he recollected having unbuckled it, and thrown it aside as he came in from exercising a troop of horse but a few hours before the council had assembled. " It was in a chair behind me," thought he, and " perhaps is there yet"—But how should he discover whether it was or not? He dares not shift his eye for a single instant from the Indian. But might he not amuse him for a moment, and grope for it without being perceived? How bravely the old man's spirit mounted in the endeavour!

He made the search; but his implacable foe, like one that delights in toying and trifling with, and mocking his victim, permitted the eager and trembling hand but to touch the hilt, not to grasp it—that were not so prudent. . . . The moment, therefore, that the searching fingers approached the hilt, the blanket fell from the shoulders of the Indian, and the bloody bayonet gleamed suddenly athwart the ceiling and flashed in the governor's eyes. The hand was withdrawn, as if smitten with electricity, from the distant sword; all defence and hope forgotten, and he locked his thin hands upon his bosom, bowed his head to the expected sacrifice, and fell upon his knees.

The countenance of the Indian could not be seen, but his solid proportions, like a block of shadow, could be distinguished in the uncertain light of the distant and dying lamps suspended from the ceiling—a bold, great outline, and sublime bearing, the more awful for their indistinctness; the more

appalling as they resembled those of a colossal shadow only. . . .

At this instant, a red light flashed across the court-yard, and streaming through the open window, touched the countenance of the Indian, and passed off like the reflection of crimson drapery, suddenly illuminated by lightning; voices were heard in a distant building, and iron hoofs rattled over the broad flag-stones of the far gateway. A few brief words were interchanged, and a shot was fired; the Indian's hand was upon the bayonet again, but the sounds passed away; . . . and the prostrate governor, who had kept an anxious eye upon the heavy doors of the hall, expecting, yet scarcely daring to pray for an approaching step, was beginning to yield anew to his terrible fate—when another step was heard, and a hand was laid upon the lock. The rattling of military accoutrements was heard, as the guard stepped aside and gave a countersign to some one approaching; and then a brief and stern echo, in the tone of unqualified authority, rang along the vaulted staircase, and the word *pass!* was heard.

Yes, yes! a hand *was* now upon the lock! The light in the apartment streamed fitfully up for a moment, and flared in the breeze from the window, so as to fill the whole room with shifting shadows.

The Indian motioned impatiently with his hand toward the door, and the governor, while his heart sank within him, arose on his feet and prepared to repel the intruder, whoever he might be—but he could not speak—his voice had gone—

The door was yielding to the hurried attempts of some one fumbling about for the lock;—and voices, in clamorous dispute, were heard approaching.

The governor tried again—" Begone! begone! for God's sake!" he cried, mingling the tone of habitual command with that of entreaty, and then recovering himself, with a feeling of shame added, in his most natural and assured manner, " Begone, whoever you are, begone!"

The noise ceased. The hand was withdrawn; and step by step, with the solid and prompt tread of a strong man, a soldier, in his youth, and accustomed to obedience, the intruder was heard descending.

There was another long silence, which each seemed unwilling to interrupt, while each numbered the departing footfalls. The chamber grew dark. It was impossible longer to distinguish objects. A low conference was held between the two. Tones of angry remonstrance, horror—threats—defiance—suppressed anguish—and then all was silent again as the house of death.

The governor spoke again—in a whisper at first, and then louder—a slight motion was heard near him—and he raised his voice. In vain, and the mysterious and death-like silence, he found more insupportable than all that he had yet endured. Where was his foe at that instant?—how employed?—ready perhaps to strike the bayonet through and through his heart at the very next breath! He could not endure it—no mortal could—he uttered a loud cry, and fell upon his face in convulsions. . . .

In the morning, just as the dappled east began to redden with the new daylight, after a night of feverish and wild dreaming, the good old governor awoke exceedingly refreshed, and lay with his eyes shut, revolving the mysterious adventure of the preceding night in his mind. It was all in vain. He could remember nothing distinctly. That an apparition had been before him; that, somehow or other he had been engaged in mortal strife, he had a kind of dim and wavering, shadowy and uncertain recollection, but all else, with whom, and where, had been held the battle—all! —was gone, in the terror of the interview, and the long insensibility and agitation that succeeded. What he had dreamed appeared reality; and the real, as he strove in vain to recall the particular features, took the fantastic and shifting proportions of a dream.

The effort grew painful to him. He became weary with the intensity of his own reminiscence, and, was fast relapsing again into a disturbed and broken slumber, half-conscious that it was better for him to sleep, and half-yielding to the delicious influence of such consciousness, and yet occasionally starting and grasping with a sudden and convulsive hand whatever happened to be nearest him, like one that, overcome by drowsiness upon a precipice, partially yields to it, grappling at the weeds and grass, and starts and shrieks as he feels his hold relaxing, and dreams that he is falling.

POETRY.
FROM RANDOLPH.

Poetry is the naked expression of power and eloquence. But for many hundred years poetry has been confounded with false music, measure, and cadence; the soul with the body, the thought with the language, the manner of speaking with the mode of thinking. The secondary qualities of poetry have been mistaken for the primary ones.

What I call poetry has nothing to do with art or learning. It is a natural music—the music of woods and waters; not that of the orchestra. It is a fine volatile essence, which cannot be extinguished or confined while there is one drop of blood in the human heart, or any sense of Almighty God among the children of men. I do not mean this irreverently—I mean precisely what I say—that poetry is a religion as well as a music. Nay, it is eloquence. It is whatever affects, touches, or disturbs the animal or moral sense of man. I care not how poetry may be expressed, nor in what language, it is still poetry; as the melody of the waters, wherever they may run, in the desert or the wilderness, among the rocks or the grass, will always be melody. It is not artificial music, the music of the head, of learning, or of science, but it is one continual voluntary of the heart; to be heard everywhere, at all times, by day and by night, whenever men will stay their hands, for a moment, or lift up their heads and listen. It is not the composition of a master; the language of art, painfully and entirely exact; but is the wild, capricious melody of *nature*, pathetic or brilliant, like the roundelay of innumerable birds whistling all about you, in the wind and water, sky and air; or the coquetting of a river breeze over the fine strings of an Eolian harp, concealed among green leaves and apple blossoms.

All men talk poetry at some time or other in their lives; even the most reasonable, cold-hearted, mathematical, and phlegmatic; but most of them without knowing it; and women yet more frequently than men: and young children too talk it perpetually, when alarmed or delighted. Yet they never talk in rhyme; nay, nor in blank verse. Even the writers of tragedy—the most perverse of God's creatures—do now and then stumble upon this truth—for in all their passionate and deepest passages they do all that they can to get rid of the foolish restraint of rhythm. And when they do not, they are, to the full, as absurd as the opera-singer, who murders and makes love by the gamut.

Poetry, too, is the natural language of the human heart—its *mother-tongue ;* and is just as naturally resorted to, on any emergency or distress, by the devout, the terrified, the affectionate, the tender-hearted, and the loving; the widowed and the afflicted, as a man's native tongue is, when, after having been a great while among strangers, where he has learned a strange language, good enough for all the common purposes of life, he is called upon by some signal and unexpected calamity to pray aloud, or to cry out with a broken and bowed spirit or a crushed heart. Instantly that a man overleaps all time and space, and falls down before the woman he loves, or his Maker, with the very language that his mother taught him, when he fell upon his little knees and lisped the dictated prayer after her, syllable by syllable. Just so it is with poetry. Prose will do for common people, or for all the common occasions of life even with uncommon people. We cannot drive a better bargain or make a better argument in poetry than in prose. . . .

I speak of this matter freely and boldly, because I know that I am competent to speak of it—and fully authorized to bear witness against the mischievous and perverted tendencies of poetical thought, when it is put, like a beautiful child or a strong giant, into shackles and gyves, hand-cuffs and pinions. Some men affect to talk about it and to give rule for it who never had a poetical idea in their heads. Fools! they might as well learn eloquence from an automaton, or swimming by seeing other people swim, as how to make poetry by reading and studying the great masters, and listening to the jackasses who are called critics, not one in a million of whom ever was or ever will be a poet. Why! because if a man be a poet, he will lack, nine hundred and ninety-nine times out of a thousand, either the judgment or the moral courage or the honesty to criticise boldly, and to speak of poetry as it deserves; and more than that, if he be a *poet* he will be above the practice of criticism.

My notion, in one word, is that poetry is the natural language of every human heart when it is roused, or inflamed, or agitated, or affected : and that prose, on the contrary, is the natural language of every human heart on all other occasions ; and that rhyme, or blank verse, or *regular* rhythm, is altogether as artificial, unnatural, and preposterous a mode of expression for the true poet as the use of a foreign idiom or foreign phrase is to the true home-bred man. The Romans affected to talk Greek, the Germans do talk French, as if they were ashamed of their mother languages ; and so do poets talk in rhyme or blank verse ; but let them all talk ever so beautifully, one can always discover that it is not natural to either of them. . . .

To put this in another light, one example will do more than a volume of abstract reasoning. Could you possibly hold out to read any poem by the greatest poet that ever lived which should contain as many words as one of the Waverly novels ? It would be about five or six times as long as Paradise Lost. If it were the best of poetry would you not get the sooner tired of it ? Assuredly. In the confusion of such a beautiful and confounding exhibition of power and brightness your senses would lose all their activity ; they would reel under it, and retain no distinct impression at all. It would be like seeing a multitude of beautiful women at the same moment, in a place crowded with august personages, innumerable pictures, statuary, delicious music, and fire-works. What would you remember of the whole ?——nothing.

---◆---

THE DUEL.
FROM ERRATA.

"I PROMISED to tell you," said Hammond, slowly, after a silence of half an hour, during which we had set together in his chamber till it had grown so dark that we could not see each other's faces : and just then the door suddenly opened. A man entered and began stirring the fire. "Leave it," said Hammond, " begone and leave it."

"Shall I bring a light, sir ?" said the servant. . . . "No—begone."

"No light !" said I, involuntarily. "No light !" echoed Hammond. "Are you afraid of the dark ?"

I know not what I was afraid of ; but I confess that I did not much like the opening of the story. Was he afraid to let me see his face while he told it ? I was very silent, and he began.

"I promised to tell you," said he in a voice so deep and sepulchral that I should not have known it had I heard it in another place ; and then he stopped. I waited some minutes, oppressed with an unaccountable sensation, to hear it again ; and at last his breathing had become so loud as to alarm me. "Hammond," said I, going to him and laying my hand upon his head, " dear Hammond, speak to me. What ails you ! what has happened !"

He tore away his locked fingers from his forehead, sprung upon his feet with a cry of horror, and pressed my hands to his heart, as if he would crush them bone and joint. I could hardly suppress a shriek—and I observed that his palms were wet, as if he had been weeping. What ! the dwarf weeping ! Hammond, the dwarf, said I to myself ; O, no—it is only sweat, or blood ! it cannot be tears.

"Hammond !" I said again to him, as I really felt, affectionately.

He attempted to rise, staggered and fell back into his seat. "What ! what ! was it only you, William ?" said he, "only you. Give me your hand—here ! here ! (placing it upon his temples among the damp hair,) do you feel any moisture there ?"

"Yes—the flesh is wet, and the hair saturated."

"Locks of the raven, boy, locks of the raven ! black and glossy as her wing ; yet, William Adams, they have been touched—there are gray spots upon them—ha ! ha !" He was choking. "Gray spots, my boy ; in the form too of a human hand !"

I shuddered at his voice ; and I remembered a strange appearance upon one side of his head, where there were several gray locks lying amid the jet black hair. "How happened it ?" said I, with a feeling of mysterious gloom that I cannot describe.

"Happened it ! He came to my bedside at night and stood there ; and put his cold hand deliberately upon my head ; and all the moisture of my brain fled from the pressure. I awoke, and the feeling of the hand, as of cold iron, was there yet—and—damn it, how your teeth chatter—what are you afraid of ? Have *you* blood upon *your* hands ? For shame—for shame. Look at me—you see how I bear it. I went to bed with locks black, . . . black as death. I arose the next day with gray hair upon my temples—I——"

I remembered now that Elizabeth had told me never to speak of that appearance : and, dark as it was, I fancied that I could see the livid hand of the spectre there yet, like an impression upon wax.

"It was not grief, nor sorrow, nor old age that did it," said the dwarf, almost inarticulate, and sobbing while he spoke ; " no, no ! but he came to me in my sleep and hooped my heart round, and my temples, with rough iron, till I feared to breathe, lest I should be lacerated. I knew it all —saw it all—the whole process, through my shut eyelids ; and on the morning, when I awoke, I was an old man.". . .

His voice—it was like something martial and alarming when he began, but when he ended it was the mournful, sweet, melancholy wailing of a fond heart broken. . . . I was willing to turn off his thought from the affliction. . . .

"Presently," said he, "presently. Let us talk of something else awhile. Only one thing upon this earth can disturb me—talk to me—say something—any thing—talk ! will you ?"

"You are disordered, Hammond," said I. "You have studied till your nerves are all vibrating with over tension."

"Oh, no—*no*, you are mistaken. My time of hard study has gone by.". . .

"I am sure, my dear Hammond," said I, deeply affected at his manner—it was so like one trying to drive away sorrow and madness by an affected hilarity—"that you are nervous from excessive application."

"No, no, I am not. *Nervous!* Albert Hammond nervous! No, no, it is something worse than that; but talk—talk—as fast as you can—my blood is curdling—come nearer—yes, yes—hush! do you hear nothing? Ah! what is that? There! there! Hush! I told you so—now you will believe me! Hush! hush!"

As he said this, he leaped upright, and I—I knew not where I was—I felt all the childish terror of a nursery. "Hammond!" said I, feigning to be indignant, while in truth I was frightened, "Come back! come back, and let us reason together like men. What is this?"

"What! did he not touch you? didn't you feel the hand?"

Some minutes passed before I could prevail upon him to sit down. I stirred the fire then, and his countenance, in the red flashing of the embers, when the disturbed sparks rushed like a torrent of fire up the chimney, was frightful and appalling. Had the devil himself been there, he could not have set more naturally upon his haunches, or looked through his huge knotted fingers with more fiery and troubled eyes. . . .

"They had all toasted their women," said Hammond, abruptly . . . "*all!*—and then he—*he*—he uttered the name of Elizabeth. The name thrilled through me. They all drank it standing. 'Elizabeth!' echoed through the whole room. I covered my ears, with a feeling of profanation. But that was nothing—nothing! 'Elizabeth who?' cried one; 'Aye,' cried another; 'let us have it.'

"'*Elizabeth Adams*,' answered the madman, in a loud voice, throwing off another bumper, which was followed by the whole company. Your blood boils, I see, William Adams, to hear me *tell* it; judge then what I felt to hear her blessed name uttered by such a man, in such a company, associated with the lewd and blaspheming. I stood thunderstruck for a moment, and then tried two or three times to get my breath; to gasp; to cry out; to speak to him; but I could not. I could not see plainly; I could not utter a sound. The company began to take notice of it; and all the noise, and laugh, and song, and riot, instantly died away into a stillness more awful than death, while every eye was turned upon me. I was leaning toward him, and I whispered very faintly, so faintly that I did not hear my own voice; but it came from the deepest place of all my heart, and he understood the motion of my lips—*he* heard me. 'Elizabeth Adams, of D——?' said I. 'Yes,' he haughtily replied, 'Elizabeth Ad——.' 'You are a scoundrel!' said I, jumping up—I would not let him finish it—dwelling on every syllable—'you are a scoundrel and a villain!' A glass decanter whizzed by my head as I spoke, and narrowly missed dashing my brains out. We rushed at each other, and he grasped a carving-knife, but it was wrenched from him, and we were separated till

the room was cleared, a circle formed, and swords put into our hands; but mine was a miserable cut and thrust, and in receiving one of his blows, before I could make a pass, it was shattered to the hilt. We closed, and I was very severely cut in the hand. No other sword could be obtained, and we stood, leaning against the wall, panting like spent tigers, till the company had agreed to escort us to a wood, just out of the town, and leave us to our fate with pistols. Some objected to this; but at last the business was arranged; how I know not; and the next thing that I recollect is, that we were together—his friend with us—that it was just daylight, and that I had just levelled and fired at his heart, and that I saw the ball strike him—but he stood still.

"'You are wounded,' said his second, approaching me. 'No,' said I, 'I am *not*, but your friend is—look to him.' When I said this he fell. It was wonderful how I escaped. He was a great shot. But when we levelled there was a strange darkness about me for a moment, and I felt as if already a ball had passed through me—coldness and numbness—but I caught his eye just then, and observed that as I dropped *my* pistol his eye followed it, till it was just opposite his breast. I fired before he had recovered himself, and the result was what I have told you.". . .

"Look here, William Adams," said he, lifting his black-matted locks, "look here!—it wasn't grief that did it—no, nor old age—but his hand! Three thousand miles were we apart. Yet at the moment, the very moment when he died, the very moment! these locks turned white! I felt his hot hand there in my sleep. I awoke with a scream that startled the household broad awake. It was midnight—but not a soul could sleep again that night. You may smile, William, but no—you do not—you look serious. Are you really so? Speak to me. Can you believe me?"

"*I do.*"

"It is impossible. You cannot. You believe that I am disordered. What! that at the moment of his death—the very moment! he should appear to me, and put his hand upon my temples and awake me!"

TALENT AND GENIUS.

FROM THE SAME.

His ambition was rather a diseased appetite for present notoriety than the gallant longing of a great heart for an imperishable and distant reputation. To his view the present was immortality; and he was foolish enough to believe that the future must echo to the voice of the present. He was, emphatically, a man of genius, though not a man of talent; but of such a genius as I would not that a brother or a son of mine should have for all the world. It was a kingly shadow, with the shadow of regal habiliments about it, which, when you approached them, fell of, and faded into brilliant exhalation, like coloured ice in the sunshine. Talent is substance: genius is show. Talent is a primary quality of things, like weight: genius the secondary quality, like colour.

A BOY'S REVERIES
FROM THE SAME.

Look where I would, these brilliant creatures were incessantly in play among the stars, which were reflected in the depth below me, as if heaven had been showering them down like blossoms into the habitations of the waters.

Ah, I cannot describe the stillness that was about me. It was awful. It was like that of death. The sky was bluer than I had ever seen it, and much further off, it appeared to me, and the solemn stars were multiplied in the water till my head ached with the temptation of their influence; and I was on the point, child that I was, of plunging after them. Do not smile. Many drowned women and children have felt the same fascination, I have no doubt, drawing them as it were by a song and a spell into the bosom of the deep; and I have felt it more than once, neither as a woman nor as a child; but on this night it was more like an attraction, an irresistible, secret allurement, a delightful influence, winning and persuading me into a voluntary self-destruction. It was more like some unknown affinity operating upon my blood, upon the spiritual part of me, like a charm, than like what I have felt, as a strong hand, pressing me into the water by main force. At one time—the time that I allude to—we were upon the high seas, a few starved and desperate men, . . . and were drifting, with our helm lashed down and topsail flying in the wind far and wide, like—O, unlike any thing ever seen upon the waters!—more like a floating hospital of lunatics and murderers, than a gallant ship, well-manned and obedient to the helm, and out upon the ocean, instinct with spirit, as if it had a soul and a will of its own. . . . I was lying, I remember, in the hot sunshine upon the half-burnt deck, with my head over the side of the ship, gasping, giddy, and sick, and deadly faint, looking blindly down into the sea, and ready to give up the ghost with every sick, impatient sob, when, all at once there was a terrific explosion below me—a strong light flashed into my brain—my veins tingled—my blood was all in confusion—and the great deep heaved and roared, and broke up and vanished! vanished like a dream from my sight. And where it had been there came up a dizzy wilderness of beauty, and flowers, and greenness. The winds blew and the trees rustled all over, and waved their rich branches, and the birds flew about and the flowers fell, and everywhere, through the short thick grass and out of the old rocks, which were spotted with shining moss—the greenest in the world—the waters gushed and bounced, and sparkled and rattled, and then wandered away singing the self-same tune that the birds were all singing, in a labyrinth of brightness, with a reality so unspeakably tempting that I had well-nigh leaped down into the bosom of the apparition. . . . I attempted to stand upon my feet, they said, and threw up my arms with a cry of transport, just as the vessel heeled—and I should have been overboard but for the dwarf, who plucked me back and held me like a giant.

41

CHILDREN—WHAT ARE THEY?
FROM THE TOKEN.

What are children? Step to the window with me. The street is full of them. Yonder a school is let loose, and here just within reach of our observation are two or three noisy little fellows, and there another party mustering for play. Some are whispering together, and plotting so loudly and so earnestly as to attract everybody's attention, while others are holding themselves aloof, with their satchels gaping so as to betray a part of their plans for to-morrow afternoon, or laying their heads together in pairs for a trip to the islands. Look at them, weigh the question I have put to you, and then answer it as it deserves to be answered: *What are children?*

To which you reply at once, without any sort of hesitation, perhaps,—"Just as the twig is bent, the tree's inclined;" or "Men are but children of a larger growth," or, peradventure, "The child is father of the man." And then perhaps you leave me, perfectly satisfied with yourself and with your answer, having "plucked out the heart of the mystery," and uttered without knowing it a string of glorious truths. . . .

Among the children who are now playing *together*, like birds among the blossoms of earth, haunting all the green shadowy places thereof, and rejoicing in the bright air, happy and beautiful creatures, and as changeable as happy, with eyes brimful of joy and with hearts playing upon their little faces like sunshine upon clear waters. Among those who are now idling together on that slope, or pursuing butterflies together on the edge of that wood, a wilderness of roses, you would see not only the gifted and the powerful, the wise and the eloquent, the ambitious and the renowned, the long-lived and the long-to-be-lamented of another age; but the wicked and the treacherous, the liar and the thief, the abandoned profligate and the faithless husband, the gambler and the drunkard, the robber, the burglar, the ravisher, the murderer and the betrayer of his country. *The child is father of the man.*

Among them and that other little troop just appearing, children with yet happier faces and pleasanter eyes, the blossoms of the future—the mothers of nations—you would see the founders of states and the destroyers of their country, the steadfast and the weak, the judge and the criminal, the murderer and the executioner, the exalted and the lowly, the unfaithful wife and the broken-hearted husband, the proud betrayer and his pale victim, the living and breathing portents and prodigies, the imbodied virtues and vices of another age and of another world, *and all playing together!* Men are but children of a larger growth.

Pursuing the search, you would go forth among the little creatures as among the types of another and a loftier language, the mystery whereof had been just revealed to you, a language to become universal hereafter, types in which the autobiography of the Future was written ages and ages ago. Among the innocent and helpless creatures that are called *children*, you would see warriors with their garments rolled in blood, the spectres of kings and princes, poets with golden harps and illuminated eyes, historians and painters, architects and sculptors, mechanics and merchants, preachers and lawyers; here a grave-digger flying a kite with his future customers; there a physician playing at marbles with his; here the predestined to an early and violent death for cowardice, fighting the battles of a whole neighbourhood; there a Cromwell, or a Cæsar, a Napoleon, or a Washington, hiding themselves for fear, enduring reproach or insult with patience; a Benjamin Franklin higgling for nuts or gingerbread, or the "old Parr" of another generation, sitting apart in the sunshine and shivering at every breath of wind that reaches him. Yet we are told that "just as the twig is bent the tree's inclined.". . . .

Even fathers and mothers look upon children with a strange misapprehension of their dignity. Even with the poets, they are only the flowers and blossoms, the dew-drops or the playthings of earth. Yet "of such is the kingdom of heaven." The Kingdom of Heaven! with all its principalities and powers, its hierarchies, dominations, thrones! The Saviour understood them better; to him their true dignity was revealed. Flowers! They are the flowers of the invisible world; indestructible, self-perpetuating flowers, with each a multitude of angels and evil spirits underneath its leaves, toiling and wrestling for dominion over it! Blossoms! They are the blossoms of another world, whose fruitage is angels and archangels. Or dew-drops! They are dew-drops that have their source, not in the chambers of the earth, nor among the vapours of the sky, which the next breath of wind, or the next flash of sunshine may dry up for ever, but among the everlasting fountains and inexhaustible reservoirs of mercy and love. Playthings! God! If the little creatures would but appear to us in their true shape for a moment! We should fall upon our faces before them, or grow pale with consternation, or fling them off with horror and loathing.

What would be our feelings to see a fair child start up before us a maniac or a murderer, armed to the teeth? to find a nest of serpents on our pillow? a destroyer, or a traitor, a Harry the Eighth, or a Benedict Arnold asleep in our bosom! A Catharine or a Peter, a Bacon, a Galileo, or a Bentham, a Napoleon, or a Voltaire, clambering up our knees after sugar-plums! Cuvier labouring to distinguish a horse-fly from a blue bottle, or dissecting a spider with a rusty nail! La Place trying to multiply his own apples, or to subtract his playfellow's gingerbread? What should we say to find ourselves romping with Messalina, Swedenbourg, and Madame de Staël! or playing bo-peep with Murat, Robespierre, and Charlotte Corday? or puss puss in the corner with George Washington, Jonathan Wild, Shakspeare, Sappho, Jeremy Taylor, Alfieri, and Harriet Wilson? Yet stranger things have happened. These were all children but the other day, and clambered about the knees, and rummaged in the pockets, and nestled in the laps of people no better than we are.

But *if* they could have appeared in their true shape for a single moment, while they were playing together! what a scampering there would have been among the grown folks! How their fingers would have tingled!

Now to me there is no study half so delightful as that of these little creatures, with hearts fresh from the gardens of the sky, in their first and fairest and most unintentional disclosures, while they are indeed a mystery, a fragrant, luminous and beautiful mystery. And I have an idea that if we only had a name for the study, it might be found as attractive and as popular; and perhaps—though I would not go too far—*perhaps* about as advantageous in the long run to the future fathers and mothers of mankind, as the study of shrubs and flowers, or that of birds and fishes. And why not? They are the cryptogamia of another world, the infusoria of the skies.

Then why not pursue the study for yourself? The subjects are always before you. No books are needed, no costly drawings, no lectures, neither transparencies nor illustrations. Your specimens are all about you. They come and go at your bidding. They are not to be hunted for, along the edge of a precipice, on the borders of the wilderness, in the desert, nor by the sea-shore. They abound not in the uninhabited or unvisited place, but in your very dwelling-houses, about the steps of your doors, in every street of every village, in every green field, and every crowded thoroughfare. They flourish bravely in snow-storms, in the dust of the trampled highway, where drums are beating and colours flying, in the roar of cities. They love the sounding sea-breeze and the open air, and may always be found about the wharves and rejoicing before the windows of toy-shops. They love the blaze of fireworks and the smell of gunpowder, and where that is they are, to a dead certainty.

You have but to go abroad for half an hour in pleasant weather, or to throw open your doors or windows on a Saturday afternoon, if you live anywhere in the neighbourhood of a school-house, or a vacant lot with here and there a patch of green or a dry place in it; and steal behind the curtains, or draw the blinds and let the fresh wind blow through and through the chambers of your heart for a few minutes, winnowing the dust and scattering the cobwebs that have gathered there while you were asleep, and lo! you will find it ringing with the voices of children at play, and all alive with the glimmering phantasmagoria of leap-frog, prison-base, or knock-up-and-catch.

Let us try the experiment. There! I have opened the windows, I have drawn the blinds, and hark! already there is the sound of little voices afar off, like "sweet bells jangling." Nearer and nearer come they, and now we catch a glimpse of bright faces peeping round the corners, and there, by that empty enclosure, a general mustering and swarming, as of bees about a newly-discovered flower-garden. But the voices we now hear proceed from two little fellows who have withdrawn from the rest. One carries a large basket, and his eyes are directed to my window; he doesn't half like the blinds being drawn. The other follows him with a tattered book under his arm, rapping the posts, one after the other, as he goes along. He is clearly on bad terms with himself. And now we can see their faces. Both are grave, and one rather pale, and trying to look ferocious. And hark! now we are able to distinguish their words. "Well, I ain't skeered o' you," says the foremost and the larger boy. "Nor I ain't skeered o' you," retorts the other; "but you needn't say you meant to lick me." And so I thought. Another, less acquainted with children, might not be able to see the connection; but I could—it was worthy of Aristotle himself or John Locke. "I *didn't* say I meant to lick ye," rejoined the first; "I said I *could* lick ye, and so I can." To which the other replies, glancing first at my window and then all up and down street, "I should like to see you try it." Whereupon the larger boy begins to move away, half-backwards, half-sideways, muttering just loud enough to be heard, "Ah, you want to fight now, jest 'cause you're close by your own house." And here the dialogue finished, and the babies moved on, shaking their little heads at each other and muttering all the way up street. Men are but children of a larger growth! Children but empires in miniature....

"Ah, ah, hourra! hourra! here's a fellow's birthday!" cried a boy in my hearing once. A number had got together to play ball, but one of them having found a birth-day, and not only the birthday, but the very boy to whom it belonged, they all gathered about him as if they had never witnessed a conjunction of the sort before. The very fellows for a committee of inquiry!—into the affairs of a national bank if you please.

Never shall I forget another incident which occurred in my presence between two other boys. One was trying to jump over a wheel-barrow. Another was going by; he stopped, and after considering a moment, spoke. "I'll tell you what you can't do," said he. "Well, what is it?" "You can't jump down your own throat." "Well, *you* can't." "*Can't I* though!" The simplicity of "Well, you can't," and the roguishness of "Can't I though!" tickled me prodigiously. They reminded me of a sparring I had seen elsewhere—I should not like to say where—having a great respect for the temples of justice and the halls of legislation....

I saw three children throwing sticks at a cow. She grew tired of her share in the game at last, and holding down her head and shaking it, demanded a new deal. They cut and ran. After getting to a place of comparative security, they stopped, and holding by the top of a board fence began to reconnoitre. Meanwhile, another troop of children hove in sight, and arming themselves with brickbats, began to approach the same cow. Whereupon two of the others called out from the fence. "You, Joe! you better mind! that's our cow!" The plea was admitted without a demurrer; and the

cow was left to be tormented by the legal owners. Hadn't these boys the law on their side?...

But children have other characters. At times they are creatures to be afraid of. Every case I give is a fact within my own observation. There are children, and I have had to do with them, whose very eyes were terrible; children who, after years of watchful and anxious discipline, were as indomitable as the young of the wild beast, dropped in the wilderness, crafty and treacherous and cruel. And others I have known who, if they live, *must* have dominion over the multitude, being evidently of them that from the foundations of the world have been always thundering at the gates of power.

WORDSWORTH.

WORDSWORTH is a great, plain-hearted, august simpleton: a gifted creature, of prodigious power: a devout dreamer, who cannot, for the soul of him, tell when he *is* awake; a strong man with the organs of a child; whose ample and profound thought can find no correspondent diction. He thinks like an angel, but speaks something less than a man. He is a giant, blind of both eyes, and deaf as a post, who has blundered, somehow or other, into Nature's laboratory, and there goes groping and rummaging about, most unprofitably for *himself*, among all the beautiful elixirs of immortality and crucibles for transmutation—wading into oceans of uncongealed precious stones—ploughing through heaps of rough gold, hardly cool from the furnace —waking strange, subterranean music, at every step, as he tumbles along, first one way and then another, among the sources of sound and harmony, totally insensible to all, one would think; while the very dust that he brings away upon his garments never fails to enrich those who have the first scouring of them, and picking of *him*—a matter that keeps a mob of retail dealers in poetry watching after him, as they watch, in China, after people who are seen to make wry faces; and when they get him in a corner, they never fail to beguile him of his old clothes, heavy with unknown spoil, and wash him clean even to the hair of his head, all the time talking baby-talk to him, and profaning his *simple majesty* with all sorts of idle and wicked mockery. In short, Wordsworth is not a little like the lump of fresh meat that Sinbad found—rolling about among diamonds— wounding and tearing itself continually—without any profit to anybody but the creatures that grow dizzy in waiting for him. Wordsworth is altogether a natural poet. Education has done nothing for him, except to make him tedious, childish, obscure, and metaphysical. His *talent* is more sublimated, simple, and clear-sighted than that of any other man—*sentiment* angelic—*imagination* altogether subordinate, quite common-place—*tas'e* too pure, periodical, subject to accident, time, place, and the moon—*industry* none at all—misunderstood and misapplied.

WILLIAM CULLEN BRYANT.

[Born 1794.]

FOR a more particular account of Mr. Bryant than will here be given the reader is referred to the eighth edition of the Poets and Poetry of America. He was born in Cummington, Hampshire county, Massachusetts, on the third of November, 1794. His ancestors, for three generations, were physicians. His father, one of the most eminent members of the profession in his day, who added to thorough scientific and classical scholarship refined taste and pleasing manners,

> "taught his youth
> The art of verse and in the bud of life
> Offered him to the muses."

The Embargo is quite equal in vigour and harmony to any thing accredited to the most precocious of the old poets at thirteen; and Thanatopsis was never surpassed in grandeur and solemnity, or in felicity of language, by an author so young as he when it was written.

From 1815 to 1825 Mr. Bryant was an attorney and counsellor at Great Barrington. It may be supposed that he had little relish for the abstruse doctrines and subtle reasonings of the jurists, and that the conflicts of the bar clashed often with his poetical and moral sensibilities, but it is known that his legal knowledge was extensive and accurate, and that he was a successful and highly respected lawyer. The occasional poems and prose writings he had published in the North American Review, and his longer poem, The Ages, delivered before the Phi Beta Kappa Society of Harvard College, in 1821, had however won for him a high reputation through all the country as a man of letters, and after ten years of experience in the courts he determined to abandon his profession for the more congenial one of an author, and with this view removed to New York, then, as now, the centre of intelligence nd enterprise in America.

There was in New York at this time an unusual number of men of literary taste and talent. Mr. Sands, Mr. Verplanck, and one or two others, had formed an association several years before under the name of the Literary Confederacy, which had issued at one time a miscellany of humour and playful satire, but

more recently had contributed articles to the Atlantic Magazine, of which Sands was editor. Soon after Mr. Bryant's arrival in the city this periodical was changed somewhat in its character, was named The New York Review, and he was engaged as an editor. He assisted in conducting it until it was merged in the United States Literary Gazette, at Boston, and wrote for it, besides his Hymn to Death, and other poems, many elaborate papers in prose, among which are A Pennsylvania Legend, and reviewals of Hadad by Hillhouse, Lives of the Provensal Poets by Nostrodamus, Moore's Life of Sheridan, and Percival's Poem before the Phi Beta Kappa Society. He continued to write for the United States Review and Literary Gazette, as the new magazine was styled, and among his contributions in 1827 we find two tales, one entitled A Narrative of Some Extraordinary Circumstances that Happened more than Twenty Years Since, and the other, A Border Tradition.

About this time he became one of the editors of the Evening Post. He however found time for the cultivation of elegant literature, and joined Verplanck and Sands in writing the Talisman, which was published under the name of an imaginary author, Francis Herbert, Esquire, for the years 1827, 1828 and 1829. The share which Sands had in this work, the cleverest of the illustrated literary annuals ever published in the country, is indicated by the contents of the collection of his writings since published,* and Mr. Verplanck's papers have been pointed out in the notice of that author contained in the present volume. The principal contributions of Mr. Bryant, besides his poems, which he has incorporated into his Poetical Works, are An Adventure in the East Indies, The Cascade of Melsingah, Recollections of the South of Spain, A Story of the Island of Cuba, The Indian Spring, The Whirlwind, Early Spanish Poetry, Phanette des Gantelmes, and The Marriage Blunder.

---

* The Writings of Robert C. Sands, in two volumes, octavo. New York, 1835.

In 1832 Mr. Bryant engaged in another scheme of joint stock authorship, with Miss Sedgwick, Mr. Sands, Mr. Paulding, and Mr. Leggett,* who had now become his associate in the editorship of the Evening Post. Sands, who was very fond of this sort of partnerships, probably suggested the work and brought its parts together. It was called Tales of Glauber Spa, and Mr. Bryant's contributions were The Skeleton Cave, and Medfield, stories not superior to some of his earlier publications in this line, but exhibiting in a somewhat striking manner the characteristics of his mind, his minute observation, and his tendency to trace effects to their causes.

In 1834 and 1835 he travelled with his family in Europe; the spring of 1843 was passed in the valley of the Mississippi, the Floridas, and the southern Atlantic states; and in 1844 he made a second visit to Great Britain, France, Germany, and Italy. He wrote letters descriptive of these various tours, which were published during his absence in the Evening Post, and are among the most interesting accounts of travel that have appeared in this country; graphic, original, judicious, and marked by the independence of feeling and taste in expression which might be expected to distinguish his compositions.

But by far the most important of Mr. Bryant's prose writings are those which have appeared in the columns of the Evening Post, in the ordinary course of his editorial labours. It is now twenty years since he became one of the conductors of that journal, and during all this period he has taken an active part in political controversies, and exerted a powerful influence over public opinion. A strict interpreter of the powers granted by the constitution to the federal government, he has opposed internal improvements, and been a sleepless and an active enemy of a national bank; in favour of perfect freedom of trade, both at home and in our intercourse with foreign nations, he has assailed constantly and earnestly all special charters for business purposes, and the policy of protecting our industry by discriminating tariffs; and an advocate of unre-

stricted liberty in discussion, he has denounced with fervid eloquence the blind servility to sections or to parties which has prevented at any time the proper canvassing of political, social, or religious principles, and the cowardly apathy of the magistracy which has so often permitted public meetings to be disturbed, and the lives of the asserters of unpopular doctrines to be endangered, by that portion of the community which by mob power enacts its treasons against humanity.

Mr. Bryant is the leading journalist of his party, which is honoured in having so illustrious a person among its champions. The force and honesty of his mind enable him to triumph over custom and prejudice. He is nearly always in advance of his colleagues in the avowal of doctrines and the advocacy of measures, and his unquestioned ability and unbending independence check continually the schemes of the less able and more unscrupulous whose rules are plunder and expediency instead of principle.

His style is clear and pointed, his sentences smooth and compact, his illustrations frequent and happily conceived, and his articles have a manifest sincerity and integrity of purpose which secure attention and respect from readers of all opinions.

So much is now said of nationality in literature, and by a certain sort of critics it is so constantly and with such offensive arrogance denied that there is any thing national in the productions of the American mind, that I cannot forbear an allusion to this quality in Mr. Bryant's writings. It may be truly said that, whatever is in them of intrinsic truth, the views of Mr. Bryant on every subject respecting which the intelligent in all countries do not agree, are essentially American, born of and nurtured by our institutions, experience and condition, and held only by ourselves and by those who look to us for instruction and example. This is the true Americanism. There is nothing forced or obtrusive in his nationality, but it is a spontaneous and ever present element in his works.

Mr. Bryant's published works are two complete editions of his Poems, illustrated, each in 1vol., 8vo., also a library edition in 3 vols., 12mo.; 2 vols. of Letters of a Traveller; An Address on Irving; Life of Fitz Greene Halleck; Life of Gulian C. Verplanck; and a new translation of Homer's Iliad, 2 vols., 8vo., 1870.

* William Leggett was author of Leisure Hours at Sea; Tales by a Country Schoolmaster; Sketches of the Sea; The Block House, in Tales of Glauber Spa, etc. He was also editor of The Critic, and The Plaindealer, two weekly gazettes which were nearly all written by himself; and was for several years associated with Mr. Bryant in the Evening Post. A collection of his Political Writings, in two volumes, has been published since his death.—See Poets and Poetry of America.

2 E

THREE NIGHTS IN A CAVERN.

FROM TALES OF GLAUBER-SPA.

[THE characters of The Skeleton's Cave one of the contributions of Mr. Bryant to the Tales of Glauber-Spa, are Father Ambrose, an aged Catholic priest; Le Maire, a gay sportsman, of French origin; and his niece, a young Anglo-American. The following extracts will convey some impression of the style and spirit of the story.]

INTRODUCTION.

WE hold our existence at the mercy of the elements; the life of man is a state of continual vigilance against their warfare. The heats of noon would wither him like the severed herb; the chills and dews of night would fill his bones with pain; the winter frost would extinguish life in an hour; the hail would smite him to death, did he not seek shelter and protection against them. His clothing is the perpetual armour he wears for his defence, and his dwelling the fortress to which he retreats for safety. Yet, even there the elements attack him; the winds overthrow his habitation; the waters sweep it away. The fire, that warmed and brightened it within, seizes upon its walls and consumes it, with his wretched family. The earth, where she seems to spread a paradise for his abode, sends up death in exhalations from her bosom; and the heavens dart down lightnings to destroy him. The drought consumes the harvests on which he relied for sustenance, or the rains cause the green corn to "rot ere its youth attains a beard." A sudden blast ingulfs him in the waters of the lake or bay from which he seeks his food; a false step, or a broken twig, precipitates him from the tree which he had climbed for its fruit; oaks falling in the storm, rocks toppling down from the precipices are so many dangers which beset his life. Even his erect attitude is a continual affront to the great law of gravitation, which is sometimes fatally avenged when he loses the balance preserved by constant care, and falls on a hard surface. The very arts on which he relies for protection from the unkindness of the elements betray him to the fate he would avoid, in some moment of negligence, or by some misdirection of skill, and he perishes miserably by his own inventions. Amid these various causes of accidental death, which thus surround us at every moment, it is only wonderful that their proper effect is not oftener produced—so admirably has the Framer of the universe adapted the faculties by which man provides for his safety, to the perils of the condition in which he is placed. Yet there are situations in which all his skill and strength are vain to protect him from a violent death, by some unexpected chance which executes upon him a sentence as severe and inflexible as the most pitiless tyranny of human despotism.

THE PARTY.

The ecclesiastic had taken the hat from his brow that he might enjoy the breeze which played lightly about the cliffs; and the coolness of which was doubly grateful after the toil of the ascent. In doing this he uncovered a high and ample forehead, such as artists love to couple with the features of old age, when they would represent a countenance at once noble and venerable. This is the only feature of the human face which Time spares: he dims the lustre of the eye; he shrivels the cheek, he destroys the firm or sweet expression of the mouth; he thins and whitens the hairs; but the forehead, that temple of thought, is beyond his reach, or rather, it shows more grand and lofty for the ravages which surround it.

The two persons whom he addressed were much younger. One of them was in the prime of manhood and personal strength, rather tall, and of a vigorous make. He wore a hunting-cap, from the lower edge of which curled a profusion of strong dark hair, rather too long for the usual mode in the Atlantic states, shading a fresh-coloured countenance, lighted by a pair of full black eyes, the expression of which was compounded of boldness and good-humour. His dress was a blue frock-coat trimmed with yellow fringe, and bound by a sash at the waist, deer-skin pantaloons, and deer-skin moccasins. He carried a short rifle on his left shoulder; and wore on his left side a leathern bag of rather ample dimensions, and on his right a powder-flask. It was evident that he was either a hunter by occupation, or at least one who made hunting his principal amusement; and there was something in his air and the neatness of his garb and equipments that bespoke the latter.

On the arm of this person leaned the third individual of the party, a young woman apparently about nineteen or twenty years of age, slender and graceful as a youthful student of the classic poets might imagine a wood-nymph. She was plainly attired in a straw hat and a dress of russet-colour, fitted for a ramble through that wild forest. The faces of her two companions were decidedly French in their physiognomy; hers was as decidedly Anglo-American. Her brown hair was parted away from a forehead of exceeding fairness, more compressed on the sides than is usual with the natives of England; and showing in the profile that approach to the Grecian outline which is remarked among their descendants in America. To complete the picture, imagine a quiet blue eye, features delicately moulded, and just colour enough on her cheek to make it interesting to watch its changes, as it deepened or grew paler with the varying and flitting emotions which slight cause will call up in a youthful maiden's bosom.

THE APPROACH TO THE CAVE.

The spot on which they now stood commanded a view of a wide extent of uncultivated and uninhabited country. An eminence interposed to hide from sight the village they had left; and on every side were the summits of the boundless forest, here and there diversified with a hollow of softer and richer verdure, where the hurricane, a short time before, had descended to lay prostrate the gigantic trees, and a young growth had shot up in their stead. Solitary savannas opened in the depth of the woods, and far off a lonely stream was flowing away in silence, sometimes among venerable trees, and sometimes through natural meadows, crimson with blossoms. All around them was the might, the majesty of vegetable life, untamed by the hand of man, and pampered by the genial elements into boundless luxuriance. The ecclesiastic pointed out to his companions the peculiarities of the scenery ; he expatiated on the flowery beauty of those unshorn lawns; and on the lofty growth, and the magnificence and variety of foliage which distinguish the American forests, so much the admiration of those who have seen only the groves of Europe....

THE ENTRANCE, AND INTERIOR.

The circumstance which first struck the attention of the party was the profound and solemn stillness of the place. The most quiet day has under the open sky its multitude of sounds—the lapse of waters, the subtle motions of the apparently slumbering air among forests, grasses, and rocks, the flight and note of insects, the voices of animals, the rising of exhalations, the mighty process of change, of perpetual growth and decay, going on all over the earth, produce a chorus of noises which the hearing cannot analyze—which, though it may seem to you silence, is not so; and when from such a scene you pass directly into one of the rocky chambers of the earth, you perceive your error by the contrast. As the three went forward they passed through a heap of dry leaves lightly piled, which the winds of the last autumn had blown into the cave from the summit of the surrounding forest, and the rustling made by their steps sounded strangely loud amid that death-like silence. A spacious cavern presented itself to their sight, the roof of which near the entrance was low, but several paces beyond it rose to a great height, where the smoke of the torch, ascending, mingled with the darkness, but the flame did not reveal the face of the vault.

THE RETURN—THE STORM—THE IMPRISONMENT.

On reaching again the mouth of the cave, they were struck with the change in the aspect of the heavens. Dark heavy clouds, the round summits of which were seen one beyond the other, were rapidly rising in the west; and through the grayish blue haze which suffused the sky before them, the sun appeared already shorn of his beams. A sound was heard afar of mighty winds contending with the forest, and the thunder rolled at a distance.

"We may stay at least until the storm is over," said Father Ambrose; "it would be upon us before we could descend these cliffs. Let us watch it from where we stand above the tops of these old woods : I can promise you it will be a magnificent spectacle."

Emily, though she would gladly have left the cave, could say nothing against the propriety of this advice; and even Le Maire, notwithstanding that he declared he had rather see a well-loaded table at that moment than all the storms that ever blew, preferred remaining to the manifest inconvenience of attempting a descent. In a few moments the dark mass of clouds swept over the face of the sun, and a tumult in the woods announced the coming of the blast. The summits of the forest waved and stooped before it, like a field of young flax in the summer breeze,—another and fiercer gust descended,—another and stronger convulsion of the forest ensued. The trees rocked backward and forward, leaned and rose, and tossed and swung their branches in every direction, and the whirling air above them was filled with their leafy

spoils. The roar was tremendous,—the noise of the ocean in a tempest is not louder,—it seemed as if that innumerable multitude of giants of the wood raised a universal voice of wailing under the fury that smote and tormented them. At length the rain began to fall, first in large and rare drops, and then thunder burst over head, and the waters of the firmament poured down in torrents, and the blast that howled in the woods fled before them as if from an element that it feared. The trees again stood erect, and nothing was heard but the rain beating heavily on the immense canopy of leaves around, and the occasional crashings of the thunder, accompanied by flashes of lightning, that threw a vivid light upon the walls of the cavern. The priest and his companions stood contemplating this scene in silence, when a rushing of water close at hand was heard. Father Ambrose showed the others where a stream, formed from the rains collected on the highlands above, descended on the crag that overhung the mouth of the cavern, and shooting clear of the rocks on which they stood, fell in spray to the broken fragments at the base of the precipice.

A gust of wind drove the rain into the opening where they stood, and obliged them to retire farther within. The priest suggested that they should take this opportunity to examine that part of the cave which, in going to the skeleton's chamber, they had passed on their left, observing, however, that he believed it was no otherwise remarkable than for its narrowness and its length. Le Maire and Emily assented, and the former taking up the torch which he had stuck in the ground, they went back into the interior. They had just reached the spot where the two passages diverged from each other, when a hideous and intense glare of light filled the cavern, showing for an instant the walls, the roof, the floor, and every crag and recess, with the distinctness of the broadest sunshine. A frightful crash accompanied it, consisting of several sharp and deafening explosions, as if the very heart of the mountain was rent asunder by the lightning, and immediately after a body of immense weight seemed to fall at their very feet with a heavy sound, and a shock that caused the place where they stood to tremble as if shaken by an earthquake. A strong blast of air rushed by them, and a suffocating odour filled the cavern.

Father Ambrose had fallen upon his knees in mental prayer, at the explosion; but the blast from the mouth of the cavern threw him to the earth. He raised himself, however, immediately, and found himself in utter silence and darkness, save that a livid image of that insufferable glare floated yet before his eyeballs. He called first upon Emily, who did not answer, then upon Le Maire, who replied from the ground a few paces nearer the entrance of the cave. He also had been thrown prostrate, and the torch he carried was extinguished. It was but the work of an instant to kindle it again, and they then discovered Emily extended near them in a swoon.

"Let us bear her to the mouth of the cavern," said Le Maire; "the fresh air from without will revive her." He took her in his arms, but on arriving at the spot he placed her suddenly on the ground, and raising both hands, exclaimed, with an accent of despair, "The rock is fallen!—the entrance is closed!" It was but too evident,—Father Ambrose needed but a single look to convince him of its truth,—the huge rock which impended over the entrance had been loosened by the thunderbolt, and had fallen upon the floor of the cave, closing all return to the outer world.

THE THIRD DAY.

On the third day the cavern presented a more gloomy spectacle than it had done at any time since the fall of the rock took place. It was now about eleven o'clock in the morning, and the shrill singing of the wind about the cliffs, and through the crevice, which now admitted a dimmer light than on the day previous, announced the approach of a storm from the south. The hope of relief from without was growing fainter and fainter as the time passed on; and the sufferings of the prisoners became more poignant. The approach of the storm, too, could only be regarded as an additional misfortune, since it would probably prevent or obstruct for that day the search which was making for them. They were all three in the outer and larger apartment of the cave. Emily was at a considerable distance from the entrance reclining on a kind of seat formed of large loose stones, and overspread with a covering of withered leaves. There was enough of light to show that she was exceedingly pale; that her eyes were closed, and that the breath came thick and pantingly through her parted lips, which alone of all her features retained the colour of life. Faint with watching, with want of sustenance, and with anxiety, she had lain herself down on this rude couch, which the care of her companions had provided for her, and had sunk into a temporary slumber. The priest stood close to the mouth of the cave leaning against the wall, with his arms folded, himself scarcely changed in appearance, except that his cheek seemed somewhat more emaciated, and his eyes were lighted up with a kind of solemn and preternatural brightness. Le Maire, with a spot of fiery red on each cheek,—his hair staring wildly in every direction, and his eyes bloodshot, was pacing the cavern floor to and fro, carrying his rifle, occasionally stopping to examine the priming, or to peck the flint; and sometimes standing still for a moment, as if lost in thought.....

"My good friend," said the priest, approaching him, "you forget what grounds of hope yet remain to us; indeed, the probability of our escape is scarcely less to-day than it was yesterday. The fall of the rock may be discovered by some one passing this way, and he may understand that it is possible we are confined here. While our existence is prolonged there is no occasion for despair. You should endeavour, my son, to compose yourself, and to rely on the goodness of that Power who has never forsaken you."

"Compose myself!" answered Le Maire, who had listened impatiently to this exhortation; "compose myself! Do you not know that there are those here who will not suffer me to be tranquil for a moment? Last night I was twice awakened, just as I had fallen asleep, by a voice pronouncing

my name, as audibly as I heard yours just now; and the second time, I looked to where the skeleton lies, and the foul thing had half-raised itself from the rock, and was beckoning me to come and place myself by its side. Can you wonder if I slept no more after that?"

"My son, these are but the dreams of a fever."

"And then, whenever I go by myself, I hear low voices and titterings of laughter from the recesses of the rocks. They mock me, that I, a free hunter, a denizen of the woods and prairies, a man whose liberty was never restrained for a moment, should be entrapped in this manner, and made to die like a buffalo in a pit, or like a criminal in the dungeons,—that I should consume with thirst in a land bright with innumerable rivers and springs, —that I should wither away with famine, while the woods are full of game and the prairies covered with buffaloes. I could face famine if I had my liberty. I could meet death without shrinking in the sight of the sun and the earth, and in the fresh open air. I should strive to reach some habitation of my fellow-creatures; I should be sustained by hope; I should travel on till I sank down with weakness and fatigue, and died on the spot. But famine made more frightful by imprisonment and inactivity, and these dreams, as you call them, that dog me asleep and awake, they are more than I can bear. Hark!" he exclaimed, after a short pause, and throwing quick and wild glances around him; "do you hear them yonder—do you hear how they mock me!—give me the rifle."

"No," said the priest, who instantly comprehended his purpose: "I must keep the piece till you are more composed."

Le Maire seemed not to hear the answer, but laying his grasp on the rifle, was about to pluck it from the old man's hands. Father Ambrose saw that the attempt to retain possession of it against his superior strength, would be vain; he therefore slipped down his right hand to the lock, and cocking it, touched the trigger, and discharged it in an instant. The report awoke Emily, who came trembling and breathless to the spot.

"What is the matter?" she asked.

"There is no harm done, my child," answered the priest, assuming an aspect of the most perfect composure. "I discharged the rifle, but it was not aimed at any thing, and I beg pardon for interrupting your repose at a time when you so much need it. Suffer me to conduct you back to the place you have left. Le Maire, will you assist?"

Supported by Le Maire on one side, and by the priest on the other, Emily, scarcely able to walk from weakness, was led back to her place of repose. Returning with Le Maire, Father Ambrose entreated him to consider how much his niece stood in need of his assistance and protection. He bade him recollect that his mad haste to quit the world before called by his Maker would leave her, should she ever be released from the cavern, alone and defenceless, or at least with only an old man for her friend, who was himself hourly expecting the summons of death. He exhorted him to reflect how much, even now, in her present condition of weakness and peril, she stood in need of his aid, and conjured him not to be guilty of a pusillanimous and cowardly desertion of one so lovely, so innocent, and so dependent upon him.

Le Maire felt the force of this appeal. A look of human pity passed across the wild expression of his countenance. He put the rifle into the hands of Father Ambrose. "You are right," said he; "I am a fool, and I have been, I suspect, very near becoming a madman. You will keep this until you are entirely willing to trust me with it. I will endeavour to combat these fancies a little longer."

THE ESCAPE.

In the mean time the light from the aperture grew dimmer and dimmer, and the eyes of the prisoners, though accustomed to the twilight of the cavern, became at length unable to distinguish objects at a few paces from the entrance. The priest and Le Maire had placed themselves by the couch of Emily, but rather, as it seemed, from that instinct of our race which leads us to seek each other's presence, than for any purpose of conversation, for each of the party preserved a gloomy silence. The topics of speculation on their condition had been discussed to weariness, and no others had now any interest for their minds. It was no unwelcome interruption to that melancholy silence, when they heard the sound of a mighty rain pouring down upon the leafy summits of the woods, and beating against the naked walls and shelves of the precipice. The roar grew more and more distinct, and at length it seemed that they could distinguish a sort of shuddering of the earth above them, as if a mighty host was marching heavily over it. The sense of suffering was for a moment suspended in a feeling of awe and curiosity.

That, likewise, is the rain," said Father Ambrose, after listening for a moment. "The clouds must pour down a perfect cataract, when the weight of its fall is thus felt in the heart of the rock."

"Do you hear that noise of running water?" asked Emily, whose quick ear had distinguished the rush of the stream formed by the collected rains over the rocks without at the mouth of the cave.

"Would that its channel were through this cavern," exclaimed Le Maire, starting up. "Ah! here we have it—we have it!—listen to the drooping of water from the roof near the entrance. And here at the aperture!" He sprang thither in an instant. A little stream detached from the main current, which descended over rocks that closed the mouth of the cave, fell in a thread of silver amid the faint light that streamed through the opening; he knelt for a moment, received it between his burning lips, and then hastily returning, bore Emily to the spot. She held out her hallowed palm, white, thin, and semi-transparent, like a pearly shell, used for dipping up the waters from one of those sweet fountains that rise by the very edge of the sea—and as fast as it filled with the cool, bright element, imbibed it with an eagerness and delight inexpressible. The priest followed her example; Le Maire also drank from the little stream as it fell, bathed in it his feverish brow, and suffered it to fall upon his sinewy neck.

42

"It has given me a new hold on life," said Le Maire, his chest distending with several full and long breathings. "It has not only quenched that hellish thirst, but it has made my head less light, and my heart lighter. I will never speak ill of this element again—the choicest grapes of France never distilled any thing so delicious, so grateful, so life-giving. Take notice, Father Ambrose, I retract all I have ever said against water and water-drinkers. I am a sincere penitent, and shall demand absolution."

Father Ambrose had begun gently to reprove Le Maire for his unseasonable levity, when Emily cried out—"The rock moves!—the rock moves! Come back—come further into the cavern!" Looking up to the vast mass that closed the entrance, he saw plainly that it was in motion, and he had just time to draw Le Maire from the spot where he had stooped down to take another draught of the stream, when a large block, which had been wedged in overhead, gave way, and fell in the very place where he left the prints of his feet. Had he remained there another instant, it must have crushed him to atoms. The prisoners, retreating within the cavern far enough to avoid the danger, but not too far for observation, stood watching the event with mingled apprehension and hope. The floor of the cave, just at the edge, on which rested the fallen rock, yawned at the fissures, where the earth with which they were filled had become saturated and swelled with water, and unable any longer to support the immense weight, settled away, at first slowly, under it, and finally, along with its incumbent load, fell suddenly and with a tremendous crash, to the base of the precipice, letting the light of day and the air of heaven into the cavern. The thunder of that disruption was succeeded by the fall of a few large fragments of rock on the right and left, after which the priest and his companions heard only the fall of the rain and the heavy sighing of the wind in the forest.

Father Ambrose and Emily knelt involuntarily in thanksgiving at their unexpected deliverance. Le Maire, although unused to the devotional mood, observing their attitude, had bent his knee to imitate it, when a glance at the outer world now laid open to his sight, made him start again to his feet with an exclamation of delight. The other two arose, also, and turned to the broad opening which now looked out from the cave over the forest. On one side of this opening rushed the torrent whose friendly waters had undermined the rock at the entrance, and now dashed themselves against its shivered fragments below. It is not for me to attempt to describe how beautiful appeared to their eyes that world which they feared never again to see, or how grateful to their senses was that fresh and fragrant air of the forests which they thought never to breathe again. The light, although the sky was thick with clouds and rain, was almost too intense for their vision, and they shaded their brows with their hands as they looked forth upon that scene of woods and meadows and waters, fairer to their view than it had ever appeared in the most glorious sunshine.

2 E 2

EDWARD EVERETT.

[Born 1794. Died 1865.]

EDWARD EVERETT, a younger brother of Alexander H. Everett,* and one of the most eminent of American scholars and rhetoricians, was born in Dorchester, near Boston, in 1794, and at the early age of thirteen entered Harvard University, where he graduated in 1811, with an extraordinary reputation for abilities and acquirements. He at first turned his attention to the law, but yielding to the wishes of his friends decided to study theology, and had been two years in the divinity school at Cambridge, when Boston was thrown into mourning by the death of the youthful and eloquent Buckminster, and he was chosen to succeed him as minister of the church in Brattle street. He was now but nineteen years of age, and his society, perhaps the largest and most intellectual in the city, had been accustomed to hear one of the most remarkable orators of modern times; but his success was still such as to justify the most sanguine anticipations of his friends. In addition to his ordinary and arduous professional labours, in the first eight months of his ministry he wrote and published, in a volume of nearly five hundred pages, a very able Defence of Christianity, against a work which had then just appeared under the title of The Grounds of Christianity Examined, by Comparing the New Testament with the Old.

In 1815, before he was twenty-one years of age, he was elected professor of the Greek Language and Literature† in the University, with permission to visit Europe for the improvement of his health, which had been impaired by severe application to his pastoral duties. He embarked at Boston soon after the peace, intending to proceed immediately to Germany, but on arriving in Liverpool ascertained that Napoleon had escaped from Elba, and so was detained in England until after the battle of Waterloo. He then went to Göttingen, where he acquired the German language, and afterward visited the principal universities of the country to inquire into the state of learning and the prevailing modes of instruction. In the autumn of 1817 he reached Paris, where he passed the following winter in preparation for his duties in the University, and became acquainted with many eminent men, one of whom was Coray, whose writings had so powerfully contributed to the regeneration of modern Greece. The summer of 1818 he spent in England, Scotland and Wales, the autumn in France, Switzerland and Italy, and the winter in Rome, where he became acquainted with Canova, then engaged on his statue of Washington, and studied ancient literature in the library of the Vatican. In the spring of 1819, carrying letters from Lord Byron to Ali Pacha, he went to the Ionian Islands, and Greece, to Troy, Constantinople, and Adrianople, and proceeding through Vienna and Paris to London, returned to the United States, having been absent about four years and a half.

He immediately entered upon the duties of his professorship at Cambridge, where he delivered courses of lectures on the History of Greek Literature, on Antiquities, and on Ancient Art, and published a Greek Grammar, from the German of Buttmann, and a Greek Reader, on the basis of the one by Jacobs.

The North American Review had now passed from the possession of the club under whose auspices it was established, and at the request of the new proprietors Mr. Everett became its editor. The first number issued under his direction was that for January, 1820, and he conducted it with an industry and ability which soon won for it an unprecedented popularity. In the four years of his editorship he wrote for it about fifty articles, making nearly one-half of the entire work for that period, and afterward, while it was under the charge of his brother, or his successors, contributed altogether some sixty articles, among which are many of the most elaborate and powerful that have ever appeared in its pages. All of them, it should be remembered, were the product only of leisure moments, amidst other occupations which had a prior claim upon him.

---

* See ante, page 284.

† M. Cousin, who was with Mr. Everett in Germany, informed a friend of ours that he was the best Grecian he ever knew, and the translator of Plato must have known a good many of the very best.—The [London] Quarterly Review.

This was particularly the case while he was editor, as he was then engaged in the active duties of his professorship. About the time his editorial connection with the Review ceased, he became a member of Congress, and also began to be called upon frequently to deliver public addresses. Although as a member of Congress he spoke but rarely, he did a great deal of labour in the committee room, generally drafting the reports on all matters of business, even when in a political minority. After having been ten years in the House of Representatives, Mr. Everett was in 1836 elected Governor of Massachusetts, and was reëlected in 1837, 1838 and 1839. In this period his special engagements left him very little leisure for literary pursuits, and his contributions to the Review are much less frequent than before. Some of his hundred articles, thrown off *currente calamo*, are undoubtedly ill arranged and superficial, but altogether they evince a variety and depth of learning, and a degree of feeling, fancy, energy and power, rarely combined in an individual. The happy wit and good temper shown in his reviewals of German and English travellers in America; the æsthetic cultivation indicated in his articles on Canova and the Epochs of Plastic Art; the fine enthusiasm which animates the paper on Coray's Aristotle and the rest of that brilliant series which electrified the country in behalf of the Greeks during their war for independence; and the statesmanlike views which mark the papers on Reform in Europe; with the familiar knowledge of the great masters of antiquity, the ready apprehension of truth and beauty, the exuberant illustration, and copious and forcible diction, which characterize his essays generally, show that literature suffered no common loss when he entered the arena of politics.

In 1836 Mr. Everett published a collection of twenty-seven Orations and Speeches delivered by him on various occasions in the preceding eleven years. It embraced, with others, those on the motives to intellectual exertion in America, the landing of the Pilgrims, the arrival of Winthrop, the battles of Concord, Lexington, Bunker Hill, and Bloody Brook, and those which he delivered at public dinners given to him at Nashville in Tennessee, Lexington, in Kentucky, and other places, during his tour through the Valley of the Mississippi to New Orleans in 1829. His speeches on political occasions, and historical and literary discourses delivered since 1836, would fill another volume equal in extent, variety, and interest. As an orator he has living very few equals. He is graceful and fervid in a remarkable degree, and his ready copiousness and felicity of illustration and quotation show how extensive and thorough has been his research, how retentive is his memory, and with what rapidity are made the decisions of his taste. He is eminently picturesque in grouping and narration, and his classical allusions have the charm of a perfect familiarity with the richest stores of learning.

In 1841 Mr. Everett was appointed Minister Plenipotentiary to the court of London, at which he resided about five years. While in England the degree of Doctor of Laws was conferred upon him by the University of Cambridge. On his return to the United States he was elected to the presidency of Harvard University, and was inaugurated on the thirtieth of April, 1846. The position of head of the oldest, wealthiest and most respectable institution of learning on this continent, is one of great dignity and importance; and no person could be found better qualified for it than the distinguished scholar whose youth and early manhood were spent in her halls as a student and professor of written learning, and whose middle age has been as fruitful of opportunities to study mankind.

Mr. Everett has scarcely fulfilled the expectations which were awakened by his first brilliant essays. He came completely armed and thoroughly trained into the lists, but has never attempted any achievement that would test the full capacity of his skill, the full might of his nature. He has been industrious; no man indeed has been more so; his discourses and reviews alone would have occupied the lifetime of an author of more than ordinary fertility; and they have been produced amid engagements that would have exhausted the energies and resources of a common mind; they have been the mere pastimes of a laborious student and statesman. Had the same activity, facility and strength been concentrated upon two or three continuous works, his reputation would be as enduring as it has been brilliant. It may be said of him that he has been perfectly successful in every thing that he has undertaken; but he has written and spoken to the present generation. The country still looks for his Life Poem.

He resigned the presidency of Harvard in 1849, and was succeeded by Jared Sparks. On the decease of Daniel Webster, Mr. Everett was appointed, Nov., 1852, Secretary of State under President Filmore, and in 1853 he succeeded Hon. John Davis as a national Senator, but resigned his seat on account of ill health, the following year.

In 1855, Mr. Everett commenced the crowning work of his life, the delivery of his great oration on Washington. This splendid oration was first delivered Feb. 22, 1856, before the Boston Mercantile Library, and the proceeds devoted to the purchase of a copy of Stuart's portrait. "The Ladies' Mount Vernon Association" for the purchase of the estate at Mount Vernon, having accepted his offer to deliver this oration for its benefit, invitations from every quarter poured in upon him, and for three years much of his time was spent in delivering it, and always to crowded audiences. It was repeated 119 times, of which four were in Philadelphia, and four in New York, producing $57,000. In the midst of this engrossing occupation he also found time to write 53 essays for the New York Ledger, which produced $10,000 for the same fund. His address on "Charity and Charitable Institutions," fifteen times repeated, raised for beneficial purposes $13,500. Another oration on "The Early Days of Franklin" also produced a large sum. Altogether his labor of about three years, for benevolent purposes, realized nearly $90,000.

In 1860, he wrote a Memoir of Washington for the Encyclopedia Britannica, which was republished in this country. His orations and speeches were published in 3 vols., 8vo.

In 1860, he was nominated for Vice President of the U. S., and received about one-eighth of the electoral vote; Lincoln's election was the signal for the defection of the Southern States. Mr. Everett was prompt to recognize the new issue, and aided the cause by various orations, and in 1863, was invited by nineteen Governors of the loyal States to deliver the oration at the consecration of the cemetery of Gettysburg. His last public appearance was at a meeting held in Boston, shortly before his death, for the relief of the people of Savannah, who were suffering privations caused by the war. He died Jan. 15th, 1865, of apoplexy. President Lincoln ordered appropriate honors to his memory

AMERICA AND GREECE

FROM "THE AFFAIRS OF GREECE." AN ARTICLE IN THE NORTH AMERICAN REVIEW.

. . . . What a monstrous complication of calamity, to have the best, the worthiest, the purest designs and actions, loaded with all the consequences of vice and crime; to be deprived not only of all that makes life joyous, but to be punished for doing well, and to be forced to go privately about those good deeds, to which men, in other countries, are exhorted as to a source of praise and honour. These things ought to be considered; and a reprehensible apathy prevails as to their reality. If liberty, virtue, and religion, were not words on our lips, without a substance in our hearts, it would be hardly possible to pursue our little local interests with such jealousy; to be all on fire in one state, for fear Congress should claim the power of internal improvements, and up in arms in another against a change of the tariff, and carried away in all, with a controversy between rival candidates for an office, which all would administer in much the same way; if a narrow selfishness did not lie at the bottom of our conduct, we could not do all this, while men, Christians as good as we, who have nerves to smart, minds to think, hearts to feel, like ourselves, are waging unaided, single-handed, at perilous odds, a war of extermination against tyrants, who deny them not only the blessings of liberty, but the mercies of slavery.

But we hope better things of our country. In the great Lancastrian school of the nations, liberty is the lesson, which we are appointed to teach. Masters we claim not, we wish not, to be, but the Monitors we are of this noble doctrine. It is taught in our settlement, taught in our Revolution, taught in our government; and the nations of the world are resolved to learn. It may be written in sand and effaced, but it will be written again and again, till hands now fettered in slavery shall boldly and fairly trace it, and lips that now stammer at the noble word, shall sound it out in the ears of their despots, with an emphasis to waken the dead. Some will comprehend it and practise it at the first; others must wrestle long with the old slavish doctrines; and others may abuse it to excess, and cause it to be blasphemed awhile in the world. But it will still be taught and still be repeated, and must be learned by all; by old and degenerate communities to revive their youth; by springing colonies to hasten their progress. With the example before them of a free representative government—of a people governed by themselves,—it is no more possible that the nations will long bear any other, than that they should voluntarily dispense with the art of printing or the mariner's compass. It is therefore plainly no age for Turks to be stirring. It is as much as men can do, to put up with Christian, with civilized, yea, with legitimate masters. The Grand Seignior is a half-century too late in the world. It requires all people's patience to be oppressed and ground to the dust, by the parental sway of most faithful, most catholic, most Christian princes. Fatigued as they are with the Holy Alliance, it were preposterous to suppose they can long submit to a horde of Tartarian infidels. The idea that the most honorable, the most responsible, the most powerful office in the state, can, like a vile heirloom, follow the chance of descent, is quite enough to task the forbearance of this bold and busy time. What then shall become of viziers and sultans, when ministers are bewildered in their cabinets, and kings are shaken on their thrones? Instead of arming their misbelieving host against a people who have taken hold of liberty, and who will be free, let them rejoice that great and little Bucharia are still vacant, and take up their march for the desert.

ARISTOCRACY.
FROM THE PROSPECTS OF REFORM IN EUROPE.

No man in the Catholic Church can take the first degrees of saintship, under a century, nor be fully canonized under two. It requires a hundred years to raise human weakness to beatific purity;—but the hundred years, if circumstances are favourable, will do it. What subsists to-day by violence, continues to-morrow by acquiescence, and is perpetuated by tradition; till at last the hoary abuse shakes the gray hairs of antiquity at us, and gives itself out as the wisdom of ages. Thus the clearest dictates of reason are made to yield to a long succession of follies. And this is the foundation of the aristocratic system at the present day. Its stronghold, with all those not immediately interested in it, is the reverence of antiquity.

By this system we mean the aggregate of all the institutions which a people, supposing them to be virtuous and well informed, and meeting together free from all prejudices, to organize themselves into a political community, and capable of foreseeing consequences, would reject, as not tending to promote the greatest happiness of the greatest number. We will assume that a people thus assembling would decide, that it was best to have an efficient civil government; composed of the legislative, executive, and judicial departments; that they would provide for the choice of the man whom the majority should think best qualified, as chief magistrate, and that they would furnish this executive officer with all the requisite means to enable him to discharge his functions. We do not, therefore, view a vigorous and well organized executive government a part of the abusive aristocratic system. But the people would plainly see, that their chief magistrate was not only constituted for their advantage, but derived his authority from their choice; consequently if any one started the idea that he possessed it by birth or divine right, the suggestion would be instantly rejected as groundless; it might even be derided as absurd. We therefore regard hereditary monarchy as a part of the system which is founded in abuse. Sooner or later, we doubt not, the time will come, when the absurdity of such a system will be as generally felt, as that of the establishment to which

Fletcher of Saltoun compares it,—an hereditary professorship of divinity, which he says he heard of in some part of Germany.

This assembly would no doubt constitute a legislative body, and would probably (supposing it, as we have stated, gifted with the foresight of what experience has taught us) organize it into two separate chambers of legislation; but of this we speak with less confidence, as the experiment of one has never been fairly tried. But whether one or two, the people would of course arrange a plan of election, by which the members of the legislature should be designated by the people. If membership were viewed as a privilege, it ought not to be monopolized; if as a burden, not to be permanently borne by one: consequently provision would he made for a limited tenure of the representative office, and an exercise, at marked intervals, of the popular choice. If any one should intimate, that in both or either of the houses, the right and duty of legislation ought to be hereditary; that when one legislator died, his place should be taken by his oldest son, or his nephew, or, in default of nearer kin, by the most distant assignable heir, (who may be, perhaps, the most stupid, the most vicious, the most contemptible person in the community); and should remain wholly vacant if he had no heir, —as if his family alone were endowed with special grace to fill it,—such an intimation would be received with astonishment and disgust, and apprehensions for the sanity of the man who made it. We therefore regard an hereditary House of Lords as a part of the aristocratic system, founded on the most flagrant abuse. By the same test of principle, we should arrive at the same conclusion, in respect to an established Church, the law of primogeniture, and all antiquated, unequal, and abusive corporate monopolies, in civil or ecclesiastical, public or private affairs.

DIVINE RIGHT AND TRADITION.
FROM THE SAME.

WAS it all mere arrogant assumption; all gratuitous fraud upon a credulous age, which taught that the establishment of crown and church was *jure divino?* Far from it. It was a calculation of the deepest worldly wisdom, a provision of the most consummate selfish sagacity. Starting from the simple and undoubted principle that civil government is approved by Providence, and that Christianity is a revelation of Divine truth, men were trained on to the toleration, and at last to the reverence of an established church and an hereditary crown, subsisting by the grace of God. The subtle spirits who reared this fabric knew well that it could rest on no other foundation. The great master principle of human weakness, man's dread of the mysterious unknown, his self-prostration before the Infinite, was resorted to, by the authors of these institutions, because no other principle was strong enough to subdue him to these institutions. They looked round for shoulders broad enough to bear this yoke. Chivalry rattled her sword at the very suggestion of it. The great barons looked over their battlements, and laughed at their fellow baron, the king, who, claiming to be greater than the greatest, was sometimes weaker than the weakest; but Superstition offered his sturdy back to the burden, and bore it like the strong ass in the Bible, for centuries. But those centuries are passed. The divine right of the crown and an established church are exploded, and on what foundation do they now rest?... They are the traditionary institutions of England; the pillars of the British monarchy. They are now, if you will, erect, but their basis is insecure. It is not two centuries since the great usurper heaved them from their foundation, and showed that their substructions, as the historian says of those of the Roman capitol, were insane. The era of the elder political fanaticism has gone by. A milder delusion succeeded, and the revolting features of the ancient toryism are now hidden under the mask of *tradition*. The sanctity of that tradition is in its turn assailed, and in it the only conservative principle of the British Constitution. We do not say, that the British Constitution is doomed to irremediable abuse,—to the forced toleration of any and every existing evil. But we humbly apprehend, that the only principle of reform, which is consistent with its preservation, is the temperate correction of practical evils, by specific remedies applied to the individual case. General and theoretic remedies are inadmissible; for theoretically the whole monarchy is an abuse.

THE LANDING OF THE MAYFLOWER.

FROM A CENTENNIAL ADDRESS AT BARNSTABLE.

Do you think, sir, as we repose beneath this splendid pavilion, adorned by the hand of taste, blooming with festive garlands, wreathed with the stars and stripes of this great republic, resounding with strains of heart-stirring music, that, merely because it stands upon the soil of Barnstable, we form any idea of the spot as it appeared to Captain Miles Standish, and his companions, on the 15th or 16th of November, 1620? Oh, no, sir. Let us go up for a moment, in imagination, to yonder hill, which overlooks the village and the bay, and suppose ourselves standing there on some bleak, ungenial morning, in the middle of November of that year. The coast is fringed with ice. Dreary forests, interspersed with sandy tracts, fill the background. Nothing of humanity quickens on the spot, save a few roaming savages, who, ill-provided with what even they deem the necessaries of life, are digging with their fingers a scanty repast out of the frozen sands. No friendly lighthouses had as yet hung up their cressets upon your headlands; no brave pilot-boat was hovering like a sea-bird on the tops of the waves, beyond the Cape, to guide the shattered bark to its harbour; no charts and soundings made the secret pathways of the deep as plain as a gravelled road through a lawn; no comfortable dwellings along the line of the shore, and where are now your well-inhabited streets, spoke a

welcome to the Pilgrim; no steeple poured the music of Sabbath morn into the ear of the fugitive for conscience' sake. Primeval wildness and native desolation brood over sea and land; and from the 9th of November, when, after a most calamitous voyage, the Mayflower first came to anchor in Provincetown harbour, to the end of December, the entire male portion of the company was occupied, for the greater part of every day, and often by night as well as by day, in exploring the coast and seeking a place of rest, amidst perils from the savages, from the unknown shore, and the elements, which it makes one's heart bleed to think upon.

But this dreary waste, which we thus contemplate in imagination, and which they traversed in sad reality, is a chosen land. It is a theatre upon which an all-glorious drama is to be enacted. On this frozen soil,—driven from the ivy-clad churches of their mother land,—escaped, at last, from loathsome prisons,—the meek fathers of a pure church will lay the spiritual basement of their temple. Here, on the everlasting rock of liberty, they will establish the foundation of a free State. Beneath its ungenial wintry sky, principles of social right, institutions of civil government, shall germinate, in which, what seemed the Utopian dreams of visionary sages, are to be more than realized.

But let us contemplate, for a moment, the instruments selected by Providence, for this political and moral creation. However unpromising the field of action, the agents must correspond with the excellence of the work. The time is truly auspicious. England is well supplied with all the materials of a generous enterprise. She is in the full affluence of her wealth of intellect and character. The age of Elizabeth has passed and garnered up its treasures. The age of the commonwealth, silent and unsuspected, is ripening towards its harvest of great men. The Burleighs and Cecils have sounded the depths of statesmanship; the Drakes and Raleighs have run the whole round of chivalry and adventure; the Cokes and Bacons are spreading the light of their master-minds through the entire universe of philosophy and law. Out of a generation of which men like these are the guides and lights, it cannot be difficult to select the leaders of any lofty undertaking; and, through their influence, to secure to it the protection of royalty. But, alas, for New England! No, sir, happily for New England, Providence works not with human instruments. Not many wise men after the flesh, not many mighty, not many noble, are called. The stars of human greatness, that glitter in a court, are not destined to rise on the lowering horizon of the despised Colony. The feeble company of Pilgrims is not to be marshalled by gartered statesmen, or mitred prelates. Fleets will not be despatched to convoy the little band, nor armies to protect it. Had there been honours to be won, or pleasures to be enjoyed, or plunder to be grasped, hungry courtiers, mid-summer friends, godless adventurers, would have eaten out the heart of the enterprise. Silken Buckinghams and Somersets would have blasted it with their patronage. But, safe amidst their unenvied perils, strong

in their inoffensive weakness, rich in their untempt-
ing poverty, the patient fugitives are permitted to
pursue unmolested the thorny paths of tribulation;
and, landed at last on the unfriendly shore, the
hosts of God, in the frozen mail of December, en-
camp around the dwellings of the just;

"Stern famine guards the solitary coast.
And winter barricades the realms of frost."

While Bacon is attuning the sweetest strains of
his honeyed eloquence to soothe the dull ear of a
crowned pedant, and his great rival, only less obsequious, is on his knees to deprecate the royal
displeasure, the future founders of the new republic beyond the sea are training up for their illustrious mission, in obscurity, hardship, and weary exile in a foreign land.

And now,—for the fulness of time is come,—
let us go up once more, in imagination, to yonder
hill, and look out upon the November scene. That
single dark speck, just discernible through the perspective glass, on the waste of waters, is the fated
vessel. The storm moans through her tattered
canvas, as she creeps, almost sinking, to her anchorage in Provincetown harbour; and there she
lies, with all her treasures, not of silver and gold,
(for of these she has none,) but of courage, of patience, of zeal, of high spiritual daring. So often
as I dwell in imagination on this scene; when I
consider the condition of the Mayflower, utterly incapable, as she was, of living through another gale;
when I survey the terrible front presented by our
coast to the navigator who, unacquainted with its
channels and roadsteads, should approach it in the
stormy season, I dare not call it a mere piece of
good fortune, that the general north and south
wall of the shore of New England should be
broken by this extraordinary projection of the
Cape, running out into the ocean a hundred miles,
as if on purpose to receive and encircle the precious vessel. As I now see her, freighted with the
destinies of a continent, barely escaped from the
perils of the deep, approaching the shore precisely
where the broad sweep of this most remarkable
headland presents almost the only point, at which,
for hundreds of miles, she could, with any ease,
have made a harbour, and this, perhaps, the very
best on the seaboard, I feel my spirit raised above
the sphere of mere natural agencies. I see the
mountains of New England rising from their
rocky thrones. They rush forward into the ocean,
settling down as they advance; and there they
range themselves, as a mighty bulwark around the
Heaven-directed vessel. Yes, the everlasting God
himself stretches out the arm of his mercy and his
power, in substantial manifestation, and gathers the
meek company of his worshippers as in the hollow
of his hand.

THE PROGRESS OF DISCOVERY.
FROM AN ADDRESS AT AMHERST COLLEGE.

WE are confirmed in the conclusion that the popular diffusion of knowledge is favourable to the
growth of science, when we reflect that, vast as is
the domain of learning is, and extraordinary as is
the progress which has been made in almost every
branch, we may assume as certain, I will not say that
we are in its infancy, but that the discoveries which
have been already made, wonderful as they are, bear
but a small proportion to those that will hereafter
be effected; and that in every thing that belongs
to the improvement of man, there is yet a field of
investigation broad enough to satisfy the most eager
thirst for knowledge, and diversified enough to suit
every variety of taste, order of intellect, or degree
of qualification. For the peaceful victories of the
mind, that unknown and unconquered world, for
which Alexander wept, is for ever near at hand;
hidden indeed, as yet, behind the veil with which
nature shrouds her undiscovered mysteries, but
stretching all along the confines of the domain of
knowledge, sometimes nearest when least suspected.
The foot has not yet pressed, nor the eye beheld
it; but the mind, in its deepest musings, in its
wildest excursions, will sometimes catch a glimpse
of the hidden realm—a gleam of light from the
Hesperian island—a fresh and fragrant breeze from
off the undiscovered land—

"Sabæan odours from the spicy shore,"

which happier voyagers, in after times, shall approach, explore and inhabit. Who has not felt,
when, with his very soul concentrated in his eyes,
while the world around him is wrapped in sleep,
he gazes into the holy depths of the midnight heavens, or wanders in contemplation among the
worlds and systems that sweep through the immensity of space—who has not felt as if their mystery
must yet more fully yield to the ardent, unwearied,
imploring research of patient science? Who does
not, in those choice and blessed moments, in which
the world and its interests are forgotten, and the
spirit retires into the inmost sanctuary of its own
meditations, and there, unconscious of every thing
but itself and the infinite Perfection, of which it
is the earthly type, and kindling the flame of thought
on the altar of prayer—who does not feel, in moments like these, as if it must at last be given to
man, to fathom the great secret of his own being—
to solve the mighty problem

"Of providence, foreknowledge, will and fate?"

When I think in what slight elements the great
discoveries that have changed the condition of the
world have oftentimes originated; on the entire
revolution in political and social affairs which has
resulted from the use of the magnetic needle; on
the world of wonders, teeming with the most important scientific discoveries, which has been opened
by the telescope; on the all-controlling influence
of so simple an invention as that of movable metallic types; on the effects of the invention of gunpowder, no doubt the casual result of some idle
experiment in alchemy; on the consequences that
have resulted and are likely to result, from the application of the vapour of boiling water to the manufacturing arts, to navigation, and transportation by
land; on the results of a single sublime conception in the mind of Newton, on which he erected,
as on a foundation, the glorious temple of the sys
tem of the heavens; in fine, when I consider how,
from the great master-principle of the philosophy

of Bacon—the induction of Truth from the observation of Fact—has flowed, as from a living fountain, the fresh and still swelling stream of modern science, I am almost oppressed with the idea of the probable connection of the truths already known, with great principles which remain undiscovered,—of the proximity in which we may unconsciously stand, to the most astonishing, though yet unrevealed mysteries of the material and intellectual world.

If, after thus considering the seemingly obvious sources from which the most important discoveries and improvements have sprung, we inquire into the extent of the field, in which farther discoveries are to be made, which is no other and no less than the entire natural and spiritual creation of God—a grand and lovely system, even as we imperfectly apprehend it, but no doubt most grand, lovely and harmonious, beyond all that we now conceive or imagine ; when we reflect that the most insulated, seemingly disconnected, and even contradictory parts of the system are, no doubt, bound together as portions of one stupendous whole ; and that those which are at present the least explicable, and which most completely defy the penetration hitherto bestowed upon them, are as intelligible, in reality, as that which seems most plain and clear ; that as every atom in the universe attracts every other atom, and is attracted by it, so every truth stands in harmonious connection with every other truth ; we are brought directly to the conclusion, that every portion of knowledge now possessed, every observed fact, every demonstrated principle, is a clew, which we hold by one end in the hand, and which is capable of guiding the faithful inquirer farther and farther into the inmost recesses of the labyrinth of nature. Ages and ages may elapse, before it conduct the patient intellect to the wonders of science to which it will eventually lead him ; and perhaps with the next step he takes, he will reach the goal, and principles destined to affect the condition of millions beam in characters of light upon his understanding. What was at once more unexpected and more obvious than Newton's discovery of the origin of light? Every living being, since the creation of the world, had gazed on the rainbow ; to none had the beautiful mystery revealed itself. And even the great philosopher himself, while dissecting the solar beam, while actually untwisting the golden and silver threads that compose the ray of light, laid open but half its wonders. And who shall say that to us, to whom, as we think, modern science has disclosed the residue, truths more wonderful than those now known will not yet be revealed ?

It is therefore by no means to be inferred, because the human mind has seemed to linger for a long time around certain results—as ultimate principles—that they and the principles closely connected with them are not likely to be pushed much farther , nor, on the other hand, does the intellect always require much time to bring its noblest truths to seeming perfection. It was, I suppose, two thousand years from the time when the peculiar properties of the magnet were first observed, be-

fore it became, through the means of those qualities, the pilot which guided Columbus to the American continent. Before the invention of the compass could take full effect, it was necessary that some navigator should practically and boldly grasp the idea that the globe is round. The two truths are apparently without connection ; but in their application to practice, they are intimately associated. Hobbes says that Dr. Harvey, the illustrious discoverer of the circulation of the blood, is the only author of a great discovery who ever lived to see it universally adopted. To the honour of subsequent science, this remark could not now, with equal truth, be made. Nor was Harvey himself without some painful experience of the obstacles, arising from popular ignorance, against which truth sometimes forces its way to general acceptance. When he first proposed the beautiful doctrine,.his practice fell off; people would not continue to trust their lives in the hands of such a dreamer. When it was firmly established and generally received, one of his opponents published a tract *de circulo sanguinis Salomoneo*, and proved from the twelfth chapter of Ecclesiastes, that the circulation of the blood was no secret in the time of Solomon. The whole doctrine of the Reformation may be found in the writings of Wiclif ; but neither he nor his age felt the importance of his principles, nor the consequences to which they led. Huss had studied the writings of Wiclif in manuscript, and was in no degree behind him, in the boldness with which he denounced the papal usurpations. But his voice was not heard beyond the mountains of Bohemia ; and he expired in agony at the stake, and his ashes were scattered upon the Rhine. A hundred years passed away. Luther, like an avenging angel, burst upon the world, and denounced the corruptions of the church, and rallied the host of the faithful, with a voice which might almost call up those ashes from their watery grave, and form and kindle them again into a living witness of the truth.

Thus Providence, which has ends innumerable to answer, in the conduct of the physical and intellectual, as well as of the moral world, sometimes permits the great discoverers fully to enjoy their fame, sometimes to catch but a glimpse of the extent of their achievements, and sometimes sends them dejected and heart-broken to the grave, unconscious of the importance of their own discoveries, and not merely undervalued by their contemporaries, but by themselves. It is plain that Copernicus, like his great contemporary, Columbus, though fully conscious of the boldness and the novelty of his doctrine, saw but a part of the changes it was to effect in science. After harbouring in his bosom for long, long years that pernicious heresy—the solar system—he died on the day of the appearance of his book from the press. The closing scene of his life, with a little help from the imagination, would furnish a noble subject for an artist. For thirty-five years he has revolved and matured in his mind his system of the heavens. A natural mildness of disposition, bordering on timidity, a reluctance to encounter controversy, and a dread of persecution. have led him to withhold his work from the press, and make known his system but to a few confidential disciples and friends. At length he draws near his end; he is seventy-three years of age, and he yields his work on " The Revo'utions of the Heavenly Orbs" to his friends for publication. The day at last has come, on which it is to be ushered into the world. It is the twenty-fourth of May, 1543. On that day—the effect, no doubt, of the intense excitement of his mind, operating upon an exhausted frame—an effusion of blood brings him to the gates of the grave. His last hour has come; he lies stretched upon the couch from which he will never rise, in his apartment at the Canonry at Frauenberg, East Prussia. The beams of the setting sun glance through the Gothic windows of his chamber; near his bedside is the armillary sphere, which he has contrived to represent his theory of the heavens; his picture, painted by himself, the amusement of his earlier years, hangs before him; beneath it are his astrolabe and other imperfect astronomical instruments; and around him are gathered his sorrowing disciples. The door of the apartment opens;—the eye of the departing sage is turned to see who enters: it is a friend, who brings him the first printed copy of his immortal treatise. He knows that in that book he contradicts all that had ever been distinctly taught, by former philosophers; he knows that he has rebelled against the sway of Ptolemy, which the scientific world had acknowledged for a thousand years; he knows that the popular mind will be shocked by his innovations; he knows that the attempt will be made to press even religion into the service against him; but he knows that his book is true. He is dying, but he leaves a glorious truth, as his dying bequest to the world. He bids the friend who has brought it place himself between the window and his bedside, that the sun's rays may fall upon the precious volume, and he may behold it once more, before his eye grows dim. He looks upon it, takes it in his hands, presses it to his breast, and expires. But no, he is not wholly gone. A smile lights up his dying countenance; a beam of returning intelligence kindles in his eye; his lips move; and the friend, who leans over him, can hear him faintly murmur the beautiful sentiments which the Christian lyrist of a later age has so finely expressed in verse:

Ye golden lamps of heaven, farewell, with all your feeble light;
Farewell, thou ever-changing moon, pale empress of the night;
And thou refulgent orb of day, in brighter flames array'd,
My soul which springs beyond thy sphere, no more demands thy aid.
Ye stars are but the shining dust of my divine abode,
The pavement of those heavenly courts, where I shall reign with God

So died the great Columbus of the heavens.

EXTENSION OF THE REPUBLIC.
FROM AN ORATION BEFORE THE PHI BETA KAPPA SOCIETY.

In the grand and steady progress of our country, the career of duty and usefulness will be run by all its children, under a constantly increasing

43

excitement. The voice, which, in the morning of life, shall awaken the patriotic sympathy of the land, will be echoed back by a community, incalculably swelled in all its proportions, before that voice shall be hushed in death. The writer, by whom the noble features of our scenery shall be sketched with a glowing pencil, the traits of our romantic early history gathered up with filial zeal, and the peculiarities of our character seized with delicate perception, cannot mount so entirely and rapidly to success, but that ten years will add new millions to the numbers of his readers. The American statesman, the orator, whose voice is already heard in its supremacy, from Florida to Maine, whose intellectual empire already extends beyond the limits of Alexander's, has yet new states and new nations starting into being, the willing tributaries to his sway.

This march of our population westward has been attended with consequences in some degree novel in the history of the human mind. It is a fact somewhat difficult of explanation, that the refinement of the ancient nations seemed almost wholly devoid of an elastic and expansive principle. The arts of Greece were enchained to her islands and her coasts; they did not penetrate the interior, at least not in every direction. The language and literature of Athens were as much unknown to the north of Pindus, at a distance of two hundred miles from the capital of Grecian refinement, as they were in Scythia. Thrace, whose mountain tops may almost be seen from the porch of the temple of Minerva at Sunium, was the proverbial abode of barbarism. Though the colonies of Greece were scattered on the coasts of Italy, of France, of Spain, and of Africa, no extension of their population far into the interior took place, and the arts did not penetrate beyond the walls of the cities where they were cultivated. How different is the picture of the diffusion of the arts and improvements of civilization, from the coast to the interior of America! Population advances westward with a rapidity which numbers may describe indeed, but cannot represent, with any vivacity, to the mind. The wilderness, which one year is impassable, is traversed the next by the caravans of the industrious emigrants, who go to follow the setting sun, with the language, the institutions, and the arts of civilized life. It is not the irruption of wild barbarians, sent to visit the wrath of God on a degenerate empire; it is not the inroad of disciplined banditti, marshalled by the intrigues of ministers and kings. It is the human family, led out to possess its broad patrimony. The states and nations, which are springing up in the valley of the Missouri, are bound to us, by the dearest ties of a common language, a common government, and a common descent. Before New England can look with coldness on their rising myriads, she must forget that some of the best of her own blood is beating in their veins; that her hardy children, with their axes on their shoulders, have been literally among the pioneers in this march of humanity; that young as she is, she has become the mother of populous states. What generous mind

2 F

would sacrifice to a selfish preservation of local preponderance, the delight of beholding civilized nations rising up in the desert; and the language,
the manners, the institutions, to which he has been
reared, carried with his household gods to the foot
of the Rocky Mountains? Who can forget that
this extension of our territorial limits is the extension of the empire of all we hold dear; of our
laws, of our character, of the memory of our ancestors, of the great achievements in our history?
Whithersoever the sons of the thirteen states shall
wander, to southern or western climes, they will
send back their hearts to the rocky shores, the battle fields, and the intrepid councils of the Atlantic
coast. These are placed beyond the reach of vicissitude. They have become already matter of history, of poetry, of eloquence:

The love, where death has set his seal,
    Nor age can chill, nor rival steal,
    Nor falsehood disavow.

Divisions may spring up, ill blood may burn,
parties be formed, and interests may seem to clash;
but the great bonds of the nation are linked to
what is passed. The deeds of the great men, to
whom this country owes its origin and growth, are
a patrimony, I know, of which its children will
never deprive themselves. As long as the Mississippi and the Missouri shall flow, those men and
those deeds will be remembered on their banks.
The sceptre of government may go where it will;
but that of patriotic feeling can never depart from
Judah. In all that mighty region which is drained
by the Missouri and its tributary streams—the valley co-extensive with the temperate zone—will
there be, as long as the name of America shall
last, a father, that will not take his children on his
knee and recount to them the events of the twenty-second of December, the nineteenth of April,
the seventeenth of June, and the fourth of July?
This then is the theatre on which the intellect
of America is to appear, and such the motives to
its exertion; such the mass to be influenced by its
energies, such the crowd to witness its efforts, such
the glory to crown its success. If I err in this
happy vision of my country's fortunes, I thank
God for an error so animating. If this be false,
may I never know the truth. Never may you, my
friends, be under any other feeling, than that a great,
a growing, an immeasurably expanding country is
calling upon you for your best services. The
name and character of our Alma Mater have always been carried by some of our brethren thousands of miles from her venerable walls; and thousands of miles still farther westward, the communities of kindred men are fast gathering, whose
minds and hearts will act in sympathy with yours.
The most powerful motives call on us, as scholars,
for those efforts, which our common country demands of all her children. Most of us are of that
class, who owe whatever of knowledge has shone
into our minds, to the free and popular institutions
of our native land. There are few of us, who
may not be permitted to boast, that we have been
reared in an honest poverty or a frugal competence,
and owe every thing to those means of education

which are equally open to all. We are summoned
to new energy and zeal by the high nature of the
experiment we are appointed in Providence to
make, and the grandeur of the theatre on which it
is to be performed. When the old world afforded
no longer any hope, it pleased Heaven to open
this last refuge of humanity. The attempt has
begun, and is going on, far from foreign corruption,
on the broadest scale, and under the most benignant prospects; and it certainly rests with us to solve
the great problem in human society, to settle, and
that for ever, that momentous question—whether
mankind can be trusted with a purely popular
system? One might almost think, without extravagance, that the departed wise and good of all
places and times are looking down from their happy
seats to witness what shall now be done by us; that
they who lavished their treasures and their blood
of old, who laboured and suffered, who spake and
wrote, who fought and perished, in the one great
cause of freedom and truth, are now hanging
from their orbs on high, over the last solemn experiment of humanity. As I have wandered over
the spots, once the scene of their labours, and
mused among the prostrate columns of their senate houses and forums, I have seemed almost to
hear a voice from the tombs of departed ages; from
the sepulchres of the nations, which died before
the sight. They exhort us, they adjure us to be
faithful to our trust. They implore us, by the
long trials of struggling humanity, by the blessed
memory of the departed; by the dear faith, which
has been plighted by pure hands, to the holy cause
of truth and man; by the awful secrets of the
prison houses, where the sons of freedom have
been immured; by the noble heads which have
been brought to the block; by the wrecks of time,
by the eloquent ruins of nations, they conjure us
not to quench the light which is rising on the
world. Greece cries to us, by the convulsed lips
of her poisoned, dying Demosthenes; and Rome
pleads with us, in the mute persuasion of her
mangled Tully.

THREE PICTURES OF BOSTON.

FROM AN ADDRESS BEFORE THE MERC. LIB. ASSOCIATION.

To understand the character of the commerce
of our own city, we must not look merely at one
point, but at the whole circuit of country, of
which it is the business centre. We must not
contemplate it only at this present moment of
time, but we must bring before our imaginations,
as in the shifting scenes of a diorama, at least three
successive historical and topographical pictures;
and truly instructive I think it would be to see
them delineated on canvas. We must survey the
first of them in the company of the venerable
John Winthrop, the founder of the state. Let us
go up with him, on the day of his landing, the seventeenth of June, 1630, to the heights of yonder
peninsula, as yet without a name. Landward
stretches a dismal forest; seaward, a waste of waters,

unspotted with a sail, except that of his own ship. At the foot of the hill you see the cabins of Walford and the Spragues, who—the latter a year before, the former still earlier—had adventured to this spot, untenanted else by any child of civilization. On the other side of the river lies Mr. Blackstone's farm. It comprises three goodly hills, converted by a spring-tide into three wood-crowned islets; and it is mainly valued for a noble spring of fresh water which gushes from the northern slope of one of these hills, and which furnished, in the course of the summer, the motive for transferring the seat of the infant settlement. This shall be the first picture.

The second shall be contemplated from the same spot—the heights of Charleston—on the same day, the eventful seventeenth of June, one hundred and forty-five years later, namely, in the year 1775. A terrific scene of war rages on the top of the hill. Wait for a favourable moment, when the volumes of fiery smoke roll away, and over the masts of that sixty-gun ship, whose batteries are blazing upon the hill, you behold Mr. Blackstone's farm changed to an ill-built town of about two thousand dwelling houses, mostly of wood, with scarce any public buildings, but eight or nine churches, the old State House, and Faneuil Hall; Roxbury beyond, an insignificant village; a vacant marsh in all the space now occupied by Cambridgeport and East Cambridge, by Chelsea and East Boston; and beneath your feet the town of Charlestown, consisting in the morning of a line of about three hundred houses, wrapped in a sheet of flames at noon, and reduced at eventide to a heap of ashes.

But those fires are kindled on the altar of Liberty. American independence is established. American commerce smiles on the spot; and now from the top of one of the triple hills of Mr. Blackstone's farm, a stately edifice arises, which seems to invite us as to an observatory. As we look down from this lofty structure, we behold the third picture—a crowded, busy scene. We see beneath us a city containing eighty or ninety thousand inhabitants, and mainly built of brick and granite. Vessels of every description are moored at the wharves. Long lines of commodious and even stately houses cover a space which, within the memory of man, was in a state of nature. Substantial blocks of warehouses and stores have forced their way to the channel. Faneuil Hall itself, the consecrated and unchangeable, has swelled to twice its original dimensions. Athenæums, hopitals, asylums and infirmaries, adorn the streets. The school-house rears its modest front in every quarter of the city, and sixty or seventy churches attest that the children are content to walk in the good old ways of their fathers. Connected with the city by eight bridges, avenues, or ferries, you behold a range of towns, most of them municipally distinct, but all of them in reality forming, with Boston, one vast metropolis, animated by one commercial life. Shading off from these, you see that most lovely back-ground, a succession of happy settlements, spotted with villas, farm houses and cottages; united to Boston by a constant intercourse; sustaining the capital from

their fields and gardens, and prosperous in the reflux of the city's wealth. Of the social life included within this circuit, and of all that in times past has adorned and ennobled it, commercial industry has been an active element, and has exalted itself by its intimate association with every thing else we hold dear. Within this circuit what memorials strike the eye!—what recollections—what institutions—what patriotic treasures and names that cannot die! There lie the canonized precincts of Lexington and Concord; there rise the sacred heights of Dorchester and Charlestown; there is Harvard, the ancient and venerable, foster-child of public and private liberality in every part of the state; to whose existence Charlestown gave the first impulse, to whose growth and usefulness the opulence of Boston has at all times ministered with open hand. Still farther on than the eye can reach, four lines of communication by railroad and steam have within our own day united with the capital, by bands of iron, a still broader circuit of towns and villages. Hark to the voice of life and business which sounds along the lines! While we speak, one of them is shooting onward to the illimitable west, and all are uniting with the other kindred enterprises, to form one harmonious and prosperous whole, in which town and country, agriculture and manufactures, labour and capital, art and nature—wrought and compacted into one grand system—are constantly gathering and diffusing, concentrating and radiating the economical, the social, the moral blessings of a liberal and diffusive commerce.

EXAMPLES OF PATRIOTISM IN OUR OWN HISTORY.

THE national character, in some of its most important elements, must be formed, elevated, and strengthened from the materials which history presents. Are we to be eternally ringing the changes upon Marathon and Thermopylæ; and going back to find in obscure texts of Greek and Latin the great exemplars of patriotic virtue? I rejoice that we can find them nearer home, in our own country, on our own soil;—that strains of the noblest sentiment that ever swelled in the breast of man are breathing to us out of every page of our country's history, in the native eloquence of our mother tongue;—that the colonial and the provincial councils of America exhibit to us models of the spirit and character which gave Greece and Rome their name and their praise among the nations. Here we ought to go for our instruction; the lesson is plain, it is clear, it is applicable. When we go to ancient history, we are bewildered with the difference of manners and institutions. We are willing to pay our tribute of applause to the memory of Leonidas, who fell nobly for his country, in the face of the foe. But when we trace him to his home, we are confounded at the reflection, that the same Spartan heroism to which he sacrificed himself at Thermopylæ, would have led him to tear his only child, if it happened to be a sickly babe,—

2 F 2

the very object for which all that is kind and good in man rises up to plead,—from the bosom of its mother, and carry it out to be eaten by the wolves of Taygetus. We feel a glow of admiration at the heroism displayed at Marathon by the ten thousand champions of invaded Greece; but we cannot forget that the tenth part of the number were slaves, unchained from the workshops and door-posts of their masters, to go and fight the battles of freedom. I do not mean that these examples are to destroy the interest with which we read the history of ancient times; they possibly increase that interest, by the singular contrast they exhibit. But they do warn us, if we need the warning, to seek our great practical lessons of patriotism at home; out of the exploits and sacrifices of which our own country is the theatre; out of the characters of our own fathers. Them we know, the high-souled, natural, unaffected, the citizen heroes. We know what happy firesides they left for the cheerless camp. We know with what pacific habits they dared the perils of the field. There is no mystery, no romance, no madness, under the name of chivalry, about them. It is all resolute, manly resistance—for conscience' and liberty's sake—not merely of an overwhelming power, but of all the force of long-rooted habits, and the native love of order and peace.

LUTHER.

IN the solemn loneliness, in which Luther found himself, he called around him not so much the masters of the Greek and Latin wisdom through the study of the ancient languages, as he did the mass of his own countrymen, by his translation of the Bible. It would have been a matter of tardy impression and remote efficacy, had he done no more than awake from the dusty alcoves of the libraries the venerable shades of the classic teachers. He roused up a population of living, sentient men, his countrymen, his brethren. He might have written and preached in Latin to his dying day, and the elegant Italian scholars, champions of the church, would have answered him in Latin better than his own; and with the mass of the people, the whole affair would have been a contest between angry and loquacious priests. "Awake all antiquity from the sleep of the libraries!" He awoke all Germany and half Europe from the scholastic sleep of an ignorance worse than death. He took into his hands not the oaten pipe of the classic muse; he moved to his great work, not

——————to the Dorian mood
Of flutes and soft recorders;—

He grasped the iron trumpet of his mother tongue, —the good old Saxon from which our own is descended, the language of noble thought and high resolve,—and blew a blast that shook the nations from Rome to the Orkneys. Sovereign, citizen,

and peasant, started at the sound; and, in a few short years, the poor monk, who had begged his bread for a pious canticle in the streets of Eisenach,—no longer friendless,—no longer solitary,— was sustained by victorious armies, countenanced by princes, and, what is a thousand times more precious than the brightest crown in Christendom, revered as a sage, a benefactor, and a spiritual parent, at the firesides of millions of his humble and grateful countrymen.

LITERATURE AND LIBERTY.

LITERATURE is the voice of the age and the state. The character, energy, and resources of the country are reflected and imaged forth in the conceptions of its great minds. They are organs of the time; they speak not their own language, they scarce think their own thoughts; but under an impulse like the prophetic enthusiasm of old, they must feel and utter the sentiments which society inspires. They do not create, they obey the spirit of the age; the serene and beautiful spirit descended from the highest heaven of liberty, who laughs at our preconceptions, and, with the breath of his mouth, sweeps before him the men and the nations that cross his path. By an unconscious instinct, the mind, in the action of its powers, adapts itself to the number and complexion of the other minds with which it is to enter into communion or conflict. As the voice falls into the key which is suited to the space to be filled, the mind, in the various exercises of its creative faculties, strives with curious search for that master-note, which will awaken a vibration from the surrounding community, and which, if it do not find it, is itself too often struck dumb.

For this reason, from the moment in the destiny of nations, that they descend from their culminating point, and begin to decline, from that moment the voice of creative genius is hushed, and at best, the age of criticism, learning, and imitation succeeds. When Greece ceased to be independent, the forum and the stage became mute. The patronage of Macedonian, Alexandrian, and Pergamean princes was lavished in vain. They could not woo the healthy Muses of Hellas, from the cold mountain tops of Greece, to dwell in their gilded halls. Nay, though the fall of greatness, the decay of beauty, the waste of strength, and the wreck of power have ever been among the favourite themes of the pensive muse, yet not a poet arose in Greece to chant her own elegy; and it is after near three centuries, and from Cicero and Sulpicius, that we catch the first notes of pious and pathetic lamentation over the fallen land of the arts. The freedom and genius of a country are invariably gathered into a common tomb, and there

——————can only strangers breathe
The name of that which was beneath.

JOHN PENDLETON KENNEDY.

[Born 1795. Died 1870.]

Mr. KENNEDY was born in Baltimore on the twenty-fifth of October, 1795. His mother was of the Pendleton family, in Virginia. His father was a prosperous merchant in Baltimore. He is the eldest of four sons, two now deceased; his brother Anthony represented Maryland, in the United States Senate, for six years. He went through the usual course of instruction in the schools of his native town, and finally was graduated at the Baltimore College, in 1812. He was just old enough to bear arms when General Ross invaded Maryland, and was among the volunteers who fought at Bladensburg and North Point, where he had sufficient military experience to serve the purposes of authorship.

He studied law, was admitted to the bar in 1816, and continued to practise with great success until he went into Congress, from which period he took an unreluctant farewell of a pursuit which he appears never to have liked, notwithstanding the eminence he attained in it. Swallow Barn shows that he had a greater affection for lawyers than for the law.

Mr. Kennedy's professional life was from first to last mixed with literature and politics. Through every stage of it he wrote a great deal of both grave and gay, the principal portion of which has been published either in the newspapers or in pamphlets, though he occasionally appeared in more ambitious volumes. At no time, however, has his application to letters been so earnest or exclusive as to give him a place in the *class* of literary men, a class which, until very recently, had no existence in this country, and which is still very small here.

His first work was a joint-stock affair, in two volumes, called The Red Book, in its character not unlike the Salmagundi of Irving and Paulding. With a very dear friend, and one of the most gifted scholars of our country, Mr. Peter Hoffman Cruse, it was thrown off in numbers, with an interval of about a fortnight between them, in Baltimore, in 1818 and 1819. It was of local and temporary in-terest, but it contained much neat and playful satire by Kennedy, and some exceedingly clever poetry by Cruse,* which will prevent its being forgotten.

Swallow Barn, or a Sojourn in the Old Dominion, was published in 1832. "I have had the greatest difficulty," he says in the preface, "to keep myself from writing a novel." It appears to have been commenced as a series of detached sketches of old or lower Virginia, exhibiting the habits, customs and opinions of the people of that region, and to have grown into something with the coherence of a story before it was finished. The plan of it very much resembles that of Bracebridge Hall, but it is purely American, and has more fidelity as an exhibition of rural life, while it is scarcely inferior in spirit and graceful humour. Miss Sedgwick has given us some delightful sketches of primitive customs and feelings in New England; Mrs. Kirkland has described with remarkable accuracy the "new homes" of Michigan; Judge Hall has been successful in delineating the border experiences of Illinois; Judge Longstreet has painted up to nature in his humorous Georgia Scenes; and Mr. Thorpe, Mr. Hooper, and others, have lifted the veil from the lodge of the hunter and the cabin of the settler in the far south-west; but none of our pictures of

* P. H. Cruse fell a victim to the cholera in 1832. He died before he had achieved in letters that distinguished reputation which all who knew him predicted for him. He was born in Baltimore in 1793, was educated at Princeton College, New Jersey, and prepared himself for the practice of the law, to which, however, he never devoted himself, preferring rather to follow the bent of his inclination in a life of literary study. He thus became an accomplished scholar, and one of the purest writers of our language. What he published is confined chiefly to the Reviews, of the ten years previous to his death, and to the Baltimore American, the editorial department of which was for several years under his charge. He possessed the most graceful wit, combined, as it usually is, with a taste of the most classical purity, and was always greatly remarked for the extraordinary vivacity and brilliancy of his conversation. These traits appear, though in less degree, in his writings. An agreeable volume might be furnished from his published and unpublished works, and I hope Mr. Kennedy will ere long lay such a one before the public.

local manners surpass, in truthful minuteness
or easy elegance of diction, these transcripts
of life in Virginia.

In 1835 Mr. Kennedy published his next
work, Horse Shoe Robinson, a Tale of the
Tory Ascendancy. He had spent a part of
the winter of 1818–19 in the Pendleton District of South Carolina, and there met his
hero, from whom he heard some extraordinary
details of his personal adventures. The novel
was suggested by this meeting, and he has
introduced into it almost a verbatim repetition
of Horse Shoe's escape from Charleston after
its surrender. No works could be more unlike each other than this and Swallow Barn.
They have no resemblance in style, in construction, or in spirit; but Horse Shoe Robinson was even more successful than its predecessor. Frank Meriwether the country gentleman, the shrewd and good-humoured old
lawyer Philpot Wart, and other characters, in
the first, are sketched with singular skill and
felicity, but they are less essentially creations
than the free-hearted, sagacious, and heroic
partisan yeoman, who quits his anvil at the
commencement of the civil war, and acts an
important though humble part through its
scenes of excitement and daring until the
Whigs are triumphant. There are in the
second work other original and admirably
executed characters, whose individuality is
distinct and perfectly sustained amid all varieties of circumstance; and skilful under-
plots, in which are imbodied beautifully-
wrought scenes of love and touching incidents of sorrow.

In 1838 appeared Rob of the Bowl, a Legend of St. Inigoe's. This novel was evidently written with much more care than the
others, but it was less successful. Though
dealing largely in invention, it is, like Horse
Shoe Robinson, of an historical character, and
may be regarded as an attempt to illustrate
the annals of Maryland under the rule of the
lord proprietary Cecilius Calvert, when the
colony was distracted by feuds between the
Protestants and Catholics. The characters
are numerous, various, and strongly marked;
but several of them are so prominent and so
elaborately finished that the interest is much
divided, and it has been remarked with some
reason, that the story wants a hero. The
historical impression which it conveys is as
accurate as the most careful study of the

incidents and temper of the times enabled the
author to render it; the costume throughout
is exact and in keeping; and the descriptions
of scenery are spirited and picturesque in an
eminent degree.

Mr. Kennedy's next work, published in
1840, was the Annals of Quodlibet, suggested
by the presidential canvass then just closed.
It is full of wit, humour, and pungent irony,
but is too exclusive in its reference to events
of the day to possess much interest now when
those events are nearly forgotten.

Each of the four works that have been mentioned is marked by distinct and happy peculiarities, and from internal evidence it probably
would never have been surmised that they were
by one author.

Mr. Kennedy was elected from Baltimore
to the Maryland House of Delegates in 1820,
1821, and 1822. In 1824 he received from
President Monroe the appointment of Secretary of Legation to Chili, which he resigned
before the sailing of the mission. He was
three times chosen a member of the House
of Representatives of the United States, for
the twenty-fifth, twenty-seventh, and twenty-
eighth congresses; and in 1846 was again
elected to the House of Delegates of Maryland. In the national legislature he soon rose
to a commanding position, and few members
enjoyed a higher degree of respect, or exerted
a more powerful influence, during the six years
for which he was a member. In the course
of his political career and connections he has
written and published many tracts on the more
engrossing questions of public economy and
policy to which the agitations of the time have
given rise, among which may be mentioned
several speeches and official reports in Congress, and numerous dissertations on public
affairs. One of his earliest performances was
a pamphlet under the signature of Mephisto-
philes, in which he reviews with great ability
Mr. Cambreling's somewhat celebrated Report
on Commerce. This was published in 1830,
and in the following year, as a member of the
Convention of the friends of American Industry, held in New York, he wrote conjointly
with Mr. Warren Dutton of Massachusetts,
and Mr. Charles Jared Ingersoll of Pennsylvania, the address which that body issued to
the people of the United States. Mr. Kennedy's last volume is A Defence of the Whigs,
published in 1844. This work is purely po-

litical, and is remarkable for clearness, vigour, and amplitude of statement and illustration. It embraces an outline of the origin and growth of the Whig party, coupled with a history of the twenty-seventh Congress, and a vindication of the Whigs in that body.

He was Speaker of the House of Delegates of Maryland. In 1852, he was Secretary of the Navy under Fillmore, and fitted out the Expedition to Japan under Perry; that for the exploration of Behring's Straits; the one to the River Platte; the one to the Coast of Africa by Lynch; and Dr. Kane's Expedition to the Arctic Ocean.

Among the other minor publications of Mr. Kennedy are an Address delivered before the Baltimore Horticultural Society in 1833, an eulogium on the life and character of his friend William Wirt in 1834, and a discourse at the dedication of the Green Mount Cemetery, in 1839. He died in 1870.

Mr. Kennedy is altogether one of our most genial, lively, and agreeable writers. His style is airy, easy, and graceful, but various, and always in keeping with his subject. He excels both as a describer and as a raconteur. His delineations of nature are picturesque and truthful, and his sketches of character are marked by unusual freedom and delicacy. He studies the periods which he attempts to illustrate with the greatest care, becomes thoroughly imbued with their spirit, and writes of them with the enthusiasm and the apparent sincerity and earnestness of a contemporary and an actor. He pays an exemplary regard to the details of costume, manners, and opinion, and is scarce ever detected in any kind of anachronism. There are some inequalities in his works, arising perhaps from the interruptions to which a man in active public life is liable; there is occasional diffuseness and redundance of incident as well as of expression; but his faults are upon the surface, and could be easily removed.

He published in 1849, Life of Wm. Wirt, 2 vols., 8vo., and later 2 vols., 12mo. At the breaking out of the Rebellion, he issued, The Border States, their Power and Duty; The Great Drama; and Ambrose's Letters on the Rebellion.

A COUNTRY GENTLEMAN.
FROM SWALLOW BARN.

FRANK MERIWETHER is now in the meridian of life;—somewhere close upon forty-five. Good cheer and a good temper both tell well upon him. The first has given him a comfortable full figure, and the latter certain easy, contemplative habits, that incline him to be lazy and philosophical. He has the substantial planter look that belongs to a gentleman who lives on his estate, and is not much vexed with the crosses of life.

I think he prides himself on his personal appearance, for he has a handsome face, with a dark blue eye, and a high forehead that is scantily embellished with some silver-tipped locks that, I observe, he cherishes for their rarity: besides, he is growing manifestly attentive to his dress, and carries himself erect, with some secret consciousness that his person is not bad. It is pleasant to see him when he has ordered his horse for a ride into the neighbourhood, or across to the court-house. On such occasions, he is apt to make his appearance in a coat of blue broadcloth, astonishingly new and glossy, and with a redundant supply of plaited ruffle strutting through the folds of a Marseilles waistcoat: a worshipful finish is given to this costume by a large straw hat, lined with green silk. There is a magisterial fulness in his garments that betokens condition in the world, and a heavy bunch of seals, suspended by a chain of gold, jingles as he moves, pronouncing him a man of superfluities.

It is considered rather extraordinary that he has never set up for Congress; but the truth is, he is an unambitious man, and has a great dislike to currying favour—as he calls it. And, besides, he is thoroughly convinced that there will always be men enough in Virginia willing to serve the people, and therefore does not see why he should trouble his head about it. Some years ago, however, there was really an impression that he meant to come out. By some sudden whim, he took it into his head to visit Washington during the session of Congress, and returned, after a fortnight, very seriously distempered with politics. He told curious anecdotes of certain secret intrigues which had been discovered in the affairs of the capital, gave a pretty clear insight into the views of some deep-laid combinations, and became all at once painfully florid in his discourse, and dogmatical to a degree that made his wife stare. Fortunately, this orgasm soon subsided, and Frank relapsed into an indolent gentleman of the opposition; but it had the effect to give a much more decided cast to his studies, for he forthwith discarded the Whig and took to the Enquirer, like a man who was not to be disturbed by doubts; and as it was morally impossible to believe what was written on both sides, to prevent his mind from being abused, he, from this time forward, gave an implicit assent to all the facts that set against Mr. Adams. The consequence of this straightforward and confiding deportment was an unsolicited and complimentary notice of him by the executive of the state. He was put into the commission of the peace, and having thus become a public man against his will, his opinions were observed to undergo some essential changes. He now thinks that a good citizen ought neither to solicit nor decline office ; that the magistracy of Virginia is the sturdiest pillar that supports the fabric of the constitution ; and that the people, " though in their opinions they may be mistaken, in their sentiments they are never wrong,"—with some other such dogmas, that, a few years ago, he did not hold in very good repute. In this temper, he has of late embarked upon the mill-pond of county affairs, and, notwithstanding his amiable and respectful republicanism, I am told he keeps the peace as if he commanded a garrison, and administers justice like a cadi.

He has some claim to supremacy in this last department ; for during three years of his life he smoked segars in a lawyer's office at Richmond ; sometimes looked into Blackstone and the Revised Code ; was a member of a debating society that ate oysters once a week during the winter ; and wore six cravats and a pair of yellow-topped boots as a blood of the metropolis. Having in this way qualified himself for the pursuits of agriculture, he came to his estate a very model of landed gentlemen. Since that time, his avocations have had a certain literary tincture ; for having settled himself down as a married man, and got rid of his superfluous foppery, he rambled with wonderful assiduity through a wilderness of romances, poems, and dissertations, which are now collected in his library, and, with their battered blue covers, present a lively type of an army of continentals at the close of the war, or an hospital of veteran invalids. These have all, at last, given way to the newspapers—a miscellaneous study very enticing to gentlemen in the country—that have rendered Meriwether a most discomfiting antagonist in the way of dates and names.

He has great suavity of manners, and a genuine benevolence of disposition that makes him fond of having his friends about him ; and it is particularly gratifying to him to pick up any genteel stranger within the purlieus of Swallow Barn and put him to the proof of a week's hospitality, if it be only for the pleasure of exercising his rhetoric upon him. He is a kind master, and considerate toward his dependants, for which reason, although he owns many slaves, they hold him in profound reverence, and are very happy under his dominion. All these circumstances make Swallow Barn a very agreeable place, and it is accordingly frequented by an extensive range of his acquaintances.

There is one quality in Frank that stands above the rest. He is a thoroughbred Virginian, and consequently does not travel much from home, except to make an excursion to Richmond, which he considers emphatically as the centre of civilization. Now and then he has gone beyond the mountain, but the upper country is not much to his taste, and in his estimation only to be resorted to when the fever makes it imprudent to remain upon the tide. He thinks lightly of the mercantile interest, and in fact undervalues the manners of the cities generally :—he believes that their inhabitants are all hollow-hearted and insincere, and altogether wanting in that substantial intelligence and honesty that he affirms to be characteristic of the country. He is a great admirer of the genius of Virginia, and is frequent in his commendation of a toast in which the state is compared to the mother of the Gracchi :—indeed, it is a familiar thing with him to speak of the aristocracy of talent as only inferior to that of the landed interest,—the idea of a freeholder inferring to his mind a certain constitutional pre-eminence in all the virtues of citizenship, as a matter of course.

The solitary elevation of a country gentleman, well to do in the world, begets some magnificent notions. · He becomes as infallible as the pope ; gradually acquires a habit of making long speeches ; is apt to be impatient of contradiction, and is always very touchy on the point of honour. There is nothing more conclusive than a rich man's logic anywhere, but in the country, amongst his dependants, it flows with the smooth and unresisted course of a gentle stream irrigating a verdant meadow, and depositing its mud in fertilizing luxuriance. . Meriwether's sayings, about Swallow Barn, import absolute verity—but I have discovered that they are not so current out of his jurisdiction. Indeed, every now and then, we have some obstinate discussions when any of the neighbouring potentates, who stand in the same sphere with Frank, come to the house ; for these worthies have opinions ot their own, and nothing can be more dogged than the conflict between them. They sometimes fire away at each other with a most amiable and unconvincible hardihood for a whole evening, bandying interjections, and making bows, and saying shrewd things with all the courtesy imaginable : but for unextinguishable pertinacity in argument, and utter impregnability of belief, there is no disputant like your country gentleman who reads the newspapers. When one of these discussions fairly gets under weigh, it never comes to an anchor again of its own accord—it is either blown out so far to sea as to be given up for lost, or puts into port in distress for want of documents,—or is upset by a call for the boot-jack and slippers—which is something like the previous question in Congress.

If my worthy cousin be somewhat over-argumentative as a politician, he restores the equilibrium of his character by a considerate coolness in religious matters. He piques himself upon being a high-churchman, but he is only a rare frequenter of places of worship, and very seldom permits himself to get into a dispute upon points of faith. · If Mr. Chub, the Presbyterian tutor in the family, ever succeeds in drawing him into this field, as he occasionally has the address to do, Meriwether is sure to fly the course :—he gets puzzled with scripture names, and makes some odd mistakes between Peter and Paul, and then generally turns the parson over to his wife, who, he says, has an astonishing memory.

Meriwether is a great breeder of blooded horses ; and, ever since the celebrated race between Eclipse and Henry, he has taken to this occupation with a renewed zeal, as a matter affecting the reputation of the state. It is delightful to hear him expatiate upon the value, importance, and patriotic bearing of this employment, and to listen to all his technical lore touching the mystery of horse-craft. He has some fine colts in training, that are committed to the care of a pragmatical old negro, named 'Carey, who, in his reverence for the occupation, is the perfect shadow of his master. He and Frank hold grave and momentous consultations upon the affairs of the stable, and in such a sagacious strain of equal debate, that it would puzzle a spectator to tell which was the leading member in the council. Carey thinks he knows a great deal more upon the subject than his master, and their frequent intercourse has begot a familiarity in the old negro that is almost fatal to Meriwether's supremacy. The old man feels himself authorized to maintain his positions according to the freest parliamentary form, and sometimes with a violence of asseveration that compels his master to abandon his ground, purely out of faint-heartedness. Meriwether gets a little nettled by Carey's doggedness, but generally turns it off in a laugh. I was in the stable with him, a few mornings after my arrival, when he ventured to expostulate with the venerable groom upon a professional point, but the controversy terminated in its customary way. "Who set you up, Master Frank, to tell me how to fodder that 'ere cretur, when I as good as nursed you on my knee?" "Well, tie up your tongue, you old mastiff," replied Frank, as he walked out of the stable, "and cease growling, since you will have it your own way;"—and then, as we left the old man's presence, he added, with an affectionate chuckle—"a faithful old cur, too, that licks my hand out of pure honesty; he has not many years left, and it does no harm to humour him!"

OLD LAWYERS.
FROM THE SAME.

I HAVE a great reverence for the profession of the law and its votaries; but especially for that part of the tribe which comprehends the old and thorough-paced stagers of the bar. The feelings, habits, and associations of the bar in general, have a very happy influence upon the character. It abounds with good fellows: And, take it altogether, there may be collected from it a greater mass of shrewd, observant, droll, playful and generous spirits, than from any other equal numbers of society. They live in each other's presence like a set of players; congregate in the courts like the former in the green room; and break their unpremeditated jests, in the interval of business, with that sort of undress freedom that contrasts amusingly with the solemn and even tragic seriousness with which they appear, in turn, upon the boards. They have one face for the public, rife with the saws and learned gravity of the profession, and another for themselves, replete with broad mirth, sprightly wit, and gay thoughtlessness. The intense mental toil and fatigue of business give them a peculiar relish for the enjoyment of their hours

of relaxation, and, in the same degree, incapacitate them for that frugal attention to their private concerns which their limited means usually require. They have, in consequence, a prevailing air of unthriftiness in personal matters, which, however it may operate to the prejudice of the pocket of the individual, has a mellow and kindly effect upon his disposition.

In an old member of the profession,—one who has grown gray in the service, there is a rich unction of originality, that brings him out from the ranks of his fellow-men in strong relief. His habitual conversancy with the world in its strangest varieties, and with the secret history of character, gives him a shrewd estimate of the human heart. He is quiet and unapt to be struck with wonder at any of the actions of men. There is a deep current of observation running calmly through his thoughts, and seldom gushing out in words: the confidence which has been placed in him, in the thousand relations of his profession, renders him constitutionally cautious. His acquaintance with the vicissitudes of fortune, as they have been exemplified in the lives of individuals, and with the severe afflictions that have "tried the reins" of many, known only to himself, makes him an indulgent and charitable apologist of the aberrations of others. He has an impregnable good humour, that never falls below the level of thoughtfulness into melancholy. He is a creature of habits; rising early for exercise; temperate from necessity, and studious against his will. His face is accustomed to take the ply of his pursuits with great facility, grave and even severe in business, and readily rising into smiles at a pleasant conceit. He works hard when at his task; and goes at it with the reluctance of an old horse in a bark-mill. His common-places are quaint and professional: they are made up of law maxims, and first occur to him in Latin. He measures all the sciences out of his proper line of study, (and with these he is but scantily acquainted,) by the rules of law. He thinks a steam-engine should be worked with *due diligence*, and without *laches*: a thing little likely to happen, he considers as *potentia remotissima*; and what is not yet in existence, or *in esse*, as he would say, is *in nubibus*. He apprehends that wit best that is connected with the affairs of the term; is particularly curious in his anecdotes of old lawyers, and inclined to be talkative concerning the amusing passages of his own professional life. He is, sometimes, not altogether free of outward foppery; is apt to be an especial good liver, and he keeps the best company. His literature is not much diversified; and he prefers books that are bound in plain calf, to those that are much lettered and gilded. He garners up his papers with a wonderful appearance of care; ties them in bundles with red tape; and usually has great difficulty to find them when he wants them. Too much particularity has perplexed him; and just so it is with his cases: they are well assorted, packed and laid away in his mind, but are not easily to be brought forth again without labour. This makes him something of a procrastinator, and rather to

44

delight in new business than finish his old. He
is, however, much beloved, and affectionately considered by the people.

———◆———

A RANGERS' DINNER.

FROM HORSE SHOE ROBINSON.

———

THE day was hot, and it was with a grateful
sense of refreshment that our wayfarers, no less
than their horses, found themselves, as they approached the lowland, gradually penetrating the
deep and tangled thicket and the high wood which
hung over and darkened the channel of the small
stream that rippled through the valley. Their
road lay along this stream and frequently crossed
it at narrow fords, where the water fell from rock
to rock in small cascades, presenting natural basins
of the limpid flood, hemmed in with the laurel and
the alder, and giving forth that gurgling, busy music which is one of the pleasantest sounds that can
assail the ear of a wearied and overheated traveller.

Butler said but little to his companion, except
now and then to express a passing emotion of admiration for the natural embellishments of the
region; until, at length, the road brought them to a
huge mass of rock, from whose base a clear fountain
issued forth over a bed of gravel, and soon lost itself
in the brook hard by. A small strip of bark, which
some friend of the traveller had placed there, caught
the pure water as it was distilled from the rock,
and threw it off in a spout some few inches above
the surface of the ground. The earth trodden
around this spot showed it to be a customary halt-
ing place for those who journeyed the road.

Here Butler checked his horse, and announced
to his comrade his intention to suspend, for awhile,
the toil of travel. "There is one thing, Galbraith,"
said he, as he dismounted, "wherein all philosophers agree,—a man must eat when he is hungry,
and rest when he is weary. We have now been
some six hours on horseback, and as this fountain
seems to have been put here for our use, it would
be sinfully slighting the bounties of providence not
to do it the honour of a halt. Get down, man:
rummage your havresac, and let us see what you
have there."

Robinson was soon upon his feet, and taking
the horses a little distance off, he fastened their
bridles to the impending branches of a tree; then
opening his saddle-bags, he produced a wallet with
which he approached the fountain where Butler
had thrown himself at full length upon the grass.
Here, as he successively disclosed his stores, he
announced his bill of fare with suitable deliberation
between each item, in the following terms:

"I don't march without provisions, you see, captain—or major, I suppose I must call you now.
Here's the rear division of a roast pig; and along
with it, by way of flankers, two spread eagles,
(holding up two broiled fowls,) and here are four
slices from the best end of a ham. Besides these,
I can throw in two apple-jacks, a half-dozen of
rolls, and—"

"I cry your mercy, sergeant! your wallet
is as bountiful as a conjurer's bag: It is a perfect cornucopia. How did you come by all this
provender?"

"It isn't so overmuch, major, when you come
to consider," said Robinson. "The old landlady
at Charlottesville is none of your heap-up, shake-
down, and running-over measures,—and when I
signified to her that we mought want a snack upon
the road, she as much as gave me to understand
that there wa'n't nothing to be had. But I took
care to make fair weather with her daughter,—as
I always do amongst the creatures,—and she let
me into the pantry, where I made bold to stow
away these few trifling articles, under the denomination of pillage.—If you are fond of Indian
corn bread, I can give you a pretty good slice of
that."

"Pillage, Galbraith! You forget you are not
in an enemy's country. I directed you scrupulously to pay for every thing you got upon the
road.—I hope you have not omitted it to-day?"

"Lord, sir! what do these women do for the
cause of liberty but cook, and wash, and mend!
I told the old Jezebel to charge it all to the continental congress."

"Out upon it, man! Would you bring us into
discredit with our best friends by your villanous
habits of free quarters—"

"I am not the only man, major, that has been
spoiled in his religion, by these wars. I had both
politeness and decency till we got to squabbling
over our chimney corners in Carolina. But when
a man's conscience begins to get hard, it does it
faster than any thing in nature: it is, I may say,
like the boiling of an egg; it is very clear at first,
but as soon as it gets cloudy, one minute more
and you may cut it with a knife."

"Well, well! let us fall to, sergeant; this is no
time to argue points of conscience."

"You seem to take no notice of this here bottle
of peach brandy, major," said Robinson. "It's a
bird that came out of the same nest. To my
thinking, it's a sort of a file leader to an eatable—
if it ar'n't an eatable itself."

"Peace, Galbraith;—it is the vice of the army
to set too much store by this devil brandy."

The sergeant was moved by an inward laugh
that shook his head and shoulders.

"Do you suppose, major, that Troy town was
taken without brandy? It's drilling and counter-
marching and charging with the bagnet, all three,
sir. But before we begin, I will just strip our
horses. A flurry of cool air on the saddle spot is
the best thing in nature for a tired horse."

Robinson now performed this office for their
jaded cattle; and having given them a mouthful
of water at the brook, returned to his post, and
soon began to despatch, with a laudable alacrity,
the heaps of provision before him. Butler partook
with a keen appetite of this sylvan repast, and
was greatly amused to see with what relish his
companion caused slice after slice to vanish, until
nothing was left of this large supply but a few
fragments.

A RUSE DE GUERRE.

FROM THE SAME.

On the morning that succeeded the night in which Horse Shoe Robinson arrived at Musgrove's, the stout sergeant might have been seen, about eight o'clock, leaving the main road from Ninety-Six, at the point where that leading to David Ramsay's s parated from it, and cautiously urging his way into the deep forest by the more private path into which he had entered. The knowledge that Innis was encamped along the Ennoree, within a short distance of the mill, had compelled him to make an extensive circuit to reach Ramsay's dwelling, whither he was now bent; and he had experienced considerable delay in his morning journey, by finding himself frequently in the neighbourhood of small foraging parties of tories, whose motions he was obliged to watch for fear of an encounter. He had once already been compelled to use his horse's heels in, what he called, "fair flight,"—and once to ensconce himself, a full half hour, under cover of the thicket afforded him by a swamp. He now, therefore, according to his own phrase, "dived into the little road that scrambled down through the woods toward Ramsay's, with all his eyes about him, looking out as sharply as a fox on a foggy morning:" and with this circumspection, he was not long in arriving within view of Ramsay's house. Like a practised soldier, whom frequent frays has taught wisdom, he resolved to reconnoitre before he advanced upon a post that might be in possession of an enemy. He therefore dismounted, fastened his horse in a fence corner, where a field of corn concealed him from notice, and then stealthily crept forward until he came immediately behind one of the out-houses. From this position he was enabled to satisfy himself that no danger was to be apprehended from his visit. He accordingly approached and entered the dwelling, where he soon found himself in the presence of its mistress.

"Mistress Ramsay," said he, walking up to the dame, who was occupied at a table, with a large trencher before her; in which she was plying some household thrift—"luck to you, ma'am, and all your house! I hope you havn't none of these clinking and clattering bullies about you, that are as thick over this country as the frogs in the kneading troughs—that they tell of."

"Good lack—Mr. Horse Shoe Robinson!" exclaimed the matron, offering the sergeant her hand. "What has brought you here? What news? Who are with you? For patience sake, tell me!"

"I am alone," said Robinson, "and a little wettish, mistress," he added, as he took off his hat and shook the water from it; "it has just sot up a rain, and looks as if it was going to give us enough on't. You don't mind doing a little dinner-work of a Sunday, I see—shelling of beans, I s'pose, is tantamount to dragging a sheep out of a pond, as the preachers allow on the Sabbath—ha, ha! Where's Davy?"

"He's gone over to the meeting-house on Ennoree, hoping to hear something of the army at Camden; perhaps you can tell us the news from that quarter?"

"Faith, that's a mistake, mistress Ramsay. Though I don't doubt that they are hard upon the scratches by this time. But, at this present speaking, I command the flying artillery. We have but one man in the corps—and that's myself; and all the guns we have got is this piece of ordnance that hangs in this old belt by my side, (pointing to his sword)—and that I captured from the enemy at Blackstock's. I was hoping I mought find John Ramsay at home—I have need of him as a recruit."

"Ah, Mr. Robinson, John has a heavy life of it, over there with Sumpter. The boy is often without his natural rest, or a meal's victuals; and the general thinks so much of him, that he can't spare him to come home. I hav'nt the heart to complain, as long as John's service is of any account, but it does seem, Mr. Robinson, like needless tempting of the mercies of providence. We thought that he might have been here to-day; yet I am glad he didn't come—for he would have been certain to get into trouble. Who should come in, this morning, just after my husband had cleverly got away on his horse, but a young cock-a-whoop ensign, that belongs to Ninety-Six, and four great Scotchmen with him, all in red coats; they had been out thieving, I warrant, and were now going home again. And who but they!—Here they were, swaggering all about my house—and calling for this, and calling for that—as if they owned the fee simple of every thing on the plantation. And it made my blood rise, Mr. Horse Shoe, to see them turn out in the yard and catch up my chickens and ducks, and kill as many as they could string about them—and I not daring to say a word: though I did give them a piece of my mind, too."

"Who is at home with you?" inquired the sergeant eagerly.

"Nobody but my youngest boy, Andrew," answered the dame. "And then, the filthy, toping rioters," she continued, exalting her voice.

"What arms have you in the house?" asked Robinson, without heeding the dame's rising anger.

"We have a rifle, and a horseman's pistol that belongs to John. They must call for drink, too, and turn my house, of a Sunday morning, into a tavern"—

"They took the route toward Ninety-Six, you said, mistress Ramsay?"

"Yes, they went straight forward upon the road. But, look you, Mr. Horse Shoe, you're not thinking of going after them?"

"Isn't there an old field, about a mile from here, on that road?" inquired the sergeant, still intent upon his own thoughts.

"Certain," replied the hostess. "You must remember the cobbler that died of drink on the road side!"

"There is a shabby, racketty cabin in the middle of the field;—am I right, good woman?"

"Yes."

"And nobody lives in it. It has no door to it?"

"There ha'n't been a family there these seven years."

"I know the place very well," said the sergeant thoughtfully, "there is woods just on this side of it."

"That's true," replied the dame:—"but what is it you are thinking about, Mr. Robinson?"

"How long before this rain began, was it that they quitted this house?"

"Not above fifteen minutes."

"Mistress Ramsay—bring me the rifle and pistol both—and the powder-horn and bullets."

"As you say, Mr. Horse Shoe," answered the dame as she turned round to leave the room,—"but I am sure I can't suspicion what you mean to do."

In a few moments the woman returned with the weapons, and gave them to the sergeant.

"Where is Andy?" asked Horse Shoe.

The hostess went to the door and called her son; almost immediately afterward, a sturdy boy, of about twelve or fourteen years of age, entered the apartment,—his clothes dripping with rain. He modestly and shyly seated himself on a chair near the door, with his soaked hat flapping down over a face full of freckles, and not less rife with the expression of an open, dauntless hardihood of character.

"How would you like a scrummage, Andy, with them Scotchmen that stole your mother's chickens this morning?" asked Horse Shoe.

"I'm agreed," replied the boy, "if you will tell me what to do."

"You are not going to take the boy out on any of your desperate projects, Mr. Horse Shoe?" said the mother, with the tears starting instantly into her eyes. "You wouldn't take such a child as that into danger?"

"Bless your soul, Mistress Ramsay, there ar'n't no danger about it!—Don't take on so. It's a thing that is either done at a blow, or not done,—and there's an end of it. I want the lad only to bring home the prisoners for me, after I have took them."

"Ah, Mr. Robinson, I have one son already in these wars. God protect him! and you men don't know how a mother's heart yearns for her children in these times. I cannot give another," she added, as she threw her arms over the shoulders of the youth and drew him to her bosom.

"Oh, it aint nothing," said Andrew, in a sprightly tone. "It's only snapping of a pistol, mother,—pooh! If I'm not afeard, you oughtn't to be."

"I give you my honour, Mistress Ramsay," said Robinson, "that I will bring or send your son safe back in one hour; and that he shan't be put in any sort of danger whatsomedever:—come, that's a good woman!"

"You are not deceiving me, Mr. Robinson?" asked the matron, wiping away a tear. "You wouldn't mock the sufferings of a weak woman in such a thing as this?"

"On the honesty of a sodger, ma'am," replied Horse Shoe, "the lad shall be in no danger, as I said before—whatsomedever."

"Then I will say no more," answered the mother. "But Andy, my child, be sure to let Mr. Robinson keep before you."

Horse Shoe now loaded the fire-arms, and having slung the pouch across his body, he put the pistol into the hands of the boy; then shouldering his rifle, he and his young ally left the room. Even on this occasion, serious as it might be deemed, the sergeant did not depart without giving some manifestation of that light-heartedness which no difficulties ever seemed to have power to conquer. He thrust his head back into the room, after he had crossed the threshold, and said with an encouraging laugh, "Andy and me will teach them, Mistress Ramsay, Pat's point of war—we will *surround* the ragamuffins."

"Now Andy, my lad," said Horse Shoe, after he had mounted Captain Peter, "you must get up behind me. Turn the lock of your pistol down," he continued, as the boy sprang upon the horse's rump, "and cover it with the flap of your jacket, to keep the rain off. It won't do to hang fire at such a time as this."

The lad did as he was directed, and Horse Shoe having secured his rifle in the same way, put his horse up to a gallop and took the road in the direction that had been pursued by the soldiers.

As soon as our adventurers had gained a wood, at a distance of about half a mile, the sergeant relaxed his speed and advanced at a pace but little above a walk.

"Andy," he said, "we have got rather a ticklish sort of a job before us—so I must give you your lesson, which you will understand better by knowing something of my plan. As soon as your mother told me that these thieving villains had left her house about fifteen minutes before the rain came on, and that they had gone along upon this road, I remembered the old field up here, and the little log hut in the middle of it; and it was natural to suppose that they had just got about near that hut when this rain came up,—and then it was the most supposable case in the world, that they would naturally go into it as the driest place they could find. So now you see it's my calculation that the whole batch is there at this very point of time. We will go slowly along until we get to the other end of this wood, in sight of the old field —and then, if there is no one on the look-out, we will open our first trench:—you know what that means, Andy?"

"It means, I s'pose, that we'll go right smack at them," replied Andrew.

"Pretty exactly," said the sergeant. "But listen to me. Just at the edge of the woods you will have to get down, and put yourself behind a tree: I'll ride forward, as if I had a whole troop at my heels,—and if I catch them, as I expect, they will have a little fire kindled, and, as likely as not, they'll be cooking some of your mother's fowls."

"Yes,—I understand," said the boy eagerly.

"No you don't," replied Horse Shoe; "but you will when you hear what I am going to say. If I get at them onawares, they'll be mighty apt to think they are surrounded, and will bellow, like fine fellows, for quarters. And thereupon, Andy, I'll cry out, 'Stand fast,' as if I was speaking to my own men; and when you hear that, you must come up full tilt,—because it will be a signal to you that the enemy has surrendered. Then it will be your business to run into the house and bring out the muskets as quick as a rat runs through a kitchen: and when you have done that, —why, all's done. But if you should hear any popping of firearms,—that is, more than one shot, which I may chance to let off—do you take that for a bad sign, and get away as fast as you can heel it. You comprehend?"

"Oh yes," replied the lad, "and I'll do what you want,—and more too, may be, Mr. Robinson."

"*Captain* Robinson, remember, Andy; you must call me captain, in the hearing of these Scotsmen."

"I'll not forget that neither," answered Andrew.

"By the time these instructions were fully impressed upon the boy, our adventurous forlorn hope, as it may fitly be called, had arrived at the place which Horse Shoe had designated for the commencement of active operations. They had a clear view of the old field; and it afforded them a strong assurance that the enemy was exactly where they wished him to be, when they discovered smoke arising from the chimney of the hovel. Andrew was instantly posted behind a tree, and Robinson only tarried a moment to make the boy repeat the signals agreed on, in order to ascertain that he had them correctly in his memory. Being satisfied from this experiment that the intelligence of young Ramsay might be depended upon, he galloped across the intervening space, and, in a few seconds, abruptly reined up his steed in the very doorway of the hut. The party within was gathered around a fire at the further end; and, in the corner opposite the door, were four muskets thrown together against the wall. To spring from his saddle, thrust himself one pace inside of the door, and to level his rifle at the group beside the fire, was a movement which the sergeant executed in an instant,—shouting at the same time—

"Surrender to Captain Robinson of the Free Will Volunteers, and to the Continental Congress, —or you are all dead men! Halt," he vociferated in a voice of thunder, as if speaking to a corps under his command; "file off, cornet, right and left, to both sides of the house. The first man that budges a foot from that there fireplace, shall have fifty balls through his body."

"To arms!" cried the young officer who commanded the squad inside of the house. "Leap to your arms, men! Why do you stand, you villains!" he added, as he perceived his men hesitate to move toward the corner where the muskets were piled.

"I don't want your blood, young man," said Robinson, coolly, as he still levelled his rifle at the officer, "nor that of your people:—but, by my father's son, I'll not leave one of you to be put upon a muster-roll, if you move an inch!"

Both parties now stood for a brief space eyeing each other, in a fearful suspense, during which there was an expression of mixed doubt and anger visible on the countenances of the soldiers, as they surveyed the broad proportions, and met the stern glance of the sergeant; whilst the delay, also, began to raise an apprehension in the mind of Robinson that his stratagem would be discovered.

"Upon him, at the risk of your lives!" cried the officer: and, on the instant, one of the soldiers moved rapidly toward the farther wall; upon which the sergeant, apprehending the seizure of the weapons, sprang forward in such a manner as would have brought his body immediately before them,— but a decayed plank in the floor caught his foot and he fell to his knee. It was a lucky accident,— for the discharge of a pistol, by the officer, planted a bullet in the log of the cabin, which would have been lodged full in the square breast of the gallant Horse Shoe, if he had retained his perpendicular position. His footing, however, was recovered almost as soon as it was lost, and the next moment found him bravely posted in front of the firearms, with his own weapon thrust almost into the face of the foremost assailant. The hurry, confusion, and peril of the crisis did not take away his self-possession; but he now found himself unexpectedly thrown into a situation of infinite difficulty, where all the chances of the fight were against him.

"Back, men, and guard the door," he cried out, as if again addressing his troop. "Sir, I will not be answerable for consequences, if my troopers once come into this house. If you hope for quarter, give up on the spot."

"His men have retreated," cried one of the soldiers. "Upon him, boys!" and instantly two or three pressed upon the sergeant, who, seizing his rifle in both hands, bore them back by main force, until he had thrown them prostrate on the floor. He then leaped toward the door with the intention of making good his retreat.

"Shall I let loose upon them, captain?" said Andrew Ramsay, now appearing, most unexpectedly to Robinson, at the door of the hut. "Come on, my brave boys!" he shouted as he turned his face toward the field.

"Keep them outside of the door—stand fast," cried the doughty sergeant again, with admirable promptitude, in the new and sudden posture of his affairs caused by this opportune appearance of the boy. "Sir, you see that you are beaten: let me warn you once more to save the lives of your men—it's oppossible for me to keep my people off a minute longer. What signifies fighting five to one!"

During this appeal the sergeant was ably seconded by the lad outside, who was calling out first on one name, and then on another, as if in the presence of a troop. The device succeeded, and the officer within, believing the forbearance of Robinson to be real, at length said—

"Lower your rifle, sir. In the presence of a superior force, taken by surprise and without arms, it is my duty to save bloodshed. With the promise of fair usage and the rights of prisoners of war, I surrender this little foraging party under my command."

"I'll make the terms agreeable," replied the sergeant. "Never doubt me, sir. Right hand file, advance, and receive the arms of the prisoners!"

"I'm here, captain," said Andrew, in a conceited tone, as if it were a mere occasion of merriment; and the lad quickly entered the house and secured the weapons, retreating with them some paces from the door.

"Now, sir," said Horse Shoe, to the ensign, "your sword, and whatever else you mought have about you of the ammunitions of war!"

The officer delivered up his sword and a pair of pocket pistols.

"Your name?—if I mought take the freedom."

"Ensign St. Jermyn, of his majesty's seventy-first regiment of light infantry."

"Ensign, your sarvant," added Horse Shoe, aiming at an unusual exhibition of politeness. "You have defended your post like an old sodger, although you ha'n't much beard upon your chin; I'll certify for you. But, seeing you have given up, you shall be treated like a man who has done his duty. You will walk out now, and form yourselves in line at the door. I'll engage my men shall do you no harm:—they are of a marciful breed."

When the little squad of prisoners submitted to this command, and came to the door, they were stricken with the most profound astonishment to find, in place of the detachment of cavalry they expected to see, nothing but one horse, one man, and one boy. Their first emotions were expressed in curses, which were even succeeded by laughter from one or two of the number. There seemed to be a disposition, on the part of some, to resist the authority that now controlled them; and sundry glances were exchanged which indicated a purpose to turn upon their captors. The sergeant no sooner perceived this than he halted, raised his rifle to his breast, and, at the same instant, gave Andrew Ramsay an order to retire a few paces, and to fire one of the captured pieces at the first man who opened his lips:

"By my hand," he said, "if I find any trouble in taking you, all five, safe away from this here house, I will thin your numbers with your own muskets! And that's as good as if I had sworn to it."

"You have my word, sir," said the ensign. "Lead on—we'll follow."

"By your leave, my pretty gentleman, you will lead, and I'll follow," replied Horse Shoe. "It may be a new piece of drill to you—but the custom is to give the prisoners the post of honour, and to walk them in front."

"As you please," answered the ensign. "Where do you take us?"

"You will march back the road you came," said the sergeant.

Finding the conqueror determined to execute summary martial law upon the first who should mutiny, the prisoners now marched in double files from the hut, back toward Ramsay's,—Horse Shoe, with Captain Peter's bridle dangling over his arm, and his gallant young auxiliary Andrew, laden with double the burden of Robinson Crusoe, (having all the fire-arms packed upon his shoulders,) bringing up the rear. In this order victors and vanquished returned to David Ramsay's.

"Well, I have brought you your ducks and chickens back, mistress," said the sergeant, as he halted his prisoners at the door, "and what's more, I have brought home a young sodger that's worth his weight in gold."

"Heaven bless my child! my boy, my brave boy!" cried the mother, seizing the lad Andrew in her arms, and unheeding any thing else in the present perturbation of her feelings. "I feared ill would come of it: but Heaven has preserved him. Did he behave handsomely, Mr. Robinson? But I am sure he did."

"A little more venturesome, ma'am, than I wanted him to be," replied Horse Shoe. "But he did excellent sarvice. These are his prisoners, Mistress Ramsay—I should never have got them, if it hadn't been for Andy. In these drumming and fifing times the babies suck in quarrel with their mother's milk. Show me another boy in America that's made more prisoners than there was men to fight them with—that's all! He's a first rate chap, Mistress Ramsay—take my word for it."

DAUNTREES AND MISTRESS WEASEL.
FROM ROB OF THE BOWL.

"Mistress Dorothy," said Captain Dauntrees, "at your leisure, pray step this way."

The dame tarried no longer than was necessary to complete a measure she was filling for a customer, and then went into the room to which she had been summoned. This was a little parlour where the captain of musqueteers had been regaling himself for the last hour over a jorum of ale, in solitary rumination. An open window gave to his view the full expanse of the river, now glowing with the rich reflections of sunset; and a balmy October breeze played through the apartment and refreshed without chilling the frame of the comfortable captain. He was seated near the window in a large easy chair when the hostess entered.

"Welcome dame," he said, without rising from his seat, at the same time offering his hand, which was readily accepted by the landlady.—"By St. Gregory and St. Michael both, a more buxom and tidy piece of flesh and blood hath never sailed between the two headlands of Potomac than thou art! You are for a junketing, Mistress Dorothy; you are tricked out like a queen this evening! I have never seen thee in thy new suit before. Thou art as gay as a marygold: and I wear thy colours, thou laughing mother of mischief! Green is the livery of thy true knight. Has your goodman, honest Garret, come home yet, dame?"

"What would you with my husband. Master Baldpate? There is no good in the wind when you throw yourself into the big chair of this parlour."

"In truth, dame, I only came to make a short night of it with you and your worthy spouse..... Tell Matty to spread supper for me in this parlour. ... and if the veritable and most authentic head of this house—I mean yourself, mistress—have no need of Garret, I would entreat to have him in company. By the hand of thy soldier, Mistress Dorothy! I am glad to see you thrive so in your calling. You will spare me Garret, dame? Come, I know you have not learnt how to refuse me a boon."

" You are a saucy Jack, Master Captain," replied the dame. "I know you of old : you would have a rouse with that thriftless babe, my husband. You sent him reeling home only last night. How can you look me in the face, knowing him, as you do, for a most shallow vessel, Captain Dauntrees ?"

" Fie on thee, dame ! You disgrace your own flesh and blood by such speech. Did you not choose him for his qualities ?—ay, and with all circumspection, as a woman of experience. You had two husbands before Garret, and when you took him for a third, it was not in ignorance of the sex. Look thee in the face ! I dare,—yea, and at thy whole configuration. Faith, you wear most bravely, Mistress Weasel ! Stand apart and let me survey : turn thy shoulders round," he added, as by a sleight he twirled the dame upon her heel so as to bring her back to his view—" thou art a woman of ten thousand, and I envy Garret such store of womanly wealth."

" If Garret were the man I took him for, Master Captain," said the dame with a saucy smile, " you would have borne a broken head long since. But he has his virtues, such as they are,—though they may lie in an egg-shell : and Garret has his frailties, too, like other men : alack, there is no denying it !"

" Frailties, forsooth ! Which of us has not, dame ? Garret is an honest man ;—somewhat old—a shade or so : yet it is but a shade. For my sake, pretty hostess, you will allow him to sup with us ! Speak it kindly, sweetheart—good old Garret's jolly, young wife !"

" Thou wheedling devil !" said the landlady ; " Garret is no older than thou art. But, truly, I may say he is of little account in the tap-room ; so he shall come to you, captain. But, look you, he is weak, and must not be overcharged."

" He shall not, mistress—you have a soldier's word for that. I could have sworn you would not deny me. Hark you, dame,—bring thine ear to my lips ;—a word in secret."

The hostess bent her head down, when the captain desired, when he said in a half-whisper, " Send me a flask of the best,—you understand ! And there's for thy pains !" he added as he saluted her cheek with a kiss.

"And there's for thy impudence, saucy captain !" retorted the spirited landlady as she bestowed the palm of her hand on the side of his head and fled out of the apartment.

Dauntrees sprang from his chair and chased the retreating dame into the midst of the crowd of the tap-room, by whose aid she was enabled to make her escape. Here he encountered Garret Weasel, with whom he went forth in quest of Arnold and the Indian, who were to be his guests at supper.

In the course of the next half hour the captain and his three comrades were assembled in the little parlour around the table, discussing their evening meal. When this was over, Matty was ordered to clear the board, and to place a bottle of wine and glasses before the party, and then to leave the room.

" You must know, Garret," said Dauntrees when the serving-maid had retired, " that we go to-night to visit the Wizard's Chapel by his lordship's order ; and as I would have stout fellows with me, I have come down here on purpose to take you along."

" Heaven bless us, Master Jasper Dauntrees !" exclaimed Garret, somewhat confounded with this sudden appeal to his valour, which was not of that prompt complexion to stand so instant a demand, and yet which the publican was never willing to have doubted—" truly there be three of you, and it might mar the matter to have too many on so secret an outgoing"——

" Tush, man,—that has been considered. His lordship especially looks to your going : you cannot choose but go."

" But my wife, Captain Dauntrees"——

" Leave that to me," said the captain ; " I will manage it as handsomely as the taking of Troy Worthy Garret, say naught against it—you must go, and take with you a few bottles of canary and a good luncheon of provender in the basket. You shall be our commissary. I came on set purpose to procure the assistance of your experience and store of comfortable sustenance. Get the bottles, Garret,—his lordship pays the scot to-night."

" I should have my nag," said Garret, " and the dame keeps the key of the stable, and will in nowise consent to let me have it. She would suspect us for a rouse if I but asked the key."

" I will engage for that, good Weasel," said Dauntrees : " I will cozen the dame with some special invention which shall put her to giving the key of her own motion : she shall be coaxed with a device that shall make all sure—only say you will obey his lordship's earnest desire." ...

" My heart is big enough," said Weasel, " for any venture ; but, in truth, I fear the dame. It will be a livelong night carouse, and she is mortal against that. What will she say in the morning ?"

" What can she say, when all is come and gone, but, perchance, that thou wert rash and hot-headed ? That will do you no harm : but an hour ago she swore to me that you were getting old—and sighed, too, as if she believed her words."

" Old, did she say ? Ho, mistress, I will show you my infirmities ! A fig for her scruples ! the heyday blood yerks yet, Master Captain. I will go with thee, comrades : I will follow you to any goblin's chapel twixt St. Mary's and Christina."

" Well said, brave vintner !" exclaimed the captain ; " now stir thee ! And when you come back to the parlour, Master Weasel, you shall find the dame here. Watch my eye and take my hint, so that you play into my hand when need shall be. I will get the nag out of the stable if he were covered with bells. Away for the provender !"

The publican went about his preparations, and had no sooner left the room than the captain called the landlady, who at his invitation showed herself at the door.

" Come in, sweetheart. Good Mistress Daffodil," he said, " I called you that you may lend us your help to laugh : since your rufflers are dispersed, your smokers obnubilated in their own clouds, your tipplers strewed upon the benches, and nothing more left for you to do in the tap-room, we would have your worshipful and witty company here in the parlour. So come in, my princess of pleasant thoughts, and make us merry with thy fancies."

"There is nothing but clinking of cans and swaggering speeches where you are, Captain Dauntrees," said the hostess. "An honest woman had best be little seen in your company. It is a wonder you ever got out of the Low Countries, where, what with drinking with boors and quarrelling with belted bullies, your three years' service was enough to put an end to a thousand fellows of your humour."

"There's destiny in it, dame. I was born to be the delight of your eyes. It was found in my horoscope, when my nativity was cast, that a certain jolly mistress of a most-especially-to-be-commended inn, situate upon a delectable point of land in the New World, was to be greatly indebted to me, first, for the good fame of her wines amongst worshipful people; and, secondly, for the sufficient and decent praise of her beauty. So was it read to my mother by the wise astrologer. . . .

At this moment Garret Weasel returned to the room. A sign from him informed the captain that the preparation he had been despatched to make was accomplished.

"How looks the night, Garret?" inquired Dauntrees: "when have we the moon?"

"It is a clear starlight and calm,' replied the publican; "the moon will not show herself till near morning."

"Have you heard the news, mistress?" inquired the captain, with an expression of some eagerness; "there is pleasant matter current concerning the mercer's wife at the Blue Triangle. But you must have heard it before this?"

"No, truly, not I," replied the hostess.

"Indeed!" said Dauntrees, "then there's a month's amusement for you. You owe the sly jade a grudge, mistress."

"In faith I do," said the dame, smiling, "and would gladly pay it."

"You may pay it off with usury now," added the captain, "with no more trouble than telling the story. It is a rare jest, and will not die quickly."

"I pray you tell it to me, good captain—give me all of it," exclaimed the dame, eagerly.

"Peregrine Cadger, the mercer, you know," said the captain—"but it is a long story, and will take time to rehearse it. Garret, how comes it that you did not tell this matter to your wife, as I charged you to do?" he inquired, with a wink at the publican.

"I resolved to tell it to her," said Weasel, "but, I know not how, it ran out of my mind—the day being a busy one"——

"A busy day to thee!" exclaimed the spouse. "Thou, who hast no more to do than a stray in the pound, what are you fit for, if it be not to do as you are commanded? But go on, captain; the story would only be marred by Garret's telling—go on yourself—I am impatient to hear it."

"I pray you, what o'clock is it, mistress?" asked the captain.

"It is only near nine. It matters not for the hour—go on."

"Nine!" exclaimed Dauntrees; "truly, dame, I must leave the story for Master Garret. Nine, said you? By my sword, I have overstayed my time! I have business with the Lord Proprietary before he goes to his bed. There are papers at the fort which should have been delivered to his lordship before this."

"Nay, captain," said the hostess, "if it be but the delivery of a packet, it may be done by some other hand. There is Driving Dick in the taproom: he shall do your bidding in the matter. Do not let so light a business as that take you away."

"To-morrow, dame, and I will tell you the tale."

"To-night, captain—to-night."

"Truly, I must go; the papers should be delivered by a trusty hand—I may not leave it to an ordinary messenger. Now, if Garret—but I will ask no such service from the good man at this time of night; it is a long way. No, no, I must do my own errand."

"There is no reason upon earth," said the landlady, "why Garret should not do it: it is but a step to the fort and back."

"I can take my nag and ride there in twenty minutes," said Garret. "I warrant you his lordship will think the message wisely intrusted to me."

"Then get you gone, without parley," exclaimed the dame.

"The key of the stable, wife," said Garret.

"If you will go, Master Garret," said Dauntrees —"and it is very obliging of you—do it quickly. Tell Nicholas Verbrack to look in my scritoire; he will find the packet addressed to his lordship. Take it, and see it safely put into his lordship's hands. Say to Nicholas, moreover, that I will be at the fort before ten to-night. You comprehend?"

"I comprehend," replied Garret, as his wife gave him the key of the stable, and he departed from the room.

"Now, captain."

"Well, mistress: you must know that Peregrine Cadger, the mercer, who in the main is a discreet man"——

"Yes."

"A discreet man—I mean, bating some follies which you wot of; for this trading and trafficking naturally begets foresight. A man has so much to do with the world in that vocation, and the world, Mistress Dorothy, is inclined by temper to be somewhat knavish, so that they who have much to do with it learn cautions which other folks do not. Now, in our calling of soldiership, caution is a sneaking virtue which we soon send to the devil; and thereby you may see how it is that we are more honest than other people. Caution and honesty do not much consort together."

"But of the mercer's wife, captain."

"Ay, the mercer's wife—I shall come to her presently. Well, Peregrine, as you have often seen, is a shade or so jealous of that fussock, his wife, who looks, when she is tricked out in her new russet grogram cloak, more like a brown haycock in motion than a living woman."

"Yes," interrupted the dame, laughing, "and

with a sunburnt top. Her red hair on her shoulders is no better, I trow."

" Her husband, who at best is but a cotquean—one of those fellows who has a dastardly fear of his wife, which, you know, Mistress·Dorothy, truly makes both man and wife to be laughed at. A husband should have his own way, and follow his humour, no matter whether the dame rails or not. You agree with me in this, Mistress Weasel?"

" In part, captain. I am not for stinting a husband in his lawful walks; but the wife should have an eye to his ways: she may counsel him."

" Oh, in reason, I grant; but she should not chide him, I mean, nor look too narrowly into his hours, that's all. Now Peregrine's dame hath a free foot, and the mercer himself somewhat of a sulky brow. Well, Halfpenny, the chapman, who is a mad wag for mischief, and who is withal a sure customer of the mercer's in small wares, comes yesternight to Peregrine Cadger's house, bringing with him worshipful Master Lawrence Hay, the Viewer."

At this moment the sound of horse's feet from the court-yard showed that Garret Weasel had set forth on his ride.

" Arnold, I am keeping you waiting," said Dauntrees. " Fill up another cup for yourself and Pamesack, and go your ways. Stay not for me, friends; or if it pleases you, wait for me in the tap-room. I will be ready in a brief space."

The ranger and the Indian, after swallowing another glass, withdrew.

" The Viewer," continued Dauntrees, " is a handsome man,—and a merry man on occasion, too. I had heard it whispered before—but not liking to raise a scandal upon a neighbour, I kept my thoughts to myself—that the mercer's wife had rather a warm side for the viewer. But be that as it may: there was the most laughable prank played on the mercer by Halfpenny and the viewer together, last night, that ever was heard of. It was thus: they had a game at Hoodman blind, and when it fell to Lawrence to be the seeker, somehow the fat termagant was caught in his arms, and so the hood next came to her. Well, she was blindfolded; and there was an agreement all round that no one should speak a word."

" Ay, I understand—I see it," said the hostess, eagerly drawing her chair nearer to the captain.

" No, you would never guess," replied Dauntrees, " if you cudgelled your brains from now till Christmas. But I can show you, Mistress Dorothy, better by the acting of the scene. Here, get down on your knees, and let me put your kerchief over your eyes."

" What can that signify ?" inquired the dame.

" Do it, mistress—you will laugh at the explosion. Give me the handkerchief. Down, dame, upon your marrow-bones:—it is an excellent jest and worth the learning."

The landlady dropped upon her knees, and the captain secured the bandage round her eyes.

" How many fingers, dame ?" he asked, holding his hand before her face.

" Never a finger can I see, captain."

45

" It is well. Now stand up—forth and away ! That was the word given by the viewer. Turn, Mistress Dorothy, and grope through the room. Oh, you shall laugh at this roundly. Grope, grope, dame."

The obedient and marvelling landlady began to grope through the apartment, and Dauntrees, quietly opening the door, stole off to the tap-room, where being joined by his comrades, they hied with all speed toward the fort, leaving the credulous dame floundering after a jest, at least until they got beyond the hail of her voice.

GREEN MOUNT CEMETERY.
FROM AN ADDRESS DELIVERED AT ITS DEDICATION.

I know not where the eye may find more pleasing landscapes than those which surround us. Here, within our enclosures, how aptly do these sylvan embellishments harmonize with the design of the place !—this venerable grove of ancient forest; this lawn shaded with choicest trees; that green meadow, where the brook creeps through the tangled thicket begemmed with wild flowers; these embowered alleys and pathways hidden in shrubbery, and that grassy knoll studded with evergreens and sloping to the cool dell where the fountain ripples over its pebbly bed :—all hemmed in by yon natural screen of foliage which seems to separate this beautiful spot from the world and devote it to the tranquil uses to which it is now to be applied. Beyond the gate that guards these precincts we gaze upon a landscape rife with all the charms that hill and dale, forest-clad heights, and cultivated fields may contribute to enchant the eye. That stream which northward cleaves the woody hills, comes murmuring to our feet, rich with the reflections of the bright heaven and the green earth; thence leaping along between its granite banks, hastens toward the city whose varied outline of tower, steeple, and dome, gilded by the evening sun and softened by the haze, seems to sleep in perspective against the southern sky: and there, fitly stationed within our view, that noble column, destined to immortality from the name it bears, lifts high above the ancient oaks that crown the hill, the venerable form of the Father of his Country, a majestic image of the deathlessness of virtue.

Though scarce an half hour's walk from yon living mart, where one hundred thousand human beings toil in their noisy crafts, here the deep quiet of the country reigns, broken by no ruder voice than such as marks the tranquillity of rural life,—the voice of " birds on branches warbling,"—the lowing of distant cattle, and the whetting of the mower's scythe. Yet tidings of the city not unpleasantly reach the ear in the faint murmur which·at intervals is borne hither upon the freshening breeze, and more gratefully still in the deep tones· of that cathedral bell,

Swinging slow, with sullen roar,

as morning and noon, and richer at eventide, it flings its pealing melody across these shades with an invocation that might charm the lingering visiter to prayer

2 G 2

GEORGE BUSH.

[Born 1796. Died 1859.]

GEORGE BUSH, one of the most profound and ingenious scholars of the present age, was born at Norwich, in the eastern part of Vermont, on the twelfth of June, 1796, and entered Dartmouth College in the eighteenth year of his age, far advanced in classical learning, and distinguished for graces of style in literary composition at that time unusual even among the veterans of the pulpit and the press. Among his classmates of Dartmouth were the late Dr. Marsh, of the University of Vermont, so eminent as a scholar, a philosopher, and a Christian; Thomas C. Upham, who has won an enviable reputation by his metaphysical writings;* and Rufus Choate, who at the bar and in the senate has been among the most conspicuous for learning, wisdom, and fervid eloquence. Mr. Choate was his "chum," and at this time their pursuits as well as their tastes were congenial; but religious influences changed the intentions of Mr. Bush, and after graduating, with the highest honours, in 1818, he entered the Theological Seminary, at Princeton, to prepare himself for the ministry. In due time he received ordination in the Presbyterian church, and having passed a year as tutor in Princeton College, he in 1824 went to Indiana, under the auspices of the Home Missionary Society, and settled at Indianapolis. In the following year he was married to a daughter of the Honourable Lewis Condict of Morristown, in New Jersey. He acquired considerable reputation as a preacher, professorships were offered him in several colleges, and prospects of the satisfaction of all his ambition seemed opening before him; but in 1827, when he had been four years in Indiana, his wife died, and he returned to the East.

He had already written occasionally for the literary and theological journals, but now he determined to consecrate his life to letters and

learning; and in the various departments of dogmatical and ethical theology, general commentary, biblical antiquities, hermeneutics and criticism, the fruits of his industrious pen have ever since engaged the attention of scholars and thinking men. His election to the professorship of Hebrew and Oriental Literature in the University of the city of New York, in 1831, may have had some influence on the direction of his studies, but the field upon which he entered would under any circumstances have been preferred by him, and is the one in which he was fitted to acquire the greatest influence and reputation.

The first work of Professor Bush was his Life of Mohammed, published in 1832.* This was followed in the next year by his celebrated Treatise on the Millennium, in which he has assumed the position that the millennium, strictly so called, is past. But by the millennium he does not understand the golden age of the church, which, in common with nearly all good men, he regards as a future era. He contends that as the memorable period of the thousand years of the apocalypse is distinguished mainly by the binding of the symbolical dragon, we must determine by the legitimate canons of interpretation what is shadowed forth by this mystic personage, before we can assure ourselves of the true character of the millennial age. The dragon, he supposes, is the grand hieroglyphic of paganism; the "binding of the dragon," but a figurative phrase for the suppression of paganism within the limits of the Roman empire, a fulfilment which he contends commenced in the reign of Constantine, and was consummated in that of Theodosius, his successor. He draws largely on the pages of Gibbon in support of his theory, assuming all along the great foundation principle that the apocalypse of John is but a series of pictured emblems, shadowing forth the ecclesiastical and civil history of the world. As a merely literary performance, this work received the highest

---

* The Elements of Mental Philosophy, Treatise on the Will, Outlines of Imperfect and Disordered Mental Action, Principles of the Interior or Hidden Life, and other philosophical and religious works, in which he has bited sound learning, good judgment, and candour.

---

* The tenth volume of Harpers' Family Library

commendations of the critics; and though not generally assented to, it has never been disproved.

In 1835 he published his Hebrew Grammar, of which a second edition appeared in 1838. It has been highly approved wherever used. It is better adapted than any other to elementary instruction.

In 1840 he commenced the publication of his commentaries on the Old Testament, of which eight volumes, Genesis, Exodus, Leviticus, Numbers, Joshua, and Judges, have been completed. His careful study, his scrupulous fidelity in eliciting the exact meaning of the original, and his peculiar tact in explaining it, have made his commentaries everywhere popular, so that before the completion of the series some of the volumes have passed through many editions. In all of them will be found discussions on the most important points of biblical science, extending far beyond the ordinary dimensions of expository notes, and amounting, indeed, to elaborate dissertations of great value. Among the subjects thus treated are, in Genesis, the temptation and the fall, the dispersion from Babel, the prophecies of Noah, the character of Melchizedec, the destruction of Sodom and Gomorrah, the history of Joseph, and the prophetical benedictions of Jacob; in Exodus, the hardening of the heart of Pharaoh, the miracles of the magicians, the pillar of cloud as the seat of the Shekinah, the decalogue, and the Hebrew theocracy; in Leviticus, a clear and minute specification of the different sacrifices, the law of marriage, including the case of marriage with a deceased wife's sister, very largely considered, and a full account of the Jewish festivals. The sixth volume contains an ample and erudite exposition of the Song of Deborah, and an extended discussion on the subject of Jephthah's vow, with a view to determine whether the Jewish warrior really sacrificed his daughter.

In 1844 he published the Hierophant, a monthly magazine, in which he enters elaborately into the nature of the prophetic symbols, and in one of the numbers brings out some grand results as to the physical destiny of the globe. He assumes that a fair construction of the language of the prophets is far from countenancing the common opinions respecting the literal conflagration of the heavens and the earth, and does not even teach

that such a catastrophe is ever to take place. He denies not that this may possibly be the finale which awaits our planet and the solar system, but contends that if so, it is to be gathered rather from astronomy than revelation, from the apocalypse of Newton, Laplace and Herschel, than from that of John. The Letters in The Hierophant to Professor Stuart, on the Double Sense of Prophecy, have been regarded as among the finest specimens of critical discussion.

The next work of Professor Bush, and the one which has excited the most attention and controversy, was Anastasis, or the Doctrine of the Resurrection of the Body Rationally and Spiritually Considered, published in 1844. There is a true and perceptible progress in our knowledge of nature, with which our knowledge of the revelation also advances. The discoveries of the geologists have made necessary a new interpretation of the scriptural genesis of the earth, and the astronomers have taught us that the old opinions of the miraculous suspension of the sun are erroneous; but while science thus modifies ideas in regard to things physical, the great moral truths of the Bible are not affected by it, and the law of conscience remains immutable. Professor Bush contends that the commonly received doctrine of the resurrection of the dead, which implies a reunion of the identical particles of matter which in our present state compose the human body, and that, however widely scattered, and however diverse the forms in which they may exist, these particles shall mysteriously be made again to live in connection with the soul, is sanctioned by neither reason nor revelation. " The ancient and accredited technicalities of religion, hallowed as they are by long usage, and wedded to the heart by early association," are clung to however with unyielding tenacity, and the more spiritual and reasonable view of the resurrection was assailed, in a manner scarcely consistent with Christian courtesy, in many of the leading religious journals, and in various tracts and volumes, to which Professor Bush replied in his work entitled The Resurrection of Christ, in Answer to the Question whether he rose in a Spiritual and Celestial, or in a Material and Earthly Body, and in The Soul, or an Inquiry into Scriptural Psychology, as developed in the use of the terms Soul, Spirit, Life, &c, viewed in its bearings on the Doctrine of the

Resurrection. Very few theological writings have been more read in so short a period, either by the laity or the clergy, and it is not to be denied that with the former at least his reasonings have been very generally convincing.

In 1845 Professor Bush avowed a full belief and candid adoption of the doctrines and disclosures of Emanuel Swedenborg, and he has since devoted himself almost exclusively to their exposition and defence. He has translated Swedenborg's Diary, from the Latin; published most of his other works, with copious original notes; made a Statement of Reasons for joining the " new church," and his new church Miscellanies maintained with an eloquence and earnestness with which they were never maintained before, the principles of the "inspired philosopher" of Upsal.

The last work of Professor Bush is on the higher phenomena of Mesmerism, in which also he is a believer, and is designed to show that the laws of spiritual intercourse developed in the magnetic state afford a striking confirmation of the truths of Swedenborg's revelations on the same subject: so much so, that if the asserted mental phenomena of Mesmerism be facts, Swedenborg's claim to communion with spirits is established.

In 1857 appeared his work, Priesthood and Clergy unknown to Christianity, or the Church a community of co-equal Brethren; and later, an Exposition of the Four Gospels according the Internal Sense; but this work was never finished.

" The inquiry after truth, which is the love-making or wooing of it; the knowledge of truth, which is the presence of it, and the belief of truth, which is the enjoying of it," Lord Bacon says, "is the sovereign good of human nature." There was never a more sincere lover of truth than George Bush; few have sought it with more earnestness and humbleness; and that he has discovered it he seems to have the evidence of a profound satisfaction. He looks for the grandest moral, political, and intellectual movements that man has ever seen; indeed thinks they are now taking place; that the race is swinging loose from its ancient moorings, and is launching upon an unexplored sea, where are no charts for its guidance, where the azimuth must be often plied and the plummet often thrown into the wide ocean, on which floats the vessel freighted with the weal of the world; but the age, with all its voices, bids him hope; the wide reprehension of wrong, the deep-seated feeling of right, the diffusion of learning and religion, the giving way of barbarous usages to order and law, the extension of man's dominion over the elements, by which space and time are removed from between nations, all give promise to him of the last and most glorious act in the drama of the earth, and while he labours he sings, Eureka !

The extent and variety of his learning, his rare courage, the unpretending simplicity and the kindness of his manners, his fervent and trustful piety, insure for him respect and affection, and render him the fittest instrument for the propagation of a new faith, that has appeared, perhaps, in the nineteenth century.

Professor Bush appears to " see darkly" something beyond the limits of the old doctrines, but his new ideas want solidity and coherence. The world will hardly believe that Emanuel Swedenborg was a divinely commissioned destroyer and recreator, though a man of extraordinary genius, who may have perceived some grand truths in physics and philosophy by a sort of spiritual sight, the nature of which he did not himself understand, and made such wise report as by some discreet and cautious men to be regarded as a prophet. Mesmerism, in its lower phenomena practised much by charlatans, who have given abundant excuse for unbelief, embraces substantial and mysterious truth; and since it has been seen that its wonders may explain those of Swedenborg, without a necessity of acknowledging any supernaturalism, the new creed has been progressive; and for the same causes and in the same ratio the importance of its author has diminished.

Much study impaired his health, and he died at Rochester, Sept. 19, 1859. In 1860, was published at Boston, Memoirs and Reminiscences of the late Prof. Geo. Bush; being for the most part, voluntary contributions from different friends. His fine library, rich in biblical, classic, and oriental literature, was sold at auction, in New York.

CATHARINE M. SEDGWICK

CATHERINE M. SEDGWICK.

[Born 1789. Died 1867.]

MISS SEDGWICK was one of the first Americans of her sex who were distinguished in the republic of letters, and in the generous rivalry of women of genius which marks the present age she continues to occupy a conspicuous and most honourable position. She is of a family which has contributed some of its brightest names to Massachusetts. Her father, who was descended from one of the major-generals in the service of Cromwell, enjoyed a high reputation as a statesman and a jurist, and was successively an officer in the revolutionary army, a representative and senator in Congress, and a judge of the supreme court of his state. Her brother Henry, who died in 1831, was an able lawyer and political writer, and another brother, the late Theodore Sedgwick, was also distinguished as a statesman and an author.[*]

Miss Sedgwick was born in the beautiful rural village of Stockbridge, on the river Housatonic, to which her father had removed in 1787. Judge Sedgwick died in 1813, before his daughter had given any indications of literary ability, but her brother Theodore, who had been among the first to appreciate the genius of Bryant,[†] soon discovered and encouraged the development of her dormant powers. The earliest of her published works was the New England Tale, originally intended to appear as a religious tract, but which grew beyond the limits of such a design, and was given to the world in a volume, in 1822. This was followed, in 1824, by Redwood, a novel which was immediately and widely popular; in 1827 by Hope Leslie or Early Times in Massachusetts, by which her reputation was yet more extended; in 1830 by Clarence, a Tale of our own Times, which was inferior in merit, though received with equal favour;

in 1832 by Le Bossu, one of the Tales of Glauber Spa, and in 1835 by The Linwoods, or "Sixty Years Since" in America, the last and in some respects the best of her novels. In the same year she also published a collection of tales and sketches which had previously appeared in various periodicals.

In 1836 Miss Sedgwick gave the public the first of a new and admirable series of illustrations of common life, Home, 18mo., and The Poor Rich Man and the Rich Poor Man, which was followed in 1837 by Live and Let Live, and subsequently by Means and Ends or Self Training, A Love Token for Children, and Stories for Young Persons, and Wilton Harvey.

In the spring of 1839, she went to Europe, and in the year which she spent in travelling wrote her Letters from Abroad to Kindred at Home, which were published in two volumes.

She also wrote Morals of Manners; Mt. Rhigi Boy; The Irish Girl; Married or Single, 2 vols.; Memoir of Joseph Curtis; A Life of Lucretia M. Davidson; and many contributions to annuals and literary magazines.

Miss Sedgwick has marked individuality. She commands as much respect by her virtues as she does admiration by her talents. Indeed the rare endowments of her mind depend in an unusual degree upon the moral qualities with which they are united for their value. She writes with a higher object than merely to amuse. Animated by a cheerful philosophy, and anxious to pour its sunshine into every place where there is lurking care or suffering, she selects for illustration the scenes of everyday experience, paints them with exact fidelity, and seeks to diffuse over the mind a delicious serenity, and in the heart kind feelings and sympathies, and wise ambition, and steady hope. A truly American spirit pervades her works. She speaks of our country as one "where the government and institutions are based on the *gospel principle* of equal rights and equal privileges to all," and denies that honour and shame depend upon condition. She is the champion of the virtuous poor, and selecting her heroes and

---

[*] The most considerable work of Mr. Sedgwick is his Public and Private Economy, in three volumes, published by Harpers.

[†] It was chiefly through the influence of Theodore Sedgwick's persuasions that Mr. Bryant was induced to remove to New York, from the neighbouring village of Great Barrington, where he was engaged in the uncongenial pursuits of a country lawyer; and it was through Mr Sedgwick's means that he first became connected with the Evening Post.

heroines from humble life, does not deem it necessary that by tricks upon them in the cradle they have been only temporarily banished from a patrician caste and estate to which they were born.

Her style is colloquial, picturesque, and marked by a facile grace which is evidently a gift of nature. Her characters are nicely drawn and delicately contrasted. Her Deborah Lenox has remarkable merit as a creation and as an impersonation, and it is perfectly indigenous. The same can be said of several others. Miss Sedgwick's delineations of New England manners are decidedly the best that have appeared, and show both a careful study and a just appreciation. Died July 31, 1867.

THE SABBATH IN NEW ENGLAND.
FROM HOPE LESLIE.

THE observance of the Sabbath began with the Puritans, as it still does with a great portion of their descendants, on Saturday night. At the going down of the sun on Saturday, all temporal affairs were suspended; and so zealously did our fathers maintain the letter, as well as the spirit of the law, that, according to a vulgar tradition in Connecticut, no beer was brewed in the latter part of the week, lest it should presume to *work* on Sunday.

It must be confessed, that the tendency of the age is to laxity; and so rapidly is the wholesome strictness of primitive times abating, that, should some antiquary, fifty years hence, in exploring his garret rubbish, chance to cast his eye on our humble pages, he may be surprised to learn, that, even now, the Sabbath is observed, in the interior of New England, with an almost Judaical severity.

On Saturday afternoon an uncommon bustle is apparent. The great class of procrastinators are hurrying to and fro to complete the lagging business of the week. The good mothers, like Burns' matron, are plying their needles, making " auld claes look amaist as weel's the new;" while the domestics, or *help*, (we prefer the national descriptive term,) are wielding, with might and main, their brooms and *mops*, to make all *tidy* for the Sabbath.

As the day declines, the hum of labour dies away, and, after the sun is set, perfect stillness reigns in every well-ordered household, and not a foot-fall is heard in the village street. It cannot be denied, that even the most scriptural, missing the excitement of their ordinary occupations, anticipate their usual bed-time. The obvious inference from this fact is skilfully avoided by certain ingenious reasoners, who allege, that the constitution was originally so organized as to require an extra quantity of sleep on every seventh night. We recommend it to the curious to inquire, how this peculiarity was adjusted, when the first day of the week was changed from Saturday to Sunday.

The Sabbath morning is as peaceful as the first hallowed day. Not a human sound is heard without the dwellings, and, but for the lowing of the herds, the crowing of the cocks, and the gossiping of the birds, animal life would seem to be extinct, till, at the bidding of the church-going bell, the old and young issue from their habitations, and, with solemn demeanôr, bend their measured steps to the meeting-house ;—the families of the minister, the squire, the doctor, the merchant, the modest gentry of the village, and the mechanic and labourer, all arrayed in their best, all meeting on even ground, and all with that consciousness of independence and equality, which breaks down the pride of the rich, and rescues the poor from servility, envy, and discontent. If a morning salutation is reciprocated, it is in a suppressed voice; and if, perchance, nature, in some reckless urchin, burst forth in laughter—" My dear, you forget it's Sunday," is the ever ready reproof.

Though every face wears a solemn aspect, yet we once chanced to see even a deacon's muscles relaxed by the wit of a neighbour, and heard him allege, in a half-deprecating, half-laughing voice, " The squire is so droll, that a body must laugh, though it be Sabbath-day."

·The farmer's ample wagon, and the little one-horse vehicle, bring in all who reside at an inconvenient walking distance,—that is to say, in our riding community, half a mile from the church. It is a pleasing sight, to those who love to note the happy peculiarities of their own land, to see the farmers' daughters, blooming, intelligent, well-bred, pouring out of these homely coaches, with their nice white gowns, prunel shoes, Leghorn hats, fans and parasols, and the spruce young men, with their plaited ruffles, blue coats, and yellow buttons. The whole community meet as one religious family, to offer their devotions at the common altar. If there is an outlaw from the society, —a luckless wight, whose vagrant taste has never been subdued,—he may be seen stealing along the margin of some little brook, far away from the condemning observation and troublesome admonitions of his fellows.

Towards the close of the day, (or to borrow a phrase descriptive of his feelings, who first used it,) " when the Sabbath begins to *abate*," the children cluster about the windows. Their eyes wander from their catechism to the western sky, and, though it seems to them as if the sun would never disappear, his broad disk does slowly sink behind the mountain; and, while his last ray still lingers on the eastern summits, merry voices break forth, and the ground resounds with bounding footsteps. The village belle arrays herself for her twilight walk; the boys gather on " the green;" the lads and girls throng to the "singing school;" while some coy maiden lingers at home, awaiting her expected suitor; and all enter upon the pleasures of the evening with as keen a relish as if the day had been a preparatory penance.

BESSIE LEE.

FROM THE LINWOODS.

[At the beginning of the Revolution a widow named Lee resides with her children in a rural village of Connecticut. Her son, a thoughtful and chivalrous youth, enters the army, distinguishes himself, and becomes a captain; her daughter, a beautiful, gentle, and affectionate girl, deserted by her lover, Jasper Meredith, passes from trusting hope through anxiety, doubt, and melancholy to a touching madness, and escapes from her friends to find her way alone to New York, with the object of restoring to him some tokens he had given of his love, an act which her disordered fancy assures her will effect her disenthralment from passion. The following extracts are from the account of the fulfilment of her mission, which is conceived and executed with singular felicity, though much of its effect will be lost by its separation from the context.]

COMMENCEMENT OF THE JOURNEY.

It was long before the dawn of one of the few soft days of October, 1779, that Bessie Lee left her safe home to begin a perilous journey. The light of reason was not quite extinct, and with some forecast she took a few coins, keepsakes, that had long lain idly in a drawer, and transferred them to her pocket; then placing in her bosom the little ivory box containing, as she wildly fancied, the charms that bound her to Jasper Meredith, she equipped herself for her journey. A regard to dress is an innate idea in woman that no philosopher can deny to the sex. In all her mutations, that remains......

Bessie, after looking over her moderate wardrobe, selected the only gala dress it contained—a white silk petticoat and blue bodice; but after dressing herself in them, either from the instinct of neatness or from the glimmering of the unfitness of such travelling apparel, she took off the silk petticoat, and after tying it in a handkerchief with some more essential articles, she laced the bodice over a dimity skirt, and put over that a long linen nightgown. Delighted with her own provident sagacity in arraying herself for day and night, she threw over the whole a brown silk cardinal, and a chip gipsy hat tied down with a blue gauze handkerchief. "He always told me I had inspiration in dress," she said, as she gave a pleased, parting glance at the glass. In passing her mother's door, she paused: "I have heard it was a bad sign," thought she, "to leave home without your parent's blessing, but I go forth with Heaven's, and hers must follow." She then proceeded to equip her horse, and set out on the New York road, which she pursued unerringly. She fancied that the same providential exemption from the necessity of sustenance vouchsafed to her was extended to her horse Steady, and the animal, happening to be full-fed, sturdy and of hard-working habits, seemed to acquiesce in his supposed destiny, save now and then, when he resolutely halted at a stream of water to slake his thirst. The part of New England through which Bessie's route lay was sterile and sparsely settled. She was unmolested, and for the most part unobserved. She would sometimes pass a house where the children would pause from their play, stare, and ask, one of the other, who that pretty lady could be? and wonder, that with such a nice cloak, she should

ride without gloves! Once a kind-hearted farmer stopped her, and after asking her numberless questions to which he received no satisfactory replies, he earnestly begged her to stop at his house for some refreshment. She declined his hospitality with the assurance that she did not need it, and a smile that so little harmonized with her blanched cheek, and wild and melancholy eye, that the good man said her looks haunted him. In truth, so unearthly was her appearance, that two gossips, whom she passed on the road, stopped, drew nearer to each other, and without speaking, gazed after her till she was out of sight; and then, with feminine particularity, compared their observations.

"She's master beautiful!" exclaimed one of them.

"Call you that beautiful!" replied her companion; "why, she has neither flesh nor blood—I felt a chill when I looked at her."

"And I felt my blood rush to my heart, as if I had seen something out of nature. I might have taken her for an angel but for her silk cardinal, and her horse, that looked more like our old roan than like the horses in Revelations."

Nancy was less imaginative. "I did not see nothing mysterious," she said, "but her pale little hands, that looked as if they could hardly hold a thread of silk."

"My! did not you see those long curls that streamed down below the hood of her cloak, looking as bright and as soft as Judith's baby when we laid it out—poor thing! and the colour of her cheeks, that were as white as my poor man's fresh tombstone—and her eyes, that shone like stars of a frosty night! don't tell me, Nancy! we must expect to see visions, and dream dreams when there's war in the land and famine at the door!" The unconscious subject of this colloquy went on, her innocent heart dilating with a hope as assured and buoyant as that of a penitent on her way to a shrine where absolution and peace await her.

It was late in the afternoon when, emerging from a wood, she observed that at a short distance before her the road forked.....

Bessie's horse fortunately selected the right direction, and obeyed his mistress's signals to hasten onward. These signals she reiterated from an impression of some indefinite danger pursuing her. By degrees, however, a languor stole over her that prevented her from observing Steady's motions. From a fast trot he had slackened to a walk, and after thus creeping on for a mile or two, he stood stock still.

Bessie sat for a while as it waiting his pleasure, and then looking at the setting sun, she said, "Well, Steady, you have done your day's duty, and I'll not be unmerciful to you. I too have a tired feeling," and she passed her hand over her throbbing temples; "but, Steady, we will not stay here by the roadside, for I think there be bad people on this road, and besides, it is better to be alone where only God is."

The country through which Bessie was now passing was rocky, hilly, and woody, excepting narrow intervals and some few cleared and cultivated slopes. She had just passed a brook, that glided quietly through a very green little meadow on her left, but which on her right, though screened from sight, sounded its approach as in the glad spirit of its young life it came leaping and dancing down a rocky gorge. Bessie, as it would seem, from the instinct of humanity, let down some bars to allow her hungry steed admittance to the meadow, saying as she did so, "You shall have the green pastures and still waters, Steady, where those home-looking willows are turning up their silvery leaves as if to kiss the parting sunbeams, and the sunflower and the golden-rod are still flaunting in their pride—poor things! but I will go on the other side, where the trees stand bravely up, to screen and guard me—and the waterfall will sing me to sleep."

She crossed the road and plunged into the wood, and, without even a footpath to guide her, she scrambled along the irregular margin of the brook; sometimes she swung herself round the trunk of a tree by grasping the tough vines encircling it; sometimes, when a bald perpendicular rock projected over the water, she surmounted it as if the danger of wetting her feet must be avoided at all pains and risks; then, a moss-covered rock imbedded in the stream attracting her eye, she would spring on to it, drop her feet into the water, doff her little chip hat, and bathe her burning temples in the cold stream: and when she again raised her head, shook back her curls and turned her face heavenward, her eye glowing with preternatural brightness, she might have been mistaken for a wanderer from the celestial sphere gazing homeward. After ascending the stream for about a hundred yards, she came to a spot which seemed to her excited imagination to have been most graced

"By the sovereign planter when he formed
All things for man's delightful use;"

and, in truth, it was a resting-place for the troubled spirit, far more difficult to find than a bed of down for the wearied body.

The thicket here expanded and spread its encircling arms around a basin worn into the earth by the force of the stream, which leaped into it over a rock some thirty feet in height. Here and there a rill straggled away from the slender column of water, and as it caught the sun's slant ray, dropped down the rock in sparkling gems. The trees were wreathed with grape-vines, whose clusters peeped through the brown leaves into the mirror below. The leaves of the topmost branches of the trees were touched with the hues of autumn, and hung over the verdant tresses below them like a wreath of gorgeous flowers. The sky was clear, and the last rays of the setting sun stole in obliquely, sweet and sad, as the parting smile of a friend, glancing along the stems of the trees and flashing athwart the waterfall.

"Here will I lay me down and rest," said Bessie, rolling up with her foot a pillow of crisp crimson leaves, that had fallen from a young delicate tree, fit emblem of herself, stricken by the first touch of adversity. "But first I will say my prayers, for I think this is one of God's temples."

She knelt and murmured forth the broken aspirations of her pure heart, and then laying herself down, she said, "I wish mother and Eliot could see me now—they would be so satisfied!"

Once she raised her head, gazed at the soft mist that was curling up from the water, and seemed intently listening. "I have somewhere read," she said, "that

'Millions of spiritual creatures walk the earth.
Unseen, both when we wake and when we sleep.'

I believe it!" again her head fell back on its sylvan pillow, and utterly incapable of farther motion or thought, she sank to deep repose. Night came on, the watchful stars shone down upon her, the planets performed their nightly course, the moon rose and set, and still the unconscious sufferer slept on. . . . .

BESSIE'S ARRIVAL IN THE CITY.

Isabelle Linwood, at her aunt's summons, had gone to her house. She met Mrs. Archer at her street door. Her face spoke of startling intelligence before she uttered it. "My dear Belle," she said, "I have the strangest news for you. I went to your father's while you were out; and just as my foot was on your door-step, a man drove up in a wagon with a girl as pale as death—such a face! The moment he stopped she sprang from the wagon. At once I knew her, and exclaimed, 'Bessie Lee!'"

"Bessie Lee! Gracious Heaven!"

"Yes; she asked eagerly if you were at home. I perceived the inconvenience—the impossibility of your taking care of her in the present state of your family. I felt anxious to do any thing and every thing for the sister of young Lee; I therefore told her you were not at home, but she could see you at my house; and I persuaded her to come home with me."

"Dear Bessie! can it be possible that she is here?"

"Yes, I have left her in that room. Her attendant told me that she arrived this morning at Kingsbridge, with a decent man and woman, who had passports from La Fayette, and a letter from him to the commander of that post, commending the unfortunate person to his humanity, and entreating him to convey her, under a proper escort, to Mr. Linwood's."

"Poor Bessie! Heaven has miraculously guided her into the best hands. How does she appear?"

"With scarcely enough mortality to shield her troubled spirit; fluttering and gentle as a stricken dove—pale, unnaturally, deadly pale—a startling brightness in her deep blue eye—her cheeks sunken; but still her features preserve the exquisite symmetry we used to think so beautiful, when a pensive, quiet little girl, she stole round after you like a shadow. And her voice, oh Belle, you cannot hear it without tears. She is mild and submissive; but restless, and excessively impatient to see you and Jasper Meredith. Twice she has come to the door to go out in search of him. I have ordered the blinds to be closed, and the candles lighted, to make it appear darker without than it really is.

I could only quiet her by the assurance that I would send for him immediately."

" Have you done so ?"

" No; I have waited to consult you."

The house Mrs. Archer occupied was of the common construction of the best houses of that day, being double, the two front apartments separated by a wide hall, a drawing-room in the rear, and a narrow cross-passage opening into a carriage-way to the yard. A few moments before Isabella arrived, a person had knocked at the door and asked to see Mrs. Archer; and being told that she was particularly engaged, he asked to be shown to a room where he might await her convenience, as he had business of importance with her. He was accordingly shown into an apartment opposite to that occupied at the moment by Mrs. Archer and Bessie.

There he found the blind children, Ned and Lizzy, so absorbed in a game of chess, that although he went near them, and overlooked them, they seemed just conscious of his presence, but not in the least disturbed by it. They went on playing and managing their game with almost as much facility as if they had their eyesight, till after a closely-fought battle Lizzy declared a checkmate. Ned was nettled by his unexpected defeat, and gave vent to his vexation by saying, " Anyhow, Miss Lizzy, you would not have beaten if I had not thought it was my knight, instead of yours, on number four."

" Oh, Ned !"

" You would not; you know I always get puzzled about the knights—I always said it was the only fault in the chessmen—I always said I wished Captain Lee had made them more different."

" That fault is easily rectified," said the looker-on.

" Captain Lee !" exclaimed Ned, whose memory was true to a voice once heard, and who never, in any circumstances, could have forgotten the sound of Eliot's voice.

" Hush, my dear little fellow, for Heaven's sake, hush !" cried Eliot, aware of the imprudence he had committed ; but it was too late.

Ned's feelings were as susceptible as his hearing. He impetuously sprang forward, and opening the door into the entry, where Mrs. Archer had just uttered the last sentence we reported of her conversation with Isabella, he cried out, " Oh, mamma, Captain Lee is here !"

Eliot involuntarily doffed his fox-skin cap, and advanced to them. Both ladies most cordially gave him their hands at the same moment, while their brows clouded with the thought of the sad tidings they had to communicate. Conscious of the precarious position he occupied, he naturally interpreted the concern so evident on their faces as the expression of a benevolent interest in his safety. " Do not be alarmed, ladies," he said; " I have nothing to fear if my little friends here be quiet; and that I am certain they will be, when they know my life depends on my remaining unknown."

' Oh, what have I done ?" exclaimed Ned,

46

bursting into tears ; but he was soon soothed by Eliot's assurances that no harm as yet was done.

Mrs. Archer withdrew the children, while Miss Linwood communicated to Eliot, as briefly as possible, the arrival and condition of his sister; and he, rather relieved than distressed by the information, told her that his deepest interest in coming to the city was the hope of obtaining some tidings of the poor wanderer. They then consulted how and when they had best present themselves before her; and it was decided that Miss Linwood should first go into the apartment, and prepare her to see Eliot.

Eliot retreated, and stood still and breathless to catch the first sound of Bessie's voice; but he heard nothing but the exclamation, " She is not here !" Eliot sprang forward. The door of the apartment which led into the side passage and the outer door were both open, and Eliot, forgetful of every thing but his sister, was rushing into the street, when Bessie entered the street door with Jasper Meredith. Impelled by her ruling purpose to see Meredith, she had, on her first discovery of the side passage, escaped into the street, where the first person she encountered was he whose image had so long been present to her, that seeing him with her bodily organ seemed to make no new impression, nor even to increase the vividness of the image stamped on her memory. She had thrown on her cloak, but had nothing on her head ; and her hair fell in its natural fair curls over her face and neck. Singular as it was for the delicate, timid Bessie to appear in this guise in the public street, or to appear there at all, and much as he was startled by her faded, stricken form, the truth did not at once occur to Meredith. The wildness of her eye was subdued in the dim twilight; she spoke in her accustomed quiet manner; and after answering to his first inquiry that she was perfectly well now, she begged him to go into Mrs. Archer's with her, as she had something there to restore to him. He endeavoured to put her off with a commonplace evasion—" he was engaged now, would come some other time," &c., but she was not to be deluded ; and seeing some acquaintances approaching, whose observation he did not care to encounter, he ascended Mrs. Archer's steps, and found himself in the presence of those whom he would have wished most to avoid ; but there was no retreat.

THE INTERVIEW.

Bessie now acted with an irresistible energy. " This way," said she, leading Meredith into the room she had quitted—" come all of you in here," glancing her eye from Meredith to Isabella and Eliot, but without manifesting the slightest surprise or emotion of any sort at seeing them, but simply saying, with a smile of satisfaction, as she shut the door and threw off her cloak, " I expected this—I knew it would be so. In visions by day and dreams by night, I always saw you together."

It was a minute before Eliot could command his voice for utterance. He folded his arms around Bessie, and murmured, " My sister !—my dear sister !"

She drew back, and placing her hands on his

2 H

shoulders and smiling, said, "Tears, Eliot, tears! Oh, shame, when this is the proudest, happiest moment of your sister's life!"

"Is she mad?" asked Meredith of Isabella.

Bessie's ear caught his last word. "Mad!" she repeated—"I think all the world is mad; but I alone am not! I have heard that whom the gods would destroy they first make mad; men and angels have been employed to save me from destruction.'

"It is idle to stay here to listen to these ravings," said Meredith, in a low voice, to Miss Linwood; and he was about to make his escape, when Isabella interposed: "Stay for a moment, I entreat you," she said; "she has been very eager to see you, and it is sometimes of use to gratify these humours."

In the mean time Eliot, his heart burning within him at his sister's being gazed at as a spectacle by that man of all the world from whose eye he would have sheltered her, was persuading her, as he would a wayward child, to leave the apartment. She resisted his importunities with a sort of gentle pity for his blindness, and a perfect assurance that she was guided by light from Heaven. "Dear Eliot," she said, "you know not what you ask of me. For this hour my life has been prolonged, my strength miraculously sustained. You have all been assembled here—you, Eliot, because a brother should sustain his sister, share her honour, and partake her happiness; Jasper Meredith to receive back those charms and spells by which my too willing spirit was bound; and you, Isabella Linwood, to see how, in my better mind, I yield him to you."

She took from her bosom a small ivory box, and opening it, she said, advancing to Meredith, and showing him a withered rose-bud, "Do you remember this? You plucked it from a little bush that almost dipped its leaves in that cold spring on the hill-side—do you remember? It was a hot summer's afternoon, and you had been reading poetry to me; you said there was a delicate praise in the sweet breath of flowers that suited me, and some silly thing you said, Jasper, that you should not, of wishing yourself a flower that you might breathe the incense that you were not at liberty to speak; and then you taught me the Persian language of flowers. I kept this little bud: it faded, but was still sweet. Alas!—alas! I cherished it for its Persian meaning." Her reminiscence seemed too vivid, her voice faltered, and her eye fell from its fixed gaze on Meredith; but suddenly her countenance brightened, and she turned to Isabella, who stood by the mantelpiece resting her throbbing head on her hand, and added, "Take it, Isabella, it is a true symbol to you."

Eliot for the first time turned his eye from his sister, and even at that moment of anguish a thrill of joy shot through every vein when he saw Isabella take the bud, pull apart its shrivelled leaves, and throw them from her. Meredith stood lean-ing against the wall, his arms folded, and his lips curled into a smile that was intended to express scornful unconcern. He might have expressed it,

he might possibly have felt it towards Bessie Lee; but when he saw Isabella throw away the bud, when he met the indignant glance of her eye flashing through the tears that suffused it, a livid paleness spread around his mouth, and that feature, the most expressive and truest organ of the soul, betrayed his inward conflict. He snatched his hat to leave the room; Bessie laid her hand on his arm: "Oh, do not go; I shall be cast back into my former wretchedness if you go now."

"Stay, sir," said Eliot; "my sister shall not be crossed."

"With all my heart; I have not the slightest objection to playing out my dumb show between vapouring and craziness."

"Villain!" exclaimed Eliot—the young men exchanged glances of fire. Bessie placed herself between them, and stretching out her arms, laid a hand on the breast of each, as if to keep them apart.—"Now this is unkind—unkind in both of you. I have come such a long and wearisome journey to make peace for all of us; and if you will but let me finish my task, I shall lay me down and sleep—for ever, I think."

Eliot pressed her burning hand to his lips. "My poor, dear sister," he said, "I will not speak an-other word, if I die in the effort to keep silence."

"Thanks, dear Eliot," she replied; and putting both her arms around his neck, she added, in a whisper, "do not be angry if he again call me crazy . there be many that have called me so—they mis take inspiration for madness, you know." Never was Eliot's self-command so tested; and retiring to the farthest part of the room, he stood with knit brows and compressed lips, looking and feeling like a man stretched on the rock, while Bessie pursued her fancied mission. "Do you remember this chain?" she asked, as she opened a bit of paper, and let fall a gold chain over Meredith's arm. He startled as if he were stung. "It cannot harm you," she said, faintly smiling, as she noticed his recoiling. "This was the charm." She smoothed the paper envelope. "As often as I looked at it, the feeling with which I first read it shot through my heart—strange, for there does not seem much in it." She murmured the words pencilled by Meredith on the envelope,

"'Can she who weaves electric chains to bind the heart,
  Refuse the golden links that boast no mystic art?'

"Oh, well do I remember," she cast up her eyes as one does who is retracing the past, "the night you gave me this; Eliot was in Boston; mother was—I don't remember where, and we had been all the evening sitting on the porch. The honey-suckles and white roses were in bloom, and the moon shone in through their leaves. It was then you first spoke of your mother in England, and you said much of the happy destiny of those who were not shackled by pride and avarice; and when you went away, you pressed my hand to your heart, and put this little packet in it. Yet" (turn-ing to Isabella) "he never said he loved me. It was only my over-credulous fancy. Take it, Isa bella; it belongs to you, who really weave the chain that binds the heart."

Meredith seized the chain as she stretched out her hand, and crushed it under his foot. Bessie looked from him to Isabella, and seemed for a moment puzzled; then said, acquiescingly, " Ah, it's all well; symbols do not make our change realities. This little brooch," she continued, steadily pursuing her purpose, and taking from the box an old-fashioned brooch, in the shape of a forget-me-not, " I think was powerless. What need had I of a forget-me-not, when memory devoured every faculty of my being? No, there was no charm in the forget-me-not; but oh, this little pencil," she took from the box the end of a lead pencil, " with which we copied and scribbled poetry together. How many thoughts has this little instrument unlocked—what feelings has it touched—what affections have hovered over its point, and gone thrilling back through the heart! You must certainly take this, Isabella, for there is yet a wonderful power in this magical little pencil—it can make such revelations."

" Dear Bessie, I have no revelations to make."

" Is my task finished?" asked Meredith.

" Not yet—not quite yet—be patient—patience is a great help; I have found it so. Do you remember this?" She held up before Meredith a tress of her own fair hair, tied with a raven lock of his in a true-love knot. " Ah, Isabella, I know very well it was not maidenly of me to tie this; I knew it then, and I begged it of him with many tears, did I not, Jasper? but I *kept* it—that was wrong too. Now, Mr. Meredith, you will help me to untie it!"

" Pardon me; I have no skill in such matters."

" Ah, is it easier to tie than to untie a true-love knot? Alas, alas! I have found it so. But you must help me. My head is growing dizzy, and I am so faint here!" She laid her hand on her heart. " It must be parted—dear Isabella, you will help me—you can untie a true-love's not!"

" I can sever it," said Isabella, with an emphasis that went to the heart of more than one that heard her. She took a pair of scissors from the table, and cut the knot. The black lock fell on the floor; the pretty tress of Bessie's hair curled around her finger:—" I will keep this for ever, my sweet Bessie," she said; " the memorial of innocence, and purity, and much-abused trust."

" Oh, I did not mean that—I did not mean that, Isabella. Surely I have not accused him; I told you he never *said* he loved me. I am not angry with him—you must not be. You cannot be long if you love him; and surely you do love him."

" Indeed, indeed, I do not."

" Isabella Linwood! you *have* loved him." She threw one arm around Isabella's neck, and looked with a piercing gaze in her face. Isabella would at this moment have given worlds to have answered with truth—" No, *never!*" She would have given her life to have so answered the treacherous blood, that, rushing to her neck, cheeks, and temples, answered unequivocally Bessie's ill-timed question.

Meredith's eye was riveted to her face, and the transition from the humiliation, the utter abasement of the moment before, to the undeniable and manifested certainty that he had been loved by the all-exacting, the unattainable Isabella Linwood, was more than he could bear, without expressing his exultation. " I thank you, Bessie Lee," he cried; " this triumph is worth all I have endured from your raving and silly drivelling. Your silent confession, Miss Linwood, is *satisfactory*, full, and plain enough; but it has come a thought too late. Good-evening to you—a fair good-night to you, sir. I advise you to take care that your sister sleep more and *dream* less."

There is undoubtedly a pleasure, transient it may be, but real it is, in the gratification of the baser passions. Meredith was a self-idolater; and at the very moment when his divinity was prostrate, it had been revived by the sweetest, the most unexpected incense. No wonder he was intoxicated. How long his delirium lasted, and what were its effects, are still to be seen. His parting taunt was lost on those he left behind.

Bessie believed that her mission was fulfilled and ended. The artificial strength which, while she received it as the direct gift of Heaven, her highly-wrought imagination had supplied, was exhausted. As Meredith closed the door, she turned to Eliot, and locking her arms around him, gazed at him with an expression of natural tenderness, that can only be imagined by those who have been so fortunate as to see Fanny Kemble's exquisite personation of Ophelia; and who remember (who could forget it?) her action at the end of the flower-scene, when reason and nature seeming to overpower her wild fancies, she throws her arms around Laertes's neck, and with one flash of her all-speaking eyes, makes every chord of the heart vibrate.

The light soon faded from Bessie's face, and she lay as helpless as an infant in her brother's arms. Isabella hastened to Mrs. Archer; and Eliot, left alone and quite unmanned, poured out his heart over this victim of vanity and heartlessness.

Mrs. Archer was prompt and efficient in her kindness. Bessie was conveyed to bed, and Eliot assured that every thing should be done for her that human tenderness and vigilance could do. After obtaining a promise from Mrs. Archer that she would write a letter to his mother, and forward it with some despatches which he knew were to be sent to Boston on the following day; and after having arranged matters for secret visits to his sister, he left her, fervently thanking God for the kind care that watched over her flickering lamp of life.

THREE YEARS AFTER.

Bessie Lee, restored to her excellent mother, and to her peaceful and now most happy home at Westbrook, was enjoying her renovated health and " rectified spirit." She lived for others, and chiefly to minister to the sick and sorrowful. She no longer suffered herself; but the chord of suffering had been so strained that it was weakened, and vibrated at the least touch of the miseries of others. Her pilgrimage was not a long one; and when it ended, the transition was gentle from the heaven she made on earth to that which awaited her in the bosom of the Father.

FRANCIS WAYLAND.

[Born 1796. Died 1865.]

FRANCIS WAYLAND was born in the city of New York on the eleventh of March, 1796, and in the seventeenth year of his age was graduated at Union College in Schenectady. After spending three years in the study of medicine, at Troy, a change of his views in regard to a profession led him in 1817 to enter the Theological Seminary at Andover, which he left at the end of a year, to become a tutor in Union College. In 1821 he accepted a call to the pastoral care of the First Baptist Church in Boston, which situation he held for five years. In 1826 he returned to Schenectady as professor of mathematics and natural philosophy, and before the close of the year removed to Providence, having been elected to the presidency of Brown University, into which office he was inducted in February, 1827.

The first publication of President Wayland was a Sermon on the Moral Dignity of the Missionary Enterprise, delivered in Boston, in 1823. To this succeeded in 1825 Two Discourses on the Duties of an American Citizen; in 1830 a Discourse before the American Institute of Instruction; in 1831 a Discourse on the Philosophy of Analogy, and a Sermon at the Installation of William Hague; in 1833 Occasional Discourses, and a Sermon at the Ordination of William R. Williams; in 1834 The Moral Conditions of Success in the Promulgation of the Gospel; in 1835 a Discourse at the Dedication of Manning Hall, Brown University, and The Elements of Moral Science (of which an abridgment, for the use of schools, was issued in the following year;) in 1837 Discourses on the Moral Law of Accumulation, and The Elements of Political Economy, (of which an abridgment appeared in 1840;) in 1838 a Discourse at the Opening of the Providence Athenæum, and The Limitations of Human Responsibility; in 1841 an Address before the Rhode Island Society for the Encouragement of Domestic Industry, and a Discourse on the Life and Character of the Honourable Nicholas Brown; in 1842 Thoughts on the Present Collegiate System in the United States, a Sermon on the Affairs

of Rhode Island, and a Thanksgiving Discourse; in 1843 The Claims of Whalemen on Christian Benevolence; in 1845 Domestic Slavery considered as a Scriptural Institution, in a Correspondence with the Reverend Richard Fuller, D. D. of South Carolina; and in 1846 a Discourse on the Life and Services of William C. Goddard. Besides these works, and his Intellectual Philosophy, he published in 1853, his Life of the Missionary, Dr. Judson, 2 vols.; Notes on the Principles and Practices of the Baptists; and Sermons to the Churches, (1858.) Several of his discourses have passed through many editions both at home and abroad, and of his Political Economy many thousand, and of his Moral Science, nearly ninety thousand copies have been sold.

The characteristic of Dr. Wayland's philosophical system consists in the harmonizing of the intellectual with the moral: it is logic applied to the theory of duty. That subject which by some writers is treated as a mysterious impulse of the sentiments, and by others as a transcendent law, to be obeyed but not understood, becomes in his pages a great scheme of reason. Sympathy is disciplined and enlightened, and understanding is warmed into superior sensibility, till the two are made one in the completeness of rational virtue. In this reduction into unity of processes before always distinct and sometimes conflicting, the popular morality undergoes some important rectifications. I think Dr. Wayland entitled to the name of a creator in moral science: not that he has suggested new principles or disclosed new motives, but that he has defined the limits and positions of subjects in which indistinctness is practically equivalent to uncertainty. By making the standard convenient he has made the obligation cogent, and in showing that we need not go beyond the line of practicability, has left no excuse for not coming up to it. When the philosophy of social relations shall reassume that importance in the public attention, which in the prevailing anarchy of opinions it cannot assert, I think that his Treatise on Human Responsibility will be looked upon as one of the great guiding monuments of human thought in the department to which it refers.

The same combination of analytical with moral perception explains the peculiarity of his genius and determines the estimate of his literary character. His productions exhibit as much brilliancy as vigour; but it is not the brilliancy of fancy, or sentiment, or rhetorical art. He inherits none of that efflorescent imagination which clustered around the understanding of Bacon with gorgeous beauty; his argumentation is almost as severe and single as Locke's. It seems to me that the intellectual processes of his mind are saved from hardness and aridity by the interfused energy of moral susceptibility; that they glow with a living and sympathetic interest because they are charged with the ardours of conscience, and are instinct with a spiritual life. That richness of lustre which in a critical point of view invests his productions, arises from two parallel rays of intelligence being refracted into one, and thrown in their blended splendour over the subject.

Few works which have so little ornament are as attractive and agreeable as those of this able thinker. They have the natural charm which belongs to the display of active, various and ready strength. Every thing that proceeds from his pen has a character of originality; not because he deals in novelty or is inclined to paradox, for there never was a more loyal servant of the truth; but because all that he produces shows the mould and stamp of his own peculiar and capacious mind.

In 1850, he inaugurated an important reform in the distribution of the college studies, extending the benefits of the college, by introducing a partial course to be pursued by such as were not intended for professional life, and conferring degrees according to the attainments made. He also identified himself with the advocacy of lay preaching, and a better adaptation of the training of candidates to the work of the ministry. The college was eminently successful under his presidency, but wearied with his long care of it, he resigned in 1855, and resided in Providence until his death on Saturday Sep. 30, 1865. His life was written by his son in 2 vols.

~~~~~~~~~

THE OBJECT OF MISSIONS.
FROM THE MORAL DIGNITY OF THE MISSIONARY ENTERPRISE.

Our object will not have been accomplished till the tomahawk shall be buried for ever, and the tree of peace spread its broad branches from the Atlantic to the Pacific; until a thousand smiling villages shall be reflected from the waves of the Missouri, and the distant valleys of the West echo with the song of the reaper; till the wilderness and the solitary place shall have been glad for us, and the desert has rejoiced, and blossomed as the rose.

Our labours are not to cease, until the last slave-ship shall have visited the coast of Africa, and, the nations of Europe and America having long since redressed her aggravated wrongs, Ethiopia, from the Mediterranean to the Cape, shall have stretched forth her hand unto God.

How changed will then be the face of Asia! Bramins, and sooders, and castes, and shasters, will have passed away, like the mist which rolls up the mountain's side before the rising glories of a summer's morning, while the land on which it rested, shining forth in all its loveliness, shall, from its numberless habitations, send forth the high praises of God and the Lamb. The Hindoo mother will gaze upon her infant with the same tenderness which throbs in the breast of any one of you who now hears me, and the Hindoo son will pour into the wounded bosom of his widowed parent the oil of peace and consolation.

In a word, point us to the loveliest village that smiles upon a Scottish or New England landscape, and compare it with the filthiness and brutality of a Caffrarian kraal, and we tell you, that our object is to render that Caffrarian kraal as happy and as gladsome as that Scottish or New England village. Point us to the spot on the face of the earth, where liberty is best understood and most perfectly enjoyed, where intellect shoots forth in its richest luxuriance, and where all the kindlier feelings of the heart are constantly seen in their most graceful exercise; point us to the loveliest, and happiest neighbourhood in the world on which we dwell, and we tell you, that our object is to render this whole earth, with all its nations, and kindreds, and tongues, and people, as happy, nay, happier than that neighbourhood.

We do believe, that God so loved the world, that he gave his only begotten Son, that whosoever believeth in him should not perish, but have everlasting life. Our object is to convey to those who are perishing the news of this salvation. It is to furnish every family upon the face of the whole earth with the word of God written in its own language, and to send to every neighbourhood a preacher of the cross of Christ. Our object will not be accomplished until every idol temple shall have been utterly abolished, and a temple of Jehovah erected in its room; until this earth, instead of being a theatre, on which immortal beings are preparing by crime for eternal condemna-

2 H 2

tion, shall become one universal temple, in which the children of men are learning the anthems of the blessed above, and becoming meet to join the general assembly and church of the first born, whose names are written in heaven. Our design will not be completed until

> "One song employs all nations, and all cry,
> 'Worthy the Lamb, for he was slain for us;'
> The dwellers in the vales and on the rocks
> Shout to each other; and the mountain tops
> From distant mountains catch the flying joy;
> Till, nation after nation taught the strain,
> Earth rolls the rapturous hosanna round."

The object of the missionary enterprise embraces every child of Adam. It is vast as the race to whom its operations are of necessity limited. It would confer upon every individual on earth all that intellectual or moral cultivation can bestow. It would rescue the world from the indignation and wrath, tribulation and anguish, reserved for every son of man that doeth evil, and give it a title to glory, honour, and immortality. You see, then, that our object is, not only to affect every individual of the species, but to affect him in the momentous extremes of infinite happiness and infinite wo. And now, we ask, what object, ever undertaken by man, can compare with this same design of evangelizing the world? Patriotism itself fades away before it, and acknowledges the supremacy of an enterprise, which seizes, with so strong a grasp, upon both the temporal and eternal destinies of the whole family of man.

And now, my hearers, deliberately consider the nature of the missionary enterprise. Reflect upon the dignity of its object; the high moral and intellectual powers which are to be called forth in its execution; the simplicity, benevolence, and efficacy, of the means by which all this is to be achieved; and we ask you, Does not every other enterprise to which man ever put forth his strength, dwindle into insignificance before that of preaching Christ crucified to a lost and perishing world?

THE IDEA OF THE SUBLIME.
FROM THE SAME.

PHILOSOPHERS have speculated much concerning a process of sensation, which has commonly been denominated the emotion of sublimity. Aware that, like any other simple feeling, it must be incapable of definition, they have seldom attempted to define it; but, content with remarking the occasions on which it is excited, have told us that it arises in general from the contemplation of whatever is vast in nature, splendid in intellect, or lofty in morals: or, to express the same idea somewhat varied, in the language of a critic of antiquity, "That alone is truly sublime, of which the conception is vast, the effect irresistible, and the remembrance scarcely, if ever, to be erased."

But, although philosophers alone have written about this emotion, they are far from being the only men who have felt it. The untutored peasant, when he has seen the autumnal tempest collecting between the hills, and, as it advanced, enveloping in misty obscurity village and hamlet, forest and meadow, has tasted the sublime in all its reality; and, whilst the thunder has rolled and the lightning flashed around him, has exulted in the view of nature moving forth in her majesty. The untaught sailor boy, listlessly hearkening to the idle ripple of the moonlight wave, when on a sudden he has thought upon the unfathomable abyss beneath him, and the wide waste of waters around him, and the infinite expanse above him, has enjoyed to the full the emotion of sublimity, whilst his inmost soul has trembled at the vastness of its own conceptions. But why need I multiply illustrations from nature? Who does not recollect the emotion he has felt while surveying aught, in the material world, of terror or of vastness?

And this sensation is not produced by grandeur in material objects alone. It is also excited on most of those occasions in which we see man tasking to the uttermost the energies of his intellectual or moral nature. Through the long lapse of centuries, who, without emotion, has read of Leonidas and his three hundred's throwing themselves as a barrier before the myriads of Xerxes, and contending unto death for the liberties of Greece?

But we need not turn to classic story to find all that is great in human action; we find it in our own times, and in the history of our own country. Who is there of us that, even in the nursery, has not felt his spirit stir within him, when, with childlike wonder, he has listened to the story of Washington? And although the terms of the narrative were scarcely intelligible, yet the young soul kindled at the thought of one man's working out the delivery of a nation. And as our understanding, strengthened by age, was at last able to grasp the detail of this transaction, we saw that our infantile conceptions had fallen far short of its grandeur. Oh! if an American citizen ever exults in the contemplation of all that is sublime in human enterprise, it is when, bringing to mind the men who first conceived the idea of this nation's independence, he beholds them estimating the power of her oppressor, the resources of her citizens, deciding in their collected might that this nation should be free, and, through the long years of trial that ensued, never blenching from their purpose, but freely redeeming the pledge they had given, to consecrate to it "their lives, their fortunes, and their sacred honour."

> "Patriots have toiled, and, in their country's cause,
> Bled nobly, and their deeds, as they deserve,
> Receive proud recompense. We give in charge
> Their names to the sweet lyre. The historic Muse,
> Proud of her treasure, marches with it down
> To latest times: and Sculpture in her turn
> Gives bond, in stone and ever-during brass,
> To guard them, and immortalize her trust."

It is not in the field of patriotism alone that deeds have been achieved, to which history has awarded the palm of moral sublimity. There have lived men, in whom the name of patriot has been merged in that of philanthropist, who, looking with an eye of compassion over the face of the earth, have felt for the miseries of our race, and have put forth their calm might to wipe off one blot from the marred and stained escutcheon of human nature, to strike off one form of suffering from the catalogue of human wo. Such a man was Howard. Surveying our world like a spirit of the blessed, he beheld the misery of the captive—he heard the groaning of the prisoner. His determination was fixed. He resolved, single-handed, to gauge and to measure one form of unpitied, unheeded wretchedness, and, bringing it out to the sunshine of public observation, to work its utter extermination. And he well knew what this undertaking would cost him. He knew what he had to hazard from the infection of dungeons, to endure from the fatigues of inhospitable travel, and to brook from the insolence of legalized oppression. He knew that he was devoting himself to the altar of philanthropy, and he willingly devoted himself. He had marked out his destiny, and he hasted forward to its accomplishment, with an intensity, " which the nature of the human mind forbade to be more, and the character of the individual forbade to be less." Thus he commenced a new era in the history of benevolence. And hence, the name of Howard will be associated with all that is sublime in mercy, until the final consummation of all things.

Such a man is Clarkson, who, looking abroad, beheld the miseries of Africa, and, looking at home, saw his country stained with her blood. We have seen him, laying aside the vestments of the priesthood, consecrate himself to the holy purpose of rescuing a continent from rapine and murder, and of erasing this one sin from the book of his nation's iniquities. We have seen him and his fellow philanthropists, for twenty years, never waver from their purpose. We have seen them persevere amidst neglect and obloquy, and contempt, and persecution, until, the cry of the oppressed having roused the sensibilities of the nation, the "Island Empress" rose in her might, and said to this foul traffic in human flesh, Thus far shalt thou go, and no farther.

THE BIBLE AND THE ILIAD.
FROM DISCOURSES ON THE DUTIES OF AN AMERICAN CITIZEN.

As to the powerful, I had almost said miraculous, effect of the Sacred Scriptures, there can no longer be a doubt in the mind of any one on whom fact can make an impression. That the truths of the Bible have the power of awakening an intense moral feeling in man under every variety of character, learned or ignorant, civilized or savage; that they make bad men good, and send a pulse of healthful feeling through all the domestic, civil, and social relations; that they teach men to love right, to hate wrong, and to seek each other's welfare, as the children of one common parent; that they control the baleful passions of the human heart, and thus make men proficients in the science of self-government; and, finally, that they teach him to aspire after a conformity to a Being of infinite holiness, and fill him with hopes infinitely more purifying, more exalted, more suited to his nature, than any other which this world has ever known,—are facts incontrovertible as the laws of philosophy, or the demonstrations of mathematics. Evidence in support of all this can be brought from every age, in the history of man, since there has been a revelation from God on earth. We see the proof of it everywhere around us. There is scarcely a neighbourhood in our country, where the Bible is circulated, in which we cannot point you to a very considerable portion of its population, whom its truths have reclaimed from the practice of vice, and taught the practice of whatsoever things are pure, and honest, and just, and of good report.

That this distinctive and peculiar effect is produced upon every man to whom the gospel is announced, we pretend not to affirm. But we do affirm, that, besides producing this special renovation, to which we have alluded, upon a part, it, in a most remarkable degree, elevates the tone of moral feeling throughout the whole community. Wherever the Bible is freely circulated, and its doctrines carried home to the understandings of men, the aspect of society is altered; the frequency of crime is diminished; men begin to love justice, and to administer it by law; and a virtuous public opinion, that strongest safeguard of right, spreads over a nation the shield of its invisible protection. Wherever it has faithfully been brought to bear upon the human heart, even under most unpromising circumstances, it has, within a single generation, revolutionized the whole structure of society; and thus, within a few years, done more for man than all other means have for ages accomplished without it. For proof of all this, I need only refer you to the effects of the gospel in Greenland, or in South Africa, in the Society Islands, or even among the aborigines of our own country.

But before we leave this part of the subject, it may be well to pause for a moment, and inquire whether, in addition to its moral efficacy, the Bible may not exert a powerful influence upon the intellectual character of man.

And here it is scarcely necessary that I should remark, that, of all the books with which, since the invention of writing, this world has been deluged, the number of those is very small which have produced any perceptible effect on the mass of human character. By far the greater part have been, even by their cotemporaries, unnoticed and unknown. Not many a one has made its little mark upon the generation that produced it, though it sunk with that generation to utter forgetfulness. But, after the ceaseless toil of six thousand years, how few have been the works, the adamantine basis of whose reputation has stood unhurt amid the fluctuations of time, and whose impression can be traced through successive centuries, on the history of our species.

When, however, such a work appears, its effects are absolutely incalculable; and such a work, you are aware, is the Iliad of Homer. Who can estimate the results produced by the incomparable efforts of a single mind; who can tell what Greece owes to this first-born of song? Her breathing marbles, her solemn temples, her unrivalled eloquence, and her matchless verse, all point us to that transcendent genius, who, by the very splendour of his own effulgence, woke the human intellect from the slumber of ages. It was Homer who gave laws to the artist; it was Homer who inspired the poet; it was Homer who thundered in the senate; and, more than all, it was Homer who was sung by the people; and hence a nation was cast into the mould of one mighty mind, and the land of the Iliad became the region of taste, the birth-place of the arts.

Nor was this influence confined within the limits of Greece. Long after the sceptre of empire had passed westward, genius still held her court on the banks of the Ilyssus, and from the country of Homer gave laws to the world. The light, which the blind old man of Scio had kindled in Greece, shed its radiance over Italy; and thus did he awaken a second nation into intellectual existence. And we may form some idea of the power which this one work has to the present day exerted over the mind of man, by remarking, that "nation after nation, and century after century, has been able to do little more than transpose his incidents, new-name his characters, and paraphrase his sentiments."

But, considered simply as an intellectual production, who will compare the poems of Homer with the Holy Scriptures of the Old and New Testament? Where in the Iliad shall we find simplicity and pathos which shall vie with the narrative of Moses, or maxims of conduct to equal in wisdom the Proverbs of Solomon, or sublimity which does not fade away before the conceptions of Job, or David, of Isaiah or St. John? But I cannot pursue this comparison. I feel that it is doing wrong to the mind which dictated the Iliad, and to those other mighty intellects on whom the light of the holy oracles never shined. Who that has read his poem has not observed how he strove in vain to give dignity to the mythology of his time? Who has not seen how the religion of his country, unable to support the flight of his imagination, sunk powerless beneath him? It is the unseen world, where the master spirits of our race breathe freely, and are at home; and it is mournful to behold the intellect of Homer striving to free itself from the conceptions of materialism, and then sinking down in hopeless despair, to weave idle tales about Jupiter and Juno, Apollo and Diana. But the difficulties under which he laboured are abundantly illustrated by the fact, that the light which poured upon the human intellect taught other ages how unworthy was the religion of his day of the man who was compelled to use it. "It seems to me," says Longinus, "that Homer, when he describes dissensions, jealousies, tears, imprisonments, and other afflictions to his deities, bath, as much as was in his power, made the men of the Iliad gods, and the gods men. To men, when afflicted, death is the termination of evils; but he hath made not only the nature, but the miseries, of the gods eternal."

If, then, so great results have flowed from this one effort of a single mind, what may we not expect from the combined efforts of several, at least his equals in power over the human heart? If that one genius, though groping in the thick darkness of absurd idolatry, wrought so glorious a transformation in the character of his countrymen, what may we not look for from the universal dissemination of those writings, on whose authors was poured the full splendour of eternal truth? If unassisted human nature, spell-bound by the instinctive desire gy, have done so much, what may we not hope for from the supernatural efforts of pre-eminent genius, which spake as it was moved by the Holy Ghost?

GLORY.

FROM A DISCOURSE ON THE DEATH OF NICHOLAS BROWN.

THE crumbling tombstone and the gorgeous mausoleum, the sculptured marble, and the venerable cathedral, all bear witness to the instinctive desire within us to be remembered by coming generations. But how short-lived is the immortality which the works of our hands can confer! The noblest monuments of art that the world has ever seen are covered with the soil of twenty centuries. The works of the age of Pericles lie at the foot of the Acropolis in indiscriminate ruin. The ploughshare turns up the marble which the hand of Phidias had chiselled into beauty, and the Mussulman has folded his flock beneath the falling columns of the temple of Minerva. But even the works of our hands too frequently survive the memory of those who have created them. And were it otherwise, could we thus carry down to distant ages the recollection of our existence, it were surely childish to waste the energies of an immortal spirit in the effort to make it known to other times, that a being whose name was written with certain letters of the alphabet, once lived, and flourished, and died. Neither sculptured marble, nor stately column, can reveal to other ages the lineaments of the spirit; and these alone can embalm our memory in the hearts of a grateful posterity. As the stranger stands beneath the dome of St. Paul's, or treads, with religious awe, the silent aisles of Westminster Abbey, the sentiment, which is breathed from every object around him, is, the utter emptiness of sublunary glory......The fine arts, obedient to private affection or public gratitude, have here imbodied, in every form, the finest conceptions of which their age was capable. Each one of these monuments has been watered by the tears of the widow, the orphan, or the patriot. But generations have passed away, and mourners and mourned have sunk together into forgetfulness. The aged crone, or the smooth-tongued beadle, as now he hurries you through aisles and chapel, utters, with measured cadence and unmeaning tone, for the thousandth time, the name and lineage of the once honoured dead; and then gladly dismisses you, to repeat again his well-conned lesson to another group of idle passers-by. Such, in its most august form, is all the immortality that matter can confer.....It is by what we ourselves have done, and not by what others have done for us, that we shall be remembered by after ages. It is by thought that has aroused my intellect from its slumbers, which has "given lustre to virtue, and dignity to truth," or by those examples which have inflamed my soul with the love of goodness, and not by means of sculptured marble, that I hold communion with Shakspeare and Milton, with Johnson and Burke, with Howard and Wilberforce.

Painted by Ames   Engraved by Gross

Wm. H. Prescott

WILLIAM H. PRESCOTT.

[Born 1796. Died 1859.]

THIS eminent historian was born in Salem, Massachusetts, on the fourth of May, 1796. His father, William Prescott, LL. D., who died at the good old age of eighty-two, in the last month of 1844, was a lawyer, and ranked among the noblest ornaments of his profession; and the general grief of the community at his loss, when he had so long been withdrawn from business and public life, afforded the most touching and honourable tribute to his intellectual and moral worth.* His grandfather was Colonel William Prescott, who commanded the American forces stationed in the redoubt at the memorable Battle of Bunker Hill, on the seventeenth of June, 1775, and with the undisciplined New England militia twice broke the ranks of the British grenadiers and light infantry, and drove them in confusion and dismay to their boats.† His great-grandfather was also a man of much consideration, and was chosen the agent of the province to the English court in 1738, but declined the office, which was subsequently filled by Edmund Quincy. Few men have more reason to take an honest pride in their descent.

In his twelfth year Mr. Prescott removed with his family to Boston, and was there placed under the care of the Reverend Dr. Gardiner, one of the pupils of the celebrated Dr. Parr, by whom he was carefully instructed in the ancient classics, and carried through a range of study in the Latin and Greek authors, quite beyond the limits usually reached at that time in our public seminaries. After entering Harvard University, which he did in 1811, one year in advance, he continued his predi-

lections for the ancient masters; and while he gave little attention to the mathematics and the sister sciences, he employed his leisure hours, especially in the latter portion of his college life, exclusively in the study of his favourite authors. It was a matter of taste with him, but considering his subsequent occupations, he has not had reason to repent it. The chaste richness of his style could have resulted only from the happiest union of learning with genius.

On his leaving the university, in 1814, he embraced the study of the law, but prepared to give a preliminary year to more general reading. He had already made good progress in a course of historical study, when he was stopped by a violent rheumatic inflammation of the eye, occasioned probably by a too free use of it, especially at night, in the study of the Greek historians, with which he chiefly occupied himself. An accidental blow in college had previously deprived him of the sight of one of his eyes, though this is not apparent from any change in the appearance of it. This threw the whole burden of study on the remaining eye, which gave way more easily on that account. After a severe illness, in which, for a while, he was perfectly blind, he recovered his vision, but so much enfeebled that he was compelled to abandon his profession and reading altogether.

In the autumn of 1815 he went to Europe, and passed two years in England, France, and Italy; too young to derive a lasting profit from his travels, but yet, probably, enjoying the novel scenes opened to him with higher relish than he would at a later period. On the classic ground of Italy he revelled as in a land of enchantment. But his associations were wholly with the ancient people, who had passed away, and he felt an enthusiasm which might have cooled under the criticism of a riper age, as he trod the soil of Cicero and the Cæsars. After a gay dream of two years in the transatlantic countries, he returned to Boston, but not to resume his studies, or even to open a volume, for his eye was still

* The late William Prescott presented to his associates, throughout a long life, whether at the bar, or on the bench, or in the dignified retirement of his late years, such an eminent example of modest talent, substantial learning, and unpretending wisdom, with affable manners, strong social affections, absolute fidelity in every relation of life, and probity beyond the slightest suspicion of reproach, as rarely adorns even the highest walks of professional excellence. Concerning whom may it be more appropriately asked than of him,

"Cui Pudor, et Justitiæ soror,
Incorrupta Fides, nudaque Veritas,
Quando ullum invenient parem?"—*Daniel Webster.*

† Dr. Young's Discourse, occasioned by the Death of the Honourable William Prescott, LL.D

47

too susceptible of inflammation. In the course of a few years he was married to a lady of his own city, and he remarks in a letter before me, that " contrary to the assertion of La Bruyère, who somewhere says that ' the most fortunate husband finds reason to regret his condition, at least once in every twenty-four hours,' I may truly say that I have found no such day in the quarter of a century that Providence has spared us to each other."

In the beautiful library of Mr. Prescott at Boston, so richly stored with the rare printed works and manuscripts used in the composition of his histories, with portraits of the Catholic sovereigns and their servants who are his heroes, and with trophies more glorious than have been won in the tented fields of war which have been sent him by admiring scholars in foreign nations, I observed suspended over one of the book-cases two swords, crossed with an Indian calumet, and was told that they were worn at Bunker Hill by the great-grandsires of his children, one in the people's service, the other in the king's. Would that the two countries might for ever be united in as firm a bond of peace as that which binds these descendants of their two champions on that memorable day.

As Mr. Prescott grew older the inflammatory tendency of the system diminished, and his eye became less sensible to the fatigue of study. At first he used it sparingly, but in a few years he so far recovered it that he was enabled to indulge his taste for books to a very reasonable extent, and the deficiency was made up by a reader. He now devoted himself to the study of the continental languages and literatures, taking copious notes, and exercising his pen very freely in critical and miscellaneous essays, chiefly in the North American Review. A selection of thirteen of the papers written in this period has recently been published, and they are remarkable for the sustained ease and felicity of expression, the fine enthusiasm and natural brilliancy, which in a still more eminent degree distinguish his later productions. The first article is a memoir of Charles Brockden Brown, to which I have been indebted in preparing the notice of that novelist in the present volume. Mr. Prescott does full justice to the remarkable series of fictions which " constitute an epoch in the ornamental literature of America," though I disagree with him, as I

have elsewhere intimated, upon some points in his criticism of Wieland. The subjects of the other papers are the Asylum for the Blind, Irving's Conquest of Granada, Cervantes, Molière, Chateaubriand's English Literature, Sir Walter Scott, Scottish Song, Bancroft's United States, Italian Narrative Poetry, Poetry and Romance of the Italians, and Da Ponte's Observations on Italian Literature. They but imperfectly indicate the range of his studies and attainments in literary and social history, as I find by consulting some of his other contributions to the Review; but they show that he was always equal to his theme in research, hearty appreciation, and acute critical judgment. The book is " affectionately dedicated" to George Ticknor, to " remind him of studies pursued together in earlier days."*

Mr. Prescott kept before his dreaming vision the hopes of one day entering the arena of history, and achieving something that posterity might not willingly let die. Aspirations to this effect are in his diary as far back as 1819. He there allows ten years for preliminary studies, and ten more for the investigation and preparation of some specific historical work. The event nearly corresponded with this preconceived arrangement, and considering the lapse of time embraced by it, it is singular.

The subject which he selected for his first performance, the reign of the sovereigns under whose auspices the existence of this continent was first revealed to Europe, was a suitable one for an American. The period in which lived Isabella of Castile, the statesman Ximenes, the soldier Cordova, and the navigator Columbus; in which the empire of the Moors was subdued, the Inquisition was established, the Jews were driven from Spain, and a new world was discovered and colonized, was not lacking in interest or importance, indeed, to tempt the most eminent historians to its illustration: yet the ground may be said to have been untrodden, since the only

* I should do myself injustice if I neglected to pay some tribute of respect to this gentleman, whose extraordinary erudition and elegant taste are so well known among contemporary scholars. He has published little, but that little makes us anxious for the appearance of some compositions upon which he is understood to have been many years engaged, among which is an elaborate History of the Spanish Language and Literature. His eminent qualifications, and the fulness of his resources, warrant the belief that this will be one of the most admirable works in our literature.

lives of Ferdinand and Isabella that had appeared are the meagre and unsatisfactory ones of the Abbé Mignot and Rupert Becker, one published in Paris in 1766, and the other in Prague in 1790.

Mr. Alexander H. Everett was our minister at the court of Spain when Mr. Prescott decided upon the choice of his subject, and through his aid and that of two other American gentlemen residing at the time in the Peninsula, he succeeded in obtaining whatever was known to exist that could not be supplied by the public and private libraries of his own city. Among the works thus procured were some brought to light by the researches of recent Spanish scholars, in the peculiar freedom of inquiry they have enjoyed, which gave him a great advantage over previous historians. In his preface he refers particularly to Llorente's History of the Inquisition, the analysis of the political institutions of the kingdom by such writers as Marina, Sempere, and Capmany; the version of the Spanish-Arab chronicles by Conde; the collections of Navarette, and the illustrations of the reign of Isabella by Clemencin, the Secretary of the Royal Academy of History; besides which he succeeded in obtaining various contemporary manuscripts, covering the whole ground of the narrative, none of which had been printed, and some of which were but little known to Spanish scholars.

When these literary treasures reached him, Mr. Prescott was not able to read even the title-pages of the volumes. He had strained the nerve of his eye by careless use of it, and it was several years before it recovered so far as to allow him to tax it again. By the sight of his Spanish treasures lying unexplored before him, he was filled with despair. He determined to try whether he could make the ears do the work of the eyes. He taught his reader, unacquainted with any language but his own, to pronounce the Spanish, though not exactly in the accent of the Court of Madrid. He read at a slow and stumbling pace, while the historian listened with painful attention. Practice at length made the work easier for both, though the reader never understood a word of his author. In this way they ploughed along patiently through seven Spanish quartos. He found at last he could go over about two-thirds as much in an hour as he could when read to in English. The ex-

periment was made, and he became convinced of the practicability of substituting the ear for the eye. He was overjoyed, for his library was no longer to consist of sealed volumes.

He now obtained the services of a secretary acquainted with the different ancient and modern languages. Still there were many impediments to overcome. His eye, however, gradually improved, and he could use it by daylight, (never again in the evening,) a few hours; though this was not till after some years, and then with repeated intervals of weeks, and sometimes months of debility. Many a chapter, and some of the severest, in Ferdinand and Isabella, were written almost wholly with the aid of the eyes of his secretary. His *modus operandi* was necessarily peculiar. He selected, first, all the authorities in the different languages that could bear on the topic to be discussed. He then listened to the reading of them, one after another, dictating very copious notes on each. When the survey was completed, a large pile of notes was amassed, which were read to him over and over again, until the whole had been embraced by his mind, when they were fused down into the consecutive contents of a chapter. When the subject was complex, and not pure narrative, requiring a great variety of reference, and sifting of contradictory authorities, the work must have been very difficult. But it strengthened memory, kept his faculties wide awake, and taught him to generalize; for the little details slipped through the holes in the memory.

His labour did not end with this process. He found it as difficult to write as to read, and procured in London a writing-case for the blind. This he could use in the dark as well as in the light. The characters, indeed, might pass for hieroglyphics, but they were deciphered by his secretary, and transferred by him to a legible form in a fair copy. Yet I have heard him say his hair sometimes stood on end at the woful blunders and misconceptions of the original, which every now and then, escaping detection, found their way into the first proof of the printer.

Amid such difficulties was the composition of Ferdinand and Isabella heroically completed, at the end of something less than ten years from its commencement. He remembered that Johnson says Milton gave up his History of England because it was scarcely possible to write history with the eyes of others;* and was stimulated in the midst of his embarrassments to overcome them. Well might he feel a proud satisfaction in conquering the obstacles of nature.

Mr. Prescott had four copies of the History first printed for himself, and had so little confidence in its immediate success, that he had thought of postponing the publication till after his death, but his father told him "the man who writes a book which he is afraid to publish is a coward." This decided him. The work was published in the beginning of 1838. Its reception in his own country and in all parts of Europe was such as to repay him, if any thing could, for the long night of toil by which it had been produced. It quickly made its appearance in London. It was praised in the Quarterly and Edinburgh Reviews, and in the leading journals, and has since gone through many editions in England, and twenty in the United States. It was republished in Paris, and translated into Spanish, German, and Italian. It was everywhere recognised at once as a great history. The voice of posterity was anticipated : by the unanimous judgment of the learned it was admitted without probation into the circle of immortal works.

Mr. Prescott allowed himself but short repose. He was not content to rest upon his laurels, nor fearful of endangering his great reputation by a second effort. The success of his first work gave him advantages he had not before possessed of collecting materials. He was made a member of the Royal Academy of Madrid, and its rich collections by Muñoz, the historiographer of the Indies, by Ponçe, from the archives at Seville, and by Navarette, its president, were thrown open to him, with permission to have copies of whatever he desired. From these collections, the results of half a century's diligent and intelligent researches, he obtained a mass of authentic and original documents relating to the conquest and settlement of Mexico and Peru, comprising altogether about eight thousand folio pages, some of which were of the highest interest and importance. The descendant and representative of Cortes, also, the Duke

of Monteleone, of Sicily, opened to him the archives of his family, from which were obtained some interesting particulars respecting the conquestador's biography. His friend, the accomplished and highly respected Don Calderon de la Barca, now resident minister at Washington from the court of Madrid, was at that time in the same capacity in Mexico, where his estimable qualities had their natural effect in securing to him every privilege he desired, and through him he obtained such materials illustrative of his subject as were existing in the country itself. The manuscripts of the Tezcucan historian Ixtlilxochitl, described as the "Livy of Anahuac;" the works of Veytia, Sahagun, Boturini, and Camargo; with the splendid pictorial works of Dupaix and Kingsborough, and whatever else was published, were also gathered round him before he entered fully upon his studies.

The History of the Conquest of Mexico was written under much greater advantages of eyesight, which had been so far improved that he was enabled to do most of the reading himself, restricting always this part of labour to the day. His writing was still conducted in the same manner as has been already described, for he had ever found the process of writing a severe tax on the eye.

Mr. Prescott's second historical work was even more successful than the first. Messrs. Harpers of New York sold nearly seven thousand copies of it in a single year. It was published at the same time in London, where it quickly passed to a second edition. It was reprinted in Paris, and was translated there, as well as in Berlin, Rome, Madrid, and Mexico. The Mexican translator, a person of some consideration in that country, advertised that he should accommodate the offensive opinions in religion and politics to the more received ideas of the Mexicans! But the version which appeared in Madrid being faithful, the Spanish Americans have perhaps had an opportunity to see the work in an unmutilated form. Among the evidences of its success abroad was the election of Mr. Prescott into the Institute of France.

The death of the venerable father of the historian for a time interrupted his studies, or The Conquest of Peru, upon which he was engaged when that event occured, was published in 1847. In 1850, Mr. Prescott visited England, Scotland and the Continent.

---

* The words of Johnson are. "To compile a history from various authors, when they can only be consulted by other eyes, is not easy, nor possible, but with more skilful and attentive help than can be commonly obtained."—*Life of Milton, quoted in preface to Ferdinand and Isabella.*

In December, 1855, appeared vols. 1 and 2 of his History of Philip the Second, and in December, 1858, vol. 3d. For this work he had assembled the largest mass of materials, and upon it he proposed to employ the last ten years of his historical life, but which he never lived to complete. The Life of Charles the V., after his Abdication, being a supplement to the work of Robertson, was published with the original work in 3 vols., 8vo., in 1857. Early in 1858, Mr. Prescott had a slight stroke of paralysis from the effect of which he never entirely recovered. On the 28th of January, 1859, he rose apparently well; a few hours afterward he was seized with a second stroke of paralysis, and expired about 2 o'clock in the afternoon, leaving a widow, two sons, and a daughter.

Mr. Prescott is undoubtedly entitled to a prominent place in the first rank of historians. With extraordinary industry he explores every source of information relating to his subjects, and with sagacity as remarkable decides between conflicting authorities and rejects improbable relations. His judgment of character is calm, comprehensive, and profoundly just. He enters into the midst of an age, and with all its influences about him, estimates its actors and its deeds. His arrangement of facts is always effective, and his style flowing, familiar, singularly transparent, and marked throughout with the most felicitous expressions.

Whatever may be the comparative merits of the four great histories he has already published, as intellectual efforts, there is little room to doubt that The Conquest of Mexico will continue to be the most popular. It is justly remarked in the Edinburgh Review, that, considered merely as a work of amusement, it will bear a favourable comparison with the best romances in the language. The careful, judicious, and comprehensive essay on the Aztec civilization, with which it opens, is not inferior in interest to the wonderful drama to which it is an epilogue. The scenery, which is sketched with remarkable vividness and accuracy, is wonderful, beautiful, and peculiar. The characters are various, strongly marked, and not more numerous than is necessary for the purposes of art. Cortez himself is a knight errant, "filled with the spirit of romantic enterprise," yet a skilful general, fruitful of resources, and of almost superhuman energies; of extraordinary cunning, but without any rectitude of judgment; a bigoted churchman, yet having no sympathy with virtue; of kind manners, but remorseless in his cruelties. His associates, Valasquez, Ordaz, Sandoval, Alvarado, and Guatemozin, the last of the priest Olmedo, the heroine Doña Marina, and others of whom we have glimpses more or less distinct, seem to have been formed as well to fill their places in the written history, as to act their parts in the crusade. And the philosophical king of Tezcuco, and Montezuma, whose character and misfortunes are reflected in his mild and melancholy face, and Guatemozin, the last of the emperors, and other Aztecs, in many of the higher qualities of civilization superior to their invaders, and inferior in scarcely any thing but a knowledge of the art of war, are grouped and contrasted most effectively with such characters as are more familiar in the scenes of history.

The biographical and bibliographical information and criticism contained in notes and addenda to the different books of Ferdinand and Isabella and The Conquest of Mexico, form one of the most attractive of their features, and would alone sustain a high reputation for learning and judgment.

Mr. Prescott perhaps excels most in description and narration, but his histories combine in a high degree almost every merit that can belong to such works. They are pervaded by a truly and profoundly philosophical spirit, the more deserving of recognition because it is natural and unobtrusive, and are distinguished above all others for their uniform candour, a quality which might reasonably be demanded of an American writing of early European policy and adventure.

In private life I may be permitted to add to this account, no man was more admired and beloved than Mr. Prescott. He was not more remarkable for his abilities and acquirements than for his amiability, simplicity, and highbred courtesy. He was one of those men who are a blessing as well as an honour to the community in which they live. I deem it not improper thus to state what every Bostonian feels to be true, because it adds very greatly in my opinion to the value of any work of history, to know that its author, to research, discrimination, and love of his subject, adds a truly conscientious spirit.

ISABELLA OF SPAIN AND ELIZABETH OF ENGLAND.

FROM FERDINAND AND ISABELLA.

It is in the amiable qualities of her sex that Isabella's superiority becomes most apparent over her illustrious namesake, Elizabeth of England,* whose history presents some features parallel to her own. Both were disciplined in early life by the teachings of that stern nurse of wisdom, adversity. Both were made to experience the deepest humiliation at the hands of their nearest relative, who should have cherished and protected them. Both succeeded in establishing themselves on the throne after the most precarious vicissitudes. Each conducted her kingdom, through a long and triumphant reign, to a height of glory which it had never before reached. Both lived to see the vanity of all earthly grandeur, and to fall the victims of an inconsolable melancholy; and both left behind an illustrious name, unrivalled in the subsequent annals of the country.

But with these few circumstances of their history, the resemblance ceases. Their characters afford scarcely a point of contact. Elizabeth, inheriting a large share of the bold and bluff King Harry's temperament, was haughty, arrogant, coarse, and irascible; while with these fiercer qualities she mingled deep dissimulation and strange irresolution. Isabella, on the other hand, tempered the dignity of royal station with the most bland and courteous manners. Once resolved, she was constant in her purposes; and her conduct in public and private life was characterized by candour and integrity. Both may be said to have shown that magnanimity which is implied by the accomplishment of great objects in the face of great obstacles. But Elizabeth was desperately selfish; she was incapable of forgiving, not merely a real injury, but the slightest affront to her vanity; and she was merciless in exacting retribution. Isabella, on the other hand, lived only for others,— was ready at all times to sacrifice self to considerations of public duty; and, far from personal resentments, showed the greatest condescension and kindness to those who had most sensibly injured her; while her benevolent heart sought every means to mitigate the authorized severities of the law, even toward the guilty.

Both possessed rare fortitude. Isabella, indeed, was placed in situations which demanded more frequent and higher displays of it than her rival; but no one will doubt a full measure of this quality in the daughter of Henry the Eighth. Elizabeth was better educated, and every way more highly accomplished than Isabella. But the latter knew enough to maintain her station with dignity; and she encouraged learning by a munificent patronage. The masculine powers and passions of Elizabeth seemed to divorce her in a great measure from the peculiar attributes of her sex; at least from those which constitute its peculiar charm; for she had abundance of its foibles—a coquetry

* Isabel, the name of the Catholic queen, is correctly rendered into English by that of Elizabeth.

and love of admiration which age could not chill; a levity most careless, if not criminal; and a fondness for dress and tawdry magnificence of ornament, which was ridiculous, or disgusting, according to the different periods of life in which it was indulged. Isabella, on the other hand, distinguished through life for decorum of manners and purity beyond the breath of calumny, was content with the legitimate affection which she could inspire within the range of her domestic circle. Far from a frivolous affectation of ornament or dress, she was most simple in her own attire, and seemed to set no value on her jewels, but as they could serve the necessities of the state; when they could be no longer useful in this way, she gave them away to her friends.

Both were uncommonly sagacious in the selection of their ministers; though Elizabeth was drawn into some errors in this particular by her levity, as was Isabella by religious feeling. It was this, combined with her excessive humility, which led to the only grave errors in the administration of the latter. Her rival fell into no such errors; and she was a stranger to the amiable qualities which led to them. Her conduct was certainly not controlled by religious principle; and, though the bulwark of the Protestant faith, it might be difficult to say whether she were at heart most a Protestant or a Catholic. She viewed religion in its connection with the state, in other words, with herself; and she took measures for enforcing conformity to her own views, not a whit less despotic, and scarcely less sanguinary, than those countenanced for conscience' sake by her more bigoted rival.

This feature of bigotry, which has thrown a shade over Isabella's otherwise beautiful character, might lead to a disparagement of her intellectual power compared with that of the English queen. To estimate this aright, we must contemplate the results of their respective reigns. Elizabeth found all the materials of prosperity at hand, and availed herself of them most ably to build up a solid fabric of national grandeur. Isabella created these materials. She saw the faculties of her people locked up in a deathlike lethargy, and she breathed into them the breath of life for those great and heroic enterprises which terminated in such glorious consequences to the monarchy. It is when viewed from the depressed position of her early days, that the achievements of her reign seem scarcely less than miraculous. The masculine genius of the English queen stands out relieved beyond its natural dimensions by its separation from the softer qualities of her sex. While her rival's, like some vast, but symmetrical edifice, loses in appearance somewhat of its actual grandeur from the perfect harmony of its proportions.

The circumstances of their deaths, which were somewhat similar, displayed the great dissimilarity of their characters. Both pined amidst their royal state, a prey to incurable despondency rather than any marked bodily distemper. In Elizabeth it sprung from wounded vanity, a sullen conviction that she had outlived the admiration on which she had so long fed,—and even the solace of friendship and the attachment of her subjects. Nor did she seek consolation, where alone it was to be found, in that sad hour. Isabella, on the other hand, sunk under a too acute sensibility to the sufferings of others. But, amidst the gloom which gathered around her, she looked with the eye of faith to the brighter prospects which unfolded of the future; and when she resigned her last breath, it was amidst the tears and universal lamentations of her people.

THE KING OF TEZCUCO.
FROM THE CONQUEST OF MEXICO.

NEZAHUALCOYOTL divided the burden of government among a number of departments, as the council of war, the council of finance, the council of justice. This last was a court of supreme authority, both in civil and criminal matters, receiving appeals from the lower tribunals of the provinces, which were obliged to make a full report, every four months, or eighty days, of their own proceedings to this higher judicature. In all these bodies, a certain number of citizens were allowed to have seats with the nobles and professional dignitaries. There was, however, another body, a council of state, for aiding the king in the despatch of business, and advising him in matters of importance, which was drawn altogether from the highest order of chiefs. It consisted of fourteen members; and they had seats provided for them at the royal table.

Lastly, there was an extraordinary tribunal, called the council of music, but which, differing from the import of its name, was devoted to the encouragement of science and art. Works on astronomy, chronology, history, or any other science, were required to be submitted to its judgment before they could be made public..... This body, which was drawn from the best instructed persons in the kingdom, with little regard to rank, had supervision of all the productions of art, and of the nicer fabrics. It decided on the qualifications of the professors in the various branches of science, on the fidelity of their instructions to their pupils, the deficiency of which was severely punished, and it instituted examinations of these latter. In short, it was a general board of education for the country. On stated days, historical compositions, and poems treating of moral or traditional topics, were recited before it by their authors. Seats were provided for the three crowned heads of the empire, who deliberated with the other members on the respective merits of the pieces, and distributed prizes of value to the successful competitors.

Such are the marvellous accounts transmitted to us of this institution; an institution certainly not to have been expected among the Aborigines of America. It is calculated to give us a higher idea of the refinement of the people than even .he noble architectural remains which still cover some parts of the continent. Architecture is, to a certain extent, a sensual gratification. It addresses itself to the eye, and affords the best scope for the parade of barbaric pomp and splendour. It is the form in which the revenues of a semi-civilized people are most likely to be lavished. The most gaudy and ostentatious specimens of it, and sometimes the most stupendous, have been reared by such hands. It is one of the first steps in the great march of civilization. But the institution in question was evidence of still higher refinement. It was a literary luxury; and argued the existence of a taste in the nation, which relied for its gratification on pleasures of a purely intellectual character.

The influence of this academy must have been most propitious to the capital, which became the nursery, not only of such sciences as could be compassed by the scholarship of the period, but of various useful and ornamental arts. Its historians, orators, and poets were celebrated throughout the country. Its archives, for which accommodations were provided in the royal palace, were stored with the records of primitive ages. Its idiom, more polished than the Mexican, was indeed the purest of all the Nahuatlac dialects; and continued, long after the Conquest, to be that in which the best productions of the native races were composed. Tezcuco claimed the glory of being the Athens of the Western World.

Among the most illustrious of her bards was the emperor himself,—for the Tezcucan writers claim this title for their chief, as head of the imperial alliance. He, doubtless, appeared as a competitor before that very academy where he so often sat as a critic. Many of his odes descended to a late generation, and are still preserved, perhaps, in some of the dusty repositories of Mexico or Spain. The historian, Ixtlilxochitl, has left a translation, in Castilian, of one of the poems of his royal ancestor. It is not easy to render his version into corresponding English rhyme without the perfume of the original escaping in this double filtration. They remind one of the rich breathings of Spanish-Arab poetry, in which an ardent imagination is tempered by a not unpleasing and moral melancholy. But, though sufficiently florid in diction, they are generally free from the meretricious ornaments and hyperbole with which the minstrelsy of the East is usually tainted. They turn on the vanities and mutability of human life; a topic very natural for a monarch who had himself experienced the strangest mutations of fortune. There is mingled in the lament of the Tezcucan bard, however, an Epicurean philosophy, which seeks relief from the fears of the future in the joys of the present. "Banish care," he says; "if there are bounds to pleasure, the saddest life must also have an end. Then weave the chaplet of flowers, and sing thy songs in praise of the all-powerful God; for the glory of this world soon fadeth away. Rejoice in the green freshness of thy spring; for the day will come when thou shalt sigh for these joys in vain; when the sceptre shall pass from thy hands, thy servants shall wander desolate in thy courts, thy sons, and the sons of thy nobles, shall drink the dregs of distress, and all the pomp of thy victories and triumphs shall live only in their recollection. Yet the remembrance of the just shall not pass away from the nations, and the good thou hast done shall ever be held in honour. The goods of this life, its glories and its riches, are but lent to us, its substance is but an illusory shadow, and the things of to-day shall change on the coming of the morrow. Then gather the fairest flowers from thy gardens to bind round thy brow, and seize the joys of the present ere they perish."

But the hours of the Tezcucan monarch were not all passed in idle dalliance with the Muse, nor in the sober contemplations of philosophy, as at a later period. In the freshness of youth and early manhood he led the allied armies in their annual expeditions, which were certain to result in a wider extent of territory to the empire. In the intervals of peace he fostered those productive arts which are the surest sources of public prosperity. He encouraged agriculture above all; and there was scarcely a spot so rude, or a steep so inaccessible, as not to confess the power of cultivation. The land was covered with a busy population, and towns and cities sprung up in places since deserted, or dwindled into miserable villages.

From resources thus enlarged by conquest and domestic industry, the monarch drew the means for the large consumption of his own numerous household, and for the costly works which he executed for the convenience and embellishment of the capital. He filled it with stately edifices for his nobles, whose constant attendance he was anxious to secure at his court. He erected a magnificent pile of buildings which might serve both for a royal residence and for the public offices. It extended, from east to west, twelve hundred and thirty-four yards, and from north to south nine hundred and seventy-eight. It was encompassed by a wall of unburnt bricks and cement, six feet wide and nine high, for one-half of the circumference, and fifteen feet high for the other half. Within this enclosure were two courts. The outer one was used as the great market-place of the city; and continued to be so until long after the Conquest,—if, indeed, it is not now. The interior court was surrounded by the council-chambers and halls of justice. There were also accommodations there for the foreign ambassadors; and a spacious saloon, with apartments opening into it for men of science and poets, who pursued their studies in this retreat, or met together to hold converse under its marble porticoes. In this quarter, also, were kept the public archives; which fared better under the Indian dynasty than they have since under their European successors.

Adjoining this court were the apartments of the king, including those for the royal harem, as liberally supplied with beauties as that of an eastern sultan. Their walls were incrusted with alabasters and richly tinted stucco, or hung with gorgeous tapestries of variegated feather-work. They led through long arcades, and through intricate labyrinths of shrubbery, into gardens where baths and sparkling fountains were overshadowed by tall groves of cedar and cypress. The basins of water were well stocked with fish of various kinds, and the aviaries with birds glowing in all the gaudy plumage of the tropics. Many birds and animals, which could not be obtained alive, were represented in gold and silver so skilfully, as to have furnished the great naturalist, Hernandez, with models for his work.

Accommodations on a princely scale were provided for the sovereigns of Mexico and Tlacopan, when they visited the court. The whole of this lordly pile contained three hundred apartments, some of them fifty yards square. The height of the building is not mentioned. It was probably not great; but supplied the requisite room by the immense extent of ground which it covered. The interior was doubtless constructed of light materials, especially of the rich woods, which, in that country, are remarkable, when polished, for the brilliancy and variety of their colours. That the more solid materials of stone stucco were also liberally employed is proved by the remains at the present day; remains which have furnished an inexhaustible quarry for the churches and other edifices since erected by the Spaniards on the site of the ancient city.

We are not informed of the time occupied in building this palace. But two hundred thousand workmen, it is said, were employed on it! However this may be, it is certain that the Tezcucan monarchs, like those of Asia and ancient Egypt, had the control of immense masses of men, and would sometimes turn the whole population of a conquered city, including the women, into the public works. The most gigantic monuments of architecture which the world has witnessed would never have been reared by the hands of freemen.

Adjoining the palace were buildings for the king's children, who by his various wives amounted to no less than sixty sons and fifty daughters. Here they were instructed in all the exercises and accomplishments suited to their station; comprehending, what would scarcely find a place in a royal education on the other side of the Atlantic, the arts of working in metals, jewelry, and feather-mosaic. Once in every four months, the whole household, not excepting the youngest, and including all the officers and attendants on the king's person, assembled in a grand saloon of the palace to listen to a discourse from an orator, probably one of the priesthood. The princes, on this occasion, were all dressed in *nequen*, the coarsest manufacture of the country. The preacher began by enlarging on the obligations of morality, and of respect for the gods, especially important in persons whose rank gave such additional weight to example. He occasionally seasoned his homily with a pertinent application to his audience, if any member of it had been guilty of a notorious delinquency. From this wholesome admonition the monarch himself was not exempted, and the orator boldly reminded him of his paramount duty to show respect for his own laws. The king, so far from taking umbrage, received the lesson with humility; and the audience, we are assured, were often melted into tears by the eloquence of the preacher. This curious scene may remind one of similar usages in the Asiatic and Egyptian despotisms, where the sovereign occasionally condescended to stoop from his pride of place, and allow his memory to be refreshed with the conviction of his own mortality. It soothed the feelings of the subject to find himself thus placed, though but for a moment, on a level with his king; while it cost little to the latter, who was removed too far from his people to suffer any thing by this short-lived familiarity. It is probable that such an act of public humiliation would have found less favour with a prince less absolute.

Nezahualcoyotl's fondness for magnificence was shown in his numerous villas, which were embellished with all that could make a rural retreat delightful. His favourite residence was at Tezcotzinco; a conical hill about two leagues from the capital. It was laid out in terraces, or hanging gardens, having a flight of steps five hundred and twenty in number, many of them hewn in the natural porphyry. In the garden on the summit was a reservoir of water, fed by an aqueduct that was carried over hill and valley, for several miles, on huge buttresses of masonry. A large rock stood in the midst of this basin, sculptured with the hieroglyphics representing the years of Nezahualcoyotl's reign and his principal achievements in each. On a lower level were three other reservoirs, in each of which stood a marble statue of a woman, emblematical of the three states of the empire. Another tank contained a winged lion,(?) cut out of the solid rock, bearing in his mouth the portrait of the emperor. His likeness had been executed in gold, wood, feather-work, and stone, but this was the only one which pleased him.

From these copious basins the water was distributed in numerous channels through the gardens, or was made to tumble over the rocks in cascades, shedding refreshing dews on the flowers and odoriferous shrubs below. In the depths of this fragrant wilderness, marble porticoes and pavilions were erected, and baths excavated in the solid porphyry, which are still shown by the ignorant natives as the "Baths of Montezuma!" The visiter descended by steps cut in the living stone, and polished so bright as to reflect like mirrors. Toward the base of the hill, in the midst of cedar groves, whose gigantic branches threw a refreshing coolness over the verdure in the sultriest seasons of the year, rose the royal villa with its light arcades and airy halls, drinking in the sweet perfumes of the gardens. Here the monarch often retired to throw off the burden of state, and refresh his wearied spirits in the society of his favourite wives, reposing during the noontide heats in the embowering shades of his paradise, or mingling, in the cool of the evening, in their festive sports and dances. Here he entertained his imperial brothers of Mexico and Tlacopan, and followed the hardier pleasures of the chase in the noble woods that stretched for miles around his villa, flourishing in all their primeval majesty. Here, too, he often repaired in the latter days of his life, when age

48

had tempered ambition and cooled the ardour of his blood, to pursue in solitude the studies of philosophy and gather wisdom from meditation.

The extraordinary accounts of the Tezcucan architecture are confirmed, in the main, by the relics which still cover the hill of Tezcotzinco, or are half-buried beneath its surface. They attract little attention, indeed, in the country, where their true history has long since passed into oblivion; while the traveller, whose curiosity leads him to the spot, speculates on their probable origin, and, as he stumbles over the huge fragments of sculptured porphyry and granite, refers them to the primitive races who spread their colossal architecture over the country long before the coming of the Acolhuans and the Aztecs.

The Tezcucan princes were used to entertain a great number of concubines. They had but one lawful wife, to whose issue the crown descended. Nezahualcoyotl remained unmarried to a late period. He was disappointed in an early attachment, as the princess, who had been educated in privacy to be the partner of his throne, gave her hand to another. The injured monarch submitted the affair to the proper tribunal. The parties, however, were proved to have been ignorant of the destination of the lady; and the court, with an independence which reflects equal honour on the judges who could give, and the monarch who could receive the sentence, acquitted the young couple. This story is sadly contrasted by the following.

The king devoured his chagrin in the solitude of his beautiful villa of Tezcotzinco, or sought to divert it by travelling. On one of his journeys he was hospitably entertained by a potent vassal, the old lord of Tepechpan, who, to do his sovereign more honour, caused him to be attended at the banquet by a noble maiden, betrothed to himself, and who, after the fashion of the country, had been educated under his own roof. She was of the blood royal of Mexico, and nearly related, moreover, to the Tezcucan monarch. The latter, who had all the amorous temperament of the South, was captivated by the grace and personal charms of the youthful Hebe, and conceived a violent passion for her. He did not disclose it to any one, however, but, on his return home, resolved to gratify it, though at the expense of his own honour, by sweeping away the only obstacle which stood in his path.

He accordingly sent an order to the chief of Tepechpan to take command of an expedition set on foot against the Tlascalans. At the same time he instructed two Tezcucan chiefs to keep near the person of the old lord, and bring him into the thickest of the fight, where he might lose his life. He assured them this had been forfeited by a great crime, but that, from regard for his vassal's past services, he was willing to cover up his disgrace by an honourable death.

The veteran, who had long lived in retirement on his estates, saw himself, with astonishment, called so suddenly and needlessly into action, for which so many younger men were better fitted. He suspected the cause, and, in the farewell enter

2 1 2

tainment to his friends, uttered a presentiment of his sad destiny. His predictions were too soon verified; and a few weeks placed the hand of his virgin bride at her own disposal.

Nezahualcoyotl did not think it prudent to break his passion publicly to the princess so soon after the death of his victim. He opened a correspondence with her through a female relative, and expressed his deep sympathy for her loss. At the same time, he tendered the best consolation in his power, by an offer of his heart and hand. Her former lover had been too well stricken in years for the maiden to remain long inconsolable. She was not aware of the perfidious plot against his life; and, after a decent time, she was ready to comply with her duty, by placing herself at the disposal of her royal kinsman.

It was arranged by the king, in order to give a more natural aspect to the affair, and prevent all suspicion of the unworthy part he had acted, that the princess should present herself in his grounds at Tezcotzinco to witness some public ceremony there. Nezahualcoyotl was standing in a balcony of the palace when she appeared, and inquired, as if struck with her beauty for the first time, "who the lovely young creature was in his gardens." When his courtiers had acquainted him with her name and rank, he ordered her to be conducted to the palace, that she might receive the attention due to her station. The interview was soon followed by a public declaration of his passion; and the marriage was celebrated not long after with great pomp, in the presence of his court, and of his brother monarchs of Mexico and Tlacopan.

This story, which furnishes so obvious a counterpart to that of David and Uriah, is told with great circumstantiality, both by the king's son and grandson, from whose narratives Ixtlilxochitl derived it. They stigmatize the action as the basest in their great ancestor's life. It is indeed too base not to leave an indelible stain on any character, however pure in other respects, and exalted.

The king was strict in the execution of his laws, though his natural disposition led him to temper justice with mercy. Many anecdotes are told of the benevolent interest he took in the concerns of his subjects, and of his anxiety to detect and reward merit, even in the most humble. It was common for him to ramble among them in disguise, like the celebrated caliph in the "Arabian Nights," mingling freely in conversation, and ascertaining their actual condition with his own eyes.

On one such occasion, when attended only by a single lord, he met with a boy who was gathering sticks in a field for fuel. He inquired of him "why he did not go into the neighbouring forest, where he would find a plenty of them." To which the lad answered, "It was the king's wood, and he would punish him with death if he trespassed there." The royal forests were very extensive in Tezcuco, and were guarded by laws full as severe as those of the Norman tyrants in England. "What kind of man is your king?" asked the monarch, willing to learn the effect of these prohibitions on his own popularity. "A very hard man," answered the boy, "who denies his people what God has given them." Nezahualcoyotl urged him not to mind such arbitrary laws, but to glean his sticks in the forest, as there was no one present who would betray him. But the boy sturdily refused, bluntly accusing the disguised king, at the same time, of being a traitor, and of wishing to bring him into trouble.

Nezahualcoyotl, on returning to the palace, ordered the child and his parents to be summoned before him. They received the orders with astonishment, but, on entering the presence, the boy at once recognised the person with whom he had discoursed so unceremoniously, and he was filled with consternation. The good-natured monarch, however, relieved his apprehensions by thanking him for the lesson he had given him, and, at the same time, commended his respect for the laws, and praised his parents for the manner in which they had trained their son. He then dismissed the parties with a liberal largess; and afterward mitigated the severity of the forest laws so as to allow persons to gather any wood they might find on the ground, if they did not meddle with the standing timber.

Another adventure is told of him with a poor woodman and his wife, who had brought their little load of billets for sale to the market-place of Tezcuco. The man was bitterly lamenting his hard lot, and the difficulty with which he earned a wretched subsistence, while the master of the palace before which they were standing lived an idle life, without toil, and with all the luxuries in the world at his command.

He was going on in his complaints, when the good woman stopped him, by reminding him he might be overheard. He was so, by Nezahualcoyotl himself, who, standing, screened from observation, at a latticed window which overlooked the market, was amusing himself, as he was wont, with observing the common people chaffering in the square. He immediately ordered the querulous couple into his presence. They appeared trembling and conscience-struck before him. The king gravely inquired what they had said. As they answered him truly, he told them they should reflect, that, if he had great treasures at his command, he had still greater calls for them; that, far from leading an easy life, he was oppressed with the whole burden of government; and concluded by admonishing them "to be more cautious in future, as walls had ears." He then ordered his officers to bring a quantity of cloth and a generous supply of cacao, (the coin of the country,) and dismissed them. "Go," said he, "with the little you now have, you will be rich; while, with all my riches, I shall still be poor."

It was not his passion to hoard. He dispensed his revenues munificently, seeking out poor, but meritorious objects, on whom to bestow them. He was particularly mindful of disabled soldiers, and those who had in any way sustained loss in the public service; and, in case of their death, extended assistance to their surviving families. Open mendicity was a thing he would never tolerate, but chastised it with exemplary rigour.

It would be incredible that a man of the enlarged mind and endowments of Nezahualcoyotl should acquiesce in the sordid superstitions of his countrymen, and still more in the sanguinary rites borrowed by them from the Aztecs. In truth, his humane temper shrunk from these cruel ceremonies, and he strenuously endeavoured to recall his people to the more pure and simple worship of the ancient Toltecs. A circumstance produced a temporary change in his conduct.

He had been married some years to the wife he had so unrighteously obtained, but was not blessed with issue. The priests represented that it was owing to his neglect of the gods of his country, and that his only remedy was to propitiate them by human sacrifice. The king reluctantly consented, and the altars once more smoked with the blood of slaughtered captives. But it was all in vain; and he indignantly exclaimed, "These idols of wood and stone can neither hear nor feel; much less could they make the heavens, and the earth, and man the lord of it. These must be the work of the all-powerful, unknown God, Creator of the universe, on whom alone I must rely for consolation and support."

He then withdrew to his rural palace of Tezcotzinco, where he remained forty days, fasting and praying at stated hours, and offering up no other sacrifice than the sweet incense of copal, and aromatic herbs and gums. At the expiration of this time, he is said to have been comforted by a vision assuring him of the success of his petition. At all events, such proved to be the fact; and this was followed by the cheering intelligence of the triumph of his arms in a quarter where he had lately experienced some humiliating reverses.

Greatly strengthened in his former religious convictions, he now openly· professed his faith, and was more earnest to wean his subjects from their degrading superstitions, and to substitute nobler and more spiritual conceptions of the Deity. He built a temple in the usual pyramidal form, and on the summit a tower nine stories high, to represent the nine heavens; a tenth was surmounted by a roof painted black, and profusely gilded with stars on the outside, and incrusted with metals and precious stones within. He dedicated this to "*the unknown God, the Cause of causes.*" It seems probable, from the emblem on the tower, as well as from the complexion of his verses, as we shall see, that he mingled with his reverence for the Supreme the astral worship which existed among the Toltecs. Various musical instruments were placed on the top of the tower, and the sound of them, accompanied by the ringing of a sonorous metal struck by a mallet, summoned the worshippers to prayers at regular seasons. No image was allowed in the edifice as unsuited to the "invisible God;" and the people were expressly prohibited from profaning the altars with blood, or any other sacrifices than that of the perfume of flowers and sweet-scented gums.

The remainder of his days was chiefly spent in his delicious solitudes of Tezcotzinco, where he devoted himself to astronomical and, probably, astrological studies, and to meditation on his immortal destiny,—giving utterance to his feelings in songs, or rather hymns, of much solemnity and pathós. An extract from one of these will convey some idea of his religious speculations. The pensive tenderness of the verses quoted in a preceding page is deepened here into a mournful, and even gloomy colouring; while the wounded spirit, instead of seeking relief in the convivial sallies of a young and buoyant temperament, turns for consolation to the world beyond the grave.

"All things on earth have their term, and, in the most joyous career of their vanity and splendour, their strength fails, and they sink into the dust. All the round world is but a sepulchre; and there is nothing, which lives on its surface, that shall not be hidden and entombed beneath it. Rivers, torrents, and streams move onward to their destination. Not one flows back to its pleasant source. They rush onward, hastening to bury themselves in the deep bosom of the ocean. The things of yesterday are no more to-day; and the things of to-day shall cease, perhaps, on the morrow. The cemetery is full of the loathsome dust of bodies once quickened by living souls, who occupied thrones, presided over assemblies, marshalled armies, subdued provinces, arrogated to themselves worship, were puffed up with vain-glorious pomp, and power, and empire.

"But these glories have all passed away, like the fearful smoke that issues from the throat of Popocatepetl, with no other memorial of their existence than the record on the page of the chronicler.

"The great, the wise, the valiant, the beautiful, —alas! where are they now? They are all mingled with the clod; and that which has befallen them shall happen to us, and to those that come after us. Yet let us take courage, illustrious nobles and chieftains, true friends and loyal subjects, —*let us aspire to that heaven, where all is eternal, and corruption cannot come.* The horrors of the tomb are but the cradle of the Sun, and the dark shadows of death are brilliant lights for the stars." The mystic import of the last sentence seems to point to that superstition respecting the mansions of the Sun, which forms so beautiful a contrast to the dark features of the Aztec mythology.

At length, about the year 1470, Nezahualcoyotl, full of years and honours, felt himself drawing near his end. Almost half a century had elapsed since he mounted the throne of Tezcuco. He had found his kingdom dismembered by faction, and bowed to the dust beneath the yoke of a foreign tyrant He had broken that yoke; had breathed new life into the nation, renewed its ancient institutions, extended wide its domain; had seen it flourishing in all the activity of trade and agriculture, gathering strength from its enlarged resources, and daily advancing higher and higher in the great march of civilization. All this he had seen, and might fairly attribute no small portion of it to his own wise and beneficent rule. His long and glorious day was now drawing to its close; and he contemplated the event with the same serenity which he had shown under the clouds of its morning and in its meridian splendour.

A short time before his death, he gathered around him those of his children in whom he most confided, his chief counsellors, the ambassadors of Mexico and Tlacopan, and his little son, the heir to the crown, his only offspring by the queen. He was then not eight years old; but had already given, as far as so tender a blossom might, the rich promise of future excellence.

After tenderly embracing the child, the dying monarch threw over him the robes of sovereignty. He then gave audience to the ambassadors, and, when they had retired, made the boy repeat the substance of the conversation. He followed this by such counsels as were suited to his comprehension, and which, when remembered through the long vista of after years, would serve as lights to guide him in his government of the kingdom. He besought him not to neglect the worship of "the unknown God," regretting that he himself had been unworthy to know him, and intimating his conviction that the time would come when he should be known and worshipped throughout the land.

He next addressed himself to that one of his sons in whom he placed the greatest trust, and whom he had selected as the guardian of the realm. "From this hour," said he to him, "you will fill the place that I have filled, of father to this child; you will teach him to live as he ought; and by your counsels he will rule over the empire. Stand in his place, and be his guide till he shall be of age to govern for himself." Then, turning to his other children, he admonished them to live united with another, and to show all loyalty to their prince, who, though a child, already manifested a discretion far above his years. "Be true to him," he added, "and he will maintain you in your rights and dignities."

Feeling his end approaching, he exclaimed, "Do not bewail me with idle lamentations. But sing the song of gladness and show a courageous spirit, that the nations I have subdued may not believe you disheartened, but may feel that each one of you is strong enough to keep them in obedience!" The undaunted spirit of the monarch shone forth even in the agonies of death. That stout heart, however, melted as he took leave of his children and friends, weeping tenderly over them, while he bade each a last adieu. When they had withdrawn, he ordered the officers of the palace to allow no one to enter it again. Soon after, he expired, in the seventy-second year of his age, and the forty-third of his reign.

Thus died the greatest monarch, and, if one foul blot could be effaced, perhaps the best, who ever sat upon an Indian throne. His character is delineated with tolerable impartiality by his kinsman, the Tezcucan chronicler. "He was wise, valiant, liberal; and, when we consider the magnanimity of his soul, the grandeur and success of his enterprises, his deep policy, as well as daring, we must admit him to have surpassed every other prince and captain of this New World. He had few failings himself, and rigorously punished those of others. He preferred the public to his private interest; was most charitable in his nature, often buying articles

at double their worth, of poor and honest persons, and giving them away again to the sick and infirm. In seasons of scarcity he was particularly bountiful, remitting the taxes of his vassals, and supplying their wants from the royal granaries. He put no faith in the idolatrous worship of the country. He was well instructed in moral science, and sought, above all things, to obtain light for knowing the true God. He believed in one God only, the Creator of heaven and earth, by whom we have our being, who never revealed himself to us in human form, nor in any other; with whom the souls of the virtuous are to dwell after death, while the wicked will suffer pains unspeakable. He invoked the Most High, as 'He by whom we live,' and 'Who has all things in himself.' He recognised the Sun for his father, and the Earth for his mother. He taught his children not to confide in idols, and only to conform to the outward worship of them from deference to public opinion. If he could not entirely abolish human sacrifices, derived from the Aztecs, he, at least, restricted them to slaves and captives."

FIRST SIGHT OF THE VALLEY OF MEXICO BY THE SPANIARDS.
FROM THE SAME.

THE troops, refreshed by a night's rest, succeeded, early on the following day, in gaining the crest of the sierra of Ahualco, which stretches like a curtain between the two great mountains on the north and south. Their progress was now comparatively easy, and they marched forward with a buoyant step as they felt they were treading the soil of Montezuma.

They had not advanced far, when, turning an angle of the sierra, they suddenly came on a view which more than compensated the toils of the preceding day. It was that of the Valley of Mexico, or Tenochtitlan, as more commonly called by the natives; which, with its picturesque assemblage of water, woodland, and cultivated plains, its shining cities and shadowy hills, was spread out like some gay and gorgeous panorama before them. In the highly rarefied atmosphere of these upper regions, even remote objects have a brilliancy of colouring and a distinctness of outline which seem to annihilate distance. Stretching far away at their feet were seen noble forests of oak, sycamore, and cedar, and beyond, yellow fields of maize and the towering maguey, intermingled with orchards and blooming gardens; for flowers, in such demand for their religious festivals, were even more abundant in this populous valley than in other parts of Anahuac. In the centre of the great basin were beheld the lakes, occupying then a much larger portion of its surface than at present; their borders thickly studded with towns and hamlets, and, in the midst,—like some Indian empress with her coronal of pearls, —the fair city of Mexico, with her white towers and pyramidal temples, reposing, as it were, on the bosom of the waters,—the far-famed "Venice of the Aztecs." High over all rose the royal hill of Chapoltepec, the residence of the Mexican monarchs, crowned with the same grove of gigantic cypresses, which at this day fling their broad shadows over the land. In the distance beyond the blue waters of the lake, and nearly screened by intervening foliage, was seen a shining speck, the rival capital of Tezcuco, and, still further on, the dark belt of porphyry, girdling the Valley around like a rich setting which Nature had devised for the fairest of her jewels.

Such was the beautiful vision which broke on the eyes of the Conquerors. And even now, when so sad a change has come over the scene; when the stately forests have been laid low, and the soil, unsheltered from the fierce radiance of a tropical sun, is in many places abandoned to sterility; when the waters have retired, leaving a broad and ghastly margin white with the incrustation of salts, while the cities and hamlets on their borders have mouldered into ruins;—even now that desolation broods over the landscape, so indestructible are the lines of beauty which Nature has traced on its features, that no traveller, however cold, can gaze on them with any other emotions than those of astonishment and rapture.

What, then, must have been the emotions of the Spaniards, when, after working their toilsome way into the upper air, the cloudy tabernacle parted before their eyes, and they beheld these fair scenes in all their pristine magnificence and beauty! It was like the spectacle which greeted the eyes of Moses from the summit of Pisgah, and, in the warm glow of their feelings, they cried out, "It is the promised land!"

THE PROFESSION OF LITERATURE.
FROM A PAPER ON SCOTT.

It is not very easy to see on what this low estimate of literature rested. As a profession, it has too little in common with more active ones to afford much ground for running a parallel. The soldier has to do with externals; and his contests and triumphs are over matter in its various forms, whether of man or material nature. The poet deals with the bodiless forms of air, of fancy lighter than air. His business is contemplative, the other's is active, and depends for its success on strong moral energy and presence of mind. He must, indeed, have genius of the highest order to effect his own combinations, anticipate the movements of his enemy, and dart with eagle eye on his vulnerable point. But who shall say that this practical genius, if we may so term it, is to rank higher in the scale than the creative power of the poet, the spark from the mind of divinity itself?

The orator would seem to afford better ground for comparison, since, though his theatre of action is abroad, he may be said to work with much the same tools as the writer. Yet how much of his success depends on qualities other than intellectual! "Action," said the father of eloquence, "action, action are the three most essential things to an orator." How much depends on the look, the gesture, the magical tones of voice, modulated to the passions he has stirred; and how much on the contagious sympathies of the audience itself which drown

every thing like criticism in the overwhelming tide of emotion! If any one would know how much, let him, after patiently standing

"till his feet throb,
And his head thumps, to feed upon the breath
Of patriots bursting with heroic rage,"

read the same speech in the columns of a morning newspaper, or in the well-concocted report of the orator himself. The productions of the writer are subjected to a fiercer ordeal. He has no excited sympathies of numbers to hurry his readers along over his blunders. He is scanned in the calm silence of the closet. Every flower of fancy seems here to wither under the rude breath of criticism; every link in the chain of argument is subjected to the touch of prying scrutiny, and if there be the least flaw in it, it is sure to be detected. There is no tribunal so stern as the secret tribunal of a man's own closet, far removed from all the sympathetic impulses of humanity. Surely there is no form in which *intellect* can be exhibited to the world so completely stripped of all adventitious aids as the form of written composition. But, says the practical man, let us estimate things by their utility. "You talk of the poems of Homer," said a mathematician, "but, after all, what do they *prove?*" A question which involves an answer somewhat too voluminous for the tail of an article. But if the poems of Homer were, as Heeren asserts, the principal bond which held the Grecian states together, and gave them a national feeling, they "prove" more than all the arithmeticians of Greece—and there were many cunning ones in it—ever proved. The results of military skill are indeed obvious. The soldier, by a single victory, enlarges the limits of an empire; he may do more—he may achieve the liberties of a nation, or roll back the tide of barbarism ready to overwhelm them. Wellington was placed in such a position and nobly did he do his work; or, rather, he was placed at the head of such a gigantic moral and physical apparatus as enabled him to do it. With his own unassisted strength, of course, he could have done nothing. But it is on his own solitary resources that the great writer is to rely. And yet, who shall say that the triumphs of Wellington have been greater than those of Scott, whose works are familiar as household words to every fireside in his own land, from the castle to the cottage; have crossed oceans and deserts, and, with healing on their wings, found their way to the remotest regions; have helped to form the character, until his own mind may be said to be incorporated into those of hundreds of thousands of his fellow-men? Who is there that has not, at some time or other, felt the heaviness of his heart lightened, his pains mitigated, and his bright moments of life made still brighter by the magical touches of his genius? And shall we speak of his victories as less real, less serviceable to humanity, less truly glorious than those of the greatest captain of his day? The triumphs of the warrior are bounded by the narrow theatre of his own age; but those of a Scott or a Shakspeare will be renewed with greater and greater lustre in ages yet unborn, when the victorious chieftain shall be forgotten, or shall live only in the song of the minstrel and the page of the chronicler.

EDWARD ROBINSON.

[Born 1794. Died 1863.]

THIS eminent scholar, who is descended from the famous John Robinson of Leyden, is a native of Connecticut, and was educated at Hamilton College, in New York, where he graduated in 1816.

The names of Edward Robinson and Moses Stuart stand at the head of the catalogue of learned men who have cultivated biblical literature in America. We are indebted mainly for our advancement in this great field of learning to the theological seminaries of Andover and Princeton. From both these institutions works have issued within a few years which have attained the highest reputation, not only in our own country but in Europe : which embrace more that is valuable and profound than in the same period has been produced elsewhere in the world. It is in this department that our authors command the greatest respect and admiration: an auspicious fact, for a nation whose scholars begin with this strong sympathy with the highest truth, and bring so successfully the strength of their intellects to its cultivation, if this impulse be maintained, will excel in every other field of investigation and reflection.

In antiquities, in criticism, in exegesis, in philology, in commentaries, and general biblical learning, much more has been done than can here be stated even in the most general manner. "It delights me," said Professor Lee of the English University of Cambridge, so long ago as 1831, "and all my Cambridge and other friends, to find that our American neighbours are really outstripping us in the cause of biblical literature." This was said in reference particularly to the Biblical Repository, (commenced by Dr. Robinson in that ear, and edited by him until 1838,) and to the labours of Professor Stuart. The Biblical Repository was indeed a most important publication, and it stands among the earliest and richest contributions made in this country to the treasures of sacred scholarship. The celebrated Professor Tholuck, of Halle, said to Dr. Robinson, "Should you succeed in making the contents of your Repository hereafter

as rich and valuable as they have been hitherto, it will become a classical book for the study of theology in America, and will be the commencement of a new era." It was held in the highest estimation abroad, and with other American works of a similar character was particularly valued for the successful combination which it presented of the spirit of piety with profound investigation and sound judgment. It introduced to our students the best results of theological erudition in Germany, and had a most important effect in continuing the impulse in sacred learning given by the earlier works of the editor and his principal colaborateur. These were, Stuart's Hebrew Grammar, first published in 1823 ; Stuart's and Robinson's Greek Grammar of the New Testament, in 1825 ; Robinson's Greek and English Lexicon, from the Clavis Philologica of Wahl, in 1826 ; Stuart's Hebrew Chrestomathy, in 1829 ; and Stuart's Course of Hebrew Study, in 1830.

Professor Stuart's Commentary on the Epistle to the Hebrews had appeared in 1827, and had been received everywhere as an accession to the body of permanent theological literature. It was spoken of in England as "the most valuable philological aid" that had been published "for the critical study of that important and in many respects difficult book ;" and Dr. Pye Smith, one of the first biblical, theological, and classical scholars in Great Britain, stated, that he felt it to be his duty to describe it as "the most important present to the cause of sound biblical interpretation that had ever been made in the English language." In Germany also it secured for Professor Stuart the highest consideration ; and it continues in all countries to be regarded as one of the noblest examples of philological theology and exegetical criticism.

In 1832 Professor Stuart gave to the world another great work of a similar character: his Commentary on the Epistle to the Romans. It was distinguished for a profoundness of research, for an intensity and minuteness of philological labour, and a singleness of purpose to arrive at the meaning of the apostle, without regard to any preconceived or partisan opinions, which obtained for it a regard as an authority equal to that awarded to its predecessor. In 1845 he published a Commentary on the Apocalypse: a profoundly learned and critical work, in which the interpretation of this difficult book varies much from that which has been most generally received. In the same year he also gave to the church a Critical History and Defence of the Old Testament Canon.

Dr. Robinson's translation of the improved edition of the Hebrew Lexicon by Gesenius appeared in 1836, and again in 1843. For this work he had prepared himself by a residence of several years in Germany, where he had gone through a wide range of study in the Shemitish languages; and the general and hearty applause of the best scholars was evidence of his success.

He soon after brought out a new edition of his Greek and English Lexicon of the New Testament, with all the improvements which years of additional labor had enabled him to give to it; and in 1845 his Harmony of the Four Gospels, in Greek, newly arranged, and with notes.

But the great work of Dr. Robinson, and his most valuable addition to our literature, is his Researches in Palestine, published in Boston, in 1841. This was the fruit of many years of study and investigation, at home and in Europe, preparatory to and consequent upon his journeyings and examinations in the Holy Land. His plans were partially formed in 1832, while the Reverend Eli Smith, an American missionary stationed at Beirût, was on a visit to the United States; but he did not set out upon his travels until the middle of July, 1837. The summer was passed in England and on the continent; in November he met Gesenius, Tholuck, Roediger, and other orientalists, in Germany; and passing through Italy, he embarked at Trieste for Alexandria. The first two months of the following year were spent in Egypt, where he was joined by Mr. Smith, and in March they set off for Jerusalem. The topographical investigations were completed in December, and Dr. Robinson resided in Berlin the two following years, where he had access to the best public and private libraries relating to the east, occupied in preparing his manuscripts for the press. The Biblical Researches were received by scholars

of all countries with demonstrations of the highest approbation. The work was recognised as one of the most learned and judicious produced in the world in this century. For patient, systematic, and sagacious investigation, it was ranked with Niebuhr's History. The great German geographer, Professor Ritter, who has himself written one of the best books on Palestine, says, "It lays open unquestionably one of the richest discoveries, one of the most important scientific conquests that has been made in the field of geography and biblical archæology.....What noble confirmation the truth of the Holy Scriptures receives from so many passages of these investigations, in a manner altogether unexpected, and often surprising, even in particulars seemingly the most trivial and unimportant !....Now first begins, since the days of Reland, the second great era of our knowledge of the Promised Land."

The latest productions of Dr. Robinson that have been given to the public are embraced in his periodical, entitled Bibliotheca Sacra, established in 1843, and of which a volume has since appeared for every year.

Our contributions to biblical literature, with few exceptions, have been made by persons connected with the colleges and theological seminaries. Professor Hodge, of Princeton, has distinguished himself by his Commentary on the Epistle to the Romans; Dr. Alexander, of the same institution, by his Commentary on Isaiah; and Professor Norton of the Divinity School at Cambridge, and Professor Bush of the University of New York, as has been stated in another part of this volume, have laboured diligently and successfully in the same department. The most remarkable exception to the rule is presented by the Reverend Albert Barnes, of Philadelphia, whose practical Notes on the New Testament have had a very large sale in this country and Great Britian, and who has published a similar work on Job, and a more extended Commentary on Isaiah, Daniel and the Psalms.

In the fields of literature and learning connected with religion, we have from the beginning had representatives whose proper station was with the most celebrated of older nations Those who are mentioned in this volume ar but types of classes, to whom more prominence would be given but that the range of these notices is in some degree limited to works of taste.

ELIZA LESLIE.

[Born 1787. Died 1858.]

MISS LESLIE is a native of Philadelphia. Her great-grandfather emigrated from Scotland, about the year 1745, and settled in Cecil county, Maryland. Her father was engaged in business in Philadelphia, and being a very ingenious man, fond of mathematics and natural philosophy, became familiarly acquainted with Franklin, Rittenhouse, Jefferson, and others of kindred tastes who at that time resided here. He was among the first to perceive the merit of the great invention of John Fitch, and was a steadfast and liberal friend of that eccentric and unfortunate man. Miss Leslie was the eldest of his children, and while she was quite young, leaving his affairs in charge of a partner, he went to reside in London, where he remained seven years. Two of his children were born here, one of whom was Charles Robert Leslie,* now one of the most eminent of living painters. He made choice of his profession at an early age, and in 1813 went abroad to study in the British and continental academies. He has since resided in England, except during the short period in which he was connected with the United States Military Academy, though he has always considered himself an American citizen. The family returned to Philadelphia in 1800, and Mr. Leslie the father died in 1804.

The education of women was managed much better than now in that period which our fathers are wont to describe as the golden age of America. Among the institutions that flourished here then were cooking-schools, in which the most important of sciences was taught in a manner that contributed largely to the comfort of the people. Miss Leslie was graduated in the famous one kept in Philadelphia for thirty years by Mrs. Goodfellow; and her first publication, a book for housekeepers, entitled Seventy-five Receipts, as well as her more recent and elaborate performances of the same kind, was scarcely less popular than Monsieur Ude's or Dr. Kitchener's.

The Seventy-five Receipts were followed by a series of volumes for juvenile readers, entitled The Mirror, The Young Americans, Atlantic Tales, Stories for Emma, Stories for Adelaide, and The American Girl's Book, all of which were found very profitable to the publishers and delightful to the new generation: they are scarcely inferior to any thing of their kind that has yet appeared.

The work by which Miss Leslie first became known in the literary world was Pencil Sketches, or Outlines of Character and Manners, published in 1833. This volume contained Mrs. Washington Potts, and about a dozen other pieces of similar character and merit. In 1835 she gave the public a second, and in 1837 a third series; and in 1841 the longest of her stories, under the title of Althea Vernon. Since then she has written enough tales and sketches for the magazines and annuals to fill four or five additional volumes.

Miss Leslie has much individuality, and in all her writings has exhibited decided talent. Her style is natural and spirited, her fable sufficiently simple and probable, her characters boldly and clearly and perhaps in all cases accurately drawn, and her description, narrative, and dialogue, uniformly well managed. Her sketches are more or less entertaining, according to the constitution of the reader's mind; but many of them are satirical; the subjects are such as we have no delight in remembering, and they are executed with a minuteness and distinctness that are sometimes truly painful. It must be confessed however that she is discriminating, that she is the satirist of the vulgar only, and presents in happy contrasts to their pretension, the intelligence and refinement of good society.

—She also published Amelia; The Dennings; American Girl's Book; Russel and Sidney; and The Behavior Book; several Cook Books; and partially wrote a Life of John Fitch. She died January 2, 1858.

---

* C. R. Leslie, R. A., was born in October, 1794. His most celebrated productions are May Day in the Reign of Elizabeth, Slender Courting Anne Page, Lady Jane Gray prevailed on to accept the Crown, Sancho relating his Adventures to the Duchess, Falstaff Dining at the House of Page, and the Coronation of Victoria. All the Leslie family are distinguished for their skill in drawing.

THAT GENTLEMAN.

FROM PENCIL SKETCHES.

On the third day, we were enabled to lay our course with a fair wind and a clear sky: the coast of Cornwall looking like a succession of low white clouds ranged along the edge of the northern horizon. Towards evening we passed the Lizard, to see land no more till we should descry it on the other side of the Atlantic. As Mr. Fenton and myself leaned over the taffrail, and saw the last point of England fade dimly from our view, we thought with regret of the shore we were leaving behind us, and of much that we had seen, and known, and enjoyed in that country of which all that remained to our lingering gaze was a dark spot so distant and so small as to be scarcely perceptible. Soon we could discern it no longer: and nothing of Europe was now left to us but the indelible recollections that it has impressed upon our minds. We turned towards the region of the descending sun—

> "To where his setting splendours burn
> Upon the western sea-maid's urn,"

and we vainly endeavoured to direct all our thoughts and feelings towards our home beyond the ocean—our beloved American home.

On that night, as on many others, when our ship was careering through the sea, with her yards squared, and her sails all trimmed to a fresh and favouring breeze, while we sat on a sofa in the lesser cabin, and looked up through the open skylight at the stars that seemed flying over our heads, we talked of the land we had so recently quitted. We talked of her people, who, though differing from ours in a thousand minute particulars, are still essentially the same. Our laws, our institutions, our manners, and our customs are derived from theirs: we are benefited by the same arts, we are enlightened by the same sciences. Their noble and copious language is fortunately ours—their Shakspeare also belongs to us; and we rejoice that we can possess ourselves of his "thoughts that breathe and words that burn" in all their original freshness and splendour, unobscured by the mist of translation. Though the ocean divides our dwelling-places; though the sword and the cannon-shot have sundered the bonds that once united us to her dominion; though the misrepresentations of travelling adventurers have done much to foster mutual prejudices, and to embitter mutual jealousies, still we share the pride of our parent in the glorious beings she can number among the children of her island home, for

> "Yet lives the blood of England in our veins."

On the fourth day of our departure from the Isle of Wight, we found ourselves several hundred miles from land, and consigned to the solitudes of that ocean-desert, "dark-heaving—boundless—endless—and sublime"—whose travellers find no path before them, and leave no track behind. But the wind was favourable, the sky was bright, the passengers had recovered their health and spirits, and for the first time were all able to present themselves at the dinner-table; and there was really what might be termed "a goodly company."

It is no longer the custom in American packet ships for ladies to persevere in what is called a sea-dress: that is, a sort of dishabille prepared expressly for the voyage. Those who are not well enough to devote some little time and attention to their personal appearance, rarely come to the general table, but take their meals in their own apartment. The gentlemen, also, pay as much respect to their toilet as when on shore......

Our passengers were not too numerous. The lesser cabin was appropriated to three other ladies and myself. It formed our drawing-room; the gentlemen being admitted only as visiters. One of the ladies was Mrs. Calcott, an amiable and intelligent woman, who was returning with her husband from a long residence in England. Another was Miss Harriet Audley, a very pretty and very lively young lady from Virginia, who had been visiting a married sister in London, and was now on her way home under the care of the captain, expecting to meet her father in New York. We were much amused during the voyage, with the coquetry of our fair Virginian as she aimed her arrows at nearly all the single gentlemen in turn; and with her frankness in openly talking of her designs and animadverting on their good or ill success. The gentlemen, with the usual vanity of their sex, always believed Miss Audley's attacks on their hearts to be made in earnest, and that she was deeply smitten with each of them in succession; notwithstanding that the smile in her eye was far more frequent than the blush on her cheek; and notwithstanding that rumour had asserted the existence of a certain cavalier in the neighbourhood of Richmond, whose constancy it was supposed she would eventually reward with her hand, as he might be considered, in every sense of the term, an excellent match.

Our fourth female passenger was Mrs. Cummings, a plump, rosy-faced old lady of remarkably limited ideas, who had literally passed her whole life in the city of London. Having been recently left a widow, she had broken up housekeeping, and was now on her way to join a son established in New York, who had very kindly sent for her to come over and live with him. The rest of the world was almost a sealed book to her, but she talked a great deal of the Minories, the Poultry, the Old Jewry, Cheapside, Long Acre, Bishopsgate Within and Bishopsgate Without, and other streets and places with appellations equally expressive.

The majority of the male passengers were pleasant and companionable—and we thought we had seen them all in the course of the first three days—but on the fourth, we heard the captain say to one of the waiters, "Juba, ask that gentleman if I shall have the pleasure of taking wine with him." My eyes now involuntarily followed the direction of Juba's movements, feeling some curiosity to know who "that gentleman" was, as I now recollected having frequently heard the epithet within the last few days. For instance, when almost every one was confined by sea-sickness to their state-rooms, I had seen the captain despatch a servant to inquire of that gentleman if he would have any thing sent to him from the table. Also, I had heard Hamilton, the steward, call out—"There, boys, don't you hear that gentleman ring his bell—why don't you run spontaneously—jump, one of you, to number eleventeen." I was puzzled for a moment to divine which state-room bore the designation of eleventeen, but concluded it to be one of the many unmeaning terms that characterize the phraseology of our coloured people. Once or twice, I wondered who that gentleman could be; but something else happened immediately to divert my attention.

Now when I heard Captain Santlow propose taking wine with him, I concluded, that, of course, that gentleman must be visible in propria persona, and casting my eyes towards the lower end of the table, I perceived a genteel looking man whom I had not seen before. He was apparently of no particular age, and there was nothing in his face that could lead any one to guess at his country. He might have been English, Scotch, Irish or American; but he had none of the characteristic marks of either nation. He filled his glass, and bowing his head to Captain Santlow, who congratulated him on his recovery, he swallowed his wine in silence. There was an animated conversation going on near the head of the table, between Miss Audley and two of her beaux, and we thought no more of him.

At the close of the dessert, we happened to know that he had quitted the table and gone on deck, by one of the waiters coming down, and requesting Mr. Overslaugh (who was sitting atilt, while discussing his walnuts, with his chair balanced on one leg, and his head leaning against the wainscot) to let him pass for a moment, while he went into No. eleventeen for that gentleman's overcoat. I now found that the servants had converted No. 13 into eleventeen. By-the-bye, that gentleman had a state-room all to himself, sometimes occupying the upper and sometimes the under birth.

"Captain Santlow," said Mr. Fenton, "allow me to ask you the name of that gentleman."

"Oh! I don't know," replied the captain, trying to suppress a smile, "at least I have forgotten it—some English name; for he is an Englishman—he came on board at Plymouth, and his indisposition commenced immediately. Mrs. Cummings, shall I have the pleasure of peeling an orange for you?"

I now recollected a little incident which had set me laughing soon after we left Plymouth, and when we were beating down the coast of Devonshire. I had been trying to write at the table in the ladies' cabin, but it was one of those days when

"Our paper, pen and ink, and we
Roll up and down our ships at sea."

And all I could do was to take refuge in my berth, and endeavour to read, leaving the door open for light and air. My attention, however, was continually withdrawn from my book by the sound of something that was dislodged from its place, sliding or falling, and frequently suffering destruction; though sometimes miraculously escaping unhurt. While I was watching the progress of two pitchers that had been tossed out of the washing-stand, and after deluging the floor with water, had met in the ladies' cabin, and were rolling amicably side by side, without happening to break each other, I saw a barrel of flour start from the steward's pantry, and running across the dining-room, stop at a gentleman that lay extended in a lower berth with his room door open, and pour out its contents upon him, completely enveloping him in a fog of meal. I heard the steward, who was busily engaged in mopping up the water that had flowed from the pitchers, call out, "Run, boys, run, that gentleman's smothering up in flour—go take the barrel off him—jump, I tell you."

How that gentleman acted while hidden in the cloud of flour, I could not perceive, and immediately the closing of the folding doors shut out the scene.

For a few days after he appeared among us, there was some speculation with regard to this nameless stranger, whose taciturnity seemed his chief characteristic. One morning while we were looking at the gambols of a shoal of porpoises that were tumbling through the waves and sometimes leaping out of them, my husband made some remark on the clumsy antics of this unsightly fish, addressing himself, for the first time, to the unknown Englishman, who happened to be standing near him. That gentleman smiled affably, but made no reply. Mr. Fenton pursued the subject—and that gentleman smiled still more affably, and walked away.

Nevertheless, he was neither deaf nor dumb, nor melancholy, but had only "a great talent for silence," and as is usually the case with persons whose genius lies that way, he was soon left entirely to himself, no one thinking it worth while to take the trouble of extracting words from him. In truth, he was so impracticable, and at the same time so evidently insignificant, and so totally uninteresting, that his fellow-passengers tacitly conveyed him to Coventry; and in Coventry he seemed perfectly satisfied to dwell. Once or twice Captain Santlow was asked again if he recollected the name of that gentleman; but he always replied with a sort of smile, "I cannot say I do—not exactly, at least—but I'll look at my manifest and see"—and he never failed to turn the conversation to something else.

The only person that persisted in occasionally talking to that gentleman, was old Mrs. Cummings; and she confided to him her perpetual alarms at "the perils of the sea," considering him a good hearer, as he never made any reply, and was always disengaged, and sitting and standing about, apparently at leisure, while the other gentlemen were occupied in reading, writing, playing chess, walking the deck, &c.

Whenever the ship was struck by a heavy sea, and after quivering with the shock, remained motionless for a moment before she recovered herself and rolled the other way, poor Mrs. Cummings supposed that we had run against a rock, and could not be convinced that rocks were not dispersed everywhere about the open ocean. And as that gentleman never attempted to undeceive her on this or any other subject, but merely listened with a placid smile, she believed that he always thought precisely as she did. She not unfrequently discussed to him, in an under tone, the obstinacy and incivility of the captain, who, she averred, with truth, had never in any one instance had the politeness to stop the ship, often as she had requested, nay, implored him to do so even when she was suffering with sea-sickness, and actually tossed out of her berth by the violence of the storm, though she was holding on with both hands......

In less than a fortnight after we left the English Channel we were off the banks of Newfoundland; and, as is frequently the case in their vicinity, we met with cold foggy weather. It cleared a little about seven in the morning, and we then discovered no less than three icebergs to leeward. One of them, whose distance from us was perhaps a mile, appeared higher than the main-mast head, and as the top shot up into a tall column, it looked like a vast rock with a light-house on its pinnacle. As the cold and watery sunbeams gleamed fitfully upon it, it exhibited in some places the rainbow tints of a prism—other parts were of a dazzling white, while its sharp angular projections seemed like masses of diamonds glittering upon snow.

The fog soon became so dense that in looking over the side of the ship we could not discern the sea. Fortunately, it was so calm that we scarcely moved, or the danger of driving on the icebergs would have been terrific. We had now no other means of ascertaining our distance from them, but by trying the temperature of the water with a thermometer.

In the afternoon the fog gathered still more thickly round us, and dripped from the rigging, so that the sailors were continually swabbing the deck. I had gone with Mr. Fenton to the round-house, and looked a while from its windows on the comfortless scene without. The only persons then on the main-deck were the captain and the first mate. They were wrapped in their watch-coats, their hair and whiskers dripping with the fog dew. Most of the passengers went to bed at an early hour, and soon all was awfully still; Mrs. Cumming being really too much frightened to talk, only that she sometimes wished herself in Shoreditch, and sometimes in Houndsditch. It was a night of real danger. The captain remained on deck till morning, and several of the gentlemen bore him company, being too anxious to stay below.

About day-break, a heavy shower of rain dispersed the fog—'The conscious vessel waked as from a trance"—A breeze sprung up that carried us out of danger from the icebergs, which were soon diminished to three specks on the horizon, and the sun rose bright and cheerfully.

Towards noon, the ladies recollected that none of them had seen that gentleman during the last twenty-four hours, and some apprehension was expressed lest he should have walked overboard in the fog. No one could give any account of him, or remember his last appearance; and Miss Audley professed much regret that now in all probability we should never be able to ascertain his name, as, most likely, he had "died and made no sign." To our shames be it spoken, not one of us could cry a tear at his possible fate. The captain had turned into his berth, and was reposing himself after the fatigue of

last night; so we could make no inquiry of him on the subject of our missing fellow-passenger.

Mrs. Cummings called the stewart, and asked him how long it was since he had seen any thing of that gentleman. "I really can't tell, madam"—replied Hamilton—"I can't pretend to charge my memory with such things. But I conclude he must have been seen yesterday—at least I rather expect he was."

The waiter Juba was now appealed to. "I believe, madam," said Juba—"I remember something of handing that gentleman the bread-basket yesterday at dinner—but I would not be qualified as to whether the thing took place or not, my mind being a good deal engaged at the time."

Solomon, the third water, disclaimed all positive knowledge of this or any other fact, but sagely remarked, "that it was very likely that gentleman had been about all yesterday as usual; yet still it was just as likely he might not; and there was only one thing certain, which was, that if he was not nowhere, he must, of course, be somewhere."

"I have a misgiving," said Mrs. Cummings, "that he will never be found again."

"I'll tell you what I can do, madam," exclaimed the steward, looking as if suddenly struck with a bright thought—"I can examine into No. eleventeen, and see if I can perceive him there." And softly opening the door of the state-room in question, he stepped back and said with a triumphant flourish of his hand—"There he is, ladies, there he is, in the upper berth, fast asleep in his double cashmere dressing gown. I opinionate that he was one of the gentlemen that stayed on deck all night, because they were afraid to go to sleep on account of the icebergers—of course nobody noticed him—but there he is now, safe enough." ·

Instantly we proceeded en masse towards No. eleventeen, to convince ourselves: and there indeed we saw that gentleman lying sleep in his double cashmere dressing gown. He opened his eyes, and seemed surprised, as well he might, at seeing all the ladies and all the servants ranged before the door of his room, and gazing in at him: and then we all stole off, looking foolish enough.

"Well," said Mrs. Cummings, "he is not dead, however,—so, we have yet a chance of knowing his name from himself, if we choose to ask him. But I'm determined I'll make the captain tell it me, as soon as he gets up. It's all nonsense, this making a secret of a man's name."......

Among the numerous steerage passengers was a young man whose profession was that of a methodist preacher. Having succeeded in making some religious impressions on the majority of his companions, he one Sunday obtained their consent to his performing divine service that evening in the steerage: and respectfully intimated that he would be highly gratified by the attendance of any of the cabin passengers that would condescend to honour him so far. Accordingly, after tea, we all descended to the steerage at early candle-light, and found every thing prepared for the occasion. A barrel, its head covered with a piece of sailcloth, served as a desk, lighted by two yellowish dip-candles placed in empty porter bottles. But as there was considerable motion, it was found that the bottles would not rest in their stations; therefore they were held by two boys. The chests and boxes nearest to the desk were the seats allotted to the ladies and gentlemen: and the steerage people ranged themselves behind.

A hymn was sung to a popular tune. The prayer and sermon were delivered in simple but impressive language; for the preacher, though a poor and illiterate man, was not deficient either in sense or feeling, and was evidently imbued with the sincerest piety. There was something solemn and affecting in the aspect of the whole scene, with all its rude arrangement; and also in the idea of the lonely and insulated situation of our little community with "one wide water all around us." And when the preacher, in his homely but fervent language, returned thanks for our hitherto prosperous voyage, and prayed for our speedy and safe arrival at our destined port, tears stood in the eyes of many of his auditors. I thought, when it was over, how frequently such scenes must have occurred between the decks of the May-flower, during the long and tempestuous passage of that pilgrim band who finally

"moored their bark
On the wild New England shore,"
and how often

Amid the storm they sung,
And the stars heard, and the sea—
when the wise and pious Brewster lifted his voice in exhortation and prayer, and the virtuous Carver, and the gallant Standish, bowed their heads in devotion before him.......

After crossing the Banks we seemed to feel ourselves on American ground, or rather on American sea. As our interest increased on approaching the land of our destination, that gentleman was proportionally overlooked and forgotten. He "kept the even tenor of his way," and we had become scarcely conscious that he was still among us : till one day when there was rather a hard gale, and the waves were running high, we were startled, as we surrounded the luncheon table, by a tremendous noise on the cabin staircase, and the sudden bursting open of the door at its foot. We all looked up, and saw that gentleman falling down-stairs, with both arms extended, as he held in one hand a tall cane stool, and in the other the captain's barometer, which had hung just within the upper door; he having involuntarily caught hold of both these articles, with a view of saving himself. "While his head, as he tumbled, went nicketty nock," his countenance, for once, assumed a new expression, and the change from its usual unvarying sameness was so striking, that, combined with his ludicrous attitude, it set us all to laughing. The waiters ran forward and assisted him to rise; and it was then found that the stool and the barometer had been the greatest sufferers; one having lost a leg, and the other being so shattered that the stair-carpet was covered with globules of quicksilver. However, he retired to his state-room, and whether or not he was seen again before next morning, I cannot positively undertake to say.

On the edge of the Gulf Stream we had a day of entire calm, when "there was not a breath the blue wave to curl." A thin veil of haziness somewhat softened the fires of the American sun, (as it was now called by the European passengers,) and we passed the whole day on deck, in a delightful state of idle enjoyment; gazing on the inhabitants of the deep, that like ourselves seemed to be taking a holyday. Dolphins, horse-mackerel, and porpoises were sporting round the vessel, and the flying-fish "with brine still dropping from its wings," was darting up into the sun-light; while flocks of petrels, their black plumage tinged with flame-colour, seemed to rest on the surface of the water; and the nautilus, "the native pilot of his little bark," glided gaily along the dimpling mirror that reflected his tiny oars and gauzy sail. We fished up large clusters of sea-weed, among which were some beautiful specimens of a delicate purple colour, which, when viewed through a microscope, glittered like silver, and were covered with little shell-fish so minute as to be invisible to the naked eye.

It was a lovely day. The lieutenant and his family were all on deck, and looked happy. That gentleman looked as usual. Towards evening, a breeze sprung up directly fair, and filled the sails, which all day had been clinging idly to the masts; and before midnight we were wafted along at the rate of nine knots an hour, "while round the waves phosphoric brightness broke," the ship seeming, as she cleaved the foam, to draw after her in her wake a long train of stars.

Next day we continued to proceed rapidly, with a fair wind, which we knew would soon bring us to the end of our voyage. The ladies' cabin was now littered with trunks and boxes, brought from the baggage room that we might select from them such articles as we thought we should require when we went on shore.

But we were soon attracted to the deck, to see the always interesting experiment of sounding with the deep-sea lead. To our great joy it came up (though from almost immeasurable depth) with a little sand adhering to the cake of tallow at the bottom of the plummet. The breeze was increasing, and Mr. Overslaugh, whose pretensions to nautical knowledge were considered very shallow by his fellow amateurs, remarked to my husband, "If this wind holds, I should not wonder if we are aground in less than two hours."......

We remained on deck the whole evening, believing it probably the last we should spend together; and the close companionship of four weeks in the very circumscribed limits of a ship had made us seem like one family. We talked of the morrow, and I forgot that that gentleman was among us, till I saw him leave the deck to retire for the night. The thought then struck me, that another day, and we should cease perhaps to remember his existence.

I laid my head on my pillow with the understanding that land would be discovered before morning, and I found it impossible to sleep. Mr. Fenton went on deck about midnight, and remained there till dawn......

Near one o'clock I heard a voice announcing the

light on the island of Neversink, and in a short time all the gentlemen were on deck. At daybreak Mr. Fenton came to ask me if I would rise and see the morning dawn upon our own country. We had taken a pilot on board at two o'clock, had a fine fair breeze to carry us into the bay of New York, and there was every probability of our being on shore in a few hours.

Soon after sunrise we were visited by a newsboat, when there was an exchange of papers, and much to inquire and much to tell.

We were going rapidly through the Narrows, when the bell rung for breakfast, which Captain Santlow had ordered at an early hour, as we had all been up before daylight. Chancing to look towards his accustomed seat, I missed that gentleman, and inquired after him of the captain. "Oh!" he replied, "that gentleman went on shore in the news-boat; did ·you not see him depart? He bowed all round before he went down the side."

"No," was the general reply, "we did not see him go." In truth we had all been too much interested in hearing, reading, and talking of the news brought by the boat.

"Then he is gone for ever," exclaimed Mrs. Cummings—"and we shall never know his name."

"Come, Captain Santlow," said Mr. Fenton, "try to recollect it.—'Let it not,' as Grumio says, 'die in oblivion, while we return to our graves inexperienced in it.'"

Captain Santlow smiled, and remained silent. "Now, captain," said Miss Audley, "I will not quit the ship till you tell me that gentleman's name. —I cannot hold out a greater threat to you, as I know you have had a weary time of it since I have been under your charge. Come, I set not my foot on shore till I know the name of that gentleman, and also why you cannot refrain from smiling whenever you are asked about it."

"Well, then," replied Captain Santlow, "though his name is a very pretty one when you get it said, there is a little awkwardness in speaking it. So I thought I would save myself and my passengers the trouble. And partly for that reason, and partly to teaze you all, I have withheld it from your knowledge during the voyage. But I can assure you he is a baronet."

"A baronet," cried Miss Audley—"I wish I had known that before, I should certainly have made a dead set at him. A baronet would have been far better worth the trouble of a flirtation, than you Mr. Williams, or you Mr. Sutton, or you Mr. Belfield, or any of the other gentlemen that I have been amusing myself with during the voyage."

"A baronet!" exclaimed Mrs. Cummings, "well, really—and have I been four weeks in the same ship with a baronet—and sitting at the same table with him,—and often talking to him face to face.— I wonder what Mrs. Thimbleby of Threadneedle street would say if she knew that I am now acquainted with a baronet?"

"But what is his name, captain?"—said Mr. Fenton; "still you do not tell us."

"His name," answered the Captain, "is Sir St. John St. Ledger."

"Sir St. John St. Ledger!" was repeated oy each of the company.

"Yes," resumed Captain Santlow—"and you see how difficult it is to say it smoothly. There is more sibilation in it than in any name I know.— Was I not right in keeping it from you till the voyage was over, and thus sparing you the trouble of articulating it, and myself the annoyance of hearing it. See, here it is in writing."

The captain then took his manifest out of his pocket-book, and showed us the words, "Sir St. John St. Ledger, of Sevenoaks, Kent."

"Pho!" said Mrs. Cummings. "Where's the trouble in speaking that name, if you only knew the right way—I have heard it a hundred times— and even seen it in the newspapers. This must be the very gentleman that my cousin George's wife is always talking about. She has a brother that lives near his estate, a topping apothecary. Why, 'tis easy enough to say his name, if you say it as we do in England."

"And how is that?" asked the captain; "wha can you make of Sir St. John St. Ledger?"

"Why, Sir Singeon Sillinger, to be sure," replied Mrs. Cummings—"I am confident he would have answered to that name. Sir Singeon Sillinger of Sunnock—cousin George's wife's brother lives close by Sunnock in a yellow house with a red door."

"And have I," said the captain laughing, "so carefully kept his name to myself, during the whole passage, for fear we should have had to call him Sir St. John St. Ledger, when all the while we might have said Sir Singeon Sillinger."

"To be sure you might," replied Mrs. Cummings, looking proud of the opportunity of displaying her superior knowledge of something. "With all your striving after sense you Americans are very ignorant people, particularly of the right way of speaking English. Since I have been on board, I have heard you all say the oddest things—though I thought there would be no use in trying to set you right. The other day there was Mr. Williams talking of the church of St. Mary le bon—instead of saying Marrow bone. Then Mr. Belfield says, Lord Cholmondeley, instead of Lord Chumley, and Col. Sinclair instead of Col. Sinkler; and Mr. Sutton says Lady Beauchamp, instead of Lady Beachum; and you all say Birmingham instead of Brummagem. The truth is, you know nothing about English names. Now that name, Trollope, that you all sneer at so much, and think so very low, why Trollope is quite genteel in England, and so is Hussey. The Trollopes and Husseys belong to great families. But I have no doubt of finding many things that are very elegant in England, counted quite vulgar in America, owing to the ignorance of your people. For my part, I was particularly brought up to despise all manner of ignorance."

In a short time a steamboat came alongside, into which we removed ourselves, accompanied by the captain and the letter bags; and we proceeded up to the city, where Mr. Fenton and myself were met on the wharf, I need not tell how, and by whom.

2 K 2

HUGH SWINTON LEGARÉ.

[Born 1797. Died 1843.]

THIS eminent scholar was descended from one of the French Huguenots who settled in South Carolina about the year 1695. He was born in Charleston on the second of January, 1797, and in the eleventh year of his age was placed in the Charleston College, then under the presidency of the learned and accomplished Mr. Mitchell King, whose judicious instruction and counsel doubtless had a large influence in the formation of his tastes and character. Early in his fifteenth year he entered the South Carolina College at Columbia, where his previous attainments, the astonishing facility with which he added to them, and the eager industry with which he devoted himself to his studies, gave him at once a lead, which, Mr. Preston says, "he maintained throughout his course, until he had graduated, not only with the highest honours of the college, but with a reputation throughout the state." The end which he proposed to himself, and which he never for a moment lost sight of, was a thorough understanding of the philosophy of legislation and the constitution of society, including all the influences, political, judicial, and moral, that effect the destinies of the human family, and how to turn that knowledge to account in the actual service of the state. Acquiring at an early period the Italian, French and German languages, he read largely in their respective authors, but continued to the end of his life to regard the literature of England as the best in the world with the single exception of the Greek. Of Milton and Shakspeare, in whom he delighted from his youth, he says in a recently published letter, that the man who has made himself a complete master of them " possesses a treasure of thought, knowledge, and sublime poetry, to be equaled in no other language ever spoken by man." He subsequently read the great writers of the British Commonwealth, Whitelock, Prynne, Harrington, and Sidney, with Hobbes, Clarendon, and others of the Jure Divino side, and those of a later day, Locke, and Hoadly, and indeed all the sound thinkers who have written in our mother tongue.

On the completion of his academical course at Columbia he returned to Charleston, and for three years applied himself diligently to the study of the law, under the direction of Mr. King, who was now one of the leading counsellors and advocates of the state. At twenty-one I believe he was admitted to the bar, but he had no idea of entering at that time upon the practice of his profession. His scheme of preparation embraced years of study in the foreign schools, and in the spring of 1818 he went to Paris, where he spent the summer in perfecting himself in the French and Italian, and in making himself acquainted as much as his leisure permitted with the world, which is seen in all its phases in that motley city. It had been his intention before leaving Charleston to go to Gottingen, and he appears afterward to have regretted that he did not do so, but he now decided upon Edinburgh, and leaving Paris about the close of September he arrived there in time to enter for the winter term the classes of civil law, natural philosophy and mathematics. His chief attention was given to juridical philosophy, and Mr. Preston, who was here as in Paris his fellow student, assures us that he addressed himself to his labours " with a quiet diligence, sometimes animated into a sort of intellectual joy." In the spring of 1819 he made an excursion through Scotland and England, and after passing some time' in London crossed over once more to France, and occupied the autumn in seeing that country, Belgium, Holland, the Rhine and the Alps. In the following winter he returned to Charleston, by way of New York and Washington.

After a short stay in the city he retired to the estate of his mother on John's Island, where he spent two years as a planter, still however devoting his leisure to the pursuit of his favourite studies. In the fall of 1820 he was elected from his parish to the state legislature, in which he continued two years. At the end of this period he removed with his family to Charleston, and entered upon the practice of his profession, with a very high reputation undoubtedly, but it appears with something less than the success he had anticipated. The estimation in which he was held, however, secured his election to the legislature as one of the representatives of the city, in 1824, and he held a seat in that body and took a leading part in its deliberations until he was made Attorney General of the state, in 1830.

In 1827 The Southern Quarterly Review was established at Charleston, partly for the exposition and defence of southern opinions and measures in politics, but chiefly as a journal of literature; and in this work, which owed its reputation mainly to his contributions, he commenced his career of authorship. His most important articles are those on Classical Learning, Roman Literature, Cicero de Republica, the Public Economy of Athens, the Life and Works of D'Aguesseau, Jeremy Bentham and the Utilitarians, Codification, Kent's Commentaries, Early Spanish Ballads, the Miscellaneous Writings of Sir Philip Sidney, Lord Byron's Character and Poems, Byron's Letters and Journals, Hall's Travels in America, the Travels of the Duke of Saxe Weimer, the Disowned and Tales of the Great St. Bernard, and the Miscellanies of William Crafts; but he wrote many others, of less importance. It is not too much to say of some of these essays that they will bear a favourable comparison with the best productions of their kind; yet they are certainly inferior to the more carefully prepared papers which he gave to the world at a subsequent period.

His appointment to the office of Attorney General of South Carolina was regarded as eminently honourable to him, inasmuch as it was conferred by a legislature in which his political opponents had a powerful ascendency. The applause which crowned his first appearance before the supreme bench at Washington vindicated to his friends their support of him, and to himself the devotion of so many years to the noble studies by which he had been fitted for the office. Mr. Livingston, who was then Secretary of State, impressed by his eloquence, the compass and solidity of his learning, and his ambition to infuse into the common law the enlarged and liberal principles and just morality of the civilians, tendered him the place of Chargé d'Affaires at the court of Brussels, with a view to the advantages it would give him in a further prosecution which he desired to make in his studies, and he sailed

for this post in the spring of 1833. The presence of much good society in Brussels rendered his stay there very agreeable to him, but did not prevent the devotion of a large portion of his time to jurisprudence, political economy, and the general reading of good authors. He returned home in 1836, and was immediately chosen a member of Congress from the Charleston district. He came into the House of Representatives at the commencement of Mr. Van Buren's administration, but his conservative principles, especially his opposition to the Sub-Treasury, which was the favourite scheme of the democratic party, prevented his reëlection in 1838, and he again entered upon the practice of his profession.

It was in this period that he wrote the masterly articles which contributed so largely to his reputation as a scholar and a man of letters in the New York Review, under the titles of The Constitutional History of Greece; Demosthenes, the Man, the Orator, and the Statesman; and The Origin, History and Influence of Roman Legislation.

He was eminently successful at the bar, and in the great canvass which preceded the election of General Harrison to the presidency he took an active part, and increased his popularity by some of the most powerful speeches made at New York, Richmond, and other cities, against the policy of the incumbent executive. On the resignation of the whig cabinet after the death of General Harrison, Mr. Tyler bestowed on Mr. Legaré the office of Attorney General of the United States. This was the office for which he was most ambitious, and "there was a universal acquiescence in the propriety of the appointment."* There are abundant testimonies of the ability with which he performed his duties in this department. Of his diligence we have his own declaration that he was so much occupied with business as to be obliged to study twelve hours a day. When Mr. Webster withdrew from the cabinet, Mr. Tyler selected Mr. Legaré to be Secretary of State ad interim, and he exhibited extraordinary energies and resources in the discharge of the double duties which now devolved upon him, rendered more oppressive by the presence in his family of death, which within a few months deprived him of a sister and his mother, to whom he was bound by the tenderest affec-

* Mr. Preston's Eulogy.

tion. His own end approached, and perhaps was accelerated by this weight of blended public and private cares. In the summer of 1843 he attended the President on a visit to Boston, to assist in the celebration of the completion of the monument on Bunker Hill. He arrived in that city on the sixteenth of June, was seized with a painful and dangerous illness the same evening, and on the morning of the twentieth breathed his last, at the house of his old classmate and steadfast friend, Mr. George Ticknor.

In 1846 a collection of the writings of Mr. Legaré was published in two large and closely printed octavo volumes, in Charleston. It consists of a Diary kept at Brussels, a Journal on the Rhine, Extracts from his Private and Diplomatic Correspondence, Orations and Speeches, and Contributions to the New York and Southern Reviews, prefaced by a memoir of his life. The collection of his previously published writings is incomplete, but the selection in the main is judicious. The private letters which are here given us are generally interesting, but they are not in all cases such as his more discreet friends cared to see in print. The diaries which he kept while abroad were evidently designed exclusively for the amusement of himself and his intimate associates, and nothing can justify their publication, at least during the lives of many of the persons mentioned in them. In the " Diary of Brussels" he himself remarks of something of the same sort, that " these attacks on ladies, and trespasses on the sanctity of private life, appeared to" him " quite shocking." This sentence should have been a warning to his literary executors.

The impression left by his collected writings is, that his mind was of the first order, but that it did not hold in that order a very prominent place. He had that rectitude of judgment, that pervading good sense, that constant natural sympathy with truth, which is a characteristic of the best class of intellects, but he was wanting in richness, fervour, and creative vigour. He possessed the forms of fine understanding, but the force of intellectual passion, or the fire of genius, are not found. His perception of truth was superior to his power of illustrating it. We follow the difficult and somewhat languid processes of his thoughts, and, surprised at last at finding him in possession of such admirable opinions on all subjects, we imagine that he must have discovered his conclusions by different faculties from those which he uses to demonstrate them. That splendid fusion of reason, imagination, and feeling, which constitutes the inspiration of the great, is not visible: the display is meagre, laborious, and painful. He fills the measure of his subject, but it is by the utmost stretch of his abilities : we do not observe the abounding power, the exuberant resources, the superfluous energy, which mark the foremost of the first.

In his own profession Mr. Legaré had, with many, discredited his reputation by the devotion which he avowed to the civil law. It is understood that no one who has been able thoroughly to master and comprehend the common law, is disposed to give much time to the civilians. I am inclined to believe that no man ever yet took up the Code, because having sounded the common law through its depths, he had found it wanting : many have cheaply sought the praise of having gone through the common law, by appearing to have attained to something beyond it, upon the principle that if you "quote Lycophron, they will take it for granted that you have read Homer." In Mr. Legaré's case, such suspicions are probably without justice. He was attracted to the " first collection of written reason" chiefly by the interest which the scholar feels in that majestic philosophy of morals which is the " imperium sine fine" of Rome. His remarks in a review of Kent's Commentaries, show that he understood what advantages the common law had attained over the civil law, as a practical system, by its constant regard for certainty, convenience, and policy. As a common lawyer Mr. Legaré was respectable; and in great cases, his elaborate style of preparation made him a formidable opponent.

As a statesman I think the finest monument of his powers is his speech in Congress on the Sub-Treasury. It is formal, elementary, and scholastic, but able, and at times brilliant. His politics, as displayed in various essays and reviews, were profound and intelligent; but it always seemed as if he had settled his views of the present times upon opinions derived from history, and not that, like Machiavelli, he had informed his judgment on occurrences in history by suggestions drawn from his own observation. Still, by any method to have formed sound principles on government and society, in the unfavourable circumstances in which he was placed, was an indication of extraordinary powers. He triumphed over disadvantages of position, connections, and party; and was among the wisest men of the south. Yet he appears, like Mr. Hamilton, and Mr. Ames, to have been of a too desponding temperament, to have magnified dangers that threatened our young energies, and to have lacked faith in our system, after it had passed some of the strongest trials to which it was reasonable to suppose it would ever be subjected.

As a classical scholar Mr. Legaré made great pretension, but there is nothing in his works to prove that he was here superior or even equal to several of his countrymen. His proficiency partook of the dryness and severity of his character. He studied rather as a grammarian than as a man of taste. He may have been accurate, but he was not elegant.

He writes often about the Greeks and Latins, but he had never caught the spirit and sentiment of classical enthusiasm. We miss the fine felicity of illustration, the apt quotation, the brilliant allusion, which are so attractive in the writings of one whose heart and fancy have dwelt familiarly in the clime of antiquity. He is not betrayed as a visitor to the halls of the past by the smell of aloes and cassia hanging about his garments, caught from the ivory palaces whereby they have made him glad. We know the fact by his constantly informing us of it, and because he describes the localities with the precision of one who must have observed, chiefly for the purpose of making a report. The most striking passage in his writings on a classical subject is that relating to Catullus, in his criticism of Dunlap's History of Ancient Literature. The remarks on that poet are original, beautiful, and undoubtedly just.

LIBERTY AND GREATNESS.
FROM CHARACTERISTICS OF THE AMERICAN REVOLUTION.

THE name of REPUBLIC is inscribed upon the most imperishable monuments of the species, and it is probable that it will continue to be associated, as it has been in all past ages, with whatever is heroic in character, and sublime in genius, and elegant and brilliant in the cultivation of arts and letters. It would not have been difficult to prove that the base hirelings who, in this age of legitimacy and downfall, have so industriously inculcated a contrary doctrine, have been compelled to falsify history and abuse reason. I might have "called up antiquity from the old schools of Greece" to show that these apostles of despotism would have passed at Athens for barbarians and slaves. I might have asked triumphantly, what land had even been visited with the influences of liberty, that did not flourish like the spring? What people had ever worshipped at her altars, without kindling with a loftier spirit and putting forth more noble energies? Where she had ever acted, that her deeds had not been heroic? Where she had ever spoken, that her eloquence had not been triumphant and sublime? It might have been demonstrated that a state of society in which nothing is obtained by patronage—nothing is yielded to the accidents of birth and fortune—where those who are already distinguished, must exert themselves lest they be speedily eclipsed by their inferiors, and these inferiors are, by every motive, stimulated to exert themselves that they may become distinguished—and where, the lists being open to the whole world, without any partiality or exclusion, the champion who bears off the prize, must have tasked his powers to the very uttermost, and proved himself the first of a thousand competitors—is necessarily more favourable to a bold, vigorous and manly way of thinking and acting, than any other. I should have asked with Longinus—who but a Republican could have spoken the philippics of Demosthenes? and what has the patronage of despotism ever done to be compared with the spontaneous productions of the Attic, the Roman, and the Tuscan muse?

With respect to ourselves, who have been so systematically vilified by British critics—if any answer were expected to be given to their shallow and vulgar sophistry, and there was not a sufficient practical refutation of it, in the undoubted success of some of the artists and writers that are springing up in our own times—we should be perfectly safe, in resting, upon the operation of general causes and the whole analogy of history, our anticipation of the proudest success, in all the pursuits of a high and honourable ambition. That living, as we do, in the midst of a forest, we have been principally engaged in felling and improving it; and that those arts, which suppose wealth and leisure and a crowded population, are not yet so flourishing amongst us as they will be in the course of a century or two, is so much a matter of course, that instead of exciting wonder and disgust, one is only surprised how it should even have attracted notice; but the question, whether we are destitute of genius and sensibility and loftiness of character, and all the aspirings that prompt to illustrious achievements, and all the elements of national greatness and glory, is quite a distinct thing, and we may appeal, with confidence, to what we have done and to what we are, to the Revolution we are

this day celebrating, to the career we have since
run, to our recent exploits upon the flood and in
the field, to the skill of our diplomacy, to the comprehensive views and undoubted abilities of our
statesmen, to the virtues and prosperity of our people, to the exhibition on every occasion of all the
talents called for by its exigencies and admitted by
its nature; nay, to the very hatred—the vehement
and irrepressible hatred, with which these revilers
themselves have so abundantly honoured us—to
show that nothing can be more preposterous than
the *contempt* with which they have sometimes
affected to speak of us.

And, were there no *other* argument, as there are
many, to prove that the character of the nation is altogether worthy of its high destinies, would it not
be enough to say that we live under a form of
government and in a state of society to which the
world has never yet exhibited a parallel? Is it
then *nothing* to be *free?* How many nations, in
the whole annals of human kind, have proved
themselves worthy of being so? Is it nothing that
we are Republicans? Were all men as enlightened, as brave, as *proud* as they ought to be, would
they suffer themselves to be insulted with any other
title? Is it nothing, that so many independent
sovereignties should be held together in such a confederacy as ours? What does history teach us of
the difficulty of instituting and maintaining such
a polity, and of the glory that, of consequence,
ought to be given to those who enjoy its advantages in so much perfection and on so grand a
scale? For, can any thing be more striking and
sublime, than the idea of an IMPERIAL REPUBLIC,
spreading over an extent of territory, more immense than the empire of the Cæsars, in the accumulated conquests of a thousand years—without
præfects or proconsuls or publicans—founded on
the maxims of common sense—employing within
itself no arms, but those of reason—and known to
its subjects only by the blessings it bestows or perpe-
tuates, yet capable of directing, against a foreign foe,
all the energies of a military despotism—a Republic, in which men are completely insignificant, and
principles and *laws* exercise, throughout its vast dominion, a peaceful and irresistible sway, blending
in one divine harmony such various habits and
conflicting opinions, and mingling in our institutions the light of philosophy with all that is dazzling in the associations of heroic achievement and
extended domination, and deep-seated and formidable power!

ENGLAND AMERICA, AND THE CRE-
DIT SYSTEM.

FROM THE SPIRIT OF THE SUB-TREASURY.

LET us look at the experience of the two other
countries in which the system exists, as we are told,
in its most vicious state—England and the United
States. Look at the result. I have no faith at
all in speculative politics. A theorist in government is as dangerous as a theorist in medicine, or
in agriculture, and for precisely the same reason—

the subjects are too complicated and too obscure
for simple and decisive experiments. I go for undisputed results in the long run. Now surely a
philosophic inquirer into the history of the commerce and public economy of nations, if he saw a
people preëminently distinguished in those particulars above all others, would be inclined to ascribe their superiority to what was *peculiar* in their
institutions; at least, whatever might be his ideas
à priori on such subjects, he would be very slow to
deny to any remarkable peculiarity in those institutions its full importance as one of the probable
causes of the success which he witnessed, unless
he could clearly show the contrary. Then, sir, by
what example are we to be guided in such matters
if not by that of England—by far the most magnificent manifestation, that the world, in any age
of it, has ever beheld, of the might and the grandeur of civilized life? Sir, I have weighed every syllable that I utter—I express a deliberate conviction,
founded upon a patient inquiry and a comparison
as complete as my limited knowledge has enabled
me to make it, between the past and the present
condition of mankind, and between the great nation of which I am speaking and those which surround her. Sir, there is a gulph between them—
that narrow channel separates worlds—it is an
ocean more than three thousand miles wide. I appeal to any one who has been abroad, whether going
from England to any part of the continent—be not
descending immensely in the scale of civilization.
I know, sir, that that word is an ambiguous one.
I know that, in some of the graces of polished
society, in some of the arts of an elegant imagination, that, in the exact sciences and in mere
learning and general intellectual cultivation, some
nations have excelled, perhaps, many equalled,
England. But, in that civilization, which, as I
have said before, it is the great end of modern political economy to promote, and which is immediately connected with the subject before you—which
at once springs out of, and leads to, the accumulation of capital and the distribution of wealth and
comfort through all classes of a community, with
an immense aggregate of national power and resources—that civilization which enables man to
" wield these elements, and arm him with the force
of all their legions," which gives him dominion
over all other creatures, and makes him emphatically the Lord of the Universe—that civilization
which consists not in music, not in playing on the
flute, as the Athenian hero said, but in turning a
small city into a great one; in that victorious, triumphant, irresistible civilization, there is nothing
recorded in the annals of mankind that does not
sink into the shades of the deepest eclipse by the
side of England. I say nothing of her recent
achievements on the land and the sea; of her fleets,
her armies, her subsidized allies. Look at the
Thames crowded with shipping; visit her arsenals,
her docks, her canals, her railways, her factories,
her mines, her warehouses, her roads, and bridges;
go through the streets of that wonderful metropolis, the bank, the emporium, and the exchange of
the whole world; converse with those merchants

who conduct and control, as far as it is possible to control, the commerce of all nations, with those manufacturers who fill every market with their unrivalled products; go into that bank which is the repository of the precious metals for all Europe; consider its notes as well as the bills of private bankers, at a premium everywhere, more valuable than specie, symbols not merely of gold, but of what is far more precious than gold, yea, than fine gold, of perfect good faith, of unblemished integrity, of sagacious enterprise, of steadfast, persevering industry, of boundless wealth, of business coextensive with the earth, and of all these things possessed, exercised, enjoyed, protected under a system of liberty chastened by the law which maintains it, and of law softened and mitigated by the spirit of liberty which it breathes throughout. Sir, I know, as well as any one, what compensations there are for all this opulence and power, for it is the condition of our being that we " buy our blessings at a price." I know that there are disturbing causes which have hitherto marred, in some degree, the effect of this high and mighty civilization ; but the hand of reform has been already applied to them, and every thing promises the most auspicious results. I have it on the most unquestionable authority, because, from an unwilling witness, that within the memory of man, never were the labouring classes of England so universally employed, and so comfortably situated as at the beginning of the present year.

But I said that there was another nation that had some experience in banking and its effects. Sir, I dare not trust myself to speak of my country with the rapture which I habitually feel when I contemplate her marvellous history. But this I will say, that on my return to it, after an absence of only four years, I was filled with wonder at all I saw and all I heard. What upon earth is to be compared with it ? I found New York grown up to almost double its former size, with the air of a great capital, instead of a mere flourishing commercial town, as I had known it. I listened to accounts of voyages of a thousand miles in magnificent steamboats on the waters of those great lakes, which, but the other day, I left sleeping in the primeval silence of nature, in the recesses of a vast wilderness; and I felt that there is a grandeur and a majesty in this irresistible onward march of a race, created, as I believe, and elected to possess and people a continent, which belong to few other objects, either of the moral or material world. We may become so much accustomed to such things that they shall make as little impression on our minds as the glories of the Heavens above us; but, looking on them, lately, as with the eye of the stranger, I felt, what a recent English traveller is said to have remarked, that, far from being without poetry, as some have vainly alleged, our whole country is one great poem. Sir, it is so; and if there be a man that can think of what is doing, in all parts of this most blessed of all lands, to embellish and advance it, who can contemplate that living mass of intelligence, activity and improvement as it rolls on, in its sure and steady progress,

to the uttermost extremities of the west; who can see scenes of savage desolation transformed, almost with the suddenness of enchantment, into those of fruitfulness and beauty ; crowned with flourishing cities, filled with the noblest of all populations ; if there be a man, I say, that can witness all this passing under his very eyes, without feeling his heart beat high, and his imagination warmed and transported by it, be sure, sir, that the raptures of song exist not for him ; he would listen in vain to Tasso or Camoens, telling a tale of the wars of knights and crusaders, or of the discovery and conquest of another hemisphere.

Sir, thinking as I do of these things ; not doubting, for a moment, the infinite superiority of our race in every thing that relates to a refined and well ordered public economy, and in all the means and instruments of a high social improvement, it strikes me as of all paradoxes the most singular, to hear foreign examples seriously proposed for our imitation in the very matters wherein that superiority has ever appeared to me to be most unquestionable. The reflection has occurred to me a thousand times in travelling over the continent of Europe. as I passed through filthy ill-paved villages, through towns in which there is no appearance of an improvement having been made since the Reformation, as I have looked at the wretched hovel of the poor peasant or artisan, or seen him at his labours with his clumsy implements and coarse gear—what a change would take place in the whole aspect of the country, if it were to fall in the hands of Americans for a single generation !

But is it paper money and the credit system alone that have achieved all these wonders? I do not say so, sir ; but can you say, can any one presume to say, that they have not done much of all this? I know that the cardinal spring and source of our success is freedom—freedom, with the peculiar character that belongs to it in our race—freedom of thought, freedom of speech, freedom of action, freedom of commerce, freedom not merely from the oppressions, but from those undue restraints and that impertinent interference of government in the interests properly belonging to individuals, which stand in the way of all improvement in the nations of continental Europe. It is this vital principle, the animating element of social equality, tempered and sobered by a profound respect for the authority of the laws, and for the rights of others, and acting upon that other prominent characteristic of the Anglo-Norman race, the strong instinct of *property*, with the personal independence and personal *comfort* that belong to it, that explains our unrivalled and astonishing progress. But of this rational, diffusive liberty, among a people so intelligent as ours, the credit system is the natural fruit, the inseparable companion, the necessary means and instrument. It is part and parcel of our existence. Whoever heard of CREDIT in a despotism, or an anarchy ? It implies *confidence*— confidence in yourself, confidence in your neighbour, confidence in your government, confidence in the administration of the laws, confidence in the sagacity, the integrity, the discretion of those with whom you have to deal; confidence, in a word, in your destiny, and your fortune, in the destinies and the fortune of the country to which you belong; as, for instance, in the case of a great national debt. It is the fruit, I say, of all that is most precious in civilized life, and to quarrel with it is to be ungrateful to God for some of the greatest blessings he has vouchsafed to man. Compare Asia with Europe; hoarding has been the usage of the former from time immemorial, because it is slavish, oppressed and barbarous; and it is curious to see the effect of English laws in breaking up (as they are doing) that system in Hindoostan. Depend upon it, sir, all such ideas are utterly alien to our way of thinking—to all the habitudes of our people, and all the interests of the country. My friends from beyond the mountains are familiar with the great principle, the magical effect of credit in a young and progressive country. They know that miracles are wrought by a small advance of money to enable enterprise and industry to bring into cultivation a virgin soil. They know how soon the treasures of its unworn fertility enable them to pay off a loan of that sort with usurious interest, and make them proprietors of estates rising in value with the lapse of every moment. Compare the great western country now, with what it was twenty years ago—sell it *sub hasta*—and compute, if the powers of arithmetic will enable you to do so, the augmentation of its riches. Sir, this is one of the phenomena of our situation to which attention has hardly ever been called—the manner in which the mere increase of population acts upon the value of property. To be struck with the prodigious results produced in this simple way, you have only to compare the estimated taxable property in Pennsylvania and New York, when it was returned for direct taxation in '99, with the returns of the same property, for the same purpose, in 1813, after an interval of fourteen years—you will see how it is that our people have been enriched by debt, and " by owing, owe not"—how with a balance of payments almost continually against them from the first settlement of the country, they have grown in riches beyond all precedent or parallel. You will appreciate all the blessings of the credit system—and imagine, perhaps, how this wonderful progress would have been impeded and embarrassed by the difficulties of a metallic circulation.

CATULLUS.
FROM AN ESSAY ON ROMAN LITERATURE.

In reference to the merits of any merely *literary* composition, a foreigner must ever distrust his own opinions when they do not entirely coincide with those of native critics. For this reason, we feel bound to admit that we probably overrate Catullus and Lucretius in considering them (for we profess to have always considered them)—as in point of original genius, the two first poets of ancient Rome. The critics of their own country say nothing that is not in their favour, but it is plain that they do not entertain so exalted an opinion of their excellence as we have ventured to express. When we speak of "the poet," says Justinian, in the begin-

ning of his Institutes, we mean Homer among the Greeks, and Virgil among the Romans; and there are others besides the Mantuan bard, who seem in the same way to take precedence of our favourites in the estimation of ancient writers.

Catullus had, among the poets of his own country, the title of *doctus*, or learned; for what reason, is not quite clear. If we are to suppose, however, with some of the commentators, that it was because of his familiar acquaintance with the Greek language and literature, we must do him the justice to say, that of all imitators he has the most originality—that of all erudite men he retains the greatest share of the playfulness, the buoyancy, and the vigour of natural talent. There is no constraint whatever in his movements—no parade or pedantry in his style. On the contrary, there never was a poet—we do not even except Shakspeare—who seemed to write more as the mood happened to prompt, and whose verses are stamped with such a decided character of facility and of spontaneity. This, indeed, is the great, and among the Latin poets, the peculiar charm of Catullus. Of all the Romans, he is most of a Greek, not by study and imitation, but by nature. His lively wit, his voluptuous character, his hearty affections, his powerful imagination, seem naturally to overflow in verse and " voluntary wake harmonious numbers." Julius Cæsar Scaliger, who finds fault with every thing, disputed this poet's pretensions to learning, and denounced his works as stuffed with nothing but vulgarity and ribaldry, but he afterwards sung a palinodia, declaring the Galliambic ode a most noble composition, and the Epithalamium of Thetis and Peleus worthy to be placed by the side of the Eneid. Other writers have been equally lavish of their praise for other excellencies; Martial, for instance, ascribes to him an unrivalled superiority in the epigram. It is impossible to imagine any two things from the same pen more entirely unlike each other, than the ode just mentioned, and the sweet and delicate effusion upon Lesbia's Sparrow, nor any falling off so sudden as from either of these to the vulgarity and nastiness of some of the Hendecasyllables. His amatory poetry is less tender than that of Tibullus, and less gay and *gallant* than that of Ovid; but it is more simple, more cordial, more voluptuous than either. A modern reader would be very much disappointed if he expected to find in it that delicacy of sentiment; that *culte des femmes ;* that distant, mysterious, and adoring love which inspired the muse of Dante and Petrarch, and which has ever since characterized the amorous ditties of our sonnetteers. The passion of Catullus had not a particle of Platonic abstraction in it—it was as far as possible from being metaphysical. It is deeply tinged with sensuality, but it has absolute possession of his whole being; he seems to be smitten to the bottom of his heart with its power—to be quite intoxicated with its delicious raptures. It is that " drunkenness of soul," of which Byron speaks, from an imagination excited and exalted by visions of bliss and images of beauty—with every feeling absorbed in one devoted passion, and all the senses dissolved in a dream of love.

The sensibility of Catullus, however, is not confined to the subjects of amatory song. There are several of his poems, on various occasions, which are full of tenderness and deep pathos. Quando leggete, says Flaminio, his imitator and almost his rival—" non vi sentite voi liquefare il cuore di dolcezza." Nothing can be more true to nature and more touching than his address to the Peninsula of Sirmio—his home, and perhaps his birth-place. The Carmen Nuptiale has been often imitated, and is committed to memory by every scholar, and the Epithalamium of Julius and Manlius may be regarded as perfect in its kind. But the noblest specimen, beyond comparison, of poetry and pathos which the works of Catullus present—the most powerful appeal to the sympathies of the human bosom as the liveliest picture of its hidden workings and intensest agonies, is that Galliambic ode to which we have already alluded. The subject is, to be sure, a very affecting one. Under the influence of a frenzied enthusiasm, a young man forsakes his home and his country, for the purpose of dedicating himself to the service of the Idæan Goddess. The vow of chastity which a monk may break, was rendered inviolable to the Gallæ (for so the priests of Cybele were called) by the same means which, in later times, a father of the church adopted to disarm the temptations of the flesh. Atys, in the frenzy of his first excitement, is regularly initiated. He rushes madly forth to mingle in the revelry of the Gallæ, whom he arouses by the trump and the timbrel, and wildly exhorts to follow him to the lofty groves of the goddess. Their frantic demeanor, the Bacchanalian dances, their shrill and piercing howls are painted with a force of colouring which nothing can surpass. The imitative harmony of the versification is perfect—it is abrupt, irregular, disordered. You hear it in the hurried step, the clashing cymbal, the resounding timbrel. To all this commotion and disorder, a moment of repose—of soft but fatal repose—succeeds. The Mænades, exhausted by their furious excitement, sink down at the threshold of the temple to sleep. A beautiful morning rises upon them, and Atys wakes—to despair. His lament is affecting beyond the power of language to describe. It seems wrung from a broken heart and is fraught with all its agony and desolation. All the poetry of all ages may be safely challenged to produce any thing more painfully interesting and pathetic.

GREEK LANGUAGE AND LITERATURE.

FROM AN ESSAY ON CLASSICAL LEARNING.

It is impossible to contemplate the annals of Greek literature and art, without being struck with them, as by far the most extraordinary and brilliant phenomena in the history of the human mind. The very language—even in its primitive simplicity, as it came down from the rhapsodists who celebrated the exploits of Hercules and Theseus, was as great a wonder as any it records. All the other tongues that civilized man has spoken are poor and feeble, and barbarous, in comparison with it. Its compass and flexibility, its riches and its powers, are altogether unlimited. It not only expresses with precision all that is thought or known at any given period, but it enlarges itself naturally, with the progress of science, and affords, as if without an effort, a new phrase, or a systematic nomenclature whenever one is called for. It is equally adapted to every variety of style and subject—to the most shadowy subtlety of distinction, and the utmost exactness of definition, as well as to the energy and the pathos of popular eloquence—to the majesty, the elevation, the variety of the epic, and the boldest license of the dithyrambic, no less than to the sweetness of the elegy, the simplicity of the pastoral, or the heedless gaiety and delicate characterization of comedy. Above all, what is an unspeakable charm—a sort of naiveté is peculiar to it, which appears in all those various styles, and is quite as becoming and agreeable in a historian or a philosopher—Xenophon for instance—as in the light and jocund numbers of Anacreon. Indeed, were there no other object in learning Greek but to see to what perfection language is capable of being carried, not only as a medium of communication, but as an instrument of thought, we see not why the time of a young man would not be just as well bestowed in acquiring a knowledge of it—for all the purposes, at least, of a liberal or elementary education—as in learning algebra, another specimen of a language or arrangement of signs perfect in its kind. But this wonderful idiom happens to have been spoken, as was hinted in the preceding paragraph, by a race as wonderful. The very first monument of their genius—the most ancient relic of letters in the western world—stands to this day altogether unrivalled in the exalted class to which it belongs. What was the history of this immortal poem and of its great fellow? Was it a single individual, and who was he, that composed them? Had he any master or model? What had been his education, and what was the state of society in which he lived? These questions are full of interest to a philosophical inquirer into the intellectual history of the species, but they are especially important with a view to the subject of the present discussion. Whatever causes account for the matchless excellence of these primitive poems, and for that of the language in which they are written, will go far to explain the extraordinary circumstance, that the same favoured people left nothing unattempted in philosophy, in letters and in arts, and attempted nothing without signal, and in some cases, unrivalled success. Winkleman undertakes to assign some reasons for this astonishing superiority of the Greeks, and talks very learnedly about a fine climate, delicate organs, exquisite susceptibility, the full development of the human form by gymnastic exercises, &c. For our own part, we are content to explain the phenomenon after the manner of the Scottish school of metaphysicians, in which we learned the little that we profess to know of that department of philosophy, by resolving it at once in an original law of nature : in other words, by substantially, but decently, confessing it to be inexplicable.

2 L

WILLIAM WARE.

[Born 1797. Died 1852.]

WILLIAM WARE was born at Hingham in Massachusetts on the third of August, 1797. He is a descendant in the fifth generation from Robert Ware, one of the earliest settlers of the colony, who came from England about the year 1644. His father was Henry Ware, D. D., many years honourably distinguished by his connection with the Divinity School at Cambridge, and the late Henry Ware, jr., D. D., was his elder brother. His only living brother is Dr. John Ware, who also shares of the literary tastes and talents of his family.

William Ware was graduated at Harvard University in 1816. After reading theology the usual term he was settled over the Unitarian society of Chambers street, New York, where he remained about sixteen years. He gave little to the press except a few sermons, and four numbers of a religious miscellany called The Unitarian, until near the close of this period, when he commenced the publication in the Knickerbocker Magazine of those brilliant papers which in the autumn of 1836 were given to the world under the title of Zenobia or the Fall of Palmyra, an Historical Romance. Before the completion of this work he had resigned his pastoral office and removed to Brookline, near Boston.

The romance of Zenobia is in the form of letters to Marcus Curtius, at Rome, from Lucius Manlius Piso, a senator, who is supposed to have been led by circumstances of a private nature to visit Palmyra toward the close of the third century, to have become acquainted with the queen and her court, to have seen the City of the Desert in its greatest magnificence, and to have witnessed its destruction by the Emperor Aurelian. For the purposes of romantic fiction the subject is perhaps the finest that had not been appropriated in all ancient history; and the treatment of it, which is highly picturesque and dramatic throughout, shows that the author has been a successful student of the institutions, manners and social life of the age he has attempted to illustrate.

Mr. Ware's second romance, Probus, or Rome in the Third Century, was published in

the summer of 1838. It is a sort of sequel to the Zenobia, and is composed of letters purporting to be written by Piso from Rome to Fausta, the daughter of Gracchus, one of the old Palmyrene ministers. • In the first work Piso meets with Probus, a Christian teacher, and is partially convinced of the truth of his doctrine; he is now a disciple, and a sharer of the persecutions which marked the last days of the reign of Aurelian. The characters in Probus are skilfully drawn and contrasted, and with a deeper moral interest, from the frequent discussions of doctrine which it contains, the romance has the classical style and spirit which characterized its predecessor.

Mr. Ware's third work is entitled Julian, or Scenes in Judea, and was published in 1841. The hero is a Roman, of Hebrew descent, who visits the land of his ancestors, to gratify a liberal curiosity, during the last days of the Saviour. Every thing connected with Palestine at this period is so familiar that the ground might seem to be sacred to History and Religion; but it has often been invaded by the romancer, and perhaps never with more success than in the present instance. Although Julian has less freshness than Zenobia, it has an air of truth and sincerity that renders it scarcely less interesting.

Mr. Ware was several years editor of the Christian Examiner, the very able journal of religion and letters published at Boston, and he was till 1845 minister of the Unitarian Society at West Cambridge, but ill health has since compelled him to relinquish all kinds of occupation. He died, Feb. 19, 1852.

The writings of Mr. Ware betray a familiarity with the civilization of the ancients, and are written in a graceful, pure and brilliant style. In our literature they are peculiar, and they will bear a favourable comparison with the most celebrated historical romances relating to the same scenes and periods which have been written abroad. They have passed through many editions in Great Britain, and have been translated into German and other languages of the continent.

THE JOURNEY TO PALMYRA.

FROM ZENOBIA.

I WILL not detain you long with our voyage, but will only mark out its course. Leaving the African shore, we struck across to Sicily, and coasting along its eastern border, beheld with pleasure the towering form of Ætna, sending up into the heavens a dull and sluggish cloud of vapours. We then ran between the Peloponnesus and Crete, and so held our course till the Island of Cyprus rose like her own fair goddess from the ocean, and filled our eyes with a beautiful vision of hill and valley, wooded promontory, and glittering towns and villas. A fair wind soon withdrew us from these charming prospects, and after driving us swiftly and roughly over the remainder of our way, rewarded us with a brighter and more welcome vision still—the coast of Syria and our destined port, Berytus.

As far as the eye could reach, both toward the north and the south, we beheld a luxuriant region, crowded with villages, and giving every indication of comfort and wealth. The city itself, which we rapidly approached, was of inferior size, but presented an agreeable prospect of warehouses, public and private edifices, overtopped here and there by the lofty palm, and other trees of a new and peculiar foliage. Four days were consumed here in the purchase of slaves, camels, and horses, and in other preparations for the journey across the desert. Two routes represented themselves, one more, the other less direct; the last, though more circuitous, appeared to me the more desirable, as it would take me within sight of the modern glories and ancient remains of Heliopolis. This, therefore, was determined upon; and on the morning of the fifth day we set forward upon our long march. Four slaves, two camels, and three horses, with an Arab conductor, constituted our little caravan; but for greater safety we attached ourselves to a much larger one than our own, consisting of travellers and traders from all parts of the world, and who were also on their way to Palmyra, as a point whence to separate to various parts of the vast east. It would delight me to lay before you, with the distinctness and minuteness of a picture, the whole of this novel and to me interesting route; but I must content myself with a slight sketch, and reserve fuller communications to the time when, once more seated with you upon the Cœlian, we enjoy the freedom of social converse.

Our way through the valleys of Libanus was like one long wandering among the pleasure grounds of opulent citizens. The land was everywhere richly cultivated, and a happier peasantry, as far as the eye of the traveller could judge, nowhere exists. The most luxuriant valleys of our own Italy are not more crowded with the evidences of plenty and contentment. Upon drawing near to the ancient Baalbec, I found, on inquiry of our guide, that we were not to pass through it, as I had hoped, nor even very near it, not nearer than between two and three miles. So that in this I had been

clearly deceived by those of whom I had made the most exact inquiries at Berytus. The event proved, however, that it was not for nothing; for soon after we had started on our journey, on the morning of the second day, turning suddenly around the projecting rock of a mountain ridge, we all at once beheld, as if a vail had been lifted up, Heliopolis and its suburbs spread out before us in all their various beauty. The city lay about three miles distant. I could only therefore identify its principle structure, the Temple of the Sun, as built by the first Antonine. This towered above the walls and over all the other buildings, and gave vast ideas of the greatness of the place, leading the mind to crowd it with other edifices that should bear some proportion to this noble monument of imperial magnificence. As suddenly as the view of this imposing scene had been revealed, so suddenly was it again eclipsed by another short turn in the road, which took us once more into the mountain valleys. But the overhanging and impenetrable foliage of a Syrian forest shielding me from the fierce rays of a burning sun, soon reconciled me to my loss—more especially as I knew that in a short time we were to enter upon the sandy desert which stretches from the Anti-Libanus almost to the very walls of Palmyra.

Upon this boundless desert we now soon entered. The scene which it presented was more dismal than I can describe. A red, moving sand —or hard and baked by the heat of a sun such as Rome never knows—low, gray rocks just rising here and there above the level of the plain, with now and then the dead and glittering trunk of a vast cedar, whose roots seemed as if they had outlasted centuries—the bones of camels and elephants, scattered on either hand, dazzling the sight by reason of their excessive whiteness—at a distance occasionally an Arab of the desert, for a moment surveying our long line, and then darting off to his fastnesses—these were the objects which, with scarce any variation, met our eyes during the four wearisome days that we dragged ourselves over this wild and inhospitable region. A little after the noon of the fourth day, as we started on our way, having refreshed ourselves and our exhausted animals, at a spring which here poured out its warm but still grateful waters to the traveller, my ears received the agreeable news that toward the east there could now be discerned the dark line which indicated our approach to the verdant tract that encompasses the great city. Our own excited spirits were quickly imparted to our beasts, and a more rapid movement soon revealed into distinctness the high land and waving groves of palm trees which mark the site of Palmyra.

It was several miles before we reached the city, that we suddenly found ourselves—landing as it were from a sea upon an island or continent—in a rich and thickly peopled country. The roads indicated an approach to a great capital in the increasing numbers of those who thronged them, meeting and passing us, overtaking us, or crossing our path. Elephants, camels, and the dromedary, which I had before seen only in the amphitheatres,

I here beheld as the native inhabitants of the soil. Frequent villas of the rich and luxurious Palmyrenes to which they retreat from the greater heats of the city now threw a lovely charm over the scene. Nothing can exceed the splendour of the sumptuous palaces. Italy itself has nothing which surpasses them. The new and brilliant costumes of the persons whom we met, together with the rich housings of the animals they rode, served greatly to add to all this beauty. I was still entranced, as it were, by the objects around me, and buried in reflection, when I was aroused by the shout of those who led the caravan, and who had attained the summit of a little rising ground, saying, " Palmyra ! Palmyra !" I urged forward my steed, and in a moment the most wonderful prospect I ever beheld—no, I cannot except even Rome—burst upon my sight. Flanked by hills of considerable elevation on the east, the city filled the whole plain below as far as the eye could reach, both toward the north and toward the south. This immense plain was all one vast and boundless city. It seemed to me to be larger than Rome. Yet I knew very well that it could not be, that it was not. And it was some time before I understood the true character of the scene before me, so as to separate the city from the country and the country from the city, which here wonderfully interpenetrate each other and so confound and deceive the observer. For the city proper is so studded with groups of lofty palm trees, shooting up among its temples and palaces, and on the other hand, the plain in its immediate vicinity is so thickly adorned with magnificent structures of the purest marble, that it is not easy, nay it is impossible at the distance at which I contemplated the whole, to distinguish the line which divided the one from the other. It was all city and all country, all country and all city. Those which lay before me I was ready to believe were the Elysian Fields. I imagined that I saw under my feet the dwellings of purified men and of gods. Certainly they were too glorious for the mere earthborn. There was a central point, however, which chiefly fixed my attention, where the vast Temple of the Sun stretched upward its thousand columns of polished marble to the heavens, in its matchless beauty casting into the shade every other work of art of which the world can boast. I have stood before the Parthenon, and have almost worshipped that divine achievement of the immortal Phidias. But it is a toy by the side of this bright crown of the eastern capital. I have been at Milan, at Ephesus, at Alexandria, at Antioch ; but in neither of these renowned cities have I beheld any thing that I can allow to approach in united extent, grandeur, and most consummate beauty, this almost more than work of man. On each side of this, the central point, there rose upward slender pyramids—pointed obelisks—domes of the most graceful proportions, columns, arches, and lofty towers, for number, and for form, beyond my power to describe. These buildings, as well as the walls of the city, being all either of white marble or of some stone as white, and being everywhere in their whole extent interspersed, as I have already said, with mul-

titudes of overshadowing palm trees, perfectly filled and satisfied my sense of beauty, and made me feel for the moment, as if in such a scene I should love to dwell and there end my days. Nor was I alone in these transports of delight. All my fellow-travellers seemed equally affected : and from the native Palmyrenes, of whom there were many among us, the most impassioned and boastful exclamations broke forth. " What is Rome to this ?" they cried. " Fortune is not constant. Why may not Palmyra be what Rome has been—mistress of the world ? Who more fit to rule than the great Zenobia ? A few years may see great changes. Who can tell what shall come to pass ?" These, and many such sayings, were uttered by those around me, accompanied by many significant gestures and glances of the eye. I thought of them afterward. We now descended the hill, and the long line of our caravan moved on toward the city.

THE DESTRUCTION OF PALMYRA.
FROM THE SAME.

AFTER one day of preparation and one of assault the city had fallen, and Aurelian again entered in triumph ; this time in the spirit of revenge and retaliation. It is evident, as we look on, horror-struck, that no quarter is given, but that a general massacre has been ordered, both of soldier and citizen. We can behold whole herds of the defenceless populace escaping from the gates or over the walls, only to be pursued—hunted—and slaughtered by the remorseless soldiers. And thousands upon thousands have we seen driven over the walls, or hurled from the battlements of the lofty towers to perish, dashed upon the rocks below.

No sooner had the evening of this fatal day set in, than a new scene of terrific sublimity opened before us, as we beheld flames beginning to ascend from every part of the city. They grew and spread till they presently appeared to wrap all objects alike in one vast sheet of fire. Towers, pinnacles and domes, after glittering awhile in the fierce blaze, one after another fell and disappeared in the general ruin. The Temple of the Sun stood long untouched, shining almost with the brightness of the sun itself, its polished shafts and sides reflecting the surrounding fires with an intense brilliancy. We hoped that it might escape, and were certain that it would, unless fired from within—as from its insulated position the flames from the neighbouring buildings could not reach it. But we watched not long ere from its western extremity the fire broke forth, and warned us that that peerless monument of human genius, like all else, would soon crumble to the ground. To our amazement however and joy, the flames, after having made great progress, were suddenly arrested, and by some cause extinguished ; and the vast pile stood towering in the centre of the desolation, of double size as it seemed, from the fall and disappearance of so many of the surrounding structures......

On the third day after the capture of the city

and the massacre of the inhabitants, the army of the "conqueror and destroyer" withdrew from the scene of its glory, and again disappeared beyond the desert. I sought not the presence of Aurelian while before the city, for I cared not to meet him drenched in the blood of women and children. But as soon as he and his legions were departed, we turned toward the city, as children to visit the dead body of a parent.

No language which I can use can give you any just conception of the horrors which met our view on the way to the walls and in the city itself. For more than a mile before we reached the gates, the roads and the fields, on either hand, were strewed with the bodies of those who, in their attempts to escape, had been overtaken by the enemy and slain. Many a group of bodies did we notice, evidently those of a family, the parents and the children, who, hoping to reach in company some place of security, had all—and without resistance apparently—fallen a sacrifice to the relentless fury of their pursuers. Immediately in the vicinity of the walls and under them the earth was concealed from the eye by the multitudes of the slain, and all objects were stained with the one hue of blood. Upon passing the gates and entering within those walls which I had been accustomed to regard as embracing in their wide and graceful sweep the most beautiful city of the world, my eye met naught but black and smoking ruins, fallen houses and temples, the streets choked with piles of still blazing timbers and the half-burned bodies of the dead. As I penetrated farther into the heart of the city, and to its better built and more spacious quarters, I found the destruction to be less—that the principal streets were standing, and many of the more distinguished structures. But everywhere—in the streets—upon the porticoes of private and public dwellings—upon the steps and within the very walls of the temples of every faith—in all places, the most sacred as well as the most common, lay the mangled carcasses of the wretched inhabitants. None apparently had been spared. The aged were there, with their bald or silvered heads—little children and infants—women, the young, the beautiful, the good—all were there, slaughtered in every imaginable way, and presenting to the eye spectacles of horror and of grief enough to break the heart and craze the brain. For one could not but go back to the day and the hour when they died, and suffer with these innocent thousands a part of what they suffered, when the gates of the city giving way, the infuriated soldiery poured in, and with death written in their faces and clamouring on their tongues, their quiet houses were invaded, and resisting or unresisting, they all fell together beneath the murderous knives of the savage foe. What shrieks then rent and filled the air—what prayers of agony went up to the gods for life to those whose ears on mercy's side were adders'—what piercing supplications that life might be taken and honour spared! The apartments of the rich and the noble presented the most harrowing spectacles, where the inmates, delicately nurtured, and knowing of danger, evil and wrong, only by name

and report, had first endured all that nature most abhors, and then, there where their souls had died, were slain by their brutal violators with every circumstance of most demoniac cruelty. Happy for those who, like Gracchus, foresaw the tempest and fled. These calamities have fallen chiefly upon the adherents of Antiochus; but among them, alas! were some of the noblest and most honoured families of the capital. Their bodies now lie blackened and bloated upon their door-stones—their own halls have become their tombs.....

The silence of death and of ruin rests over this once and but so lately populous city. As I stood upon a high point which overlooked a large extent of it, I could discern no signs of life, except here and there a detachment of the Roman guard dragging forth the bodies of the slaughtered citizens, and bearing them to be burned or buried. This whole people is extinct. In a single day these hundred thousands have found a common grave. Not one remains to bewail or bury the dead. Where are the anxious crowds, who, when their dwellings have been burned, eagerly rush in as the flames have spent themselves to sorrow over their smoking altars, and pry with busy search among the hot ashes, if perchance they may yet rescue some lamented treasure, or bear away at least the bones of a parent or a child, buried beneath the ruins? They are not here. It is broad day, and the sun shines bright, but not a living form is seen lingering about these desolated streets and squares. Birds of prey are already hovering round, and alighting without apprehension of disturbance wherever the banquet invites them; and soon as the shadows of evening shall fall, the hyena of the desert will be here to gorge himself upon what they have left, having scented afar off upon the tainted breeze the fumes of the rich feast here spread for him. These Roman grave-diggers from the legion of Bassus, are alone upon the ground to contend with them for their prize. O, miserable condition of humanity! Why is it that to man have been given passions which he cannot tame, and which sink him below the brute! Why is it that a few ambitious are permitted by the Great Ruler, in the selfish pursuit of their own aggrandizement, to scatter in ruin, desolation, and death, whole kingdoms—making misery and destruction the steps by which they mount up to their seats of pride! O, gentle doctrine of Christ! doctrine of love and of peace, when shall it be that I and all mankind shall know thy truth, and the world smile with a new happiness under thy life-giving reign!

DEDICATION OF THE TEMPLE OF THE SUN.

FROM PROBUS.

Vast preparations had been making for the dedication for many days or even months preceding, and the day arose upon a city full of expectation of the shows, ceremonies and games that were to reward their long and patient waiting. For the season of the year the day was hot, unnaturally so; and the sky filled with those massive clouds, piled like mountains of snow one upon another, which, while they both please the eye by their forms and veil the fierce splendours of the sun as they now and then sail across his face, at the same time portend wind and storm. All Rome was early astir. It was ushered in by the criers traversing the streets and proclaiming the rites and spectacles of the day, what they were and where to be witnessed, followed by troops of boys imitating in their grotesque way the pompous declarations of the men of authority, not unfrequently drawing down upon their heads the curses and the batons of the insulted dignitaries. ....

At the appointed hour we were at the palace of Aurelian on the Palatine, where a procession, pompous as art and rank and numbers could make it, was formed, to move thence by a winding and distant route to the temple near the foot of the Quirinal. Julia repaired with Portia to a place of observation near the temple—I to the palace to join the company of the emperor. Of the gorgeous magnificence of the procession I shall tell you nothing. It was in extent and variety of pomp and costliness of decoration, a copy of that of the late triumph, and went even beyond the captivating splendour of the example. Roman music—which is not that of Palmyra—lent such charms as it could to our passage through the streets to the temple, from a thousand performers.

As we drew near to the lofty fabric, I thought that no scene of such various beauty and magnificence had ever met my eye. The temple itself is a work of unrivalled art. In size it surpasses any other building of the same kind in Rome, and for the excellence in workmanship and purity of design, although it may fall below the standard of Hadrian's age, yet for a certain air of grandeur and luxuriance of invention in its details, and lavish profusion of embellishment in gold and silver, no temple or other edifice of any preceding age ever perhaps resembled it. Its order is the Corinthian, of the Roman form, and the entire building is surrounded by its slender columns, each composed of a single piece of marble. Upon the front is wrought Apollo surrounded by the Hours. The western extremity is approached by a flight of steps of the same breadth as the temple itself. At the eastern there extends beyond the walls to a distance equal to the length of the building a marble platform, upon which stands the altar of sacrifice, and which is ascended by various flights of steps, some little more than a gently rising plain, up which the beasts are led that are destined to the altar.

When this vast extent of wall and column of the most dazzling brightness came into view, everywhere covered, together with the surrounding temples, palaces and theatres, with a dense mass of human beings, of all climes and regions, dressed out in their richest attire—music from innumerable instruments filling the heavens with harmony—shouts of the proud and excited populace every few moments and from different points, as Aurelian advanced, shaking the air with its thrilling din—the neighing of horses, the frequent blasts of the trumpet—the

whole made more solemnly imposing by the vast masses of cloud which swept over the sky, now suddenly unveiling and again eclipsing the sun, the great god of this idolatry, and from which few could withdraw their gaze ;—when at once this all broke upon my eye and ear, I was like a child who before had never seen aught but his own village and his own rural temple, in the effect wrought upon me, and the passiveness with which I abandoned myself to the sway of the senses. Not one there was more ravished by the outward circumstance and show. I thought of Rome's thousand years, of her power, her greatness and universal empire, and for a moment my step was not less proud than that of Aurelian. But after that moment—when the senses had had their fill, when the eye had seen the glory, and the ear had fed upon the harmony and the praise, then I thought and felt very differently ; sorrow and compassion for these gay multitudes were at my heart ; prophetic forebodings of disaster, danger, and ruin to those to whose sacred cause I had linked myself, made my tongue to falter in its speech and my limbs to tremble. I thought that the superstition that was upheld by the wealth and the power, whose manifestations were before me, had its roots in the very centre of the earth—far too deep down for a few like myself ever to reach them. I was like one whose last hope of life and escape is suddenly struck away.

I was roused from these meditations by our arrival at the eastern front of the temple. Between the two central columns, on a throne of gold and ivory, sat the emperor of the world, surrounded by the senate, the colleges of augurs and haruspices, and by the priests of the various temples of the capital, all in their peculiar costume. Then Fronto, the priest of the temple, when the crier had proclaimed that the hour of worship and sacrifice had come, and had commanded silence to be observed —standing at the altar, glittering in his white and golden robes like a messenger of light—bared his head, and lifting his face up toward the sun, offered in clear and sounding tones the prayers of dedication. As he came toward the close of his prayer, he, as is so usual, with loud and almost frantic cries and importunate repetition, called upon the god to hear him, and then with appropriate names and praises invoked the Father of gods and men to be present and hear. Just as he had thus solemnly invoked Jupiter by name, and was about to call upon the other gods in the same manner, the clouds, which had been deepening and darkening, suddenly obscured the sun ; a distant peal of thunder rolled along the heavens, and at the same moment from the dark recesses of the temple a voice of preternatural power came forth, proclaiming so that the whole multitude heard the words—" God is but one ; the king eternal, immortal, invisible." It is impossible to describe the horror that seized those multitudes. Many cried out with fear, and each seemed to shrink behind the other. Paleness sat upon every face. The priest paused as if struck by a power from above. Even the brazen Fronto was appalled. Aurelian leaped from his seat, and by his countenance, white and awe-struck, showed that to him it came as a voice from the gods. He spoke not, but stood gazing at the dark entrance into the temple from which the sound had come. Fronto hastily approached him, and whispering but one word as it were into his ear, the emperor started; the spell that bound him was dissolved; and recovering himself—making indeed as though a very different feeling had possessed him—cried out in fierce tones to his guards:

"Search the temple; some miscreant hid away among the columns profanes thus the worship and the place. Sieze him and drag him forth to instant death."

The guards of the emperor and the servants of the temple rushed in at that bidding and searched in every part the interior of the building. They soon emerged, saying that the search was fruitless. The temple in all its aisles and apartments was empty.

The ceremonies, quiet being again restored, then went on. Twelve bulls, of purest white and of perfect forms, their horns bound about with fillets, were now led by the servants of the temple up the marble steps to the front of the altar, where stood the cultrarii and haruspices, ready to slay them and examine their entrails. The omens as gathered by the eyes of all from the fierce strugglings and bellowings of the animals as they were led toward the place of sacrifice—some even escaping from the hands of those who had the management of them—and from the violent and convulsive throes of others as the blow fell upon their heads, or the knife severed their throats, were of the darkest character, and brought a deep gloom upon the brow of the emperor. The report of the haruspices upon examination of the entrails was little calculated to remove that gloom. It was for the most part unfavourable. Especially appalling was the sight of a heart so lean and withered that it scarce seemed possible it should ever have formed a part of a living animal. But more harrowing than all was the voice of Fronto, who prying with the haruspices into the smoking carcass of one of the slaughtered bulls, suddenly cried out with horror that "no heart was to be found."

The emperor, hardly to be restrained by those near him from some expression of anger, ordered a more diligent search to be made.

"It is not in nature that such a thing should be," he said. "Men are, in truth, sometimes without hearts; but brutes, as I think, never."

The report was however confidently confirmed. Fronto himself approached, and said that his eye had from the first been upon the beast, and the exact truth had been stated.

The carcasses, such parts as were for the flames, were then laid upon the vast altar, and the flames of the sacrifice ascended.

The heavens were again obscured by thick clouds, which, accumulating into dark masses, began now nearer and nearer to shoot forth lightning and roll their thunders. The priest commenced the last office, prayer to the god to whom the new temple had been thus solemnly consecrated. He again bowed his head, and again lifted up his voice. But no sooner had he invoked the god of the temple and besought his ear, than again from its dark interior the same awful sounds issued forth, this time saying "Thy gods, O Rome, are false and lying gods. God is but one."

Aurelian, pale as it seemed to me with superstitious fear, strove to shake it off, giving it artfully and with violence the appearance of offended dignity. His voice was a shriek rather than a human utterance, as he cried out,

"This is but a Christian device; search the temple till the accursed Nazarene be found, and hew him piecemeal—" more he would have said, but at the instant a bolt of lightning shot from the heavens, and lighting upon a large sycamore which shaded a part of the temple court, clove it in twain. The swollen cloud at the same moment burst, and a deluge of rain poured upon the city, the temple, the gazing multitudes, and the just kindled altars. The sacred fires went out in hissing and darkness; a tempest of wind whirled the limbs of the slaughtered victims into the air, and abroad over the neighbouring streets. All was confusion, uproar, terror and dismay. The crowds sought safety in the houses of the nearest inhabitants, and the porches of the palaces. Aurelian and the senators, and those nearest him, fled to the interior of the temple. The heavens blazed with the quick flashing of the lightning, and the temple itself seemed to rock beneath the voice of the thunder. I never knew in Rome so terrific a tempest. The stoutest trembled, for life hung by a thread. Great numbers, it has now been found, in every part of the capitol, fell a prey to the fiery bolts. The capitol itself was struck, and the brass statue of Vespasian in the forum thrown down and partly melted. The Tiber in a few hours overran its banks, and laid much of the city on its borders under water.

But ere long the storm was over. The retreating clouds, but still sullenly muttering in the distance as they rolled away, were gaily lighted up by the sun, which again shone forth in his splendour. The scattered limbs of the victims were collected and again laid upon the altar. Dry wood being brought, the flames quickly shot upward and consumed to the last joint and bone the sacred offerings. Fronto once more stood before the altar, and now, uninterrupted, performed the last office of the ceremony. Then around the tables spread within the temple to the honour of the gods, feasting upon the luxuries contributed by every quarter of the earth, and filling high with wine, the adverse omens of the day were by most forgotten. But not by Aurelian. No smile was seen to light up his dark countenance. The jests of Varus and the wisdom of Porphyrius alike failed to reach him. Wrapped up in his own thoughts, he brooded gloomily over what had happened, and strove to read the interpretation of portents so unusual and alarming.

GEORGE BANCROFT.

[Born 1800.]

MR. BANCROFT was born in Worcester, Massachusetts, in the year 1800. His father, the Reverend Aaron Bancroft, D. D., who died at an advanced age in 1839, after having been for more than half a century minister of a Congregational church in that town, was a theological and historical writer of some reputation, and was eminently distinguished for the liberality of his views, the kindness of his manners, and the spotless purity of his character. His Life of Washington, of which many editions have been published, appeared originally in 1807, and his devotion to American history at this period doubtless had some influence in kindling that intellectual passion in his son which has since produced such honourable fruits.

At the early age of thirteen Mr. Bancroft entered Harvard College, where he graduated in 1817, with the first honours of his class. He had determined to study theology, and his essay on this occasion, for which he received from the corporation one of the Bowdoin prizes, was on the Use and Necessity of Revelation. In the following year, he went to Germany, and devoted himself two years to the study of history and philology, under Professor Heeren, at Göttingen, where he received the degree of Doctor of Philosophy. He then went to Berlin, where he cultivated the society of learned men, (among others of Varnhagen von Ense, one of the most brilliant of contemporary German authors,) and next to Heidelberg, where he became acquainted with Schlosser, the first of German historians, who awakened his taste for history. Before his return he also visited Italy and France, and stayed a short time in London.

He had not entirely abandoned his design of entering the ministry. Indeed he preached a few times, in a manner that induced predictions that he would greatly distinguish himself in the pulpit. But he was disposed to devote himself to literature and learning, and cherished dreams of successful authorship. His first book was a small collection of Poems,

404

chiefly illustrative of his experiences and observations abroad, which appeared in 1823. In the following year he gave the public his translation of the Reflections on the Politics of Ancient Greece, by Professor Heeren, with whom, at Göttingen, he had been accustomed to live on terms of intimacy, and soon after, he opened the Round Hill School, at Northampton, and devoted himself assiduously to teaching. Here he translated several books on the study of the ancient languages, from the German, and in 1828, Heeren's histories of the States of Antiquity, and of the Political System of Europe and its Colonies, from the Discovery of America to the Independence of the American Continent. These versions demanded and evinced not only a thorough knowledge of the German language, but a wide range of classical and general learning.

He now began to give more and more attention to politics. At first he was a Whig, but during his residence at Northampton he went over to the Democracy, and in an article in the Boston Quarterly Review, on the Progress of Civilization, attempted to show that the natural association of men of letters is with that party.

In 1834 Mr. Bancroft published the first volume of his History of the Colonization of the United States, which was everywhere received with the liveliest applause. The reputation which he acquired by this and other literary labours, and the ability he exhibited as a politician, commended him to the notice of the dispensers of place and patronage in Washington, and he was appointed to the lucrative post of Collector of the Customs at Boston. His official duties did not divert him from his studies, and in 1837 he gave to the press the second and in 1840 the third volume of his History, completing the first part of it, and introducing, as a youthful surveyor in the service of Virginia, the hero of the second, which is to embrace the period and appear under the title of The History of the Revolution.

On the election of General Harrison to the

Presidency Mr. Bancroft was superseded as Collector of Boston, but the democrats came into power again in 1844, and he was then called into the Cabinet, as Secretary of the Navy. Here he was a bold and fearless reformer, in a department in which much reform was needed, and though many of his recommendations respecting the Navy were not adopted, for reasons quite independent of their inherent character, no minister has exerted a more powerful or advantageous influence upon this branch of the public service.* He resigned his place in the cabinet in September, 1846, was immediately after appointed Minister Plenipotentiary to Great Britain, and in the month of October arrived in London, where he resided until 1849.

Mr. Bancroft's History of the United States is one of the great works of the present age, stamped more plainly with its essential character than any other of a similar sort that has been written. The subject of the birth and early experiences of a radically new and thoroughly independent nation, has a deep philosophical interest, which to the historian is in stead of that dramatic attraction of which the few incidents in the progress of many small communities, scattered over a continent, independent of each other, and all dependent on a foreign power, are necessarily destitute. This Mr. Bancroft perceives, and entering deeply into the spirit of the times, he becomes insensibly the advocate of the cause of freedom, which invalidates his testimony. He suffers too much "his passion to instruct his reason." He is more mastered by his subject than himself master of it. Liberty with him is not the result of an analytical process, but the basis of his work, and he builds upon it synthetically.

When Mr. Bancroft commenced his labours, the very valuable but incomplete history by Judge Marshall was the only work on the subject by a native author that was deserving of much praise. Grahame's faithful history of the Colonization, and the brilliant account of the Revolution by Botta, were acknowledged to be the best histories of the country for their respective periods. This fact alone was sufficient to guide an American historian

* Among many things for which the country is indebted to Mr. Bancroft the Secretary, are the Nautical School of Alexandria and the Astronomical Observatory of Washington.

in the choice of his theme, had he been less deeply imbued than Mr. Bancroft with the principles which our history illustrates.— Whatever may be the merit of some of Mr. Bancroft's opinions, there are in the volumes he has published no signs of a superficial study of events. His narrative is based on contemporary documents, and he has shown remarkable patience in collecting, and in assorting, comparing and arranging them. In this respect his work is singularly faithful.

In regard to the characters and adventures of many of the early discoverers, the principles and policies of the founders of several of the states, and the peculiarities and influences of the various classes of colonists, the details are full and the reflections eminently philosophical. The languages, religions, and rural and warlike customs of the Indians, are also treated in a manner that evinces much research and ingenuity.

Mr. Bancroft's style is elaborate, scholarly, and forcible, though sometimes not without a visible effort at eloquence, and there is occasionally a dignity of phrase that is not in keeping with the subject matter. It lacks the delightful ease and uniform *proportion* which mark the diction of Prescott.

He is evidently sincere in the principles he advocates, though in a few points of minor importance he has evinced some unsteadiness of conviction. Altogether his work is equal to its great reputation in general ability, research and originality, and it is eminently American, in the best sense of that word as used in regard to literature.

Mr. Bancroft's History has been translated into several foreign languages, and the German version recently passed to a fourth edition. It has been republished in its original language in London and Paris.

The fourth and fifth volumes of the History being the first and second volumes of the History of the Revolution, were published in 1852–3, vol. 6th in 1854, vol. 7th in 1858, vol. 8th in 1860, vol. 9th in 1866, and the 10th is preparing. He is now minister to Prussia.

Besides the works of Mr. Bancroft which I have mentioned, he has published an abridgment of his History of the Colonization of the United States, several orations, articles in the North American and Boston Quarterly Reviews, and a vol. of Miscellanies.

VIRGINIA.

FROM THE HISTORY OF THE UNITED STATES.

VIRGINIA had long been the home of its inhabitants. "Among many other blessings," said their statute-book, "God Almighty hath vouchsafed increase of children to this colony; who are now multiplied to a considerable number," and the huts in the wilderness were as full as the birds-nests of the woods.

The genial climate and transparent atmosphere delighted those who had come from the denser air of England. Every object in nature was new and wonderful. The loud and frequent thunder-storms were phenomena that had been rarely witnessed in the colder summers of the north; the forests, majestic in their growth, and free from underwood, deserved admiration for their unrivalled magnificence; the purling streams and the frequent rivers, flowing between alluvial banks, quickened the ever-pregnant soil into an unwearied fertility; the strangest and the most delicate flowers grew familiarly in the fields; the woods were replenished with sweet barks and odours; the gardens matured the fruits of Europe, of which the growth was invigorated and the flavour improved by the activity of the virgin mould. Especially the birds, with their gay plumage and varied melodies, inspired delight; every traveller expressed his pleasure in listening to the mocking-bird, which carolled a thousand several tunes, imitating and excelling the notes of all its rivals. The humming-bird, so brilliant in its plumage and so delicate in its form, quick in motion yet not fearing the presence of man, haunting about the flowers like the bee gathering honey, rebounding from the blossoms into which it dips its bill, and as soon returning "to renew its many addresses to its delightful objects," was ever admired as the smallest and the most beautiful of the feathered race. The rattle-snake, with the terrors of its alarms and the power of its venom; the opossum, soon to become as celebrated for the care of its offspring as the fabled pelican; the noisy frog, booming from the shallows like the English bittern; the flying-squirrel; the myriads of pigeons, darkening the air with the immensity of their flocks, and, as men believed, breaking with their weight the boughs of trees on which they alighted,—were all honoured with frequent commemoration and became the subjects of the strangest tales. The concurrent relation of all the Indians justified the belief, that, within ten days' journey toward the setting of the sun, there was a country where gold might be washed from the sand, and where the natives themselves had learned the use of the crucible; but definite and accurate as were the accounts, inquiry was always baffled, and the regions of gold remained for two centuries an undiscovered land.

Various were the employments by which the calmness of life was relieved. George Sandys, an idle man, who had been a great traveller, and who did not remain in America, a poet whose verse was tolerated by Dryden and praised by Izaak Walton, beguiled the ennui of his seclusion by translating the whole of Ovid's Metamorphoses. To the man of leisure, the chase furnished a perpetual resource. It was not long before the horse was multiplied in Virginia; and to improve that noble animal was early an object of pride, soon to be favoured by legislation. Speed was especially valued; and "the planter's pace" became a proverb.

Equally proverbial was the hospitality of the Virginians. Labour was valuable; land was cheap; competence promptly followed industry. There was no need of a scramble; abundance gushed from the earth for all. The morasses were alive with water-fowl; the creeks abounded with oysters, heaped together in inexhaustible beds; the rivers were crowded with fish; the forests were nimble with game; the woods rustled with covies of quails and wild-turkies, while they rung with the merry notes of the singing birds; and hogs, swarming like vermin, ran at large in troops. It was "the best poor man's country in the world." "If a happy peace be settled in poor England," it had been said, "then they in Virginia shall be as happy a people as any under heaven." But plenty encouraged indolence. No domestic manufactures were established; every thing was imported from England. The chief branch of industry, for the purpose of exchanges, was tobacco-planting; and the spirit of invention was enfeebled by the uniformity of pursuit.

CONNECTICUT.

FROM THE SAME.

CONNECTICUT, from the first, possessed unmixed popular liberty. The government was in honest and upright hands; the little strifes of rivalry never became heated; the magistrates were sometimes persons of no ordinary endowments; but though gifts of learning and genius were valued, the state was content with virtue and single-mindedness; and the public welfare never suffered at the hands of plain men. Roger Williams had ever been a welcome guest at Hartford; and "that heavenly man, John Haynes," would say to him, "I think, Mr. Williams, I must now confess to you, that the most wise God hath provided and cut out this part of the world as a refuge and receptacle for all sorts of consciences." There never existed a persecuting spirit in Connecticut; while "it had a scholar to their minister in every town or village." Education was cherished; religious knowledge was carried to the highest degree of refinement, alike in its application to moral duties, and to the mysterious questions on the nature of God, of liberty, and of the soul. A hardy race multiplied along the alluvion of the streams, and subdued the more rocky and less inviting fields; its population for a century doubled once in twenty years, in spite of considerable emigration; and if, as has often been said, the ratio of the increase of population is the surest criterion of public happiness, Connecticut was long the happiest state in the world. Religion united with the pursuits of agriculture, to give to the land the aspect of salubrity. The domestic wars were discussions of knotty points in theology; the concerns of the parish, the merits of the minister, were the weightiest affairs; and a church reproof the heaviest calamity. The strifes of the parent country, though they sometimes occasioned a levy among the sons of the husbandmen, yet never brought an enemy within their borders; tranquillity was within their gates, and the peace of God within their hearts. No fears of midnight ruffians could disturb the sweetness of slumber; the best house required no fastening but a latch, lifted by a string; bolts and locks were unknown.

There was nothing morose in the Connecticut character. It was temperate industry enjoying the abundance which it had created. No great inequalities of condition excited envy, or raised political feuds; wealth could display itself only in a larger house and a fuller barn; and covetousness was satisfied by the tranquil succession of harvests. There was venison from the hills; salmon, in their season, not less than shad, from the rivers; and sugar from the trees of the forest. For a foreign market little was produced beside cattle; and in return for them but few foreign luxuries stole in. Even so late as 1713, the number of seamen did not exceed one hundred and twenty. The soil had originally been justly divided, or held as common property in trust for the public, and for new comers. Forestalling was successfully resisted; the brood of speculators in land inexorably turned aside. Happiness was enjoyed unconsciously; beneath the rugged exterior humanity wore its sweetest smile. There was for a long time hardly a lawyer in the land. The husbandman who held his own plough, and fed his own cattle, was the great man of the age; no one was superior to the matron, who, with her busy daughters, kept the hum of the wheel incessantly alive, spinning and weaving every article of their dress. Fashion was confined within narrow limits; and pride, which aimed at no grander equipage than a pillion, could exult only in the common splendor of the blue and white linen gown, with short sleeves, coming down to the waist, and in the snow-white flaxen apron, which, primly starched and ironed, was worn on public days by every woman in the land. For there was no revolution except from the time of sowing to the time of reaping; from the plain dress of the week day to the more trim attire of Sunday.

Every family was taught to look upward to God, as to the Fountain of all good. Yet life was not sombre. The spirit of frolic mingled with innocence: religion itself sometimes wore the garb of gayety; and thanksgiving to God was, from primitive times, as joyous as it was sincere. Nature always asserts her rights, and abounds in means of gladness.

The frugality of private life had its influence on public expenditure. Half a century after the concession of the charter, the annual expenses of the government did not exceed eight hundred pounds, or four thousand dollars; and the wages of the chief justice were ten shillings a day while on service. In each county a magistrate acted as judge of probate, and the business was transacted with small expense to the fatherless.

Education was always esteemed a concern of deepest interest, and there were common schools from the first. Nor was it long before a small college, such as the day of small things permitted, began to be established; and Yale owes its birth "to ten worthy fathers, who, in 1700, assembled at Branford, and each one, laying a few volumes on a table, said, 'I give these books for the founding of a college in this colony.'"

But the political education of the people is due to the happy organization of towns, which here, as indeed throughout all New England, constituted each separate settlement a little democracy of itself. It was the natural reproduction of the system, which the instinct of humanity had imperfectly revealed to our Anglo-Saxon ancestors. In the ancient republics, citizenship had been an hereditary privilege. In Connecticut, citizenship was acquired by inhabitancy, was lost by removal. Each town-meeting was a little legislature, and all inhabitants, the affluent and more needy, the wise and the foolish, were members with equal franchises. There the taxes of the town were discussed and levied; there the village officers were chosen; there roads were laid out, and bridges voted; there the minister was elected, the representatives to the assembly were instructed. The debate was open to all; wisdom asked no favours; the churl abated nothing of his pretensions. Whoever reads the records of these village democracies, will be perpetually coming upon some little document of political wisdom, which breathes the freshness of rural legislation, and wins a disproportioned interest, from the justice and simplicity of the times. As the progress of society required exertions in a wider field, the public mind was quickened by associations that were blended with early history; and when Connecticut emerged from the quiet of its origin, and made its way into scenes where a new political world was to be created, the sagacity that had regulated the affairs of the village, gained admiration in the field and in council.

———◆———

CHIVALRY AND PURITANISM.
FROM THE SAME.

HISTORIANS have loved to eulogize the manners and virtues, the glory and the benefits, of chivalry. Puritanism accomplished for mankind far more. If it had the sectarian crime of intolerance, chivalry had the vices of dissoluteness. The knights were brave from gallantry of spirit; the Puritans from the fear of God. The knights were proud of loyalty; the Puritans of liberty. The knights did homage to monarchs, in whose smile they beheld honour, whose rebuke was the wound of disgrace; the Puritans, disdaining ceremony, would not bow at the name of Jesus, nor bend the knee to the King of kings. Chivalry delighted in outward show, favoured pleasure, multiplied amusement, and degraded the human race by an exclusive respect for the privileged classes; Puritanism bridled the passions, commanded the virtues of self-denial, and rescued the name of man from disho-nour. The former valued courtesy; the latter, jus-tice. The former adorned society by graceful re-finements; the latter founded national grandeur on universal education. The institutions of chivalry were subverted by the gradually-increasing weight, and knowledge, and opulence of the industrious classes; the Puritans, rallying upon those classes, planted in their hearts the undying principles of democratic liberty.

THE HUGUENOTS IN CAROLINA.
FROM THE SAME.

WHAT need of describing the stripes, the roast-ings by slow fires, the plunging into wells, the gashes from knives, the wounds from red-hot pin-cers, and all the cruelties employed by men who were only forbidden not to ravish nor to kill? The loss of lives cannot be computed. How many thousands of men, how many thousands of chil-dren and women, perished in the attempt to escape, who can tell? An historian has asserted that ten thousand perished at the stake, or on the gibbet and the wheel.

But the efforts of tyranny were powerless. Truth enjoys serenely her own immortality; and opinion, which always yields to a clearer convic-tion, laughs violence to scorn. The unparalleled persecution of vast masses of men for their reli-gious creed, occasioned but a new display of the power of humanity; the Calvinists preserved their faith over the ashes of their churches, and the bodies of their murdered ministers. The power of a brutal soldiery was defied by whole companies of faith-ful men, that still assembled to sing their psalms; and from the country and the city, from the com-fortable homes of wealthy merchants, from the abodes of an humbler peasantry, from the work-shops of artisans, hundreds of thousands of men rose up, as with one heart, to bear testimony to the indefeasible, irresistible right to freedom of mind.

Every wise government was eager to offer a re-fuge to the upright men who would carry to other countries the arts, the skill in manufactures, and the wealth of France. Emigrant Huguenots put a new aspect on the north of Germany, where they filled entire towns and sections of cities, introduc-ing manufactures before unknown. A suburb of London was filled with French mechanics; the prince of Orange gained entire regiments of sol-diers, as brave as those whom Cromwell led to vic-tory; a colony of them reached even the Cape of Good Hope. In our American colonies they were welcome everywhere. The religious sympathies of New England were awakened; did any arrive in poverty, having barely escaped with life?—the towns of Massachusetts contributed liberally to their support, and provided them with lands. Others repaired to New York; but the warmer climate was more inviting to the exiles of Languedoc, and South Carolina became the chief resort of the Huguenots. What though the attempt to emigrate was by the

law of France a felony? In spite of every pre-caution of the police, five hundred thousand souls escaped from their country. The unfortunate were more wakeful to fly than the ministers of tyranny to restrain....

Escaping from a land where the profession of their religion was a felony, where their estates were liable to be confiscated in favour of the apostate, where the preaching of their faith was a crime to be expiated on the wheel, where their children might be torn from them, to be subjected to the nearest Catholic relation—the fugitives from Lan-guedoc on the Mediterranean, from Rochelle, and Saintange, and Bordeaux, the provinces on the Bay of Biscay, from St. Quentin, Poictiers, and the beautiful valley of Tour, from St. Lo and Dieppe, men who had the virtues of the English Puritans, without their bigotry, came to the land to which the tolerant benevolence of Shaftesbury had invited the believer of every creed. From a land that had suffered its king, in wanton bigotry, to drive half a million of its best citizens into exile, they came to the land which was the hospitable re-fuge of the oppressed; where superstition and fa-naticism, infidelity and faith, cold speculation and animated zeal, were alike admitted without ques-tion, and where the fires of religious persecution were never to be kindled. There they obtained an assignment of lands, and soon had tenements; there they might safely make the woods the scene of their devotions, and join the simple incense of their psalms to the melodies of the winds among the ancient groves. Their church was in Charles-ton; and thither, on every Lord's day, gathering from their plantations upon the banks of the Cooper, and taking advantage of the ebb and flow of the tide, they might all regularly be seen, the parents with their children, whom no bigot could now wrest from them, making their way in light skiffs along the river, through scenes so tranquil, that silence was broken only by the rippling of oars, and the hum of the flourishing village that gemmed the confluence of the rivers.

NEW NETHERLANDS AND NEW YORK.
FROM THE SAME.

SOMBRE forests shed a melancholy grandeur over the useless magnificence of nature, and hid in their deep shades the rich soil which the sun had never warmed. No axe had levelled the giant progeny of the crowded groves, in which the fantastic forms of withered limbs, that had been blasted and riven by lightning, contrasted strangely with the ver-dant freshness of a younger growth of branches. The wanton grape-vine, seeming by its own power to have sprung from the earth, and to have fas-tened its leafy coils on the top of the tallest fo-rest tree, swung in the air with every breeze, like the loosened shrouds of a ship. Trees might every-where be seen breaking from their root in the marshy soil, and threatening to fall with the first rude gust; while the ground was strown with the ruins of former forests, over which a profusion of wild flowers wasted their freshness in mockery of the gloom. Reptiles sported in the stagnant pools, or crawled unharmed over piles of mouldering trees. The spotted deer couched among the thickets; but not to hide, for there was no pursuer; and there were none but wild animals to crop the uncut herbage of the productive prairies. Silence reigned, broken, it may have been, by the flight of land-birds or the flapping of water-fowl, and rendered more dismal by the howl of beasts of prey. The streams, not yet limited to a channel, spread over sand-bars, tufted with copses of willow, or waded through wastes of reeds; or slowly but surely undermined the groups of sycamores that grew by their side. The smaller brooks spread out into sedgy swamps, that were overhung by clouds of mosquitoes; masses of decaying vegetation fed the exhalations with the seeds of pestilence, and made the balmy air of the summer's evening as deadly as it seemed grateful. Vegetable life and death were mingled hideously together. The horrors of corruption frowned on the fruitless fertility of uncultivated nature.

And man, the occupant of the soil, was wild as the savage scene, in harmony with the rude nature by which he was surrounded; a vagrant over the continent, in constant warfare with his fellow-man; the bark of the birch his canoe; strings of shells his ornaments, his record, and his coin; the roots of the forest among his resources for food; his knowledge in architecture surpassed both in strength and durability by the skill of a beaver; bended saplings the beams of his house; the branches and rind of trees its roof; drifts of forest-leaves his couch; mats of bulrushes his protection against the winter's cold; his religion the adoration of nature; his morals the promptings of undisciplined instinct; disputing with the wolves and bears the lordship of the soil, and dividing with the squirrel the wild fruits with which the universal woodlands abounded....

And how changed is the scene from that on which Hudson gazed! The earth glows with the colours of civilization; the banks of the streams are enamelled with richest grasses; woodlands and cultivated fields are harmoniously blended; the birds of spring find their delight in orchards and trim gardens, variegated with choicest plants from every temperate zone; while the brilliant flowers of the tropics bloom from the windows of the greenhouse and the saloon. The yeoman, living like a good neighbour near the fields he cultivates, glories in the fruitfulness of the valleys, and counts with honest exultation the flocks and herds that browse in safety on the hills. The thorn has given way to the rosebush; the cultivated vine clambers over rocks where the brood of serpents used to nestle; while industry smiles at the changes she has wrought, and inhales the bland air which now has health on its wings.

And man is still in harmony with nature, which he has subdued, cultivated, and adorned. For him the rivers that flow to remotest climes mingle their waters; for him the lakes gain new outlets to the ocean; for him the arch spans the flood, and

science spreads iron pathways to the recent wilderness; for him the hills yield up the shining marble and the enduring granite; for him the forests of the interior come down in immense rafts; for him the marts of the city gather the produce of every clime, and libraries collect the works of genius of every language and every age. The passions of society are chastened into purity; manners are made benevolent by civilization; and the virtue of the country is the guardian of its peace. Science investigates the powers of every plant and mineral, to find medicines for disease; schools of surgery rival the establishments of the Old World. An active daily press, vigilant from party interests, free even to dissoluteness, watches the progress of society, and communicates every fact that can interest humanity; the genius of letters begins to unfold his powers in the warm sunshine of public favour. And while idle curiosity may take its walk in shady avenues by the ocean side, commerce pushes its wharves into the sea, blocks up the wide rivers with its fleets, and, sending its ships, the pride of naval architecture, to every clime, defies every wind, outrides every tempest, and invades every zone.

———◆———

JOHN LOCKE AND WILLIAM PENN.

FROM THE SAME.

PENN, despairing of relief in Europe, bent the whole energy of his mind to accomplish the establishment of a free government in the New World. For that "heavenly end," he was prepared by the severe discipline of life, and the love, without dissimulation, which formed the basis of his character. The sentiment of cheerful humanity was irrepressibly strong in his bosom; as with John Eliot and Roger Williams, benevolence gushed prodigally from his ever-flowing heart; and when, in his late old age, his intellect was impaired, and his reason prostrated by apoplexy, his sweetness of disposition rose serenely over the clouds of disease. Possessing an extraordinary greatness of mind, vast conceptions, remarkable for their universality and precision, and "surpassing in speculative endowments;" conversant with men, and books, and governments, with various languages, and the forms of political combinations, as they existed in England and France, in Holland, and the principalities and free cities of Germany, he yet sought the source of wisdom in his own soul. Humane by nature and by suffering; familiar with the royal family; intimate with Sunderland and Sydney; acquainted with Russel, Halifax, Shaftesbury, and Buckingham; as a member of the Royal Society, the peer of Newton and the great scholars of his age,—he valued the promptings of a free mind more than the awards of the learned, and reverenced the single-minded sincerity of the Nottingham shepherd more than the authority of colleges and the wisdom of philosophers. And now, being in the meridian of life, but a year older than was Locke, when, twelve years before, he had framed a constitution for Carolina, the Quaker legislator was come to the New World to lay the foundations of states. Would he imitate the vaunted system of the great philosopher? Locke, like William Penn, was tolerant; both loved freedom; both cherished truth in sincerity. But Locke kindled the torch of liberty at the fires of tradition; Penn at the living light in the soul. Locke sought truth through the senses and the outward world; Penn looked inward to the divine revelations in every mind. Locke compared the soul to a sheet of white paper, just as Hobbes had compared it to a slate, on which time and chance might scrawl their experience; to Penn, the soul was an organ which of itself instinctively breathes divine harmonies, like those musical instruments which are so curiously and perfectly framed, that, when once set in motion, they of themselves give forth all the melodies designed by the artist that made them. To Locke, "Conscience is nothing else than our own opinion of our own actions;" to Penn, it is the image of God, and his oracle in the soul. Locke, who was never a father, esteemed "the duty of parents to preserve their children to not be understood without reward and punishment;" Penn loved his children, with not a thought for the consequences. Locke, who was never married, declares marriage an affair of the senses; Penn reverenced woman as the object of fervent, inward affection, made, not for lust, but for love. In studying the understanding, Locke begins with the sources of knowledge; Penn with an inventory of our intellectual treasures. Locke deduces government from Noah and Adam, rests it upon contract, and announces its end to be the security of property; Penn, far from going back to Adam, or even to Noah, declares that "there must be a people before a government," and, deducing the right to institute government from man's moral nature, seeks its fundamental rules in the immutable dictates "of universal reason," its end in freedom and happiness. The system of Locke lends itself to contending factions of the most opposite interests and purposes; the doctrine of Fox and Penn, being but the common creed of humanity, forbids division, and insures the highest moral unity. To Locke, happiness is pleasure; things are good and evil only in reference to pleasure and pain; and to "inquire after the highest good is as absurd as to dispute whether the best relish be in apples, plums, or nuts;" Penn esteemed happiness to lie in the subjection of the baser instincts to the instinct of Deity in the breast, good and evil to be eternally and always as unlike as truth and falsehood, and the inquiry after the highest good to involve the purpose of existence. Locke says plainly, that, but for rewards and punishments beyond the grave, "it is *certainly right* to eat and drink, and enjoy what we delight in;" Penn, like Plato and Fenelon, maintained the doctrine so terrible to despots, that God is to be loved for his own sake, and virtue to be practised for its intrinsic loveliness. Locke derives the idea of infinity from the senses, describes it as purely negative, and attributes it to nothing but space, duration and number; Penn derived the idea from the soul, and ascribed it to truth, and virtue, and God. Locke

declares immortality a matter with which reason has nothing to do, and that revealed truth must be sustained by outward signs and visible acts of power; Penn saw truth by its own light, and summoned the soul to bear witness to its own glory. Locke believed "not so many men in wrong opinions as is commonly supposed, because the greatest part have no opinions at all, and do not know what they contend for;" Penn likewise vindicated the many, but it was because truth is the common inheritance of the race. Locke, in his love of tolerance, inveighed against the methods of persecution as "Popish practices;" Penn censured no sect, but condemned bigotry of all sorts as inhuman. Locke, as an American lawgiver, dreaded a too numerous democracy, and reserved all power to wealth and the feudal proprietaries; Penn believed that God is in every conscience, his light in every soul; and therefore, stretching out his arms, he built—such are his own words—"a free colony for all mankind." This is the praise of William Penn, that, in an age which had seen a popular revolution shipwreck popular liberty among selfish factions; which had seen Hugh Peters and Henry Vane perish by the hangman's cord and the axe; in an age when Sydney nourished the pride of patriotism rather than the sentiment of philanthropy, when Russel stood for the liberties of his order, and not for new enfranchisements, when Harrington, and Shaftesbury, and Locke, thought government should rest on property,—Penn did not despair of humanity, and, though all history and experience denied the sovereignty of the people, dared to cherish the noble idea of man's capacity for self-government. Conscious that there was no room for its exercise in England, the pure enthusiast, like Calvin and Descartes, a voluntary exile, was come to the banks of the Delaware to institute "THE HOLY EXPERIMENT."

WILLIAM THE THIRD.

FROM THE SAME.

THE character of the new monarch of Great Britain could mould its policy, but not its constitution. True to his purposes, he yet wins no sympathy. In political sagacity, in force of will, far superior to the English statesmen who environed him; more tolerant than his ministers or his parliaments, the childless man seems like the unknown character in algebra which is introduced to form the equation, and dismissed when the problem is solved. In his person thin and feeble, with eyes of a hectic lustre, of a temperament inclining to the melancholic, in conduct cautious, of a self-relying humour, with abiding impressions respecting men, he sought no favour, and relied for success on his own inflexibility and the greatness and maturity of his designs. Too wise to be cajoled, too firm to be complaisant, no address could sway his resolve. In Holland, he had not scrupled to derive an increase of power from the crimes of rioters and assassins; in England, no filial respect diminished the energy of his ambition. His exterior was chilling; yet he had a passionate delight in horses and the chase. In conversation he was abrupt, speaking little and slowly, and with repulsive dryness; in the day of battle, he was all activity, and the highest energy of life, without kindling his passions, animated his frame. His trust in Providence was so connected with faith in general laws, that, in every action, he sought the principle which should range it on an absolute decree. Thus, unconscious to himself, he had sympathy with the people, who always have faith in Providence. "Do you dread death in my company?" he cried to the anxious sailors, when the ice on the coast of Holland had almost crushed the boat that was bearing him to the shore. Courage and pride pervaded the reserve of the prince who, spurning an alliance with a bastard daughter of Louis XIV., had made himself the centre of a gigantic opposition to France. For England, for the English people, for English liberties, he had no affection, indifferently employing the whigs, who found their pride in the revolution, and the tories, who had opposed his elevation, and who yet were the fittest instruments "to carry the prerogative high." One great passion had absorbed his breast—the independence of his native country. The harsh encroachments of Louis XIV., which, in 1672, had made William of Orange a revolutionary stadtholder, now assisted to constitute him a revolutionary king, transforming the impassive champion of Dutch independence into the defender of the liberties of Europe.

DISCOVERY OF THE MISSISSIPPI BY MARQUETTE.

FROM THE SAME.

BEHOLD, in 1673, on the tenth day of June, the meek, single-hearted, unpretending, illustrious Marquette, with Joliet for his associate, five Frenchmen as his companions, and two Algonquins as guides, lifting their two canoes on their backs, and walking across the narrow portage that divides the Fox River from the Wisconsin. They reach the watershed;—uttering a special prayer to the immaculate Virgin, they leave the streams that, flowing onwards, could have borne their greetings to the castle of Quebec;—already they stand by the Wisconsin. "The guides returned," says the gentle Marquette, "leaving us alone, in this unknown land, in the hands of Providence." France and Christianity stood in the valley of the Mississippi. Embarking on the broad Wisconsin, the discoverers, as they sailed west, went solitarily down the stream, between alternate prairies and hill-sides, beholding neither man nor the wonted beasts of the forest: no sound broke the appalling silence, but the ripple of their canoe, and the lowing of the buffalo. In seven days, "they entered happily the Great River, with a joy that could not be expressed;" and the two birch-bark canoes, raising their happy sails under new skies and to unknown breezes, floated down the calm magnificence of the ocean stream, over the broad, clear sand-bars, the resort of innumerable waterfowl,—gliding past

islets that swelled from the bosom of the stream, with their tufts of massive thickets, and between the wide plains of Illinois and Iowa, all garlanded with majestic forests, or checkered by island groves and the open vastness of the prairie.

About sixty leagues below the mouth of the Wisconsin, the western bank of the Mississippi bore on its sands the trail of men; a little footpath was discerned leading into a beautiful prairie; and, leaving the canoes, Joliet and Marquette resolved alone to brave a meeting with the savages. After walking six miles, they beheld a village on the banks of a river, and two others on a slope, at a distance of a mile and a half from the first. The river was the Mou-in-gou-e-na, or Moingona, of which we have corrupted the same into Des Moines. Marquette and Joliet were the first white men who trod the soil of Iowa. Commending themselves to God, they uttered a loud cry. The Indians hear; four men advance slowly to meet them, bearing the peace-pipe brilliant with many coloured plumes. "We are Illinois," said they,— that is, when translated, "We are men;" and they offered the calumet. An aged chief received them at his cabin with upraised hands, exclaiming, "How beautiful is the sun, Frenchmen, when thou comest to visit us! Our whole village awaits thee; thou shalt enter in peace into all our dwellings." And the pilgrims were followed by the devouring gaze of an astonished crowd.

At the great council, Marquette published to them the one true God, their Creator. He spoke, also, of the great captain of the French, the governor of Canada, who had chastised the Five Nations and commanded peace; and he questioned them respecting the Mississippi and the tribes that possessed its banks. For the messengers, he announced the subjection of the Iroquóis, a magnificent festival was prepared of hominy, and fish, and the choicest viands from the prairies.

After six days' delay, and invitations to new visits, the chieftain of the tribe, with hundreds of warriors, attended the strangers to their canoes; and, selecting a peace-pipe embellished with the head and neck of brilliant birds, and all feathered over with plumage of various hues, they hung round Marquette the mysterious arbiter of peace and war, the sacred calumet, a safeguard among the nations.

The little group proceeded onwards. "I did not fear death," says Marquette; "I should have esteemed it the greatest happiness to have died for the glory of God." They passed the perpendicular rocks, which wore the appearance of monsters; they heard at a distance the noise of the waters of the Missouri, known to them by its Algonquin name of Pekitanoni; and, when they came to the most beautiful confluence of rivers in the world,—where the swifter Missouri rushes like a conqueror into the calmer Mississippi, dragging it, as it were, hastily to the sea,—the good Marquette resolved in his heart, anticipating Lewis and Clarke, one day to ascend the mighty river to its source; to cross the ridge that divides the oceans, and descending a westerly flowing stream, to publish the gospel to all the people of this New World.

In a little less than forty leagues, the canoes floated past the Ohio, which was then, and long afterwards, called the Wabash. Its banks were tenanted by numerous villages of the peaceful Shawnees, who quailed under the incursions of the Iroquois.

The thick canes begin to appear so close and strong, that the buffalo could not break through them; the insects become intolerable; as a shelter against the suns of July, the sails are folded into an awning. The prairies vanish; and forests of whitewood, admirable for their vastness and height, crowd even to the skirts of the pebbly shore. It is also observed that, in the land of the Chickasas, the Indians have guns.

Near the latitude of thirty-three degrees, on the western bank of the Mississippi, stood the village of Mitchigamea, in the region that had not been visited by Europeans since the days of De Soto. "Now," thought Marquette, "we must, indeed, ask the aid of the Virgin." Armed with bows and arrows, with clubs, axes, and bucklers, amidst continual whoops, the natives, bent on war, embark in vast canoes made out of the trunks of hollow trees; but, at the sight of the mysterious peace-pipe held aloft, God touched the hearts of the old men, who checked the impetuosity of the young; and, throwing their bows and quivers into the canoes, as a token of peace, they prepared a hospitable welcome.

The next day, a long, wooden canoe, containing ten men, escorted the discoverers, for eight or ten leagues to the village of Akansea, the limit of their voyage. They had left the region of the Algonquins, and, in the midst of the Sioux and Chickasas, could speak only by an interpreter. A half league above Akansea, they were met by two boats, in one of which stood the commander, holding in his hand the peace-pipe, and singing as he drew near. After offering the pipe, he gave bread of maize. The wealth of his tribe consisted in buffalo skins; their weapons were axes of steel,—a proof of commerce with Europeans.

Thus had our travellers descended below the entrance of the Arkansas, to the genial climes that have almost no winter but rains, beyond the bound of the Huron and Algonquin languages, to the vicinity of the Gulf of Mexico, and to tribes of Indians that had obtained European arms by traffic with Spaniards or with Virginia.

So, having spoken of God, and the mysteries of the Catholic faith; having become certain that the Father of Rivers went not to the ocean east of Florida, nor yet to the Gulf of California, Marquette and Joliet left Akansea, and ascended the Mississippi.

At the thirty-eighth degree of latitude, they entered the River Illinois, and discovered a country without its paragon for the fertility of its beautiful prairies, covered with buffaloes and stags,—for the loveliness of its rivulets, and the prodigal abundance of wild duck and swans, and of a species of parrots and wild turkeys. The tribe of Illinois, that tenanted its banks, entreated Marquette to come and reside among them. One of their chiefs, with their young men, conducted the party, by way of Chicago, to Lake Michigan; and, before the end of September, all were safe in Green Bay.

Joliet returned to Quebec to announce the discovery, of which the fame, through Talon, quickened the ambition of Colbert; the unaspiring Marquette remained to preach the gospel to the Miamis, who dwelt in the north of Illinois, round Chicago. Two years afterward, sailing from Chicago to Mackinaw, he entered a little river in Michigan. Erecting an altar, he said mass after the rites of the Catholic church; then, begging the men who conducted his canoe to leave him alone for a half hour,

"In the darkling wood,
Amidst the cool and silence, he knelt down,
And offered to the Mightiest solemn thanks
And supplication."

At the end of the half-hour, they went to seek him, and he was no more. The good missionary, discoverer of a world, had fallen asleep on the margin of the stream that bears his name. Near its mouth, the canoemen dug his grave in the sand. Ever after, the forest rangers, if in danger on Lake Michigan, would invoke his name. The people of the west will build his monument.

CHARACTER OF FRANKLIN.

FROM THE SAME.

WITH placid tranquillity, Benjamin Franklin looked quietly and deeply into the secrets of nature. His clear understanding was never perverted by passion, or corrupted by the pride of theory. The son of a rigid Calvinist, the grandson of a tolerant Quaker, he had from boyhood been familiar not only with theological subtilties, but with a catholic respect for freedom of mind. Skeptical of tradition as the basis of faith, he respected reason rather than authority; and, after a momentary lapse into fatalism, escaping from the mazes of fixed decrees and free will, he gained, with increasing years, an increasing trust in the overruling providence of God. Adhering to none "of all the religions" in the colonies, he yet devoutly, though without form, adhered to religion. But though famous as a disputant, and having a natural aptitude for metaphysics, he obeyed the tendency of his age, and sought by observation to win an insight into the mysteries of being. Loving truth, without prejudice and without bias, he discerned intuitively the identity of the laws of nature with those of which humanity is conscious; so that his mind was like a mirror, in which the universe, as it reflected itself, revealed her laws. He was free from mysticism, even to a fault. His morality, repudiating ascetic severities, and the system which enjoins them, was indulgent to appetites of which he abhorred the sway; but his affections were of a calm intensity; in all his career, the love of man gained the mastery over personal interest. He had not the imagination which inspires the bard or kindles the orator; but an exquisite propriety, parsimonious of ornament, gave ease of expression and graceful simplicity even to his most careless writings. In life, also, his tastes were delicate. Indifferent to the pleasures of the table, he relished the delights of music and harmony, of which he enlarged the instruments. His blandness of temper, his modesty, the benignity of his manners, made him the favourite of intelligent society ; and, with healthy cheerfulness, he derived pleasure from books, from philosophy, from conversation,—now calmly administering consolation to the sorrower, now indulging in the expression of light-hearted gayety. In his intercourse, the universality of his perceptions bore, perhaps, the character of humour ; but, while he clearly discerned the contrast between the grandeur of the universe and the feebleness of man, a serene benevolence saved him from contempt of his race, or disgust at its toils. To superficial observers, he might have seemed as an alien from speculative truth, limiting himself to the world of the senses ; and yet, in study, and among men, his mind always sought, with unaffected simplicity, to discover and apply the general principles by which nature and affairs are controlled,—now deducing from the theory of caloric improvements in fireplaces and lanterns, and now advancing human freedom by firm inductions from the inalienable rights of man. Never professing enthusiasm, never making a parade of sentiment, his practical wisdom was sometimes mistaken for the offspring of selfish prudence ; yet his hope was steadfast, like that hope which rests on the Rock of Ages, and his conduct was as unerring as though the light that led him was a light from heaven. He never anticipated action by theories of self-sacrificing virtue ; and yet, in the moments of intense activity, he, from the highest abodes of ideal truth, brought down and applied to the affairs of life the sublimest principles of goodness, as noiselessly and unostentatiously as became the man who, with a kite and hempen string, drew the lightning from the skies. He separated himself so little from his age, that he has been called the representative of materialism ; and yet, when he thought on religion, his mind passed beyond reliance on sects to faith in God ; when he wrote on politics, he founded the freedom of his country on principles that know no change ; when he turned an observing eye on nature, he passed always from the effect to the cause, from individual appearances to universal laws ; when he reflected on history, his philosophic mind found gladness and repose in the clear anticipation of the progress of humanity.

THE YOUTH OF WASHINGTON.
FROM THE SAME.

AFTER long years of strife, of repose, and of strife renewed, England and France solemnly agreed to be at peace. The treaties of Aix la Chapelle had been negotiated, by the ablest statesmen of Europe, in the splendid forms of monarchical diplomacy. They believed themselves the arbiters of mankind, the pacificators of the world,—reconstructing the colonial system on a basis which should endure for ages,—confirming the peace of Europe by the nice adjustment of material forces. At the very time of the congress of Aix la Chapelle, the woods of Virginia sheltered the youthful George Washington, the son of a widow. Born by the side of the Potomac, beneath the roof of a Westmoreland

farmer, almost from infancy his lot had been the lot of an orphan. No academy had welcomed him to its shades, no college crowned him with its honours : to read, to write, to cipher—these had been his degrees in knowledge. And now, at sixteen years of age, in quest of an honest maintenance, encountering intolerable toil ; cheered onward by being able to write to a schoolboy friend, " Dear Richard, a doubloon is my constant gain every day, and sometimes six pistoles ;" " himself his own cook, having no spit but a forked stick, no plate but a large chip ;" roaming over spurs of the Alleghenies, and along the banks of the Shenandoah ; alive to nature, and sometimes " spending the best of the day in admiring the trees and richness of the land ;" among skin-clad savages, with their scalps and rattles, or uncouth emigrants, " that would never speak English ;" rarely sleeping in a bed ; holding a bearskin a splendid couch ; glad of a resting-place for the night upon a little hay, straw, or fodder, and often camping in the forests, where the place nearest the fire was a happy luxury ;—this stripling surveyor in the woods, with no companion but his unlettered associates, and no implements of science but his compass and chain, contrasted strangely with the imperial magnificence of the congress of Aix la Chapelle. And yet God had selected, not Kaunitz, nor Newcastle, not a monarch of the house of Hapsburg, nor of Hanover, but the Virginia stripling, to give an impulse to human affairs, and, as far as events can depend on an individual, had placed the rights and the destinies of countless millions in the keeping of the widow's son.

PURITAN INTOLERANCE.
FROM THE SAME.

To the colonists the maintenance of their religious unity seemed essential to their cordial resistance to English attempts at oppression. And why, said they, should we not insist upon this union ? We have come to the outside of the world for the privilege of living by ourselves ; why should we open our asylum to those in whom we can repose no confidence ? The world cannot call this persecution. We have been banished to the wilderness ; is it an injustice to exclude our oppressors, and those whom we dread as their allies, from the place which is to shelter us from their intolerance ? Is it a great cruelty to expel from our abode the enemies of our peace, or even the doubtful friend ? Will any man complain at being driven from among banished men, with whom he has no fellowship ; of being refused admittance to a gloomy place of exile ? The wide continent of America invited colonization ; they claimed their own narrow domains of " the brethren." Their religion was their life ; they welcomed none but its adherents ; they could not tolerate the scoffer, the infidel, or the dissenter ; and the presence of the whole people was required in their congregation. Such was the system inflexibly established and regarded as the only adequate guarantee of the rising liberties of Massachusetts.

2 M 2

GEORGE P. MARSH.

[Born 1801.]

GEORGE P. MARSH, late envoy of the United States at Constantinople, was born in the pleasant village of Woodstock, in that state, in the month of March, 1801, and was educated at Dartmouth college, in New Hampshire, where he graduated with a high reputation for natural abilities and scholarship, in 1820. He soon after removed to Burlington, in Vermont, (the seat of the University of that state, of which his cousin, the late learned and reverend James Marsh,* was soon after made president,) and entered upon the study of the law ; and since his admission to the bar he has resided there, in the successful practice of his profession, except when attending to the duties which have been devolved upon him from time to time in the state and national legislatures. He was a representative in Congress from 1842 to 1849.

Mr. Marsh is known as a scholar of profound and various erudition, and as a writer of strongly marked individuality and nationality. His sympathies are with the Goths, whose presence he recognizes in whatever is grand and pecu-

liar in the characters of the founders of New England, and in whatever gives promise of her integrity, greatness, and permanence. He is undoubtedly better versed than any American in the fresh and vigorous literature of the north of Europe, and perhaps is so also in that fruit of a new birth of genius and virtue, the Puritan literature of Great Britain and continental Europe. In the Goths in New England, (published in 1836,) he has contrasted in a striking manner the characters of the Goths and the Romans, and traced the presence and influence of the former in the origin and growth of this republic ; and in a Discourse recently delivered before the New England Society of the city of New York, he enters again upon the subject, and points to the growth among us, of the Roman element which is as antagonistical to freedom as it is to Gothicism.

In New England, more than in any other part of the country, the popular character is distinctive and may be regarded as settled. The seed from the May Flower fell upon good ground, and sprung up, and the new fruit, modified by climate, and other influences, constitutes a variety by itself. No one seems to have been so successful as Mr. Marsh, in resolving the New England character into its elements, and in discerning in it what is transient and what is permanent; or with so sharp and well instructed a vision to have seen so much to justify hope of the future destinies of the country.

Mr. Marsh's acquaintance with the fine arts is very extensive and accurate, and we have few better linguists. Among the fruits of his devotion to Gothic learning are A Compendious Grammar of the Old Northern or Icelandic Language, (modestly announced on the title page as "compiled and translated from the grammar of Rask," though it is in many respects an original work,) and various essays, literary and historical, relating to the Goths, and their connexion with this country.

Mr. Marsh has also published The Camel, his introduction into the U. S. ; 2 vols. of Lectures on the English Language ; and Man and Nature, or Physical geography modified.

* James Marsh, D. D., who has been several times referred to in this volume, was born at Hartford in Vermont in 1794, was graduated at Dartmouth College in 1817, and soon after entered the seminary at Andover, where he studied divinity, about one year, at the end of which time he accepted an invitation to return to Hanover as a tutor. He again went to Andover in 1820, to complete his professional studies, and while there wrote a few articles for the North American Review, one of which is that on Italian Literature, in the thirty-sixth number. From 1823 to 1826 he was Professor of Languages in Hampden Sydney College in Virginia. In the latter year he was appointed President of the University of Vermont, but afterward resigned this office to accept that of Professor of Philosophy. He published at Burlington in 1829 the first American edition of Coleridge's Aids to Reflection, with an elaborate Preliminary Essay, which attracted a great deal of attention among thinking men by its lucid and powerful exposition and assertion of the highest principles in philosophy. In 1830 he published Selections from Old English Writers on Practical Theology ; in 1833 his translation of Herder on the Spirit of Hebrew Poetry, and at various times many articles on religion and philosophy in the periodicals. He died in the forty-eighth year of his age, in 1842. His Remarks on Psychology, Discourses on Sin, Conscience, and some other subjects, with a selection from his tracts and letters, were published in Boston in 1843. He was undoubtedly the first of our metaphysicians except Edwards.

THE GOTH AND THE ROMAN.

FROM THE GOTHS IN NEW ENGLAND.

I shall do my audience the justice to suppose, that they are too well instructed to be the slaves of that antiquated and vulgar prejudice, which makes Gothicism and barbarism synonymous. The Goths, the common ancestors of the inhabitants of North Western Europe, are the noblest branch of the Caucasian race. We are their children. It was the spirit of the Goth that guided the May-Flower across the trackless ocean; the blood of the Goth that flowed at Bunker's Hill.

Nor were the Goths the savage and destructive devastators that popular error has made them. They indeed overthrew the dominion of Rome, but they renovated her people; they prostrated her corrupt government, but they respected her monuments; and Theodoric the Goth not only spread but protected many a precious memorial, which Italian rapacity and monkish superstition have since annihilated. The old lamentation, *Quod non fere-runt barbari, fecere Barberini*, contains a world of truth, and had not Rome's own sons been her spoilers, she might have shone at this day in all the splendour of her Augustan age.

England is Gothic by birth, Roman by adoption. Whatever she has of true moral grandeur, of higher intellectual power, she owes to the Gothic mother; while her grasping ambition, her material energies, her spirit of exclusive selfishness, are due to the Roman nurse.

The Goth is characterized by the reason, the Roman by the understanding; the one by imagination, the other by fancy; the former aspires to the spiritual, the latter is prone to the sensuous. The Gothic spirit produced a Bacon, a Shakspeare, a Milton; the Roman, an Arkwright, a Brindley, and a Locke. It was a Roman, that gathered up the coals on which St. Lawrence had been broiled; a Goth, who, when a fellow disciple of the great Swiss reformer had rescued his master's heart from the enemy, on the field where the martyr fell, snatched that heart from its preserver, and hurled it, yet almost palpitating with life, into the waters of a torrent, lest some new superstition should spring from the relics of Zwingli.

Rome, it is said, thrice conquered the world; by her arms, by her literature and art, by her religion. But Rome was essentially a nation of robbers. Her territory was acquired by unjust violence. She plundered Greece of the choicest productions of the pencil and the chisel, and her own best literature and highest art are but imperfect copies of the masterpieces of the creative genius of the Greek. She not only sacked the temples, but removed to the imperial city the altars, and adopted the Gods of the nations she conquered. Tiberius even prepared a niche for the Christian Saviour among the heathen idols in the Pantheon, and when Constantine made Christianity the religion of the state, he sanctioned the corruptions which Rome had engrafted upon it, and handed it down to his successors, contaminated with the accumulated superstitions of the whole heathen world.

The Goth has thrice broken her sceptre. The Goth dispelled the charm that made her arms invincible. The Goth overthrew her idolatrous altar, and the Goth is now surpassing her proudest works in literature and in art.

The cardinal distinction between these conflicting elements, as exemplified in literature and art, government, and religion, may be thus stated. The Roman mistakes the means for the end, and subordinates the principle to the form. The Goth, valuing the means only as they contribute to the advancement of the end, looks beneath the form, and seeks the in-dwelling, life-giving principle, of which he holds the form to be but the outward expression. With the Goth, the idea of life is involved in the conception of truth, and though he recognises life as an immutable principle, yet he perceives that its forms of expression, of action, of suffering, are infinitely diversified, agreeing however in this, that all its manifestations are characterized by development, motion, progress. To him truth is symbolized by the phenomena of organic life. The living plant or animal, that has ceased to grow, has already begun to die. Living truth, therefore, though immutable in essence, he regards as active, progressive in its manifestations; and he rejects truths which have lost their vitality, forms divorced from their spirituality, symbols which have ceased to be expressive. With the Goth, all truth is an ever-living principle, whence should spring the outward expression, fluctuating, varying, according to the circumstances which call it forth; with the Roman, its organic life is petrified, frozen into inflexible forms, inert. To the one it is a perennial fountain, a living stream, which murmurs, and flows, and winds " at its own sweet will," refreshing all life within the sphere of its influence, and perpetually receiving new accessions from springs that are fed by the showers of heaven, as it hastens onward to that unfathomable ocean of divine knowledge, which is both its primeval source and its ultimate limit. To the other, it is a current congealed to ice by the rigour of winter, chilling alike the landscape and the spectator, or a pool, that stagnates, putrefies, breeds its countless swarms of winged errors.

In literature and art the Goth pursues the development of a principle, the expression of a thought, the realization of an ideal; the Roman seeks to fix the attention, and excite the admiration, of the critic or the spectator, by the material and sensuous beauties of his work.

Thus, in poetry, the Roman aims at smoothness of versification, harmonious selection and arrangement of words, and brilliancy of imagery; the Goth strives to give utterance to " thoughts that breathe, in words that burn."

In plastic and pictorial art, the Roman attracts the spectator by the grace and the voluptuous beauty of the external form, the harmony of colouring, the fitness and proportion of the accessories, the excellence of keeping; the Goth regards these but as auxiliaries, and subordinates or even sacrifices them all to the expression of the thought or passion, which dictates the action represented.

The Goth holds that goverment springs from the

people, is instituted for their behoof, and is limited to the particular objects for which it was originally established; that the legislature is but an organ for the solemn expression of the deliberate will of the nation, that the coercive power of the executive extends only to the enforcement of that will, and that penal sanctions are incurred only by resistance to it as expressed by the proper organ. The Roman views government as an institution imposed from without, and independent of the people, and holds, that it is its vocation not to express but to control the public will; and hence, by a ready corruption, government comes to be considered as established for the private advantage of the ruler, who asserts not only a proprietary right to the emoluments of office, but an ultimate title to all the possessions, both of the state and of the individual citizen.

To the same source may be referred the poor fiction of divine indefeasible right, and that other degrading doctrine, which supposes all the powers of government, legislative, judicial and executive, to have been originally lodged in the throne, allowing to the subject such political rights only, as have been conceded to him by the sovereign; and hence too that falsest and most baneful of errors, the incubus of the British constitution, which consolidates or rather confounds church and state, conceding to the civil ruler supreme authority in spiritual matters, and ascribing temporal power to religious functionaries and ecclesiastical jurisdictions. So in spiritual things we find a like antagonism....

INFLUENCE OF THE BIBLE ON LITE-RATURE AND ART.

FROM AN ADDRESS BEFORE THE NEW ENGLAND SOCIETY.

It was long ago said, that the most efficient mental training is the thorough and long continued study of some one production of a master mind, and it has become proverbial, that the most irresistible of intellectual gladiators is the man of one book, he that wields but a single weapon. If such be the effect of appropriating, and as it were, assimilating and making connatural with ourselves, the fruits of a fellow creature's mental efforts, what may we not expect from the study and comprehension of that book which is a revelation, nay, a reflection, of the mind of our Maker? What can withstand a champion who wields a naked faulchion drawn from the armory of the most High? With our Puritan ancestors the Bible was the text-book of parental instruction; it was regarded with fond and reverent partiality as the choicest classic of the school, it was the companion of the closet, the pillow of the lonely wayfarer, the only guide to happiness beyond the tomb. Of all Christian sects, the Puritans were most profoundly versed in the sacred volume; of all men they have best exemplified the spirit of its doctrines; of all religious communities, they have most abundantly enjoyed those blessings wherewith God has promised to crown his earthly church.

It is to early familiarity with the Bible, to its perse-

vering study, and its daily use, that we must chiefly ascribe the great intellectual power of the English Puritans of the seventeenth century, and the remarkable metaphysical talent of many of their American descendants. Intellectual philosophy, the knowledge of the spiritual in man, is literally, as well as figuratively, a *divine* science. It can be successfully pursued only where the divine word, undistorted by any gloss of human authority, may be both freely read and openly discussed, and where the relations of man to God and all other divine things are subject to investigation, checked by no fear of legal restraints, the condemnation of councils, or the anathema of the priest. Where the doctrine of overruling human jurisdiction in matters of faith is received, there may be scholastic subtlety indeed, but no metaphysical acuteness or depth. The tone and character of abstract speculation are always influenced by the subjects with which it is conversant, and the mind, which, through fear of trenching on forbidden ground, is forced to exert its busy energies on airy trifles, or questions of impossible solution, will soon become as frivolous, or as incapable of determination as the puzzles it idly unriddles, or the problems it vainly seeks to resolve. All higher philosophy is essentially religious, and its fearless, yet reverent study, as a science, implied if not revealed in the Scriptures, is

"Not harsh and crabbed, as dull fools suppose,"

but it is the fittest preparation both for achieving and appreciating the highest triumphs of human genius, whether in the sublimest flights of poesy, or the glorious creations of plastic and pictorial art.

It has been falsely charged upon Puritanism, that it is hostile to taste, to refinement, and to art; and this because its equal polity, its simple rites, and its humble temples, adorned with no pomp of sculptured imagery, no warm creations of the voluptuous pencil, minister not to the ambitious passions of those who serve at the altar, or of those who "only stand and wait;" and because it finds the loftiest poetry, the most glowing eloquence, the most terrible sublimity, the tenderest pathos, and the most ravishing beauty, in the visions of the Psalmist and the Prophets, the promises and menaces of the old and new covenant, the life and passion of the Saviour, the gospel delineations of the happiness of the blessed.... But if it be asked, what human spirit has been most keenly alive to feel, and most abundantly endowed with the creative power to realize, in living and imperishable forms, all that is lovely or terrible in nature, all that is grand or beautiful in art, all that is noble or refined in feeling, all that is glorious in humanity, and all that is sublime in religion, all men unhesitatingly answer, the soul of John Milton, the Christian and the Puritan. The source whence Milton drew his inspiration was the Sacred Book. Without a thorough familiarity with that volume, such poetry and such prose as that of Milton can neither be produced, nor comprehended, for the knowledge of the Bible is not merely suggestive of the loftiest conceptions, but, in awakening the mind to the idea of the infinite, it confers the power of originating as well as of appreciating them.

HERMAN HOOKER.

[Born 1804. Died 1865.]

Mr. Hooker is a native of Poultney, Rutland county, Vermont. He was·graduated at Middlebury College in 1825, and soon after entered upon the study of divinity at the Presbyterian Theological Seminary in Princeton. He subsequently took orders in the Episcopal Church, and acquired considerable reputation as a preacher; but at the end of a few years ill health compelled him to abandon the pulpit, and he has since resided in Philadelphia.

Mr. Hooker published in 1835 The Portion of the Soul, or Thoughts on its Attributes and Tendencies as Indications of its Destiny; in the same year Popular Infidelity, which in later editions is entitled, The Philosophy of Unbelief in Morals and Religion, as discernible in the Faith and Character of Men; and in 1846 The Uses of Adversity and the Provisions of Consolation. Besides these volumes, he has published much in reviews and religious miscellanies. Thoughts and Maxims. 1847.

Upon meeting with qualities like Mr. Hooker's in one not known among the popular authors of the country, we are prompted to say with Wordsworth, "Strongest minds are often those of whom the world hears least," or in the bolder words of Henry Taylor, "The world knows nothing of its greatest men." It is surprising that a voice like his should have awakened no echoes. He deserves a place among the first religious writers of the age: for he has been faithful to the great mission laid upon the priesthood, which is, not to labour upon "forms, modes, shews" of devotion, nor to dispute of systems, schools and theories of faith, but to be witnesses of a law above the world, and prophets of a consolation that is not of mortality. When we take up one of his books we could imagine that we had fallen upon one of those great masters in divinity who in the seventeenth century illustrated the field of moral relations and affections with a power and splendour peculiar to that age. These great writers possessed an apprehension of spiritual subjects, sensitive, yet profoundly rational; a vision on which the rays of a higher consciousness streamed in lustre so transcend-ing that the light of earth seemed like a shadow thrown across its course; which differed from inspiration in degree rather than in kind. The resemblance of Mr. Hooker to these great authors is obviously not an affectation. It is not confined to style, but reaches to the constitution and tone of the mind. His productions indicate the same temper of deep thoughtfulness upon man's estate and destiny; the same union of a personal sympathy with a judicial superiority, which suffers in all the human weaknesses which it detects and condemns; the same earnest sense of their subjects as realities, clear, present and palpable; the same quick feeling, toned into dignity by pervading, essential wisdom; and that direct cognisance of the substances of religion, which does not deduce its great moral truths as consequences of an assumed theory, but seizes them as primary elements that verify themselves and draw the theories after them by a natural connection. Fretted and wearied with metaphysical theologies; vexed by the self-illustration, the want of candour, the fierceness, the ungenial and unsatisfying hollowness of popular religionism, we turn with a grateful relief to this soothing and impressive system which speculates not, wrangles not, reviles not, but, while it every-where testifies of the degradation we are under, touches our spirits to power and purity by the constant exhortation of "sursum corda!"

The style of Mr. Hooker abounds in spontaneous interest and unexpected graces. It seems to result immediately from his character, and to be an inseparable part of it. It is free from all the commonplaces of fine writing; has nothing of the formal contrivance of the rhetorician, the balanced period, the pointed turn, the recurring cadence. Yet the charms of a genuine simplicity, of a directness almost quaint, of primitive gravity, and calm, native good sense, renders it singularly agreeable to a cultivated taste. Undoubtedly there is in spiritual sensibility something akin to genius, and like it tending to utterance in language significant and beautiful. We meet at times in Mr. Hooker's writings with phrases of the rarest felicity and of great delicacy and expressiveness; in which we know not whether most to admire the vigour which has conceived so striking a thought, or the refinement of art which has fixed it in words so beautifully exact. He died, 1865.

INFIDELITY AND GUILT INFERRED FROM THE VIRTUES OF MEN.
FROM THE PHILOSOPHY OF UNBELIEF.

If you take from them the diction and metre of fashion, the thoughts and affections which are bred in worldly fancies and amusements, what do you leave them but empty vessels, mansions whose great inhabitants are kept in chains by usurpers, or presented as strung up in bones, with no heart, no flashes of wit and conscience, shadowing life and hope. They are " without God in the world ;" that is, they are without that influence from him, entering into their affections, joys, plans, hopes, and shaping the conduct, which a belief of his word would impart. They are infidels, no better in condition and prospect, than those who acknowledge they are so ; and if they do not know it, it is because they have not taken the trouble to be informed : they want the reflection necessary to conviction......

Sin, considered abstractly, is no evil in their view. They never think that its nature is to obstruct all faith in the word of God,—that low apprehensions of its evil nature tend directly to produce diminishing impressions of the excellency of the divine law, and of the worth of the privileges and blessings of the gospel. In short, their views make "the manifold wisdom of God" in the great plan of redemption by the sufferings and death of Christ, foolishness, a downright misconception of their condition and necessities. Entertaining these notions of sin, and affected by them in this manner, no wonder they are not troubled by it, and do not seek deliverance from it. Who will apply for grace when he feels that he has strength enough without it ? Who that is whole will seek a physician ? Who that is in no danger will fly to a refuge ? Who can be penetrated with shame and sorrow for that which he deems no crime, or discredit to himself ? Who will learn to depend on a foreign agency to live virtuously, when virtue is his boast, and considered to be his birthright ? No persons are in greater danger of falling into these views of sin, and the unbelief they engender, than those to whom we have alluded. They are not, generally, addicted to distinguished iniquities,—things that expose themselves, abash pride, and endanger character. They are strict observers of decency and moderation in sinning. They are only devoted to pleasures and amusements called innocent. They are not pious to be sure, but that is no crime, not a thing to be repented of or alarmed at. Nothing is more common, say they, and we may safely and without reproach go with the multitude in one respect, if we shun their vices in others. Thus they are confident; no temptations scare them, no danger of being brought near great offences along an inclined road of evil is apprehended, and the only wonder is, that they last so long, that they do not sooner and oftener slide, break through all restraint, and stand out as matured criminals. There is criminality in all they do, for they do nothing well ; and not to do well, is to do wrong. Their great error is, that they do not see the sinfulness of sin in their forgetfulness of God ; in their not rating and loving objects according to the measure of their worth and excellence. These things show that their nature has run wild from goodness,—that they are estranged from God ; and to be estranged from him is the sum and essence of all sin, the very heart of infidelity,— that keeper of the conscience that shuts out the entrance of truth, and cries peace, peace, when all the peace there is, is only that, when pains and fears give way to death.

If we examine the best virtues of unconverted men generally, and particularly of such as we have last described, we shall find new light on the subject. It requires no great insight into human nature, to discover the remnants of a now fallen, but once glorious, structure ; and, what is most remarkable, to see that the remains of this ancient greatness are more apt to be quickened and drawn out by their semblances and qualities, found in creatures, than by the bright and full perfection of them which is in the Creator ;—that the heart puts on its most benign face, and sends forth prompt returns of gratitude and love to creatures who have bestowed on us favour and displayed other amiable qualities, while He, whose goodness is so great, so complete, so pervading, that there is none besides it, is unrequited, unheeded, unseen, though hanging out his glory from the heavens, and coming down to us in streams of compassion and love, which have made an ocean on earth that is to overflow and fill it. How strange it is, that all this love, so wonderful in itself, so undeserved, so diffused, that we see it in every beauty, and taste it in every enjoyment,—should be lost on creatures whose love for the gentler and worthier qualities of each other, runs so often into rapture and devotion ! How strange that they should be so delighted with streams which have gathered such admixtures of earth, which cast up such "mire and dirt," and have such shallows and falls that we often wreck our hopes in them,—as not to be reminded by them of the great and unmixed fountain whence they have flowed, or of the great ocean, to whose dark and unbottomed depths they will at last settle, as too earthy to rise to its pure and glorious surface ! There are many mysteries in human nature, but none greater than this : for while it shows man is so much a creature of sense and so devoid of faith, that objects, to gain his attention and affection, must not only be present to him, but have something of sense and self in them, we are still left to wonder how he could, with such manifestations of divine goodness in him, around him, and for him, have failed to see and adore them, and become so like a brute, as not to think of God, the original of all that is lovely, when thinking of those his qualities which so please and affect him in creatures; and this, though they be so soiled and defaced by sin, that his unmixed fondness for any the most agreeable of them, instead of being an accomplishment, is a sure indication of a mind sunk greatly below the standard allotted to it by the Creator.

Our wonder will be raised higher still, if we consider that our nature, when most corrupt and perverse, is not wholly lost to all sense of gratitude, but may be wrought upon by human kindness, when all the amazing compassion and love of God fail to affect it; if we consider that the very worst of men who set their faces against the heavens, affronting the mercy and defying the majesty thereof, are sometimes so softened with a sense of singular and undeserved favours, that their hearts swell with grateful sentiments towards their benefactors, and something akin to virtue is kindled up where nothing of the kind was seen before; we might think it incredible, if there was any doubting of what we see and know. When we see such men so ready to acknowledge their obligations to their fellows, and to return service for service; so impatient of being thought ungrateful, when they have any character or interest to promote by it, and sometimes, when they have not; so strongly affected with the goodness of him who has interposed between them and temporal danger or death, and yet so little moved by the love of God in Christ, which has undertaken their rescue from eternal and deserved woes, and not merely their rescue, but their exaltation to fellowship with himself, and to the pleasures for evermore at his right hand,—a love compared with which the greatest love of creatures is as a ray of light to the sun, and that ray mixed and darkened, while this is so disinterested and free in the grounds and motives of it, that it is exercised towards those who have neither merit to invite, nor disposition to receive it; when we see this, and find that this love, so worthy in itself, so incomprehensible in its degree and in the benefits it would confer, is the only love to which they make no returns of thankfulness or regard, we may ascribe as much of it as we please to the hardness and corruption of their hearts, but that will not account for such conduct. Depravity, considered by itself, will not enable us fully to understand it. Depraved, sensual, and perverse as they are, they have something in them that is kindled by human kindness, and why should it not be kindled by the greater "kindness of God our Saviour?" It is not because it is a divine kindness; not that it is less needed—not that it is bestowed in less measure, or at less expense. And if it is because they do not apprehend this kindness, do not feel their need of it, do not see any thing affecting in the measure and expense of it, this is infidelity; and it grows out of an entire misconception of their own character, and of the character and law of God. It is a total blindness to distant and invisible good and evil. It is a ven-

turing of every thing most important to themselves on an uncertainty, which they would not and could not do, if they had any understanding of the value of the interests at stake. They really see nothing important but the gratifications of sense and time: still they have the remains of a capacity for something higher. These may be contemplated with profit, if not with admiration. They resemble the motions in the limbs and heart of animals, when the head is severed from the body. They are symptoms of a life that of itself must come to nothing; a life that is solely pouring itself out on the ground. But as this is all the life they have, an image of life, and that only of life in death; and as the motions of it are only excited by the creature's kindness, we discover in their best virtues, or rather, in their only breathings and indications of virtue, the evidence of a faithless heart.

The different classes of people brought to our view in this chapter, generally consider themselves very innocent; some, because they are free from great vices, and others, because great vices have blinded their eyes to guilt. But it is observable that the ground of this supposed innocence is the same in all, and lies in mistaken views of the evil nature of sin, and of the gospel plan of delivering them both from its pollution and curse; so that the most virtuous one of them is as much an infidel in this as the most vicious, that he does not believe himself to be totally ruined by sin, totally destitute of any thing acceptable to a holy God, and totally dependent on him for grace to renew and fit the soul for the bliss of heaven. Their virtues, too, though in some more clearly manifested than in others, are in all the same as to the grounds and objects of them. They are such as love, gratitude, sympathy with the distresses, and patient endurance of the welfare, of others. We see much of these in one way and another, and sometimes very attractive examples of them. But, as has been shown, their aptest, if not their only exercise, is in view of the favours, claims, and virtues of creatures. These display acts of love, gratitude, and self-denial, strongly fastening on and ending in the creatures, while they are in no degree moved by the greater occasions and excitements of these virtues, found in the dispensations and perfections of the Creator. These very virtues, then, which are more the distinction of some than of others, yet in some way the boast of all, are, as truly as their vices, the proof of rank infidelity— that mixture of folly and estrangement which seems to say, "there is no God."

THE VICTORIES OF LOVE.
FROM THE USES OF ADVERSITY.

Love is represented as the fulfilling of the aw —a creature's perfection. All other graces, all divine dispensations contribute to this, and are lost in it as in a heaven. It expels the dross of our nature; it overcomes sorrow; it is the full joy of our Lord. Let us contemplate its capacities and resources as applied to the experience of life. Property and business may fail, and still the eye of hope may fix itself on other objects, and confidence may strengthen itself in other schemes, but when death enters into our family and loved ones are missing from our sight, though God may have made their bed in sickness, and established their hope in death, nothing can then relieve us but trust and love. Philosophy and pleasure do but intrude upon and aggravate our grief. But love, the light of God, may chase away the gloom of this hour, and start up in the soul trusts, which give the victory over ourselves. The harp of the spirit, though its cords be torn, never yields such sweet notes, such swelling harmony, as when the world can draw no music from it. How often do we see strokes fall on the heart, which it would be but mockery for man to attempt to relieve, and which yet served to unlock the treasures of that heart and reveal a sweetness to it, which it had not known before. See that mother. She loves and mourns as none but a mother can. Behold the greatness and the sweetness of her grief! Her child is dead, and she says "It is well with me, and it is well with my child. It is well because God has taken him; He has said ' of such is the kingdom of heaven,' that he doth not willingly afflict, and I know it must be well." Can there be any greatness greater than this? Did ever any prince at the head of invincible armies win a victory like it! Her heart is in heaviness and her home is desolated, but she has been to her heavenly Father and unbosomed her griefs before him. There is peace on her saddened countenance, peace in her gentle words, the peace of God has come down and is filling her trusting soul. How sweet and soft is her sorrow, and how it softens and awes without agitating others!

It is related that on a small, and rocky, and almost inaccessible island, is the residence of a poor widow. The passage of the place is exceedingly dangerous to vessels, and her cottage is called the "Lighthouse," from the fact that she uniformly keeps a lamp burning in her little window at night. Early and late she may be seen trimming her lamp with oil, lest some misguided bark may perish through her neglect. For this she asks no reward. But her kindness stops not here. When any vessel is wrecked, she rests not till the chilled mariners come ashore to share her little board, and be warmed by her glowing fire. This poor woman in her younger, perhaps not happier days, though happy they must have been, for sorrow cannot lodge in such a heart, witnessed her husband struggling with the waves and swallowed up by the remorseless billows,

"In sight of home and friends who thronged to save."

This directed her benevolence towards those who brave the dangers of the deep; this prompted her present devoted and solitary life, in which her only, b er sufficient enjoyment is in doing good. Sweet and blessed fruit of bereavement! What beauty is here! a loveliness I would little speak of, but more revere! a flower crushed indeed, yet sending forth its fragrance to all around! Truly, as the sun seems greatest in his lowest estate, so did sorrow enlarge her heart and make her appear the more noble, the lower it brought her down. We cannot think she was unhappy, though there was a remembered grief in her heart. A grieved heart may be a richly stored one. Where charity abounds, misery cannot.

"Such are the tender woes of love,
   Fost'ring the heart, they bend."

A pious lady who had lost her husband, was for a time inconsolable. She could not think, scarcely could she speak of any thing but him. Nothing seemed to take her attention but the three promising children he had left her, imaging to her his presence, his look, his love. But soon these were all taken ill and died within a few days of each other, and now the childless mother was calmed even by the greatness of the stroke. The hand of God was thus made visible to her. She could see nothing in the dispensation. Thus was the passion of her grief allayed. Her indisposition to speak of her loss, her solemn repose, was the admiration of all beholders. The Lord had not slain her; he had slain what to some mothers is more than life, that in which the sweets of life were treasured up, that which she would give life to redeem, and yet could she say, "I will trust in Him." As the lead that goes quickly down to the ocean's depth, ruffles its surface less than lighter things, so the blow which was strongest, did not so much disturb her calm of mind, but drove her to its proper trust.

We had a friend loved and lovely. He had genius and learning. He had all qualities, great and small, blending in a most attractive whole—a character as much to be loved as admired, as truly gentle as it was great, and so combining opposite excellencies that each was beautified by the other. Between him and her who survives him there was a reciprocity of taste and sympathy—a living in each other, so that her thoughts seemed but the pictures of his—her mind but a glass that showed the very beauty that looked into it, or rather became itself that beauty. Dying in his dying, she did not all die. Her love, the heart's animation, lifted her up; but her sense of loss was merged for a while in her love and confidence of his good estate. In strong and trusting thoughts of him as a happy spirit, and of God as his and her portion, she rested as in a cloud. A falling from this elevation, was truly a coming to one's self from God—a leaving of heaven for earth. Let her tell the rest in words as beautiful as they are true to nature. "My desolating loss I realize more and more. For many weeks his peaceful and triumphant departure left such an elevating influence on my mind. that I could only think of him as a pure and happy spirit. But now my feelings have become more selfish, and I long for the period to arrive, when I may lie down by his side and be reunited in a nobler and more enduring union than even that which was ours here."

Thus does the mind, when it ceases to look upward, fall from its elevation. Thus is the low note of sadness heard running through all the music of life, when ourselves are the instruments we play upon. The sorrow that deepens not love, and runs not off with it, must ever flood the spirit and bear it down. Our best and sweetest life, that which we live in the good of others, is richly stocked with charities. The life which we live in ourselves, that which depends on our stores, is master only of chaff and smoke, when they are taken away, and destitute of that last relieving accommodation, a resigned spirit. The young man whom Jesus told to sell all his goods and give to the poor, and he should have treasure in heaven, should be truly enriched—"was sad at that saying." He understood not the riches of love, which never feels itself so wealthy as when it has expended all in obedience to the commands it honours; never so well furnished against want and sorrow, as when best assured of the approbation of its object. In that we are creatures, we see how poor we must be, having nothing laid up in the Creator. Selfishness is poverty; it is the most utter destitution of a human being. It can bring nothing to his relief; it adds soreness to his sorrows; it sharpens his pains; it aggravates all the losses he is liable to endure, and when goaded to extremes, often turns destroyer and strikes its last blows on himself. It gives us nothing to rest in or to fly to, in trouble; it turns our affections on ourselves, self on self, as the sap of a tree descending out of season from its heavenward branches, and making not only its life useless, but its growth downward,

If there is any thing about us which good hearts will reverence, it is our grief on the loss of those we love. It is a condition in which we seem to be smitten by a Divine hand, and thus made sacred. It is a grief, too, which greatly enriches the heart, when rightly borne. There may be no rebellion of the will, the sweetest sentiments towards God and our fellow beings may be deepened, and still the desolation caused in the treasured sympathies and hopes of the heart gives a new colour to the entire scene of life. The dear affections which grew out of the consanguinities and connections of life, next to those we owe to God, are the most sacred of our being; and if the hopes and revelations of a future state did not come to our aid, our grief would be immoderate and inconsolable, when these relations are broken by death.

But we are not left to sorrow in darkness. Death is as the foreshadowing of life. We die that we may die no more. So short too is our life here, a mortal life at best, and so endless is the life on which we enter at death, an immortal life, that the consideration may well moderate our sorrow at parting. All who live must be separated by the great appointment, and if the change is their gain, we poorly commend our love to them, more poorly our love to Christ, who came to redeem them and us, for the end of taking us to his rest, if we refuse to be comforted. Yes, it is selfish to dwell on our griefs, as though some strange thing had happened to us, as though they were too important to be relieved, or it were a virtue to sink under them. I would revere all grief of this kind, yet I would say there is such a thing as a will of cherishing it, which makes it rather killing than improving in its effect. This may be done under a conceit of duty or gratitude to the dead. It may be done as a sacrifice to what we deem is expected of us, or as a thing becoming in the eyes of others. But that bereavement seems rather sanctified which saddens not the heart over much, and softens without withering it; which refuses no comfort or improvement we can profitably receive, and imposes no restraints on the rising hopes of the heart; which, in short, gives way and is lost in an overgrowth of kind and grateful affections.

OUR ONLY SATISFYING PORTION.
FROM THE PORTION OF THE SOUL.

WE have generous and noble emotions, we are capable of a devotion to one of our kind that makes us forget all that is due to ourselves, and exacts nothing but the reception of its gifts and honours, and yet all this treasure, more than we are, and more far than we can call our own or have a right to bestow, may be treated as a trifle; the perishable work of our hands may be more prized than the purest, the largest devisings of the heart; yea, what we are, and more than we can ever be in affection, may be rejected and despised as less than nothing; but let one such aspiring thought go out after God, and he will fly to meet it as of more value than all treasures. He will call in angels to rejoice over it, will reward it with what, yea more than, it intends towards him, and give it a place in his bosom. Our best aims towards him can never fail of their end; towards all other objects they must fall short of it, if not entirely yet partially, for their incapacity to impart that happiness which our devotion would expect as well as confer. No creature can reward so great a capacity as that we have; and the suffering it may cause us may equal in degree the happiness it craves. There are wrongs and losses, of which our nature is capable, which disqualify the mind and heart for their proper place and influence, and cast a gloom upon every prospect, and which we should be quite unable to bear, if we were obliged to estimate them as annihilations, or suspensions of the proper and rightful interests of our being. The smallest injury of this description could never occur in a just government, without an equivalent provided somewhere, and to be realized, we may not know in what manner. The view, however, that has been taken of this subject, promises not merely an equivalent, but a gain, and this, though it cannot take away pain, endows submission with reason, and relieves our darkness with the sun-light of hope.

THOUGHTS.

SELF-LOVE is the parent of presumption. We are never so bad or so old but self-love may keep us in favour with ourselves.

Vanity is a refined selfishness, which is ever exacting homage, but never paying any.

If a vain person flatter you, it is to try his power on you, and you must be made his tool, or he your enemy.

2 N

ORESTES A. BROWNSON.

[Born about 1802.]

Mr. Brownson is a native of Windsor county in Vermont. Except that he lost his father while he was an infant I know little of his early life. It is understood however that it was passed in scenes foreign to the pursuits of literature, and that he owes nothing to the culture of the schools. He was at one time a minister of the Presbyterian church, then a Universalist, then a Deist. The sermon preached by Dr. Channing at the ordination of Mr. Farley, in 1828, awakened in his mind a train of thought which led him again to believe himself a Christian, and resume his profession as a preacher. One Abner Kneeland, an infidel of the more vulgar description, had been for some time exciting considerable attention in Boston by harangues against the Christian religion, and Mr. Brownson, who had now outlived this sort of stuff, went to that city to oppose him, with his own experience and reason, and to gather about him such as were troubled with doubts and asking for more certain grounds of religious faith. It is a proof of his success, that the infidel organization was broken up, its press stopped, and its leader compelled to find a new home.

About this time Mr. Brownson became an admirer and a student of the contemporary French philosophers, and introduced himself to the public as a writer by a series of bold and eloquent articles in the Christian Examiner. In 1836 he published a small volume entitled New Views of Christianity, Society, and the Church. In the following year we find that he was minister of a "Society for Christian Union and Progress," some of his discourses before which were printed and had a wide circulation. In 1838 he commenced the Boston Quarterly Review, and in 1840 published Charles Elwood, or the Infidel Converted, a metaphysical novel, which was intended to be substantially the history of his own religious experience. He has since given to the press many discourses, letters, and other tracts, upon metaphysical, theological, and political subjects, but by far the largest portion of his writings has appeared in the Boston Quarterly

Review. This work he conducted almost single-handed for five years, with a freedom and an energy which gained him a wide reputation. At the close of the volume for 1842 he was induced to merge it in the Democratic Review, published in New York, "on condition of becoming a free and independent contributor to its pages for two years." The character of his articles proved unacceptable to a large portion of the subscribers to that work, and his connection with it ceased before the expiration of the time agreed upon. In the beginning of 1844 he revived his own periodical under the title of Brownson's Quarterly Review, and has ever since continued it, writing himself nearly all its contents. He had modified his politics, and philosophy, and changed his religion; and in the Roman Catholic church, with which he now united himself, he found a new audience, more numerous than any he had before addressed.

When our attention is first engaged by this ardent and earnest schemer, we are caught by the luxuriance of mental production with which his pages appear to be teeming. There is a profusion of speculative suggestion, a prodigality of bright hypothesis, and a seeming energy of logical analysis, which make us believe for the moment that we have met with an inexhaustible storehouse of thought. But when the perusal of one of his papers is ended, we are surprised to observe how little we have appropriated of that which we have read; how slightly our own faculties have been either enriched or strengthened by what they have gone through; to how small an extent the speculations of the author have become assimilated with our mental consciousness. The operations of Mr. Brownson's mind want a relation to definite and settled reason. They lack some pervading principle or quality by which they might be linked to the general sense of men. We desire to give them a fixity in the field of human interests by determining from what element of nature they take their origin, or in what results of life they propose to terminate. As it is, they seem to be lost in the infinitude of mental space. His reflective faculties are morbidly susceptible to every suggestion that comes upon the field of their action. He possesses an irritability of intelligence that reacts on every subject with an energy as quick as it is copious. But that common sense, which is the unison of the individual intellect with the general reason of life,—the organizing influence which tends to ally particular speculations to the great body of human understanding,—the magnetism of mind by which thought is inclined always to move around the axis of truth—that great, rationalizing power is wanting. The mind of Mr. Brownson displays a preternatural activity. But its action is heated, and the play of the judgment sometimes a little irregular. It is not the energy of health, but the restlessness of fever; he is ever moving onward, because he has lost the ability to remain in repose. He inquires, not to satisfy reason, but to stimulate speculation; and his processes contemplate, not the establishment of truth, but the generation of theories. He is acute, even to super-subtlety; but is wanting in comprehensiveness of view. He sees far along a narrow line of vision, but the capacity of seeing many different things at the same time, and of embracing in one expanded conception a great compass of considerations,—which is the royal faculty of Understanding,—he does not possess. His faculties are intensely " vital in every part;" but want that calmness, that self-balanced composure, that spontaneous tendency to simple, permanent principles, which give to human intelligence an aspect of greatness.

With regard to Mr. Brownson's merits as a cultivator of that philosophy of society which he professes, a candid estimate would probably determine that his own contributions to it amount to nothing : we cannot discover any one element of opinion, any one definite view, any single principle of arrangement or detail, which a future historian will refer to his name as connected with its first appearance in the science. It is indeed a little difficult for minds of that extreme susceptibility which we have noted in Mr. Brownson ever to be original: they are so impressible to the force of others, that they rarely can develope forms from their own reason against surrounding things; they multiply the suggestions of others into a thousand variations, but they do not invent. Accordingly, through life, he has played the part of a parasite mind, which passes on from system to system, clasping each in succession as a part of itself. · Arranged in the order of time, his writings now constitute a sort of Philosophical Almanac, with a new scheme of truth for every day in the year : but the explanation is to be found in that absence of genuineness which I have just referred to. It would be impossible to link his former opinions with his present ones, by any connexion, either logical or psychological. No method of reasoning could derive one from the other ; and no process of mental experience can be conceived of by which an understanding adapted to originate the former class of views could be matured into a capacity to originate the later class. But in fact neither in one case nor in the other was Mr. Brownson writing his own opinions. He once wrote La Mennais ; he afterward wrote Jouffroy ; and now he writes Comte. The development of the last phase of his views is more creditable to his judgment than to his candour; for I do not recollect that he has once mentioned the name of an author from whom he has rather compiled than borrowed. Those who are familiar with one of the greatest productions which the intellect of Europe has evolved since the Novum Organon, will not fail to recognise in Mr. Brownson's theories of the organic unity of the human race, the progressive development of society, and its subordination to inherent laws, the necessity of government, the fallacy of obedience to the will of the majority, and many other similar positions, imperfect and confused renderings of those great views that appear in a power so irresistible, an order so majestic, and a precision and certainty so absolute, in the Cours de Philosophie Positive. But in the papers of Mr. Brownson the beautiful conceptions of M. Comte are depraved by the metaphysical propension of a mind incapable of apprehending truth in a purely positive form ; in the reproduction, for example, of the French writer's views, in the article on The Community System, the scientific conception of the social unity of the race degenerates into the chimera of Platonic ideas. That method, of which the philosophical character was defined by Bacon, which was first applied to social phenomena by the prophetical sagacity of Vico, and which is illustrated with system-

atic extension in the comprehensive expositions of Comte, undoubtedly is the scheme
upon which in future times truth will be developed and society arranged: it is to be
regretted that its discoveries in politics first
became known to American readers in this
fragmentary and imperfect manner, curtailed
of their fair proportions, marred and defeatured
by the confusing dimness of the medium in
which they are reflected. Mr. Brownson's
mind is essentially an imitative one, and in
all its displays shows the stamp of a secondary character.

The style of Mr. Brownson has some good
qualities. It is commonplace, without purity,
and destitute of any characteristic brilliancy or
elegance; but it is natural, direct, and plain.
It is that simple and unaffected manner which
has the appearance of being formed, not upon
any plan, but merely by practice and use.
Occasionally his better taste is overcome by
the faults of Carlyle, or some other favourite
of the hour; but when he uses his own style, it
would be difficult to name an author who renders abstruse subjects so familiar, or conducts
the most arduous discussions with greater ease.

IMMORTALITY.

FROM CHARLES ELWOOD.

I PASS over several months in which nothing I
can bring myself to relate, of much importance occurred. Elizabeth and I met a few times after the
interview I have mentioned. She was ever the
same pure-minded, affectionate girl; but the view
which she had taken of her duty to God, and the
struggle which thence ensued between religion
and love, surrounded as she was by pious friends,
whose zeal for the soul hereafter far outran their
knowledge of what would constitute its real well-
being here, preyed upon her health, and threatened
the worst results. From those results I raise not
the veil.

One tie alone was left me, one alone bound me
to my race and to virtue. My mother, bowed with
years and afflictions, still lived, though in a distant
part of the country. A letter from a distant relative with whom she resided, informed me that she
was very ill, and demanded my presence, as she
could not survive many days. I need not say this
letter afflicted me. I had not seen my mother for
several years; not because I wanted filial affection,
but I had rarely been able to do as I would. Poverty is a stern master, and when combined with
talent and ambition, often compels us to seem
wanting in most of the better and more amiable
affections of our nature. I had always loved and
reverenced my mother; but her image rose before
me now as it never had before. It looked mournfully upon me, and in the eloquence of mute sorrow seemed to upbraid me with neglect, and to tell
me that I had failed to prove myself a good son.

I lost no time in complying with my mother's
request. I found her still living, but evidently near
her last She recognised me, brightened up a moment, thanked me for coming to see her, thanked
her God that he had permitted her to look once
more upon the face of her son, her only child, and
to God, the God in whom she believed, who had
protected her through life, and in whom she had
found solace and support under all her trials and
sorrows, she commended me, with all the fervour
of undoubting piety and the warmth of maternal

love, for time and eternity. The effort exhausted
her; she sunk into a sort of lethargy, which in a
few hours proved to be the sleep of death.

I watched by the lifeless body; I followed it to
its resting-place in the earth: went at twilight and
stood by the grave which had closed over it. Do
you ask what were my thoughts and feelings?

I was a disbeliever, but I was a man, and had a
heart; and not the less a heart because few shared
its affections. But the feelings with which professed believers and unbelievers meet death, either
for themselves or for others, are very nearly similar.
When death comes into the circle of our friends
and sunders the cords of affection, it is backward
we look, not forward, and we are with the departed
as he lives in our memories, not as he may be in
our hopes. The hopes nurtured by religion are
very consoling when grief exists only in anticipation, or after time has hallowed it; but they have
little power in the moment when it actually breaks
in upon the soul, and pierces the heart. Besides,
there are few people who know how to use their
immortality. Death to the great mass of believers
as well as of unbelievers comes as the king of terrors, in the shape of a Total Extinction of being.
The immortality of the soul is assented to rather
than believed,—believed rather than lived. And
withal it is something so far in the distant future,
that till long after the spirit has left the body, we
think and speak of the loved ones as no more.
Rarely does the believer find that relief in the doctrine of immortality, which he insists on with so
much eloquence in his controversy with unbelievers. He might find it, he ought to find it, and
one day will; but not till he learns that man is
immortal, and not merely is to be immortal.

I lingered several weeks around the grave of my
mother, and in the neighbourhood where she had
lived. It was the place where I had passed my
own childhood and youth. It was the scene of
those early associations which become the dearer
to us as we leave them the farther behind. I stood
where I had sported in the freedom of early childhood; but I stood alone, for no one was there with
whom I could speak of its frolics. One feels singularly desolate when he sees only strange faces,

and hears only strange voices in what was the home of his early life.

I returned to the village where I resided when I first introduced myself to my readers. But what was that spot to me now? Nature had done much for it, but nature herself is very much what we make her. There must be beauty in our souls, or we shall see no loveliness in her face; and beauty had died out of my soul. She who might have recalled it to life, and thrown its hues over all the world was —— but of that I will not speak.

It was now that I really needed the hope of immortality. The world was to me one vast desert, and life was without end or aim. The hope of immortality is not needed to enable us to bear grief, to meet great calamities. These can be, as they have been, met by the atheist with a serene brow and a tranquil pulse. We need not the hope of immortality in order to meet death with composure. The manner in which we meet death depends altogether more on the state of our nerves than the nature of our hopes. But we want it when earth has lost its gloss of novelty, when our hopes have been blasted, our affections withered, and the shortness of life and the vanity of all human pursuits have come home to us, and made us exclaim, "Vanity of vanities, all is vanity;" we want then the hope of immortality to give to life an end, an aim.

We all of us at times feel this want. The infidel feels it early in life. He learns all too soon, what to him is a withering fact, that man does not complete his destiny on earth. Man never completes any thing here. What then shall he do if there be no hereafter? With what courage can I betake myself to my task? I may begin—but the grave lies between me and the completion. Death will come to interrupt my work, and compel me to leave it unfinished. This is more terrible to me than the thought of ceasing to be. I could *almost*,—at least, I think I could—consent to be no more, after I had finished my work, achieved my destiny; but to die before my work is completed, while that destiny is but begun,—this is the death which comes to me indeed as a "King of Terrors."

The hope of another life to be the complement of this, steps in to save us from this death, to give us the courage and the hope *to begin*. The rough sketch shall hereafter become the finished picture, the artist shall give it the last touch at his easel; the science we had just begun shall be completed, and the incipient destiny shall be achieved. Fear not to begin, thou hast eternity before thee in which to end.

I wanted, at the time of which I speak, this hope. I had no future. I was shut up in this narrow life as in a cage. All for whom I could have lived, laboured, and died, were gone, or worse than gone. I had no end, no aim. My affections were driven back to stagnate and become putrid in my own breast. I had no one to care for. The world was to me as if it were not; and yet a strange restlessness came over me. I could be still nowhere. I roved listlessly from object to object, my body was carried from place to place, I knew not why, and asked not myself wherefore. And yet change of object, change of scene wrought no change within me. I existed, but did not live. He who has no future, has no life.

———◆———

THE BIBLE.

FROM THE BOSTON QUARTERLY REVIEW.

I REMEMBER well the time when the Bible was to me a revolting book, when I could find no meaning in it, and when I could not believe that religious people could honestly regard it as they professed to regard it. Its very style and language were offensive, and if I was called upon to write upon religious topics, I took good care to avoid, as much as possible, the use of its phraseology. But it is not so with me now. Life has developed within me wants which no other book can satisfy. Say nothing now of the divine origin of the Bible; take it merely as an ancient writing which has come down to us, and it is to me a truly wonderful production. I take up the writings of the most admired geniuses of ancient or modern times; I read them, and relish them; and yet there is a depth in my experience they do not fathom. This is much, I say; but I have lived more than is here; I have wants this does not meet; it records only a moiety of my experience. But with the Bible it is not so. Whatever my state, its authors seem to have anticipated it. Whatever anomaly in my experience I note, they seem to have recorded it. What experience these men had, if indeed they spoke from experience! It is well called the Book, for it is the book in which seems to be registered all that the individual or the race ever has lived, or ever can live. It is all here. If I would bow down with sorrow for sin, and pour out my soul in deep contrition for my wanderings, here are the very words I want, and words terribly expressive. If I would break forth in thanksgiving for release from the bonds of iniquity, and shout in exulting strains my forgiveness, here is the hymn already composed, which exactly meets the temper of my mind. Then, again, even the language of our common English version, ridiculed as it often has been, is after all the only language in which I can utter the spiritual facts which are developed within me. I seek to vary the expression, to select what I may regard as an equivalent but more elegant term, and some how or other the soul of the passage escapes, and I find remaining nothing but a lifeless form of words. It does not therefore seem strange to me now, though it once did, the attachment the Christian world has to this venerable Book, nor the tenacity with which they, who speak the English tongue, hold on to our common version, in spite of the defects which criticism justly points out.

LYDIA M. CHILD.

[Born 18—.]

LYDIA MARIA FRANCIS, now Mrs. DAVID LEE CHILD, commenced her literary life with Hobomok, a Tale of Early Times, published in 1824. She had resided several years in Maine, far removed from all literary associations, but was then on a visit to her brother, the Reverend Conyers Francis, minister of the Unitarian church in Watertown, and now of Harvard University. One Sunday noon, soon after her arrival there, she took up a number of the North American Review, and read Doctor Palfrey's article on Yamoyden, in which he eloquently describes the adaptation of early New England history to the purposes of fiction. She had never written a word for the press,—never had dreamed of turning author,—but the spell was on her, and seizing a pen, before the bell rung for the afternoon meeting she had composed the first chapter of the novel, just as it is printed. When it was shown to her brother, her young ambition was flattered by the exclamation, " But, Maria, did you *really* write this? do you mean what you say, that it is *entirely* your own?" The excellent doctor little knew the effect of his words. Her fate was fixed: in six weeks Hobomok was finished. It is a story of the Pilgrim times, and the scene is chiefly in Salem and Plymouth. Among the characters are Lady Arabella Johnson, Governor Endicott, and others known in history. They are very well drawn, and the sketches of manners and scenery are truthful and spirited. But the plot is unnatural, and is not very skilfully managed. There were then, however, very few American books of this sort; Cooper had just begun his brilliant career, and Miss Sedgwick's first novel had been out but two or three weeks; and Hobomok therefore attracted much attention. It was followed, in the next year, by The Rebels, a Tale of the Revolution, which has about the same kind and degree of merit. It is worth mentioning, that the speech of James Otis, in this novel, which is often quoted in school books, and has found its way into histories, as authentic, as well as Whitfield's celebrated sermon, in the same work, was coined entirely by Mrs. Child.

In 1831 she published The Mother's Book, and in 1832 The Girl's Book, two volumes designed to exhibit the reciprocal duties of parent and child, in their several relations to each other, which had a large and well deserved success.

About the same time, for the Ladies' Family Library, published in Boston, of which she was editor, she wrote Lives of Madame de Staël and Roland, in one volume; Lives of Lady Russel and Madame Guyon, in one volume; Biographies of Good Wives, in one volume; and The History and Condition of Women, in two volumes. These are all interesting and valuable books, exhibiting taste and judgment, but marked by little of the individuality which distinguishes her more original productions.

In 1833 Mrs. Child published The Coronal, a collection of miscellaneous pieces in prose and verse, many of which had before been printed, in the literary annuals; and in the same year her Appeal for that Class of Americans called Africans, which was the first work that appeared in this country in favour of the immediate emancipation of the slaves. It was earnest and able, and was read with deep interest both at home and in Europe. A copy of it falling into the hands of Doctor Channing, who had not before been acquainted with her, he walked from Boston to Roxbury to introduce himself and to thank her for writing it.

In 1835 appeared the most beautiful of her works, Philothea, a romance of Greece in the days of Pericles. It had been four or five years in its progress, " for the practical tendencies of the age, and particularly of the country in which I lived," she says in her preface, " have so continually forced me into the actual, that my mind has seldom obtained freedom to rise into the ideal." She had made a strong effort to throw herself into the spirit of the times, " which is prone to neglect beautiful and fragrant flowers, unless their roots will answer for vegetables, and their leaves for herbs." But there were seasons when her soul felt restless in this bondage; in these she abandoned herself to pursuits of a more congenial sort; and, led by love of the romantic and beautiful, among

"The intelligible forms of ancient poets,
    The fair humanities of old religion,"

she attempted to depict the life of Athens in its most glorious age, when Pericles presided over the destinies of the state, Plato taught in the Academy, Phidias built temples and carved statues of the gods, and Aspasia captivated sages by her beauty, and overthrew the severity of female manners by appearing unveiled at the symposia of the wits. Except Mr. Ware's Zenobia and Probus, Philothea is the only classical romance deserving any consideration that has been produced in this country, and it is worthy to be ranked with those admirable works. The scenery is purely Grecian; all the externals are in keeping; the narrative is interesting and clearly defined; and the style is elevated and chaste, abounding in unlooked-for turns and spontaneous beauties. But the author seems hardly to have caught the antique spirit: the philosophical tone of Philothea reminds us quite as much of Boston as of Athens.

In 1841 Mr. and Mrs. Child went to reside in New York, where they conducted for some time The National Anti-Slavery Standard, a weekly gazette of which the title indicated the object and general character. For this she wrote much, not of the subject of slavery only, but of many others that belong to the country and to the age, and in all her articles showed an earnest spirit, generous sympathies, and wide knowledge. In the summer of 1841 she commenced a series of Letters to the editor of the Boston Courier, which were so fresh, so spirited, and familiar, and had about them so much of pleasing individuality, that they were reprinted in all parts of the country, and came to be looked for with as much interest as the new numbers of the magazines. Upon the publication of the fortieth letter they were collected and issued in a volume, under the title of Letters from New York. None of the booksellers seemed willing to publish them, but the indications of their popularity were such as could not be mistaken by the author, and she therefore printed the first edition on her own account; and the rapid sale of thousand after thousand copies, secured a ready market for the second series, which appeared in 1845.

These Letters are on every variety of subjects that would be suggested to a thoughtful, earnest and benevolent mind, in the houses, thoroughfares, and public assemblies of a city, in a period of excitement and transition, and every one of them strikes a chord to which the heart of some reader will vibrate in unison.

Fact and Fiction, the last fiction which Mrs. Child has given to the public, is a collection of tales, of various kinds, but all characteristic and excellent, which she had previously published in the periodicals. The Children of Mount Ida, and A Legend of the Apostle John, relate to classical times, and have the marble polish and chasteness of her Philothea. To another, Hilda Silfverling, a fantasy, she has imparted the interest and imagery that belong to Scandinavian manners and scenery. But perhaps those which have most of her own individuality are The Neighbour-in-Law, an admirable illustration of the power of kindness in softening and moulding natures beyond all other influences, and the Beloved Tune, an expression of mental experiences, resembling some of the fine pieces of imagination interspersed with the second series of her Letters from New York.

Mrs. Child has a large acquaintance with common life, which she describes with a genial sympathy and fidelity,—a generous love of freedom, extreme susceptibility of impressions of beauty, and an imagination which bodies forth her feelings in forms of peculiar distinctness and freshness. Her works abound in bright pictures and fanciful thoughts, which seem to be of the atmosphere in which she lives. She transfuses into them something of her own spirit, which, though meditative and somewhat mystical, is always cheerful and radiant. In her revelations on music, illustrations of the doctrine of correspondences, and all the more speculative parts of her various writings, she has shown that fine perception of the mysterious analogy which exists between the physical and moral world, and of the mode in which the warp and woof of life are mingling, which is among the first attributes of the true poet.

She also published, Flowers for Children, 3 parts; The Frugal Housewife; The Family Nurse; Power of Kindness; Rose Marion; Life of Isaac T. Hopper; and the Progress of Religious Ideas through successive Ages, 1855, 3 vols., the most elaborate of all her works, of which a new edition was issued in 1869.

A BANQUET AT ASPASIA'S.

FROM PHILOTHEA.

THE room in which the guests were assembled, was furnished with less of Asiatic splendour than the private apartment of Aspasia; but in its magnificent simplicity, there was a more perfect manifestation of ideal beauty. It was divided in the middle by eight Ionic columns alternately of Phrygian and Pentelic marble. Between the central pillars stood a superb statue from the hand of Phidias, representing Aphrodite guided by love and crowned by the goddess of Persuasion. Around the walls were Phœbus and Hermes in Parian marble, and the nine Muses in ivory. A fountain of perfumed water from the adjoining room diffused coolness and fragrance as it passed through a number of concealed pipes, and finally flowed into a magnificent vase, supported by a troop of Naiades.

In a recess stood the famous lion of Myron, surrounded by infant loves, playing with his paws, climbing his back, and decorating his neck with garlands. This beautiful group seemed actually to live and move in the clear light and deep shadows derived from a silver lamp suspended above.

The walls were enriched with some of the choicest paintings of Apollodorus, Zeuxis, and Polygnotus. Near a fine likeness of Pericles, by Aristolaus, was Aspasia, represented as Chloris scattering flowers over the earth, and attended by winged Hours.

It chanced that Pericles himself reclined beneath his portrait, and though political anxiety had taken from his countenance something of the cheerful freshness which characterized the picture, he still retained the same elevated beauty—the same deep, quiet expression of intellectual power. At a short distance, with his arm resting on the couch, stood his nephew, Alcibiades, deservedly called the handsomest man in Athens. He was laughing with Hermippus, the comic writer, whose shrewd, sarcastic and mischievous face was expressive of his calling. Phidias slowly paced the room, talking of the current news with the Persian Artaphernes. Anaxagoras reclined near the statue of Aphrodite, listening and occasionally speaking to Plato, who leaned against one of the marble pillars, in earnest conversation with a learned Ethiopian.

The gorgeous apparel of the Asiatic and African guests contrasted strongly with the graceful simplicity of Grecian costume. A saffron-coloured mantle and a richly embroidered Median vest glittered on the person of the venerable Artaphernes. Tithonus, the Ethiopian, wore a skirt of ample folds, which scarcely fell below the knee. It was of the glorious Tyrian hue, resembling a crimson light shining through transparent purple. The edge of the garment was curiously wrought with golden palm leaves. It terminated at the waist in a large roll, twined with massive chains of gold, and fastened by a clasp of the far-famed Ethiopian topaz. The upper part of his person was uncovered and unornamented, save by broad bracelets of gold, which formed a magnificent contrast with

the sable colour of his vigorous and finely-proportioned limbs.

As the ladies entered, the various groups came forward to meet them; and all were welcomed by Aspasia with earnest cordiality and graceful self-possession. While the brief salutations were passing, Hipparete, the wife of Alcibiades, came from an inner apartment, where she had been waiting for her hostess. She was a fair, amiable young matron, evidently conscious of her high rank. The short blue tunic, which she wore over a lemon-coloured robe, was embroidered with golden grasshoppers; and on her forehead sparkled a jewelled insect of the same species. It was the emblem of unmixed Athenian blood; and Hipparete alone, of all the ladies present, had a right to wear it. Her manners were an elaborate copy of Aspasia; but deprived of the powerful charm of unconsciousness, which flowed like a principle of life into every motion of that beautiful enchantress....

At a signal from Plato, slaves filled the goblets with wine, and he rose to propose the usual libation to the gods. Every Grecian guest joined in the ceremony, singing in a recitative tone:

Dionysus, this to thee,
God of warm festivity!
Giver of the fruitful vine,
To thee we pour the rosy wine!

Music, from the adjoining room, struck in with the chorus, and continued for some moments after it had ceased.

For a short time, the conversation was confined to the courtesies of the table, as the guests partook of the delicious viands before them. Plato eat olives and bread only; and the water he drank was scarcely tinged with Lesbian wine. Alcibiades rallied him upon this abstemiousness; and Pericles reminded him that even his great pattern, Socrates, gave Dionysus his dues, while he worshipped the heaven-born Pallas.

The philosopher quietly replied, " I can worship the fiery God of Vintage only when married with Nymphs of the Fountain."

"But tell me, O Anaxagoras and Plato," exclaimed Tithonus, "if, as Hermippus hath said, the Grecian philosophers discard the theology of the poets? Do you not believe in the gods?"

Plato would have smiled, had he not reverenced the simplicity that expected a frank and honest answer to a question so dangerous. Anaxagoras briefly replied, that the mind which did not believe in divine beings, must be cold and dark indeed.

"Even so," replied Artaphernes devoutly; " blessed be Oromasdes, who sends Mithras to warm and enlighten the world! But what surprises me most is, that you Grecians import new divinities from other countries as freely as slaves, or papyrus, or marble. The sculptor of the gods will scarcely be able to fashion half their images."

"If the custom continues," rejoined Phidias, " it will indeed require a lifetime as long as that conferred upon the namesake of Tithonus."

"Thanks to the munificence of artists, every deity has a representative in my dwelling," observed Aspasia.

"I have heard strangers express their surprise

that the Athenians have never erected a statue to the principle of *Modesty*," said Hermippus.

"So much the more need that we enshrine her image in our own hearts," rejoined Plato.

The sarcastic comedian made no reply to this quiet rebuke. Looking toward Artaphernes, he continued: "Tell me, O servant of the great king, wherein the people of your country are more wise in worshipping the sun than we who represent the same divinity in marble?"

"The principles of the Persian religion are simple, steady, and uniform," replied Artaphernes; "but the Athenian are always changing. You not only adopt foreign gods, but sometimes create new ones, and admit them into your theology by solemn act of the great council. The circumstances have led me to suppose that you worship them as mere forms. The Persian Magi do indeed prostrate themselves before the rising Sun; but they do it in the name of Oromasdes, the universal Principle of Good, of whom that great luminary is the visible symbol. In our solemn processions, the chariot sacred to Oromasdes precedes the horse dedicated to Mithras; and there is deep meaning in the arrangement. The Sun and the Zodiac, the Balance and the Rule, are but emblems of truths, mysterious and eternal. As the garlands we throw on the sacred fire feed the flame, rather than extinguish it, so the sublime symbols of our religion are intended to preserve, not to conceal, the truths within them."

"Though you disclaim all images of divinity," rejoined Aspasia, "yet we hear of your Mithras pictured like a Persian king, trampling on a prostrate ox."

With a smile, Artaphernes replied, "I see, lady, that you would fain gain admittance to the Mithraic cave; but its secrets, like those of your own Eleusis, are concealed from all save the initiated."

"They tell us," said Aspasia, "that those who are admitted to the Eleusinian mysteries die in peace, and go directly to the Elysian fields; while the uninitiated wander about in the infernal abyss."

"Of course," said Anaxagoras, "Alcibiades will go directly to Elysium, though Solon groped his way in darkness."

The old philosopher uttered this with imperturbable gravity, as if unconscious of satirical meaning; but some of the guests could scarcely repress a smile, as they recollected the dissolute life of the young Athenian.

"If Alcibiades spoke his real sentiments," said Aspasia, "I venture to say he would tell us that the mystic baskets of Demeter, covered with long purple veils, contain nothing half so much worth seeing, as the beautiful maidens who carry them."

She looked at Pericles, and saw that he again cautioned her, by raising the rose toward his face, as if inhaling its fragrance.

There was a brief pause; which Anaxagoras interrupted, by saying, "The wise can never reverence images merely as images. There is a mystical meaning in the Athenian manner of supplicating the gods with garlands on their heads, and bearing in their hands boughs of olive twined with wool. Pallas, at whose birth we are told gold rained upon the earth, was unquestionably a personification of wisdom. It is not to be supposed that the philosophers of any country consider the sun itself as any thing more than a huge ball of fire; but the sight of that glorious orb leads the contemplative soul to the belief in one Pure Intelligence, one Universal Mind, which in manifesting itself produces order in the material world, and preserves the unconfused distinction of infinite varieties."

"Such, no doubt, is the tendency of all reflecting minds," said Phidias; "but in general, the mere forms are worshipped, apart from the sacred truths they represent. The gods we have introduced from Egypt are regarded by the priests of that learned land as emblems of certain divine truths brought down from ancient times. They are like the Hermæ at our doors, which outwardly appear to rest on inexpressive blocks of stone; but when opened, they are found to contain beautiful statues of the gods within them. It is not so with the new fables which the Greeks are continually mixing with their mythology. Pygmalion, as we all know, first departed from the rigid outline of ancient sculpture, and impressed life and motion upon marble. The poets, in praise of him, have told us that his ardent wishes warmed a statue into a lovely and breathing woman. The fable is fanciful and pleasing in itself; but will it not hereafter be believed as reality? Might not the same history be told of much that is believed? It is true," added he, smiling, "that I might be excused for favouring a belief in images, since mortals are ever willing to have their own works adored."

"What! does Plato respond to the inquiries of Phidias?" asked Artaphernes.

The philosopher replied: "Within the holy mysteries of our religion is preserved a pure and deep meaning, as the waters of Arethusa flow uncontaminated beneath the earth and the sea. I do not presume to decide whether all that is believed has the inward significancy. I have ever deemed such speculations unwise. If the chaste daughter of Latona always appears to my thoughts veiled in heavenly purity, it is comparatively unimportant whether I can prove that Acteon was torn by his dogs, for looking on the goddess with wanton eyes. Anaxagoras said wisely that material forms lead the contemplative mind to the worship of ideal good, which is in its nature immortal and divine. Homer tells us that the golden chain resting upon Olympus reaches even to the earth. Here we see but a few of the last links, and those imperfectly. We are like men in the subterranean cave, so chained that they can look only forward to the entrance. Far above and behind us is a glowing fire: and beautiful beings, of every form, are moving between the light and we poor fettered mortals. Some of these bright beings are speaking, and others are silent. We see only the shadows cast on the opposite wall of the cavern, by the reflection of the fire above; and if we hear the echo of voices, we suppose it belongs to those passing shadows. The soul, in its present condition, is an exile from the orb of light; its ignorance is forgetfulness; and whatever we can perceive of truth, or imagine of beauty, is but a reminiscence of our former more glorious state of being. He who reverences the gods, and subdues his own passions, returns at last to the blest condition from which he fell. But to talk, or think, about these things with proud impatience, or polluted morals, is like pouring pure water into a miry trench; he who does it disturbs the mud, and thus causes the clear water to become defiled. When Odysseus removed his armor from the walls, and carried it to an inner apartment, invisible Pallas moved before him with her golden lamp, and filled the place with radiance divine. Telemachus, seeing the light, exclaimed, 'Surely, my father, some of the celestial gods are present.' With deep wisdom, the king of Ithaca replied, 'Be silent. Restrain your intellect, and speak not.'"

"I am rebuked, O Plato," answered Phidias; "and from henceforth, when my mind is dark and doubtful, I will remember that transparent drops may fall into a turbid well. Nor will I forget that sometimes, when I have worked on my statues by torch-light, I could not perceive their real expression, because I was carving in the shadow of my own hand."

"Little can be learned of the human soul and its connection with the Universal Mind," said Anaxagoras; "these sublime truths seem vague and remote, as Phœacia appeared to Odysseus like a vast shield floating on the surface of the distant ocean."

"The glimmering uncertainty attending all such speculations, has led me to attach myself to the Ionic sect, who devote themselves entirely to the study of outward nature."

"And this is useful," rejoined Plato : "The man who is to be led from a cave will more easily see what the heavens contain by looking to the light of the moon and the stars, than by gazing on the sun at noon-day."

THE BELOVED TUNE.
FRAGMENTS OF A LIFE, IN SMALL PICTURES.
FROM FACT AND FICTION.

A child, a friend, a wife, whose soft heart sings
In unison with ours, breeding its future wings.—*Leigh Hunt.*

IN a pleasant English garden, on a rustic chair of intertwisted boughs, are seated two happy human beings. Beds of violets perfume the air, and the verdant hedge-rows stand sleepily in the moonlight. A guitar lies on the greensward, but it is silent now, for all is hushed in the deep stillness of the heart. That youthful pair are whispering their first acknowledgment of mutual love. With them is now unfolding life's best and brightest blossom, so beautiful and so transient, but leaving, as it passes into fruit, a fragrance through all the paths of memory.

And now the garden is alone in the moonlight. The rustic bench, and the whispering foliage of the tree, tell each other no tales of those still kisses,

those gentle claspings, and all the fervent language of the heart. But the young man has carried them away in his soul; and as he sits alone at his chamber window, gazing in the mild face of the moon, he feels, as all do who love and are beloved, that he is a better man, and will henceforth be a wiser and a purer one. The worlds within and without are veiled in transfigured glory, and breathe together in perfect harmony. For all these high aspirations, this deep tide of tenderness, this fulness of beauty, there is but one utterance; the yearning heart must overflow in music. Faint and uncertain come the first tones of the guitar, breathing as softly as if they responded to the mere touch of the moonbeams. But now the rich manly voice has united with them, and a clear spiritual melody flows forth, plaintive and impassioned, the modulated breath of indwelling life and love. All the secrets of the garden, secrets that painting and poetry had no power to reveal, have passed into the song.

At first, the young musician scarcely noticed the exceeding beauty of the air he was composing. But a passage that came from the deepest of the heart, returned to the heart again, and filled it with its own sweet echoes. He lighted a lamp, and rapidly transferred the sounds to paper. Thus has he imbodied the floating essence of his soul, and life's brightest inspiration cannot pass away with the moonlight and the violet-fragrance that veiled its birth.

But obstacles arise in the path of love. Dora's father has an aversion to foreigners, and Alessandro is of mingled Italian and German parentage. He thinks of worldly substance, as fathers are wont to do; and Alessandro.is simply leader of an orchestra, and a popular composer of guitar music. There is a richer lover in question, and the poor musician is sad with hope deferred, though he leans ever trustfully on Dora's true heart. He labours diligently in his vocation, gives lessons day by day, and listens with all patience to the learner's trip-hammer measurement of time, while the soul within him yearns to pour itself forth in floods of improvised melody. He composes music industriously, too; but it is for the market, and slowly and reluctantly the offended tones take their places per order. Not thus came they in that inspired song, where love first breathed its bright but timid joy over vanished doubts and fears. The manuscript of that melody is laid away, and seldom can the anxious lover hear its voice.

But two years of patient effort secures his prize. The loved one has come to his humble home, with her bridal wreath of jessamine and orange-buds. He sits at the same window, and the same moon shines on him; but he is no longer alone. A beautiful head leans on his breast, and a loving voice says, "Dearest Alessandro, sing me a song of thine own composing." He was at that moment thinking of the rustic seat in her father's garden, of violets breathing to the moonlight, of Dora's first bashful confession of love; and smiling with a happy consciousness, he sought for the written voice of that blissful hour. But he will not tell her when it was composed, lest it should not say so much to her heart, as it does to his. He begins by singing other songs, which drawing-room misses love for their tinkling sweetness. Dora listens well pleased, and sometimes says, "That is pretty, Alessandro; play it again." But now comes the voice of melting, mingling souls. That melody, so like sunshine, and rainbows, and bird-warbling, after a summer shower, with rain-drops from the guitar at intervals, and all subsiding into blissful, dreamy moonlight. Dora leans forward, gazing earnestly in his face, and with beaming tearful eyes, exclaims, "Oh, that is very beautiful! That is *my* tune." "Yes, it is indeed thy tune," replied the happy husband; and when she had heard its history, she knew why it had seemed so like echoes of her own deepest heart.

Time has passed, and Alessandro sits by Dora's bed-side, their eyes looking into each other through happy tears. Their love is crowned with life's deepest, purest joy, its most heavenly emotion. Their united lives have re-appeared in a new existence; and they feel that without this rich experience the human heart can never know one-half its wealth of love. Long sat the father in that happy stillness, and wist not that angels near by smiled when he touched the soft down of the infant's arm, or twined its little finger over his, and looked his joyful tenderness into the mother's eyes. The tear-dew glistened on those long dark fringes, when he took up his guitar and played the beloved tune. He had spoken no word to his child. These tones were the first sounds with which he welcomed her into the world.

A few months glide away, and the little Fioretta knows the tune for herself. She claps her hands and crows at sight of the guitar, and all changing emotions show themselves in her dark melancholy eyes, and on her little tremulous lips. Play not too sadly, thou fond musician; for this little soul is a portion of thine own sensitive being, more delicately tuned. Ah, see now the grieved lip, and the eyes swimming in tears! Change, change to a gayer measure! for the little heart is swelling too big for its bosom. There, now she laughs and crows again! Yet plaintive music is her choice, and especially the beloved tune. As soon as she can toddle across the room, she welcomes papa with a shout, and runs to bring the guitar, which mother must help her carry, lest she break it in her zeal. If father mischievously tries other tunes than her favourites, she shakes her little curly head, and trots her feet impatiently. . But when he touches the first notes he ever played to her, she smiles and listens seriously, as if she heard her own being prophesied in music. As she grows older, the little lady evinces a taste right royal; for she must needs eat her supper to the accompaniment of sweet sounds. It is beautiful to see her in her night-gown, seated demurely in her small arm-chair, one little naked foot unconsciously beating time to the tune. But if the music speaks too plaintively, the big tears roll silently down, and the porringer of milk, all unheeded, pours its treasures on the floor. Then come smothering kisses from the happy father and mother, and love-claspings with her little

soft arms. As the three sit thus intertwined, the musician says playfully, "Ah, this is the perfect chord!"

Three years pass away, and the scene is changed. There is discord now where such sweet harmony prevailed. The light of Dora's eyes is dim with weeping, and Fioretta "has caught the trick of grief, and sighs amid her playthings." Once, when she had waited long for the beloved father, she ran to him with the guitar, and he pushed her away, saying angrily, "Go to bed; why did your mother keep you up so long?" The sensitive little being, so easily repulsed, went to her pillow in tears; and after that, she no more ran to him with music in her hand, in her eye, and in her voice. Hushed now is the beloved tune. To the unhappy wife it seems a mockery to ask for it; and Alessandro seldom touches his guitar; he says he is obliged to play enough for his bread, without playing to his family at home. At the glee-club the bright wine has tempted him, and he is slowly burying heart and soul in the sepulchre of the body. Is there no way to save this beautiful son of genius and feeling? Dora at first pleads with him tenderly; but made nervous with anxiety and sorrow, she at last speaks words that would have seemed impossible to her when she was so happy, seated on the rustic chair, in the moonlighted garden; and then comes the sharp sorrow, which a generous heart always feels when it *has* so spoken to a cherished friend. In such moments of contrition, memory turns with fond sadness to the beloved tune. Fioretta, whose little fingers must stretch wide to reach an octave, is taught to play it on the piano, while mother sings to her accompaniment, in their lonely hours. After such seasons, a tenderer reception always greets the wayward husband; but his eyes, dulled by dissipation, no longer perceive the delicate shadings of love in those home pictures, once so dear to him. The child is afraid of her father, and this vexes him; so a strangeness has grown up between the two playmates, and casts a shadow over all their attempts at joy. One day, Alessandro came home as twilight was passing into evening. Fioretta had eaten her supper, and sat on her mother's lap, chatting merrily; but the little clear voice hushed, as soon as father's step was heard approaching. He entered with flushed cheek and unsteady motions, and threw himself full length on the sofa, grumbling that it was devilish dismal there. Dora answered hastily, "When a man has made his home dismal, if he don't like it, he had better stay where he finds more pleasure." The next moment, she would have given worlds if she had not spoken such words. Her impulse was to go and fall on his neck, and ask forgiveness; but he kicked over Fioretta's little chair with such violence that the kindly impulse turned back, and hid itself in her widowed heart. There sat they silently in the twilight, and Dora's tears fell on the little head that rested on her bosom. I know not what spirit guided the child; perhaps in her busy little heart she remembered how her favourite sounds used to heighten all love, and cheer all sorrow; perhaps angels came and took her by the hand. But so it was, she slipped down from mother's lap, and scrambling up on the music-stool, began to play the tune which had been taught her in private hours, and which the father had not heard for many months. Wonderfully the little creature touched the keys with her tiny fingers, and ever and anon her weak but flexible voice chimed in with a pleasant harmony. Alessandro raised his head, and looked and listened. "God bless her dear little soul!" he exclaimed; "can *she* play it! God bless her! God bless her!" He clasped the darling to his breast, and kissed her again and again. Then seeing the little overturned chair, once so sacred to his heart, he caught it up, kissed it vehemently, and burst into a flood of tears. Dora threw her arms round him, and said softly, "Dear Alessandro, forgive me that I spoke so unkindly." He pressed her hand, and answered in a stifled voice, "Forgive *me*, Dora. God bless the little angel! Never again will father push away her little chair." As they stand weeping on each other's necks, two little soft arms encircle their knees, and a small voice says, "Kiss Fietta." They raise her up, and fold her in long embraces. Alessandro carries her to her bed, as in times of old, and says cheerfully, "No more wine, dear Dora; no more wine. Our child has saved me."

But when discord once enters a domestic paradise, it is not easily dispelled. Alessandro occasionally wants the want of the stimulus to which he has become accustomed, and the corroding appetite sometimes makes him gloomy and petulant. Dora does not make sufficient allowance for this, and her own nature being quick and sensitive, she sometimes gives abrupt answers, or betrays impatience by hasty motions. Meanwhile Alessandro is busy, with some secret work. The door of his room is often locked, and Dora is half-displeased that he will not tell her why; but all her questions he answers only with a kiss and a smile. And now the Christmas morning comes, and Fioretta rises bright and early to see what Santa Claus has put in her stocking. She comes running with her apron full, and gives mother a package, on which is written, "A merry Christmas, and a Happy New Year to my beloved wife." She opens it, and reads "Dearest Dora, I have made thee a music-box. When I speak hastily to my loved ones, I pray thee wind it up; and when I see the spark kindling in thy eyes, I will do the same. Thus, dearest, let memory teach patience unto love." Dora winds up the music-box, and lo, a spirit sits within, playing the beloved tune! She puts her hand within her husband's, and they look at each other with affectionate humility. But neither of them speak the resolution they form, while the voice of their early love falls on their ears, like the sounds of a fairy guitar.

Memory, thus aided, does teach patience unto love. No slackened string now sends discord through the domestic tune. Fioretta is passing into maidenhood, beautiful as an opening flower. She practises on the guitar, while the dear good father sits with his arm across her chair, singing from a manuscript tune of her own composing. In his eyes,

this first effort of her genius cannot seem otherwise than beautiful. Ever and anon certain notes recur, and they look at each other and smile, and Dora smiles also. "Fioretta could not help bringing in *that* theme," she says, "for it was sung to her in her cradle." The father replies, "But the variations are extremely pretty and tasteful;" and a flush of delight goes over the expressive face of his child. The setting sun glances across the guitar, and just touches a rose in the maiden's bosom. The happy mother watches the dear group earnestly, and sketches rapidly on the paper before her. And now she, too, works privately in her own room, and has a secret to keep. On Fioretta's fifteenth birth-day, she sends by her hands a covered present to the father. He opens it, and finds a lovely picture of himself and daughter, the rose and the guitar. The sunlight glances across them in a bright shower of fine soft rays, and touches on the manuscript, as with a golden finger, the few beloved notes, which had made them smile. As the father shrined within his divine art the memory of their first hour of mutual love, so the mother has embalmed in *her* beautiful art the first musical echo from the heart of their child.

But now the tune of life passes into a sadder mode. Dora, pale and emaciated, lies propped up with pillows, her hand clasped within Fioretta's, her head resting on her husband's shoulder.

All is still—still. Their souls are kneeling reverently before the Angel of Death. Heavy sunset guns, from a neighbouring fort, boom through the air. The vibrations shake the music-box, and it starts up like a spirit, and plays the cherished tune. Dora presses her daughter's hand, and she, with a faint smile, warbles the words they have so often sung. The dying one looks up to Alessandro, with a deep expression of unearthly tenderness. Gazing thus, with one long-drawn sigh, her affectionate soul floats away on the wings of that etherial song. The memory that taught endurance unto love leaves a luminous expression, a farewell glory, on the lifeless countenance. Attendant angels smile, and their blessing falls on the mourners' hearts, like dew from heaven. Fioretta remains to the widowed one, the graceful blossom of his lonely life, the incarnation of his beloved tune.

A STREET SCENE.

FROM LETTERS FROM NEW YORK.

THE other day, as I came down Broome-street, I saw a street musician, playing near the door of a genteel dwelling. The organ was uncommonly sweet and mellow in its tones, the tunes were slow and plaintive, and I fancied that I saw in the woman's Italian face an expression that indicated sufficient refinement to prefer the tender and the melancholy, to the lively "trainer tunes" in vogue with the populace. She looked like one who had suffered much, and the sorrowful music seemed her own appropriate voice. A little girl clung to her scanty garments, as if afraid of all things but her mother. As I looked at them, a young lady of pleasing countenance opened the window, and oegan to sing like a bird, in keeping with the street organ. Two other young girls came and leaned on her shoulder; and still she sang on. Blessings on her gentle heart! It was evidently the spontaneous gush of human love and sympathy. The beauty of the incident attracted attention. A group of gentlemen gradually collected round the organist; and ever as the tune ended, they bowed respectfully toward the window, waved their hats, and called out, "More, if you please!" One, whom I knew well for the kindest and truest soul, passed round his hat; hearts were kindled, and the silver fell in freely. In a minute, four or five dollars were collected for the poor woman. She spoke no word of gratitude, but she gave *such* a look! "Will you go to the next street, and play to a friend of mine!" said my kind-hearted friend. She answered, in tones expressing the deepest emotion, "No, sir, God bless you all—God bless you *all*," (making a courtesy to the young lady, who had stept back, and stood sheltered by the curtain of the window,) "I will play no more to-day; I will go *home*, now." The tears trickled down her cheeks, and as she walked away, she had ever and anon wiped her eyes with the corner of her shawl. The group of gentlemen lingered a moment to look after her, then turning toward the now closed window, they gave three enthusiastic cheers, and departed, better than they came. The pavement on which they stood had been a church to them; and for the next hour, at least, their hearts were more than usually prepared for deeds of gentleness and mercy. Why are such scenes so uncommon? Why do we thus repress our sympathies, and chill the genial current of nature, by formal observances and restraints?

UNSELFISHNESS.
FROM THE SAME.

I found the Battery unoccupied, save by children, whom the weather made as merry as birds. Every thing seemed moving to the vernal tune of
"Brignal banks are fresh and fair,
And Greta woods are green."
To one who was chasing her hoop, I said, smiling, "You are a nice little girl." She stopped, looked up in my face, so rosy and happy, and laying her hand on her brother's shoulder, exclaimed earnestly, "And *he* is a nice little boy, too!" It was a simple, child-like act, but it brought a warm gush into my heart. Blessings on all unselfishness! on all that leads us in love to prefer one another. Here lies the secret of universal harmony; this is the diapason, which would bring us all into tune. Only by losing ourselves can we find ourselves. How clearly does the divine voice within us proclaim this, by the hymn of joy it sings, whenever we witness an unselfish deed, or hear an unselfish thought. Blessings on that loving little one! She made the city seem a garden to me. I kissed my hand to her, as I turned off in quest of

the Brooklyn ferry. The sparkling waters, swarmed with boats, some of which had taken a big ship by the hand, and were leading her out to sea, as the prattle of childhood often guides wisdom into the deepest and broadest thought.

FLOWERS.
FROM THE SAME.

How the universal heart of man blesses flowers! They are wreathed round the cradle, the marriage altar, and the tomb. The Persian in the far East, delights in their perfume, and writes his love in nosegays; while the Indian child of the far west clasps his hands with glee, as he gathers the abundant blossoms—the illuminated scripture of the prairies. The Cupid of the ancient Hindoos tipped his arrows with flowers, and orange buds are the bridal crown with us, a nation of yesterday. Flowers garlanded the Grecian altar, and they hang in votive wreaths before the Christian shrine.

All these are appropriate uses. Flowers should deck the brow of the youthful bride, for they are in themselves a lovely type of marriage. They should twine round the tomb, for their perpetually renewed beauty is a symbol of the resurrection. They should festoon the altar, for their fragrance and their beauty ascend in perpetual worship before the Most High.

THE SELF-CONSCIOUS AND THE UNCONSCIOUS.

WITH whizz and glare the rocket rushed upward proclaiming to all men, "Lo, I am coming! Look at *me!*" Gracefully it bent in the air, and sprinkled itself in shining fragments; but the gem-like sparks went out in the darkness, and a stick on the ground was all that remained of the rocket.

High above the horizon a radiant star shone in quiet glory, making the night time beautiful. Men knew not when it rose; for it went up in the stillness.

In a rich man's garden stands a pagoda. The noise of the hammers told of its progress, and all men knew how much was added to it day by day. It was a pretty toy, with curious carving and gilded bells. But it remained as skill had fashioned it, and grew not, nor cast seed into the future.

An oak noiselessly dropped an acorn near by, and two leaves sprang from the ground, and became a fair young tree. The gardener said to the hawthorn, "When did the oak go above you?" The hawthorn answered, "I do not know; for it passed quietly by in the night."

Thus does mere talent whizz and hammer, to produce the transient forms of things, while genius unconsciously evolves the great and the beautiful, and "casts it silently into everlasting time."

ROBERT MONTGOMERY BIRD.

[Born 1803. Died 1854.]

DR. BIRD was born at Newcastle, in Delaware, and received his classical and professional education in Philadelphia. It is now seven or eight years' since, after about as long a period of active and various literary employment, he laid aside his pen, apparently with an intention never to resume it, and retired from the city to the quiet of his native town.

His history is in this respect somewhat peculiar. After the production of three tragedies,* each successful on the stage, and one permanently so, for it has maintained possession of the theatre for nearly fourteen years, and is still acted with applause; with no failure to annoy him and, at that time, no rival; still in youth, and full of resources; with a portfolio filled with plays, written and half-written, and plans, plots, and fables, without number; in the midst of his popularity; he suddenly deserted the drama altogether, resisting the persuasions of his friends, and rejecting numerous liberal offers which were made to him by actors and managers. Turning from the drama to prose fiction, and seeming to be as much at home in one field of composition as the other, he produced in rapid succession his various romances, writing and publishing the fourteen volumes of which they consist within a period of five years, at the end of which he suddenly and without any apparent reason, entirely abandoned the field of letters.†

The first work which Dr. Bird published,—for not one of his plays has even yet been given to the press,—was Calavar, or the Knight of the Conquest, a Romance of Mexico, which appeared in 1834. The scene was before untried by the novelist, and the events and characters, which are chiefly historical, are admirably adapted to the purposes of fiction. Mr. Prescott, in a note to his History of the Conquest, alluding to this picturesque romance, remarks that the author "has studied with great care the costume, manners, and military usages of the natives," and "has done for them what Cooper has done for the wild tribes of the north,—touched their rude features with the bright colouring of a poetic fancy. He has been equally fortunate in his delineation of the picturesque scenery of the land," Mr. Prescott continues, "and if he has been less so in attempting to revive the antique dialogue of the Spanish cavalier, we must not be surprised: nothing is more difficult than the skilful execution of a modern antique." I quote this as the judgment of the most competent of all critics respecting whatever relates to Spanish-American history. Dr. Bird evidently prepared himself in the most thorough manner for his task, and until the appearance of the admirable history of Mr. Prescott, there was perhaps in the English language no work from which could be obtained a more just impression of the subjugation of the empire of Aztecs than from Calavar.

Early in 1835 Dr. Bird published The Infidel, or the Fall of Mexico, a romance in which reappear many of the characters of his earlier work, and which may be regarded as its sequel, although each is independent and complete. The Infidel is marked by the traits which distinguished Calavar, but was apparently written with much more care. A colloquy at its beginning brings all the persons of the drama in a masterly manner before the reader,—each with his peculiar lineaments, with his passions, interests, and designs,—and their individuality is happily preserved throughout the work, which abounds in dramatic situations, brilliantly executed dialogues, and graphic descriptions of nature. It has more concentration of action and a more ingeniously contrived plot than Calavar, and was less successful only because the subject had now lost something of its novelty.

The Hawks of Hawk Hollow, a Tradition of Pennsylvania, appeared in the same year

---

* The Gladiator, Oraloosa, and the Broker of Bogota.
† It is probable that Dr. Bird, like many others in this country, was compelled by the foolish and wicked law of literary piracy which deprives the foreign author of copyright, to abandon the field. It will be observed that his latest work appeared about the time of the commencement of the system of cheap publishing, since which there have been comparatively few original books issued in America.

434

and is as different in style as in subject from the romances of Mexico. It contains some vigorous writing, and original and powerful sketches of character; but more of the tumult and brutality of border life than is worth preserving in literature.

Sheppard Lee came out anonymously in New York in 1836, and though never claimed or acknowledged by Dr. Bird, I have reasons for being confident that he is its author. The hero, when first introduced to the reader, is a New Jersey farmer, in moderate circumstances, envious of every one richer or happier than himself, and dreaming of wealth and ease which he lacks the industry and wit to acquire. He at last resolves to search for buried treasures, and just as he fancies that a fortune is within his grasp, an accident stretches him a corpse upon the scene of his labours. His spirit enters into the body of a sporting squire, who had broken his neck just in time, and who had been, when living, the object of Lee's especial envy. He soon finds that some things in his new sphere are less agreeable than he had supposed; and that he may have the largest experience of conditions, his soul is adroitly shifted into new forms, until, having been a dandy, a miser, a quaker philanthropist, a slave, and a planter, he once more becomes plain Sheppard Lee, with thirty acres of the soil of New Jersey, and enough skill as a ploughman to turn it to good account. The book abounds with whim and burlesque, pointed but playful satire, and felicitous sketches of society. The various metempsychoses, in the end, are declared by the hero's sister to be the result of delirium, occasioned by harassing pecuniary difficulties; but Mr. Lee has some doubt upon the subject, and determines to make public his own version of the matter, with a view of letting everybody decide for himself.

In the spring of 1837 Dr. Bird gave to the public, through his regular publishers in Philadelphia, Nick of the Woods, or the Jibbenainosay. It is a tale of early border life, the period of its incidents being about ten years before the admission of Kentucky to the Union; and its characters present such motley contrasts as are brought together in the tessellated society of our extreme western frontier. One of them is Roaring Ralph Stackpole, a wild, lawless fellow, and the original, as the author surmises, of a race since very numerous, and known on the Mississippi as creatures of the half horse and half alligator species, or " ringtail roarers from Salt River." The Indians of Dr. Bird are very different from those of Mr. Cooper, and it may be, as has been often contended, that they are more accurately drawn; but I think not. Brown gave us glimpses of Indian life; and they were remarkably picturesque and truthful. Since he wrote, Cooper's Indian characters are the most natural as well as the most interesting that have appeared in our fictitious literature, unless the tribes of the Mississippi region are essentially unlike those of the St. Lawrence and the Mohawk. Bird's Nick of the Woods is, however, a singularly original and bold conception, executed with remarkable ability.

Under the title of Peter Pilgrim, or a Rambler's Recollections, Dr. Bird, in 1838, published a collection of magazine papers, among which are an account of the Mammoth Cave, and various stories illustrative of life on the western border.

In 1839 appeared the last of his novels, The Adventures of Robin Day. The hero, who relates his own story, came ashore with the wreck of a schooner, one wild night in the month of September, 1796, upon the coast of New Jersey, and lives a life

"Of most disastrous chances,
Of moving accidents by flood and field,"

until he is enabled by some happy accidents to settle in peace and affluence, and write his "travel's history."

Dr. Bird's historical romances have the merit of truthfulness, a phrase which implies fidelity, not merely of narrative, but of impersonation, feeling and manners, and a nice observance of all the elements which contribute to the costume and develope the spirit of an age. His characters are well sketched and shaded, and his scenes have an air of verisimilitude that impresses the reader with an idea that he is perusing a narrative of real events. There is in each of his novels a plot, ingenious, intricate, and so managed as to produce an intense curiosity, and a succession of surprises in its development. His style is varied with the nature of his subjects. In Calavar and The Infidel it has a certain stateliness and occasional pomp which is suitable to scenes so grand and romantic, and to the characters of the time and country. Of his other works, the diction is simple and familiar, and sometimes needlessly careless and inelegant. He died in 1854..

FIRST APPROACH TO MEXICO FROM THE MOUNTAINS.

FROM CALAVAR.

"I HAVE heard that the cold which freezes men to death, begins by setting them to sleep. Sleep brings dreams; and dreams are often most vivid and fantastical, before we have yet been wholly lost in slumber. Perhaps 'tis this most biting and benumbing blast, that brings me such phantoms. Art thou not very cold?"

"Not very, señor: methinks we are descending; and now the winds are not so frigid as before."

"I would to heaven, for the sake of us all, that we were descended yet lower; for night approaches, and still we are stumbling among these clouds, that seem to separate us from earth, without yet advancing us nearer to heaven."

While the cavalier was yet speaking, there came from the van of the army, very far in the distance, a shout of joy, that was caught up by those who toiled in his neighbourhood, and continued by the squadrons that brought up the rear, until finally lost among the echoes of remote cliffs. He pressed forward with the animation shared by his companions, and, still leading Jacinto, arrived, at last, at a place where the mountain dipped downwards with so sudden and so precipitous a declivity, as to interpose no obstacle to the vision. The mists were rolling away from his feet in huge wreaths, which gradually, as they became thinner, received and transmitted the rays of an evening sun, and were lighted up with a golden and crimson radiance, glorious to behold, and increasing every moment in splendour. As this superb curtain was parted from before him, as if by cords that went up to heaven, and surged voluminously aside, he looked over the heads of those that thronged the side of the mountain beneath, and saw, stretching away like a picture touched by the hands of angels, the fair valley imbosomed among those romantic hills, whose shadows were stealing visibly over its western slopes, but leaving all the eastern portion dyed with the tints of sunset. The green plains studded with yet greener woodlands; the little mountains raising their fairy-like crests: the lovely lakes, now gleaming like floods of molten silver, where they stretched into the sunshine, and now vanishing away, in a shadowy expanse, under the gloom of the growing twilight; the structures that rose, vaguely and obscurely, here from their verdant margins, and there from their very bosom, as if floating on their placid waters, seeming at one time to present the image of a city crowned with towers and pinnacles, and then again broken by some agitation of the element, or confused by some vapour swimming through the atmosphere, into the mere fragments and phantasms of edifices, —these, seen in that uncertain and fading light, and at that misty and enchanting distance, unfolded such a spectacle of beauty and peace as plunged the neophyte into a revery of rapture. The trembling of the page's hand, a deep sigh that breathed from his lips, recalled him to consciousness, without however dispelling his delight.

"By the cross which I worship!" he cried, "it fills me with amazement, to think that this cursed and malefactious earth doth contain a spot that is so much like a paradise! Now do I remember me of the words of the Señor Gomez, that 'no man could conceive of heaven, till he had looked upon the valley of Mexico,'—an expression which, at that time, I considered very absurd, and somewhat profane; yet, if I am not now mistaken, I shall henceforth, doubtless, when figuring to my imagination the seats of bliss, begin by thinking of this very prospect."

A NIGHT VIEW IN MEXICO.

FROM THE SAME.

"TURN, señor, from these pigmy vases to the great censers, which God has himself raised to his majesty!"

As De Morla spoke, he turned from the altars, and Don Amador, following with his eyes the direction in which he pointed, beheld a spectacle which instantly drove from his mind the thought of the idolatrous urns. Far away in the southwest, at the distance of eight or ten leagues, among a mass of hills that upheld their brows in gloomy obscurity, a colossal cone elevated its majestic bulk to heaven, while the snows which invested its resplendent sides glittered in the fires that crowned its summit. A pillar of smoke, of awful hue and volume, rose to an enormous altitude above its head, and then parting and spreading on either side through the serene heaven, lay still and solemn, like a funeral canopy, over its radiant pedestal. From the crater, out of which issued this portentous column, arose also, time by time, great flames with a sort of lambent playfulness, in strange and obvious contrast with their measureless mass and power; while ever and anon globes of fire, rushing up through the pillar of vapour, as through a transparent cylinder, burst at the top, and spangled the grim canopy with stars. No shock creeping through the earth, no heavy roar stealing along the atmosphere, attested the vigour of this sublime furnace; but all in silence and solemn tranquillity, the spectacle went on,—now darkling, now waxing temporarily into an oppressive splendour, as if for the amusement of those shadowy phantoms who seemed to sit in watch upon the neighbouring peaks.

"This is indeed," said Don Amador, reverently, "if God should require an altar of fire, such a high place as might be meeter for his worship than any shrine raised by the hands of man. God is very great and powerful! The sight of such a spectacle doth humble me in mine own thoughts: for what is man, though full of vanity and arrogance, in the sight of Him who builds the fire-mountains?"

"Padre Olmedo," said his companion, "will ask you, what is this fire-mountain, though to the eye so majestic, and to appearance so eternal, to the creeping thing whose spark of immortality will burn on, when the flames of yonder volcano are quenched for ever?"

"It is very true," said the neophyte, "the moun

tains burn away, the sea wastes itself into air, but the soul that God has given us consumes not. The life of the body passes away like these flames; the vitality that is in the spirit is a gift that heaven has not extended to the stars!"

RALPH STACKPOLE AND THE QUAKER.

FROM NICK OF THE WOODS.

Roaring Ralph was a stout, bandy-legged, broad-shouldered, and bull-headed tatterdemalion, ugly, mean, and villanous of look; yet with an impudent, swaggering, joyous self-esteem traced in every feature and expressed in every action of body, that rather disposed the beholder to laugh than to be displeased at his appearance. An old blanket-coat, or wrap-rascal, once white, but now of the same muddy brown hue that stained his visage, and once also of sufficient length to defend his legs, though the skirts had long since been transferred to the cuffs and elbows, where they appeared in huge patches, covered the upper part of his body; while the lower boasted a pair of buckskin breeches and leather wrappers, somewhat its junior in age, but its rival in mud and maculation. An old round fur hat, intended originally for a boy, and only made to fit his head by being slit in sundry places at the bottom, thus leaving a dozen yawning gaps, through which, as through the chinks of a lattice, stole out as many stiff bunches of black hair, gave to the capital excrescence an air as ridiculous as it was truly uncouth, which was not a little increased by the absence of one side of the brim, and by a loose fragment of it hanging down on the other. To give something martial to an appearance in other respects so outlandish and ludicrous, he had his rifle, and other usual equipments of a woods-man, including the knife and tomahawk, the first of which he carried in his hand, swinging it about at every moment, with a vigour and apparent care-lessness well fit to discompose a nervous person, had any such happened among his auditors. As if there was not enough in his figure, visage, and attire to move the mirth of beholders, he added to his other attractions a variety of gestures and antics of the most extravagant kinds, dancing, leaping and dodging about, clapping his hands and cracking his heels together, with the activity, restlessness, and, we may add, the grace of a jumping-jack......

Had the gallant captain of horse-thieves boasted the blood, as he afterwards did the name, of an "alligator half-breed," he could have scarce con-ducted himself in a way more worthy of his pa-rentage. He leaped into the centre of the throng, where, having found elbow-room for his purpose, he performed the gyration mentioned before, fol-lowing it up by other feats expressive of his hostile humour. He flapped his wings and crowed, until every chanticleer in the settlement replied to the note of battle; he snorted and neighed like a horse; he bellowed like a bull; he barked like a dog; he yelled like an Indian; he whined like a panther;

he howled like a wolf, until one would have thought he was a living menagerie, comprising within his single body the spirit of every animal noted for its love of conflict. Then, not content with such a display of readiness to fight the field, he darted from the centre of the area allowed him for his ex-ercise, and invited the lookers-on individually to battle. "Whar's your buffalo-bull," he cried, "to cross horns with the roarer of Salt River! Whar's your full-blood colt that can shake a saddle off! h'yar's an old nag can kick off the top of a buck-eye! Whar's your cat of the Knobs? your wolf of the Rolling Prairies? h'yar's the old brown b'ar can claw the bark off a gum-tree! H'yar's a man for you, Tom Bruce! Same to you, Sim Roberts! to you, and to you, and to you! Ar'n't I a ring-tailed squealer! Can go down Salt on my back, and swim up the Ohio! Whar's the man to fight Roaring Ralph Stackpole!"

Now, whether it happened that there were none present inclined to a contest with such a champion, or whether it was that the young men looked upon the exhibition as a mere bravado meant rather to amuse them than to irritate, it so occurred that not one of them accepted the challenge; though each, when personally called on, did his best to add to the roarer's fury, if fury it really were, by letting off sundry jests in relation to borrowed horses and regulators.*

"If you're rarely ripe for a fight, Roaring Ralph," cried Tom Bruce the younger, who had shown, like the others, a greater disposition to jest than to do battle with the champion, "here comes the very man for you. Look, boys, thar comes Bloody Na-than!" At which formidable name there was a loud shout set up, with an infinite deal of laughing and clapping of hands.

"Whar's the feller?" cried Captain Stackpole, springing six feet into the air, and uttering a whoop of anticipated triumph. "I've heerd of the brute, and, 'tarnal death to me, but I'm his super-supe-rior! Show me the crittur, and let me fly! Cock-a-doodle-do!"

"Hurrah for Roaring Ralph Stackpole!" cried the young men, some of whom proceeded to pat him on the back in compliment to his courage, while others ran forward to hasten the approach of the expected antagonist.

The appearance of the comer, at a distance, promised an equal match to the captain of horse-thieves;...... but when one came to survey him a little more closely, he could not avoid suspecting that the soubriquet, instead of being given to indi-cate warlike and dangerous traits of character, had been bestowed out of pure wantonness and derision. His visage, seeming to belong to a man of at least forty-five or fifty years of age, was hollow, and al-most as weather-worn as his apparel, with a long hooked nose, prominent chin, a wide mouth ex-ceedingly straight and pinched, with a melancholy

---

* It is scarce necessary to inform the reader, that by this term must be understood those public-spirited citi-zens, amateur jack-ketches, who administer lynch-law in districts where regular law is but inefficiently, or not at all, established.

or contemplative twist at the corners, and a pair of black staring eyes that beamed a good-natured, humble, and perhaps submissive, simplicity of disposition. His gait, too, as he stumbled along up the hill, with a shuffling, awkward, hesitating step, was more like that of a man who apprehended injury and insult, than of one who possessed the spirit to resist them. · The fact, moreover, of sustaining on his own shoulders a heavy pack of deer and other skins, to relieve the miserable horse which he led, betokened a merciful temper, scarce compatible with the qualities of a man of war and contention......

On the whole, the appearance of the man was any thing in the world but that of the bulky and ferocious ruffian whom the nickname had led Roland to anticipate; and he scarce knew whether to pity him, or to join in the laugh with which the young men of the settlement greeted his approach. Perhaps his sense of the ridiculous would have disposed the young soldier to merriment; but the wistful look with which, while advancing, Nathan seemed to deprecate the insults he evidently expected, spoke volumes of reproach to his spirit, and the half-formed smile faded from his countenance.

"Thar!" exclaimed Tom Bruce, slapping Stackpole on the shoulder, with great glee, "thar's the man that calls himself Dannger! At him, for the honour of Salt River; but take care of his fore-legs, for, I tell you, he's the Pennsylvania war-horse."

"And ar'n't I the ramping tiger of the Rolling Fork?" cried Captain Ralph; "and can't I eat him, hoss, dog, dirty jacket, and all? Hold me by the tail, while I devour him!"

With that he executed two or three escapades, demivoltes, curvets, and other antics of a truly equine character, and galloping up to the amazed Nathan, saluted him with a neigh so shrill and hostile that even White Dobbin pricked up his ears, and betrayed other symptoms of alarm.

"Surely, colonel, you will not allow that mad ruffian to assail the poor man?"

"Oh, Ralph won't hurt him; he's never ambitious, except among Injuns and horses. He's only for skearing the old feller."

"And who may the old fellow be? and why do you call him Bloody Nathan?"

"We call him Bloody Nathan," replied the commander, "because he's the only man in all Kentucky, that won't fight! and thar's the way he beats us all hollow. Lord, captain, you'd hardly believe it, but he's nothing more than a poor Pennsylvania Quaker; and what brought him out to Kentucky, whar thar's nar another creatur' of his tribe, thar's no knowing. Some say he war dishonest, and so had to cut loose from Pennsylvania; but I never heerd of him stealing any thing in Kentucky: I reckon thar's too much of the chicken about him for that. Some say he is hunting rich lands; which war like enough for any body that war not so poor and lazy. And some say his wits are unsettled, and I hold that that's the truth of the creatur'; for he does nothing but go wandering up and down the country, now h'yar and now thar, hunting for meat and skins; and that's pretty much

the way he makes a living. Thar's them that's good-natur'd, that calls him Wandering Nathan, because of his being h'yar, and thar, and everywhar. He don't seem much afear'd of the Injuns; but, they say, the red brutes never disturbs the Pennsylvania Quakers. Howsomever, he makes himself useful; for sometimes he finds Injun sign whar thar's no Injuns thought of, and so he gives information; but he always dues it, as he says, to save bloodshed, not to bring on a fight. He comes to me once, thar's more than three years ago, and instead of saying, 'Cunnel, thar's twenty Injuns lying on the road at the lower fort of Salt, whar you may nab them;' says he, says he, 'Friend Thomas, thee must keep the people from going nigh the ford, for thar's Injuns thar that will hurt them;' and then he takes himself off; whilst I rides down thar with twenty-five men and exterminates them, killing six, and driving the others the Lord knows whar. He has had but a hard time of it among us, poor creatur'; for it used to make us wrathy to find thar war so little fight in him, that he wouldn't so much as kill a murdering Injun. I took his gun from him once; for why, he wouldn't attend muster when I had enrolled him. But I pitied the brute; for he war poor, and thar war but little corn in his cabin, and nothing to shoot meat with; and so I gave it back, and told him to take his own ways for an old fool."

While Colonel Bruce was thus delineating the character of Nathan Slaughter, the latter found himself surrounded by the young men of the station, the but of a thousand jests, and the victim of the insolence of the captain of horse-thieves. It is not to be supposed that Roaring Ralph was really the bully and madman that his extravagant freaks and expressions seemed to proclaim him. These, like any other "actions that a man might play," were assumed, partly because it suited his humour to be fantastic, and partly because the putting of his antic disposition on, was the only means which he, like many of his betters, possessed of attracting attention, and avoiding the neglect and contempt to which his low habits and appearance would have otherwise justly consigned him. There was, therefore, little really hostile in the feelings with which he approached the non-combatant; though it was more than probable, the disgust he, in common with the other warlike personages, entertained toward the peaceable Nathan, might have rendered him a little more malicious than usual.

"Bloody Nathan!" said he, as soon as he had concluded his neighing and curvetting, "if you ever said your prayers, now's the time. Down with your pack,—for I can't stand deer's ha'r sticking in my swallow, no how!"

"Friend," said Bloody Nathan, meekly, "I beg thee will not disturb me. I am a man of peace and quiet."

And so saying he endeavoured to pass onwards, but was prevented by Ralph, who, seizing his heavy bundle with one hand, applied his right foot to it with a dexterity that not only removed it from the poor man's back, but sent the dried skins scattering over the road. This feat was rewarded by the spectators with loud shouts, all which, as well as the insult itself, Nathan bore with exemplary patience.

"Friend," he said, "what does thee seek of me, that thee treats me thus?"

"A fight!" replied Captain Stackpole, uttering a war-whoop; "a fight, strannger, for the love of heaven!"

"Thee seeks it of the wrong person," said Nathan; "and I beg thee will get thee away."

"What!" said Stackpole, "ar'nt thee the Pennsylvania war-horse, the screamer of the meeting-house, the bloody-mouthed b'ar of Yea-Nay-and-Verily?"

"I am a man of peace," said the submissive Slaughter.

"Yea verily, verily and yea!" cried Ralph, snuffling through the nostrils, but assuming an air of extreme indignation; "Strannger, I've heerd of you! You're the man that holds it agin duty and conscience to kill Injuns, the red-skin screamers,— that refuses to defend the women, the splendiferous creaturs! and the little children, the squal-a-baby d'ars! And wharfo'! Bec'ause as how you're a man of peace and no fight, you superiferous, long-legged, no-souled crittur! But I'm the gentleman to make a man of you. So down with your gun, and 'tarnal death to me, I'll whip the cowardly devil out of you." .

"Friend," said Nathan, his humility yielding to a feeling of contempt, "thee is theeself a cowardly person, or thee wouldn't seek a quarrel with one, thee knows, can't fight thee. Thee would not be so ready with thee match."

With that, he stooped to gather up his skins, a proceeding that Stackpole, against whom the laugh was turned by this sally of Nathan's, resisted, by catching him by the nape of the neck, twirling him round, and making as if he really would have beaten him.

Even this the peaceful Nathan bore without anger or murmuring; but his patience fled, when Stackpole, turning to the little dog, which by bristling its back and growling, expressed a half inclination to take up its master's quarrel, applied his foot to its ribs with a violence that sent it rolling some five or six yards down the hill, where it lay for a time yelping and whining with pain.

"Friend!" said Nathan, sternly, "thee is but a dog theeself, to harm the creature! What will thee have with me!"

"A fight! a fight, I tell thee!" replied Captain Ralph, "till I teach thy leatherified conscience the new doctrines of Kentucky."

"Fight thee I cannot, and dare not," said Nathan; and then added, "but if thee must have thee deserts, thee *shall* have them. Thee prides theeself upon thee courage and strength—will thee adventure with me a friendly fall?"

"Hurrah for Bloody Nathan!" cried the young men, vastly delighted at this unwonted spirit, while Captain Ralph himself expressed his pleasure, by leaping into the air, crowing, and dashing off his hat, which he kicked down the hill with as much good will as he had previously bestowed upon the little dog.

"Off with your leather night-cap, and down with your rifle," he cried, giving his own weapon into the hands of a looker-on, "and scrape some of the grease off your jacket; for, 'tarnal death to me, I shall give you the Virginny lock, fling you headfo'most, and you'll find yourself, in a twinkling, sticking fast right in the centre of the 'arth!"

"Thee may find theeself mistaken," said Nathan, giving up his gun to one of the young men, but instead of rejecting his hat, pulling it down tight over his brows. "There is locks taught among the mountains of Bedford that may be as good as them learned on the hills of Virginia.—I am ready for thee."

"Cock-a-doodle-doo!" cried Ralph Stackpole, springing towards his man, and clapping his hands, one on Nathan's left shoulder, the other on his right hip: "Are you ready?"

"I am," replied Nathan.

"Down then, you go, war you a buffalo!" And with that the captain of horse-thieves put forth his strength, which was very great, in an effort that appeared to Roland quite irresistible; though, as it happened, it scarce moved Nathan from his position.

"Thee is mistaken, friend!" he cried, exerting his strength in return, and with an effect that no one had anticipated. By magic, as it seemed, the heels of the captain of horse-thieves were suddenly seen flying in the air, his head aiming at the earth, upon which it as suddenly descended with the violence of a bomb-shell; and there it would doubtless have burrowed, like the aforesaid implement of destruction, had the soil been soft enough for the purpose, or exploded into a thousand fragments, had not the shell been double the thickness of an ordinary skull.

"Huzza! Bloody Nathan for ever!" shouted the delighted villagers.

"He has killed the man," said Forrester; "but bear witness, all, the fellow provoked his fate."

"Thanks to you, strannger! but not so dead as you reckon," said Ralph, rising to his feet and scratching his poll, with a stare of comical confusion. "I say, strannger, here's my shoulders—but whar's my head?—Do you reckon I had the worst of it?"

"Huzza for Bloody Nathan Slaughter! He has whipped the ramping tiger of Salt River;" cried the young men of the station.

"Well, I reckon he has," said the magnanimous Captain Ralph, picking up his hat: then walking up to Nathan, who had taken his dog into his arms, to examine into the little animal's hurts, he cried, with much good-humoured energy,—"Thar's my fo'-paw, in token I've had enough of you, and want no mo'. But I say, Nathan Slaughter," he added, as he grasped the victor's hand, "it's no thing you can boast of, to be the strongest man in Kentucky, and the most sevagarous at a tussel,—h'yar among murdering Injuns and scalping runnegades, and keep your fists off their top-nots. Thar's my idea: for I go for the doctrine, that every able-bodied man should sarve his country and his neighbours, and fight their foes; and them that does is men and gentlemen, and them that don't is cowards and rascals, that's my idea. And so, fawwell."

RALPH WALDO EMERSON.

[Born 1803.]

THE development of the transcendental philosophy in New England is deserving of more consideration than can here be bestowed upon it. I can remember the period when the general principles of Locke, with a slight infusion of Reid and Dugald Stuart, constituted the orthodox philosophical creed of New England. The first shock given to that system was Professor Marsh's calm, profound and luminous exposition of the doctrines of Coleridge, in his prefaces to the American editions of The Friend and the Aids to Reflection. This was followed by Mr. Brownson's various writings and lectures, developing, in a popular form, the philosophy of Victor Cousin and the French school. Almost everybody who attended a lecture or a sermon by Mr. Brownson, was at once transformed into a metaphysician, and could discourse very decisively on the essential distinction between reason and reasoning, and could look with compassion on all who held to the old philosophy, or were defective in insight. Cousin was very grateful to his American disciple, and repeatedly spoke of him as the first metaphysician in the United States. But there have been changes of the moon since then, and it is needless to say that Mr. Brownson now shines in the light of a different system.

Contemporary with Mr. Brownson, though very different in mind and character, was Mr. Emerson, the transcendentalist *par eminence*, and the most original of the school. Neither Coleridge nor Cousin was sufficient for him, but in subtlety and daring he rather approaches Fichte. He is the son of a Unitarian clergyman of Boston, and in 1821, when about seventeen years of age, was graduated at Harvard University. Having turned his attention to theology, he was ordained minister of one of the congregations of his native city, but embracing soon after some peculiar views in regard to the forms of worship, he abandoned his profession, and retiring to the quiet village of Concord, after the manner of an Arabian prophet, gave himself up to "thinking," preparatory to his appearance as a revelator. His oration entitled Man-Thinking, delivered before the Phi Beta Kappa Society in the summer of 1837, attracted a great deal of attention, but less than his address before the senior class in Divinity College at Cambridge in the following year. He began now to be understood. His peculiarity was not so much his system as his point of view. He did not pretend to reason, but to discover; he was not a logician, but a seer; he announced, not argued. His prominent doctrine is, that the deity is impersonal,—mere being, and comes to *self-consciousness* only in individuals. The distinction of this from pantheism is this, that while pantheism "sinks man and nature in God," Mr. Emerson "sinks God and nature in man."

In 1838 Mr. Emerson published Literary Ethics, an oration, and in the following year a small volume entitled Nature. In 1840 he commenced The Dial, a magazine of literature, philosophy and religion, which was continued four years; in 1841 he published The Method of Nature, an oration; Man the Reformer, a lecture on some of the prominent features of the present age; three Lectures on the Times, and the first series of his Essays. In the next two or three years he published little except his papers in The Dial, but in 1844 he gave to the public lectures on New England Reformers, the Young American, and Negro Emancipation in the West Indies, and the second series of his Essays. He has since delivered lectures on Swedenborg, Napoleon, New England, and other subjects, which are regarded by some who have heard them as decidedly the finest of his works; and in December, 1846, he published a volume of Poems, which have peculiar and remarkable merits.

Mr. Emerson is "a seeker with no Past at his back." He evidently aims to break the moulds of popular beliefs, and to get at the heart of the matter, to look around and within with the fresh vision of "a first man," and like Adam in the garden to put his own names upon what he sees. He has none of the ill humour which denies because others affirm; he simply takes leave to look for himself. While therefore he continually sees and represents things in singular lights, and sometimes inverts them, so that it would seem to be an inevitable conclusion that either he is crazy or we, on the other hand he regenerates our faith, by giving us an original testimony to great truths. Thus, his essay on The Over-Soul, notwithstanding its unscriptural title, is as orthodox as St. Paul.

Whatever appearances there may be to the contrary, Mr. Emerson is no destructive. He is a builder, a born and anointed poet. His demand is Truth. He must stand face to face with the Absolute. Insatiable as is his craving for truth, he is always orderly and serene. He gives no sign that any deterring considerations have ever occurred to him. Whatever suggestions of fear or policy there may be, they are less than cobwebs to him. They cannot impede, they do not even tease him. He is as self-possessed and assured as if he carried in his pocket a commission, signed and sealed of all mankind, to say just the thing that he is saying. Mr. Emerson is never commonplace. Hence we infer that he is a genuine worker. He cannot, like a host of others, write in his sleep. Every thing is wrought out by his own thought. I have sometimes fancied that he must, in his listless moments, repine at the stubbornness of his genius, which can bear to be mute, but which cannot declaim, nor tolerate in him any attempt at "fine writing." There is a very common talent, passing for a great deal more than it is worth,—the sole talent of many quite distinguished writers,—which lies in the putting of words together so fitly and musically that they seem to sing a new truth, when it is "an old song," with no variations. Mr. Emerson is utterly deficient in this power. He cannot juggle with words. He has no bank-notes: nothing but bullion. If he states an old and world-known truth, he does it with that felicity of expression which gives us a fresh sense of its value, and we confess that the same thing was never before so well said. He fits his word to his thought, consulting no ear but his own.

In reading Mr. Emerson's works we must observe Coleridge's admirable rule : " When you cannot understand an author's ignorance, account yourself ignorant of his understanding." At the slightest glance we shall find here and there in them much to inspire respect for his sagacity and admiration for his genius. When therefore he seems to be unintelligible, or absurd, modesty dictates that we should at least entertain the question whether the defect

be in him or us. If we cannot explain his ignorance, we shall do wisely to distrust our own understanding. It is possible, nay, it is in a very high degree probable, not only that he really has a meaning, but that he has a very good and a very great meaning, and that he has expressed it in the very best form, so that, were we as keen-sighted as he, we should recognise the beauty both of the thought and the expression.

An ingenious friend and admirer of Mr. Emerson, a few years since, put forth some very amusing pencil sketches illustrative of his hard sayings. They were caricatures, it is true ; but they implied a great compliment. How many of our writers of established fame use language sufficiently picturesque to admit of such illustrations ?

—In connection with the opposition to the old school of metaphysics may be mentioned Doctor Walker, the Professor of Philosophy in Harvard University ; the Reverend Theodore Parker, and the Reverend William B. Greene. Doctor Walker delivered in Boston a few years ago three series of lectures on Natural Religion, in which he steered between the extremes of both parties, confined himself to no particular system, but in his general principles coincided very nearly with Cousin, as modified by Jouffroy. Mr. Parker may also be classed with the school of Cousin, but his metaphysics are confusedly blended with radical notions regarding government, and heretical notions regarding religion,—a kind of aggregation in one mind of what is most offensive in the different French and German schools. Mr. Greene is a powerful and original thinker, with no other point of agreement with the transcendentalists than the negative one of rejection of Locke.

Opposed to all these is Mr. Bowen, the well-known editor of the North American Review, who hates transcendentalism in all its forms, deeming it, as developed in New England, a monstrosity, made up of cant, sentimentalism, and unreason. A receiver of the general principles of Locke, as modified by the progress of philosophical discovery, he enforces them with great energy and determination. Though I dissent from many of his opinions, and question the validity of his positions, I still think that his disquisitions evince a strength, breadth, and acuteness of understanding, a knowledge of his subjects, and a directness of style which place them very high among American contri butions to the science of metaphysics.

BEAUTY.

FROM NATURE.

THE presence of a higher, namely, of the spiritual element is essential to its perfection. The high and divine beauty which can be loved without effeminacy, is that which is found in combination with the human will, and never separate. Beauty is the mark God sets upon virtue. Every natural action is graceful. Every heroic act is also decent, and causes the place and the bystanders to shine. We are taught by great actions that the universe is the property of every individual in it. Every rational creature has all nature for his dowry and estate. It is his, if he will. He may divest himself of it; he may creep into a corner, and abdicate his kingdom, as most men do; but he is entitled to the world by his constitution. In proportion to the energy of his thought and will, he takes up the world into himself. " All those things for which men plough, build, or sail, obey virtue;" said an ancient historian. " The winds and waves," said Gibbon, "are always on the side of the ablest navigators." So are the sun and moon and all the stars of heaven. When a noble act is done,—perchance in a scene of great natural beauty; when Leonidas and his three hundred martyrs consume one day in dying, and the sun and moon come each and look at them once in the steep defile of Thermopylæ; when Arnold Winkelried, in the high Alps, under the shadow of the avalanche, gathers in his side a sheaf of Austrian spears to break the line for his comrades; are not these heroes entitled to add the beauty of the scene to the beauty of the deed? When the bark of Columbus nears the shore of America;—before it, the beach lined with savages, fleeing out of all their huts of cane; the sea behind; and the purple mountains of the Indian Archipelago around, can we separate the man from the living picture? Does not the New World clothe his form with her palm-groves and savannahs as fit drapery? Ever does natural beauty steal in like air, and envelope great actions. When Sir Harry Vane was dragged up the Tower-hill, sitting on a sled, to suffer death, as the champion of the English laws, one of the multitude cried out to him, "You never sate on so glorious a seat." Charles II., to intimidate the citizens of London, caused the patriot Lord Russel to be drawn in an open coach, through the principal streets of the city, on his way to the scaffold. " But," to use the simple narrative of his biographer, "the multitude imagined they saw liberty and virtue sitting by his side." In private places, among sordid objects, an act of truth or heroism seems at once to draw to itself the sky as its temple, the sun as its candle. Nature stretcheth out her arms to embrace man, only let his thoughts be of equal greatness. Willingly does she follow his steps with the rose and the violet, and bend her lines of grandeur and grace to the decoration of her darling child. Only let his thoughts be of equal scope, and the frame will suit the picture. A virtuous man is in unison with her works, and makes the central figure of the visible sphere.

POETRY AND NATURE.

FROM LITERARY ETHICS.

BY Latin and English poetry, we were born and bred in an oratorio of praises of nature,—flowers, birds, mountains, sun, and moon; yet the naturalist of this hour finds that he knows nothing, by all their poems, of any of these fine things; that he has conversed with the merest surface and show of them all: and of their essence, or of their history, knows nothing. Further inquiry will discover that nobody,—that not these chanting poets themselves, knew any thing sincere of these handsome natures they so commended; that they contented themselves with the passing chirp of a bird that they saw one or two mornings, and listlessly looked at sunsets, and repeated idly these few glimpses in their song. But, go into the forest, you shall find all new and undescribed. The screaming of the wild geese, flying by night; the thin note of the companionable titmouse, in the winter day; the fall of swarms of flies in autumn, from combats high in the air, pattering down on the leaves like rain; the angry hiss of the wood-birds; the pine throwing out its pollen for the benefit of the next century; the turpentine exuding from the tree—and, indeed, any vegetation—any animation, any and all are alike unattempted. The man who stands on the sea-shore, or who rambles in the woods, seems to be the first man that ever stood on the shore, or entered a grove, his sensations and his world are so novel and strange. Whilst I read the poets, I think that nothing new can be said about morning and evening; but when I see the daybreak, I am not reminded of these Homeric, or Shakspearian, or Miltonic, or Chaucerian pictures. No; but I feel, perhaps, the pain of an alien world,—a world not yet subdued by the thought; or, I am cheered by the moist, warm, glittering, budding, melodious hour, that takes down the narrow walls of my soul, and extends its life and pulsation to the very horizon. That is morning, to cease for a bright hour to be a prisoner of this sickly body, and to become as large as nature.

The noonday darkness of the American forest, the deep, echoing, aboriginal woods, where the living columns of the oak and fir tower up from the ruins of the trees of the last millennium; where, from year to year, the eagle and the crow see no intruder; the pines, bearded with savage moss, yet touched with grace by the violets at their feet; the broad, cold lowland, which forms its coat of vapour with the stillness of subterranean crystallization; and where the traveller, amid the repulsive plants that are native in the swamp, thinks with pleasing terror of the distant town; this beauty,—haggard and desert beauty, which the sun and the moon, the snow and the rain repaint and vary, has never been recorded by art, yet is not indifferent to any passenger. All men are poets at heart. They serve nature for bread, but her loveliness overcomes them sometimes. What mean these journeys to Niagara; these pilgrims to the White Hills? Men believe in the adaptations of utility, always. In the mountains, they may believe in the adaptations of the eye. Undoubtedly, the changes of geology have a relation to the prosperous sprouting of the corn and peas in my kitchen garden; but not less is there a relation of beauty between my soul and the dim crags of Agiocochook up there in the clouds. Every man, when this is told, hearkens with joy, and yet his own conversation with nature is still unsung.

THE POWER OF LOVE.

FROM AN ESSAY ON LOVE.

BE our experience in particulars what it may, no man ever forgot the visitations of that power to his heart and brain, which created all things new; which was the dawn in him of music, poetry and art; which made the face of nature radiant with purple light, the morning and the night varied enchantments; when a single tone of one voice could make the heart beat, and the most trivial circumstance associated with one form, is put in the amber of memory: when we became all eye when one was present, and all memory when one was gone; when the youth becomes a watcher of windows, and studious of a glove, a veil, a ribbon, or the wheels of a carriage; when no place is too solitary, and none too silent for him who has richer company and sweeter conversation in his new thoughts, than any old friends, though best and purest, can give him; for, the figures, the motions, the words of the beloved object are not like other images written in water, but, as Plutarch said, "enamelled in fire," and make the study of midnight.

"Thou art not gone being gone, where'er thou art,
Thou leav'st in him thy watchful eyes, in him thy loving heart."

In the noon and the afternoon of life, we still throb at the recollection of days when happiness was not happy enough, but must be drugged with the relish of pain and fear; for he touched the secret of the matter, who said of love,

"All other pleasures are not worth its pains:"

and when the day was not long enough, but the night too must be consumed in keen recollections; when the head boiled all night on the pillow with the generous deed it resolved on; when the moonlight was a pleasing fever, and the stars were letters, and the flowers ciphers, and the air was coined into song; when all business seemed an impertinence, and all the men and women running to and fro in the streets, mere pictures.

The passion remakes the world for the youth. It makes all things alive and significant. Nature grows conscious. Every bird on the boughs of the tree sings now to his heart and soul. Almost the notes are articulate. The clouds have faces, as he looks on them. The trees of the forest, the waving grass and the peeping flowers have grown intelligent; and almost he fears to trust them with the secret which they seem to invite. Yet nature soothes and sympathizes. In the green solitude he finds a dearer home than with men.

"Fountain heads and pathless groves,
Places which pale passion loves,

Moonlight walks, when all the fowls
Are safely housed, save bats and owls,
A midnight bell, a passing groan,
These are the sounds we feed upon."

Behold there in the wood the fine madman! He is a palace of sweet sounds and sights; he dilates; he is twice a man; he walks with arms akimbo; he soliloquizes; he accosts the grass and the trees; he feels the blood of the violet, the clover and the lily in his veins; and he talks with the brook that wets his foot.

The causes that have sharpened his perceptions of natural beauty, have made him love music and verse. It is a fact often observed, that men have written good verses under the inspiration of passion, who cannot write well under any other circumstances.

The like force has the passion over all his nature. It expands the sentiment; it makes the clown gentle, and gives the coward heart. Into the most pitiful and abject it will infuse a heart and courage to defy the world, so only it have the countenance of the beloved object. In giving him to another, it still more gives him to himself. He is a new man, with new perceptions, new and keener purposes, and a religious solemnity of character and aims. He does not longer appertain to his family and society. He is somewhat. He is a person. He is a soul.

GENIUS.

FROM THE METHOD OF NATURE.

AND what is Genius but finer love, a love impersonal, a love of the flower and perfection of things, and a desire to draw a new picture or copy of the same? It looks to the cause and life: it proceeds from within outward, whilst talent goes from without inward. Talent finds its models and methods and ends in society, exists for exhibition, and goes to the soul only for power to work. Genius is its own end, and draws its means and the style of its architecture from within, going abroad only for audience and spectator, as we adapt our voice and phrase to the distance and character of the ear we speak to. All your learning of all literatures would never enable you to anticipate one of its thoughts or expressions, and yet each is natural and familiar as household words. Here about us coils for ever the ancient enigma, so old and so unutterable. Behold! there is the sun, and the rain, and the rocks: the old sun, the old stones. How easy were it to describe all this fitly: yet no word can pass. Nature is a mute, and man, her articulate speaking brother, lo! he also is a mute. Yet when genius arrives, its speech is like a river, it has no straining to describe, more than there is straining in nature to exist. When thought is best, there is most of it. Genius sheds wisdom like perfume, and advertises us that it flows out of a deeper source than the foregoing silence, that it knows so deeply and speaks so musically because it is itself a mutation of the thing it describes. It is sun and moon and wave and fire in music, as astronomy is thought and harmony in masses of matter.

THE COMPENSATIONS OF CALAMITY.
FROM AN ESSAY ON COMPENSATION.

THE changes which break up at short intervals the prosperity of men, are advertisements of a nature whose law is growth. Evermore it is the order of nature to grow, and every soul is by this intrinsic necessity quitting its whole system of things, its friends, and home, and laws, and faith, as the shell-fish crawls out of its beautiful but stony case, because it no longer admits of its growth, and slowly forms a new house. In proportion to the vigour of the individual, these revolutions are frequent, until in some happier mind they are incessant, and all worldly relations hang very loosely about him, becoming, as it were, a transparent fluid membrane through which the form is always seen, and not as in most men an indurated heterogeneous fabric of many dates, and of no settled character, in which the man is imprisoned. Then there can be enlargement, and the man of to-day scarcely recognises the man of yesterday. And such should be the outward biography of man in time, a putting off of dead circumstances day by day, as he renews his raiment day by day. But to us, in our lapsed estate, resting not advancing, resisting not coöperating with the divine expansion, this growth comes by shocks.

We cannot part with our friends. We cannot let our angels go. We do not see that they only go out, that archangels may come in. We are idolaters of the old. We do not believe in the riches of the soul, in its proper eternity and omnipresence. We do not believe there is any force in to-day to rival or re-create that beautiful yesterday. We linger in the ruins of the old tent, where once we had bread and shelter and organs, nor believe that the spirit can feed, cover, and nerve us again. We cannot again find aught so dear. so sweet, so graceful. But we sit and weep in vain. The voice of the Almighty saith, "Up and onward for evermore!" We cannot stay amid the ruins. Neither will we rely on the new; and so we walk ever with reverted eyes, like those monsters who look backwards.

And yet the compensations of calamity are made apparent to the understanding also, after long intervals of time. A fever, a mutilation, a cruel disappointment, a loss of wealth, a loss of friends seems at the moment unpaid loss, and unpayable. But the sure years reveal the deep remedial force that underlies all facts. The death of a dear friend, wife, brother, lover, which seemed nothing but privation, somewhat later assumes the aspect of a guide or genius; for it commonly operates revolutions in our way of life, terminates an epoch of infancy or of youth which was waiting to be closed, breaks up a wonted occupation, or a household, or style of living, and allows the formation of new ones more friendly to the growth of character. It permits or constrains the formation of new acquaintances, and the reception of new influences that prove of the first importance to the next years; and the man or woman who would have remained a sunny garden flower, with no room for its roots and too much sunshine for its head, by the falling of the walls and the neglect of the gardener, is made the banian of the forest, yielding shade and fruit to wide neighbourhoods of men.

TRAVELLING.
FROM ESSAY ON SELF-RELIANCE.

IT is for want of self-culture that the idol of travelling, the idol of Italy, of England, of Egypt, remains for all educated Americans. They who made England, Italy, or Greece venerable in the imagination, did so not by rambling round creation as a moth round a lamp, but by sticking fast where they were, like an axis of the earth. In manly hours, we feel that duty is our place, and that the merrymen of circumstance should follow as they may. The soul is no traveller: the wise man stays at home with the soul, and when his necessities, his duties, on any occasion call him from his house, or into foreign lands, he is at home still, and is not gadding abroad from himself, and shall make men sensible by the expression of his countenance, that he goes the missionary of wisdom and virtue, and visits cities and men like a sovereign, and not like an interloper or a valet.

I have no churlish objection to the circumnavigation of the globe, for the purposes of art, of study, and benevolence, so that the man is first domesticated, or does not go abroad with the hope of finding somewhat greater than he knows. He who travels to be amused, or to get somewhat which he does not carry, travels away from himself, and grows old even in youth among old things. In Thebes, in Palmyra, his will and mind have become old and dilapidated as they. He carries ruins to ruins.

Travelling is a fool's paradise. We owe to our first journeys the discovery that place is nothing. At home I dream that at Naples, at Rome, I can be intoxicated with beauty, and lose my sadness. I pack my trunk, embrace my friends, embark on the sea, and at last wake up at Naples, and there beside me is the stern fact, the sad self, unrelenting, identical, that I fled from. I seek the Vatican, and the palaces. I affect to be intoxicated with sights and suggestions, but I am not intoxicated. My giant goes with me wherever I go.

But the rage of travelling is itself only a symptom of a deeper unsoundness affecting the whole intellectual action. The intellect is vagabond, and the universal system of education fosters restlessness. Our minds travel when our bodies are forced to stay at home. We imitate; and what is imitation but the travelling of the mind? Our houses are built with foreign taste; our shelves are garnished with foreign ornaments; our opinions, our tastes, our whole minds lean, and follow the past and the distant, as the eyes of a maid follow her mistress. The soul created the arts wherever they have flourished. It was in his own mind that the artist sought his model. It was an application of his own thought to the thing to be done and the conditions to be observed. And why need we copy the Doric or the Gothic model? Beauty, convenience, grandeur of thought, and quaint expression are as near to us as to any, and if the American artist will study with hope and love the precise thing to be done by him, considering the climate, the soil, the length of the day, the wants of the people, the habit and form of the government, he will create a house in which all these will find themselves fitted, and taste and sentiment will be satisfied also.

Insist on yourself; never imitate. Your own gift you can present every moment with the cumulative force of a whole life's cultivation ; but of the adopted talent of another, you have only an extemporaneous, half possession. That which each can do best, none but his Maker can teach him. No man yet knows what it is, nor can, till that person has exhibited it. Where is the master who could have taught Shakspeare ? Where is the master who could have instructed Franklin, or Washington, or Bacon, or Newton ? Every great man is a unique. The Scipionism of Scipio is precisely that part he could not borrow. If anybody will tell me whom the great man imitates in the original crisis when he performs a great act, I will tell him who else than himself can teach him. Shakspeare will never be made by the study of Shakspeare. Do that which is assigned thee, and thou canst not hope too much or dare too much. ¹ There is at this moment, there is for me an utterance bare and grand as that of the colossal chisel of Phidias, or trowel of the Egyptians, or the pen of Moses, or Dante, but different from all these. Not possibly will the soul all rich, all eloquent, with thousand-cloven tongue, deign to repeat itself; for if I can hear what these patriarchs say, surely I can reply to them in the same pitch of voice : for the ear and the tongue are two organs of one nature. Dwell up there in the simple and noble regions of thy life, obey thy heart, and thou shalt reproduce the Foreworld again.

STATELINESS AND COURTESY.

FROM AN ESSAY ON MANNERS.

I LIKE that every chair should be a throne, and hold a king. I prefer a tendency to stateliness, to an excess of fellowship. Let the incommunicable objects of nature and the metaphysical isolation of man teach us independence. Let us not be too much acquainted. I would have a man enter his house through a hall filled with heroic and sacred sculptures, that he might not want the hint of tranquillity and self-poise. We should meet each morning, as from foreign countries, and spending the day together, should depart at night, as into foreign countries. In all things I would have the island of a man inviolate. Let us sit apart as the gods, talking from peak to peak all round Olympus. No degree of affection need invade this religion. This is myrrh and rosemary to keep the other sweet. Lovers should guard their strangeness. If they forgive too much, all slides into confusion and meanness. It is easy to push this deference to a Chinese etiquette ; but coolness and absence of heat and haste indicate fine qualities. A gentleman makes no noise: a lady is serene.

Proportionate is our disgust at those invaders who fill a studious house with blast and running, to secure some paltry convenience. Not less I dislike a low sympathy of each with his neighbour's needs. Must we have a good understanding with one another's palates ? as foolish people, who have lived long together, know when each wants salt or sugar. I pray my companion, if he wishes for bread, to ask me for bread, and if he wishes for sassafras or arsenic, to ask me for them, and not to hold out his plate, as if I knew already. Every natural function can be dignified by deliberation and privacy. Let us leave hurry to slaves. The compliments and ceremonies of our breeding should signify, however remotely, the recollection of the grandeur of our destiny.

The flower of courtesy does not very well bide handling, but if we dare to open another leaf, and explore what parts go to its conformation, we shall find also an intellectual quality. To the leaders of men, the brain as well as the flesh and the heart must furnish a proportion. Defect in manners is usually the defect of fine perceptions. Men are too coarsely made for the delicacy of beautiful carriage and customs. It is not quite sufficient to good-breeding, a union of kindness and independence. We imperatively require a perception of, and a homage to beauty in our companions. Other virtues are in request in the field and workyard, but a certain degree of taste is not to be spared in those we sit with. I could better eat with one who did not respect the truth or the laws, than with a sloven and unpresentable person. Moral qualities rule the world, but at short distances, the senses are despotic. The same discrimination of fit and fair runs out, if with less rigour, into all parts of life. The average spirit of the energetic class is good sense, acting under certain limitations and to certain ends. It entertains every natural gift. Social in its nature, it respects every thing which tends to unite men. It delights in measure. The love of beauty is mainly the love of measure or proportion. The person who screams, or uses the superlative degree, or converses with heat, puts whole drawing-rooms to flight. If you wish to be loved, love measure. You must have genius, or a prodigious usefulness, if you will hide the want of measure. This perception comes in to polish and perfect the parts of the social instrument. Society will pardon much to genius and special gifts, but, being in its nature a convention, it loves what is conventional, or what belongs to coming together. That makes the good and bad of manners, namely, what helps or hinders fellowship. For, fashion is not good sense absolute, but relative ; not good sense private, but good sense entertaining company. It hates corners and sharp points of character, hates quarrelsome, egotistical, solitary, and gloomy people ; hates whatever can interfere with total blending of parties ; whilst it values all peculiarities as in the highest degree refreshing, which can consist with good fellowship. And besides the general infusion of wit to heighten civility, the direct splendour of intellectual power is ever welcome in fine society as the costliest addition to its rule and its credit.

2 P

TRUTH AND TENDERNESS.
FROM AN ESSAY ON FRIENDSHIP.

I do not wish to treat friendships daintily, but with roughest courage. When they are real, they are not glass threads or frost-work, but the solidest thing we know. For now, after so many ages of experience, what do we know of nature, or of ourselves? Not one step has man taken toward the solution of the problem of his destiny. In one condemnation of folly stand the whole universe of men. But the sweet sincerity of joy and peace, which I draw from this alliance with my brother's soul, is the nut itself whereof all nature and all thought is but the husk and shell. Happy is the house that shelters a friend! It might well be built, like a festal bower or arch, to entertain him a single day. Happier, if he know the solemnity of that relation, and honour its law! It is no idle band, no holiday engagement. He who offers himself a candidate for that covenant, comes up, like an Olympean, to the great games, where the first-born of the world are the competitors. He proposes himself for contests where Time, Want, Danger are in the lists, and he alone is victor who has truth enough in his constitution to preserve the delicacy of his beauty from the wear and tear of all these. The gifts of fortune may be present or absent, but all the hap in that contest depends on intrinsic nobleness, and the contempt of trifles. There are two elements that go to the composition of friendship, each so sovereign that I can detect no superiority in either, no reason why either should be first named. One is Truth. A friend is a person with whom I may be sincere. Before him, I may think aloud. I am arrived at last in the presence of a man so real and equal, that I may drop even those undermost garments of dissimulation, courtesy, and second thought, which men never put off, and may deal with him with the simplicity and wholeness, with which one chemical atom meets another. Sincerity is the luxury allowed, like diadems and authority, only to the highest rank, that being permitted to speak truth, as having none above it to court or conform unto. Every man alone is sincere. At the entrance of a second person, hypocrisy begins. We parry and fend the approach of our fellow man by compliments, by gossip, by amusements, by affairs. We cover up our thought from him under a hundred folds. I knew a man who, under a certain religious frenzy, cast off his drapery, and omitting all compliment and commonplace, spoke to the conscience of every person he encountered, and that with great insight and beauty. At first he was resisted, and all men agreed he was mad. But persisting, as indeed he could not help doing, for some time in this course, he attained to the advantage of bringing every man of his acquaintance into true relations with him. No man would think of speaking falsely with him, or of putting him off with any chat of markets or reading-rooms. But every man was constrained by so much sincerity to face him, and what love of nature, what poetry, what symbol of truth he had, he did certainly show him. But to most of us society shows not its face and eye, but its side and its back. . . . . We can seldom go erect. Almost every man we meet requires some civility, requires to be humoured ;—he has some fame, some talent, some whim of religion or philanthropy in his head that is not to be questioned, and so spoils all conversation with him. But a friend is a sane man who exercises not my ingenuity but me. My friend gives me entertainment without requiring me to stoop, or to lisp, or to mask myself. A friend, therefore, is a sort of paradox in nature. I who alone am, I who see nothing in nature whose existence I can affirm with equal evidence to my own, behold now the resemblance of my being in all its height, variety and curiosity, reiterated in a foreign form; so that a friend may well be reckoned the masterpiece of nature.

The other element of friendship is Tenderness. We are holden to men by every sort of tie, by blood, by pride, by fear, by hope, by lucre, by lust, by hate, by admiration, by every circumstance and badge and trifle, but we can scarce believe that so much character can subsist in another as to draw us by love. Can another be so blessed, and we so pure, that we can offer him tenderness? When a man becomes dear to me, I have touched the goal of fortune. I find very little written directly to the heart of this matter in books. And yet I have one text which I cannot choose but remember. My author says, "I offer myself faintly and bluntly to those whose I effectually am, and tender myself least to him to whom I am the most devoted." I wish that friendship should have feet, as well as eyes and eloquence. It must plant itself on the ground, before it walks over the moon. I wish it to be a little of a citizen, before it is quite a cherub. We chide the citizen because he makes love a commodity. It is an exchange of gifts, of useful loans; it is good neighbourhood ; it watches with the sick; it holds the pall at the funeral; and quite loses sight of the delicacies and nobility of the relation. But though we cannot find the god under this disguise of a sutler, yet, on the other hand, we cannot forgive the poet if he spins his thread too fine, and does not substantiate his romance by the municipal virtues of justice, punctuality, fidelity, and pity. I hate the prostitution of the name of friendship to signify modish and worldly alliances. I much prefer the company of plough-boys and tin-pedlars, to the silken and perfumed amity which only celebrates its days of encounter by a frivolous display, by rides in a curricle, and dinners at the best taverns. The end of friendship is a commerce the most strict and homely that can be joined; more strict than any of which we have experience. It is for aid and comfort through all the relations and passages of life and death. It is fit for serene days, and graceful gifts, and country rambles, but also for rough roads and hard fare, shipwreck, poverty, and persecution. It keeps company with the sallies of the wit and the trances of religion. We are to dignify to each other the daily needs and offices of man's life, and embellish it by courage, wisdom and unity. It should never fall into something usual and settled, but should be alert and inventive, and add rhyme and reason to what was drudgery.

THEODORE S. FAY.

[Born 1807.]

MR. THEODORE S. FAY is a native of New York, and was educated for the bar. In 1832 he published Dreams and Reveries of a Quiet Man, containing The Little Genius, and other essays, written for the New York Mirror, of which he was at that time one of the editors. It is a collection of agreeable papers on a great variety of subjects, indicating delicacy of taste and feeling, and is very well described by the title.

In 1833 Mr. Fay went to Europe where he remained three years. In this period he wrote his pleasant journal of travels entitled The Minute Book, and his first novel, Norman Leslie, a Tale of the Present Times, founded upon a domestic tragedy which a few years before had excited intense interest in the city of New York. It was published in 1835, and was very successful, passing to a second edition within a few months. In 1837 he was appointed Secretary of Legation for the United States at the court of Berlin, and in 1853 minister to Switzerland ; at Berlin he wrote The Countess Ida, which was published in New York and London in June, 1840. His object, as stated in a short preface, is " to illustrate a principle, and to record his protest against a useless and barbarous custom, which, to the shame of his own country, exists here in a less modified form than the good sense and good taste of European communities, to say nothing of their moral and religious feeling, would sanction." This custom is duelling, and the plot is so constructed as to show the possibility of resisting a practice founded upon a false sense of honour, and of meeting calmly and bearing patiently the taunts, the contempt, and the infamy which a conscientious regard to duty, in defiance of the prejudices of society, never fails to bring upon the man who dares to be called a coward. The principal character is Claude Wyndham, an English gentleman, travelling in Prussia. Vindicating his character for courage by the most intrepid bearing in perilous situations, he refuses to fight, after receiving every species of wrong and insult, even to a blow, and his

friends, the dearest, wisest, best of them even, desert him. Of course he in the end has a " happy issue out of his difficulties," and poetical justice is done to all the parties. The story is skilfully managed, and some of the scenes are exceedingly effective. It may be that, as in most works of a didactic aim, the good characters are somewhat too heavenly minded, and the bad as much below a reasonable degree of wickedness, but if so it detracts more from the artistical beauty of the work than from its moral effect.

Mr. Fay's next work was Hoboken, a Romance of New York, published in 1843. As in Norman Leslie and The Countess Ida, he has endeavoured in this novel to awaken the feelings of the heart and array the convictions of the judgment against duelling. Henry and Franklin Lenox are sons of a popular lawyer, and lovers of Fanny Elton, by whom they are both rejected. Subsequently the younger Lenox resents an insult offered to her by a Captain Glendenning of the British army, by knocking him down in the theatre, and a duel follows, in which his bullet passes through the hat of his adversary, who fires into the air, and makes an apology. The parties become friends, and Glendenning returns to Montreal, where he is taunted by Colonel Nicholson, his commanding officer, with having too precipitately adjusted his quarrel. He revisits New York, and in a second meeting with Lenox kills him. The elder brother, on being rejected by Miss Elton, goes abroad, and while travelling on the continent with the Earl of Middleton, previously introduced to the reader as Colonel Nicholson, encounters Glendenning, whose life has been embittered by his unhappy affair in New York, and who now in his presence accuses the earl of having forced him to the fatal duel with Franklin Lenox. He ascertains the truth of the charge, challenges Middleton, and kills him. Returning to America he learns that his rejection by Fanny Elton was caused by the slanders of an enemy, and is married to her. Woven with the main plot is the history o
447

the gradual conversion of Henry Lenox from deism to the true faith and a holy life. The plot is ingenious, and the incidents natural and dramatic, but the novel is on the whole inferior to the Countess Ida.

Mr. Fay has since published Robert Rueful, and Sydney Clifton, two short Tales; and Ulric, or the voices, a poetical romance. He has also prepared a History of Switzerland, and a series of Geography and Astronomy.

A DUEL.

FROM THE COUNTESS IDA.

[CLAUDE WYNDHAM is in Berlin, where he has been the subject of continued persecutions by a *soi-disant* Lord Elkington. who, after many unsuccessful efforts to bring about a hostile meeting. finally *strikes* him at a court ball. Denham, a friend to Wyndham, just arrived from London, witnesses the act, and while our hero, stung almost to madness by the injury, is endeavouring, in the privacy of a night walk in the *Thiergarten*, to regain the mastery of his passions, he gives the duellist a meeting.]

CLAUDE went back to his hotel in a state of mind bordering on distraction, but it had the effect to divert him from the consideration of himself. It seemed that a fatal duel on his account, in return for an insult which he had declined to resent, was all that was necessary to sink him to the lowest depths in the world's esteem, if not in his own. But that was a less insupportable reflection than the situation of Mrs. Denham and the sweet little girl, who were, probably, yet locked in peaceful slumber, unconscious of the thunder-bolt about to fall upon them. He would have gone again to the police, but he had no precise information to give, and he felt sure, too, that it was too late for interference. There was, however, still a *hope*. It was possible either that chance might interrupt the meeting—or that Elkington might fall—or that, if Denham should receive a wound, it might not be mortal. But then the utter recklessness of Denham—his knowledge of Elkington's affair with the cards—and the unerring skill, as well as remorseless character of the latter, recurred to him with an agonizing force. As he entered the hotel he saw that there was an unusual confusion. Several waiters were running to and fro. One of them came up to him quickly as soon as he saw him.

"You had better go to Madam Denham."

"Has any thing happened?"

"Mr. Denham has gone off."

"And not yet returned?"

"No."

He breathed again. He had felt an unutterable fear on approaching the house.

"Thank God!" he said, "all may yet be well."

"The lady is in a bad way, sir; she's very ill."

At this moment a voice from a servant at the top of the stairs called out,

"Has Mr. Wyndham come in yet?"

"You'd better go to her, sir," said the landlord. "I fear something very dreadful has—"

Claude recovered from a momentary faintness, nerved his heart, and entered the room. All that he had imagined of horrible was surpassed by Mrs. Denham. She was pale as death herself. Her hair hung in disorder about her beautiful and lightly clothed person. Her eyes were distended with

terror, and the little Ellen clung to her bosom, weeping aloud, and winding her arms around her neck affectionately, and repeating,

"Dear sister, my dear, dear sister. He will come, he will come. He will indeed, indeed he will!"

Mrs. Denham's eyes were perfectly dry and starting from her head. She looked an image of tragedy itself. The moment Claude entered she saw him, for her wild eyes were fixed on the door; she sprang up with an hysterical laugh, and, rushing upon him as a lioness on one who had robbed her of her young, she uttered, in tones that pierced his heart and froze his blood, the dreadful words:

"Ah! and now then! *where's Charles ?*"

"He is—he is—"

"Is he here? Is he here?"

"No—not here—not this instant."

"Where is he, then? *What* have you done with him?"

"My dearest madam—"

"Is he *dead?*"

"No, no—God grant—I hope—not—not dead," muttered Claude, trembling beneath the powerful agitation of this scene.

"Is he safe? Will he come? What do *you* know? Is there any hope?"

"I think—I believe—"

"What do you *know?* Speak—as before your God. *If* you deceive me!"

Claude turned away, and, pressing his extended hand against his forehead, shook as one by the bed of the beloved and the dying.

She released her hold on him, and her hands fell nerveless by her side.

"Then he is *dead.* Oh God—oh God—I have often feared this." She sank back into a chair.

"Charles—my husband—it is a dream—it is impossible."

Claude approached her, and took her cold hand in his.

"My dear friend, hear me. It is too late to deceive you as to what has occurred. Your husband *has* gone out to comply with a strange custom, but we have no news of him, upon my honour. It is very possible he may return—alive—unhurt. Believe me, dearest madam, there are many reasons to hope—indeed, indeed there are."

"I'm sure there are," said Ellen, climbing up and again winding her arms around her neck, and covering her lips, forehead, and face with kisses.

"You do not *know* any thing, then?"

"Nothing."

"And he *may* return! His step may be heard —his beloved image may once more bless my eyes! Hark—hark"—her face lighted up with intense pleasure—"it is—it is—ha, ha! ha, ha!" She screamed with joy, and darted toward the door, which opened and admitted—a stranger.

The shock was too much for the poor girl. She would have fallen at full length upon the floor had not Claude caught her on his arm. He lifted her to the sofa, and, consigning her to the care of the maid, turned to the new-comer.

"Who are you, sir—and what is your message?"

"Sir," said the man, "I am a Commissioner of the Hotel. I have been sent to the lodgings of Lord Elkington with directions to let you know when he returned."

"And he *has* returned?" said Claude, in a low tone, and with a shudder of inexpressible horror.

"He has."

"Alone?"

"Alone."

[Wyndham repairs to the hotel of Lord Elkington, who offe.s, as *satisfaction*, for the murder of his friend, to fight him—a proposition which is declined. An intimation follows that the presence of a man who has so little respect for the usages of society is unwelcome, and he goes back to his own lodgings.]

"Has he come home? Is he here? Have you seen him? Have you heard any thing of him?" were the fearful questions from every lip as Claude returned to his hotel.

"Madam Denham is nearly distracted," said the landlord. "She calls for you. Pray go to her."

"I dare not," said Claude, with a shudder.

"She has demanded to be informed the instant you come in," said the man. "She is in a state of intense excitement and agony. She walks the floor with frantic steps, as pale as a sheet. Sometimes she groans and weeps, sometimes she prays. She's in a terrible way. It's quite dreadful—and the poor little girl, too, is so distressed. My God! what sort of a man must her husband be, to leave her in such a condition?"

A servant here came for Mr. Wyndham. He must go instantly to Madam Denham. It was with a faltering heart that Claude complied with this request, and once more approached the door where so lately he bade adieu to the friend who, perhaps, was now in eternity. As he did so, he heard the hasty steps of the bereaved widow—her deep groans—her bursting sobs. He entered. Her look made him shudder.

"Speak!" cried she. "Charles—"

"I know nothing," said Claude.

"Have you seen Lord Elkington?"

Claude hesitated.

"Is he living?"

"He is."

"Oh, Mr. Wyndham, for the love of God, tell me all. You know, I am sure you do. I can bear it better than this suspense. Tell me—my husband is wounded—is perhaps—she clasped her hand with quivering lips and sobbed convulsively —"*dead!*"

"I do not know. I have heard nothing distinctly. He may be alive—"

"Oh, God bless you for that word. He may yet live. But *where* is he? Why does he not return? Perhaps he is wounded. Perhaps he is this instant dying!"

She pressed her hands against her brain.

"Ah, cruel, cruel Charles! Is it you who have abandoned me thus? you, who have torn my heart —inflicted these horrid pangs? I will no longer wait. I will go seek him."

She rushed to the door.

"My dear, dear sister," said Ellen, "you cannot go. You do not know where he is. You are not dressed. If he were in the street, he would soon be here. If not, where would you go? Stay with me, my dear, dear sister. God will take care of us;" and the sweet child again folded her in her arms, and pressed her ashy cheek against her little bosom.

"He might come, too, during your absence," said the maid respectfully.

"Oh yes! true!" she said, with a frightful smile.

Hours passed away as if they were ages. Noon —evening—night—and still Denham came not— and no news. Claude had again addressed himself to the police. They were abroad in search of the parties, but they could obtain no intelligence as to where they had gone, or what had become of them. Elkington was not at his lodgings—Lady Beverly had left town the day before for Hamburg, as if in anticipation of some difficulty. It was reported, too, that Elkington, early in the morning, had also gone, but whither no one knew. His escape had been connived at by so many gentlemen, who thought they were aiding a gallant fellow out of an unjust danger, that the police could get no trace of him. Indeed, from many considerations, they conducted the pursuit with no great activity. Although duelling was strictly prohibited in Prussia, and particularly by the great Frederic, whose clear mind had seen all its folly and wickedness, the crime was then—as we fear, alas, it is now —considered as one of those genteel misdemeanours of which a large class of educated, and many excellent men, are rather proud than ashamed. The magistrate who sternly sentences a poor, ignorant creature for having stolen wherewithal to support fainting life, cannot condemn the passionate fool who submits his disagreements with his friends to the chances of mortal combat, and who shows so little respect for himself—his adversary—society— and God, as to stake two lives on a throw, and thus sanction one crime by joining it with another. The police also felt that the parties were Englishmen—that securing a surviver in such a case would place them in an awkward dilemma. Lord Elkington's rank and fortune, moreover, threw a sort of exemption over his actions in the public opinion, and it was understood also that the injury had been words offensive to his *honour* as a *gentleman*.

Poor Mrs. Denham. It seemed impossible that she could endure the interminable length of this day; but the very intensity of her apprehensions prevented her from sinking into the insensibility which nature would otherwise have provided for her relief. As the night approached, her agony had reached a state of nervous excitement, which rendered it necessary to call in a physician; but she would take nothing, and permit no remedies to be adopted, till she should receive direct intelligence of Mr. Denham.

2 P 2

Nine o'clock struck—ten—eleven—twelve; still Denham came not, and no news of him could be obtained. It was now near one. The widow—for all felt that she was such except herself, and she still hoped—was almost deprived of her senses. At every whisper she started, at every step in the street she trembled. Sometimes the sound of horses' feet would advance from the distance. Her features would light up: the noise approached, and seemed about to stop at the door, but went on, and was lost again in the distance; now a shout in the street startled her—now an oath. Sometimes she heard the tramping of the soldiers' feet, as the guard were led round to their posts; and once a party of riotous young men went by, and, by a cruel coincidence, stopped immediately beneath the window, shouting forth a glee, which was interrupted by peals of laughter. Then they departed singing, their voices softening as they retreated, and dying at last utterly away; leaving, they little knew what—silence, solitude, and despair behind them.

"Mr. Wyndham," said Mrs. Denham, suddenly, in a voice of sternness, which made him think her senses were failing, " you are the cause of this !"

"My dearest madam—"

" You—coward !"

"Great Heaven !"

" You knew my husband had the heart of a lion. You knew he couldn't see his friend abused, and you—you meanly took a blow—a blow ! a base, blasting blow ! and yet you live—coward ! and he, my brave, my noble, my lion-hearted Charles, for your infamy has risked his life—which, God in his mercy be praised, is but a risk. He will not perish. It is impossible. He will come. He is wounded, doubtless, but what do I care for wounds ? He will come, or he will send for me. I shall nurse him. He will recover; but you, sir, must never look for his friendship again; nor his, nor mine, nor the world's esteem, nor your own. You are a dishonoured man. I had rather be Elkington than you. A blow ! coward !"

There was suddenly a knock at the door. Mrs. Denham fell back in her chair, laughing hysterically. The intruder was a messenger of the police, to know whether any news had been received of the affair.

One o'clock. The heavy peal went floating and quivering over the silent town, and struck into the hearts of all present, for they now foreboded the worst. The solemn sound, as it died away, called forth new groans, sobs, and hysterical screams. All conversation ceased. There was as little room for remark as for hope or consolation. They sat like those unhappy beings we sometimes read of on a wreck, waiting in mute despair till the broken hulk goes down with them for ever.

Two o'clock struck. Mrs. Denham had sunk into a state of exhaustion, when a sharp, heavy knock announced an end of this suspense. There was decision in it. The door was opened by a servant, and a step was heard in the hall, quick, light, buoyant. It approached, and all eyes were turned toward the door.

"Ah God ! he is here at last," cried Mrs. Denham, with a smile of ineffable happiness, and gasping for breath. The new-comer entered. It was again a stranger. A start of horror went round the room, and a low shudder was heard from Mrs. Denham, who buried her face in her hands.

"Mr. Wyndham ?" said the stranger, who was a gentleman in dress and appearance.

Claude stepped forward and recognised Beaufort.

"I beg your pardon," said that gentleman, with a polite smile; "will you permit me to have one word with you ?"

He cast a glance around upon the rest of the company, but without in the least changing his manner. He was a man of the world, and well knew what he was going to see when he undertook the mission.

Claude followed him into an adjoining chamber.

"Devilish painful duty, my dear fellow—disagreeable thing—in fact, d—d awkward—but—"

"Speak out, and tell me what has happened," said Claude, sternly; " I also have my duties."

"Sir !" said Beaufort, "your tone is very extraordinary, but your excitement excuses any liberty ; I have promised to let you know that your friend is hurt."

"Hurt ! Oh, Beaufort ! Oh, Heaven be praised ! is he only hurt ?"

"Why, his wound is bad—d—d bad. He—he —in short, he's—dead, sir."

"Dead !" said Claude, with awe, with horror unutterable. "Denham ! my friend !"

"Yes, dead enough, sir. This is possibly rather annoying to you. I'm devilish sorry—I am, positively."

"Dead !" echoed Claude, the sound of his friend's living voice ringing in his ears ; his beaming, laughing eyes flashing full before his imagination.

"To say the truth, this morning at P——. He behaved very well—devilish well—I'm quite sure you'll be glad to hear that. The thing was perfectly well managed, I assure you. Perfectly. Nothing could be handsomer or fairer. Elkington missed him the first shot. Devilish odd, too—wasn't it ? The second he hit him. He's a terrible dog. The ball went directly through the heart. He leaped six feet in the air, and he was a dead man before he came down. I protest I never saw any thing so handsomely done."

"And I am to bear this news to his wife !"

"Certainly ! I've done my part. I stood by him to the last, and have brought the corpse in town. It will be here in—let me see, half past two—it'll certainly be three. By-the-way, madam is a fine-looking creature. Devilish pretty in that dress. Poor girl! I'm devilish sorry. You'll take good care of her, Wyndham ! Egad, you're a lucky dog ! Where are you going to have the body put ?"

"Did—did my friend leave me no message ?"

"Oh, apropos—what a forgetful dog I am ! Certainly—a note for you."

"Give it me."

"Yes, devilish queer that I should forget that, as the poor man isn't likely to trouble me with another in a hurry. He put it in my hand the very last thing. He behaved immensely well, positively. I really thought at first that he was going to touch Elkington ; his ball grazed his sleeve. Elkington smoked a segar through the whole affair. He's a capital fellow. Why—I've lost your letter —no—yes, I have—no—ah, here it is."

" Who has the body ?"

" Two men. We hired 'em to bring it in town in the carriage. Egad ! it's been all day in a windmill. We had to disperse, you see. Elkington's gone this morning at twelve ; I start to-night. I shall run over to Carlsbad. This cursed German *cuisine* plays the devil with one's stomach. Won't you smoke ?"

Claude did not answer. He was reading the note he had just received, which struck his nerves and soul with an agony of horror and grief, traced, as it was, by one now in the grave.

" Well—adieu," said Beaufort. " *Leben sie wohl, mein freund ! Au revoir !"*

And the young man, lighting his segar and arranging the curls around his forehead, went out.

POVERTY.

FROM THE SAME.

PERHAPS of all the evils which can befall a man, poverty, if not the very worst, is, as society is constructed, the most difficult to endure with cheerfulness, and the most full of bitter humiliations and pains. Sickness has its periods of convalescence, and even guilt of repentance and reformation. For the loss of friends time affords relief, and religion and philosophy open consolation. But poverty is unremitting misery, perplexity, restlessness, and shame. It is the vulture of Prometheus. It is the rock of Sisyphus. It throws over the universal world an aspect which only the poor can see and know. The woes of life become more terrible, because they fall unalleviated upon the heart ; and its pleasures sicken even more than its woes as they are beheld by those who cannot enjoy them. The poor man in society is almost a felon. The cold openly sneer, and the arrogant insult with impunity. The very earth joins his enemies, and spreads verdant glades and tempting woods where his foot may never tread. The very sky, with a human malice, when his fellow-beings have turned him beneath its dome, bites him with bitter winds and drenches him with pitiless tempests. He almost ceases to be a man, and yet he is lower than the brute ; for they are clothed and fed, and have their dens ; but the penniless wanderer, turned with suspicion from the gate of the noble or the thatched roof of the poor, is helplessly adrift amid more dangers and pains as befall any other creature.

CROSSING THE ALPS.

FROM THE MINUTE BOOK.

OUR journey across the Splugen was, to us, a day memorable for ever. Our recollections are of grandeur—gloomy vastness—awful solitude. The road winds up, and up, and up—a mad stream, white with foam, thundering all day by its side—amid slopes and cliffs, forests and vales—then a plain and poor hut, or a ragged town and some beggars. You pause and rest ; and then, again, up and up—winding and turning—sometimes through tremendous ravines—sometimes by magnificent waterfalls—sometimes along giddy and yawning gulfs—yet, still, always up and up. Then the face of the earth changes, and the grass fades nearly away, and the naked, everlasting rocks lift their gray backs through the soil. The tempest of six thousand years have beaten against them. Now, the road steals through a desert of endless stones, broken and scattered about—now through a long, dark gallery, wet and dripping—now at the brink of a tremendous precipice, which your imagination would receive as the summit of any mountain ; but, anon, the toiling, panting, sweating horses drag you around an angle of rock ; and, lo ! above you overhang other cliffs and other mountains in the sky ; piles, swells and pyramids of snow and ice ; an l, so near their awful heights as to *startle* you, the white line runs yet higher and higher, and you believe not that it is your path still so far above you —and yet it is. The earth is now totally changed, and the temperature, and atmosphere, and heavens are changed. You wrap your heavy cloak around you in the biting cold. Dark clouds are rolling gloomily over your path, and the white snow shines beneath you, and the winter winds shakes violently the closed glasses of your carriage ; and, as the road, still mounting and bending up and up, turns your face now to the right—now to the left—you catch, far below, such awful gleamings of sublime scenery—such dim, wild depths of azure—such forms of cold blue lifted and built up around you in the eternal silence, and shrouded in mist and storm, that your very soul is hushed and chilled, and you feel as if the King of Terrors had here fixed his home ; and, were a *spectre* to stand in your path, or to lean and beckon to you from his car of rolling mist, you would behold him, without starting, for your imagination can scarcely be more excited. A cataract, which, on the plain, would draw all Europe to it, is here no curiosity. Its lonely thunder swells and dies away in the interminable solitude. Twenty times we thought ourselves at the height of this stupendous road, and yet its zigzag course appeared ever mounting far before us up and up, till the cold grew extreme, and the darkness of night overlooked us ; and we were completely lost and enveloped in heavy, wet clouds, rolling around us like a mighty ocean.

GEORGE B. CHEEVER.

THE Reverend GEORGE B. CHEEVER, D. D., is a native of Hallowell in Maine, and was graduated at Bowdoin College in that state in 1825. After completing his theological studies he was for several years minister of a Congregational church in Salem, Massachusetts, where he made his first appearance as an author in the allegory of Deacon Giles's Distillery, which is as happy in its invention and execution as it is severe and just in its satire. In 1828 he published Studies in Poetry, and in 1829 and 1832 selections from our Poets and Prose Writers, which indicated a large acquaintance and fine taste in literature. In the last mentioned year he prefixed to an edition of the works of Leighton, remarks on the life, character, and writings of that prelate, and became a contributor to the North American Review, his best articles in which are on Bunyan, Coleridge, Hebrew Poetry, and the Letters of Junius. He has since written largely in the American Monthly Magazine, The Biblical Repository, The Christian Spectator, The American Quarterly Register, The Literary and Theological Review, and other periodicals, on various subjects of religion and letters, with a keenness of discrimination, force of logic, and elegance of diction, which commanded for his articles the attention of cultivated and thoughtful minds.

In 1837 he went abroad, and passed two years and a half chiefly in Egypt, Turkey, and Southern Europe. On his return he became pastor of the Allen Street Presbyterian Church in the city of New York.

In 1841 he published God's Hand in America; in 1842 Essays on Capital Punishment; in 1843, The Characteristics of a Christian Philosopher, a Discourse in commemoration of the Virtues and Attainments of James Marsh, and The Elements of National Greatness, a Discourse before the New England Society; in 1844 Lectures on Hierarchical Despotism; and in 1845 Lectures on The Pilgrim's Progress and the Life and Times of John Bunyan. The general character of all these works will be rightly inferred from the titles. That on Bunyan is the longest, and in a literary point of view much the best. It is a genial and very able commentary on the life, character, and writings of the greatest genius except Milton who lived in England in the age of the Puritans. It was perhaps suggested by a work of Southey, who was unfitted by political and ecclesiastical prejudices for doing justice to the unordained priest of Bedford, with whom Dr. Cheever had on nearly every point a very hearty sympathy.

In 1845 Dr. Cheever made a second visit to Europe, and on his return published The Pilgrim in the Shadow of Mont Blanc, and a few months after, The Pilgrim in the Shadow of the Jungfrau. These are souvenirs of wanderings among the Alps and the cities from which they can be discerned, written in a style singularly glowing and picturesque, and indicating a quick perception and enthusiastic love of the grand and beautiful in nature. It has been complained of Dr. Cheever that he introduces too frequently his religious opinions, and is too apt to find "sermons" in every thing he hears or sees. But a traveller who has no individuality has no merit; one who does not worship when he comes into the presence of the sublimest works of God is no Christian; and one who can regard without a feeling of indignation a people oppressed and debased by a political and religious despotism is no American. "A pilgrim may wander all over the earth," says Dr. Cheever, "and find no spot where men are bound to God by so many ties of mercy as we are in our own dear native country, or where old and young, rich and poor, have so much cause for heartfelt rejoicing." He sees all other lands in the light of his own, and in this respect contrasts finely with those weak-minded Americans who excite so much contempt when abroad by obtrusive exhibitions of their want of patriotism. Dr. Cheever's other works are; The Hill Difficulty ; Windings of the River of Life ; Voices of Nature to the Soul of Man ; Bible in Common Schools; Lectures on Cowper; Powers of the World to come; God against Slavery.

452

MONT BLANC FROM THE COL DE BALME.

FROM THE WANDERINGS OF A PILGRIM.

The Col de Balme is about seven thousand feet high, and lying as it does across the vale of Chamouny at the end toward Martigny and the valley of the Rhone, through which runs the grand route of the Simplon from Switzerland to Italy, you have from it one of the most perfect of all views both of Mont Blanc and the vale of Chamouny, with all the other mountain ridges on every side. You have, as it were, an observatory erected for you, seven thousand feet high, to look at a mountain of sixteen thousand....

Till we arrived within a quarter of an hour of the summit, the atmosphere was clear, and Mont Blanc rose to the view with a sublimity which it seemed at every step could scarcely be rivalled, and which yet at every step was increasing. The path is a winding ascent, practicable only for mules or on foot. A north-east wind, in this last quarter of an hour, was driving the immensity of mist from the other side of the mountain over the summit, enveloping all creation in a thick frosty fog, so that when we got to the solitary house, we were surrounded by an ocean of cold gray cloud, that left neither mountain nor the sun itself distinguishable. And such, thought we, is the end of all our morning's starvation, perils, and labours ; not to see an inch before us ; all this mighty prospect, for which alone one might worthily cross the Atlantic, hidden from us, and quite shut out ! We could have wept, perhaps, if we had not been too cold and too hungry. Our host burned up the remainder of his year's supply of wood to get us a fire, and then most hospitably provided us with a breakfast of roast potatoes, whereby all immediate danger of famishing was deferred to a considerable distance. But our bitter disappointment in the fog was hard to be borne, and we sat brooding and mourning over the gloomy prospect for the day, and wondering what we had best do with ourselves, when suddenly, on turning toward the window, Mont Blanc was flashing in the sunshine.

Such an instantaneous and extraordinary revelation of splendour we never dreamed of. The clouds had vanished, we could not tell where, and the whole illimitable vast of glory in this, the heart of Switzerland's Alpine grandeurs, was disclosed ; the snowy Monarch of Mountains, the huge glaciers, the jagged granite peaks, needles, and rough enormous crags congregated and shooting up in every direction, with the long beautiful vale of Chamouny visible from end to end, far beneath, as still and shining as a picture ! Just over the longitudinal ridge of mountains on one side was the moon in an infinite depth of ether ; it seemed as if we could touch it ; and on the other the sun was exulting as a bridegroom coming out of his chamber. The clouds still sweeping past us, now concealing, now partially veiling, and now revealing the view, added to its power by such sudden alternations.

Far down the vale floated in mid air beneath us a few fleeces of cloud, below and beyond which lay the valley with its villages, meadows, and winding paths, and the river running through it like a silver thread. Shortly the mists congregated away beyond this scene, rolling masses upon masses, penetrated and turned into fleecy silver by the sunlight, the whole body of them gradually retreating over the south-western end and barrier of the valley. In our position we now saw the different gorges in the chain of Mont Blanc lengthwise, Charmontiere, Du Bois, and the Glacier du Bosson protruding its whole *enorme* from the valley. The grand Mulet, with the vast snow-depths and *crevasses* of Mont Blanc were revealed to us. That sublime summit was now for the first time seen in its solitary superiority, at first appearing round and smooth, white and glittering with perpetual snow, but as the sun in his higher path cast shadows from summit to summit, and revealed ledges and chasms, we could see the smoothness broken. Mont Blanc is on the right of the valley, looking up from the Col de Balme ; the left range being much lower, though the summit of the Buet is near ten thousand feet in height. Now on the Col de Balme we are midway in these sublime views, on an elevation of seven thousand feet, without an intervening barrier of any kind to interrupt our sight.

On the Col itself we are between two loftier heights, both of which I ascended, one of them being a ridge so sharp and steep, that though I got up without much danger, yet on turning to look about me and come down, it was absolutely frightful. A step either side would have sent me sheer down a thousand feet ; and the crags by which I had mounted appeared so loosely perched, as if I could shake and tumble them from their places by my hand. The view in every direction seemed infinitely extended, chain behind chain, ridge after ridge, in almost endless succession.

But the hour of most intense splendour in this day of glory was the rising of the clouds in Chamouny, as we could discern them like stripes of amber floating in an azure sea. They rested upon, and floated over the successive glacier gorges of the mountain range on either hand, like so many islands of the blest, anchored in mid-heaven below us ; or like so many radiant files of the white-robed heavenly host floating transversely across the valley. This extended through its whole length, and it was a most singular phenomenon ; for through these ridges of cloud we could look as through a telescope down into the vale and along to its farther end ; but the intensity of the light flashing from the snows of the mountains and reflected in these fleecy radiances, almost as so many secondary suns, hung in the clear atmosphere, was well-nigh blinding.

The scene seemed to me a fit symbol of celestial glories ; and I thought if a vision of such intense splendour could be arrayed by the divine power out of mere earth, air, and water, and made to assume such beauty indescribable at a breath of the wind, a movement of the sun, a slight change in the elements, what mind could even dimly and distantly form to itself a conception of the splendours of the world of heavenly glory.

MONT BLANC FROM THE VAL D'AOSTE.

FROM THE SAME.

MONT BLANC from the Italian side, from the Val d'Aoste, is presented to the eye in a greater unity of sublimity, with a more undivided and overwhelming impression than from any other point. In the vale of Chamouny you are almost too near; you are under the mountain, and not before it; and from the heights around it there are other objects that command a portion of your admiration. But here Mont Blanc is the only object, as it were, between you and eternity. It is said that on this side the mountain rises in almost a sheer perpendicular precipice thirteen thousand feet high; an object that quite tyrannizes over the whole valley, so that you see nothing else; and in a day of such glowing brilliancy as I am writing of, you desire to see nothing else, for it seems as if heaven's splendours were coming down upon you!

It was between four and five in the afternoon that I came upon this view—and I gazed, and gazed, and gazed, almost wishing that I could spend as many days as there were minutes in the same position, and full of regret to leave a spot of such glorious beauty. The splendour was almost blinding. A brilliant sun, a few fleecy clouds around the mountain, a clear transparent atmosphere, the valley invested with the richest verdure, range after range of mountains retreating behind one another, tints softening from shade to shade, the light mingling with, and, as it were, entering into, the green herbage and forming with it a soft, luminous composition, dim ridges of hazy light, and at the close of this perspective of magnificence, Mont Blanc sheeted with snow, and flashing like a type of the Celestial City!

Coming suddenly upon such a scene, you think that no other point of view can possibly be equal to this, and you are tempted not to stir from the spot till sundown; but, looking narrowly, you see that the road scales the cliffs at some distance beyond, at an overhanging point where Mont Blanc will still be in full view; so you pass on, plunging for a few moments into a wood of chestnuts, and losing Mont Blanc entirely. Then you emerge, admiring the rich scene through which you have been advancing, until you gain the point which you observed from a distance, where the road circles the jagged, outjutting crags of the mountain at a great distance above the bottom of the valley, and then again the vision of glory bursts upon you. What combinations! Forests of the richest, deepest green, vast masses of foliage below you, as fresh and glittering in the sunlight as if just washed in a June shower, mountain crags towering above, the river Doire thundering far beneath you, down black, jagged, savage ravines; behind you, at one end of the valley, a range of snow-crowned mountains; before you, the same vast and magnificent perspective which arrested your admiration at first, with its infolding and retreating ranges of verdure and sunlight, and at the close, Mont Blanc flashing as lightning, as it were a mountain of pure alabaster.

The fleecy clouds that here and there circled and touched it, or like a cohort of angels brushed its summit with their wings, added greatly to the glory; for the sunlight reflected from the snow upon the clouds, and from the clouds upon the snow, made a more glowing and dazzling splendour. The outlines of the mountains being so sharply defined against the serene blue of the sky, you might deem the whole mass to have been cut out from the ether. You have this view for hours, as you pass up the valley, but at this particular point it is the most glorious.

It was of such amazing effulgence at this hour, that no language can give any just idea of it. Gazing steadfastly and long upon it, I began to comprehend what Coleridge meant when he said that he almost lost the sense of his own being in that of the mountain, so that it seemed to be a part of him and he of it. Gazing thus, your sense almost becomes dizzy in the tremulous effulgence. And then the sunset! The rich hues of sunset upon such a scene! The golden light upon the verdure, the warm crimson tints upon the snow, the crags glowing like jasper, the masses of shade cast from summit to summit, the shafts of light shooting past them into the sky, and all this flood of rich magnificence succeeded so rapidly by the cold gray of the snow, and gone entirely when the stars are visible above the mountains, and it is night!

THE MER DE GLACE.

FROM THE SAME.

AT Montanvert you find yourself on the extremity of a *plateau*, so situated, that on one side you may look down into the dread frozen sea, and on the other, by a few steps, into the lovely, green vale of Chamouny. What astonishing variety and contrast in the spectacle! Far beneath, a smiling and verdant valley, watered by the Arve, with hamlets, fields and gardens, the abode of life, sweet children and flowers:—far above, savage and inaccessible crags of ice and granite, and a cataract of stiffened billows, stretching away beyond sight—the throne of Death and Winter.

From the bosom of the tumbling sea of ice, enormous granite needles shoot into the sky, objects of singular sublimity, one of them rising to the great height of thirteen thousand feet, seven thousand above the point where you are standing. This is more than double the height of Mount Washington in our country, and this amazing pinnacle of rock looks like the spire of an interminable colossal cathedral, with other pinnacles around it. No snow can cling to the summits of these jagged spires; the lightning does not splinter them; the tempests rave round them; and at their base, those eternal drifting ranges of snow are formed, that sweep down into the frozen sea, and feed the perpetual, immeasurable masses of the glacier. Meanwhile, the laughing verdure, sprinkled with flowers, plays upon the edges of the enormous masses of ice—so near, that you may almost touch the ice with one hand, and with the other pluck the violet. So, oftentimes, the ice and the verdure are mingled in our earthly pilgrimage;— so, sometimes, in one and the same family you may see the exquisite refinements and the crabbed repugnancies of human nature. So, in the same house of God, on the same bench, may sit an angel and a murderer; a villain, like a glacier, and a man with a heart like a sweet running brook in the sunshine.

The impetuous arrested cataract seems as if it were ploughing the rocky gorge with its turbulent surges. Indeed the ridges of rocky fragments along the edges of the glacier, called *moraines*, do look precisely as if a colossal iron plough had torn them from the mountain, and laid them along in one continuous furrow on the frozen verge. It is a scene of stupendous sublimity. These mighty granite peaks, hewn and pinnacled into Gothic towers, and these rugged mountain walls and buttresses,—what a cathedral! with this cloudless sky, by starlight, for its fretted roof—the chanting wail of the tempest, and the rushing of the avalanche for its organ. How grand the thundering sound of the vast masses of ice tumbling from the roof of the Arve-cavern at the foot of the glacier! Does it not seem, as it sullenly and heavily echoes, and rolls up from so immense a distance below, even more sublime than the thunder of the avalanche above us?

AVALANCHES OF THE JUNGFRAU.
FROM THE SAME.

ORDINARILY, in a sunny day at noon, the avalanches are falling on the Jungfrau about every ten minutes, with the roar of thunder, but they are much more seldom visible, and sometimes the traveller crosses the Wengern Alp without witnessing them at all. But we were so very highly favoured as to see two of the grandest avalanches possible in the course of about an hour, between twelve o'clock and two. One cannot command any language to convey an adequate idea of their magnificence. You are standing far below, gazing up to where the great disc of the glittering Alp cuts the heavens, and drinking in the influence of the silent scene around. Suddenly an enormous mass of snow and ice, in itself a mountain, seems to move; it breaks from the toppling outmost mountain ridge of snow, where it is hundreds of feet in depth, and in its first fall of perhaps two thousand feet, is broken into millions of fragments. As you first see the flash of distant artillery by night, then hear the roar, so here you may see the white flashing mass majestically bowing, then hear the astounding din. A cloud of dusty, misty, dry snow rises into the air from the concussion, forming a white volume of fleecy smoke, or misty light, from the bosom of which thunders forth the icy torrent in its second prodigious fall over the rocky battlements. The eye follows it delighted as it ploughs through the path which preceding avalanches have worn, till it comes to the brink of a vast ridge of bare rock, perhaps more than two thousand feet perpendicular. Then pours the whole cataract over the gulf with a still louder roar of echoing thunder, to which nothing but the noise of Niagara in its sublimity is comparable. Nevertheless, you may think of the tramp of an army of elephants, of the roar of multitudinous cavalry marching to battle, of the whirlwind tread of ten thousand bisons sweeping across the prairie, of the tempest surf of ocean beating and shaking the continent, of *the sound of torrent floods or of a numerous host*, or of the voice of the Trumpet on Sinai, exceeding loud, and waxing louder and louder, so that all the people in the camp trembled, or of the rolling orbs of that fierce chariot described by Milton,

Under whose burning wheels
The steadfast empyrean shook throughout.

It is with such a mighty shaking tramp that the avalanche down thunders. Another fall of still greater depth ensues, over a second similar castellated ridge or reef in the face of the mountain, with an awful majestic slowness, and a tremendous crash, in its concussion, awakening again the reverberating peals of thunder. Then the torrent roars on to another smaller fall, till at length it reaches a mighty groove of snow and ice, like the slide down the Pilatus, of which Playfair has given so powerfully graphic a description. Here its progress is slower, and last of all you listen to the roar of the falling fragments as they drop out of sight with a dead weight into the bottom of the gulf, to rest there for ever. Now figure to yourself a cataract like that of Niagara, (for I should judge the volume of one of these avalanches to be probably every way superior in bulk to the whole of the Horse-shoe fall,) poured in foaming grandeur, not merely over one great precipice of two hundred feet, but over the successive ridgy precipices of two or three thousand, in the face of a mountain eleven thousand feet high, and tumbling, crashing, thundering down, with a continuous din of far greater sublimity than the sound of the grandest cataract. Placed on the slope of the Wengern Alp, right opposite the whole visible side of the Jungfrau, we have enjoyed two of these mighty spectacles, at about half an hour's interval between them. The first was the most sublime, the second the most beautiful. The roar of the falling mass begins to be heard the moment it is loosened from the mountain; it pours on with the sound of a vast body of rushing water; then comes the first great concussion, a booming crash of thunders, breaking on the still air in mid heaven; your breath is suspended as you listen and look; the mighty glittering mass shoots headlong over the main precipice, and the fall is so great that it produces to the eye that impression of dread majestic slowness, of which I have spoken, though it is doubtless more rapid than Niagara. But if you should see the cataract of Niagara itself coming down five thousand feet above you in the air, there would be the same impression. The image remains in the mind, and can never fade from it; it is as if you had seen an alabaster cataract from heaven.

CHARLES FENNO HOFFMAN.

[Born 1806.]

CHARLES FENNO HOFFMAN, son of Judge Josiah Ogden Hoffman, was born in the city of New York, in the year 1806. 'The name FENNO he derives from his maternal grandfather, a distinguished politician of the federal party in Philadelphia, during the administration of Washington. His father's family came to New York from Holland, before the days of Peter Stuyvesant, and have ever held an honourable position in the state. His father, in his younger days, was often the successful competitor of Hamilton, Burr, Pinkney, and other professional giants, for the highest honours of the legal forum, and his brother, Mr. Ogden Hoffman, still maintains the family reputation at the bar.

When six years old, he was sent to a Latin grammar-school in New York, from which, at the age of nine, he was transferred to the Poughkeepsie Academy, a seminary upon the Hudson, about eighty miles from the city, which at that time enjoyed great reputation. The harsh treatment he received here induced him to run away, and his father, finding that he had not improved under a course of severity, did not insist upon his return, but placed him under the care of an accomplished Scottish gentleman in one of the rural villages of New Jersey. During a visit home from this place, when about twelve years of age, he met with an injury which involved the necessity of the immediate amputation of his right leg, above the knee. The painful circumstances are minutely detailed in The New York Evening Post, of the twenty-fifth of October, 1817, from which it appears, that while, with other lads, attempting the dangerous feat of leaping aboard a steamer as she passed a pier, under full way, he was caught between the vessel and the wharf. The steamer swept by, and left him clinging by his hands to the pier, crushed in a manner too frightful for description. This deprivation, instead of acting as a disqualification for the manly sports of youth, and thus turning the subject of it into a retired student, seems rather to have given young Hoffman an especial ambition to excel in field sports and pastimes, to the still further neglect of perhaps more useful acquirements. At fifteen he entered Columbia College, and here, as at preparatory schools, was noted rather for success in gymnastic exercises than in those of a more intellectual character. His reputation, judging from his low position in his class, contrasted with the honours that were awarded him by the college societies at their anniversary exhibitions, was greater with the students than with the faculty, though the honorary degree of Master of Arts, conferred upon him under peculiarly gratifying circumstances, after leaving the institution in his third or junior year without having graduated, clearly implies that he was still a favourite with his *alma mater.*

Immediately after leaving college—being then eighteen years old—he commenced the study of the law with Mr. Harmanus Bleecker, of Albany. When twenty-one, he was admitted to the bar, and in the succeeding three years he practised in the courts of the city of New York. During this period he wrote anonymously for the New York American—having made his first essay as a writer for the gazettes while in Albany—and soon after, I believe, became associated with Mr. Charles King in the editorship of that paper. Certainly he gave up the legal profession, for the successful prosecution of which he appears to have been unfitted by his love of books, society, and the rod and gun, and since that time has devoted his attention almost constantly to literature.

In October, 1833, Mr. Hoffman left New York to travel in the western states and territories; and arriving at Detroit by way of Pennsylvania and Ohio, directed his course through the peninsula of Michigan and the northern parts of Indiana and Illinois to the Prairie du Chien, on the upper Mississippi, which was the northern and western limit of his journey. On his return he passed through Missouri, Kentucky, Tennessee, and Virginia, and reached home near the close of June, 1834. Of this tour he gave a very interesting account

450

CHARLES FENNO HOFFMAN.

CHARLES FENNO HOFFMAN, son of Judge Josiah Ogden Hoffman, was born in the city of New York, in the year 1806. The family of Fenno is descended from his maternal grandfather, a distinguished politician of the federal party in Philadelphia, during the administration of Washington. His father's family came to New York from Holland ...

... of Peter Stuyvesant ... honourable ... in his youth ... competitor ... other ... nours of the ... his brother, Mr. Ogden H... ... the family reputation ...

... sent to a Latin grammar ... York, from which ... at G... transferred to the Poughkeepsie ... a seminary upon the Hudson ... miles from the city, which ... great reputation. The ... received here induced him to ... his father, finding that he had ... a course of severity, did not ... him, but placed him under the care of ... accomplished Scottish gentleman ... villages of New Jersey. ... from this place, when about ... age, he met with an injury which ... necessity of the immediate ... of the right leg, above the knee. The circumstances are minutely detailed in the New York Evening Post, of the twentieth of ... 1817, from which it appears, that with some other lads, attempting the dangerous feat of leaping aboard a steamer as she passed a pier ... he was caught between the ... and the wharf. The vessel swept ... ... clinging by his ... to the pier ... in a manner too ... his description. This deprivation, instead of acting as a damp ... ... for the manly sports of youth, and thus turning the subject of it into a retired student, seems rather to have given young Hoffman an especial ambition to excel in field sports and

... to the still ... ... more useful acquire... entered Columbia College ... paratory schools, was not ... in gymnastic exercises th... intellectual character. ... after his low positio... ... with the honours ... college societ... ... was grea... ... th... ... leaving ... year without ... plied that he was still ... class under.

Immediately after leav... then eighteen years ol... study of the law with Mr... of Albany. When twe... mitted to the bar, and fo... years he practised in the ... New York. During th... anonymously for the N... having made his first es... gazettes while in Alban... believes, became associa... King in the editorship... tainly he gave up the l... successful prosecution ... to have been unfitted b... society, and the rod and ... time has devoted his ... stantly to literature.

In October, 1833, Mr ... York to travel in the w... prisc, and arriving at ... Pennsylvania and Ohio, ... through the peninsula of ... northern parts of Indian... Prairie du Chien, on the ... which was the northern ... his journey. On his ret... Missouri, Kentucky, Tenn... and reached home near the ... Of this tour he gave a ver...

494

in two volumes, entitled, A Winter in the West, published in New York and London early in 1835. Although Mr. Irving soon after gave to the public his Tour on the Prairies, in which he has described, with his customary felicity, similar scenes and characters, Mr. Hoffman's work retained the popular favour with which it was originally received. It has since passed through several editions, and will continue to be admired so long as graphic delineations of nature, spirited sketches of men and manners, and richness and purity of style, are appreciated.

Mr. Hoffman's second work, Wild Scenes in the Forest and the Prairie, appeared originally in London, in 1837, and an impression of it, embracing some important additions, was printed in New York, in 1843. In this he has given some very happy and original scenic and legendary illustrations of American subjects, and has been equally successful in the tender and the humorous.

It was followed, in 1840, by Greyslaer, a Romance of the Mohawk, founded on the celebrated criminal trial of Beauchamp,* for the murder of Colonel Sharpe, the Solicitor General of Kentucky, the particulars of which, softened away in the novel, are minutely detailed in the appendix to his Winter in the West. Some of the English critics pronounced the scenes between Greyslaer and Alida de Roos melodramatic and improbable; but the authenticated facts of the tragedy are stranger than the fiction. In transferring the scene of his tale from Kentucky to the valley of the Mohawk, and at the same time carrying back the date of it half a century, little violence is done to the probabilities of the story, as the reader will be satisfied when he reflects upon the changes which fifty years have wrought since New York was a frontier state, exposed to the border warfare of the Indians. Balt, the Hunter, in this novel, is a well-conceived and admirably sustained character, American, in the genuine sense of the word. Greyslaer has so many traits about him which find a response in our consciousness, that we cannot but think his original existed somewhere else than in the imagination of the novelist. I do not refer so much to his habits and manners, as to his idiosyn-

cracies—his ways of feeling and thinking. No one who has not reflected upon his emotions, and indulged often in self-meditation, can fully recognise the chief merit of this character, considered as a type of real humanity.

The Knickerbocker Magazine was first issued under the editorial auspices of Mr. Hoffman, and he subsequently became the proprietor of the American Monthly, one of the ablest literary periodicals ever published in this country. While editor of this work he also conducted, for one year, the New York Mirror, and wrote a series of zealous and able papers in favour of a law of international copyright for The New Yorker.

In 1843 he published The Vigil of Faith, a Legend of the Andirondack Mountains, of which several editions have since appeared in this country and England. It contains much fine description and sentiment; the narrative is remarkably well managed, and in no other poem has Indian superstition or tradition been used with more skill or success. But his reputation as a poet rests mainly on his songs, which are unquestionably the finest that have been produced in this country. They are simple, entire and glowing, and evidently grew out of his own experiences and observation. The Myrtle and Steel, Sparkling and Bright, Rosalie Clare, and others, have a spontaneous lyrical flow, an earnest sincerity of feeling, and an inherent delicacy that distinguish only the best works of this description.

A few years ago Mr. Hoffman wrote a novel under the title of The Red Spur of Ramapo, of which high expectations were formed by his friends, from the knowledge they had of his enthusiasm in regard to the scenes and characters introduced into it, and the unusual degree of labour he had bestowed upon its composition. Just after the completion of his arrangements with the publishers, and when it had been announced as in the press, he was taken ill, and before his recovery the servant who attended his chambers, had "used all the paper that was written on to kindle fires, and carefully preserved, in the gentleman's portfolio, all the pieces that were unsoiled!"

The imperfect state of Mr. Hoffman's health for some years past has prevented him from making any additions to the literature of the country.

* Mr. William Gilmore Simms has, since the publication of Greyslaer, written a novel entitled Beauchampe, which is founded on the same history.

BEN BLOWER'S STORY;
OR HOW TO RELISH A JULEP.

"ARE you sure that's THE FLAME over by the shore?"

"Certing, manny! I could tell her pipes acrost the Mazoura."*

"And you will overhaul her?"

"Won't we though! I tell ye, Strannger, so sure as my name's Ben Blower, that that last tar bar'l I hove in the furnace has put jist the smart chance of go-ahead into us to cut off The Flame from yonder pint, or send our boat to kingdom come."

"The devil!" exclaimed a bystander who, intensely interested in the race, was leaning the while against the partitions of the boiler-room. "I've chosen a nice place to see the fun, near this infernal powder-barrel!"

"Not so bad as if you were in it!" coolly observed Ben, as the other walked rapidly away.

"As if he were in it! in what? in the boiler?"

"Certing! Don't folks sometimes go into bilers, manny?"

"I should think there'd be other parts of the boat more comfortable."

"That's right; poking fun at me at once't; but wait till we get through this brush with the old Flame, and I'll tell ye of a regular fixin scrape that a man may get into. It's true, too, every word of it—as sure as my name's Ben Blower."......

"You have seen the Flame then afore, Strannger? Six year ago, when new upon the river, she was a raal out and outer, I tell ye. I was at that time a hand aboard of her. Yes, I belonged to her at the time of her great race with the 'Go-liar.' You've heern, mayhap, of the blow-up by which we lost it? They made a great fuss about it; but it was nothing but a mere fiz of hot water after all. Only the springing of a few rivets, which loosened a biler plate or two, and let out a thin spirting upon some niggers that hadn't sense enough to get out of the way. Well, the 'Go-liar' took off our passengers, and we ran into Smasher's Landing to repair damages, and bury the poor fools that were killed. Here we laid for a matter of thirty hours or so, and got things to rights on board for a bran new start. There was some carpenters' work yet to be done, but the captain said that that might be fixed off jist as well when we were under way— we had worked hard—the weather was sour, and we needn't do any thing more jist now—we might take that afternoon to ourselves, but the next morning he'd get up steam bright and airly, and we'd all come out new. There was no temperance society at Smasher's Landing, and I went ashore upon a lark with some of the hands."

I omit the worthy Benjamin's adventures upon land, and, despairing of fully conveying his language in its original Doric force, will not hesitate to give the rest of his singular narrative in my own words, save where, in a few instances, I can recall his precise phraseology, which the reader will easily recognise.

---

* The name "Missouri" is thus generally pronounced upon the western waters.

"The night was raw and sleety when I regained the deck of our boat. The officers, instead of leaving a watch above, had closed up every thing, and shut themselves in the cabin. The fire-room only was open. The boards dashed from the outside by the explosion had not yet been replaced. The floor of the room was wet, and there was scarcely a corner which afforded a shelter from the driving storm. I was about leaving the room, resigned to sleep in the open air, and now bent only upon getting under the lee of some bulkhead that would protect me against the wind. In passing out I kept my arms stretched forward to feel my way in the dark, but my feet came in contact with a heavy iron lid; I stumbled, and, as I fell, struck one of my hands into the 'manhole,' (I think this was the name he gave to the oval-shaped opening in the head of the boiler,) through which the smith had entered to make his repairs. I fell with my arm thrust so far into the aperture that I received a pretty smart blow in the face as it came in contact with the head of the boiler, and I did not hesitate to drag my body after it, the moment I recovered from this stunning effect, and ascertained my whereabouts. In a word I crept into the boiler, resolved to pass the rest of the night there. The place was dry and sheltered. Had my bed been softer, I would have had all that man could desire; as it was, I slept, and slept soundly.

"I should mention though, that, before closing my eyes, I several times shifted my position. I had gone first to the farthest end of the boiler, then again I had crawled back to the manhole, to put my hand out and feel that it was really still open. The warmest place was at the farther end, where I finally established myself, and that I knew from the first. It was foolish in me to think that the opening through which I had just entered could be closed without my hearing it, and that, too, when no one was astir but myself; but the blow on the side of my face made me a little nervous perhaps; besides, I never could bear to be shut up in any place—it always gives a wild-like feeling about the head. You may laugh, Stranger, but I believe I should suffocate in an empty church, if I once felt that I was so shut up in it that I could not get out. I have met men afore now just like me, or worse rather—much worse. Men that it made sort of furious to be tied down to any thing, yet so soft-like and contradictory in their natures that you might lead them anywhere so long as they didn't feel the string. Stranger, it takes all sorts of people to make a world! and we may have a good many of the worst kind of white-men here out west. But I have seen folks upon this river—quiet looking chaps, too, as ever you see—who were so teetotally carankterankterous that they'd shoot the doctor who'd tell them they couldn't live when ailing, and make a die of it, just out of spite, when told they must get well. Yes, fellows as fond of the good things of earth as you and I, yet who'd rush like mad right over the gang-plank of life, if once brought to believe that they had to stay in this world whether they wanted to leave it or not. Thunder and bees! if such a fellow as that had heard the cocks crow as I did—awakened to find darkness about him—darkness so thick you might cut it with a knife—heard other sounds, too, to tell that it was morning, and scrambling to fumble for that manhole, found it, too, black—closed—black and even as the rest of the iron coffin around him, closed, with not a rivet-hole to let God's light and air in—why—why—he'd 'a *swounded* right down on the spot, as I did, and I ain't ashamed to own it to no white-man."

The big drops actually stood upon the poor fellow's brow, as he now paused for a moment in the recital of his terrible story. He passed his hand over his rough features, and resumed it with less agitation of manner.

"How long I may have remained there senseless I don't know. The doctors have since told me it must have been a sort of fit—more like an apoplexy than a swoon, for the attack finally passed off in sleep.—Yes, I slept; I know *that*, for I dreamed—dreamed a heap o' things afore I awoke,—there is but one dream, however, that I have ever been able to recall distinctly, and that must have come on shortly before I recovered my consciousness. My resting-place through the night had been, as I have told you, at the far end of the boiler. Well, I now dreamed that the manhole was still open—and, what seems curious, rather than laughable, if you take it in connection with other things, I fancied that my legs had been so stretched in the long walk I had taken the evening before, that they now reached the whole length of the boiler, and extended through the opening.

"At first, (in my dreaming reflections,) it was a comfortable thought, that no one could now shut up the manhole without awakening me. But soon it seemed as if my feet, which were on the outside, were becoming drenched in the storm which had originally driven me to seek this shelter. I felt the chilling rain upon my extremities. They grew colder and colder, and their numbness gradually extended upward to other parts of my body. It seemed, however, that it was only the under side of my person that was thus strangely visited. I laid upon my back, and it must have been a species of nightmare that afflicted me, for I knew at last that I was dreaming, yet felt it impossible to rouse myself. A violent fit of coughing restored, at last, my powers of volition. The water, which had been slowly rising around me, had rushed into my mouth; I awoke to hear the rapid strokes of the pump which was driving it into the boiler!

"My whole condition—no—not all of it—not yet—my *present* condition flashed with new horror upon me. But I did not again swoon. The choking sensation which had made me faint, when I first discovered how I was entombed, gave way to a livelier, though less overpowering emotion. I shrieked even as I started from my slumber. The previous discovery of the closed aperture, and the instant oblivion that followed, seemed only a part of my dream, and I threw my arms about and looked eagerly for the opening by which I had entered the horrid place—yes, looked for it, and felt for it, though it was the terrible conviction that it

was closed—a second time brought home to me—which prompted my frenzied cry. Every sense seemed to have tenfold acuteness, yet not one to act in unison with another. I shrieked again and again —imploringly—desperately—savagely. I filled the hollow chamber with my cries, till its iron walls seemed to tingle around me. The dull strokes of the accursed pump seemed only to mock at, while they deadened my screams.

"At last I gave myself up. It is the struggle against our fate which frenzies the mind. We cease to fear when we cease to hope. I gave myself up, and then I grew calm!

"I was resigned to die—resigned even to my mode of death. It was not, I thought, so very new after all, as to awaken unwonted horror in a man. Thousands have been sunk to the bottom of the ocean shut up in the holds of vessels—beating themselves against the battened hatches—dragged down from the upper world shrieking, not for life, but for death only beneath the eye and amid the breath of heaven. Thousands have endured that appalling kind of suffocation. I would die only as many a better man had died before me. I *could* meet such a death. I said so—I thought so—I felt so—felt so, I mean, for a minute—or more; ten minutes it may have been—or but an instant of time. I know not—nor does it matter if I could compute it. There *was* a time, then, when I was resigned to my fate. But, good God! was I resigned to it in the shape in which next it came to appal? Stranger, I felt that water growing hot about my limbs, though it was yet mid-leg deep. I felt it, and, in the same moment, heard the roar of the furnace that was to turn it into steam before it could get deep enough to drown one!

"You shudder,—It was hideous. But did I shrink and shrivel, and crumble down upon that iron floor, and lose my senses in that horrid agony of fear?—No!—though my brain swam and the life-blood that curdled at my heart seemed about to stagnate there for ever, still *I knew!* I was too hoarse—too hopeless, from my previous efforts, to cry out more. But I struck—feebly at first, and then strongly—frantically with my clenched fist against the sides of the boiler. There were people moving near who *must* hear my blows! Could not I hear the grating of chains, the shuffling of feet, the very rustle of a rope—hear them all, within a few inches of me? I did—but the gurgling water that was growing hotter and hotter around my extremities, made more noise within the steaming chaldron, than did my frenzied blows against its sides.

"Latterly I had hardly changed my position, but now the growing heat of the water made me plash to and fro; lifting myself wholly out of it was impossible, but I could not remain quiet. I stumbled upon something—it was a mallet!—a chance tool the smith had left there by accident. With what wild joy did I seize it—with what eager confidence did I now deal my first blows with it against the walls of my prison! But scarce had I intermitted them for a moment when I heard the clang of the iron door as the fireman flung it wide to feed the flames that were to torture me. My knocking was unheard, though I could hear him toss the sticks into the furnace beneath me, and drive to the door when his infernal oven was fully crammed.

"Had I yet a hope? I had, but it rose in my mind side by side with the fear that I might now become the agent of preparing myself a more frightful death—Yes! when I thought of that furnace with its fresh-fed flames curling beneath the iron upon which I stood—a more frightful death even than that of being boiled alive! Had I discovered that mallet but a short time sooner—but no matter, I would by its aid resort to the only expedient now left.

"It was this:—I remembered having a marline-spike in my pocket, and in less time than I have taken in hinting at the consequences of thus using it, I had made an impression upon the sides of the boiler, and soon succeeded in driving it through. The water gushed through the aperture—would they see it?—No; the jet could only play against a wooden partition which must hide the stream from view—it must trickle down upon the decks before the leakage would be discovered. Should I drive another hole to make that leakage greater? Why, the water within seemed already to be sensibly diminished—so hot had become that which remained—should more escape, would I not fear it bubble and hiss upon the fiery plates of iron that were already scorching the soles of my feet? ······

"Ah! there is a movement—voices—I hear them calling for a crowbar:—The bulkhead cracks as they pry off the planking. They have seen the leak—they are trying to get at it!—Good God! why do they not first dampen the fire?—Why do they call for the—the—

"Stranger, look at that finger! it can never regain its natural size—but it has already done all the service that man could expect from so humble a member, *Sir, that hole would have been plugged up on the instant,* unless *I had jammed my finger through!*

"I heard the cry of horror as they saw it without—the shout to drown the fire—the first stroke of the cold water-pump. They say, too, that I was conscious when they took me out—but I—I remember nothing more till they brought a julep to my bed-side afterwards, AND *that julep!—*"

"Cooling! was it?"

"STRANGER!!!"

Ben turned away his head and wept—He could no more.

THE FLYING HEAD.
A LEGEND OF SACONDAGA LAKE.
FROM WILD SCENES IN THE FOREST AND PRAIRIE.

"The Great God hath sent us signs in the sky! we have heard uncommon noise in the heavens, and have seen HEADS fall down upon the earth!" *Speech of Tahaya-doris, a Mohawk sachem, at Albany,* Oct. 25th, 1689.—COLDEN'S *Five Nations.*

It hath tell-tale tongues;—this casing air
That walls us in—and their wandering breath
Will whisper the horror everywhere.
That clings to that ruthless deed of death.
And a vengeful eye from the gory tide
Will open to blast the parricide.

THE country about the head-waters of the great

Mohegan, (as the Hudson is sometimes called,) though abounding in game and fish, was never, in the recollection of the oldest Indians living, nor in that of their fathers' fathers, the permanent residence of any one tribe. From the black mountain tarns, where the eastern fork takes its rise, to the silver strand of Lake Pleasant, through which the western branch makes its way after rising in Sacondaga Lake, the wilderness that intervenes, and all the mountains round about the fountain-heads of the great river, have, from time immemorial, been infested by a class of beings with whom no good man would ever wish to come in contact.

The young men of the Mohawk have, indeed, often traversed it, when, in years gone by, they went on the war path after the hostile tribes of the north; and the scattered and wandering remnants of their people, with an occasional hunting-party from the degenerate bands that survive at St. Regis, will yet occasionally be tempted over these haunted grounds in quest of the game that still finds a refuge in that mountain region. The evil shapes that were formerly so troublesome to the red hunter, seem, in these later days, to have become less restless at his presence; and, whether it be that the day of their power has gone by, or that their vindictiveness has relented at witnessing the fate which seems to be universally overtaking the people whom they once delighted to persecute—certain it is, that the few Indians who now find their way to this part of the country are never molested, except by the white settlers who are slowly extending their clearings among the wild hills of the north.

The "FLYING HEAD," which is supposed to have first driven the original possessors of these hunting-grounds, whosoever they were, from their homes, and which, as long as tradition runneth back, in the old day before the whites came hither, guarded them from the occupancy of every neighbouring tribe, has not been seen for many years by any credible witness, though there are those who insist that it has more than once appeared to them, hovering, as their fathers used to describe it, over the lake in which it first had its birth. The existence of this fearful monster, however, has never been disputed. Rude representations of it are still occasionally met with in the crude designs of those degenerate aborigines who earn a scant subsistence by making birchen baskets and ornamented pouches for such travellers as are curious in their manufacture of wampum and porcupine quills; and the origin and history of the Flying Head survives, while even the name of the tribe whose crimes first called it into existence, has passed away for ever.

It was a season of great severity with that forgotten people whose council-fires were lighted on the mountain promontory that divides Sacondaga from the sister lake into which it discharges itself.[*]

A long and severe winter, with but little snow, had killed the herbage at its roots, and the moose and deer had trooped off to the more luxuriant

* A hamlet is now growing up on this beautiful mountain slope, and the scenery in the vicinity is likely to be soon better known, from the late establishment of a line of post-coaches between Sacondaga Lake and Saratoga Springs.

pastures along the Mohawk, whither the hunters of the hills dared not follow them. The fishing, too, failed; and the famine became so devouring among the mountains, that whole families, who had no hunters to provide for them, perished outright. The young men would no longer throw the slender product of the chase into the common stock, and the women and children had to maintain life as well as they could upon the roots and berries the woods afforded them.

The sufferings of the tribe became at length so galling, that the young and enterprising began to talk of migrating from the ancient seat of their people; and, as it was impossible, surrounded as they were by hostile tribes, merely to shift their hunting-grounds for a season and return to them at some more auspicious period, it was proposed that if they could effect a secret march to the great lake off to the west of them, they should launch their canoes upon Ontario, and all move away to a new home beyond its broad waters. The wild rice, of which some had been brought into their country by a runner from a distant nation, would, they thought, support them in their perilous voyage along the shores of the great water, where it grows in such profusion; and they believed that, once safely beyond the lake, it would be easy enough to find a new home abounding in game upon those flowery plains which, as they had heard, lay like one immense garden beyond the chain of inland seas.

The old men of the tribe were indignant at the bare suggestion of leaving the bright streams and sheltered valleys, amid which their spring-time of life had passed so happily. They doubted the existence of the garden regions of which their children spoke; and they thought that if there were indeed such a country, it was madness to attempt to reach it in the way proposed. They said, too, that the famine was a scourge which the Master of Life inflicted upon his people for their crimes; that if its pains were endured with the constancy and firmness that became warriors, the visitation would soon pass away; but that those who fled from it would only war with their destiny, and that chastisement would follow them, in some shape, wheresoever they might flee. Finally, they added that they would rather perish by inches on their native hills—they would rather die that moment, than leave them for ever, to revel in plenty upon stranger plains.

"Be it so; they have spoken!" exclaimed a fierce and insolent youth, springing to his feet and casting a furious glance around the council as the aged chief, who had thus addressed it, resumed his seat. "Be the dotard's words their own, my brothers; let them die for the words they have even now acknowledged. We know of none; our unsullied summers have nothing to blush for. It is they that have drawn this curse upon our people: it is for them that our vitals are consuming with anguish, while our strength wastes away in the search of sustenance we cannot find; or which, when found, we are compelled to share with those for whose misdeeds the Great Spirit hath placed it far from us. They have spoken—let them die. Let them die,

if we are to remain to appease the angry Spirit; and the food that now keeps life lingering in their shrivelled and useless carcases, may then nerve the limbs of our young hunters, or keep our children from perishing. Let them die, if we are to move hence, for their presence will but bring a curse upon our path: their worn-out frames will give way upon the march; and the raven that hovers over their corses will guide our enemies to the spot, and scent them like wolves upon our trail. Let them die, my brothers; and, because they are still our tribesmen, let us give them the death of warriors, and that before we leave this ground."

And with these words the young barbarian, pealing forth a ferocious whoop, buried his tomahawk in the head of the old man nearest to him. The infernal yell was echoed on every side; a dozen flint hatchets were instantly raised by as many remorseless arms, and the massacre was wrought before one of those thus horribly sacrificed could interpose a plea of mercy. But for mercy they would not have pleaded, had opportunity been afforded them; for even in the moment that intervened between the cruel sentence and its execution, they managed to show that stern resignation to the decrees of fate which an Indian warrior ever exhibits when death is near; and each of the seven old men that perished thus barbarously, drew his wolf-skin mantle around his shoulders and nodded his head, as if inviting the death-blow that followed.

The parricidal deed was done! and it now became a question how to dispose of the remains of those whose lamp of life, while twinkling in the socket, had been thus fearfully quenched for ever. The act, though said to have been of not unfrequent occurrence among certain Indian tribes at similar exigencies, was one utterly abhorrent to the nature of most of our aborigines; who, from their earliest years, are taught the deepest veneration for the aged. In the present instance, likewise, it had been so outrageous a perversion of their customary views of duty among this simple people, that it was thought but proper to dispense with their wonted mode of sepulture, and dispose of the victims of famine and fanaticism in some peculiar manner. They wished in some way to sanctify the deed, by offering up the bodies of the slaughtered to the Master of Life, and that without dishonouring the dead. It was, therefore, agreed to decapitate the bodies and burn them; and as the nobler part could not, when thus dissevered, be buried with the usual forms, it was determined to sink the heads together to the bottom of the lake.

The soulless trunks were accordingly consumed, and the ashes scattered to the winds. The heads were then deposited singly, in separate canoes, which were pulled off in a kind of procession from the shore. The young chief who had suggested the bloody scene of the sacrifice, rowed in advance, in order to designate the spot where they were to disburden themselves of their gory freight. Resting then upon his oars, he received each head in succession from his companions, and proceeded to tie them together by their scalp-locks, in order to sink

2 Q 2

the whole, with a huge stone, to the bottom. But the vengeance of the Master of Life overtook the wretch before his horrid office was accomplished; for no sooner did he receive the last head into his canoe than it began to sink, his feet became entangled in the hideous chain he had been knotting together, and, before his horror-stricken companions could come to his rescue, he was dragged, shrieking, to the bottom. The others waited not to see the water settle over him, but pulled with their whole strength for the shore.

The morning dawned calmly upon that unhallowed water, which seemed at first to show no traces of the deed it had witnessed the night before. But gradually, as the sun rose up higher, a few gory bubbles appeared to float over one smooth and turbid spot, which the breeze never crisped into a ripple. The parricides sat on the bank watching it all the day; but sluggish, as at first, that sullen blot upon the fresh blue surface still remained. Another day passed over their heads, and the thick stain was yet there. On the third day the floating slime took a greener hue, as if coloured by the festering mass beneath; but coarse fibres of darker dye marbled its surface, and on the fourth day these began to tremble along the water like weeds growing from the bottom, or the long tresses of a woman's scalp floating in a pool when no wind disturbs it. The fifth morning came, and the conscience-stricken watchers thought that the spreading-scalp—for such now all agreed it was—had raised itself from the water, and become rounded at the top, as if there were a head beneath it. Some thought, too, that they could discover a pair of hideous eyes glaring beneath the dripping locks. They looked on the sixth, and there indeed was a monstrous HEAD floating upon the surface, as if anchored to the spot, around which the water—notwithstanding a blast which swept the lake—was calm and motionless as ever.

Those bad Indians then wished to fly; but the doomed parricides had not now the courage to encounter the warlike bands through which they must make their way in fleeing from their native valley. They thought, too, that, as nothing about the head, except the eyes, had motion, it could not harm them, resting quietly, as it did, upon the bosom of the waters. And, though it was dreadful to have that hideous gaze fixed for ever upon their dwellings, yet they thought that if the Master of Life meant this as an expiation for their phrenzied deed, they would strive to live on beneath those unearthly glances without shrinking or complaint.

But a strange alteration had taken place in the floating head on the morning of the seventh day. A pair of broad wings, ribbed, like those of a bat, and with claws appended to each tendon, had grown out during the night; and, buoyed up by these, it seemed to be now resting on the water. The water itself appeared to ripple more briskly near it, as if joyous that it was about to be relieved of its unnatural burden; but still, for hours, the head maintained its first position. At last the wind began to rise, and, driving through the trough of the waves, beneath their expanded membrane, raised the

wings from the surface, and seemed for the first time to endow them with vitality. They flapped harshly once or twice upon the billows, and the head rose slowly and heavily from the lake.

An agony of fear seized upon the gazing parricides, but the supernatural creation made no movement to injure them. It only remained balancing itself over the lake, and casting a shadow from its wings that wrapped the valley in gloom. But dreadful was it beneath their withering shade to watch that terrific monster, hovering like a falcon for the stoop, and know not upon what victim it might descend. It was then that they who had sown the gory seed from which it sprung to life, with one impulse sought to escape its presence by flight. Herding together like a troop of deer when the panther is prowling by, they rushed in a body from the scene. But the flapping of the demon pinions was soon heard behind them, and the winged head was henceforth on their track wheresoever it led.

In vain did they cross one mountain barrier after another, plunge into the rocky gorge, or thread the mazy swamp, to escape their fiendish watcher. The Flying Head would rise on tireless wings over the loftiest summit, or dart in arrowy flight through the narrowest passages without furling its pinions: while their sullen threshing would be heard even in those vine-webbed thickets where the little ground bird can scarcely make its way. The very caverns of the earth were no protection to the parricides from its presence; for scarcely would they think they had found a refuge in some sparry cell, when, poised midway between the ceiling and the floor, they would behold the Flying Head glaring upon them. Sleeping or waking, the monster was ever near; they paused to rest, but the rushing of its wings, as it swept around their resting-place in never-ending circles, prevented them from finding forgetfulness in repose; or if, in spite of those blighting pinions that ever fanned them, fatigue did at moments plunge them in uneasy slumbers, the glances of the Flying Head would pierce their very eyelids, and steep their dreams in horror.

What was the ultimate fate of that band of parricides, no one has ever known. Some say that the Master of Life kept them always young, in order that their capability of suffering might never wear out; and these insist that the Flying Head is still pursuing them over the great prairies of the far-west. Others aver that the glances of the Flying Head turned each of them gradually into stone; and these say that their forms, though altered by the wearing of the rains in the lapse of long years, may still be recognised in those upright rocks which stand like human figures along the shores of some of the neighbouring lakes; though most Indians have another way of accounting for these figures. Certain it is, however, that the Flying Head always comes back to this part of the country about the times of the equinox; and some say even that you may always hear the flapping of its wings whenever such a storm as that we have just weathered is brewing.

CAROLINE M. KIRKLAND.

[Born 18—. Died 1864.]

MRS. KIRKLAND, formerly Miss Caroline M. Stansbury, is a native, I believe, of New York. On her marriage with the late amiable and accomplished William Kirkland,* soon after his return from Europe, (where he had spent some time for the purpose of improving his knowledge of modern languages,) he resigned a professorship which he held in Hamilton College, and established a school in the beautiful village of Geneva, on the Seneca Lake, where they resided several years. They subsequently removed into Michigan, where Mrs. Kirkland wrote A New Home: Who'll Follow! or Glimpses of Western Life, by Mrs. Mary Clavers, an Actual Settler, and Forest Life, the first of which was published in 1839, and the last in 1842. No works of their class were ever more brilliantly successful than these original and admirable pictures of frontier scenery, woodcraft, and domestic experience. For genial humour, graphic description, and shrewd sense, "Mrs. Clavers" proved herself equal to any writers of her sex, while in delicacy, nice perception of character, and all the more feminine qualities of authorship, there was no one in this country at least to be preferred to her. In 1845 she published

* William Kirkland, son of the Honourable Joseph Kirkland, was born in New Hartford, near Utica, in New York, in the year 1800. He was originally educated for the ministry, but some conscientious scruples kept him from entering upon its sacred duties, and he was appointed first a tutor and then a professor in Hamilton College. He visited Europe for the gratification of a liberal curiosity, and to gain a more perfect mastery of the languages of the continent, and while abroad resided nearly two years in Gottingen. He removed to New York, from Michigan, in 1842, and in that city devoted his attention chiefly to literature. In October, 1846, he established a religious journal which promised to be very successful; but on the nineteenth of that month his friends were surprised at the intelligence of his sudden and melancholy death. His body was on that day recovered from the Hudson river, near Fishkill. He was returning from a visit to his little son, in the neighbourhood of Newburgh, the previous evening, and being deaf and very near-sighted, he probably made a misstep in the dark, fell into the river, and was rapidly swept away by the current, while the noise of the departing boat prevented those on board from hearing any cries for assistance. He was a fine scholar, an elegant and able writer, and was very much beloved for his many gentlemanly qualities.

Western Clearings, a collection of tales and sketches illustrative of the same sort of life. It has the strength, freshness, effect and brilliancy, which we associate with the best conception of our native character, and is uniformly saved from those kindred faults which lie so fatally near to this bold class of virtues, by the inborn refinement, practised taste, ready tact, and varied resources which are her special and rare accomplishment. In the roughest scenes she is never coarse; amidst the least cultivated society she never is vulgar. She interests us in the wild men and in the wild occurrences of border life, by identifying them with the fortunes and feelings of that humanity of which we are a part. Her sympathies are sensitive and various in their range, but always sound and healthful, and neither extravagant in their objects nor excessive in their degree. The constant presence of strong active sense on the part of the author carries us through the monotonous incidents of western settlement with animation, amusement and instruction. These narratives have throughout that simplicity, vigour, and inherent beauty, which a superior mind, if it be faithful to the great law of genuineness and honesty, never fails of attaining in its representations of the actual. Laying aside factitious models, and seeking only to apprehend the subject before her in its just and permanent characteristics, and to express those views with sincerity and directness, Mrs. Kirkland has attained a success which may well serve as a monitor and guide to those who, upon less judicious plans, are labouring to create an American literature. There is but one way in which we can be, rightly and advantageously, free from the tyranny of British examples. Truth of understanding and truth of feeling must be the only directors to real excellence in untried courses.

She also wrote, Essay on Spenser; Holidays Abroad; The Evening Book; Home Book of Beauty; A Book for the Home Circle; The Helping Hand; Autumn Hours; Garden Walks with the Poets; and Memoirs of Washington She died in April, 1864.

MR. AND MRS. DOUBLEDAY.

FROM A NEW HOME.

I HAVE been frequently reminded of one of Johnson's humorous sketches. A man returning a broken wheelbarrow to a Quaker, with "Here, I've broke your rotten wheelbarrow, usin' on 't. I wish you'd get it mended right off, 'cause I want to borrow it again this afternoon." The Quaker is made to reply, "Friend, it shall be done';" and I wish I possessed more of his spirit.

But I did not intend to write a chapter on involuntary loans; I have a story to tell.

One of my best neighbours is Mr. Philo Doubleday, a long, awkward, honest, hard-working Maineman, or Mainiote, I suppose one might say; so good-natured, that he might be mistaken for a simpleton; but that must be by those that do not know him. He is quite an old settler, came in four years ago, bringing with him a wife, who is to him as vinegar-bottle to oil-cruet, or as mustard to the sugar, which is used to soften its biting qualities. Mrs. Doubleday has the sharpest eyes, the sharpest nose, the sharpest tongue, the sharpest elbows, and, above all, the sharpest voice, that ever " penetrated the interior" of Michigan. She has a tall, straight, bony figure, in contour somewhat resembling two hard-oak planks fastened together and stood on end; and, strange to say! she was full five-and-thirty when her mature graces attracted the eye and won the affections of the worthy Philo. What eclipse had come over Mr. Doubleday's usual sagacity, when he made choice of his Polly, I am sure I never could guess; but he is certainly the only man in the wide world who could possibly have lived with her; and he makes her a most excellent husband.

She is possessed with a neat devil; I have known many such cases; her floor is scoured every night, after all are in bed but the unlucky scrubber, Betsey, the maid of all work; and wo to the unfortunate "indiffidle," as neighbour Jenkins says, who first sets dirty boot on it in the morning. If men come in to talk over road business, for Philo is much sought when "the public" has any work to do, or school business, for that, being very troublesome, and quite devoid of profit, is often conferred upon Philo, Mrs. Doubleday makes twenty errands into the room, expressing in her visage all the force of Mrs. Raddle's inquiry, "Is them wretches going?" And when, at length, their backs are turned, out comes the bottled vengeance. The sharp eyes, tongue, elbow, and voice, are all in instant requisition.

"Fetch the broom, Betsey! and the scrub-broom, Betsey! and the mop, and that 'ere dish of soap, Betsey! And why on earth didn't you bring some ashes? You didn't expect to clean such a floor as this without ashes, did you?"—"What time are you going to have dinner, my dear?" says the imperturbable Philo, who is getting ready to go out.

"Dinner! I'm sure I don't know! there's no time to cook dinner in this house! nothing but slave, slave, slave, from morning till night, cleaning up after a set of nasty, dirty," &c., &c.

"Phew!" says Mr. Doubleday, looking at his fuming help-mate with a calm smile, "It'll all rub out when it's dry, if you'll only let it alone."

"Yes, yes; and it would be plenty clean enough for you if there had been forty horses in here."

Philo, on some such occasion, waited till his Polly had stepped out of the room, and then, with a bit of chalk, wrote, on the broad black walnut mantelpiece,—

> "Bolt and bar hold gate of wood,
> Gate of iron springs make good,
> Bolt nor spring can bind the flame,
> Woman's tongue can no man tame,"

and then took his hat and walked off.

This is his favourite mode of vengeance,—"poetical justice," as he calls it; and, as he is never at a loss for a rhyme of his own or other people's, Mrs. Doubleday stands in no small dread of these efforts of genius. Once, when Philo's crony, James Porter, the blacksmith, had left the print of his blackened knuckles on the outside of the oft-scrubbed door, and was the subject of some rather severe remarks from the gentle Polly, Philo, as he left the house with his friend, turned and wrote, over the offended spot,—

> "Knock not here!
> Or dread my dear.—P. D."

and the very next person that came was Mrs. Skinner, the merchant's wife, all dressed in her red merino, to make a visit. Mrs. Skinner, who did not possess an unusual share of tact, walked gravely round to the back door, and left Mrs. Doubleday up to the eyes in soap making. Dire was the mortification, and point blank were the questions, as to how the visiter came to go round that way; and when the warning couplet was produced in justification, we must draw a veil over what followed, as the novelists say.

Sometimes these poeticals came in aid of poor Betsey; as once, when on hearing a crash in the little shanty-kitchen, Mrs. Doubleday called, in her shrillest tones, "Betsey! what on earth's the matter!" Poor Betsey, knowing what was coming, answered, in a deprecatory whine, "The cow's kicked over the buckwheat batter!"

When the clear, hilarous voice of Philo, from the yard where he was chopping, instantly completed the triplet;—

"Take up the pieces and throw'm at her!" for once the grim features of his spouse relaxed into a smile, and Betsey escaped her scolding.

Yet Mrs. Doubleday is not without her excellent qualities as a wife, a friend, and a neighbour. She keeps her husband's house and stockings in unexceptionable trim. Her *emptins* are the envy of the neighbourhood. Her vinegar is,—as how could it fail!—the *ne plus ultra* of sharpness; and her pickles are greener than the grass of the field. She will watch night after night with the sick, perform the last sad offices for the dead, or take to her home and heart the little ones whose mother is removed for ever from her place at the fire-side. All this she can do cheerfully, and she will not repay herself, as many good people do, by recounting every word of the querulous sick man, or the desolate mourner, with added hints of tumbled drawers, closets all in heaps, or *awful* dirty kitchens.

I was sitting one morning with my neighbour, Mrs. Jenkins, who is a sister of Mr. Doubleday, when Betsey, Mrs. Doubleday's "hired girl," came in with one of the shingles of Philo's handiwork in her hand, which bore, in Mr. Doubleday's well-known chalk marks,—

> " Come quick, Fanny!
> And bring the granny;
> For Mrs. Double-
> day's in trouble."

And the next intelligence was of a fine, new pair of lungs, at that hitherto silent mansion. I called very soon after to take a peep at the " latest found;" and if the suppressed delight of the new papa was a treat, how much more was the softened aspect, the womanized tone of the proud and happy mother. I never saw a being so completely transformed. She would almost forget to answer me, in her absorbed watching of the breath of the little sleeper. Even when trying to be polite, and to say what the occasion demanded, her eyes would not be withdrawn from the tiny face. Conversation on any subject but the ever-new theme of "babies," was out of the question. Whatever we began upon, whirled round sooner or later to the one point. The needle may tremble, but it turns not with the less constancy to the pole.

As I pass for an oracle in the matter of paps and possets, I had frequent communication with my now happy neighbour, who had forgotten to scold her husband, learned to let Betsey have time to eat, and omitted the nightly scouring of the floor, lest so much dampness might be bad for the baby. We were in deep consultation, one morning, on some important point touching the well-being of this sole object of Mrs. Doubleday's thoughts and dreams, when the very same little Ianthe Howard, dirty as ever, presented herself. She sat down and stared a while without speaking, *à l'ordinaire,* and then informed us, that her mother " wanted Mrs. Doubleday to let her have her baby for a little while, 'cause Benny's".…—but she had no time to finish the sentence.

" Lend my baby ! ! !"—and her utterance failed. The new mother's feelings were fortunately too big for speech, and Ianthe wisely disappeared before Mrs. Doubleday found her tongue. Philo, who entered on the instant, burst into one of his electrifying laughs, with—

> " Ask my Polly,
> To lend her dolly !—"

and I could not help thinking, that one must come " West," in order to learn a little of every thing.

ARISTOCRACY.

FROM WESTERN CLEARINGS.

THE great ones of the earth might learn many a lesson from the little. What has a certain dignity on a comparatively large scale, is so simply laughable when it is seen in miniature, (and, unlike most other things, perhaps, its real features are better distinguished in the small,) that it must be wholesome to observe how what we love appears in those whom we do not admire. The monkey and the magpie are imitators; and when the one makes a thousand superfluous bows and grimaces, and the other hoards what can be of no possible use to him, we may, even in those, see a far off reflex of certain things prevalent among ourselves. Next in order come little children ; and the boy will put a napkin about his neck for a cravat, and the girl supply her ideal of a veil by pinning a pocket handkerchief to her bonnet, while we laugh at the self-deception, and fancy that we value only realities. But what affords us most amusement, is the awkward attempt of the rustic, to copy the airs and graces which have caught his fancy as he saw them exhibited in town ; or, still more naturally, those which have been displayed on purpose to dazzle him, during the stay of some " mould of fashion" in the country. How exquisitely funny are his efforts and their failure! How the true hugs himself in full belief that the gulf between himself and the *pseudo* is impassable! Little dreams he that his own ill-directed longings after the *distingué* in air or in position seem to some more fortunate individual as far from being accomplished as those of the rustic to himself, while both, perhaps, owe more to the tailor and milliner than to any more dignified source.

The country imitates the town, most sadly ; and it is really melancholy, to one who loves his kind, to see how obstinately people will throw away real comforts and advantages in the vain chase of what does not belong to solitude and freedom. The restraints necessary to city life are there compensated by many advantages resulting from close contact with others ; while in the country those restraints are simply odious, curtailing the real advantages of the position, yet entirely incapable of substituting those which belong to the city.

Real refinement is as possible in the one case as in the other. Would it were more heartily sought in both !

In the palmy days of alchemy, when the nature and powers of occult and intangible agents were deemed worthy the study of princes, the art of sealing hermetically was an essential one ; hence many a precious elixir would necessarily become unmanageable and useless if allowed to wander in the common air. This art seems now to be among the lost, in spite of the anxious efforts of cunning projectors ; and at the present time a subtle essence, more volatile than the elixir of life—more valuable than the philosopher's stone—an invisible and imponderable but most real agent, long bottled up for the enjoyment of a privileged few, has burst its bounds and become part of our daily atmosphere. Some mighty sages still contrive to retain within their own keeping important portions of this treasure ; but there are regions of the earth where it is open to all, and, in the opinion of the exclusive, sadly desecrated by having become an object of pursuit to the vulgar. Where it is still under a degree of control, the seal of Hermes is variously represented. In Russia, the supreme will of 'he autocrat regulates the distribution of the " airy good;" in other parts of the Continent, ancient prescription has still the power to keep it within its due reservoirs. In France, its uses and advantages have been publicly denied and repudiated; yet it is said that practically everybody stands open-mouthed where it is known to be floating in the air, hoping to inhale as much as possible without the odium of seeming to grasp at what has been decided to be worthless. In England we are told that the precious fluid is still kept with great solicitude in a dingy receptacle called Almack's, watched ever by certain priestesses, who are self-consecrated to an attendance more onerous than that required for maintaining the Vestal fire, and who yet receive neither respect nor gratitude for their pains. Indeed, the fine spirit has become so much diffused in England that it reminds us of the riddle of Mother Goose—

A house-full, a hole-full,
But can't catch a bowl-full.

If such efforts in England amuse us, what shall we say of the agonized pursuit everywhere observable in our own country? We have denounced the fascinating gas as poisonous—we have staked our very existence upon excluding it from the land, yet it is the breath of our nostrils—the soul of our being—the one thing needful—for which we are willing to expend mind, body, and estate. We exclaim against its operations in other lands, but it is the purchaser decrying to others the treasure he would appropriate to himself. We take much credit to ourselves for having renounced what all the rest of the world were pursuing, but our practice is like that of the toper who had forsworn drink, yet afterward perceiving the contents of a brother sinner's bottle to be spilt, could not forbear falling on his knees to drink the liquor from the frozen hoof-prints in the road; or that other votary of indulgence, who, having once had the courage to pass a tavern, afterward turned back that he might "treat resolution." We have satisfied our consciences by theory; we feel no compunction in making our practice just like that of the rest of the world.

This is true of the country generally; but it is nowhere so strikingly evident as in these remote regions which the noise of the great world reaches but at the rebound—as it were in faint echoes; and these very echoes changed from their original, as Paddy asserts of those of the Lake of Killarney. It would seem that our *elixir vitæ*—a strange anomaly—becomes stronger by dilution. Its power of fascination, at least, increases as it recedes from the fountain head. The Russian noble may refuse to let his daughter smile upon a suitor whose breast is not covered with orders; the German dignitary may insist on sixteen quarterings; the well-born Englishman may sigh to be admitted into a coterie not half as respectable or as elegant as the one to which he belongs—all this is consistent enough; but we must laugh when we see the managers of a city ball admit the daughters of *wholesale* merchants, while they exclude the families of merchants who sell at *retail*; and still more when we come to the "new country" and observe that Mrs. Pen-

niman, who takes *in* sewing, utterly refuses to associate with her neighbour Mrs. Clapp, because she goes *out* sewing by the day; and that our friend Mr. Diggins, being raised a step in the world by the last election, signs all his letters of friendship, "D. Diggins, Sheriff."

THE LAND-FEVER.

FROM THE SAME.

[In 1835 and 1836, a fever of speculation in lands took place in the far West. Both the speculators, and the "land-lookers" who helped them in the business of their purchases, were odious to the actual settlers, because, by thus buying up land, they threatened to maintain a wilderness round the clearings for years—a serious disadvantage to these already too solitary men. So much being premised, and with the additional knowledge that the backwoodsmen are generally very hospitable, the reader will apprehend the humour of the following sketch. It was at the height of the fever that Mr. Willoughby, a respectable-looking middle-aged man, riding a jaded horse, and carrying with him blankets, valise, saddle-bags, and holsters, stopped in front of a rough log-house, and accosted its tall and meagre tenant.]

THIS individual and his dwelling resembled each other in an unusual degree. The house was, as we have said, of the roughest; its ribs scarcely half filled in with clay; its "looped and windowed raggedness" rendered more conspicuous by the tattered cotton sheets which had long done duty as glass, and which now fluttered in every breeze; its roof of oak shingles, warped into every possible curve; and its stick chimney, so like its owner's hat, open at the top, and jammed in at the sides; all shadowed forth the contour and equipments of the exceedingly easy and self-satisfied person who leaned on the fence, and snapped his long cart-whip, while he gave such answers as suited him to the gentleman in the India-rubbers, taking especial care not to invite him to alight.

"Can you tell me, my friend,——" civilly began Mr. Willoughby.

"Oh! friend!" interrupted the settler; "who told you that I was your friend? Friends is scuss in these parts."

"You have at least no reason to be otherwise," replied the traveller, who was blessed with a very patient temper, especially where there was no use in getting angry.

"I don't know that," was the reply. "What fetch'd you into these woods?"

"If I should say 'my horse,' the answer would perhaps be as civil as the question."

"Jist as you like," said the other, turning on his heel, and walking off.

"I wished merely to ask you," resumed Mr. Willoughby, talking after the nonchalant son of the forest, "whether this is Mr. Pepper's land."

"How do you know it a'n't mine?"

"I'm not likely to know at present it seems," said the traveller, whose patience was getting a little frayed. And taking out his memorandum-book, he ran over his minutes: "South half of north-west quarter of section fourteen——Your name is Leander Pepper, is it not?"

"Where did you get so much news? You a'n't the sheriff, be ye?"

"Pop!" screamed a white-headed urchin from the house, "Mam says supper's ready."

"So a'n't I," replied the papa; "I've got all my chores to do yet." And he busied himself at a log pig-stye on the opposite side of the road, half as large as the dwelling-house. Here he was soon surrounded by a squealing multitude, with whom he seemed to hold a regular conversation.

Mr. Willoughby looked at the westering sun, which was not far above the dense wall of trees that shut in the small clearing; then at the heavy clouds which advanced from the north, threatening a stormy night; then at his watch, and then at his note-book; and after all, at his predicament—on the whole, an unpleasant prospect. But at this moment a female face showed itself at the door. Our traveller's memory reverted at once to the testimony of Ledyard and Mungo Park; and he had also some floating and indistinct poetical recollections of woman's being useful when a man was in difficulties, though hard to please at other times. The result of these reminiscences, which occupied a precious second, was, that Mr. Willoughby dismounted, fastened his horse to the fence, and advanced with a brave and determined air, to throw himself upon female kindness and sympathy.

He naturally looked at the lady, as he approached the door, but she did not return the compliment. She looked at the pigs, and talked to the children, and Mr. Willoughby had time to observe that she was the very duplicate of her husband; as tall, as bony, as ragged, and twice as cross-looking.

"Malviny Jane!" she exclaimed, in no dulcet treble, "be done a-paddlin' in that 'ere water! If I come there, I'll——"

"You'd better look at Sophrony, I guess!" was the reply.

"Why, what's she a-doin'?"

"Well, I guess if you look, you'll see!" responded Miss Malvina, coolly, as she passed into the house, leaving at every step a full impression of her foot in the same black mud that covered her sister from head to foot.

The latter was saluted with a hearty cuff, as she emerged from the puddle; and it was just at the propitious moment when her shrill howl aroused the echoes, that Mr. Willoughby, having reached the threshold, was obliged to set about making the agreeable to the mamma. And he called up for the occasion all his politeness.

"I believe I must become an intruder on your hospitality for the night, madam," he began. The dame still looked at the pigs. Mr. Willoughby tried again, in less courtly phrase.

"Will it be convenient for you to lodge me tonight, ma'am? I have been disappointed in my search for a hunting-party, whom I had engaged to meet, and the night threatens a storm."

"I don't know nothin' about it; you must ask the old man," said the lady, now for the first time taking a survey of the new comer; "with my will, we'll lodge nobody."

This was not very encouraging, but it was a poor night for the woods; so our traveller persevered, and making so bold a push for the door that

the lady was obliged to retreat a little, he entered, and said he would await her husband's coming.

And in truth he could scarcely blame the cool reception he had experienced, when he beheld the state of affairs within those muddy precincts. The room was large, but it swarmed with human beings. The huge open fire-place, with its hearth of rough stone, occupied nearly the whole of one end of the apartment; and near it stood a long cradle, containing a pair of twins, who cried—a sort of hopeless cry, as if they knew it would do no good, yet could not help it. The schoolmaster, (it was his week,) sat reading a tattered novel, and rocking the cradle occasionally, when the children cried too loud. An old gray-headed Indian was curiously crouched over a large tub, shelling corn on the edge of a hoe; but he ceased his noisy employment when he saw the stranger, for no Indian will ever willingly be seen at work, though he may be sometimes compelled by the fear of starvation or the longing for whisky, to degrade himself by labour. Near the only window was placed the work-bench and entire paraphernalia of the shoemaker, who in these regions travels from house to house, shoeing the family and mending the harness as he goes, with various interludes of songs and jokes, ever new and acceptable. This one, who was a little, bald, twinkling-eyed fellow, made the smoky rafters ring with the burden of that favourite ditty of the west:

"All kinds of game to hunt, my boys, also the buck and doe,
All down by the banks of the river O-hi-o ;"

and children of all sizes, clattering in all keys, completed the picture and the concert.

The supper-table, which maintained its place in the midst of this living and restless mass, might remind one of the square stone lying bedded in the bustling leaves of the acanthus; but the associations would be any but those of Corinthian elegance. The only object which at that moment diversified its dingy surface was an iron hoop, into which the mistress of the feast proceeded to turn a quantity of smoking hot potatoes, adding afterward a bowl of salt, and another of pork fat, by courtesy denominated gravy: plates and knives dropped in afterward, at the discretion of the company.

Another call of "Pop! pop!" brought in the host from the pig-stye; the heavy rain which had now begun to fall, having, no doubt, expedited the performance of the chores. Mr. Willoughby, who had established himself resolutely, took advantage of a very cloudy assent from the proprietor, to lead his horse to a shed, and to deposit in a corner his cumbrous outer gear; while the company used in turn the iron skillet which served as a wash basin, dipping the water from a large trough outside, overflowing with the abundant drippings of the eaves. Those who had no pocket handkerchiefs, contented themselves with a nondescript article which seemed to stand for the family towel; and when this ceremony was concluded, all seriously addressed themselves to the demolition of the potatoes. The grown people were accommodated with chairs and chests; the children prosecuted a series of flying raids upon the good cheer, snatching a potato now and then as they could find an opening under the raised arm of one of the family, and then retreating to the chimney corner, tossing the hot prize from hand to hand, and blowing it stoutly the while. The old Indian had disappeared.

To our citizen, though he felt inconveniently hungry, this primitive meal seemed a little meagre; and he ventured to ask if he could not be accommodated with some tea.

"A'n't my victuals good enough for you?"

"Oh!—the potatoes are excellent, but I am very fond of tea."

"So be I, but I can't have every thing I want—can you?"

This produced a laugh from the shoemaker, who seemed to think his patron very witty, while the schoolmaster, not knowing but the stranger might happen to be one of his examiners next year, produced only a faint giggle, and then reducing his countenance instantly to an awful gravity, helped himself to his seventh potato.

The rain which now poured violently, not only outside but through many a crevice in the roof, naturally kept Mr. Willoughby; and finding that dry potatoes gave him the hiccups, he withdrew from the table, and seating himself on the shoemaker's bench, took a survey of his quarters.

Two double beds and the long cradle seemed all the sleeping apparatus; but there was a ladder which doubtless led to a lodging above. The sides of the room were hung with abundance of decent clothing, and the dresser was well stored with the usual articles, among which a tea-pot and canister shone conspicuous; so that the appearance of inhospitality could not arise from poverty, and Mr. Willoughby concluded to set it down to the account of rustic ignorance.

The eating ceased not until the hoop was empty, and then the company rose and stretched themselves, and began to guess it was about time to go to bed. Mr. Willoughby inquired what was to be done with his horse.

"Well! I s'pose he can stay where he is."

"But what can he have to eat?"

"I reckon you won't get nothing for him, without you turn him out on the mash."

"He would get off to a certainty!"

"Tie his legs."

The unfortunate traveller argued in vain. Hay was "scuss," and potatoes were "scusser;" and in short the "mash" was the only resource, and these natural meadows afford but poor picking after the first of October. But to the "mash" was the good steed despatched, ingloriously hampered with the privilege of munching wild grass in the rain, after his day's journey.

Then came the question of lodging for his master. The lady, who had by this time drawn out a trundle-bed, and packed it full of children, said there was no bed for him, unless he could sleep "up chamber" with the boys.

Mr. Willoughby declared that he should make out very well with a blanket by the fire.

"Well! just as you like," said his host; "but

Solomon sleeps there, and if you like to sleep by Solomon, it is more than I should."

This was the name of the old Indian, and Mr. Willoughby once more cast woful glances toward the ladder.

But now the schoolmaster, who seemed rather disposed to be civil, declared that he could sleep very well in the long cradle, and would relinquish his place beside the shoemaker to the guest, who was obliged to content himself with this arrangement, which was such as was most usual in these times.

The storm continued through the night, and many a crash in the woods attested its power. The sound of a storm in the dense forest is almost precisely similar to that of a heavy surge breaking on a rocky beach; and when our traveller slept, it was only to dream of wreck and disaster at sea, and to wake in horror and affright. The wild rain drove in at every crevice, and wet the poor children in the loft so thoroughly, that they crawled shivering down the ladder, and stretched themselves on the hearth, regardless of Solomon, who had returned after the others were in bed.

But morning came at last; and our friend, who had no desire farther to test the vaunted hospitality of a western settler, was not among the latest astir. The storm had partially subsided; and although the clouds still lowered angrily, and his saddle had enjoyed the benefit of a leak in the roof during the night, Mr. Willoughby resolved to push on as far as the next clearing, at least, hoping for something for breakfast besides potatoes and salt. It took him a weary while to find his horse, and when he saddled him, and strapped on his various accoutrements, he entered the house, and inquired what he was to pay for his entertainment—laying somewhat of a stress on the last word.

His host, nothing daunted, replied that he guessed he would let him off for a dollar.

Mr. Willoughby took out his purse, and as he placed a silver dollar in the leathern palm outspread to receive it, happened to look toward the hearth, and perceiving the preparations for a very substantial breakfast, the long pent-up vexation burst forth.

"I really must say, Mr. Pepper——" he began: his tone was certainly that of an angry man, but it only made his host laugh.

"If this is your boasted western hospitality, I can tell you——"

"You'd better tell me what the dickens you are peppering me up this fashion for! My name isn't Pepper, no more than yours is! May be that is your name; you seem pretty warm."

"Your name not Pepper! Pray, what is it then?"

"Ah! there's the thing now! You land-hunters ought to know sich things without asking."

"Land-hunter! I'm no land-hunter!"

"Well! you're a land-shark, then—swallowin' up poor men's farms. The less I see of such cattle, the better I'm pleased."

"Confound you!" said Mr. Willoughby, who waxed warm, "I tell you I've nothing to do with land. I wouldn't take your whole state for a gift."

"What did you tell my woman you was a land-hunter for, then?"

And now the whole matter became clear in a moment; and it was found that Mr. Willoughby's equipment, with the mention of a "hunting-party," had completely misled both host and hostess. And to do them justice, never were regret and vexation more heartily expressed.

"You needn't judge our new country folks by me," said Mr. Handy, for such proved to be his name; "any man in these parts would as soon bite off his own nose, as to snub a civil traveller that wanted a supper and a night's lodging. But somehow or other, your lots o' fixin', and your askin' after that 'ere Pepper—one of the worst land-sharks we've ever had here—made me mad; and I know I treated you worse than an Indian."

"Humph!" said Solomon.

"But," continued the host, "you shall see whether my old woman can't set a good breakfast, when she's a mind to. Come, you shan't stir a step till you've had breakfast; and just 'take back this plaguey dollar. I wonder it did't burn my fingers when I took it."

Mrs. Handy set forth her very best, and a famous breakfast it was, considering the times. And before it was finished, the hunting party made their appearance, having had some difficulty in finding their companion, who had made no very uncommon mistake as to section corners and town-lines.

"I'll tell ye what," said Mr. Handy, confidentially, as the cavalcade with its baggage-ponies, loaded with tents, gun-cases, and hampers of provisions, was getting into order for a march to the prairies, "I'll tell ye what; if you've occasion to stop anywhere in the Bush, you'd better tell 'em at the first goin' off that you a'n't land-hunters."

But Mr. Willoughby had already had "a caution."

LAZY PEOPLE.
FROM THE SAME.

You may see him, if you are an early riser, setting off, at peep of dawn, on a fishing expedition. He winds through the dreary woods, yawning portentously, and stretching as if he were emulous of the height of the hickory trees. Dexterously swaying his long rod, he follows the little stream till it is lost in the bosom of the woodland lake; if unsuccessful from the bank, he seeks the frail skiff, which is the common property of laborious idlers like himself. and, pushing off shore, sits dreaming under the sun's wilting beams, until he has secured a supply for the day. Home again—an irregular meal at any time of day—and he goes to bed with the ague; but he murmurs not, for fishing is not work.....

Then come the whortleberries; not the little, stunted, seedy things that grow on dry uplands and sandy commons; but the produce of towering bushes in the plashy meadow; generous, pulpy berries, covered with a fine bloom; the "blae-berry" of Scotland; a delicious fruit, though of humble reputation, and, it must be confessed, somewhat enhanced in value by the scarcity of the more refined productions of the garden. We scorn thee not, oh! bloom-covered neighbour! but gladly buy whole bushels of thy prolific family from the lounging Indian, or the still lazier white man. We must not condemn the gatherers of whortleberries, but it is a melancholy truth that they do not get rich......

Baiting for wild bees beguiles the busy shunner of work into many a wearisome tramp, many a night-watch, and many a lost day. This is a most fascinating chase, and sometimes excites the very spirit of gambling. The stake seems so small in comparison with the possible prize—and gamblers and honey-seekers think all possible things probable—that some, who are scarcely ever tempted from regular business by any other disguise of idleness, cannot withstand a bee-hunt. A man whose arms and axe are all-sufficient to insure a comfortable livelihood for himself and his family, is chopping, perhaps, in a thick wood, where the voices of the locust, the cricket, the grasshopper, and the wild bee, with their kindred, are the only sounds that reach his ear from sunrise till sunset. He feels lonely and listless; and as noon draws on, he ceases from his hot toil, and, seating himself on the tree which has just fallen beneath his axe, he takes out his lunch of bread and butter, and, musing as he eats, thinks how hard his life is, and how much better it must be to have bread and butter without working for it. His eye wanders through the thick forest, and follows, with a feeling of envy, the winged inhabitants of the trees and flowers, till at length he notes among the singing throng some half dozen of bees.

The lunch is soon despatched; a honey tree must be near; and the chopper spends the remainder of the daylight in endeavouring to discover it. But the cunning insects scent the human robber, and will not approach their home until nightfall. So our weary wight plods homeward laying plans for their destruction.

The next morning's sun, as he peeps above the horizon, finds the bee-hunter burning honey-comb and old honey near the scene of yesterday's inkling. Stealthily does he watch his line of bait, and cautiously does he wait until the first glutton that finds himself sated with the luscious feast sets off in a "bee-line"—"like arrow darting from the bow"—blind betrayer of his home, like the human inebriate. This is enough. The spoiler asks no more; and the first moonlight night sees the rich hoard transferred to his cottage; where it sometimes serves, almost unaided, as food for the whole family, until the last drop is consumed. One hundred and fifty pounds of honey are sometimes found in a single tree, and it must be owned the temptation is great; but the luxury is generally dearly purchased, if the whole cost and consequences be counted. To be content with what supplies the wants of the body for the present moment, is, after all, the characteristic rather of the brute than of the man; and a family accustomed to this view of life will grow more and more idle and thriftless, until poverty and filth and even beggary lose all their terrors. It is almost proverbial among farmers that bee-hunters are always behindhand.

2 R

NATHANIEL HAWTHORNE.

[Born about 1807. Died 1864.]

THIS admirable author was born in Salem, Massachusetts, and is of a family which for several generations has "followed the sea." Among his ancestors, I believe, was the "bold Hawthorne" who is celebrated in a revolutionary ballad as commander of the "Fair American." He was educated at Bowdoin College in Maine, where he graduated in 1825. One of his classmates here was Mr. Longfellow.

In 1837 Mr. Hawthorne published the first and in 1842 the second volume of his Twice Told Tales, so named because they had previously appeared in the periodicals. In 1845 he edited The Journal of an African Cruiser, and in 1846 published Mosses from an Old Manse, a second collection of his magazine papers.

In the introduction to the last work he has given some delightful glimpses of his personal history. He had been several years in the Custom house at Boston, while Mr. Bancroft was collector, and afterward had joined that remarkable association, the "Brook Farm Community," at West Roxbury, where, with others, he appears to have been reconciled to the old ways, as quite equal to the inventions of Fourier, St Simon, Owen, and the rest of that ingenious company of schemers who have been so intent upon a reconstruction of the foundations of society. In 1843 he went to reside in the pleasant village of Concord, in the "Old Manse," which had never been profaned by a lay occupant until he entered it as his home. In the Introduction, to which allusion has been made, he says—

"A priest had built it; a priest had succeeded to it; other priestly men, from time to time, had dwelt in it; and children, born in its chambers, had grown up to assume the priestly character. It was awful to reflect how many sermons must have been written there. The latest inhabitant alone—he, by whose translation to Paradise the dwelling was left vacant—had penned nearly three thousand discourses, besides the better, if not the greater number, that gushed living from his lips. How often, no doubt, had he paced to and fro along the avenue, attuning his meditations, to the sighs and gentle murmurs, and deep and solemn peals of the wind, among the lofty tops of the trees! In that variety of natural utterances, he could find something accordant with every passage of his sermon, were it of tenderness or reverential fear. The boughs over my head seemed shadowy with solemn thoughts, as well as with rustling leaves. I took shame to myself for having been so long a writer of idle stories, and ventured to hope that wisdom would descend upon me with the falling leaves of the avenue; and that I should light upon an intellectual treasure in the Old Manse, well worth those hoards of long hidden gold,
470

which people seek for in moss-grown houses. Profound treatises of morality—a layman's unprofessional, and therefore unprejudiced views of religion;—histories (such as Bancroft might have written, had he taken up his abode here, as he once purposed), bright with picture, gleaming over a depth of philosophic thought,—these were the works that might fitly have flowed from such a retirement. In the humblest event, I resolved at least to achieve a novel, that should evolve some deep lesson, and should possess physical substance enough to stand alone. In furtherance of my design, and as if to leave me no pretext for not fulfilling it, there was, in the rear of the house, the most delightful little nook of a study that ever offered its snug seclusion to a scholar. It was here that Emerson wrote 'Nature;' for he was then an inhabitant of the Manse, and used to watch the Assyrian dawn and the Paphian sunset and moonrise, from the summit of our eastern hill. When I first saw the room, its walls were blackened with the smoke of unnumbered years, and made still blacker by the grim prints of puritan ministers that hung around. These worthies looked strangely like bad angels, or, at least, like men who had wrestled so continually and so sternly with the devil, that somewhat of his sooty fierceness had been imparted to their own visages. They had all vanished now; a cheerful coat of paint, and golden tinted paper hangings, lighted up the small apartment; while the shadow of a willow-tree, that swept against the overhanging eves, attempered the cheery Western sunshine. In place of the grim prints there was the sweet and lovely head of one of Raphael's Madonnas, and two pleasant little pictures of the Lake of Como. The only other decorations were a purple vase of flowers, always fresh, and a bronze one containing graceful ferns. My books (few, and by no means choice; for they were chiefly such walls as chance had thrown in my way) stood in order about the room, seldom to be disturbed."

In his home at Concord, thus happily described, in the midst of a few congenial friends, Hawthorne passed three years; and, "in a spot so sheltered from the turmoil of life's ocean," he says, "three years hasten away with a noiseless flight, as the breezy sunshine chases the cloud-shadows across the depths of a still valley." But at length his repose was invaded, by that "spirit of improvement," which is so constantly marring the happiness of quiet-loving people, and he was compelled to look out for another residence.

"Now came hints, growing more and more distinct, that the owner of the old house was pining for his native air. Carpenters next appeared, making a tremendous racket among the outbuildings, strewing green grass with pine shavings and chips of chestnut joists, and vexing the whole antiquity of the place with their discordant renovations. Soon, moreover, they divested our abode of the veil of woodbine which had crept over a large portion of its southern face. All the aged mosses were cleared unsparingly away; and there were horrible whispers about brushing up the external walls with a coat of paint—a purpose as little to my taste as might be that of rouging the venerable cheeks of one's grandmother. But the hand that renovates is always more sacrilegious than that which destroys. In fine, we gathered up our household goods, drank a farewell cup of tea in our pleasant little breakfast-room—delicately fragrant tea, an unpurchasable luxury, one of the many angel-gifts that had fallen like dew upon us—and passed forth between the tall stone gate-posts, as uncertain as the wandering Arabs where our tent might next be pitched. Providence took me by the hand, and—an oddity of dispensation which, I trust, there is no irreverence in smiling at—has led me, as the newspapers announce while I am writing, from the Old Manse into a Custom House! As a storyteller, I have often contrived strange vicissitudes for my imaginary personages, but none like this. The treasure of intellectual gold, which I had hoped to find in our secluded dwelling, had never come to light. No profound treatise of ethics—no philosophic history—no novel, even, that could stand unsupported on its edges—all that I had to show, as a man of letters, were these few tales and essays, which had blossomed out like flowers in the calm summer of my heart and mind."

The Mosses from an Old Manse he declares are the last offering of their kind it is his purpose ever to put forth, saying, modestly, "unless I could do better I have done enough in this kind." So will say no reader who can appreciate their grace and beauty, or the wisdom with which they are pervaded.

, The characteristics of Hawthorne which first arrest the attention are imagination and reflection, and these are exhibited in remarkable power and activity in tales and essays, of which the style is distinguished for great simplicity, purity and tranquillity. His beautiful story of Rappacini's Daughter was originally published in the Democratic Review, as a translation from the French of one M. de l'Aubepine, a writer whose very name, he remarks in a brief introduction, (in which he gives in French the titles of some of his tales, as *Contes deux foix racontées, Le Culte du Feu,* etc.) "is unknown to many of his countrymen, as well as to the student of foreign literature." He describes himself, under this *nomme de plume,* as one who—

"Seems to occupy an unfortunate position between the transcendentalists (who under one name or another have their share in all the current literature of the World), and the great body of pen-and-ink men who address the intellect and sympathies of the multitude. If not too refined, at all events too remote, too shadowy and unsubstantial, in his modes of development, to suit the taste of the latter class, and yet too popular to satisfy the spiritual or metaphysical requisitions of the former, he must necessarily find himself without an audience, except here and there an individual, or possibly an isolated clique."

His writings, to do them justice, he says—

"Are not altogether destitute of fancy and originality; they might have won him greater reputation but for an inveterate love of allegory, which is apt to invest his plots and characters with the aspect of scenery and people in the clouds, and to steal away the human warmth out of his conceptions. His fictions are sometimes historical, sometimes of the present day, and sometimes, so far as can be discovered, have little or no reference either to time or space. In any case he generally contents himself with a very slight embroidery of outward manners,—the faintest possible counterfeit of real life,—and endeavours to create an interest by some less obvious peculiarity of the subject. Occasionally a breath of nature, a rain-drop of pathos and tenderness, or a gleam of humour, will find its way into the midst of his fantastic imagery, and make us feel as if, after all, we were yet within the limits of our native earth. We will only add to this cursory notice, that M de l'Aubépine's productions, if the reader chance to take them in precisely the proper point of view, may amuse a leisure hour as well as those of a brighter man, if otherwise they can hardly fail to look excessively like nonsense."

Hawthorne is as accurately as he is happily described in this curious piece of criticism, though no one who takes his works in the "proper point of view," will by any means agree to the modest estimate which, in the perfect sincerity of his nature, he has placed upon them. He is original, in invention, construction, and expression, always picturesque, and sometimes in a high degree dramatic. His favourite scenes and traditions are those of his own country, many of which he has made classical by the beautiful associations that he has thrown around them. Every thing to him is suggestive, as his own pregnant pages are to the congenial reader. All his productions are life-mysteries, significant of profound truths. His speculations, often bold and striking, are presented with singular force, but with such a quiet grace and simplicity as not to startle until they enter in and occupy the mind. The gayety with which his pensiveness is occasionally broken, seems more than any thing else in his works to have cost some effort. The gentle sadness, the "half-acknowledged melancholy," of his manner and reflections, are more natural and characteristic.

His style is studded with the most poetical imagery, and marked in every part with the happiest graces of expression, while it is calm, chaste, and flowing, and transparent as water. There is a habit among nearly all the writers of imaginative literature, of adulterating the conversations of the poor with barbarisms and grammatical blunders which have no more fidelity than elegance. Hawthorne's integrity as well as his exquisite taste prevented him from falling into this error. There is not in the world a large rural population that speaks its native language with a purity approaching that with which the English is spoken by the common people of New England. The vulgar words and phrases which in other states are supposed to be peculiar to this part of the country are unknown east of the Hudson, except to the readers of foreign newspapers, or the listeners to low comedians who find it profitable to convey such novelties into Connecticut, Massachusetts, and Vermont. We are glad to see a book that is going down to the next ages as a representative of national manners and character in all respects correct.

—Since the above was written, Mr. Hawthorne has added to his fame by the publication of The Scarlet Letter, and The House of Seven Gables, which have confirmed his rank as one of the great masters in romantic art.

A RILL FROM THE TOWN PUMP.

FROM THRICE-TOLD TALES.

SCENE—*the corner of two principal streets. The* TOWN PUMP *talking through its nose.*)

Noon, by the north clock! Noon, by the east! High noon, too, by these hot sunbeams, which fall, scarcely aslope, upon my head, and almost make the water bubble and smoke, in the trough under my nose. Truly, we public characters have a tough time of it! And, among all the town officers, chosen at March meeting, where is he that sustains, for a single year, the burden of such manifold duties as are imposed, in perpetuity, upon the Town Pump? The title of "town treasurer" is rightfully mine, as guardian of the best treasure that the town has. The overseers of the poor ought to make me their chairman, since I provide bountifully for the pauper, without expense to him that pays taxes. I am at the head of the fire department, and one of the physicians to the board of health. As a keeper of the peace, all water-drinkers will confess me equal to the constable. I perform some of the duties of the town clerk, by promulgating public notices, when they are posted on my front. To speak within bounds, I am the chief person of the municipality, and exhibit, moreover, an admirable pattern to my brother officers, by the cool, steady, upright, downright, and impartial discharge of my business, and the constancy with which I stand to my post. Summer or winter, nobody seeks me in vain; for, all day long, I am seen at the busiest corner, just above the market, stretching out my arms, to rich and poor alike; and at night, I hold a lantern over my head, both to show where I am, and keep people out of the gutters.

At this sultry noontide, I am cupbearer to the parched populace, for whose benefit an iron goblet is chained to my waist. Like a dramseller on the mall, at muster day, I cry aloud to all and sundry, in my plainest accents, and at the very tiptop of my voice. Here it is, gentlemen! Here is the good liquor! Walk up, walk up, gentlemen, walk up, walk up! Here is the superior stuff! Here is the unadulterated ale of father Adam—better than Cognac, Hollands, Jamaica, strong beer, or wine of any price; here it is by the hogshead or the single glass, and not a cent to pay! Walk up, gentlemen, walk up, and help yourselves!

It were a pity, if all this outcry should draw no customers. Here they come. A hot day, gentlemen! Quaff, and away again, so as to keep yourselves in a nice cool sweat. You, my friend, will need another cup-full, to wash the dust out of your throat, if it be as thick there as it is on your cowhide shoes. I see that you have trudged half a score of miles to-day; and, like a wise man, have passed by the taverns, and stopped at the running brooks and well-curbs. Otherwise, betwixt heat without and fire within, you would have been burnt to a cinder, or melted down to nothing at all, in the fashion of a jelly-fish. Drink, and make room for that other fellow, who seeks my aid to quench the fiery fever of last night's potations, which he drained from no cup of mine. Welcome,

most robicund sir! You and I have been great strangers, hitherto; nor, to confess the truth, will my nose be anxious for a closer intimacy, till the fumes of your breath be a little less potent. Mercy on you, man! the water absolutely hisses down your red-hot gullet, and is converted quite to steam, in the miniature tophet, which you mistake for a stomach. Fill again, and tell me, on the word of an honest toper, did you ever, in cellar, tavern, or any kind of a dram-shop, spend the price of your children's food, for a swig half so delicious? Now, for the first time these ten years, you know the flavour of cold water. Good-by; and, whenever you are thirsty, remember that I keep a constant supply, at the old stand. Who next? Oh, my little friend, you are let loose from school, and come hither to scrub your blooming face, and drown the memory of certain taps of the ferule, and other schoolboy troubles, in a draught from the Town Pump. Take it, pure as the current of your young life. Take it, and may your heart and tongue never be scorched with a fiercer thirst than now! There, my dear child, put down the cup, and yield your place to this elderly gentleman, who treads so tenderly over the paving-stones, that I suspect he is afraid of breaking them. What! he limps by, without so much as thanking me, as if my hospitable offers were meant only for people who have no wine cellars. Well, well, sir—no harm done, I hope! Go draw the cork, tip the decanter; but, when your great toe shall set you a-roaring, it will be no affair of mine. If gentlemen love the pleasant titillation of the gout, it is all one to the Town Pump. This thirsty dog, with his red tongue lolling out, does not scorn my hospitality, but stands on his hind legs, and laps eagerly out of the trough. See how lightly he capers away again! Jowler, did your worship ever have the gout?

Are you all satisfied? Then wipe your mouths, my good friends; and, while my spout has a moment's leisure, I will delight the town with a few historical reminiscences. In far antiquity, beneath a darksome shadow of venerable boughs, a spring bubbled out of the leaf-strown earth, in the very spot where you now behold me, on the sunny pavement. The water was as bright and clear, and deemed as precious, as liquid diamonds. The Indian sagamores drank of it, from time immemorial, till the fatal deluge of the fire-water burst upon the red men, and swept their whole race away from the cold fountains. Endicott, and his followers, came next, and often knelt down to drink, dipping their long beards in the spring. The richest goblet, then, was of birch bark. Governor Winthrop, after a journey afoot from Boston, drank here, out of the hollow of his hand. The elder Higginson here wet his palm, and laid it on the brow of the first town-born child. For many years it was the watering-place, and, as it were, the wash-bowl of the vicinity—whither all decent folks resorted, to purify their visages, and gaze at them afterwards—at least the pretty maidens did—in the mirror which it made. On Sabbath days, whenever a babe was to be baptized, the sexton filled his basin here, and placed it on the communion-table of the humble meeting-house, which partly covered the site of yonder stately brick one. Thus, one generation after another was consecrated to Heaven by its waters, and cast their waxing and waning shadows into its glassy bosom, and vanished from the earth, as if mortal life were but a flitting image in a fountain. Finally, the fountain vanished also. Cellars were dug on all sides, and cart-loads of gravel flung upon its source, whence oozed a turbid stream, forming a mudpuddle, at the corner of two streets. In the hot months, when its refreshment was most needed, the dust flew in clouds over the forgotten birthplace of the waters, now their grave. But, in the course of time, a Town Pump was sunk into the source of the ancient spring; and when the first decayed, another took its place—and then another, and still another—till here stand I, gentlemen and ladies, to serve you with my iron goblet. Drink, and be refreshed! The water is pure and cold as that which slaked the thirst of the red sagamore, beneath the aged boughs, though now the gem of the wilderness is treasured under these hot stones, where no shadow falls, but from the brick buildings. And be it the moral of my story, that, as this wasted and long-lost fountain is now known and prized again, so shall the virtues of cold water, too little valued since your fathers' days, be recognised by all.

Your pardon, good people! I must interrupt my stream of eloquence, and spout forth a stream of water, to replenish the trough for this teamster and his two yoke of oxen, who have come from Topsfield, or somewhere along that way. No part of my business is pleasanter than the watering of cattle. Look! how rapidly they lower the watermark on the sides of the trough, till their capacious stomachs are moistened with a gallon or two apiece, and they can afford time to breathe it in, with sighs of calm enjoyment. Now they roll their quiet eyes around the brim of their monstrous drinking-vessel. An ox is your true toper.

But I perceive, my dear auditors, that you are impatient for the remainder of my discourse. Impute it, I beseech you, to no defect of modesty, if I insist a little longer on so fruitful a topic as my own multifarious merits. It is altogether for your good. The better you think of me, the better men and women will you find yourselves. I shall say nothing of my all-important aid on washing days; though, on that account alone, I might call myself the household god of a hundred families. Far be it from me also, to hint, my respectable friends, at the show of dirty faces, which you would present, without my pains to keep you clean. Nor will I remind you how often, when the midnight bells make you tremble for your combustible town, you have fled to the Town Pump, and found me always at my post, firm, amid the confusion, and ready to drain my vital current in your behalf. Neither is it worth while to lay much stress on my claims to a medical diploma, as the physician, whose simple rule of practice is preferable to all the nauseous lore which has found men sick or left them so, since the days of Hippocrates. Let us take a broader view of my beneficial influence on mankind.

No; these are trifles, compared with the merits which wise men concede to me—if not in my single self, yet as the representative of a class—of being the grand reformer of the age. From my spout, and such spouts as mine, must flow the stream, that shall cleanse our earth of the vast portion of its crime and anguish, which has gushed from the fiery fountains of the still. In this mighty enterprise, the cow shall be my great confederate. Milk and water! The Town Pump and the Cow! Such is the glorious copartnership, that shall tear down the distilleries and brewhouses, uproot the vineyards, shatter the cider-presses, ruin the tea and coffee trade, and, finally monopolize the whole business of quenching thirst. Blessed consummation! Then, Poverty shall pass away from the land, finding no hovel so wretched, where her squalid form may shelter itself. Then Disease, for lack of other victims, shall gnaw its own heart, and die. Then Sin, if she do not die, shall lose half her strength. Until now, the phrensy of hereditary fever shall have raged in the human blood, transmitted from sire to son, and rekindled, in every generation, by fresh draughts of liquid flame. When that inward fire shall be extinguished, the beat of passion cannot but grow cool, and war—the drunkenness of nations—perhaps will cease. At least, there will be no war of households. The husband and wife, drinking deep of peaceful joy—a calm bliss of temperate affections—shall pass hand in hand through life, and lie down, not reluctantly, at its protracted close. To them, the past will be no turmoil of mad dreams, nor the future an eternity of such moments as follow the delirium of the drunkard. Their dead faces shall express what their spirits were, and are to be, by a lingering smile of memory and hope.

Ahem! Dry work, this speechifying; especially to an unpractised orator. I never conceived, till now, what toil the temperance lecturers undergo for my sake. Hereafter, they shall have the business to themselves. Do, some kind Christian, pump a stroke or two, just to wet my whistle. Thank you, sir! My dear hearers, when the world shall have been regenerated, by my instrumentality, you will collect your useless vats and liquor casks into one great pile, and make a bonfire, in honour of the Town Pump. And, when I shall have decayed, like my predecessors, then, if you revere my memory, let a marble fountain, richly sculptured, take my place upon the spot. Such monuments should be erected everywhere, and inscribed with the names of the distinguished champions of my cause. Now listen; for something very important is to come next.

There are two or three honest friends of mine—and true friends, I know, they are—who, nevertheless, by their fiery pugnacity in my behalf, do put me in fearful hazard of a broken nose, or even a total overthrow upon the pavement, and the loss of the treasure which I guard. I pray you, gentlemen, let this fault be amended. Is it decent, think you, to get tipsy with zeal for temperance, and take up the honourable cause of the Town Pump, in the style of a toper, fighting for his brandy bottle?

Or, can the excellent qualities of cold water be no otherwise exemplified, than by plunging, slapdash, into hot water, and wofully scalding yourselves and other people? Trust me, they may. In the moral warfare, which you are to wage—and, indeed, in the whole conduct of your lives—you cannot choose a better example than myself, who have never permitted the dust and sultry atmosphere, the turbulence and manifold disquietudes of the world around me, to reach that deep, calm well of purity, which may be called my soul. And whenever I pour out that soul, it is to cool earth's fever, or cleanse its stains.

One o'clock! Nay, then, if the dinner-bell begins to speak, I may as well hold my peace. Here comes a pretty young girl of my acquaintance, with a large stone pitcher for me to fill. May she draw a husband, while drawing her water, as Rachel did of old. Hold out your vessel, my dear! There it is, full to the brim; so now run home, peeping at your sweet image in the pitcher, as you go; and forget not, in a glass of my own liquor, to drink— "Success to the Town Pump!"

——◆——

DAVID SWAN.—A FANTASY.

FROM THE SAME.

We can be but partially acquainted even with the events which actually influence our course through life, and our final destiny. There are innumerable other events, if such they may be called, which come close upon us, yet pass away without actual results, or even betraying their near approach, by the reflection of any light or shadow across our minds. Could we know all the vicissitudes of our fortunes, life would be too full of hope and fear, exultation or disappointment, to afford us a single hour of true serenity. This idea may be illustrated by a page from the secret history of David Swan.

We have nothing to do with David, until we find him, at the age of twenty, on the high road from his native place to the city of Boston, where his uncle, a small dealer in the grocery line, was to take him behind the counter. Be it enough to say, that he was a native of New Hampshire, born of respectable parents, and had received an ordinary school education, with a classic finish by a year at Gilmanton academy. After journeying on foot, from sunrise till nearly noon of a summer's day, his weariness and the increasing heat determined him to sit down in the first convenient shade, and await the coming up of the stage-coach. As if planted on purpose for him, there soon appeared a little tuft of maples, with a delightful recess in the midst, and such a fresh bubbling spring, that it seemed never to have sparkled for any wayfarer but David Swan. Virgin or not, he kissed it with his thirsty lips, and then flung himself along the brink, pillowing his head upon some shirts and a pair of pantaloons, tied up in a striped cotton handkerchief. The sunbeams could not reach him; the dust did not yet rise from the road, after the heavy rain of yesterday; and his grassy lair suited the young man better than a bed of down. The spring murmured drowsily beside him; the branches waved dreamily across the blue sky, overhead; and a deep sleep, perchance hiding dreams within its depths, fell upon David Swan. But we are to relate events which he did not dream of.

While he lay sound asleep in the shade, other people were wide awake, and passed to and fro, a-foot, on horseback, and in all sorts of vehicles, along the sunny road by his bedchamber. Some looked neither to the right hand nor the left, and knew not that he was there; some merely granted that way, without admitting the slumberer among their busy thoughts; some laughed to see how soundly he slept; and several, whose hearts were brimming full of scorn, ejected their venomous superfluity on David Swan. A middle-aged widow, when nobody else was near, thrust her head a little way into the recess, and vowed that the young fellow looked charming in his sleep. A temperance lecturer saw him, and wrought poor David into the texture of his evening's discourse, as an awful instance of dead drunkenness by the road-side. But, censure, praise, merriment, scorn, and indifference, were all one, or rather all nothing, to David Swan.

He had slept only a few moments, when a brown carriage, drawn by a handsome pair of horses, bowled easily along, and was brought to a standstill, nearly in front of David's resting-place. A linch-pin had fallen out, and permitted one of the wheels to slide off. The damage was slight, and occasioned merely a momentary alarm to an elderly merchant and his wife, who were returning to Boston in the carriage. While the coachman and a servant were replacing the wheel, the lady and gentleman sheltered themselves beneath the maple trees, and there espied the bubbling fountain, and David Swan asleep beside it. Impressed with the awe which the humblest sleeper usually sheds around him, the merchant trod as lightly as the gout would allow; and his spouse took good heed not to rustle her silk gown lest David should start up, all of a sudden.

"How soundly he sleeps!" whispered the old gentleman. "From what a depth he draws that easy breath! Such sleep as that brought on without an opiate, would be worth more to me than half my income; for it would suppose health, and an untroubled mind."

"And youth, besides," said the lady. "Healthy and quiet age does not sleep thus. Our slumber is no more like his than our wakefulness."

The longer they looked, the more did this elderly couple feel interested in the unknown youth, to whom the way-side and the maple shade were as a secret chamber, with the rich gloom of damask curtains brooding over him. Perceiving that a stray sunbeam glimmered down his face, the lady contrived to twist a branch aside, so as to intercept it. And having done this little act of kindness, she began to feel like a mother to him.

"Providence seems to have laid him here," whispered she to her husband, "and to have brought us hither to find him, after our disappointment in our cousin's son. Methinks I can see a likeness to our departed Henry. Shall we awaken him?"

"To what purpose?" said the merchant, hesitating. "We know nothing of the youth's character."

"That open countenance!" replied his wife, in the same hushed voice, yet earnestly. "This innocent sleep!"

While these whispers were passing, the sleeper's heart did not throb, nor his breath become agitated, nor his features betray the least token of interest. Yet Fortune was bending over him, just ready to let fall a burden of gold. The old merchant had lost his only son, and had no heir to his wealth, except a distant relative, with whose conduct he was dissatisfied. In such cases, people sometimes do stranger things than to act the magician, and awaken a young man to splendour, who fell asleep in poverty.

"Shall we not awaken him?" repeated the lady, persuasively.

"The coach is ready, sir," said the servant, behind.

The old couple started, reddened, and hurried away, mutually wondering, that they should ever have dreamed of doing any thing so very ridiculous. The merchant threw himself back in the carriage, and occupied his mind with the plan of a magnificent asylum for unfortunate men of business. Meanwhile, David Swan enjoyed his nap.

The carriage could not have gone above a mile or two, when a pretty young girl came along, with a tripping pace, which danced precisely how her little heart was dancing in her bosom. Perhaps it was this merry kind of motion that caused—is there any harm in saying it?—her garter to slip its knot. Conscious that the silken girth, if silk it were, was relaxing its hold, she turned aside into the shelter of the maple trees, and there found a young man asleep by the spring! Blushing, as red as any rose, that she should have intruded into a gentleman's bed-chamber, and for such a purpose too, she was about to make her escape on tiptoe. But, there was peril near the sleeper. A monster of a bee had been wandering overhead—buzz, buzz, buzz—now among the leaves, now flashing through the strips of sunshine, and now lost in the dark shade, till finally he appeared to be settling on the eyelid of David Swan. The sting of a bee is sometimes deadly. As free-hearted as she was innocent, the girl attacked the intruder with her handkerchief, brushed him soundly, and drove him from beneath the maple shade. How sweet a picture! This good deed accomplished, with quickened breath, and a deeper blush, she stole a glance at the youthful stranger, for whom she had been battling with a dragon in the air.

"He is handsome!" thought she, and blushed redder yet.

How could it be that no dream of bliss grew so strong within him, that, shattered by its very strength, it should part asunder, and allow him to perceive the girl among its phantoms? Why, at least, did no smile of welcome brighten upon his face? She was come, the maid whose soul, according to the old and beautiful idea, had been severed from his own, and whom, in all his vague but passionate desires, he yearned to meet. Her, only, could he love with perfect love—him, only, could she receive into the depths of her heart—and now her image was faintly blushing in the fountain, by his side; should it pass away, its happy lustre would never gleam upon his life again.

"How sound he sleeps!" murmured the girl.

She departed, but did not trip along the road so lightly as when she came.

Now, this girl's father was a thriving country merchant in the neighbourhood, and happened, at that identical time, to be looking out for just such a young man as David Swan. Had David formed a way-side acquaintance with the daughter, he would have become the father's clerk, and all else in natural succession. So here, again, had good fortune—the best of fortunes—stolen so near, that her garments brushed against him; and he knew nothing of the matter.

The girl was hardly out of sight, when two men turned aside beneath the maple shade. Both had dark faces, set off by cloth caps, which were drawn down aslant over their brows. Their dresses were shabby, yet had a certain smartness. These were a couple of rascals, who got their living by whatever the devil sent them, and now, in the interim of other business, had staked the joint profits of their next piece of villany on a game of cards, which was to have been decided here under the trees. But, finding David asleep by the spring, one of the rogues whispered to his fellow—

"Hist!—Do you see that bundle under his head?"

The other villain nodded, winked, and leered.

"I'll bet you a horn of brandy," said the first, "that the chap has either a pocketbook, or a snug little hoard of small change, stowed away amongst his shirts. And if not there, we shall find it in his pantaloons' pocket."

"But how if he wakes?" said the other.

His companion thrust aside his waistcoat, pointed to the handle of a dirk, and nodded.

"So be it!" muttered the second villain.

They approached the unconscious David, and, while one pointed the dagger toward his heart, the other began to search beneath the bundle his head. Their two faces, grim, wrinkled, and ghastly with guilt and fear, bent over their victim, looking horrible enough to be mistaken for fiends, should he suddenly awake. Nay, had the villains glanced aside into the spring, even they would hardly have known themselves, as reflected there. But David Swan had never worn a more tranquil aspect, even when asleep on his mother's breast.

"I must take away the bundle," whispered one.

"If he stirs, I'll strike," muttered the other.

But, at this moment, a dog, scenting along the ground, came in beneath the maple trees, and gazed alternately at each of these wicked men, and then at the quiet sleeper. He then lapped out of the fountain.

"Pshaw!" said one villain. "We can do nothing now. The dog's master must be close behind."

"Let's take a drink, and be off," said the other.
The man, with the dagger, thrust back the weapon into his bosom, and drew forth a pocket-pistol, but not of that kind which kills by a single discharge. It was a flask of liquor, with a block-tin tumbler screwed upon the mouth. Each drank a comfortable dram, and left the spot, with so many jests, and such laughter at their unaccomplished wickedness, that they might be said to have gone on their way rejoicing. In a few hours, they had for-gotten the whole affair, nor once imagined that the recording angel had written down the crime of mur-der against their souls, in letters as durable as eter-nity. As for David Swan, he still slept quietly, neither conscious of the shadow of death when it hung over him, nor of the glow of renewed life, when that shadow was withdrawn.

He slept, but no longer so quietly as at first. An hour's repose had snatched, from his elastic frame, the weariness with which many hours of toil had burdened it. Now, he stirred—now, moved his lips, without a sound—now, talked, in an in-ward tone, to the noonday spectres of his dream. But a noise of wheels came rattling louder and louder along the road, until it dashed through the dispersing mist of David's slumber—and there was the stage-coach. He started up, with all his ideas about him.

"Halloo, driver!—Take a passenger?" shouted he.

"Room on top!" answered the driver.

Up mounted David, and bowled away merrily toward Boston, without so much as a parting glance at that fountain of dreamlike vicissitude. He knew not that a phantom of Wealth had thrown a golden hue upon its waters—nor that one of Love had sighed softly through their murmur—nor that one of Death had threatened to crimson them with his blood—all, in the brief hour since he lay down to sleep. Sleeping or waking, we hear not the airy footsteps of the strange things that almost happen. Does it not argue a superintending Providence, that, while viewless and unexpected events thrust themselves continually athwart our path, there should still be regularity enough, in mortal life, to render foresight even partially available?

THE CELESTIAL RAILROAD.

FROM MOSSES FROM AN OLD MANSE.

NOT a great while ago, passing through the gate of dreams, I visited that region of the earth in which lies the famous city of Destruction. It in-terested me much to learn that, by the public spirit of some of the inhabitants, a railroad has recently been established between this populous and flou-rishing town, and the Celestial City. Having a little time upon my hands, I resolved to gratify a liberal curiosity to make a trip thither. Accord-ing-ly, one fine morning, after paying my bill at the hotel, and directing the porter to stow my luggage behind a coach, I took my seat in the vehicle and set out for the Station-house. It was my good for-tune to enjoy the company of gentlemen—one Mr. Smooth-it-away—who, though he had never actu-ally visited the Celestial City, yet seemed as well acquainted with its laws, customs, policy, and sta-tistics, as with those of the city of Destruction, of which he was a native townsman. Being, more-over, a director of the railroad corporation, and one of its largest stockholders, he had it in his power to give me all desirable information respecting that praiseworthy enterprise.

Our coach rattled out of the city, and at a short distance from its outskirts, passed over a bridge, of elegant construction, but somewhat too slight, as I imagined, to sustain any considerable weight. On both sides lay an extensive quagmire, which could not have been more disagreeable either to sight or smell, had all the kennels of the earth emptied their pollution there.

"This," remarked Mr. Smooth-it-away, "is the famous Slough of Despond—a disgrace to all the neighbourhood; and the greater, that it might so easily be converted into firm ground."

"I have understood," said I, "that efforts have been made for that purpose, from time immemorial. Bunyan mentions that above twenty thousand cart-loads of wholesome instructions had been thrown in here, without effect."

"Very probably!—and what effect could be an-ticipated from such unsubstantial stuff?" cried Mr. Smooth-it-away. "You observe this convenient bridge. We obtained a sufficient foundation for it by throwing into the Slough some editions of books of morality, volumes of French philosophy and German rationalism, tracts, sermons, and essays of modern clergymen, extracts from Plato, Confu-cius, and various Hindoo sages, together with a few ingenious commentaries upon texts of Scrip-ture—all of which, by some scientific process, have been converted into a mass like granite. The whole bog might be filled up with similar matter."

It really seemed to me, however, that the bridge vibrated and heaved up and down in a very formi-dable manner; and, in spite of Mr. Smooth-it-away's testimony to the solidity of its foundation, I should be loth to cross it in a crowded omnibus; especially, if each passenger were encumbered with as heavy luggage as that gentleman and myself. Nevertheless, we got over without accident, and soon found ourselves at the Station-house. This very neat and spacious edifice is erected on the site of the little Wicket-Gate, which formerly, as all old pilgrims will recollect, stood directly across the highway, and, by its inconvenient narrowness, was a great obstruction to the traveller of liberal mind and expansive stomach. The reader of John Bun-yan will be glad to know, that Christian's old friend Evangelist, who was accustomed to supply each pilgrim with a mystic roll, now presides at the ticket office. Some malicious persons, it is true, deny the identity of this reputable character with the Evangelist of old times, and even pretend to bring competent evidence of an imposture. Without in-volving myself in a dispute, I shall merely observe, that, so far as my experience goes, the square pieces of pasteboard, now delivered to passengers, are much more convenient and useful along the road, than the antique roll of parchment. Whether they will be as readily received at the gate of the Celestial City, I decline giving an opinion.

A large number of passengers were already at the Station-house, awaiting the departure of the cars. By the aspect and demeanour of these persons, it was easy to judge that the feelings of the community had undergone a very favourable change, in reference to the celestial pilgrimage. It would have done Bunyan's heart good to see it. Instead of a lonely and ragged man, with a huge burden on his back, plodding along sorrowfully on foot, while the whole city hooted after him, here were parties of the first gentry and most respectable people in the neighbourhood, setting forth toward the Celestial City, as cheerfully as if the pilgrimage were merely a summer tour. Among the gentlemen were characters of deserved eminence, magistrates, politicians, and men of wealth, by whose example religion could not but be greatly recommended to their meaner brethren. In the ladies' apartment, too, I rejoiced to distinguish some of those flowers of fashionable society, who are so well fitted to adorn the most elevated circles of the Celestial City. There was much pleasant conversation about the news of the day, topics of business, politics, or the lighter matters of amusement; while religion, though indubitably the main thing at heart, was thrown tastefully into the back-ground. Even an infidel would have heard little or nothing to shock his sensibility.

One great convenience of the new method of going on pilgrimage, I must not forget to mention. Our enormous burdens, instead of being carried on our shoulders, as had been the custom of old, were all snugly deposited in the baggage-car, and, as I was assured, would be delivered to their respective owners at the journey's end. Another thing, likewise, the benevolent reader will be delighted to understand. It may be remembered that there was an ancient feud, between Prince Beelzebub and the keeper of the Wicket-Gate, and that the adherents of the former distinguished personage were accustomed to shoot deadly arrows at honest pilgrims, while knocking at the door. This dispute, much to the credit as well of the illustrious potentate above-mentioned, as of the worthy and enlightened Directors of the railroad, has been pacifically arranged, on the principle of mutual compromise. The Prince's subjects are now pretty numerously employed about the Station-house, some in taking care of the baggage, others in collecting fuel, feeding the engines, and such congenial occupations; and I can conscientiously affirm, that persons more attentive to their business, more willing to accommodate, or more generally agreeable to the passengers, are not to be found on any railroad. Every good heart must surely exult at so satisfactory an arrangement of an immemorial difficulty.

"Where is Mr. Great-heart?" inquired I. "Beyond a doubt, the Directors have engaged that famous old champion to be chief conductor on the railroad?"

"Why, no," said Mr. Smooth-it-away, with a dry cough. "He was offered the situation of brakeman; but, to tell you the truth, our friend Great-heart has grown preposterously stiff and narrow in his old age. He has so often guided pilgrims over the road, on foot, that he considers it a sin to travel in any other fashion. Besides, the old fellow had entered so heartily into the ancient feud with Prince Beelzebub, that he would have been perpetually at blows or ill language with some of the prince's subjects, and thus have embroiled us anew. So, on the whole, we were not sorry when honest Great-heart went off to the Celestial City, in a huff, and left us at liberty to choose a more suitable and accommodating man. Yonder comes the conductor of the train. You will probably recognise him at once."

The engine at this moment took its station in advance of the cars, looking, I must confess, much more like a sort of mechanical demon that would hurry us to the infernal regions, than a laudable contrivance for smoothing our way to the Celestial City. On its top sat a personage almost enveloped in smoke and flame, which—not to startle the reader—appeared to gush from his own mouth and stomach, as well as from the engine's brazen abdomen.

"Do my eyes deceive me?" cried I. "What on earth is this! A living creature?—if so, he is own brother to the engine he rides upon!"

"Poh, poh, you are obtuse!" said Mr. Smooth-it-away, with a hearty laugh. "Don't you know Apollyon, Christian's old enemy, with whom he fought so fierce a battle in the Valley of Humiliation? He was the very fellow to manage the engine; and so we have reconciled him to the custom of going on pilgrimage, and engaged him as chief conductor."

"Bravo, bravo!" exclaimed I, with irrepressible enthusiasm, "this shows the liberality of the age; this proves, if any thing can, that all musty prejudices are in a fair way to be obliterated. And how will Christian rejoice to hear of this happy transformation of his old antagonist! I promise myself great pleasure in informing him of it, when we reach the Celestial City."

The passengers being all comfortably seated, we now rattled away merrily, accomplishing a greater distance in ten minutes than Christian probably trudged over in a day. It was laughable while we glanced along, as it were, at the tail of a thunderbolt, to observe two dusty foot-travellers, in the old pilgrim-guise, with cockle-shell and staff, their mystic rolls of parchment in their hands, and their intolerable burdens on their backs. The preposterous obstinacy of these honest people, in persisting to groan and stumble along the difficult pathway, rather than take advantage of modern improvements, excited great mirth among our wiser brotherhood. We greeted the two pilgrims with many pleasant gibes and a roar of laughter; whereupon, they gazed at us with such woful and absurdly compassionate visages, that our merriment grew tenfold more obstreperous. Apollyon, also, entered heartily into the fun, and contrived to flirt the smoke and flame of the engine, or of his own breath, into their faces, and envelope them in an atmosphere of scalding steam. These little practical jokes amused us mightily, and doubtless afforded the pilgrims the gratification of considering themselves martyrs.

At some distance from the railroad, Mr. Smooth-it-away pointed to a large, antique edifice, which, he observed, was a tavern of long standing, and had formerly been a noted stopping-place for pilgrims. In Bunyan's road-book it is mentioned as the Interpreter's House.

"I have long had a curiosity to visit that old mansion," remarked I.

"It is not one of our stations, as you perceive," said my companion. "The keeper was violently opposed to the railroad; and well he might be, as the track left his house of entertainment on one side, and thus was pretty certain to deprive him of all his reputable customers. But the foot-path still passes his door; and the old gentleman now and then receives a call from some simple traveller, and entertains him with fare as old-fashioned as himself."

Before our talk on this subject came to a conclusion, we were rushing by the place where Christian's burden fell from his shoulders, at the sight of the Cross. This served as a theme for Mr. Smooth-it-away, Mr. Live-for-the-world, Mr. Hide-sin-in-the-heart, Mr. Scaly-conscience, and a knot of gentlemen from the town of Shun-repentance, to descant upon the inestimable advantages resulting from the safety of our baggage. Myself, and all the passengers indeed, joined with great unanimity in this view of the matter; for our burdens were rich in many things esteemed precious throughout the world; and especially we each of us possessed a great variety of favourite Habits, which we trusted would not be out of fashion, even in the polite circles of the Celestial City. It would have been a sad spectacle to see such an assortment of valuable articles tumbling into the sepulchre. Thus pleasantly conversing on the favourable circumstances of our position, as compared with those of past pilgrims, and of narrow-minded ones at the present day, we soon found ourselves at the foot of the Hill of Difficulty. Through the very heart of this rocky mountain a tunnel has been constructed, of most admirable architecture, with a lofty arch and a spacious double-track; so that, unless the earth and rocks chance to crumble down, it will remain an eternal monument of the builder's skill and enterprise. It is a great though incidental advantage, that the materials from the heart of the Hill of Difficulty have been employed in filling up the Valley of Humiliation; thus obviating the necessity of descending into that disagreeable and unwholesome hollow.

"This is a wonderful improvement, indeed," said I. "Yet I should have been glad of an opportunity to visit the Palace Beautiful, and be introduced to the charming young ladies—Miss Prudence, Miss Piety, Miss Charity, and the rest—who have the kindness to entertain pilgrims there."

"Young ladies!" cried Mr. Smooth-it-away, as soon as he could speak for laughing. "And charming young ladies! Why, my dear fellow, they are old maids, every soul of them—prim, starched, dry, and angular—and not one of them, I will venture to say, has altered so much as the fashion of her gown since the days of Christian's pilgrimage."

"Ah, well," said I, much comforted, "then I can very readily dispense with their acquaintance."

The respectable Apollyon was now putting on the steam at a prodigious rate; anxious, perhaps, to get rid of the unpleasant reminiscences connected with the spot where he had so disastrously encountered Christian. Consulting Mr. Bunyan's road-book, I perceived that we must now be within a few miles of the Valley of the Shadow of Death; into which doleful region, at our present speed, we should plunge much sooner than seemed at all desirable. In truth, I expected nothing better than to find myself in the ditch on one side, or the quag on the other. But on communicating my apprehensions to Mr. Smooth-it-away, he assured me that the difficulties of this passage, even in its worst condition, had been vastly exaggerated, and that, in its present state of improvement, I might consider myself as safe as on any railroad in Christendom.

Even while we were speaking, the train shot into the entrance of this dreaded Valley. Though I plead guilty to some foolish palpitations of the heart, during our headlong rush over the causeway here constructed, yet it were unjust to withhold the highest encomiums on the boldness of its original conception, and the ingenuity of those who executed it. It was gratifying, likewise, to observe how much care had been taken to dispel the everlasting gloom, and supply the defect of cheerful sunshine; not a ray of which has ever penetrated among these awful shadows. For this purpose, the inflammable gas, which exudes plentifully from the soil, is collected by means of pipes, and thence communicated to a quadruple row of lamps, along the whole extent of the passage. Thus a radiance has been created, even out of the fiery and sulphurous curse that rests for ever upon the Valley; a radiance hurtful, however, to the eyes, and somewhat bewildering, as I discovered by the changes which it wrought in the visages of my companions. In this respect, as compared with natural daylight, there is the same difference as between truth and falsehood; but if the reader have ever travelled through the dark Valley, he will have learned to be thankful for any light that he could get; if not from the sky above, then from the blasted soil beneath. Such was the red brilliancy of these lamps, that they appeared to build walls of fire on both sides of the track, between which we held our course of lightning speed, while a reverberating thunder filled the Valley with its echoes. Had the engine run off the track—a catastrophe, it is whispered, by no means unprecedented—the bottomless pit, if there be any such a place, would undoubtedly have received us. Just as some dismal fooleries of this nature had made my heart quake, there came a tremendous shriek, careering along the Valley as if a thousand devils had burst their lungs to utter it, but which proved to be merely the whistle of the engine, on arriving at a stopping-place.

The spot, where we had now paused, is the same that our friend Bunyan—truthful man, but infected with many fantastic notions—has designated, in terms plainer than I like to repeat, as the mouth of the infernal region. This, however, must be a mistake; inasmuch as Mr. Smooth-it-away, while he remained in the smoky and lurid cavern, took occasion to prove that Tophet has not even a metaphorical existence. The place, he assured us, is no other than the crater of a half-extinct volcano, in which the Directors had caused forges to be set up, for the manufacture of railroad iron. Hence, also, is obtained a plentiful supply of fuel for the use of the engines. Whoever has gazed into the dismal obscurity of the broad cavern-mouth, whencever and anon darted huge tongues of dusky flame,—and had seen the strange, half-shaped monsters, and visions of faces horribly grotesque, into which the smoke seemed to wreathe itself,—and had heard the awful murmurs, and shrieks, and deep shuddering whispers of the blast, sometimes forming themselves into words almost articulate,—would have seized upon Mr. Smooth-it-away's comfortable explanation, as greedily as we did. The inhabitants of the cavern, moreover, were unlovely personages, dark, smoke-begrimed, generally deformed, with mis-shapen feet, and a glow of dusky redness in their eyes; as if their hearts had caught fire, and were blazing out of the upper windows. It struck me as a peculiarity, that the labourers at the forge, and those who brought fuel to the engine, when they began to draw short breath, positively emitted smoke from their mouth and nostrils.

Among the idlers about the train, most of whom were puffing cigars which they had lighted at the flame of the crater, I was perplexed to notice several who, to my certain knowledge, had heretofore set forth by railroad for the Celestial City. They looked dark, wild, and smoky, with a singular resemblance, indeed, to the native inhabitants; like whom, also, they had a disagreeable propensity to ill-natured gibes and sneers, the habit of which had wrought a settled contortion of their visages. Having been on speaking terms with one of these persons—an indolent, good-for-nothing fellow, who went by the name of Take-it-easy—I called him, and inquired what was his business there.

"Did you not start," said I, "for the Celestial City?"

"That's a fact," said Mr. Take-it-easy, carelessly puffing some smoke into my eyes. "But I heard such bad accounts, that I never took pains to climb the hill, on which the city stands. No business doing—no fun going on—nothing to drink, and no smoking allowed—and a thrumming of church-music from morning till night! I would not stay in such a place, if they offered me houseroom and living free."

"But, my good Mr. Take-it-easy,' cried I, "why take up your residence here, of all places in the world?"

"Oh," said the loafer, with a grin, "it is very warm hereabouts, and I meet with plenty of old acquaintances, and altogether the place suits me.

I hope to see you back again, some day soon. A pleasant journey to you!"

While he was speaking, the bell of the engine rang, and we dashed away, after dropping a few passengers, but receiving no new ones. Rattling onward through the Valley, we were dazzled with the fiercely gleaming gas-lamps as before. But sometimes, in the dark of intense brightness, grim faces, that bore the aspect and expression of individual sins, or evil passions, seemed to thrust themselves through the veil of light, glaring upon us, and stretching forth a great dusky hand, as if to impede our progress. I almost thought, that they were my own sins that appalled me there. These were freaks of imagination—nothing more, certainly,—mere delusions, which I ought to be heartily ashamed of—but, all through the Dark Valley, I was tormented, and pestered, and dolefully bewildered, with the same kind of waking dreams. The mephitic gases of that region intoxicate the brain. As the light of natural day, however, began to struggle with the glow of the lanterns, these vain imaginations lost their vividness, and finally vanished with the first ray of sunshine that greeted our escape from the Valley of the Shadow of Death. Ere we had gone a mile beyond it, I could well-nigh have taken my oath, that this whole gloomy passage was a dream.

At the end of the Valley, as John Bunyan mentions, is a cavern, where, in his days, dwelt two cruel giants, Pope and Pagan, who had strewn the ground about their residence with the bones of slaughtered pilgrims. These vile old troglodytes are no longer there; but in their deserted cave another terrible giant has thrust himself, and makes it his business to seize upon honest travellers, and fat them for his table with plentiful meals of smoke, mist, moonshine, raw potatoes, and saw-dust. He is a German by birth, and is called Giant Transcendentalist; but as to his form, his features, his substance, and his nature generally, it is the chief peculiarity of this huge miscreant, that neither he for himself, nor anybody for him, has ever been able to describe them. As we rushed by the cavern's mouth, we caught a hasty glimpse of him, looking somewhat like an ill-proportioned figure, but considerably more like a heap of fog and duskiness. He shouted after us, but in so strange a phraseology, that we knew not what he meant, nor whether to be encouraged or affrighted.

It was late in the day, when the train thundered into the ancient city of Vanity, where Vanity Fair is still at the height of prosperity, and exhibits an epitome of whatever is brilliant, gay, and fascinating, beneath the sun. As I purposed to make a considerable stay here, it gratified me to learn that there is no longer the want of harmony between the townspeople and pilgrims, which impelled the former to such lamentably mistaken measures as the persecution of Christian, and the fiery martyrdom of Faithful. On the contrary, as the new railroad brings with it great trade and a constant influx of strangers, the lord of Vanity Fair is its chief patron, and the capitalists of the city are among the largest stockholders. Many passen

gers stop to take their pleasure or make their profit in the Fair, instead of going onward to the Celestial City. Indeed, such are the charms of the
place, that people often affirm it to be the true and
only heaven; stoutly contending that there is no
other, that those who seek further are mere dreamers, and that, if the fabled brightness of the Celestial City lay but a bare mile beyond the gates of
Vanity, they would not be fools enough to go
thither. Without subscribing to these, perhaps,
exaggerated encomiums, I can truly say, that my
abode in the city was mainly agreeable, and my
intercourse with the inhabitants productive of much
amusement and instruction.

Being naturally of a serious turn, my attention
was directed to the solid advantages derivable from
a residence here, rather than to the effervescent
pleasures, which are the grand object with too many
visitants. The Christian reader, if he have had
no accounts of the city later than Bunyan's time,
will be surprised to hear that almost every street
has its church, and that the reverend clergy are
nowhere held in higher respect than at Vanity
Fair. And well do they deserve such honourable
estimation; for the maxims of wisdom and virtue
which fall from their lips, come from as deep a
spiritual source, and tend to as lofty a religious aim,
as those of the sagest philosophers of old. In justification of this high praise, I need only mention
the names of the Rev. Mr. Shallow-deep; the Rev.
Mr. Stumble-at-Truth; that fine old clerical character, the Rev. Mr. This-to-day, who expects shortly to resign his pulpit to the Rev. Mr. That-to-mor-
row; together with the Rev. Mr. Bewilderment;
the Rev. Mr. Clog-the-spirit; and, last and greatest, the Rev. Dr. Wind-of-doctrine. The labours
of these eminent divines are aided by those of innumerable lecturers, who diffuse such a various
profundity, in all subjects of human or celestial
science, that any man may acquire an omnigenous
erudition, without the trouble of even learning to
read. Thus literature is etherealized by assuming
for its medium the human voice; and knowledge,
depositing all its heavier particles—except, doubtless, its gold—becomes exhaled into a sound, which
forthwith steals into the ever-open ear of the community. These ingenious methods constitute a sort
of machinery, by which thought and study are done
to every person's hand, without his putting himself
to the slightest inconvenience in the matter. There
is another species of machine for the wholesale
manufacture of individual morality. This excellent result is effected by societies for all manner of
virtuous purposes; with which a man has merely
to connect himself, throwing, as it were, his quota
of virtue into the common hoard; and the president and directors will take care that the aggregate
amount be well applied. All these, and other wonderful improvements in ethics, religion, and literature, being made plain to my comprehension, by
the ingenious Mr. Smooth-it-away, inspired me
with a vast admiration of Vanity Fair.

It would fill a volume, in an age of pamphlets,
were I to record all my observations in this great
capital of human business and pleasure. There

was an unlimited range of society—the powerful,
the wise, the witty, and the famous in every walk of
life—princes, presidents, poets, generals, artists, actors, and philanthropists, all making their own market at the Fair, and deeming no price too exorbitant
for such commodities as hit their fancy. It is well
worth one's while, even if he had no idea of buying or selling, to loiter through the bazaars, and
observe the various sorts of traffic that were going
forward.

Some of the purchasers, I thought, made very
foolish bargains. For instance, a young man having inherited a splendid fortune, laid out a considerable portion of it in the purchase of diseases,
and finally spent all the rest for a heavy lot of repentance and a suit of rags. A very pretty girl
bartered a heart as clear as crystal, and which
seemed her most valuable possession, for another
jewel of the same kind, but so worn and defaced
as to be utterly worthless. In one shop, there
were a great many crowns of laurel and myrtle,
which soldiers, authors, statesmen, and various
other people, pressed eagerly to buy; some purchased these paltry wreaths with their lives; others
by a toilsome servitude of years; and many sacrificed whatever was most valuable, yet finally slunk
away without the crown. There was a sort of
stock or scrip, called Conscience, which seemed to
be in great demand, and would purchase almost
any thing. Indeed, few rich commodities were to
be obtained without paying a heavy sum in this particular stock, and a man's business was seldom very
lucrative, unless he knew precisely when and how
to throw his hoard of Conscience into the market.
Yet as this stock was the only thing of permanent
value, whoever parted with it was sure to find himself a loser, in the long run. Several of the speculations were of a questionable character. Occasionally, a member of Congress recruited his
pocket by the sale of his constituents; and I was
assured that public officers have often sold their
country at a very moderate price. Thousands sold
their happiness for a whim. Gilded chains were in
great demand, and purchased at almost any sacrifice.
In truth, those who desired, according to the old
adage, to sell any thing valuable for a song, might
find customers all over the Fair; and there were
innumerable messes of pottage, piping hot, for such
as chose to buy them with their birthrights. A
few articles, however, could not be found genuine
at the Vanity Fair. If a customer wished to renew his stock of youth, the dealers offered him a
set of false teeth and an auburn wig; if he demanded peace of mind, they recommended opium
or a brandy-bottle.

Tracts of land and golden mansions, situate in
the Celestial City, were often exchanged, at very
disadvantageous rates, for a few years' lease of
small, dismal, inconvenient tenements in Vanity
Fair. Prince Beelzebub himself took great interest in this sort of traffic, and sometimes condescended to meddle with smaller matters. I once
had the pleasure to see him bargaining with a miser
for his soul, which, after much ingenious skirmish-
ing on both sides, his Highness succeeded in ob-

taining at about the value of sixpence. The prince remarked, with a smile, that he was loser by the transaction.

Day after day, as I walked the streets of Vanity, my manners and deportment became more and more like those of the inhabitants. The place began to seem like home ; the idea of pursuing my travels to the Celestial City was almost obliterated from my mind. I was reminded of it, however, by the sight of the same pair of simple pilgrims at whom we had laughed so heartily, when Apollyon puffed smoke and steam into their faces, at the commencement of our journey. There they stood amid the densest bustle of Vanity—the dealers offering them their purple, and fine linen, and jewels; the men of wit and humour gibing at them; a pair of buxom ladies ogling them askance ; while the benevolent Mr. Smooth-it-away whispered some of his wisdom at their elbows, and pointed to a newly-erected temple,—but there were these worthy simpletons, making the scene look wild and monstrous, merely by their sturdy repudiation of all part in its business or pleasures.

One of them—his name was Stick-to-the-right—perceived in my face, I suppose, a species of sympathy and almost admiration, which, to my own great surprise, I could not help feeling for this pragmatic couple. It prompted him to address me.

"Sir," inquired he, with a sad, yet mild and kindly voice, "do you call yourself a pilgrim?"

"Yes," I replied, "my right to that appellation is indubitable. I am merely a sojourner here in Vanity Fair, being bound to the Celestial City by the new railroad."

"Alas, friend," rejoined Mr. Stick-to-the-right, "I do assure you, and beseech you to receive the truth of my words, that that whole concern is a bubble. You may travel on it all your lifetime, were you to live thousands of years, and yet never get beyond the limits of Vanity Fair! Yea; though you should deem yourself entering the gates of the Blessed City, it will be nothing but a miserable delusion."

"The Lord of the Celestial City," began the other pilgrim, whose name was Mr. Foot-it-to-Heaven, "has refused, and will ever refuse, to grant an act of incorporation for this railroad; and unless that be obtained, no passenger can ever hope to enter his dominions. Wherefore, every man, who buys a ticket, must lay his account with losing the purchase-money—which is the value of his own soul."

"Poh, nonsense!" said Mr. Smooth-it-away, taking my arm and leading me off, "these fellows ought to be indicted for a libel. If the law stood as it once did in Vanity Fair, we should see them grinning through the iron bars of the prison window."

This incident made a considerable impression on my mind, and contributed with other circumstances to indispose me to a permanent residence in the city of Vanity ; although, of course, I was not simple enough to give up my original plan of gliding along easily and commodiously by railroad. Still, I grew anxious to be gone. There was one strange

thing that troubled me ; amid the occupations or amusements of the fair, nothing was more common than for a person—whether at a feast, theatre, or church, or trafficking for wealth and honours, or whatever he might be doing, and however unseasonable the interruption—suddenly to vanish like a soap-bubble, and be never more seen of his fellows ; and so accustomed were the latter to such little accidents, that they went on with their business, as quietly as if nothing had happened. But it was otherwise with me.

Finally, after a pretty long residence at the Fair, I resumed my journey toward the Celestial City, still with Mr. Smooth-it-away at my side. At a short distance beyond the suburbs of Vanity, we passed the ancient silver mine, of which Demas was the first discoverer, and which is now wrought to great advantage, supplying nearly all the coined currency of the world. A little further onward was the spot where Lot's wife had stood for ages, under the semblance of a pillar of salt. Curious travellers have long since carried it away piecemeal. Had all regrets been punished as rigorously as this poor dame's were, my yearning for the relinquished delights of Vanity Fair might have produced a similar change in my own corporeal substance, and left me a warning to future pilgrims.

The next remarkable object was a large edifice, constructed of moss-grown stone, but in a modern and airy style of architecture. The engine came to a pause in its vicinity with the usual tremendous shriek.

"This was formerly the castle of the redoubted giant Despair," observed Mr. Smooth-it-away ; "but, since his death, Mr. Flimsy-faith has repaired it, and now keeps an excellent house of entertainment here. It is one of our stopping-places."

"It seems but slightly put together," remarked I, looking at the frail, yet ponderous walls. "I do not envy Mr. Flimsy-faith his habitation. Some day it will thunder down upon the heads of the occupants."

"We shall escape, at all events," said Mr. Smooth-it-away ; "for Apollyon is putting on the steam again."

The road now plunged into a gorge of the Delectable Mountains, and traversed the field where, in former ages, the blind men wandered and stumbled among the tombs. One of these ancient tombstones had been thrust across the track, by some malicious person, and gave the train of cars a terrible jolt. Far up the rugged side of a mountain, I perceived a rusty iron door, half overgrown with bushes and creeping plants, but with smoke issuing from its crevices.

"Is that," inquired I, "the very door in the hillside, which the shepherds assured Christian was a by-way to Hell?"

"That was a joke on the part of the shepherds," said Mr. Smooth-it-away, with a smile. "It is neither more nor less than the door of a cavern, which they use as a smoke-house for the preparation of mutton hams."

My recollections of the journey are now, for a

little space, dim and confused, inasmuch as a singular drowsiness here overcame me, owing to the fact that we were passing over the enchanted ground, the air of which encourages a disposition to sleep. I awoke, however, as soon as we crossed the borders of the pleasant land of Beulah. All the passengers were rubbing their eyes, comparing watches, and congratulating one another on the prospect of arriving so seasonably at the journey's end. The sweet breezes of this happy clime came refreshingly to our nostrils; we beheld the glimmering gush of silver fountains, overhung by trees of beautiful foliage and delicious fruit, which were propagated by grafts from the celestial gardens. Once, as we dashed onward like a hurricane, there was a flutter of wings, and the bright appearance of an angel in the air, speeding forth on some heavenly mission. The engine now announced the close vicinity of the final Station-house, by one last and horrible scream, in which there seemed to be distinguishable every kind of wailing and wo, and bitter fierceness of wrath, all mixed up with the wild laughter of a devil or a madman. Throughout our journey, at every stopping-place, Apollyon had exercised his ingenuity in screwing the most abominable sounds out of the whistle of the steam-engine; but in this closing effort he outdid himself, and created an infernal uproar, which, besides disturbing the peaceful inhabitants of Beulah, must have sent its discord even through the celestial gates.

While the horrid clamor was still ringing in our ears, we heard an exulting strain, as if a thousand instruments of music, with height, and depth, and sweetness in their tones, at once tender and triumphant, were struck in unison, to greet the approach of some illustrious hero, who had fought the good fight and won a glorious victory, and was come to lay aside his battered arms for ever. Looking to ascertain what might be the occasion of this glad harmony, I perceived, on alighting from the cars, that a multitude of shining ones had assembled on the other side of the river, to welcome two poor pilgrims, who were just emerging from its depths. They were the same whom Apollyon and ourselves had persecuted with taunts and gibes, and scalding steam, at the commencement of our journey—the same whose unworldly aspect and impressive words had stirred my conscience, amid the wild revelries of Vanity Fair.

"How amazingly well those men have got on!" cried I to Mr. Smooth-it-away. "I wish we were secure of as good a reception."

"Never fear—never fear!" answered my friend. "Come—make haste; the ferry-boat will be off directly; and in three minutes you will be on the other side of the river. No doubt you will find coaches to carry you up to the city gates."

A steam ferry-boat, the last improvement on this important route, lay at the river side, puffing, snorting, and emitting all those other disagreeable utterances, which betoken the departure to be immediate. I hurried on board with the rest of the passengers, most of whom were in great perturbation; some brawling out for their baggage; some tearing their hair and exclaiming that the boat would explode or sink; some already pale with the heaving of the stream; some gazing affrighted at the ugly aspect of the steersman; and some still dizzy with the slumberous influences of the Enchanted Ground. Looking back to the shore, I was amazed to discern Mr. Smooth-it-away waving his hand in token of farewell!

"Don't you go over to the Celestial City?" exclaimed I.

"Oh, no!" answered he with a queer smile, and that same disagreeable contortion of visage which I had remarked in the inhabitants of the Dark Valley. "Oh, no! I have come thus far only for the sake of your pleasant company. Good-bye! We shall meet again."

And then did my excellent friend, Mr. Smooth-it-away, laugh outright; in the midst of which cachinnation, a smoke-wreath issued from his mouth and nostrils, while a twinkle of lurid flame darted out of either eye, proving indubitably that his heart was all of a red blaze. The impudent fiend! To deny the existence of Tophet, when he felt its fiery tortures raging within his breast! I rushed to the side of the boat, intending to fling myself on shore. But the wheels, as they began their revolutions, threw a dash of spray over me, so cold—so deadly cold, with the chill that will never leave those waters, until Death be drowned in his own river—that, with a shiver and a heart-quake, I awoke. Thank heaven, it was a Dream!

SPRING.

FROM THE SAME.

THANK Providence for Spring! The earth—and man himself, by sympathy with his birth-place—would be far other than we find them, if life toiled wearily onward, without this periodical infusion of the primal spirit. Will the world ever be so decayed, that spring may not renew its greenness? Can man be so dismally age-stricken, that no faintest sunshine of his youth may revisit him once a year? It is impossible. The moss on our time-worn mansion brightens into beauty; the good old pastor, who once dwelt here, renewed his prime, regained his boyhood, in the genial breezes of his ninetieth spring. Alas for the worn and heavy soul, if, whether in youth or age, it have outlived its privilege of spring-time sprightliness! From such a soul, the world must hope no reformation of its evil—no sympathy with the lofty faith and gallant struggles of those who contend in its behalf. Summer works in the present, and thinks not of the future; Autumn is a rich conservative; Winter has utterly lost its faith, and clings tremulously to the remembrance of what has been; but Spring, with its outgushing life, is the true type of the Movement!

N. P. WILLIS.

[Born 1807. Died 1867.]

NATHANIEL PARKER WILLIS was born in Portland on the twentieth of January, 1807. While he was a child his family removed to Boston, and in the Latin School of that city, and the Phillips Academy of Andover he was fitted for college. At Yale, which he entered in the seventeenth year of his age, he distinguished himself by a series of graceful poems, on sacred subjects, which made his name widely familiar, and immediately after he graduated, in 1827, he was engaged by Mr. S. G. Goodrich (then a publisher in Boston, and since " world renowned" as author of the excellent books which have appeared under the *nomme de plume* of Peter Parley,) to edit The Legendary, and The Token. In 1828 he established The American Monthly Magazine, which he conducted two years, at the end of which time it was merged in The New York Mirror, and he went to Europe. On his arrival in France he was attached to the American legation by Mr. Rives, then our minister at the court of Versailles, and with a diplomatic passport he travelled in that country, Italy, Greece, Asia Minor, Turkey, and last of all in England, where he remained two years, and was married. The letters which he wrote while abroad, under the title of Pencillings by the Way, were first published in the New York Mirror, and have since been collected into volumes, in which shape they have passed through numerous editions. In 1835 he published Inklings of Adventure, a series of tales and sketches which appeared originally in a London Magazine under the signature of Philip Slingsby. In 1837 he returned to the United States, and retired to a pleasant seat on the Susquehanna, where he resided two years. Early in 1839 he bécame one of the editors of The Corsair, a literary gazette, in New York, and in the autumn of that year he went again to London, where in the following winter he published Loiterings of Travel, in three volumes, and Two Ways of Dying for a Husband, comprising the plays of Bianca Visconti and Tortesa the Usurer. In 1840 appeared an illustrated edition of his

Poems, and his Letters from Under a Bridge, and about the same time he wrote the descriptive parts of the beautiful pictorial works entitled American Scenery, and Ireland. In 1843, with Mr. George P. Morris, he revived The New York Mirror, (which had been discontinued for several years,) first as a weekly and afterward as a daily gazette, but withdrew from it upon the death of his wife, in 1844, and made another visit to England, where he published Dashes at Life with a Free Pencil, consisting of stories and sketches illustrative of contemporary European and American society.* On his return to New York he issued his Complete Works, in a close-printed imperial octavo volume of nine hundred pages, containing about as much as twenty common duodecimos. In October, 1846, he was married to a daughter of the Honourable Mr. Grinnell, of Massachusetts, and in the following month he settled in New York, where he was once more associated with Mr. Morris as an editor, in conducting The Home Journal, a weekly gazette devoted principally to literature.

The popularity of the poems of Mr. Willis has led to their publication in numerous editions, and a complete collection of them, illustrated by one of the most distinguished of our artists, F. O. C. Darley, was published in 1852, by Carey & Hart.

Mr. Willis is a brilliant and delicate colourist in art. He does not communicate his conceptions by any process like drawing or

* In the preface to the London edition of his Dashes at Life, Mr. Willis makes the following remarks upon the effect in his own case of the denial of copy money to foreigners:

"Like the sculptor who made toys of the fragments of his unsaleable Jupiter, the author, in the following collection of brief tales, gives material, that, but for a single objection, would have been moulded into works of larger design That objection is the unmarketableness of American books in America, owing to our defective law of copyright. The foreign author being allowed no property in his books, the American publisher gets for nothing every new novel brought out in England. Of course, while he can have for publication, *gratis*, the new novels of Bulwer, D'Israeli, James, and others, he will not *pay* an American author for a new book, even if it were equally good. The consequence is, that we must either write books to give a way, or take some vein of literature where the competition is more equal—an alternative which makes almost all American authors mere contributors of short papers to periodicals."

moulding; he paints them. He belongs to the Venetian school in letters. The attraction of his writings consists not in the outline or general cast of the whole work, nor even in the grandeur or gracefulness of particular scenes or ideas or passages within it, nor yet in the showy elegance of sentences or even of phrases,—but in the magical, illuminating effect of a single word, which, chosen from a treasury of gems, and disposed with consummate skill toward every ray of sympathy, blazes with various lustre, and kindles a whole paragraph into pictorial brightness and warmth. The affinity between form and colour, and the extent to which under particular circumstances one is suggested by the other, rank among the mysteries of our mental organization; yet it is certain that the most defined conceptions, and the most distinct impressions of shape may be surprised into the mind by the illusory play of tints,—which communicate with the consciousness by signals that cheat the eye. There is not a more remarkable illustration of this, in literature, than is furnished by Mr. Willis. It is a consequence of these peculiarities that the beauties of his writings are chiefly those of detail. In his narratives, fascinated by the almost excessive loveliness which beams upon us from a thousand points as we pass along, we forget to observe that the story as a whole has little probability, consistency, or dignity. The fabric in which he deals is the finest valenciennes; in which all consideration of the figure or plan is merged and lost in the richness of finish that glitters from every part.

A delicate ideality is the characteristic of his genius: a faculty, in him, not impetuous or energetic, but copious and constant. He views his subjects always from the picturesque point, to borrow a term from landscape painting; and if the subject naturally is not susceptible of such a view, he elevates and disposes it in its relations to other objects, so as to create such a point of observation. He looks at all objects through a poetical medium. It is this which lends so unfading a charm to all his productions; and it is this, especially,

which tinges his language with such mysterious lustre. His sensibility to the imaginative impression of a scene in nature, or a situation in society, is exquisite; and his skill in rendering it in words, with precision and distinctness, is singularly felicitous. By such a faculty he has accomplished the description of landscapes with power and splendour so extraordinary. He does not delineate and define the picture, but seizes the sentiments, or ideas, or moral images, which are the mental antitypes, as it were, of the scene, and reproduces them with all the hues of fancy. His portraitures of scenery, therefore, are more vivid than accurate; and the connection between the different parts is according to the truth of the mind rather than the truth of nature.

The life and fertility of the mind of Mr. Willis are very remarkable. His spirits and faculties seem to have been bathed in perpetual freshness. The stream of thought and feeling, in him, is like the bubbling out-spring of a natural fountain, which flows forth with gayety and freedom, if it flows at all. His powers seem never to be lessened by exhaustion. His fancy is never soiled by fatigue. He never copies others, and he never repeats himself; but always prompt, and always vivid, his mind acts with the certainty of a natural prism which turns every ray that reaches it into peculiar beauty.

The triumph of his literary fortunes is his having reconciled and joined the broadest and most pervading popularity with the admiration of the most highly refined. At first sight he might seem to have written for only polished and fastidious tastes,—for a state of society in which an extreme cultivation borders on effeminacy and affectation; yet the strongest response to his genius is from the strenuous and busy world of excitement and action. To the objection which has sometimes been made, that the delicacies of his genius are too subtle, and that his taste is somewhat tinged with quaintness and conceits, his friends make the ready answer, that no writer commands the attention and holds the sympathies of the public with greater power.

A newly arranged edition of his writings was published in 1855 & seq: in 11 vols., 12mo., viz.: Rural Letters, People I have met, Life Here and There, Hurry-Graphs, Pencillings by the way, A summer cruise in the Mediterranean, Fun Jottings, A Health Trip to the Tropics, Letters from Idlewild, Famous Persons and Places, and the Rag Bag. An edition of his Poems, illustrated with wood-cuts, is issued in 8vo.; a plain edition in 16mo. and 32 mo., also, his Sacred Poems, beautifully illustrated, in square 12mo. He died Jan. 21, 1867.

THE CHEROKEE'S THREAT.

FROM INKLINGS OF ADVENTURE.

`AT the extremity' of a green lane in the outer skirt of the fashionable suburb of New Haven stood a rambling old Dutch house, built probably when the cattle of Mynheer grazed over the present site of the town. It was a wilderness of irregular rooms, of no describable shape in its exterior, and from its southern balcony, to use an expressive Gallicism, " gave upon the bay." Long Island sound, the great highway from the northern Atlantic to New York, weltered in alternate lead and silver, (oftener like the brighter metal, for the climate is divine,) between the curving lip of the bay and the interminable and sandy shore of the island some six leagues distant; the procession of ships and steamers stole past with an imperceptible progress; the ceaseless bells of the college chapel came deadened through the trees from behind, and (the day being one of golden autumn, and myself and St. John waiting while black Agatha answered the door-bell) the sun-steeped precipice of East Rock, with its tiara of blood-red maples flushing like a Turk's banner in the light, drew from us both a truant wish for a ramble and a holyday. I shall have more to say anon of the foliage of an American October: but just now, while I remember it, I wish to record a belief of my own, that if, as philosophy supposes, we have lived other lives—if

. . . . . . "our star
Hath had elsewhere its setting,
And cometh from afar"—

it is surely in the days tempered like the one I am remembering and describing—profoundly serene, sunny as the top of Olympus, heavenly pure, holy, and more invigorating and intoxicating than luxurious or balmy; the sort of air that the visiting angels might have brought with them to the tent of Abraham—it is on such days, I would record, that my own memory steps back over the dim threshold of life, (so it seems to me,) and on such days only. It is worth the translation of our youth and our household gods to a sunnier land, if it were alone for those immortal revelations.

In a few minutes from this time were assembled in Mrs. Ilfrington's drawing-room the six or seven young ladies of my more particular acquaintance among her pupils, of whom one was a newcomer, and the object of my mingled curiosity and admiration. It was the one day of the week when morning visiters were admitted, and I was there, in compliance with an unexpected request from my friend, to present him to the agreeable circle of Mrs. Ilfrington. As an *habitué* in her family, this excellent lady had taken occasion to introduce to me, a week or two before, the newcomer of whom I have spoken above—a departure from the ordinary rule of the establishment, which I felt to be a compliment, and which gave me, I presumed, a tacit claim to mix myself up in that young lady's destiny as deeply as I should find agreeable. The newcomer was the daughter of an Indian chief, and her name was Nunu.

The wrongs of civilization to the noble aborigines of America are a subject of much poetical feeling in the United States, and will ultimately become the poetry of the nation. At present the sentiment takes occasionally a tangible shape, and the transmission of the daughter of a Cherokee chief to New Haven, to be educated at the expense of the government, and of several young men of the same high birth to different colleges, will be recorded among the evidences in his history that we did not plough the bones of their fathers into our fields without some feelings of compunction. Nunu had come to the seaboard under the charge of a female missionary, whose pupil she had been in one of the native schools of the west, and was destined, though a chief's daughter, to return as a teacher to her tribe when she should have mastered some of the higher accomplishments of her sex. She was an apt scholar, but her settled melancholy, when away from her books, had determined Mrs. Ilfrington to try the effect of a little society upon her, and hence my privilege to ask for her appearance in the drawing-room.

As we strolled down in the alternate shade and sunshine of the road, I had been a little piqued at the want of interest, and the manner of course, with which St. John had received my animated descriptions of the personal beauty of the Cherokee.

" I have hunted with the tribe," was his only answer, " and know their features."

" But she is not like them," I replied, with a tone of some impatience; " she is the beau ideal of a red skin, but it is with the softened features of an Arab or an Egyptian. She is more willowy than erect, and has no higher cheek-bones than the plaster Venus in your chambers. If it were not for the lambent fire in her eye, you might take her, in the sculptured pose of her attitudes, for an immortal bronze of Cleopatra. I tell you she is divine."

St. John called to his dog, and we turned along the green bank above the beach, with Mrs. Ilfrington's house in view, and so opens a new chapter in my story.

In the united pictures of Paul Veronese and Raphael, steeped as their colours seem to have been in the divinest age of Venetian and Roman female beauty, I have scarcely found so many lovely women, of so different models and so perfect, as were assembled during my sophomore year under the roof of Mrs. Ilfrington. They went about in their evening walks, graceful and angelic, but, like the virgin pearls of the sea, they poured the light of their loveliness on the vegetating oysters about them, and no diver of fashion had yet taught them their value. Ignorant myself in those days of the scale of beauty, their features are enamelled in my memory, and I have tried insensibly by that standard (and found wanting) of every court in Europe the dames most worshipped and highest born. Queen of the Sicilies, loveliest in your own realm of sunshine and passion! Pale and transparent princess—pearl of the court of Florence—than whom the creations on the immortal walls of the Pitti less discipline our eye for the shapes of heaven! Gipsy of the Pactolus! Jewess of the Thracian Gallipolis! Bright and gifted cynosure

of the aristocracy of England!—ye are five women
I have seen in as many years' wandering over the
world, lived to gaze upon, and live to remember
and admire—a constellation, I almost believe, that
has absorbed all the intensest light of the beauty
of a hemisphere—yet, with your pictures coloured
to life in my memory, and the pride of rank and
state thrown over most of you like an elevating
charm, I go back to the school of Mrs. Ilfrington,
and (smile if you will!) they were as lovely, and
stately, and as worthy of the worship of the world.

I introduced St. John to the young ladies as they
came in. Having never seen him, except in the
presence of men, I was little curious to know whether his singular *aplomb* would serve him as well
with the other sex, of which I was aware he had
had a very slender experience. My attention was
distracted for the moment of mentioning his name
to a lovely little Georgian, (with eyes full of the
liquid sunshine of the south,) by a sudden bark of
joy from the dog, who had been left in the hall;
and as the door opened, and the slight and graceful Indian girl entered the room, the usually unsocial animal sprang bounding in, lavishing caresses on her, and seemingly wild with the delight
of a recognition.

In the confusion of taking the dog from the
room, I had again lost the moment of remarking
St. John's manner, and on the entrance of Mrs.
Ilfrington, Nunu was sitting calmly by the piano,
and my friend was talking in a quiet undertone
with the passionate Georgian.

"I must apologize for my dog," said St. John,
bowing gracefully to the mistress of the house;
"he was bred by Indians, and the sight of a Cherokee reminded him of happier days—as it did his
master."

Nunu turned her eyes quickly upon him, but
immediately resumed her apparent deep study of
the abstruse figures in the Kidderminster carpet.

"You are well arrived, young gentlemen," said
Mrs. Ilfrington; "we press you into our service
for a botanical ramble. Mr. Slingsby is at leisure,
and will be delighted, I am sure. Shall I say as
much for you, Mr. St. John?"

St. John bowed, and the ladies left the room for
their bonnets—Mrs. Ilfrington last. The door was
scarcely closed when Nunu reappeared and checking herself with a sudden feeling at the first step
over the threshold, stood gazing at St. John, evidently under very powerful emotion.

"Nunu!" he said, smiling slowly and unwillingly, and holding out his hand with the air of one
who forgives an offence.

She sprang upon his bosom with the bound of
a leveret, and between her kisses broke the
endearing epithets of her native tongue, in words
that I only understood by their passionate and
thrilling accent. The language of the heart is
universal.

The fair scholars came in one after another, and
we were soon on our way through the green fields
to the flowery mountain-side of East Rock; Mrs.
Ilfrington's arm and conversation having fallen to
my share, and St. John rambling at large with the

rest of the party, but more particularly beset by
Miss Temple, whose Christian name was Isabella,
and whose Christian charity had no bowels for
broken hearts.

The most sociable individuals of the party for a
while were Nunu and Lash; the dog's recollection
of the past seeming, like those of wiser animals,
more agreeable than the present. The Cherokee
astonished Mrs. Ilfrington by an abandonment to
joy and frolic which she had never displayed before—sometimes fairly outrunning the dog at full
speed, and sometimes sitting down breathless upon
a green bank, while the rude creature overpowered
her with his caresses. The scene gave origin to
a grave discussion between that well-instructed
lady and myself, upon the singular force of childish
association—the extraordinary intimacy between
the Indian and the trapper's dog being explained
satisfactorily (to her, at least) on that attractive
principle. Had she but seen Nunu spring into
the bosom of my friend half an hour before, she
might have added a material corollary to her proposition. If the dog and the chief's daughter
were not old friends, the chief's daughter and St.
John certainly *were*.

As well as I could judge by the motions of two
people walking before me, St. John was advancing
fast in the favour and acquaintance of the graceful
Georgian. Her southern indolence was probably
an apology in Mrs. Ilfrington's eyes for leaning
heavily on her companion's arm; but in a momentary halt, the capricious beauty disembarrassed
herself of the bright scarf that had floated over her
shoulders, and bound it playfully around his waist.
This was rather strong on a first acquaintance, and
Mrs. Ilfrington was of that opinion.

"Miss Temple!" said she, advancing to whisper
a reproof to the beauty's ear.

Before she had taken a second step, Nunu
bounded over the low hedge, followed by the dog,
with whom she had been chasing a butterfly, and
springing upon St. John with eyes that flashed fire,
she tore the scarf into shreds, and stood trembling
and pale, with her feet on the silken fragments.

"Madam!" said St. John, advancing to Mrs.
Ilfrington, after casting on the Cherokee a look of
surprise and displeasure, "I should have told you
before that your pupil and myself are not new acquaintances. Her father is my friend. I have
hunted with the tribe, and have hitherto looked
upon Nunu as a child. You will believe me, I
trust, when I say her conduct surprises me, and I
beg to assure you that any influence I may have
over her will be in accordance with your own
wishes exclusively."

His tone was cold, and Nunu listened with fixed
lips and frowning eyes.

"Have you seen her before since her arrival?"
asked Mrs. Ilfrington.

"My dog brought me yesterday the first intelligence that she was here: he returned from his
morning ramble with a string of wampum about
his neck which had the mark of the tribe. He
was her gift," he added, patting the head of the
dog, and looking with a softened expression at

Nunu, who dropped her head upon her bosom, and walked on in tears.

The chain of the Green mountains, after a gallop of some five hundred miles, from Canada to Connecticut, suddenly pulls up on the shore of Long Island sound, and stands rearing with a bristling mane of pine-trees, three hundred feet in air, as if checked in mid career by the sea. Standing on the brink of this bold precipice, you have the bald face of the rock in a sheer perpendicular below you; and, spreading away from the broken masses at its feet lies an emerald meadow, inlaid with a crystal and rambling river, across which, at a distance of a mile or two, rise the spires of the university, from what else were a thick-serried wilderness of elms. Back from the edge of the precipice extends a wild forest of hemlock and fir, ploughed on its northern side by a mountain-torrent, whose bed of marl, dry and overhung with trees in the summer, serves as a path and a guide from the plain to the summit. It were a toilsome ascent but for that smooth and hard pavement, and the impervious and green thatch of pine tassels overhung.

Antiquity in America extends no further back than the days of Cromwell, and East Rock is traditionary ground with us—for there harboured the regicides Whalley and Goffe, and many a breath-hushing tale is told of them over the smouldering log-fires of Connecticut. Not to rob the historian, I pass on to say that this cavernous path to the mountain-top was the resort in the holyday summer afternoons of most of the poetical and otherwise well-disposed gentlemen sophomores, and, on the day of which I speak, of Mrs. Ilfrington and her seven-and-twenty lovely scholars. The kind mistress ascended with the assistance of my arm, and St. John drew stoutly between Miss Temple and a fat young lady with an incipient asthma. Nunu had not been seen since the first cluster of hanging flowers had hidden her from our sight, as she bounded upward.

The hour or two of slanting sunshine, poured in upon the summit of the precipice from the west, had been sufficient to induce a fine and silken moss to show its fibres and small blossoms above the carpet of pine-tassels; and emerging from the brown shadow of the wood, you stood on a verdant platform, the foliage of sighing trees overhead, a fairies' velvet beneath you, and a view below that you may as well (if you would not die in your ignorance) make a voyage over the water to see. We found Nunu lying thoughtfully near the brink of the precipice, and gazing off over the waters of the sound, as if she watched the coming or going of a friend under the white sails that spotted its bosom. We recovered our breath in silence, I alone, perhaps, of that considerable company gazing with admiration at the lithe and unconscious figure of grace lying in the attitude of the Grecian Hermaphrodite on the brow of the rock before us. Her eyes were moist and motionless with abstraction, her lips just perceptibly curved in an expression of mingled pride and sorrow, her small hand buried and clinched in the moss, and her left foot and ankle, models of spirited symmetry, escaped carelessly from her dress, the high instep strained back as if recovering from a leap, with the tense control of emotion.

The game of the coquettish Georgian was well played. With a true woman's pique, she had redoubled her attentions to my friend from the moment that she found it gave pain to another of her sex; and St. John, like most men, seemed not unwilling to see a new altar kindled to his vanity, though a heart he had already won was stifling with the incense. Miss Temple was very lovely. Her skin, of that taint of opaque and patrician white which is found oftenest in Asian latitudes, was just perceptibly warmed toward the centre of the cheek with a glow like sunshine through the thick white petal of a magnolia; her eyes were hazel, with those inky lashes which enhance the expression a thousand-fold, either of passion or melancholy; her teeth were like strips from the lily's heart; and she was clever, captivating, graceful, and a thorough coquette. St. John was mysterious, romantic-looking, superior, and, just now, the only victim in the way. He admired, as all men do, those qualities which, to her own sex, rendered the fair Isabella unamiable; and yielded himself, as all men will, a satisfied prey to enchantments of which he knew the springs were the pique and vanity of the enchantress. How singular it is that the highest and best qualities of the female heart are those with which men are the least captivated!

A rib of the mountain formed a natural seat a little back from the pitch of the precipice, and here sat Miss Temple, triumphant in drawing all eyes upon herself and her tamed lion; her lap full of flowers, which he had found time to gather on the way, and her white hands employed in arranging a bouquet of which the destiny was yet a secret. Next to their own loves, ladies like nothing on earth like mending or marring the loves of others; and while the violets and already-dropping wild flowers were coquettishly chosen or rejected by those slender fingers, the sun might have swung back to the east like a pendulum, and those seven-and-twenty misses would have watched their lovely schoolfellow the same. Nunu turned her head slowly around at last, and silently looked on. St. John lay at the feet of the Georgian, glancing from the flowers to her face, and from her face to the flowers, with an admiration not at all equivocal. Mrs. Ilfrington sat apart, absorbed in finishing a sketch of New Haven; and I, interested painfully in watching the emotions of the Cherokee, sat with my back to the trunk of a hemlock—the only spectator who comprehended the whole extent of the drama.

A wild rose was set in the heart of the bouquet at last, a spear of riband-grass added to give it grace and point, and nothing was wanting but a string. Reticules were searched, pockets turned inside out, and never a bit of riband to be found. The beauty was in despair.

"Stay," said St. John, springing to his feet. "Lash! Lash!"

The dog came coursing in from the wood, and crouched to his master's hand.

"Will a string of wampum do?" he asked, feeling under the long hair on the dog's neck, and untying a fine and variegated thread of many-coloured beads, worked exquisitely.

The dog growled, and Nunu sprang into the middle of the circle with the fling of an adder, and seizing the wampum as he handed it to her rival, called the dog, and fastened it once more around his neck.

The ladies rose in alarm; the belle turned pale, and clung to St. John's arm; the dog, with his hair bristling upon his back, stood close to her feet in an attitude of defiance; and the superb Indian, the peculiar genius of her beauty developed by her indignation, her nostrils expanded, and her eyes almost showering fire in their flashes, stood before them like a young Pythoness, ready to strike them dead with regard.

St. John recovered from his astonishment after a moment, and leaving the arm of Miss Temple, advanced a step, and called to his dog.

The Cherokee patted the animal on his back, and spoke to him in her own language; and, as St. John still advanced, Nunu drew herself to her fullest height, placed herself before the dog, who slunk growling from his master, and said to him, as she folded her arms. "The wampum is mine."

St. John coloured to the temples with shame.

"Lash!" he cried, stamping with his feet, and endeavouring to fright him from his protectress.

The dog howled and crept away, half-crouching with fear, toward the precipice; and St. John shooting suddenly past Nunu, seized him on the brink, and held him down by the throat.

The next instant, a scream of horror from Mrs. Ilfrington, followed by a terrific echo from every female present, started the rude Kentuckian to his feet.

Clear over the abyss, hanging with one hand by an ashen sapling, the point of her tiny foot just poising on a projecting ledge of rock, swung the desperate Cherokee, sustaining herself with perfect ease, but with all the determination of her iron race collected in calm concentration on her lips.

"Restore the wampum to his neck," she cried, with a voice that thrilled the very marrow with its subdued fierceness, "or my blood rest on your soul!"

St. John flung it toward the dog, and clasped his hands in silent horror.

The Cherokee bore down the sapling till its slender stem cracked with the tension, and rising lightly with the rebound, alit like a feather upon the rock. The subdued student sprang to her side; but with scorn on her lip, and the flush of exertion already vanished from her cheek, she called to the dog, and with rapid strides took her way alone down the mountain.

———

Five years had elapsed. I had put to sea from the sheltered river of boyhood—had encountered the very storms of a first entrance into life—had trimmed my boat, shortened sail, and, with a sharp eye to windward, was lying fairly on my course. Among others from whom I had parted company was Paul St. John, who had shaken hands with me at the university gate, leaving me, after four years' intimacy, as much in doubt as to his real character and history as the first day we met. I had never heard him speak of either father or mother, nor had he, to my knowledge, received a letter from the day of his matriculation. He passed his vacations at the university; he had studied well, yet refused one of the highest college honours offered him with his degree; he had shown many good qualities, yet some unaccountable faults; and, all in all, was an enigma to myself and the class. I knew him, clever, accomplished, and conscious of superiority; and my knowledge went no farther. The coach was at the gate, and I was there to see him off; and, after four years' constant association, I had not an idea where he was going, or to what he was destined. The driver blew his horn.

"God bless you, Slingsby!"

"God bless you, St. John!"

And so we parted.

It was five years from this time, I say, and, in the bitter struggles of first manhood, I had almost forgotten there was such a being in the world. Late in the month of October, in 1829, I was on my way westward, giving myself a vacation from the law. I embarked, on a clear and delicious day, in the small steamer which plies up and down the Cayuga lake, looking forward to a calm feast of scenery, and caring little who were to be my fellow-passengers. As we got out of the little harbour of Cayuga, I walked astern for the first time, and saw the not very unusual sight of a group of Indians standing motionless by the wheel. They were chiefs returning from a diplomatic visit to Washington.

I sat down by the companion-ladder, and opened soul and eye to the glorious scenery we were gliding through. The first severe frost had come, and the miraculous change had passed upon the leaves which is known only in America. The blood-red sugar maple, with a leaf brighter and more delicate than a Circassian lip, stood here and there in the forest like the Sultan's standard in a host—the solitary and far-seen aristocrat of the wilderness; the birch, with its spiritlike and amber leaves, ghosts of the departed summer, turned out along the edges of the woods like a lining of the palest gold; the broad sycamore and the fan-like catalpa flaunted their saffron foliage in the sun, spotted with gold like the wings of a lady-bird; the kingly oak, with its summit shaken bare, still hid its majestic trunk in a drapery of sumptuous dyes, like a stricken monarch, gathering his robes of state about him to die royally in his purple; the tall poplar, with its minaret of silver leaves, stood blanched like a coward in the dying forest, burdening every breeze with its complainings; the hickory paled through its enduring green; the bright berries of the mountain-ash flushed with a more sanguine glory in the unobstructed sun; the gaudy tulip-tree, the Sybarite of vegetation, stripped of its golden cups, still drank the intoxicating light of noonday in leaves than which the lip of an Indian shell was never more delicately teinted; the still deeper-dyed vines of the lavish wilderness, perishing with the noble things whose summer they had shared, outshone them in their decline, as woman in her death is heavenlier than the being on whom in life she leaned; and alone and unsympathizing in this universal decay, outlaws from Nature, stood the fir and the hemlock, their frowning and sombre heads darker and less lovely than ever, in contrast with the death-struck glory of their companions.

The dull colours of English autumnal foliage give you no conception of this marvellous phenomenon. The change here is gradual; in America it is the work of a night—of a single frost!

Oh, to have seen the sun set on hills bright in the still green and lingering summer, and to wake in the morning to a spectacle like this!

It is as if a myriad of rainbows were laced through the tree-tops—as if the sunsets of a summer—gold, purple, and crimson—had been fused in the alembic of the west, and poured back in a new deluge of light and colour over the wilderness. It is as if every leaf in those countless trees had been painted to outflush the tulip—as if, by some electric miracle, the dyes of the earth's heart had struck upward, and her crystals and ores, her sapphires, hyacinths, rubies, had let forth their imprisoned colours to mount through the roots of the forest, and, like the angels that in olden time entered the body of the dying, reanimate the perishing leaves, and revel an hour in their bravery.

I was sitting by the companion-ladder, thinking to what on earth these masses of foliage could be resembled, when a dog sprang upon my knees, and, the moment after, a hand was laid on my shoulder.

"St. John! Impossible!"

"Bodily!" answered my quondam classmate.

I looked at him with astonishment. The soigné man of fashion I had once known was enveloped in a kind of hunter's frock, loose and large, and girded to his waist by a belt; his hat was exchanged for a cap of rich otter skin; his pantaloons spread with a slovenly carelessness over his feet; and, altogether, there was that in his air which told me at a glance that he had renounced the world. Lash had recovered his leanness, and, after wagging out his joy, he crouched between my feet, and lay looking into my face, as if he was brooding over the more idle days in which we had been acquainted.

"And where are you bound?" I asked, having answered the same question for myself.

"Westward with the chiefs!"

"For how long?"

"The remainder of my life."

I could not forbear an exclamation of surprise.

"You would wonder less," said he, with an impatient gesture, "if you knew more of me. And, by-the-way," he added with a smile, "I think I never told you the first half of the story—my life up to the time I met you."

"It was not for want of a catechist,' I answered, settling myself in an attitude of attention.

"No; and I was often tempted to gratify your curiosity: but from the little intercourse I had had with the world, I had adopted some precocious principles; and one was, that a man's influence over others was vulgarized and diminished by a knowledge of his history."

I smiled, and as the boat sped on her way over the calm waters of the Cayuga, St. John went on leisurely with a story which is scarce remarkable enough for a repetition. He believed himself the natural son of a western hunter, but only knew that he had passed his early youth on the borders of civilization, between whites and Indians, and that he had been more particularly indebted for protection to the father of Nunu. Mingled ambition and curiosity had led him eastward while still a lad, and a year or two of a most vagabond life in the different cities had taught him the caution and bitterness for which he was so remarkable. A fortunate experiment in lotteries supplied him with the means of education, and, with singular application in a youth of such wandering habits, he had applied himself to study under a private master, fitted himself for the university in half the usual time, and cultivated, in addition, the literary taste which I have remarked upon.

"This," he said, smiling at my look of astonishment, "brings me up to the time when we met. I came to college at the age of eighteen with a few hundred dollars in my pocket, some pregnant experience of the rough side of the world, great confidence in myself, and distrust of others, and, I believe, a kind of instinct of good manners, which made me ambitious of shining in society. You were a witness to my début. Miss Temple was the first highly educated woman I had ever known, and you saw her effect on me."

"And since we parted?"

"Oh, since we parted my life has been vulgar enough. I have ransacked civilized life to the bottom, and found it a heap of unredeemed falsehoods. I do not say it from common disappointment, for I may say I succeeded in every thing I undertook——"

"Except Miss Temple," I said, interrupting, at the hazard of wounding him.

"No; she was a coquette, and I pursued her till I had my turn. You see me in my new character now. But a month ago I was the Apollo of Saratoga, playing my own game with Miss Temple. I left her for a woman worth ten thousand of her—and here she is."

As Nunu came up the companion-way from the cabin, I thought I had never seen breathing creature so exquisitely lovely. With the exception of a pair of brilliant moccasins on her feet, she was dressed in the usual manner, but with the most absolute simplicity. She had changed in those five years from the child to the woman, and, with a round and well-developed figure, additional height, and manners at once gracious and dignified, she walked and looked the chieftain's daughter. St. John took her hand, and gazed on her with moisture in his eyes.

"That I could ever have put a creature like this," he said, "into comparison with the dolls of civilization!"

We parted at Buffalo; St. John with his wife and the chiefs to pursue their way westward by Lake Erie, and I to go moralizing on my way to Niagara.

NAHANT.
FROM THE SAME.

If you can imagine a buried Titan lying along the length of a continent with one arm stretched out into the midst of the sea, the place to which I would transport you, reader mine! would lie as it were in the palm of the giant's hand. The small promontory to which I refer, which becomes an island in certain states of the tide, is at the end of one of the long capes of Massachusetts, and is still called by its Indian name, *Nahant.* Not to make you uncomfortable, I beg to introduce you at once to a pretentious hotel, "squat like a toad" upon the unsheltered and highest point of this citadel in mid sea, and a very great resort for the metropolitan New Englanders. Nahant is perhaps, liberally measured, a square half-mile; and it is distant from what may fairly be called mainland, perhaps a league.

Road to Nahant there is none. The *oi polloi* go there by steam; but when the tide is down, you may drive there with a thousand chariots over the bottom of the sea. As I suppose there is not such another place in the known world, my tale will wait while I describe it more fully. If the Bible had been a fiction, (not to speak profanely,) I should have thought the idea of the destruction of Pharaoh and his host had its origin in some such wonder of nature.

Nahant is so far out in the ocean, that what is called the "ground swell," the majestic heave of its great bosom going on for ever like respiration, (though its face may be like a mirror beneath the sun, and wind may not have crisped its surface for days and weeks,) is as broad and powerful within a rood of the shore as is a thousand miles at sea.

The promontory itself is never wholly left by the ebb; but, from its western extremity, there runs a narrow ridge, scarce broad enough for a horse-path, impassable for the rocks and sea-weed of which it is matted, and extending at just high-water mark from Nahant to the mainland. Seaward from this ridge, which is the only connection of the promontory with the continent, descends an expanse of sand, left bare six hours out of the twelve by the retreating sea, as smooth and hard as marble, and as broad and apparently as level as the plain of the Hermus. For three miles it stretches away without shell or stone, a surface of white, fine-grained sand, beaten so hard by the eternal hammer of the surf, that the hoof of a horse scarce marks it, and the heaviest wheel leaves it as printless as a floor of granite. This will be easily understood when you remember the tremendous rise and fall of the ocean swell, from the very bosom of which, in all its breadth and strength, roll in the waves of the flowing tide, breaking down on the beach, every one, with the thunder of a host precipitated from the battlements of a castle. Nothing could be more solemn and anthem-like than the succession of these plunging surges. And when the "tenth wave" gathers, far out at sea, and rolls onward to the shore, first with a glassy and heaving swell as if some mighty monster were lurching inland beneath the water, and then, bursting up into foam, with a front like an endless and sparry crystal wall, advances and overwhelms every thing in its progress, till it breaks with a centupled thunder on the beach—it has seemed to me, standing there, as if thus might have beaten the first surge on the shore after the fiat which "divided sea and land." I am no Cameronian, but the sea (myself on shore) always drives me to Scripture for an illustration of my feelings.

The promontory of Nahant must be based on the earth's axle, else I cannot imagine how it should have lasted so long. In the mildest weather, the ground-swell of the sea gives it a fillip at every heave that would lay the "castled crag of Drachenfels" as low as Memphis. The wine trembles in your beaker of claret as you sit after dinner at the hotel; and if you look out at the eastern balcony, (for it is a wooden pagoda, with balconies, verandahs, and colonnades *ad libitum*,) you will see the grass breathless in the sunshine upon the lawn, and the ocean as polished and calm as *Miladi's* brow beyond, and yet the spray and foam dashing fifty feet into the air between, and enveloping the "Devil's Pulpit" (a tall rock split off from the promontory's front) in a perpetual kaleidoscope of mists and rainbows. Take the trouble to transport yourself there! I will do the remaining honours on the spot. A cavern as cool (not as silent) as those of Trophonius lies just under the brow of yonder precipice, and the waiter shall come after us with our wine. You have dined with the Borromeo in the grotto of Isola Bella, I doubt not, and know the perfection of *art*—I will show you that of *nature*. (I should like to transport you for a similar contrast from Terni to Niagara, or from San Giovanni Laterano to an aisle in a forest of Michigan; but the Dædalian mystery, alas! is unsolved. We "fly not yet.")

Here we are, then, in the "Swallow's Cave." The floor descends by a gentle declivity to the sea, and from the long dark cleft stretching outward you look forth upon the broad Atlantic—the shores of Ireland the first *terra firma* in the path of your eye. Here is a dark pool left by the retreating tide for a refrigerator, and with the champagne in the midst, we will recline about it like the soft Asiatics of whom we learned pleasure in the east, and drink to the small-featured and purple-lipped "Mignons" of Syria—those fine-limbed and fiery slaves, adorable as Peris, and by turns languishing and stormy, whom you buy for a pinch of piastres. (say 5*l.* 5*s.*) in sunny Damascus. Your drowsy Circassian, faint and dreamy, or your crockery Georgian—fit dolls for the sensual Turk—is, to him who would buy *soul,* dear at a *para* the hecatomb.

We recline, as it were, in an ebon pyramid, with a hundred feet of floor and sixty of wall, and the fourth side open to the sky. The light comes in mellow and dim, and the sharp edges of the rocky portal seem let into the pearly arch of heaven. The tide is at half-ebb, and the advancing and retreating waves, which at first just lifted the fringe of crimson dulse at the lip of the cavern, now dash their spray-pearls on the rock below, the "tenth" surge alone rallying as if in scorn of its retreating follows, and, like the chieftain of Culloden Moor, rushing back singly to the contest. And now that the waters reach the entrance no more, come forward and look on the sea! The swell lifts!—would you not think the bases of the earth rising beneath it? It falls!—would you not think the foundation of the deep had given way? A plain, broad enough for the navies of the world to ride at large, heaves up evenly and steadily as if it would lie against the sky, rests a moment spell-bound in its place, and falls again as far—the respiration of a sleeping child not more regular and full of slumber. It is only on the shore that it chafes. Blessed emblem! it is at peace with itself! The rocks war with a nature so unlike their own, and the hoarse din of their border onsets resounds through the caverns they have rent open; but beyond, in the calm bosom of the ocean, what heavenly dignity! what godlike unconsciousness of alarm! I did not think we should stumble on such a moral in the cave! By the deeper base of its hoarse organ, the sea is now playing upon its lowest stops, and the tide is down. Hear! how it rushes in beneath the rocks, broken and stilled in its tortuous way, till it ends with a washing and dull hiss among the sea-weed, and, like a myriad of small tinkling bells, the dripping from the crags is audible. There is fine music in the sea!

And now the beach is bare. The cave begins to cool and darken, and the first gold teint of sunset is stealing into the sky, and the sea looks of a changing opal, green, purple, and white, as if its floor were paved with pearl, and the changing light struck up through the waters. And there heaves a ship into the horizon, like a white-winged bird lying with dark breast on the waves, abandoned of the sea-breeze within sight of port, and repelled even by the spicy breath that comes with a welcome off the shore. She comes from " merry England." She is freighted with more than merchandise. The home-sick exile will gaze on her snowy sail as she sets in with the morning breeze, and bless it; for the wind that first filled it on its way swept through the green valley of his home! What links of human affection brings she over the sea? How much comes in her that is not in her " bill of lading," yet worth, to the heart that is waiting for it, a thousand times the purchase of her whole venture! *Mais montons nous!* I hear the small hoofs of Thalaba; my stanhope waits; we will leave this half bottle of champagne, that "remainder biscuit," and the echoes of our philosophy, to the Naiads who have lent us their drawing-room. Undine, or Egeria! Lurly, or Arethusa! whatever thou art called, nymph of this shadowy cave! adieu!

Slowly, Thalaba! Tread gingerly down this rocky descent! So! Here we are on the floor of the vasty deep! What a glorious race-course! The polished and printless sand spreads away before you as far as the eye can see, the surf comes in below, breast-high ere it breaks, and the white fringe of the sliding wave shoots up the beach, but leaves room for the marching of a Persian phalanx on the sands it has deserted. Oh, how noiselessly runs the wheel, and how dreamily we glide along, feeling our motion but in the resistance of the wind, and by the trout-like pull of the ribands by the excited animal before us. Mark the colour of the sand! White at high-water mark, and thence deepening to a silvery gray as the water has evaporated less—a slab of Egyptian granite in the obelisk of St. Peter's not more polished and unimpressible. Shell or rock, weed or quicksand, there is none; and mar or deface its bright surface as you will, it is ever beaten down anew, and washed even of the dust of the foot of man, by the returning sea. You may write upon its fine-grained face with a crowquill—you may course over its dazzling expanse with a troop of chariots.

Most wondrous and beautiful of all, within twenty yards of the surf, or for an hour after the tide has left the sand, it holds the water without losing its firmness, and is like a gray mirror, bright as the bosom of the sea. (By your leave, Thalaba!) And now lean over the dasher, and see those small fetlocks striking up from beneath—the flying mane, the thoroughbred action, the small and expressive head, as perfect in the reflection as in the reality; like Wordsworth's swan, he

" *Trots double, horse* and shadow."

You would swear you were skimming the surface of the sea; and the delusion is more complete as the white foam of the " tenth wave" skims in beneath wheel and hoof, and you urge on with the treacherous element gliding away visibly beneath you.

We seem not to have driven fast, yet three miles, fairly measured, are left behind, and Thalaba's blood is up. Fine creature! I would not give him

" For the best horse the Sun has in his stable."

We have won champagne ere now, Thalaba and I, trotting on this silvery beach; and if ever old age comes on me, and I intend it never shall on aught save my mortal coil, (my spirit vowed to perpetual youth,) I think these vital breezes, and a trot on these exhilarating sands, would sooner renew my prime than a rock in St. Hilary's cradle, or a dip in the well of Kanathos. May we try the experiment together, gentle reader?

I am not settled in my own mind whether this description of one of my favourite haunts in America was written most to introduce the story that is to follow, or the story to introduce the description. Possibly the latter, for having consumed my callow youth in wandering "to and fro in the earth," like Sathanas of old, and looking on my country now with an eye from which all the minor and temporary features have gradually faded, I find my pride in it (after its glory as a republic) settling principally on the superior handiwork of nature in its land and water. When I talk of it now, it is looking through another's eyes—his who listens. I do not describe it after my own memory of what it *was once to me*, but according to my idea of what it will *seem now to a stranger*. Hence I speak not of the friends I made, rambling by lake or river. The lake and the river are there, but the friends are changed—to themselves and me. I speak not of the lovely and loving ones that stood by me, looking on glen or waterfall. The glen and the waterfall are romantic still, but the form and the heart that breathed through it are no longer lovely or loving. I should renew my joys by the old mountain and river, for, all they ever were I should find them still, and never seem to myself grown old, or cankered of the world, or changed in form or spirit, while they reminded me but of my youth, with their familiar sunshine and beauty. But the friends that I knew—*as* I knew them—are dead. They look no longer the same; they have another heart in them; the kindness of the eye, the smilingness of the lip, are no more there. Philosophy tells me the material and living body changes and renews, particle by particle, with time; and experience—cold-blooded and stony monitor—tells me, in his frozen monotone, that heart and spirit change with it and renew! But the name remains, mockery that it is! and the memory sometimes; and so these apparitions of the past—that we almost fear to question when they encounter us, lest the change they have undergone should freeze our blood—stare coldly on us, yet call us by name, and answer, though coldly to their own, and have that terrible similitude to what they were, mingled with their unsympathizing and hollow mummery, that we wish the grave of the past, with all that it contained of kind or lovely, had been sealed for ever. The heart we have lain near before our birth (so read I the book of human life) is the only one that cannot forget that it has loved us. Saith well and affectionately an American poet, in some birthday verses to his mother—

"Mother! dear mother! the feelings nurst
As I hung at thy bosom, *clung round thee first*—
'Twas the earliest link in love's warm chain,
'Tis the only one that will long remain
And as, year by year, and day by day,
Some friend, still trusted, drops away,
Mother! dear mother! oh, *dost thou see
How the shortened chain brings me nearer thee!*"

UNWRITTEN MUSIC.
FROM THE SAME.

MEPHISTOPHELES could hardly have found a more striking amusement for Faust than the passage of three hundred miles in the canal from Lake Erie to the Hudson. As I walked up and down the deck of the packet-boat, I thought to myself, that if it were not for thoughts of things that come more home to one's "business and bosom," (particularly "bosom,") I could be content to retake my berth at Schenectady, and return to Buffalo for amusement. The Erie canal-boat is a long and very pretty drawing-room afloat. It has a library, sofas, a tolerable cook, curtains or Venetian blinds, a civil captain, and no smell of steam or perceptible motion. It is drawn generally by three horses at a fair trot, and gets you through about a hundred miles a day, as softly as if you were witched over the ground by Puck and Mustard-seed. The company (say fifty people) is such as pleases Heaven; though I must say (with my eye all along the shore, collecting the various dear friends I have made and left on that long canal)

there are few highways on which you will meet so many lovely and loving fellow-passengers. On this occasion my star was bankrupt—Job Smith being my only civilized companion—and I was left to the unsatisfactory society of my own thoughts and the scenery.

Discontented as I may seem to have been, I remember, through eight or ten years of stirring and thickly-sown manhood, every moment of that lonely evening. I remember the progression of the sunset, from the lengthening shadows and the first gold upon the clouds, to the deepening twilight and the new-sprung star hung over the wilderness. And I remember what I am going to describe—a twilight anthem in the forest—as you remember an air of Rossini's, or a transition in the half-fiendish, half-heavenly creations of Meyerbeer. I thought time dragged heavily then, but I wish I had as light a heart and could feel as vividly now!

The Erie canal is cut a hundred or two miles through the heart of the primeval wilderness of America, and the boat was gliding on silently and swiftly, and never sailed a lost cloud through the abyss of space on a course more apparently new and untrodden. The luxuriant soil had sent up a rank grass that covered the horse-path like velvet; the Erie water was clear as a brook in the winding canal; the old shafts of the gigantic forest spurred into the sky by thousands, and the yet unscared eagle swung off from the dead branch of the pine, and skimmed the tree-tops for another perch, as if he had grown to believe that gliding spectre a harmless phenomenon of nature. The horses drew steadily and unheard at the end of the long line; the steersman stood motionless at the tiller, and I lay on a heap of baggage in the prow, attentive to the slightest breathing of nature, but thinking, with an ache at my heart, of Edith Linsey, to whose feet (did I mention it?) I was hastening with a lover's proper impatience. I might as well have taken another turn in my "fool's paradise."

The gold of the sunset had glided up the dark pine tops and disappeared, like a ring taken slowly from an Ethiop's finger; the whip-poor-will had chanted the first stave of his lament; the bat was abroad, and the screech-owl, like all bad singers, commenced without waiting to be importuned, though we were listening for the nightingale. The air, as I said before, had been all day breathless; but as the first chill of evening displaced the warm atmosphere of the departed sun, a slight breeze crisped the mirrored bosom of the canal, and then commenced the night anthem of the forest, audible, I would fain believe, in its soothing changes, by the dead tribes whose bones whiten amid the perishing leaves. First, whisperingly yet articulately, the suspended and wavering foliage of the birch was touched by the many-fingered wind, and, like a faint prelude, the silver-lined leaves rustled in the low branches; and, with a moment's pause, when you could hear the moving of the vulture's claws upon the bark, as he turned to get his breast to the wind, the increasing breeze swept into the pine-tops, and drew forth from their fringe-like and myriad tassels a low monotone like the refrain of a far-off dirge; and still as it murmured, (seeming to you sometimes like the confused and heart-broken responses of the penitents on a cathedral floor,) the blast strengthened and filled, and the rigid leaves of the oak, and the swaying fans and chalices of the magnolia, and the rich cups of the tulip-trees, stirred and answered with their different voices like many-toned harps; and when the wind was fully abroad, and every moving thing on the breast of the earth was roused from its daylight repose, the irregular and capricious blast, like a player on an organ of a thousand stops, lulled and strengthened by turns, and from the hiss in the rank grass, low as the whisper of fairies, to the thunder of the impinging and groaning branches of the larch and the fir, the anthem went ceaselessly through its changes, and the harmony (though the owl broke in with his scream, and though the overblown monarch of the wood came crashing to the earth) was still perfect and without a jar. It is strange that there is no sound of nature out of tune. The roar of the waterfall comes into this anthem of the forest like an accompaniment of bassoons, and the occasional bark of the wolf, or the scream of a night-bird, or even the deep-throated croak of the frog, is no more discordant than the outburst of an octave flute above the even melody of an orchestra; and it is surprising how the large raindrops, pattering on the leaves, and the small voice of the nightingale (singing, like nothing but himself, sweetest in the darkness) seems an intensitive and a low burden to the general anthem of the earth—as it were, a single voice among instruments.

I had what Wordsworth calls a "couchant ear" in my youth, and my story will wait, dear reader, while I tell you of another harmony that I learned to love in the wilderness.

There will come sometimes in the spring—say in May, or whenever the snow-drops and sulphur butterflies are tempted out by the first timorous sunshine—there will come, I say, in that yearning and youth-renewing season, a warm shower at noon. Our tent shall be pitched on the skirts of a forest of young pines, and the evergreen foliage, if foliage it may be called, shall be a daily refreshment to our eye while watching, with the west wind upon our cheeks, the unclothed branches of the elm. The rain descends softly and warm; but with the sunset the clouds break away, and it grows suddenly cold enough to freeze. The next morning you shall come out with me to a hillside looking upon the south, and lie down with your ear to the earth. The pine tassels hold in every four of their fine fingers a drop of rain frozen like a pearl in a long ear-ring, sustained in their loose grasp by the rigidity of the cold. The sun grows warm at ten, and the slight green fingers begin to relax and yield, and by eleven they are all drooping their icy pearls upon the dead leaves with a murmur through the forest like the swarming of the bees of Hybla. There is not much variety in its music, but it is a pleasant monotone for thought, and if you have a restless fever in your bosom, (as I had, when I learned to love it, for the travel which has corrupted the heart and the ear that it

soothed and satisfied then,) you may lie down with a crooked root under your head in the skirts of the forest, and thank Heaven for an anodyne to care. And it is better than the voice of your friend, or the song of your lady-love, for it exacts no gratitude, and will not desert you ere the echo dies upon the wind.

Oh, how many of these harmonies there are!—how many that we hear, and how many that are "too constant to be heard!" I could go back to my youth, now, with this thread of recollection, and unsepulture a hoard of simple and long-buried joys that would bring the blush upon my cheek to think how my senses are dulled since such things could give me pleasure! Is there no "well of Kanathos" for renewing the youth of the soul?—no St. Hilary's cradle? no elixir to cast the slough of heart-sickening and heart-tarnishing custom? Find me an alchymy for *that*, with your alembic and crucible, and you may resolve to dross again your philosopher's stone!

———

TRENTON FALLS.
FROM THE SAME.

TRENTON Falls is rather a misnomer. I scarcely know what you would call it, but the wonder of nature which bears the name is a tremendous torrent, whose bed, for several miles, is sunk fathoms deep into the earth—a roaring and dashing stream, so far below the surface of the forest in which it is lost, that you would think, as you come suddenly upon the edge of its long precipice, that it was a river in some inner world, (coiled within ours, as we in the outer circle of the firmament,) and laid open by some Titanic throe that had cracked clear asunder the crust of this " shallow earth." The idea is rather assisted if you happen to see below you, on its abysmal shore, a party of adventurous travellers; for, at that vast depth, and in contrast with the gigantic trees and rocks, the same number of well-shaped pismires, dressed in the last fashions, and philandering upon your parlour floor, would be about of their apparent size and distinctness.

They showed me at Eleusis the well by which Proserpine ascends to the regions of day on her annual visit to the plains of Thessaly—but with the *genius loci* at my elbow in the shape of a Greek girl as lovely as Phryné, my memory reverted to the bared axle of the earth in the bed of this American river, and I was persuaded (looking the while at the *feronière* of gold sequins on the Phidian forehead of my Katinka) that supposing Hades at the centre of the earth, you are nearer to it by some fathoms at Trenton. I confess I have had, since my first descent into those depths, an uncomfortable doubt of the solidity of the globe—how the deuse it can hold together with such a crack in its bottom!

It was a night to play Endymion, or do any Tom-foolery that could be laid to the charge of the moon, for a more omnipresent and radiant atmosphere of moonlight never sprinkled the wilderness with silver. It was a night in which to wish it might never be day again—a night to be enamoured of the stars, and bid God bless them like human creatures on their bright journey—a night to love in, to dissolve in—to do every thing but what night is made for—sleep! Oh heaven! when I think how precious is life in such moments; how the aroma—the celestial bloom and flower of the soul —the yearning and fast-perishing enthusiasm of youth—waste themselves in the solitude of such nights on the senseless and unanswering air; when I wander alone, unloving and unloved, beneath influences that could inspire me with the elevation of a seraph, were I at the ear of a human creature that could summon forth and measure my limitless capacity of devotion—when I think this, and feel this, and so waste my existence in vain yearnings, I could extinguish the divine spark within me like a lamp on an unvisited shrine, and thank Heaven for an assimilation to the animals I walk among! And that is the substance of a speech I made to Job as a sequitur of a well-meant remark of his own, that "it was a pity Edith Linsey was not there." He took the clause about the "animals" to himself, and made an apology for the same a year after. We sometimes give our friends, quite innocently, such terrible knocks in our rhapsodies!

Most people talk of the *sublimity* of Trenton, but I have haunted it by the week together for its mere loveliness. The river, in the heart of that fearful chasm, is the most varied and beautiful assemblage of the thousand forms and shapes of running water that I know in the world. The soil and the deep-striking roots of the forest terminate far above you, looking like a black rim on the enclosing precipices; the bed of the river and its sky-sustaining walls are of solid rock, and, with the tremendous descent of the stream—forming for miles one continuous succession of falls and rapids—the channel is worn into curves and cavities which throw the clear waters into forms of inconceivable brilliancy and variety. It is a sort of half-twilight below, with here and there a long beam of sunshine reaching down to kiss the lip of an eddy or form a rainbow over a fall, and the reverberating and changing echoes,

"Like a ring of bells whose sound the wind still alters,"

maintain a constant and most soothing music, varying at every step with the varying phase of the current. Cascades of from twenty to thirty feet, over which the river flies with a single and hurrying leap, (not a drop missing from the glassy and bending sheet,) occur frequently as you ascend; and it is from these that the place takes its name. But the falls, though beautiful, are only peculiar from the dazzling and unequalled rapidity with which the waters come to the leap. If it were not for the leaf which drops wavering down into the abysm from trees apparently painted on the sky, and which is caught away as if the lightning had suddenly crossed it, you would think the vault of the steadfast heavens a flying element as soon. The spot in that long gulf of beauty that I best remember is a smooth descent of some hundred yards, where the river in full and undivided volume skims over a plane as polished as a table of scagliola, looking, in its invisible speed, like one mirror of gleaming but motionless crystal. Just above, there is a sudden turn in the glen which sends the water like a catapult against the opposite angle of the rock, and, in the action of years, it has worn out a cavern of unknown depth, into which the whole mass of the river plunges with the abandonment of a flying fiend into hell, and, reappearing like the angel that has pursued him, glides swiftly but with divine serenity on its way. (I am indebted for that last figure to Job, who travelled with a Milton in his pocket, and had a natural redolence of "Paradise Lost" in his conversation.)

Much as I detest water in small quantities, (to drink,) I have a hydromania in the way of lakes, rivers, and waterfalls. It is, by much, the *belle* in the family of the elements. *Earth* is never tolerable unless disguised in green. *Air* is so thin as only to be visible when she borrows drapery of water; and *Fire* is so staringly bright as to be unpleasant to the eyesight; but water, soft, pure, graceful water! there is no shape into which you can throw her that she does not seem lovelier than before. She can borrow nothing of her sisters. Earth has no jewels in her lap so brilliant as her own spray pearls or emeralds; Fire has no rubies like that what she steals from the sunset; Air has no robes like the grace of her fine-woven and ever-changing drapery of silver. A health (in wine!) to WATER!

Who is there that did not love some stream in his youth? Who is there in whose vision of the past there does not sparkle up, from every picture of childhood, a spring or a rivulet woven through the darkened and torn woof of first affections like a thread of unchanged silver? How do you interpret the instinctive yearning with which you search for the river-side or the fountain in every scene of nature—the clinging unaware to the river's course when a truant in the fields in June —the dull void you find in every landscape of which it is not the ornament and the centre? For myself, I hold with the Greek: "Water is the first principle of all things: we were made from it and we shall be resolved into it."

CAUTERSKILL FALLS.
FROM THE SAME.

A MILE or two back from the mountain-house, on nearly the same level, the gigantic forest suddenly sinks two or three hundred feet into the earth, forming a tremendous chasm, over which a bold stag might almost leap, and above which the rocks hang on either side with the most threatening and frowning grandeur. A mountain-stream creeps through the forest to the precipice, and leaps as suddenly over, as if, Arethusa-like, it fled into the earth from the pursuing steps of a satyr. Thirty paces from its brink, you would never suspect, but for the hollow reverberation of the plunging stream, that any thing but a dim and mazy wood was within a day's journey. It is visited as a great curiosity in scenery, under the name of Cauterskill Falls.

Henry W. Longfellow.

HENRY W. LONGFELLOW.

[Born 1807.]

HENRY WADSWORTH LONGFELLOW, a son of the Honourable Stephen Longfellow, of Portland, was born in that city on the twenty-seventh of February, 1807. At the early age of fourteen he entered Bowdoin College, and at the close of the usual period of four years, he was graduated, with high honours, and an unusual reputation for moral as well as intellectual elevation. For a few months, in 1825, he was a law student, in the office of his father, but being offered a professorship of modern languages, which it was proposed to found in Bowdoin College, he was relieved from this uncongenial pursuit to prepare himself for its duties by a visit to Europe, and accordingly left home and passed three years and a half, travelling or residing in France, Italy, Spain, Germany, Holland and England. He returned home in 1829, eminently fitted for his office, upon which he immediately entered. The youthful professor was a great favourite with the collegians; when not engaged in the labours of instruction he was himself a student, or, as sometimes happened, a weaver of those beautiful verses, in which he has exhibited so much both of genius and cultivation; and in a few years he became known through all the country as one of the most graceful poets and most elegant and accomplished scholars of whom we could boast, so that when Mr. George Ticknor, in 1835, resigned the professorship of modern languages and belles-lettres, in the oldest and most distinguished of our universities, there was no hesitation in calling to the vacant post Mr. Longfellow, who had already something of the fame of a veteran in teaching, though yet scarcely twenty-eight years of age. He now therefore resigned his professorship at Brunswick, and again went abroad, with a view of becoming more thoroughly acquainted with the languages and literatures of the north of Europe. He passed more than a year in Denmark, Sweden, Germany and Switzerland, and returning to America, in the autumn of 1836, entered immediately upon his duties at Cambridge, where he has ever since resided, except during a short visit to Europe, for the restoration of his health, in 1842.

As has been intimated above, Professor Longfellow commenced his literary life, and acquired an enviable reputation, at an early age. Indeed while he was an undergraduate he wrote many tasteful and carefully finished poems, for the United States Literary Gazette, and in æsthetic criticism, he soon after exhibited abilities of a very high order, in various articles which he contributed to the North American Review. In 1833 he published his translation from the Spanish of the celebrated poem of Don Jorge Manrique on the death of his father, with a beautiful introductory essay on the moral and religious poetry of Spain; in 1835 his Outre-Mer, or a Pilgrimage beyond the Sea; in 1839 Hyperion, a romance; in 1840 Voices of the Night, his first collection of poems; in 1831 Ballads and other Poems, (embracing The Children of the Lord's Supper, from the Swedish of Tegnér); in 1842 The Spanish Student, a play; in 1843 Poems on Slavery; in 1845 The Poets and Poetry of Europe, with introductions and biographical notices; and in 1846 two complete editions of his Poetical Works, one of which is beautifully illustrated by the best artists of the country.

As a poet Mr. Longfellow's merits are of a very high though not of the highest order. Nothing can be more graceful and tender than some of his Voices of the Night; or more picturesque and dramatical than some of his Ballads; or more simple, chaste, and beautifully wise than the greater part of his short poems, which seem to be painted experiences of both the mind and heart. They have that stamp of nature which commends them alike to the rudest and the most cultivated. Every one can understand them, and in every one they are sure to awaken some responsive feeling. Yet he seems to want a certain freshness and creative energy, perhaps on account of that absence of self-reliance, which is commonly observable in men, in the formation of whose characters the study of books has had more than a due influence.

495

The first prose work of Professor Longfellow was a collection of tales and sketches illustrating the impressions of a youthful scholar as he wanders leisurely through southern Europe. Hyperion is in a similar spirit, but has a unity of purpose, and is bolder and more sustained. The scholar, here, with his delicate fancy and extreme susceptibility, is exposed to trials. But his life is in obedience to the impressive motto of the romance, " Look not mournfully into the Past: It comes not back again. Wisely improve the Present: It is thine. Go forth to meet the shadowy Future, without fear, and with a manly heart." Here is the moral, which is wrought out ingeniously and with exquisite taste, though with little constructive talent, for the plot is very simple, and the incidents are barely sufficient to give life to the sentiments. It is a poem, full of beautiful thoughts and illustrations; a painting of conceptions that float in the solitary mind of a man of genius, refinement and feeling.

THE VILLAGE OF AUTEUIL.
FROM OUTRE-MER.

The sultry heat of summer always brings with it, to the idler and the man of leisure, a longing for the leafy shade and the green luxuriance of the country. It is pleasant to interchange the din of the city, the movement of the crowd, and the gossip of society, with the silence of the hamlet, the quiet seclusion of the grove, and the gossip of a woodland brook. As is sung in the old ballad of Robin Hood,—

"In somer, when the shawes be sheyn,
  And leves be large and long,
Hit is full mery in feyre foreste,
  To hear the foulys song;
To se the dere draw to the dale
  And leve the hilles hee,
And shadow hem in the leves grene,
  Vnder the grene wode tre."

It was a feeling of this kind that prompted me, during my residence in the north of France, to pass one of the summer months at Auteuil, the pleasantest of the many little villages that lie in the immediate vicinity of the metropolis. It is situated on the outskirts of the Bois de Boulogne, a wood of some extent, in whose green alleys the dusty cit enjoys the luxury of an evening drive, and gentlemen meet in the morning to give each other satisfaction in the usual way. A cross-road, skirted with green hedgerows, and overshadowed by tall poplars, leads you from the noisy highway of St. Cloud and Versailles to the still retirement of this suburban hamlet. On either side the eye discovers old châteaux amid the trees, and green parks, whose pleasant shades recall a thousand images of La Fontaine, Racine, and Molière; and on an eminence, overlooking the windings of the Seine, and giving a beautiful though distant view of the domes and gardens of Paris, rises the village of Passy, long the residence of our countrymen Franklin and Count Rumford.

I took up my abode at a *maison de santé;* not that I was a valetudinarian, but because I there found some one to whom I could whisper, " How sweet is solitude !" Behind the house was a garden filled with fruit trees of various kinds, and adorned with gravel-walks and green arbours, furnished with tables and rustic seats, for the repose of the invalid and the sleep of the indolent. Here the inmates of the rural hospital met on common ground, to breathe the invigorating air of morning, and while away the lazy noon or vacant evening with tales of the sick chamber.

The establishment was kept by Dr. Dentdelion, a dried-up little fellow, with red hair, a sandy complexion, and the physiognomy and gestures of a monkey. His character corresponded to his outward lineaments; for he had all a monkey's busy and curious impertinence. Nevertheless, such as he was, the village Æsculapius strutted forth the little great man of Auteuil. The peasants looked up to him as to an oracle; he contrived to be at the head of every thing, and laid claim to the credit of all public improvements in the village; in fine, he was a great man on a small scale.

It was within the dingy walls of this little potentate's imperial palace that I chose my country residence. I had a chamber in the second story, with a solitary window, which looked upon the street, and gave me a peep into a neighbour's garden. This I esteemed a great privilege; for, as a stranger, I desired to see all that was passing out of doors; and the sight of green trees, though growing on another's ground, is always a blessing. Within doors—had I been disposed to quarrel with my household gods—I might have taken some objection to my neighbourhood; for, on one side of me was a consumptive patient, whose graveyard cough drove me from my chamber by day; and on the other, an English colonel, whose incoherent ravings, in the delirium of a high and obstinate fever, often broke my slumbers by night; but I found ample amends for these inconveniences in the society of those who were so little indisposed as hardly to know what ailed them, and those who, in health themselves, had accompanied a friend or relative to the shades of the country in pursuit of it. To these I am indebted for much courtesy; and particularly to one who, if these pages should ever meet her eye, will not, I hope, be unwilling to accept this slight memorial of a former friendship.

It was, however, to the Bois de Boulogne that I looked for my principal recreation. There I took my solitary walk, morning and evening; or, mounted on a little mouse-coloured donkey, paced demurely along the woodland pathway. I had a favourite seat beneath the shadow of a venerable oak, one of the few hoary patriarchs of the wood which had survived the bivouacs of the allied armies. It stood upon the brink of a little glassy pool, whose tranquil bosom was the image of a quiet and secluded life, and stretched its parental arms over a rustic bench, that had been constructed beneath it for the accommodation of the foot traveller, or, perchance, some idle dreamer like myself. It seemed to look round with a lordly air upon its old hereditary domain, whose stillness was no longer broken by the tap of the martial drum, nor the discordant clang of arms; and, as the breeze whispered among its branches, it seemed to be holding friendly colloquies with a few of its venerable contemporaries, who stooped from the opposite bank of the pool, nodding gravely now and then, and gazing at themselves with a sigh in the mirror below.

In this quiet haunt of rural repose I used to sit at noon, hear the birds sing, and "possess myself in much quietness." Just at my feet lay the little silver pool, with the sky and the woods painted in its mimic vault, and occasionally the image of a bird, or the soft, watery outline of a cloud, floating silently through its sunny hollows. The water-lily spread its broad, green leaves on the surface, and rocked to sleep a little world of insect life in its golden cradle. Sometimes a wandering leaf came floating and wavering downward, and settled on the water; then a vagabond insect would break the smooth surface into a thousand ripples, or a green-coated frog slide from the bank, and, plump! dive headlong to the bottom.

I entered, too, with some enthusiasm, into all the rural sports and merrimakes of the village. The holydays were so many little eras of mirth and good feeling; for the French have that happy and sunshine temperament,—that merry-go-mad character, —which renders all their social meetings scenes of enjoyment and hilarity. I made it a point never to miss any of the *fêtes champêtres*, or rural dances, at the wood of Boulogne; though I confess it sometimes gave me a momentary uneasiness to see my rustic throne beneath the oak usurped by a noisy group of girls, the silence and decorum of my imaginary realm broken by music and laughter, and, in a word, my whole kingdom turned topsy-turvy with romping, fiddling, and dancing. But I am naturally, and from principle, too, a lover of all those innocent amusements which cheer the labourer's toil, and, as it were, put their shoulders to the wheel of life, and help the poor man along with his load of cares. Hence I saw with no small delight the rustic swain astride the wooden horse of the *carrousel*, and the village maiden whirling round and round in its dizzy car; or took my stand on a rising ground that overlooked the dance, an idle spectator in a busy throng. It was just where the village touched the outward border of the wood. There a little area had been levelled beneath the trees, surrounded by a painted rail, with a row of benches inside. The music was placed in a slight balcony, built around the trunk of a large tree in the centre; and the lamps, hanging from the branches above, gave a gay, fantastic, and fairy

look to the scene. How often in such moments did I recall the lines of Goldsmith, describing those "kinder skies" beneath which "France displays her bright domain," and feel how true and masterly the sketch,—

"Alike all ages; dames of ancient days
Have led their children through the mirthful maze,
And the gray grandsire, skilled in gestic lore,
Has frisked beneath the burden of threescore."

Nor must I forget to mention the *fête patronale*, —a kind of annual fair, which is held at mid-summer, in honour of the patron saint of Auteuil. Then the principal street of the village is filled with booths of every description; strolling players, and rope-dancers, and jugglers, and giants, and dwarfs, and wild beasts, and all kinds of wonderful shows, excite the gaping curiosity of the throng; and in dust, crowds, and confusion, the village rivals the capital itself. Then the goodly dames of Passy descend into the village of Auteuil; then the brewers of Billancourt and the tanners of Sèvres dance lustily under the green-wood tree; and then, too, the sturdy fishmongers of Brétigny and Saint-Yon regale their fat wives with an airing in a swing, and their customers with eels and crawfish; or, as is more poetically set forth in an old Christmas carol,—

"Vous eussiez vu venir tous ceux de Saint-Yon,
Et ceux de Bretigny apportant du poisson,
Les barbeaux et gardons, anguilles et carpettes
Etoient à bon marché
Croyez,
A cette journee-là,
Là, là,
Et aussi les perchettes."

I found another source of amusement in observing the various personages that daily passed and repassed beneath my window. The character which most of all arrested my attention was a poor blind fiddler, whom I first saw chanting a doleful ballad at the door of a small tavern near the gate of the village. He wore a brown coat, out at elbows, the fragment of a velvet waistcoat, and a pair of tight nankeens, so short as hardly to reach below his calves. A little foraging cap, that had long since seen its best days, set off an open, good-humoured countenance, bronzed by sun and wind. He was led about by a brisk, middle-aged woman, in straw hat and wooden shoes; and a little bare-footed boy, with clear, blue eyes and flaxen hair, held a tattered hat in his hand, in which he collected eleëmosynary sous. The old fellow had a favourite song, which he used to sing with great glee to a merry, joyous air, the burden of which ran "*Chantons l'amour et le plaisir!*" I often thought it would have been a good lesson for the crabbed and discontented rich man to have heard this remnant of humanity,—poor, blind, and in rags, and dependent upon casual charity for his daily bread, singing in so cheerful a voice the charms of existence, and, as it were, fiddling life away to a merry tune.

I was one morning called to my window by the sound of rustic music. I looked out and beheld a procession of villagers advancing along the road, attired in gay dresses, and marching merrily on in the direction of the church. I soon perceived that it was a marriage-festival. The procession was led by a long orang-outang of a man, in a straw hat and white dimity bobcoat, playing on an asthmatic clarionet, from which he contrived to blow unearthly sounds, ever and anon squeaking off at right angles from his tune, and winding up with a grand flourish on the guttural notes. Behind him, led by his little boy, came the blind fiddler, his honest features glowing with all the hilarity of a rustic bridal, and, as he stumbled along, sawing away upon his fiddle till he made all crack again. Then came the happy bridegroom, dressed in his Sunday suit of blue, with a large nosegay in his button-hole; and close beside him his blushing bride, with downcast eyes, clad in a white robe and slippers, and wearing a wreath of white roses in her hair. The friends and relatives brought up the procession; and a troop of village urchins came shouting along in the rear, scrambling among themselves for the largess of sous and sugar-plums that now and then issued in large handfuls from the pockets of a lean man in black, who seemed to officiate as master of ceremonies on the occasion. I gazed on the procession till it was out of sight; and when the last wheeze of the clarionet died upon my ear, I could not help thinking how happy were they who were thus to dwell together in the peaceful bosom of their native village, far from the pestilential vices of the town.

On the evening of the same day, I was sitting by the window, enjoying the freshness of the air and the beauty and stillness of the hour, when I heard the distant and solemn hymn of the Catholic burial-service, at first so faint and indistinct that it seemed an illusion. It rose mournfully on the hush of evening,—died gradually away,—then ceased. Then it rose again, nearer and more distinct, and soon after a funeral procession appeared, and passed directly beneath my window. It was led by a priest, bearing the banner of the church, and followed by two boys, holding long flambeaux in their hands. Next came a double file of priests in their surplices, with a missal in one hand and a lighted wax taper in the other, chanting the funeral dirge at intervals,—now pausing, and then again taking up the mournful burden of their lamentation, accompanied by others, who played upon a rude kind of bassoon, with a dismal and wailing sound. Then followed various symbols of the church, and the bier borne on the shoulders of four men. The coffin was covered with a velvet pall, and a chaplet of white flowers lay upon it, indicating that the deceased was unmarried. A few of the villagers came behind, clad in mourning robes, and bearing lighted tapers. The procession passed slowly along the same street that in the morning had been thronged by the gay bridal company. A melancholy train of thought forced itself home upon my mind. The joys and sorrows of this world are so strikingly mingled! Our mirth and grief are brought so mournfully in contact! We laugh while others weep,—and others rejoice when we are sad! The light heart and the heavy walk side by side and go about together! Beneath the same roof are spread the wedding-feast and the funeral-

pall! The bridal-song mingles with the burial-hymn! One goes to the marriage-bed, another to the grave; and all is mutable, uncertain, and transitory.

It is with sensations of pure delight that I recur to the brief period of my existence which was passed in the peaceful shades of Auteuil. There is one kind of wisdom which we learn from the world, and another kind which can be acquired in solitude only. In cities we study those around us; but in the retirement of the country we learn to know ourselves. The voice within us is more distinctly audible in the stillness of the place; and the gentler affections of our nature spring up more freshly in its tranquillity and sunshine.—nurtured by the healthy principle which we inhale with the pure air, and invigorated by the genial influences which descend into the heart from the quiet of the sylvan solitude around, and the soft serenity of the sky above.

———

SPRING.
FROM HYPERION.

It was a sweet carol, which the Rhodian children sang of old in spring, bearing in their hands, from door to door, a swallow, as herald of the season;

"The swallow is come!
The swallow is come!
O fair are the seasons, and light
Are the days that she brings,
With her dusky wings,
And her bosom snowy white."

A pretty carol, too, is that, which the Hungarian boys, on the islands of the Danube, sing to the returning stork in spring;

"Stork! stork! poor stork!
Why is thy foot so bloody?
A Turkish boy hath torn it;
Hungarian boy will heal it,
With fiddle, fife, and drum."

But what child has a heart to sing in this capricious clime of ours, where spring comes sailing in from the sea, with wet and heavy cloud-sails, and the misty pennon of the eastwind nailed to the mast! Yet even here, and in the stormy month of March even, there are bright warm mornings, when we open our windows to inhale the balmy air. The pigeons fly to and fro, and we hear the whirring sound of wings. Old flies crawl out of the cracks, to sun themselves; and think it is summer. They die in their conceit; and so do our hearts within us, when the cold sea-breath comes from the eastern sea; and again,

"The driving hail
Upon the window beats with icy flail."

The red-flowering maple is first in blossom, its beautiful purple flowers unfolding a fortnight before the leaves. The moose-wood follows, with rose-coloured buds and leaves; and the dogwood, robed in the white of its own pure blossoms. Then comes the sudden rain storm; and the birds fly to and fro, and shriek. Where do they hide themselves in such storms? at what firesides dry their feathery cloaks? At the fireside of the great, hospitable sun, to-morrow, not before,—they must sit in wet garments until then.

In all climates spring is beautiful. In the south it is intoxicating, and sets a poet beside himself. The birds begin to sing;—they utter a few rapturous notes, and then wait for an answer in the silent woods. Those green-coated musicians, the frogs, make holiday in the neighbouring marshes. They, too, belong to the orchestra of nature; whose vast theatre is again opened, though the doors have been so long bolted with icicles, and the scenery hung with snow and frost, like cobwebs. This is the prelude, which announces the rising of the broad green curtain. Already the grass shoots forth. The waters leap with thrilling pulse through the veins of the earth; the sap through the veins of the plants and trees; and the blood through the veins of man. What a thrill of delight in spring-time! What a joy in being and moving! Men are at work in gardens; and in the air there is an odour of the fresh earth. The leaf-buds begin to swell and blush. The white blossoms of the cherry hang upon the boughs like snow-flakes, and ere long our next-door neighbours will be completely hidden from us by the dense green foliage. The May flowers open their soft blue eyes. Children are let loose in the fields and gardens. They hold butter-cups under each others' chins, to see if they love butter. And the little girls adorn themselves with chains and curls of dandelions; pull out the yellow leaves to see if the schoolboy loves them, and blow the down from the leafless stalk, to find out if their mothers want them at home.

And at night so cloudless and so still! Not a voice of living thing,—not a whisper of leaf or waving bough,—not a breath of wind,—not a sound upon the earth nor in the air! And overhead bends the blue sky, dewy and soft, and radiant with innumerable stars, like the inverted bell of some blue flower, sprinkled with golden dust, and breathing fragrance. Or if the heavens are overcast, it is no wild storm of wind and rain; but clouds that melt and fall in showers. One does not wish to sleep; but lies awake to hear the pleasant sound of the dropping rain.

SUMMER-TIME.
FROM THE SAME.

THEY were right,—those old German minnesingers,—to sing the pleasant summer-time! What a time it is! How June stands illuminated in the calendar! The windows are all wide open; only the Venetian blinds closed. Here and there a long streak of sunshine streams in through a crevice. We hear the low sound of the wind among the trees; and, as it swells and freshens, the distant doors clap to, with a sudden sound. The trees are heavy with leaves; and the gardens full of blossoms, red and white. The whole atmosphere is laden with perfume and sunshine. The birds sing. The cock struts about, and crows loftily. Insects chirp in the grass. Yellow butter-cups stud the green carpet like golden buttons, and the red blossoms of the clover like rubies. The elm-trees reach their long, pendulous branches almost to the ground. White clouds sail aloft; and vapours fret the blue sky with silver threads. The white village gleams afar against the dark hills. Through the meadow winds the river,—careless, indolent. It seems to love the country, and is in no haste to reach the sea. The bee only is at work,—the hot and angry bee. All things else are at play; he never plays, and is vexed that any one should.

People drive out from town to breathe, and to be happy. Most of them have flowers in their hands; bunches of apple-blossoms, and still oftener lilacs. Ye denizens of the crowded city, how pleasant to you is the change from the sultry streets to the open fields, fragrant with clover-blossoms! how pleasant the fresh breezy country air, dashed with brine from the meadows! how pleasant, above all, the flowers, the manifold beautiful flowers!

It is no longer day. Through the trees rises the red moon, and the stars are scarcely seen. In the vast shadow of night, the coolness and the dews descend. I sit at the open window to enjoy them; and hear only the voice of the summer wind. Like black hulks, the shadows of the great trees ride at anchor on the billowy sea of grass. I cannot see the red and blue flowers, but I know that they are there. Far away in the meadow gleams the silver Charles. The tramp of horses' hoofs sounds from the wooden bridge. Then all is still, save the continuous wind of the summer night. Sometimes I know not if it be the wind or the sound of the neighbouring sea. The village clock strikes; and I feel that I am not alone.

How different is it in the city! It is late, and the crowd is gone. You step out upon the balcony, and lie in the very bosom of the cool, dewy night, as if you folded her garments about you. The whole starry heaven is spread out overhead. Beneath lies the public walk with trees, like a fathomless, black gulf, into whose silent darkness the spirit plunges and floats away, with some beloved spirit clasped in its embrace. The lamps are still burning up and down the long street. People go by, with grotesque shadows, now fore-shortened and now lengthening away into the darkness and vanishing, while a new one springs up behind the walker, and seems to pass him on the sidewalk. The iron gates of the park shut with a jangling clang. There are footsteps, and loud voices,—tumult,—a drunken brawl,—an alarm of fire;—then silence again. And now at length the city is asleep, and we can see the night. The belated moon looks over the roofs, and finds no one to welcome her. The moonlight is broken. It lies here and there in the squares, and the opening of streets,—angular, like blocks of white marble.

TELL me, my soul, why art thou restless? Why dost thou look forward to the future with such strong desire? The present is thine,—and the past;—and the future shall be!

LIVES OF SCHOLARS.

FROM THE SAME.

WHAT a strange picture a university presents to the imagination. The lives of scholars in their cloistered stillness;—literary men of retired habits, and professors who study sixteen hours a day, and never see the world but on a Sunday. Nature has, no doubt, for some wise purpose, placed in their hearts this love of literary labour and seclusion. Otherwise, who would feed the undying lamp of thought? But for such men as these, a blast of wind through the chinks and crannies of this old world, or the flapping of a conqueror's banner, would blow it out for ever. The light of the soul is easily extinguished. And whenever I reflect upon these things I become aware of the great importance, in a nation's history, of the individual fame of scholars and literary men. I fear, that it is far greater than the world is willing to acknowledge; or, perhaps, I should say, than the world has thought of acknowledging. Blot out from England's history the names of Chaucer, Shakspeare, Spenser, and Milton only, and how much of her glory would you blot out with them! Take from Italy such names as Dante, Petrarch, Boccaccio, Michel Angelo, and Raphael, and how much would still be wanting to the completeness of her glory! How would the history of Spain look if the leaves were torn out, on which are written the names of Cervantes, Lope de Vega, and Calderon! What would be the fame of Portugal, without her Camoens; of France, without her Racine, and Rabelais, and Voltaire; or Germany, without her Martin Luther, her Gœthe, and Schiller!—Nay, what were the nations of old, without their philosophers, poets, and historians! Tell me, do not these men in all ages and in all places, emblazon with bright colours the armorial bearings of their country? Yes, and far more than this; for in all ages and all places they give humanity assurance of its greatness; and say, Call not this time or people wholly barbarous; for thus much, even then and there, could the human mind achieve! But the boisterous world has hardly thought of acknowledging all this. Therein it has shown itself somewhat ungrateful. Else, whence the great reproach, the general scorn, the loud derision, with which, to take a familiar example, the monks of the middle ages are regarded. That they slept their lives away is most untrue. For in an age when books were few,—so few, so precious, that they were often chained to their oaken shelves with iron chains, like galley-slaves to their benches, these men, with their laborious hands, copied upon parchment all the lore and wisdom of the past, and transmitted it to us. Perhaps it is not too much to say, that, but for these monks, not one line of the classics would have reached our day. Surely, then, we can pardon something to those superstitious ages, perhaps even the mysticism of the scholastic philosophy, since, after all, we can find no harm in it, only the mistaking of the possible for the real, and the high aspirings of the human mind

after a long-sought and unknown somewhat. I think the name of Martin Luther, the monk of Wittemberg, alone sufficient to redeem all monkhood from the reproach of laziness! If this will not, perhaps the vast folios of Thomas Aquinas will;—or the countless manuscripts, still treasured in old libraries, whose yellow and wrinkled pages remind one of the hands that wrote them, and the faces that once bent over them.

WHERE SHOULD THE SCHOLAR LIVE?

FROM THE SAME.

WHERE should the scholar live? In solitude or in society? In the green stillness of the country, where he can hear the heart of nature beat, or in the dark, gray city, where he can hear and feel the throbbing heart of man? I will make answer for him, and say, in the dark gray city. Oh, they do greatly err, who think, that the stars are all the poetry which cities have; and therefore that the poet's only dwelling should be in sylvan solitudes, under the green roof of trees. Beautiful, no doubt, are all the forms of nature, when transfigured by the miraculous power of poetry; hamlets and harvest fields, and nut-brown waters, flowing ever under the forest, vast and shadowy, with all the sights and sounds of rural life. But after all, what are these but the decorations and painted scenery in the great theatre of human life? What are they but the coarse materials of the poet's song? Glorious indeed, is the world of God around us, but more glorious the world of God within us. There lies the land of song; there lies the poet's native land. The river of life, that flows through streets tumultuous, bearing along so many gallant hearts, so many wrecks of humanity;—the many homes and households, each a little world in itself, revolving round its fireside, as a central sun; all forms of human joy and suffering, brought into that narrow compass;—and to be in this and be a part of this; acting, thinking, rejoicing, sorrowing, with his fellow-men;—such, such should be the poet's life. If he would describe the world, he should live in the world. The mind of the scholar, also, if you would have it large and liberal, should come in contact with other minds. It is better that his armour should be somewhat bruised even by rude encounters, than hang for ever rusting on the wall. Nor will his themes be few or trivial, because apparently shut in between the walls of houses, and having merely the decorations of street scenery. A ruined character is as picturesque as a ruined castle. There are dark abysses and yawning gulfs in the human heart, which can be rendered passable only by bridging them over with iron nerves and sinews, as Challey bridged the Savine in Switzerland, and Telford the sea between Anglesea and England, with chain bridges. These are the great themes of human thought; not green grass, and flowers, and moonshine. Besides, the mere external forms of nature we make our own, and carry with us into the city, by the power of memory.

MEN OF GENIUS.

FROM THE SAME.

It has become a common saying, that men of genius are always in advance of their age; which is true. There is something equally true, yet not so common; namely, that, of these men of genius, the best and bravest are in advance not only of their own age, but of every age. As the German prose poet says, every possible future is behind them. We cannot suppose, that a period of time will ever come, when the world, or any considerable portion of it, shall have come up abreast with these great minds, so as fully to comprehend them. And oh! how majestically they walk in history; some like the sun, with all his travelling glories round him; others wrapped in gloom, yet glorious as a night with stars. Through the else silent darkness of the past, the spirit hears their slow and solemn footsteps. Onward they pass, like those hoary elders seen in the sublime vision of an earthly paradise, attendant angels bearing golden lights before them, and, above and behind, the whole air painted with seven listed colours, as from the trail of pencils!

And yet, on earth, these men were not happy, —not all happy, in the outward circumstance of their lives. They were in want, and in pain, and familiar with prison bars, and the damp, weeping walls of dungeons! Oh, I have looked with wonder upon those, who, in sorrow and privation, and bodily discomfort, and sickness, which is the shadow of death, have worked right on to the accomplishment of their great purposes; toiling much, enduring much, fulfilling much;—and then, with shattered nerves, and sinews all unstrung, have laid themselves down in the grave, and slept the sleep of death,—and the world talks of them, while they sleep.

It would seem, indeed, as if all their sufferings had but sanctified them! As if the death-angel, in passing, had touched them with the hem of his garment, and made them holy! As if the hand of disease had been stretched out over them only to make the sign of the cross upon their souls. And as in the sun's eclipse we can behold the great stars shining in the heavens, so in this life eclipse have these men beheld the lights of the great eternity, burning solemnly and for ever!

LIFE.

FROM THE SAME.

Life is one, and universal; its forms many and individual. Throughout this beautiful and wonderful creation there is never-ceasing motion, without rest by night or day, ever weaving to and fro. Swifter than a weaver's shuttle it flies from birth to death, from death to birth; from the beginning seeks the end, and finds it not, for the seeming end is only a dim beginning of a new out-going and endeavour after the end. As the ice upon the mountain, when the warm breath of the summer's sun breathes upon it, melts, and divides into drops, each of which reflects an image of the sun; so life, in the smile of God's love, divides itself into separate forms, each bearing in it and reflecting an image of God's love. Of all these forms the highest and most perfect in its god-likeness is the human soul. The vast cathedral of nature is full of holy scriptures, and shapes of deep, mysterious meaning; but all is solitary and silent there; no bending knee, no uplifted eye, no lip adoring, praying. Into this vast cathedral comes the human soul, seeking its Creator; and the universal silence is changed to sound, and the sound is harmonious, and has a meaning, and is comprehended and felt. It was an ancient saying of the Persians, that the waters rush from the mountains and hurry forth into all the lands to find the lord of the earth; and the flame of the fire, when it awakes, gazes no more upon the ground, but mounts heavenward to seek the lord of heaven; and here and there the earth has built the great watch-towers of the mountains, and they lift their heads far up into the sky, and gaze ever upward and around, to see if the Judge of the World comes not! Thus in nature herself, without man, there lies a waiting, and hoping, a looking and yearning, after an unknown somewhat. Yes; when, above there, where the mountain lifts its head over all others, that it may be alone with the clouds and storms of heaven, the lonely eagle looks forth into the gray dawn, to see if the day comes not! when, by the mountain torrent, the brooding raven listens to hear if the chamois is returning from his nightly pasture in the valley; and when the soon uprising sun call out the spicy odours of the thousand flowers, th Alpine flowers, with heaven's deep blue and th blush of sunset on their leaves;—then there awake in nature, and the soul of man can see and com prehend it, an expectation and a longing for a fu ture revelation of God's majesty. It awakens, also, when in the fulness of life, field and forest rest at noon, and through the stillness is heard only the song of the grasshopper and the hum of the bee; and when at evening the singing lark, up from the sweet-swelling vineyards rises, or in the later hours of night Orion puts on his shining armour, to walk forth in the fields of heaven. But in the soul of man alone is this longing changed to certainty and fulfilled. For lo! the light of the sun and the stars shines through the air, and is nowhere visible and seen; the planets hasten with more than the speed of the storm through infinite space, and their footsteps are not heard, but where the sunlight strikes the firm surface of the planets, where the stormwind smites the wall of the mountain cliff, there is the one seen and the other heard. Thus is the glory of God made visible, and may be seen, where in the soul of men it meets its likeness changeless and firm-standing. Thus, then, stands man;—a mountain on the boundary between two worlds;—its foot in one, its summit far-rising into the other. From this summit the manifold landscape of life is visible, the way of the past and perishable, which we have left behind us; and, as we evermore ascend, bright glimpses of the daybreak of eternity beyond us!

PAUL FLEMMING RESOLVES.
FROM THE SAME.

AND now the sun was growing high and warm. A little chapel, whose door stood open, seemed to invite Flemming to enter and enjoy the grateful coolness. He went in. There was no one there. The walls were covered with paintings and sculpture of the rudest kind, and with a few funeral tablets. There was nothing there to move the heart to devotion; but in that hour the heart of Flemming was weak,—weak as a child's. He bowed his stubborn knees and wept. And oh! how many disappointed hopes, how many bitter recollections, how much of wounded pride, and unrequited love, were in those tears, through which he read on a marble tablet in the chapel wall opposite, this singular inscription :—

"Look not mournfully into the past: It comes not back again. Wisely improve the present: It is thine. Go forth to meet the shadowy future, without fear, and with a manly heart."

It seemed to him, as if the unknown tenant of that grave had opened his lips of dust, and spoken to him the words of consolation, which his soul needed, and which no friend had yet spoken. In a moment the anguish of his thoughts was still. The stone was rolled away from the door of his heart; death was no longer there, but an angel clothed in white. He stood up, and his eyes were no more bleared with tears; and, looking into the bright, morning heaven, he said —

"I will be strong!"

Men sometimes go down into tombs, with painful longings to behold once more the faces of their departed friends; and as they gaze upon them, lying there so peacefully with the semblance that they wore on earth, the sweet breath of heaven touches them, and the features crumble and fall together, and are but dust. So did his soul then descend for the last time into the great tomb of the past, with painful longings to behold once more the dear faces of those he had loved; and the sweet breath of heaven touched them, and they would not stay, but crumbled away and perished as he gazed. They, too, were dust. And thus, far-sounding, he heard the great gate of the past shut behind him as the divine poet did the gate of paradise; when the angel pointed him the way up the holy mountain; and to him likewise was it forbidden to look back.

In the life of every man, there are sudden transitions of feeling, which seem almost miraculous. At once, as if some magician had touched the heavens and the earth, the dark clouds melt into the air, the wind falls, and serenity succeeds the storm. The causes which produce these sudden changes may have been long at work within us, but the changes themselves are instantaneous, and apparently without sufficient cause. It was so with Flemming and from that hour forth he resolved, that he would no longer veer with every shifting wind of circumstance; no longer be a child's plaything in the hands of fate, which we ourselves do make or mar. He resolved henceforward not to lean on others; but to walk self-confident and self-possessed; no longer to waste his years in vain regrets, nor wait the fulfilment of boundless hopes and indiscreet desires; but to live in the present wisely, alike forgetful of the past, and careless of what the mysterious future might bring. And from that moment he was calm, and strong; he was reconciled with himself! His thoughts turned to his distant home beyond the sea. An indescribable, sweet feeling rose within him.

"Thither will I turn my wandering footsteps," said he; "and be a man among men, and no longer a dreamer among shadows. Henceforth be mine a life of action and reality! I will work in my own sphere, nor wish it other than it is. This alone is health and happiness. This alone is life.

'Life that shall send
    A challenge to its end,
And when it comes, say, Welcome, friend!'

Why have I not made these sage reflections, this wise resolve, sooner? Can such a simple result spring only from the long and intricate process of experience? Alas! it is not till time, with reckless hand, has torn out half the leaves from the book of human life, to light the fires of passion with, from day to day, that man begins to see, that the leaves which remain are few in number, and to remember, faintly at first, and then more clearly, that, upon the earlier pages of that book, was written a story of happy innocence, which he would fain read over again. Then come listless irresolution, and the inevitable inaction of despair; or else the firm resolve to record upon the leaves that still remain, a more noble history than the child's story, with which the book began."

THE GLACIER OF THE RHONE.
FROM THE SAME.

ERE long he reached the magnificent glacier of the Rhone; a frozen cataract, more than two thousand feet in height, and many miles broad at its base. It fills the whole valley between two mountains, running back to their summits. At the base it is arched, like a dome; and above, jagged and rough, and resembles a mass of gigantic crystals, of a pale emerald tint, mingled with white. A snowy crust covers its surface; but at every rent and crevice the pale green ice shines clear in the sun. Its shape is that of a glove, lying with the palm downwards, and the fingers crooked and close together. It is a gauntlet of ice, which, centuries ago, winter, the king of these mountains, threw down in defiance to the sun; and year by year the sun strives in vain to lift it from the ground on the point of his glittering spear.

WILLIAM GILMORE SIMMS.

[Born 1806. Died 1870.]

THIS industrious and prolific author is a native of Charleston. His mother died while he was an infant, and his father, failing soon after as a merchant, emigrated to the western country, leaving him to the care of an aged grandmother, with a small maternal property, which she hoarded so carefully as to withhold the appropriations necessary for his education. He received therefore no other instruction than such as are given in one of the grammar schools of the city, which constitutional feebleness and frequent confinement by sickness prevented him from attending with much regularity. Ill health however had its advantages. Incapable of joining in the more hardy sports of his age, he was driven to books for amusement, and read with never-failing zest whatever came in his way, of poetry, romance, biography, or history, and with particular avidity gleaned from travels and tradition all that related to the colonial and revolutionary periods in the Carolinas. He grew apace, in physical and intellectual strength, wrote for the press on all varieties of subjects, and on his twenty-first birthday, was admitted to practise in the courts of Charleston as an attorney and counsellor at law.

Mr. Simms published his first book, Lyrical and Other Poems, in 1825, when he was about eighteen years of age. It was followed in 1827 by Early Lays, in 1829 by The Vision of Cortez and other Poems, and in 1830 by The Tri-Color, or Three Days of Blood in Paris. There are gleams of sunshine in all these youthful essays, and some of the songs and other short pieces have a dash and spirit, and genuine feeling in them which promised much from a judicious culture; but he had not even then patience for revision, and perhaps his best performances should be regarded as below the level of his powers.

As soon as Mr. Simms came into possession of his inherited property he purchased The Charleston City Gazette, and with ambition, energy, and confidence, entered upon the difficult profession of an editor. It was an unfortunate period for the experiment, and doubly so for one of his principles, and unhesitating independence of character. He was a Unionist, and for a considerable period his paper was the only one in the state to breast the storm of Nullification. His failure, under the circumstances, was a matter of course. At the end of a few years he found that he had exhausted his pecuniary resources and involved himself in debt. He disposed of his establishment, therefore, and nothing daunted by the past, decided suddenly and finally upon his future pursuits. It was a bold undertaking, but he determined to retrieve his fortune by literature, and immediately entered upon measures of preparation.

By this time he had lost his father, and his wife, whom he had married before he was of age. He had made two long journeys through the south and west, impressing on his mind views of their wildest and most beautiful scenery, to be transferred to the pages of dreamed-of poems and romances, and in the spring of 1832 he visited for the first time the north. After travelling through the most interesting portions of the country he paused at the rural village of Hingham, in Massachusetts, and there prepared for the press the longest and best of his poems, Atalantis, a Story of the Sea, which was published in the following winter in New York. This was succeeded in 1833 by Martin Faber, the Story of a Criminal,* and the Book of my Lady; in 1834 by Guy Rivers, a Tale of Georgia; in 1835 by The Yemassee, a Romance of Carolina, and The Partisan, a Tale of the Revolution; in 1836 by Mellichampe, a Legend of the Santee; in 1837 by a collection of Tales

---

* Martin Faber, a gloomy and passionate tale, appeared soon after the English novel entitled Miserimus, and was instantly declared by reviewers here and abroad to be an imitation of that work. But they were at fault in this, as they are in nine-tenths of this sort of charges. Martin Faber was expanded from a tale, which Mr. Simms published ten years before, in a magazine in Charleston, containing all the distinguishing traits and scenes of the subsequent romance. It belongs to the family of which Godwin's Caleb Williams is the best known model; but those who read the two works will fail to find any imitation on the part of the American author.

503

published with a new edition of Martin Faber; in 1838 by Pelayo a Story of the Goth, Richard Hurdis or the Avenger of Blood, a Tale of Alabama, and Carl Werner, with other Tales of the Imagination; in 1839 by The Damsel of Darien, and Southern Passages and Pictures, a collection of poems; in 1840 by Border Beagles, a Tale of Mississippi, and The History of South Carolina; in 1841 by The Kinsmen or the Black Riders of the Congaree, and Confession or the Blind Heart, a Domestic Story; in 1842 by Beauchampe or the Kentucky Tragedy, a Tale of Passion; in 1843 by Donna Florida, a Tale, (in four cantos;) in 1844 by the Life and Times of Francis Marion; in 1845 by Grouped Thoughts and Scattered Fancies, a collection of sonnets, Helen Halsey or the Swamp State of Conelachita, a Tale of the Borders, Castle Dismal or the Bachelor's Christmas, a Domestic Legend, The Wigwam and the Cabin, a collection of tales, and Views and Reviews of American Literature, History, and Fiction; in 1846 by Count Julian, the Last Days of the Goth, Ayretos, or Songs of the South, second series of The Wigwam and the Cabin, second series of Views and Reviews of American Literature, History and Fiction, and the Life of John Smith, the founder of Virginia. We have here of poetry: Lyrical and other Poems, Early Lays, The Vision of Cortez, The Tri-Color, Atalantis, Southern Passages and Pictures, Donna Florida, Grouped Thoughts and Scattered Fancies, and Ayretos, &c. 14 volumes; of the more purely imaginative fiction: The Book of My Lady, Martin Faber, Carl Werner, Castle Dismal, The Wigwam and the Cabin,—eight volumes; of domestic border novels: Guy Rivers, Richard Hurdis, Border Beagles, Beauchampe, Helen Halsey,—nine volumes; of historical romance: The Yemasee, Damsel of Darien, Pelayo, Count Julian, —eight volumes; of revolutionary stories:

The Partisan, Mellichampe, The Kinsmen,— six volumes; of history and biography: The History of South Carolina, The Life of Marion, The Life of John Smith,—four volumes; of essays and criticism: Views and Reviews, —two volumes: In all sixty-three volumes, in about forty years,—besides which, in the same period, Mr. Simms has written much for quarterly reviews, monthly magazines, and other periodicals, was for several years editor of The Magnolia, and its successor, The Southern and Western Monthly Magazine, and has published various orations and addresses.

Mr. Simms writes at times with great power. His descriptions of persons and places are often graphic. His characters have marked and generally well-sustained individuality, and some of them, particularly of the Indian and negro races, are eminently original. His novels are interesting, but the interest arises more from situation than from character. Our attention is engrossed by actions, but we feel little sympathy with the actors. He gives us too much of ruffianism. The coarseness and villany of many of his characters has no attraction in works of the imagination. If true to nature, which may be doubted, it is not true to nature as we love to contemplate it, and it serves no good purpose in literature. It may be regarded as the chief fault of Mr. Simms, that he does not discriminate between what is irredeemably base and revolting, and what by the hand of art may be made subservient to the exhibition of beauty, which should be the prime aim of the writer of poetical and romantic fiction. Crime is a cheap element of interest, but like powder or steam it is one of danger as well as of power, to be used carefully, by those familiar with its possible effects, and very rarely by any except for the purposes of contrast and shadow.

Mr. Simms's paintings of southern border scenery are vivid and natural; but he has little repose. He delights in action, whether of men or of the elements, and is most successful in strife, storm, and tumult. It is worth mentioning, that the German author Seatsfield has borrowed very largely from his works, and that whole pages which he has translated almost literally from Guy Rivers, have been praised abroad as superior to any thing done by Americans in describing their own country. The action of his novels is generally rapid, and the style, especially of those in which

of some of his works, a number of editions have appeared, others he has suppressed, some have been republished in England, and several have been translated into German and French. The standard edition of his select works illustrated by Darley, was completed in 1859, in 20 vols. A new edition in cheaper form is being published. During the war his house was burnt, and a number of manuscripts were destroyed, which may account for his having published only a few magazine articles since.—Ed.

the narrative is in the first person, is vehement and passionate. His later style is much better than that with which he commenced, but in all his prose compositions it has marks of haste.

The shorter stories of Mr. Simms are his best works. They have unity, completeness, and strength, and though not written with elegance, are comparatively free from redundancies and weighty offences against taste. The collection entitled The Wigwam and the Cabin,* is deeply interesting, and on many accounts must be regarded as a valuable contribution to our literature. Of his reviews I think less favourably, not agreeing with what is peculiar in his principles as a critic; but they are elaborate and have uniformly an air of independence and integrity.

By his skill in analysis, his knowledge of the movements of character and the secret springs of action, his sympathy with what is true and honourable, his acquaintance with history and letters, and his broad field of observation, with a certain philosophical tone of judging of men and measures by other than local and temporary standards, and the unwearied industry by which in various departments he is constantly exhibiting these resources, Mr. Simms is entitled to a large share of public attention.

He had been several years a prominent member of the legislature, and in December, 1846, was defeated by but one vote as a candidate for the office of lieutenant-governor of the State. He died at Savannah, June 11th, 1870.

GRAYLING:
OR, "MURDER WILL OUT."
FROM THE WIGWAM AND THE CABIN.
—
CHAPTER I.

THE world has become monstrous matter-of-fact in latter days. We can no longer get a ghost story, either for love or money. The materialists have it all their own way; and even the little urchin, eight years old, instead of deferring with decent reverence to the opinions of his grandmamma, now stands up stoutly for his own. He believes in every "ology" but pneumatology. "Faust" and the "Old Woman of Berkeley" move his derision only, and he would laugh incredulously, if he dared, at the Witch of Endor. The whole armoury of modern reasoning is on his side; and, however he may admit at seasons that belief can scarcely be counted a matter of will, he yet puts his veto on all sorts of credulity. That cold-blooded demon called Science has taken the place of all the other demons. He has certainly cast out innumerable devils, however he may still spare the principal. Whether we are the better for his intervention is another question. There is reason to apprehend that in disturbing our human faith in shadows, we have lost some of those wholesome moral restraints which might have kept many of us virtuous, where the laws could not.

The effect, however, is much the more seriously evil in all that concerns the romantic. Our story-tellers are so resolute to deal in the real, the actual only, that they venture on no subjects the details of which are not equally vulgar and susceptible of proof. With this end in view, indeed, they too commonly choose their subjects among convicted felons, in order that some of those may avail themselves of the evidence which led to their conviction; and, to

prove more conclusively their devoted adherence to nature and the truth, they depict the former not only in her condition of nakedness, but long before she has found out the springs of running water. It is to be feared that some of the coarseness of modern taste arises from the too great lack of that veneration which belonged to, and elevated to dignity, even the errors of preceding ages. A love of the marvellous belongs, it appears to me, to all those who love and cultivate either of the fine arts. I very much doubt whether the poet, the painter, the sculptor, or the romancer, over yet lived, who had not some strong bias—a leaning, at least,—to a belief in the wonders of the invisible world. Certainly, the higher orders of poets and painters, those who create and invent, must have a strong taint of the superstitious in their composition. But this is digressive, and leads us from our purpose.

It is so long since we have been suffered to see or hear of a ghost, that a visitation at this time may have the effect of novelty, and I propose to narrate a story which I heard more than once in my boyhood, from the lips of an aged relative, who succeeded, at the time, in making me believe every word of it; perhaps, for the simple reason that she convinced me she believed every word of it herself. My grandmother was an old lady who had been a resident of the seat of most frequent war in Carolina during the Revolution. She had fortunately survived the numberless atrocities which she was yet compelled to witness; and, a keen observer, with a strong memory, she had in store a thousand legends of that stirring period, which served to beguile me from sleep many and many a long winter night. The story which I propose to tell was one of these; and when I say that she not only devoutly believed it herself, but that it was believed by sundry of her contemporaries, who were themselves privy to such of the circumstances as could be known to third parties, the gravity with which I repeat the legend will not be considered very astonishing.

The revolutionary war had but a little while been concluded. The British had left the country ; but peace did not imply repose. The community was still in that state of ferment which was natural enough to passions, not yet at rest, which had been brought into exercise and action during the protracted seven years' struggle through which the nation had just passed. The state was overrun by idlers, adventurers, profligates, and criminals. Disbanded soldiers, half-starved and reckless, occupied the highways,—outlaws, emerging from their hiding-places, skulked about the settlements with an equal sentiment of hate and fear in their hearts ;—patriots were clamouring for justice upon the tories, and sometimes anticipating its course by judgments of their own ; while the tories, those against whom the proofs were too strong for denial or evasion, buckled on their armour for a renewal of the struggle. Such being the condition of the country, it may easily be supposed that life and property lacked many of their necessary securities. Men generally travelled with weapons, which were displayed on the smallest provocation : and few who could provide themselves with an escort ventured to travel any distance without one.

There was, about this time, said my grandmother, and while such was the condition of the country, a family of the name of Grayling, that lived somewhere upon the skirts of "Ninety-six" district. Old Grayling, the head of the family, was dead. He was killed in Buford's massacre. His wife was a fine woman, not so very old, who had an only son named James, and a little girl, only five years of age, named Lucy. James was but fourteen when his father was killed, and that event made a man of him. He went out with his rifle in company with Joel Sparkman, who was his mother's brother, and joined himself to Pickens's Brigade. Here he made as good a soldier as the best. He had no sort of fear. He was always the first to go forward ; and his rifle was always good for his enemy's button at a long hundred yards. He was in several fights both with the British and tories ; and just before the war was ended he had a famous brush with the Cherokees, when Pickens took their country from them. But though he had no fear, and never knew when to stop killing while the fight was going on, he was the most bashful of boys that I ever knew ; and so kind-hearted that it was almost impossible to believe all we heard of his fierce doings when he was in battle. But they were nevertheless quite true for all his bashfulness.

Well, when the war was over, Joel Sparkman, who lived with his sister, Grayling, persuaded her that it would be better to move down into the low country. I don't know what reason he had for it, or what they proposed to do there. They had very little property, but Sparkman was a knowing man, who could turn his hand to a hundred things ; and as he was a bachelor, and loved his sister and her children just as if they had been his own, it was natural that she should go with him wherever he wished. James, too, who was restless by nature—and the taste he had enjoyed of the wars had made him more so—he was full of it ; and so, one sunny morning in April, their wagon started for the city. The wagon was only a small one, with two horses, scarcely larger than those that are employed to carry chickens and fruit to the market from the Wassamaws and thereabouts. It was driven by a negro fellow named Clytus, and carried Mrs. Grayling and Lucy. James and his uncle loved the saddle too well to shut themselves up in such a vehicle ; and both of them were mounted on fine horses which they had won from the enemy. The saddle that James rode on, —and he was very proud of it,—was one that he had taken at the battle of Cowpens from one of Tarleton's own dragoons, after he had tumbled the owner. The roads at that season were excessively bad, for the rains of March had been frequent and heavy, the track was very much cut up, and the red clay gullies of the hills of "Ninety-six" were so washed that it required all shoulders, twenty times a day, to get the wagon-wheels out of the bog. This made them travel very slowly,—perhaps, not more than fifteen miles a day. Another cause for slow travelling was, the necessity of great caution, and a constant look-out for enemies both up and down the road. James and his uncle took it by turns to ride a-head, precisely as they did when scouting in war, but one of them always kept along with the wagon. They had gone on this way for two days, and saw nothing to trouble and alarm them. There were few persons on the high-road, and these seemed to the full as shy of them as they probably were of strangers. But just as they were about to camp, the evening of the second day, while they were splitting lightwood, and getting out the kettles and the frying-pan, a person rode up and joined them without much ceremony. He was a short, thick-set man, somewhere between forty and fifty : had on very coarse and common garments, though he rode a fine black horse of remarkable strength and vigour. He was very civil of speech, though he had but little to say, and that little showed him to be a person without much education and with no refinement. He begged permission to make one of the encampment, and his manner was very respectful and even humble ; but there was something dark and sullen in his face—his eyes, which were of a light gray colour, were very restless, and his nose turned up sharply, and was very red. His forehead was excessively broad, and his eyebrows thick and shaggy—white hairs being freely mingled with the dark, both in them and upon his head. Mrs. Grayling did not like this man's looks, and whispered her dislike to her son ; but James, who felt himself equal to any man, said, promptly—

"What of that, mother! we can't turn the stranger off and say 'no ;' and if he means any mischief, there's two of us, you know."

The man had no weapons—none, at least, which were then visible ; and deported himself in so humble a manner, that the prejudice which the party had formed against him when he first appeared, if it was not dissipated while he remained, at least failed to gain any increase. He was very quiet, did not mention an unnecessary word, and seldom permitted his eyes to rest upon those of any of the party, the females not excepted. This, perhaps, was the only circumstance, that, in the mind of Mrs. Grayling, tended to confirm the hostile impression which his coming had originally occasioned. In a little while the temporary encampment was put in a state equally social and warlike. The wagon was wheeled a little way into the woods, and off the road; the horses fastened behind it in such a manner that any attempt to steal them would be difficult of success, even were the watch neglectful which was yet to be maintained upon them. Extra guns, concealed in the straw at the bottom of the wagon, were kept well loaded. In the foreground, and between the wagon and the highway, a fire was soon blazing with a wild but cheerful gleam; and the worthy dame, Mrs. Grayling, assisted by the little girl, Lucy, lost no time in setting on the frying-pan, and cutting into slices the haunch of bacon, which they had provided at leaving home. James Grayling patroled the woods, meanwhile, for a mile or two round the encampment, while his uncle, Joel Sparkman, foot to foot with the stranger, seemed—if the absence of all care constitutes the supreme of human felicity—to realize the most perfect conception of mortal happiness. But Joel was very far from being the careless person that he seemed. Like an old soldier, he simply hung out false colours, and concealed his real timidity by an extra show of confidence and courage. He did not relish the stranger from the first, any more than his sister; and having subjected him to a searching examination, such as was considered, in those days of peril and suspicion, by no means inconsistent with becoming courtesy, he came rapidly to the conclusion that he was no better than he should be.

"You are a Scotchman, stranger," said Joel, suddenly drawing up his feet, and bending forward to the other with an eye like that of a hawk stooping over a covey of partridges. It was a wonder that he had not made the discovery before. The broad dialect of the stranger was not to be subdued; but Joel made slow stages and short progress in his mental journeyings. The answer was given with evident hesitation, but it was affirmative.

"Well, now, it's mighty strange that you should ha' fou't with us and not agin us," responded Joel Sparkman. "There was a precious few of the Scotch, and none that I knows on, saving yourself, perhaps,—that did'nt go dead agin us, and for the tories, through thick and thin. That 'Cross Creek settlement' was a mighty ugly thorn in the sides of us whigs. It turned out a raal bad stock of varmints. I hope,—I reckon, stranger,—you aint from that part."

"No," said the other; "oh no! I'm from over the other quarter. I'm from the Duncan settlement above."

"I've hearn tell of that other settlement, but I never know'd as any of the men fou't with us. What gineral did you fight under? What Carolina gineral?"

"I was at Gum Swamp when General Gates was defeated," was the still hesitating reply of the other.

"Well, I thank God, I warn't there, though I reckon things wouldn't ha' turned out quite so bad, if there had been a leetle sprinkling of Sumter's, or Pickens's, or Marion's men, among them two-legged critters that run that day. They did tell that some of the regiments went off without ever once emptying their rifles. Now, stranger, I hope you warn't among them fellows."

"I was not," said the other with something more of promptness.

"I don't blame a chap for dodging a bullet if he can, or being too quick for a bagnet, because, I'm thinking, a live man is always a better man than a dead one, or he can become so; but to run without taking a single crack at the inimy, is downright cowardice. There's no two ways about it, stranger."

This opinion, delivered with considerable emphasis, met with the ready assent of the Scotchman, but Joel Sparkman was not to be diverted, even by his own eloquence, from the object of his inquiry.

"But you ain't said," he continued, "who was your Carolina gineral. Gates was from Virginny, and he stayed a mighty short time when he come. You didn't run far at Camden, I reckon, and you joined the army agin, and come in with Greene. Was that the how?"

To this the stranger assented, though with evident disinclination.

"Then, moutbe, we sometimes went into the same scratch together? I was at Cowpens and 'Ninety-Six,' and seen sarvice at other odds and eends, where there was more fighting than fun. I reckon you must have been at 'Ninety-Six,'—perhaps at Cowpens, too, if you went with Morgan?"

The unwillingness of the stranger to respond to these questions appeared to increase. He admitted, however, that he had been at "Ninety-Six," though, as Sparkman afterwards remembered, in this case, as in that of the defeat of Gates at Gum Swamp, he had not said on which side he had fought. Joel, as he discovered the reluctance of his guest to answer his questions, and perceived his growing doggedness, forbore to annoy him, but mentally resolved to keep a sharper look-out than ever upon his motions. His examination concluded with an inquiry, which, in the plain-dealing regions of the south and south-west, is not unfrequently put first.

"And what mout be your name, stranger?"

"Macnab," was the ready response, "Sandy Macnab."

"Well, Mr. Macnab, I see that my sister's got supper ready for us; so we mout as well fall to upon the hoecake and bacon."

Sparkman rose while speaking, and led the way

to the spot, near the wagon, where Mrs. Grayling had spread the feast. "We're pretty nigh on to the main road, here, but I reckon there's no great danger now. Besides, Jim Grayling keeps watch for us, and he's got two as good eyes in his head as any scout in the country, and a rifle that, after you once know how it shoots, 'twould do your heart good to hear its crack, if so be that twa'n't your heart that he drawed sight on. He's a perdigious fine shot, and as ready to shoot and fight as if he had a nateral calling that way."

"Shall we wait for him before we eat?" demanded Macnab, anxiously.

"By no sort o' reason, stranger," answered Sparkman. "He'll watch for us while we're eating, and after that I'll change shoes with him. So fall to, and don't mind what's a coming."

Sparkman had just broken the hoecake, when a distant whistle was heard.

"Ha! That's the lad now!" he exclaimed, rising to his feet. "He's on trail. He's got a sight of an inimy's fire, I reckon. 'Twon't be onreasonable, friend Macnab, to get our we'pons in readiness;" and, so speaking, Sparkman bid his sister get into the wagon, where the little Lucy had already placed herself, while he threw open the pan of his rifle, and turned the priming over with his finger. Macnab, meanwhile, had taken from his holsters, which he had before been sitting upon, a pair of horseman's pistols, richly mounted with figures in silver. These were large and long, and had evidently seen service. Unlike his companion, his proceedings occasioned no comment. What he did seemed a matter of habit, of which he himself was scarcely conscious. Having looked at his priming, he laid the instruments beside him without a word, and resumed the bit of hoecake which he had just before received from Sparkman. Meanwhile, the signal whistle, supposed to come from James Grayling, was repeated. Silence ensued then for a brief space, which Sparkman employed in perambulating the grounds immediately contiguous. At length, just as he had returned to the fire, the sound of a horse's feet was heard, and a sharp quick halloo from Grayling informed him that all was right. The youth made his appearance a moment after, accompanied by a stranger on horseback; a tall, fine-looking young man, with a keen flashing eye, and a voice whose lively clear tones, as he was heard approaching, sounded cheerily like those of a trumpet after victory. James Grayling kept along on foot beside the new-comer; and his hearty laugh, and free, glib, garrulous tones, betrayed to his uncle, long ere he drew nigh, enough to declare the fact, that he had met unexpectedly with a friend, or, at least, an old acquaintance.

"Why, who have you got there, James?" was the demand of Sparkman, as he dropped the butt of his rifle upon the ground.

"Why, who do you think, uncle? Who but Major Spencer—our own major?"

"You don't say so!—what!—well! Li'nel Spencer, for sartin! Lord bless you, major, who'd ha' thought to see you in these parts; and

jest mounted too, for all natur, as if the war was to be fou't over agin. Well, I'm raal glad to see you. I am, that's sartin!"

"And I'm very glad to see you, Sparkman," said the other, as he alighted from his steed, and yielded his hand to the cordial grasp of the other.

"Well, I knows that, major, without you saying it. But you've jest come in the right time. The bacon's frying, and here's the bread;—let's down upon our haunches, in right good airnest, camp fashion, and make the most of what God gives us in the way of blessings. I reckon you don't mean to ride any further to-night, major?"

"No," said the person addressed, "not if you'll let me lay my heels at your fire. But who's in your wagon? My old friend, Mrs. Grayling, I suppose?"

"That's a true word, major," said the lady herself, making her way out of the vehicle with good-humoured agility, and coming forward with extended hand.

"Really, Mrs. Grayling, I'm very glad to see you." And the stranger, with the blandness of a gentleman and the hearty warmth of an old neighbour, expressed his satisfaction at once more finding himself in the company of an old acquaintance. Their greetings once over, Major Spencer readily joined the group about the fire, while James Grayling—though with some reluctance—disappeared to resume his toils of the scout while the supper proceeded.

"And who have you here?" demanded Spencer, as his eye rested on the dark, hard features of the Scotchman. Sparkman told him all that he himself had learned of the name and character of the stranger, in a brief whisper, and in a moment after formally introduced the parties in this fashion—

"Mr. Macnab, Major Spencer. Mr. Macnab says he's true blue, major, and fou't at Camden, when General Gates run so hard to 'bring the d—d militia back.' He also fou't at 'Ninety-Six,' and Cowpens—so I reckon we had as good as count him one of us."

Major Spencer scrutinized the Scotchman keenly—a scrutiny which the latter seemed very ill to relish. He put a few questions to him on the subject of the war, and some of the actions in which he allowed himself to have been concerned; but his evident reluctance to unfold himself—a reluctance so unnatural to the brave soldier who has gone through his toils honourably—had the natural effect of discouraging the young officer, whose sense of delicacy had not been materially impaired amid the rude jostlings of military life. But, though he forbore to propose any other questions to Macnab, his eyes continued to survey the features of his sullen countenance with curiosity and a strangely increasing interest. This he subsequently explained to Sparkman, when, at the close of supper, James Grayling came in, and the former assumed the duties of the scout.

"I have seen that Scotchman's face somewhere, Sparkman, and I'm convinced at some interesting moment; but where, when, or how, I cannot call to mind. The sight of it is even associated in my mind with something painful and unpleasant; where could I have seen him?"

"I don't somehow like his looks myself," said Sparkman, "and I mislists he's been rether more of a tory than a whig; but that's nothing to the purpose now; and he's at our fire, and we've broken hoecake together; so we cannot rake up the old ashes to make a dust with."

"No, surely not," was the reply of Spencer. "Even though we knew him to be a tory, that cause of former quarrel should occasion none now. But it should produce watchfulness and caution. I'm glad to see that you have not forgot your old business of scouting in the swamp."

"Kin I forget it, major?" demanded Sparkman, in tones which, though whispered, were full of emphasis, as he laid his ear to the earth to listen.

"James has finished supper, major—that's his whistle to tell me so; and I'll jest step back to make it cl'ar to him how we're to keep up the watch to-night."

"Count me in your arrangements, Sparkman, as I am one of you for the night," said the major.

"By no sort of means," was the reply. "The night must be shared between James and myself. Ef so be you wants to keep company with one or t'other of us, why, that's another thing, and, of course, you can do as you please."

"We'll have no quarrel on the subject, Joel," said the officer, good-naturedly, as they returned to the camp together.

CHAPTER II.

The arrangements of the party were soon made. Spencer renewed his offer at the fire to take his part in the watch; and the Scotchman, Macnab, volunteered his services also; but the offer of the latter was another reason why that of the former should be declined. Sparkman was resolute to have every thing his own way; and while James Grayling went out upon his lonely rounds, he busied himself in cutting bushes and making a sort of tent for the use of his late commander. Mrs. Grayling and Lucy slept in a wagon. The Scotchman stretched himself with little effort before the fire; while Joel Sparkman, wrapping himself up in his cloak, crouched under the wagon body, with his back resting partly against one of the wheels. From time to time he arose and thrust additional brands into the fire, looked up at the night, and round upon the little encampment, then sunk back to his perch and stole a few moments, at intervals, of uneasy sleep. The first two hours of the watch were over, and James Grayling was relieved. The youth, however, felt in no mood for sleep, and taking his seat by the fire, he drew from his pocket a little volume of Easy Reading Lessons, and by the fitful flame of the resinous light-wood, he prepared, in this rude manner, to make up for the precious time which his youth had lost of its legitimate employments, in the stirring events of the preceding seven years

consumed in war. He was surprised at this employment by his late commander, who, himself sleepless, now emerged from the bushes and joined Grayling at the fire. The youth had been rather a favourite with Spencer. They had both been reared in the same neighbourhood, and the first military achievements of James had taken place under the eye, and had met the approbation of his officer. The difference of their ages was just such as to permit of the warm attachment of the lad without diminishing any of the reverence which should be felt by the inferior. Grayling was not more than seventeen, and Spencer was perhaps thirty-four—the very prime of manhood. They sat by the fire and talked of old times and told old stories with the hearty glee and good-nature of the young. Their mutual inquiries led to the revelation of their several objects in pursuing the present journey. Those of James Grayling were scarcely, indeed, to be considered his own. They were plans and purposes of his uncle, and it does not concern this narrative that we should know more of their nature than has already been revealed. But, whatever they were, they were as freely unfolded to his hearer as if the parties had been brothers, and Spencer was quite as frank in his revelations as his companion. He, too, was on his way to Charleston, from whence he was to take passage for England.

"I am rather in a hurry to reach town," he said, "as I learn that the Falmouth packet is preparing to sail for England in a few days, and I must go in her."

"For England, major!" exclaimed the youth with unaffected astonishment.

"Yes, James, for England. But why—what astonishes you?"

"Why, lord!" exclaimed the simple youth, "if they only knew there, as I do, what a cutting and slashing you did use to make among their red coats, I reckon they'd hang you to the first hickory."

"Oh, no! scarcely," said the other, with a smile.

"But I reckon you'll change your name, major!" continued the youth.

"No," responded Spencer, "if I did that, I should lose the object of my voyage. You must know, James, that an old relative has left me a good deal of money in England, and I can only get it by proving that I am Lionel Spencer; so you see I must carry my own name, whatever may be the risk."

"Well, major, you know best; but I do think if they could only have a guess of what you did among their sodgers at Hobkirk's and Cowpens, and Eutaw, and a dozen other places, they'd find some means of hanging you up, peace or no peace. But I don't see what occasion you have to be going cl'ar away to England for money, when you've got a sight of your own already."

"Not so much as you think for," replied the major, giving an involuntary and uneasy glance at the Scotchman, who was seemingly sound asleep on the opposite side of the fire. "There

is, you know, but little money in the country at
any time, and I must get what I want for my expenses when I reach Charleston. I have just
enough to carry me there."

"Well, now, major, that's mighty strange. I
always thought that you was about the best off of
any man in our parts; but if you're strained so
close, I'm thinking, major,—if so be you wouldn't
think me too presumptuous,—you'd better let me
lend you a guinea or so that I've got to spare, and
you can pay me back when you get the English
money."

And the youth fumbled in his bosom for a little
cotton wallet, which, with its limited contents, was
displayed in another instant to the eyes of the
officer.

"No, no, James," said the other, putting back
the generous tribute; "I have quite enough to
carry me to Charleston, and when there I can
easily get a supply from the merchants. But I
thank you, my good fellow, for your offer. You
are a good fellow, James, and I will remember
you."

It is needless to pursue the conversation farther. The night passed away without any alarms,
and at dawn of the next day the whole party was
engaged in making preparation for a start. Mrs.
Grayling was soon busy in getting breakfast in
readiness. Major Spencer consented to remain
with them until it was over: but the Scotchman,
after returning thanks very civilly for his accommodation of the night, at once resumed his journey. His course seemed, like their own, to lie
below; but he neither declared his route nor betrayed the least desire to know that of Spencer.
The latter had no disposition to renew those inquiries from which the stranger seemed to shrink
the night before, and he accordingly suffered him
to depart with a quiet farewell, and the utterance
of a good-natured wish, in which all the parties
joined, that he might have a pleasant journey.
When he was fairly out of sight, Spencer said to
Sparkman,

"Had I liked that fellow's looks, nay, had I not
positively disliked them, I should have gone with
him. As it is, I will remain and share your
breakfast."

The repast being over, all parties set forward;
but Spencer, after keeping along with them for a
mile, took his leave also. The slow wagon-pace
at which the family travelled, did not suit the high-
spirited cavalier; and it was necessary, as he assured them, that he should reach the city in two
nights more. They parted with many regrets, as
truly felt as they were warmly expressed; and
James Grayling never felt the tedium of wagon
travelling to be so severe as throughout the whole
of that day when he separated from his favourite
captain. But he was too stout-hearted a lad to
make any complaint; and his dissatisfaction only
showed itself in his unwonted silence, and an over-
anxiety, which his steed seemed to feel in common with himself, to go rapidly ahead. Thus the
day passed, and the wayfarers at its close had
made a progress of some twenty miles from sun

to sun. The same precautions marked their encampment this night as the last, and they rose in
better spirits with the next morning, the dawn of
which was very bright and pleasant, and encouraging. A similar journey of twenty miles brought
them to the place of bivouac as the sun went
down; and they prepared as usual for their securities and supper. They found themselves on the
edge of a very dense forest of pines and scrubby
oaks, a portion of which was swallowed up in a
deep bay—so called in the dialect of the country
—a swamp-bottom, the growth of which consisted
of mingled cypresses and bay-trees, with tupola,
gum, and dense thickets of low stunted shrubbery, cane grass, and dwarf willows, which filled
up every interval between the trees, and to the
eye most effectually barred out every human intruder. This bay was chosen as the background
for the camping party. Their wagon was wheeled
into an area on a gently rising ground in front,
under a pleasant shade of oaks and hickories, with
a lonely pine rising loftily in occasional spots
among them. Here the horses were taken out,
and James Grayling prepared to kindle up a fire;
but, looking for his axe, it was unaccountably
missing, and after a fruitless search of half an
hour, the party came to the conclusion that it had
been left on the spot where they had slept last
night. This was a disaster, and, while they meditated in what manner to repair it, a negro boy
appeared in sight, passing along the road at their
feet, and driving before him a small herd of cattle.
From him they learned that they were only a
mile or two from a farmstead where an axe might
be borrowed; and James, leaping on his horse,
rode forward in the hope to obtain one. He
found no difficulty in his quest; and, having obtained it from the farmer, who was also a tavern-
keeper, he casually asked if Major Spencer had
not stayed with him the night before. He was
somewhat surprised when told that he had not.

"There was one man stayed with me last
night," said the farmer, "but he did'nt call himself
a major, and didn't much look like one."

"He rode a fine sorrel horse,—tall, bright
colour, with white fore foot, didn't he?" asked
James.

"No, that he didn't! He rode a powerful
black, coal black, and not a bit of white about
him."

"That was the Scotchman! But I wonder
the major didn't stop with you. He must have
rode on. Isn't there another house near you,
below?"

"Not one. There's ne'er a house either above
or below for a matter of fifteen miles. I'm the
only man in all that distance that's living on this
road; and I don't think your friend could have
gone below, as I should have seen him pass. I've
been all day out there in that field before your
eyes, clearing up the brush."

CHAPTER III.

SOMEWHAT wondering that the major should
have turned aside from the track, though without

attaching to it any importance at that particular moment, James Grayling took up the borrowed axe and hurried back to the encampment, where the toil of cutting an extra supply of light-wood to meet the exigencies of the ensuing night, sufficiently exercised his mind as well as his body, to prevent him from meditating upon the seeming strangeness of· the circumstance. But when he sat down to his supper over the fire that he had kindled, his fancies crowded thickly upon him, and he felt a confused doubt and suspicion that something was to happen, he knew not what. His conjectures and apprehensions were without form, though not altogether void; and he felt a strange sickness and a sinking at the heart which was very unusual with him. He had, in short, that lowness of spirits, that cloudy apprehensiveness of soul which takes the form of presentiment, and makes us look out for danger even when the skies are without a cloud, and the breeze is laden, equally and only, with balm and music. His moodiness found no sympathy among his companions. Joel Sparkman was in. the best of humours, and his mother was so cheery and happy, that when the thoughtful boy went off into the woods to watch, he could hear her at every moment breaking out into little catches of a country ditty, which the gloomy events of the late war had not yet obliterated from her memory.

"It's very strange !" soliloquized the youth, as he wandered along the edges of the dense bay or swamp-bottom, which we have passingly referred to,—" it's very strange what troubles me so ! I feel almost frightened, and yet I know I'm not to be frightened easily, and I don't see any thing in the woods to frighten me. It's strange the major didn't come along this road ! Maybe he took another higher up that leads by a different settlement. I wish I had asked the man at the house if there's such another road. I reckon there must be, however, for where could the major have gone ?"

The unphilosophical mind of James Grayling did not, in his farther meditations, carry him much beyond this starting point; and with its continual recurrence in soliloquy, he proceeded to traverse the margin of the bay, until he came to its junction with, and termination at, the highroad. The youth turned into this, and, involuntarily departing from it a moment after, soon found himself on the opposite side of the bay thicket. He wandered on and on, as he himself described it, without any power to restrain himself. He knew not how far he went; but, instead of maintaining his watch for two hours only, he was gone more than four; and, at length, a sense of weariness which overpowered him all of a sudden, caused him to seat himself at the foot of a tree, and snatch a few moments of rest. He denied that he slept in this time. He insisted to the last moment of his life that sleep never visited his eyelids that night,—that he was conscious of fatigue and exhaustion, but not drowsiness,— and that this fatigue was so numbing as to be painful, and effectually kept him from any sleep.

While he sat thus beneath the tree, with a body weak and nerveless, but a mind excited, he knew not how or why, to the most acute degree of expectation and attention, he heard his name called by the well-known voice of his friend, Major Spencer. The voice called him three times,— "James Grayling !—James !—James Grayling !" before he could muster strength enough to answer. It was not courage he wanted,—of that he was positive, for he felt sure, as he said, that something had gone wrong, and he was never more ready to fight in his life than at that moment, could he have commanded the physical capacity; but his throat seemed dry to suffocation,—his lips effectually sealed up as if with wax, and when he did answer, the sounds seemed as fine and soft as the whisper of some child just born.

"Oh ! major, is it you ?"

Such, he thinks, were the very words he made use of in reply; and the answer that he received was instantaneous, though the voice came from some little distance in the bay, and his own voice he did not hear. He only knows what he meant to say. The answer was to this effect.

"It is, James !—It is your own friend, Lionel Spencer, that speaks to you; do not be alarmed when you see me ! I have been shockingly murdered !"

James asserts that he tried to tell him that he would not be frightened, but his own voice was still a whisper, which he himself could scarcely hear. A moment after he had spoken, he heard something like a sudden breeze that rustled through the bay bushes at his feet, and his eyes were closed without his effort, and indeed in spite of himself. When he opened them, he saw Major Spencer standing at the edge of the bay, about twenty steps from him. Though he stood in the shade of a thicket, and there was no light in the heavens save that of the stars, he was yet enabled to distinguish perfectly, and with great ease, every lineament of his friend's face.

He looked very pale, and his garments were covered with blood; and James said that he strove very much to rise from the place where he sat and approach him;—"for, in truth," said the lad, "so far from feeling any fear, I felt nothing but. fury in my heart; but I could not move a limb. My feet were fastened to the ground; my hands to my sides; and I could only bend forward and gasp. I felt as if I should have died with vexation that I could not rise; but a power which I could not resist made me motionless, and almost speechless. I could only say, 'Murdered !'—and that one word I believe I must have repeated a dozen times.

"'Yes, murdered !—murdered by the Scotchman who slept with us at your fire the night before last. James, I look to you to have the murderer brought to justice ! James !—do you hear me, James ?'

"These," said James, "I think were the very words, or near about the very words, that I heard; and I tried to ask the major to tell me how it was, and how I could do what he required; but I didn't hear myself speak, though it would appear that he did, for almost immediately after I had tried to speak what I wished to say, he answered me just as if I had said it. He told me that the Scotchman had waylaid, killed, and hidden him in that very bay; that his murderer had gone to Charleston; and that if I made haste to town, I would find him in the Falmouth packet, which was then lying in the harbour and ready to sail for England. He farther said that every thing depended on my making haste,—that I must reach town by to-morrow night if I wanted to be in season, and go right on board the vessel and charge the criminal with the deed. 'Do not be afraid,' said he, when he had finished; 'be afraid of nothing, James, for God will help and strengthen you to the end.' When I heard all, I burst into a flood of tears, and then I felt strong. I felt that I could talk, or fight, or do almost any thing; and I jumped up to my feet, and was just about to run down to where the major stood, but, with the first step which I made forward, he was gone. I stopped and looked all around me, but I could see nothing; and the bay was just as black as midnight. But I went down to it, and tried to press in where I thought the major had been standing; but I couldn't get far, the brush and bay bushes were so close and thick. I was now bold and strong enough, and I called out, loud enough to be heard half a mile. I didn't exactly know what I called for, or what I wanted to learn, or I have forgotten. But I heard nothing more. Then I remembered the camp, and began to fear that something might have happened to mother and uncle, for I now felt, what I had not thought of before, that I had gone too far round the bay to be of much assistance, or, indeed, to be in time for any, had they been suddenly attacked. Besides, I could not think how long I had been gone; but it now seemed very late. The stars were shining their brightest, and the thin white clouds of morning were beginning to rise and run towards the west. Well, I bethought me of my course,—for I was a little bewildered and doubtful where I was; but, after a little thinking, I took the back track, and soon got a glimpse of the camp-fire, which was nearly burnt down; and by this I reckoned I was gone considerably longer than my two hours. When I got back into the camp, I looked under the wagon, and found uncle in a sweet sleep, and though my heart was full almost to bursting with what I had heard, and the cruel sight I had seen, yet I wouldn't waken him; and I beat about and mended the fire, and watched, and waited, until near daylight, when mother called to me out of the wagon, and asked who it was. This wakened my uncle, and then I up and told all that had happened, for if it had been to save my life, I couldn't have kept it in much longer. But though mother said it was very strange, Uncle Sparkman considered that I had been only dreaming; but he couldn't persuade me of it; and when I told him I intended to be off at daylight, just as the major had told me to do, and ride my best all the way to Charleston, he laughed, and said I was a fool. But I felt that I was no fool, and I was solemn certain that I hadn't been dreaming; and though both mother and he tried their hardest to make me put off going, yet I made up my mind to it, and they had to give up. For, wouldn't I have been a pretty sort of a friend to the major, if, after what he told me, I could have stayed behind, and gone on only at a wagon-pace to look after the murderer! I don't think if I had done so that I should ever have been able to look a white man in the face again. Soon as the peep of day, I was on horseback. Mother was mighty sad, and begged me not to go, but Uncle Sparkman was mighty sulky, and kept calling me fool upon fool, until I was almost angry enough to forget that we were of blood kin. But all his talking did not stop me, and I reckon I was five miles on my way before he had his team in traces for a start. I rode as briskly as I could get on without hurting my nag. I had a smart ride of more than forty miles before me, and the road was very heavy. But it was a good two hours from sunset when I got into town, and the first question I asked of the people I met was, to show me where the ships were kept. When I got to the wharf they showed me the Falmouth packet, where she lay in the stream, ready to sail as soon as the wind should favour."

CHAPTER IV.

JAMES GRAYLING, with the same eager impatience which he has been suffered to describe in his own language, had already hired a boat to go on board the British packet, when he remembered that he had neglected all those means, legal and otherwise, by which alone his purpose might be properly effected. He did not know much about legal process, but he had common sense enough, the moment that he began to reflect on the subject, to know that some such process was necessary. This conviction produced another difficulty; he knew not in which quarter to turn for counsel and assistance; but here the boatman who saw his bewilderment, and knew by his dialect and dress that he was a back-countryman, came to his relief, and from him he got directions where to find the merchants with whom his uncle, Sparkman, had done business in former years. To them he went, and without circumlocution, told the whole story of his ghostly visitation. Even as a dream, which these gentlemen at once conjectured it to be, the story of James Grayling was equally clear and curious; and his intense warmth and the entire absorption, which the subject had effected, of his mind and soul, was such that they judged it not improper, at least to carry out the search of the vessel which he contemplated. It would certainly, they thought, be a curious coincidence—believing James to be a veracious youth —if the Scotchman should be found on board. But another test of his narrative was proposed by one of the firm. It so happened that the business agents of Major Spencer, who was well known in Charleston, kept their office but a few rods distant from their own; and to them all parties at once proceeded. But here the story of James was encountered by a circumstance that made somewhat against it. These gentlemen produced a letter from Major Spencer, intimating the utter impossibility of his coming to town for the space of a month, and expressing his regret that he should be unable to avail himself of the opportunity of the foreign vessel, of whose arrival in Charleston, and proposed time of departure, they had themselves advised him. They read the letter aloud to James and their brother merchants, and with difficulty suppressed their smiles at the gravity with which the former related and insisted upon the particulars of his vision.

"He has changed his mind," returned the impetuous youth; "he was on his way down, I tell you,—a hundred miles on his way,—when he camped with us. I know him well, I tell you, and talked with him myself half the night."

"At least," remarked the gentlemen who had gone with James, "it can do no harm to look into the business. We can procure a warrant for searching the vessel after this man, Macnab; and should he be found on board the packet, it will be a sufficient circumstance to justify the magistrates in detaining him, until we can ascertain where Major Spencer really is."

The measure was accordingly adopted, and it was nearly sunset before the warrant was procured, and the proper officer in readiness. The impatience of a spirit so eager and so devoted as James Grayling, under these delays, may be imagined; and when in the boat, and on his way to the packet where the criminal was to be sought, his blood became so excited that it was with much ado he could be kept in his seat. His quick, eager action continually disturbed the trim of the boat, and one of his mercantile friends, who had accompanied him, with that interest in the affair which curiosity alone inspired, was under constant apprehension lest he would plunge overboard in his impatient desire to shorten the space which lay between. The same impatience enabled the youth, though never on shipboard before, to grasp the rope which had been flung at their approach, and to mount her sides with catlike agility. Without waiting to declare himself or his purpose, he ran from one side of the deck to the other, greedily staring, to the surprise of officers, passengers, and seamen, in the faces of all of them, and surveying them with an almost offensive scrutiny. He turned away from the search with disappointment. There was no face like that of the suspected man among them. By this time, his friend, the merchant, with the sheriff's officer, had entered the vessel, and were in conference with the captain. Grayling drew nigh in time to hear the latter affirm that there was no man of the name of Macnab, as stated in the warrant, among his passengers or crew.

"He is—he must be!" exclaimed the impetuous youth. "The major never lied in his life, and couldn't lie after he was dead. Macnab is here—he is a Scotchman—"

The captain interrupted him—

"We have, young gentleman, several Scotchmen on board, and one of them is named Macleod—"

"Let me see him—which is he!" demanded the youth.

By this time, the passengers and a goodly portion of the crew were collected about the little party. The captain turned his eyes upon the group, and asked,

"Where is Mr. Macleod?"

"He is gone below—he's sick!" replied one of the passengers.

"That's he! That must be the man!" exclaimed the youth. "I'll lay my life that's no other than Macnab. He's only taken a false name."

It was now remembered by one of the passengers, and remarked, that Macleod had expressed himself as unwell, but a few moments before, and had gone below even while the boat was rapidly approaching the vessel. At this statement, the captain led the way into the cabin, closely followed by James Grayling and the rest.

"Mr. Macleod," he said with a voice somewhat elevated, as he approached the berth of that person, "you are wanted on deck for a few moments."

"I am really too unwell, captain," replied a feeble voice from behind the curtain of the berth.

"It will be necessary," was the reply of the captain. "There is a warrant from the authorities of the town, to look after a fugitive from justice."

Macleod had already begun a second speech declaring his feebleness, when the fearless youth, Grayling, bounded before the captain and tore away, with a single grasp of his hand, the curtain which concealed the suspected man from their sight.

"It is he!" was the instant exclamation of the youth, as he beheld him. "It is he—Macnab, the Scotchman—the man that murdered Major Spencer!"

Macnab,—for it was he,—was deadly pale. He trembled like an aspen. His eyes were dilated with more than mortal apprehension, and his lips were perfectly livid. Still, he found strength to speak, and to deny the accusation. He knew nothing of the youth before him—nothing of Major Spencer—his name was Macleod, and he had never called himself by any other. He denied, but with great incoherence, every thing which was urged against him.

"You must get up, Mr. Macleod," said the captain: "the circumstances are very much against you. You must go with the officer!"

"Will you give me up to my enemies?" demanded the culprit. "You are a countryman—a Briton. I have fought for the king, our master, against these rebels, and for this they seek my life. Do not deliver me into their bloody hands!"

"Liar!" exclaimed James Grayling—"Didn't you tell us at our own camp-fire that you were with us! that you were at Gates's defeat, and 'Ninety-Six!'"

"But I didn't tell you," said the Scotchman, with a grin, "which side I was on!"

"Ha! remember that!" said the sheriff's officer. "He denied, just a moment ago, that he knew this young man at all; now, he confesses that he did see and camp with him."

The Scotchman was aghast at the strong point which, in his inadvertence, he had made against himself; and his efforts to excuse himself, stammering and contradictory, served only to involve him more deeply in the meshes of his difficulty. Still he continued his urgent appeals to the captain of the vessel, and his fellow-passengers, as citizens of the same country, subjects to the same monarch, to protect him from those who equally hated and would destroy them all. In order to move their national prejudices in his behalf, he boasted of the immense injury which he had done, as a tory, to the rebel cause; and still insisted that the murder was only a pretext of the youth before him, by which to gain possession of his person, and wreak upon him the revenge which his own fierce performances during the war had naturally enough provoked. One or two of the passengers, indeed, joined with him in entreating the captain to set the accusers adrift and make sail at once; but the stout Englishman who was in command, rejected instantly the unworthy counsel. Besides, he was better aware of the dangers which would follow any such rash proceeding. Fort Moultrie, on Sullivan's Island, had been already refitted and prepared for an enemy; and he was lying, at that moment, under the formidable range of grinning teeth, which would have opened upon him, at the first movement, from the jaws of Castle Pinckney.

"No, gentlemen," said he, "you mistake your man. God forbid that I should give shelter to a murderer, though he were from my own parish."

"But I am no murderer," said the Scotchman.

"You look cursedly like one, however," was the reply of the captain. "Sheriff, take your prisoner."

The base creature threw himself at the feet of the Englishman, and clung, with piteous entreaties, to his knees. The latter shook him off, and turned away in disgust.

"Steward," he cried, "bring up this man's luggage."

He was obeyed. The luggage was brought up from the cabin and delivered to the sheriff's officer, by whom it was examined in the presence of all, and an inventory made of its contents. It consisted of a small new trunk, which, it afterwards appeared, he had bought in Charleston, soon after his arrival. This contained a few changes of raiment, twenty-six guineas in money, a gold watch, not in repair, and the two pistols which he had shown while at Joel Sparkman's camp fire; but, with this difference, that the stock of one was broken off short just above the grasp, and the butt was entirely gone. It was not found among his chattels. A careful examination of the articles in his trunk did not result in any thing calculated to strengthen the charge of his criminality; but there was not a single person present who did not feel as morally certain of his guilt as if the jury had already declared the fact. That night he slept—if he slept at all—in the common jail of the city.

CHAPTER V.

HIS accuser, the warm-hearted and resolute James Grayling, did not sleep. The excitement, arising from mingling and contradictory emotions, —sorrow for his brave young commander's fate, and the natural exultation of a generous spirit at the consciousness of having performed, with signal success, an arduous and painful task, combined to drive all pleasant slumbers from his eyes; and with the dawn he was again up and stirring, with his mind still full of the awful business in which he had been engaged. We do not care to pursue his course in the ordinary walks of the city, nor account for his employments during the few days which ensued, until, in consequence of a legal examination into the circumstances which anticipated the regular work of the sessions, the extreme excitement of the young accuser had been renewed. Macnab or Macleod,—and it is possible that both names are fictitious,—as soon as he recovered from his first terrors, sought the aid of an attorney—one of those acute, small, chopping lawyers, to be found in almost every community, who are willing to serve with equal zeal the sinner and the saint, provided that they can pay with equal liberality. The prisoner was brought before the court under habeas corpus, and several grounds submitted by his counsel with the view to obtaining his discharge. It became necessary to ascertain, among the first duties of the state, whether Major Spencer, the alleged victim, was really dead. Until it could be established that a man should be imprisoned, tried, and punished for a crime, it was first necessary to show that a crime had been committed, and the attorney made himself exceedingly merry with the ghost story of young Grayling. In those days, however, the ancient Superstition was not so feeble as she has subsequently become. The venerable judge was one of those good men who had a decent respect for the faith and opinions of his ancestors; and though he certainly would not have consented to the hanging of Macleod under the sort of testimony which had been adduced, he yet saw enough, in all the circumstances, to justify his present detention. In the mean time, efforts were to be made, to ascertain the whereabouts of Major Spencer; though, were he even missing,—so the counsel for Macleod contended,—his death could be by no means assumed in consequence. To this the judge shook his head doubtfully. "'Fore God!" said he, "I would not have you to be too sure of that." He was an Irishman, and proceeded after the fashion of his country. The reader will therefore *bear* with his *bull*. "A man may properly be hung for murdering another, though the murdered man be not dead; ay, before God, even though he be actually unhurt and uninjured, while the murderer is swinging by the neck for the bloody deed!"

The judge,—who it must be understood was a real existence, and who had no small reputation in his day in the south,—proceeded to establish the correctness of his opinions by authorities and argument, with all of which, doubtlessly, the bar were exceedingly delighted; but, to provide them in this place would only be to interfere with our own progress. James Grayling, however, was not satisfied to wait the slow processes which were suggested for coming at the truth. Even the wisdom of the judge was lost upon him, possibly, for the simple reason that he did not comprehend it. But the ridicule of the culprit's lawyer stung him to the quick, and he muttered to himself. more than once, a determination " to lick the life out of that impudent chap's leather." But this was not his only resolve. There was one which he proceeded to put into instant execution, and that was to seek the body of his murdered friend in the spot where he fancied it might be found— namely, the dark and dismal bay where the spectre had made its appearance to his eyes.

The suggestion was approved—though he did not need this to prompt his resolution—by his mother and uncle, Sparkman. The latter determined to be his companion, and he was farther accompanied by the sheriff's officer who had arrested the suspected felon. Before daylight, on the morning after the examination before the judge had taken place, and when Macleod had been remanded to prison, James Grayling started on his journey. His fiery zeal received additional force at every added moment of delay, and his eager spurring brought him at an early hour after noon, to the neighbourhood of the spot through which his search was to be made. When his companions and himself drew nigh, they were all at a loss in which direction first to proceed. The bay was one of those massed forests, whose wall of thorns, vines, and close tenacious shrubs, seemed to defy invasion. To the eye of the townsman it was so forbidding that he pronounced it absolutely impenetrable. But James was not to be baffled. He led them round it, taking the very course which he had pursued the night when the revelation was made him; he showed them the very tree at whose foot he had sunk when the supernatural torpor—as he himself esteemed it— began to fall upon him; he then pointed out the spot, some twenty steps distant, at which the spectre made his appearance. To this spot they then proceeded in a body, and essayed an entrance, but were so discouraged by the difficulties at the outset, that all, James not excepted, concluded that neither the murderer nor his victim could possibly have found entrance there.

But, lo! a marvel! Such it seemed, at the first blush, to all the party. While they stood confounded and indecisive, undetermined in which way to move, a sudden flight of wings was heard, even from the centre of the bay, at a little distance above the spot where they had striven for entrance. They looked up, and beheld about fifty buzzards— those notorious domestic vultures of the south— ascending from the interior of the bay, and perch-

ing along upon the branches of the loftier trees by which it was overhung. Even were the character of these birds less known, the particular business in which they had just then been engaged, was betrayed by huge gobbets of flesh which some of them had borne aloft in their flight, and still continued to rend with beak and bill, as they tottered upon the branches where they stood. A piercing scream issued from the lips of James Grayling as he beheld this sight, and strove to scare the offensive birds from their repast.

. " The poor major! the poor major!" was the involuntary and agonized exclamation of the youth. " Did I ever think he would come to this!"

The search, thus guided and encouraged, was pressed with renewed diligence and spirit; and, at length, an opening was found through which it was evident that a body of considerable size had but recently gone. The branches were broken from the small shrub trees, and the undergrowth trodden into the earth. They followed this path, and, as is the case commonly with waste tracts of this description, the density of the growth diminished sensibly at every step they took, till they reached a little pond, which, though circumscribed in area, and full of cypresses, yet proved to be singularly deep. Indeed, it was an alligator-hole, where, in all probability, a numerous tribe of these reptiles had their dwelling. Here, on the edge of the pond, they discovered the object which had drawn the keen-sighted vultures to their feast, in the body of a horse, which James Grayling at once identified as that of Major Spencer. The carcass of the animal was already very much torn and lacerated. The eyes were plucked out, and the animal completely disembowelled. Yet, on examination, it was not difficult to discover the manner of his death. This had been effected by fire-arms. Two bullets had passed through his skull, just above the eyes, either of which must have been fatal. The murderer had led the horse to the spot, and committed the cruel deed where his body was found. The search was now continued for that of the owner, but for some time it proved ineffectual. At length, the keen eyes of James Grayling detected, amidst a heap of moss and green sedge that rested beside an overthrown tree, whose branches jutted into the pond, a whitish, but discoloured object, that did not seem native to the place. Bestriding the fallen tree, he was enabled to reach this object, which, with a burst of grief, he announced to the distant party was the hand and arm of his unfortunate friend, the wristband of the shirt being the conspicuous object which had first caught his eye. Grasping this, he drew the corse, which had been thrust beneath the branches of the tree, to the surface; and, with the assistance of his uncle, it was finally brought to the dry land. Here it underwent a careful examination. The head was very much disfigured; the skull was fractured in several places by repeated blows of some hard instrument, inflicted chiefly from behind. A closer inspection revealed a bullet-hole in the abdomen, the first wound, in all probability, which the unfortunate gentleman received, and by which he was, perhaps, tumbled from his horse. The blows on the head would seem to have been unnecessary, unless the murderer—whose proceedings appeared to have been singularly deliberate,—was resolved upon making "assurance doubly sure." But, as if the watchful Providence had meant that nothing should be left doubtful which might tend to the complete conviction of the criminal, the constable stumbled upon the butt of the broken pistol which had been found in Macleod's trunk. This he picked up on the edge of the pond in which the corse had been d.scovered, and while James Grayling and his uncle, Sparkman, were engaged in drawing it from the water. The place where the fragment was discovered at once denoted the pistol as the instrument by which the final blows were inflicted. "'Fore God," said the judge to the criminal, as these proofs were submitted on the trial, " you may be a very innocent man after all, as, by my faith, I do think there have been many murderers before you; but you ought, nevertheless, to be hung as an example to all other persons who suffer such strong proofs of guilt to follow their innocent misdoings. Gentlemen of the jury, if this person, Macleod or Macnab, didn't murder Major Spencer, either you or I did; and you must now decide which of us it is! I say, gentlemen of the jury, either you, or I, or the prisoner at the bar, murdered this man; and if you have any doubts which of us it was, it is but justice and mercy that you should give the prisoner the benefit of your doubts; and so find your verdict. But, before God, should you find him not guilty, Mr. Attorney there can scarcely do any thing wiser than to put us all upon trial for the deed."

The jury, it may be scarcely necessary to add, perhaps under certain becoming fears of an alternative such as his honour had suggested, brought in a verdict of "Guilty," without leaving the panel ; and Macnab, *alias* Macleod, was hung at White Point, Charleston, somewhere about the year 178-.

"And here," said my grandmother, devoutly, " you behold a proof of God's watchfulness to see that murder should not be hidden, and that the murderer should not escape. You see that he sent the spirit of the murdered man—since, by no other mode could the truth have been revealed—to declare the crime, and to discover the criminal. But for that ghost, Macnab would have got off to Scotland, and probably have been living to this very day on the money that he took from the person of the poor major."

As the old lady finished the ghost story, which, by the way, she had been tempted to relate for the fiftieth time, in order to combat my father's ridicule of such superstitions, the latter took up the thread of the narrative.

"Now, my son," said he, " as you have heard all that your grandmother has to say on this subject, I will proceed to show you what you have to believe, and what not. It is true that Macnab

murdered Spencer in the manner related; that James Grayling made the discovery and prosecuted the pursuit; found the body and brought the felon to justice; that Macnab suffered death, and confessed the crime; alleging that he was moved to do so, as well because of the money that he suspected Spencer to have in his possession, as because of the hate which he felt for a man who had been particularly bold and active in cutting up a party of Scotch loyalists to which he belonged, on the borders of North Carolina. But the appearance of the spectre was nothing more than the work of a quick imagination, added to a shrewd and correct judgment. James Grayling saw no ghost, in fact, but such as was in his own mind; and, though the instance was one of a most remarkable character, one of singular combination, and well depending circumstances, still, I think it is to be accounted for by natural and very simple laws."

The old lady was indignant.

"And how could he see the ghost just on the edge of the same bay where the murder had been committed, and where the body of the murdered man even then was lying?"

My father did not directly answer the demand, but proceeded thus :—

"James Grayling, as we know, mother, was a very ardent, impetuous, sagacious man. He had the sanguine, the race-horse temperament. He was generous, always prompt and ready, and one who never went backward. What he did, he did quickly, boldly, and thoroughly! He never shrank from trouble of any kind: nay, he rejoiced in the constant encounter with difficulty and trial; and his was the temper which commands and enthrals mankind. He felt deeply and intensely whatever occupied his mind, and when he parted from his friend he brooded over little else than their past communion and the great distance by which they were to be separated. The dull travelling wagon-gait at which he himself was compelled to go, was a source of annoyance to him; and he became sullen, all the day, after the departure of his friend. When, on the evening of the next day, he came to the house where it was natural to expect that Major Spencer would have slept the night before, and he learned the fact that no one stopped there but the Scotchman, Macnab, we see that he was struck with the circumstance. He mutters it over to himself, " Strange, where the major could have gone !" His mind then naturally reverts to the character of the Scotchman ; to the opinions and suspicions which had been already expressed of him by his uncle, and felt by himself. They had all, previously, come to the full conviction that Macnab was, and had always been, a tory, in spite of his protestations. His mind next, and very naturally, reverted to the insecurity of the highways; the general dangers of travelling at that period ; the frequency of crime, and the number of desperate men who were everywhere to be met with. The very employment in which he was then engaged, in scouting the woods for the protection of the camp, was calculated to bring such reflections to his mind. If these precautions were considered necessary for the safety of persons so poor, so wanting in those possessions which might prompt cupidity to crime, how much more necessary were precautions in the case of a wealthy gentleman like Major Spencer! He then remembered the conversation with the major at the camp-fire, when they fancied that the Scotchman was sleeping. How natural to think then, that he was all the while awake; and, if awake, he must have heard him speak of the wealth of his companion. True, the major, with more prudence than himself, denied that he had any money about him, more than would bear his expenses to the city; but such an assurance was natural enough to the lips of a traveller who knew the dangers of the country. That the man, Macnab, was not a person to be trusted, was the equal impression of Joel Sparkman and his nephew from the first. The probabilities were strong that he would rob and perhaps murder, if he might hope to do so with impunity; and as the youth made the circuit of the bay in the darkness and solemn stillness of the night, its gloomy depths and mournful shadows, naturally gave rise to such reflections as would be equally active in the mind of a youth, and of one somewhat familiar with the arts and usages of strife. He would see that the spot was just the one in which a practised partisan would delight to set an ambush for an unwary foe. There ran the public road, with a little sweep, around two-thirds of the extent of its dense and impenetrable thickets. The ambush could lie concealed, and at ten steps command the bosom of its victim. Here, then, you perceive that the mind of James Grayling, stimulated by an active and sagacious judgment, led by gradual and reasonable stages come to these conclusions: that Major Spencer was an object to tempt a robber; that the country was full of robbers; that Macnab was one of them; that this was the very spot in which a deed of blood could be most easily committed, and most easily concealed; and, one important fact, that gave strength and coherence to the whole, that Major Spencer had not reached a well-known point of destination, while Macnab had.

"With these thoughts, thus closely linked together, the youth forgets the limits of his watch and his circuit. This fact, alone, proves how active his imagination had become. It leads him forward, brooding more and more on the subject, until, in the very exhaustion of his body, he sinks down beneath a tree. He sinks down and falls asleep; and in his sleep, what before was plausible conjecture, becomes fact, and the creative properties of his imagination give form and vitality to all his fancies. These forms are bold, broad, and deeply coloured, in due proportion with the degree of force which they receive from probability. Here, he sees the image of his friend; but, you will remark—and this should almost conclusively satisfy any mind that all that he sees is the work of his imagination,—that, though Spencer tells him that he is murdered, and by Macnab, he does not tell him how, in what manner, or with what weapons. Though he sees him pale and ghostlike, he does not see, nor can he say, where his wounds are! He sees his pale features distinctly, and his garments are bloody. Now, had he seen the spectre in the true appearances of death, as he was subsequently found, he would not have been able to discern his features, which were battered, according to his own account, almost out of all shape of humanity, and covered with mud; while his clothes would have streamed with mud and water, rather than with blood."

"Ah!" exclaimed the old lady, my grandmother, "it's hard to make you believe any thing that you don't see; you are like Saint Thomas in the Scriptures; but how do you propose to account for his knowing that the Scotchman was on board the Falmouth packet? Answer to that!"

"That is not a more difficult matter than any of the rest. You forget that in the dialogue which took place between James and Major Spencer at the camp, the latter told him that he was about to take passage for Europe in the Falmouth packet, which then lay in Charleston harbour, and was about to sail. Macnab heard all that."

"True enough, and likely enough," returned the old lady; "but, though you show that it was Major Spencer's intention to go to Europe in the Falmouth packet, that will not show that it was also the intention of the murderer."

"Yet what more probable, and how natural for James Grayling to imagine such a thing! In the first place he knew that Macnab was a Briton; he felt convinced that he was a tory; and the inference was immediate, that such a person would scarcely have remained long in a country where such characters laboured under so much odium, disfranchisement, and constant danger from popular tumults. The fact that Macnab was compelled to disguise his true sentiments, and affect those of the people against whom he fought so vindictively, shows what was his sense of the danger which he incurred. Now, it is not unlikely that Macnab was quite as well aware that the Falmouth packet was in Charleston, and about to sail, as Major Spencer. No doubt he was pursuing the same journey, with the same object, and had he not murdered Spencer, they would, very likely, have been fellow-passengers together to Europe. But, whether he knew the fact before or not, he probably heard it stated by Spencer while he seemed to be sleeping; and, even supposing that he did not then know, it was enough that he found this to be the fact on reaching the city. It was an after-thought to fly to Europe with his ill-gotten spoils; and whatever may have appeared a politic course to the criminal, would be a probable conjecture in the mind of him by whom he was suspected. The whole story is one of strong probabilities which happened to be verified. . . . . He never, my son, saw any other ghosts than those of his own making!"

I heard my father with great patience to the end, though he seemed very tedious. He had taken a great deal of pains to destroy one of my greatest sources of pleasure. I need not add that I continued to believe in the ghost, and, with my grandmother, to reject the philosophy.

2 X

JOSEPH C. NEAL.

[Born 1807. Died 1847.]

THE author of Charcoal Sketches was born in Greenland in New Hampshire on the third of February, 1807. His father had been for many years principal of a popular academy in Philadelphia, and was now minister of a Congregational church,—a retirement to the country and from the arduous duties in which he had been engaged having been rendered necessary by ill health. He died when our author, his only son, was about two years of age, and his family soon after returned to Philadelphia.

Mr. Neal resided several years in the village of Pottsville, but in 1831 he settled in Philadelphia as editor of The Pennsylvanian, a journal which has since been conspicuous for its influence on the political character of the state, and for a certain liveliness and courtesy which do not commonly distinguish the organs of contending parties. For about ten years his devotion to the arduous duties of his profession was unremitted; but at length his health failed, and, in 1841, he travelled in Europe and Africa in the hope of deriving benefit from relaxation and change of scene. He returned in the following year, and was able to resume his occupation; but he finally retired from the Pennsylvanian in 1844, to enter upon the lighter and more congenial business of conducting a weekly literary miscellany which he established in the autumn of that year under the title of Neal's Saturday Gazette. The reputation he had acquired during his long connection with the press, particularly as a writer of wit and humour, secured for this periodical an immediate success which has rarely been paralleled; and it appears to have grown steadily in the popular favour, as every week has brought increase of its circulation.

Mr. Neal's first compositions, of that class for which he is chiefly distinguished, appeared under the title of City Worthies, in The Pennsylvanian, soon after the establishment of that journal, and were reprinted and praised in a large proportion of the newspapers of the country. In 1837 he published Charcoal Sketches, or Scenes in a Metropolis, in which

he drew, with remarkable spirit and fidelity, a class of characters always floating near the bottom in great cities. Of this work several large editions have been sold in the United States, and it was republished in London, under the auspices of Mr. Dickens. In 1844 he published Peter Ploddy and other Oddities, and he has since given to the public a new series of Charcoal Sketches in his Gazette.

The effect of many of Mr. Neal's portraitures is injured by the use of descriptive names, such as "Fydget Fixington," "Tippleton Tipps," "Shiverton Shakes," and "Slyder Downehylle," in which there is exhibited no humour, and but a puerile invention. This sort of nomenclature prevents the interest which might arise from the gradual discovery of a person's peculiarities from conversation and action, and shows a consciousness of a want of power to individualize in any other manner. The system is allowable only in allegory, and even in this sort of writing should be used with great caution and judgment. Mr. Neal is a very good moral philosopher, of a certain sort, or rather, a moral historian, who is not so careful of the dignity of his subject as to refrain from an occasional exhibition of it in undress. It is sometimes apparent, however, that he is a describer and narrator only, without that genial sympathy with his own creations which is necessary to give them an actual existence to the mind. His style is compact and pointed, abounding in droll combinations, and peculiar phrases, which have the ease and naturalness of transcripts of real conversations.

Mr. Neal's style in other compositions is neat and graceful, and frequently sparkling and witty. He had too much good nature to be caustic, and too much refinement to be coarse. It evinces ingenuousness, sincerity, and manly feeling.

—Mr. Neal continued in the editorship of The Saturday Gazette, until the third of July, 1848, when he died, very suddenly, in Philadelphia. A second series of his Charcoal Sketches has since been published by his widow.

A PRETTY TIME OF NIGHT.

FROM SECOND SERIES OF CHARCOAL SKETCHES.

W E know it to be theoretical in certain schools—in the kitchen, for instance, which is the most orthodox and sensible of the schools—that, as a general rule, the leading features of character are indicated by the mode in which we pull a bell; and that, to a considerable extent, we may infer the kind of person who is at the door—just as we do the kind of fish that bobs the cork—by the species of vibration which is given to the wire. Rash, impetuous, choleric and destructive, what chance has the poor little bell in such hands? But the considerate, modest, lowly and retiring—do you ever know such people to break things? Depend upon it, too, that our self-estimate is largely indicated by our conduct in this respect. If it does not betray what we really are, it most assuredly discloses the temper of the mind at the moment of our ringing.

" Tinkle !"

Did you hear ?

Nothing could be more amiable or more unobtrusive than that. It would scarcely disturb the nervous system of a mouse ; and whoever listened to it, might at once understand, that it was the soft tintinnabulary whisper of a gentleman of the convivial turn and of the " locked out" description, who, conscious probably of default, is desirous of being admitted to his domiciliary comforts, upon the most pacific and silent terms that can be obtained from those who hold the citadel and possess the inside of the door.

" Tinkle !"

Who can doubt that he—Mr. Tinkle—would take off his boots and go up stairs in his stocking-feet, muttering rebuke to every step that creaked ? What a deprecating mildness there is in the deportment of the " great locked out !" How gently do they tap, and how softly do they ring ; while perchance, in due proportion to their enjoyment in untimely and protracted revel, is the penitential aspect of their return. There is a " never-do-so-any-more-ishness"all about them—yea—even about the bully boys " who would'nt go home till morning—till daylight does appear," singing up to the very door ; and when they

" Tinkle !"

It is intended as a hint merely, and not as a broad annunciation—insinuated—not proclaimed aloud—that somebody who is very sorry—who " didn't go to help it," and all that—is at the threshold, and that if it be the same to you, he would be exceeding glad to come in, with as little of scolding and rebuke as may be thought likely to answer the purpose. There is a hope in it—a subdued hope—

" Tinkle !"

—that perchance a member of the family—good-natured as well as insomnolent—may be spontaneously awake, and disposed to open the door without clamouring up Malcolm, Donalbain, and the whole house. Why should every one know ? But—

" Tinkle—tankle !"

Even patience itself—on a damp, chilly, unwholesome night—patience at the street door, all alone by itself and disposed to slumber—as patience is apt to be after patience has been partaking of potations and of collations—even patience itself cannot be expected to remain tinkling there— " pianissimo"—hour after hour, as if there were nothing else in this world worthy of attention but the ringing of bells. Who can be surprised, that patience at last becomes reckless and desperate, let the consequences—rhinoceroses or Hyrcan tigers—assume what shape they may ?

There is a furious stampede upon the marble—a fierce word or two of scathing Saxon, and then— "Rangle—ja-a-a-ngle—ra-a-a-ng!!!"—the sound being of that sharp, stinging, excruciating kind, which leads to the conclusion that somebody is " worse," and is getting in a rage.

That one, let me tell you, was Mr. Dawson Dawdle, in whom wrath had surmounted discretion, and who, as a forlorn hope, had now determined to make good his entrance—assault, storm, escalade—at any hazard and at any cost. Dawson Dawdle was furious now—" sevagerous"—as you have been, probably, when kept at the door till your teeth rattled like castanets and cachuchas.

Passion is picturesque in attitude as well as poetic in expression. Dawson Dawdle braced his feet one on each side of the door-post, as a purchase, and tugged at the bell with both hands, until windows flew up in all directions, and night-capped heads in curious variety were projected into the gloom. Something seemed to be the matter at Dawdle's.

" Who's sick !" cried one.

" Where's the fire ?" asked another.

" The Mexicans are come !" shouted a third. But Dawson Dawdle had reached that state of intensity, which is regardless of every consideration but that of the business in hand, and he continued to pull away, as if at work by the job, while several observing watchmen stood by in admiration of his zeal. Yet there was no answer to this pealing appeal for admittance—not that Mrs. Dawson Dawdle was deaf—not she—nor dumb either. Nay, she had recognised Mr. Dawdle's returning step —that husband's " foot," which should, according to the poet,

"Have music in't,
As he comes up the stair."

But Dawdle was allowed to make his music in the street, while his wife—obdurate—listened with a smile bordering, we fear, a little upon exultation, at his progressive lessons and rapid improvements in the art of ringing " triple-bob-majors."

" Let him wait," remarked Mrs. Dawson Dawdle; " let him wait—'twill do him good. I'm sure I've been waiting long enough for him."

And so she had ; but, though there be a doubt whether this process of waiting had " done good" in her own case, yet if there be truth or justice in the vengeful practice which would have us act towards others precisely as they deport themselves to us,—and every one concedes that it is very agreeable, however wrong, to carry on the war after this fashion,—Mrs. Dawson Dawdle could have little difficulty in justifying herself for the course adopted.

Only to think of it, now!

Mrs. Dawson Dawdle is one of those natural and proper people, who become sleepy of evenings, and who are rather apt to yawn after tea. Mr. Dawson Dawdle, on the other hand, is of the unnatural and improper species, who are not sleepy or yawny of evenings—never so, except of mornings. Dawson insists on it that he is no chicken to go to roost at sundown; while Mrs. Dawson Dawdle rises with the lark. The larks he prefers, are larks at night. Now, as a corrective to these differences of opinion, Dawson Dawdle had been cunningly deprived of his pass-key, that he might be induced "to remember not to forget" to come home betimes—a thing he was not apt to remember, especially if good companionship intervened.

Thus, Mrs. Dawdle was "waiting up" for him.···

To indulge in an episode here, *apropos* to the general principle involved, it may be said, pertinently enough, that this matter of waiting, if you have nerves—"waiting up," or "waiting down"—choose either branch of the dilemma—is not to be ranged under the head of popular amusements, or classified in the category of enlivening recreation. To wait—who has not waited?—fix it as we will—is always more or less of a trial; and whether the arrangement be for "waiting up"—disdainful of sleep—or for "waiting down"—covetous of dozes—it rarely happens that the intervals are employed in the invocation of other than left-handed blessings, on the head of those who have caused this deviation from comfortable routine; or that, on their tardy arrival—people conscious of being waited for, always stay out as long and as provokingly as they can—we find ourselves at all disposed to amiable converse, or complimentary expression.

And reason good. If we lie down, for instance, when my young lady has gone to a "Polka party," or my young gentleman has travelled away to an affair of the convivialities, do we ever find it conducive to refreshing repose, this awkward consciousness, overpending like the sword of Damocles, that sooner or later the disturbance must come, to call us startingly from dreams? Nor, after we have tossed and tumbled into a lethargy, is it to be set down as a pleasure to be aroused, all stupid and perplexed, to scramble down the stairway, for the admission of delinquents, who—the fact admits of no exception—ring, ring, ring, or knock, knock, knock away, long after you have heard them, and persist in goading you to frenzies, by peal upon peal, when your very neck is endangered by rapidity of movement in their behalf. It is a lucky thing for them when they so ungratefully ask "why you didn't make haste," as they always do, or mutter about being "kept there all night," as they surely will, that despotic powers are unknown in these regions, and that you are not invested with supreme command. But now get thee to sleep again, as quickly as thou canst, though it may be that the task is not the easiest in the world.

"Waiting up," too; this likewise has its delecta-

tions. The very clock seems at last to have entered into the conspiracy—the hands move with sluggish weariness, and there is a laggard sound in the swinging of the pendulum, which almost says that time itself is tired, as it ticks its progress to the drowsy ear. There is a bustle in the street, no doubt, as you sit down doggedly to wakefulness; and many feet are pattering from the theatre and circus. For a time the laugh is heard, and people chatter as they pass, boy calling unto boy, or deepmouthed men humming an untuned song. Now doors are slammed, and shutters closed, and bolts are shooting, in earnest of retirements for the night. Forsaken dogs bark round and round the house, and vocal cats beset the portico. The rumbling of the hack dwindles in the distance, as the cabs roll by from steamboat wharf and railroad depot. You are deserted and alone—tired of book—sated with newspaper—indisposed to thought. You nod—ha! ha!—bibetty bobetty!—as your hair smokes and crackles in the lamp. But it is folly now to peep forth. Will they never come? No—do they ever, until all reasonable patience is exhausted?—Yes —here they are!—Pshaw!—sit still—it is but a straggling step; and hour drags after hour, until you have resolved it o'er and o'er again, that this shall be the last of your vigils, let who will request it as a favour that you will be good enough to sit up for them. I wouldn't do it!

So it is not at all to be marvelled at that Mrs. Dawson Dawdle—disposed as we know her to be, to sleepiness at times appropriate to sleep—was irate at the non-appearance of Mr. Dawson Dawdle, or that after he had reached home, she detained him vengefully at the street door, as an example to such dilatoriness in general, for it is a prevailing fault in husbandry, and that, in particular, being thus kept out considerably longer than he wished to keep out—too much of a good thing being good for nothing—he might be taught better, on the doctrine of curing an evil by aggravation—both were aggravated.

But the difficulty presents itself here, that Mr. Dawson Dawdle has a constitutional defect, beyond reach of the range of ordinary remedial agents. Being locked out, is curative to some people, for at least a time—till they forget it, mostly. But Dawson Dawdle is the man who is always too late—he must be too late—he would not know himself if he were not too late—he would not be he, if he were not too late. Too late is to him a matter of course—a fixed result in his nature. He had heard of "soon," and he believed that perhaps there might occasionally be something of the sort—spasmodic and accidental—but, for his own part, he had never been there himself. And as for "too soon;" he regarded it as imaginative altogether—an incredibility. The presumption is, that he must have been born an hour or so too late, and that he had never been able to make up the difference. In fact, Dawson Dawdle is a man to be relied on—no mistake as to Dawson Dawdle. Whenever he makes an appointment, you are sure he will not keep it, which saves a deal of trouble on your side of the question: and at the best, if an early hour be set, any time will answer, in the latter part of the day. Dawson Dawdle forgets, too;—how complimentary it is to be told that engagements in which we are involved are so readily forgotten! Leave it to the Dawdles to forget; and never double the affront by an excuse that transcends the original offence.—Or else, Dawson Dawdle did not know it was so late; and yet Dawson might have been sure of it. When was it otherwise than late with the late Mr. Dawson Dawdle!

"Well," said he at the bell-handle all this time, "Well, I suppose it's late again—it rings as if it was late; and somehow or other it appears to me that it always is late, especially and particularly when my wife tells me to be sure to be home early —'you, Dawson, come back soon; d'ye hear!' and all that sort o' thing. I wish she wouldn't—it puts me out, to keep telling me what I ought to do; and when I have to remember to come home early, it makes me forget all about it, and discomboberates my ideas so that I'm a great deal later than I would be if I was left to my own sagacity. Let me alone, and I'm great upon sagacity; but yet what is sagacity when it has no key and the dead-latch is down? What chance has sagacity got when sagacity's wife won't let sagacity in? I'll have another pull at the bell—exercise is good for one's health."

This last peal—as peals, under such circumstances, are apt to be—was louder, more sonorous, and in all respects more terrific than any of its "illustrious predecessors," practice in this respect tending to the improvement of skill on the one hand, just as it adds provocation to temper on the other. For a moment, the fate of Dawson Dawdle quivered in the scale, as the eye of his exasperated lady glanced fearfully round the room for a means of retaliation and redress. Nay, her hand rested for an instant upon a pitcher, while thoughts of hydropathies, douches, showerbaths, Graefenbergs, and Priessnitzes, in their medicinal application to dilatory husbands, presented themselves in quick aquatic succession, like the rushings of a cataract. Never did man come nearer to being drowned than Mr. Dawson Dawdle.

"But no," said she, relenting; "if he were to ketch his death o' cold, he'd be a great deal more trouble than he is now—husbands with bad colds —coughing husbands and sneezing husbands—are the stupidest and tiresomest kind of husbands—bad as they may be, ducking don't improve 'em. I'll have recourse to moral suasion; and if that won't answer, I'll duck him afterwards."

Suddenly and in the midst of a protracted jangle, the door flew widely open, and displayed the form of Mrs. Dawson Dawdle, standing sublime—silent —statuesque—wrapped in wrath and enveloped in taciturnity. Dawdle was appalled.

"My dear!" and his hand dropped nervelessly from the bell-handle. "My dear, it's me—only me!"

Not a word of response to the tender appeal— the lady remained obdurate in silence—chilly and voiceless as the marble, with her eyes sternly fixed upon the intruder. Dawson Dawdle felt himself running down.

66

"My dear—he! he!" and Dawson laughed with a melancholy quaver—"it's me that's come home —you know me—it's late, I confess—it's most always late—and I—ho! ho!—why don't you say something, Mrs. Dawson Dawdle?—Do you think I'm going to be skeered, Mrs. Dawdle?"

As the parties thus confronted each other, Mrs. Dawdle's "masterly inactivity" proved overwhelming. For reproaches, Dawson was prepared—he could bear part in a war of opinion—the squabble is easy to most of us—but where are we when the antagonist will not deign to speak, and environs us, as it were, in an ambuscade, so that we fear the more because we know not what to fear?

"Why don't she blow me up?" queried Dawdle to himself, as he found his valour collapsing—"why don't she blow me up like an affectionate woman and a loving wife, instead of standing there in that ghostified fashion?"

Mrs. Dawdle's hand slowly extended itself towards the culprit, who made no attempt at evasion or defence—slowly it entwined itself in the folds of his neck-handkerchief, and, as the unresisting Dawson had strange fancies relative to bow-strings, he found himself drawn inward by a sure and steady grasp. Swiftly was he sped through the darksome entry and up the winding stair, without a word to comfort him in his stumbling progress.

"Dawson Dawdle!—Look at the clock!—A pretty time of night, indeed, and you a married man. Look at the clock, I say, and see."

Mrs. Dawson Dawdle, however, had, for the moment, lost her advantage in thus giving utterance to her emotion; and Mr. Dawson Dawdle, though much shaken, began to recover his spirits.

"Two o'clock, Mr. Dawdle—two!—isn't it two, I ask you?"

"If you are positive about the fact, Mrs. Dawdle, it would be unbecoming in me to call your veracity in question, and I decline looking. So far as I am informed, it generally is two o'clock just about this time in the morning—at least, it always has been whenever I stayed up to see. If the clock is right, you'll be apt to find it two just as it strikes two—that's the reason it strikes, and I don't know that it could have a better reason."

"A pretty time!"

"Yes—pretty enough!" responded Dawdle; "when it don't rain, one time of night is as pretty as another time of night—it's the people that's up in the time of night, that's not pretty; and you, Mrs. Dawdle, are a case in pint—keeping a man out of his own house. It's not the night that's not pretty, Mrs. Dawdle, but the goings on, that's not—and you are the goings on. As for me, I'm for peace—a dead-latch key and peace; and I move that the goings on be indefinitely postponed, because, Mrs. Dawdle, I've heard it all before—I know it like a book; and if you insist on it, Mrs. Dawdle, I'll save you trouble, and speak the whole speech for you right off the reel, only I can't cry good when I'm jolly."

But Dawson Dawdle's volubility, assumed for the purpose of hiding his own misgivings, did not answer the end which he had in view; for Mrs.

2 x 2

Dawson Dawdle, having had a glimpse at its effects, again resorted to the "silent system" of connubial management. She spoke no more that night, which Dawson, perchance, found agreeable enough; but she would not speak any more the day after, which perplexed him when he came down too late for breakfast, or returned too late for dinner.

"I do wish she would say something," muttered Dawdle; "something cross, if she likes—any thing, so it makes a noise. It makes a man feel bad, after he's used to being talked to, not to be talked to in the regular old-fashioned way. When one's so accustomed to being blowed up, it seems as if he was lost or didn't belong to anybody, if no one sees to it that he's blowed up at the usual time. Bachelors, perhaps, can get along well enough without having their comforts properly attended to in this respect.—What do they know, the miserable creatures, about such warm receptions, and such little endearments? When they are out too late, nobody's at home preparing a speech for them; but I feel just as if I was a widower, if I'm not talked to for not being at home in time." ......

CORNER LOUNGERS.
FROM PETER PLODDY AND OTHER ODDITIES.

"COMMON people, Billy—low, onery, common people, can't make it out when natur's raised a gentleman in the family—a gentleman all complete, only the money's been forgot. If a man won't work all the time—day in and day out—if he smokes by the fire or whistles out of the winder, the very gals bump agin him and say 'get out of the way loaf!'"

"But, Billy, my son, never mind, and keep not a lettin' on," continued Nollikins, and a beam of hope irradiated his otherwise saturnine countenance; "the world's a railroad and the cars is comin'—all we'll have to do is to jump in, chalked free. There will be a time—something must happen. Rich widders are about yet, though they are snapped up so fast. Rich widders, Billy, are 'special providences,' as my old boss used to say when I broke my nose in the entry, sent here like rafts to pick up deservin' chaps when they can't swim no longer. When you've bin down twy'st, Billy, and are jist off agin, then comes the widder a floatin' along. Why, splatterdocks is nothin' to it, and a widder is the best of all life-preservers, when a man is most a case, like you and me."

"Well, I'm not perticklar, not I, nor never was. I'll take a widder, for my part, if she's got the mint drops, and never ask no questions. I'm not proud—never was harrystocratic—I drinks with anybody, and smokes all the cigars they give me. What's the use of bein' stuck up, stiffy? It's my principle that other folks are nearly as good as we, if they're not constables nor aldermen. I can't stand them sort."

"No, Billy," said Nollikins, with an encouraging smile, "no, Billy, such indiwidooals as them don't know human natur'—but, as I was goin' to say, if there happens to be a short crop of widders, why can't somebody leave us a fortin?—That will do as well, if not better. Now look here—what's easier than this? I'm standin' on the wharf—the rich man tries to go aboard of the steamboat—the niggers push him off the plank—in I jumps, ca-splash! The old gentleman isn't drowned; but he might have been drowned but for me, and if he had a bin, where's the use of his money then? So he gives me as much as I want now, and a great deal more when he defuncts riggler, accordin' to law and the practice of civilized nations. You see—that's the way the thing works. I'm at the wharf every day—can't afford to lose a chance, and I begin to wish the old chap would hurra about comin' along. What can keep him?"

"If it 'ud come to the same thing in the end," remarked Billy Bunkers, "I'd rather the niggers would push the old man's little boy into the water, if it's all the same to him. Them fat old fellers are so heavy when they're skeered, and hang on so—why, I might get drowned before I had time to go to bank with the check! But what's the use of waitin'? Couldn't we shove 'em in some warm afternoon, ourselves? Who'd know in the crowd?"

"I've thought of that, Bunkers, when a man was before me that looked like the right sort. I've often said to myself, 'My friend, how would you like to be washed for nothin'?'—but, Billy, there might be mistakes—perhaps, when you got him out, he couldn't pay. What then?"

"Why, keep a puttin' new ones in to soak every day, till you do fish up the right one."

"It won't do, my friend—they'd smoke the joke—all the riff-raff in town would be pushin' old gentlemen into the river, and the elderly folks would have to give up travellin' by the steamboat. We must wait, I'm afeared, till the real thing happens. The right person will be sure to come along."

"I hope so; and so it happens quick, I don't much care whether it's the old man, or his little boy, or that rich widder, that gets a ducking. I'm not proud." ....

"Then you'll see me come the nonsense over the old folks—who's loafer now!—and my dog will bite their cat—who's ginger-pop and jam spruce beer, at this present writin', I'd like to know?" ...

Thus, wrapped in present dreams and future anticipations—a king that is to be—lives Nicholas Nollikins—the grand exemplar of the corner loungers. There he stations himself; for hope requires a boundless prospect and a clear look-out, that, by whatever route fortune chooses to approach, she may have a prompt reception. Nicholas and his tribe exist but for to-morrow, and rely firmly upon that poetic justice, which should reward those who wait patiently until the wheel of fortune turns up a prize. They feel, by the generous expansion of their souls, by their impatience of ignoble toil, by their aspirations after the beautiful and nice, that their present position in society is the result of accident and inadvertency, and that, if they are not false to the nature that is within them, the time must come when the mistake will be rectified, and "they shall walk in silk attire and siller hae to spare," which is not by any means the case at present. All that can be expected just now, is, that they should spare other people's "siller."

EDGAR A. POE.

[Born 1811. Died 1849.]

EDGAR A. POE, born in Baltimore in January, 1811, was the second son of David and Elizabeth Arnold Poe, of the theatre, both of whom died in Richmond, in 1815, leaving three children in homeless poverty. He was adopted by Mr. Allan, a merchant, who in the following year placed him at a school near London, from which in 1822 he was removed to the University of Virginia, where he graduated with distinction in 1826. His irregularities at college caused a disagreement with his patron, and he joined an expedition to assist the Greeks; but after proceeding as far as St. Petersburg, on the way to Athens, he returned, and a reconciliation with Mr. Allan having been effected, he was enabled to enter the Military Academy at West Point. Here he made his first essays in literature, in a small volume of Poems, printed in 1830, about which time he left the Academy, and Mr. Allan having died without making any provision for him in his will, he was compelled afterward to rely entirely upon his pen for support. Securing attention with two literary prizes at Baltimore, he was in 1835 engaged by the proprietor of The Southern Literary Messenger, at Richmond, to assist in editing that magazine; in 1838, he removed to Philadelphia, where he was connected as editor with Burton's Magazine one year, and with Graham's a year and a half; and he continued in the latter city until 1844, during which time he published Tales of the Grotesque and the Arabesque, in two volumes; and Arthur Gordon Pym, a nautical romance, in one volume; besides many of his finest criticisms, and other tales and poems, in periodicals. He went next to New York, where he was employed several months as a reviewer of books for the Home Journal, and was first an associate and afterward the sole editor of the Broadway Journal. In the winter of 1848, while at Fordham, a few miles from the city, he suffered much from poverty, and his wife, to whom he had been married about twelve years, died in the following spring. He had already published new collections of his Poems and Tales, and the magazine

sketches of the Literati, and in 1849 he gave to the world Eureka, a Prose Poem, intended to illustrate his views of the constitution of the Universe. In the summer of 1849 he revisited Virginia, and it was believed that he had entirely mastered his habits of dissipation; but on the fourth of October he set out for New York, to fulfil a literary engagement, and to prepare for his second marriage. Arriving in Baltimore, he gave his trunk to a porter, with directions to convey it to the cars which were to leave in an hour or two for Philadelphia, and went into a tavern to obtain some refreshment. Here he met acquaintances who invited him to drink: his resolutions and duties were forgotten; in a few hours he was in such a state as is commonly induced only by long-continued intoxication; after a night of insanity and exposure, he was carried to a hospital; and there, on the evening of the seventh of October, 1849, he died, at the age of thirty-eight years.

Soon afterward, having been appointed his literary executor, I collected and published his various works, in three volumes, for the benefit of his family. In the third volume I have given an account of his life, with opinions of his genius. His realm was on the shadowy confines of human experience, among the abodes of crime, gloom, and horror, and there he delighted to surround himself with images of beauty and of terror, to raise his solemn palaces and towers and spires in a night upon which should rise no sun. His minuteness of detail, refinement of reasoning, and propriety and power of language—the perfect keeping and apparent good faith, with which he managed the evocation and exhibition of his strange and spectral and revolting creations—gave him an astonishing mastery over his readers, so that his books were closed as one would lay aside nightmare or the spells of opium. The analytical subtlety evinced in his works has frequently been overestimated, because it has not been sufficiently considered that his mysteries were composed with the express design of being dissolved. When Poe attempted the illustration of the pro-

523

founder operations of the mind, as displayed in written reason or in real action, he frequently failed entirely. In poetry, as in prose, he was eminently successful in the metaphysical treatment of the passions. His poems are constructed with wonderful ingenuity, and finished with consummate art. They display a sombre and weird imagination, and a taste almost faultless in the apprehension of that sort of beauty which was most agreeable to his temper. But they evince little genuine feeling, and less of that spontaneous ecstacy which gives its freedom, smoothness, and naturalness to immortal verse. He was not remarkably original in invention. Indeed some of his plagiarisms are scarcely paralleled for audacity: for instance,

in The Pit and the Pendulum, the complicate machinery upon which the interest depends is borrowed from a story entitled Vivenzio, in Blackwood's Magazine. In his Marginalia he also borrowed largely, especially from Coleridge. As a critic, he rarely ascended from the particular to the general, from subjects to principles; he was familiar with the microscope but never looked through the telescope. His criticisms are of value to the degree in which they are demonstrative, but his unsupported assertions and opinions were so apt to be influenced by friendship or enmity, by the desire to please or the fear to offend, or by his constant ambition to surprise, or produce a sensation, that they should be received in all cases with distrust of their fairness.

THE FALL OF THE HOUSE OF USHER.

DURING the whole of a dull, dark, and soundless day in the autumn of the year, when the clouds hung oppressively low in the heavens, I had been passing alone on horseback, through a singularly dreary tract of country; and at length found myself, as the shades of the evening drew on, within view of the melancholy House of Usher. I know not how it was—but, with the first glimpse of the building, a sense of insufferable gloom pervaded my spirit. I say insufferable; for the feeling was unrelieved by any of that half-pleasurable, because poetic, sentiment, with which the mind usually receives even the sternest natural images of the desolate or terrible. I looked upon the scene before me—upon the mere house, and the simple landscape features of the domain—upon the bleak walls—upon the vacant eyelike windows—upon a few rank sedges—and upon a few white trunks of decayed trees—with an utter depression of soul which I can compare to no earthly sensation more properly than to the after-dream of the reveller upon opium—the bitter lapse into everyday life—the hideous dropping off of the veil. There was an iciness, a sinking, a sickening of the heart—an unredeemed dreariness of thought which no goading of the imagination could torture into aught of the sublime. What was it so unnerved me in the contemplation of the House of Usher? It was a mystery all insoluble; nor could I grapple with the shadowy fancies that crowded upon me as I pondered. I was forced to fall back upon the unsatisfactory conclusion, that while, beyond a doubt, there *are* combinations of very simple natural objects which have the power of thus affecting us, still the analysis of this power lies among considerations beyond our depth. It was possible, I reflected, that a mere different arrangement of the particulars of the scene, of the details of the picture, would be sufficient to molify, or perhaps to annihilate its capacity for sorrowful impression; and acting upon this idea, I

reined my horse to the precipitous brink of a black and lurid tarn that lay in unruffled lustre by the dwelling, and gazed down—but with a shudder even more thrilling than before—upon the remodelled and inverted images of the gray sedge, and the ghastly tree-stems, and the vacant and eye-like windows.

Nevertheless, in this mansion of gloom I now proposed to myself a sojourn of some weeks. Its proprietor, Roderick Usher, had been one of my boon companions in boyhood; but many years had elapsed, since our last meeting. A letter, however, had lately reached me in a distant part of the country—a letter from him—which, in its wildly importunate nature, had admitted of no other than a personal reply. The MS. gave evidence of nervous agitation. The writer spoke of acute bodily illness—of a mental disorder which oppressed him —and of an earnest desire to see me, as his best, and indeed his only personal friend, with a view of attempting, by the cheerfulness of my society, some alleviation of his malady. It was the manner in which all this, and much more, was said—it was the apparent *heart* that went with his request—which allowed me no room for hesitation; and I accordingly obeyed forthwith what I still considered a very singular summons.

Although, as boys, we had been even intimate associates, yet I really knew little of my friend. His reserve had been always excessive and habitual. I was aware, however, that his very ancient family had been noted, time out of mind, for a peculiar sensibility of temperament, displaying itself, through long ages, in many works of exalted art, and manifested, of late, in repeated deeds of munificent yet unobtrusive charity, as well as in a passionate devotion to the intricacies, perhaps even more than to the orthodox and easily recognisable beauties, of musical science. I had learned, too, the very remarkable fact, that the stem of the Usher race, all time-honoured as it was, had put forth, at no period, any enduring branch; in other words, that the entire family lay in the direct line of descent, and had always, with very trifling and very temporary variation, so lain. It was this deficiency, I considered, while running over in thought the perfect keeping of the character of the premises with the accredited character of the people, and while speculating upon the possible influence which the one, in the long lapse of centuries, might have exercised upon the other—it was this deficiency, perhaps, of collateral issue, and the consequent undeviating transmission, from sire to son, of the patrimony with the name, which had, at length, so identified the two as to merge the original title of the estate in the quaint and equivocal appellation of the "House of Usher"—an appellation which seemed to include, in the minds of the peasantry who used it, both the family and the family mansion.

I have said that the sole effect of my somewhat childish experiment—that of looking down within the tarn—had been to deepen the first singular impression. There can be no doubt that the consciousness of the rapid increase of my superstition —for why should I not so term it?—served mainly to accelerate the increase itself. Such, I have long known, is the paradoxical law of all sentiments having terror as a basis. And it might have been for this reason only, that, when I again uplifted my eyes to the house itself, from its image in the pool, there grew in my mind a strange fancy— a fancy so ridiculous, indeed, that I but mention it to show the vivid force of the sensations which oppressed me. I had so worked upon my imagination as really to believe that the whole mansion and domain there hung an atmosphere peculiar to themselves and their immediate vicinity—an atmosphere which had no affinity with the air of heaven, but which had reeked up from the decayed trees, and the gray wall, and in the silent tarn—a pestilent and mystic vapour, dull, sluggish, faintly discernible, and leaden-hued.

Shaking off from my spirit what *must* have been a dream, I scanned more narrowly the real aspect of the building. Its principal feature seemed to be that of an excessive antiquity. The discoloration of ages had been great. Minute fungi overspread the whole exterior, hanging in a fine tangled web-work from the eaves. Yet all this was apart from any extraordinary dilapidation. No portion of the masonry had fallen; and there appeared to be a wild inconsistency between its still perfect adaptation of parts, and the crumbling condition of the individual stones. In this there was much that reminded me of the spacious totality of old woodwork which has rotted for long years in some neglected vault, with no disturbance from the breath of the external air. Beyond this indication of extensive decay, however, the fabric gave little token of instability. Perhaps the eye of a scrutinizing observer might have discovered a barely perceptible fissure, which, extending from the roof of the building in front, made its way down the wall in a zigzag direction, until it became lost in the sullen waters of the tarn.

Noticing these things, I rode over a short cause-way to the house. A servant in waiting took my horse, and I entered the Gothic archway of the hall. A valet, of stealthy step, thence conducted me, in silence, through many dark and intricate passages in my progress to the *studio* of his master. Much that I encountered on the way contributed, I know not how, to heighten the vague sentiments of which I have already spoken. While the objects around me—while the carvings of the ceilings, the sombre tapestries of the walls, the ebon blackness of the floors, and the phantasmagoric armorial trophies which rattled as I strode, were but matters to which, or to such as which, I had been accustomed from my infancy—while I hesitated not to acknowledge how familiar was all this—I still wondered to find how unfamiliar were the fancies which ordinary images were stirring up. On one of the staircases, I met the physician of the family. His countenance, I thought, wore a mingled expression of low cunning and perplexity. He accosted me with trepidation and passed on. The valet now threw open a door and ushered me into the presence of his master.

The room in which I found myself was very large and lofty. The windows were long, narrow, and pointed, and at so vast a distance from the black oaken floor as to be altogether inaccessible from within. Feeble gleams of encrimsoned light made their way through the trellised panes, and served to render sufficiently distinct the more prominent objects around; the eye, however, struggled in vain to reach the remoter angles of the chamber, or the recesses of the vaulted and fretted ceiling. Dark draperies hung upon the walls. The general furniture was profuse, comfortless, antique, and tattered. Many books and musical instruments lay scattered about, but failed to give any vitality to the scene. I felt that I breathed an atmosphere of sorrow. An air of stern, deep, and irredeemable gloom hung over and pervaded all.

Upon my entrance, Usher arose from a sofa on which he had been lying at full length, and greeted me with a vivacious warmth which had much in it, I at first thought, of an overdone cordiality—of the constrained effort of the *ennuyé* man of the world. A glance, however, at his countenance convinced me of his perfect sincerity. We sat down; and for some moments, while he spoke not, I gazed upon him with a feeling half of pity, half of awe. Surely, man had never before so terribly altered, in so brief a period, as had Roderick Usher! It was with difficulty that I could bring myself to admit the identity of the wan being before me with the companion of my early boyhood. Yet the character of his face had been at all times remarkable. A cadaverousness of complexion; an eye large, liquid, and luminous beyond comparison; lips somewhat thin and very pallid, but of a surpassingly beautiful curve; a nose of a delicate Hebrew model, but with a breadth of nostril unusual in similar formations; a finely moulded chin, speaking, in its want of prominence, of a want of moral energy; hair of a more than web-like softness and tenuity; these features, with an inordinate expansion above the regions of the temple, made up altogether a countenance not easily to be forgotten. And now in the mere exaggeration of the prevailing character of these features, and of the expression they were wont to convey, lay so much of change that I doubted to whom I spoke. The now ghastly pallor of the skin, and the now miraculous lustre of the eye, above all things startled and even awed me. The silken hair, too, had been suffered to grow all unheeded, and as, in its wild gossamer texture, it floated rather than fell about the face, I could not, even with effort, connect its Arabesque expression with any idea of simple humanity.

In the manner of my friend I was at once struck with an incoherence—an inconsistency; and I soon found this to arise from a series of feeble and futile struggles to overcome an habitual trepidancy—an excessive nervous agitation. For something of this nature I had indeed been prepared, no less by his letter, than by reminiscences of certain boyish traits, and by conclusions deduced from his peculiar physical conformation and temperament. His action was alternately vivacious and sullen. His voice varied rapidly from a tremulous indecision (when the animal spirits seemed utterly in abeyance) to that species of energetic concision—that abrupt, weighty, unhurried, and hollow-sounding enunciation—that leaden, self-balanced and perfectly modulated guttural utterance, which may be observed in the lost drunkard, or the irreclaimable eater of opium, during the periods of his most intense excitement.

It was thus that he spoke of the object of my visit, of his earnest desire to see me, and of the solace he expected me to afford him. He entered, at some length, into what he conceived to be the nature of his malady. It was, he said, a constitutional and a family evil, and one for which he despaired to find a remedy—a mere nervous affection, he immediately added, which would undoubtedly soon pass off. It displayed itself in a host of unnatural sensations. Some of these, as he detailed them, interested and bewildered me; although, perhaps, the terms, and the general manner of the narration had their weight. He suffered much from a morbid acuteness of the senses; the most insipid food was alone endurable; he could wear only garments of certain texture; the odours of all flowers were oppressive; his eyes were tortured by even a faint light; and there were but peculiar sounds, and these from stringed instruments, which did not inspire him with horror.

To an anomalous species of terror I found him a bounden slave. "I shall perish," said he, "I *must* perish in this deplorable folly. Thus, thus, and not otherwise, shall I be lost. I dread the events of the future, not in themselves, but in their results. I shudder at the thought of any, even the most trivial, incident, which may operate upon this intolerable agitation of soul. I have, indeed, no abhorrence of danger, except in its absolute effect—in terror. In this unnerved—in this pitiable condition—I feel that the period will sooner or later arrive when I must abandon life and reason together, in some struggle with the grim phantasm, FEAR."

I learned, moreover, at intervals, and through broken and equivocal hints, another singular feature of his mental condition. He was enchained by certain superstitious impressions in regard to the dwelling which he tenanted, and whence, for many years, he had never ventured forth—in regard to an influence whose supposititious force was conveyed in terms too shadowy here to be re-stated—an influence which some peculiarities in the mere form and substance of his family mansion, had, by dint of long sufferance, he said, obtained over his spirit—an effect which the *physique* of the gray walls and turrets, and of the dim tarn into which they all looked down, had, at length, brought about upon the *morale* of his existence.

He admitted, however, although with hesitation, that much of the peculiar gloom which thus afflicted him could be traced to a more natural and far more palpable origin—to the severe and long-continued illness—indeed to the evidently approaching dissolution—of a tenderly beloved sister—his sole companion for long years—his last and only relative on earth. "Her decease," he said, with a bitterness which I can never forget, "would leave him (him the hopeless and the frail) the last of the ancient race of the Ushers." While he spoke, the lady Madeline (for so was she called) passed slowly through a remote portion of the apartment, and, without having noticed my presence, disappeared. I regarded her with an utter astonishment not unmingled with dread—and yet I found it impossible to account for such feelings. A sensation of stupor oppressed me, as my eyes followed her retreating steps. When a door, at length, closed upon her, my glance sought instinctively and eagerly the countenance of the brother—but he had buried his face in his hands, and I could only perceive that a far more than ordinary wanness had overspread the emaciated fingers through which trickled many passionate tears.

The disease of the lady Madeline had long baffled the skill of her physicians. A settled apathy, a gradual wasting away of the person, and frequent although transient affections of a partially cataleptical character, were the unusual diagnosis. Hitherto she had steadily borne up against the pressure of her malady, and had not betaken herself finally to bed; but, on the closing in of the evening of my arrival at the house, she succumbed (as her brother told me at night with inexpressible agitation) to the prostrating power of the destroyer; and I learned that the glimpse I had obtained of her person would thus probably be the last I should obtain—that the lady, at least while living, would be seen by me no more.

For several days ensuing, her name was unmentioned by either Usher or myself: and during this period I was busied in earnest endeavours to alleviate the melancholy of my friend. We painted and read together; or I listened, as if in a dream, to the wild improvisations of his speaking guitar. And thus, as a closer and still closer intimacy admitted me more unreservedly into the recesses of his spirit, the more bitterly did I perceive the futility of all attempt at cheering a mind from which darkness, as if an inherent positive quality, poured forth upon all objects of the moral and physical universe, in one unceasing radiation of gloom.

I shall ever bear about me a memory of the many solemn hours I thus spent alone with the master of the House of Usher. Yet I should fail in any attempt to convey an idea of the exact character of the studies, or of the occupations, in which he involved me, or led me the way. An excited and highly distempered ideality threw a sulphureous lustre over all. His long improvised dirges will ring for ever in my ears. Among other things, I hold painfully in mind a certain singular perversion and amplification of the wild air of the last waltz of Von Weber. From the paintings over which his elaborate fancy brooded, and which grew, touch by touch, into vaguenesses at which I shuddered the more thrillingly, because I shuddered knowing not why;—from these paintings (vivid as their images now are before me) I would in vain endeavour to educe more than a small portion which should lie within the compass of merely written words. By the utter simplicity, by the nakedness of his designs, he arrested and over-awed attention. If ever mortal painted an idea, that mortal was Roderick Usher. For me at least —in the circumstances then surrounding me— there arose out of the pure abstractions which the hypochondriac contrived to throw upon his canvas, an intensity of intolerable awe, no shadow of which felt I ever yet in the contemplation of the certainly glowing yet too concrete reveries of Fuseli.

One of the phantasmagoric conceptions of my friend, partaking not so rigidly of the spirit of abstraction, may be shadowed forth, although feebly, in words. A small picture presented the interior of an immensely long and rectangular vault or tunnel, with low walls, smooth, white, and without interruption or device. Certain accessory points of the design served well to convey the idea that this excavation lay at an exceeding depth below the surface of the earth. No outlet was observed in any portion of its vast extent, and no torch, or other artificial source of light was discernible; yet a flood of intense rays rolled throughout, and bathed the whole in a ghastly and inappropriate splendour.

I have just spoken of that morbid condition of the auditory nerve which rendered all music intolerable to the sufferer, with the exception of certain effects of stringed instruments. It was, perhaps, the narrow limits to which he thus confined himself upon the guitar, which gave birth, in great measure, to the fantastic character of his perform-ances. But the fervid *facility* of his *impromptus* could not be so accounted for. They must have been, and were, in the notes, as well as in the words of his wild fantasias, (for he not unfrequent-ly accompanied himself with rhymed verbal im-provisations,) the result of that intense mental col-lectedness and concentration to which I have pre-viously alluded as observable only in particular mo-ments of the highest artificial excitement. The words of one of these rhapsodies I have easily re-membered. I was, perhaps, the more forcibly im-pressed with it, as he gave it, because, in the under or mystic current of its meaning, I fancied that I perceived, and for the first time, a full conscious-ness on the part of Usher, of the tottering of his lofty reason upon her throne. The verses, which were entitled "The Haunted Palace," ran very nearly, if not accurately, thus:

In the greenest of our valleys,
  By good angels tenanted,
Once a fair and stately palace—
  Radiant palace—reared its head.
In the monarch Thought's dominion—
  It stood there!
Never seraph spread a pinion
  Over fabric half so fair.

Banners yellow, glorious, golden,
  On its roof did float and flow;
(This—all this—was in the olden
  Time long ago)
And every gentle air that dallied,
  In that sweet day,
Along the ramparts plumed and pallid,
  A winged odour went away.

Wanderers in that happy valley
  Through two luminous windows saw
Spirits moving musically
  To a lute's well-tuned law,
Round about a throne, where sitting
  (Porphyrogene!)
In state his glory well befitting,
  The ruler of the realm was seen.

And all with pearl and ruby glowing
  Was the fair palace door,
Through which came flowing, flowing, flowing,
  And sparkling evermore,
A troop of Echoes whose sweet duty
  Was but to sing,
In voices of surpassing beauty,
  The wit and wisdom of their king.

But evil things, in robes of sorrow,
  Assailed the monarch's high estate;
(Ah, let us mourn, for never morrow
  Shall dawn upon him desolate!)
And, round about his home, the glory
  That blushed and bloomed
Is but a dim-remembered story
  Of the old time entombed.

And travellers now within that valley,
  Through the red-litten windows, see
Vast forms that move fantastically
  To a discordant melody;
While, like a rapid ghastly river,
  Through the pale door,
A hideous throng rush out for ever,
  And laugh—but smile no more.

I well remember that suggestions arising from this ballad, led us into a train of thought wherein there became manifest an opinion of Usher's which I mention not so much on account of its novelty, (for other men have thought thus,) as on account of the pertinacity with which he maintained it. This opinion, in its general form, was that of the sentience of all vegetable things. But, in his dis-ordered fancy, the idea had assumed a more daring character, and trespassed, under certain conditions, upon the kingdom of inorganization. I lack words to express the full extent, or the earnest *abandon* of his persuasion. The belief, however, was con-nected (as I have previously hinted) with the gray stones of the home of his forefathers. The condi-tions of the sentience had been here, he imagined, fulfilled in the method of collocation of these stones —in the order of their arrangement, as well as in that of the many *fungi* which overspread them and of the decayed trees which stood around—above all, in the long undisturbed endurance of this arrangement, and in its reduplication in the still waters of the tarn. Its evidence—the evidence of the sentience—was to be seen, he said, (and I here started as he spoke,) in the gradual yet certain condensation of an atmosphere of their own about the waters and the walls. The result was discoverable, he added, in that silent, yet importunate and terrible influence which for centuries had moulded the destinies of his family, and which made *him* what I now saw him—what he was. Such opinions need no comment, and I will make none.

Our books—the books which, for years, had formed no small portion of the mental existence of the invalid—were, as might be supposed, in strict keeping with this character of phantasm. We pored together over such works as the Ververt et Charteuse of Gresset; the Belphegor of Machiavelli; the Heaven and Hell of Swedenborg; the Subterranean Voyage of Nicholas Klimm by Holberg; the Chiromancy of Robert Flud, of Jean D'Indaginé, and of De la Chambre; the Journey into the Blue Distance of Tieck; and the City of the Sun of Campanella. One favourite volume was a small octavo edition of the *Directorium Inquisitorium*, by the Dominican Eymeric de Gironne; and there were passages in Pomponius Mela, about the old African Satyrs and Œgipans, over which Usher would sit dreaming for hours. His chief delight, however, was found in the perusal of an exceedingly rare and curious book in quarto Gothic—the manual of a forgotten church—the *Vigiliae Mortuorum secundum Chorum Ecclesiae Maguntinae.*

I could not help thinking of the wild ritual of this work, and of its probable influence upon the hypochondriac, when, one evening, having informed me abruptly that the lady Madeline was no more, he stated his intention of preserving her corpse for a fortnight, (previously to its final interment,) in one of the numerous vaults within the main walls of the building. The worldly reason, however, assigned for this singular proceeding, was one which I did not feel at liberty to dispute. The brother had been led to his resolution (so he told me) by consideration of the unusual character of the malady of the deceased, of certain obtrusive and eager inquiries on the part of her medical men, and of the remote and exposed situation of the burial-ground of the family. I will not deny that when I called to mind the sinister countenance of the person whom I met upon the staircase, on the day of my arrival at the house, I had no desire to oppose what I regarded as at best but a harmless, and by no means an unnatural, precaution.

At the request of Usher, I personally aided him in the arrangements for the temporary entombment. The body having been encoffined, we two alone bore it to its rest. The vault in which we placed it (and which had been so long unopened that our torches, half smothered in its oppressive atmosphere, gave us little opportunity for investigation) was small, damp, and entirely without means of admission for light; lying, at great depth, immediately beneath that portion of the building in which

was my own sleeping apartment. It had been used, apparently, in remote feudal times, for the worst purposes of a donjon-keep, and, in later days, as a place of deposit for powder, or some other highly combustible substance, as a portion of its floor, and the whole interior of a long archway through which we reached it, were carefully sheathed with copper. The door, of massive iron, had been, also, similarly protected. Its immense weight caused an unusually sharp grating sound, as it moved upon its hinges.

Having deposited our mournful burden upon tressels within this region of horror, we partially turned aside the yet unscrewed lid of the coffin, and looked upon the face of the tenant. A striking similitude between the brother and sister now first arrested my attention; and Usher, divining, perhaps, my thoughts, murmured out some few words from which I learned that the deceased and himself had been twins, and that sympathies of a scarcely intelligible nature had always existed between them. Our glances, however, rested not long upon the dead—for we could not regard her unawed. The disease which had thus entombed the lady in the maturity of youth, had left, as usual in all maladies of a strictly cataleptical character, the mockery of a faint blush upon the bosom and the face, and that suspiciously lingering smile upon the lip which is so terrible in death. We replaced and screwed down the lid, and, having secured the door of iron, made our way, with toil, into the scarcely less gloomy apartments of the upper portion of the house.

And now, some days of bitter grief having elapsed, an observable change came over the features of the mental disorder of my friend. His ordinary manner had vanished. His ordinary occupations were neglected or forgotten. He roamed from chamber to chamber with hurried, unequal, and objectless step. The pallor of his countenance had assumed, if possible, a more ghastly hue—but the luminousness of his eye had utterly gone out. The once occasional huskiness of his tone was heard no more; and a tremulous quaver, as if of extreme terror, habitually characterized his utterance. There were times, indeed, when I thought his unceasingly agitated mind was labouring with some oppressive secret, to divulge which he struggled for the necessary courage. At times again, I was obliged to resolve all into the mere inexplicable vagaries of madness, for I beheld him gazing upon vacancy for long hours, in an attitude of the profoundest attention, as if listening to some imaginary sound. It was no wonder that his condition terrified—that it infected me. I felt creeping upon me, by slow yet certain degrees, the wild influences of his own fantastic yet impressive superstitions.

It was, especially, upon retiring to bed late at night of the seventh or eighth day after the placing of the lady Madeline within the donjon, that I experienced the full power of such feelings. Sleep came not near my couch—while the hours waned and waned away. I struggled to reason off the nervousness which had dominion over me. I endeavoured to believe that much, if not all of what I felt, was due to the bewildering influence of the gloomy furniture of the room—of the dark and tattered draperies, which, tortured into motion by the breath of a rising tempest, swayed fitfully to and fro upon the walls, and rustled uneasily about the decorations of the bed. But my efforts were fruitless. An irrepressible tremor gradually pervaded my frame; and, at length, there sat upon my very heart an incubus of utterly causeless alarm. Shaking this off with a gasp and a struggle, I uplifted myself upon the pillows, and, peering earnestly within the intense darkness of the chamber, hearkened—I know not why, except that an instinctive spirit prompted me—to certain low and indefinite sounds which came, through the pauses of the storm, at long intervals, I knew not whence. Overpowered by an intense sentiment of horror, unaccountable yet unendurable, I threw on my clothes with haste, (for I felt I should sleep no more during the night,) and endeavoured to arouse myself from the pitiable condition into which I had fallen, by pacing rapidly to and fro through the apartment.

I had taken but few turns in this manner, when a light step on an adjoining staircase arrested my attention. I presently recognised it as that of Usher. In an instant afterward he rapped, with a gentle touch, at my door, and entered, bearing a lamp. His countenance was, as usual, cadaverously wan—but, moreover, there was a species of mad hilarity in his eyes—an evidently restrained *hysteria* in his whole demeanor. His air appalled me—but any thing was preferable to the solitude which I had so long endured, and I even welcomed his presence as a relief.

"And you have not seen it?" he. said abruptly, after having stared about him for some moments in silence—"you have not then seen it?—but, stay! you shall." Thus speaking, and having carefully shaded his lamp, he hurried to one of the casements, and threw it freely open to the storm.

The impetuous fury of the entering gust nearly lifted us from our feet. It was, indeed, a tempestuous yet sternly beautiful night, and one wildly singular in its terror and its beauty. A whirlwind had apparently collected its force in our vicinity; for there were frequent and violent alterations in the direction of the wind; and the exceeding density of the clouds (which hung so low as to press upon the turrets of the house) did not prevent our perceiving the life-like velocity with which they flew careering from all points against each other, without passing away into the distance. I say that even their exceeding density did not prevent our perceiving this—yet we had no glimpse of the moon or stars—nor was there any flashing forth of the lightning. But the under surfaces of the huge masses of agitated vapour, as well as all terrestrial objects immediately around us, were glowing in the unnatural light of a faintly luminous and distinctly visible gaseous exhalation which hung about and ·enshrouded the mansion.

"You must not—you shall not behold this!" said I, shudderingly, to Usher, as I led him, with a gentle violence, from the window to a seat. "These

appearances, which bewilder you, are merely electrical phenomena not uncommon—or it may be that they have their ghastly origin in the rank miasma of the tarn. Let us close this casement;—the air is chilling and dangerous to your frame. Here is one of your favourite romances. I will read and you shall listen;—and so we will pass away this terrible night together."

The antique volume which I had taken up was the "Mad Trist" of Sir Launcelot Canning; but I had called it favourite of Usher's more in sad jest than in earnest; for, in truth, there is little in its uncouth and unimaginative prolixity which could have had interest for the lofty and spiritual ideality of my friend. It was, however, the only book immediately at hand; and I indulged a vague hope that the excitement which now agitated the hypochondriac might find relief (for the history of mental disorder is full of similar anomalies) even in the extremeness of the folly which I should read. Could I have judged, indeed, by the wild overstrained air of vivacity with which he hearkened, or apparently hearkened, to the words of the tale, I might well have congratulated myself upon the success of my design.

I had arrived at that well-known portion of the story where Ethelred, the hero of the Trist, having sought in vain for peaceable admission into the dwelling of the hermit, proceeds to make good an entrance by force. Here, it will be remembered, the words of the narrative run thus:

"And Ethelred, who was by nature of a doughty heart, and who was now mighty withal, on account of the powerfulness of the wine which he had drunken, waited no longer to hold parley with the hermit, who, in sooth, was of an obstinate and maliceful turn, but, feeling the rain upon his shoulders, and fearing the rising of the tempest, uplifted his mace outright, and, with blows, made quickly room in the plankings of the door for his gauntleted hand; and now pulling therewith sturdily, he so cracked, and ripped, and tore all asunder, that the noise of the dry and hollow-sounding wood alarumed and reverberated throughout the forest."

At the termination of this sentence I started, and, for a moment, paused; for it appeared to me (although I at once concluded that my excited fancy had deceived me)—it appeared to me that, from some very remote portion of the mansion, there came, indistinctly, to my ears, what might have been, in its exact similarity of character, the echo (but a stifled and dull one certainly) of the very cracking and ripping sound which Sir Launcelot had so particularly described. It was, beyond doubt, the coincidence alone which had arrested my attention; for, amid the rattling of the sashes of the casements, and the ordinary commingled noises of the still increasing storm, the sound, in itself, had nothing, surely, which should have interested or disturbed me. I continued the story ·

"But the good champion Ethelred, now entering within the door, was sore enraged and amazed to perceive no signal of the maliceful hermit; but, in the stead thereof, a dragon of a scaly and prodigious demeanor, and of a fiery tongue, which sate in guard before a palace of gold, with a floor of silver; and upon the wall there hung a shield of shining brass with this legend enwritten—

Who entereth herein. a conqueror hath bin;
Who slayeth the dragon, the shield he shall win;

And Ethelred uplifted his mace and struck upon the head of the dragon, which fell before him, and gave up his pesty breath, with a shriek so horrid and harsh, and withal so piercing, that Ethelred had fain to close his ears with his hands against the dreadful noise of it, the like whereof was never before heard."

Here again I paused abruptly, and now with a feeling of wild amazement—for there could be no doubt whatever that, in this instance, I did actually hear (although from what direction it proceeded I found it impossible to say) a low and apparently distant, but harsh, protracted, and most unusual screaming or grating sound—the exact counterpart of what my fancy had already conjured up for the dragon's unnatural shriek as described by the romancer.

Oppressed, as I certainly was, upon the occurrence of this second and most extraordinary coincidence, by a thousand conflicting sensations, in which wonder and extreme terror were predominant, I still retained sufficient presence of mind to avoid exciting, by any observation, the sensitive nervousness of my companion. I was by no means certain that he had noticed the sounds in question; although, assuredly, a strange alteration had, during the last few minutes, taken place in his demeanor. From a position fronting my own, he had gradually brought round his chair, so as to sit with his face to the door of the chamber; and thus I could but partially perceive his features, although I saw that his lips trembled as if he were murmuring inaudibly. His head had dropped upon his breast—yet I knew that he was not asleep, from the wide and rigid opening of the eye as I caught a glance of it in profile. The motion of his body, too, was at variance with this idea—for he rocked from side to side with a gentle yet constant and uniform sway. Having rapidly taken notice of all this, I resumed the narrative of Sir Launcelot, which thus proceeded:

"And now, the champion, having escaped from the terrible fury of the dragon, bethinking himself of the brazen shield, and of the breaking up of the enchantment which was upon it, removed the carcass from out of the way before him, and approached valorously over the silver pavement of the castle to where the shield was upon the wall; which in sooth tarried not for his full coming, but fell down at his feet upon the silver floor, with a mighty great and terrible ringing sound."

No sooner had these syllables passed my lips, than—as if a shield of brass had indeed, at the moment, fallen heavily upon a floor of silver—I became aware of a distinct, hollow, metallic, and clangorous, yet apparently muffled reverberation. Completely unnerved, I leaped to my feet, but the measured rocking movement of Usher was undisturbed. I rushed to the chair in which he sat. His eyes were bent fixedly before him, and throughout his whole countenance there reigned a stony rigidity. But, as I placed my hand upon his shoulder, there came a strong shudder over his whole person; a sickly smile quivered about his lips; and I saw that he spoke in a low, hurried, and gibbering murmur, as if unconscious of my presence. Bending closely over him, I at length drank in the hideous import of his words.

"Not hear it!—yes, I hear it, and *have* heard it. Long—long—long—many minutes, many hours, many days, have I heard it—yet I dared not—oh, pity me, miserable wretch that I am!—I dared not —I *dared* not speak! *We have put her living in the tomb!* Said I not that my senses were acute? I *now* tell you that I heard her first feeble movements in the hollow coffin. I heard them—many, many days ago—yet I dared not—*I dared not speak!* And now—to-night—Ethelred—ha! ha! —the breaking of the hermit's door, and the deathcry of the dragon, and the clangor of the shield! —say, rather, the rending of her coffin, and the grating of the iron hinges of her prison, and her struggles within the coppered archway of the vault! Oh whither shall I fly? Will she not be here anon? Is she not hurrying to upbraid me for my haste? Have I not heard her footstep on the stair? Do I not distinguish that heavy and horrible beating of her heart? Madman!"—here he sprang furiously to his feet, and shrieked out his syllables, as if in the effort he were giving up his soul—"*Madman! I tell you that she now stands without the door!*"

As if in the superhuman energy of his utterance there had been found the potency of a spell —the huge antique pannels to which the speaker pointed, threw slowly back, upon the instant, their ponderous and ebony jaws. It was the work of the rushing gust—but then without those doors there *did* stand the lofty and enshrouded figure of the lady Madeline of Usher. There was blood upon her white robes, and the evidence of some bitter struggle upon every portion of her emaciated frame. For a moment she remained trembling and reeling to and fro upon the threshold—then, with a low moaning cry, fell heavily inward upon the person of her brother, and in her violent and now final death-agonies, bore him to the floor a corpse, and a victim to the terrors he had anticipated.

From that chamber, and from that mansion, I fled aghast. The storm was still abroad in all its wrath as I found myself crossing the old causeway. Suddenly there shot along the path a wild light, and I turned to see whence a gleam so unusual could have issued; for the vast house and its shadows were alone behind me. The radiance was that of the full, setting, and blood-red moon, which now shone vividly through that once barely-discernible fissure, of which I have before spoken as extending from the roof of the building, in a zigzag direction, to the base. While I gazed, this fissure rapidly widened—there came a fierce breath of the whirlwind—the entire orb of the satellite burst at once upon my sight—my brain reeled as I saw the mighty walls rushing asunder—there was a long tumultuous shouting sound like the voice of a thousand waters—and the deep and dank tarn at my feet closed sullenly and silently over the fragments of the "*House of Usher.*"

HENRY T. TUCKERMAN.

[Born 1813.]

HENRY THEODORE TUCKERMAN, one of our most genial and elegant essayists, and a very graceful and pleasing poet, was born in Boston on the twentieth of April, 1813. His health having somewhat failed, when he was about nineteen years of age, by the advice of his physicians he relinquished his studies to test the influence of travel in the milder climate of southern Europe. He passed the autumn of 1833, and the following winter and spring in Italy, and having returned to America, published early in 1835 his first work, under the title of The Italian Sketch Book, of which a second edition appeared in 1837. This is not so much a description of the scenery, antiquities, or condition of the country, as an echo of the feelings which they awakened. It exhibited a fine vein of sentiment, and a delicate ideality that justified the favourable auguries of the critics concerning the author's future distinction.

Mr. Tuckerman resumed and for a time prosecuted his academical studies, but again experiencing the injurious effects of a sedentary life and continued mental application, he embarked in the fall of 1837 for the Mediterranean. After visiting Gibraltar and Malta he made the tour of Sicily, and having passed a winter in Palermo, proceeded to Florence, where he remained the chief part of the ensuing year. On his return, in 1839, he published Isabel, or Sicily, a Pilgrimage, in which, adopting the guise of a romance to avoid the egotistical tone of a formal journal, he has given many interesting descriptions and reflections incident to a residence in Sicily. It is a graceful and ingenuous book, graphic and suggestive, and indicative of refinement, pure sympathies, and a cultivated taste.

In the autumn of 1841 he published a volume of miscellanies under the title of Rambles and Reveries, and in 1846 appeared his best and most characteristic work, Thoughts on the Poets. This volume embraces essays on twenty-six* Italian, English and American poets. It exhibits a taste skilled in the fine influences of language, a subtle apprehension of ideal beauty, and great independence in literary and personal judgments. In considering an author's character he has a just regard to his peculiar circumstances and history, and in examining his productions assumes as much as possible his spirit, is moved by the influences which give a direction to his genius, and looks upon life and nature with his eyes. The essays on Goldsmith, Burns, Shelley and Alfieri are instances of this wise candor and intellectual sympathy. His investigations seem to be alike genial, and his comments on all to be marked by the same loving disposition and unpretending but acute critical judgment.

The latest of Mr. Tuckerman's writings are a series of agreeable papers entitled, Leaves from the Diary of a Dreamer, a melange of description, speculation and sentiment.

His principal poem, entitled The Spirit of Poetry, was published in 1843. It is didactic and critical, carefully studied and highly finished. His minor pieces have more fancy and feeling. Some of them are passionate and tender, and they generally evince much delicacy, and a manly sincerity of disposition.

He wrote a series of criticisms, which were published under the title of Artist Life, or Sketches of American Painters; also, a Memoir of Horatio Greenough; Characteristics of Literature, illustrated by the Genius of Distinguished Men; Mental Portraits, or Studies of Character; Life of Commodore Silas Talbot; The Character and Services of De Witt Clinton; The Optimist, a collection of Essays; Essays, Biographical and Critical, on Character; The Rebellion, its Latent Causes, and True Significance; A Sheaf of Verse bound for the Fair; America and her Commentators, with a critical sketch of Travel in the U. S.; Memorial of the Life and Character of Jno. W. Francis, Jr.; and a Memoir of Dr. Jno. W. Francis. He has written much on literature and art for the magazines, which has not been collected.

---

*Petrarch, Goldsmith. Gray, Collins, Pope, Burns, Alfieri, Thomson, Cowper, Young. Crabbe, Coleridge, Shelley, Byron, Keats, Hunt, Moore, Rogers, Wordsworth, Campbell, Hemans, Proctor, Tennyson, Barrett, Drake, Bryant.

A DEFENCE OF ENTHUSIASM.

FROM AN ESSAY ENTITLED NEW ENGLAND PHILOSOPHY.

LET us recognise the beauty and power of true enthusiasm ; and whatever we may do to enlighten ourselves and others, guard against checking or chilling a single earnest sentiment. For what is the human mind, however enriched with acquisitions or strengthened by exercise, unaccompanied by an ardent and sensitive heart ? Its light may illumine, but it cannot inspire. It may shed a cold and moonlight radiance upon the path of life, but it warms no flower into bloom ; it sets free no ice-bound fountains. Dr. Johnson used to say, that an obstinate rationality prevented him from being a papist. Does not the same cause prevent many of us from unburdening our hearts and breathing our devotions at the shrines of nature ? There are influences which environ humanity too subtle for the dissecting knife of reason. In our better moments we are clearly conscious of their presence, and if there is any barrier to their blessed agency, it is a formalized intellect. Enthusiasm, too, is the very life of gifted spirits. Ponder the lives of the glorious in art or literature through all ages. What are they but records of toils and sacrifices supported by the earnest hearts of their votaries ? Dante composed his immortal poem amid exile and suffering, prompted by the noble ambition of vindicating himself to posterity ; and the sweetest angel of his paradise is the object of his early love. The best countenances the old painters have bequeathed to us are those of cherished objects intimately associated with their fame. The face of Raphael's mother blends with the angelic beauty of all his madonnas. Titian's daughter and the wife of Corregio again and again meet in their works. Well does Foscolo call the fine arts the children of love. The deep interest with which the Italians hail gifted men, inspires them to the mightiest efforts. National enthusiasm is the great nursery of genius. When Cellini's statue of Perseus was first exhibited on the Piazza at Florence, it was surrounded for days by an admiring throng, and hundreds of tributary sonnets were placed upon its pedestal. Petrarch was crowned with laurel at Rome for his poetical labours, and crowds of the unlettered may still be seen on the Mole at Naples, listening to a reader of Tasso. Reason is not the only interpreter of life. The fountain of action is in the feelings. Religion itself is but a state of the affections. I once met a beautiful peasant woman in the valley of the Arno, and asked the number of her children. "I have three here and two in paradise," she calmly replied, with a tone and manner of touching and grave simplicity. Her faith was of the heart. Constituted as human nature is, it is in the highest degree natural that rare powers should be excited by voluntary and spontaneous appreciation. Who would not feel urged to high achievement, if he knew that every beauty his canvas displayed, or every perfect note he breathed, or every true inspiration of his lyre, would find an instant response in a thousand breasts ? Lord Brougham calls the word "impossible" the mother-tongue of little souls. What, I ask, can counteract self-distrust, and sustain the higher efforts of our nature but enthusiasm ? More of this element would call forth the genius, and gladden the life of New England. While the mere intellectual man speculates, and the mere man of acquisition cites authority, the man of feeling acts, realizes, puts forth his complete energies. His earnest and strong heart will not let his mind rest; he is urged by an inward impulse to imbody his thought. He must have sympathy ; he must have results. And nature yields to the magician, acknowledging him as her child. The noble statue comes forth from the marble, the speaking figure stands out from the canvas, the electric chain is struck in the bosoms of his fellows. They receive his ideas, respond to his appeal, and reciprocate his love.

Constant supplies of knowledge to the intellect, and the exclusive culture of reason may, indeed, make a pedant and logician ; but the probability is, these benefits, if such they are, will be gained at the expense of the soul. Sentiment, in its broadest acceptation, is as essential to the true enjoyment and grace of life as mind. Technical information, and that quickness of apprehension which New Englanders call smartness, are not so valuable to a human being as sensibility to the beautiful, and a spontaneous appreciation of the divine influences which fill the realms of vision and of sound, and the world of action and feeling. The tastes, affections and sentiments, are more absolutely the man than his talent or acquirements. And yet it is by and through the latter that we are apt to estimate character, of which they are at best but fragmentary evidences. It is remarkable that, in the New Testament, allusions to the intellect are so rare, while the "heart" and the "spirit we are of" are ever appealed to. Sympathy is the "golden key" which unlocks the treasures of wisdom ; and this depends upon vividness and warmth of feeling. It is therefore that Tranio advises— "In brief, sir, study what you most affect." A code of etiquette may refine the manners, but the "heart of courtesy," which, through the world, stamps the natural gentleman, can never be attained but through instinct ; and in the same manner, those enriching and noble sentiments which are the most beautiful and endearing of human qualities, no process of mental training will create. To what end is society, popular education, churches, and all the machinery of culture, if no living truth is elicited which fertilizes as well as enlightens ? Shakspeare undoubtedly owed his marvellous insight into the human soul to his profound sympathy with man. He might have conned whole libraries on the philosophy of the passions; he might have coldly observed facts for years, and never have conceived of jealousy like Othello's, the remorse of Macbeth, or love like that of Juliet. When the native sentiments are once interested, new facts spring to light. It was under the excitement of wonder and love, that Byron, tossed on the lake of Geneva, thought that "Jura answered from her misty shroud," responsive to the thunder of the

Alps. With 'no eye of mere curiosity did Bryant follow the lonely flight of the waterfowl. Veneration prompted the inquiry,

"Whither 'midst falling dew
When glow the heavens with the last steps of day,
Far through their rosy depths dost thou pursue
Thy solitary way ?"

Sometimes, in musing upon genius in its simpler manifestations, it seems as if the great art of human culture consisted chiefly in preserving the glow and freshness of the heart. It is certain that in proportion as its merely mental strength and attainment takes the place of natural sentiment, in proportion as we acquire the habit of receiving all impressions through the reason, the teachings of nature grow indistinct and cold, however it may be with those of books. That this is the tendency of the New England philosophy of life and education, I think can scarcely be disputed. I have remarked that some of our most intelligent men speak of mastering a subject, of comprehending a book, of settling a question, as if these processes involved the whole idea of human cultivation. The reverse of all this is chiefly desirable. It is when we are overcome, and the pride of intellect vanquished before the truth of nature, when, instead of coming to a logical decision, we are led to bow in profound reverence before the mysteries of life, when we are led back to childhood, or up to God, by some powerful revelation of the sage or minstrel, it is then our natures grow. To this end is all art. Exquisite vocalism, beautiful statuary and painting, and all true literature, have not for their great object to employ the ingenuity of prying critics, or furnish the world with a set of new ideas, but to move the whole nature by the perfection and truthfulness of their appeal. There is a certain atmosphere exhaled from the inspired page of genius, which gives vitality to the sentiments, and through these quickens the mental powers. And this is the chief good of books. Were it otherwise, those of us who have bad memories might despair of advancement. I have heard educated New Englanders boast of the quantity of poetry they have read in a given time, as if rich fancies and elevated thoughts are to be despatched as are beefsteaks on board our steamboats. Newspapers are estimated by their number of square feet, as if this had any thing to do with the quality of their contents. Journeys of pleasure are frequently deemed delightful in proportion to their rapidity, without reference to the new scenery or society they bring into view. Social gatherings are not seldom accounted brilliant in the same degree that they are crowded. Such would not be the case, if what the phrenologists call the affective powers, were enough considered; if the whole soul, instead of the "meddling intellect" alone, was freely developed; if we realized the truth thus expressed by a powerful writer—"within the entire circle of our intellectual constitution, we value nothing but emotion; it is not the powers, but the fruit of those powers, in so much feeling of a lofty kind as they will yield."

One of the most obvious consequences of these traits appears in social intercourse. Foreigners have ridiculed certain external habits of Americans, but these were always confined to the few, and where most prevalent have yielded readily to censure. There are incongruities of manners still more objectionable, because the direct exponents of character and resulting from the philosophy of life. Delicacy and self-respect are the fruits, not so much of intellect as sensibility. We are considerate towards others in proportion as our own consciousness gives us insight. The sympathies are the best teachers of politeness; and these are ever blunted by an exclusive reliance on perception. Nothing is more common than to find educated New Englanders unconsciously invading the privacy of others, to indulge their idle curiosity, or giving a personal turn to conversation in a way that outrages all moral refinement. This is observable in society professedly intellectual. It is scarcely deemed rude to allude to one's personal appearance, health, dress, circumstances, or even most sacred feelings, although neither intimacy nor confidence lend the slightest authority to the proceeding. Such violation of what is due to others, is more frequently met with among the cultivated of this than any other country. It is comparatively rare here to encounter a natural gentleman. A New England philosopher, in a recent work,* betrays no little fear of "excess of fellowship." In the region he inhabits there is ground for the apprehension. No standard of manners will correct the evil. The peasantry of southern Europe, and the most ignorant Irishwomen often excel educated New Englanders in genuine courtesy. Their richer feelings teach them how to deal with others. Reverence and tenderness (not self-possession and intelligence) are the hallowed avenues through which alone true souls come together. The cool satisfaction with which character is analyzed and defined in New England, is an evidence of the superficial test which observation alone affords. A Yankee dreams not of the world which is revealed only through sentiment. Men, and especially women, shrink from unfolding the depths of their natures to the cold and prying gaze which aims to explore them only as an intellectual diversion. It is the most presumptuous thing in the world, for an unadulterated New Englander, however 'cute and studious, to pretend to know another human being, if nobly endowed; for he is the last person to elicit latent and cherished emotions. He may read mental capacities and detect moral tendencies, but no familiarity will unveil the inner temple; only in the vestibule will his prying step be endured.

Another effect of this exaggerated estimate of intellect is, that talent and character are often regarded as identical. This is a fatal but very prevalent error. A gift of mind, let it ever be remembered, is not a grace of soul. Training, or native skill, will enable any one to excel in the machinery of expression. The phrase—artistical, whether in reference to statuary, painting, literature, or manners, implies only aptitude and dexterity.

* Emerson's Essays, second series.
2 Y 2

Who is not aware, for instance, of the vast difference between a merely scientific knowledge of music and that enlistment of the sympathies in the art which makes it the eloquent medium of passion, sentiment, and truth? And in literature, how often do we find the most delicate perception of beauty in the writer, combined with a total want of genuine refinement in the man! Art is essentially imitative; and its value, as illustrative of character, depends not upon the mental endowments, but upon the moral integrity of the artist. The idea of talent is associated more or less with the idea of success; and on this account, the lucrative creed of the New Englander recognises it with indiscriminate admiration; but there is a whole armory of weapons in the human bosom, of more celestial temper. It is a nobler and a happier thing to be capable of self-devotion, loyalty, and generous sympathies, to cherish a quick sense of honour and find absolute comfort only in being lost in another, than to have an eye for colour, whereby the rainbow can be transferred to canvas, or a felicity of diction that can embalm the truest pictures in immortal numbers. Not only or chiefly in what he does, resides the significance of a human being. His field of action and the availability of his powers depend upon health, education, self-reliance, position, and a thousand other agencies; what he *is* results from the instincts of his soul, and for these alone he is truly to be loved. It is observable among New Englanders, that an individual's qualities are less frequently referred to as a test of character than his performances. It is very common for them to sacrifice social and private to public character, friendship to fame, sympathy to opinion, love to ambition, and sentiment to propriety. There is an obvious disposition among them to appraise men and women at their market rather than their intrinsic value. A lucky speculation, a profitable invention, a saleable book, an effective rhetorical effort, or a sagacious political ruse—some fact which proves, at best, only adroitness and good fortune, is deemed the best escutcheon to lend dignity to life, or hang as a lasting memorial upon the tomb. Those more intimate revelations and ministries which deal with the inmost gifts of mind, and warmest emotions of the heart, and through which alone love and truth are realized, are but seldom dreamt of in their philosophy.

There is yet another principle which seems to me but faintly recognised in the New England philosophy of life, however it may be occasionally cultivated as a department of literature; and yet it is one which we should deem essentially dear to man, a glorious endowment, a crowning grace of humanity. It is that principle through which we commune with all that is lovely and grand in the universe, which mellows the pictures of memory into pensive beauty, and irradiates the visions of hope with unearthly brightness; which elevates our social experience by the glow of fancy, and exhibits scenes of perfection to the soul that the senses can never realize. It is the poetical principle. If this precious gift could be wholly annihilated amid the commonplace and the actual, we should lose the interest of life. The dull routine of daily experience, the tame reality of things, would weigh like a heavy and permanent cloud upon our hearts. But the office of this divine spirit is to throw a redeeming grace around the objects and the scenes of being. It is the breeze that lifts the weeds on the highway of time and brings to view the violets beneath. It is the holy water which, sprinkled on the Mosaic pavement of life, makes vivid its brilliant tints. It is the mystic harp upon whose strings the confused murmur of toil, gladness and grief, loses itself in music. But it performs a yet higher function than that of consolation. It is through the poetical principle that we form images of excellence, a notion of progress that quickens every other faculty to rich endeavour. All great men are so, chiefly through unceasing effort to realize in action, or imbody in art, sentiments of deep interest or ideas of beauty. As colours exist in rays of light, so does the ideal in the soul, and life is the mighty prism which refracts it. Shelley maintains that it is only through the imagination that we can overleap the barriers of self and become identified with the universal and the distant, and, therefore, that this principle is the true fountain of benevolent affections and virtue. I know it is sometimes said that the era of romance has passed; that with the pastoral, classic, and chivalrous periods of the world, the poetic element died out. But this is manifestly a great error. The forms of society have greatly changed, and the methods of poetical development are much modified, but the principle itself is essential to humanity. No! mechanical as is the spirit of the age, and wide as is the empire of utility, as long as the stars appear nightly in the firmament, and golden clouds gather around the departing sun; as long as we can greet the innocent smile of infancy and the gentle eye of woman; as long as this earth is visited by visions of glory and dreams of love and hopes of heaven; while life is encircled by mystery, brightened by affection, and solemnized by death, so long will the poetical spirit be abroad, with its fervent aspirations and deep spells of enchantment. Again, it is often urged that the poetical spirit belongs appropriately to a certain epoch of life, and that its influence naturally ceases with youth. But this can only be the case through self-apostasy. The poetical element was evidently intended to mingle with the whole of human experience; not only to glow in the breast of youth, but to dignify the thought of manhood, and make venerable the aspect of age. Its purpose clearly is to relieve the sternness of necessity, to lighten the burden of toil, and throw sacredness and hope even around suffering—as the old painters were wont to depict groups of cherubs above their martyrdoms. Nor can I believe that the agency of this principle is so confined and temporary as many suppose. It is true our contemplation of the beautiful is of short duration, our flights into the ideal world brief and occasional. We can but bend in passing at the altar of beauty, and pluck a flower hastily by the way-side;—but may there not be an instinct which eagerly appropriates even these transitory associations? May they not be unconsciously absorbed into the essence of our life, and gradually refine and exalt the spirit within us? I cannot think that such rich provision for the poetic sympathies is intended for any casual or indifferent end. Rather let us believe there is a mystic language in the flowers, and a deep meaning in the stars, that the transparency of the winter air and the long sweetness of summer twilight pass, with imperceptible power, over the soul; rather let us cherish the thought that the absorbing emotions of love, the sweet excitement of adventure and the impassioned solemnity of grief, with a kind of spiritual chemistry, combine and purify the inward elements into nobler action and more perfect results. Of the poetical principle, the philosophy of life in New England makes little account. Emblems of the past do not invite our gaze down the vistas of time. Reverence is seldom awakened by any object, custom, or association. The new, the equal, the attainable, constantly deaden our faith in infinite possibilities. Life rarely seems miraculous, and the commonplace abounds. There is much to excite, and little to chasten and awe. We need to see the blessedness of a rational conservatism, as well as the inspiring call for reform. There are venerable and lovely agencies in this existence of ours which it is sacrilege to scorn. The wisdom of our renowned leaders in all departments is too restless and conscious to be desirable; and it would be better for our boasted " march of mind," if, like the quaint British essayist, a few more " were dragged along in the procession." An extravagant spirit of utility invades every scene of life however sequestered. We attempt not to brighten the grim features of care, or relieve the burdens of responsibility. The daughter of a distinguished law professor in Europe was in the habit of lecturing in her father's absence. To guard against the fascination of her charms, which it was feared would divert the attention of the students, a curtain was drawn before the fair teacher, from behind which she imparted her instructions. Thus do we carefully keep out of sight the poetical and veil the spirit of beauty, that we may worship undisturbed at the shrine of the practical. We ever seek the light of knowledge; but are content that no fertilizing warmth lend vitality to its beams.

When the returning pilgrim approaches the shores of the new world, the first sign of the vicinity of his native land is traced in hues of rare glory on the western sky. The sunsets grow more and more gorgeous as he draws near, and while he leans over the bulwarks of a gallant vessel, (whose matchless architecture illustrates the mechanical skill of her birth-place,) and watches their shifting brilliancy, it associates itself with the fresh promise and young renown of his native land; and when from the wide solitude of the Atlantic, he plunges once more amid her eager crowds, it is with the earnest and I must think patriotic wish, that with her prosperous activity might mingle more of the poetry of life!

But what the arrangements of society fail to provide, the individual is at liberty to seek. No-where are natural beauty and grandeur more lavishly displayed than on this continent. In no part of the world are there such noble rivers, beautiful lakes, and magnificent forests. The ermine robe of winter is, in no land, spread with more dazzling effect, nor can the woodlands of any clime present a more varied array of autumnal tints. Nor need we resort to the glories of the universe alone. Domestic life exists with us in rare perfection; and it requires but the heroism of sincerity and the exercise of taste, to make the fireside as rich in poetical associations as the terrace and verandah of southern lands. Literature, too, opens a rich field. We can wander through Eden to the music of the blind bard's harp, or listen in the orange groves of Verona, beneath the quiet moonlight, to the sweet vows of Juliet. Let us, then, bravely obey our sympathies, and find in candid and devoted relations with others, freedom from the constraints of prejudice and form. Let us foster the enthusiasm which exclusive intellectual cultivation would extinguish. Let us detach ourselves sufficiently from the social machinery to realize that we are not integral parts of it; and thus summon into the horizon of destiny those hues of beauty, love and truth, which are the most glorious reflections of the soul!

LOVE.

FROM THOUGHTS ON THE POETS.

MANY live and die knowing nothing of love except through their intellect. Their ideas on the subject are fanciful, because it has never been revealed by consciousness. Yet it were to question the benignity of God, to believe that an element of our being so operative and subtle, and one that abounds chiefly in the good and the gifted, is of light import or not susceptible of being explained by reason, justified by conscience, and hallowed by religion, and thus made to bear a harvest not only of delight but of virtue. Love, Petrarch maintains, is the crowning grace of humanity, the holiest right of the soul, the golden link which binds us to duty and truth, the redeeming principle that chiefly reconciles the heart to life, and is prophetic of eternal good. It is a blessing of a glorious experience, according to the soul in which it is engendered. Let us endeavour to define its action and vindicate its worth, as set forth in the sonnets of Petrarch.

All noble beings live in their affections. While this important fact has been ever illustrated by poets, it is seldom fully recognised in moral systems or popular theology. Yet if we would truly discern the free, genuine elements of character, the history of the heart affords the only authentic ground of judgment. Love has been, and is, so mightily abused, that in the view of superficial reasoners it becomes identified rather with feebleness than strength. Yet, in point of fact, its highest significance can alone be realized by natures of singular depth and exaltation. To the unperverted soul, instead of a pastime it is a discipline. Once elevated from a blind instinct to a conscious principle, it is the mighty tide which sways all that is solemn and eternal in life. To love, in one sense, is, indeed, little more than an animal necessity; but to love nobly, profoundly—to love, as Madame de Stael expresses it, "at once with the mind and with the heart," to dedicate to another mature sympathies, is the noblest function of a human being. The fever of passion, the ignoble motives, the casual impulses which belong to our nature, blend, it is true, with the exercise of all affection, but love, in its deepest and genuine import, is the highest and most profound interest of existence. This is a truth but imperfectly understood; but there are few spirits so utterly bereft of celestial affinities as not to respond, more or less cordially, to every sincere appeal to a capacity so divine. All the folly of vain imaginations, all the coarseness of vulgar sensuality, all the scorn of mental hardihood, while they profane the name, can never violate the sacred realities of love. There have been, and there ever will be earnest and uncompromising hearts, who bravely vindicate a faith too native and actuating ever to be eradicated. Such natures can only realize themselves through love, and in proportion to their integrity will be their consciousness of the glory of this attribute. They intuitively anticipate its pervading influence upon their character and happiness. They feel that within it lies the vital points of their destiny, and through it their access to truth. The world may long present but glimpses of what they ever watch to decry. Life may seem barren of a good never absent from their inward sense. At times, from very weariness, they may be half inclined to believe that the love for which they pray is but a poetic invention, having no actual type. Witnessing so much apparent renunciation, they may, at last, regard themselves as vain dreamers, and look back with bitter regret upon years of self-delusion. But, the great want, the haunting vision, the prophetic need, assert themselves still; and when, through self-denial and fervent trust, the dawn glimmers upon their souls, the lonely vigil and restless fears of the night are forgotten in "a peace which the world can neither give nor take away." To some minds it may appear sacrilegious thus to identify love with religion, but the sentiments rightly understood, are too intimately allied to be easily divided. It is through the outward universe that natural theology points us to a Supreme Intelligence; and it is through the creature that spirits of lofty mould most nearly approach the Creator. Coleridge describes love as the absorption of self in an idea dearer than self. This is doubtless the only process by which the problem of human life is solved to exalted natures. It is vain that you bid them find content, either in the pleasures of sense or the abstractions of wisdom, however keen their perceptions, or ardent their passions. They know themselves born to find completion through another. A subtle and pleading expectance foretells the advent of a Messiah. They seek not, but wait. It is no romantic vision, no extravagant desire, but a clear and deep conviction that speaks in their bosoms. This is the germ of the sweetest flower that shall

adorn their being; this is their innate pledge of immortality, and ceaselessly invokes them to self-respect and glory.

There is something essentially shallow in the play of character, until feeling gives it shape and intensity. The office of love is to induce a strong and permanent motive, and it is this process which concentrates all the faculties of the soul. Hence the satisfaction which follows;—a condition wholly different from what was previously regarded as enjoyment. Through vanity and the senses, partial delight may have been obtained; but it was a graft upon, rather than a product of the heart. The blessedness of true love springs from the soul itself, and is felt to be its legitimate and holiest fruit. Thus, and thus alone, is human nature richly developed, and the best interests of life wisely embraced. Shadows give way to substance, vague wishes to permanent aims, indifferent moods to endearing associations, and vain desire to a "hope full of immortality." Man is for the first time revealed to himself, and absolutely known to another; for entire sympathy, not friendly observation, is the key to our individual natures; and when this has fairly opened the sacred portal, we are alone no more for ever!

AUTHORSHIP.
FROM THE SAME.

If we look narrowly into the history of those with whose thoughts and feelings literature has made us most intimate, it will often appear that in them there was combined a degree of sensibility and reflection which absolutely, by the very law of the soul, must find a voice, and that it was the pressure of some outward necessity, or the pain of some inward void that made that voice—(fain to pour itself out in low and earnest tones)—audible to all mankind. Some one has said that fame is love disguised. The points of a writer are usually those wherein he has been most alone; and they owe their effect to the vividness of expression which always results from conscious self-reliance. Literary vanity is a subject of frequent ridicule: but many confound a thirst for recognition with a desire for praise. The former is a manly as well as a natural sentiment. Indeed there is something noble in the feeling which leads an ardent mind—looking in vain for a response to its oracles among the friends amid whom its lot is cast—to appeal to a wider circle and send its messages abroad on the wings of the press, in the hope and faith that some heart will leap at the tidings and accept them as his own. I am persuaded that this truly human craving for sympathy and intelligent communion, is frequently mistaken for a weaker and more selfish appetite—the morbid love of fame. High-toned and sensitive beings invariably find their most native aliment in personal associations. They are sufficiently aware that notoriety profanes, that the nooks, and not the arena of life afford the best refreshment. It is usually because poverty, ill health, domestic trial, political tyranny, or misplaced affection has deprived their hearts of a complete sanctuary, that they seek for usefulness and honour in the fields of the world.

MARGARET FULLER D'OSSOLI.

[Born 1810. Died 1850.]

SARAH MARGARET FULLER, by marriage Marchioness of Ossoli, was born in Cambridge, Massachusetts, May 23, 1810. Her father, Mr. Timothy Fuller, was a lawyer, and from 1817 to 1825 a representative in Congress. At the close of his career as a legislator he retired to a farm near Cambridge, where he died soon after, leaving a widow and six children, of whom Margaret was the eldest.

At a very early age she exhibited unusual abilities, and was particularly distinguished for an extraordinary facility in acquiring languages. Her father, proud of the displays of her intelligence, prematurely stimulated it to a degree that was ultimately injurious to her physical constitution. In her ninth year he was accustomed to require of her the composition of a number of Latin verses every day, while her studies in philosophy, history, general science, and current literature were pressed to the limit of her capacities. When he first went to Washington he was accustomed to speak of her as one " better skilled in Greek and Latin than half of the professors ;" and in one of her essays she herself observes that in childhood she had well-nigh forgotten her English while constantly reading in other tongues.

Soon after the death of her father she applied herself to teaching, as a vocation, first in Boston, then in Providence, and afterward in Boston again. She made her first appearance as an author, in a translation of Eckermann's Conversations with Goethe, in 1839. When Mr. Emerson, the next year, established The Dial, she became one of the principal contributors to that remarkable periodical, in which she wrote many of the most striking papers on literature, art, and society. In the summer of 1843, she made a journey to the Sault St. Marie, and in the next spring published in Boston reminiscences of her tour, under the title of Summer on the Lakes. The Dial having been discontinued, she went to reside in New York, where she had charge of the literary department of the Tribune, which acquired a great accession of reputation from her critical essays. Here, in 1845, she published Woman in the Nineteenth Century, an eloquent expression of her discontent at having been created female ; and in 1846, Papers on Literature and Art, in two volumes, consisting of essays and reviews, reprinted from periodicals.

In the summer of 1845, she accompanied the family of a friend to Europe, visiting England, Scotland, and France, and passing through Italy to Rome, where they spent the ensuing winter. The following spring she proceeded with her friends to the north of Italy, and there stopped, spending most of the summer at Florence, and returning, at the approach of winter, to Rome, where she was soon after married to Giovanni, Marquis d'Ossoli, who made her acquaintance during her first winter in that city. They resided in the Roman states until the summer of 1850, when, after the surrender of Rome to the French army, they deemed it expedient to go to Florence, both having taken an active part in the republican movement. They left Florence in June, and at Leghorn embarked in the ship Elizabeth for New York. The passage commenced auspiciously, but at Gibraltar the master of the ship died of small-pox, and they were detained at the quarantine there some time in consequence of this misfortune, but finally set sail again on the eighth of June, and arrived on the American coast during a terrible thunder-storm on the eighteenth and nineteenth of August, when, in the midst of darkness, rain, and a terrific gale, the ship was hurled on the breakers off Fire Island, near Long Island, and in a few hours was broken in pieces. Margaret Fuller d'Ossoli, the Marquis d'Ossoli, and their son, with several others, lost their lives.

Madame d'Ossoli had completed for the press an extended work on The Recent Revolutions in Europe, which was lost in the wreck. She also wrote, while abroad, a series of brilliant Letters for the Tribune, under the title of Scenes and Thoughts in Europe. Her Woman in the Nineteenth Century is one of the most brilliant of the many books

on the intellectual and social position of woman that has been published. It is difficult,
however, to understand what is its real import, further than to the extent that the
author was ill satisfied that there should be
difference in the rank and opportunity of the
sexes. That there should be some difference
in their sphere she seemed not unwilling to
allow. Like the rest of that diverting company of women who have contemplated a nullification of certain of the statutes of nature, she
would but have choice of places and vocations.

Summer on the Lakes evinces considerable
descriptive power, and contains some good
verses. Her remarks in this work upon the
Indians, and that part of our ethnological literature which relates to them, are very superficial and incautious. She says of Mr. Schoolcraft's Algic Researches, that "a worse book
could hardly have been made of such fine materials;" that "had the mythological or hunting stories of the Indians been written down
exactly as they were received from the lips of
the narrators, the collection could not have
been surpassed in interest," but that, as it
is, "the phraseology in which they were expressed has been entirely set aside, and the
flimsy graces common to the style of the
annuals and souvenirs substituted for the
Spartan brevity and sinewy grasp of Indian
speech." Nothing can be more absurd than
this characteristic sentence. The phraseology of the tales has of course been "set aside"
in translating them into a language radically
different, but the antique simplicity of the originals has been as well preserved as the genius
of the English tongue permitted. The wife
of the learned author thus assailed, herself
of the aboriginal race, and distinguished for
whatever is peculiar in their character, wrote
down and translated many of these myths
and traditions, and it is amusing to see even
her part of the work ranked on the score of
fidelity below the few stories written out by
Mrs. Jameson, who, however excellent as a
critic of art, was here quite out of her depth
—almost as ignorant as Miss Fuller herself,
who when this was composed had been about
one week west of Buffalo, and had seen perhaps a dozen vagabond Indians across the
streets of Detroit and Chicago.

The Papers on Literature and Art contain
a short essay on Critics, in which she gives
a brief exposition of her views of criticism.
It is followed by some dozen papers, several
of which are admirable in their way. They
are all forcible, and brilliant in a degree;
but frequently pointed with pique or prejudice.

She was fond of epigram, and showed everywhere a willingness to advance any opinion
for the sake of making a point. Thus, in a
review of Mr. Poe's writings, she makes the
observation that " no form of literary activity
has so terribly degenerated among us as the
tale," because it gave opportunity to remark
" that everybody who wants a new hat or bonnet takes this way to earn one from the magazines or annuals." But no fact is more generally understood by those who have paid
any attention to the advancement and condition of letters here, than that the exact reverse of this is true. She rarely attempted
particular or analytical criticism, but commended or censured all books with about an
equal degree of earnestness, being generally
most severe upon those of home production,
excepting a few by personal friends.

She had remarkable quickness, but not
much subtlety of apprehension; general, but
not solid acquirements; and an astonishing
facility in the use of her intellectual furniture, which secured her the reputation of
being one of the best talkers of the age.
Her written style is generally excellent,—
various, forcible, and picturesque,—though
sometimes pedantic and careless,—very much
like that of her conversation, and probably a
result of but the same degree of labour.

<hr>

NIAGARA.
—

We have not been fortunate in weather, for there
cannot be too much, or too warm sunlight for this
scene, and the skies have been lowering with cold,
unkind winds. My nerves, too much braced up by
such an atmosphere, do not well bear the continual
stress of sight and sound. For here there is no
escape from the weight of a perpetual creation; all
other forms and motions come and go, the tide rises
and recedes, the wind, at its mightiest, moves in
gales and gusts, but here is really an incessant, an
indefatigable motion. Awake or asleep, there is
no escape, still this rushing round you and through
you. It is in this way I have most felt the grandeur—somewhat eternal, if not infinite.

At times a secondary music rises; the cataract seems to seize its own rhythm and sing it over again, so that the ear and soul are roused by a double vibration. This is some effect of the wind, causing echoes to the thundering anthem. It is very sublime, giving the effect of a spiritual repetition through all the spheres. ...

All great expression, which, on a superficial survey, seems so easy as well as so simple, furnishes, after a while, to the faithful observer its own standard by which to appreciate it. Daily these proportions widened and towered more and more upon my sight, and I got, at last, a proper foreground for these sublime distances. Before coming away, I think I really saw the full wonder of the scene. After awhile it so drew me into itself as to inspire an undefined dread, such as I never knew before, such as may be felt when death is about to usher us into a new existence. The perpetual trampling of the waters seized my senses. I felt that no other sound, however near, could be heard, and would start and look behind me for a foe. I realized the identity of that mood of nature in which these waters were poured down with such absorbing force, with that in which the Indian was shaped on the same soil. For continually upon my mind came, unsought and unwelcome, images, such as never haunted it before, of naked savages stealing behind me with uplifted tomahawks; again and again this illusion recurred, and even after I had thought it over, and tried to shake it off, I could not help starting and looking behind me....

The rapids enchanted me far beyond what I expected; they are so swift that they cease to seem so; you can think only of their beauty. The fountain beyond the Moss Islands, I discovered for myself, and thought it for some time an accidental beauty which it would not do to leave, lest I might never see it again. After I found it permanent, I returned many times to watch the play of its crest. In the little waterfall beyond, nature seems, as she often does, to have made a study for some larger design. She delights in this,—a sketch within a sketch, a dream within a dream. Wherever we see it, the lines of the great buttress in the fragment of stone, the hues of the waterfall, copied in the flowers that star its bordering mosses, we are delighted; for all the lineaments become fluent, and we mould the scene in congenial thought with its genius....

As I rode up to the neighbourhood of the falls, a solemn awe imperceptibly stole over me, and the deep sound of the ever-hurrying rapids prepared my mind for the lofty emotions to be experienced. When I reached the hotel, I felt a strange indifference about seeing the aspiration of my life's hopes. I lounged about the rooms, read the stage bills upon the walls, looked over the register, and, finding the name of an acquaintance, sent to see if he was still there. What this hesitation arose from, I know not; perhaps it was a feeling of my unworthiness to enter this temple which nature has erected to its God.

At last, slowly and thoughtfully I walked down to the bridge leading to Goat Island, and when I stood upon this frail support, and saw a quarter of a mile of tumbling, rushing rapids, and heard their everlasting roar, my emotions overpowered me, a choking sensation rose to my throat, a thrill rushed through my veins, " my blood ran rippling to my finger's ends." This was the climax of the effect which the falls produced upon me—neither the American nor the British fall moved me as did these rapids. For the magnificence, the sublimity of the latter I was prepared by descriptions and by paintings. When I arrived in sight of them I merely felt, " ah, yes, here is the fall, just as I have seen it in picture." When I arrived at the terrapin bridge, I expected to be overwhelmed, to retire trembling from this giddy eminence, and gaze with unlimited wonder and awe upon the immense mass rolling on and on, but, somehow or other, I thought only of comparing the effect on my mind with what I had read and heard. I looked for a short time, and then with almost a feeling of disappointment, turned to go to the other points of view to see if I was not mistaken in not feeling any surpassing emotion at this sight. But from the foot of Biddle's stairs, and the middle of the river, and from below the table rock, it was still " barren, barren all." And, provoked with my stupidity in feeling most moved in the wrong place, I turned away to the hotel, determined to set off for Buffalo that afternoon. But the stage did not go, and, after nightfall, as there was a splendid moon, I went down to the bridge, and leaned over the parapet, where the boiling rapids came down in their might. It was grand, and it was also gorgeous; the yellow rays of the moon made the broken waves appear like auburn tresses twining around the black rocks. But they did not inspire me as before. I felt a foreboding of a mightier emotion to rise up and swallow all others, and I passed on to the terrapin bridge. Every thing was changed, the misty apparition had taken off its many-coloured crown which it had worn by day, and a bow of silvery white spanned its summit. The moonlight gave a poetical indefiniteness to the distant parts of the waters, and while the rapids were glancing in her beams, the river below the falls was black as night, save where the reflection of the sky gave it the appearance of a shield of blued steel. No gaping tourists loitered, eyeing with their glasses, or sketching on cards the hoary locks of the ancient river god. All tended to harmonize with the natural grandeur of the scene. I gazed long. I saw how here mutability and unchangeableness were united. I surveyed the conspiring waters rushing against the rocky ledge to overthrow it at one mad plunge, till, like toppling ambition, o'erleaping themselves, they fall on t'other side, expanding into foam ere they reach the deep channel where they creep submissively away.

Then arose in my breast a genuine admiration, and an humble adoration of the Being who was the architect of this and of all. Happy were the first discoverers of Niagara, those who could come unawares upon this view and upon that, whose feelings were entirely their own.

J. T. HEADLEY.

[Born 1814.]

THE first American ancestor of Mr. HEAD-LEY was the eldest son of an English baronet, who came to this country in consequence of a domestic quarrel, and ultimately refused the family estate, which is now held by Sir Francis Headley, the author of a work of some note on chemistry. Mr. Headley was born on the thirtieth of December, 1814, at Walton, in New York, where his father was settled as a clergyman. It is a wild and romantic spot, on the banks of the Delaware, and his early familiarity with its scenery doubtless occasioned much of his love of mountain climbing, and indeed his descriptive power. He commenced his studies with the law in view, but changed his plan, and after graduating, at Union College, became a student of theology, at Auburn. He was licensed in New York, and a church was offered him in that city, but his health was feeble, and his physician dissuaded him from attempting to preach. Unwilling, however, to abandon his profession without an effort, he took charge of a small church in Stockbridge, in Massachusetts, where he thought he could give himself the most favourable trial, but after two years and a half, broke down completely, and planned a European tour and residence for his recovery. He went to Italy in the summer of 1842, intending to spend the winter there, the summer in Switzerland, and the next winter in the East. The state of his health, however, led to some modification of his design: he remained in Italy only about eight months, travelled some time in Switzerland, passed through Germany and the Netherlands, went into Belgium, thence to France, then over England and Wales, and finally home, having been absent less than two years. His health being worse than when he went abroad, he gave up all idea of following his profession, and turned his attention to literature.

His first publication was a translation from the German, which appeared anonymously, in 1844. In the following year he gave to the press Letters from Italy and the Alps and the Rhine, and in 1846, Napoleon and his Marshals, and The Sacred Mountains.

Mr. Headley is one of the most promising of the youthful writers of this country. He has shown his capacity to write an agreeable book, and to write a popular one. His Letters from Italy is a work upon which a man of taste will be gratified to linger. It possesses the unfatiguing charms of perfect simplicity and truth. It exhibits a thousand lively traits, of an ingenuous nature, which, formed in a sincere and unsophisticated society, and then brought into the midst of the old world, retains all its freshness and distinctiveness, and observes with native intelligence every thing that is striking in the life and manners and scenery around it. There is a graceful frankness pervades the composition, which engages the interest of the reader in the author as well as in the subject. We meet, everywhere, the evidences of manly feeling, pure sympathies, and an honourable temper. In many of the passages there is a quiet and almost unconscious humour, which reminds us of the delicate raillery of The Spectator. The style is delightfully free from every thing bookish and commonplace; it is natural, familiar, and idiomatic. It approaches, as a work of that design ought to do, the animation, variety, and ease, of spoken language.

The work called Napoleon and his Marshals was written to be popular. The author obviously contemplated nothing but effect. In that point of view, it displays remarkable talent for accomplishing a proposed object. The figures and scenes are delineated with that freedom and breadth of outline, and in that vivid and strongly contrasted style of colouring, which are well calculated to attract and delight the people. If it were regarded as a work written to satisfy his own ideas of excellence, and as the measure of his best abilities, it could not be considered as adding any thing to his reputation. He has taken the subject up with ardour, but with little previous preparation: the work therefore indicates imperfect information, immature views of character, and many hasty and unconsidered opinions. The style has the same melodramatic exaggeration which the whole design of the work exhibits. Yet unquestionably there is power manifested even in the faults of these brilliant sketches. There is that exuberant copiousness of imagination and passion, which, if it be not admirable in itself. is interesting as the excess of youthful genius. We accept it as a promise, but are not satisfied with it as a production. If it be true, however, as has been stated, that some five thousand copies of this book have been disposed of in the few months that have elapsed since its publication, Mr. Headley has many motives to disregard the warnings which may be mingled with his triumph.

I am unwilling to trust myself in a detailed criticism of Mr. Headley's latest work,—The Sacred Mountains. He may readily be acquitted of intentional irreverence; but he has displayed a most unfortunate want of judgment, and a singular insensibility to the character of the subjects which he undertook to handle. The attempt to approximate and familiarize the incidents of the Deluge, to illustrate the Transfiguration by historical contrasts, and to heighten the agony and awe of the Crucifixion by the extravagancies of rhetoric, has produced an effect that is purely displeasing. As events in the annals of the world, those august occurrences "stand solitary and sublime," and are only to be viewed through the passionless ether of the inspired narrative. As mysteries of faith, and symbols of a truth before which our nature bows down, they recede into the infinite distance of sanctity and worship. In a literary point of view Mr. Headley's design has much the same success that would attend an effort to represent the stars of heaven, the horror of an eclipse, or the roseate beauty of an evening sky, by the whiz and crackle of artificial fireworks.

We think so highly of Mr. Headley's natural powers, that we feel a concern in their proper direction and development. The fascination of strong writing, the love of rhetorical effect, have proved the "*torva voluptas*" by which American genius has often been betrayed and sacrificed. It is to be hoped that Mr. Headley will recover in time from the dangerous intoxication. He should remember that the spirit of literary art is essentially natural, simple, and calm; that it is advanced, not by sympathy with the passions of the multitude, but by lonely communion with that high idea of excellence, which is pure, permanent, and sacred; that it dwells not in excitement,

and the fervent endeavour after an outward result, but in the quiet yet earnest development of those inward instincts of grace and beauty which are the creative energy of genius. Mr. Headley's first move in literature was a commendable and successful one, and he could not do better for his true fame than to retrace his steps, and recover the line of his earliest efforts.

—Besides the works above mentioned Mr. Headley has published several orations and many able articles in the reviews.

The extraordinary sale of Napoleon and his Marshals, stamped Mr. Headley as one of the most popular of American authors, and he in the next year followed it up with a similar work on Washington and his Generals, a series of very spirited biographical sketches, but which did not meet with the same measure of success as the Napoleon. This was followed in 1848 by Oliver Cromwell, a life, based mainly upon Carlyle's researches; and in 1851, by the Imperial Guard of Napoleon, founded upon a popular French history by St. Hilaire. In 1852, appeared Lives of Gens. Scott and Jackson; in 1853, a History of the War of 1812; and in 1854, a Pictorial Life of Washington, first written for Graham's magazine.

His Adirondack; or, Life in the Woods, whither he went for his health in 1848, is a spirited volume of travelling sketches, the result of his summer excursion, and of which a new edition, enlarged by material gained by several later trips, was republished in 1869. It is decidedly, so far, the most agreeable and informing book on the subject, though not possessing the romancing tendencies of Rev. Mr. Murray's book.

Besides those mentioned above, he has written Sacred Scenes and Characters, a companion to his Sacred Mountains; and a volume of Miscellanies, Sketches, and Rambles; a Life of Gen. Havelock, written at the time so much interest was excited by the India War, in 1859; The Chaplains and Clergy of the Revolution, 1861; and Grant and Sherman, their Campaigns and Generals.

Mr. Headley was for some years the Representative of his district in the Legislature of New York, and in 1855, was chosen Secretary of the State. His popularity as an author was owing to his tact in selecting subjects of absorbing interest to the people, to the vigor of his pen, and his power of grouping his scenes and representing them in brilliant and dazzling language to the reader.

NAPLES.

FROM LETTERS FROM ITALY.

To-NIGHT we arrived from Castellamare. Our road wound along the bay—near Pompeii, through Torre del Greco, into the city. The sky was darkly overcast—the wind was high and angry, and the usually quiet bay threw its aroused and rapid swell on the beach. Along the horizon, between the sea and sky, hung a storm-cloud blacker than the water. Here and there was a small sailing-craft, or fisherman's boat, pulling for the shore, while those on the beach were dragging their boats still farther up on the sand, in preparation for the rapidly-gathering storm. There is always something fearful in this bustling preparation for a tempest. It was peculiarly so here. The roar of the surge was on one side; on the other lay a buried city—a smoking mountain; while our very road was walled with lava, that cooled on the spot where it stood. The column of smoke that Vesuvius usually sent so calmly into the sky, now lay on a level with the summit, and rolled rapidly inland, before the fierce sea-blast. It might have been fancy; but, amid such elements of strength, and such memories and monuments of their fury, it *did* seem as if it wanted but a single touch to send valley, towns, mountain, and all, like a fired magazine into the air. Clouds of dust rolled over us, blotting out even the road from our view; while the dull report of cannon from Naples, coming at intervals on our ears, added to the confusion and loneliness of the scene. As we entered the city and rode along the port, the wild tossing of the tall masts as the heavy hulls rocked on the waves, the creaking of the timbers, and the muffled shouts of seamen, as they threw their fastenings, added to the gloom of the evening; and I went to my room, feeling that I should not be surprised to find myself aroused at any moment by the rocking of an earthquake under me. The night did not disappoint the day, and set in with a wildness and fury, that these fire-countries alone exhibit. My room overlooked the bay and Vesuvius. The door opened upon a large balcony. As I stood on this, and heard the groaning of the vessels below, reeling in the darkness, and the sullen sound of the surge, as it fell on the beach, while the heavy thunder rolled over the sea, and shook the city on its foundations,—I felt I would not live in Naples. Ever and anon a vivid flash of lightning would throw distant Vesuvius in bold relief against the sky, with his forehead completely wrapped in clouds that moved not to the blast, but clung there, as if in solemn consultation with the mountain upon the night. Overhead the clouds were driven in every direction, and nature seemed bestirring herself for some wild work. At length the heavy rain-drops began to fall, one by one, as if pressed from the clouds; and I turned to my room, feeling that the storm would weep itself away.

THE MISERERE AT ROME.

FROM THE SAME.

THE night on which our Saviour is supposed to have died is selected for this service. The Sistine Chapel is dimly lighted, to correspond with the gloom of the scene shadowed forth.... The ceremonies commenced with the chanting of the Lamentations. Thirteen candles, in the form of an erect triangle, were lighted up in the beginning, representing the different moral lights of the ancient church of Israel. One after another was extinguished as the chant proceeded, until the last and brightest one at the top, representing *Christ*, was put out. As they one by one slowly disappeared in the deepening gloom, a blacker night seemed gathering over the hopes and fate of man, and the lamentation grew wilder and deeper. But as the Prophet of prophets, the Light, the Hope of the world, disappeared, the lament suddenly ceased. Not a sound was heard amid the deepening gloom. The catastrophe was too awful, and the shock too great to admit of speech. He who had been pouring his sorrowful notes over the departure of the good and great seemed struck suddenly dumb at this greatest wo. Stunned and stupified, he could not contemplate the mighty disaster. I never felt a heavier pressure on my heart than at this moment. The chapel was packed in every inch of it, even out of the door far back into the ample hall, and yet not a sound was heard. I could hear the breathing of the mighty multitude, and amid it the suppressed half-drawn sigh. Like the chanter, each man seemed to say, "Christ is gone, we are orphans —all orphans!" The silence at length became too painful. I thought I should shriek out in agony, when suddenly a low wail, so desolate and yet so sweet, so despairing and yet so tender, like the last strain of a broken heart, stole slowly out from the distant darkness and swelled over the throng, that the tears rushed unbidden to my eyes, and I could have wept like a child in sympathy. It then died away as if the grief were too great for the strain. Fainter and fainter, like the dying tone of a lute, it sunk away as if the last sigh of sorrow was ended, when suddenly there burst through the arches a cry so piercing and shrill that it seemed not the voice of song, but the language of a wounded and dying heart in its last agonizing throb. The multitude swayed to it like the forest to the blast. Again it ceased, and broken sobs of exhausted grief alone were heard. In a moment the whole choir joined their lament and seemed to weep with the weeper. After a few notes they paused again, and that sweet, melancholy voice mourned on alone. Its note is still in my ear. I wanted to see the singer. It seemed as if such sounds could come from nothing but a broken heart. Oh !· how unlike the joyful, the triumphant anthem that swept through the same chapel on the morning that symbolized the resurrection.

CORNELIUS MATHEWS.

[Born 1817.]

MR. MATHEWS was born in New York in 1817, and was graduated at the university of that city when about twenty years of age. He soon after entered upon the study of the law, and in due time was admitted to practise as an attorney and counsellor. His attention, however, has been mainly given to literature, and probably no one of our younger authors has written more largely. From 1835 to 1838 he was a contributor to the Knickerbocker and American Monthly magazines, in which appeared some of his best sketches of life and manners. In 1838 he published The Motley Book, a series of tales and sketches, of a humorous character. In 1839 he delivered an Address on the True Aims of Life, before the alumni of the New York University; and in the same year appeared his Behemoth, a Legend of the Mound Builders, in which he endeavoured to make the gigantic relics which have been discovered in the central parts of the continent subservient to the purposes of the imagination. The conception was a fine one, but the execution, although the work embraces some good passages, was generally bad, evincing a want of both taste and power. In 1840 he gave the public The Politicians, a Comedy, in five acts, designed to exhibit the various humours attending the election of an alderman in the city of New York, and in the same year, with his friend Mr. E. A. Duyckinck, a man of much cultivation and an agreeable style of writing, he commenced Arcturus, a monthly magazine, which was continued a year and a half. In its pages appeared his Wakondah, the Master of Life, a poetical fragment founded upon an Indian tradition; and The Career of Puffer Hopkins, a novel, of which three or four editions have since been issued. In 1842 he published several pamphlets on International Copyright, and in the following year, Poems on Man, in the American Republic, which, though unfinished and rough, are terse, and evince reflection and manly feeling. In 1843 also appeared a complete edition of his various writings, up to that period. His last work, Big Abel and the Little

Manhattan, was published in Wiley and Putnam's Library of American Books, in 1845.

The longest, most ambitious, and best known of the works of Mr. Mathews, is The Career of Puffer Hopkins. The object appears to be to illustrate the every-day life of the middling and lower classes in New York. The main story is that of the public advancement of a vulgar politician; but it is interrupted by many scenes and incidents that in no way assist in arriving at the conclusion, in which are introduced the inhabitants and frequenters of the dens of crime and wretchedness in the city. The book has some merits. The characters are drawn with considerable vigour and distinctness, and they are very well sustained, in dialogue and action. But Puffer Hopkins is no more a representative of life in New York than it is of life in Dublin. From beginning to end it has scarcely a gleam of vraisemblance. Its whole spirit is low and base, and as untrue as it is revolting. If, as the author intimates in his preface, it was his hope to produce a book " characteristic and national in its features," surely no hope was ever more completely disappointed.

Big Abel and the Little Manhattan is a suggestive parallel between the present and primitive condition of New York. A great-grandson of the navigator Hudson, and the heir of the last chief of the Mannahatoes, are supposed to have in contemplation a suit against the corporation of the city, for the whole of its territory, and are represented as wandering about its streets and squares, agreeing upon a division of the property they expect to acquire.

The style of Mr. Mathews is unnatural, and in many places indicates a mind accustomed to the contemplation of vulgar depravity. Who would think of finding such names as " Hobbleshank," " Greasy Peterson," " Fishblatt," or " Flab," in Washington Irving or Nathaniel Hawthorne? but they are characteristic of Puffer Hopkins. His language is sometimes affectedly quaint, and when more natural, though comparatively fresh, it is rude and uncouth. Some writers are said to advance on stilts; our author may be said to proceed difficultly, strainingly, jerkingly through mire.

The charge of a want of nationality is somewhat stale, but as copies of the works of Mr. Mathews have gone abroad, it is proper to say that nothing has ever been printed in this country that exhibits less the national character. It is not intended here to say that The Politicians and Puffer Hopkins are German, French, or English, but merely that they are not in any kind or degree *American*. The most servile of all our copyists have thus far been those who have talked most of originality, as if to divert attention from their felt deficiencies in this respect. Our "Young America" had not wit enough to coin for itself a name, but must parody one used in England; and in its *pronunciamento* in favour of a fresh and vigorous literature, it adopts a quaint phraseology, that so far from having been born here, or even naturalized, was never known among us, except to the readers of very old books and the Address of the Copyright Club. In all its reviews of literature and art, the standards are English, which would be well enough, perhaps, if they were English standards, but they are the fifth rate men with whose writings only their own can be compared. Their very clamor about Americanism is borrowed from the most worthless foreign scribblers, and has reference chiefly to the comparatively unimportant matter of style. Of genuine nationality they seem to have no just apprehension. It has little to do with any peculiar collocation of words, but is the pervading feeling and opinion of a country, leavening all its written thought. And the prime argument in favour of an international recognition of copyright (aside from that of justice to the pillaged author) arises from the fact that under the present system the real education of the popular heart is yielded too exclusively to men taught by a different experience and under different institutions. The absurdest of all schemes is that of creating a national literature by inventing tricks of speech, or by any sort of forced originality. Of which, proof enough may be found in the writings of Mr. Mathews, who wrote very good English and very good sense until he was infected with the disease of building up a national literature.

~~~~~~~~~~~~~~~~~~

THE MISSION OF HOBBLESHANK.

FROM PUFFER HOPKINS.

THERE was one that toiled in Puffer's behalf more like a spirit than a man; a little shrunken figure, that was everywhere, for days before the canvas; a universal presence, breathing in every ear the name of Puffer. There was not a tap-room that he did not haunt; no obscure alley into which he did not penetrate, and make its reeking atmosphere vocal with his praises. Wherever a group of talkers or citizens were gathered, the little old man glided in and dropped a word that might bear fruit at the ballot-box. At nightfall he would mix with crowds of shipwrights' prentices and labourers, and kindle their rugged hearts with the thought of the young candidate.

He stopped not with grown men and voters, but seizing moments when he could, he whispered the name in children's ears, that, being borne to parents by gentle lips, it might be mixed with kindly recollections, and so be made triumphant.

It was given out that the Blinkerites had established or discovered, in some under-ground tenements that never saw light of day, a great warren of voters. When the toilsome old man learned of this burrow that was to be sprung against his favourite, he looked about for an equal mine, whence voters might be dug in scores, at a moment's notice, should occasion demand. With this in view, one afternoon, he entered Water street, at Peck slip, like a skilful miner, as though a great shaft had been sunk just there.

A strange climate it was that he was entering; one where the reek and soil are so thick and fertile, that they seem to breed endless flights of great white overcoats, and red-breasted shirts, and flying blue trowsers, that swarm in the air, and fix, like so many bats, against the house sides.

Tropical too, for there's not a gaudy colour, green, or red, or orange-yellow, that the sun, shining through the smoky atmosphere, does not bring out upon the house fronts; and for inhabitants of the region, there are countless broad-backed gentlemen, who, plucking from some one of the neighbouring depositories a cloth roundabout, and a black tarpaulin, sit in the doorways launching their cigars upon the street, or gather within.

Hobbleshank, a resident of the inland quarter of the city, certainly came upon these, with his frock and eye-glass, as a traveller and landsman from far in the interior; and when he first made his appearance in their thoroughfare, looking hard about with his single eye, it could not be cause of surprise that they wondered aloud as he passed, where the little old blubber had come from......

But when, as he got accustomed to the place, he accosted them with a gentle voice, said a complimentary word for their sign-board, with its full-length sailor's lass—Hope upon her anchor, or sturdy Strength, standing square upon his pins—they began at once to have a fancy for the old man.

He passed from house to house, making friends in each. Sometimes he made his way into the bar-room, where, seated against the wall, on benches all around the sanded floor, with dusty bamboo rods, alligator skins, outlandish eggs, and sea-weeds plucked among the Caribees or the Pacific islands, or some far-off shore, he would linger by the hour, listening with all the wondering patience of a child, to their ocean-talk. And when they were through, he would draw a homely similitude between their story—the perils their ship had crossed—with the good ship of state; and then tell them of a young friend of his, who was on trial before the ship's crew for a master's place. Before he left, in nine cases of ten, they gave their hands for Puffer, sometimes even rising and confirming it with a cheer that shook the house, and brought their messmates thronging in from the neighbourhood, when the story would be recited to them by a dozen voices, and new recruits to Puffer's side enrolled.

Then, again, he would be told of an old sick sailor in an upper chamber—tied there by racking pains in his joints, answering, they would say, each wrench to the trials his old ship's timbers were passing through on the voyage she was now out upon—and mounting up, he would find him busy in his painful leisure, building a seventy-six, razeed to the size of a cock-boat, for the landlord's mantle. Gaining upon him by degrees, Hobbleshank would sit at his side; and by-and-by, when he saw it would be kindly taken, gathering up a thread of twine or two, and helping to form a length of cable or rigging. By the time a dozen ropes were fashioned, he would have a promise from the old sea-dog that he would show his teeth at the polls when roll-call came.

There were some, too, engaged in boisterous mirth and jollity in back parlors, just behind the bar; where a plump little fellow, in his blue roundabout, duck trowsers supported by the hips, and tarpaulin hat, with a flying riband that touched the floor and shortened him in appearance by a foot, broke down in a hornpipe to the sound of an ancient fiddle, that broke down quite as fast as he did. In the enthusiasm that held him, Hobbleshank even joined in, and with some comic motions and strange contortions of the visage, carried the day so well that he won the back parlor's heart at once; and they promised him whatever he asked.

The little old man—true to the interest he had first shown—bent himself with such hearty good will to his task, that when, after many days' labour, he left Water street, at its other extremity, there was not a ripe old salt that was not gathered, nor a tall young sailor that was not harvested, for the cause. And so he pursued the task he had set to himself without faltering, without a moment's pause. For days before the contest came on, he was out at sunrise, moving about wherever a vote

could be found; nursing and maturing it for the polling day, as a gardener would a tender plant; watching and tending many out-of-the-way places, and by a skilful discourse, a chance word, an apt story, ripening it against the time when it was to be gathered.

Late at night, when others, who might have been expected to be stirring and making interest for themselves, slumbered, Hobbleshank taking his rounds through the city with the watchmen, with more than the pains of an industrious clear-starcher, smoothed the placards on the fences; jumping up where they were beyond his height, as was often the case, and brushing them down, both ways, with out-spread hands, so that they should read plain and free to the simplest passer-by. Was there ever one that toiled so, with the faith and heart of an angel, in the dusty road that time-servers use to travel!

THE MOUND BUILDERS.

FROM BEHEMOTH.

Upon the summit of a mountain which beetled in the remote west over the dwellings and defences of a race long since vanished, stood, at the close of a midsummer's day, a gigantic shape whose vastness darkened the whole vale beneath. The sunset purpled the mountain-top, and crimsoned with its deep, gorgeous tints the broad occident; and as the huge figure leaned against it, it seemed like a mighty image cut from the solid peak itself, and framed against the sky. Below, in a thousand groups were gathered, in their usual evening worship, a strange people, who have left upon hills and prairies so many monuments of their power, and who yet, by some mighty accident, have taken the trumpet out of the hand of Fame, and closed for ever, as regards their historical and domestic character, the busy lips of tradition. Still we can gather vaguely, that the mound builders accomplished a career in the west, corresponding, though less severe and imposing, with that which the Greeks and Romans accomplished, in what is styled by courtesy the old world. The hour has been when our own west was thronged with empires. Over that archipelago of nations the Dead Sea of time has swept obliviously, and subsiding, has left their graves only the greener for a new people in this after age to build their homes thereon. But at the present time, living thousands and ten thousands of the ancient people were paying homage to their deity; and as they turned their eyes together to bid their customary solemn adieu to the departing sun, they beheld the huge shape blotting it from sight. The first feeling which sprang in their bosoms as they looked upon the vision was, that this was some monstrous prodigy, exhibited by the powers of the air or the powers of darkness to astonish and awe them.

Mr. Matthews has also written Witchcraft, a Tragedy; Jacob Leisler, a Play; Moneypenny, or the Heart of the World, a Romance; Chanticleer, a Thanksgiving story of the Peabody family and a Pen-and-Ink Panorama of New York City, 18mo., 1853.

T. B. THORPE.

[Born 1815.]

WE have promise of a rich and peculiar literature in the south-west and south. The excellent story of Mike Fink, the last of the Boatmen, by the late Mr. Morgan Neville, of Cincinnati, has been followed by many others of a similar character, from the Valley of the Mississippi, which have given a raciness, all their own, to two or three of our periodicals. The first collection of these appeared in Philadelphia in 1835, under the title of The Big Bear of Arkansas by T. B. Thorpe, and other Tales by Various Authors, edited by Mr. William T. Porter, the well-known conductor of the New York Spirit of the Times. It was followed, in 1846, by The Mysteries of the Backwoods, entirely by Mr. Thorpe, and Captain Simon Suggs, late of the Talapoosa Volunteers, together with Taking the Census, and other Alabama Sketches, by Mr. Johnson J. Hooper ; and A Quarter Race in Kentucky, with other Tales, chiefly from contributions to the Spirit of the Times,—all of which contain passages of bold, original and indigenous, though sometimes not very delicate humour.*

Mr. Thorpe (the son of a clergyman who died with a brilliant reputation at the early age of twenty-six) was born in Westfield, Massachusetts, in 1815. While he was an infant his parents removed to New York, where he resided until he left the north to settle in Louisiana. He early exhibited a taste for the fine arts, and chose historical painting as a profession. When but seventeen years of age his picture of the Bold Dragoon† was exhibited at the New York Academy of Fine Arts, and was very highly praised by the late Colonel Trumbull, for its original design and happily told story. Circumstances led to the abandonment of his pencil, and he entered the Wesleyan University at Middletown, in Connecticut, where he spent three years ; and when he was twenty-one years of age, his health being somewhat impaired, he sought a more congenial climate in Louisiana, in which state he resided until 1853. The characteristics of her scenery and population, and the romance of her history, he has exhibited with singular felicity in some of his writings.

The last book of Mr. Thorpe, Our Army on the Rio Grande, was published in the summer of 1846, and contained a record of the observations of the author while accompanying the forces under General Taylor into the territory of Mexico, illustrated with engravings from drawings made by himself.

In 1853, Mr. Thorpe removed to New York, and published a collection of his sketches, entitled The Hive of the Bee-Hunter. He has since contributed sketches to Harper's magazine.

Mr. Thorpe may serve as a type of the class of writers that has been referred to.* He has a genuine relish for the sports and pastimes of southern frontier life, and describes them with remarkable freshness and skill of light and shade. No one enters more heartily into all the whims and grotesque humours of the backwoodsman, or brings him more actually and clearly before us. He has fixed upon his pages one of the evanescent phases of American life, with a distinctness and fidelity that will make his books equally interesting as works of art or history.

Mr. Thorpe's style is simple, animated and picturesque, but has marks of carelessness, which, perhaps, result from mistakes of the printers, as he has never been able to superintend the passage of any of his writings through the press.

---

* These volumes are illustrated by Mr. F. O. C. Darley, of Philadelphia, a young artist who in his line, I believe. has now no superior. His drawings are remarkably spirited and life-like, and are perfect reproductions of the characters and scenes of his authors.

† Now in possession of Mr. Washington Irving.

546

---

* The limits of this volume are so nearly filled that I shall be unable to give the space I had intended to Judge Longstreet, author of the amusing volume entitled Georgia Scenes ; to Mr Briggs, who has evinced both wit and humour of a high order in his Harry Franco, and other novels and sketches ; to the late William P. Hawes, whose Sporting Scenes, edited by a congenial spirit, Henry W. Herbert, have been praised by all who have read them ; and to several others who have appeared as witnesses of the fact that there is humour of the richest description in the country.

TOM OWEN, THE BEE-HUNTER.
FROM MYSTERIES OF THE BACKWOODS.

As a country becomes cleared up and settled, bee-hunters disappear; consequently they are seldom if ever noticed in literature. Among this backwoods fraternity have flourished men of genius, in their way, who have died unwept and unsung, while the heroes of the turf and of the chase have been lauded to the skies for every trivial superiority they have displayed in their respective pursuits. To chronicle the exploits of sportsmen is commendable : the custom began as early as the days of the antediluvians, for we read that " Nimrod was a mighty hunter before the Lord." Familiar, however, as Nimrod's name may be, or even Davy Crockett's, what does it amount to, when we reflect that Tom Owen, the bee-hunter, is comparatively unknown !

Yes, the " mighty" Tom Owen has hunted from the time he could stand alone, until the present, and not a pen has inked paper to record his exploits. " Solitary and alone" has he traced his game through the mazy labyrinth of ether, marked, *I hunted, I found, I conquered,* upon the carcasses of his victims, and then marched homeward with his spoils, quietly and satisfiedly sweetening his path through life, and by its very obscurity adding the principal element of the sublime.

It was on a beautiful southern October morning, at the hospitable mansion of a friend, where I was staying to drown dull care, that I first had the pleasure of seeing Tom Owen. He was straggling, on this occasion, on the rising ground that led to the hospitable mansion of mine host, and the difference between him and ordinary men was visible at a glance. Perhaps it showed itself as much in the perfect contempt of fashion he displayed in the adornment of his outward man, as it did in the more elevated qualities of his mind that were visible in his face. His head was adorned with an outlandish pattern of a hat; and his nether limbs were ensconced in a pair of inexpressibles, beautifully fringed by the brier-bushes through which they were often drawn. Coats and vests he considered as superfluities. Hanging upon his back were a couple of pails; and he had an axe in his right hand. Such were the varieties that characterized the corpus of Tom Owen. As is usual with great men, he had his partisans, and with a courtier-like humility they depended upon the expression of his face for all their hopes of success. The common salutations of meeting were sufficient to draw me within the circle of his influence, and I at once became one of his most ready followers. " See yonder!" said Tom, stretching his long arm into the air; " See yonder—there's a bee." We all *looked* in the direction he indicated, but that was the extent of our observation. " It was a fine bee," continued Tom, " black body, yellow legs, and into that tree,"--pointing to a towering oak, blue in the distance. " In a clear day I can see a bee over a mile, easy !" When did Coleridge " talk" like that ? And yet Tom Owen uttered such a saying with perfect ease.

After a variety of meanderings through the thick woods, and clambering over fences, we came to our place of destination as pointed out by Tom...... The felling of a great tree is a sight that calls up a variety of emotions; and Tom's game was lodged in one of the finest in the forest. But " the axe was laid at the root of the tree," which, in his mind, was made expressly for bees to build their nests in, that he might cut it down, and obtain possession of the honey. The sharp sounds of the axe as it played in the hands of Tom, was replied to by a stout negro from the opposite side; and by the rapidity of their strokes they fast gained upon the heart of the lordly sacrifice. There was a little poetry in the thought, that long before this mighty empire of states was formed, Tom Owen's " bee-hive" had stretched its brawny arms to the winter's blast, and grown green in the summer's sun. Yet such was the case; and how long I might have moralized I know not, had not the enraged buzzing about my ears convinced me that the occupants of the tree were not going to give up their home and treasure without showing considerable practical fight. No sooner had the little insects satisfied themselves that they were about to be attacked, than they began one after another to descend from their airy abode, and fiercely pitch into our faces; anon a small company, headed by an old veteran, would charge with its entire force upon all parts of our body at once. It need not be said that the better part of valour was displayed by a precipitate retreat from such attacks.

In the midst of this warfare, the tree began to tremble with the fast-repeated strokes of the axe, and then might have been seen a hive of stingers precipitating themselves from above on the unfortunate hunter beneath. Now it was that Tom shone in his glory.

His partisans, like many hangers-on about great men, began to desert him on the first symptoms of danger; and when the trouble thickened, they one and all took to their heels, and left only our hero and Sambo to fight their adversaries. Sambo however soon dropped his axe, and fell into all kinds of contortions; first he would seize the back of his neck with his hands, then his shins, and yell with pain. " Don't holler, nigger, till you get out of the woods," said the sublime Tom, consolingly ; but writhe he did, until he broke, and left Tom " alone in his glory."

Cut-thwack ! sounded through the confused hum at the foot of the tree, marvellously reminding me of the interruptions that occasionally broke in upon the otherwise monotonous hours of my school days. A sharp cracking finally told me the chopping was done; and looking aloft, I saw the mighty tree balancing in the air. Slowly and majestically it bowed for the first time towards its mother earth, gaining velocity as it descended, shivering the trees that interrupted its course, and falling with thundering sound, splintering its gigantic limbs, and burying them deeply in the ground.

The sun, for the first time in at least two centuries, broke uninterruptedly through the chasm made in the forest, and shone with splendour upon the magnificent Tom standing, a conqueror, among his spoils.

As might have been expected, the bees were very much astonished and confused, and by their united voices they would have proclaimed death, had it been in their power, to all their foes, not, of course, excepting Tom Owen himself. But the wary hunter was up to the tricks of his trade, and, like a politician, he knew how easily an enraged mob could be quelled with smoke; and smoke he tried until his enemies were completely destroyed. We, Tom's hangers-on, now approached his treasure. It was a rare one, and, as he observed, "contained a rich chance of plunder." Nine feet, by measurement, of the hollow of the tree was full, and this afforded many pails of pure honey. Tom was liberal, and supplied us all with more than we wanted, and " toted," by the assistance of Sambo, his share to his own home, soon to be devoured, and replaced by the destruction of another tree and another nation of bees.

Thus Tom exhibited within himself an unconquerable genius which would have immortalized him, had he directed it in following the sports of Long Island or New-Market.

We have seen Colonel Bingaman, the Napoleon of the southern turf, glorying amid the victories of his favourite sport; we have heard the great Crockett detail the soul-stirring adventures of a bear-hunt, we have listened, with almost suffocating interest, to the tale of a Nantucket seaman, while he portrayed the death of the whale; and we have also seen Tom Owen, triumphantly engaged in a bee-hunt. We beheld and wondered at the sports of the turf, the field, and the sea, because the objects acted on by man were terrible indeed when their instincts were aroused; but in the bee-hunt of Tom Owen and its consummation, the grandeur *visible* was imparted by the mighty mind of Tom Owen himself.

FAT GAME.

FROM THE BIG BEAR OF ARKANSAS.

[The narrator is supposed to be in a cabin of one of the splendid steamers on the Mississippi. After the boat has left the wharf, the "Big Bear of Arkansas" enters, takes a chair, puts his feet on the stove, and looking back over his shoulder passes the general and familiar salute of "Strangers, how are you?" avowing himself as much at home as if he had been at "the Forks of Cypress," and "prehaps a little more so " Some of the company at this familiarity look a little angry, and some astonished; but in a moment every face is wreathed in a smile. There is something about the intruder that wins the heart on sight. He appears to be a man enjoying perfect health and contentment, his eyes are as sparkling as diamonds, and good-natured to simplicity. Then his perfect confidence in himself is irresistibly droll. He relates that he has been to New Orleans for the first time, and has been inquired of by some of the "perlite chaps" respecting the game in his part of the country]

" GAME, indeed! that's what city folks call it; maybe such trash live in my diggins, but I arn't noticed them yet: a bird any way is too trifling. I never did shoot at but one, and I'd never forgiven myself for that, had it weighed less than forty pounds. I wouldn't draw a rifle on any thing less than that; and when I meet with another wild turkey of the same weight, I will drap him.'

" A wild turkey weighing forty pounds !" exclaimed twenty voices in the cabin at once.

" Yes, strangers, and wasn't it a whopper? You see, the thing was so fat that it couldn't fly far; and when he fell out of the tree, after I shot him, on striking the ground he bust open behind, and the way the pound gobs of tallow rolled out of the opening was perfectly beautiful."

" Where did all that happen?" asked a cynical-looking Hoosier.

" Happen! happened in Arkansaw: where else could it have happened, but in the creation state, the finishing-up country—a state where the *sile* runs down to the centre of the 'arth, and government gives you a title to every inch of it? Then its airs—just breathe them, and they will make you snort like a horse. It's a state without a fault, it is."····

" What season of the year do your hunts take place?" inquired a gentlemanly foreigner, who, from some peculiarities of his baggage, I suspected to be an Englishman, on some hunting expedition, probably at the foot of the Rocky Mountains.

" The season for bar hunting, stranger," said the man of Arkansaw, " is generally all the year round, and the hunts take place about as regular. I read in history that varmints have their fat season, and their lean season. That is not the case in Arkansaw, feeding as they do upon the *spontenacious* productions of the sile, they have one continued fat season the year round : though in winter things in this way is rather more greasy than in summer, I must admit. For that reason bar with us run in warm weather, but in winter they only waddle. Fat, fat! it's an enemy to speed; it tames every thing that has plenty of it. I have seen wild turkeys, from its influence, as gentle as chickens. Run a bar in this fat condition, and the way it improves the critter for eating is amazing; it sort of mixes the ile up with the meat, until you can't tell t'other from which. I've done this often. I recollect one perty morning in particular, of putting an old fellow on the stretch, and considering the weight he carried, he run well. But the dogs soon tired him down; and when I came up with him wasn't he in a beautiful sweat—I might say fever ; and then to see his tongue sticking out of his mouth a feet, and his sides sinking and opening like a bellows, and his cheeks so fat he couldn't look cross. In this fix I blazed at him, and pitch me naked into a briar patch if the steam didn't come out of the bullet-hole ten foot in a straight line. The fellow, I reckon, was made on the high-pressure system, and the lead sort of bust his biler."

" That column of steam was rather curious, or else the bear must have been *warm*," observed the foreigner, with a laugh.

" Stranger, as you observe, that bar was WARM, and the blowing off of the steam showed it, and also how hard the varmint had been run. I have no doubt if he had kept on two miles farther, his insides would have been stewed ; and I expect to meet with a varmint yet of extra bottom, who will run himself into a skin-full of bar's grease : it is possible ; much onlikelier things have happened."

DOGS AND GUNS.
FROM THE SAME.

A TIMID little man near me inquired if the bear in Arkansaw ever attacked the settlers in numbers. "No," said our hero, warming with the subject; "no, stranger, for you see it ain't the natur of bar to go in droves; but the way they squander about in pairs and single ones is edifying. And then the way I hunt them—the old black rascals know the crack of my gun as well as they know a pig's squealing. They grow thin in our parts,—it frightens them so, and they do take the noise dreadfully, poor things. That gun of mine is a perfect *epidemic among bar:* if not watched closely, it will go off as quick on a warm scent as my dog Bowieknife will: and then that dog—whew! why the fellow thinks that the world is full of bar, he finds them so easy. It's lucky he don't talk as well as think; for with his natural modesty, if he should suddenly learn how much he is acknowledged to be ahead of all other dogs in the universe, he would be astonished to death in two minutes. Strangers, that dog knows a bar's way as well as a horse-jockey knows a woman's: he always barks at the right time, bites at the exact place, and whips without getting a scratch. I never could tell whether he was made expressly to hunt bar, or whether bar was made expressly for him to hunt: any way, I believe they were ordained to go together as naturally as Squire Jones says a man and woman is, when he moralizes in marrying a couple. In fact, Jones once said, said he, 'Marriage according to law is a civil contract of divine origin; it's common to all countries as well as Arkansaw, and people take to it as naturally as Jim Doggett's Bowieknife takes to bar.'"

A FARM IN ARKANSAS.
FROM THE SAME.

JUST stop with me, stranger, a month or two, or a year if you like,—and you will appreciate my place. I can give you plenty to eat; for beside hog and hominy, you can have bar-ham, and bar-sausages, and a mattress of bar-skins to sleep on, and a wildcat-skin, pulled off hull, stuffed with cornshucks, for a pillow. That bed would put you to sleep if you had the rheumatics in every joint in your body. I call that ar bed a *quietus.* Then look at my land—the government ain't got another such a piece to dispose of. Such timber, and such bottom land! why you can't preserve any thing natural you plant in it unless you pick it young, things thar will grow out of shape so quick. I once planted in those diggins a few potatoes and beets: they took a fine start, and after that an ox-team couldn't have kept them from growing. About that time I went off to old Kentuck on bisiness, and did not hear from them things in three months, when I accidentally stumbled on a fellow who had stopped at my place, with an idea of buying me out. "How did you like things?" said I. "Pretty well!" said he; "the cabin is convenient, and the timber land is good; but that bottom land ain't worth the first red cent." "Why?" said I.

"'Cause," said he. "'Cause what?" said I. "'Cause it's full of cedar stumps and Indian mounds," said he, "and *it can't be cleared!*" "Lord!" said I; "them ar 'cedar stumps' is beets, and them ar 'Indian mounds' ar tater hills." As I expected, the crop was overgrown and useless: the sile is too rich, *and planting in Arkansaw is dangerous.* I had a good-sized sow killed in that same bottom land. The old thief stole an ear of corn, and took it down where she slept at night to eat. Well, she left a grain or two on the ground, and lay down on them; before morning the corn shot up, and the percussion killed her dead. I don't plant any more: natur intended Arkansaw for a hunting-ground, and I go according to natur.

DEATH OF THE BIG BEAR.
FROM THE SAME.

I TOLD my neighbours, that on Monday morning —naming the day—I would start THAT BAR, and bring him home with me, or they might divide my settlement among them, the owner having disappeared. Well, stranger, on the morning previous to the great day of my hunting expedition, I went into the woods near my house, taking my gun and Bowie-knife along, just *from habit,* and there sitting down also from habit, what should I see, getting over my fence, but *the bar!* Yes, the old varmint was within a hundred yards of me, and the way he walked *over that fence*—stranger, he loomed up like a *black mist,* he seemed so large, and he walked right towards me. I raised myself, took deliberate aim, and fired. Instantly the varmint wheeled, gave a yell, and *walked through the fence* like a falling tree would through a cobweb. I started after, but was tripped up by my inexpressibles, which either from habit, or the excitement of the moment, were about my heels; and before I had really gathered myself up, I heard the old varmint groaning in a thicket near by, like a thousand sinners, and by the time I reached him he was a corpse. Stranger, it took five niggers and myself to put that carcase on a mule's back, and old long-ears waddled under his load, as if he was foundered in every leg of his body; and with a common whopper of a bar, he would have trotted off, and enjoyed himself. 'Twould astonish you to know how big he was: I made a *bed-spread of his skin,* and the way it used to cover my bar-mattress, and leave several feet on each side to tuck up, would have delighted you. It was in fact a creation bar, and if it had lived in Samson's time, and had met him, in a fair fight, it would have licked him in the twinkling of a dice-box. But, stranger, I never liked the way I hunted him, *and missed him.* There is something curious about it, I could never understand,—and I never was satisfied at his giving in so *easy at last.* Perhaps, he had heard of my preparations to hunt him the next day, so he just come in, like Capt. Scott's coon, to save his wind to grunt with in dying; but that ain't likely. My private opinion is, that that bar was an *unhuntable bar, and died when his time come*

E. P. WHIPPLE.

[Born 1819.]

THE youngest and last of the authors I shall notice in this volume is Mr. E. P. WHIPPLE, who has exhibited remarkable powers, both discriminating and comprehensive, in many critical essays which have appeared in the reviews and magazines, and gives promise of occupying a higher rank than has been attained by any other American in this department. Mr. Whipple was born in Gloucester, Massachusetts, on the eighth of March, 1819. When he was four years of age his family removed to Salem, where he attended various schools until he was fifteen, when he entered The Bank of General Interest in that city as a clerk. In 1837, being then in his eighteenth year, he went to Boston, where he has ever since resided, occupied mainly with commercial pursuits.

Although from the age of fourteen Mr. Whipple has been a writer for the press, occasionally producing articles which evinced an extraordinary fulness of information, maturity of judgment and command of language, it was not until 1843, when he published in the Boston Miscellany a paper on Macaulay, rivalling in analysis and reflection and richness of diction the best productions of that brilliant essayist, that he became individually known as a writer to any but his few associates and confidants. He has since published in the North American Review articles on the Puritans, the American Poets, Daniel Webster as an Author, the Old English Dramatists, the British Critics, South's Sermons, Byron, Wordsworth, Talfourd, James the Novelist, Sydney Smith, and other subjects; in the American Review on Beaumont and Fletcher, English Poets of the Nineteenth Century, and Coleridge as a Philosophical Critic; and in other periodicals essays and reviewals sufficient to form several volumes, some of the most striking of which are on Words, Egotism in Great and Little Men, the Ludicrous Side of Life, and the Literature of the Present Day.

Criticism in this age has been made an art, and many of the best writers of this and other nations have chiefly employed themselves in examining into and discovering the worth of what has previously been accomplished. There is danger that this fascinating pursuit will be made too exclusive, and leave us without such imbodied evidences of the power and greatness of our own generation as can be produced only by a loving and long continued devotion to a single object. It cannot be denied however that among its fruits is much of the most agreeable and some of the most brilliant literature in our language.

The scope of Mr. Whipple's studies is in some degree indicated by the titles of his articles. His favourite authors appear to be those of the golden age of English literature. His style is sensuous, flowing, and idiomatic, abounding in unforced antitheses, apt illustrations, and natural graces. Though he is no copyist, some of his articles suggest a fusion of the strength of the Areopagitica with the ease and liveliness of The Spectator. The characteristics of his criticism are its genuine insight and catholic liberality. He enters deeply into the spirit of the work he examines, is peculiarly sensitive to its beauties and excellencies, and writes of them with keen discrimination, cheerful confidence, and unhesitating freedom. His apprehension is both quick and profound, and none of our critics is more successful in illustrating truth or producing a fair and distinct impression of an author.

Since the above was written, Mr. Whipple has been prominently before the public as a critic and lecturer, in the leading journals, and at the chief halls in the country. He has published, Lectures on Subjects connected with Literature and Life; Essays and Reviews, 2 vols.; Washington and the Revolution; Character and Characteristic Men; and the Literature of the Age of Elizabeth. His lectures are philosophical in their texture, marked by nice discrimination, occasionally pushing a favorite theory to the verge of paradox; and when the reasoning faculties of his audience are exhausted, relieving the discussion by frequent picked anecdotes, and pointed thrusts of wit and satire. His friends and admirers had hoped with his abilities, for some work of permanent value from his pen.

THE POWER OF WORDS.
FROM AN ESSAY ON WORDS.

WORDS are most effective when arranged in that order which is called style. The great secret of a good style, we are told, is to have proper words in proper places. To marshal one's verbal battalions in such order that they may bear at once upon all quarters of a subject, is certainly a great art. This is done in different ways. Swift, Temple, Addison, Hume, Gibbon, Johnson, Burke, are all great generals in the discipline of their verbal armies, and the conduct of their paper wars. Each has a system of tactics of his own, and excels in the use of some particular weapon. The tread of Johnson's style is heavy and sonorous, resembling that of an elephant or a mail-clad warrior. He is fond of levelling an obstacle by a polysyllabic battering-ram. Burke's words are continually practising the broad-sword exercise, and sweeping down adversaries with every stroke. Arbuthnot " plays his weapon like a tongue of flame." Addison draws up his light infantry in orderly array, and marches through sentence after sentence, without having his ranks disordered or his line broken. Luther is different. His words are " half battle ;" "his smiting idiomatic phrases seem to cleave into the very secret of the matter." Gibbon's legions are heavily armed, and march with precision and dignity to the music of their own tramp. They are splendidly equipped, but a nice eye can discern a little rust beneath their fine apparel, and there are suttlers in his camp who lie, cog, and talk gross obscenity. Macaulay, brisk, lively, keen and energetic, runs his thoughts rapidly through his sentence, and kicks out of the way every word which obstructs his passage. He reins in his steed only when he has reached his goal, and then does it with such celerity that he is nearly thrown backwards by the suddenness of his stoppage. Gifford's words are moss-troopers, that waylay innocent travellers and murder them for hire. Jeffrey is a fine " lance," with a sort of Arab swiftness in his movement, and runs an iron-clad horseman through the eye before he has had time to close his helmet. John Wilson's camp is a disorganized mass, who might do effectual service under better discipline, but who under his lead are suffered to carry on a rambling and predatory warfare, and disgrace their general by flagitious excesses. Sometimes they steal, sometimes swear, sometimes drink and sometimes pray. Swift's words are porcupine's quills, which he throws with unerring aim at whoever approaches his lair. All of Ebenezer Elliot's words are gifted with huge fists, to pummel and bruise. Chatham and Mirabeau throw hot shot into their opponents' magazines. Talfourd's forces are orderly and disciplined, and march to the music of the Dorian flute ; those of Keats keep time to the tones of the pipe of Phœbus ; and the hard, harsh-featured battalions of Maginn, are always preceded by a brass band. Hallam's word-infantry can do much execution, when they are not in each other's way. Pope's phrases are either daggers or rapiers. Willis's words are often tipsy with the champaign of the fancy, but even when they reel and stagger they keep the line

of grace and beauty, and though scattered at first by a fierce onset from graver cohorts, soon reunite without wound or loss. John Neal's forces are multitudinous and fire briskly at every thing. They occupy all the provinces of letters, and are nearly useless from being spread over too much ground. Everett's weapons are ever kept in good order, and shine well in the sun, but they are little calculated for warfare, and rarely kill when they strike. Webster's words are thunder-bolts, which sometimes miss the Titans at whom they are hurled, but always leave enduring marks when they strike. Hazlitt's verbal army is sometimes drunk and surly, sometimes foaming with passion, sometimes cool and malignant, but drunk or sober are ever dangerous to cope with. Some of Tom Moore's words are shining dirt, which he flings with excellent aim. This list might be indefinitely extended, and arranged with more regard to merit and chronology. My own words, in this connection, might be compared to ragged, undisciplined militia, which could be easily rooted by a charge of horse, and which are apt to fire into each other's faces.

THE POETRY OF HOLMES.
FROM A REVIEW AL OF THE POETS AND POETRY OF AMERICA.

To write good comic verse is a different thing from writing good comic poetry. A jest or a sharp saying may be easily made to rhyme ; but to blend ludicrous ideas with fancy and imagination, and display in their conception and expression the same poetic qualities usually exercised in serious composition, is a rare distinction. Among American poets, we know of none who excels Holmes in this difficult branch of the art. Many of his pleasant lyrics seem not so much the offspring of wit, as of fancy and sentiment turned in a humorous direction. His manner of satirizing the foibles, follies, vanities, and affectations of conventional life is altogether peculiar and original. He looks at folly and pretension from the highest pinnacle of scorn. They never provoke his indignation, for to him they are too mean to justify anger, and hardly worthy of petulance. His light, glancing irony and fleering sarcasm are the more effective, from the impertinence of his benevolent sympathies. He wonders, hopes, wishes, titters, and cries with his victims. He practises on them the legerdemain of contempt. He kills with a sly stab, and proceeds on his way as if " nothing in particular" had happened. He picks his teeth with cool unconcern, while looking down on the captives of his wit, as if their destruction conferred no honour upon himself, and was unimportant to the rest of mankind. He makes them ridicule themselves, by giving a voice to their motions and manners. He translates the conceited smirk of the coxcomb into felicitous words. The vacant look and trite talk of the bore he links with subtle analogies. He justifies the egotist unto himself by a series of mocking sophisms. He expresses the voiceless folly and affectation of the ignorant and brainless by cunningly contrived phrases and apt imagery. He idealizes nonsense, pertness, and aspiring dulness. The movement of his wit is so swift, that its presence is known only when it strikes. He will sometimes, as it were, blind the eyes of his victims with diamond dust, and then pelt them pitilessly with scoffing compliments. He passes from the sharp, stinging gibe to the most grotesque exaggerations of drollery, with a bewildering rapidity.

Holmes is also a poet of sentiment and passion. "Old Ironsides," "The Steamboat," "Qui Vive," and numerous passages of "Poetry," display a lyrical fire and inspiration which should not be allowed to decay for want of care and fuel. In those poems of fancy and sentiment, where the exceeding richness and softness of his diction seem trembling on the verge of meretricious ornament, he is preserved from slipping into Della Cruscanism by the manly energy of his nature and his keen perception of the ridiculous. Those who know him only as a comic lyrist, as the libellous laureat of chirping folly and presumptuous egotism, would be surprised at the clear sweetness and skylark thrill of his serious and sentimental compositions.

THE PURITANS.
FROM A REVIEWAL OF NEAL'S HISTORY

The Puritans—there is a charm in that word which will never be lost on a New England ear. It is closely associated with all that is great in New England history. It is hallowed by a thousand memories of obstacles overthrown, of dangers nobly braved, of sufferings unshrinkingly borne, in the service of freedom and religion. It kindles at once the pride of ancestry, and inspires the deepest feelings of national veneration. It points to examples of valour in all its modes of manifestation,—in the hall of debate, on the field of battle, before the tribunal of power, at the martyr's stake. It is a name which will never die out of New England hearts. Wherever virtue resists temptation, wherever men meet death for religion's sake, wherever the gilded baseness of the world stands abashed before conscientious principle, there will be the spirit of the Puritans. They have left deep and broad marks of their influence on human society. Their children, in all times, will rise up and call them blessed. A thousand witnesses of their courage, their industry, their sagacity, their invincible perseverance in well-doing, their love of free institutions, their respect for justice, their hatred of wrong, are all around us, and bear grateful evidence daily to their memory. We cannot forget them, even if we had sufficient baseness to wish it. Every spot of New England earth has a story to tell of them; every cherished institution of New England society bears the print of their minds. The strongest element of New England character has been transmitted with their blood. So intense is our sense of affiliation with their nature, that we speak of them universally as our "fathers." And though their fame everywhere else were weighed down with calumny and hatred, though the principles for which they contended, and the noble deeds they performed, should become the scoff of sycophants and oppressors, and be blackened by the smooth falsehoods of the selfish and the cold, there never will be wanting hearts in New England to kindle at their virtues, nor tongues and pens to vindicate their name.

NEED OF A NATIONAL LITERATURE.
FROM AN ARTICLE ON THE AMERICAN POETS.

In order that America may take its due rank in the commonwealth of nations, a literature is needed which shall be the exponent of its higher life. We live in times of turbulence and change. There is a general dissatisfaction, manifesting itself often in rude contests and ruder speech, with the gulf which separates principles from actions. Men are struggling to realize dim ideals of right and truth, and each failure adds to the desperate earnestness of their efforts. Beneath all the shrewdness and selfishness of the American character, there is a smouldering enthusiasm which flames out at the first touch of fire,—sometimes at the hot and hasty words of party, and sometimes at the bidding of great thoughts and unselfish principles. The heart of the nation is easily stirred to its depths; but those who rouse its fiery impulses into action are often men compounded of ignorance and wickedness, and wholly unfitted to guide the passions which they are able to excite. There is no country in the world which has nobler ideas imbodied in more worthless shapes. All our factions, fanaticisms, reforms, parties, creeds, ridiculous or dangerous though they often appear, are founded on some aspiration or reality which deserves a better form and expression. There is a mighty power in great speech. If the sources of what we call our fooleries and faults were rightly addressed, they would echo more majestic and kindling truths. We want a poetry which shall speak in clear, loud tones to the people; a poetry which shall make us more in love with our native land, by converting its ennobling scenery into the images of lofty thoughts; which shall give visible form and life to the abstract ideas of our written constitutions; which shall confer upon virtue all the strength of principle and all the energy of passion; which shall disentangle freedom from cant and senseless hyperbole, and render it a thing of such loveliness and grandeur as to justify all self-sacrifice; which shall make us love man by the new consecrations it sheds on his life and destiny; which shall force through the thin partitions of conventionalism and expediency; vindicate the majesty of reason; give new power to the voice of conscience, and new vitality to human affection; soften and elevate passion; guide enthusiasm in a right direction; and speak out in the high language of men to a nation of men.

FROM AN AMBROTYPE BY REHN

ENG^D BY A B WALTER

Chs. D. Cleveland

SUPPLEMENT.

1870.

SUPPLEMENT
TO THE PRECEDING SKETCH.

SINCE the preceding sketch of American Literature was written in 1846, nearly a quarter of a century has passed by. The author, RUFUS WILMOT GRISWOLD, died in New York in 1857, aged forty-two years. After travelling extensively in his own country and Europe, he studied theology and became a preacher in the Baptist denomination. He was soon favorably known as interested in literature, having connected himself editorially with the *New Yorker*, the *Brother Jonathan*, the *New World*, and other journals. In 1842, he was the editor of *Graham's Magazine*. In 1852, he projected, and conducted till 1852, the *International Monthly Magazine*. Besides these services of encouragement to American literature, six or eight works on history and biography partly written by himself, a novel, "seven discourses on historical and philosophical subjects, and contributions to magazines and newspapers sufficient to fill a dozen octavo volumes," he produced a numerous series of books, most of them connected prominently and very usefully with American authorship. We condense a list found in Allibone's valuable "Dictionary of Authors," namely:—1. Poems, 1841. —2. Sermons, 1841.—3. The Biographical Annual for 1842.—4. Curiosities of American Literature. (Published as an appendix to an American edition of D'Israeli's Curiosities of Literature).—5. The Poets and Poetry of America, 1842. A highly commended work, which has passed through sixteen editions.—6. The Prose Writers of America, 1846. Of the last two named works, Duyckinck says, " they were the first comprehensive illustrations of the literature of the country, and have exerted an important influence through their criticisms, on the reputation of the numerous authors included, in their reception at home and abroad." It was also warmly commended by Prescott, Bryant, Tuckerman, Poe, the *Knickerbocker Magazine*, and Horace Binney Wallace ; the last named of whom, in his Literary Criticisms, thus said :—" He has done a useful work, and he has done it well. The book now before us is more than respectable : it is executed ably and in

many parts brilliantly. In some respects it is an extraordinary work ; such
as few men in America perhaps, besides its author, could have produced, and
he only after years of sedulous investigation, and under many advantages of
circumstance or accident. He has shown himself to be of Cicero's mind :
' *Mihi quidem nulli satis eruditi videntur quibus nostra ignota sunt.*' The distribution of the various orders into their classes, and the selection of representatives of each class or type, exhibit much skill. Many passages present
fine specimens of acute, original, and just criticism. We differ from Mr.
Griswold sometimes, but never without feeling that we owe it to the public in
all cases to give a reason why we do not assent to the conclusions of so candid and discriminating a judge."—7. The Female Poets of America, 1848.
—8. The Prose Works of John Milton, with a Critical Memoir, 1845.—9.
Washington and the Generals of the American Revolution, 1847, (edited
and partly written by Griswold).—10. Napoleon and the Marshals of the
Empire, 1847, (in conjunction with H. B. Wallace.)—11. Scenes in the
Life of the Saviour, by Poets and Painters (edited).—12. The Sacred Poets
of England and America, (edited) 1849.—13. The Poets and Poetry of
England in the Nineteenth Century.—14. Memoir of Edgar A. Poe, in an
edition of his works, 1856.—15. The Republican Court; or, American
Society in the days of Washington, with twenty-one portraits of distinguished women.

It remains for us, following the order in which our author has reviewed
the departments of American literature, to give a sketch of the losses
by death, and of the new names which have filled and are filling their
places in our literary ranks.

Of Theological and Religious writers who were named as Griswold's
cotemporaries, Archibald, James Waddel, and Joseph Addison Alexander;
George Bush, John Henry Hopkins, Samuel Farmer Jarvis, Andrews
Norton, Edward Robinson, Moses Stuart, Leonard Woods, and James
Marsh are no longer among the living. Other distinguished names of those
who have passed away, may now be added, as Lyman Beecher, some of
whose sermons and addresses are of extraordinary ability and eloquence;
John McClintock, whose name, made prominent heretofore by his useful
religious and philological writings, is now likely to be long regarded
with high esteem and gratitude for his labors in that excellent work,
McClintock and Strong's Cyclopædia of Biblical Literature, a great library
in a compact form; Theodore Parker, whose extraordinary genius, learning,

and destructive free-thinking, made him the most eminent of American rationalists, so-called; George W. Bethune, shown to be of rare scholarship, eloquence, and vigor of thought, by his various discourses. Among his larger works, his "Expository Lectures on the Heidelberg Catechism," have gained him, perhaps, a permanent distinction as a doctrinal writer.— Robert Baird, "the international preacher," whose earnest writings, as well as other labors, have been widely spread over Europe and America; George W. Burnap, Lyman H. Atwater, Prof. B. B. Edwards, Samuel H. Turner, Hubbard Winslow, Nathaniel West, Hiram Mattison,— on all whose names, of good esteem in literature, it would be worth while to linger longer than is here allowed. There remain to us Albert Barnes, the most popular of modern commentators; George P. Fisher, whose able essays on the Supernatural Origin of Christianity stand well in scholarship and philosophy; William G. T. Shedd, a writer of valuable essays and treatises, among which his History of Christian Doctrine is in deservedly high reputation; Philip Schaff, who has eminently fulfilled the prediction of his teacher, Neander, in the fame of profound learning, evinced in many important works, among which his great History of the Christian Church deserves especial mention; Andrew P. Peabody, whose beautiful, impressive, and vigorous style worthily clothes earnest, clear, and abundant thought; James Walker, whose writings, though few of them have yet come into print, are widely respected in appreciation of the lucid, impressive, simple language of deeply penetrating thought, and, as it were, oracular wisdom; Henry Ward Beecher, a wonderfully fruitful worker and writer, whose sermons, now for several years past published every week, and read by thousands, to say nothing of his essays, lectures, and other works, make his genius too well known to be dwelt upon here; Henry A. Boardman, a writer of many eloquent, vigorous, clear, and interesting discourses and books; Horace Bushnell, whose productions have commanded remarkable attention for power, originality, ingenuity, and masterly style; William R. Alger, the chief of whose learned works, a "Critical History of the Doctrine of a Future Life," is well pronounced "a monument of learned industry"; besides others, whose literary eminence calls for more especial mention than our space allows; as, Charles Hodge, Joseph P. Thompson, James Freeman Clarke, Gardiner Spring, Austin Phelps, Howard Malcom, Richard S. Storrs, Cyrus A. Bartol, Edmund H. Sears, Robert J. Breckenridge,

Frederick Hedge, Leonard Bacon, Edwards A. Park, Stephen H. Tyng,* B. F. Crocker.

Of all the eminent Historians named in the preceding sketch, but one remains alive—George Bancroft. Prescott added his "Conquest of Peru," "Philip the Second," "Charles the Fifth," and "Biographical and Critical Miscellanies"; Sparks his "Correspondence of the American Revolution": Cooper, Wheaton, and Irving, wrote no more histories before their lamented departure.—Other historical writers who have passed away, having come into grateful public notice within recent years, are Richard Hildreth, who wrote an elaborate History of the United States, in six volumes, admirably free from irrelevant matter, being clearly, honestly, and usefully told; George Tucker, author of an able Political History of the United States. Thomas H. Benton industriously wrought noble records of American Constitutional History; Richard Rush left some valuable miscellaneous contributions to historical and diplomatic literature. Samuel M. Schmucker, numerous works enjoying much popular favor. Dr. John W. Francis, in his "Old New York," and other pleasing essays in the interest of American history and literature, justified the high esteem in which he was regarded as a man of letters. Amos Dean has left a voluminous "History of Civilization," now in process of publication, the fruit of long industry, and believed to be a work of much merit and usefulness. David O. Allen contributed "India, Ancient and Modern." Harvey Newcomb wrote one hundred and five volumes, of which several are historical, his "Cyclopedia of Missions" being especially valuable. Samuel G. Goodrich, the popular "author and editor of about one hundred and seventy volumes—one hun-

---

* It is important to add also some mention of writers on *Morals*, or subjects connected with the second commandment, and the list would properly include a great number of writers on political, social, and educational reform. We may here name Joseph Alden, Leonard Bacon, Henry B. Bascom, J. Bascom, H. W. Bellows, Francis Bowen, Elihu Burritt, Henry Ward Beecher, William Ellery Channing, J. T. Champlin, Caroline H. Dall, Orville Dewey, Ralph Waldo Emerson, R. G. Hazard, J. G. Holland, Mark Hopkins, Francis Lieber, Margaret Fuller Ossoli, Thomas C. Upham, James Walker, Francis Wayland, Hubbard Winslow. Valuable writers in the cause of Education have been Horace Mann, some of whose remarkable writings deserve a permanent place in literature; Warren Burton, J. S. Hart, Stephen Olin, J. P. Wickersham, and many others.

To this mention of Ethics we may append an allusion to American *Metaphysics*, if only for the sake of naming Noah Porter's great treatise on the "Human Intellect," which is an honor to the country. Haven, Wayland, and Upham have written well concerning Mental Philosophy. *Logic* also has found able expositors in Francis Bowen, Charles C. Everett, H. N. Day, and, if we may now proudly claim him as made over to America, James McCosh.

dred and sixteen bearing the name of Peter Parley," wrote more than twenty
historical books.—Among the living there is at least one great historian,
namely, John Lothrop Motley, who, in Everett's esteem, is placed "by the
side of our great American historical trio—Bancroft, Irving and Prescott."
The latter, whose own historic field Motley's path crossed, bore his distinguished "testimony to the extent of Motley's researches, and the accuracy
with which he had given the results of them to the public." His Rise of
the Dutch Republic, and History of the United Netherlands, came before
the public view like a fair cosmos all at once produced out of a stupendous
labyrinth of rude and chaotic material, as if a tangled forest of records were,
through masterly industry, judgment, and love, laid out into a rich garden
of history in charming order under the sun, so that the general reader may
run or linger with delight: and explorers the most thoroughly conversant
with Motley's chosen field, continually admire fruits of historic erudition
undiscovered before.—John G. Palfrey has gratefully (whatever we may
feel on a few minor points,) revived "the image of the eminent virtue of
New England" in one of the most important and extensive of his valuable
works, "The History of New England," written with great devotion and
painstaking in a style of considerable vigor and vivacity. Francis Parkman's highly interesting, attractive, and valuable works on early American
history in its connection with Indians of the West, do great credit to the
recent literary talent of America. Henry C. Lea has lately taken the first
rank among ecclesiastical historians. "Very great learning and admirable impartiality" has lately been acknowledged by Lecky, in his History
of European Morals, as manifest in "'Lea's History of Sacerdotal Celibacy,'
which is certainly," he continues, "one of the most valuable works that
America has produced. Since the great history of Dean Milman, I know
no-work in English which has thrown more light on the moral condition
of the Middle Ages, and none which is more fitted to dispel the gross illusions concerning that period which Positive writers, and writers of a certain
ecclesiastical school, have conspired to sustain." Samuel Hopkins, in his
graphic account of the Puritans in the Reign of Queen Elizabeth, has skilfully bedecked a substantial framework of history with the drapery of
romance. Samuel Eliot has produced a valuable "History of Liberty,"
and other works. Henry B. Smith's "History of the Church of Christ in
Chronological Tables" is an admirably arranged and a most useful condensation of an immense amount of ecclesiastical history for convenient
71

reference. Edward McPherson has produced a good compend of the Political History of the Rebellion. Many other histories of the recent civil war in the United States have been written, of which we may name, as among the most important of them, Horace Greeley's "Great American Conflict," which has had a large circulation; Frank Moore's "Rebellion Record," published in frequent numbers during the war, and now making twelve octavo volumes, containing every important item, document, or account which could be gathered at the time, that might serve to aid the future historian of that great crisis in civilization; Alexander H. Stephens' "Constitutional View of the Late War between the States"; John W. Draper's "History of the American Civil War," the first considerable attempt at an elaborate, philosophical history of that event, and written with great ability, clearness, and vigor, though in some points rather to be called theoretical than philosophical. His other works, as the "History of the Intellectual Development of Europe," and "Thoughts on the Future Civil Policy of America," the former of which has been translated into several European languages, are remarkable for much vigor, breadth, and depth of thought. Though, as must be expected of a philosopher, his productions are read with various degrees of approbation on the part of thinking men, yet they generally secure a very attentive examination. But we have not space to mention what our many other valuable writers of history have well done; as, Abel Stevens, an eminent historian of American Methodism; J. H. Kurtz, estimable in church history; Benson J. Lossing, the successful artist-historian; George W. Greene, author of "Historical View of the American Revolution," "History and Geography of the Middle Ages," "Historical Studies," and various essays; B. F. De Costa, an inquirer into the Pre-Columbian Discovery of America; Henry B. Dawson, Lorenzo Sabine, John W. Thornton, John Russell Bartlett, John R. Brodhead, James Savage; Charles Guyarré, who has produced an excellent history of Louisiana; Samuel G. Drake, of learned diligence in early New England history; Parke Godwin, who has published a volume of a "History of France" which promises to be a valuable work.

Historical Biography has lost (of authors not already named as deceased) Marshall, Tudor, Wirt, Wheaton, Josiah Quincy, and Richard Biddle. Additional names of biographers who also have departed are Calvin Colton, writer of a Life of Henry Clay; William Gilmore Simms, who wrote lives of Putnam, Greene, Marion, and Smith; Matthew L. Davis, writer of Memoirs of Aaron Burr; John L. Blake, favorably known for his useful Biographical Dictionary; Henry J. Raymond, who wrote a life of Abraham Lincoln, but was best made known as one of the greatest of American journalists.

Perhaps the greatest work on general biography for comprehensiveness, indefatigable industry, and encyclopedic and accurate learning which the English language can boast, is Dr. Joseph Thomas's "Universal Pronouncing Dictionary of Biography and Mythology," now issuing from the press, and received with almost the warmest and highest praise by even the most exacting critics. Another monument of stupendous industry and research, and a most valuable boon to the literary world, is Allibone's great and excellent Dictionary of British and American Authors, all but the third volume of which is now published. Regarded with similar admiration is William B. Sprague's "Annals of the American Pulpit; or, Commemorative Notices of Distinguished American Clergymen of Various Denominations, from the early settlement of the country to the close of the year 1805; with Historical Introductions." Another product of wonderful industry (twenty years') is James Savage's Genealogical Dictionary of the First Settlers of New England.

James Parton, as a biographical author, stands clearly the first among American, and, so far as we know, among living writers, in genius to depict a seemingly animate portrait of the course of a life which had passed out of sight. And this he does, not altogether by vivid imagination and that lively sympathy by which he enters into the life which he describes, and speaks from within it as if it were his own for the time, but also by virtue of unwearied industry in searching out facts and circumstances. The interesting material thus diligently rescued from oblivion, and constructed into a biography now reproduced in letters, from the original once written on fleeting time, is clothed in a style pleasing, lively, and of sufficiently warm coloring. Important biographies also have been written as follows: that of Jefferson, by Henry S. Randall—also one by Hamilton W. Pierson, and one by George Tucker; Lyman Beecher's by his son Charles, Wirt's by John P. Kennedy, Judge Story's by his son William W. Story, who has also gained celebrity as a sculptor, essayist, and writer of legal treatises; William Ellery Channing's by his nephew Wm. Henry Channing, General Greene's by George W. Greene, that of Chief Justice Parsons by his son Theophilus Parsons, Governor Winthrop's by Robert C. Winthrop, Theodore Parker's by John Weiss, Washington Irving's by Pierre M. Irving, his nephew; Margaret Fuller Ossoli's by R. W. Emerson, Wm. H. Channing, and J. F. Clarke; Martin Van Buren's by William Allen Butler, Edward Irving's by Margaret Oliphant, Edward Livingstone's by Charles H. Hunt, Madison's by Wm. C. Rives, Dr. Wayland's by his sons F. and H. L. Wayland, Josiah Quincy's by his son Edmund Quincy, Rufus Choate's by Samuel Gilman Brown, Washington's by Irving.

All those who were named as distinguished orators—Webster, Clay, Calhoun, John Quincy Adams, Everett, Legaré, and Burgess—have since died. Perhaps no great orator has passed away who was endowed with more eminent and varied powers of eloquence than Rufus Choate, though, like Pinckney's, a great part of the triumphant efforts of his brilliant genius, masterly reason, ornate learning, impressive and thrilling delivery, have escaped public observation and permanent literature, by being heard only at the Bar. Yet much remains imperishable in American letters, delivered by him on literary, historical, and legal occasions, some of which, as his oration on Webster, is considered "worthy to be compared with the consummate masterpieces of Greek and Latin eloquence." Others who knew how to make the people hear as well as read, whether as orators, public speakers, or rhetoricians, were Justice Story, Chancellor Kent, Francis Wayland, Dr. John W. Francis, Josiah Quincy, Alexander H. Everett, James A. Hillhouse, George W. Bethune, Sargent S. Prentiss, Thomas H. Benton, Gulian C. Verplanck.

Of the modern political history of the United States, the speeches of Charles Sumner, soon to be re-printed in ten large volumes, which will comprise his published literary works, are likely to be looked upon and studied by posterity as an inseparable part. While a life so devoted to redeeming the promises of the Declaration of Independence must have the most enduring monument in the downfall of American slavery, yet it will have also a lasting literary monument in "the power and splendor of his speeches, the dignity of their tone, their affluence in learning, the lucidness and force of their logic, the artistic unity of each, their uniform correctness and magnificence of diction." Of perhaps a more uniformly terse and pointed diction, as less encumbered by occasional exuberance of learning, is the forcible and accomplished oratory of Wendell Phillips, by which polished arrows not only of wit and sarcasm, but of earnest conviction also, are sent straight to their mark. Not ornate, but earnest, vigorous, and efficient, have been the many public speeches of Henry Wilson, in the same cause of freedom. Those of William H. Seward are likely also to occupy an important place in the history of that to which he gave the appellation, "irrepressible conflict." The eulogist of Sumner, above quoted, has observed also, (yet we do not adopt the somewhat ungenerous assertion, except for the general comparison suggested) that not one of his contemporaries in the Senate, except Seward, "has left a solitary speech which can now be read through without languor and reluctance." Richard H. Dana, Jr., a patriot learned in law and accomplished in letters, has made valuable and eloquent public speeches. Robert C. Winthrop has given several noble historical and literary orations. Horace Bushnell, Orville Dewey, Peleg Sprague, Horace Binney, E. P. Whipple, and George S. Hillard, like many others eminent also in unspoken literature, have given public addresses, much to general admiration and profit.

The great masters of Political Philosophy before named have been gathered to the other fathers of a grateful country. And though a genuine statesman may here or there be sifted out of the mass of our politicians, though admired writers on constitutional jurisprudence are still left to this generation; it is for history, and not for us, to add any modern name to the list of political sages who could give to the country a Constitution and a Federalist.

Political Economy has lost from its roll of living writers Gallatin, Raguet, Thomas Cooper, Clay, Webster, Hamilton, Madison, Calhoun, Matthew Carey, A. H. Everett, Clement Biddle, Legget, Professors Dew, Vethake, Wayland, Colton, Raymond. While Greeley, Amasa Walker, and Henry C. Carey have continued to write on this subject. Carey is said to be "considered throughout Europe as the only person who has mastered, and therefore who has been able clearly to explain, the principles of Political Economy." There are a great number of able writers of essays for reviews and other periodicals on subjects connected with Political Economy. Of those who have written considerable treatises we have the names of Bascom, Colwell, Dr. Wm. Elder, Professors Bowen and Perry. Professor Bowen's recent work forcibly and clearly discusses those phases of the subject which have now become most interesting to Americans.

All those eminent writers on Jurisprudence who have been named, are gone from this life, except the venerable Horace Binney. It was lately acknowledged by eminent British authority, that on several important points of Jurisprudence no satisfactory treatises had been written except in America. Edmund Burke also said of the American Colonies, in his speech on Conciliation with America: " In no country in the world, perhaps, is the law so general a study; the greater number of the deputies sent to Congress were lawyers; but all who read, and most do read, endeavor to retain some smattering of that science. I have been told by an eminent bookseller, that in no branch of his business, after treatises on popular science, were so many books as those on law exported to the plantations; the Colonists have now fallen into their way of printing them for their own use. I hear that they have sold nearly as many of ' Blackstone's Commentaries' in America as in England." Kent's Commentaries, as a juridical classic of admired wisdom and masterly learning, are regarded, in the opinion of English as well as American jurists, as a rival and almost a substitute for Blackstone's. Lord Campbell has said: " I really hardly know any name which we can so much boast of as the Americans may of that of Professor Story, and Chancellor Kent, and others of very great distinction." Francis Lieber's works have received the highest eulogies from men eminent in jurisprudence in Europe and America. John Bouvier, George T. Curtis, Theodore Woolsey, William Whiting, J. N. Pomeroy, Timothy Walker, and several others at least as profoundly learned and of as high authority in law, but whose treatises are chiefly professional, rather than national, have produced legal works of great merit.

Of before-named writers in Biblical Criticism, we miss J. A. Alexander, George Bush, Andrews Norton, Edward Robinson, Moses Stuart. In addition we have lost at least two excellent Hebraists, George R. Noyes and Isaac Leeser. Several other Biblical scholars have risen to the first rank, as Horatio B. Hackett; Ezra Abbot, whose learning is said to be almost without superior in matters of Bibliography and Textual Criticism; Thomas J. Conant, Taylor Lewis, Wm. Henry Greene, Philip Schaff.

Classical scholars have lost from their number Felton,* Robinson, Anthon; and, not before named, E. A. Andrews, Peter Bullions, and John J.

---

* As a Greek scholar, Felton is said to have been "unsurpassed by any other in the country. He had a love of art which was cultivated by his devotion to a language and literature so calculated to improve and perfect the taste. He was deeply interested in everything that concerned Greece, her poets, orators, historians, and philosophers, but especially her monuments of art, and whatever reminded him of her ancient glory, or enabled him to understand more fully the meaning of her ancient writers. His works are numerous and of great value." Over fifty articles in the *North American Review*, and several in the *New American Cyclopædia*, are from his pen.

Owen. It appears safe to say that Americans have, among them, no more profoundly learned Grecian, by scholarship as well as by nation, than E. A. Sophocles, the writer of several works of highest authority, and now lately again benefactor to Greek learning by his "Greek Lexicon of the Roman and Byzantine Periods"—a work which stands alone on the ground it covers, a treasure of ripe scholarship, great patriotic learning, and withal good sense. The following have published excellent works which bear testimony to high attainments in Greek or Latin scholarship: Professors Boise, Champlin, Chase, Crosby, Drisler, Feuling, Frieze, Goodwin, Hackett, Hadley, Harkness, Johnson, Lewis, Lincoln, Short, Tyler, E. R. Humphreys and Samuel H. Taylor.

In more general Philology, we have names worthy to be compared with any in the English language: William D. Whitney, the author of "Language and the Study of Language," and (more especially in English Philology) George P. Marsh, who has done as much as any other master-scholar to throw light on the history and nature of our own language; to whom we may now add Francis A. March, for his very scholarly Comparative Grammar of the Anglo-Saxon Language, and his excellent Method of Philological Study of the English Language. Francis J. Child and Hiram Corson have labored with distinguished learning and merit in a similar field. Schele de Vere's interesting Studies in English, together with other linguistic productions, and William C. Fowler's and Benjamin W. Dwight's meritorious works evince accomplished scholarship. "You Americans," said a distinguished foreign scholar, quoted in W. C. Fowler's excellent work on the English language, "have a taste and talent for language. Your dictionaries, and grammars, and exegetical works do great credit to your national literature." William Henry Greene has made useful contributions to the study of Hebrew. E. G. Squier appears alone among our learned writers on the native languages of South and Central America—for we know not whether Porter C. Bliss has published much of his knowledge in that department. For evidences of rare acquaintance with North American Indian languages, we may record the names of J. H. Trumbull, said to be the only man who can read Eliot's Indian Bible; Thomas Hurlburt, who has preached in the Cree and Ojibway languages for thirty years—and, for that matter, many missionaries to the Indians might perhaps be named, yet irrelevantly, here; and S. S. Haldeman, a writer on languages and ethnology of North American Indians. We have to record the death of Josiah

W. Gibbs, a useful contributor to the study of comparative philology; of Goold Brown, the estimable author of a "Grammar of English Grammars"; of William W. Turner, who contributed much to Hebrew and Oriental learning, as well as to the study of American Indian languages; of Nathan L. Lindsay, Miron Winslow, Levi Janvier, and Isador Löwenthal.

In addition to our great Lexicographers, Webster and Pickering, Worcester is also among the eminent departed. John Russell Bartlett has given us a valuable Dictionary of Americanisms. Several good linguistic and other dictionaries have been made by certain above-mentioned authors, in their respective departments of study, and by others. Ripley and Dana have ably edited that colossal and excellent literary enterprise, Appleton's American Cyclopædia, completed in sixteen volumes.

In Mathematics many new names have arisen, from whom are departed H. N. Robinson, William M. Gillespie, John Gummere, A. D. Bache, Benjamin Greenleaf. Benjamin Peirce has produced great fruits of the profoundest mathematical gifts. Other distinguished names are Davies, Loomis, Chauvenet, Mahan, Maury—and, indeed, we know not where to end our list of them.

Astronomy has parted with George P. Bond, William C. Bond, O. M. Mitchell, and Olmstead. Well known writers in this science are Hannah M. Bouvier, W. A. Norton, B. A. Gould, and C. H. Davis. Bache, Newton, Maury, Wilkes, Blodget, and Loomis have also rendered distinguished service to *Meteorology*, which has lost that of Redfield, Espy, and Dr. Hare. In *Natural Philosophy*, eminent names are Olmstead, Snell, Ewbank, Renwick (deceased). The chief ranks of noted names in *Chemistry* before given have been refilled by Cooke, Storer, Eliot, Hosford, Youmans, Rogers, Knapp, Biddle, Porter, Wells. The last named was, until recently, the highly competent editor of the "Annual of Scientific Discovery." His able successors are Samuel Kneeland and John Trowbridge. Professor Dana is still left, the Nestor of American Mineralogists and Geologists. Overman, Shepard, Hitell, and Alger (deceased), have also added greatly to the knowledge of *Mineralogy*. *Geology* has lost the following master-laborers Hitchcock, Silliman, Emmons, Vanuxem, Rogers, Woost, Maclure, Houghton, Cotting; and has happily gained, besides Dana, a Whitney, Hall, Owen, Percival, Jackson, Mather, Adams, Foster, Isaac Lea, Loomis, Lynch, Trask, Blake, Norwood, Lieber, Winchell, Hayden, and many more. Gray has continued making admirable additions to the literature of

Botany. Wood's botanical treatises are also widely useful. Nuttall, Leavenworth, and others have contributed valuable knowledge of this "amiable science." *Zoology* can now hardly be thought of without the great name of Agassiz; and a noble company of other zoologists have highly exalted American science, among whom are Gould, Leidy, Cope, Hagan, Stimpson, Hall, Clark, Lea, Walter, Harvey, Holmes, Kneeland, Conrad, Morse, Orton, Hart, De Kay.* Alexander Wilson, the great *Ornithologist,* and his successors, Bonaparte, Audubon, Nuttall, and Cassin, are gone; Elliot and Spencer Baird remain. Excellent works on *Entomology* have been written by Harris,* Packard, Trimble, and Verrill. Baird and Gill are noted in *Ichthyology;* Adams, Binney, and Bland in *Conchology.* *Ethnology* has lost Schoolcraft, Gallatin, and Morton. Other contributors thereto are J. R. Bartlett, Squier, Brace, Brinton, Gliddon, Nott, and Hayden. *Geographical literature* is indebted first to Guyot, and also in an eminent degree to Colton, Mitchell, Page, Pickering, and Marsh.

The following are the names noticed by Griswold of writers of Fiction, of whose subsequent death we have account: Paulding, Cooper, Sedgwick, Simms, Dr. Bird, Wm. Ware, Allston, Irving, Hawthorne, Willis, Poe, Kirkland. These have been followed by Theodore Winthrop, Caroline Lee Hentz, Thomas Bulfinch, Eliza Leslie, J. V. Huntingdon.—But the field (now became a vast hot-bed beyond measure) of romantic fiction, which was spoken of by Griswold as thronged with laborers, is now too much crowded to suffocation to allow any detailed allusion to the merits of even the workmen that need least to be ashamed, disposed to rear fair flowers rather than foster these abounding multitudes of meretricious weeds. If the "*intellectual* condition and *prospects* of the country" were to be judged according to our people's eager patronage of this department of literature, we confess a fear that our young nation's brain bids fair to reel or soften with the artificial excitement of fast youth, rather than be invigorated with manly discipline of more temperate nurture, seasoned with truth and health, in other departments of our noble literature. Our disproportionate fictitious literature seems to be both a cause and effect of American haste, impatience of discipline, and superficiality, whether in scholarship, or business, or truly baptismal religion. Even "Sunday-school" children, to look at their usual libraries, are as likely to drink of the distillery of fiction, as to be fed with

* Deceased.

72

the sincere milk of the word. Yet our reading of stimulants, so intimately connected with our high-pressure living, has a strong antidote in the Philistinism of this busy country, teeming with undeveloped material resources, and enforcing, on water and land and beneath, that sturdy, practical grappling with imperative labor, which takes much nonsense out of our novel readers and links our iron age to the heroic, even though romantic excitement adds a spice of the tragic.

Among the best writers of fiction are Harriet Beecher Stowe, whose " Uncle Tom's Cabin " produced an impression throughout our country that remains without parallel in the history of our literature, and it is believed to have hastened the day of freedom in the land ; numerous works of high reputation from her pen have followed ;—Sarah Jane Lippincott ("Grace Greenwood") whose writings, says Henry Giles, " are eminently characteristic ; they are strictly national ; they are likewise decisively individual ;"—Elizabeth Stuart Phelps, recently introduced to wide-spread notice by her somewhat remarkable book, " The Gates Ajar " ; subsequent stories from her pen also meet with very favorable reception ; and (merely to mention well-known names without comment, and in indiscriminate order), Louisa M. Alcott, Donald G. Mitchell (" Ik Marvel "), Ann S. Stephens, Thomas Bulfinch, Bayard Taylor, Edward Everett Hale, J. G. Holland, Oliver Wendell Holmes, George William Curtis, J. R. Gilmore ("Edmund Kirke "), Virginia F. Townsend, Virginia C. Terhune ("Marion Harland"), Mary A. Denison, T. S. Arthur, Emma D. E. N. Southworth, Emily Judson (Fanny Forrester), J. T. Trowbridge, Wm. T. Adams (" Oliver Optic"), Meta Landor, Harriet Prescott Spofford, Richard P. Kimball, Mary J. Holmes, Elizabeth Stoddard, Margaret Hosmer, James K. Hosmer, Anna E. Porter, John Esten Cook, Charles G. Leland, Anna Cora Ritchie, Paul Preston, Rebecca Harding Davis, Harriet B. McKeever, Caroline E. K. Davis, and others.

Contributors to our Humorous, Comic, and Satirical literature who have passed away,—besides, among those already mentioned, Irving, Paulding, Sands, Verplanck, Willis Gaylord Clarke, Joseph C. Neal, Mrs. Gilman, Seba Smith (" Jack Downing "), and Halleck,—are Charles F. Browne, known as "Artemus Ward" ; Henry P. Leland, author of " The Gray Bay Mare" ; Frederick S. Cozzens, writer of the " Sparrow-grass Papers" ; Mortimer Thompson, known as J. Q. Philander Doesticks,—" Artemus Ward " was a genuine humorist, independently of the laughable spelling of his words—a cheap feature in funny writing adopted also by D. R. Locke ("Petroleum V. Nasby,") Henry G. Shaw ("Josh Billings,") and a number of inferior imitators. "Nasby" and "Josh Billings," while perhaps little inferior as humorists to "A. Ward," merit more respect for earnestness of moral purpose, writing not principally for public amusement, but for persuasion of certain heartfelt principles of individual or political morality.—The highest place in our choice literature of Wit may be accorded to Oliver Wendell Holmes,* and among humorists to James Russell Lowell.†—George William Curtis in his "Potiphar Papers" has produced a series of satirical sketches of fashionable society which have been highly commended for their "gayety of humor" as well as for their "polished invective."—George D. Prentice, (deceased) an accomplished editor, has a fame in America by reason of many witty sayings of his in print.—S. Clemens, widely known of late as "Mark Twain", is causing many hearty laughs not unmingled with moral profit, by several popular productions of his wit, humor, and good sense.—Charles G. Leland, author of the famous "Hans Breittmann" Ballads, though they are in verse, shall be mentioned here, as an accomplished humorist through the medium of the German-American

---

* "Neither of these kinds of [Holmes's] verse has prepared us for anything so good, so sustained, so national, and yet so akin to our finest humorists as is the 'Autocrat of the Breakfast Table'; a very delightful book . . . . A book to possess two copies of; one to be read and marked, thumbed and dog-eared; and one to stand up in its pride of place with the rest on the shelves, all ranged in shining rows, as dear old friends, not merely as nodding acquaintances. Not at all like that ponderous and overbearing autocrat, Dr. Johnson, is our Yankee friend. He has more of Goldsmith's sweetness and lovability. He is a true lover of elegance and high-bred grace, dainty fancies, and all-pleasurable things, as was Leigh Hunt; he has more worldly sense without the moral languor; but there is the same boy-heart, beating in a manly breast, beneath the poet's singing robe. For he is a poet as well as a humorist. Indeed, although this book is written in prose, it is full of poetry, with the 'beaded bubbles' of humor dancing up through the hippocrene, and 'winking at the brim', with a winning look of invitation shining in their merry eyes."—*North British Review*, 1860.

* "The greatest of all American humorists is James Russell Lowell; and the greatest of all American books of humor is the 'Biglow Papers.' If Holmes can match the Queen Anne men in their genial way, with a pleasant tincture of Montaigne, Lowell reminds us more of the lusty strength and boundless humor of that great Elizabethan literature. Not that he imitates them, or follows in their footsteps; for if there be an American book that might have existed as an indigenous growth, independently of an European literature, we feel that book to be the Biglow Papers . . . . The humor is 'audible and full of vent', racy in hilarious hyperbole, and it has that infusion of poetry necessary to the richest and deepest humor. The book is a national birth, and it possesses that element of nationality which has been the most enduring part of all the best and greatest births in literature and art . . . . And the crowning quality of Lowell's book is that it was found at home. It could not have been written in any other country than America."—*North British Review*, 1860.

dialect admirably managed by him—a skilful linguist; and his productions are so warmly welcomed by intelligent readers both in England and here, as to seem possessed of an unusually permanent fame.—B. P. Shillaber has made the name of "Mrs. Partington" scarcely ever to be heard without a smile. Robert H. Newell, author of the "Orpheus C. Kerr" papers, George Harris, and C. H. Webb are also of fair prominence.

Our list of new writers of Essays, as must be expected, is very large. Our vast periodical literature comprises the larger part of what is written in this department, yet very much appears in book form. Most writers of important contributions to literature are also writers of essays or "articles" on their favorite subjects. Emerson, Hillard, Sumner, Tuckerman, Whipple, Lowell, have remained among the most gifted of our essayists, continually adding brilliant, valuable, or able productions to our national literature. The past twenty-five years have added to the public gratification and profit, such names as Leonard Bacon, Robert Baird,* Joseph T. Buckingham,* Thomas Bulfinch,* Prof. Samuel G. Brown, Charles A. Bristed, George H. Calvert, George B. Cheever, Lydia Maria Child, Charles D. Cleveland,* another excellent laborer in the promotion of the knowledge of American Literature, and also of English; G. T. Congdon, Hiram Corson, Edward T. Channing,* whose instructions have doubtless been the seed of much that is excellent in the style of many writers; George William Curtis, T. L. Cuyler, E. A. and G. L. Duyckinck, whose excellent "Cyclopædia of American Literature" has perhaps made up by magnitude and completeness as much as Griswold's work accomplished by priority and general circulation, in making American literature known at home and abroad; Abigail E. Dodge ("Gail Hamilton"), B. B. Edwards,* William Everett, Theodore S. Fay, Cornelius C. Felton, Henry Giles, Oliver Wendell Holmes, W. D. Howells, Thomas Wentworth Higginson, Caleb Sprague Henry, Fitz Greene Halleck,* J. S. Hart, Nathaniel Hawthorne,* J. G. Holland ("Timothy Titcomb"), Henry James, James Jackson Jarves, Emily Judson* ("Fanny Forrester"), Thomas Starr King,* Richard B. Kimball, Henry C. Lea, Charles G. Leland, H. W. Longfellow, George P. Marsh, Robert S. Mackenzie, O. M. Mitchell,* Walter Mitchell, Charles Eliot Norton, Edwards A. Park, James Parton, Sara P. Parton ("Fanny Fern"), James K. Paulding,* Calvin Pease,* Andrew P. Peabody, Wendell Philips, Josiah Quincy,* George Ripley, Dr. James Rush,* Richard Rush,* Theo-

---

* Deceased.

dore Sedgwick,* Lydia H. Sigourney,* W. W. Story, H. B. Stowe, George
Ticknor, author of the excellent "History of Spanish Literature" which is
recognized in Europe as a "permanent authority", Henry D. Thoreau,*
Horace Binney Wallace,* John G. Whittier, whose prose writings alone,
would ensure him a high position in literature; and Theodore Winthrop.*

The list of writers of Voyages and Travels has been increased by the
following well-known names: H. N. Bishop, author of "One Thousand
Miles' Walk across South America"; Du Chaillu, C. C. Coffin, Walter
Colton, J. C. Fletcher, in connection with D. P. Kidder, writer of Brazil
and Brazilians; Louis Grout, author of "Zulu Land"; Capt. Charles
Francis Hall and J. I. Hayes, distinguished writers on Arctic travel; W.
D. Howells, the accomplished writer of "Venetian Life", and several other
productions which have recently placed him in the foremost rank of elegant
literature; Thomas Starr King, author of a charming work on the "White
Hills; their Legends, Landscape, and Scenery"; the lamented Dr. Elisha
Kent Kane, writer of "one of the most remarkable records", says Prescott,
"I ever met with, of difficulties, and of the power of a brave spirit to overcome them"; Frederick Law Olmsted, author of the "Cotton Kingdom";
James Orton, author of "The Andes and the Amazon"; Com. M. C. Perry,
the excellent narrator of his noted expedition to the China Seas and Japan;
Raphael Pumpelly, whose recent work, "Across America and Asia", is
remarkably well received; and Bayard Taylor, the foremost name in American literature of travel. Many names might well be added to this list.

Conscious of the meagreness and omissions of a statement so condensed
as the above has to be, of the most noticeable additions to American literature since Griswold's day, we leave our task, with a sense of grateful satisfaction and proper pride in the noble and successful literary achievements
of our country during the brief period here glanced over; believing that
no words of ours could add to the conviction which even such a record must
enforce, that the intellectual condition and prospects of the country are in
most encouraging prosperity.

---

* Deceased.

JAMES KENT, LL.D.

[Born 1763. Died 1847.]

JAMES KENT LL.D., one of the most eminent of modern jurists, was born July 31, 1763, at Fredericks, Putnam Co., N. Y. He graduated at Yale, 1781; commenced the practice of law, 1785; elected a member of the N. Y. State Assembly, 1790 and '92; Professor of law at Columbia College, N. Y., 1793–98; Master in Chancery, and member of the Legislature, 1796; Recorder of the City, 1797; Puisne Judge of the Supreme Court of N. Y., 1798; Chief Justice of the same Court, 1804–1814; Chancellor of N. Y., 1814–1823; during this latter period he resided at Albany. In his 60th year, by the Constitution of the State, his term of office expired, just when he was in the prime of his powers and usefulness. He removed in 1823, back to N. Y., and resumed the Law Professorship at Columbia College. Part of his lectures before this Institution were published. He also helped to edit the Revised Laws of the State of N. Y., 1802, 2 vols., 8vo.; delivered an anniversary address before the Historical Society, 1828; Address before the Phi Beta Kappa of Yale, 1831, and one before the Law Association of N. Y., 1836. He drew up a Course of Reading for young men, for the benefit of the Mercantile Library, 1840; of which a new edition, enlarged by President Charles King, LL. D. and Henry A. Oakley, was published, 1853. A portion of his decisions as Chancellor, selected by himself, will be found in Johnson's Chancery Reports, 7 vols.,1814–23; decisions that must forever remain a monument of judicial wisdom, learning, and eloquence,
without superior in those of any country or of any age.

His greatest, and one of the most important works ever issued in this country, is Commentaries upon American Law, 4 vols., 1826–30, of which he revised the 6th edition shortly before his death. Eight editions were sold up to 1855, yielding a profit to the author and his heirs of over $135,000; and the sales have been steady and large ever since. Several abridgments have appeared, all of which are used as Text Books, and are the standards on the subject of American Law. Judge Story declares Kent's Commentaries will range on the same shelf with the classical work of Blackstone, an opinion supported by the most eminent jurists of the country. While even as a library book of reference for the historical student, or general reader, its importance can hardly be overrated.

A Memoir and Letters of Chancellor Kent, was written by his son, Wm. Kent. Judge Duer delivered a Discourse on his Life, Character, and Public Services, in which he says, "Great as our country is in all the elements of a just renown, and illustrious as its annals have become by the labors, and by the exploits of statesmen and of heroes, it may yet be doubted whether, hitherto, it has produced a man more worthy of its entire veneration, gratitude, and love, than him whose services to his country and to his race, we are this day met to commemorate."

THE LAW OF NATIONS.

FROM THE COMMENTARIES ON AMERICAN LAW.

BY this law we are to understand that code of public instruction, which defines the rights and prescribes the duties of nations, in their intercourse with each other. The faithful observance of this law is essential to national character, and to the happiness of mankind. According to the observation of Montesquieu, it is founded on the principle, that different nations ought to do each other as much good in peace, and as little harm in war, as possible, without injury to their true interests. But as the precepts of this code are not defined in every case with perfect precision, and as nations have no common civil tribunal to resort to for the interpretation and execution of this law, it is often very difficult to ascertain, to the satisfaction of the parties concerned, its precise injunctions and extent; and a still greater difficulty is the want of adequate pacific means to secure obedience to its dictates.

There has been a difference of opinion among writers, concerning the foundation of the law of nations. It has been considered by some as a mere system of positive institutions, founded upon consent and usage; while others have insisted that it was essentially the same as the law of nature, applied to the conduct of nations, in the character of moral persons, susceptible of obligations and laws. We are not to adopt either of these theories as exclusively true. The most useful and practical part of the law of nations is, no doubt, instituted or positive law, founded on usage, consent, and agreement. But it would be improper to separate this law entirely from natural jurisprudence, and not to consider it as deriving much of its force and dignity from the same principles of right reason, the same views of the nature and constitution of man, and the same sanction of Divine revelation, as those from which the science of morality is deduced. There is a natural and a positive law of nations. By the former, every state, in its relations with other states, is bound to conduct itself with justice, good faith, and benevolence; and this application of the law of nature has been called by Vattel the necessary law of nations, because nations are bound by the law of nature to observe it; and it is termed by others the internal law of nations, because it is obligatory upon them in point of conscience.

We ought not, therefore, to separate the science of public law from that of ethics, nor encourage the dangerous suggestion, that governments are not so strictly bound by the obligations of truth, justice, and humanity, in relation to other powers, as they are in the management of their own local concerns. States, or bodies politic, are to be considered as moral persons, having a public will, capable and free to do right and wrong, inasmuch as they are collections of individuals, each of whom carries with him into the service of the community the same binding law of morality and religion which ought to control his conduct in private life. The law of nations is a complex system, composed of various ingredients. It consists of general principles of right and justice, equally suitable to the government of individuals in a state of natural equality, and to the relations and conduct of nations; of a collection of usages, customs, and opinions, the growth of civilization and commerce; and of a code of conventional or positive law. In the absence of these latter regulations, the intercourse and conduct of nations are to be governed by principles fairly to be deduced from the rights and duties of nations, and the nature of moral obligation; and we have the authority of the lawyers of antiquity, and of some of the first masters in the modern school of public law, for placing the moral obligation of nations and of individuals on similar grounds, and for considering individual and national morality as parts of one and the same science.

The law of nations, so far as it is founded on the principles of natural law, is equally binding in every age, and upon all mankind. But the Christian nations of Europe, and their descendants on this side of the Atlantic, by the vast superiority of their attainments in arts, and science, and commerce, as well as in policy and government; and, above all, by the brighter light, the more certain truths, and the more definite sanction which Christianity has communicated to the ethical jurisprudence of the ancients, have established a law of nations peculiar to themselves. They form together a community of nations united by religion, manners, morals, humanity, and science, and united also by the mutual advantages of commercial intercourse, by the habit of forming alliances and treaties with each other, of interchanging ambassadors, and of studying and recognizing the same writers and systems of public law.

The law of nations, as understood by the European world, and by us, is the offspring of modern times. The most refined states among the ancients seem to have had no conception of the moral obligations of justice and humanity between nations, and there was no such thing in existence as the science of international law. They regarded strangers and enemies as nearly synonymous, and considered foreign persons and property as lawful prize. Their laws of war and peace were barbarous and deplorable. So little were mankind accustomed to regard the rights of persons or property, or to perceive the value and beauty of public order, that in the most enlightened ages of the Grecian republics, piracy was regarded as an honorable employment. There were powerful Grecian states that avowed the practice of piracy; and the fleets of Athens, the best disciplined and most respectable naval force in all antiquity, were exceedingly addicted to piratical excursions. It was the received opinion, that Greeks, even as between their own cities and states, were bound to no duties, nor by any moral law, without compact; and that prisoners taken in war, had no rights, and might lawfully be put to death, or sold into perpetual slavery, with their wives and children.

There were, however, many feeble efforts, and some successful examples, to be met with in Grecian history, in favor of national justice. The object of the Amphictyonic council was to institute a law of nations among the Greeks, and settle contests between Grecian states by a pacific adjustment. It was also a law of nations among them, and one which was very religiously observed, to allow to the vanquished the privilege of burying their own dead, and to grant the requisite truce for that purpose. Some of these states had public ministers resident at the courts of others, and there were some distinguished instances of great humanity shown to prisoners of war. During a cessation of arms in the course of the Peloponnesian war, Athens and Sparta agreed to an exchange or mutual surrender of prisoners. The sound judgment and profound reflections of Aristotle, naturally raised his sense of right above the atrocious maxims and practices of his age, and he perceived the injustice of that doctrine of Grecian policy, that, by the laws of war, the vanquished became the absolute property of the victor.

ALEXANDER WILSON.

[Born 1766. Died 1813]

ALEXANDER WILSON, the first to claim the title of the American Ornithologist, and the one who has so thoroughly maintained it by his charming and accurate descriptions, and the best and most natural drawings of birds ever published, was born at Paisley, Scotland, July 6, 1766. His parents were persons in humble but respectable circumstances; his father was a weaver, and bore a high character as a man of strict honesty and industrious habits, united to much good sense and superior intelligence. He fondly hoped Alexander, his eldest son, would become a minister of the Gospel, and placed him with a clergyman for that purpose; but the death of his mother when he was ten years old, leaving a large family, needing motherly care, induced his father to marry again, and his family increasing, he was obliged to suspend his son's education. Alexander had made good use of his time; he says in a letter in 1811, "for my success, I have to thank the goodness of a kind father whose attention to my education in early life, as well as the books then put into my hands, first gave my mind a bias towards relishing the paths of literature, and the charms and magnificence of nature."

At the age of 13, he was apprenticed to a weaver, with whom he remained from 1779 to 1782. He then worked four years longer at his trade, writing poetry during his spare moments. Of an active turn of mind and body, he was glad to give up weaving, and start out as a peddler, pursuing this occupation for three years, visiting most of the romantic and literary objects of interest in Scotland. In 1789, he made arrangements with a publisher for an edition of his poems, for which he issued a poetical prospectus and hand-bill, which he distributed on his pedestrian tour. The subscription part was a failure, though the book was printed in July, 1790, and he started out again to sell copies. Meeting with but little success, he resumed the loom at Paisley. Hearing of a literary discussion at Edinburgh, he studied for it, wrote a poem called the Laurel Disputed, worked hard for the means to travel to that city, and read it at the time and place of discussion. Though the audience did not agree with him, he made many friends, and became a contributor to the Bee, edited by Dr. Anderson.

Before leaving town, he recited two other poems, Rab and Ringan, and the Loss of the Pack, and published his poem in blank verse, the Laurel Disputed, or, the Merits of Robert Ferguson and Allan Ramsay contrasted. On returning to Paisley, when his funds were exhausted, his Edinburgh success induced him to bring out a new edition of his poems, entitled, Poems, Humorous, Satirical, and Serious, and the author again attempted to be his own bookseller, and again failed.

In 1792, his poem of Watty and Meg, published anonymously, met with great success— one hundred thousand copies being sold in a few weeks—and received the high honor of being attributed to Burns. This was a great gratification to the author, who entertained a high regard for the great poet, and had previously made his acquaintance by a letter which he wrote to Burns on the first publication of his poems, in which he objected to some on the score of immorality. Burns replied he was so accustomed to such communications, that he usually paid no attention to them ; but that as Wilson showed himself to be a good poet, he would, in this instance, vindicate himself. Wilson afterwards visited Burns at Ayrshire.

A dispute arising between the manufacturers and weavers of Paisley, Wilson wrote several satirical poems, for one of which, the Shark, or, Long Mills Detected, he was sentenced to jail for a few days, and to burn the poem in public, on February 6th, 1793. This occurrence, with his sympathy with the democratic spirit of the early days of the French Revolution, which caused him to be suspected by the authorities, the hopelessness of bettering his condition in the old world, and the alluring prospect of political and pecuniary independence, held out by the new, were the motives of his emigration to America. After living four months at the rate of a shilling a week, he saved money enough for his passage, walked to Port Patrick, sailed to Belfast, and thence embarked for America.

He landed at New Castle, Delaware, July 14, 1794, and proceeded to Philadelphia, 33 miles, on foot, shooting on the way a red-headed woodpecker, the commencement of his ornithological pursuits. On his arrival at the city, he worked at copper plate printing, and afterward at weaving and peddling. These were abandoned in 1795, for school keeping near Frankford, and afterward at Milestown, Pa., where he remained a few years, diligently employed in acquiring as well as imparting information. He also took a hand at politics, and delivered an oration on the Power and Value of National Liberty, and wrote the song entitled Jefferson and Liberty.

In 1802, he took charge of a seminary near Gray's Ferry, on the Schuylkill, four miles from Philadelphia. This brought him into communication with two valuable friends, Wm. Bartram the Botanist, and Lawson the Engraver. His leisure hours were now devoted to the pursuit to which he was becoming more and more attached—that of Ornithology. A letter he wrote about this time, June, 1803, says, "close application to the duties of my profession, which I have followed since Nov., 1795, has deeply injured my constitution; the more so, that my rambling disposition was the worst calculated of any one's in the world for the austere regularity of a teacher's life. I have had many pursuits since I left Scotland —mathematics, the German language, music, drawing, etc., and I am now about to make a collection of all our finest birds." He wrote for Chas. Brockden Brown's Literary Magazine, the Solitary Tutor, and other poems.

In October, 1804, Wilson, with two friends, made a pedestrian-tour to the Falls of Niagara. Winter overtook them on their return, in November, near Cayuga Lake. One of his companions tarried with his relatives till Spring; the other availed himself of a less fatiguing mode of transportation than that of his legs; while Wilson trudged home with his gun on his shoulder, through the snow "mid-leg deep", and arrived there in December, after a journey of 1257 miles, and an absence of 59 days. One result of his trip was his fine poem of the Foresters, published in the Portfolio, and afterwards reprinted in a 16mo. volume; another to confirm him in the resolution he had taken, "Feeling more eager than ever to commence some more extensive expedition, where scenes and subjects, entirely new and generally unknown, might reward my curiosity; and where perhaps my humble acquisitions might add something to the stores of knowledge."

Seeing the imperfections of books on the subject of the birds of our country, how incorrectly and often falsely they were represented in drawings, he determined to devote his life to Ornithology.

Wilson now employed his leisure hours in perfecting himself in drawing and coloring. He also practiced the art of etching, and endeavored to engage his friend Lawson in his projected publication on American Ornithology, but without success. Obstacles did not, however, change his purpose. He declared his intention to go on, though the effort cost him his life. "If so, I shall at least leave a small beacon to point out where I perished." He wrote to Jefferson in 1806, requesting employment in the expeditions fitting out for the survey of the western territory. No reply was received; but private enterprise was now about to furnish means for the execution of his long cherished project. Wm. Bradford, the publisher, engaged Wilson to superintend a new edition of Rees's Cyclopedia. The liberal salary received enabled Wilson to give up school-keeping, and devote himself to this work, which progressed so well in his hands that the publisher agreed to undertake the Ornithology. He worked so unremittingly in preparing for the press, that his health began to fail. As a relaxation, he undertook a pedestrian tour through Pennsylvania, in August, 1807, from which he returned with new vigor to his desk.

The first of the nine volumes of the great work was published in Sept., 1808, the edition consisting of 200 copies. The plates were well engraved by Lawson, and colored by his daughters from patterns made by Wilson. In the same month, the author set out for the eastward to procure subscribers. He travelled as far as Maine, and returned through Vermont, by the way of Albany to Philadelphia. Visiting "many thousands who have examined my book—among men of the first character for taste and literature—I have heard nothing but expressions of the highest admiration and esteem"; but getting few subscribers for "a work too good for the country." During the winter he travelled southward. Returning with a few subscribers, 300 additional copies were struck off. The price was one hundred and twenty dollars per copy of 9 vols. Volume II appeared in Jan., 1810, and the author having seen it through the press, set out on a tour down the Ohio and Mississippi, in quest of new materials and new subscribers. From Pittsburg he descended the river in an open skiff, which though perilous, recommended itself for its economy and freedom of action. During this descent of the Ohio, a voyage of 720 miles, he wrote the poem of the Pilgrim.

From Louisville, he made his way to Nashville, and thence through the Indian country to Natchez. On the 6th of June, he reached New Orleans, 252 miles from Natchez. Here, in a fortnight, he procured 60 new subscribers. He took passage in a ship for New York, where he arrived, July 30th. He returned to Philadelphia, on the 2d of August, after a seven months' tour, during which he had spent only $450, but had obtained an abundant supply of materials for his work, including several beautiful, and hitherto unknown birds.

In 1812, he was made a member of the American Philosophical Society. The greater part of the years 1811–12, were spent by him at the Botanical garden of his friend, Mr. Bartram. There, removed from the noise and bustle of the town, he enjoyed complete freedom from interruption, and was able to dispose of his time to the best advantage, while he recruited his overworn and sinking frame by happy rambles through the neighboring woods. Here the publication of his Ornithology progressed rapidly, and he now tasted the satisfaction of knowing that his labors had not been in vain, and that the value of his great work, was becoming more and more generally appreciated.

In September, he made a short excursion to the eastward for the purpose of visiting his subscribers, settling accounts with his agents and pursuing his investigations. At Haverhill the good people observing a stranger among them of very inquisitive habits, arrested him as a spy from Canada, taking sketches to facilitate British invasion; but on finding out the truth, dismissed him with many apologies. He also made several short excursions to different parts, and five times visited the coast of New Jersey, in pursuit of the waders and web-footed tribes. The aggregate of his peregrinations amounted to upwards of 10,000 miles. In the early part of 1813, the seventh volume of the Ornithology was completed, and soon after its publication, he again set out, on an expedition to Egg Harbor, to procure materials for the 8th volume, principally the marine water-fowl. This was his last expedition, and occupied nearly four months. On his return to Philadelphia, he applied himself with the greatest diligence to prepare the letter press of the forthcoming volume, which he thought would nearly terminate his labors, and bring him to the completion of a work on which he had risked his reputation, his fortune, and his earthly all. Unhappily this object was attended with such an excess of toil, as brought on one of his old complaints, which had gradually been becoming more frequent when mind or body was harrassed and agitated in the prosecution of any favorite object. The dysentery, his former foe, resumed its deadly assaults, and after a few days illness, Wilson expired, August 23, 1813, in the 48th year of his age.

Sir William Jardine says, " In his birthplace, a society has been formed by his admirers, who meet annually to talk over past recollections, when the merits of his works and the remembrance of the deceased poet and naturalist are commemorated in a speech or an ode." Surely America has reason to do him honor.

It is mentioned by Mr. Ord, his friend and biographer, that Wilson had proposed, on the completion of his Ornithology, to publish an edition in four volumes, 8vo., the figures to be engraved on wood. He also contemplated a work on the Quadrupeds of the U. S., to be printed in the same style as the Ornithology. Part of the eighth volume, having been put through the press while the author was living, the remainder was edited by Mr. Ord, and the 8th and 9th volumes were published in January, 1814; though the illustrations had all been prepared under Wilson's supervision before his death. Mr. Ord had been Wilson's assistant in his rambles, and was well qualified to complete his work. He accompanied the 9th volume with a life of its author. Subsequently four additional volumes were given to the world by Charles Lucien Bonaparte

Prince of Musignano. They appeared in 1828, the first of which was edited by Dr. John D. Godman, the eminent naturalist, who himself wrote a very able work on American Quadrupeds, which passed through a number of editions; the last three volumes were edited by Wm. Cooper. A new edition of Wilson's Ornithology, the letter press in 3 vols. 8 vo., and the plates in 1 vol., royal 4to., was published in 1825, by Harrison Hall. An edition in one vol., octavo, edited by Dr. Brewer, with notes, was published in Boston, in 1841. A new edition in 3 vols., imperial 8vo., with an atlas of over three hundred carefully colored plates from Wilson's original plates in folio, is about to be reprinted in Philadelphia, 1870, by Porter and Coates, and will be an ornament and a valuable addition to any library. It is the Classic on the subject. Several editions of the work, with and without plates, have been issued in England.

When we think of the limited opportunities Wilson had of acquiring information, and examine the result of his life-long endeavor to leave something behind him, which the world would not willingly let die, we know not whether most to admire his indomitable perseverance, his great self-reliance, or the natural ardor of his mind, which could carry through to a successful termination, through all the difficulties he surmounted, a work of such magnitude. His descriptions are so truthful, and so full of the charm of nature, as at once to attract the most casual reader by the brilliant sweetness of his style, while his drawings, unrivalled for their accuracy of engraving and coloring, represent each bird so faithfully, as to size and color, and the most likely position the bird is usually seen in, that the most careless observer, at once recognizes any bird he may ever have been acquainted with, even if so long ago as his boyish days. Another great merit in his plates is, that all the birds are represented the size of life, where possible, while the others are drawn to an accurate scale, which is of vast use in understanding his descriptions, or recognizing the bird when seen.

The poems of Wilson reflect his sympathies, his sensibilities, his love of humorous observation among men; as his prose, with its quick, lively step and minute discrimination, so freshly pictures the feathered world. He has his song for love and beauty, and his similar choice of subject in ludicrous tale or ballad, with a smarting sense of wrong and poverty; while an early observation in natural history, and his pursuit of descriptive poetry, belong especially to Wilson the Naturalist. We may add that at his death, Burns wrote one of his sweetest songs upon Wilson, invoking the birds to join in mourning "wham we deplore." Speaking to a friend one day on the subject of death, Wilson expressed a wish that his body should repose in some rural spot sacred to peace and solitude, and where the birds might sing over his grave. He was buried in the cemetery of the old Swedes' Church in Southwark, Philadelphia, and a plain marble tomb marks the place where he is laid.

In his personal appearance, Wilson was tall and handsome; rather slender than athletic in form. His countenance was exprsssive and thoughtful, his eye powerful and intelligent, and his conversation remarkable for quickness and originality. He was warm-hearted and generous in his affections, and through life displayed a constant attachment to his friends, even after many years of separation.

Few examples can be found in literary history equal to that of Wilson. Though fully aware of the difficulty of the enterprise in which he engaged, his heart never for a moment really failed him. His success was complete, for his work on Birds has secured him immortal honor. We conclude with a quotation from Burns:

* * * * * * * * * * *

Thee, Wilson, Nature's sel shall mourn
By wood and wild,
Where, haply, pity strays forlorn,
Frae man exil'd.
Mourn, ye wee songsters o' the wood;
Ye groups that crop the heather bud;
Ye curlews calling thro' a clud;
Ye whistling plover;
And mourn, ye whirring paitrick brood;
He's gane for ever!
Mourn, clam'ring craiks at close o' day,
'Mang fields o' flow'ring clover gay;
And when ye wing your annual way
Frae our cauld shore,
Tell thae far warls, wha lies in clay,
Wham we deplore.

THE BLUE-BIRD

FROM THE AMERICAN ORNITHOLOGY. [1]

THE pleasing manners and sociable disposition of this little bird entitle him to particular notice. As one of the first messengers of spring, bringing the charming tidings to our very doors, he bears his own recommendation always along with him, and meets with a hearty welcome from every body.

Though generally accounted a bird of passage, yet so early as the middle of February, if the weather be open, he usually makes his appearance about his old haunts, the barn, orchard and fence-posts. Storms and deep snows sometimes succeeding, he disappears for a time; but about the middle of March is again seen, accompanied by his mate, visiting the box in the garden, or the hole in the old apple-tree, the cradle of some generations of his ancestors. "When he first begins his amours," says a curious and correct observer, "it is pleasing to behold his courtship, his solicitude to please and to secure the favor of his beloved female. He uses the tenderest expressions, sits close by her, caresses and sings to her his most endearing warblings. When seated together, if he espies an insect delicious to her taste, he takes it up, flies with it to her, spreads his wing over her and puts it in her mouth." If a rival makes his appearance, (for they are ardent in their loves,) he quits her in a moment, attacks and pursues the intruder, as he shifts from place to place, in tones that bespeak the jealousy of his affection, conducts him with many reproofs beyond the extremities of his territory, and returns to warble out his transports of triumph beside his beloved mate. The preliminaries being thus settled, and the spot fixed on, they begin to clean out the old nest, and the rubbish of the former year, and to prepare for the reception of their future offspring. Soon after this another sociable little pilgrim (*Motacilla domestica*, House Wren), also arrives from the south, and finding such a snug birth pre-occupied, shows his spite, by watching a convenient opportunity, and in the absence of the owner popping in and pulling out sticks; but takes special care to make off as fast as possible.

The female lays five, and sometimes six, eggs, of a pale blue color; and raises two, and sometimes three broods in a season; the male taking the youngest under his particular care while the female is again sitting. Their principal food are insects, particularly large beetles, and others of the coleopterous kinds that lurk among old dead and decaying trees. Spiders are also a favorite repast with them. In fall they occasionally regale themselves on the berries of the sour gum; and as winter approaches, on those of the red cedar, and on the fruit of a rough hairy vine that runs up and cleaves fast to the trunks of trees. Ripe persimmons is another of their favorite dishes; and many other fruits and seeds which I have found in their stomachs at that season, which, being no botanist, I am unable to particularize. They are frequently pestered with a species of tape-worm, some of which I have taken from their intestines of an extraordinary size, and in some cases in great numbers. Most other birds are also plagued with these vermin; but the Blue-bird seems more subject to them than any I know, except the Wood-cock. An account of the different species of vermin, many of which I doubt not are non-descripts, that infest the plumage and intestines of our birds, would of itself form an interesting publication; but as this belongs more properly to the entomologist, I shall only, in the course of this work, take notice of some of the most remarkable; and occasionally represent them in the same plate with those birds on which they are usually found.

The usual spring and summer song of the Blue-bird is a soft, agreable and oft-repeated warble, uttered with open quivering wings, and is extremely pleasing. In his motions and general character he has great resemblance to the Robin Red-breast of Britain; and had he the brown olive of that bird, instead of his own blue, could scarcely be distinguished from him. Like him he is known to almost every child; and shows as much confidence in man by associating with him in summer, as the other by his familiarity in winter. He is also of a mild and peaceful disposition, seldom fighting or quarrelling with other birds. His society is courted by the inhabitants of the country, and few farmers neglect to provide for him, in some suitable place, a snug little summer house, ready fitted and rent-free. For this he more than sufficiently repays them by the cheerfulness of his song, and the multitude of injurious insects which he daily destroys. Towards fall, that is the month of October, his song changes to a single plaintive note, as he passes over the yellow, many colored woods; and his melancholy air recalls to our minds the approaching decay of the face of nature. Even after the trees are stript of their leaves, he still lingers over his native fields, as if loth to leave them. About the middle or end of November few or none of them are seen; but with every return of mild and open weather we hear his plaintive note amidst the fields, or in the air, seeming to deplore the devastations of winter. Indeed, he appears scarcely ever totally to forsake us; but to follow fair weather through all its journeyings till the return of spring.

Such are the mild and pleasing manners of the Blue-bird, and so universally is he esteemed, that I have often regretted that no pastoral muse has yet arisen in this western woody world, to do justice to his name, and endear him to us still more by the tenderness of verse, as has been done to his representative in Britain, the Robin Red-breast. A small acknowledgment of this kind I have to offer, which the reader I hope will excuse as a tribute to rural innocence.

When winter's cold tempests and snows are no more,
Green meadows and brown furrow'd fields re-appearing,
The fishermen hauling their shad to the shore,
And cloud-cleaving geese to the Lakes are a-steering;
When first the lone butterfly flits on the wing;
When red glow the maples, so fresh and so pleasing,
O then comes the Blue-bird, the HERALD OF SPRING!
And hails with his warblings the charms of the season.

Then loud piping frogs make the marshes to ring;
Then warm glows the sunshine, and fine is the weather;
The blue woodland flowers just beginning to spring,
And, spicewood and sassafras budding together:
O then to your gardens ye housewives repair!
Your walks border up ; sow and plant at your leisure ;
The Blue-bird will chant from his box such an air,
That all your hard toils will seem truly a pleasure.

He flits through the orchard, he visits each tree,
The red flowering peach and the apple's sweet blossoms;
He snaps up *destroyers* wherever they be,
And seizes the caitiffs that lurk in their bosoms;
He drags the vile *grub* from the corn he devours;
The worms from their webs where they riot and welter ;
His song and his services freely are ours,
And all that he asks is, in summer a shelter.

The ploughman is pleased when he gleams in his train,
Now searching the furrows—now mounting to cheer him ;
The gardener delights in his sweet simple strain,
And leans on his spade to survey and to hear him ;
The slow ling'ring schoolboys forget they'll be chid,
While gazing intent as he warbles before 'em
In mantle of sky-blue, and bosom so red,
That each little loiterer seems to adore him.

When all the gay scenes of the summer are o'er,
And autumn slow enters so silent and sallow,
And millions of warblers, that charmed us before,
Have fled in the train of the sun-seeking swallow;
The Blue-bird, forsaken, yet true to his home,
Still lingers, and looks for a milder to-morrow,
Till forced by the horrors of winter to roam,
He sings his adieu in a lone note of sorrow.

While spring's lovely season, serene, dewy, warm,
The green face of earth, and the pure blue of heav'n,
Or love's native music have influence to charm,
Or sympathy's glow to our feelings are giv'n,
Still dear to each bosom the Blue-bird shall be,
His voice, like the thrillings of hope, is a tre'asure;
For, through bleakest storms if a calm he but see,
He comes to remind us of sunshine and pleasure!

The Blue-bird, in summer and fall, is fond of frequenting open pasture fields; and there perching on the stalks of the great *mullein*, to look out for passing insects. A whole family of them are often seen, thus situated, as if receiving lessons of dexterity from their more expert parents, who can espy a beetle crawling among the grass, at a considerable distance ; and after feeding on it, instantly resume their former position. But whoever informed Dr. Latham that "this bird is never seen on trees, though it makes its nest in the holes of them !" might as well have said, that the Americans are never seen in the streets, though they build their houses by the sides of them. For what is there in the construction of the feet and claws of this bird to prevent it from perching? Or what sight more common to an inhabitant of this country than the Blue-bird perched on the top of a peach or apple-tree ; or among the branches of those reverend broadarmed chestnut trees, that stand alone in the middle of our fields, bleached by the rains and blasts of ages?

The blue-bird is six inches and three quarters in length, the wings remarkably full and broad ; the whole upper parts are of a rich sky blue, with purple reflections ; the bill and legs are black ; inside the mouth and soles of the feet yellow, resembling the color of a ripe persimmon ; the shafts of all the wing and tail feathers are black ; throat, neck, breast, and sides partially under the wings, chestnut ; wings dusky black at the tips ; belly and vent white ; sometimes the secondaries are

exteriorly light brown, but the bird has in that case not arrived at his full color. The female is easily distinguished by the duller cast of the back, the plumage of which is skirted with light brown, and by the red on the breast being much fainter, and not descending near so low as in the male ; the secondaries are also more dusky. This species is found over the whole United States ; in the Bahama islands where many of them winter; as also in Mexico, Brazil, and Guiana.

Mr. Edwards mentions that the specimen of this bird which he was favored with, was sent from the Bermudas ; and as these islands abound with the cedar, it is highly probable that many of those birds pass from our continent thence, at the commencement of winter, to enjoy the mildness of that climate as well as their favorite food.

As the Blue-bird is so regularly seen in winter, after the continuance of a few days of mild and open weather, it has given rise to various conjectures as to the place of his retreat. Some supposing it to be in close sheltered thickets, lying to the sun ; others the neighborhood of the sea, where the air is supposed to be more temperate, and where the matters thrown up by the waves furnish him with a constant and plentiful supply of food. Others trace him to the dark recesses of hollow trees, and subterraneous caverns, where they suppose he dozes away the winter, making, like Robinson Crusoe, occasional reconnoitring excursions from his castle, whenever the weather happens to be favorable. But amidst the snows and severities of winter I have sought for him in vain in the most favorable sheltered situations of the middle states ; and not only in the neighborhood of the sea, but on both sides of the mountains. I have never, indeed, explored the depths of caverns in search of him, because I would as soon expect to meet with tulips and butterflies there, as Blue-birds, but among hundreds of woodmen, who have cut down trees of all sorts, and at all seasons, I have never heard one instance of these birds being found so immured in winter; while in the whole of the middle and eastern states, the same general observation seems to prevail that the Blue-bird always makes his appearance in winter after a few days of mild and open weather. On the other hand, I have myself found them numerous in the woods of North and South Carolina, in the depth of winter, and I have also been assured by different gentlemen of respectability, who have resided in the islands of Jamaica, Cuba, and the Bahamas and Bermudas, that this very bird is common there in winter. We also find, from the works of Hernandes Piso and others, that it is well known in Mexico, Guiana and Brazil ; and if so, the place of its winter retreat is easily ascertained, without having recourse to all the trumpery of holes and caverns, torpidity, hybernation, and such ridiculous improbabilities.

Nothing is more common in Pennsylvania than to see large flocks of these birds in spring and fall, passing, at considerable heights in the air; from the south in the former, and from the north in the latter season. I have seen, in the month of October, about an hour after sun-rise, ten or fifteen of them descend from a great height and settle on the top of a tall detached tree, appearing, from their silence and sedateness, to be strangers, and fatigued. After a pause of a few minutes they began to dress and arrange their plumage, and continued so employed for ten or fifteen minutes more; then, on a few warning notes being given, perhaps by the leader of the party, the whole remounted to a vast height, steering in a direct line for the southwest. In passing along the chain of the Bahamas towards the West Indies, no great difficulty can occur from the frequency of these islands; nor even to the Bermudas, which are said to be 600 miles from the nearest part of the continent. This may seem an extraordinary flight for so small a bird; but it is nevertheless a fact that it is performed. If we suppose the Blue-bird in this case to fly only at the rate of a mile per minute, which is less than I have actually ascertained him to do over land, ten or eleven hours would be sufficient to accomplish the journey; besides the chances he would have of resting places by the way, from the number of vessels that generally navigate those seas. In like manner, two days at most, allowing for numerous stages for rest, would conduct him from the remotest regions of Mexico to any part of the Atlantic states. When the natural history of that part of the continent and its adjacent isles, are but known, and the periods at which its birds of passage arrive and depart, are truly ascertained, I have no doubt but these suppositions will be fully corroborated.

THE BALD EAGLE,
FROM THE SAME.

THIS bird has been long known to naturalists, being common to both continents; and occasionally met with from a very high northern latitude, to the borders of the torrid zone, but chiefly in the vicinity of the sea and along the shores and cliffs of our lakes and large rivers. Formed by nature for braving the severest cold; feeding equally on the produce of the sea, and of the land; possessing powers of flight, capable of outstripping even the tempests themselves; unawed by anything but man, and, from the ethereal heights to which he soars, looking abroad at one glance, on an immeasurable expanse of forests, fields, lakes and ocean, deep below him; he appears indifferent to the little localities of change of seasons; as, in a few minutes he can pass from summer to winter, from the lower to the higher regions of the atmosphere, the abode of eternal cold; and thence descend at will to the torrid or the arctic regions of the earth. He is therefore found at all seasons in the countries he inhabits; but prefers such places as have been mentioned above, from the great partiality he has for fish.

In procuring these he displays, in a very singular manner, the genius and energy of his character, which is fierce, contemplative, daring and tyranni-

cal; attributes not exerted but on particular occasions; but, when put forth, overwhelming all opposition. Elevated on a high dead limb of some gigantic tree, that commands a wide view of the neighboring shore and ocean, he seems calmly to contemplate the motions of the various feathered tribes that pursue their busy avocations below: the snow-white Gulls, slowly winnowing the air; the busy Tringæ, coursing along the sands; trains of Ducks, streaming over the surface; silent and watchful Cranes, intent and wading; clamorous crows, and all the winged multitudes that subsist by the bounty of this vast liquid magazine of nature. High over all these hovers one, whose action instantly arrests all his attention. By his wide curvature of wing, and sudden suspension in air, he knows him to be the *Fish-Hawk*, settling over some devoted victim of the deep. His eye kindles at the sight, and balancing himself, with half-opened wings, on the branch, he watches the result. Down, rapid as an arrow from heaven, descends the distant object of his attention, the roar of its wings reaching the ear as it disappears in the deep, making the surges foam around! At this moment the looks of the Eagle are all ardor; and, levelling his neck for flight, he sees the Fish-Hawk once more emerge, struggling with his prey, and mounting in the air with screams of exultation. These are the signal for our hero, who, launching into the air, instantly gives chase, soon gains on the Fish-Hawk. Each exerts his utmost to mount above the other, displaying, in these rencounters, the most elegant and sublime aerial evolutions. The unencumbered Eagle rapidly advances, and is just on the point of reaching his opponent, when, with a sudden scream, probably of despair and honest execration, the latter drops his fish; the Eagle, poising himself for a moment as if to take a more certain aim, descends like a whirlwind, snatches it in his grasp ere it reaches the water, and bears his ill-gotten booty silently away to the woods.

These predatory attacks. and defensive manœuvres, of the Eagle and the Fish-Hawk, are matters of daily observation along the whole of our sea-coast, from Florida to New England; and frequently excite great interest in the spectators. Sympathy, however, on this, as on most other occasions, generally sides with the honest and laborious sufferer, in opposition to the attacks of power, injustice and rapacity; qualities for which our hero is so generally notorious, and which, in his superior *man*, are certainly detestable. As for the feelings of the poor fish, they seem altogether out of the question.

When driven, as he sometimes is, by the combined courage and perseverance of the Fish-Hawks from their neighborhood, and forced to hunt for himself, he retires more inland, in search of young pigs, of which he destroys great numbers. In the lower parts of Virginia and North Carolina, where the inhabitants raise vast herds of those animals, complaints of this kind are very general against him. He also destroys young lambs in the early part of spring; and will sometimes attack old sickly sheep, aiming furiously at their eyes.

BENJAMIN SILLIMAN.

[Born 1779. Died 1864.]

PROFESSOR BENJAMIN SILLIMAN, the son of G. S. Silliman, a lawyer of distinction, and a Revolutionary patriot and soldier, was born in North Stratford, now Trumbull, Conn., August 8, 1779. He entered Yale College, in 1791, and graduated in 1796; for a time he studied the law; in 1799 he was appointed a tutor in the College; and has since been prominent in its faculty—his professorship of Chemistry, Mineralogy, and Geology, dating from 1804. He devoted himself to these sciences at the suggestion of President Dwight; studied some time in New Haven; spent two seasons in Philadelphia; and perfected himself in Edinburgh and London, where he purchased scientific books and apparatus for the college. He had given a partial course of lectures before he went abroad, and gave his first full course in Yale, in 1806-7. In 1810 he published his Journal of Travels in England, Holland, and Scotland, and two passages on the Atlantic, which was received with great favor, and passed through several editions. It was one of the first of which an account was published, in the United States. Nearly fifty years later he crossed the Atlantic again, and has contrasted his observations after this interval in the two volumes which he published in 1853, with the title, A Visit to Europe in 1851. Another record of his travels, is Remarks made in a short tour between Hartford and Quebec, in the autumn of 1819. Uniting mineralogy and geology to chemistry, he made a geological survey of Connecticut; observed the fall of a meteorite; constructed, with the aid of Professor Hare, a compound blowpipe, and repeated the experiments of Sir Humphry Davy. In the course of his college engagement, he has published Elements of Chemistry in the order of the lectures in Yale College, in 1830; and has edited Henry's Chemistry, and Bakewell's Geology. His lectures on Chemistry, to which the public have been admitted, at Yale, and which he has delivered in the chief cities of the country, have gained him much reputation, which has been extended at home and abroad by his able editorship of the American Journal of Science, of which he commenced the publication in 1818.

This important journal was commenced in July, 1818, and was sustained for many years at the private expense of Prof. Silliman. In April, 1838, Benj. Silliman, Jr., became associate editor. The first series of the Journal was completed in 1846, in 50 vols., the last one being a full Index to the others. A second series followed with Prof. Jas. D. Dana, as associate editor, with whom others have since been connected.

This Journal is well known and appreciated throughout the learned world, and has become a very extensive repository of the scientific labors of our countrymen, and will ever remain a permanent monument of the editor's zeal and perseverance in his studies.

In 1853, Prof. Silliman resigned his office as a Professor in Yale College, on account of growing infirmities of age, and was complimented with the title of "Professor Emeritus." He was succeeded in the Department of Geology by Prof. Jas. D. Dana, and in that of Chemistry, by his son, B. Silliman, Jr., who has proved himself a worthy successor of his father, not only as a Professor, but as a scientific man and author. He has published, First Principles of Chemistry; and First Principles of Physics or Natural Philosophy; both of which have been largely introduced as Text Books.

Prof. Silliman, who had been for nearly three-quarters of a century identified with the history and progress of Yale College, died at his residence, in New Haven, on the morning of a National Thanksgiving, Nov. 24, 1864. Though far advanced in life, dying at the age of 85, time had laid its hand gently upon him; his form was erect, and his faculties were unimpaired to the last, adding a new instance to the many recorded of the genial old age of naturalists and men of science, and the favorable influence on mind and body of their pursuits. His integrity and amiability gained him the universal respect of his friends and associates, as his services to the cause of science, made his name regarded with interest throughout the world.

EXCURSION TO MONT BLANC.

FROM A VISIT TO EUROPE IN 1851.

MONTAGNE VERT AND THE MER DE GLACE.
—In reference to this ascent. we secured the two
guides esteemed the best in Chamouni—Auguste
Balmat and David Coutet—the same that have
been already alluded to. We were early on our
saddles, upon strong mules, but not with decrepit
horse furniture, as in some former mountain journeys; all was now so strong and good as to command our confidence. The guides went on foot.
The ladies were furnished with fortified saddles
to guard against falling off, and they had each
an extra attendant walking by the side of the
mule.

This mountain is very steep, and rocky; it is
exceedingly encumbered with its own immense
ruins, which, in the course of ages, have rolled
down from its summit and lodged either at its
base or on its flanks. There are piles on piles of
rocks, and some of them are of great dimensions;
among which, to clear even a mule path has evidently been a work of great labor and difficulty.
The zigzag ascent winds around turns, which are
very abrupt and frequent. They often pass along
the edge of fearful precipices, where a false step
would send the mule and the rider to destruction.
It often seems as if the apparently perverse, but
really skilful little animal, was about to walk deliberately off, as, in order that his feet may find
their proper position, his head and neck are projected beyond the road, and overhang the precipice.
But do not interfere with the nice balancing of
your mule; he knows better than you can instruct
him how to proceed, and has not the least inclination to roll down the mountain, although the
wrong pulling up of a rein, or the sudden change
of position of a heavy man on the saddle, may
force him and yourself to that result. Trust a
good Providence, and the mule, as the instrument, and you will pass safely along the mountain
steeps.

The ascent occupied two hours and a half, when
we arrived at the hotel near the top of the mountain, which falls but a few hundred feet short of
being as high as Mount Washington in New
Hampshire. We found that several strangers had
already arrived, like us, to see the glacier; our position enabled us to look down upon the Mer de
Glace, and, being furnished each with an alpenstock, we cautiously descended the bank of the
mountain, which inclines with a gentle slope down
to the sea of ice.

THE MER DE GLACE.—We were again favored
by fine weather, and the sun shone bright. In a
rain, it would be dangerous to walk on the slippery
ice, and in a fog or snow-storm (for on the high
Alps snow-storms occur in all the months of the
year) in such circumstances the adventurer would
be in constant danger of falling into the yawning
crevasses.

Arrived upon its immense and cold bosom, we
looked eagerly around, and saw that it was indeed
a sea of ice; or rather, it is like a great river suddenly congealed in the midst of a tempest. By
a little practice with our poles pointed with iron,
we acquired confidence, and made excursions in
various directions. This glacier is, indeed, a wonder. From the mountain top it descends more
than 20 miles, and has an extent, as our guides
assured us, of more than 50, if all the ramifica-
tions are included; it reaches quite down into the
valley of Chamouni. The breadth of this glacier,
in that portion which was under our immediate
inspection, is from half a mile to a mile. It is, at
present, much divided by cross fissures or crevasses,
which grow more numerous as the season advances. The glacier, by moving downward, at the
rate of more than a foot in a day, is impeded by
the rocky bottom, and as the ice, thus hooked and
grappled by the pointed rocks, hangs there in opposition to gravity, which is constantly urging the
mass downward, it cracks, forming those open fissures which the French call crevasses. An intelligible description of a glacier is not an easy
thing. It is not, as one might suppose, a smooth
glassy surface, like that on a quiet, congealed lake;
possibly in the very elevated regions it may have
that appearance, but in these lower regions it is a
continuous series of masses connected, indeed, below, but so separated above by the fissures, that
the portions appear like vast white rocks—white
originally, but the fine fragments and dust of the
granite and other rocks, disintegrated by the
weather on the exposed cliffs, and blown down
upon the surface of the glaciers, gives them that
soiled and dingy aspect which they present. It
has often been remarked by those who have examined the glaciers, that rocks and stones, falling
upon them, are buried in the falling snows of the
higher regions, and by the melting and freezing
of the snow, they become eventually buried in solid
ice. In the progress of years, and in the succession of summers, as the glacier advances downward,
bearing along these rocks and stones, they are disclosed by the melting of their covering, and thus
they come into view as if they had actually risen.
Sometimes they so effectually cover and protect
the ice on which they lie, that it does not sensibly
melt beneath them, while the general surface all
around is lowered by the melting, and thus it happens that a rock may stand on a pedestal of ice sometimes several feet or yards above the general level
—and many such rocks may be in view at once,
but eventually the pedestals give way, and the elevated rocks fall to the common level.

The fissures and crevasses are so numerous and
deep, and their edges are so slippery, that great
care is requisite at all times to avoid falling into
them; when they are concealed by snow, arched
over them, the danger becomes imminent, and in
such cases the cautious guides try the soundness of
the footing by applying the iron-pointed alpenstock.
The sides of the crevasses are of a splendid blue-
green color, and the ice often contains pools of pel-
lucid water; the more superficial cavities or little
lakes, accessible without danger, and the water, from
its purity and coldness, is very refreshing to the
traveller. Rills of water, coursing over the surface

74

plunge into the crevasses and are lost, all but the musical murmur of their fall.

Even the masses, which externally are soiled and dirty, on being broken exhibit pure and transparent ice, looking like the most perfect rock crystal. Every morning the hotels are supplied by resorting to the lower end of the glaciers. They need wish for nothing purer; and thus they have an unfailing supply from these great natural icehouses—sources which are perennial and inexhaustible.

The first appearance of the glaciers is like that of a fearfully agitated ocean, tossed by violent, and conflicting, and eddying winds, congealed ere the billows have had time to subside, and thus preserving all its high ridges, its peaks, and deep hollows. Still, there is a degree of regularity in the confusion: the tumult has observed a law which has opened the fissures, in curves, parallel, and nearly at right angles to the rocky banks, the convexity being downwards from its source.

MORAINES.—This is the name given of old to the piles of rocks, and stones, and ruins which are crowded along the sides of the glaciers, forming *lateral* moraines; and the name includes also those still more considerable piles that are both borne along by the glacier and pushed before it in its descending course, forming *terminal* moraines. From our present point of view, we could see only the lateral moraines of the Mer da Glace; the terminal we reserved for another occasion. The lateral accumulations are here very great; they form a high and rough border of granite rocks, which are, in some instances, very large; and as they often lie high above the glacier, forming a train along the naked rocky sides, they prove that the glacier has been anciently much thicker, and has descended at a higher elevation.

ROCKS BORNE ALONG on the surface of the glacier are very numerous, and, like those arranged along the sides, they are granite, often in enormous blocks. They either lie upon the glacier, or repose in its crevasses, or are frozen into it in mass; and as they move downward, with a progress slow indeed, but sure, they will eventually find their place in the lower country, or they will be piled up along the sides in lateral moraines.

The theory of glaciers cannot be adequately discussed in these rapid popular remarks; but the writings of Agassiz, Charpentier, Forbes of Edinburgh, Guyot, and other eminent Alpine travellers and writers, afford ample information. The transportation of rocks by glaciers to great distances is a fact fully established. The rocks have fallen from the higher cliffs, and have been borne along downward. The masses of rocks and stones that are pressed beneath the glacier during the season of its motion, in the summer, or between it and the lateral walls, produce those furrows, scratches, and grooves, and those polished surfaces, which are observed in all the countries where glaciers exist, and often also where they are not found at the present day. The erratic rocks, called boulders, have often the same origin as those on the back of the great and little Salève, near Geneva.

Floating icebergs have also been efficient in the transportation of the erratics. This necessarily implies submergence of the countries over which the bergs have passed; just as they are, in fact, floated in the present era from the polar regions of both hemispheres; and, therefore, we must admit the existence of elevated ice-bound cliffs to form the icebergs, and to afford masses of rock.

Currents and deluges of water, especially when favored by gravity, may have been, to a certain extent, auxiliary to the movement of rocks; but they are not of themselves competent to place the boulders where we often find them, perched high on mountain tops, or reclining on their declivities; and often the boulders, as we have recently seen on the Salève, are not only of an entirely different nature from the mountain on which they lie, but they offer no proof of friction, their sharp and angular outline being still well defined.

"A glacier," says Professor Forbes, " is an endless scroll—a stream of time, upon whose stainless ground is engraven the succession of events, whose dates far transcend the memory of living man.

"At the usual rate of descent, a rock which fell upon a high glacier 200 years ago, may only just now have reached its final resting-place in the lower country; and a block larger than the largest of Egyptian obelisks may occupy the time of six generations of men in its descent, before it is laid low in the common grave of its predecessors."

The glaciers often terminate so abruptly that corn has been seen to grow next to the glacier, and the inhabitants have gathered ripe cherries, while standing with one foot on the tree and the other on the glacier.

THE SCENERY AROUND THE MER DE GLACE.—The aspect of the mountains here is very sublime. Far, very far above the observer, the snowy ridges, peaks and domes rise in solemn grandeur, mantled with ever-during ice. Before and around the observer are the naked Aiguilles, needle-shaped mountains, composed of rocks whose sides are so steep that snow will not lie upon them. They are rude, acute cones, sometimes solitary and again grouped, rising many thousand feet above the Mer de Glace, and so very precipitous that they cannot be climbed. Only birds of the most powerful wing can scale their walls, or gain their summit. The Aiguille de Dru is the most remarkable. It rose before us to-day in solitary grandeur. It is exceedingly acute, is very high, perhaps 6000 feet, above the glacier, and is garnished with many subordinate bristling points, which appear like delicate Gothic turrets, or minarets of Saracenic architecture.

One of our party remarked, that the Val del Bove was here repeated, although on a greatly diminished scale; instead, however, of an amphitheatre of lava it was an amphitheatre of ice, piled up in the same wild confusion. The immense mountains of snow above, the rocky walls of the yawning gulf, and the groups of Aiguilles, included an amphitheatrical area, depressed thousands of feet, like the volcanic floor of the Val del Bove, and, like that, having a still lower outlet of communication with the nether world.

GEORGE TICKNOR.

[Born 1791.]

GEORGE TICKNOR was born in Boston, August 1, 1791, and graduated at Dartmouth College at sixteen. He occupied himself the next three years in Boston with a diligent study of the ancient classics, when he engaged in the study of the law, and was admitted to the bar in 1813. The tastes of the scholar, however, prevailed over the practice of the profession, and in 1815, Mr. Ticknor sailed for Europe, to accomplish himself in the thorough course of instruction of a German University. He passed five years in studying the languages and literature of Europe, residing at Gottingen, Paris, Madrid, Lisbon, Rome, and Edinburgh, making the acquaintance of eminent scholars on the Continent and Great Britain, among others of Sir Walter Scott, and Robert Southey, who admired his scholarship, and stock of curious Spanish lore, maintaining afterwards intimate correspondence and association in similar pursuits and scholarship. Scott, whom he visited at Abbotsford in 1819, speaks of Mr. Ticknor in one of his letters, as " a wondrous fellow for romantic lore and antiquarian research."

Mr. Ticknor returned home in 1820, to enter upon the duties of a new Professorship of Modern Languages and Literature, in Harvard University, to which he had been appointed during his absence. Well qualified, he became actively engrossed in its duties, delivering lectures on French and Spanish literature; on particular authors, as Dante and Gœthe; on the English poets, and other kindred topics. Mr. Prescott says, " The influence of this instruction was soon visible in the higher education as well as the literary ardor shown by the graduates. So decided was the impulse thus given to the popular sentiment, that considerable apprehension was felt, lest modern literature was to receive a disproportionate share of attention in the scheme of collegiate education."

After fifteen years passed in these liberal duties at Harvard, Mr. Ticknor, in 1835, resigned his professorship, and with his family paid a second visit to Europe. He passed three years in England and on the Continent; collecting books on Spanish literature. In 1840, after his return to America, completely armed by his studies in Europe, the mental experience of his previous course of lectures, and with the rich resources of an unexampled collection of Castilian literature in his library, Mr. Ticknor commenced his important work on Spanish literature.

The History of Spanish Literature was published in 1849, in London and New York, in 3 vols., 8vo., uniform with Prescott's Works. It at once arrested the attention of scholars on both sides the Atlantic, and received the highest encomiums from the principal Journals and Reviews of England and the Continent, as a standard contribution to the history of literature. The extent of its research was universally admired, and its style at once modest and dignified, and associated with a sound judgment, followed the subject without prejudice, or those affectations which are the besetting sins of writers on taste. He illustrates the work by the personal history of the authors mentioned, and this again by the history of the times in which they lived. The History was translated into the Spanish and German languages.

Besides this important work, Mr. Ticknor has published, the Remains of Nathaniel Appleton Haven, with a Memoir; and a Life of Lafayette, enlarged from his article in the North American Review, that has passed through several editions, and was translated in France and Germany. He has also written one of the most admirable pieces of biography, a Life of his friend, Wm. H. Prescott; the first edition was published in 1864, sumptuously in 4to., and has passed through several editions in 8vo.

He has written a number of articles for periodicals, and also taken great interest in the cause of education. His noble library, one of the finest in the country, particularly on certain subjects, has always been opened to the scholar in search of anything, which its treasures could impart.

DON QUIXOTE.

FROM HISTORY OF SPANISH LITERATURE.

At the very beginning of his work, Cervantes announces it to be his sole purpose to break down the vogue and authority of books of chivalry, and, at the end of the whole, he declares anew, in his own person, that " he had had no other desire than to render abhorred of men the false and absurd stories contained in books of chivalry ;" exulting in his success, as an achievement of no small moment. And such, in fact, it was; for we have abundant proof that the fanaticism for these romances was so great in Spain, during the sixteenth century, as to have become matter of alarm to the more judicious. At last, they were deemed so noxious, that, in 1553, they were prohibited by law from being printed or sold in the American colonies, and in 1555 the same prohibition, and even the burning of all copies of them extant in Spain itself, was earnestly asked for by the Cortes. The evil, in fact, had become formidable, and the wise began to see it.

To destroy a passion that had struck its roots so deeply in the character of all classes of men, to break up the only reading which at that time could be considered widely popular and fashionable, was certainly a bold undertaking, and one that marks anything rather than a scornful or broken spirit, or a want of faith in what is most to be valued in our common nature. The great wonder is, that Cervantes succeeded. But that he did there is no question. No book of chivalry was written after the appearance of Don Quixote, in 1605; and from the same date, even those already enjoying the greatest favor ceased, with one or two unimportant exceptions, to be reprinted ; so that, from that time to the present, they have been constantly disappearing, until they are now among the rarest of literary curiosities ;—a solitary instance of the power of genius to destroy, by a single well-timed blow, an entire department, and that, too, a flourishing and favored one, in the literature of a great and proud nation.

The general plan Cervantes adopted to accomplish this object, without, perhaps, foreseeing its whole course, and still less all its results, was simple as well as original. In 1605, he published the First Part of Don Quixote, in which a country gentleman of La Mancha—full of genuine Castilian honor and enthusiasm, gentle and dignified in his character, trusted by his friends, and loved by his dependants—is represented as so completely crazed by long reading the most famous books of chivalry, that he believes them to be true, and feels himself called on to become the impossible knight-errant they describe,—nay, actually goes forth into the world to defend the oppressed and avenge the injured, like the heroes of his romances.

To complete his chivalrous equipment,—which he had begun by fitting up for himself a suit of armor strange to his century,—he took an esquire out of his neighborhood ; a middle-aged peasant, ignorant and credulous to excess, but of great good-nature; a glutton and a liar; selfish and gross, yet attached to his master ; shrewd enough occasionally to see the folly of their position, but always amusing, and sometimes mischievous, in his interpretations of it. These two sally forth from their native village in search of adventures, of which the excited imagination of the knight, turning windmills into giants, solitary inns into castles, and galley-slaves into oppressed gentlemen, finds abundance wherever he goes ; while the esquire translates them all into the plain prose of truth with an admirable simplicity, quite unconscious of its own humor, and rendered the more striking by its contrast with the lofty and courteous dignity and magnificent illusions of the superior personage. There could, of course, be but one consistent termination of adventures like these. The knight and his esquire suffer a series of ridiculous discomfitures, and are at last brought home, like madmen, to their native village, where Cervantes leaves them, with an intimation that the story of their adventures is by no means ended.

*   *   *   *   *   *

The latter half of Don Quixote is a contradiction of the proverb Cervantes cites in it,—that several parts were never yet good for much. It is, in fact, better than the first. It shows more freedom and vigor ; and, if the carricature is sometimes pushed to the very verge of what is permitted, the invention, the style of thought, and, indeed, the materials throughout, are richer, and the finish is more exact. The character of Samson Carrasco, for instance, is a very happy, though somewhat bold, addition to the original persons of the drama ; and the adventures at the castle of the Duke and Duchess, where Don Quixote is fooled to the top of his bent ; the managements of Sancho as governor of his island ; the visions and dreams of the cave of Montesinos ; the scenes with Roque Guinart, the freebooter, and with Gines de Passamonte, the galley-slave and puppet-show man ; together with the mock-heroic hospitalities of Don Antonio Moreno at Barcelona, and the final defeat of the knight there, are all admirable. In truth, every thing in this Second Part, especially its general outline and tone, show that time and a degree of success he had not before known had ripened and perfected the strong manly sense and sure insight into human nature which are visible everywhere in the works of Cervantes, and which here become a part, as it were, of his peculiar genius, whose foundations had been laid, dark and deep, amidst the trials and sufferings of his various life.

But throughout both parts, Cervantes shows the impulses and instincts of an original power with most distinctness in his development of the characters of Don Quixote and Sancho ; characters in whose contrast and opposition is hidden the full spirit of his peculiar humor, and no small part of what is most characteristic of the entire fiction. They are his prominent personages. He delights, therefore, to have them as much as possible in the front of his scene. They grow visibly upon his favor as he advances, and the fondness of his liking for them makes him constantly produce them in lights and relations as little foreseen by himself as they are by his readers. The knight, who seems to have been originally intended for a parody of the Amadis, becomes gradually a detached, separate, and wholly independent personage, into whom is infused so much of a generous and elevated nature, such gentleness and delicacy, such a pure sense of honor, and such a warm love for whatever is noble and good, that we feel almost the same attachment to him that the barber and the curate did, and are almost as ready as his family was to mourn over his death.

The case of Sancho is again very similar, and perhaps in some respects stronger. At first, he is introduced as the opposite of Don Quixote, and used merely to bring out his master's peculiarities in a more striking relief. It is not until we have gone through nearly half of the First Part that he utters one of those proverbs which form afterwards the staple of his conversation and humor; and it is not till the opening of the Second Part, and, indeed, not till he comes forth, in all his mingled shrewdness and credulity, as governor of Barataria, that his character is quite developed and completed to the full measure of its grotesque, yet congruous, proportions.

Cervantes, in truth, came, at last, to love these creations of his marvellous power, as if they were real, familiar personages, and to speak of them and treat them with an earnestness and interest that tend much to the illusion of his readers. Both Don Quixote and Sancho are thus brought before us, like such living realities, that, at this moment, the figures of the crazed, gaunt, dignified knight and of his round, selfish, and most amusing esquire dwell bodied forth in the imaginations of more, among all conditions of men throughout Christendom, than any other of the creations of human talent.

PRESCOTT'S METHOD OF LIVING.

FROM THE SAME.

That Mr. Prescott, under his disheartening infirmities,—I refer not only to his imperfect sight, but to the rheumatism from which he was seldom wholly free,—should, at the age of five-and-twenty or thirty, with no help but this simple apparatus, have aspired to the character of an historian dealing with events that happened in times and countries far distant from his own, and that are recorded chiefly in foreign languages and by authors whose conflicting testimony was often to be reconciled by laborious comparison, is a remarkable fact in literary history. It is a problem the solution of which was, I believe, never before undertaken; certainly never before accomplished. Nor do I conceive that he himself could have accomplished it, unless to his uncommon intellectual gifts had been added great animal spirits, a strong, persistent will, and a moral courage which was to be daunted by no obstacle that he might deem it possible to remove by almost any amount of effort.

That he was not insensible to the difficulties of his undertaking, we have partly seen, as we have witnessed how his hopes fluctuated while he was struggling through the arrangements for beginning to write his "Ferdinand and Isabella," and, in fact, during the whole period of its composition. But he showed the same character, the same fertility of resource, every day of his life, and provided, both by forecast and self-sacrifice, against the embarrassments of his condition as they successively presented themselves.

The first thing to be done, and the thing always to be repeated day by day, was to strengthen, as much as possible, what remained of his sight, and at any rate, to do nothing that should tend to exhaust its impaired powers. In 1821, when he was still not without some hope of its recovery, he made this memorandum. "I will make it my principal purpose to restore my eye to its primitive vigor, and will do nothing habitually that can seriously injure it." To this end he regulated his life with an exactness that I have never known equalled. Especially in whatever related to the daily distribution of his time, whether in regard to his intellectual labors, to his social enjoyments, or to the care of his physical powers, including his diet, he was severely exact,—managing himself, indeed, in this last respect, under the general directions of his wise medical adviser, Dr. Jackson, but carrying out these directions with an ingenuity and fidelity all his own.

He was an early riser, although it was a great effort for him to be such. From boyhood it seemed to be contrary to his nature to get up betimes in the morning. He was, therefore, always awaked, and after silently, and sometimes slowly and with reluctance, counting twenty, so as fairly to arouse himself, he resolutely sprang out of bed; or, if he failed, he paid a forfeit, as a memento of his weakness, to the servant who knocked at his chamber-door. His failures, however, were rare. When he was called, he was told the state of the weather and of the thermometer. This was important, as he was compelled by his rheumatism—almost always present, and, when not so, always apprehended—to regulate his dress with care; and, finding it difficult to do so in any other way, he caused each of its heavier external portions to be marked by his tailor with the number of ounces it weighed, and then put them on according to the temperature, sure that their weight would indicate the measure of warmth and protection they would afford.

As soon as he was dressed, he took his early exercise in the open air. This, for many years, was done on horseback, and, as he loved a spirited horse and was often thinking more of his intellectual pursuits than of anything else while he was riding, he sometimes caught a fall. But he was a good rider, and was sorry to give up this form of exercise and resort to walking or driving, as he did, by order of his physician, in the last dozen years of his life. No weather, except a severe storm, prevented him at any period from thus, as he called it, "winding himself up." Even in the coldest of our very cold winter mornings, it was his habit, so long as he could ride, to see the sun rise on a particular spot three or four miles from town. In a letter to Mrs. Ticknor, who was then in Germany, dated March, 1836,—at the end of a winter memorable for its extreme severity,—he says, " You will give me credit for some spunk when I tell you that I have not been frightened by the cold a single morning from a ride on horseback to Jamaica Plain and back again before breakfast. My mark has been to see the sun rise by Mr. Greene's school, if you remember where that is." When the rides here referred to were taken, the thermometer was often below zero of Fahrenheit.

On his return home, after adjusting his dress anew, with reference to the temperature within doors, he sat down, almost always in a very gay humor, to a moderate and even spare breakfast,— a meal he much liked, because, as he said, he could then have his family with him in a quiet way, and so begin the day happily. From the breakfast-table he went at once to his study. There, while busied with what remained of his toilet, or with the needful arrangements for his regular occupations, Mrs. Prescott read to him, generally from the morning papers, but sometimes from the current literature of the day. At a fixed hour— seldom later than ten—his reader, or secretary, came. In this, as in everything, he required punctuality; but he noted tardiness only by looking significantly at his watch; for it is the testimony of all his surviving secretaries, that he never spoke a severe word to either of them in the many years of their familiar intercourse.

When they had met in the study, there was no thought but of active work for about three hours. His infirmities, however, were always present to warn him how cautiously it must be done, and he was extremely ingenious in the means he devised for doing it without increasing them. The shades and shutters for regulating the exact amount of light which should be admitted; his own position relatively to its direct rays, and to those that were reflected from surrounding objects; the adaptation of his dress and of the temperature of the room to his rheumatic affections; and the different contrivances for taking notes from the books that were read to him, and for impressing on his memory, with the least possible use of his sight, such portions of each as were needful for his immediate purpose,—were all of them the result of painstaking experiments, skilfully and patiently made. But their ingenuity and adaptation were less remarkable than the conscientious consistency with which they were employed for forty years.

He never liked to work more than three hours consecutively. At one o'clock, therefore, he took a walk of about two miles, and attended to any little business abroad that was incumbent on him, coming home generally refreshed and exhilarated, and ready to lounge a little and gossip. Dinner followed, for the greater part of his life about three o'clock, although, during a few years, he dined in winter at five or six, which he preferred, and which he gave up only because his health demanded the change. In the summer he always dined early, so as to have the late afternoon for driving and exercise during our hot season.

He enjoyed the pleasures of the table, and even its luxuries, more than most men. But be restricted himself carefully in the use of them, adjusting everything with reference to its effect on the power of using his eye immediately afterwards, and especially on his power of using it the next day. Occasional indulgence when dining out or with friends at home he found useful, or at least not injurious, and was encouraged in it by his medical counsel. But he dined abroad, as he did everything of the sort, at regulated intervals, and not only determined beforehand in what he should deviate from his settled habits, but often made a record of the result for his future government.

The most embarrassing question, however, as to diet, regarded the use of wine, which, if at first it sometimes seemed to be followed by bad consequences, was yet, on the whole, found useful, and was prescribed to him. To make everything certain, and settle the precise point to which he should go, he instituted a series of experiments, and between March, 1818, and November, 1820,—a period of two years and nine months,—he recorded the exact quantity of wine that he took every day, except the few days when he entirely abstained. It was Sherry or Madeira. In the great majority of cases—four fifths, I should think—it ranged from one to two glasses, but went up sometimes to four or five, and even to six. He settled at last, upon two, or two and a half as the quantity best suited to his case, and persevered in this as his daily habit, until the last year of his life, during which a peculiar regimen was imposed upon him from the peculiar circumstances of his health. In all this I wish to be understood that he was rigorous with himself,—much more so than persons thought who saw him only when he was dining with friends, and when, but equally upon system and principle, he was much more free.

He generally smoked a single weak cigar after dinner, and listened at the same time to light reading from Mrs. Prescott. A walk of two miles —more or less—followed; but always enough, after the habit of riding was given up, to make the full amount of six miles walking for the day's exercise, and then, between five and eight, he took a cup of tea, and had his reader with him for work two hours more.

The labors of the day were now definitively ended. He came down from his study to his library, and either sat there or walked about while Mrs. Prescott read to him from some amusing book, generally a novel, and, above all other novels, those of Scott and Miss Edgeworth. In all this he took great solace. He enjoyed the room as well as the reading, and, as he moved about, would often stop before the books,—especially his favorite books, —and be sure that they were all in their proper places, drawn up exactly to the front of their respective shelves, like soldiers on a dress-parade,— sometimes speaking of them, and almost to them, as if they were personal friends. At half past ten, having first taken nearly another glass of wine, he went to bed, fell asleep quickly, and slept soundly and well.

EDWARD HITCHCOCK.

[Born 1793. Died 1864.]

EDWARD HITCHCOCK, D. D., LL.D., an eminent Geologist, was born at Deerfield, Mass., May 24, 1793; became a teacher in 1816, and was afterwards pastor of the Congregational Church at Conway, Mass.; Professor of Chemistry and Natural History in Amherst College, 1825; appointed to make a Geological Survey of Mass., in 1830 and 1837; President of Amherst College, and Professor of Natural Theology and Geology, 1844, which he resigned in 1854; Agricultural Commissioner for Mass., to visit the Agricultural Schools of Europe, 1850.

Among Dr. Hitchcock's early literary labors were the preparation of an almanac for four years, 1815–18; and the composition of a Tragedy, the Downfall of Bonaparte. He has since then given to the world a number of works which have conferred upon him a distinguished reputation both in Europe and America. The following are their titles: Geology of the Connecticut Valley; Catalogue of Plants within twenty miles of Amherst; Dyspepsia forestalled and resisted; An Argument for early Temperance; Four Reports on the Geology, Zoology, and Botany of Massachusetts; A Wreath for a Tomb; Elementary Geology, which passed through many editions in this country and England, where it was edited by Dr. J. Pye Smith, and highly praised by Dr. Mantell, Dr. Buckland, and other eminent Geologists; Fossil Footsteps in the U. S.; History of a Zoological Temperance Convention in Central Africa; Religious Lectures on the Phenomena of the four seasons; The Religion of Geology and its connected Sciences, reprinted in several editions in England; Report on the Agricultural Schools of Europe;

Memoir of Mary Lyon; Lectures on Diet, Regimen, and Employment; Outlines of the Geology of the Globe, and of the United States in particular; Religious Truth illustrated from Science; Illustrations of Surface Geology; Report to the Massachusetts Government on the Ichnology of New England; Report on the Geology of Vermont in 1860; and his last work, Reminiscences of Amherst College, historical, scientific, biographical, and autobiographical; also, of other and wider Life Experiences. This work, including an account of the growth and development of the College, its museums and scientific resources, with much of a personal character, is a most valuable contribution to the history of education in America. The list of his publications exhibits an extraordinary degree of intellectual activity, continued through a long life, and includes 171 articles, 24 being distinct volumes, and the remainder, contributions to reviews, pamphlets, occasional sermons, etc., about eight thousand pages. Most of his writings, he adds, were produced "not with the expectation that they would go down to posterity, but to aid a little in advancing present knowledge—in adding some items that should go into the general stock; so that, although the works themselves should be forgotten, some feeble influence, at least, might remain upon the great cause of learning and religion." He had hoped to write a great work on Natural Theology. His health gradually failing, for the last few years of his life, though his intellectual activity continued unabated, he died at Amherst, Feb. 27, 1864, aged seventy.

SCIENCE AND THE BIBLE.
FROM THE RELIGION OF GEOLOGY.

If the geological interpretation of Genesis be true, then it should be taught to all classes of the community. It is, indeed, unwise to alter received interpretations of Scripture without very strong reasons. We should be satisfied that the new light, which has come to us, is not that of a trans-

ient meteor, but of a permanent luminary. We should, also, be satisfied that the proposed change is consistent with the established rules of philology. If we introduce change of this sort before these points are settled, even upon passages that have no connection with fundamental moral principles, we shall distress many an honest and pious heart, and expose ourselves to the necessity of further change But on the other hand, if we delay the change

long after these points are fairly settled, we shall
excite the suspicion that we dread to have the
light of science fall upon the Bible. Nor let it be
forgotten how disastrous has ever been the influence of the opinion that theologians teach one
thing, and men of science another. Now, in the
case under consideration, is there any reason to
doubt the high antiquity of the globe, as demonstrated by geology ? If any point, not capable of
mathematical demonstration in physical science,
is proved, surely this truth is established. And
how easily reconciled to the inspired record, by an
interpretation entirely consistent with the rules of
philology, and with the scope of the passage, and
the tenor of the Bible ! It seems to me far more
natural, and easy to understand, than that interpretation which it became necessary to introduce
when the Copernican system was demonstrated to
be true. The latter must have seemed to conflict
strongly with the natural and most obvious meaning of certain passages of the Bible, at a time when
men's minds were ignorant of astronomy, and, I
may add, of the true mode of interpreting the language of Scripture respecting natural phenomena.
Nevertheless, the astronomical exegesis prevailed,
and every child can now see its reasonableness.
So it seems to me that the child can easily apprehend the geological interpretation and its reasons.
Why, then, should it not be taught to children,
that they may not be liable to distrust the whole
Bible, when they come to the study of geology ?
I rejoice, however, that the fears and prejudices of
the pious and the learned are so fast yielding to
evidence; and I anticipate the period, when, on
this subject, the child will learn the same thing in
the Sabbath school and the literary institution.
Nay, I anticipate the time as not distant, when
the high antiquity of the globe will be regarded as
no more opposed to the Bible than the earth's
revolution round the sun and on its axis. Soon
shall the horizon, where geology and revelation
meet, be cleared of every cloud, and present only
an unbroken and magnificent circle of truth.

GEOLOGY AND RELIGION.
FROM THE SAME.

If we may trust the facts and reasonings of geology as to the antiquity of the globe, the mind is
almost overwhelmed in attempting to run back
over the mighty periods of its existence. Chronology has no measuring line long enough to stretch
over them ; and Imagination tires on her wing in
attempting the daring flight. And yet all along
that almost interminable line we discover the footsteps of Jehovah. In every change, mechanical,
chemical, or organic,—and how numerous they
have been !—we see the energizing and controlling
power of Divinity. Every step is but the development of some plan worthy of infinite Wisdom ;
every new *tableau* in the opening series gives a

brighter display, till the harmonies become complete in man.

From the past we may derive at least a strong
presumption as to the future. If in all past periods
change has been the higher and controlling law
of our world,—the essential means of its preservation and of the happiness of sentient beings,—if,
in fact, it is the great law of the material universe,
what reason have we to suppose that the process
will stop now ? Rather may we presume that
other changes are to succeed. And since we know
of no example of the annihilation of a particle of
matter, but only of its metamorphosis, where
shall we set limits to the expanding series ? Why
may not change, through all eternity, be, as in all
past time it has been, an essential means of happiness to created natures ?

Thus standing on this middle point of existence
which we now occupy, we can look back through
the glass which geology holds before us, almost to
the birth of time, and see successive systems rising
and gradually unfolding the great plans and purposes of Jehovah ; and as we turn the glass forward,
imagination can discover no end to the developments that are to follow. We can see many links
of the chain, and we know that it has a beginning ; but the extremities lie too deeply buried in
the past and the future to be seen by mortal
vision.

Are not these ennobling views ? Do they not
give us exalted conceptions of God's government
and operations ? What wider vistas into space
does astronomy open than this its kindred science
opens into duration ? What Christian will hesitate
to give up his soul to the liberalizing, purifying,
and elevating influences of these grand disclosures !
For having felt their interest and power on earth,
he may surely hope that their deeper and more
thorough study will form a part of the employments
and enjoyments of heaven.

From all that has been advanced we may safely
say, that no other science, nay, perhaps not all the
other sciences, touch religion at so many points as
geology. And at what connecting point do we
discover collision ? If upon a few of them some
obscurity still rests, yet with nearly all how clear
the harmony—how strong the mutual corrobora-
tion ! With how much stronger faith do we cling
to the Bible when we find so many of its principles
thus corroborated ! From many a science has the
supposed viper come forth and fastened itself upon
the hand of Christianity. But instead of falling
down dead, as an unbelieving world expected, how
calmly have they seen her shake off the beast and
feel no harm ! Surely it is time that unbelievers,
like the ancient heathen, should confess the divinity of the Bible when they see how invulnerable
it is to every assault. Surely it is time for the believer to cease fearing that any deadly influence
will emanate from geology and fasten itself upon
his faith, and learn to look upon this science only
as an auxiliary and friend.

SAMUEL GRISWOLD GOODRICH.

[Born 1793   Died 1860.]

SAMUEL G. GOODRICH, better known as Peter Parley, the most prolific and popular of American authors, was born at Ridgefield, Conn., August 19, 1793. He commenced in early life the publication of historical, geographical, and other school books at Hartford, and became, in the same department, a writer so prolific, that it is impossible for us to even name them here, but he published a list and a full account of them, together with a list of spurious works claimed to be written by him, in an Appendix to his Recollections of a Lifetime, the bare recital of the titles alone occupying six closely printed pages. "I stand before the public, as the author and editor of about 170 volumes—116 bearing the name of Peter Parley. Of all these about 7,000,000 of volumes have been sold; about 300,000 vols. are now sold annually." They may be summed up as follows:—Miscellaneous works, including 14 vols. of the Token, 30 vols.; School books, 27 vols.; Peter Parley's Tales, 36 vols.; Parley's Historical Compends, 36 vols.; Parley's Miscellanies, 70 vols.

In 1823–1824, he visited Europe, and on his return established himself as a publisher in Boston, where he commenced the Token, which he edited for a number of years, the contributions and illustrations being the productions of American authors and artists; Mr. Goodrich furnishing poems and sketches, and rendering a further service to the public, by his encouragement of young and unknown authors, among whom were Everett, Longfellow, Sedgwick, Sigourney, Willis, and Nathaniel Hawthorne, the finest of whose Twice Told Tales were first told in the Token. The famous Peter Parley series was commenced about the same time; Mr. Goodrich turning to good account, in his little square volumes, his recent travels in Europe, and his tact in arrangement and illustration. The Geography was an especial favorite.

He has found time, amid his constant labor as a compiler, to assert his claims as an original author, by the publication, in 1837, of The Outcast and other Poems; in 1841, of

a selection of his contributions to the Token, Sketches from a Student's Window; and in 1851, by an elegantly illustrated edition of his Poems. In 1838, Mr. Goodrich published Fireside Education, a volume of judicious counsel to parents, presented in a popular and attractive manner, composed in sixty days, while the author was occupied with important duties as a member of the Massachusetts Senate.

He was editor of Parley's Magazine for one year, a work which he started, but was obliged to give up from ill health and an affection of his eyes. He began Merry's Museum, and continued it from 1841 to 1854.

In 1851, President Fillmore appointed Mr. Goodrich Consul to Paris. In 1855, he returned to New York, where he resided until his death, which occurred from heart disease, suddenly, on the 9th of May, 1860.

While in Paris, he made arrangements for the translation and introduction of his Peter Parley series into France.

On his return from France, he published in 1856, two most interesting volumes of autobiographical Recollections of a Life-time; or, Men and Things I have seen, historical, biographical, anecdotical, and descriptive. Commencing with an easy colloquial narrative of the experiences of his boyhood in Connecticut, presenting many curious details of a simplicity which has almost passed away. As he proceeds, various New England personages of consequence are brought upon the scene, and we have some valuable notices of the war of 1812. The literary men of that time are introduced. Then comes the author's first journey to England, and his acquaintance with various celebrities. His active literary career at home succeeds, followed by his consulship at Paris, which included the period of the revolution of 1848.

While in Paris, he purchased electrotypes of a number of beautifully engraved cuts of Animals and Birds, etc., for which he prepared the letter press of an Illustrated Natural History; it was published in two elegant imperial 8vo. volumes in 1859, meeting with a large sale.

THE COUP D'ETAT.
FROM RECOLLECTIONS OF A LIFE-TIME.

On Monday evening, the 1st of December, 1852, I was present at the Elysée, and was then first introduced to Louis Napoleon. The room was tolerably full, the company consising, as is usual in such cases, of diplomats, military officers, and court officials, with a sprinkling of citizens in black coats —for hitherto the requisition of a court uniform had not been imposed. This, you will remember, was under the Republic; the rule which raised the black coat to a question of state, grew out of the Empire. Nevertheless, I was forcibly struck by the preponderance of soldiers in the assembly, and I said several times to my companions, that it seemed more like a camp than a palace. The whole scene was dull; the President himself appeared preoccupied, and was not master of his usual urbanity; Gen. Magnan walked from room to room with a ruminating air, occasionally sending his keen glances around, as if searching for something which he could not find. There was no music, no dancing. That gayety which almost always pervades a festive party in Paris, was wholly wanting. There was no ringing laughter, no merry hum of conversation. I noticed all this, but I did not suspect the cause. At eleven o'clock the assembly broke up, and the guests departed. At twelve, the conspirators gathered for their several tasks, commenced their operations.

About four in the morning, the leading members of the Assembly were seized in their beds, and hurried to prison. Troops were distributed at various points, so as to secure the city. When the light of day came, proclamations were posted at the corners of the streets announcing to the citizens that the National Assembly was dissolved, that universal suffrage was decreed, that the Republic was established! Such was the general unpopularity of the Assembly, that the first impression of the people was that of delight at its overthrow. Throughout the first day, the streets of Paris were like a swarming hive, filled with masses of people, yet for the most part in good-humor. The second day they had reflected, and began to frown, but yet there was no general spirit of revolt. A few barricades were attempted, but the operators were easily dispersed. The third day came, and although there was some agitation among the masses, there was evidently no preparation, no combination for general resistance. As late as ten o'clock in the forenoon, I met one of the republicans whom I knew, and asked him what was to be done. His reply was:

"We can do nothing: our leaders are in prison; we are bound hand and foot. I am ready to give my life at the barricades, if with the chance of benefit; but I do not like to throw it away. We can do nothing!"

Soon after this, I perceived heavy columns of troops, some four thousand men, marching through the Rue de la Paix, and then proceeding along the Boulevards toward the Porte St. Denis. These were soon followed by a body of about a thousand horse. I was told that similar bodies were moving to the same point through other avenues of the city. In a short time the whole Boulevard, from the Rue de la Paix to the Place de la Bastille, an extent of two miles, was filled with troops. My office was on the Boulevard des Italiens, and was now fronted by a dense body of lancers, each man with his cocked pistol in his hand. Except the murmur of the horses' hoofs, there was a general stillness over the city. The sidewalks were filled with people, and though there was no visible cause for alarm, there was still a vague apprehension which cast pallor and gloom upon the faces of all.

Suddenly a few shots were heard in the direction of the Boulevard Montmartre, and then a confused hum, and soon a furious clatter of hoofs. A moment after, the whole body of horse started into a gallop, and rushed by as if in flight; presently they halted, however, wheeled slowly, and gradually moved back, taking up their former position. The men looked keenly at the houses on either side, and pointed their pistols threateningly at all whom they saw at the windows. It afterward appeared, that when the troops had been drawn out in line and stationed along the Boulevard, some half dozen shots were fired into them from the tops of buildings and from windows, this created a sudden panic; the troops ran, and crowding upon others, caused the sudden movement I have described. In a few moments, the heavy, sickening sound of muskets came from the Porte St. Denis. Volley succeeded volley, and after some time the people were seen rushing madly along the pavements of the Boulevard as if to escape. The gate of our hotel was now closed, and at the earnest request of the throng that had gathered for shelter in the court of the hotel, I put out the "Stars and Stripes"—the first and last time that I ever deemed it necessary. The dull roar of muskets, with the occasional boom of cannon, continued at intervals for nearly half an hour. Silence at last succeeded, and the people ventured into the streets. About four in the afternoon, I walked for a mile along the Boulevard. The pavements were strewn with the fragments of shattered windows, broken cornices, and shivered doorways. Many of the buildings, especially those on the southern side of the street, were thickly spattered with bullet-marks, especially around the windows. One edifice was riddled through and through with cannon-shot. Frequent spots of blood stained the sidewalk, and along the Boulevard Montmartre, particularly around the doorways, there were pools like those of the shambles; it being evident that the reckless soldiers had shot down in heaps the fugitives who, taken by surprise, strove to obtain shelter at the entrances of the hotels upon the street. It was a sight to sicken the heart, especially of an American, who is not trained to these scenes of massacre. Toward evening a portion of the troops moved away; the rest remained, and bivouacked in the streets for the night. At ten o'clock, I again visited the scene, and was greatly struck with the long line of watch-fires, whose fitful lights, reflected by dark groups of armed men, only rendered the spectacle more ghastly and gloomy.

Engraved by John Sartain Phila

Henry B Lacey

... the organs of that taught by Kay
... their successors. It was also
... Swedish, at Stockholm, and ex-
... abroad. For several years
... composed all the leading articles,
... the Plough, the Loom and the
... were afterwards collected in a
... entitled the Harmony of Interests; and
... a pamphlet, called the Prospect, agri-
... manufacturing, commercial, and finan-
... of 1851. He issued in 1853,
... domestic and foreign; and,
... International Copyright. In 1804, the
... the South; and in 1858, Principles of
... 3 vols., 8vo., and Letters to the
... of the U. S., one vol., 12mo.; a
... on topics of Political Economy,
... W. C. Bryant, in 1860; and
... to Hon. Schuyler Colfax, in 1865.
... Mr. Carey's works have been translated
... Swedish, German, French, and
... have commanded attention, not
... vigor with which his ideas are
... but from the novelty and ability
... positions, placing him among the
... political economists.

... great work, Principles of Social Science,
... doctrines of all his previous publications,
... the fruits of a quarter of a century's studies
... digested, systematized, and condensed. Mr.
Carey, not only in his own country, but through-
... Europe, where his writings have been exten-
... studied, is the acknowledged founder
... head of a new school of Political Economy.
The doctrines which he proclaimed are eminently hopeful, progressive, and democratic,
and those who accepted them, are with a
... of significance styled of the American
school. For an able discrimination between
... and that in undisputed sway with
... contributions to social science
... (Dismal)...
... in Philadelphia...

HENRY C. CAREY.

[Born 1793.]

THIS prolific and able writer on Political Economy, whose praise is in both hemispheres, is the son of Matthew Carey, who was born in Dublin, in 1760, and emigrating to this country early in life, became an extensive publisher, which business he carried on successfully for nearly half a century; upon retiring from active trade, as an eminent philanthropist aiding the poor and the suffering, and an active public spirited citizen, he maintained the same eminence as he had attained in the publishing business; he died in 1839. He was the author of several works which enjoyed considerable popularity in their day. His son, Henry C. Carey, was born in Philadelphia, in 1793, and succeeded his father in business in 1821, and continued in this pursuit till 1838. He established the system of trade sales among publishers.

Mr. Carey inherited an inclination to investigate subjects in connection with political economy, and in 1836 published an Essay on the Rate of Wages, which in 1840 was expanded into the Laws of Wealth; or, Principles of Political Economy, 3 vols., 8vo. The novel positions assumed, at once attracted the attention of the European political economists, and from many of them elicited the warmest praise; it was published in Italian at Turin, and in Swedish at Upsal. Bastiat has taken from Carey, ideas that he had developed and had presented to his readers with so much skill, and with such an imposing mass of facts, as in truth to leave in suspense the decision of even the most accomplished student of his works. Carey, and after him, Bastiat, have thus introduced a formula in relation to the measure of Value, that I believe is destined to be universally adopted. In 1838, Mr. Carey published The Credit System in France, Great Britain, and the United States. In 1840, Answers to the Questions, What constitutes currency? What are the causes of its unsteadiness? etc. In 1848, the Past, the Present, and the Future. The design of this work is to show that men are everywhere now doing precisely as has heretofore been done, and that they do so in obedience to a great and universal law, directly the reverse of that taught by Ricardo, Malthus, and their successors. It was also republished in Swedish, at Stockholm, and excited great attention abroad. For several years Mr. Carey contributed all the leading articles, and others, to the Plough, the Loom and the Anvil, which were afterwards collected in a volume, entitled the Harmony of Interests; and others in a pamphlet, called the Prospect, agricultural, manufacturing, commercial, and financial, at the opening of 1851. He issued in 1853, The Slave-Trade, domestic and foreign; and, Letters on International Copyright. In 1804, the North and the South, and in 1858, Principles of Social Science, 3 vols., 8vo., and Letters to the President of the U. S., one vol., 12mo.; a Series of Letters on topics of Political Economy, addressed to W. C. Bryant, in 1860; and another series to Hon. Schuyler Colfax, in 1865. Most of Mr. Carey's works have been translated into Russian, Swedish, German, French, and Italian, and have commanded attention, not only from the vigor with which his ideas are expressed, but from the novelty and ability of his propositions, placing him among the very first of political economists.

In his great work, Principles of Social Science, the doctrines of all his previous publications, and the fruits of a quarter of a century's studies are digested, systematized, and condensed. Mr. Carey, not only in his own country, but throughout Europe, where his writings have been extensively studied, is the acknowledged founder and head of a new school of Political Economy. The doctrines which he proclaimed are eminently hopeful, progressive, and democratic, and those who accepted them, are with a fulness of significance styled of the American school. For an able discrimination between his system and that in undisputed sway when he began his contributions to social science, see an article in Allibone's Dictionary, I., 339. Mr. Carey has resided in Philadelphia all his life; is a gentleman of most polished and urbane manners, and of erect form, showing great vigor of constitution and intellect.

THE WARRIOR-CHIEF AND THE TRADER.

THE object of the warrior-chief being that of preventing the existence of any motion in society except that which centres in himself, he monopolizes land, and destroys the power of voluntary association among the men he uses as his instruments. The soldier, obeying the word of command, is so far from holding himself responsible to God or man for the observance of the rights of person or of property, that he glories in the extent of his robberies and in the number of his murders. The man of the Rocky Mountains adorns his person with the scalps of his butchered enemies; while the more civilized murderer contents himself with adding a ribbon to the decoration of his coat; but both are savages alike. The trader—equally with the soldier seeking to prevent any movement except that which centres in himself—also uses irresponsible machines. The sailor is among the most brutalized of human beings, bound, like the soldier to obey orders, at the risk of having his back seamed by the application of the whip. The human machines used by war and trade are the only ones, except the negro slave, who are now flogged.

The soldier desires labor to be cheap, that recruits may readily be obtained. The great land-owner desires it may be cheap, that he may be enabled to appropriate to himself a large proportion of the proceeds of his land; and the trader desires it to be cheap, that he may be enabled to dictate the terms upon which he will buy as well as those upon which he will sell.

The object of all being thus identical,—that of obtaining power over their fellow-men,—it is no matter of surprise that we find the trader and the soldier so uniformly helping and being helped by each other. The bankers of Rome were as ready to furnish material aid to Cæsar, Pompey, and Augustus, as are now those of London, Paris, Amsterdam, and Vienna to grant it to the Emperors of France, Austria, and Russia; and as indifferent as they in relation to the end for whose attainment it was destined to be used. War and trade, thus travel together, as is shown by the history of the world. The only difference between wars made for the purposes of conquest, and those for the maintenance of monopolies of trade, being that the virulence of the latter is much greater than is that of the former. The conqueror, seeking political power, is *sometimes* moved by a desire to improve the condition of his fellow-men; but the trader, in pursuit of power, is animated by no other idea than that of buying in the cheapest market and selling in the dearest,—cheapening merchandise in the one, even at the cost of starving the producers, and increasing his price in the other, even at the cost of starving the consumers. Both profit by whatever tends to diminution in the power of voluntary association and consequent decline of commerce. The soldier forbids the holding of meetings among his subjects. The slave-owner interdicts his people from assembling together, except at such times and in such places as meet his approbation. The shipmaster rejoices when the men of England separate from each other, and transport themselves by hundreds of thousands to Canada and Australia, because it enhances freights; and the trader rejoices, because the more widely men are scattered, the more they need the service of the middle-man, and the richer and more powerful does he become at their expense.

MAN THE SUBJECT OF SOCIAL SCIENCE.

MAN, the molecule of society, is the subject of social science. In common with all other animals, he requires to eat, drink, and sleep; but his greatest need is that of association with his fellow-men. Dependent upon the experience of himself and others for all his knowledge, he requires language to enable him either to record the results of his own observation, or to profit by those of others; and of language there can be none without association. Without language, he must remain in ignorance of the existence of powers granted to him in lieu of the strength of the ox and the horse, the speed of the hare, and the sagacity of the elephant, and must remain below the level of the brute creation. To have language, there must be association and combination of men with their fellow-men; and it is on this condition only that man can be man; on this alone that we can conceive of the being to which we attach the idea of man. "It is not good," said God, "that man should live alone;" nor do we ever find him doing so,—the earliest records of the world exhibiting to us beings living together in society, and using words for the expression of their ideas. Language escapes from man at the touch of nature herself; and the power of using words is his essential faculty, enabling him to maintain commerce with his fellow-men, and fitting him for that association without which language cannot exist. The words "society" and "language" convey to the mind separate and distinct ideas; and yet by no effort of the mind can we conceive the existence of the one without the other.

The subject of social science, then, is man, the being to whom have been given reason and the faculty of individualizing sounds so as to give expression to every variety of idea, and who has been placed in a position to exercise that faculty. Isolate him, and with the loss of the power of speech he loses the power to reason, and with it the distinctive quality of man. Restore him to society, and with the return of the power of speech he become again the reasoning man.

HORACE MANN.

[Born 1796.   Died 1859.]

THIS distinguished friend of education was born at Franklin, Mass., May 4, 1796; he graduated at Brown University, 1819; acted there as tutor till 1822; elected representative to the State Legislature for Dedham, in 1828, and for Suffolk, 1836–39; Secretary of Mass. Board of Education, 1837–48; and in the latter year succeeded John Q. Adams in the National House of Representatives. In 1853, Mr. Mann was elected President of Antioch College, at Yellow Springs, Ohio, and acted also as Professor of Political Economy, Intellectual and Moral Philosophy, Constitutional Law and Natural Theology. The college was open to both sexes, and had 400 pupils in 1854, one-third of whom were females; under the rule of Mr. Mann, it had immediate and continued success.

Mr. Mann is chiefly known as a writer, through his valuable series of twelve Annual Education Reports, stored with ingenious and pertinent discussion of the various means and machinery to be employed in the work of popular education, both intellectual and physical. Through these he has identified himself with the progress of the public school system of Massachusetts. He published as part of this series his Report of an educational Tour in Germany, Britain, et ., made in 1843.

He was eminent as a reformer and philanthropist, lecturing on temperance and kindred subjects. His lectures and addresses were vigorous and energetic, delivered in a familiar colloquial manner. In appearance, he was tall, very erect, and remarkably slender, with silvery gray hair, animated and expressive features, light complexion, and rapid pace. As an orator, his smooth, flowing style, musical voice, and graceful manner, with fertility, amplitude, and energy of diction, often adorned his subject with a graceful, rushing eloquence, that captivated the breathless audience.

Horace Mann died at Yellow Springs, in his 64th year, August 2, 1859. A posthumous volume of Twelve Sermons, delivered by him to the pupils, as head of this institution, bears witness to his interest in education, to which he had mainly devoted his life. The life of Horace Mann, by his widow, Mrs. Mary Mann, 8vo., Boston, 1865, traces his career with minuteness, and is a valuable contribution to biographical literature and the history of the times.

His published works, besides the Reports, are: Form and Arrangement of Schoolhouses; Lectures on Education; A Few Thoughts for a Young Man when Entering upon Life, 25,000 copies sold; Mann and Chase's (Pliny E.) Arithmetic practically applied, 3 vols.; Letters and Speeches on Slavery; A Few Thoughts on the Power and Duties of Woman; Report of the Educational Census of Great Britain in 1851; and various orations and addresses in pamphlet form; Tracts on Temperance Subjects; he also edited 10 vols. of the Common School Journal, Boston, 1839–48.

Edward Everett, speaking of Horace Mann, said, "he will be remembered till the history of Massachusetts is forgotten, as one of her greatest benefactors."

Mrs. Mann, formerly Miss Mary Peabody, also published, Christianity in the Kitchen; a physiological Cook Book, 1857, 12mo.; and a Primer of reading, drawing, and spelling, on a new plan, 16mo.

THE CHOICE.
FROM THOUGHTS FOR A YOUNG MAN.

ENDUED, then, with these immortal and energetic capacities to soar or sink; with these heights of glory above him, and this abysm of wretchedness below him; *whitherward shall a young man set his face, and how shall he order his steps ?*

There is a time when the youthful heir of a throne first comes to a knowledge of his mighty prerogatives; when he first learns what strength there is in his imperial arm, and what happiness or woe wait upon his voice. So there must be a time when the vista of the future, with all its possibilities of glory and of shame, first opens upon the vision of youth. Then is he summoned to make his choice between truth and treachery; between honor and dishonor; between purity and profligacy; between moral life and moral death. And as he doubts or balances between the heavenward and the hellward course; as he struggles to rise or consents to fall; is there, in all the universe of God, a spectacle of higher exultation or of deeper pathos! Within him are the appetites of a brute and the attributes of an angel; and when these meet in council to make up the roll of his destiny and seal his fate, shall the beast hound out the seraph! Shall the young man, now conscious of the largeness of his sphere and of the sovereignty of his choice, wed the low ambitions of the world, and seek, with their emptiness, to fill his immortal desires? Because he has a few animal wants that must be supplied, shall he become all animal,—an epicure and an inebriate,—and blasphemously make it the first doctrine of his catechism,—"the Chief End of Man,"—*to glorify his stomach and to enjoy it?* Because it is the law of self-preservation that he shall provide for himself, and the law of religion that he shall provide for his family when he has one, must he, therefore, cut away all the bonds of humanity that bind him to his race, forswear charity, crush down every prompting of benevolence, and if he can have the palace and the equipage of a prince, and the table of a Sybarite, become a blind man, and a deaf man, and a dumb man, when he walks the streets where hunger moans and nakedness shivers? Because he must earn his bread by the sweat of his brow, must he, therefore, become a devotee of Mammon, and worship the meanest god that dwells in Erebus? Because he has an instinct for the approval of his fellow-men, and would aspire to the honors of office, shall he, therefore, supple his principles so that they may take the Protean shape of every popular clamor; or poise his soul on what the mechanicians call a *universal joint*, which turns in every direction with indiscriminate facility? Because absurd notions, descending to us from the worst and the weakest of men, have created factitious distinctions between employments, shall he seek a sphere of life for which he is neither fitted by nature nor by culture, and spoil a good cobbler by becoming a poor lawyer; or commit the double injustice of robbing the mountain goats of a herdsman to make a faithless shepherd in the Lord's pastures? Let the young man remember there is nothing derogatory in any employment which ministers to the well-being of the race. It is the spirit that is carried into an employment that elevates or degrades it. The ploughman that turns the clod may be a Cincinnatus or a Washington, or he may be brother to the clod he turns. It is every way creditable to handle the yard-stick and to measure tape; the only discredit consists in having a soul whose range of thought is as short as the stick and as narrow as the tape. There is no glory in the act of affixing a signature by which the treasures of commerce are transferred, or treaties between nations are ratified; the glory consists in the rectitude of the purpose that approves the one, and the grandeur of the philanthropy that sanctifies the other. The time is soon coming, when, by the common consent of mankind, it will be esteemed more honorable to have been *John Pounds*, putting new and beautiful souls into the ragged children of the neighborhood, while he mended their fathers' shoes, than to have sat upon the British throne. The time now is, when, if Queen Victoria, in one of her magnificent "Progresses" through her realms, were to meet that more than American queen, Miss Dix, in her "circumnavigation of charity" among the insane, the former should kneel and kiss the hand of the latter; and the ruler over more than a hundred millions of people should pay homage to the angel whom God has sent to the maniac.

No matter what may be the fortunes or the expectations of a young man, he has no right to live a life of idleness. In a world so full as this of incitements to exertion and of rewards for achievement, idleness is the most absurd of absurdities and the most shameful of shames. In such a world as ours, the idle man is not so much a biped as a bivalve; and the wealth which breeds idleness, —of which the English peerage is an example, and of which we are beginning to abound in specimens in this country,—is only a sort of human oyster-bed where heirs and heiresses are planted, to spend a contemptible life of slothfulness in growing plump and succulent for the grave-worm's banquet.

TEMPERANCE IN EATING.
FROM THE SAME.

Vastly less depends upon the table to which we sit down, than upon the appetite which we carry to it. The palled epicure, who spends five dollars for his dinner, extracts less pleasure from his meal than many a hardy laborer who dines for a shilling. The desideratum is, not greater luxuries, but livelier *papillæ;* and if the devotee of appetite would propitiate his divinity aright, he would not send to the Yellowstone for buffaloes' tongues, nor to France for *paté de fois gras,* but would climb a mountain, or swing an axe. With health, there is no end to the quantity or the variety from which the palate can extract its pleasures. Without health, no delicacy that nature or art produces can provoke a zest. Hence, when a man destroys his health, he destroys, so far as he is concerned, whatever of sweetness, of flavor and of savor, the teeming earth can produce. To him who has poisoned his appetite by excesses, the luscious pulp of grape or peach, the nectareous juices of orange or pineapple, are but a loathing and a nausea. He has turned gardens and groves of delicious fruit into gardens and groves of ipecac, and aloes. The same vicious indulgences that blasted his health, blasted all orchards and cane-fields also. Verily, the man who is physiologically "wicked" does not live out half his days; nor is this the worst of his punishment, for he is more than half dead while he appears to live.

JOHN GORHAM PALFREY.

[Born 1796.]

JOHN GORHAM PALFREY, the son of a Boston merchant, was born in that city, May 2, 1796. He was fitted for college at Exeter Academy; graduated at Harvard in 1815; studied theology, and in 1818, was ordained over the Brattle Street Church, Boston, where he continned till 1831, when he was appointed Dexter Professor of Sacred Literature in Harvard. For six years he was editor of the North American Review; and delivered a course of lectures before the Lowell Institute, on the Evidences of Christianity, which were published in 2 vols., 8vo. He also published Lectures on Hebrew Scriptures, 4 vols.; and Sermons on Duties of Private Life; Papers on the Slave Power; Discourses on Intemperance; The New Testament conformed to Griesbach's Standard Greek Text; Grammar of Chaldee, Syriac, Samaritan, and Rabbinical; Relation between Judaism and Christianity; Official Reports of the Statistics of Mass., in 8vo. vols., 1845–48; A History of New England during the Stuart Dynasty, 3 vols., 8vo.; also, an abridged edition of the same in 2 vols., crown, 8vo., New York, 1866. Mr Palfrey, at various times, has published many pamphlet orations, sermons, etc., on temperance, slavery, historical, and religious subjects.

His History of New England will doubtless be the established history of that portion of our country. It evinces a noble and hearty appreciation of the early settlers of New England, guided by cool, impartial reason, and exhibiting throughout extensive research and a careful collation of facts.

LANDING OF THE PILGRIM FATHERS.
FROM HISTORY OF NEW ENGLAND.

THE narrow peninsula, sixty miles long, which terminates in Cape Cod, projects eastwardly from the mainland of Massachusetts, in shape resembling the human arm bent rectangularly at the elbow and again at the wrist. In the basin enclosed landward by the extreme point of this projection, in the roadstead of what is now Provincetown, the Mayflower dropped her anchor at noon on a Saturday near the close of autumn.

In the afternoon, "fifteen or sixteen men, well armed," were sent on shore to reconnoitre and collect fuel. They returned at evening, reporting that they had seen neither person nor dwelling, but that the country was well wooded, and that the appearance as to soil was promising.

Having kept their Sabbath in due retirement, the men began the labors of the week by landing a shallop from the ship and hauling it up the beach for repairs, while the women went on shore to wash clothes. While the carpenter and his men were at work on the boat, sixteen others, armed and provisioned, with Standish for their commander, set off on foot to explore the country. The only incident of this day was the sight of five or six savages, who on their approach ran away too swiftly to be overtaken. At night, lighting a fire and setting a guard, the party bivouacked at the distance, as they supposed, of ten miles from their vessel. Proceeding southward next morning, they observed marks of cultivation, some heaps of earth, which they took for signs of graves, and the remains of a hut, with "a great kettle, which had been some ship's kettle." In a heap which they opened, they found two baskets containing four or five bushels of Indian corn, of which they took as much as they could carry away in their pockets and in a kettle. Further on, they saw two canoes, and "an old fort or palisado, made by some Christians," as they thought. The second night, which was rainy, they encamped again, with more precautions than before. On Friday evening, having lost their way meanwhile, and been amused by an accident to Bradford, who was caught in an Indian deer-trap, they returned to their friends "both weary and welcome, and delivered in their corn into the store to be kept for seed, for they knew not how to come by any, and therefore were very glad, proposing, so soon as they could meet with any of the inhabitants of that place, to make them large satisfaction."

The succeeding week was spent in putting their tools in order and preparing timber for a new boat. During this time, which proved to be cold and stormy, much inconvenience was experienced from having to wade "a bow-shot" through the shallow water to the shore; and many took "coughs and colds, which afterwards turned to the scurvy." On Monday of the week next following, twenty-four of the colonists, in the shallop, which was now refitted, set out for an exploration along the coast, accompanied by Jones. the shipmaster, and ten of his people, in the long-boat. That day and the following night they suffered from a cold snow-storm, and were compelled to run into the shore for security. The next day brought them to the harbor to which the preceding journey by land had been extended, now named by them *Cold Harbor*, and ascertained to have a depth of twelve feet of water at flood-tide. Having slept under a shelter of pine-trees, they proceeded to make an examination of the spot as to its fitness for their settlement; in doing which, under the snow-covered and frozen surface, they found another parcel of corn and a bag of beans. These spoils they sent back in the shallop with Jones and sixteen of the party, who were ill, or worn out with exposure and fatigue. Marching inland five or six miles, they found a grave with a deposit of personal articles, as "bowls, trays, dishes," "a knife, a pack-needle," "a little bow," and some "strings and bracelets of fine white beads." Two wigwams were seen, which appeared to have been recently inhabited. Returning to their boat in the evening, the party hastened to rejoin their friends.

The question was discussed whether they should make a further examination of the coast, or sit down at the harbor which had been visited. The land about it had been under cultivation. The site appeared healthy, and convenient for defence, as well as for taking whales, of which numbers were daily seen. The severity of the winter season was close at hand, and the delay, fatigue, and risk of further explorations were dreaded. But on the whole, the uncertainty as to an adequate supply of water, with the insufficiency of the harbor, which, though commodious for boats, was too shallow for larger vessels, was regarded as a conclusive objection, and it was resolved to make a further examination of the bay. The mate of the Mayflower had told them of Agawam, now Ipswich, as a good harbor, with fertile land, and facilities for fishing. But, as things stood, it was thought too distant for a visit.

As soon as the state of the weather permitted, a party of ten, including Carver, Bradford, and others of the principal men, set off with eight seamen in the shallop on what proved to be the final expedition of discovery. The severity of the cold was extreme. "The water froze on their clothes, and made them many times like coats of iron." Coasting along the cape in a southerly direction for six or seven leagues, they landed and slept at a place where ten or twelve Indians had appeared on the shore. The Indians ran away on the party approached, and at night it was supposed that it was their fires which appeared at four or five miles' distance. The next day, while part of the company in the shallop examined the shore, the rest ranging about the country where are now the towns of Wellfleet and Eastham, found a burial-place, some old wigwams, and a small store of parched acorns, buried in the ground; but they met with no inhabitants. The following morning, at daylight, they had just ended their prayers, and were preparing breakfast

at their camp on the beach, when they heard a yell, and a flight of arrows fell among them. The assailants turned out to be thirty or forty Indians, who, being fired upon, retired. Neither side had been harmed. A number of the arrows were picked up, "some whereof were headed with brass, others with hart's horn, and others with eagles' claws."

Getting on board, they sailed all day along the shore in a storm of snow and sleet, making, by their estimate, a distance of forty or fifty miles, without discovering a harbor. In the afternoon, the gale having increased, their rudder was disabled, and they had to steer with oars. At length the mast was carried away, and they drifted in the dark with a flood-tide. With difficulty they brought up under the lee of a "small rise of land." Here a part of the company, suffering from wet and cold, went on shore, though not without fear of hostile neighbors, and lighted a fire by which to pass the inclement night. In the morning, "they found themselves to be on an island secure from the Indians, where they might dry their stuff, fix their pieces, and rest themselves; and, this being the last day of the week, they prepared there to keep the Sabbath."

"On Monday, they sounded the harbor, and found it fit for shipping, and marched also into the land, and found divers corn-fields and little running brooks, a place, as they supposed, fit for situation; . . . . . so they returned to their ship again with this news to the rest of their people, which did much comfort their hearts." Such is the record of that event which has made *the twenty-second of December* a memorable day in the calendar. * * * * * *

These were discouraging circumstances, but far worse troubles were to come. The labor of providing habitations had scarcely begun, when sickness set in, the consequence of exposure and bad food. Within four months it carried off nearly half their number. Six died in December, eight in January, seventeen in February, and thirteen in March. At one time during the winter, only six or seven had strength enough left to nurse the dying and bury the dead. Destitute of every provision which the weakness and the daintiness of the invalid require, the sick lay crowded in the unwholesome vessel, or in half-built cabins heaped around with snow-drifts. The rude sailors refused them even a share of those coarse sea-stores which would have given a little variety to their diet, till disease spread among the crew, and the kind ministrations of those whom they had neglected and affronted brought them to a better temper. The dead were interred in a bluff by the water-side, the marks of burial being carefully effaced, lest the natives should discover how the colony had been weakened. The imagination vainly tasks itself to comprehend the horrors of that fearful winter. The only mitigations were, that the cold was of less severity than is usual in the place, and that there was not an entire want of food or shelter.

ALBERT BARNES.

[Born 1798.]

THIS eminent Commentator was born in Rome, New York, Dec. 1, 1798. He worked with his father in the tannery until he was seventeen years old, when he entered Fairfield Academy, Conn., where he remained until 1819. He entered the Senior Class in Hamilton College, and graduated in July, 1820. He had intended studying law, but feeling it his duty to study theology, he went to the Theological Seminary at Princeton; he remained three years, and was licensed to preach April 23, 1823, by the Presbytery of New Brunswick. After preaching at various places, he took charge of the First Presbyterian Church in Morristown, N. J., Feb. 25, 1825. In 1830, he accepted a call from the First Presbyterian Church, in Philadelphia, and was installed June 25th. In both churches his ministry was highly prosperous, and his people became devotedly attached to him.

In 1835, George Junkin, D. D., preferred against Mr. Barnes charges of heresy, based on his Commentaries on the Epistle to the Romans. The Presbytery sustained Mr. Barnes, and Dr. Junkin appealed to the Synod of Philadelphia. The Synod sustained the appeal, and suspended Mr. Barnes from the ministry "until he should give evidence of repentance"; Mr. Barnes appealed to the General Assembly that met at Pittsburgh, May, 1836, and the Assembly restored him to his functions by a large majority.

During his residence at Morristown, Mr. Barnes commenced a series of Commentaries on the New Testament, designed for Sunday School teachers and family reading. The volume upon Matthew was published in 1832, and was followed, at various times, by ten other volumes, until the New Testament was completed. After he had commenced, hearing that the Rev. James W. Alexander was engaged on a similar work, he wrote to him, proposing to abandon his project in favor of his friend. On Dr. Alexander's reply—that in consequence of his feeble health he desired to transfer his work to the able hand already occupied on the same project, Mr. Barnes determined to con-

tinne. The work met with so favorable a reception that the author enlarged his design, and has since annotated several books of the Old Testament, with the same distinguished success. Besides eleven volumes on the New Testament, he has published Notes on Isaiah, 3 vols., Job, 2 vols., Daniel, 1 vol., Psalms, 3 vols., all maintaining his high reputation for profound and varied scholarship.

He also published an edition of Butler's Analogy, with an Introduction of rare ability; Sermons on Revivals; Practical Sermons; Episcopacy tested by Scripture; the Way of Salvation; Tracts on Temperance, and Slavery; the Supremacy of the Laws; Inquiry into the Scriptural Views of Slavery; the Church and Slavery; Inquiries and Suggestions in Regard to the Foundation of Faith in the Word of God; Life at Three-score, a sermon; the Atonement in its Relations to Law and Government; Manual of Family Prayers; Miscellaneous Essays and Reviews, 2 vols.; and Evidences of Christianity.

His Commentaries are eminently practical, and among the best works of the kind in the language. The high estimation in which they are held by the religious world, is evinced by the numerous editions which have been published in England as well as in this country. More than a million volumes have been sold in this country, and probably many more in England. The wonder that he was able to write so much, and so well, without interfering with his daily duties, is explained in his "Life at Three-Score," where he says: "All my Commentaries on the Scriptures have been written before nine o'clock in the morning." He was always an early riser, and a man of method, and laid down his pen as the clock struck nine, even if in the middle of a sentence. He has repeatedly refused the title of D. D. from conscientious motives.

Possessed naturally of a clear and vigorous understanding, his opinions are uniformly expressed in a brief, perspicuous manner. They are characterized by good sense, earnest piety, and the natural graces of a style remarkable for its simplicity and ease.

LIFE AT THREE-SCORE AND TEN.

FROM "LIFE AT THREE-SCORE AND TEN."

To him, however, who has reached the period of Three-Score and Ten years, no such change is possible; no such new plan is to be entered on. The purpose of life is accomplished; the changes have been all passed through. There is no new profession to be chosen; there are no new plans to be formed; there is no new distinction to be acquired; there are no books to be written, no houses to be built, no fields to be cultivated, no forests to be levelled, no works of art to be entered on. Painful as the thought may be, society, and the business walks of life, have no place for the old man; there is no place for him in the social circles of the gay, in the mercantile calling, at the bar, in the medical profession, in the pulpit, on the bench, in the senate chamber, in embassies to foreign courts. Distinctions and honors are no longer to be divided between him and his competitors; and the accumulating wealth of the world is no more to be the subject of partnership between him and others. Without plan now except as to the future world; his old companions, rivals and friends having fallen by the way; the active pursuits of life, and the offices of trust and honor now in other hands; the busy world not caring for his aid, and hoping nothing from him, it is his now, except as far as the friends of earlier years may have been spared to him, or as he may have secured the respect of the new generation that is coming on the stage of action, to tread his solitary way, already more than half forgotten, to the grave. He has had his day, and the world has nothing more to give him or to hope from him.

Most men in active life look forward, with fond anticipation, to a time when the cares of life will be over, and when they will be released from its responsibilities and burdens; if not with an absolute desire that such a time should come, yet with a feeling that it will be a relief when it does come. Many an hour of anxiety in the counting room; many an hour of toil in the workshop or on the farm; many an hour of weariness on the bench; many a burdened hour in the great offices of state, and many an hour of exhaustion and solicitude in professional life, is thus relieved by the prospect of rest—of absolute rest—of entire freedom from responsibility. What merchant and professional man, what statesman, does not look forward to such a time of repose, and anticipate a season—perhaps a long one—of calm tranquillity before life shall end; and when the time approaches, though the hope often proves fallacious, yet its approach is not unwelcome. Diocletian and Charles V. descended from their thrones to seek repose, the one in private life, and the other in a cloister; and the aged judge, merchant or pastor, welcomes the time when he feels that the burden which he has long borne may be committed to younger men.

Yet when the time comes, it is different from what had been anticipated. There is, to the surprise, perhaps, of all such men, this new—this strange—idea; an idea which they never had before, and which did not enter into their anticipations: *that they have now nothing to live for;* that they have no motive for effort; that they have no plan or purpose of life. They seem now to themselves, perhaps to others, to have no place in the world; no right in it. Society has no place for them, for it has nothing to confer on them, and they can no longer *make* a place for themselves. General Washington, when the war of Independence was over, and he had returned to Mount Vernon, is said to have felt "lost," because he had not an army to provide for daily; and Charles V., so far from finding rest in his cloister as such, amused himself, as has been commonly supposed, in trying to make clocks and watches run together, and so far from actually withdrawing from the affairs of state,—miserable in his chosen place of retreat—still busied himself with the affairs of Europe, and sought in the convent at Yuste to govern his hereditary dominions which he had professedly resigned to his son, and as far as possible still to control the empire where he had so long reigned. The retired merchant, unused to reading, and unaccustomed to agriculture or the mechanical arts, having little taste, it may be, for the fine arts or for social life, or opportunity for indulging in those tastes, finds life a burden, and sighs for his old employments and associations, for in his anticipations of this period he never allowed the idea to enter his mind that he would then have really closed all his plans of life; that he would have nothing to do; that as he had professedly done with the world, so the world has actually done with him.

How great, therefore, is the difference in the condition of a man of twenty and one of seventy years! To those in the former condition the words of Milton in relation to our first parents when they went out from Eden into the wide world may not improperly be applied:—

"The world was all before them then, where to choose
Their place of rest, and Providence their guide;"

those, in the other case, have nothing which they *can* choose. There is nothing before them but the one path—that which leads to the grave—to another world. To them the path of wealth, of fame, of learning, of ambition, is closed forever. The world has nothing more for them; they have nothing more for the world.

If an inference should be drawn from these remarks, it should *not* be one of melancholy and gloom. There are cheerful views which an aged man may take of life, perhaps not *less* cheerful than those which are taken in early years. If early life is full of hope, it is also often full of anxiety and uncertainty; if in advanced life the world has now nothing to offer to a man, it may be that much is gained by being free from the cares, the burdens, and the anxieties of earlier years; if to such an one this world has nothing now to give, there may be much more than it ever gave even in anticipation, and infinitely more than it has given in reality, in the hope of the life to come.

JACOB ABBOTT.

[Born 1803.]

Rev. Jacob Abbott was born in Hallowell, Maine, in 1803, and entered Bowdoin College at twelve years of age. After graduating, he studied theology at Andover, and, on completing his three years' course there, was appointed tutor, and afterwards Professor of Mathematics, in Amherst College, which station he filled with great success. Thence he was called to the pastoral charge of the Elliott Street Congregational Church, Boston. Mr. Abbott was very successful as a teacher in his well-known Mount Vernon School for Young Ladies, in Boston; and at a later period, when associated with his brother, John S. C. Abbott, in the Houston and Bleecker Street Schools, in New York. Since then he has devoted his time entirely to writing, and has acquired a high reputation as the author of a variety of works having for their object the moral and religious training, and the intellectual instruction of the young.

His first important literary work, The Young Christian, appeared in Boston, in 1825; it was followed in the series by The Corner Stone, The Way to do Good, and Hoaryhead and McDonner. The Young Christian series has enjoyed not only a wide circulation in this country, but numerous editions have been issued in England, Scotland, France, and Germany, translated into various languages of Europe and Asia. He wrote The Teacher, Moral Influences employed in the Instruction and Government of the Young, 12mo.

When these were completed, Mr. Abbott commenced the Rollo Series of Juvenile writings, which reached 24 vols., consisting of the Rollo Books, 14 vols.; the Lucy Books, 6 vols.; and the Jonas Books, in 4 vols. The Marco Paul Series followed, in 6 vols., and subsequently the Franconia Stories, in 10 vols. A series of Illustrated Histories, extending now to 30 vols., appeared in rapid succession from the press of Harpers, tastefully printed, and with the particular topic attractively set forth in a fluent, easy narrative. Harper's Story Books, a series of narratives written to certain cuts, were published in 36 thin volumes; also, uniform in style, The Little Learner Series, 5 vols., and, The Rainbow and Lucky series, 5 vols. He published a narrative of his travels, entitled, A Summer in Scotland. He commenced, in 1870, a new series under the title of The Juno Stories, in 4 vols.

Mr. Abbott has great skill as a story-teller for the young. He avoids particularly all ambiguity and obscurity. His page is neither encumbered by superfluous matter, nor deficient in the necessary fulness of explanation. No writer of original works for children, in this country, has attained to a wider popularity or greater sale

---

DOING OUR FATHER'S BUSINESS.
FROM THE CORNER-STONE.

If you look into the Bible, to your Savior, for an example, you will see that the first principle of action which he announced was, that he was doing his Father's business. But you say perhaps that he was sent from heaven to do a great work here, which you can not do. " I can not go," you say, "from place to place, preaching the gospel and working miracles, and giving sight to the blind and healing the sick. I would do it if I could."

It is true you can not do that. That is, you can not do your Father's business in the same way precisely, that Christ did it. Or, to explain it more fully, God has a great deal of business to be done in this world, and it is of various kinds, and the particular portion allotted to each person depends upon the circumstances in which each one is placed. You cannot do exactly what Christ did while he was here, but you can do what he would have done had he been in your place. You can not make a blind man happy by restoring his sight, but you can make your little sister happy by helping her up kindly when she has fallen down; and that last is your Father's business as much as the other. His business here is to make every one happy, and to relieve every one's suffering. You can not persuade great multitudes of men to love and obey God, as Christ endeavored to do, but you may lead your brothers and sisters to him, by your silent influence and happy example. So you can bear sufferings patiently, and

JACOB ABBOTT.

take injuries meekly, and thus exhibit the character which God desires that men should everywhere see. The light which you thus let shine may be a feeble light, and it may illuminate only a narrow circle around you; but if it is the light of genuine piety, it will be in fact the glory of God; and if it is your great object to let this light shine, you are about your Father's business as truly as Jesus was, when he preached to the thronging multitude, or brought Lazarus from the tomb.

It is very difficult for an observer to know whether an individual is acting for God or for himself. A Christian merchant, for instance, who feels that he holds a stewardship, will be as industrious, as enterprising, and as persevering in his plans as any other merchant. Only he acts as agent, while the other acts as principal. So a boy may be amiable and gentle and kind without any regard to God, or any desire to carry on *his* plans. But God sees very clearly who is working for *him*, and who is not; and there is not one, and there never has been one, in any age, who, if he had been inclined to enter God's service, would not have found enough to do for him, had he been disposed to do it. The example of Jesus Christ in this respect is an example for all mankind. It is intended for universal imitation, and they who pass through life without imitating it, must find themselves condemned when they come to their account.

And how strange it is, that there should be found so very few willing to do the work of God in this world. Even of those few, most, instead of entering into it heart and soul, do just enough to satisfy what they suppose to be the expectations of their Christian brethren. A lady will spend her life, engrossed with such objects of interest as new furniture, and fashionable dress, and the means of securing the admiration of others, for herself or her children. She thinks for days and weeks of procuring some new article of furniture, not for comfort or convenience, but for show; and when at last the long-expected acquisition is made, she is pleased and delighted, as if one of the great objects of her existence had been accomplished. She spends hours in deciding upon the color or texture of a ribbon, which as soon as it is chosen will begin to fade, and after a very brief period fall into contempt and be rejected; or she pursues, month after month, and year after year, what she calls the pleasures of society, which pleasures are often a compound of pride, vanity, envy, jealousy, and ill-will. Her husband, perhaps, in the mean-time devotes himself to pursuits equally unworthy an immortal mind. They do good occasionally, as opportunities occur, and call themselves Christians; but they seem to have no idea, that God has any great work in life for them to do.

Has he work for them to do? Yes; there is a world to be restored to holiness and happiness, and he asks their help in doing it. He has put their children almost completely in their power, so that the eternal happiness of these children might be almost certainly secured, and has given them connections with society, of which they might avail themselves in working most efficiently for him. If they would take hold of this enterprise, they would have some elevated and ennobling object before them. They would see, one after another, those connected with them, returning to God. They would see their children growing up in piety. Every night, they would feel that they had been living during the day for God; and whatever might be their difficulties and trials, they would be relieved from all sense of responsibility and care. Instead of feeling gloomy and sad, as their children were gradually separated from them, or were one by one removed by death, and as they themselves were gradually drawing toward the close of life, they would find their interest in their great business growing stronger and stronger as they approached the change which would bring them more directly into connection with their Father.

The offer, on the part of our Maker, to take us into his service, in this world, is in fact the only plan which can give human life any real dignity, or substantial value. Without it all human employments are insignificant, all pleasure is insipid, and life is a sterile waste, void of verdure or bloom. Without this, there is an entire disproportion between the lofty powers and capacities of human nature, and the low pursuits and worthless objects which are before it in its present home. An immortal spirit, capable of thoughts which explore the universe, and of feelings and desires reaching forward to eternity, spending life in seeing how many pieces of stamped metal it can get together! a mind made in the image of God, and destined to live as long as he, buried for years in thoughts about the size and beauty of a dwelling which is all the time going to decay, or about the color and fashion of dress, or the hues and carvings of rosewood or mahogany!

But let no one understand me to condemn the enjoyments, which come to us through the arts and refinements of life. It is making these things the great object of existence,—it is the eager pursuit of them, as the chief business of life, which the example of our Savior and the principles of the gospel condemn. These arts and refinements are intended to add to human happiness. They will make the most rapid progress in those countries where Christianity most perfectly prevails. Jesus Christ had a love for beauty, both of nature and art; he admired the magnificent architecture of the temple, and deeply lamented the necessity of its overthrow, and his dress was at least of such a character, that the disposal of it was a subject of importance to the well-paid soldiers who crucified him. Yes, the universal reign of Christianity will be the reign of taste, and refinement, and the arts; but while the enjoyments of men will be increased in a tenfold degree from these and other sources, their hearts will be set far less on them, than they are now. These enjoyments will be recreations by the way, to cheer and refresh those whose hearts are mainly bent on accomplishing the objects of their Father in Heaven.

HORACE BUSHNELL.

[Born 1804.]

HORACE BUSHNELL, the now eminent theologian was born in 1804, in New Preston or Washington, Litchfield Co., Conn. He was as a boy employed in a fulling mill in the village. He graduated at Yale College in 1827, was engaged as literary editor of the Journal of Commerce in New York, and in 1829, was tutor in Yale. In 1831, he studied for the law, but deserted it for theology. In May, 1833, he assumed the duties of Pastor of the North Congregational Church, at Hartford. At this time he contributed to the religious periodicals, and delivered the Phi Beta Kappa oration at New Haven, to the Class of 1837, on the Principles of Greatness.

He commenced the publication of his theological works in 1847, with his Views of Christian Nurture, and of subjects adjacent thereto, in which he presented his views of the spiritual economy of revivals, and marks out the philosophical limitations to a system which had been carried to excess. In 1849, he published, God in Christ, three Discourses on the doctrine of the Trinity, that created a great deal of discussion, and much opposition from some of his Congregational brethren, and was the cause of his being brought before the Ministerial Association. The main points of his defence were presented in his new volume, Christ in Theology; or, Character of Jesus, in 1851.

He has also achieved distinguished success in the philosophical essay, in which he mingles subtle and refined speculation with the affairs of every-day life, in a manner peculiarly his own. The titles of these essays show the bent of his mind; On Taste and Fashion; the Moral Tendencies and Results of Human History; Work and Play; Unconscious Influence; the Day of Roads; The Northern Iron; Barbarism the First Danger; Religious Music; Politics under the Law of God. In 1849, Dr.

Bushnell pronounced an oration, The Fathers of New England, before the New York New England Society; and in 1851, Speech for Connecticut, before the Legislature.

In 1858, he published Sermons for the New Life, 12mo., which is marked by the spirituality, elevated views, ingenious illustration, and fervid eloquence which characterize all his writings. In the same year, Nature and the Supernatural, as together constituting the one System of God, 12mo., undertaken mainly to establish the credibility and historic fact of what is supernatural in the Christian Gospels. In 1860, he issued Christian Nurture, 12mo., thirteen discourses on the theory and practice of Christianity, with especial relation to the family, being an enlarged edition of a previous work of the same title. In 1864, he collected a number of the essays we have mentioned above, under the title of Work and Play, or Literary Varieties, 12mo., all of a historical, literary, or philosophical character. The same year he published, Christ and his Salvation, a series of twenty-one Sermons variously related to the subject. In 1865, he issued, The Vicarious Sacrifice, grounded on Principles of Universal Obligation, 12mo.; and in 1869, Moral Uses of Dark Things; and, Women's Suffrage, the Reform against Nature. The latter upon a topic, at the time, much discussed by the press; the author takes ground that this new reform against nature, is an attempt to make trumpets out of flutes, and sunflowers out of violets.

Dr. Bushnell's writings have attracted considerable attention among theologians, from the bold and original manner in which he has presented views of the doctrines of the Calvinistic faith. The dissertation prefixed to his volume "God in Christ," contains the germ of most of what are considered his theological peculiarities.

USES OF PHYSICAL DANGER.

FROM MORAL USES OF DARK THINGS.

ABOUT the highest exhibition of power obtained or obtainable by man, is discovered in the command or sovereign mind-grapple he learns how to maintain over causes infinitely above him, as respects their physical efficiency. He is not only not cowed before the tremendous forces of the creation of God, but he steals their secret, and by means of it he actually takes them into service. And in doing it he is often moved by the stimulation of danger, going directly into the chambers where the danger lurks, and working in close precinct with it. His most striking contrivances, combinations, tools, machines, operations, discoveries, are ways found out by his intelligence for keeping at bay, or reducing to subserviency, forces that would otherwise crush him. As he must go mining underground, in halls that are filled with combustible, explosive gas, he learns by a little experiment how to fence with a fine wire-gauze, when he has a safety-lamp that commands the gas to be harmless; and walking there underground, through the valley of the shadow of death, with it in hand, he fears no evil. Beset by a dreadful plague, that breathes infection round him year by year, carrying off a third part of the world's children, he learns to steal a poison from one of his domesticated animals, and, vaccinated with a touch of this, he goes, and lets them go, directly into the bad exposure, doing it as securely as if the plague-infection were wholly at his bidding. The wild, half-demoniacal terrors of alchemy attract his search instead of repelling it, and chemistry is the result. The sea is a terrible devouring element, and the mariner goes coasting cautiously along the frightful shores for long ages, fearing not only the rocks and winds, but vastly more that he shall wander into unknown regions, and be never able to find where he is, or by what course to reach his home. By and by it is discovered, by explorative genius groping far away among the stars, that by angle and distance and calculated tables and observations, the random ship that was can find her place, at almost any time, within a mile, and set her course with reliable precision for any country or harbor on the globe. The sea again he finds a yawning gulf between him and the world; he searches it out with his mind as the fishes can net with their fins, maps the still bottom, draws his wire along it, and then sits down to think and talk serenely through three thousand miles of wave and storm. Still more sublime, because vastly more complex, is that wonderful combination of study and experience by which human society learns to organize itself in law and government, so as to keep in safe control those worst infestations of danger that are created by social wrong and passion. The problem is, how to distribute selfishness, and set bad power in balance, so as to keep it safe in the maintenance of order and justice. A very cheap, small thing it is to make out navigation tables, even though we go to the stars for our data; but to make out safe navigations for society, and steer the ark of liberty through the perilous seas of wrong and passion—this, alas! is an art that comes more slowly; and yet it comes! We shall have it by and by, the world over. And yet all these and other puttings forth of skill and adaptive discovery, in the nature-field of our life, are only types of that vastly higher and more qualified intelligence by which we are to get the worlds

of spirit and religion into our command, and bring the powers of the world to come into our service In its highest view, the great problem of religion, it is true, is not safety, but righteousness—how to be right with God; how a soul in evil may come up out of evil into God's acceptance and friendship, as being co-ordinate with him in character. And yet the first impulse to this is the felt insecurity of evil, set home and seconded by all the perils of time. From that humble beginning the soul is to get spring, and then, by its divine explorations of study, and faith, and sacrifice, it is to climb up into God's eternity, appropriating all the grandest truths and powers and celestial navigations of his realms. Nowhere does he engineer so loftily and ascend to such a grade of intelligence as here. We have almost no conception of intelligence, what it can contrive, and seize, and command, till we follow it up hither into this diviner field. Think what we may of fear, and danger, and the weakness of all such initiations of motive, they do in fact prepare us to exactly that which is the crown of intelligence, and without which it has no crown

USES OF WINTER.

FROM THE SAME.

THE contrast observable here between summer and winter life, in respect to the habit or capacity of reflection, is specially remarkable. Self-indulgence, luxury, and a free bathing of sensation in the world's temperatures and odors make soft motive for us in the summer, and lull us in a softening element. We seek the out-door shade and open air, and the motion of our being is outward, away from its own center. The songs of the morning are music in our ear. The air is laden with incense. Scenes of beauty open to the eye, and we fill ourselves all day with images of freshness and life. All which is of the highest use—it is even necessary to the furniture of the mind. But it requires a time of reflection afterward, to enable us to realize the moral benefits prepared. After the mind has received the summer into its storehouse, then it wants the winter, as a time wherein to review and con over its stores. Then let the summer wane, and the autumnal frost begin to whiten the plain. Let the songs be hushed, the verdure fall off, and the scented air breathe only cold. Let the snows spread their blanket over the dead world, and the wintry blasts howl vengefully and wild. Now the senses lose their objects, and the man, not as being moved inwardly, but frost-nipped rather without, gathers in his mind to reflection. And there he finds gathered in also all the images of the creation, himself among them present also to himself. Their meanings, monitions, suggestions, and the matter-forms of thought there is in them, throng in to his aid. He hears the whispers of his conscience, and thinks of other worlds. Every prospect without forbidding and desolate, and the in-door fire more attractive in his evenings than any walk abroad, he is shut up, in a sense, even wontedly, to his chamber, and to thoughts that relate to his own being and well-being. If he ever cogently and closely thinks, it will probably be now. If he is ever seriously bent to the very highest concernments of his nature, he is likely to be so now. There is more of tone in his moral perceptions than at other times. Truth is seen more clearly, and his soul rings like a bell under its touch, because he is undiverted by things without, and thought is single in its action.

Now, it is well understood that the mind never attains to great intellectual strength without first forming a habit of reflection. And the same is necessary to a vigorous pronouncement of the moral man—the conscience, the spiritual emotions, and the religious aspirations. Hence the well-known superficiality and the great intellectual and moral dearth of the tropical climates. Having no winter, they have no capacity of deep, well-invigorated reflection, and no firm condensation of thoughtful temperament. Their moral nature especially wants the true frigorific tension of a well wintered life and experience. For it is often observed, partly because the habit is more reflective, and partly for other reasons, that men have a stronger sense of principles in winter, than at any other time. They see them invested with a certain rigor and severity, like the season itself. Or, perhaps, without making any such comparison, they do, by a certain force of association, behold them, as they do the trunks of the forest, standing in their pure anatomy, curtained by no garniture of leaves, and stretching their bare, stiff limbs to the sky. Hence the contrast between tropical consciences, which are made more conscious of our moral and religious wants in the winter, than we are in the softer, balmier seasons. If we can judge from the feeding of the swine on the ripened products of the year; the parable of the prodigal son is a winter parable in its date. He came also to himself, and began to be in want, because it was a time of short allowance. The intimation therefore is, that the sense of guilt and hunger, in the moral nature, is the needed precondition of all highest spiritual good ; and when but in the winter shall this necessary sense of want be wakened ? Let every thing about the man be an image of the dearth and coldness of a cold heart. Surround him with winter as a counterpart to the winter of the mind. Cut him off from the diversions and half-satisfactions of his summer pleasures, take

away the sceneries and prospects that relieve the tedium of an empty heart. Shut him up to himself, leaving no resource, save what he finds in himself. And then, if ever, he will be likely to feel the stir of those sublime, everlasting wants, that put all moral natures reaching after God. In this matter, it is not the question simply, what a cold, blank soul may be put on thinking, by the experiences and sceneries of winter. We have a great many gospelings that do not come to thought, or work by thought at all, but only by the states, or impressions they beget in ways more immediate ; even as hymns do not take our head by their mere creed matter, but play themselves straightway into sentiments. And so it is that God's great ordinance of snow—the blank of it, the white of it, and the cold, and the readiness to be dissolved and pass away—is just that power on human feeling most profoundly adapted to the fit movement of the soul's immortal want. It is a kind of scenery felt to be both congenial and chill ; answering faithfully to the dreary chill of hunger that pinches the bosom within.

Analogous to this effect of winter and closely related, is the fact that we are more capable of realizing invisible sceneries and worlds in the winter, than at any other time. God is more vividly imaged to the mind, we can not but admit, in the sceneries, and showers, and dews of summer. It appears to be intimated also, that our paradise will have tropical attractions, yielding twelve manner of fruits—a fruit every month—but the time to realize these invisible things of God and his paradise, is when a pall is thrown over things visible that have a resemblance. Thus it would be very unskillful if any one, having it for his problem how to produce the most vivid impression of the beauties of paradise—the river clear as crystal, the golden sands, the trees of life blooming fast by the river—were to choose the time when spring is bursting into leaf and flower, and the odors are floating, and the music warbling on the air. In that case he will only raise an impression that the good world's delectations are about on a par with our present, which does not after all appear to be very superlatively blessed ; whereas, if he should rather choose the dreary and bleak winter, when the creation is desolate and bare, he would call on our imaginations to paint the picture, and be sure that they would make it blessed above all fact—as superlatively blessed as it need be. It must also be remembered that the invisible things of religion will be just as much more real in the winter, as the want of them is more impressively felt ; as much more real as their principles are more distinctly apprehended ; as much more real as the power of thought is more separated from the distractions of the senses.

JOHN S. C. ABBOTT.

[Born 1805.]

Rev. John S. C. Abbott, brother of Rev. Jacob Abbott, was born at Brunswick, Me., in 1805 ; graduated at Bowdoin College, 1825, and at the Theological Seminary in Andover, Mass., 1829. He is a congregational clergyman, and a writer of many successful works for the young. He also constantly contributes historical articles to Harper's Magazine.

His principal works are the Mother at Home, first published in 1833 ; a work of the utmost importance to mothers ; it takes such estimates of the maternal character, as are overwhelming in their solemnity. He has shown himself a master of his subject, and has treated it with equal delicacy and force.

This was followed by the Child at Home ; the duties and trials peculiar to the child are explained in this volume in the same clear and and attractive manner in which those of the mother are set forth in "The Mother at Home." Kings and Queens, or Life in the Palace; Practical Christianity, a Treatise designed for young men ; it is characterized by the simplicity of style and appositeness of illustration which make a book easily read and readily understood. The Histories of Marie Antoinette, Josephine, Mad. Roland, Cortez, Henri IV. of France, King Philip, and Joseph Bonaparte, part of Abbott's Historical series by himself and brother, published by Harpers.

He published a History of the French Revolution of 1789, as viewed in the Light of Republican Institutions, illustrated, 8vo. His sympathies are strongly on the side of the French people in their conflict with the throne. He regards the atrocities committed, as excesses for which the kings and court minions of preceding generations were chiefly answerable— as the inevitable reaction of a people suppressed and cramped, pillaged and outraged by weary centuries of despotism.

His largest work, however, is his Life of Napoleon, in 2 vols., royal, 8vo., profusely illustrated, first issued in Harper's Magazine, 1852–1854. This biography has been warmly criticized by the opponents of Napoleon's policy, and as stoutly defended by his admirers. Written in a popularly attractive style, with much success as a narrative ; its principal defect is, the excessive laudation of Napoleon as a demi-god, a hero without blemish. While no one can deny the extraordinary abilities of the most wonderful man that ever lived, still every candid mind must admit he had his faults ; he would not have been human, had it been otherwise. The defect of Mr. Abbott's history is that he too much endeavors to draw the veil over the darkest parts of the character of Napoleon, and displaying mostly the godlike parts of his hero. Great hero that he was, extraordinary mind as he possessed, able to almost instantly grasp the weightiest subjects in law, finance, government, politics, or military matters, there was a certain amount of selfishness in his ambition to elevate France to the loftiest pinnacle of greatness among nations, which would occasionally show forth in striking contrast to the character of our own Washington. The apparent aim of Mr. Abbott has been, not to pervert facts, but to place them in such strong lights and shades, that the lights shall play upon only such points as he wishes to be most prominent, and the reader rises from its perusal, so dazzled with the brilliancy of the subject, as hardly to be able to see mentally, anything but just what the author wants him to, and that always is what will most redound to the glorification of his hero's character. The work had great and deserved success, and was followed by Napoleon at St. Helena ; intended to give the particulars of his residence on that island, his sayings while there, and the last events of his life. It is an excellent compilation, and a necessary conclusion and accompaniment to the previous three volumes.

He edited also the Confidential Correspondence of Napoleon and Josephine, 2 vols., 12mo.

THE BATTLE OF WATERLOO.

FROM THE LIFE OF NAPOLEON.

A SERIES of unparalleled fatalities appear to have thwarted Napoleon's profoundly laid plans throughout the whole of this momentous campaign. The treachery of Bourmont rescued the enemy from that surprise which would unquestionably have secured his destruction. The neglect of Ney to take possession of Quatre-Bras, and the false intelligence sent to Napoleon that it was occupied, again snatched a decisive victory from the Emperor. And yet this great man—never disposed to quarrel with his destiny—uttered no angry complaints. He knew that Ney had intended no wrong, and he lost not a moment in useless repining. He immediately sent a friendly message to Ney, and calmly gathered up his resources to do what he could under the change of circumstances.

Night again came with its unintermitted storm. It was the night of the 16th of June. The soldiers, drenched, hungry, weary, bleeding. dying, in vain sought repose beneath that inclement sky and in those miry fields. Napoleon, at Ligny, not ten miles from Quatre-Bras, was a victor. Ney, repulsed at every point, slept upon his arms before his indomitable foe at Quatre-Bras. Blucher, with his broken battalions, retreated, unopposed, during the night, toward Wavre. Wellington, informed of this retreat, fell back to form a junction with the Prussian army at Waterloo. Napoleon dispatched Marshal Grouchy, with thirty thousand men, to pursue the retreating Prussians, to keep them continually in sight, to harass them in every way, and to press them so hotly that they should not be able to march to the aid of Wellington.

The morning of the 17th of June dawned dismally upon these exhausted and wretched victims of war, through the clouds and the rain, and the still continued wailings of the storm. The soldiers of Grouchy were so worn down by the superhuman exertions and sufferings of the last few days, that they were unable to overtake the rapidly retreating Prussians. They, however, toiled along through the miry roads with indomitable energies. Napoleon, leaving Grouchy to pursue the Prussians, immediately passed over to Quatre-Bras, to unite his forces with those of Ney, and to follow the retreat of Wellington. Their combined army amounted to about 70,000 men. With these the Emperor followed vigorously in the track of Wellington.

The Duke had retreated during the day toward Brussels, and halted on the spacious field of Waterloo, about nine miles from the metropolis. Here, having skilfully selected his ground and posted his troops. he anxiously awaited the arrival of Blucher, to whom he had sent urgent dispatches to hasten to his aid. Blucher was at Wavre, but a few hours' march from Waterloo, with 72,000 men. The junction of these forces would give Wellington an overwhelming superiority of numbers. He would then have at least 150,000 troops with whom to assail less than 70,000.

As night approached, the troops of Napoleon, toiling painfully through the storm, the darkness, and the mire, arrived also on the fatal plain. The late hour at which the several divisions of the French army reached the unknown field of battle, involved in the obscurity of darkness and the storm, embarrassed the Emperor exceedingly. As the light was fading away, he pointed toward the invisible sun, and said, " What would I not give to be this day possessed of the power of Joshua, and enabled to retard thy march for two hours!"

Napoleon, judging from the bivouac fires of the enemy that they were strongly posted and intended to give battle, reconnoitered the ground by groping over it on foot, and posted his battalions as they successively arrived. He immediately sent a dispatch to Marshal Grouchy, ordering him to press the Prussians vigorously, and to keep himself in a position to combine with the Emperor's operations. For eighteen hours the Emperor had tasted neither of sleep, repose, nor nourishment. His clothes were covered with mud and soaked with rain. But regardless of exposure and fatigue, he did not seek even to warm himself by the fires around which his drenched troops were shivering. All the night long the rain fell in torrents, and all the night long the Emperor toiled, unprotected in the storm, as he prepared for the conflict of the morrow.

Wellington's army, variously estimated at from 72,000 to 90,000 in number, was admirably posted along the brow of a gentle eminence, a mile and a half in length. A dense forest in the rear, where the ground gradually fell away, concealed from the view and the shot of the enemy all but those who stood upon the brow of the eminence. Napoleon established his troops, estimated at from 65,000 to 75,000, within cannon-shot of the foe, and on the gentle declivity of a corresponding rise of land, which extended parallel to that occupied by the English.

The dreadful night at length passed away, and the morning of the 18th of June dawned, lurid and cheerless, through the thick clouds. It was the morning of the Sabbath day. The vast field of Waterloo, plowed and sown with grain, soaked by the rains of the past week, and cut up by the wheels and the tramp of these enormous armies, was converted into a quagmire. The horses sank to their knees in the humid soil. The wheels of the guns, encumbered with adhesive clay, rolled heavily, axle-deep, in the mire. Under circumstances of such difficulty, the French were compelled to attack down one ridge of slopes, across a valley, and up another ridge, toiling through the mud, exposed all the way to point-blank discharges from the batteries and lines of the English. Wellingtou was to act simply on the defensive, endeavoring to maintain his position until the arrival of Blucher.

About eight o'clock the clouds of the long storm broke and dispersed ; the sun came out in all its glory, and one of the most bright and lovely of summer Sabbaths smiled upon Waterloo. The skies ceased to weep, and the vail of clouds was withdrawn, as if God would allow the angels to look down and witness this awful spectacle of man's inhumanity to man.

Napoleon assembled most of his general officers around him to give them his final orders. "The enemy's army," said he, "is superior to ours by nearly a fourth. There are, however, ninety chances in our favor to ten against us."

"Without doubt," exclaimed Marshal Ney, who had that moment entered, "if the Duke of Wellingtou were simple enough to wait for your Majesty's attack. But I am come to announce that his columns are already in full retreat, and are fast disappearing in the forest of Soignes."

"You have seen badly," the Emperor replied, with calm confidence. "It is too late. By such a step he would expose himself to certain ruin. He has thrown the dice; they are now for us."

At half past ten o'clock all the movements were made, and the troops were in their stations for the battle. Thus far profound silence had reigned on the field, as the squadrons moved with noiseless steps to their appointed stations. The hospitals were established in the rear. The corps of surgeons had spread out their bandages and splinters, knives and saws, and, with their sleeves rolled up, were ready for their melancholy deeds of mercy. The Emperor rode along his devoted lines. Every eye was riveted upon him. Every heart said, "God bless him !"

"One heart," says Lamartine, "beat between these men and the Emperor. In such a moment they shared the same soul and the same cause. The army was Napoleon. Never before was it so entirely Napoleon as now. At such a moment he must have felt himself more than a man, more than a sovereign. His army bent in homage to the past, the present, and the future, and welcomed victory or defeat, the throne or death with its chief. It was determined on everything, even on the sacrifice of itself, to restore him his empire, or to render his last fall illustrious. To have inspired such devotion was the greatness of Napoleon ; to evince it even to madness was the greatness of his army." Such is the reluctant concession, blended with ungenerous slurs, of Napoleon's most uncandid and most envenomed foe.

The acclamations which burst from the lips of nearly seventy thousand men, thus inspired with one affection, one hope, one soul, resounded in prolonged echoes over the field, and fell portentously on the ears of the waiting enemy.

In the English army there was probably not a man who was not proud of the renown of Old England, and proud of the genius of the Duke of Wellington. But in all those serried ranks there was perhaps not one single private who *loved* the Iron Duke. Indeed, there was so strong a sympathy with the Emperor, among the Belgian and Hanoverian troops, who were *compelled* to march under the banner of the Allies, that the Duke had great fears that they would abandon him in the heat of battle, and pass over to the generous, sympathizing, warm-hearted chieftain of the people

In reference to these German contingents, Sir Walter Scott says—in truthful utterance, though with inelegant phrase—" They were in some instances suspected to be lukewarm to the cause in which they were engaged, so that it would have been imprudent to trust more to their assistance and co-operation than could not possibly be avoided."

At eleven o'clock the horrid carnage commenced. On either side everything was done which mortal courage or energy could accomplish. Hour after hour the French soldiers, shouting " *Vive l'Empereur !*" made onset after onset, up to the very muzzles of the British guns, and were cut down by those terrific discharges like grass before the scythe. The demon of destruction and woe held its high carnival in the midst of the demoniac revelry of those bloody hours. Every discharge which blended its thunder with the roar of that awful battle, was sending widowhood and orphanage to distant homes, blinding the eyes of mothers and daughters with tears of agony, and darkening once happy dwellings with life-long wretchedness.

For many hours the whole field was swept with an unintermitted storm of balls, shells, bullets, and grape-shot ; while enormous masses of cavalry, in fluent and refluent surges, trampled into the bloody mire the dying and the dead. There were now forty thousand of the combatants weltering in gore. The wide-extended field was everywhere covered with bodies in every conceivable form of hideous mutilation. The flash of the guns, the deafening thunder of artillery and musketry, the groans and the piercing shrieks of the wounded, the dense volumes of smoke which enveloped the plain in almost midnight gloom, the delirious shouts of the assailants as they rushed upon death, the shrill whistling of the missiles of destruction, and the wild flight of the fugitives, as, in broken bands, they were pursued and sabred by the cavalry, presented the most revolting spectacle of war in all the enormity of its guilt and of its fiendish brutality. Who, before the tribunal of God, is to be held responsible for that day of blood ?

In the midst of these awful scenes, early in the afternoon, as portions of Wellington's line were giving way, and flying in dismay toward Brussels, carrying the tidings of defeat, and when Napoleon felt sure of the victory, the Emperor's quick eye discerned, far off upon his right, an immense mass of men, more than thirty thousand strong, emerging from the forest, and with rapid step deploying upon the plain. At first Napoleon was sanguine that it was Marshal Grouchy, and that the battle was decided. But in another moment their artillery balls began to plow his ranks, and the Emperor learned that it was Bulow, with the advance-guard of Blucher's army, hastening to the rescue of Wellington.

This was giving the foe a fearful preponderance of power. Napoleon had now less than sixty thousand men, while Wellington, with this reinforcement, could oppose to him a hundred thousand. But the Emperor, undismayed, turned calmly to Marshal Soult, and said, "We had ninety chances out of a hundred in our favor this morning. The arrival of Bulow makes us lose thirty. But we have still sixty against forty. And if Grouchy sends on his detachment with rapidity the victory will be thereby only the more decisive, for the corps of Bulow must, in that case, be entirely lost."

Napoleon was compelled to weaken his columns, which were charging upon the wavering lines of Wellington, by dispatching ten thousand men to beat back these fresh battalions, thirty thousand strong. The enthusiastic French, armed in the panoply of a just cause, plunged recklessly into the ranks of this new foe, and drove him back into the woods. The Emperor with his diminished columns continued his terrible charges. He kept his eye anxiously fixed upon the distant horizon, expecting every moment to see the gleaming banners of Grouchy. The Marshal heard the tremendous cannonade booming from the field of Waterloo, and yet refused, notwithstanding the entreaties of his officers, to approach the scene of the terrific strife. He has been accused of treason. Napoleon charitably ascribes his fatal inactivity to want of judgment. The couriers sent to him in the morning were either intercepted by the enemy or turned traitors. Grouchy did not receive the order. In the circumstances of the case, however, to every one but himself the path of duty seemed plain.

General Excelsmann, rode up to Marshal Grouchy, and said, "The Emperor is in action with the English army. There can be no doubt of it. A fire so terrible cannot be a skirmish. We ought to march to the scene of action. I am an old soldier of the army of Italy, and have heard General Bonaparte promulgate this principle a hundred times. If we turn to the left we shall be on the field of battle in two hours." Count Gerard joined them, and urged the same advice. Had Grouchy followed these counsels, and appeared upon the field with his division of thirty thousand men, probably not a man of the English or Prussian army could have escaped the Emperor. But Grouchy, though he had lost sight of Blucher, pleaded his orders to follow him, and refused to move.

"Do you think," said O'Meara to Napoleon at St. Helena, "that Grouchy betrayed you intentionally?"

"No! no!" the Emperor promptly replied; "but there was a want of energy on his part. There was also treason among the staff. I believe that some of the officers whom I had sent to Grouchy betrayed me, and went over to the enemy. Of this, however, I am not certain, as I have never seen Grouchy since."

As the French soldiers witnessed the prompt retreat of Bulow's reinforcement, and the Emperor was about to make a charge with the Old Guard, which never yet had charged in vain, they deemed the victory sure. Loud shouts of "*Vive l'Empereur!*" rang along their lines, which rose above the roar of the battle, and fell ominously, in prolonged echoes, upon the ears of the allied troops. A panic spread through the ranks of Wellington's army. Many of the regiments were reduced to skeletons, and some, thrown into disorder, were rushing from the field in fugitive bands. The whole rear of the English army now presented a tumultuary scene of confusion, the entire space between Waterloo and Brussels being filled with stragglers and all the *débris* of a routed army.

Wellington stood upon a gentle eminence, watching with intense anxiety for the coming of Blucher. He knew that he could hold out but a short time longer. As he saw his lines melting away, he repeatedly looked at his watch, and then fixed his gaze upon the distant hills, and as he wiped the perspiration which mental anguish extorted from his brow, exclaimed, "Would to Heaven that Blucher or night would come."

Just at this critical moment, when the Emperor was giving an order for a simultaneous attack by his whole force, two long, dark columns, of thirty thousand each, the united force of Blucher and Bulow, came pouring over the hills, down upon the torn and bleeding flank of Napoleon's exhausted troops. Thus an army of sixty thousand fresh soldiers, nearly equal to Napoleon's whole force at the commencement of the conflict, with exultant hurrahs and bugle peals, and thundering artillery, came rushing upon the plain. It was an awful moment. It was a thunderbolt of fate.

"It is almost certain," says General Jomini, who had deserted to the Allies, and was at this time aide-de-camp to Emperor Alexander, "that Napoleon would have remained master of the field of battle, but for the arrival of 65,000 Prussians on his rear."

The Emperor's wasted bands were now in the extreme of exhaustion. For eight hours every physical energy had been tasked to its utmost endurance, by such a conflict as the world had seldom seen before. Twenty thousand of his soldiers were either lying upon the ground or motionless in death. He had now less than fifty thousand men to oppose to one hundred and fifty thousand. Wellington during the day had brought up some additional forces from his rear, and could now oppose the Emperor with numbers three to one.

The intelligent French soldiers instantly perceived the desperate state of their affairs. But, undismayed, they stood firm, waiting only for the command of their Emperor. The allied army saw at a glance its advantage, and a shout of exultation burst simultaneously from their lips. The Emperor, with that wonderful coolness which never forsook him, promptly recalled the order for a general charge, and by a very rapid and skilful series of manœuvres, as by magic, so changed the front of his army as to face the Prussians advancing upon his right, and the lines of Wellington before him.

Everything depended now upon one desperate charge by the Imperial Guard, before the Prussians, trampling down their feeble and exhausted opponents, could blend their squadrons with the battalions of Wellington. The Emperor placed himself at the head of this devoted and invincible band, and advanced in front of the British lines, apparently intending himself to lead the charge. But the officers of his staff entreated him to remember that the safety of France depended solely upon him. Yielding to their solicitations, he resigned the command to Ney.

The scene now presented was one of the most sublime which war has ever furnished. The Imperial Guard had never yet moved but in the path of victory. As these renowned battalions, in two immense columns, descended the one eminence and ascended the other to oppose their bare bosoms to point-blank discharges from batteries double-shotted or loaded to the muzzle with grape, there was a moment's lull in the storm of battle. Both armies gazed with awe upon the scene. The destinies of Napoleon, of France, of Europe were suspended upon the issues of a moment. The fate of the world trembled in the balance. Not a drum beat the charge. Not a bugle uttered its inspiriting notes. Not a cheer escaped the lips of those proud, determined, indomitable men. Silently, sternly, unflinchingly they strode on till they arrived within a few yards of the batteries and bayonets which the genius of Wellington had arrayed to meet them. There was a flash as of intensest lightning gleaming along the British lines. A peal as of crashing thunder burst upon the plain. A tempest of bullets, shot, shells, and all the horrible missiles of war, fell like hailstones upon the living mass, and whole battalions melted away and were trampled in the bloody mire by the still advancing host. Defiant of death, the intrepid Guard, closing up its decimated ranks, pressed on, and pierced the British line. Every cannon, every musket which could be brought to bear, was directed to this unfaltering and terrible foe. Ney, in the course of a few moments, had five horses shot beneath him. Then, with a drawn sabre, he marched on foot at the head of his men. Napoleon gazed with intense anxiety upon the progress of this heroic band, till enveloped in clouds of smoke it was lost to sight.

At the same moment the Prussians came rushing upon the field, with infantry, cavalry, and artillery, entirely overpowering the feeble and exhausted squadrons left to oppose them. A gust of wind swept away the smoke, and as the anxious eye of Napoleon pierced the tumult of the battle to find his Guard, it had disappeared. Almost to a man they were weltering in blood. A mortal paleness overspread the cheek of the Emperor. The French army also saw that the Guard was annihilated. An instantaneous panic struck every heart. With exultant shouts the army of Blucher and of Wellington rushed upon the plain, and a scene of horror ensued at which humanity shudders. The banners of despotic Prussia and of constitutional England blended in triumph, and intertwined their folds over that gory field, where the liberties of Europe were stricken to the dust. Blucher and Wellington, with their dripping

swords, met with congratulations in the midst of the bloody arena. Each claimed the honor of the victory. Together they had achieved it. Wellington's troops were so exhausted as to be unable to follow the discomfited army. "Leave the pursuit to me," said Blucher. "I will send every man and every horse after the enemy." He fulfilled his promise with a merciless energy characteristic of this debauched and fierce dragoon. No quarter was shown. The unarmed were cut down, and even the prisoners were sabred.

The English soldiers, as usual, were generous and merciful in the hour of victory. They dispersed over the field and carried refreshments and assistance, not only to their own wounded countrymen, but also to their bleeding and dying foes.

Napoleon threw himself into a small square, which he had kept as a reserve, and urged it forward into the densest throngs of the enemy. He was resolved to perish with his Guard. Cambronne, its brave commander, seized the reins of the Emperor's horse, and said to him, in beseeching tones, "Sire, death shuns you. You will but be made a prisoner." Napoleon shook his head, and for a moment resisted. But then his better judgment told him that thus to throw away his life would be but an act of suicide. With tears filling his eyes, and grief overspreading his features, he bowed to these heroes, ready to offer themselves up in a bloody sacrifice. Faithful even to death, with a melancholy cry they shouted, " Vive l'Empereur!" These were their last words, their dying farewell. Silent and sorrowful, the Emperor put spurs to his horse, and disappeared from the fatal field. It was the commencement of his journey to St. Helena.

This one square, of two battalions, alone covered the flight of the army as a gallant rear-guard. The Prussians and the English pressed it on three sides, pouring into its bosom the most destructive discharges. Squadrons of cavalry plunged upon them, and still they remained unbroken. The flying artillery was brought up, and pitilessly pierced the heroic band with a storm of cannon balls. This invincible square, the last fragment of the Old Guard, nerved by that soul which its Imperial creator had breathed into it, calmly closing up as death thinned its ranks, slowly and defiantly retired, arresting the flood of pursuit. General Cambronne was now bleeding from six wounds. But a few scores of men, torn and bleeding, remained around him. The English and Prussians, admiring such heroism, and weary of the butchery, suspended for a moment their fire, and sent a flag of truce, demanding a capitulation. General Cambronne returned the immortal reply, "*The Guard dies, but never surrenders!*" A few more volleys of bullets from the infantry, a few more discharges of grape-shot from the artillery, mowed them all down. Thus perished, on the fatal field of Waterloo, the Old Guard of Napoleon. It was the creation of the genius of the Emperor; he had inspired it with his own lofty spirit; and the fall of the Emperor it devotedly refused to survive

CAROLINE LEE HENTZ.

[Born about 1805. Died 1856.]

MRS. CAROLINE LEE HENTZ, a daughter of Gen. John Whiting, was born in Lancaster, Mass. In 1825, she married Prof. N. M. Hentz, a French gentleman, at that time associated with Mr. Geo. Bancroft, in the Round Hill School of Northampton. Mr. Hentz was soon after appointed Professor in the College at Chapel Hill, North Carolina, where they remained for several years. They removed to Covington, Ky., and afterwards to Cincinnati, O. and Florence, Ala. Here they conducted for nine years a prosperous female Academy, and afterwards at Tuscaloosa, Tuskegee, and in 1848, at Columbus, Ga.

While at Covington, she wrote for a prize of $500, the tragedy of De Lara, or the Moorish Bride, which met with success and was published at Columbus; Lamorah, or the Western Wild, a Tragedy; Constance of Werdenberg, a Tragedy; Human and Divine Philosophy, a poem, and other poetical pieces.

Attention was first called to her as a novelist by her stories of Aunt Patty's Scrap Bag, and The Mob Cap; each of which formed the title of a series of novelettes in book form, published in 1846. These were followed by Linda, or the Pilot of the Belle Creole; Rena, or the Snow-Bird; Marcus Warland, or the Long Moss Spring; Eoline, or Magnolia Vale; Wild Jack; Helen and Arthur, or Miss Thusa's Spinning Wheel; The Planter's Northern Bride; Ugly Effie, or the Neglected one and the Beauty; Love after Marriage; The Banished Son; The Victim of Excitement; The Parlor Serpent; The Flowers of Elocution, a class-book; Robert Graham, a sequel to Linda; and Ernest Linwood.

The scenes and incidents of her stories are for the most part drawn from the Southern States; were written in the midst of her social circle, and in the intervals of the ordinary avocations of a busy life. They are sensational in their style, but written with great talent, an excellent finish, and all with some good moral purpose in view. They have met with a marked and deserved popularity, so much so that 93,000 volumes were sold in three years. They still maintain a certain amount of their popularity; a new uniform edition, in 12 volumes, 12mo., was published in 1870.

Her later years spent with her elder children in Florida, were shaded by many cares and trials, from the loss of relatives and the illness of her husband, yet she employed her pen to the last. Her latest composition, written five days before her death, was a short poem, marking her pious resignation, entitled, No Cross, No Crown. She died from an attack of pneumonia, at her home in Marianna, Florida, February 11, 1856.

Professor Hentz, after a protracted illness, did not survive her long, dying, Nov. 4, 1856. He was a gentleman of fine education, and of good attainments in the natural sciences, particularly entomology.

THE FATAL CONCERT.
FROM EOLINE; OR, MAGNOLIA VALE.

GAINING a window not far from the platform, Horace jumped on to its sill, and drawing back as far as possible in the embrasure, gazed upon a scene which seemed to him more like a dream of the imagination than a living actuality. A very elevated platform ran along the whole breadth of the hall, and was separated from it by a row of classic pillars, which were all decorated for the occasion with garlands of evergreen and flowers. Two flights of steps, covered with green cloth, one on each side, led up to this elevation, and a chandelier suspended above, mingled its lustre with the lamps burning beneath.

Miss Manly sat in the centre on a chair raised so as to resemble a throne or dais, and looked down in her majesty on the throng below. No Queen, surrounded by her court, ever bore a loftier presence or carried herself more royally, than the Principal of the Magnolia Vale Seminary. Certainly no queen ever felt more proud of her subjects, or reigned with a more absolute dominion over them. She was dressed for the evening with unusual splendor, and held her ivory fan as if it were a sceptre. On each side of her the pupils were arranged in semicircular order, standing, the taller nearer to her, and gradually diminishing in height as they diverged from the great central luminary. Their uniform was white muslin, relieved by sashes of cerulean hue, and almost all were decorated with some favorite flower. There they stood, these young girls, in their white, flowing robes and azure ribbons, with their sweet flowers, all radiant in juvenility and innocence, so bright, so joyous, that it made one's heart ache to look at them and think these morning blossoms of life should ever be exposed to the mildew and the storm, or worse than all, to the cold, bitter frost. In the centre, just in front of Miss Manly, whose lofty position prevented her from being concealed, appeared Eoline, seated at the piano, in the same celestial livery of white and blue. The music leaves unfolded before her, partially concealed her from the gaze of the audience, but this slight screen did not intercept the view of Horace, who beheld her with sensations such as woman had never before inspired in his breast. Never had she seemed so dazzlingly fair, so softly, yet resplendently lovely. He looked as Adam looked when he beheld the new-made bride of Eden, beaming on his kindling vision. He was as one waking out of a deep sleep, by a flash of conviction, intense as the lightning, and almost as scorching. When strong passions have lain dormant for a long time under a superincumbent weight of intellect, their awakening is the bound of the giant, strong, exultant and fearful. Horace trembled and glowed as the new life came rushing and flowing in, into every vein—giving him the sense of a new creation. It flashed from his eyes—it burned upon his cheek—he felt it in every fibre of his being. But the moment that revealed Eoline to him, invested with this new-born glory, this moment, the warmest, the brightest, soon proved the darkest of his life. For on the right hand stood the minstrel lover, with his pale alabaster face, brilliant eyes, and romantic-waving hair, adorned with every grace that can captivate the eye of woman. And all the time he was gazing, music was gushing forth and filling the hall and sweeping out into the starry night. They were singing an anthem of praise. *Hosanna* was the burden of the strain—" Hosanna," ascended clear and high, as the highest warblings of the flute, from the lips of Eoline—" Hosanna," repeated the youthful hand, in their sweet, bird-like contralto—" Hosanna," breathed St. Leon, in his deep melodious tenor—" Hosanna, Hosanna," resounded the whole choir, in one strong burst of jubilant harmony, while the keys quivered and sparkled under Eoline's jewelled fingers. Horace listened with an interest, an intensity that amounted to agony. As one by one, and then all in one, the *Hosannas* swept by him, and he beheld Eoline the centre of that region of light and harmony, she seemed lost to him forever—lost by his own madness. The words of little Willie rang in his ears —" How could you help loving Ela ?—What did you let her go away for ?" " Because I was a fool, dolt, maniac," thought he, " and I deserve to be punished, as I am."

There was a breathless silence after the anthem closed, then a sudden and spontaneous burst of applause. Once, twice, thrice the building shook with its thunders. During the lull that succeeded,

Miss Manly arose. Her tall figure at once arrested every eye.

" Hush, hush, the Colonel is going to speak !" ran in a whisper across the benches.

And truly the Colonel *was* going to make a speech, and a very sensible one, too.

"We thank the audience," she said, bending graciously forward, and waving her ivory fan. "We thank our friends, for their manifestations of approbation. We receive them in the spirit of kindness in which we are certain they burst forth. But as the performers are young ladies whose modesty and delicacy we feel it our duty to guard, as we would a tender flower, and as they must naturally shrink from anything like notoriety and acclamation, we would most respectfully request, that silence, expressive silence, should hereafter speak their praise."

There was a murmur, when Miss Manly resumed her seat after a dignified bow, and some boys put their hands together ready to clap, but the public respected Miss Manly, and feared her displeasure, and as her pupils had passed a splendid Examination, they were anxious to conform to her wishes, and therefore preserved silence.   *   *

The concert was winding to a close; the last anthem was announced. The white-robed choir again arranged themselves in a semi-lunar form, while Eoline and St. Leon took the same position as at the opening of the concert. Miss Manly stood up to enjoy this last act of a triumphant drama. Eoline, who missed for a moment the voice of St. Leon, looked up and saw him leaning against the piano, with his hand pressed against his side, and his face wearing the pallor of death. Giving her one earnest, thrilling glance, his eyes closed, and he fell back, perfectly insensible.

It would be difficult to describe the scene of confusion that followed. The forward pressure of the crowd impeded every breath of air, and formed an impenetrable barrier round the platform. The frightened children condensed themselves on the other side—Miss Manly, no less alarmed, for once exerting herself in vain to call them to order.

" Stand back !" exclaimed Eoline, in an agony of terror, " keep back, if you would not kill him ! He is not dead. Good Heavens !—will nobody help him ! Oh, Horace !" she cried, for he had wedged the crowd, he knew not how, and sprang upon the platform, " for God's sake get a glass of water !"

" Here is water ! and here !" cried a dozen voices, while Horace knelt and raised the lifeless St. Leon on his arm.

" Carry him to the window !" exclaimed a commanding voice, while another strong pair of arms surrounded the young man, " he will die for want of air."

It was Doctor Hale, the doctor, *par excellence*, of Montebello, whose commands had the authority of Scripture. By the copious application of water, and the current of fresh air admitted to his lungs, St. Leon revived, so as to open his eyes, and give evidence of consciousness- and that was all

RICHARD HILDRETH.

[Born 1807. Died 1865.]

RICHARD HILDRETH, was born at Deerfield, Mass., June 28, 1807. He was the son of Rev. Hosea Hildreth, who was called to Phillips Academy at Exeter, N. H., when his son was only four years old, and the family removed thither. He graduated at Harvard College, where he was distinguished for his high class-rank, and his attainments in general literature. He kept a school for a year in Concord, Mass. ; then studied law, and was admitted to practice at the Suffolk bar, in 1830. In 1832, with others he founded the Boston Atlas, upon which he was afterwards engaged at several periods of his life.

In consequence of ill health, Mr. Hildreth resided in Florida in 1834–6. While there he wrote the novel of Archy Moore, founded upon incidents of slave life that came under his observation. Upon his return it was published anonymously, met with success, and was reprinted in England. This was afterwards republished in 1852, under the title of The White Slave. In 1837–8, he was the corres-pondent at Washington, of the Boston Atlas ; he returned to Boston in 1838, and became the chief editor of that paper. He wrote a series of powerful articles against the annexa-tion of Texas, which helped to form public opinion at the time. He also contributed largely to the nomination of Gen. Harrison to the Presidency, and published a life of him in one volume, 18mo.

Abandoning journalism, Mr. Hildreth pub-lished in 1840, Despotism in America, an able work on the moral, political, and social char-acter of slavery ; a History of Banks, advocating a system of free banking, with security to bill-holders, a plan since adopted ; and a translation from the French of Dumont, of Bentham's Theory of Legislation. These were followed by a Letter on Miracles, and other controversial pamphlets on various speculative topics. These works were marked by keen and vigorous argument, but at times by an unsparing severity of language that mate-rially interfered with their popularity.

In 1840, for the benefit of his health, Mr. Hildreth went to Demarara, where he continued his literary activity by editing two newspapers. Here he also wrote his Theory of Morals, pub-lished in 1844, and his Theory of Politics, published in 1853. These two were the first of six treatises, the remaining four to have been on Wealth, Taste, Knowledge, and Edu-cation ; an attempt to apply to these subjects the inductive method of investigation, which he supposed, might be employed as suc-cessfully in ethical and kindred science, as it has been in the domain of physical discov-eries.

Finding the public too little interested in his speculative inquiries, Mr. Hildreth devoted his attention to the History of the United States, the work upon which his fame will chiefly rest. The first volume was issued in 1849, and the entire work, in 6 vols., in the three succeeding years. This elaborate history covers the period beginning with the settle-ment of the country, and concluding with the end of Monroe's first term in 1821. It met with criticisms entirely opposite to each other. He gave the history of the earliest founders of the Republic, " in their own proper persons, often rude, hard, narrow, superstitious, and mistaken, but always earnest, downright, manly, and sincere. The result of their labors is eulogy enough ; their best apology is to tell their story exactly as it was." He embodied the mature results of long-continued and exhausting labor, carried on by a mind not ill adapted to historical inquiry, acute, compre-hensive, endowed with an inflexible honesty of purpose, and never avoiding the sober duties of the historian for the sake of rhetori-cal display. It is a plain and well-written narrative of public events, mostly in the order of their occurrence, without any attempt to generalize them, or to deduce from them broader lessons of experience. But the story is conscientiously—and, as far as details go, thoroughly—told.

Japan as it Was and Is, a compilation from the best works on that country, was published in 1855 ; when he became a regular contributor to the New York Tribune, and at the close of the year removed to New York.

His last work, Atrocious Judges, or Lives of Judges infamous as tools of Tyrants and Instruments of Oppression, was published in 1856; a selection from Lord Campbell's Lives of the Chief Justices and Lives of the Chancellors, with an Appendix.

He was one of the writers for Appleton's American Cyclopedia; the amount of literary drudgery which he has performed, attests his singular mental vigor and activity, as well as the inadequate remuneration of more congenial literary labor. In 1861, he was appointed by President Lincoln, U. S. Consul at Trieste. He held this position for a time, till failing health compelled him to relinquish it. He still remained abroad, however, gradually sinking, till his feeble constitution was exhausted. He died at Florence, Italy, on the 11th of July, 1865.

EFFECT OF AMERICAN NAVAL VICTORIES.

FROM HISTORY OF THE UNITED STATES, 2D SERIES.

THE effect of these early naval encounters, whether in America or in England, was very striking. While they served to relieve the war party, mortified to the last degree by the imbecility and misfortunes of their incapable generals, the Federalists also joined to extol them as proofs that commerce was best to be defended at sea, and as justifying their ancient partiality for a navy, which now became all at once, in spite of old party prejudices, the general favorite of the nation. It was proclaimed, with many boastings, that the downfall of Great Britain must certainly be near, since at last she had found her match on the ocean; and these exultations and prophecies, however extravagant, seemed to be justified by the astonishment and mortification of the British themselves. Apprehensions were freely expressed in their newspapers of being stripped, " by a piece of striped bunting flying at the mast-heads of a few fir-built frigates, manned by a handful of bastards and outlaws "—such being the polite terms in which, with angry flourish, the American navy and people were described—of that maritime superiority, into a confession of which every nation in Europe had been successively beaten. Presently, however, recovering a little from their amazement and terror, explanations and apologies were sought for and found. The victorious American frigates, it was said, were larger ships than their opponents, with more men, more guns by half a dozen or so, and heavier metal, twenty-fours on the gun-deck instead of eighteens; and it was even pretended that they were chiefly manned by runaway British sailors. Except the British sailors, this was all true enough; but it hardly justified the exaggeration that the American frigates were seventy-fours in disguise; nor did it apply to the case of the Wasp and the Frolic, which were equally matched. The difference, indeed, was not so great as to have been much thought of in contests with ships of any other flag; nor was it at all sufficient to explain, if other things were equal, such speedy and total defeats with such disparity of loss. It was too plain that the American ships were not only larger and stronger, but better handled and better fought—a circumstance, on the supposition of a general equality in skill and courage, natural enough in a few vessels with reputations to make, insults and taunts to revenge, and sailors' rights to fight for, but, even thus explained, breaking much too rudely upon the English dream of naval invincibility to be anywise acceptable. Forethought, and with it a tendency to see the gloomy side, are the characteristics of the English mind. The harm that a few frigates could immediately do might be of little consequence; but who could tell what might happen in the future? And, indeed, even for the present, with Bonaparte, the turning and rapid descent of whose fortune hardly yet showed itself, desperately bent on the destruction of Britain and her commerce, what was not to be apprehended from the springing into existence of a new hostile naval power?

A considerable part of the inhabitants of New England, whence in former wars the greater proportion of American privateers had issued, had now serious scruples upon that point. The growing spirit of civilization and commerce had begun to view this species of warfare as little better than robbery. Jefferson had testified against it in his model treaty with Prussia, in which the contracting parties had mutually renounced this species of annoyance. Why, indeed, should not private property be as much respected on sea as on land? It shocked the moral sense of many, this seizing and appropriating the ships of their late British correspondents, who, though nationally enemies, still remained mercantile and personal friends. Most of the Federalist ship-owners and seafaring people, and some who were Democrats, refused to participate in what had so much the aspect of piracy. But the prospect of plunder, the gloss of patriotism, the thirst for revenge, and the impulse of necessity, still fitted out numerous privateers, as well from the ports of New England, especially from Salem, the head-quarters of the Massachusetts Democracy, as from New York, Philadelphia, and Baltimore. Before the close of the year, more than three hundred prizes had been made by the American cruisers, public and private, including, however, a number of American vessels sailing under British licenses.

JOHN GREENLEAF WHITTIER.

[Born 1808.]

John G. Whittier, who owes his presence in this collection, more to his celebrity as a poet, than to his merit as a prose writer, was born in 1808, in the old homestead near Haverhill, Mass.; where his ancestors of the Quaker persuasion, in spite of Puritan persecutions, settled on the banks of the Merrimack.

He lived at home until his eighteenth year, working on the farm, and occasionally at shoemaking, writing during his leisure hours verses for the Haverhill Gazette. He went to school for two years; and afterwards became editor of the American Manufacturer, a newspaper published at Boston in the tariff interest; then editor of a paper at Hartford. After a few years spent at home in farming, and representing his town in the State Legislature, he engaged in the proceedings of the American Anti-Slavery Society, of which he was elected Secretary in 1836, and edited the Pennsylvania Freeman, in Philadelphia, writing many stirring poems for it, which were afterward published in his collected poems under the heading of Voices of Freedom. The importance attached to them by the abolition party has probably thrown into the shade some of the finer qualities of his mind.

In 1840, Mr. Whittier took up his residence at Amesbury, Mass., where his best productions have been written, and where he wrote as corresponding editor, many articles for the National Era, published at Washington, many of which were collected into volumes. Since the establishing of the Atlantic Monthly, he has contributed to almost every number.

In 1830, he wrote a memoir prefixed to Brainerd's poems; 1831, a volume of poems and prose sketches, Legends of New England, representing a taste early formed by him for the quaint Indian and Colonial superstitions of the country; a sequel to this volume, the Supernaturalism of New England, was published in 1847. Moll Pitcher, one of his early poems, was of a similar character. So also was his Indian story, Mogg Megone, which derived its name from a leader among the Saco Indians in the war of 1677, and was published in 1836. In 1845, appeared the Stranger in Lowell, a series of sketches of scenery and character, suggested by that great manufacturing town. In 1848, an octavo illustrated edition of his poems was published.

In 1849, appeared his Leaves from Margaret Smith's Journal, written in the antique style brought into vogue by the clever Lady Willoughby's Diary. The fair journalist, with a taste for nature, poetry, and character, and fully sensitive to the religious influences of the spot, visits New England in 1678, and writes her account of the manners and influences of the time to her cousin in England, a gentleman to whom she is to be married. In point of delicacy and happy description, this work is full of beauties; though the unnecessary tediousness of its form will remain a permanent objection to it.

Old Portraits and Modern Sketches, appeared in 1850. It is a series of Prose essays on Bunyan, Baxter, Ellwood, Nayler, Andrew Marvell, John Roberts of the old time folks; and, Hopkins, Leggett, Rogers, and Dinsmore for the moderns; they were mostly originally published as sketches for the National Era. In the same year he published Songs of Labor and other poems; and in 1853, the Chapel of the Hermits, and other poems. He has also issued, The Panorama; Home Ballads; and, In War Time and other poems, in 1864.

He published in 1866, Literary Recreations and Miscellanies; most of the pieces were originally written for newspapers with which he had been connected; they were very varied in their character, and the subject treated of, but afford a good insight into the mind of the author. His prose writings have been collected and published in two volumes.

His most popular poems of any length, are Maud Muller, and Snow-Bound; the latter published in an illustrated volume, with its pen and pencil pictures of a New England family, has enjoyed unbounded and deserved popularity. The Tent and the Beach, a collection of poems was issued in 1868, followed in 1869, by Ballads of New England, of which an octavo edition, illustrated by American artists was published.

Of his collected poems, various editions, and of all sizes have been issued, and have met with large sales; indeed, he may be said to be second in popularity only to Longfellow, among American poets. Though boldness, energy and strength, are Whittier's leading characteristics, yet many of his prose works and poems are marked by a tenderness, a grace, and a beauty, not exceeded by those of any other American writer. Of his later poems, it is not enough to say, that they sustain the author's previous reputation. Several of them may be said to surpass his previous efforts. His verse has not lost in power as it has been mellowed by age and experience. There is the same eye for nature, love of the historic incidents of the past of New England; the same devoted patriotism and ardor for human love and freedom in the present; and there is perhaps greater condensation, and a fiery energy, all the more effective for being constrained within the bounds of art.

PILGRIM'S PROGRESS.
FROM OLD PORTRAITS AND MODERN SKETCHES.

LITTLE did the short-sighted persecutors of Bunyan dream, when they closed upon him the door of Bedford jail, that God would overrule their poor spite and envy, to his own glory and the world-wide renown of their victim. In the solitude of his prison, the ideal forms of beauty and sublimity, which had long flitted before him vaguely, like the vision of the Temanite, took shape and coloring; and he was endowed with power to reduce them to order, and arrange them in harmonious groupings. His powerful imagination, no longer self-tormenting, but under the direction of reason and grace, expanded his narrow cell into a vast theatre, lighted up for the display of its wonders.

That stony cell of his was to him like the rock of Padan-aram to the wandering Patriarch. He saw angels ascending and descending. The House Beautiful rose up before him, and its holy sisterhood welcomed him. He looked, with his Pilgrim, from the Chamber of Peace. The Valley of Humiliation lay stretched out beneath his eye, and he heard "the curious melodious note of the country birds, who sing all the day long in the spring time, when the flowers appear, and the sun shines warm, and makes the woods and groves and solitary places glad." Side by side with the good Christiana and the loving Mercy, he walked through the green and lowly valley, "fruitful as any the crow flies over," through "meadows beautiful with lilies;" the song of the poor but fresh-faced shepherd boy, who lived a merry life, and wore the herb *heart's-ease* in his bosom, sounded through his cell:

"He that is down need fear no fall;
He that is low no pride."

The broad and pleasant "river of the Water of Life" glided peacefully before him, fringed "on either side with green trees, with all manner of fruit," and leaves of healing, with "meadows beautified with lilies, and green all the year long;" he saw the Delectable Mountains, glorious with sunshine, overhung with gardens and orchards and vineyards; and beyond all, the Land of Beulah, with its eternal sunshine, its song of birds, its music of fountains, its purple clustered vines, and groves through which walked the Shining Ones, silver-winged and beautiful.

What were bars and bolts and prison walls to him, whose eyes were anointed to see, and whose ears opened to hear, the glory and the rejoicing of the City of God, when the pilgrims were conducted to its golden gates, from the black and bitter river, with the sounding trumpeters, the transfigured harpers with their crowns of gold, the sweet voices of angels, the welcoming peal of bells in the holy city, and the songs of the redeemed ones? In reading the concluding pages of the first part of Pilgrim's Progress, we feel as if the mysterious glory of the Beatific Vision was unveiled before us. We are dazzled with the excess of light. We are entranced with the mighty melody; overwhelmed by the great anthem of rejoicing spirits. It can only be adequately described in the language of Milton in respect to the Apocalypse, as "a sevenfold chorus of hallelujahs and harping symphonies."

AUTOBIOGRAPHIES.
FROM THE SAME.

COMMEND us to autobiographies! Give us the veritable notchings of Robinson Crusoe on his stick, the indubitable records of a life long since swallowed up in the blackness of darkness, traced by a hand the very dust of which has become undistinguishable. The foolishest egotist who ever chronicled his daily experiences, his hopes and fears, poor plans and vain reachings after happiness, speaking to us out of the Past, and thereby giving us to understand that it was quite as real as our Present, is in no mean sort our benefactor, and commands our attention, in spite of his folly. We are thankful for the very vanity which prompted him to bottle up his poor records, and cast them into the great sea of Time, for future voyagers to pick up. We note, with the deepest interest, that in him too was enacted that miracle of a conscious existence, the reproduction of which in ourselves awes and perplexes us. He, too, had a mother; he hated and loved; the light from old-quenched hearths shone over him; he walked in the sunshine over the dust of those who had gone before him, just as we are now walking over his. These records of him remain, the footmarks of a long-extinct life, not of mere animal organism, but of a being like ourselves, enabling us, by studying their hieroglyphic significance, to decipher and see clearly into the mystery of existence centuries ago. The dead generations live again in these old self-biographies. Incidentally, unintentionally, yet in the simplest and most natural manner, they make us familiar with all the phenomena of life in the by-gone ages. We are brought in contact with actual flesh-and-blood men and women, not the ghostly outline figures which pass for such, in what is called History. The horn lantern of the biographer, by the aid of which, with painful min-uteness, he chronicled, from day to day, his own outgoings and incomings, making visible to us his pitiful wants, labors, trials and tribulations, of the stomach and of the conscience, sheds, at times, a strong clear light upon contemporaneous activities; what seemed before half fabulous, rises up in dis-tinct and full proportions; we look at statesmen, philosophers, and poets, with the eyes of those who lived perchance their next door neighbors, and sold them beer, and mutton, and household stuffs, had access to their kitchens, and took note of the fash-ion of their wigs and the color of their breeches. Without some such light, all history would be just about as unintelligible and unreal as a dimly re-membered dream.

The journals of the early Friends or Quakers are in this respect invaluable. Little, it is true, can be said, as a general thing, of their literary merits. Their authors were plain, earnest men and women, chiefly intent upon the substance of things, and having withal a strong testimony to bear against carnal wit and outside show and ornament. Yet, even the scholar may well admire the power of certain portions of George Fox's Journal, where a strong spirit clothes its utterance in simple, down-right Saxon words; the quiet and beautiful enthu-siasm of Pennington; the torrent energy of Edward Burrough; the serene wisdom of Penn; the logical acuteness of Barclay; the honest truthfulness of Sewell; the wit and humor of John Roberts, (for even Quakerism had its apostolic jokers and drab-coated Robert Halls;) and last, not least, the sim-ple beauty of Woolman's Journal, the modest rec-ord of a life of good works and love.

MILTON AND ELLWOOD.
FROM THE SAME.

In the meantime, where is our "Master Mil-ton?" We left him deprived of his young com-panion and reader, sitting lonely in his small din-ing-room, in Jewen street. It is now the year 1665; is not the pestilence in London? A sinful and godless city, with its bloated bishops, fawning around the Nell Gwyns of a licentious and profane

Defender of the Faith; its swaggering and drunken cavaliers; its ribald jesters; its obscene ballad-sing-ers; its loathsome prisons, crowded with God-fear ing men and women; is not the measure of its in-iquity already filled up? Three years only have passed since the terrible prayer of Vane went up-ward from the scaffold on Tower Hill: "When my blood is shed upon the block, let it, oh God, have a voice afterward!" Audible to thy ear, oh bosom friend of the martyr! has that blood cried from earth; and now, how fearfully is it answered! Like the ashes which the Seer of the Hebrews cast towards Heaven, it has returned in boils and blains upon the proud and oppressive city. John Milton, sitting blind in Jewen street, has heard the toll of the death bells, and the night-long rumble of the burial-carts, and the terrible summons, "BRING OUT YOUR DEAD!" The Angel of the Plague, in yellow mantle, purple-spotted, walks the streets. Why should he tarry in a doomed city, forsaken of God! Is not the command, even to him, "Arise! and flee for thy life." In some green nook of the quiet country, he may finish the great work which his hands have found to do. He bethinks him of his old friends, the Penning-tons, and his young Quaker companion, the patient and gentle Ellwood.

DEATH OF BAXTER.
FROM THE SAME.

The circumstances of his trial before the judicial monster, Jeffries, are too well known to justify their detail in this sketch. He was sentenced to pay a fine of five hundred marks. Seventy years of age, and reduced to poverty by former persecu-tions, he was conveyed to the King's Bench pris-on. Here for two years he lay a victim to intense bodily suffering. When, through the influence of his old antagonist, Penn, he was restored to free-dom, he was already a dying man. But he came forth from prison as he entered it, unsubdued in spirit. Urged to sign a declaration of thanks to James II., his soul put on the athletic habits of youth, and he stoutly refused to commend an act of toleration which had given freedom not to him-self alone, but to Papists and Sectaries. Shaking off the dust of the Court from his feet, he retired to a dwelling in Charter-House Square, near his friend Sylvester's, and patiently awaited his deliver-ance. His death was quiet and peaceful. "I have pain," he said to his friend Mather; "there is no arguing against sense; but I have peace. I have peace." On being asked how he did, he answered, in memorable words, "*Almost well!*"

He was buried in Christ Church, where the remains of his wife and her mother had been placed. An immense concourse attended his fu-neral, of all ranks and parties.

OLIVER WENDELL HOLMES.

[Born 1809.]

OLIVER WENDELL HOLMES, M. D., the eminent poet, wit, physician, and lecturer, is the son of Rev. Abiel Holmes, D. D., of Cambridge, Mass., the author of American Annals. He was born at Cambridge, August 29, 1809, educated at Phillips Academy at Exeter, and graduated at Harvard in 1829. He studied law for a year, and wrote humorous poems for the Collegian, a periodical published by some under-graduates of Harvard, in 1830, some of which were preserved in his Collected Poems, as the Spectre Pig, Evening by a Tailor, etc. He forsook the law and poetry, and studied medicine, which he went to Paris to acquire more perfectly. Returning home in 1835, he took his degree, and commenced practice in Boston the following year.

In 1836, he delivered Poetry, a metrical Essay before the Harvard Phi Beta Kappa, which he published in the first volume of his acknowledged poems in the same year. In 1838, he was elected Professor of Anatomy and Physiology, in the Medical School of Dartmouth College. He married in 1840, resigning his professorship to establish himself in practice in Boston, where he soon became a successful and fashionable practitioner. In 1847, he was elected Parkman Professor of Anatomy and Physiology, in the Medical School of Harvard. In 1849, he relinquished practice, and has his summer residence at Pittsfield, Mass., on the remnant of 24,000 paternal acres on the Housatonic, which he calls Canoe Place; in winter he resides at Boston.

Dr. Holmes has written a number of prize medical essays, published between 1838 and 1848, and has contributed occasionally to medical journals. No one is happier at a festive occasion, whether literary, medical or social. His wit, apparently unpremeditated, bubbling over, and sparkling with true, genuine fun, hits at the absurd, and in derision of quackeries of any kind. His Terpsichore, Stethescope song, Modest Request, Urania, a Rhymed Lesson, and Astræa, are good samples delivered on such occasions. These

620

peculiarities united with a vast and ready store of learning on almost every topic, have made him one of the most popular of lecturers, to which he devotes much of his time.

In 1852, he delivered a course of lectures on the English Poets of the 19th century, in which his style was precise and animated, his criticism bold and dashing, dropping each poetaster as he comes across him with a felicitous shot. In look and manners he is the vivacious, sparkling personage his poems would indicate; his smile is easily invoked; he is fond of fun and repartee, and his conversation runs on laden with the best stores from the whole range of science and society. He is a lover of the fields, trees, and streams, and out-of-door life, and of the convivial board, where he is at home with his sallies of wit and poetry.

It is, however, as a prose writer, that it is our duty to speak of him. In 1857, the Atlantic Monthly was started in Boston as a vehicle for the thought that is so plentiful in New England, and Dr. Holmes was at once enlisted as a contributor. In November, he more fully displayed his wonderful powers by commencing a series of papers entitled The Autocrat of the Breakfast Table. This series constitutes one of the most racy, interesting and brilliant course of magazine-articles ever published. For wit, pathos, profound philosophical speculation, nice descriptive powers, keen insight into human nature, aptness and force of illustration, united to great wealth of literary, scientific, and artistic knowledge, and all in a style that is a model for the light essay, these papers have given the author a very high rank in American literature. The characters represented around the breakfast table assuming an individuality as sharply cut and defined as would be presented to the eye by the best photograph. These papers, at the end of the year, were collected into a volume, illustrated by Hoppin, and were read with avidity in their collected form by a new and larger circle of readers. Yielding to the public demand for more, the author commenced a new series under the title of The Professor at the Breakfast Table, retaining some of the same characters, but adding new ones which awakened as much interest. The papers were a thought graver in matter, with a decided leaning to theological discussion, an infusion of liberal principles, and a deeper pathos and interest in the romance of Iris, and a quaint personage, Little Boston, a creation dedicated to the pride and antiquity of that renowned city; the whole enlivened or rendered pathetic by a monthly humorous or serious copy of verses. These were collected like their predecessors into a volume.

Following these, in the magazine, appeared the Professor's Story, which, on its conclusion, was published under the title of Elsie Venner, a Romance of Destiny, in 2 vols. While this is more of the novel, with more plot and character than the previous works, it is a shrewd sketch of social life, written in a style bright, pure, and simple, idiomatic in dialogue, and a real, life-like work of fiction, happily relieved by wit and humor.

Shortly after this work, Dr. Holmes issued, in 1861, another volume of professional writings, Currents and Counter-Currents in Medical Science, with other addresses and essays; also, Border Lines in some Provinces of Medical Science. These were followed by some of his miscellaneous contributions to the magazine, entitled Soundings from the Atlantic, and later the Guardian Angel, with a new Preface, etc.

Dr. Holmes is as genial and gentle, and withal, as philosophical, an essayist as any of modern times. He is, however, somewhat more than an essayist; he is contemplative, discursive, poetical, thoughtful, philosophical, amusing, imaginative, tender,—never didactic. This is the secret of his marked success: he interests variously constituted minds and various moods of mind.

CONVERSATION.
FROM THE AUTOCRAT OF THE BREAKFAST-TABLE.

NEITHER make too much of flaws and occasional overstatements. Some persons seem to think that absolute truth, in the form of rigidly stated propositions, is all that conversation admits. This is precisely as if a musician should insist on having nothing but perfect chords and simple melodies,— no diminished fifths, no flat sevenths, no flourishes, on any account. It is fair to say, that, just as music must have all these, so conversation must have its partial truths, its embellished truths, its exaggerated truths. It is in its higher forms an artistic product, and admits the ideal element as much as pictures or statues. One man who is a little too literal can spoil the talk of a whole tableful of men of *esprit*.—"Yes," you say, "but who wants to hear fanciful people's nonsense? Put the facts to it, and then see where it is!"—Certainly, if a man is too fond of paradox,—if he is flighty and empty,—if, instead of striking those fifths and sevenths, those harmonious discords, often so much better than the twinned octaves, in the music of thought,—if. instead of striking these, he jangles the chords, stick a fact into him like a stiletto. But remember that talking is one of the fine arts,—the noblest, the most important, and the most difficult,—and that its fluent harmonies may be spoiled by the intrusion of a single harsh note. Therefore conversation which is suggestive rather than argumentative, which lets out the most of each talker's results of thought, is commonly the pleasantest and the most profitable. It is not easy, at the best, for two persons talking together to make the most of each other's thoughts, there are so many of them.

[The company looked as if they wanted an explanation.]

When John and Thomas, for instance, are talking together, it is natural enough that among the six there should be more or less confusion and misapprehension.

[Our landlady turned pale;—no doubt she thought there was a screw loose in my intellects, —and that involved the probable loss of a boarder. A severe-looking person, who wears a Spanish cloak and a sad cheek, fluted by the passions of the melodrama, whom I understand to be the professional ruffian of the neighboring theatre, alluded, with a certain lifting of the brow, drawing down of the corners of the mouth, and somewhat rasping *voce di petto*, to Falstaff's nine men in buckram. Everybody looked up. I believe the old gentleman opposite was afraid I should seize the carving-knife; at any rate, he slid it to one side, as it were carelessly.]

I think, I said, I can make it plain to Benjamin Franklin here, that there are at least six personalities distinctly to be recognized as taking part in that dialogue between John and Thomas.

Three Johns.
1. The real John; known only to his Maker.
2. John's ideal John; never the real one, and often very unlike him.
3. Thomas's ideal John; never the real John, nor John's John, but often very unlike either.

Three Thomases.
1. The real Thomas.
2. Thomas's ideal Thomas.
3. John's ideal Thomas.

Only one of the three Johns is taxed; only one

can be weighed on a platform-balance ; but the other two are just as important in the conversation. Let us suppose the real John to be old, dull, and ill-looking. But as the higher powers have not conferred on men the gift of seeing themselves in the true light, John very possibly conceives himself to be youthful, witty, and fascinating, and talks from the point of view of this ideal. Thomas, again, believes him to be an artful rogue, we will say ; therefore he *is*, so far as Thomas's attitude in the conversation is concerned, an artful rogue, though really simple and stupid. The same conditions apply to the three Thomases. It follows, that, until a man can be found who knows himself as his Maker knows him, or who sees himself as others see him, there must be at least six persons engaged in every dialogue between two. Of these, the least important, philosophically speaking, is the one that we have called the real person. No wonder two disputants often get angry, when there are six of them talking and listening all at the same time.

[A very unphilosophical application of the above remarks was made by a young fellow, answering to the name of John, who sits near me at table. A certain basket of peaches, a rare vegetable, little known to boarding-houses, was on its way to me *vid* this unlettered Johannes. He appropriated the three that remained in the basket, remarking that there was just one apiece for him. I convinced him that his practical inference was hasty and illogical, but in the meantime he had eaten the peaches.]

THE INNER NATURE.

FROM THE SAME.

EVERY person's feelings have a front-door and a side-door by which they may be entered. The front-door is on the street. Some keep it always open ; some keep it latched ; some, locked ; some, bolted,—with a chain that will let you peep in, but not get in ; and some nail it up, so that nothing can pass its threshold. This front-door leads into a passage which opens into an ante-room, and this into the interior apartments. The side-door opens at once into the sacred chambers.

There is almost always at least one key to this side-door. This is carried for years hidden in a mother's bosom. Fathers, brothers, sisters, and friends, often, but by no means so universally, have duplicates of it. The wedding-ring conveys a right to one ; alas, if none is given with it !

If nature or accident has put one of these keys into the hands of a person who has the torturing instinct, I can only solemnly pronounce the words that Justice utters over its doomed victim,— *The Lord have mercy on your soul !* You will probably go mad within a reasonable time,—or, if you are a man, run off and die with your head on a curb-

stone, in Melbourne or San Francisco,—or, if you are a woman, quarrel and break your heart, or turn into a pale, jointed petrifaction that moves about as if it were alive, or play some real life-tragedy or other.

Be very careful to whom you trust one of these keys of the side-door. The fact of possessing one renders those even who are dear to you very terrible at times. You can keep the world out from your front-door, or receive visitors only when you are ready for them ; but those of your own flesh and blood, or of certain grades of intimacy, can come in at the side-door, if they will, at any hour and in any mood. Some of them have a scale of your whole nervous system, and can play all the gamut of your sensibilities in semitones,—touching the naked nerve pulps as a pianist strikes the keys of his instrument. I am satisfied that there are as great masters of this nerve playing as Vieuxtemps or Thalberg in their lines of performance. Married life is the school in which the most accomplished artists in this department are found. A delicate woman is the best instrument ; she has such a magnificent compass of sensibilities ! From the deep inward moan which follows pressure on the great nerves of right, to the sharp cry as the filaments of taste are struck with a crashing sweep, is a range which no other instrument possesses. A few exercises on it daily at home fit a man wonderfully for his habitual labors, and refresh him immensely as he returns from them. No stranger can get a great many notes of torture out of a human soul ; it takes one that knows it well, —parent, child, brother, sister, intimate. Be very careful to whom you give a side-door key ; too many have them already.

You remember the old story of the tender-hearted man, who placed a frozen viper in his bosom, and was stung by it when it became thawed ? If we take a cold-blooded creature into our bosom, better that it should sting us and we should die than that its chill should slowly steal into our hearts ; warm it we never can ! I have seen faces of women that were fair to look upon, yet one could see that the icicles were forming round these women's hearts. I knew what freezing image lay on the white breasts beneath the laces !

A very simple *intellectual* mechanism answers the necessities of friendship, and even of the most intimate relations of life. If a watch tells us the hour and the minute, we can be content to carry it about with us for a life-time, though it has no second-hand, and is not a repeater, nor a musical watch,—though it is not enamelled nor jewelled, —in short, though it has little beyond the wheels required for a trustworthy instrument, added to a good face and a pair of useful hands. The more wheels there are in a watch or a brain, the more trouble they are to take care of. The movements of exaltation which belong to genius are egotistic by their very nature. A calm, clear mind, not subject to the spasms and crises that are so often met with in creative or intensely perceptive natures, is the best basis for love or friendship.

ORMSBY McKNIGHT MITCHEL.

[Born 1810. Died 1862.]

GENERAL MITCHELL was born of Virginia parentage in Union Co., Ky., August 28, 1810. His father died when he was about three years old, and the family removed to Lebanon, Ohio. There he received his first education, and at the age of thirteen began life as a clerk in a store. In 1825, he entered West Point; he was a bright, zealous student, and graduated with credit in the class of 1829, as Second Lieutenant of Artillery. He remained two years as assistant professor of mathematics and was then stationed at St. Augustine, Fla.

In 1832, he resigned his military commission, engaged in the study of the law, was admitted to the bar in Cincinnati, Ohio, and practised for two years; when he was appointed professor at the Cincinnati College. During a portion of this time he was Chief Engineer of the Little Miami Railroad. In 1842, he delivered a course of lectures on Astronomy, and undertook the establishment of an observatory at Cincinnati. He roused the enthusiasm of the public, collected funds, visited Europe to purchase the apparatus, and on his return superintended the construction of the building. At the completion in 1845, Prof. Mitchell began a series of astronomical observations, partly with a new declination apparatus of his own invention. In 1846, he began the publication of the Siderial Messenger. In 1848, he published a course of lectures, delivered in various cities, entitled The Planetary and Stellar Worlds; the work was written with great vigor and enthusiasm, met with considerable success, and has become a standard work on the subject. In the same year, he was appointed chief engineer of the Ohio and Mississippi railroad. In 1859, he was Director of the newly-erected Dudley Observatory, at Albany, retaining supervision of the Cincinnati Observatory. In 1860, he published a second volume of popular astronomy, A Concise Elementary Treatise on the Sun, Planets, Satellites, and Comets, in which he presented the results of his own observation, and the new methods employed in the observatories under his care.

From the successful prosecution of his favor-ite science, Prof. Mitchell was now called by the opening of the great rebellion. He hastened to offer his services to his country, which were accepted, and he assumed command of the Department of the Ohio, as Brigadier-General of volunteers. He rendered distinguished service in command of a division of Buell's army in the advance upon Bowling Green, Ky., the occupation of Nashville, Tenn., and the subsequent movements in Alabama, in the spring campaign of 1862. For his energetic capture of Huntsville, Ala., he was made a Major-General of volunteers. In the autumn of the same year he succeeded Gen. Hunter at Hilton Head, S. C., in command of the Department of the South. There, while he was engaged with his habitual ardor, he was stricken by yellow fever, and died after a few days' illness, at Beaufort, Oct. 30, 1862.

Gen. Mitchell left a third series of lectures, which were published in 1863, under the title of The Astronomy of the Bible. It is an eloquent assertion of the harmony between science and revelation, under the heads of "The Astronomical Evidences of the Being of a God; the God of the Universe is Jehovah; the Cosmogony as revealed by the present state of Astronomy; the Mosaic account of Creation; the Astronomical allusions in the Book of Job; the Astronomical Miracles of the Bible."

This energetic writer, lover of science, and devoted Christian, in his short life, made a name for himself, which will not soon sink into oblivion. His magnetic clock was first offered to the inspection of his friends in 1848, and in 1849, he added another contribution to science in his new declination apparatus. Besides the writings mentioned above, he edited an edition of Burritt's Geography of the Heavens. His first work was reprinted in England in two editions. His noble treatises on the most sublime of studies, are attractive and intelligible alike to the learned and unlearned.

He was the recipient of many honors, due to his own merits. He had filled many offices and posts. Few men of our age have exhibited a more extended genius.

THE FIRST PREDICTED ECLIPSE.

FROM "PLANETARY AND STELLAR WORLDS."

RAPIDLY have we traced the career of discovery. The toil and watching of centuries have been condensed into a few moments of time, and questions requiring ages for their solution have been asked, only to be answered. In connection with the investigations just developed, and as a consequence of their successful prosecution, the query arose whether in case science had reached to a true exposition of the causes producing the eclipse of the sun, was it not possible to stretch forward in time, and anticipate and predict the coming of these dread phenomena ?

To those who have given but little attention to the subject, even in our own day, with all the aids of modern science, the prediction of an eclipse, seems sufficiently mysterious and unintelligible. How then it was possible, thousands of years ago, to accomplish the same great object, without any just views of the structure of the system, seems utterly incredible. Follow me, then, while I attempt to reveal the train of reasoning which led to the prediction of the first eclipse of the sun, the most daring prophecy ever made by human genius. Follow in imagination, this bold interrogator of the skies to his solitary mountain summit—withdrawn from the world—surrounded by his mysterious circles, there to watch and ponder through the long nights of many—many years. But hope cheers him on, and smooths his rugged pathway. Dark and deep as is the problem, he sternly grapples with it, and resolves never to give over till victory crowns his efforts.

He has already remarked, that the moon's track in the heavens crossed the sun's, and that this point of crossing was in some way intimately connected with the coming of the dread eclipse. He determines to watch and learn whether the point of crossing was fixed, or whether the moon in each successive revolution, crossed the sun's path at a different point. If the sun in its annual revolution could leave behind him a track of fire marking his journey among the stars, it is found that this same track was followed from year to year, and from century to century with undeviating precision. But it was soon discovered, that it was far different with the moon. In case she too could leave behind her a silver thread of light sweeping round the heavens, in completing one revolution, this thread would not join, but would wind around among the stars in each revolution, crossing the sun's fiery track at a point west of the previous crossing. These points of crossing were called the *moon's nodes*. At each revolution the node occurred further west, until after a cycle of about nineteen years, it had circulated in the same direction entirely round the ecliptic. Long and patiently did the astronomer watch and wait, each eclipse is duly observed, and its attendant circumstances are recorded, when, at last, the darkness begins to give way and a ray of light breaks in upon his mind. He finds that no eclipse of the sun ever occurs unless the *new moon is in the act of crossing the sun's track*. Here

was a grand discovery.—He holds the key which he believes will unlock the dread mystery, and now, with redoubled energy, he resolves to thrust it into the wards and drive back the bolts.

To predict an eclipse of the sun, he must sweep forward, from new moon to new moon, until he finds some new *moon* which should occur, while the moon was in the act of crossing from one side to the other of the sun's track.—This certainly was possible. He knew the exact period from new moon to new moon, and from one crossing of the ecliptic to another. With eager eye he seizes the moon's place in the heavens, and her age, and rapidly computes where she will be at her next change. He finds the new moon occurring far from the sun's track; he runs round another revolution; the place of the new moon falls closer to the sun's path, and the next yet closer, until reaching forward with piercing intellectual vigor, he at last, finds a new moon which occurs precisely at the computed time of her passage across the sun's track. Here he makes his stand, and on the day of the occurrence of that new moon, he announces to the startled inhabitants of the world, that the sun shall expire in dark eclipse.—Bold prediction ! —Mysterious prophet ! with what scorn must the unthinking would have received this solemn declaration. How slowly do the moons roll away, and with what intense anxiety does the stern philosopher await the coming of that day which should crown him with victory, or dash him to the ground in ruin and disgrace. Time to him moves on leaden wings ; day after day, and at last hour after hour, roll heavily away. The last night is gone—the moon has disappeared from his eagle gaze in her approach to the sun, and the dawn of the eventful day breaks in beauty on a slumbering world.

This daring man, stern in his faith, climbs alone to his rocky home, and greets the sun as he rises and mounts the heavens, scattering brightness and glory in his path. Beneath him is spread out the populous city, already teeming with life and activity. The busy morning hum rises on the still air and reaches the watching place of the solitary astronomer. The thousands below him, unconscious of his intense anxiety, buoyant with life, joyously pursue their rounds of business, their cycles of amusement. The sun slowly climbs the heavens, round and bright and full-orbed. The lone tenant of the mountain-top almost begins to waver in the sternness of his faith, as the morning hours roll away. But the time of his triumph, long delayed, at length begins to dawn ; a pale and sickly hue creeps over the face of nature. The sun has reached his highest point, but his splendor is dimmed, his light is feeble. At last it comes !—Blackness is eating away his round disc, —onward with slow but steady pace, the dark veil, moves blacker than a thousand nights,—the gloom deepens,—the ghastly hue of death covers the universe,—the last ray is gone, and horror reigns. A wail of terror fills the murky air,—the clangor of brazen trumpets resounds,—an agony of despair dashes the stricken millions to the ground, while that lone man, erect on his rocky summit, with arms outstretched to heaven, pours forth the grateful gushings of his heart to God, who had crowned his efforts with triumphant victory. Search the records of our race, and point me, if you can, to a scene more grand, more beautiful. It is to me the proudest victory that genius ever won. It was the conquering of nature, of ignorance, of superstition, of terror, all at a single blow, and that blow struck by a single arm.— And now do you demand the name of this wonderful man! Alas! what a lesson of the instability of earthly fame are we taught in this simple recital.—He who had raised himself immeasurably above his race.—who must have been regarded by his fellows as little less than a god, who had inscribed his fame on the very heavens, and had written it in the sun, with a "pen of iron, and the point of a diamond," even this one has perished from the earth—name, age, country. are all swept into oblivion, but his proud achievement stands. The monument reared to his honor stands, and although the touch of time has effaced the lettering of his name, it is powerless, and cannot destroy the fruits of his victory.

A thousand years roll by: the astronomer stands on the watch tower of old Babylon, and writes for posterity the records of an eclipse; this record escapes destruction, and is safely wafted down the stream of time. A thousand years roll away: the old astronomer, surrounded by the fierce, but wondering Arab, again writes, and marks the day which witnesses the sun's decay. A thousand years roll heavily away: once more the astronomer writes from amidst the gay throng that crowds the brightest capital of Europe. Record is compared with record, date with date, revolution with revolution, the past and present are linked together,—another struggle commences, and another victory is won. Little did the Babylonian dream that he was observing for one who after the lapse of three thousand years, should rest upon this very record, the successful resolution of one of nature's darkest mysteries.

KEPLER'S DISCOVERY OF THE THIRD LAW.

FROM THE SAME.

NOTHING daunted, he proceeded to investigate the possible relations between the cubes of the periods and distances. Here again he was foiled: no law exhibited itself.—He returned ever fresh to the attack, and now commenced a series of trials involving the relations between the simple periods and the squares of the distances. Here a ray of hope broke in upon his dim and darkened path.

No actual relation existed, yet there was a very distant approximation, enough to excite hope.— He then tried simple multiples of the periods and the squares of the distances—all in vain. He finally abandoned the simple periods and distances, and rose to an examination of the relations

79

between the squares of these same quantities.— Gaining nothing here, he rose still higher, to the cubes of the periods and distances;—no success, until finally he tried the proportion existing between the squares of the periods in which the planets perform their revolutions and the cubes of their distances from the sun.—Here was the grand secret, but, alas! in making his numerical computations, an error in the work vitiated the results, and with the greatest discovery which the mind ever achieved in his very grasp, the heart-sick and toil-worn philosopher turned away almost in despair from his endless research.

Months rolled round, and yet his mind with a sort of keen instinct, would recur again and again to this last hypothesis. Guided by some kind angel or spirit whose sympathy had been touched by the unwearied zeal of the mortal, he returned to his former computations, and with a heaving breast, and throbbing heart, he detects the numerical error in his work, and commences anew. The square of Jupiter's period is to the square of Saturn's period as the cube of Jupiter's distance is to some fourth term, which Kepler hoped and prayed might prove to be the cube of Saturn's distance. With trembling hand, he sweeps through the maze of figures; the fourth term is obtained; he compares it with the cube of Saturn's distance.—They are the same!—He could scarcely believe his own senses. He feared some demon mocked him.— He ran over the work again and again—He tried the proportion, the square of Jupiter's period to the square of Mars' period as the cube of Jupiter's distance to a fourth term, which he found to be the cube of the distance of Mars.—Till finally full conviction burst upon his mind: he had won the goal, the struggle of seventeen long years was ended, God was vindicated, and the philosopher, in the wild excitement of his glorious triumph, exclaims:

" Nothing holds me. I will indulge my sacred fury! If you forgive me I rejoice; if you are angry I can bear it. The die is cast. The book is written, to be read either now, or by posterity, I care not which.—It may well wait a century for a reader, since God has waited six thousand years for an observer!"

More than two hundred years have rolled away since Kepler announced his great discoveries. Science has marched forward with swift and resistless energy.—The secrets of the universe have been yielded up under the inquisitorial investigations of godlike intellect. The domain of the mind has been extended wider and wider. One planet after another has been added to our system ; even the profound abyss which separates us from the fixed stars has been passed, and thousands of. rolling suns have been descried, swiftly flying. or majestically sweeping through the thronged regions of space. But the laws of Kepler bind them all, —satellite and primary—planet and sun—sun and system,—all with one accord, proclaim. in silent majesty the triumph of the hero philosopher.

HORACE GREELEY.

[Born 1811.]

HORACE GREELEY, at the head of the editorial profession in this country, was born of plain parents at Amherst, N. H., Feb. 3, 1811. He received a limited common school education, which be improved by application to private studies; his pursuit of knowledge was carried on with unwearied activity. When fourteen years old, his father removed to Vermont, and he became an apprentice in the office of the Northern Spectator, at Pultney, Vt. He returned home in 1830, at the discontinuance of the paper, but soon after, his father having removed to Chatauque Co., N. Y., on the Pennsylvania line, he became an apprentice in Erie, Pa., for fifty dollars a year. Out of this small sum, he gave his father more than one-half, and in August, 1831, started for New York, and entered the city, the scene of his future labors and triumphs, with a suit of blue cotton jean, two brown shirts, and five dollars in cash, as his working capital. He worked at his trade as journeyman printer for eighteen months. In 1834, in conjunction with Jonas Winchester, be commenced the publication of the New Yorker, a weekly paper of sixteen pages, quarto. Though conducted, for several years, with much ability as a political and literary journal, it was abandoned as unsuccessful. Mr. Greeley also conducted the Jeffersonian for the Whig Central Committee of the State, and for six months the Log Cabin, a campaign paper in the presidential election of 1840.

On Saturday, April 10, 1841, appeared the first number of his new paper, The New York Tribune, which at once took its stand as a thoroughly appointed, independent, and spirited journal.

In July, he associated with him in its management as partner, Mr. McElrath. With increased facilities, it was kept fully up to the needs of the times, and became noted for its enterprise, and its full, early, and correct news. As the organ of the tariff party, upholding anti-slavery, advocating the cause of temperance, and other prominent topics of the times, it soon became well-known, and a power in the land. Upon Mr. McElrath's retiring from the paper, a company was formed under the title of The Tribune Association, who now own and run the paper, with Mr. Greeley as chief editor. It is one of the best paying properties in the newspaper list, and mainly owing to the ability with which Mr. Greeley has conducted it.

Mr. Greeley has always taken a leading part in the politics of the country, belonging to the old Whig party. In 1848, he was elected a member of the House of Representatives. In 1851, he visited Europe, and was chosen chairman of. one of the juries of the World's Fair at London. On his return, he published Glances at Europe, letters written to the Tribune. In 1853, he edited a volume of papers from the Tribune, Art and Industry as represented in the Exhibition at the Crystal Palace, New York. Also Hints towards Reforms, addresses delivered on various occasions. Mr. J. Parton, the author of several popular biographies, wrote the Life of Horace Greeley, in one volume; well written, and displaying enthusiasm, research, and good sense. Mr. Greeley also wrote his autobiography, which had a large sale; this he lately revised and issued in octavo, with the new title of Recollections of a Busy Life.

Mr. Greeley has also published, Association, Discussed by H. Greeley and H. J. Raymond, 8vo., 1847; History of the Struggle for Slavery Extension or Restriction in the U. S. from 1787 to 1856, 8vo., which passed through several editions; and, The Tribune Almanac, a yearly mass of facts, particularly invaluable to politicians; a new issue of these photographed on stone, in 2 vols., was issued in 1869, a most remarkable event in the annals of book-making.

His great work is The American Conflict: A History of the Great Rebellion, its causes, incidents, and results; published in 2 vols., 8vo., with maps and illustrations, and sold by subscription; it reached the enormous sale of 150,000 copies. Mr. Greeley's position, both before and during the war, as one of the leading editors and politicians, with his vigorous style and flowing pen, made him peculiarly fitted to write a popular history of the great conflict, and the drift and progress of American opinion respecting Human Slavery, and the public appreciated it.

Mr. Greeley has also devoted considerable attention to agricultural matters, upon which he writes intelligently, earnestly, and with a great deal of matter-of-fact common sense. In 1869, he published, Essays designed to elucidate the Science of Political Economy, while serving to explain and defend the policy of Protection to Home Industry, as a system of National co-operation for the Elevation of Labor, 16mo.

With a shrewd, clear intellect, an astonishingly vigorous style, and a heart easily wrought up to that degree of passion necessary to the production of the best kind of writing, he fears not the quill of any man living. His widely-circulated journal contains good specimens of acute wit, critical reasoning, solid argument, brilliant invective, profound philosophy, beautiful poetry, and moving eloquence mixed with the opposite of these.

MY FARMING.

FROM RECOLLECTIONS OF A BUSY LIFE.

THOSE who have read my account of my farm will have judged that it is not well calculated to enrich its owner by large, easily produced crops, and that it was bought in full view of this fact. I wanted a place near a railroad station, and not too far from the city; my wife wanted pure air, agreeable scenery, reasonable seclusion, but, above all, a choice, never-failing spring, a cascade, and evergreen woods, as I have already stated. Having found these on the thirty-odd acres which comprised our original purchase, we were not so unreasonable as to expect to secure also the fertility and facility of a dry, gently rolling Western prairie, or of a rich intervale of the Connecticut or Hudson. We knew that our upland was in good part hard, steep, and rocky, and that its productive capacity—never remarkable—had been largely reduced by two centuries of persistent and often excessive pasturing. Sheep may thus be fed a thousand years, yet return to the soil nearly as much as they take from it; not so with milch cows, when their milk is sent away to some city, and nothing returned therefor that enriches the fields whence that milk, in the shape of grass or hay, was drawn. And so, measurably, of Fruit: whereas Apples have long been a leading staple of our region,—Newcastle having formerly boasted more Apple-trees than any township of its size in America. But an Apple-tree cannot forever draw on the Bank of Nature without having its drafts protested, if nothing is ever deposited there to its credit; and caterpillars have so long been allowed to strip most of our trees unresisted, that many have grown prematurely old and moss-covered. One year with another, Newcastle does not grow half so many Apples as her trees call for; and she never will till she feeds her trees better and fights their enemies with more persistent resolution than she has done. I have seen five thousand of those trees, in the course of a brief morning ride in June, with more caterpillars than remaining leaves per tree; and very little reflection can be needed to show that trees so neglected for a few years will have outlived their usefulness.

The woods are *my* special department. Whenever I can save a Saturday for the farm, I try to give a good part of it to my patch of forest. The axe is the healthiest implement that man ever handled, and is especially so for habitual writers and other sedentary workers, whose shoulders it throws back, expanding their chests, and opening their lungs. If every youth and man, from fifteen to fifty years old, could wield an axe two hours per day, dyspepsia would vanish from the earth, and rheumatism become decidedly scarce. I am a poor chopper; yet the axe is my doctor and delight. Its use gives the mind just enough occupation to prevent its falling into revery or absorbing trains of thought, while every muscle in the body receives sufficient, yet not exhausting, exercise. I wish all our boys would learn to love the axe.

I began by cutting out the Witch Hazels, and other trash not worth keeping, and trimming up my trees, especially the Hemlocks, which grow limbs clear to the ground, and throw them out horizontally to such a distance that several rods of ground are sometimes monopolized by a single tree. Many of these lower limbs die in the course of time, but do not fall off; on the contrary, they harden and sharpen into spikes, which threaten your face and eyes as if they were bayonets. These I have gradually cut away and transformed into fuel. Many of my Hemlocks I have trimmed to a height of at least fifty feet; and I mean to serve many others just so, if I can ever find time before old age compels me to stop climbing.

But the Hemlock so bristles throughout with limbs that it can easily be climbed by a hale man till he is seventy; and, working with a hatchet or light axe, you commence trimming at the top,— that is, as high as you choose to trim,—and, without difficulty, cut all smooth as you work your way down. Limbs to the ground may be graceful in the edge of your wood; but your tree will not make timber nearly so fast as if trimmed, and you cannot afford it so much space as it claims in the heart of your patch of forest.

If I linger proudly among my trees, consider that here most of my farm-work has been done, and here my profit has been realized, in the shape of health and vigor. When I am asked the usual question, "How has your farming paid?" I can truthfully answer that *my* part of it has paid splendidly, being all income and no outgo,—and who can show a better balance sheet than *that?*

Seriously—I believe there is money to be made by judicious tree-planting and forest-culture, now that railroads have so greatly cheapened the cost of transportation. If any man has or can buy a tract of woodland, or land too poor or broken to be profitably tilled, let him shut out cattle, and steadily plant choice trees while cutting out poorer; let him cut every tree that stops growing and begins to decay, or shed its limbs; let him not hesitate to thin as well as trim up; let him cut out Red Oak, for instance, and sow the acorns of White; let him, when half a dozen or more sprouts start from a single stump, cut away all but two or three, and by and by cut again; and I am confident that he may thus grow timber twice as rapidly as where it is neglected, and grow trees far more valuable than those that come by chance. Nay: if near a city, he can make a thousand dollars far more easily, though less quickly, by growing Timber than by growing Grain.

THE GREAT SENATORS.

FROM THE SAME.

OUR great triumvirate—Clay, Webster, Calhoun—last appeared together in public life in the Senate of 1849–50: the two former figuring conspicuously in the debates which preluded and resulted in what was termed the Compromise of that year,—Mr. Calhoun dying as they had fairly opened, and Messrs. Clay and Webster not long after their close. This chapter is, therefore, in some sort, my humble tribute to their genius and their just renown.

I best knew and loved Henry Clay: he was by nature genial, cordial, courteous, gracious, magnetic, winning. When General Glascock, of Georgia, took his seat in Congress as a Representative, a mutual friend asked, "General, may I introduce you to Henry Clay?" "No, sir!" was the stern response; "I am his adversary, and choose not to subject myself to his fascination." I think it would have been hard to constitute for three or four years a legislative body whereof Mr. Clay was a member, and not more than four sevenths were his pledged, implacable opponents, whereof he would not have been the master-spirit, and the author and inspirer of most of its measures, after the first or second year.

Mr. Webster was colder, graver, sterner, in his general bearing; though he could unbend and be sunny and blithe in his intercourse with those admitted to his intimacy. There were few gayer or more valued associates on a fishing or sailing party. His mental calibre was much the larger; I judge that he had read and studied more; though neither could boast much erudition, not even intense application. I believe each was about thirty years in Congress, where Mr. Clay identified his name with the origin or success of at least half a dozen important measures to every one thus blended with Mr. Webster's. Though Webster's was far the more massive intellect, Mr Clay as a legislator evinced far the greater creative, constructive power. I once sat in the Senate Chamber when Mr. Douglas, who had just been transferred from the House, rose, to move forward a bill in which he was interested. "We have no such practice in the Senate, sir," said Mr. Webster, in his deep, solemn voice, fixing his eye on the mover, but without rising from his seat. Mr. Douglas at once varied his motion, seeking to achieve his end in a somewhat different way. "That is not the way we do business in the Senate, sir," rejoined Mr. Webster, still more decisively and sternly. "The Little Giant" was a bold, ready man, not easily overawed or disconcerted; but, if he did not quiver under the eye and voice of Webster, then my eyesight deceived me,—and I was very near him.

Mr. Calhoun was a tall, spare, earnest, evidently thoughtful man, with stiff, iron-gray hair, which reminded you of Jackson's about the time of his accession to the Presidency. He was eminently a logician,—terse, vigorous, relentless. He courted the society of clever, aspiring young men who inclined to fall into his views, and exerted great influence over them. As he had abandoned the political faith which I distinguish and cherish as National while I was yet a school-boy, I never met him at all intimately; yet once, while I was connected with mining on Lake Superior, I called on him, as on other leading members of Congress, to explain the effect of the absurd policy then in vogue, of keeping mineral lands out of market, and attempting to collect a percentage of the mineral as rent accruing to the Government. He received me courteously, and I took care to make my statement as compact and perspicuous as I could, showing him that, even in the Lead region, where the system had attained its full development, the Treasury did not receive enough rent to pay the salaries of the officers employed in collecting it. "Enough," said Mr. Calhoun; "you are clearly right. I will vote to give away these lands, rather than perpetuate this vicious system." "We only ask, Mr. Calhoun," I rejoined, "that Congress fix on the lands whatever price it may deem just, and sell them at that price to those lawfully in possession; they failing to purchase, then to whomsoever will buy them." "That plan will have my hearty support," he responded; and it did. When the question came at length to be taken, I believe there was no vote in either House against selling the mineral lands.

HARRIET BEECHER STOWE.

[Born 1812.]

HARRIET ELIZABETH BEECHER, daughter of Rev. Lyman Beecher, D. D., an eminent theologian and father of a remarkable family, was born at Litchfield, Conn., June 14, 1812. She was educated at her sister Catherine's school, in Hartford, until fifteen years of age, when she assisted in teaching until her twentieth year, and then removed to Cincinnati, O., with her father, in the autumn of 1832. In 1833, she married Rev. Calvin E. Stowe, Professor of Languages and Biblical Literature in Lane Theological Seminary. During her residence in Cincinnati, she became deeply interested in the question of slavery, from seeing many fugitives from the Slave States and hearing from them their tales of suffering.

Her first publication was the story of Uncle Lot, printed in Judge Hall's monthly magazine at Cincinnati, in 1833, and from this time she became a frequent and popular writer in the various periodicals in the country. In 1849, a collection of her pieces was published by the Harpers, entitled the May Flower, which was much enlarged in new editions published in 1855, and in 1866; a collection of tales and essays hardly equalled for ease and naturalness of description, touching narrative, and elevating moral tone.

In 1850, Professor Stowe was called to Brunswick College, Me., and removed his family thither. The passage of the Fugitive Slave Bill in that year excited Mrs. Stowe to write Uncle Tom's Cabin, or Life among the Lowly, which she wrote with great rapidity, under a constant pressure of school and family cares, and frail health. This was originally published in weekly parts in the National Era, at Washington, from June, 1851 to April, 1852. It was published in book form in Boston, in 1852, in 2 vols., 12mo., with a few illustrations. Its success was great and immediate; 100,000 were sold in this country in eight weeks, 200,000 within a year, and 316,000 to 1870. In England its success though not at once so great, was very decided; it was published there in May, 1852, and in September, the demand had so increased that 10,000 copies

per day for four weeks, were sold by one house alone, and 1000 persons were employed in manufacturing them to keep up a supply, and by the end of the year more than one million of copies had been sold in England, of the thirty different editions issued. In France four different versions were made, one publisher alone issuing his in five different sizes; there were fourteen versions of it in Germany; two in Russia, two in Dutch, two in Welsh, three in Magyar, two in Wallachian, and one each in Italian, Spanish, Danish, Swedish, Flemish, Polish, Portugese, Wendish, Armenian, Arabic, Romaic, Chinese, and Japanese. It would be impossible to state the number of copies of this work sold, but it must amount to many millions. It was one of the most powerful blows aimed at slavery, and. it exhibits such a knowledge of human nature, such powers of description, such heart-stirring pathos, and such richness and beauty of thought and language, as to make it the most remarkable book published in this country. The Italian translation enjoys the honor of the Pope's prohibition. It has been dramatized in twenty different forms, and acted in every capital of Europé, and every town of any size in the United States, still maintaining its hold upon the stage.

In 1852, Prof. Stowe was called to the chair of Biblical Literature in Andover Theological Seminary. Though the literary merits of Uncle Tom were generally acknowledged, its conformity to truth was denied by some, and questioned by many, and it had been grossly assailed as giving too dark and false a view of slavery; Mrs. Stowe, therefore, in the following year published, A Key to Uncle Tom's Cabin, presenting the original Facts and Documents on which the story was founded, drawn chiefly from Southern authorities, which more than verified all she had depicted. Ninety thousand copies were sold in one month, and it was reprinted abroad.

In April, 1853, Mrs Stowe, with her husband, and brother, Rev. Charles Beecher, went to Europe for her health, where she was received and entertained with enthusiasm and the greatest distinction. On her return, she published Sunny Memories of Foreign Lands, being her observations and reflections on what she saw abroad; 2 vols., 12mo. The volumes met with considerable sale, due more to her previous fame, that to any merit in the work, as they did not rank with more interesting and agreeable volumes written by women of less natural ability.

In 1855, she published a Geography for My Children, which was a failure. Also, Dred, a Tale of the Dismal Swamp, 2 vols., 12mo., and reprinted in one volume in 1866, under the title of Nina Gordon. It sold to the extent of 100,000 copies in two months, and 150,000 copies to August, 1857. Though not equal to Uncle Tom's Cabin in the unity of the plot, in the simplicity of the story, in deep pathos, or in the absorbing interest it excites in the several characters, it contains many passages of powerful and beautiful writing, and is in advance of its great prototype in the withering scorn and indignant sarcasm with which it holds up before the world that sham religion that puts "sacrifice" before "mercy" and substitutes mere church-going and outward observances for practical righteousness. It was reprinted in German, French, and several other languages. In 1858, she wrote, Our Charley, and what to do with him, a juvenile book.

In the Atlantic Monthly, for Dec., 1858, Mrs. Stowe commenced the publication of The Minister's Wooing, which was issued in Oct., 1859, in one vol., 12mo., a tale, of which 30,000 were sold in six months. Followed in 1862, by the Pearl of Orr's Island, 12mo., a story of singular pathos and beauty, in her best style; and Agnes of Sorrento, a story containing many passages of graceful or picturesque description.

In 1863, "Many Thousand Women of Great Britain" issued a "Christain Address" to their sisters in America, about the Great Rebellion, in which it would be hard to say which was most prominent, their ignorance or their impudence, but which Mrs. Stowe very properly and ably answered in her Reply on behalf of the Women of America. Since then she has published a number of minor works, mostly reprints of articles contributed to the Atlantic Monthly and Our Young Folks, as, The Ravages of a Carpet, 1864; House and Home papers,

by Christopher Crowfield; Religious Poems, 1865; Stories about our Dogs; Little Foxes, or the insignificant little Habits which mar Domestic Happiness; Queer Little People, 1867; Daisy's first winter, and other stories; The Chimney-Corner, 12 papers from the Atlantic, 1868; Men of our Times, or Leading Patriots of the Day, 8vo., a work, made to sell by subscription; and, The American Woman's Home, or Principles of Domestic Science, 1869; an octavo volume got up in conjunction with her sister, Catherine E. Beecher, to be sold by subscription.

In May, 1869, she published her last Novel, Oldtown Folks, one vol., 12mo., reprinted in England, in 3 vols., 8vo., which has been deservedly successful; 25,000 copies were sold in three months.

In addition to the above writings, Mrs. Stowe is the author of The Two Altars; A word to the Sorrowful; My Expectation; My Strength; Strong Consolation; and, Things that cannot be Shaken; six tracts. She has been a frequent contributor to Hall's Monthly Magazine, Godey's Lady's Book, the New York Evangelist, the Independent, Our Young Folks, Old and New, etc. She wrote an Introduction to the American edition of Charlotte Elizabeth's Works; and contributed to the autobiography of her father, Rev. Lyman Beecher, D. D., 2 vols., 12mo. Her stanzas, Still with Thee, were published, with music, by Rev. Charles Beecher. In December, 1868, she became co-editor with Donald G. Mitchell, of a new weekly paper for the farm and fireside, Hearth and Home.

Here we should willingly close this article on Mrs. Stowe, even if it had been to announce the period of her decease, sooner than to have to add the chapter which follows, and is necessary to complete her literary history; the facts of which have so injured her popularity, her reputation, and the power for good of all her previous works. In December, 1868, there was published in London, the autobiography of the Countess Guiccioli, the mistress of Lord Byron, entitled, My Recollections of Lord Byron, and those of Eye-witnesses of his Life, in 2 vols., 8vo. This book, reviewed in Blackwood's Magazine, in July, 1869, was reprinted in America, in two editions, 8vo., and 12mo. Mrs. Stowe, taking umbrage at some statements of the Guiccioli, wrote an article, entitled, The True Story of Lady Byron's Life, which she published at the same time, September, in the Atlantic Monthly, Boston, and MacMillan's Magazine, London. This was reviewed with great severity in the Quarterly Review, the Saturday Review, London Times, Pall Mall Gazette, and many other English, American, French, and German periodicals. As an impartial chronicler, it is proper to state that we know of no instance of such sweeping censure—of such general, almost universal, condemnation—as that with which Mrs. Stowe's alleged offence was visited; and this equally by the few who believed as by the many who disbelieved her story. The publication of her article was immediately followed by other writers in defence of Lord Byron, whose character, with little or no evidence she had foully aspersed, in which they showed conclusively that she must have been misled, or else was wilfully or artfully concocting her "True Story". Here it was hoped by the respectable portion of the community she would allow the matter to rest. To the surprise of the public, she published in December, a 12mo. volume on the same subject entitled, Lady Byron vindicated, a History of the Byron Controversy from its beginning in 1816 to the Present Time; in which she reaffirmed her original statement, in a long, wordy enlargement of her original article, but without any new proofs or any substantial proof which the public were led to expect as the cause of her publishing another article on the subject. We use much milder language than most of the lady's critics when we say that this vindication is considered unsatisfactory. The book was reviewed in short articles by the leading critics, and was severely let alone by the reading public; it fell almost still-born from the press, the first supplies still oppressing the booksellers shelves, unsold. That any American woman of so much supposed good sense or morality, should have been found willing to spread into the interior of so many households, so foul a story unsupported by any reliable facts, is incredible. Even had it been true, what good was to be accomplished? Lady Byron's fame needed no vindication, and surely as the result of these articles, she does not stand so high in public estimation as before their issue; while the sale of Byron's works has been increased.

THE MOTHER'S STRUGGLE.
FROM UNCLE TOM'S CABIN.

It is impossible to conceive of a human creature more wholly desolate and forlorn than Eliza, when she turned her footsteps from Uncle Tom's Cabin.

Her husband's suffering and dangers, and the danger of her child, all blended in her mind, with a confused and stunning sense of the risk she was running, in leaving the only home she had ever known, and cutting loose from the protection of a friend whom she loved and revered. Then there was the parting from every familiar object,—the place where she had grown up, the trees under which she had played, the groves where she had walked many an evening in happier days, by the side of her young husband,—everything, as it lay in the clear, frosty starlight, seemed to speak reproachfully to her, and ask her whither could she go from a home like that?

But stronger than all was maternal love, wrought into a paroxysm of frenzy by the near approach of a fearful danger. Her boy was old enough to have walked by her side, and, in an indifferent case, she would only have led him by the hand; but now, the bare thought of putting him out of her arms made her shudder, and she strained him to her bosom with a convulsive grasp, as she went rapidly forward.

The frosty ground creaked beneath her feet, and she trembled at the sound; every quaking leaf and fluttering shadow sent the blood backward to her heart, and quickened her footsteps. She wondered within herself at the strength that seemed to become upon her; for she felt the weight of her boy as if it had been a feather, and every flutter of fear seemed to increase the supernatural power that bore her on, while from her pale lips burst forth, in frequent ejaculations, the prayer to a Friend above—"Lord, help! Lord, save me!"

If it were your Harry, mother, or your Willie, that were going to be torn from you by a brutal trader, to-morrow morning,—if you had seen the man, and heard that the papers were signed and delivered, and you had only from twelve o'clock till morning to make good your escape,—how fast could you walk? How many miles could you make in those few brief hours, with the darling at your bosom,—the little sleepy head on your shoulder,—the small, soft arms trustingly holding on to your neck?

For the child slept. At first, the novelty and alarm kept him waking; but his mother so hurriedly repressed every breath or sound, and so assured him that if he were only still she would certainly save him, that he clung quietly round her neck, only asking, as he found himself sinking to sleep,

"Mother, I don't need to keep awake, do I?"

"No, my darling; sleep, if you want to."

"But, mother, if I do get asleep, you won't let him get me?"

"No! so may God help me!" said his mother, with a paler cheek, and a brighter light in her large dark eyes.

"You're *sure*, an't you, mother?"

"Yes, *sure?*" said the mother, in a voice that startled herself; for it seemed to her to come from a spirit within, that was no part of her; and the boy dropped his little weary head on her shoulder, and was soon asleep. How the touch of those warm arms, the gentle breathings that came in her neck seemed to add fire and spirit to her movements! It seemed to her as if strength poured into her in electric streams, from every gentle touch and movement of the sleeping, confiding child. Sublime is the dominion of the mind over the body, that, for a time, can make flesh and nerve impregnable, and string the sinews like steel, so that the weak become so mighty.

The boundaries of the farm, the grove, the wood-lot, passed by her dizzily, as she walked on; and still she went, leaving one familiar object after another, slacking not, pausing not, till reddening daylight found her many a long mile from all traces of any familiar objects upon the open highway.

She had often been, with her mistress, to visit some connections, in the little village of T——, not far from the Ohio river, and knew the road well. To go thither, to escape across the Ohio river, were the first hurried outlines of her plan of escape; beyond that, she could only hope in God.

When horses and vehicles began to move along the highway, with that alert perception peculiar to a state of excitement. and which seems to be a sort of inspiration, she became aware that her headlong pace and distracted air might bring on her remark and suspicion. She therefore put the boy on the ground, and, adjusting her dress and bonnet, she walked on at as rapid a pace as she thought consistent with the preservation of appearances. In her little bundle she had provided a store of cakes and apples, which she used as expedients for quickening the speed of the child, rolling the apple some yards before them, when the boy would run with all his might after it; and this ruse, often repeated, carried them over many a half-mile.

After awhile, they came to a thick patch of woodland, through which murmured a clear brook. As the child complained of hunger and thirst, she climbed over the fence with him; and, sitting down behind a large rock which concealed them from the road, she gave him a breakfast our of her little package. The boy wondered and grieved that she could not eat; and when, putting his arms round her neck, he tried to wedge some of his cake into her mouth, it seemed to her that the rising in her throat would choke her.

"No, no, Harry darling! mother can't eat till you are safe. We must go on——on——till we come to the river!" And she hurried again into the road, and again constrained herself to walk regularly and composedly forward.

She was many miles past any neighborhood where she was personally known. If she should chance to meet any who knew her, she reflected that the well-known kindness of the family would be of itself a blind to suspicion, as making it an unlikely supposition that she could be a fugitive. As she was also so white as not to be known as of colored lineage, without a critical survey, and her child was white also, it was much easier for her to pass on unsuspected.

On this presumption, she stopped at noon at a neat farm-house, to rest herself, and buy some dinner for her child and self; for, as the danger decreased with the distance, the supernatural tension of the nervous system lessened, and she found herself both weary and hungry.

The good woman, kindly and gossiping, seemed rather pleased than otherwise with having somebody come in to talk with; and accepted, without examination, Eliza's statement, that she "was going on a little piece, to spend a week with her friends,"—all which she hoped in her heart might prove strictly true.

An hour before sunset, she entered the village of T——. by the Ohio river, weary and footsore, but still strong in heart. Her first glance was at the river, which lay, like Jordan, between her and the Canaan of liberty on the other side.

It was now early spring, and the river was swollen and turbulent; great cakes of floating ice were swinging heavily to and fro in the turbid waters. Owing to the peculiar form of the shore on the Kentucky side, the land bending far out into the water, the ice had been lodged and detained in great quantities, and the narrow channel which swept round the bend was full of ice, piled one cake over another, thus forming a temporary barrier to the descending ice, which lodged, and formed a great, undulating raft, filling up the whole river, and extending almost to the Kentucky shore.

Eliza stood, for a moment, contemplating this unfavorable aspect of things, which she saw at once must prevent the usual ferry-boat from running, and then turned into a small public house on the bank, to make a few inquiries.

The hostess, who was busy in various fizzing and stewing operations over the fire, preparatory to the evening meal, stopped, with a fork in her hand, as Eliza's sweet and plaintive voice arrested her.

"What is it?" she said.

"Isn't there any ferry or boat, that takes people over to B——, now?" she said.

"No, indeed!" said the woman; "the boats has stopped running."

Eliza's look of dismay and disappointment struck the woman, and she said, inquiringly,

"May be you're wanting to get over?—anybody sick? Ye seem mighty anxious?"

"I've got a child that's very dangerous," said Eliza. "I never heard of it till last night, and I've walked quite a piece to-day, in hopes to get to the ferry."

"Well, now, that's onlucky," said the woman

whose motherly sympathies were much aroused; I'm re'lly consarned for ye. Solomon!" she called, from the window, towards a small back building. A man, in leather apron and very dirty hands, appeared at the door.

"I say, Sol," said the woman, "is that ar man going to tote them bar'ls over to-night?"

"He said he should try, if 't was any way prudent,' said the man.

"There's a man a piece down here, that's going over with some truck this evening, if he durs'to; he'll be in here to supper to-night, so you'd better set down and wait. That's a sweet little fellow," added the woman, offering him a cake.

But the child, wholly exhausted, cried with weariness.

"Poor fellow! he isn't used to walking, and I've hurried him on so," said Eliza.

"Well, take him into this room," said the woman, opening into a small bed-room, where stood a comfortable bed. Eliza laid the weary boy upon it, and held his hands in hers till he was fast asleep. For her there was no rest. As a fire in her bones, the thought of the pursuer urged her on; and she gazed with longing eyes on the sullen, surging waters that lay between her and liberty.

Here we must take our leave of her for the present, to follow the course of her pursuers.

* * * * * *

At two o'clock Sam and Andy brought the horses up to the posts, apparently greatly refreshed and invigorated by the scamper of the morning.

Sam was there new oiled from dinner, with an abundance of zealous and ready officiousness. As Haley approached, he was boasting, in flourishing style, to Andy, of the evident and eminent success of the operation, now that he had "farly come to it."

"Your master, I s'pose, don't keep no dogs," said Haley, thoughtfully, as he prepared to mount.

"Heaps on 'em," said Sam, triumphantly; "thar's Bruno—he's a roarer! and, besides that, 'bout every nigger of us keeps a pup of some natur or uther."

"Poh!" said Haley,—and he said something else, too, with regard to the said dogs, at which Sam muttered.

"I don't see no use cussin' on 'em, no way."

"But your master don't keep no dogs (I pretty much know he don't) for trackin' out niggers."

Sam knew exactly what he meant, but he kept on a look of earnest and desperate simplicity.

"Our dogs all smells round considerable sharp. I spect they's the kind, though they han't never had no practice. They's far dogs, though, at most anything, if you'd get 'em started. Here, Bruno," he called, whistling to the lumbering Newfoundland, who came pitching tumultuously toward them.

"You go hang!" said Haley, getting up. "Come, tumble up now."

Sam tumbled up accordingly, dexterously contriving to tickle Andy as he did so, which oc-

80

casioned Andy to split out into a laugh, greatly to Haley's indignation, who made a cut at him with his riding-whip.

"I's 'astonished at yer, Andy," said Sam, with awful gravity. "This yer's a seris bisness, Andy. Yer mustn't be a makin' game. This yer an't no way to help Mas'r."

"I shall take the straight road to the river," said Haley, decidedly, after they had come to the boundaries of the estate. "I know the way of all of 'em,—they makes tracks for the underground."

"Sartin," said Sam, "dat's de idee. Mas'r Haley hits de thing right in de middle. Now, der's two roads to de river,—de dirt road and der pike,—which Mas'r mean to take?"

Andy looked up innocently at Sam, surprised at hearing this new geographical fact, but instantly confirmed what he said, by a vehement reiteration.

"Cause," said Sam, "I'd rather be 'clined to 'magine that Lizy'd take de dirt road, bein' it's the least travelled."

Haley, notwithstanding that he was a very old bird, and naturally inclined to be suspicious of chaff, was rather brought up by this view of the case.

"If ye warnt both on yer such cussed liars, now!" he said, contemplatively, as he pondered a moment.

The pensive, reflective tone in which this was spoken appeared to amuse Andy prodigiously, and he drew a little behind, and shook so as apparently to run a great risk of falling off his horse, while Sam's face was immovably composed into the most doleful gravity.

"Course," said Sam, "Mas'r can do as he'd ruther; go de straight road, if Mas'r thinks best,—it's all one to us. Now, when I study 'pon it, I think de straight road de best, deridedly."

"She would naturally go a lonesome way," said Haley, thinking aloud, and not minding Sam's remark.

"Dar an't no sayin'," said Sam; "gals is pecular; they never does nothin ye thinks they will; mose gen'lly the contrar. Gals is nat'lly made contrary; and so, if you thinks they've gone one road, it is sartin you'd better go 'tother, and then you'll be sure to find 'em. Now, my private 'pinion is, Lizy took der dirt road; so I think we'd better take de straight one."

This profound generic view of the female sex did not seem to dispose Haley particularly to the straight road; and he announced decidedly that he should go the other, and asked Sam when they should come to it.

"A little piece ahead," said Sam, giving a wink to Andy with the eye which was on Andy's side of the head; and he added, gravely, "but I've studded on de matter, and I m quite clar we ought not to go dat ar way. I nebber been over it no way. It's despit lonesome, and we might lose our way,—whar we'd come to, de Lord only knows."

"Nevertheless," said Haley, "I shall go that way."

"Now I think on't, I think I hear 'em tell

that dat ar road was all fenced up and down by der creek, and thar, an't it, Andy?"

Andy wasn't certain; he'd only "hearn tell" about that road, but never been over it. In short, he was strictly non-committal.

Haley, accustomed to strike the balance of probabilities between lies of greater or lesser magnitude, thought that it lay in favor of the dirt road aforesaid. The mention of the thing he thought he perceived was involuntary or Sam's part at first, and his confused attempts to dissuade him he set down to a desperate lying on second thoughts, as being unwilling to implicate Eliza.

When, therefore, Sam indicated the road, Haley plunged briskly into it, followed by Sam and Andy.

Now, the road, in fact, was an old one, that had formerly been a thoroughfare to the river, but abandoned for many years after the laying of the new pike. It was open for about an hour's ride, and after that it was cut across by various farms and fences. Sam knew this fact perfectly well,—indeed, the road had been so long closed up, that Andy had never heard of it. He, therefore, rode along with an air of dutiful submission, only groaning and vociferating occasionally that 't was "desp't rough, and bad for Jerry's foot."

"Now, I jest give yer warning," said Haley, "I know yer; yer won't get me to turn off this yer road, with all yer fussin—so you shet up!"

"Mas'r will go his own way!" said Sam, with rueful submission, at the same time winking most portentously to Andy, whose delight was now very near the explosive point.

Sam was in wonderful spirits,—professed to keep a very brisk look-out,—at one time exclaiming that he saw "a gal's bonnet" on the top of some distant eminence, or calling to Andy "if that thar wasn't 'Lizy' down in the hollow," always making these exclamations in some rough or craggy part of the road, where the sudden quickening of speed was a special inconvenience to all parties concerned, and thus keeping Haley in a state of constant commotion.

After riding about an hour in this way, the whole party made a precipitate and tumultuous descent into a barn-yard belonging to a large farming establishment. Not a soul was in sight, all the hands being employed in the fields; but, as the barn stood conspicuously and plainly square across the road, it was evident that their journey in that direction had reached a decided finale.

"Wan't dat ar what I telled Mas'r?" said Sam, with an air of injured innocence. "How does strange gentleman spect to know more about a country dan de natives born and raised?"

"You rascal!" said Haley, "you knew all about this."

"Didn't I tell yer I know'd, and yer wouldn't believe me! I telled Mas'r 't was all shet up, and fenced up, and I didn't spect we could get through,—Andy heard me."

It was all too true to be disputed, and the unlucky man had to pocket his wrath with the best grace he was able, and all three faced to the right

about, and took up their line of march for the highway.

In consequence of all the various delays, it was about three-quarters of an hour after Eliza had laid her child to sleep in the village tavern that the party came riding into the same place. Eliza was standing by the window, looking out in another direction, when Sam's quick eye caught a glimpse of her. Haley and Andy were two yards behind. At this crisis, Sam contrived to have his hat blown off, and uttered a loud and characteristic ejaculation, which startled her at once; she drew suddenly back; the whole train swept by the window, round to the front door.

A thousand lives seemed to be concentrated in that one moment to Eliza. Her room opened by a side door to the river. She caught her child, and sprang down the steps towards it. The trader caught a full glimpse of her, just as she was disappearing down the bank; and throwing himself from his horse, and calling loudly on Sam and Andy, he was after her like a hound after a deer. In that dizzy moment her feet to her scarce seemed to touch the ground, and a moment brought her to the water's edge. Right on behind they came; and, nerved with strength such as God gives only to the desperate, with one wild cry and flying leap, she vaulted sheer over the turbid current by the shore, on to the raft of ice beyond. It was à desperate leap—impossible to anything but madness and despair; and Haley, Sam, and Andy, instinctively cried out, and lifted up their hands, as she did it.

The huge green fragment of ice on which she alighted, pitched and creaked as her weight came on it, but she staid there not a moment. With wild cries and desperate energy she leaped to another and still another cake;—stumbling—leaping—slipping—springing upwards again! Her shoes are gone—her stockings cut from her feet—while blood marked every step; but she saw nothing, felt nothing, till dimly, as in a dream, she saw the Ohio side, and a man helping her up the bank.

"Yer a brave gal, now, whoever ye ar!" said the man, with an oath.

Eliza recognized the voice and face of a man who owned a farm not far from her old home.

"O, Mr. Symmes!—save me—do save me—do hide me!" said Eliza.

"Why, what's this?" said the man. "Why, if tan't Shelby's gal!"

"My child!—this boy!—he'd sold him! There is his Mas'r," said she, pointing to the Kentucky shore. "O, Mr. Symmes, you've got a little boy!"

"So I have," said the man, as he roughly, but kindly drew her up the steep bank. "Besides, you're a right brave gal. I like grit, wherever I see it."

When they had gained the top of the bank, the man paused.

"I'd be glad to do something for ye," said he; "but then there's nowhar I could take ye. The best I can do is to tell ye to go *thar*," said he, pointing to a large white house which stood by itself, off the main street of the village. "Go thar; they're kind folks. Thar's no kind o' danger but they'll help you,—they're up to all that sort o' thing."

"The Lord bless you!" said Eliza, earnestly.

"No 'casion, no 'casion in the world," said the man. "What I've done's of no 'count."

"And, oh, surely, sir, you won't tell any one!"

"Go to thunder gal! What do you take a fellow for? In course not, said the man. "Come, now, go along like a likely, sensible gal, as you are. You've arnt your liberty, and you shall have it, for all me."

The woman folded her child to her bosom, and walked firmly and swiftly away. The man stood and looked after her.

"Shelby, now, mebbe won't think this yer the most neighborly thing in the world; but what's a feller to do? If he catches one of my gals in the same fix, he's welcome to pay back. Somehow I never could see no kind o' critter a strivin' and pantin', and trying to clar theirselves, with the dogs arter 'em, and go agin 'em. Besides, I don't see no kind of 'casion for me to be hunter and catcher for other folks, neither."

So spoke this poor, heathenish Kentuckian, who had not been instructed m his constitutional relations, and consequently was betrayed into acting in a sort of Christianized manner which, if he had been better situated and more enlightened, he would not have been left to do.

Haley had stood a perfectly amazed spectator of the scene, till Eliza had disappeared up the bank, when he turned a blank, inquiring look on Sam and Andy.

"That ar was a tolable fair stroke of business," said Sam.

"The gal's got seven devils in her, I believe!" said Haley. "How like a wildcat she jumped!"

"Wal, now," said Sam, scratching his head, "I hope Mas'r 'll 'scuse us tryin' dat ar road. Don't think I feel spry enough for dat ar, no way!" and Sam gave a hoarse chuckle.

"You laugh!" said the trader, with a growl.

"Lord bless you, Mas'r, I couldn't help it, now," said Sam, giving way to the long pent-up delight of his soul. "She looked so curi's, a leapin' and springin'—ice a crackin'—and only to hear her,—plump! ker chunk! ker splash! Spring! Lord! how she goes it!" and Sam and Andy laughed till the tears rolled down their cheeks.

"I'll make ye laugh t'other side yer mouths!" said the trader, laying about their heads with his riding-whip.

Both ducked, and ran shouting up the bank, and were on their horses before he was up.

"Good-evening, Mas'r!" said Sam, with much gravity. "I berry much spect Missis be anxious 'bout Jerry. Mas'r Haley won't want us no longer. Missis wouldn't hear of our ridin' the critters over Lizy's bridge to-night;" and, with a facetious poke into Andy's ribs, he started off, followed by the latter, at full speed,—their shouts of laughter coming faintly on the wind.

CANDACE'S OPINIONS.
FROM THE MINISTER'S WOOING.

"I intend," said Mr. Marvyn, "to make the same offer to your husband, when he returns from work to-night."

"Laus, Mass'r,—why, Cato, he'll do jes' as I do,—dere a'n't no kind o' need o' askin' him. 'Course he will."

A smile passed round the circle, because between Candace and her husband there existed one of those whimsical contrasts which one sometimes sees in married life. Cato was a small-built, thin, softly-spoken negro, addicted to a gentle chronic cough; and, though a faithful and skilful servant, seemed, in relation to his better half, much like a hill of potatoes under a spreading apple-tree. Candace held to him with a vehement and patronizing fondness, so devoid of conjugal reverence as to excite the comments of her friends.

"You must remember, Candace," said a good deacon to her one day, when she was ordering him about at a catechizing, "you ought to give honor to your husband; the wife is the weaker vessel."

"I de weaker vessel?" said Candace, looking down from the tower of her ample corpulence on the small, quiet man whom she had been fledging with the ample folds of a worsted comforter, out of which his little head and shining bead-eyes looked, much like a blackbird in a nest,—"I de weaker vessel? Umph!"

A whole-woman's-rights' convention could not have expressed more in a day than was given in that single look and word. Candace considered a husband as a thing to be taken care of,—a rather inconsequent and somewhat troublesome species of pet, to be humored, nursed, fed, clothed, and guided in the way that he was to go,—an animal that was always losing off buttons, catching colds, wearing his best coat every day, and getting on his Sunday hat in a surreptitious manner for week-day occasions; but she often condescended to express it as her opinion that he was a blessing, and that she didn't know what she should do, if it wasn't for Cato. In fact, he seemed to supply her that which we are told is the great want in woman's situation,—an object in life. She sometimes was heard expressing herself very energetically in disapprobation of the conduct of one of her sable friends, named Jinny Stiles, who, after being presented with her own freedom, worked several years to buy that of her husband, but became afterwards so disgusted with her acquisition, that she declared she would "neber buy anoder nigger."

"Now Jinny don't know what she's talkin about," she would say. "S'pose he does cough and keep her awake nights, and take a little too much sometimes, a'n't he better'n no husband at all? A body wouldn't seem to hab nutlin to lib for, ef dey hadn't an ole man to look arter. Men is nate'lly foolish about some tings,—but dey's good deal better'n nuffin."

And Candace, after this condescending remark, would lift off with one hand a brass kettle in which poor Cato might have been drowned, and fly across the kitchen with it as if it were a feather.

THEODORE PARKER.

[Born 1812. Died 1860.]

THEODORE PARKER, the distinguished theologian, was born about 1812, at Lexington, Mass., the son of a farmer, and the grandson of a Revolutionary soldier, Capt. John Parker. He was a graduate of the Unitarian theological school at Cambridge, Mass., in 1836, and was afterwards settled as Minister of the Second Church in Roxbury. From 1840 to 1842, he was a contributor of theological papers to the Dial and Christian Examiner, which he collected in a volume of Critical and Miscellaneous writings in 1843. In 1841, he gave great offence to many of his friends, by a Discourse on the Transient and Permanent in Christianity; and in 1842, by the publication of a Discourse on matters relating to Religion; the substance of a series of lectures delivered the previous season, and a manifesto of the growing changes of the author in his doctrinal opinions, which had widely departed from points of church authority, the inspiration of the Scriptures, and the divine character of the Saviour.

Proscribed by the Unitarian societies of Boston on account of his new views, Mr. Parker organized a new congregation and independent service, and published Two Sermons on leaving an old and entering a new place of worship. His discourses were on some topic of the times or point of morality; questions of slavery, war, social and moral reforms of various kinds, were discussed with much acute analysis, and occasional effective satire. He bore a prominent part in the agitation of the Fugitive Slave Law, of which he was a vigorous denouncer.

In the winter of 1858–9, having suffered an attack of consumptive disease, he reached the island of Santa Cruz, greatly prostrated; but he slowly rallied, and in April, addressed a long letter, which his congregation published, under the title of Theodore Parker's Experience as a Minister, with some account of his Life and Education for the Ministry. Mr. Parker's health was sufficiently invigorated by his visit to the West Indies to enable him to make the voyage to Europe from Santa Cruz, with a prospect of further recovery He passed the summer of 1859, on the Continent, mainly in Switzerland, and wintered in Italy, at Rome. He enjoyed the beauties of nature, and was keenly alive, as usual, to the public questions of the day, at home and abroad. He succumbed to his disease, on his way north, at Florence, May 10, 1860. He lies buried, with a simple inscription on a tombstone, recording the day of his birth and death, in the cemetery outside the city. By his will, Mr. Parker bequeathed to the City of Boston, for the Public Library, the chief part of his library, over 11,000 vols. and 2500 pamphlets. Many eulogies were pronounced upon him by able writers and speakers, and a Life and Correspondence, 2 vols., 8vo., New York, 1864, by John Weiss, was published; a full and elaborate memoir, narrative and critical, exhibiting with much force and originality, the peculiar habits of thought, cherished opinions, and life-long studies of its subject.

His works were voluminous, and consist of, besides those mentioned above, a Critical and Historical Introduction to the Canonical Scriptures, from the German of De Wette, 2 vols., 8vo., three revised editions; Letters to the People on Slavery; Speeches, Addresses, and Occasional Sermons, 2 vols.; Discourse occasioned by the death of Daniel Webster, which gave great offence to nearly every one; Ten Sermons of Religion; Sermons on Theism, Atheism, and the Popular Theology; Old Age; Additional Speeches, Addresses, and Occasioual Sermons; Discourse on the Functions of a Teacher of Religion, in these times; Sermons on the Consequences of an Immoral Principle and False Idea of Life; Sermon on the Moral Dangers incident to Prosperity; Theodore Parker's Trial for the Misdemeanor of a Speech against Kidnapping, with the Author's Defence; New Years Sermon, what Religion may do for a man; and, Farewell Letter; together with many occasional sermons, addresses, or orations, of which we have not space for a list. Two editions of his complete works, translated into German, have been published in Germany; a German volume of Hymns suggested by his writings, has also been published there. A collective edition of his works, containing his Theological, Polemical, and Critical Writings, Sermons, Speeches, and Addresses, and Literary Miscellanies, edited by Francis Power Cobbe, was published in London, 1863–65, 12 vols., crown 8vo. A new edition of his works, 14 vols., was published in Boston, 1868-9. There was also published in London; Half-Battle Words from Theodore Parker; Prayers; Lessons from the World of Matter and the World of Mind; selected from Notes of unpublished Sermons.

THE PERISHING CLASSES OF BOSTON.
FROM SPEECHES, ADDRESSES, AND OCCASIONAL SERMONS.

WHAT will be the fate of these 2000 children? Some men are superior to circumstances; so well born they defy ill breeding. There may be children so excellent and strong they cannot be spoiled. Surely there are some who will learn with no school; boys of vast genius, whom you cannot keep from learning. Others there are of wonderful moral gifts, whom no circumstances can make vulgar; they will live in the midst of corruption and keep clean through the innate refinement of a wondrous soul. Out of these 2000 children there may be two of this sort; it were foolish to look for more than one in a thousand. The 1997 depend mainly on circumstances to help them; yes, to make their character. Send them to school and they will learn. Give them good precepts, good examples, they will also become good. Give them bad precepts, bad examples, and they become wicked. Send them half clad and uncared for into your streets, and they grow up hungry savages, greedy for crime.

What have these abandoned children to help them? Nothing, literally nothing! They are idle, though their bodies crave activity. They are poor, ill-clad, and ill-fed. There is nothing about them to foster self-respect; nothing to call forth their conscience, to awaken and cultivate their sense of religion. They find themselves beggars in the wealth of a city; idlers in the midst of its work. Yes, savages in the midst of civilization. Their consciousness is that of an outcast, one abandoned and forsaken of men. In cities, life is intense amongst all classes. So the passions and appetites of such children are strong and violent. Their taste is low; their wants clamorous. Are religion and conscience there to abate the fever of passion and regulate desire? The moral class and the cultivated shun these poor wretches, or look on with stupid wonder. Our rule is that the whole need the physician, not the sick. They are left almost entirely to herd and consort with the basest of men; they are exposed early and late to the worst influences, and their only comrades are men whom the children of the rich are taught to shun as the pestilence. To be poor is hard enough in the country, where artificial wants are few, and those easily met, where all classes are humbly clad, and none fare sumptuously every day. But to be poor in the city, where a hundred artificial desires daily claim satisfaction, and where, too, it is difficult for the poor to satisfy the natural and unavoidable wants of food and raiment; to be hungry, ragged, dirty, amid luxury, wantonness and refinement; to be miserable in the midst of abundance, that is hard beyond all power of speech. Look, I will not say at the squalid dress of these children, as you see them prowling about the markets and wharves, or contending in the dirty lanes and by-places into which the pride of Boston has elbowed so much of her misery; look at their faces! Haggard as they are, meagre and pale and wan, want is not the worst thing written there, but cunning, fraud, violence and obscenity, and worst of all, fear!

Amid all the science and refined culture of the nineteenth century, these children learn little, little that is good, much that is bad. In the intense life around them, they unavoidably become vicious, obscene, deceitful and violent. They will lie, steal, be drunk. How can it be otherwise?

If you could know the life of one of those poor lepers of Boston, you would wonder, and weep. Let me take one of them at random out of the mass. He was born, unwelcome, amid wretchedness and want. His coming increased both. Miserably he struggles through his infancy, less tended than the lion's whelp. He becomes a boy. He is covered only with rags, and those squalid with long accumulated filth. He wanders about your streets, too low even to seek employment, now snatching from a gutter half rotten fruit which the owner flings away. He is ignorant; he has never entered a school-house; to him even the alphabet is a mystery. He is young in years, yet old in misery. There is no hope in his face. He herds with others like himself, low, ragged, hungry and idle. If misery loves company, he finds that satisfaction. Follow him to his home at night; he herds in a cellar; in the same sty with father, mother, brothers, sisters, and perhaps yet other families of like degree. What served him for dress by day, is his only bed by night.

Well, this boy steals some trifle, a biscuit, a bit of rope, or a knife from a shop-window, be is seized and carried to jail. The day comes for trial. He is marched through the streets in handcuffs, the companion of drunkards and thieves, thus deadening the little self respect which Nature left even in an outcast's bosom. He sits there chained like a beast; a boy in irons! the sport and mockery of men vulgar as the common sewer. His trial comes. Of course he is convicted. The show of his countenance is witness against him. His rags and dirt, his ignorance, his vagrant habits, his idleness, all testify against him. That face so young, and yet so impudent, so sly, so writ all over with embryo villany, is evidence enough. The jury are soon convinced, for they see his temptations in his look, and surely know that in such a condition men will steal: yes, they themselves would steal. The judge represents the law, and that practically regards it a crime for a boy to be weak and poor. Much of our common law, it seems to me, is based on might, not right. So he is hurried off to jail at a tender age, and made legally the companion of felons. Now the State has him wholly in her power; by that rough adoption, has made him her own child, and sealed the indenture with the jailor's key. His handcuffs are the symbol of his sonship to the State. She shuts him in her college for the Little. What does that teach him; science, letters; even morals and religion? Little enough of this, even in Boston, and in most counties of Massachusetts, I think nothing at all, not even a trade which he can practise when his term expires!' I have been told a story, and I wish it might be falsely told, of a boy, in this city, of sixteen, sent to the house of correction for five years because he stole a bunch of keys, and coming out of that jail at twenty-one, unable to write, or read, or calculate, and with no trade but that of picking oakum. Yet he had been five years the child of the State, and in that college for the poor! Who would employ such a youth; with such a reputation; with the smell of the jail in his very breath? Not your shrewd men of business, they know the risk; not your respectable men, members of churches and all that; not they! Why it would hurt a man's reputation for piety to do good in that way. Besides, the risk is great, and it argues a great deal more Christianity than it is popular to have, for a respectable man to employ such a youth. He is forced back into crime again. I say, forced, for honest men will not employ him when the State shoves him out of the jail. Soon you will have him in the court again, to be punished more severely. Then he goes to the State-prison, and then again, and again, till death mercifully ends his career!

Who is to blame for all that? I will ask the best man among the best of you, what he would have become, if thus abandoned, turned out in childhood, and with no culture, into the streets, to herd with the wickedest of men! Somebody says, there are "organic sins" in society which nobody is to blame for. But by this sin organized in society, these vagrant children are training up to become thieves, pirates and murderers. I cannot blame them. But there is a terrible blame some-

where, for it is not the will of God that one of these little ones should perish. Who is it that organizes the sin of society?

THOUGHTS FOR A NEW YEAR
FROM THE SAME.

THIS is the first Sunday of a new year. What an hour for resolutions; what a moment for prayer! If you have sins in your bosom, cast them behind you now. In the last year, God has blessed us; blessed us all. On some his angels waited, robed in white, and brought new joys; here a wife, to bind men closer yet to Providence; and there a child, a new Messiah, sent to tell of innocence and heaven. To some his angels came clad in dark livery, veiling a joyful countenance with unpropitious wings, and bore away child, father, sister, wife, or friend. Still were they angels of good Providence, all God's own; and he who looks aright finds that they also brought a blessing, but concealed, and left it, though they spoke no word of joy. One day our weeping brother shall find that gift and wear it as a diamond on his breast.

The hours are passing over us, and with them the day. What shall the future Sundays be, and what the year? What we make them both. God gives us time. We weave it into life, such figures as we may, and wear it as we will. Age slowly rots away the gold we are set in, but the adamantine soul lives on, radiant every way in the light streaming down from God. The genius of eternity, star-crowned, beautiful, and with prophetic eyes, leads us again to the gates of time, and gives us one more year, bidding us fill that golden cup with water as we can or will. There stand the dirty, fetid pools of worldliness and sin; curdled, and mantled, film-covered, streaked and striped with many a hue, they shine there, in the slanting light of new-born day. Around them stand the sons of earth and cry: Come hither; drink thou and be saved! Here fill thy golden cup! There you may seek to fill your urn : to stay your thirst. The deceitful element, roping in your hands, shall mock your lip. It is water only to the eye. Nay, show-water only unto men half-blind. But there, hard by, runs down the stream of life, its waters never frozen, never dry; fed by perennial dews falling unseen from God. Fill there thine urn, oh, brother-man, and thou shalt thirst no more for selfishness and sin, and faint no more amid the toil and heat of day; wash there, and the leprosy of sin, its scales of blindness, shall fall off, and thou be clean for ever. Kneel there and pray; God shall inspire thy heart with truth and love, and fill thy cup with never-ending joy!

HENRY WARD BEECHER.

[Born 1813.]

It is more for his fame as an eminent preacher and eloquent lecturer, than from his ability as a writer, that Henry Ward Beecher is enrolled in our list. He was born in Litchfield, Conn., June 24, 1813. He graduated at Amherst College in 1834, and studied theology at Lane Seminary, Cincinnati, under the Presidency of his father, Rev. Lyman Beecher. He first settled as a Presbyterian minister at Lawrenceburg, Ind., 1837, and removed to Indianapolis, where he remained until 1847, when he accepted the call to the Plymouth church in Brooklyn, N. Y., an organization of Orthodox Congregational believers; which position he continues to occupy, acquiring for himself and giving to his church a position and a fame known throughout the land. As a preacher, he is said to have the largest uniform congregation in the U. S., as a lecturer he is very popular, and as a pulpit and platform orator he has few or no superiors. Nothing is apparently studied or artificial about his oratory; it is frank, natural, cordial, hearty, and fearless. He seems to feel deeply the truths that he utters, and therefore makes his audience feel them too. He was married in 1837 to a sister of the Rev. Dr. Bullard, of St. Louis, and of Rev. Asa Bullard, Boston.

Mr. Beecher's writings are few, and have mostly been collected by other hands, but chiefly with his sanction. They are; Lectures to Young Men, 16mo., 1850, many editions have been published; the style is terse and vigorous, in an earnest view of expostulation; Industry and Idleness, 18mo., 1850; The Star Papers, two series, articles collected from the Independent, which he assisted to edit; these productions are marked by an easy, tone, eloquent, and often poetic, with a practical knowledge of life, its duties and privileges, which is the secret of much of their interest. Life-Thoughts, gathered from his extemporaneous Discourses, by Edna Dean Proctor; 25,000 copies were sold within a few months; Notes from Plymouth Pulpit, a collection of memorable Passages from his Discourses, by Augusta Moore; Eyes and Ears, 12mo.; Freedom and War, discourses upon topics suggested by the times; Royal Truths; Family Prayers; and Sermons, in 2 vols., 8vo. He also edited the Plymouth collection of Hymns, published in several sizes. Plain and Pleasant Talks about Fruits, Flowers, and Farming; relate to horticultural topics and were suggested by the multifarious knowledge to be found in the works of the English gardener, Loudon; but the naked facts in Mr. Beecher's mind spring up a living growth of ideas, ornamented with cheerful and profitable associations. He always writes of the country with a lover's minuteness, and a healthy enthusiasm.

In 1862, Mr. Beecher visited England, and rendered an important service to his country by his eloquent vindication of the policy of the American Government, in the war which it was maintaining for the preservation of the Union. As the war was approaching its conclusion, in April, 1865, Mr. Beecher, at the request of the Government, delivered an oration at Fort Sumter, on the anniversary of its fall, and the formal restoration of the national flag by Major Anderson. His oration on the centennial anniversary of the birthday of Robert Burns, January, 1859, was of the highest interest.

In 1868, Mr. Beecher wrote for the New York Ledger, Norwood, or Village Life in New England, which was reprinted in one volume, 12mo., and reached a sale of 45,000 copies. It was a tale of New England life, and depicted the habits of the people of that section in a most life-like manner.

Mr. Beecher has recently undertaken the editorship of the Christian Union, a new and popular religious weekly.

Mr. Beecher's books contain rich gems of deep thought, brilliant fancy, and devotional feeling. It is impossible to do him justice by any extracts from his sermons or essays. One must hear him preach or lecture to feel his power, or to understand it. The following selections, however, will give some idea of his style, sentiments, and inexhaustible wealth of thought and illustration.

BUSINESS AND RELIGION.

FROM THE PLYMOUTH PULPIT, SECOND SERIES.

GOD says to men on the farm, in the store, on the ship, everywhere in life, "Be diligent in business, fervent in spirit." Those two things are put so near together in the Bible that nobody can get them apart. No wedge can drive them asunder. But for the most part men say, "My business is there, and my religion is here." They seek to divide them. When they go into the closet to pray, they feel, "I have had a vision of God and of heaven—oh that I could keep it all day!" You would not do half so well in business if you kept it as you would if you lost it.

Do you suppose that when a man has said "Good-by" to his dear wife, and his chubby little children, that are more to him than the blood in his own veins, and gone to his shop, he feels that he must think of his family all day long, instead of thinking of wheels, and springs, and belts, and levers, and his business? If he undertakes to think of his wife and children, every time one of them comes up to his mind, a thread snaps, and he betrays his trust. It is enough that he has a latent love which lies like a bird on its nest, and hatches singing joys. He does not care if he does not think of them once during the whole day; for he knows that the fountain will burst out and bubble up when the evening comes.

Tell me that men work for money! So they do. Tell me that they engage in the rivalries of the street! So they do. But many men are goaded to dishonesty by the love which they bear to those whom they love at home, and not because they love money so much. Home is the fountain that inspires them. And yet you know how, in spite of the inspiration of a loving home, men forget, for the time being, that home, and all that it contains, in the struggle that they are making with the world, and only at intervals come back to the memory of that which is most dear to them. And that is enough.

Now, let a man have a vision of God and heaven. It does not follow that all day long he should go thinking of the catechism, and religion, and prayer. If a man has leisure, it is a blessed thing for him to sit down, as it were, under the shadow of a great religious truth, as at midday one sits down by a fountain to take his nooning; but do by God as you do by those that you know you love on earth. Believe that love is a unit, and that that part which is hidden, and which is the inspiring part, and which gives you strength for the other parts, is just as really a part of your religious duty as any other, and that, though it may not manifest itself in the sphere of duty and labor, it is no less influential.

Let no man say, then, "Oh! if I had not my store, I could be such a good Christian!" You could not be half so good a Christian as you are now. Let no man say, "Oh! if I had not my school; if I was a minister, and could choose my own hours, and read those blessed books of theology, (I guess you never read any of them!)

how good I should be!" Do you, then, think that ministers are so much better than other people? They are men of like passions with their fellows. They are subject to pride. They are easily tempted to anger and jealousy. They are liable to faults of a thousand kinds. Having leisure to think about a religious life does not make men any better than working out their salvation in the sphere of labor to which they are called. A man can be a good Christian, and have a store or factory under his control, or an army on his hands. Whatever duty a man is called to, whether it be in the school, or in the shop, or in the mine, or on the ship, it is his business to be a Christian in the discharge of that duty. Wherever a man may be, his whole life should be animated by religion. A true man is not what he is in the prayer-meeting, nor what he is in the Sunday-school, nor what he is in his best moments, but what his average life is, in all his hours put together. This grand average tells where a man stands, and how much of a Christian he is. And it is this that leads to discouragement; because men think that if they are true Christians they ought to be in a hymn state, a psalm state, a prayer state, all the time. I do not think so. They ought to be in a state such that when, in the providence of God, it is fit that they should sing, they will be ready to sing; but you might as well say that a man ought to be in a state to dandle his babe every minute, as to say that a man should always be in an active religious state of mind.

The father is a surgeon, and has a very trying case. For an hour he has stood with a man's life trembling under his hand; and the difference of a thought, one way or the other, would have been the difference of the excision of an artery or a nerve; and, during all this time, his mind and body have been undergoing a severe strain; and do you say that, when he lays down his instruments, and the patient has been rolled upon the bed, he ought to go right out from the midst of blood, and scalpels, and saws, and sponges, and commence dandling his babe! Is there no fitness of times? Do you say that a man should run from one thing right to another, as if there were no such thing as perpendicular distances between them? How little common sense men have in religion! How wise men are in the adjustment of things outside of religion! and how foolish they are in the adjustment of things in religion!

I have heard men say that a man ought to live so as to be prepared, at any moment, to give up his account to God; and that he ought never to do anything which would not be congruous with the tremendous scenes of the judgment-day. I hold the great truth that a man should always be prepared to die; but I do not think that truth is at all the same as to say that every one of the experiences which are proper to the earth-state would be congruous with a state transcendently different from the earth-state. Do you suppose that if a man was sick, and his physician had prescribed tartar emetic, and it had just begun to work, he would be in an eminent state in which to appear at the judgment seat? Is there any sin in not being in such a state? There are many things that are proper to one condition, which would not be congruous with another condition. Any mode of criticism, therefore, which is based on the principle that we are to transfer things that are proper to one relation to another relation that is totally different; any mode of criticism which rubs out the interval, and the necessity of modification, is impertinent and absurd.

CHRIST THE DOOR.

FROM THE SAME.

If there is a sound in the household sweeter than the opening and closing door of the house where love reigns, I do not know what it is. Much as we may be educated to music, if you will recall your own experience, you will know that the sweetest sounds that you hear are not musical sounds. If in the night you wake from a troubled dream, child as you are, affrighted and trembling, the sweetest of all Beethoven's music below would not be so comforting as to hear your father clear his voice—h-e-m—in the room adjoining. You turn over, and feel that you are at home. And so, a walk in the entry, or even a cough in grandmother's room, is so surrounded with sweet associations of home, that no formulated musical sounds are half so sweet as are these incidental and very homely sounds. And the opening and shutting of the door at the right hour is one of the musical sounds of home.

All day long the father strives in the office, in the store, in the shop, in the street, along the wharves, wherever his labor calls him; and the whole day has been full of care and wrangling. The head is hot, and the hand is weary, and the pulse is feverish; and as the day draws on, the busy man prepares at last for home.

The man draws near his dwelling. The door opens to his touch. The children hear it. The elder ones run. The young prattler, motherborne, gets there first—quicker than the nimblest. Now, how his heart rejoices! Every wrinkle is rubbed out. He looks around with a sense of grateful rest, and thanks God that the sound of that shutting door was the last echo of the thunder of care and trouble. That is outside, and he is at home, with her that he loves best, and with those that are dearest to him. That door opened to let him in to love and peace and joy; it shut to keep out the turbulence of the quarrelsome world, and the influence of grinding business.

Now, is there any likeness in this to Christ Jesus? Is there any such access to Christ Jesus as may be compared to a man's experience when he repairs to his home, and, opening the door, has the full sweet welcome, and, shutting it, exiles all that disturbs and all that creates discord? "Behold, I am the door," says Christ; as if he were a householder. Opening, you shall be within the circle of love. Shutting, you shall be protected

against all turmoil and care. Perfect peace have they who put their trust in him. Joy and peace, that pass all understanding—such joy and peace as the world knows not—are to be found in Christ. My dear friends, there is a friendship in the Lord Jesus Christ which may be to us what the door of the household is to the most care-bestridden and bested of men. What the home, with all its sweet affections is to the troubled heart, that the Saviour is to those who know how to make use of him—not the Saviour didactically taught or controversially preached, but the Saviour discerned by a living and personal faith. There is such intercourse and welcome behind him as there is behind the shutting door. There is that in him which shall make every man, in the midst of the most tried and bestormed life, rest upon his bosom. Oh! if men could but find the Door, if they could but know what peace there is in Christ Jesus for them, I am sure they would not go so friendless, and harassed, and distressed.

FAULTS.

FROM THE SAME, THIRD SERIES.

A MAN has a large emerald, but it is "feathered," and he knows an expert would say, "What a pity that it has such a feather!" it will not bring a quarter as much as it otherwise would; and he cannot take any satisfaction in it. A man has a diamond; but there is a flaw in it, and it is not the diamond that he wants. A man has an opal, but it is imperfect, and he is dissatisfied with it. An opal is covered with little seams, but they must be the right kind of seams. If it has a crack running clear across, it is marred, no matter how large it is, and no matter how wonderful its reflections are. And this man is worried all the time because he knows his opal is imperfect; and it would worry him even if he knew that nobody else noticed it.

So it is in respect to dispositions, and in respect to character at large. Little cracks, little flaws, little featherings in them, take away their exquisiteness and beauty, and take away that fine finish which makes moral art. How many noble men there are who are diminished, who are almost wasted, in their moral influence! How many men are like the red maple! It is one of the most gorgeous trees, both in spring, blossoming, and in autumn, with its crimson foliage. But it stands knee-deep in swamp-water, usually. To get to it, you must wade, or leap from bog to bog, tearing your raiment, and soiling yourself. I see a great many noble men, but they stand in a swamp of faults. They bear fruit that you fain would pluck, but there are briars and thistles and thorns all about it; and to get it you must make your way through all these hindrances.

How many persons there are that are surrounded by a thousand little petty faults. They are so hedged in by these things that you lose all the comfort and joy you would otherwise have in them.

81

JOHN LOTHROP MOTLEY.

[Born 1814.]

Mr. Motley was born in Dorchester, Mass., April 15, 1814; and is a member of an old Boston family, graduating at Harvard in 1831. Afterwards he soon went to Europe, and spent several years in Germany, studying at the Universities, and acquiring a knowledge of its literature. He returned to the United States in 1835, applied himself to the study of the law, and was admitted to the Boston bar. He married Miss Benjamin in 1836; and the practice of his profession proving uncongenial, he devoted his time and talents to the pursuit of letters, which his ample means enabled him to do.

Like most young authors he commenced by writing articles for the periodicals; and in 1839 published his first work, Morton's Hope; or, the Memoirs of a Provincial, the scene of which is laid in the neighborhood of Boston, and from its scenes and incidents may be supposed to be founded on some facts and experiences of the author. This was followed by Merry-mount, a romance of the Massachusetts Colony, upon a picturesque episode of New England history presented in the narrative of Thomas Morton, in the time of Gov. Winthrop. Both of these fictions are written with spirit, the descriptions are carefully elaborated, and the narrative is enlivened with occasional flashes of genuine humor.

In 1841, Mr. Webster, an intimate friend of the father of Mr. Motley, appointed the son to the post of Secretary of Legation to Russia, under Col. Todd, where he remained two years, when he resigned and returned home. While there he contributed to the North American Review, an article on Peter the Great, which at once excited marked attention.

Finding his forte was not fiction, be resolved to apply himself to history, and in 1851, again visited Europe, residing at Dresden, Paris, and other cities, acquiring materials for, and writing his noble historical work, the Rise of the Dutch Republic, 3 vols., 8vo., a "history of the great agony through which the Republic of Holland was ushered into life." It embraces besides an Historical Introduction, the period from the abdication of Charles V., in 1855, to the death of William the Silent, Prince of Orange, in 1584. The note in the preface, of vol. 1, of Prescott's Philip II., having called attention to the forthcoming work, it was on its publication in 1856, perused with no ordinary interest on both sides of the Atlantic. It was at once favorably received by the critics of every publication of any note, and by the pens of such authors as M. Guizot, (who superintended the publication in French of a translation made in his own family) Irving, Prescott, Palfrey, Lieber, Everett, Bancroft, Sumner, and many others in Holland, France, Germany, and England. Fifteen thousand copies were sold in England in less than two years, many editions in this country; it was reprinted at Amsterdam, translated into German, at Leipsic and Dresden, translated into Dutch by the chief Archivist of the Netherlands, and into French, all of which editions also met with rapid sales. The author also received the degree of LL. D. from Harvard, of D. C. L. from the University of Oxford, and was chosen the successor of Mr. Prescott, as a corresponding member of the Institute of France.

He had not been home a year after it was published, when he resolved to continue the History in a similar work. For this purpose he again left for Europe, and took up his main quarters at the Hague, where he wrote his history of the United Netherlands, the first two volumes of which were published in 1861, followed by two more tracing the progress of events from the death of William down to the Synod of Dort, and which he hopes some day to continue through the Thirty Years' War to the Peace of Westphalia. The judgment passed upon these four volumes, by the highest critical authorities, confirms the impression made by the author in his preceding work.

The subject of Mr. Motley's histories, was one of peculiar interest, and of remarkable novelty to English and American readers. It had been little cultivated by historians, and of late several collections of original materials, presented new opportunities to the coming historian. Mr. Motley brought to the work great industry, a spirit of candor, an enthusiasm for the theme, and a style practiced in the arts of picturesque narration. His conscientiousness in the use of the vast material at his command was not less remarkable than the perseverance with which he brought it together. Insensibly the reader was delighted by its animated style and attractive illustrations of manners and character, while its research, its power, its earnest spirit, its breadth of design and successful execution, placed its author in the front rank of historians. His history presents the reader with an entirely new view of the policy and acts of the parties engaged in the great drama enacted in the Netherlands.

The motives and acts of Philip II., and of the Court of France, the diplomacy of Queen Elizabeth, of Walsingham, and of Leicester, the military genius of Parma in the siege of Antwerp, the story of the Spanish Armada, its origin and destruction, are treated with a master hand, and for the first time narrated with the fulness which their varied circumstances and relations demand. The civil history of the period is unwound with masterly skill and sagacity, the narratives of military exploits are alive with living incidents, while the spirit of the whole drama is gathered up in the central characters of William the Silent and Philip II.

In 1861, Mr. Motley was appointed Minister Plenipotentiary to Austria, and resided at Vienna. While there he rendered an important service to his country by his publication in the London Times, of an elaborate essay, entitled Causes of the American Civil War, which was republished in numerous editions, one of which was widely spread by the Union Leagues, to enlighten some American citizens, who needed it as well as those abroad. Mr. Motley, at the present time, 1870, ably represents our country at the Court of England.

THE SECOND SIEGE OF LEYDEN.

THE invasion of Louis of Nassau had, as already stated, effected the raising of the first siege of Leyden. That leaguer had lasted from the 31st of October, 1573, to the 21st of March, 1574, when the soldiers were summoned away to defend the frontier. By an extraordinary and culpable carelessness, the citizens, neglecting the advice of the Prince, had not taken advantage of the breathing time thus afforded them to victual the city and strengthen the garrison. They seemed to reckon more confidently upon the success of Count Louis than he had even done himself; for it was very probable that, in case of his defeat, the siege would be instantly resumed. This natural result was not long in following the battle of Mookerheyde.

On the 26th of May, Valdez reappeared before the place, at the head of eight thousand Walloons and Germans, and Leyden was now destined to pass through a fiery ordeal. This city was one of the most beautiful in the Netherlands. Placed in the midst of broad and fruitful pastures, which had been reclaimed by the hand of industry from the bottom of the sea, it was fringed with smiling villages, blooming gardens, fruitful orchards. The ancient and, at last, decrepit Rhine, flowing languidly towards its sandy death-bed, had been multiplied into innumerable artificial currents, by which the city was completely interlaced. These watery streets were shaded by lime trees, poplars, and willows, and crossed by one hundred and forty-five bridges, mostly of hammered stone. The houses were elegant, the squares and streets spacious, airy and clean, the churches and public edifices imposing, while the whole aspect of the place suggested thrift, industry, and comfort. Upon an artificial elevation, in the centre of the city, rose a ruined tower of unknown antiquity. By some it was considered to be of Roman origin, while others preferred to regard it as a work of the Anglo-Saxon Hengist, raised to commemorate his conquest of England. Surrounded by fruit trees, and overgrown in the centre with oaks, it afforded, from its mouldering battlements, a charming prospect over a wide expanse of level country, with the spires of neighboring cities rising in every direction. It was from this commanding height, during the long and terrible summer days which were approaching, that many an eye was to be strained anxiously seaward, watching if yet the ocean had begun to roll over the land.

Valdez lost no time in securing himself in the possession of Maeslandsluis, Vlaardingen, and the Hague. Five hundred English, under command of Colonel Edward Chester, abandoned the fortress of Valkenburg, and fled towards Leyden. Refused admittance by the citizens, who now, with reason, distrusted them, they surrendered to Valdez, and were afterwards sent back to England. In the course of a few days, Leyden was thoroughly invested, no less than sixty-two redoubts, some of them having remained undestroyed from the previous siege, now girdling the city, while the besiegers already numbered nearly eight thousand, a force to be daily increased. On the other hand, there were no troops in the town, save a small corps of "freebooters," and five companies of the burgher guard. John Van der Does, Seigneur of Nordwyck, a gentleman of distinguished family, but still more distinguished for his learning, his poetical genius, and his valor, had accepted the office of military commandant.

The main reliance of the city, under God, was on the stout hearts of its inhabitants within the walls, and on the sleepless energy of William the Silent without. The Prince, hastening to comfort and encourage the citizens, although he had been justly irritated by their negligence in having omitted to provide more sufficiently against the emergency while there had yet been time, now reminded them that they were not about to contend for themselves alone, but that the fate of their country and of unborn generations would, in all human probability, depend on the issue about to be tried. Eternal glory would be their portion if they manifested a courage worthy of their race and of the sacred cause of religion and liberty. He implored them to hold out at least three months, assuring them that he would, within that time, devise the means of their deliverance. The citizens responded, courageously and confidently, to these missives, and assured the Prince of their firm confidence in their own fortitude and his exertions.

And truly they had a right to rely on that calm and unflinching soul, as on a rock of adamant. All alone, without a being near him to consult, his right arm struck from him by the death of Louis, with no brother left to him but the untiring and faithful John, he prepared without delay for the new task imposed upon him. France, since the defeat and death of Louis, and the busy intrigues which had followed the accession of Henry III., had but small sympathy for the Netherlands. The English government, relieved from the fear of France, was more cold and haughty than ever. An Englishman, employed by Requesens to assassinate the Prince of Orange, had been arrested in Zealand, who impudently pretended that he had undertaken to perform the same office for Count John, with the full consent and privity of Queen Elizabeth. The provinces of Holland and Zealand were stanch and true, but the inequality of the contest between a few brave men, upon that handsbreadth of territory, and the powerful Spanish Empire, seemed to render the issue hopeless.

Moreover, it was now thought expedient to publish the amnesty which had been so long in preparation, and this time the trap was more liberally baited. The pardon, which had passed the seals upon the 8th of March, was formally issued by the Grand Commander on the 6th of June. By the terms of this document the King invited all his erring and repentant subjects to return to his arms, and to accept a full forgiveness for their past offences, upon the sole condition that they should once more throw themselves upon the bosom of the Mother Church. There were but few exceptions to the amnesty, a small number of individuals, all mentioned by name, being alone excluded; but although these terms were ample, the act was liable to a few stern objections. It was easier now for the Hollanders to go to their graves than to mass, for the contest, in its progress, had now entirely assumed the aspect of a religious war. Instead of a limited number of heretics in a state which, although constitutional was Catholic, there was now hardly a Papist to be found among the natives. To accept the pardon then was to concede the victory, and the Hollanders had not yet discovered that they were conquered. They were resolved, too, not only to be conquered, but annihilated, before the Roman Church should be re-established on their soil, to the entire exclusion of the Reformed worship. They responded with steadfast enthusiasm to the sentiment expressed by the Prince of Orange, after the second siege of Leyden had been commenced; "As long as there is a living man left in the country, we will contend for our liberty and our religion." The single condition of the amnesty assumed, in a phrase, what Spain had fruitlessly striven to establish by a hundred battles, and the Hollanders had not faced their enemy on land and sea for seven years to succumb to a phrase at last.

Moreover, the pardon came from the wrong direction. The malefactor gravely extended forgiveness to his victims. Although the Hollanders had not yet disembarrassed their minds of the supernatural theory of government, and felt still the reverence of habit for regal divinity, they naturally considered themselves outraged by the trick now played before them. The man who had violated all his oaths, trampled upon all their constitutional liberties, burned and sacked their cities, confiscated their wealth, hanged, beheaded, burned, and buried alive their innocent brethren, now came forward, not to implore, but to offer forgiveness. Not in sackcloth, but in royal robes; not with ashes, but with a diadem upon his head, did the murderer present himself vicariously upon the scene of his crimes. It may be supposed that, even in the sixteenth century, there were many minds which would revolt at such blasphemy. Furthermore, even had the people of Holland been weak enough to accept the pardon, it was impossible to believe that the promise would be fulfilled. It was sufficiently known how much faith was likely to be kept with heretics, notwithstanding that the act was fortified by a papal Bull, dated on the 30th of April, by which Gregory XIII. promised forgiveness to those Netherland sinners who duly repented and sought absolution for their crimes, even although they had sinned more than seven times seven.

For a moment the Prince had feared lest the pardon might produce some effect upon men wearied by interminable suffering, but the event proved him wrong. It was received with universal and absolute contempt. No man came forward to take advantage of its conditions, save one brewer in Utrecht, and the son of a refugee pedler from Leyden. With these exceptions, the only ones recorded, Holland remained deaf to the royal voice. The city of Leyden was equally cold to the messages of mercy, which were especially addressed to its population by Valdez and his agents. Certain Netherlanders, belonging to the King's party, and familiarly called "Glippers," despatched from the camp many letters to their rebellious acquaintances in the city. In these epistles the citizens of Leyden were urgently and even pathetically exhorted to submission by their loyal brethren, and were implored "to take pity upon their poor old fathers, their daughters, and their wives." But the burghers of Leyden thought that the best pity which they could show to those poor old fathers, daughters, and wives, was to keep them from the clutches of the Spanish soldiery; so they made no answer to the Glippers, save by this single line, which they wrote on a sheet of paper, and forwarded, like a letter, to Valdez;

"Fistula dulce canit, volucrem cum decipit anceps."

According to the advice early given by the Prince of Orange, the citizens had taken an account of their provisions of all kinds, including the live stock. By the end of June, the city was placed on a strict allowance of food, all the provisions being purchased by the authorities at an equitable price. Half a pound of meat and half a pound of bread was allotted to a full grown man, and to the rest, a due proportion. The city being strictly invested, no communication, save by carrier pigeons, and by a few swift and skilful messengers, called jumpers, was possible. Sorties and fierce combats were, however, of daily occurrence, and a handsome bounty was offered to any man who brought into the city gates the head of a Spaniard. The reward was paid many times, but the population was becoming so excited and so apt, that the authorities felt it dangerous to permit the continuance of these conflicts. Lest the city, little by little, should lose its few disciplined defenders, it was now proclaimed, by sound of church bell, that in future no man should leave the gates.

The Prince had his head-quarters at Delft and at Rotterdam. Between those two cities, an important fortress, called Polderwaert, secured him in the control of the alluvial quadrangle, watered on two sides by the Yssel, and the Meuse. On the 29th June, the Spaniards, feeling its value, had made an unsuccessful effort to carry this fort by storm. They had been beaten off, with the loss of several hundred men, the Prince remaining in possession of the position, from which alone he could hope to relieve Leyden. He still held in his hand the keys with which he could unlock the ocean gates and let the waters in upon the land, and he had long been convinced that nothing could save the city but to break the dykes. Leyden was not upon the sea, but he could send the sea to Leyden, although an army fit to encounter the besieging force under Valdez could

not be levied. The battle of Mookerheyde had, for the present, quite settled the question of land relief, but it was possible to besiege the besiegers with the waves of the ocean. The Spaniards occupied the coast from the Hague to Vlaardingen, but the dykes along the Meuse and Yssel were in possession of the Prince. He determined that these should be pierced, while, at the same time, the great sluices at Rotterdam, Schiedam, and Delfthaven should be opened. The damage to the fields, villages, and growing crops would be enormous, but he felt that no other course could rescue Leyden, and with it the whole of Holland from destruction. His clear expositions and impassioned eloquence at last overcame all resistance. By the middle of July the estates fully consented to his plan, and its execution was immediately undertaken. "Better a drowned land than a lost land," cried the patriots, with enthusiasm, as they devoted their fertile fields to desolation. The enterprise for restoring their territory, for a season, to the waves, from which it had been so patiently rescued, was conducted with as much regularity as if it had been a profitable undertaking. A capital was formally subscribed, for which a certain number of bonds were issued, payable at a long date. In addition to this preliminary fund, a monthly allowance of forty-five guldens was voted by the estates, until the work should be completed, and a large sum was contributed by the ladies of the land, who freely furnished their plate, jewellery, and costly furniture to the furtherance of the scheme.

Meantime, Valdez, on the 30th July, issued most urgent and ample offers of pardon to the citizens, if they would consent to open their gates and accept the King's authority, but his overtures were received with silent contempt, notwithstanding that the population was already approaching the starvation point. Although not yet fully informed of the active measures taken by the Prince, they still chose to rely upon his energy and their own fortitude, rather than upon the honied words which had formerly been heard at the gates of Harlem and of Naarden. On the 3d of August, the Prince, accompanied by Paul Buys, chief of the commission appointed to execute the enterprise, went in person along the Yssel, as far as Kappelle, and superintended the rupture of the dykes in sixteen places. The gates at Schiedam and Rotterdam were opened, and the ocean began to pour over the land. While waiting for the waters to rise, provisions were rapidly collected, according to an edict of the Prince, in all the principal towns of the neighborhood, and some two hundred vessels, of various sizes, had also been got ready at Rotterdam, Delfthaven, and other ports.

The citizens of Leyden were, however, already becoming impatient, for their bread was gone, and of its substitute malt cake, they had but slender provision. On the 12th of August they received a letter from the Prince, encouraging them to resistance, and assuring them of a speedy relief, and on the 21st they addressed a despatch to him in reply, stating that they had now fulfilled their original promise, for they had held out two months with food, and another month without food. If not soon assisted, human strength could do no more ; their malt cake would last but four days, and after that was gone, there was nothing left but starvation. Upon the same day, however, they received a letter, dictated by the Prince, who now lay in bed at Rotterdam with a violent fever, assuring them that the dykes were all pierced, and that the water was rising upon the "Land-scheiding," the great outer barrier which separated the city from the sea. He said nothing, however, of his own illness, which would have cast a deep shadow over the joy which now broke forth among the burghers.

The letter was read publicly in the market-place, and to increase the cheerfulness, burgo-master Van der Werf, knowing the sensibility of his countrymen to music, ordered the city musicians to perambulate the streets, playing lively melodies and martial airs. Salvos of cannon were likewise fired, and the starving city for a brief space put on the aspect of a holiday, much to the astonishment of the besieging forces, who were not yet aware of the Prince's efforts. They perceived very soon, however, as the water everywhere about Leyden had risen to the depth of ten inches, that they stood in a perilous position. It was no trifling danger to be thus attacked by the waves of the ocean, which seemed about to obey with docility the command of William the Silent. Valdez became anxious and uncomfortable at the strange aspect of affairs ; for the besieging army was now in its turn beleaguered, and by a stronger power than man's. He consulted with the most experienced of his officers, with the country people, with the most distinguished among the Glippers, and derived encouragement from their views concerning the Prince's plan. They pronounced it utterly futile and hopeless. The Glippers knew the country well, and ridiculed the desperate project in unmeasured terms.

Even in the city itself, a dull distrust had succeeded to the first vivid gleam of hope, while the few royalists among the population boldly taunted their fellow-citizens to their faces with the absurd vision of relief which they had so fondly welcomed. "Go up to the tower, ye Beggars," was the frequent and taunting cry, "go up to the tower, and tell us if ye can see the ocean coming over the dry land to your relief "— and day after day they did go up to the ancient tower of Hengist, with heavy heart and anxious eye, watching, hoping, praying, fearing, and at last almost despairing of relief by God or man. On the 27th they addressed a desponding letter to the estates, complaining that the city had been forgotten in its utmost need, and on the same day a prompt and warm-hearted reply was received, in which the citizens were assured that every human effort was to be made for their relief. "Rather," said the estates, "will we see

our whole land and all our possessions perish in the waves, than forsake thee, Leyden. We know full well, moreover, that with Leyden, all Holland must perish also." They excused themselves for not having more frequently written, upon the ground that the whole management of the measures for their relief had been intrusted to the Prince, by whom alone all the details had been administered, and all the correspondence conducted.

The fever of the Prince had, meanwhile, reached its height. He lay at Rotterdam, utterly prostrate in body, and with mind agitated nearly to delirium, by the perpetual and almost un-assisted schemes which he was constructing. Relief, not only for Leyden, but for the whole country, now apparently sinking into the abyss, was the vision which he pursued as he tossed upon his restless couch. Never was illness more unseasonable. His attendants were in despair, for it was necessary that his mind should for a time be spared the agitation of business. The physicians who attended him agreed, as to his disorder, only in this, that it was the result of mental fatigue and melancholy, and could be cured only by removing all distressing and perplexing subjects from his thoughts, but all the physicians in the world could not have succeeded in turning his attention for an instant from the great cause of his country. Leyden lay, as it were, anxious and despairing at his feet, and it was impossible for him to close his ears to her cry. Therefore, from his sick bed he continued to dictate words of counsel and encouragement to the city; to Admiral Boisot commanding the fleet, minute directions and precautions. To-wards the end of August a vague report had found its way into his sick chamber that Leyden had fallen, and although he refused to credit the tale, yet it served to harass his mind, and to heighten fever. Cornelius Van Mierop, Receiver-General of Holland, had occasion to visit him at Rotterdam, and strange to relate, found the house almost deserted. Penetrating, unattended, to the Prince's bed-chamber, he found him lying quite alone. Inquiring what had become of all his attendants, he was answered by the Prince, in a very feeble voice, that he had sent them all away. The Receiver-General seems, from this, to have rather hastily arrived at the conclusion that the Prince's disorder was the pest, and that his servants and friends had all deserted him from cowardice. This was very far from being the case. His private secretary and his maitre d' hotel watched, day and night, by his couch, and the best physicians of the city were in constant attendance. By a singular accident, all had been despatched on different errands, at the express desire of their master, but there had never been a suspicion that his disorder was the pest, or pestilential. Nerves of steel, and a frame of adamant could alone have resisted the constant anxiety and the consuming fatigue to which he had so long been exposed. His illness had been aggravated by the rumor of Leyden's fall, a fiction which Cornelius Mierop was now enabled flatly to contradict. The Prince began to mend from that hour. By the end of the first week of September, he wrote a long letter to his brother, assuring him of his convalescence, and expressing, as usual, a calm confidence in the divine decrees— " God will ordain for me,' said he, " all which is necessary for my good and my salvation. He will load me with no more afflictions than the fragility of this nature can sustain."

The preparations for the relief of Leyden, which, notwithstanding his exertions, had grown slack during his sickness, were now vigorously resumed. On the 1st of September, Admiral Boisot arrived out of Zealand with a small number of vessels, and with eight hundred veteran sailors. A wild and ferocious crew were those eight hundred Zealanders. Scarred, hacked, and even maimed, in the unceasing conflicts in which their lives had passed; wearing crescents in their caps, with the inscription, " Rather Turkish than Popish ;" renowned far and wide, as much for their ferocity as for their nautical skill ; the appearance of these wildest of the " Sea-beggars " was both eccentric and terrific. They were known never to give nor to take quarter, for they went to *mortal* combat only, and had sworn to spare neither noble nor simple, neither king, kaiser, nor pope, should they fall into their power.

More than two hundred vessels had been now assembled, carrying generally ten pieces of cannon, with from ten to eighteen oars, and manned with twenty-five hundred veterans, experienced both on land and water. The work was now undertaken in earnest. The distance from Leyden to the outer dyke, over whose ruins the ocean had already been admitted, was nearly fifteen miles. This reclaimed territory, however, was not maintained against the sea by these external barriers alone. The flotilla made its way with ease to the Land-scheiding, a strong dyke within five miles of Leyden, but here its progress was arrested. The approach to the city was surrounded by many strong ramparts, one within the other, by which it was defended against its ancient enemy, the ocean, precisely like the circumvallations by means of which it was now assailed by its more recent enemy, the Spaniard. To enable the fleet, however, to sail over the land, it was necessary to break through this two-fold series of defences. Between the Land-scheiding and Leyden were several dykes, which kept out the water ; upon the level territory, thus encircled, were many villages, together with a chain of sixty-two forts, which completely occupied the land. All these villages and fortresses were held by the veteran troops of the King ; the besieging force being about four times as strong as that which was coming to the rescue.

The Prince had given orders that the Land-scheiding, which was still one-and-a-half foot above water, should be taken possession of, at every hazard. On the night of the 10th and 11th of September this was accomplished, by surprise, and in a masterly manner. The few Spaniards

who had been stationed upon the dyke were all despatched or driven off, and the patriots fortified themselves upon it, without the loss of a man. As the day dawned the Spaniards saw the fatal error which they had committed in leaving this bulwark so feebly defended, and from two villages which stood close to the dyke, the troops now rushed in considerable force to recover what they had lost. A hot action succeeded, but the patriots had too securely established themselves. They completely defeated the enemy, who retired, leaving hundreds of dead on the field, and the patriots in complete possession of the Land-scheiding. This first action was sanguinary and desperate. It gave an earnest of what these people, who came to relieve their brethren, by sacrificing their property and their lives, were determined to effect. It gave a revolting proof, too, of the intense hatred which nerved their arms. A Zealander, having struck down a Spaniard on the dyke, knelt on his bleeding enemy, tore his heart from his bosom, fastened his teeth in it for an instant, and then threw it to a dog, with the exclamation, " 'Tis too bitter." The Spanish heart was, however, rescued, and kept for years, with the marks of the soldier's teeth upon it, a sad testimonial of the ferocity engendered by this war for national existence.

The great dyke having been thus occupied, no time was lost in breaking it through in several places, a work which was accomplished under the very eyes of the enemy. The fleet sailed through the gaps ; but, after their passage had been effected in good order, the Admiral found, to his surprise, that it was not the only rampart to be carried. The Prince had been informed, by those who claimed to know the country, that, when once the Land-scheiding had been passed, the water would flood the country as far as Leyden, but the " Greenway," another long dyke, three-quarters of a mile farther inward, now rose at least a foot above the water, to oppose their further progress. Fortunately, by a second and still more culpable carelessness, this dyke had been left by the Spaniards in as unprotected a state as the first had been. Promptly and audaciously Admiral Boisot took possession of this barrier also, levelled it in many places, and brought his flotilla, in triumph, over its ruins. Again, however, he was doomed to disappointment. A large mere, called the Freshwater Lake, was known to extend itself directly in his path about midway between the Land-scheiding and the city. To this piece of water, into which he expected to have instantly floated, his only passage lay through one deep canal. The sea which had thus far borne him on, now diffusing itself over a very wide surface, and under the influence of an adverse wind, had become too shallow for his ships. The canal alone was deep enough, but it led directly towards a bridge, strongly occupied by the enemy. Hostile troops, moreover, to the amount of three thousand occupied both sides of the canal. The bold Boisot, nevertheless, determined to force his passage, if possible. Selecting a few of his strongest vessels, his heaviest artillery, and his bravest sailors, he led the van himself, in a desperate attempt to make his way to the mere. He opened a hot fire upon the bridge, then converted into a fortress, while his men engaged in hand-to-hand combat with a succession of skirmishers from the troops along the canal. After losing a few men, and ascertaining the impregnable position of the enemy, he was obliged to withdraw, defeated, and almost despairing.

A week had elapsed since the great dyke had been pierced, and the flotilla now lay motionless in shallow water, having accomplished less than two miles. The wind, too, was easterly, causing the sea rather to sink than to rise. Everything wore a gloomy aspect, when, fortunately, on the 18th, the wind shifted to the northwest, and for three days blew a gale. The waters rose rapidly, and before the second day was closed the armada was afloat again. Some fugitives from Zoetermeer village now arrived, and informed the Admiral that, by making a detour to the right, he could completely circumvent the bridge and the meer. They guided him, accordingly, to a comparatively low dyke, which led between the villages of Zoetermeer and Benthuyzen. A strong force of Spaniards was stationed in each place, but, seized with a panic, instead of sallying to defend the barrier, they fled inwardly towards Leyden, and halted at the village of North Aa. It was natural that they should be amazed. Nothing is more appalling to the imagination than the rising ocean tide, when man feels himself within its power; and here were the waters, hourly deepening and closing around them, devouring the earth beneath their feet, while on the waves rode a flotilla, manned by a determined race, whose courage and ferocity were known throughout the world. The Spanish soldiers, brave as they were on land, were not sailors, and in the naval contests which had taken place between them and the Hollanders had been almost invariably defeated. It was not surprising, in these amphibious skirmishes, where discipline was of little avail, and habitual audacity faltered at the vague dangers which encompassed them, that the foreign troops should lose their presence of mind.

Three barriers, one within the other, had now been passed, and the flotilla, advancing with the advancing waves, and driving the enemy steadily before it, was drawing nearer to the beleaguered city. As one circle after another was passed, the besieging army found itself compressed within a constantly contracting field. The "Ark of Delft," an enormous vessel, with shot-proof bulwarks, and moved by paddle-wheels turned by a crank, now arrived at Zoetermeer, and was soon followed by the whole fleet. After a brief delay, sufficient to allow the few remaining villagers to escape, both Zoetermeer and Benthuyzen, with the fortifications, were set on fire, and abandoned to their fate. The blaze lighted up the desolate and watery waste around, and was seen at Leyden, where it was hailed as the beacon of hope. Without further impediment, the Armada proceeded to North Aa; the enemy retreating from this position also, and flying to Zoeterwoude, a strongly fortified village but a mile and three-quarters from the city walls. It was now swarming with troops, for the bulk of the besieging army had gradually been driven into a narrow circle of forts, within the immediate neighborhood of Leyden. Besides Zoeterwoude, the two posts where they were principally established were Lammen and Leyderdorp, each within three hundred rods of the town. At Leyderdorp were the headquarters of Valdez; Colonel Borgia commanded in the very strong fortress of Lammen.

The fleet was, however, delayed at North Aa by another barrier, called the "Kirk-way." The waters, too, spreading once more over a wider space, and diminishing under an east wind, which had again arisen, no longer permitted their progress, so that very soon the whole armada was stranded anew. The waters fell to the depth of nine inches, while the vessels required eighteen and twenty. Day after day the fleet lay motionless upon the shallow sea. Orange, rising from his sick bed as soon as he could stand, now came on board the fleet. His presence diffused universal joy; his words inspired his desponding army with fresh hope. He rebuked the impatient spirits who, weary of their compulsory idleness, had shown symptoms of ill-timed ferocity, and those eight hundred mad Zealanders, so frantic in their hatred to the foreigners who had so long profaned their land, were as docile as children to the Prince. He reconnoitered the whole ground, and issued orders for the immediate destruction of the Kirkway, the last important barrier which separated the fleet from Leyden. Then, after a long conference with Admiral Boisot, he returned to Delft.

Meantime, the city was at its last gasp. The burghers had been in a state of uncertainty for many days; being aware that the fleet had set forth for their relief, but knowing full well the thousand obstacles which it had to surmount. They had guessed its progress by the illumination from the blazing villages; they had heard its salvos of artillery, on its arrival at North Aa; but since then, all had been dark and mournful again, hope and fear, in sickening alternation, distracting every breast. They knew that the wind was unfavorable, and at the dawn of each day every eye was turned wistfully to the vanes of the steeples. So long as the easterly breeze prevailed, they felt, as they anxiously stood on towers and housetops, that they must look in vain for the welcome ocean. Yet, while thus patiently waiting, they were literally starving; for even the misery endured at Harlem had not reached that depth and intensity of agony to which Leyden was now reduced. Bread, malt cake, horse flesh, had entirely disappeared; dogs, cats, rats, and other vermin, were esteemed luxuries. A small number of cows, kept as long as possible, for their milk, still remained; but a few were killed from day to day, and distributed in minute proportions, hardly sufficient to support life among the famishing population. Starving wretches swarmed daily around the shambles where these cattle were slaughtered, contending for any morsel which might fall, and lapping eagerly the blood as it ran along the pavement; while the hides. chopped and boiled. were greedily devoured. Women and children, all day long, were seen searching gutters and dunghills for morsels of food, which they disputed fiercely with the famishing dogs. The green leaves were stripped from the trees, every living herb was converted into human food, but these expedients could not avert starvation. The daily mortality was frightful—infants starved to death on the maternal breasts, which famine had parched and withered; mothers dropped dead in the streets, with their dead children in their arms. In many a house the watchmen, in their rounds, found a whole family of corpses, father, mother, and children, side by side, for a disorder called the plague, naturally engendered of hardship and famine, now came, as if in kindness, to abridge the agony of the people. The pestilence stalked at noonday through the city, and the doomed inhabitants fell like grass beneath its scythe. From six thousand to eight thousand human beings sank before this scourge alone, yet the people resolutely held out—women and men mutually encouraging each other to resist the entrance of their foreign foe—an evil more horrible than pest or famine.

The missives from Valdez, who saw more vividly than the besieged could do, the uncertainty of his own position, now poured daily into the city, the enemy becoming more prodigal of his vows, as he felt that the ocean might yet save the victims from his grasp. The inhabitants in their ignorance, had gradually abandoned their hopes of relief, but they spurned the summons to surrender. Leyden was sublime in its despair. A few murmurs were, however, occasionally heard at the steadfastness of the magistrates, and a dead body was placed at the door of the burgomaster, as a silent witness against his inflexibility. A party of the more faint-hearted even assailed the heroic Adrian Van der Werf with threats and reproaches as he passed through the streets. A crowd had gathered around him, as he reached a triangular place in the centre of the town, into which many of the principal streets emptied themselves, and upon one side of which stood the church of Saint Pancras, with its high brick tower surmounted by two pointed turrets, and with two ancient lime trees at its entrance. There stood the burgomaster, a tall, haggard, imposing figure, with dark visage, and a tranquil but commanding eye. He waved his broad-leaved felt hat for silence, and then exclaimed, in language which has been almost literally preserved, "What would ye, my friends? Why do ye murmur that we do not break our vows and surrender the city to the Spaniards? a fate more horrible than the agony which she now endures. I tell you I have made an oath to hold the city, and may God give me strength to keep my oath! I can die but once; whether by your hands, the enemy's, or by the hand of God. My own fate is indiffer-

82

ent to me, not so that of the city intrusted to my care. I know that we shall starve if not soon relieved; but starvation is preferable to the dishonored death which is the only alternative. Your menaces move me not; my life is at your disposal; here is my sword, plunge it into my breast, and divide my flesh among you. Take my body to appease your hunger, but expect no surrender, so long as I remain alive."

. The words of the stout burgomaster inspired a new courage in the hearts of those who heard him, and a shout of applause and defiance arose from the famishing but enthusiastic crowd. They left the place, after exchanging new vows of fidelity with their magistrate, and again ascended tower and battlement to watch for the coming fleet. From the ramparts they hurled renewed defiance at the enemy. "Ye call us rat-eaters and dog-eaters," they cried, "and it is true. So long, then, as ye hear dog bark or cat mew within the walls, ye may know that the city holds out. And when all has perished but ourselves, be sure that we will each devour our left arms, retaining our right to defend our women, our liberty, and our religion, against the foreign tyrant. Should God, in his wrath, doom us to destruction, and deny us all relief, even then will we maintain ourselves forever against your entrance. When the last hour has come, with our own hands we will set fire to the city and perish, men, women, and children, together in the flames, rather than suffer our homes to be polluted, and our liberties to be crushed." Such words of defiance, thundered daily from the battlements, sufficiently informed Valdez as to his chance of conquering the city, either by force or fraud, but at the same time, he felt comparatively relieved by the inactivity of Boisot's fleet, which still lay stranded at North Aa. "As well," shouted the Spaniards, derisively, to the citizens, "as well can the Prince of Orange pluck the stars from the sky as bring the ocean to the walls of Leyden for your relief."

On the 28th of September, a dove flew into the city, bringing a letter from Admiral Boisot. In this despatch, the position of the fleet at North Aa was described in encouraging terms, and the inhabitants were assured that, in a very few days at furthest, the long-expected relief would enter their gates. The letter was read publicly upon the market-place, and the bells were rung for joy. Nevertheless on the morrow, the vanes pointed to the east, the waters so far from rising, continued to sink, and Admiral Boisot was almost in despair. He wrote to the Prince, that if the spring tide now to be expected, should not, together with a strong and favorable wind, come immediately to their relief, it would be in vain to attempt anything further, and that the expedition would, of necessity, be abandoned. The tempest came to their relief. A violent equinoctial gale, on the night of the 1st and 2d of October, came storming from the northwest, shifting after a few hours full eight points, and then blowing still more violently from the southwest. The waters of the North Sea were piled in vast masses upon the southern coast of Holland, and then dashed furiously landward, the ocean rising over the earth, and sweeping with unrestrained power across the ruined dykes.

In the course of twenty-four hours, the fleet at North Aa, instead of nine inches, had more than two feet of water. No time was lost. The Kirkway, which had been broken through according to the Prince's instructions, was now completely overflowed, and the fleet sailed at midnight, in the midst of the storm and darkness. A few sentinel vessels of the enemy challenged them as they steadily rowed towards Zoeterwoude. The answer was a flash from Boisot's cannon, lighting up the black waste of waters. There was a fierce naval midnight battle; a strange spectacle among the branches of those quiet orchards, and with the chimney stacks of half-submerged farm houses rising around the contending vessels. The neighboring village of Zoeterwoude shook with the discharges of the Zealanders' cannon, and the Spaniards assembled in that fortress knew that the rebel Admiral was at last afloat and on his course. The enemy's vessels were soon sunk, their crews hurled into the waves. On went the fleet, sweeping over the broad waters which lay between Zoeterwoude and Zweiten. As they approached some shallows, which led into the great mere, the Zealanders dashed into the sea, and with sheer strength shouldered every vessel through. Two obstacles lay still in their path— the forts of Zoeterwoude and Lammen, distant from the city five hundred and two hundred and fifty yards respectively. Strong redoubts, both well supplied with troops and artillery, they were likely to give a rough reception to the light flotilla, but the panic, which had hitherto driven their foes before the advancing patriots, had reached Zoeterwoude. Hardly was the fleet in sight when the Spaniards, in the early morning, poured out from the fortress, and fled precipitately to the left, along a road which led in a westerly direction towards the Hague. Their narrow path was rapidly vanishing in the waves, and hundreds sank beneath the constantly deepening and treacherous flood. The wild Zealanders, too, sprang from their vessels upon the crumbling dyke and drove their retreating foes into the sea. They hurled their harpoons at them, with an accuracy acquired in many a polar chase; they plunged into the waves in the keen pursuit, attacking them with boat-hook and dagger. The numbers who thus fell beneath these corsairs, who neither gave nor took quarter, were never counted, but probably not less than a thousand perished. The rest effected their escape to the Hague.

The first fortress, was thus seized, dismantled, set on fire, and passed, and a few strokes of the oars brought the whole fleet close to Lammen. This last obstacle rose formidable and frowning directly across their path. Swarming as it was with soldiers, and bristling with artillery, it seemed to defy the armada either to carry it by storm or to pass under its guns into the city. It appeared that the enterprise was, after all, to founder within sight of the long expecting and expected

haven. Boisot anchored his fleet within a respectful distance, and spent what remained of the day in carefully reconnoitring the fort, which seemed only too strong. In conjunction with Leyderdorp, the head-quarters of Valdez, a mile and a half distant on the right, and within a mile of the city, it seemed so insuperable an impediment that Boisot wrote in despondent tone to the Prince of Orange. He announced his intention of carrying the fort, if it were possible, on the following morning, but if obliged to retreat, he observed, with something like despair, that there would be nothing for it but to wait for another gale of wind. If the waters should rise sufficiently to enable them to make a wide detour, it might be possible, if, in the meantime, Leyden did not starve or surrender, to enter its gates from the opposite side.

Meantime, the citizens had grown wild with expectation. A dove had been despatched by Boisot, informing them of his precise position, and a number of citizens accompanied the burgomaster, at nightfall, toward the tower of Hengist —"Yonder," cried the magistrate, stretching out his hand towards Lammen, "yonder, behind that fort, are bread and meat, and brethren in thousands. Shall all this be destroyed by the Spanish guns, or shall we rush to the rescue of our friends?" "We will tear the fortress to fragments with our teeth and nails," was the reply, "before the relief, so long expected, shall be wrested from us." It was resolved that a sortie, in conjunction with the operations of Boisot, should be made against Lammen with the earliest dawn. Night descended upon the scene, a pitch dark night, full of anxiety to the Spaniards, to the armada, to Leyden. Strange sights and sounds occurred at different moments to bewilder the anxious sentinels. A long procession of lights issuing from the fort were seen to flit across the black face of the waters, in the dead of night, and the whole of the city wall, between the Cowgate and the Tower of Burgundy, fell with a loud crash. The horror-struck citizens thought that the Spaniards were upon them at last; the Spaniards imagined the noise to indicate a desperate sortie of the citizens. Everything was vague and mysterious.

Day dawned, at length, after the feverish night, and the Admiral prepared for the assault. Within the fortress reigned a death-like stillness, which inspired a sickening suspicion. Had the city, indeed, been carried in the night; had the massacre already commenced; had all this labor and audacity been expended in vain? Suddenly a man was described, wading breast-high through the water from Lammen towards the fleet, while at the same time, one solitary boy was seen to wave his cap from the summit of the fort. After a moment of doubt, the happy mystery was solved. The Spaniards had fled, panic struck, during the darkness. Their position would still have enabled them, with firmness, to frustrate the enterprise of the patriots, but the hand of God, which had sent the ocean and the tempest to the deliverance of Leyden, had struck her enemies with terror likewise. The lights which had been seen moving during the night were the lanterns of the retreating Spaniards, and the boy who was now waving his triumphant signal from the battlements had alone witnessed the spectacle. So confident was he in the conclusion to which it led him, that he had volunteered at daybreak to go thither all alone. The magistrates, fearing a trap, hesitated for a moment to believe the truth, which soon, however, became quite evident. Valdez, flying himself from Leyderdorp, had ordered Colonel Borgia to retire with all his troops from Lammen. Thus, the Spaniards had retreated at the very moment that an extraordinary accident had laid bare a whole side of the city for their entrance. The noise of the wall, as it fell, only inspired them with fresh alarm; for they believed that the citizens had sallied forth in the darkness, to aid the advancing flood in the work of destruction. All obstacles being now removed, the fleet of Boisot swept by Lammen, and entered the city on the morning of the 3d of October. Leyden was relieved.

The quays were lined with the famishing population, as the fleet rowed through the canals, every human being who could stand, coming forth to greet the preservers of the city. Bread was thrown from every vessel among the crowd. The poor creatures who, for two months had tasted no wholesome human food, and who had literally been living within the jaws of death, snatched eagerly the blessed gift, at last too liberally bestowed. Many choked themselves to death, in the greediness with which they devoured their bread; others became ill with the effects of plenty thus suddenly succeeding starvation;— but these were isolated cases, a repetition of which was prevented. The Admiral, stepping ashore, was welcomed by the magistracy, and a solemn procession was immediately formed. Magistrates and citizens, wild Zealanders, emaciated burgher guards, sailors, soldiers, women, children,—nearly every living person within the walls, all repaired without delay to the great church, stout Admiral Boisot leading the way. The starving and heroic city, which had been so firm in its resistance to an earthly king, now bent itself in humble gratitude before the King of kings. After prayers, the whole vast congregation joined in the thanksgiving hymn. Thousands of voices raised the song, but few were able to carry it to its conclusion, for the universal emotion, deepened by the music, became too full for utterance. The hymn was abruptly suspended, while the multitude wept like children. This scene of honest pathos terminated, the necessary measures for distributing the food and for relieving the sick were taken by the magistracy. A note dispatched to the Prince of Orange, was received by him at two o'clock, as he sat in church at Delft. It was

of a somewhat different purport from that of the letter which he had received early in the same day from Boisot; the letter in which the admiral had informed him that the success of the enterprise depended, after all, upon the desperate assault upon a nearly impregnable fort. The joy of the Prince may be easily imagined, and so soon as the sermon was concluded, he handed the letter just received to the minister, to be read to the congregation. Thus, all participated in his joy. and united with him in thanksgiving.

The next day, notwithstanding the urgent entreaties of his friends, who were anxious lest his life should be endangered by breathing, in his scarcely convalescent state, the air of the city where so many thousands had been dying of the pestilence, the Prince repaired to Leyden. He, at least, had never doubted his own or his country's fortitude. They could, therefore. most sincerely congratulate each other, now that the victory had been achieved. "If we are doomed to perish," he had said a little before the commencement of the siege, "in the name of God, be it so! At any rate, we shall have the honor to have done what no nation ever did before us, that of having defended and maintained ourselves, unaided, in so small a country. against the tremendous efforts of such powerful enemies. So long as the poor inhabitants here, though deserted by all the world, hold firm, it will still cost the Spaniards the half of Spain, in money and in men, before they can make an end of us."

The termination of the terrible siege of Leyden was a convincing proof to the Spaniards that they had not yet made an end of the Hollanders. It furnished, also, a sufficient presumption that until they had made an end of them, even unto the last Hollander, there would never be an end of the struggle in which they were engaged. It was a slender consolation to the Governor-General, that his troops had been vanquished, not by the enemy, but by the ocean. An enemy whom the ocean obeyed with such docility might well be deemed invincible by man. In the headquarters of Valdez, at Leyderdorp, many plans of Leyden and the neighborhood were found lying in confusion about the room.

Valdez had fled so speedily as to give rise to much censure and more scandal. He was even accused of having been bribed by the Hollanders to desert his post, a tale which many repeated, and a few believed. On the 4th of October, the day following that on which the relief of the city was effected, the wind shifted to the north east, and again blew a tempest. It was as if the waters, having now done their work, had been rolled back to the ocean by an Omnipotent hand, for in the course of a few days, the land was bare again, and the work of reconstructing the dykes commenced.

ANDREW JACKSON DOWNING.

[Born 1815. Died 1852.]

A. J. Downing, the pioneer and father of tasteful Rural Architecture and Landscape Gardening in this country, was born at Newburgh, on the Hudson, October 30, 1815. His father was a nursery-man, and dying in 1822, left young Downing to his own resources. His education was limited, being derived from the Academy at Montgomery, near Newburgh. At the age of sixteen, he joined his brother in the management of his nursery. When quite a young man he commenced practice with his pen, by writing Essays on Horticultural topics, and sketches of beautiful scenery, for the New York Mirror and other papers. In June, 1838, he married Miss De Wint, residing on the opposite bank of the Hudson. He commenced the practice of Architecture, by planning a beautiful Elizabethan cottage for his own residence.

In 1841, Mr. Downing published his Treatise on the Theory and Practice of Landscape Gardening, adapted to North America, with a view to the improvement of Country Residences, with remarks on Rural Architecture. Mr. Downing produced a masterly and very delightful book, in which he displayed sound criticism and refined judgment in matters of taste; he had evidently studied the works of his predecessors, taking from them the richest ore, but refining it in the crucible of his mind and applying it to the wants of this country. It was highly successful, and orders for the construction of houses and decoration of grounds, followed orders for copies to his publishers.

In 1845, he published the first full and thorough work, with systematic arrangement, on the Fruits and Fruit Trees of America, in 1 vol., 12mo., and an edition in 8vo., with many beautifully colored portraits of fruits, imported from Paris. The sale in eight years was 15,000 copies, and everywhere acknowledged the standard work on the subject; it tended much to promote the best and most judicious selection and culture of fruit trees. A new edition revised, and much enlarged by his son, Charles Downing, bringing it down to the present time, was issued in 1869, in one large volume, 8vo.

In 1846, he became editor of the Horticulturist, published at Albany, and wrote for it a monthly essay, and other articles. By his tact, and practical knowledge, he soon made it the leading magazine on the subject. In 1849, he edited an American reprint of Wightwick's Hints to Young Architects, adding Additional Notes and Hints to Persons about building in this country; in one volume, 8vo., which passed through several editions.

In 1850, he visited England, to obtain a competent assistant to assist him in his large and rapidly increasing architectural business. He spent the summer there visiting those perfect examples of his art, the great country-seats of England, to which his fame, which had already preceded him, and his winning, gentle manners, gave him access. He wrote some delightful letters and accounts of his visits, which are very attractive, and display the character and thoughts of the man, a gentleman of fine taste, and a thorough artist in his profession.

The same year he published, Architecture of Country Houses; including Designs for Cottages, Farm-houses, Villas, and Furniture, one volume, 8vo., which has passed through sixteen editions.

In 1851, he was commissioned by President Fillmore, in pursuance of an act of Congress, to lay out and plant the public grounds in Washington, surrounding the White House, Capitol, and Smithsonian Institution. The appointment gave great satisfaction to the public, as it was felt he was the man pre-eminently fitted for the work. He was engaged actively in this and other professional labors, when on the 28th of July, 1852, he embarked on board the Henry Clay steamboat for New York, en route to Newport, with his wife. On the way down the boat commenced racing with the Armenia, and was soon discovered to be on fire. In the crowd, he was separated from his wife; when last seen he was assisting others to escape, was heard to utter a prayer while in the water struggling with others clinging to him, and was seen no more. His body was recovered next day. His loss was felt by all who had interest in the subject of improving our homes to be a national one.

After his decease, his Rural Essays were collected in one volume, 8vo., prefaced by a well written and sympathetic memoir, by George W. Curtis, and A Letter to his Friends, by Miss Bremer, who had been his guest while in this country.

His writings have undoubtedly exercised a great and salutary influence on the taste for rural architecture and improvements in this country. His books still remain the standard works on the subject, though there have been many others written since. His style as an essayist, was like that of the man, pleasant, easy, and gentlemanly.

CITIZENS RETIRING TO THE COUNTRY.

FROM RURAL ESSAYS.

PERHAPS the foundation of all the miscalculations that arise, as to expenditure in forming a country residence, is, that citizens are in the habit of thinking every thing in the country *cheap*. Land in the town is sold by the foot, in the country by the acre. The price of a good house in town is, perhaps, three times the cost of one of the best farms in the country. The town buys every thing: the country raises every thing. To live on your own estate, be it one acre or a thousand, to have your own milk, butter and eggs, to raise your own chickens and gather your own strawberries, with nature to keep the account instead of your grocer and market-woman, that is something like a rational life; and more than rational, it must be cheap. So argues the citizen about retiring, not only to enjoy his *otium cum dignitate*, but to make a thousand dollars of his income, produce him more of the comforts of life than two thousand did before.

Well; he goes into the country. He buys a farm (run down with poor tenants and bad tillage). He builds a new house, with his own ignorance instead of architect and master-builder, and is cheated roundly by those who take advantage of this masterly ignorance in the matter of bricks and mortar; or he repairs an old house at the full cost of a new one, and has an unsatisfactory dwelling for ever afterwards. He undertakes high farming, and knowing nothing of the practical economy of husbandry, every bushel of corn that he raises costs him the price of a bushel and a half in the market. Used in town to a neat and orderly condition of his premises, he is disgusted with old tottering fences, half drained fields and worn-out pastures, and employs all the laboring force of the neighborhood to put his grounds in good order.

Now there is no objection to all this for its own sake. On the contrary, good buildings, good fences, and rich pasture fields are what especially delight us in the country. What then is the reason that, as the country place gets to wear a smiling aspect, its citizen owner begins to look serious and unhappy? Why is it that country life does not satisfy and content him? Is the country, which all poets and philosophers have celebrated as the Arcadia of this world,—is the country treacherous? Is nature a cheat, and do seed-time and harvest conspire against the peace of mind of the retired citizen?

Alas! It is a matter of *money*. Every thing seems to be a matter of money now-a-days. The country life of the old world, of the poets and romancers, is cheap. The country life of our republic is *dear*. It is for the good of the many that labor should be high, and it is high labor that makes country life heavy and oppressive to such men— only because it shows a balance, increasing year after year, on the wrong side of the ledger. Here is the source of all the trouble and dissatisfaction in what may be called the country life of gentlemen amateurs, or citizens, in this country—"it don't pay." Land is cheap, nature is beautiful, the country is healthy, and all these conspire to draw our well-to-do citizen into the country. But labor is dear, experience is dearer, and a series of experiments in unprofitable crops the dearest of all; and our citizen friend, himself, as we have said, is in the situation of a man who has set out on a delightful voyage, on a smooth sea, and with a cheerful ship's company; but who discovers, also, that the ship has sprung a leak—not large enough to make it necessary to call all hands to the pump—not large enough perhaps to attract any body's attention but his own, but quite large enough to make it certain that he must leave her or be swamped—and quite large enough to make his voyage a serious piece of business.

Every thing which a citizen does in the country, costs him an incredible sum. In Europe (heaven save the masses), you may have the best of laboring men for twenty or thirty cents a day. Here you must pay them a dollar, at least our amateur must, though the farmers contrive to get their labor for eight or ten dollars a month and board. The citizen's home once built, he looks upon all heavy expenditures as over; but how many hundreds— perhaps thousands, has he not paid for out-buildings, for fences, for roads, &c. Cutting down yonder hill, which made an ugly blotch in the view,—it looked like a trifling task; yet there were five hundred dollars swept clean out of his bank account, and there seems almost nothing to show for it. You would not believe now that any hill ever stood there—or at least that nature had not arranged it all (as you feel she ought to have done), just as you see it. Your favorite cattle and horses have died, and the flock of sheep have been sadly diminished by the dogs, all to be replaced— and a careful account of the men's time, labor and manure on the grain fields, shows that for some reason that you cannot understand, the crop —which is a fair one, has actually cost you a trifle more than it is worth in a good market.

To cut a long story short, the larger part of our citizens who retire upon a farm to make it a country residence, are not aware of the fact, that capital cannot be profitably employed on land in the Atlantic States *without a thorough practical knowledge of farming.* A close and systematic economy, upon a good soil, may enable, and does enable some gentlemen farmers that we could name, to make a good profit out of their land— but citizens who launch boldly into farming, hiring farm laborers at high prices, and trusting operations to others that should be managed under the master's eye—are very likely to find their farms a sinking fund that will drive them back into business again.

To be happy in any business or occupation (and country life on a farm is a matter of business), we must have some kind of *success* in it; and there is no success without profit, and no profit without practical knowledge of farming.

The lesson that we would deduce from these reflections is this; that no mere amateur should buy a large farm for a country residence, with the expectation of finding pleasure and profit in it for the rest of his life, unless, like some citizens that we have known—rare exceptions—they have a genius for all manner of business, and can master the whole of farming, as they would learn a running-hand in six easy lessons. Farming. in the older States, where the natural wealth of the soil has been exhausted, is *not* a profitable business for amateurs—but quite the reverse. And a citizen who has a sufficient income without farm- ing, had better not damage it by engaging in so expensive an amusement.

"But we must have something to do; we have been busy near all our lives, and cannot retire into the country to fold our hands and sit in the sun- shine to be idle." Precisely so. But you need not therefore ruin yourself on a large farm. Do not be ambitious of being great landed pro- prietors. Assume that you need occupation and interest, and buy a small piece of ground—a few acres only—as *few* as you please—but without any regard for profit. Leave that to those who have learned farming in a more practical school. You think, perhaps, that you can find nothing to do on a few acres of ground. But that is the greatest of mistakes. A half a dozen acres, the capacities of which are fully developed, will give you more pleasure than five hundred poorly

cultivated. And the advantage for you is, that you can, upon your few acres, spend just as little or just as much as you please. If you wish to be prudent, lay out your little estate in a simple way, with grass and trees, and a few walks, and a single man may then take care of it. If you wish to indulge your taste, you may fill it with shrub- beries, and arboretums, and conservatories, and flower-gardens, till every tree and plant and fruit in the whole vegetable kingdom, of really superior beauty and interest, is in your collection. Or, if you wish to turn a penny, you will find it easier to take up certain fruits or plants and grow them to high perfection so as to command a profit in the market, than you will to manage the various operations of a large farm. We could point to ten acres of ground from which a larger income has been produced than from any farm of five hundred acres in the country. Gardening, too, offers more variety of interest to a citizen than farming; its operations are less rude and toilsome, and its pleasures more immediate and refined. Citizens, ignorant of farming, should, therefore, buy small places, rather than large ones, if they wish to consult their own true interest and hap- piness.

But some of our readers, who have tried the thing, may say that it is a very expensive thing to settle oneself and get well established, even on a small place in the country. And so it is. if we proceed upon the fallacy, as we have said, that every thing in the *country* is cheap. Labor is dear; it costs you dearly to-day, and it will cost you dearly to-morrow, and the next year. There- fore, in selecting a site for a home in the country, always remember to choose a site where nature has done as much as possible for you. Don't say to yourself as many have done before you—"Oh! I want occupation, and I rather like the new place—raw and naked though it may be. *I will create a paradise for myself.* I will cut down yonder hill that intercepts the view, I will level and slope more gracefully yonder rude bank, I will terrace this rapid descent, I will make a lake in yonder hollow." Yes, all this you may do for occupation, and find it very delightful occupation too, if you have the income of Mr. Astor. Otherwise, after you have spent thousands in creating your paradise, and chance to go to some friend who has bought all the graceful undulations, and sloping lawns, and sheets of water, natural, ready made—as they may be bought in thousands of purely natural places in America, for a few hundred dollars, it will give you a species of plea- sure-ground-dyspepsia to see how foolishly you have wasted your money, and this, more especially, when you find, as the possessor of the most fin- ished place in America finds, that he has no want of occupation, and that far from being finished, he has only begun to elicit the highest beauty, keep- ing and completeness of which his place is capable.

RICHARD H. DANA, JR.

[Born 1815.]

RICHARD H. DANA, JR., the son of the poet of the same name, was born at Cambridge, in 1815. In his boyhood, he had a strong passion for the sea, and would have entered the Navy, if he had not taken the advice of his father, and entered Harvard. For a period he left Harvard, and was under the tutorship of Rev. Leonard Woods of Andover. On returning to Cambridge, an attack of measles affected his eyesight so as to compel him to give up his books. Clinging to his old love he resolved to go to sea, and rough it as a common sailor before the mast. Accordingly, he set sail on the 14th of August, 1834, in the brig Pilgrim, from Boston, for a voyage around Cape Horn to the western coast of North America; visited California, little thinking of what it was soon to be, performed his duty throughout the voyage with spirit. and returned in the ship in September, 1836. to Boston.

In 1840, he published his famous narrative of Two Years before the Mast, a Personal Narrative of Life at Sea, in one volume, 18mo. It was immediately successful, passing through many editions, being reprinted in London, where the British Admiralty adopted it for distribution in the navy; was also translated into several languages. It has been quoted as authority in the House of Lords. The work was written to present a true picture of a sailor's life at sea. That it has done so, is evidenced by its popularity with not only the masses but with Jack Tar himself; it is one of the most popular of books at the lending libraries and every nautical library. He says honestly how things were, and how they affected him, in the simple, straight-forward language of a disciplined mind, without any appearance of seeking for words, but those that will best answer the purpose come and fall into their proper places of their own will; good sense and good humor sum up the enduring merits of this book.

Up to this time, every work professing to give life at sea, had been written by persons who gained their experience as naval officers or passengers, persons who must take a very different view of the whole matter from that which would be taken by a common sailor. Besides the interest which every one must feel in exhibitions of life in those forms, in which he himself has never experienced it, there has been, of late years, a great deal of attention directed toward common seamen, and a strong sympathy awakened in their behalf. Yet no book had been written by one who has been of them, and can know what their life really is; no voice from the forecastle had been heard.

Mr. Dana, after his return, entered the senior class at Harvard, where he graduated in 1837, and pursued the study of the law at the Law school under Judges Story and Greenleaf. With a well disciplined and acute legal mind, his success at the bar was rapid; his book bringing him many maritime cases.

In 1850, he edited with a preface, Washington Allston's Lectures on Art and Poems.

His Seamen's Manual, is a Treatise on Practical Seamanship, with plates, a technical dictionary of sea terms, and an epitome of the laws affecting the mutual position of Master and Sailor. It is reprinted in England, and is used in both countries. In 1859, he wrote, a Vacation Voyage to Cuba and Back, one volume, 12mo. A new edition of his Two Years, has recently been published in handsome form, 12mo.

He has been a prominent member of the Free-soil party, and as such vigorously attacked the Fugitive Slave Law; he was also an able and efficient member of the State Convention for revising the Constitution of Massachusetts. He married a grand-daughter of the Rev. James Marsh.

In 1860, for his health, he visited California and the Islands of the Pacific, thence by China and through the East to Europe. As a leading member of the Republican party, he was appointed by Lincoln to the office of U. S. Attorney for the District of Massachusetts.

Besides many legal opinions, and public addresses, Mr. Dana has published his Address upon Edward Everett; a noble and interesting performance, in which he does justice to Mr. Everett's conduct and writings.

A SOUTH-EASTER.

FROM TWO YEARS BEFORE THE MAST.

THIS night, after sundown, it looked black at the southward and eastward, and we were told to keep a bright look-out. Expecting to be called up, we turned in early. Waking up about midnight, I found a man who had just come down from his watch, striking a light. He said that it was beginning to puff up from the southeast, and that the sea was rolling in, and he had called the captain; and as he threw himself down on his chest with all his clothes on, I knew that he expected to be called. I felt the vessel pitching at her anchor, and the chain surging and snapping, and lay awake, expecting an instant summons. In a few minutes it came—three knocks on the scuttle, and "All hands ahoy! bear-a-hand, up and make sail." We sprang up for our clothes, and were about half way dressed, when the mate called out, down the scuttle, "Tumble up here, men! tumble up! before she drags her anchor." We were on deck in an instant. "Lay aloft and loose the topsails!" shouted the captain, as soon as the first man showed himself. Springing into the rigging, I saw that the Ayacucho's topsails were loosed, and heard her crew singing-out at the sheets as they were hauling them home. This had probably started our captain; as "old Wilson" (the captain of the Ayacucho) had been many years on the coast, and knew the signs of the weather. We soon had the topsails loosed; and one hand remaining, as usual, in each top, to overhaul the rigging and light the sail out, the rest of us laid down to man the sheets. While sheeting home, we saw the Ayacucho standing athwart our bows, sharp upon the wind, cutting through the head sea like a knife, with her raking masts and sharp bows running up like the head of a greyhound. It was a beautiful sight. She was like a bird which had been frightened and had spread her wings in flight. After the topsails had been sheeted home, the head yards braced aback, the fore-top-mast staysail hoisted and the buoys streamed, and all ready forward, for slipping, we went aft and manned the slip-rope which came through the stern port with a turn round the timber-heads. "All ready forward?" asked the captain. "Aye, aye, sir; all ready," answered the mate. "Let go!" "All gone, sir;" and the iron cable grated over the windlass and through the hawse-hole, and the little vessel's head swinging off from the wind under the force of her backed head sails, brought the strain upon the slip-rope. "Let go aft!" Instantly all was gone, and we were under weigh. As soon as she was well off from the wind, we filled away the head yards, braced all up sharp, set the foresail and trysail, and left our anchorage well astern, giving the point a good berth. "Nye's off too," said the captain to the mate; and looking astern, we could just see the little hermaphrodite brig under sail standing after us.

It now began to blow fresh; the rain fell fast, and it grew very black; but the captain would not take in sail until we were well clear of the point. As soon as we left this on our quarter, and were standing out to sea, the order was given, and we sprang aloft. double reefed each topsail, furled the foresail, and double reefed the trysail, and were soon under easy sail. In these cases of slipping for south-easters, there is nothing to be done, after you have got clear of the coast, but to lie-to under easy sail, and wait for the gale to be over, which seldom lasts more than two days, and is often over in twelve hours; but the wind never comes back to the southward until there has been a good deal of rain fallen. "Go below the watch," said the mate; but here was a dispute which watch it should be, which the mate soon, however, settled by sending his watch below, saying that we should have our turn the next time we got under weigh. We remained on deck till the expiration of the watch, the wind blowing very fresh and the rain coming down in torrents. When the watch came up, we wore ship, and stood on the other tack, in towards land. When we came up again, which was at four in the morning, it was very dark, and there was not much wind, but it was raining as I thought I had never seen it rain before. We had on oilcloth suits and south-wester caps, and had nothing to do but to stand bolt upright and let it pour down upon us. There are no umbrellas, and no sheds to go under at sea.

While we were standing about on deck, we saw the little brig drifting by us, hove to under her fore topsail double reefed; and she glided by like a phantom. Not a word was spoken, and we saw no one on deck but the man at the wheel. Toward morning the captain put his head out of the companion-way and told the second mate, who commanded our watch, to look out for a change of wind, which usually followed a calm and heavy rain; and it was well that he did; for in a few minutes it fell dead calm, the vessel lost her steerage-way, and the rain ceased. We hauled up the trysail and courses, squared the after yards, and waited for the change, which came in a few minutes, with a vengeance, from the northwest, the opposite point of the compass. Owing to our precautions we were not taken aback, but ran before the wind with square yards. The captain coming on deck, we braced up a little and stood back for our anchorage. With the change of wind came a change of weather, and in two hours the wind moderated into the light steady breeze, which blows down the coast the greater part of the year, and, from its regularity, might be called a trade-wind. The sun came up bright, and we set royals, skysails, and studding-sails, and were under fair way for Santa Barbara. The Little Loriotte was astern of us, nearly out of sight; but we saw nothing of the Ayacucho. In a short time she appeared, standing out from Santa Rosa Island, under the lee of which she had been hove to, all night. Our captain was anxious to get in before her, for it would be a great credit to us, on the coast, to beat the Ayacucho, which had been called the best sailer in the North Pacific, in which she had been known as a trader for six years or more. * * * But he walked away, as you would haul in a line.

HENRY DAVID THOREAU.

[Born 1817. Died 1862.]

HENRY D. THOREAU was born in Concord, Mass., July 12, 1817. He graduated at Harvard in 1837. He taught school, and tried his hand at trade, but seems not to have been happy or succeeded at either. He contributed a number of papers to the Dial. He was rather of a moody, philosophically speculative, turn of mind, disliked the forms and customs of society, and perhaps with a somewhat indolent turn of character.

In 1849, he published, A Week on the Concord and Merrimack Rivers; a record of a trip he made in a boat with his brother on those rivers, in the year 1839; boating by day, and sleeping in a tent at night. It is a book of mingled essay and description, of illustrations of physical geography, of history of the settlements on the route, of botanical excursions, philosophical speculations and literary studies. It is occasionally rash and conceited, in a certain transcendental affectation of expression on religious subjects; but in many other passages remarkable for its nicety of observation, and acute literary and moral perceptions. The trip was made two years after he left college, though the book was not published for nine years later.

His next book was published with equal deliberation. Walden, or Life in the Woods, was published in Boston in 1854; it is the story of a humor of the author, to see how little a man requires, or could live on, which occupied him a term of two years and two months from March, 1845, to test it; it attracted attention more from its oddity than from any practical results. Retiring from the world, to the edge of a pond near Concord, Mass., with a borrowed axe and a capital of about twenty-five dollars, he builds himself a house, assisted in the raising by R. W. Emerson and Geo. W. Curtis, ten feet wide by fifteen feet long, costing him $28.12. His food, clothing, etc., cost him, for eight months, about $19.15, in addition to what he raised from the ground. The cost it will be observed is trifling, but, so was the quality of the fare and the living, such as would tempt no one to imitate that style of exis-tence. It gave him ample time to read, think, and observe. His descriptions of natural history are such as would delight Izaak Walton or Alexander Wilson. Mixed with considerable transcendental speculation, are shrewd humors, fresh, nice observation of books and men, with occasionally a touch of the poetic vein.

The records of this wayward genius, will be found in his books, of which several were published after his death. He died of consumption at Concord, May 7, 1862. During his life, he enjoyed the friendship and society of his neighbors, R. W. Emerson and Nathaniel Hawthorne, the former of whom wrote a biographical sketch of him, prefixed to Excursions in Field and Forest, 12mo., Boston, 1863.

Thoreau, a man of humors, led a dreamy, meditative, philosophic sort of life, apparently without any definite aim. His books are noticeable on the score of a certain quaint study of natural history and scenery, and may continue to be read as the works of a thoughtful scholar and original student of nature, who possessed peculiarities and humors of character, love of independence, a kindly vein of observation, and a happy talent of description, which invested homely and every-day subjects with new interest.

His works have been published in seven uniform volumes, viz.: A Week on the Concord and Merrimack Rivers; Walden, or Life in the Woods; Excursions in Field and Forest; The Maine Woods; Cape Cod; Letters to Various Persons; and, A Yankee in Canada.

Thoreau was bred to no profession; he never married; he lived alone; he never went to church; he never voted; he refused to pay a tax to the State; he ate no flesh, drank no wine, and never knew the use of tobacco; and though a naturalist, he used neither trap nor gun. He chose to be the bachelor of thought and Nature; to be rich, by making his wants few, and supplying them himself. There was somewhat military in his nature not to be subdued, always manly and able, but rarely tender, as if he did not feel himself except in opposition.

MY HOUSE.

FROM WALDEN.

NEAR the end of March, 1845, I borrowed an axe and went down to the woods by Walden Pond, nearest to where I intended to build my house, and began to cut down some tall arrowy white pines, still in their youth, for timber. It is difficult to begin without borrowing, but perhaps it is the most generous course thus to permit your fellow-men to have an interest in your enterprise. The owner of the axe, as he released his hold on it, said that it was the apple of his eye; but I returned it sharper than I received it. It was a pleasant hillside where I worked, covered with pine woods, through which I looked out on the pond, and a small open field in the woods where pines and hickories were springing up. The ice in the pond was not yet dissolved, though there were some open spaces, and it was all dark colored and saturated with water. There were some slight flurries of snow during the days that I worked there; but for the most part when I came out on to the railroad, on my way home, its yellow sand heap stretched away gleaming in the hazy atmosphere, and the rails shone in the spring sun, and I heard the lark and pewee and other birds already come to commence another year with us. They were pleasant spring days, in which the winter of man's discontent was thawing as well as the earth, and the life that had lain torpid began to stretch itself. One day, when my axe had come off and I had cut a green hickory for a wedge, driving it with a stone, and had placed the whole to soak in a pond hole in order to swell the wood, I saw a striped snake run into the water, and he lay on the bottom, apparently without inconvenience, as long as I staid there, or more than a quarter of an hour; perhaps because he had not yet fairly come out of the torpid state.

It appeared to me that for a like reason men remain in their present low and primitive condition; but if they should feel the influence of the spring of springs arousing them, they would of necessity rise to a higher and more ethereal life. I had previously seen the snakes in frosty mornings in my path with portions of their bodies still numb and inflexible, waiting for the sun to thaw them. On the first of April it rained and melted the ice, and in the early part of the day, which was very foggy, I heard a stray goose groping about over the pond and cackling as if lost, or like the spirit of the fog.

So I went on for some days cutting and hewing timber, and also studs and rafters, all with my narrow axe, not having many communicable or scholar-like thoughts, singing to myself,—

> Men say they know many things
> But lo! they have taken wings,—
> The arts and sciences,
> And a thousand appliances;
> The wind that blows
> Is all that anybody knows.

I hewed the main timbers six inches square, most of the studs on two sides only, and the rafters and floor timbers on one side, leaving the rest of the bark on, so that they were just as straight and much stronger than sawed ones. Each stick was carefully mortised or tenoned by its stump, for I had borrowed other tools by this time. My days in the woods were not very long ones; yet I usually carried my dinner of bread and butter, and read the newspaper in which it was wrapped, at noon, sitting amid the green pine boughs which I had cut off, and to my bread was imparted some of their fragrance, for my hands were covered with a thick coat of pitch. Before I had done I was more the friend than the foe of the pine tree, though I had cut down some of them, having become better acquainted with it. Sometimes a rambler in the wood was attracted by the sound of my axe, and we chatted pleasantly over the chips which I had made.

By the middle of April, for I made no haste in my work, but rather made the most of it, my house was framed and ready for the raising. I had already bought the shanty of James Collins, an Irishman who worked on the Fitchburg Railroad, for boards. James Collins' shanty was considered an uncommonly fine one. When I called to see it he was not at home. I walked about the outside, at first unobserved from within, the window was so deep and high. It was of small dimensions, with a peaked cottage roof, and not much else to be seen, the dirt being raised five feet all around as if it were a compost heap. The roof was the soundest part, though a good deal warped and made brittle by the sun. Door-sill there was none, but a perennial passage for the hens under the door board. Mrs. C. came to the door and asked me to view it from the inside. The hens were driven in by my approach. It was dark, and had a dirt floor for the most part, dank, clammy, and aguish, only here a board and there a board which would not bear removal. She lighted a lamp to show me the inside of the roof and the walls, and also that the board floor extended under the bed, warning me not to step into the cellar, a sort of dust hole two feet deep.

In her own words, they were "good boards overhead, good boards all around, and a good window," —of two whole squares originally, only the cat had passed out that way lately. There was a stove, a bed, and a place to sit, an infant in the house where it was born, a silk parasol, gilt-framed looking-glass, and a patent new coffee-mill nailed to an oak sapling, all told. The bargain was soon concluded, for James had in the meanwhile returned. I to pay four dollars and twenty-five cents to-night, he to vacate at five to-morrow morning, selling to nobody else meanwhile: I to take possession at six. It were well, he said, to be there early, and anticipate certain indistinct but wholly unjust claims on the score of ground rent and fuel. This he assured me was the only encumbrance. At six I passed him and his family on the road. One large bundle held their all,— bed, coffee-mill, looking-glass, hens,—all but the cat, she took to the woods and became a wild-cat, and, as I learned afterward, trod in a trap set for woodchucks, and so became a dead cat at last.

I took down this dwelling the same morning, drawing the nails, and removed it to the pond side by small cartloads, spreading the boards on the grass there to bleach and warp back again in the sun. One early thrush gave me a note or two as I drove along the woodland path. I was informed treacherously by a young Patrick that neighbor Seeley, an Irishman, in the intervals of the carting, transferred the still tolerable, straight, and drivable nails, staples, and spikes to his pocket, and then stood when I came back to pass the time of day, and look freshly up, unconcerned, with spring thoughts, at the devastation; there being a dearth of work, as he said. He was there to represent spectatordom, and help make this seemingly insignificant event one with the removal of the gods of Troy.

I dug my cellar in the side of a hill sloping to the south, where a woodchuck had formerly dug his burrow, down through sumach and blackberry roots, and the lowest stain of vegetation, six feet square by seven deep, to a fine sand where potatoes would not freeze in any winter. The sides were left shelving, and not stoned; but the sun having never shone on them, the sand still keeps its place. It was but two hours work. I took particular pleasure in this breaking of ground, for in almost all latitudes men dig into the earth for an equable temperature. Under the most splendid house in the city is still to be found the cellar where they store their roots as of old, and long after the superstructure has disappeared posterity remark its dent in the earth. The house is still but a sort of porch at the entrance of a burrow.

At length, in the beginning of May, with the help of some of my acquaintances, rather to improve so good an occasion for neighborliness than from any necessity, I set up the frame of my house. No man was ever more honored in the character of his raisers than I. They are destined, I trust, to assist at the raising of loftier structures one day.

I began to occupy my house on the 4th of July, as soon as it was boarded and roofed, for the boards were carefully feather-edged and lapped, so that it was perfectly impervious to rain; but before boarding I laid the foundation of a chimney at one end, bringing two cartloads of stones up the hill from the pond in my arms. I built the chimney after my hoeing in the fall, before a fire became necessary for warmth, doing my cooking in the mean while out of doors on the ground, early in the morning: which mode I still think is in some respects more convenient and agreeable than the usual one. When it stormed before my bread was baked, I fixed a few boards over the fire, and sat under them to watch my loaf, and passed some pleasant hours in that way. In those days, when my hands were much employed, I read but little, but the least scraps of paper which lay on the ground, my holder, or tablecloth, afforded me as much entertainment, in fact answered the same purpose as the Iliad.

It would be worth the while to build still more deliberately than I did, considering, for instance, what foundation a door, a window, a cellar, a garret, have in the nature of man, and perchance never raising any superstructure until we found a better reason for it than our temporal necessities even. There is some of the same fitness in a man's building his own house that there is in a bird's building its own nest. Who knows but if men constructed their dwellings with their own hands, and provided food for themselves and families simply and honestly enough, the poetic faculty would be universally developed, as birds universally sing when they are so engaged! But alas! we do like cowbirds and cuckoos, which lay their eggs in nests which other birds have built, and cheer no traveller with their chattering and unmusical notes. Shall we forever resign the pleasure of construction to the carpenter? What does architecture amount to in the experience of the mass of men? I never in all my walks came across a man engaged in so simple and natural an occupation as building his house. It is no the tailor alone who is the ninth part of a man; it is as much the preacher, and the merchant, and the farmer. Where is this division of labor to end? and what object does it finally serve? No doubt another may also think for me; but it is not therefore desirable that he should do so to the exclusion of my thinking for myself.

Before winter I built a chimney, and shingled the sides of my house, which were already impervious to rain, with imperfect and sappy shingles made of the first slice of the log, whose edges I was obliged to straighten with a plane.

I have thus a tight shingled and plastered house, ten feet wide by fifteen long, and eight-feet posts, with a garret and a closet, a large window on each side, two trap doors, one door at the end, and a brick fireplace opposite. The exact cost of my house, paying the usual price for such materials as I used, but not counting the work, all of which was done by myself, was as follows; and I give the details because very few are able to tell exactly what their houses cost, and fewer still, if any, the separate cost of the various materials which compose them :—

Boards,	$8 03½	mostly shanty boards.
Refuse shingles for roof and sides,	. 4 00	
Laths, . . .	. 1 25	
Two second-hand windows with glass,	. 2 43	
One thousand old brick	4 00	
Two casks of lime,	. 2 40	That was high.
Hair,	. 0 31	More than I needed.
Mantle-tree iron,	. 0 15	
Nails,	. 3 90	
Hinges and Screws,	. 0 14	
Latch, . .	. 0 10	
Chalk, . .	. 0 01	
Transportation .	. 1 40	{ I carried a good part on my back.
In all,	$28 12½	

These are all the materials excepting the timber, stones and sand, which I claimed by squatter's right. I have also a small wood-shed adjoining, made chiefly of the stuff which was left after building the house.

JAMES RUSSELL LOWELL.

[Born 1819.]

JAMES RUSSELL LOWELL, more noted as a poet than as a prose writer, was born in Cambridge, Mass., Feb. 22, 1819, at his father's country seat of Elmwood. His father, the Rev. Charles Lowell, is the author of about 20 published Discourses; a volume of Occasional Sermons; one of Practical Sermons; Meditations for the Afflicted, Sick, and Dying; and, Devotional Exercises for Communicants.

James Russell Lowell graduated at Harvard in 1838, tried law, which he soon relinquished for poetry and letters. In 1855, he succeeded Prof. Longfellow as Professor of Belles-Lettres in Harvard, and spent some months in Europe before assuming its duties. In 1841, he published his first volume, A Year's Life; and in 1843, The Pioneer, a Literary and Critical Magazine, a fashionable illustrated periodical of which only three numbers were issued. In 1844, he published the Legend of Brittany, Poems and Sonnets. In the same year he married Miss Maria White, of Watertown, a lady of fine culture, who left at her decease a number of excellent poems, which her husband had privately printed as a memorial volume.

In 1845, Mr. Lowell issued his Conversations on the Old Poets, a series of critical and æsthetic essays, displaying a subtle knowledge of English literature, in the form of dialogue, an unpleasant vehicle for introducing a liberal stock of reflections on life and literature generally. They show a deep appreciation of the poetical merit of the authors quoted, and a fineness of critical tact quite unusual in the literature of the magazines. The third series of his poems appeared in 1848, and in the same year, his Vision of Sir Launfal, founded on a legend of a search for the San Greal; and A Fable for Critics, a review article done into rhyme. It abounds in ingenious turns of expression and felicitous sketches of character: it is witty and humorous, and, for the most part in a spirit of genial appreciation; but, in a few instances, the judgments indicate too narrow a range of sympathies, and the caustic severity of others has been attributed to desires of retaliation. Both of these volumes have been

very popular; and, The Bigelow Papers, a political satire in Yankee rhyme upon the Invasion of Mexico, and Slavery. A second series of these witty poems was afterwards collected from the papers and magazines.

He published also, Fireside Travels, 16mo.; in 1868, Under the Willows, and other Poems; and in 1870, Among my Books, Essays upon Dryden, Witchcraft, Shakspeare, New England two centuries ago, Lessing, and, Rousseau and the Sentimentalists.

His collected poems were first issued in 1850, in 2 vols., 16mo., and afterwards in 32mo., and have passed through many editions. He has written many articles for the periodicals.

In 1857, he married Miss Frances Dunlap, niece of ex-Governor Dunlap, of Maine.

Lowell is generally looked upon as a serious poet, and, indeed, no one has a better claim to be so regarded, for seriousness is one of the first essentials of genuine poetry. But seriousness is not necessarily sadness. Much of his poetry overflows with mirthful and jocund feelings, and in his most pungent satire there is a bubbling up of a genial and loving nature; the brilliant flashes of his wit are softened by an evident gentleness of motive.

Lowell's prose writings are as remarkable as his poetry: the copiousness of his illustrations, the richness of his imagery, the easy flow of his sentences, the keenness of his wit, and the force and clearness of his reasoning, give to his reviews and essays, a fascinating charm that would place him in the front rank of our prose writers, if he did not occupy a similar position among our poets. He unites, in his most effective power, the dreamy, suggestive character of the transcendental bards with the philosophic simplicity of Wordsworth. He has written clever satires, good sonnets, and some long poems with fine descriptive passages. He reminds us often of Tennyson in the sentiment and the construction of his verse. Imagination and philanthropy are the dominant elements in his writings,—some of which are marked by a graceful flow and earnest tone.

NEW ENGLAND

FROM AMONG MY BOOKS.

NEW ENGLAND history has rather a gregarious than a personal interest. Here, by inherent necessity rather than design, was made the first experiment in practical democracy, and accordingly hence began that reaction of the New World upon the Old whose result can hardly yet be estimated. There is here no temptation to make a hero, who shall sum up in his own individuality and carry forward by his own will that purpose of which we seem to catch such bewitching glances in history, which reveals itself more clearly and constantly, perhaps, in the annals of New England than elsewhere, and which yet, at best, is but tentative, doubtful of itself, turned this way and that by chance, made up of instinct, and modified by circumstance quite as much as it is directed by deliberate forethought. Such a purpose, or natural craving, or result of temporary influences, may be misguided by a powerful character to his own ends, or, if he be strongly in sympathy with it, may be hastened toward its own fulfilment; but there is no such heroic element in our drama, and what is remarkable is, that, under whatever government, democracy grew with the growth of the New England Colonies, and was at last potent enough to wrench them, and the better part of the continent with them, from the mother country. It is true that Jefferson embodied in the Declaration of Independence the speculative theories he had learned in France, but the impulse to separation came from New England; and those theories had been long since embodied there in the practice of the people, if they had never been formulated in distinct propositions.

I have little sympathy with declaimers about the Pilgrim Fathers, who look upon them all as men of grand conceptions and superhuman foresight. An entire ship's company of Columbuses is what the world never saw. It is not wise to form any theory and fit our facts to it, as a man in a hurry is apt to cram his travelling-bag, with a total disregard of shape or texture. But perhaps it may be found that the facts will only fit comfortably together on a single plan, namely, that the fathers did have a conception (which those will call grand who regard simplicity as a necessary element of grandeur) of founding here a commonwealth on those two eternal bases of Faith and Work; that they had, indeed, no revolutionary ideas of universal liberty, but yet, what answered the purpose quite as well, an abiding faith in the brotherhood of man and the fatherhood of God; and that they did not so much propose to make all things new, as to develop the latent possibilities of English law and English character, by clearing away the fences by which the abuse of the one was gradually discommoning the other from the broad fields of natural right. They were not in advance of their age, as it is called, for no one who is so can ever work profitably in it; but they were alive to the highest and most earnest thinking of their time.

WITCHCRAFT.

FROM THE SAME.

AND if there are men who regret the Good Old Times, without too clear a notion of what they were, they should at least be thankful that we are rid of that misguided energy of faith which justified conscience in making men unrelentingly cruel. Even Mr. Leckie softens a little at the thought of the many innocent and beautiful beliefs of which a growing scepticism has robbed us in the decay of supernaturalism. But we need not despair; for, after all, scepticism is first cousin of credulity, and we are not surprised to see the tough doubter Montaigne hanging up his offerings in the shrine of our Lady of Loreto. Scepticism commonly takes up the room left by defect of imagination, and is the very quality of mind most likely to seek for sensual proof of supersensual things. If one came from the dead, it could not believe; and yet it longs for such a witness, and will put up with a very dubious one. So long as night is left and the helplessness of dream, the wonderful will not cease from among men. While we are the solitary prisoners of darkness, the witch seats herself at the loom of thought, and weaves strange figures into the web that looks so familiar and ordinary in the dry light of every-day. Just as we are flattering ourselves that the old spirit of sorcery is laid, behold the tables are tipping and the floors drumming all over Christendom. The faculty of wonder is not defunct, but is only getting more and more emancipated from the unnatural service of terror, and restored to its proper function as a minister of delight. A higher mode of belief is the best exorciser, because it makes the spiritual at one with the actual world instead of hostile, or at best alien. It has been the grossly material interpretations of spiritual doctrine that have given occasion to the two extremes of superstition and unbelief. While the resurrection of the body has been insisted on, that resurrection from the body which is the privilege of all has been forgotten. Superstition in its baneful form was largely due to the enforcement by the Church of arguments that involved a *petitio principii*, for it is the miserable necessity of all false logic to accept of very ignoble allies. Fear became at length its chief expedient for the maintenance of its power; and as there is a beneficent necessity laid upon a majority of mankind to sustain and perpetuate the order of things they are born into, and to make all new ideas manfully prove their right, first, to be at all, and then to be heard, many even superior minds dreaded the tearing away of vicious accretions as dangerous to the whole edifice of religion and society. But if this old ghost be fading away in what we regard as the dawn of a better day, we may console ourselves by thinking that perhaps, after all, we are not so *much* wiser than our ancestors. The rappings, the trance mediums, the visions of hands without bodies, the sounding of musical instruments without visible fingers, the miraculous inscriptions on the naked flesh, the enlivenment of furniture,—we have invented none of them, they are all heirlooms.

JOSIAH GILBERT HOLLAND, M. D.

[Born 1819.]

DR. J. G. HOLLAND was born at Belchertown, Mass., July 24, 1819. When he had partly completed his studies, preparatory to entering college, his health became enfeebled by too severe application, and he concluded, after a period of relaxation, to study medicine, which he did, in the meantime teaching as a means of support. In 1845, he took his degree of M. D., at the Berkshire Medical College, Pittsfield, Mass., and practiced about two years at Springfield, where he married Elizabeth L. Chapin. He afterwards became teacher of a private school at Richmond, Va., for three months, and then accepted the appointment of Superintendent of Public Schools in Vicksburg, Miss. While there, he wrote frequently for the press; but, after discharging the duties of his office with great satisfaction for a year and half, he accepted an offer as editor of the Springfield Republican, and removed back to Massachusetts. He has discharged his editorial duties with such tact and ability, that that paper is one of the most successful and widely known and quoted journals in the country.

In 1855, Dr. Holland published the History of Western Massachusetts, of four counties, in 2 vols., 12mo., which he had written the previous year. In 1857, appeared the Bay Path, a novel founded on some of the colonial incidents of his history; which did not meet with much success, nor at a later period when it was reissued.

In 1858, he reprinted from the Republican, Timothy Titcomb's Letters to Young People, that had an immediate and great success, and which very deservedly still continues. Eminently successful in their manner and adaptation to the wants of the country, they attracted attention for their beauty of style, purity of English, and sound common sense. The advice contained in them is excellent, entirely practical, sufficiently minute, and eminently judicious,—intended to make useful and happy men and women.

The same year he published, Bitter Sweet, a poem of New England rustic life, unique in its structure, for the most part in blank verse, of a somewhat rugged character, in keeping with the subject matter. It opens with a picture of a wild November storm raging around a country homestead on a New England Thanksgiving, at which the gathered family, after the bountiful repast and the pleasantries of the evening, talk far into the night upon questions of theology, in connection with their personal experiences of the joys and sorrows of life. It met with great success in both illustrated and plain editions.

In 1859, he issued Gold Foil Hammered from Popular Proverbs, in which, with a wider scope in its treatment of social subjects than in Titcomb's Letters, it treated of matters of the same general character in the same common sense way. This was followed by three other books of somewhat similar character; Letters to the Joneses; Lessons in Life, a series of familiar essays; and Plain Talk on Familiar Subjects.

In 1860, Dr. Holland published his second novel, Miss Gilbert's Career, a tale of American village life, well told, with some powerfully drawn characters, truthful pictures, and humorous delineations. It met with a fair share of success.

Upon the death of Mr. Lincoln, Dr. Holland wrote a very excellent biography, which had a large sale by subscription.

In 1867, he published his second long poem, Kathrina, her sorrows and mine, which at once attained to great popularity in an elegantly illustrated octavo edition, also in plain 12mo.

Dr. Holland now ranks as one of the most popular of American authors; and perhaps no American poet has met with such instant and ready recognition, such universal popularity, and with so great literary and pecuniary success. Two editions of his works are published, one in 12mo., and his most popular works in 16mo., uniform style, called the Brightwood edition.

FEMALE SOCIETY—THE WOMAN FOR A WIFE.

FROM TITCOMB'S LETTERS.

In many of the books addressed to young men, a great deal is said about the purifying and elevating influences of female society. Sentimental young men affect this kind of reading, and if anywhere in it they can find countenance for the policy of early marriage, they are delighted. Now, while I will be the last to deny the purifying and elevating influence of pure and elevated women, I do deny that there is anything in indiscriminate devotion to female society, which makes a man better or purer. Suppose a man cast away on the Cannibal Islands, and not in sufficiently good flesh to excite the appetites of the gentle epicureans among whom he has fallen. Suppose him, in fact, to be "received into society," and made the private secretary of a king without a liberal education. Suppose after a while, he feels himself subsiding into a state of barbarism, and casts around for some redeeming or conservative influence. At this moment it occurs to him that in the trunk on which he sailed ashore were a number of books. He flies to the trunk, and, in an ecstasy of delight, discovers that among them is a volume addressed to young men. He opens it eagerly, and finds the writer to declare that next to the Christian religion, there is nothing that will tend so strongly to the elevation and purification of young men, as female society. He accordingly seeks the society of women, and drinks in the marvellous influences of their presence. He finds them unacquainted with some of the most grateful uses of water, and in evident ignorance of the existence of ivory combs. About what year of the popular era is it to be supposed that he will arrive at a desirable state of purification and perfection?

Now, perhaps you do not perceive the force of this illustration. Let us get at it, then. When you find youself shut out from all female society except that which is beneath you, that society will do you just as much and no more good than that of the fair cannibals, especially if it be young. If, in all this society, you can find one old woman of sixty, who has common sense, genial good-nature, experience, some reading, and a sympathetic heart, cherish her as you would her weight in gold, but let the young trash go. You will hear nothing from them but gossip and nonsense, and you will only get disgusted with the world and yourself. Inspiration to higher and purer life always comes from above a man; and female society can only elevate and purify a man when it is higher than he is. In the element of purity, I doubt not that women generally are superior to men, but it is very largely a negative or unconscious element, and has not the power and influence of a positive virtue.

Therefore, whenever you seek for female society, as an agency in the elevation of your tastes, the preservation of your morals, and the improvement of your mind, seek for that which is above you. I do not counsel you to treat with rudeness or studied neglect such inferior female society as you are obliged to come in contact with. On the contrary, you owe such society a duty. You should stimulate it, infuse new life into it, if possible, and do for it what you would have female society do for yourself.

This matter of seeking female society above yourself you should carry still further. Never content yourself with the idea of having a common-place wife. You want one who will stimulate you, stir you up, keep you moving, show you your weak points, and make something of you. Don't fear that you cannot get such a wife. I very well remember the reply which a gentleman who happened to combine the qualities of wit and common sense, made to a young man who expressed a fear that a certain young lady of great beauty and attainments would dismiss him, if he should become serious. "My friend," said the wit, "infinitely more beautiful and accomplished women than she is, have married infinitely uglier and meaner men than you are." And such is the fact. If you are honest and honorable, if your character is spotless, if you are enterprising and industrious, if you have some grace and a fair degree of sense, and if you love appreciatingly and truly, you can marry almost anybody worth your having. So, to encourage yourself, carry in your memory the above aphorism reduced to a form something like this: "Infinitely finer women than I ever expect to marry, have loved and married men infinitely meaner than I am."

The apprehensions of women are finer and quicker than those of men. With equally early advantages, the woman is more of a woman at eighteen than a man is a man at twenty-one. After marriage, as a general thing, the woman ceases to acquire. Now, I do not say that this is necessary, or that it should be the case, but I simply state a general fact. The woman is absorbed in family cares, or perhaps devotes from ten to twenty years to the bearing and rearing of children—the most dignified, delightful, and honorable office of her life. This consumes her time, and, in a great multitude of instances, deprives her of intellectual culture.

In the meantime, the man is out, engaged in business. He comes in daily contact with minds stronger and sharper than his own. He grows and matures, and in ten years from the date of his marriage, becomes in reality, a new man. Now, if he was so foolish as to marry a woman because she had a pretty form and face, or sweet eyes, or an amiable disposition, or a pleasant temper, or wealth, he will find that he has passed entirely by his wife, and that she is really no more of a companion for him than a child would be. I know of but few sadder sights in this world than that of mates whom the passage of years has miss-mated. A woman ought to have a long start of a man, and then, ten to one the man will come out ahead in the race of a long life.

I suppose that in every young man's mind there exist the hope and the expectation of marriage. When a young man pretends to me that he has no wish to marry, and that he never expects to marry, I always infer one of two things: that he lies, and is really very anxious for marriage, or that his heart has been polluted by associations with unworthy women. In a thousand cases we shall not find three exceptions to this rule. A young man who, with any degree of earnestness, declares that he intends never to marry, confesses to a brutal nature or perverted morals.

But how shall a good wife he won? I know that men naturally shrink from the attempt to obtain companions who are their superiors; but they will find that really intelligent women, who possess the most desirable qualities, are uniformly modest, and hold their charms in modest estimation. What such women most admire in men is gallantry; not the gallantry of courts and fops, but boldness, courage, devotion, decision, and refined civility. A man's bearing wins ten superior women where his boots and brains win one. If a man stand before a woman with respect for himself and fearlessness of her, his suit is half won. The rest may safely be left to the parties most interested. Therefore, never be afraid of a woman. Women are the most harmless and agreeable creatures in the world, to a man who shows that he has got a man's soul in him. If you have not got the spirit in you to come up to a test like this, you have not got that in you which most pleases a high-souled woman, and you will be obliged to content yourself with the simple girl who, in a quiet way, is endeavoring to attract and fasten you.

But don't be in a hurry about the matter. Don't get into a feverish longing for marriage. It isn't creditable to you. Especially don't imagine that any disappointment in love which takes place before you are twenty-one years old will be of any material damage to you. The truth is, that before a man is twenty-five years old he does not know what he wants himself. So don't be in a hurry. The more of a man you become, and the more of manliness you become capable of exhibiting in your association with women, the better wife you will be able to obtain; and one year's possession of the heart and hand of a really noble specimen of her sex, is worth nine hundred and ninety-nine years' possession of a sweet creature with two ideas in her head, and nothing new to say about either of them. "Better fifty years of Europe than a cycle of Cathay." So don't be in a hurry, I say again. You don't want a wife now, and you have not the slightest idea of the kind of a wife you will want by-and-by. Go into female society if you can find that which will improve you, but not otherwise. You can spend your time better. Seek the society of good men. This is often more accessible to you than the other, and

it is through that mostly that you will find your way to good female society.

If any are disposed to complain of the injustice to woman of advice like this, and believe that it involves a wrong to her, I reply that not the slightest wrong is intended. Thorough appreciation of a good woman, on the part of a young man, is one of his strongest recommendations to her favor. The desire of such a man to possess and associate his life with such a woman, gives evidence of qualities, aptitudes, and capacities which entitle him to any woman's consideration and respect. There is something good in him; and however uncultivated he may be—however rude in manner, and rough in person—he only needs development to become worthy of her, in some respects, at least. I shall not quarrel with a woman who desires a husband superior to herself, for I know it will be well for her to obtain such an one, if she will be stimulated by contact with a higher mind to a brighter and broader development. At the same time, I must believe that for a man to marry his inferior, is to call upon himself a great misfortune; to deprive himself of one of the most elevating and refining influences which can possibly affect him. I therefore believe it to be the true policy of every young man to aim high in his choice of a companion. I have previously given a reason for this policy, and both that and this conspire to establish the soundness of my counsel.

One thing more: not the least important, but the last in this letter. No woman without piety in her heart is fit to be the companion of any man. You may get, in your wife, beauty, amiability, sprightliness, wit, accomplishments, wealth, and learning, but if that wife have no higher love than herself and yourself, she is a poor creature. She cannot elevate you above mean aims and objects, she cannot educate her children properly, she cannot in hours of adversity sustain and comfort you, she cannot bear with patience your petulance induced by the toils and vexations of business, and she will never be safe against the seductive temptations of gaiety and dress.

Then, again, a man who has the prayers of a pious wife, and knows that he has them—upheld by heaven, or by a refined sense of obligation and gratitude—can rarely become a very bad man. A daily prayer from the heart of a pure and pious wife, for a husband engrossed in the pursuits of wealth and fame, is a chain of golden words that links his name every day with the name of God. He may snap it three hundred and sixty-five times in a year, for many years, but the chances are that in time he will gather the sundered filaments, and seek to re-unite them in an everlasting bond.

HERMAN MELVILLE.

[Born 1819.]

HERMAN MELVILLE was born in New York, August 1, 1819. His father was an importer and made frequent trips across the Atlantic. Herman seemed to inherit a love for the ocean; his early boyhood was passed at Albany, and Lansingburg, in New York, and at Berkshire, Mass., where he now resides; but in his eighteenth year, he shipped as a sailor on a vessel leaving New York for Liverpool. He made a hurried visit to London, and returned home "before the mast."

He liked his marine life well enough to embark on a whaling vessel for the Pacific for the sperm fishery, Jan. 1, 1841. After eighteen months of the cruise, the vessel arrived at the Marquesas Islands, at Nukuheva. Melville with a fellow sailor, tired of the ship and its discipline, took "French leave", and hid themselves in the forest, with the intention of resorting to a peaceful tribe of natives, but mistaking their way, fell into the hands of a warlike tribe in the Typee valley. Here they were detained in a sort of captivity for four months; he was separated from his companion, and was rescued one day when on the shore, by a boat's crew from a Sidney whaler. He shipped on board the vessel, and was landed at Tahiti; from thence he went to the Sandwich Islands, stayed a few months, and then shipped as ordinary seaman on board the man-of-war, the frigate United States, then on its return voyage, and reached Boston, in October, 1844, having been absent from home three years. In 1847, he married the daughter of Chief Justice Shaw of Boston, resided in New York for a short time, and then removed to Berkshire, Mass., on a finely situated farm, adjacent to the old Melville House, in the immediate neighborhood of the residence of O. W. Holmes, the poet; he overlooks the town of Pittsfield, and its mountainous vicinity. In the fields and his study, and in the society of his family and friends, so different from his earlier experiences, he has spent his later years; and written most of his later works, which may account for the speculative and dreamy character of them.

His first book, Typee, a narrative of a residence in the Marquesas, was published in New York and London, in 1846. That he was no unobservant spectator of the peculiar phases of society which he encountered during his travels, we have ample evidence in his descriptive volumes. Typee, a peep at Polynesian Life, was a curiosity, it was the first account of a residence among those natives by a person who has lived with them in their own fashion, and as near as may be, on terms of social equality. It has such a picturesque, dreamy, glowing, air about it; such a spirited and vigorous fancy of the style; such freshness and novelty of interest; so romantic and bewitching incidents in the narrative; that it at once piqued curiosity, and arrested the attention and excited the enthusiasm of the reading public. It made a reputation for the author in a day. The Robinson-Crusoe style was heightened by the introduction of the lovely Fayaway, and his simple mode of life with her and the natives.

Mr. Melville followed up this success the next year with Omoo, a narrative of Adventure in the South Seas, which takes up the story with the escape from Typee and gives a humorous account of his adventures in Tahiti. For pleasant, easy narrative, it is the most natural and agreeable of his books. His delineations of island life and scenery, are most correctly and faithfully drawn.

In 1849, appeared Mardi, and a Voyage Thither, 2 vols., 12mo., a rambling philosophical romance, with many delicate traits and fine bursts of fancy, but which it will pay nobody to wade through, consequently it was not a success. He did better the same year, in Redburn, his first voyage; being the Sailor-boy Confessions and Reminiscences of the Son of a Gentleman, in the merchant service. The style is more natural and manly than Mardi; with less of its obscurity and nonsense; it was not very popular.

In 1850, he published, White-Jacket, or the World in a Man-of-War. A truthful and interesting work in which he says a good word for Poor Jack. This was followed in 1851, by Moby Dick, or the Whale; the details of the fishery and the natural history of the animal are well told, but the metaphysical portions of the narrative destroy its interest. He also published Pierre, or the Ambiguities; The Piazza Tales; The Confidence Man, his Masquerade; and a number of magazine articles in Putnam's and Harper's magazines.

Herman Melville is an original thinker, and boldly and unreservedly expresses his opinions, often in a way that irresistibly startles and enchains the interest of the reader. He possesses amazing powers of expression: he can be terse, copious, eloquent, brilliant, imaginative, poetical, satirical, pathetic, at will. He is never stupid, never dull; but, alas! he is often mystical and unintelligible,—not from any inability to express himself, for his writing is pure, manly English, and a child can always understand what he says,—but the ablest critic cannot always tell what he really means; solely from his incorrigible perversion of his rare and lofty gifts

---

POLYNESIAN LIFE.
FROM TYPEE.

THERE was no boat on the lake; but at my solicitation and for my special use, some of the young men attached to Marheyo's household, under the direction of the indefatigable Kory-Kory, brought up a light and tastefully carved canoe from the sea. It was launched upon the sheet of water, and floated there as gracefully as a swan. But, melancholy to relate, it produced an effect I had not anticipated. The sweet nymphs, who had sported with me before in the lake, now all fled its vicinity. The prohibited craft, guarded by the edicts of the "taboo," extended the prohibition to the waters in which it lay.

For a few days, Kory-Kory, with one or two other youths, accompanied me in my excursions to the lake, and while I paddled about in my light canoe, would swim after me shouting and gambolling in pursuit. But I was ever partial to what is termed in the "Young Men's Own Book"— "the society of virtuous and intelligent young ladies;" and in the absence of the mermaids, the amusement became dull and insipid. One morning I expressed to my faithful servitor my desire for the return of the nymphs. The honest fellow looked at me bewildered for a moment, and then shook his head solemnly, and murmured "taboo! taboo!" giving me to understand that unless the canoe was removed, I could not expect to have the young ladies back again. But to this procedure I was averse; I not only wanted the canoe to stay where it was, but I wanted the beauteous Fayaway to get into it, and paddle with me about the lake. This latter proposition completely horrified Kory-Kory's notions of propriety. He inveighed against it, as something too monstrous to be thought of. It not only shocked their established notions of propriety, but was at variance with all their religious ordinances.

However, although the "taboo" was a ticklish thing to meddle with, I determined to test its capabilities of resisting an attack. I consulted the chief Mehevi, who endeavored to persuade me from my object: but I was not to be repulsed; and accordingly increased the warmth of my solicitations.

At last he entered into a long, and I have no doubt a very learned and eloquent exposition of the history and nature of the "taboo" as affecting this particular case; employing a variety of most extraordinary words, which, from their amazing length and sonorousness, I have every reason to believe were of a theological nature. But all that he said failed to convince me: partly, perhaps, because I could not comprehend a word that he uttered; but chiefly, that for the life of me I could not understand why a woman should not have as much right to enter a canoe as a man. At last he became a little more rational, and intimated that, out of the abundant love he bore me, he would consult with the priests and see what could be done.

How it was that the priesthood of Typee satisfied the affair with their consciences, I know not; but so it was, and Fayaway's dispensation from this portion of the taboo was at length procured. Such an event I believe never before had occured in the valley; but it was high time the islanders should be taught a little gallantry, and I trust that the example I set them may produce beneficial effects. Ridiculous, indeed, that the lovely creatures should be obliged to paddle about in the water, like so many ducks, while a parcel of great strapping fellows skimmed over its surface in their canoes.

The first day after Fayaway's emancipation, I had a delightful little party on the lake—the damsel, Kory-Kory, and myself. My zealous bodyservant brought from the house a calabash of poeepoee, half a dozen young cocoa-nuts—stripped of their husks—three pipes, as many yams, and me on his back a part of the way. Something of a load; but Kory-Kory was a very strong man for his size, and by no means brittle in the spine. We had a very pleasant day; my trusty valet plied the paddle and swept us gently along the margin of the water, beneath the shades of the overhanging thickets. Fayaway and I reclined in the stern of the canoe, on the very best terms possible with one another; the gentle nymph occasionally placing her pipe to her lip, and exhaling the mild fumes of the tobacco, to which her rosy breath added a fresh perfume. Strange as it may seem, there is nothing in which a young and beautiful female appears to more advantage than in the act of smoking. How captivating is a Peruvian lady, swinging in her gaily-woven hammock of grass, extended between two orange-trees, and inhaling the fragrance of a choice cigarro! But Fayaway, holding in her delicately-formed olive hand the long yellow reed of her pipe, with its quaintly carved bowl, and every few moments languishingly giving forth light wreaths of vapor from her mouth and nostrils, looked still more engaging.

We floated about thus for several hours, when I looked up to the warm, glowing, tropical sky, and then down into the transparent depths below ; and when my eye, wandering from the bewitching scenery around, fell upon the grotesquely-tattooed form of Kory-Kory, and finally encountered the pensive gaze of Fayaway, I thought I had been transported to some fairy region, so unreal did everything appear.

This lovely piece of water was the coolest spot in all the valley, and I now made it a place of continual resort during the hottest period of the day. One side of it lay near the termination of a long, gradually expanding gorge, which mounted to the heights that environed the vale. The strong trade wind, met in its course by these elevations, circled and eddied about their summits, and was sometimes driven down the steep ravine and swept across the valley, ruffling in its passage the otherwise tranquil surface of the lake.

One day, after we had been paddling about for some time, I disembarked Kory-Kory, and paddled the canoe to the windward side of the lake. As I turned the canoe, Fayaway, who was with me, seemed all at once to be struck with some happy idea. With a wild exclamation of delight, she disengaged from her person the ample robe of tappa which was knotted over her shoulder (for the purpose of shielding her from the sun), and spreading it out like a sail, stood erect with upraised arms in the head of the canoe. We American sailors pride ourselves upon our straight clean spars, but a prettier little mast than Fayaway made was never shipped aboard of any craft.

In a moment the tappa was distended by the breeze—the long brown tresses of Fayaway streamed in the air—and the canoe glided rapidly through the water, and shot towards the shore. Seated in the stern, I directed its course with my paddle until it dashed up the soft sloping bank, and Fayaway, with a light spring, alighted on the ground.

OUTBREAK OF THE CREW.
FROM OMOO.

The purpose of Bembo had been made known to the men generally by the watch ; and now that our salvation was certain, by an instinctive impulse they raised a cry, and rushed toward him.

Just before liberated by Dunk and the steward, he was standing doggedly by the mizen-mast ; and, as the infuriated sailors came on, his blood-shot eye rolled, and his sheath-knife glittered over his head.

"Down with him !" "Strike him down !" "Hang him at the main-yard !" such were the shouts now raised. But he stood unmoved, and, for a single instant, they absolutely faltered.

"Cowards !" cried Salem, and he flung himself upon him. The steel descended like a ray of light ; but did no harm ; for the sailor's heart was beating against the Mowree's before he was aware.

They both fell to the deck, when the knife was instantly seized, and Bembo secured.

"For'ard ! for'ard with him !" was again the cry ; "give him a sea-toss !" "overboard with him !" and he was dragged along the deck, struggling and fighting with tooth and nail.

All this uproar immediately over the mate's head at last roused him from his drunken nap, and he came staggering on deck.

"What's this ?" he shouted, running right in among them.

"It's the Mowree, zur ; they are going to murder him, zur," here sobbed poor Rope Yarn, crawling close up to him.

"Avast ! avast !" roared Jermin, making a spring toward Bembo, and dashing two or three of the sailors aside. At this moment the wretch was partly flung over the bulwarks, which shook with his frantic struggles. In vain the doctor and others tried to save him : the men listened to nothing.

"Murder and mutiny, by the salt sea !" shouted the mate ; and dashing his arms right and left, he planted his iron hand upon the Mowree's shoulder.

"There are two of us now ; and as you serve him, you serve me," he cried, turning fiercely round.

"Over with them together, then," exclaimed the carpenter, springing forward ; but the rest fell back before the courageous front of Jermin, and, with the speed of thought, Bembo, unharmed, stood upon deck.

"Aft with ye !" cried his deliverer ; and he pushed him right among the men, taking care to follow him up close. Giving the sailors no time to recover, he pushed the Morwee before him, till they came to the cabin scuttle, when he drew the slide over him, and stood still. Throughout, Bembo never spoke one word.

"Now for'ard where ye belong !" cried the mate, addressing the seamen, who by this time, rallying again, had no idea of losing their victim.

"The Mowree ! the Mowree !" they shouted.

Here the doctor, in answer to the mate's repeated questions, stepped forward, and related what Bembo had been doing ; a matter which the mate but dimly understood from the violent threatenings he had been hearing.

For a moment he seemed to waver ; but at last, turning the key in the padlock of the slide, he breathed through his set teeth—"Ye can't have him ; I'll hand him over to the consul, so for'ard with ye, I say : when there's any drowning to be done, I'll pass the word ; so away with ye, ye blood-thirsty pirates !"

It was to no purpose that they begged or threatened : Jermin, although by no means sober, stood his ground manfully, and before long they dispersed, soon to forget everything that had happened.

JAMES PARTON.

[Born 1822.]

JAMES PARTON, a resident of New York, was born at Canterbury, England, Feb. 9, 1822. Brought to New York when he was five years old, he was educated in its vicinity, and afterwards taught for seven years, when he became a writer for the Home Journal.

He published his first work, the Life of Horace Greeley, in 1855, in one volume, 12mo., and enlarged it in 1869. From the popularity of his subject, and the ability of his biography, it was very successful. It is noticeable for its research, the minuteness of its statements, its picturesque incidents, a certain dashing enthusiasm, and forms an interesting contribution to the history of American journalism.

Mr. Parton, in 1855, edited the Humorous Poetry of the English Language; a spirited selection, of which many editions were sold.

In 1859, appeared his Life and Times of Aaron Burr; which, from the nature of his subject, and the manner in which he handled it, excited enough interest and criticism, to sell more than twenty editions. The author, a hearty admirer of the brilliant qualities of Burr, attempts a vindication of his character from the wholesale reproaches cast upon him. In some respects it is almost a model biography, certainly one of more than ordinary interest; contradictory enough in phenomena of good and evil; a romance in real life; or the story of an American Barry Lindon. A letter was published in the New York Observer, from a relative of Burr's family, protesting strongly against Mr. Parton's presentation of Burr's character.

In 1860, he issued his Life of Andrew Jackson, 4 vols., royal 8vo., and later editions in crown 8vo., and an abridged edition in one volume, 12mo., in 1862. Said to be the best biography of any American politician, for its unfailing spirit, its industrious research, and its air of candor and impartiality in handling the perplexing facts of the hero's career, neither transmuting the faults nor exaggerating inordinately the merits of its subject. With unwearied industry, he sought out the details of the story in the newspaper and other original

memorials of the times; sifted interests and contradictory testimony; visited localities and examined living witnesses. The style is easy and flowing, warmly colored without extravagance, and his pages are filled with striking incidents and events.

During the war, in 1863, he published: General Butler in New Orleans, History of the Administration of the Department of the Gulf in the year 1862. One stout volume, crown, 8vo. It passed through eighteen editions, also an abridged edition, in 8vo., paper, and an edition in German. Treating of subjects of the period which no writer could make uninteresting, and certainly not Mr. Parton.

In 1864, appeared his Life and Times of Benjamin Franklin, in 2 vols., crown, 8vo., in which he displays his accustomed skill, industry, love of anecdote, and perception of character, in giving a living and animated portrait of his great subject, full of interest and instruction.

In 1865, he wrote the Life of John Jacob Astor, to which is appended his will. In 1866, Manual for the Instruction of "Rings", railroad and political, 24mo.; How New York City is Governed, 16mo.; Famous Americans of Recent Times, containing Lives of Clay, Webster, Calhoun, Randolph, Girard, Bennett, Goodyear, Beecher, Vanderbilt, Theodosia Burr, and Astor. In 1868, People's Book of Biography; or, short Lives of the most interesting Persons of all Ages and Countries, 8vo., a book made to sell by subscription; Smoking and Drinking, 16mo., an article from the Atlantic Monthly. In 1869, The Danish Islands, are we bound in honor to pay for them? and a new edition of his Life of Horace Greeley, with eight additional chapters. He is now said to be engaged on the Life and Times of Voltaire; and the Life of ex-Governor Yates, of Illinois. He constantly contributes to the magazines.

His reputation is that of a painstaking, honest, and courageous historian, ardent with patriotism, but unprejudiced; his style is easy, natural, and flowing; whatever subject he undertakes the biography of is sure to be well and justly done, and his book will command attention.

Mr. Parton married in 1855, Sarah Payson Eldredge, formerly Miss Willis, a sister of N. P. Willis, but married in 1834, to Chas. H. Eldredge of Boston, who died in 1846. Under the nom-de-plume of Fanny Fern she was widely known as the author of short sketches of sparkling vivacity and piquant thoughts. Her first volume, Fern Leaves, 1st series, was issued in 1853; her second, Little Ferns for Fanny's Little Friends, in Dec., 1853; and her third, Fern Leaves, second series, in 1854; the sale of these volumes reached 200,000 copies in a year.

In 1854, Fanny Fern published her first continuous story, Ruth Hall, which had the extraordinary sale of over 50,000 copies in eight months, owing to her previous popularity and the curiosity to read a novel from her pen, and the various and sweeping criticisms which it gave rise to. In the autumn of 1855, her second novel, Rose Clark, was issued, also meeting with great success. In 1856, her second book for Juveniles, the Play-Day Book, and in 1857 her volume of Fresh Leaves, were issued. In 1868, she issued Folly as it Flies, hit at by Mrs. S. Parton; which excited but little attention. She had a permanent engagement with the New York Ledger, where most of her short articles appeared. The Life and Beauties of Fanny Fern was published in England.

HENRY CLAY'S POPULARITY.
FROM FAMOUS AMERICANS OF RECENT TIMES.

OF our public men of the sixty years preceding the war, Henry Clay, was certainly the most shining figure. Was there ever a public man, not at the head of a state, so beloved as he? Who ever heard such cheers, so hearty, distinct, and ringing, as those which his name evoked? Men shed tears at his defeat, and women went to bed sick from pure sympathy with his disappointment. He could not travel during the last thirty years of his life, but only make progresses. When he left his home the public seized him and bore him along over the land, the committee of one State passing him on to the committee of another, and the hurrahs of one town dying away as those of the next caught his ear. The country seemed to place all its resources at his disposal; all commodities sought his acceptance. Passing through Newark once, he thoughtlessly ordered a carriage of a certain pattern: the same evening the carriage was at the door of his hotel in New York, the gift of a few Newark friends. It was so everywhere and with everything. His house became at last a museum of curious gifts. There was the counterpane made for him by a lady ninety-three years of age, and Washington's camp-goblet given him by a lady of eighty; there were pistols, rifles, and fowling-pieces enough to defend a citadel; and, among a bundle of walking-sticks, was one cut for him from a tree that shaded Cicero's grave. There were gorgeous prayer-books, and Bibles of exceeding magnitude and splendor, and silver-ware in great profusion. On one occasion there arrived at Ashland the substantial present of twenty-three barrels of salt. In his old age, when his fine estate, through the misfortunes of his sons, was burdened with mortgages to the amount of thirty thousand dollars, and other large debts weighed heavily upon his soul, and he feared to be compelled to sell the home of fifty years and seek a strange abode, a few old friends secretly raised the needful sum, secretly paid the mortgages and discharged the debts, and then caused the aged orator to be informed of what had been done, but not of the names of the donors. "Could my life insure the success of Henry Clay, I would freely lay it down this day," exclaimed an old Rhode Island sea-captain on the morning of the Presidential election of 1844. Who has forgotten the passion of disappointment, the amazement and despair, at the result of that day's fatal work? Fatal we thought it then, little dreaming that, while it precipitated evil, it brought nearer the day of deliverance.

It must be confessed, however, that Henry Clay, who was for twenty-eight years a candidate for the Presidency, cultivated his popularity. Without ever being a hypocrite, he was habitually an actor; but the part which he enacted was Henry Clay exaggerated. He was naturally a most courteous man; but the consciousness of his position made him more elaborately and universally courteous than any man ever was from mere good-nature. A man on the stage must overdo his part, in order not to seem to underdo it. There was a time when almost every visitor to the city of Washington desired, above all things, to be presented to three men there, Clay, Webster, and Calhoun, whom to have seen was a distinction. When the country member brought forward his agitated constituent on the floor of the Senate-chamber, and introduced him to Daniel Webster, the Expounder was likely enough to thrust a hand at him without so much as turning his head or discontinuing his occupation, and the stranger shrunk away painfully conscious of his insignificance. Calhoun, on the contrary, besides receiving him with civility, would converse with him, if opportunity favored, and treat him to a disquisition on the nature of government and the "beauty" of nullification, striving to make a lasting impression on his intellect. Clay would rise, extend his hand with that winning grace of his, and instantly captivate him by his all-conquering courtesy. He would call him by name, inquire respecting his health, the town whence he came, how long he had been in Washington, and send him away pleased with himself and enchanted with Henry Clay. And what was his delight to receive a few weeks after, in his distant village, a copy of the Kentuckian's last speech, bearing on the cover the frank of "H. Clay"! It was almost enough to make a man think of "running for Congress"! And, what was still more intoxicating, Mr. Clay, who had a surprising memory, would be likely, on meeting this individual two years after the introduction, to address him by name.

There was a gamy flavor, in those days, about Southern men, which was very pleasing to the people of the North. Reason teaches us that the barn-yard fowl is a more meritorious bird than the game-cock; but the imagination does not assent to the proposition. Clay was at once game-cock and domestic fowl. His gestures called to mind the magnificently branching trees of his Kentucky forests, and his handwriting had the neatness and delicacy of a female copyist. There was a careless, graceful ease in his movements and attitudes, like those of an Indian chief; but he was an exact man of business, who docketed his letters, and could send from Washington to Ashland for a document, telling in what pigeon-hole it could be found. Naturally impetuous, he acquired early in life an habitual moderation of statement, an habitual consideration for other men's self-love, which made him the pacificator of his time. The great compromiser was himself a compromise. The ideal of education is to tame men without lessening their vivacity,—to unite in them the freedom, the dignity, the prowess of a Tecumseh, with the servicable qualities of the civilized man. This happy union is said to be sometimes produced in the pupils of the great public schools of England, who are savages on the play-ground and gentlemen in the school-room. In no man of our knowledge has there been combined so much of the best of the forest chief with so much of the good of the trained man of business as in Henry Clay. This was one secret of his power over classes of men so diverse as the hunters of Kentucky and the manufacturers of New England.

HENRY CLAY'S LAST YEARS.
FROM THE SAME.

IT is proof positive of a man's essential soundness, if he improves as he grows old. Henry Clay's last years were his best; he ripened to the very end. His friends remarked the moderation of his later opinions, and his charity for those who had injured him most. During the last ten years of his life no one ever heard him utter a harsh

judgment of an opponent. Domestic afflictions, frequent and severe, had chastened his heart; his six affectionate and happy daughters were dead; one son was a hopeless lunatic in an asylum; another was not what such a father had a right to expect; and, at length, his favorite and most promising son, Henry, in the year 1847, fell at the battle of Buena Vista. It was just after this last crushing loss, and probably in consequence of it, that he was baptized and confirmed a member of the Episcopal Church.

When, in 1849, he reappeared in the Senate, to assist, if possible, in removing the slavery question from politics, he was an infirm and serious, but not sad, old man of seventy-two. He never lost his cheerfulness or his faith, but he felt deeply for his distracted country. During that memorable session of Congress he spoke seventy times. Often extremely sick and feeble, scarcely able, with the assistance of a friend's arm, to climb the steps of the Capitol, he was never absent on the days when the Compromise was to be debated. It appears to be well attested, that his last great speech on the Compromise was the immediate cause of his death. On the morning on which he began his speech, he was accompanied by a clerical friend, to whom he said, on reaching the long flight of steps leading to the Capitol, "Will you lend me your arm, my friend? for I find myself quite weak and exhausted this morning." Every few steps he was obliged to stop and take breath. "Had you not better defer your speech?" asked the clergyman. "My dear friend," said the dying orator, "I consider our country in danger; and if I can be the means, in any measure, of averting that danger, my health or life is of little consequence." When he rose to speak, it was but too evident that he was unfit for the task he had undertaken. But, as he kindled with his subject, his cough left him, and his bent form resumed all its wonted erectness and majesty. He may, in the prime of his strength, have spoken with more energy, but never with so much pathos and grandeur. His speech lasted two days, and, though he lived two years longer, he never recovered from the effects of the effort. Toward the close of the second day, his friends repeatedly proposed an adjournment; but he would not desist until he had given complete utterance to his feelings. He said afterwards that he was not sure, if he gave way to an adjournment, that he should ever be able to resume.

Henry Clay was a man of honor and a gentleman. He kept his word. He was true to his friends, his party, and his convictions. He paid his debts and his son's debts. The instinct of solvency was very strong in him. He had a religion, of which the main component parts were self-respect and love of country. These were supremely authoritative with him; he would not do anything which he felt to be beneath Henry Clay, or which he thought would be injurious to the United States. Five times a candidate for the Presidency, no man can say that he ever purchased support by the promise of an office, or by any other engagement savoring of dishonor.

THE DUEL BETWEEN HAMILTON AND BURR.

FROM LIFE OF AARON BURR.

FEW of the present generation have stood upon the spot, which was formerly one of the places that strangers were sure to visit on coming to the city, and which the events of this day rendered for ever memorable. Two miles and a half above the city of Hoboken, the heights of Weehawken rise, in the picturesque form so familiar to New Yorkers, to an elevation of a hundred and fifty feet above the Hudson. These heights are rocky, very steep, and covered with small trees and tangled bushes. Under the heights, at a point half a mile from where they begin, there is, twenty feet above the water, a grassy ledge or shelf, about six feet wide, and eleven paces long. This was the fatal spot. Except that it is slightly encumbered with underbrush, it is, at this hour, precisely what it was on the 11th of July, 1804. There is an old cedar-tree at the side, a little out of range, which must have looked then very much as it does now. The large rocks which partly hem in the place are, of course, unchanged, except that they are decorated with the initials of former visitors. One large rock, breast-high, narrows the hollow in which Hamilton stood to four feet or less.

Inaccessible to foot-passengers along the river, except at low tide, with no path down to it from the rocky heights above, no residence within sight on that side of the river, unless at a great distance, it is even now a singularly secluded scene. But fifty years ago, when no prophet had yet predicted Hoboken, that romantic shore was a nearly unbroken solitude. A third of a mile below the dueling-ground there stood a little tavern, the occasional resort of excursionists; where, too, dueling parties not unfrequently breakfasted before proceeding to the ground, and where they sometimes returned to invigorate their restored friendship with the landlord's wine. A short distance above the ground, lived a fine-hearted old Captain, who, if he got scent of a duel, would rush to the place, throw himself between the combatants, and never give over persuading and threatening till he had established a peace or a truce between them. He was the owner of the ground, and spoke with authority. He never ceased to think that, if on this fatal morning, he had observed the approach of the boats, he could have prevented the subsequent catastrophe.

But, for the very purpose of preventing suspicion, it had been arranged that Colonel Burr's boat should arrive some time before the other. About half-past six, Burr and Van Ness landed, and leaving their boat a few yards down the river, ascended over the rocks to the appointed place. It was a warm, bright, July morning. The sun looks down, directly after rising, upon the Weehawken heights, and it was for that reason that the two men removed their coats before the arrival of the other party. There they stood carelessly breaking away the branches of the underwood, and looking out upon as fair, as various, as animated, as beautiful a scene, as mortal eyes in this beautiful world ever behold. The haze-crowned city; the bright, broad, flashing, tranquil river; the long reach of waters, twelve miles or more, down to the Narrows; the vessels at anchor in the harbor; misty, blue Staten Island, swelling up in superb contour from the lower bay; the verdant flowery heights around; the opposite shore of the river, then dark with forest, or bright with sloping lawn; and, to complete the picture, that remarkably picturesque promontory called Castle Point, that bends out far into the stream, a mile below Weehawken, and adds a peculiar beauty to the foreground;—all these combine to form a view, one glance at which *ought* to have sent shame and horror to the duelist's heart, that so much as the thought of closing a human being's eyes for ever on so much loveliness, had ever lived a moment in his bosom.

Hamilton's boat was seen to approach. A few minutes before seven it touched the rocks, and Hamilton and his second ascended. The principals and seconds exchanged the usual salutations, and the seconds proceeded immediately to make the usual preparations. They measured ten full paces; then cast lots for the choice of position, and to decide who should give the word. The lot, in both cases, fell to General Hamilton's second, who chose the *upper* end of the ledge for his principal, which, at that hour of the day, could not have been the best, for the reason that the morning sun, and the flashing of the river, would both interfere with the sight. The pistols were then loaded, and the principals placed, Hamilton looking over the river toward the city, and Burr turned toward the heights, under which they stood. As Pendleton gave Hamilton his pistol, he asked,

"Will you have the hair-spring set?"

"*Not this time*," was the quiet reply.

Pendleton then explained to both principals the rules which had been agreed upon with regard to the firing; after the word *present*, they were to fire as soon as they pleased. The seconds then withdrew to the usual distance.

"Are you ready?" said Pendleton.

Both answered in the affirmative. A moment's pause ensued. The word was given. Burr raised his pistol, took aim, and fired. Hamilton sprang upon his toes with a convulsive movement, reeled a little toward the heights, at which moment he involuntarily discharged his pistol, and then fell forward headlong upon his face, and remained motionless on the ground. His ball rustled among the branches, seven feet above the head of his antagonist, and four feet wide of him. Burr heard it, looked up, and saw where it had severed a twig. Looking at Hamilton, he beheld him falling, and sprang toward him with an expression of pain upon his face. But at the report of the pistols, Dr. Hosack, Mr. Davis, and the boatman, hurried anxiously up the rocks to the scene of the duel; and Van Ness, with presence of mind, seized Burr, shielded him from observation with an umbrella, and urged him down the steep to the boat

DONALD G. MITCHELL.

[Born 1822.]

Donald G. Mitchell was born in Norwich, Conn., April, 1822. His father was pastor of the Congregational Church, and his grandfather was a member of the first Congress, and Chief Justice of the Supreme Court of Conn., for many years.

Mr. Mitchell graduated at Yale in 1841. His health being feeble, he passed three years in the country, occasionally exercising his pen on agriculture, and writing letters to the Albany Cultivator. He next spent a year and a half abroad, visiting the Isle of Jersey, rambling through England on foot, visiting every county, and travelling over the Continent, writing letters on the agriculture of the countries he visited, to the Albany Cultivator. On his return, he commenced the study of law in New York; and soon after published the results of his tour in Fresh Gleanings; or a new sheaf from the Old Fields of Continental Europe, by Ik. Marvel; a pleasant volume of scholarly and leisurely observation of the principal places and sights of Europe; it attracted about the usual attention of volumes of travel.

His health again becoming feeble, he returned to Europe, and spent some of the eventful months of 1848 in Paris, and among the vineyards of France. He published on his return, in 1850, the Battle Summer, being Transcriptions from Personal Observations in Paris during the year 1848, by Ik. Marvel. This was not very successful, the style being too similar to that of Carlyle in his descriptions of the French Revolution.

His next publication was The Lorgnette, or Studies of the Town, by an Opera-goer; a periodical similar to Irving and Paulding's Salmagundi, containing essays and satires of the topics and fashions of the day by a Looker-on. It appeared anonymously and attracted for a time considerable attention among fashionable circles; it was written in a quiet, pure style, and contains some of his best passages.

During the progress of the Lorgnette, he published The Reveries of a Bachelor, a Book of the Heart, 12mo., 1850. A contemplative view of life from the slippered ease of the chimney-corner. A slight story runs through the volume, containing some pathetic scenes tenderly narrated. It was at once a decided and brilliant success, many thousand copies have been sold, and it is still in active demand; it was published in 12mo., and afterwards in an elegantly illustrated 8vo. edition by Darley, also in 16mo. It is one of the choicest specimens of half romance and half essay of a true man and a scholar; his eloquence, which gushes forth at times in a flood, could only issue from the depth of a large heart; its illustrations are such as he alone who has become thoroughly imbued with the best of the world's literature could supply. True feeling, refinement, purity, and elegance of style are the prominent characteristics of this delightful and admirably-executed volume.

This same vein was followed up the next year in, Dream Life, a Fable of the Seasons. Whether the author had exhausted his freshness, or the subject had lost some of its novelty, this volume was not as successful as the Reveries, though it had abundant success for an author less popular. It still mantains its popularity.

In 1853, Mr. Mitchell was appointed U. S. Consul at Venice. He remained there but a short time; while abroad, he gathered together materials for a History of Venice, which he has never published, if written. He travelled in Europe, and returned in 1855.

He next published, Fudge Doings; being Tony Fudge's Record of the Same; a connected series of sketches of city fashionable life, in the vein of the Lorgnette, originally published in the Knickerbocker Magazine. A rambling, though entertaining story, which will hardly add to his reputation either as a thinker or writer.

Mr. Mitchell purchased a farm in the vicinity of New Haven on which he resides. He has since devoted his time to the improvement of the place, writing articles for Harper's Magazine and the Atlantic, practicing his profession of Rural Architect and laying out grounds, and, in 1869, became editor of The Hearth and the Home, a weekly periodical of Agriculture and Domestic matters.

My Farm of Edgewood, appeared in 1863, and its sequel, Wet Days at Edgewood in 1864. The first a very pleasant description of the adventures of a gentleman in search of a farm, its acquisition, and subsequent improvement; the latter rather uninteresting sketches of the literature and past history of amateur farming and agriculture.

He has varied his agricultural pursuits by the publication of Seven Stories, with Basement and Attic; and, Doctor Johns, a novel. 2 vols., 12mo., reprinted from the Atlantic, where as a serial story, it excited considerable attention.

HAPPY AT LAST.

FROM REVERIES OF A BACHELOR.

SHE does not mistake my feelings, surely :—ah, no,—trust a woman for that! But what have I, or what am I, to ask a return? She is pure, and gentle as an angel; and I—alas—only a poor soldier in our world-fight against the Devil! Sometimes in moods of vanity, I call up what I fondly reckon my excellencies or deserts—a sorry, pitiful array, that makes me shamefaced when I meet her. And in an instant, I banish them all. And I think, that if I were called upon in some high court of justice, to say why I should claim her indulgence, or her love—I would say nothing of my sturdy effort to beat down the roughnesses of toil —nothing of such manliness as wears a calm front amid the frowns of the world,—nothing of little triumphs, in the every-day fight of life; but only, I would enter the simple plea—this heart is hers!

She leaves; and I have said nothing of what was seething within me ;—how I curse my folly! She is gone, and never perhaps will return. I recal in despair her last kind glance. The world seems blank to me. She does not know; perhaps she does not care, if I love her.—Well, I will bear it,—I say. But I cannot bear it. Business is broken; books are blurred; something remains undone, that fate declares must be done. Not a place can I find, but her sweet smile gives to it, either a tinge of gladness, or a black shade of desolation.

I sit down at my table with pleasant books; the fire is burning cheerfully; my dog looks up earnestly when I speak to him; but it will never do!

Her image sweeps away all these comforts in a flood. I fling down my book; I turn my back upon my dog; the fire hisses and sparkles in mockery of me.

Suddenly a thought flashes on my brain ;—I will write to her—I say. And a smile floats over my face,—a smile of hope, ending in doubt. I catch up my pen—my trusty pen; and the clean sheet lies before me. The paper could not be better, nor the pen. I have written hundreds of letters; it is easy to write letters. But now, it is not easy.

I begin, and cross it out. I begin again, and get on a little farther ;—then cross it out. I try again, but can write nothing. I fling down my pen in despair, and burn the sheet, and go to my

85

library for some old sour treatise of Shaftesbury, or Lyttleton; and say—talking to myself all the while; let her go !—She is beautiful, but I am strong; the world is short; we—I and my dog, and my books, and my pen, will battle it through bravely, and leave enough for a tomb-stone.

But even as I say it, the tears start ;—it is all false saying! And I throw Shaftesbury across the room, and take up my pen again. It glides on and on, as my hope glows, and I tell her of our first meeting, and of our hours in the ocean twilight, and of our unsteady stepping on the heaving deck, and of that parting in the noise of London, and of my joy at seeing her in the pleasant country, and of my grief afterward. And then I mention Bella,—her friend and mine—and the tears flow; and then I speak of our last meeting, and of my doubts, and of this very evening,—and how I could not write, and abandoned it,—and then felt something within me that made me write, and tell her————all !————"That my heart was not my own, but was wholly hers; and that if she would be mine,————I would cherish her, and love her always !"

Then, I feel a kind of happiness,—a strange, tumultuous happiness, into which doubt is creeping from time to time, bringing with it a cold shudder. I seal the letter, and carry it—a great weight—for the mail. It seems as if there could be no other letter that day; and as if all the coaches and horses, and cars, and boats were specially detailed to bear that single sheet. It is a great letter for me; my destiny lies in it.

I do not sleep well that night ;—it is a tossing sleep; one time joy—sweet and holy joy comes to my dreams, and an angel is by me ;—another time, the angel fades—the brightness fades, and I wake, struggling with fear. For many nights it is so, until the day comes, on which I am looking for a reply.

The postman has little suspicion that the letter which he gives me—although it contains no promissory notes, nor moneys, nor deeds, nor articles of trade—is yet to have a greater influence upon my life and upon my future, than all the letters he has ever brought to me before. But I do not show him this; nor do I let him see the clutch with which I grasp it. I bear it, as if it were a great and fearful burden, to my room. I lock the door, and having broken the seal with a quivering hand,—read :—

" Paul—for I think I may call you so now—I know not how to answer you. Your letter gave me great joy; but it gave me pain too. I cannot —will not doubt what you say : I believe that you love me better than I deserve to be loved; and I know that I am not worthy of all your kind praises. But it is not this that pains me; for I know that you have a generous heart, and would forgive, as you always have forgiven, any weakness of mine. I am proud too, very proud, to have won your love; but it pains me—more perhaps than you will believe—to think that I cannot write back to you, as I would wish to write ;—alas, never !"

Here I dash the letter upon the floor, and with my hand upon my forehead, sit gazing upon the glowing coals, and breathing quick and loud.— The dream then is broken !

Presently I read again :

————"You know that my father died, before we had ever met. He had an old friend, who had come from England; and who in early life had done him some great service, which made him seem like a brother. This old gentleman was my god-father, and called me daughter. When my father died, he drew me to his side, and said,— ' Carry, I shall leave you, but my old friend will be your father;' and he put my hand in his, and said—' I give you my daughter.'

" This old gentleman had a son, older than myself; but we were much together, and grew up as brother and sister. I was proud of him ; for he was tall and strong, and every one called him handsome. He was as kind too, as a brother could be; and his father was like my own father. Every one said, and believed, that we would one day be married ; and my mother, and my new father spoke of it openly. So did Laurence, for that is my friend's name.

" I do not need to tell you any more, Paul ; for when I was still a girl, we had promised, that we would one day be man and wife. Laurence has been much in England; and I believe he is there now. The old gentleman treats me still as a daughter, and talks of the time, when I shall come and live with him. The letters of Laurence are very kind; and though he does not talk so much of our marriage as he did, it is only, I think, because he regards it as so certain.

" I have wished to tell you all this before; but I have feared to tell you ; I am afraid I have been too selfish to tell you. And now what can I say ? Laurence seems most to me like a brother ;—and you, Paul————but I must not go on. For if I marry Laurence, as fate seems to have decided, I will try and love him, better than all the world.

" But will you not be a brother, and love me, as you once loved Bella ;—you say my eyes are like hers, and that my forehead is like hers ;—will you not believe that my heart is like hers too ?

" Paul, if you shed tears over this letter—I have shed them as well as you. I can write no more now.

"Adieu."

I sit long looking upon the blaze ; and when I rouse myself, it is to say wicked things against destiny. Again, all the future seems very blank. I cannot love Carry, as I loved Bella ; she cannot be a sister to me; she must be more, or nothing ! Again, I seem to float singly on the tide of life, and see all around me in cheerful groups. Everywhere the sun shines, except upon my own cold forehead. There seems no mercy in Heaven, and no goodness for me upon Earth.

I write after some days, an answer to the letter. But it is a bitter answer, in which I forget myself, in the whirl of my misfortunes—to the utterance of reproaches.

Her reply, which comes speedily, is sweet, and gentle. She is hurt by my reproaches, deeply hurt. But with a touching kindness, of which I am not worthy, she credits all my petulance to my wounded feeling ; she soothes me ; but in soothing, only wounds the more. I try to believe her, when she speaks of her unworthiness ;—but I cannot.

Business, and the pursuits of ambition or of interest, pass on like dull, grating machinery. Tasks are met, and performed with strength indeed, but with no cheer. Courage is high, as I meet the shocks, and trials of the world ; but it is a brute, careless courage, that glories in opposition. I laugh at any dangers, or any insiduous pitfalls ;—what are they to me ? What do I possess, which it will be hard to lose ? My dog keeps by me ; my toils are present ; my food is ready ; my limbs are strong ;————what need for more ?

The months slip by ; and the cloud that floated over my evening sun, passes.

Laurence wandering abroad, and writing to Caroline, as to a sister,—writes more than his father could have wished. He has met new faces, very sweet faces ; and one which shows through the ink of his later letters, very gorgeously. The old gentleman does not like to lose thus his little Carry ; and he writes back rebuke. But Laurence, with the letters of Caroline before him for data, throws himself upon his sister's kindness, and charity. It astonishes not a little the old gentleman, to find his daughter pleading in such strange way, for the son. "And what will you do then, my Carry ?"—the old man says.

————"Wear weeds, if you wish, sir ; and love you and Laurence more than ever !"

And he takes her to his bosom, and says— " Carry—Carry, you are too good for that wild fellow Laurence !"

Now, the letters are different ! Now they are full of hope—dawning all over the future sky. Business, and care, and toil, glide, as if a spirit animated them all ; it is no longer cold machine work, but intelligent, and hopeful activity. The sky hangs upon you lovingly, and the birds make music, that startles you with its fineness. Men wear cheerful faces ; the storms have a kind pity, gleaming through all their wrath.

The days approach, when you can call her yours. For she has said it, and her mother has said it ; and the kind old gentleman, who says he will still be her father, has said it too; and they have all welcomed you—won by her story—with a cordiality, that has made your cup full, to running over. Only one thought comes up to obscure your joy;—is it real? or if real, are you worthy to enjoy? Will you cherish and love always, as you have promised, that angel who accepts your word, and rests her happiness on your faith? Are there not harsh qualities in your nature, which you fear may sometime make her regret that she gave herself to your love and charity? And those friends who watch over her, as the apple of their eye, can you always meet their tenderness and approval, for your guardianship of their treasure? Is it not a treasure that makes you fearful, as well as joyful?

But you forget this in her smile: her kindness, her goodness, her modesty, will not let you remember it. She *forbids* such thoughts; and you yield such obedience, as you never yielded even to the commands of a mother. And if your business, and your labor slip by, partially neglected—what matters it? What is interest, or what is reputation, compared with that fullness of your heart, which is now ripe with joy?

The day for your marriage comes; and you live as if you were in a dream. You think well, and hope well for all the world. A flood of charity seems to radiate from all around you. And as you sit beside her in the twilight, on the evening before the day, when you will call her yours, and talk of the coming hopes, and of the soft shadows of the past; and whisper of Bella's love, and of that sweet sister's death, and of Laurence, a new brother, coming home joyful with his bride,—and lay your cheek to hers—life seems as if it were all day, and as if there could be no night!

The marriage passes; and she is yours,—yours forever.

LIGHTED WITH A COAL.
FROM THE SAME.

THAT first taste of the new smoke, and of the fragrant leaf is very grateful; it has a bloom about it, that you wish might last. It is like your first love,—fresh, genial, and rapturous. Like that, it fills up all the craving of your soul; and the light, blue wreaths of smoke, like the roseate clouds that hang over the morning of your heart life, cut you off from the chill atmosphere of mere worldly companionship, and make a gorgeous firmament for your fancy to riot in.

I do not speak now of those later, and manlier passions, into which judgment must be thrusting its cold tones, and when all the sweet tumult of your heart has mellowed into the sober ripeness of affection. But I mean that boyish burning, which belongs to every poor mortal's lifetime, and which bewilders him with the thought that he has reached the highest point of human joy, before he has tasted any of that bitterness, from which alone our highest human joys have sprung. I mean the time, when you cut initials with your jack-knife on the smooth bark of beech trees; and went moping under the long shadows at sunset; and thought Louise the prettiest name in the wide world; and picked flowers to leave at her door; and stole out at night to watch the light in her window; and read such novels as those about Helen Mar, or Charlotte, to give some adequate expression to your agonized feelings.

At such a stage, you are quite certain that you are deeply, and madly in love; you persist in the face of heaven, and earth. You would like to meet the individual who dared to doubt it.

You think she has got the tidiest, and jauntiest little figure that ever was seen. You think back upon some time when in your games of forfeit, you gained a kiss from those lips; and it seems as if the kiss was hanging on you yet, and warming you all over. And then again, it seems so strange that your lips did really touch hers! You half question if it could have been actually so,—and how you could have dared;—and you wonder if you would have courage to do the same thing again?—and upon second thought, are quite sure you would,—and snap your fingers at the thought of it.

What sweet little hats she does wear; and in the school room, when the hat is hung up—what curls —golden curls, worth a hundred Golcondas! How bravely you study the top lines of the spelling book —that your eyes may run over the edge of the cover, without the schoolmaster's notice, and feast upon her!

You half wish that somebody would run away with her, as they did with Amanda, in the Children of the Abbey;—and then you might ride up on a splendid black horse, and draw a pistol, or blunderbuss, and shoot the villains, and carry her back, all in tears, fainting, and languishing upon your shoulder;—and have her father (who is Judge of the County Court,) take your hand in both of his, and make some eloquent remarks. A great many such re-captures you run over in your mind, and think how delightful it would be to peril your life, either by flood, or fire—to cut off your arm, or your head, or any such trifle,—for your dear Louise.

You can hardly think of anything more joyous in life, than to live with her in some old castle, very far away from steamboats, and post-offices, and pick wild geraniums for her hair, and read poetry with her, under the shade of very dark ivy vines. And you would have such a charming boudoir in some corner of the old ruin, with a harp in it, and books bound in gilt, with cupids on the cover, and such a fairy couch, with the curtains hung—as you have seen them hung in some illustrated Arabian stories—upon a pair of carved doves!

SARA JANE LIPPINCOTT.

MRS. SARA JANE LIPPINCOTT, formerly Miss Clarke, better known by her nom-de-plume of Grace Greenwood, was born at Pompey, Onondaga Co., N. Y. While a school-girl she moved to Rochester and acquired most of her education there. Her father removed to New Brighton, Pa., in 1843.

Soon after her removal thither, she acquired a reputation as the author of some sprightly letters to Morris and Willis of the N. Y. Mirror, over the signature of Grace Greenwood. Some poetical effusions published under her real name, met with a favorable reception, and the identity of the authoress with the brilliant letter-writer could not long remain a secret. These were succeeded by various prose compositions, in the National Era at Washington, and in Godey's Lady's Book, which she edited for a year. She afterward, in October, 1853, at the time of her marriage, commenced the editorship of The Little Pilgrim, a periodical for youth, in which she first published most of her juvenile books.

Her first volume, Greenwood Leaves, was published in 1850, at Boston, and was a decided success. In 1851, she published her Poems, which attracted considerable attention, particularly Ariadne, The Horseback Ride, and Pygmalion. In this year, also appeared her first juvenile book, The History of my Pets, an admirable story-book, the precursor of many others. A second series of Greenwood Leaves was issued the following year; and also another juvenile work, called Recollections of my Childhood.

In the spring of 1852, she visited Europe, and spent fifteen months in England and on the Continent. Soon after her return, she published a record of her travels, entitled Haps and Mishaps of a Tour in Europe, including an enthusiastic account of numerous European friends of the author; but it was severely criticized in the London Athenæum. It reached an eighth edition.

Soon after her return from Europe, she was married to Leander K. Lippincott, who was the publisher of the Little Pilgrim, and for the next two years she busily assisted in the editing of it. In the fall of 1855, she published Merrie England, the first of a series of books of foreign travel, descriptions, tales, and historic sketches for children. In the spring of 1856, a volume entitled A Forest Tragedy, and other Tales, appeared; and in the fall of 1857, Stories and Legends of Travel and History, the second of the above series; followed by Stories from Famous Ballads; Bonnie Scotland; Records of Five Years; Stories of Many Lands; and, Stories and Sights of France and Italy.

Mrs. Lippincott's life has not been an idle one; she has kept her talent bright by use charming all her readers, both old and young, by her fine thoughts, expressed in a style of great ease, simplicity, and beauty. Her writings speak for themselves, and they have spoken widely: they are eminently characteristic; are strictly national; they are likewise decisively individual. Her prose writings are animated by a hearty spirit of out-of-door life and enjoyment, and a healthy, sprightly view of society. Her poems are the expressions of a prompt, generous nature; her Ariadne is worthy of Mrs. Norton.

THE BABY IN THE BATH-TUB.
FROM RECORDS OF FIVE YEARS.

"ANNIE! Sophie! come up quick, and see baby in her bath-tub!" cries a charming little maiden, running down the wide stairway of an old country house, and half-way up the long hall, all in a fluttering cloud of pink lawn, her soft dimpled cheeks tinged with the same lovely morning hue. In an instant there is a stir and gush of light laughter in the drawing-room, and presently, with a movement a little more majestic and elder-sisterly, Annie and Sophie float noiselessly through the hall and up the soft-carpeted ascent, as though borne on their respective clouds of blue and white drapery, and take their way to the nursery, where a novel entertainment awaits them. It is the first morning of the eldest married sister's first visit home, with her first baby; and the first baby, having slept late after its journey, is about to take its first bath in the old house.

"Well, I declare, if here isn't mother, forgetting her dairy, and Cousin Nellie, too, who must have left poor Ned all to himself in the garden, lonely and disconsolate, and I am torn from my books, and Sophie from her flowers, and all for the sake of seeing a nine-months-old baby kicking about in a bath-tub! What simpletons we are!"

Thus Miss Annie, the *proude ladye* of the family; handsome, haughty, with perilous proclivities toward grand socialistic theories, transcendentalism, and general strong-mindedness; pledged by many a saucy vow to a life of single dignity and freedom, given to studies artistic, æsthetic, philosophic, and ethical; a student of Plato, an absorber of Emerson, an exalter of her sex, a contemner of its natural enemies.

"Simpletons are we?" cries pretty Elinor Lee, aunt of the baby on the other side, and " Cousin Nellie" by love's courtesy, now kneeling close by the bath-tub, and receiving on her sunny braids a liberal baptism from the pure, plashing hands of babyhood,—" simpletons, indeed! Did I not once see thee, O Pallas-Athene, standing rapt before a copy of the ' Crouching Venus'? and this is a sight a thousand times more beautiful; for here we have color, action, radiant life, and such grace as the divinest sculptors of Greece were never able to entrance in marble. Just look at these white, dimpled shoulders, every dimple holding a tiny, sparkling drop,—these rosy, plashing feet and hands,—this laughing, roguish face,—these eyes, bright and blue and deep as lakes of fairy-land,—these ears, like dainty sea-shells,—these locks of gold, dripping diamonds,—and tell me what cherub of Titian, what Cupid of Greuze, was ever half so lovely. I say, too, that Raphael himself would have jumped at the chance of painting Louise, as she sits there, towel in hand, in all the serene pride and chastened dignity of young maternity,—of painting her as *Madonna.*"

"Why, Cousin Nellie is getting poetical for once, over a baby in a bath-tub!"

"Well, Sophie, isn't it a subject to inspire *real* poets, to call out and yet humble the genius of painters and sculptors? Isn't it an object for the reverence of ' a glorious human creature,'—such a pure and perfect form of physical life, such a starry little soul, fresh from the hands of God? If your Plato teaches otherwise, Cousin Annie, I'm glad I've no acquaintance with that distinguished heathen gentleman; if your Carlyle, with his ' soul above buttons' and babies, would growl, and your Emerson smile icily at the sight, away with them!"

"Why, Nellie, you goose, Carlyle is ' a man and a brother,' in spite of his ' Latter-Day Pamphlets,' and no ogre. I believe he is very well disposed toward babies in general; while Emerson is as tender as he is great. Have you forgotten his ' Threnody,' in which the sob of a mortal's sorrow rises and swells into an immortal's pean? I see that baby is very lovely; I think that Louise

may well be proud of her. It's a pity that she must grow up into conventionalities and all that. —perhaps become some man's plaything, or slave."

" O, *don't*, sister!—' sufficient for the day is the *worriment* thereof.' But I think you and Nellie are mistaken about the *pride*. I am conscious of no such feeling in regard to my little Florence, but only of joy, gratitude, infinite tenderness, and solicitude."

Thus the young mother,—for the first time speaking, but not turning her eyes from the bath-tub.

"Ah, coz, it won't go! Young mothers *are* the proudest of living creatures. The sweetest and saintliest among you have a sort of subdued exultation, a meek assumption, an adorable insolence, toward the whole unmarried and childless world. I have never seen anything like it elsewhere."

"*I* have, in a bantam Biddy, parading her first brood in the hen-yard, or a youthful duck, leading her first little downy flock to the water."

" Ha, blasphemer! are you there?" cries Miss Nellie, with a bright smile, and a brighter blush. Blasphemer's other name is a tolerably good one, —Edward Norton,—though he is oftenest called " our Ned." He is the sole male representative of a wealthy old New England family,—the pride and darling of four pretty sisters, " the only son of his mother, and she a widow," who adores him,— " a likely youth, just twenty-one," handsome, brilliant and standing six feet high in his stockings. Yet, in spite of all these unfavorable circumstances, he is a very good sort of a fellow. He is just home from the model college of the Commonwealth, where he learned to smoke, and, I blush to say, has a cigar in hand at this moment, just as he has been summoned from the garden by his pet sister, Kate, half wild with delight and excitement. With him comes a brother according to the law, and after the spirit,—a young, slender, fair-haired man, but with an indescribable something of paternal importance about him. He is the other proprietor of baby, and steps forward with a laugh and a " Heh, my little water-nymph, my Iris!" and, by the bath-tub kneeling, catches a moist kiss from smiling baby lips, and a sudden wilting shower on shirt-front and collar, from moister baby hands.

Young collegian pauses on the threshold, essaying the look lofty and sarcastic, for a moment. Then his eye rests on Nellie Lee's blushing face, on the red, smiling lips, the braids of gold, sprinkled with shining drops,—meets those sweet, shy eyes, and a sudden, mysterious feeling, soft and vague and tender, floods his gay, young heart. He looks at baby again. " 'Tis a pretty sight, upon my word! Let me throw away my cigar before I come nearer: it is incense too profane for such pure rites. Now give me a peep at Dian-the-less! How the little witch revels in the water! A small Undine. Jolly, isn't it, baby? Why, Louise, I did not know that Floy was so lovely, such a perfect little creature. How fair she is! Why, her flesh, where it is not rosy, is of the pure, translucent whiteness of a water-lily."

No response to this tribute, for baby has been in the water more than long enough, and must be taken out. willy, nilly. Decidedly nilly it proves; baby proceeds to demonstrate that she is not altogether cherubic, by kicking and screaming lustily, and striking out frantically with her little dripping hands. But Madonna wraps her in soft linen, rolls her and pats her, till she grows good and merry again, and laughs through her pretty tears.

But the brief storm has been enough to clear the nursery of all save grandmama and Auntie Kate, who draw nearer to witness the process of drying and dressing. Tenderly mother rubs the dainty, soft skin, till every dimple gives up its last hidden droplet; then, with many a kiss, and smile, and coo, she robes the little form in fairy-like garments of cambric, lace, flannel, soft as a moth's wing, and delicate embroidery. The small, restless feet are caught, and encased in comical little hose, and shod with Titania's own slippers. Then the light golden locks are brushed and twined into tendril-like curls, and lo! the beautiful labôr of love is finished. Baby is bathed and dressed for the day.

"Well, she *is* a beauty! I don't wonder you and Charles are proud of her. O, Louise, if your father could have seen her! She is very like our first baby, the one we lost, at nearly—yes, just about her age." Here grandmama goes out, tearful, having sped unconscious her Parthian shaft; while, with a quick sob, which is neither for the father long dead, nor the sister never known, the young mother clasps her treasure closer, and murmurs, " O, my darling, my love, my sweetest, sweetest one! stay with me always, always! O, I would that I could guard and shield you from every pain, every grief,—make your sweet life all beauty, love, and joy !"

Baby hardly understands this burst of sensibility, but the passionate embrace reminds her of something. She asks and receives. Like a bee on a lily-flower, she clings to the fair, sweet breast, murmuring contentedly now and then. Presently, the gurgling draughts grow less eager, the little hands cease to wander restlessly over the smooth, unmantled neck. The little head is thrown back, the blue eyes look with a satisfied smile into the brooding mother-face.

Next, her lips all moist with the white nectar, baby is given, with many an anxious injunction, into the eager arms of Auntie Kate, who, followed by a supernumerary nurse, bears her in triumph down hall and stairway, and out into a garden, all glorious and odorous with a thousand roses.

Here, on a shawl, gay-colored and soft, spread on the grass, under an acacia-tree, the little Queen of Hearts is deposited at last. Here she rolls and tumbles, and sends out shrill, sweet peals of laughter, as auntie and nurse pelt her with rose-buds and clover-tufts. Sometimes an adventurous spirit seizes her; she creeps energetically beyond shawl-bounds, her little province of Cashmere, makes a raid into the tall, inviting grass, clutches ruthlessly at buttercups, breaks into nunneries of pale pansies, and decapitates whole families of daisies at a grasp. Sometimes, tired of predatory incursions, she lies on her back, and listens in a luxurious, lazy ecstasy to the gush of the fountain and the song of the robin, or watches the golden butterflies, coming from and going to nobody knows where, as though they had suddenly bloomed out of the sunshine, and died away into it again.

Away down the garden, in the woodbine arbor, by the little brook, sit the young collegian and fair Nellie Lee, talking very low, but very earnestly, on a subject vastly interesting to them, doubtless, for they seem to have quite forgotten baby. Yet her presence in the garden hallows the very air for them, gives a new joy and beauty to life, new sweetness to love.

The golden summer morning wears on. Papa is away with his fishing-rod; mamma sits at a window overlooking the garden, embroidering a dainty little robe, and under her cunning fingers the love of her heart and a thousand tender thoughts grow slowly into delicate white shapes of leaf and flower; grandmama is about her household duties, the tears of sad memory wiped from her eyes, and the light of the Christian's calm hope relit therein; Annie is in the library with Plato, but unusual softness lurks about her mouth, and she looks off her book now and then, and throws about her a strange, wandering glance, dreamy and tender to sadness; her sisters are in the drawing-room at their music, gay as birds; the lovers are we know where; and baby is still under the acacia-tree. But the white lids are beginning to droop a little heavily over the sweet blue eyes, and she will soon drop away into baby dream-land.

All nature blooms, and shines, and sounds gently and lovingly, to humor her delicate senses; human love the richest and tenderest is round about her, within reach of her imperious little voice. God breathes himself into her little-heart through all things,—love, light, food, sunshine, fragrance, and soft airs. All is well within and without the child, as all should be for all children under the sun, for every sinless, helpless little immortal, the like of whom Christ the Lord took into his tender arms and blessed. But how is it, dainty baby Floy, with thousands of thy brothers and sisters, as lovely and innocent as thou? Are there not such, to whom human love and care is denied, to whom nature seems unkind, of whom God seems forgetful, for whom even Christ's blessing is made of no avail?

FRANCIS PARKMAN.

[Born 1823.]

FRANCIS PARKMAN, the son of an esteemed clergyman of the same name, was born in Boston, Sept. 16, 1823. He graduated at Harvard, in 1844, and two years later travelled upon the western prairies, with a view of studying the manners and characters of the Indians. The results of his trip he published in the Knickerbocker Magazine, under the title of The Oregon Trail, and afterwards in a volume, The California and Oregon Trail, being Sketches of Prairie and Rocky Mountain Life. A volume instinct with the spirit of the wild life which it described, written with much vivacity and good taste, conveying much accurate information of the character of the country between the Mississippi and the Pacific, and investing truth with all the attractiveness of fiction.

Familiar with Indian life and its scenes, when he turned his attention to historical composition, he naturally chose a subject in keeping. He published, in 1851, the History of the Conspiracy of Pontiac and the War of the North American Tribes against the English Colonies after the Conquest of Canada, one volume, 8vo., London edition, 2 vols., 8vo. This has passed through several editions here and in England. Prepared under great difficulties, as the author had to read and write by the eyes and the hands of another, it is an uncommonly meritorious work, and one of the best written histories that has been produced in this country. In the form of authentic and detailed record, it gives a most complete and accurate picture of Indian character and life, and of Indian warfare such as it was a century ago, written with much spirit and picturesque effect.

His next publication was of a different character, a story of the present day, presenting pictures of life on both sides of the Atlantic, entitled Vassall Morton, published in 1856. The hero is arrested by the Austrian police, on suspicion of being concerned in revolutionary plots; and his escape from prison and perilous journey on foot to an Italian seaport, form one of the most thrilling passages in the book.

He resumed the historical pen in 1865, by the publication of the first of a series of Historical Narratives, on France and England in North America; I. The Huguenots in Florida, II. Samuel de Champlain. The second volume of the series, The Jesuits in North America in the Seventeenth Century, was issued in 1867. Both of these volumes, candid and impartial, with an insight into character unclouded by any mists of prejudice, were received with great favor and increasing popularity, and have passed through several editions.

He also prefixed an Introduction to Bouquet's Expedition against the Ohio Indians in 1764, published in the Ohio Valley Historical Series of Reprints, Cincinnati, 1868.

In 1869, he published the third volume of his Historical Narratives, The Discovery of the Great West, 1 vol., 8vo. The discovery of the valleys of the Mississippi and the Lakes is a portion of our history hitherto very obscure.

LA ROCHE'S COLONY.

FROM PIONEERS OF FRANCE IN THE NEW WORLD.

YEARS rolled on. France, long tossed among the surges of civil commotion, plunged at last into a gulf of fratricidal war. Blazing hamlets, sacked cities, fields steaming with slaughter, profaned altars, ravished maidens, a carnival of steel and fire, marked the track of the tornado. There was little room for schemes of foreign enterprise. Yet, far aloof from siege and battle, the fishermen of the western ports still plied their craft on the Banks of Newfoundland. Humanity, morality, decency, might be forgotten, but cod-fish must still be had for the use of the faithful on Lent and fast days. Still the wandering Esquimaux saw the Norman and Breton sails hovering around some lonely headland, or anchored in fleets in the harbor of St. John; and still, through salt spray and driving mist, the fisherman dragged up the riches of the sea.

In 1578, there were a hundred and fifty French

fishing-vessels at Newfoundland, besides two hundred of other nations, Spanish, Portuguese, and English. Added to these were twenty or thirty Biscayan whalers. In 1607, there was an old French fisherman at Canseau who had voyaged to these seas for forty-two successive years.

But if the wilderness of ocean had its treasures, so, too, had the wilderness of woods. It needed but a few knives, beads, and trinkets, and the Indians would throng to the shore burdened with the spoils of their winter hunting. Fishermen threw up their old vocation for the more lucrative trade in bear-skins and beaver-skins. They built rude huts along the shores of Anticosti, where, at that day, the bison, it is said, could be seen wallowing in the sands. They outraged the Indians; they quarrelled with each other; and this infancy of the Canadian fur-trade showed rich promise of the disorders which marked its riper growth. Others, meanwhile, were ranging the gulf in search of walrus-tusks; and, the year after the battle of Ivry, St. Malo sent out a fleet of small craft in quest of this new prize.

In all the western seaports, merchants and adventurers turned their eyes towards America; not, like the Spaniards, seeking treasures of silver and gold, but the more modest gains of codfish and train-oil, beaver-skins and marine ivory. St. Malo was conspicuous above them all. The rugged Bretons loved the perils of the sea, and saw with a jealous eye every attempt to shackle their activity on this its favorite field. When two nephews of Cartier, urging the great services of their uncle, gained a monopoly of the American fur-trade for twelve years, such a clamor arose within the walls of St. Malo, that the obnoxious grant was promptly revoked.

But soon a power was in the field against which all St. Malo might clamor in vain. A Catholic nobleman of Brittany, the Marquis de la Roche, bargained with the King to colonize New France. On his part, he was to receive a monopoly of the trade, and a profusion of worthless titles and empty privileges. He was declared Lieutenant-General of Canada, Hochelaga, Newfoundland, Labrador, and the countries adjacent, with sovereign power within his vast and ill-defined domain. He could levy troops, declare war and peace, make laws, punish or pardon at will, build cities, forts, and castles, and grant out lands in fiefs, seigniories, counties, viscounties, and baronies. Thus was effete and cumbrous feudalism to make a lodgment in the New World. It was a scheme of high-sounding promise, but, in performance, less than contemptible. La Roche ransacked the prisons, and, gathering thence a gang of thieves and desperadoes, embarked them in a small vessel, and set sail to plant Christianity and civilization in the West. Suns rose and set, and the wretched bark, deep freighted with brutality and vice, held on her course. She was so small, that the convicts, leaning over her side, could wash their hands in the water. At length, on the gray horizon they described a long, gray line of ridgy sand. It was Sable Island, off the coast of Nova Scotia. A wreck lay stranded on the beach, and the surges broke ominously over the long, submerged arms of sand, stretched far out into the sea on the right hand and on the left.

Here La Roche landed the convicts, forty in number, while, with his more trusty followers, he sailed to explore the neighboring coasts and choose a site for the capital of his new dominion. Thither, in due time, he proposed to remove the prisoners. But suddenly a tempest from the west assailed him. The frail vessel was at its mercy. She must run before the gale, which, howling on her track, drove her off the coast, and chased her back towards France.

Meanwhile the convicts watched in suspense for the returning sail. Days passed, weeks passed, and still they strained their eyes in vain across the waste of ocean. La Roche had left them to their fate. Rueful and desperate, they wandered among the sand-hills, through the stunted whortle-berry-bushes, the rank sand-grass, and the tangled cranberry-vines which filled the hollows. Not a tree was to be seen; but they built huts of the fragments of the wreck. For food, they caught fish in the surrounding sea, and hunted the cattle which ran wild about the island, sprung, perhaps, from those left here eighty years before by the Baron de Lery. They killed seals, trapped black foxes, and clothed themselves in their skins. Their native instincts clung to them in their exile. As if not content with their inevitable miseries, they quarrelled and murdered each other. Season after season dragged on. Five years elapsed, and, of the forty, only twelve were left alive. Sand, sea, and sky,—there was little else around them; though, to break the dead monotony, the walrus would sometimes rear his half human face and glistening sides on the reefs and sand-bars. At length, on the far verge of the watery desert, they descried a rising sail. She stood on towards the island; a boat's crew landed on the beach, and the excited exiles were once more among their countrymen.

When La Roche returned to France, the fate of his followers lay heavy on his mind. But the day of his prosperity was gone forever. A host of enemies rose against him and his privileges. The Duke de Mercœur, who still made head against the crown, and claimed sovereign power in Brittany, seized him and threw him into prison. In time, however, he gained a hearing of the King, and the Norman pilot Chedotel was despatched to bring the outcasts home. When they arrived in France, Henry the Fourth summoned them into his presence. They stood before him, says an old writer, like river-gods of yore; for, from head to foot they were clothed in shaggy skins, and beards of prodigious length hung from their swarthy faces. They had accumulated, on their island, a quantity of valuable furs. Of these Chedotel had robbed them; but the pilot was forced to disgorge his prey, and, with the aid of a bounty from the King, they were enabled to embark on their own account in the Canadian trade. To their leader, fortune was less kind. Broken by disaster and imprisonment, La Roche died miserably.

GEORGE WILLIAM CURTIS.

[Born 1824.]

GEORGE WILLIAM CURTIS, the brilliant and fascinating writer, and graceful and eloquent orator, was born in Providence, R. I., in 1824. He went to school at six years of age, in Boston, and remained until he was eleven. He returned to Providence, and at the age of fifteen went to New York, his father at that time, removing his family thither. Here he spent a year in a mercantile house, then studied for two years, and at eighteen, joined the Brook Farm Association at West Roxbury, Mass., a pleasant pastoral episode in his life of a year and a half. In reference to which experience, Hawthorne in the preface to Blithedale Romance, calls upon him to become the historian of the settlement—"Even the brilliant Howadji might find as rich a theme in his youthful reminiscences of Brook Farm, and a more novel one,—close at hand as it lies,—than those which he has since made so distant a pilgrimage to seek, in Syria and along the current of the Nile."

He spent the next winter in New York, but being still enamored of the country, he went to Concord, Mass., and lived in a farmer's family, roughing it as a farmer's boy, but enjoying the intellectual society of Emerson, Hawthorne, Thoreau, Channing, and other kindred spirits, of whom Emerson endeavored to form a club, but which the individual peculiarities of its philosophic members prevented from being continued. For an account of this, see Curtis' article in "Homes of American Authors." In this volume, published in 1853, Mr. Curtis wrote the articles on Emerson, Hawthorne, Longfellow, and Bancroft. Here he remained, strengthening his body, and perfecting his mind in various literary accomplishments for two years.

In August, 1846, Mr. Curtis sailed for Europe, landing at Marseilles, visiting the southern coast of Europe, Genoa, Leghorn, and Florence, passing the winter in Rome, with Crawford, Hicks, Kensett, Cranch, Terry, Freeman, and other artists resident there. In the spring, he travelled through southern Italy, and Venice. At Milan, he met Mr. Geo. S. Hillard, and the

Rev. Frederick H. Hedge, author of The Prose Writers of Germany, and travelled with them into Germany. He studied at Berlin, and matriculated at the University in 1848, travelling through Germany, making the tour of the Danube into Hungary, passed the winter in Paris, the summer in Switzerland, then crossed into Italy, and returned home by way of Naples, Sicily, Malta, and the east, arriving in America in the summer of 1850.

In the autumn of that year, he prepared Nile Notes of a Howadji, much of which was written as it stands, on the Nile. It was published the following spring in New York and London, and at once met with success, and is still in popular demand. In this brilliant volume of Eastern travels, the genius of the youthful author, was first revealed to the public. Written in a style which combines the voluptuous softness of an Oriental atmosphere with the sunny splendors of the tropics, he takes the reader with him into rare and beautiful scenes of nature, unfolds the mysteries of Arabian life, and reproduces the strange incidents of a unique tour in language of wonderful vividness and force.

Connecting himself with the Tribune during the winter, he spent the summer in a fashionable tour of the watering places, writing letters to the Tribune, which were afterward published in 1852, with a few illustrations under the title of Lotus-Eating, a summer book. Humor, pathos, and sentiment are generally blended in its pages, its reflections are always suggestive, its brilliant word-painting is relieved by an under-current of genuine feeling, and its fresh and glowing descriptions give a new charm to familiar objects.

In the same year, he issued The Howadji in Syria, which he had written the previous autumn and winter at Providence. It abounds in picturesque descriptions of the marvels of the Holy Land, throwing fresh light on ancient localities, and imbued with the spirit of sympathy and reverence for the sacred scenes which it calls forth from the dim oblivion of the past.

Returning to New York in the autumn of 1852, he became one of the original editors of Putnam's Magazine, contributing much to its success by the publication of a series of brilliant sketches of fashionable society, which were afterwards published in a volume, in 1853, The Potiphar Papers, admirably illustrated by Hoppin. As graphic and telling descriptions of a peculiar phase of American society they are unexcelled ; they dissected the best society with fresh and sparkling wit, genial humor, and keen and truthful satire.

This was followed by Prue and I, sketches from Putnam, in which the characters, an old, simple-minded book-keeper and his amiable, common-sense wife, afford an opportunity for the author displaying the most genial humor that has graced similar essays since those of Elia. Dinner Time, My Chateaux en Espagne, and Sea from Shore, are delightful.

His next and last work was Trumps, a regular novel of fashionable society, which was well illustrated by Hoppin. The materials were drawn from the many colored exhibitions of fashionable and commercial life in New York, and they are wrought up into a cabinet of portraitures, which vividly reflect the familiar traits of the original ; the character-drawing is in admirable tone, salient and effective, without exaggeration, with scarcely a trace of the effort of composition, but completed with the most delicate effect of light and shade.

He has also contributed a number of papers to Putnam, a picturesque historical paper on Newport and some other papers, in Harper's Magazine, including tales of fashionable society by Smythe, Jr.

In 1853, Mr. Curtis entered the field as a lecturer, in which his graceful and finished style, pure taste, and fine fancy added to his graceful delivery, won him great success. In 1854, he delivered a poem before a literary society at Brown University, Providence. In 1856, he took an active part in the Fremont campaign, delivering many speeches with telling effect, from their argument and brilliant oratory. In August, he delivered an oration before the literary societies of Wesleyan University, on The Duty of the American Scholar to Politics and the Times. In 1856, Mr. Curtis ventured into business, joining a publishing house in New York, which failed in August, 1857, losing all he had invested. In November, 1856, Mr. Curtis married the daughter of Francis G. Shaw, of Boston. He has for years past edited Harper's periodicals with consummate ability. Mr. Curtis also wrote a memoir of, and edited Rural Essays by, A. J. Downing.

Mr. Curtis is a gentleman of exquisite poetic taste, refined but glowing in feeling and fancy, polished in his style, and altogether a most captivating writer. He is as thoroughly independent as he is able, in politics.

MY CHATEAUX.

FROM PRUE AND I.

I AM the owner of great estates. Many of them lie in the West ; but the greater part are in Spain. You may see my western possessions any evening at sunset when their spires and battlements flash against the horizon.

It gives me a feeling of pardonable importance, as a proprietor, that they are visible, to my eyes at least, from any part of the world in which I chance to be. In my long voyage around the Cape of Good Hope to India (the only voyage I ever made, when I was a boy and a supercargo), if I fell home-sick, or sank into a reverie of all the pleasant homes I had left behind, I had but to wait until sunset, and then looking toward the west, I beheld my clustering pinnacles and towers brightly burnished as if to salute and welcome me.

So, in the city, if I get vexed and wearied, and cannot find my wonted solace in sallying forth at dinner-time to contemplate the gay world of youth and beauty hurrying to the congress of fashion,—

or if I observe that years are deepening their tracks around the eyes of my wife, Prue, I go quietly up to the housetop, toward evening, and refresh myself with a distant prospect of my estates. It is as dear to me as that of Eton to the poet Gray ; and, if I sometimes wonder at such moments whether I shall find those realms as fair as they appear, I am suddenly reminded that the night air may be noxious, and descending, I enter the little parlor where Prue sits stitching, and surprise that precious woman by exclaiming with the poet's pensive enthusiasm ;

> "Thought would destroy their Paradise,
> No more ;—where ignorance is bliss,
>   'Tis folly to be wise."

Columbus, also, had possessions in the West, and as I read aloud the romantic story of his life, my voice quivers when I come to the point in which it is related that sweet odors of the land mingled with the sea-air, as the admiral's fleet approached the shores ; that tropical birds flew out and fluttered around the ships, glittering in the sun, the gorgeous promises of the new country; that boughs, perhaps with blossoms not all decayed, floated out to welcome the strange wood from which the craft were hollowed. Then I cannot restrain myself. I think of the gorgeous visions I have seen before I have even undertaken the journey to the West, and I cry aloud to Prue :

"What sun-bright birds, and gorgeous blossoms, and celestial odors will float out to us, my Prue, as we approach our western possessions!"

The placid Prue raises her eyes to mine with a reproof so delicate that it could not be trusted to words; and, after a moment, she resumes her knitting and I proceed.

These are my western estates, but my finest castles are in Spain. It is a country famously romantic, and my castles are all of perfect proportions, and appropriately set in the most picturesque situations. I have never been to Spain myself, but I have naturally conversed much with travellers to that country; although, I must allow, without deriving from them much substantial information about my property there. The wisest of them told me that there were more holders of real estate in Spain than in any other region he had ever heard of, and they are all great proprietors. Every one of them possesses a multitude of the stateliest castles. From conversation with them you easily gather that each one considers his own castles much the largest and in the loveliest positions. And, after I had heard this said, I verified it, by discovering that all my immediate neighbors in the city were great Spanish proprietors.

It is not easy for me to say how I know so much, as I certainly do, about my castles in Spain. The sun always shines upon them. They stand lofty and fair in a luminous, golden atmosphere, a little hazy and dreamy, perhaps, like the Indian summer, but in which no gales blow and there are no tempests. All the sublime mountains, and beautiful valleys, and soft landscape, that I have not yet seen, are to be found in the grounds. They command a noble view of the Alps; so fine, indeed, that I should be quite content with the prospect of them from the highest tower of my castle, and not care to go to Switzerland.

The neighboring ruins, too, are as picturesque as those of Italy, and my desire of standing in the Coliseum, and of seeing the shattered arches of the Aqueducts stretching along the Campagna and melting into the Alban Mount, is entirely quenched. The rich gloom of my orange groves is gilded by fruit as brilliant of complexion and exquisite of flavor as any that ever dark-eyed Sorrento girls, looking over the high plastered walls of southern Italy, hand to the youthful travellers, climbing on donkeys up the narrow lane beneath.

The Nile flows through my grounds. The Desert lies upon their edge, and Damascus stands in my garden. I am given to understand, also, that the Parthenon has been removed to my Spanish possessions. The Golden-Horn is my fish-preserve; my flocks of golden fleece are pastured on the plain of Marathon, and the honey of Hymettus is distilled from the flowers that grow in the vale of Enna—all in my Spanish domains.

From the windows of those castles look the beautiful women whom I have never seen, whose portraits the poets have painted. They wait for me there, and chiefly the fair-haired child, lost to my eyes so long ago, now bloomed into an impossible beauty. The lights that never shone, glance at evening in the vaulted halls, upon banquets that were never spread. The bands I have never collected, play all night long, and enchant the brilliant company, that was never assembled, into silence.

*   *   *   *   *   *

What then? Shall I betray a secret? I have already entertained this party in my humble little parlor at home; and Prue presided as serenely as Semiramis over her court. Have I not said that I defy time, and shall space hope to daunt me? I keep books by day, but by night books keep me. They leave me to dreams and reveries. Shall I confess, that sometimes when I have been sitting, reading to my Prue, Cymbeline, perhaps, or a Canterbury tale, I have seemed to see clearly before me the broad highway to my castles in Spain; and as she looked up from her work, and smiled in sympathy, I have even fancied that I was already there.

OUR BEST SOCIETY
FROM THE POTIPHAR PAPERS.

YET, after all, and despite the youths who are led out, and carried home, or who stumble through the "German," this is a sober matter. My friend told us we should see the "best society." But he is a prodigious wag. Who make this country? From whom is its character of unparalleled enterprise, heroism, and success derived? Who have given it its place in the respect and the fear of the world? Who, annually, recruit its energies, confirm its progress, and secure its triumph? Who are its characteristic children, the pith, the sinew, the bone, of its prosperity? Who found, and direct, and continue its manifold institutions of mercy and education? Who are, essentially, Americans? Indignant friend, these classes, whoever they may be, are the "best society," because they alone are the representatives of its character and cultivation. They are the "best society" of New York, of Boston, of Baltimore, of St. Louis, of New Orleans, whether they live upon six hundred or sixty thousand dollars a year—whether they inhabit princely houses in fashionable streets (which they often do), or not—whether their sons have graduated at Celarius's and the *Jardin Mabille*, or have never been out of their fathers' shops—whether they have "air" and "style," and are "so gentlemanly" and "so aristocratic," or not. Your shoemaker, your lawyer, your butcher, your clergymen—if they are simple and steady, and, whether rich or poor, are unseduced by the sirens of extravagance and ruinous display, help make up the "best society." For that mystic communion is not composed of the rich, but of the worthy ; and is " best " by its virtues, and not by its vices. When Johnson, Burke, Goldsmith, Garrick, Reynolds, and their friends, met at supper in Goldsmith's rooms, where was the " best society" in England ? When George the Fourth outraged humanity and decency in his treatment of Queen Caroline, who was the first scoundrel in Europe ?

Pause yet a moment, indignant friend. Whose habits and principles would ruin this country as rapidly as it has been made ? Who are enamored of a puerile imitation of foreign splendors ? Who strenuously endeavor to graft the questionable points of Parisian society upon our own ? Who pass a few years in Europe and return sceptical of republicanism and human improvement, longing and sighing for more sharply emphasized social distinctions ? Who squander, with profuse recklessness, the hard-earned fortunes of their sires ? Who diligently devote their time to nothing, foolishly and wrongly supposing that a young English nobleman has nothing to do ? Who, in fine, evince by their collective conduct, that they regard their Americanism as a misfortune, and are so the most deadly enemies of their country ? ·None but what our wag facetiously termed " the best society."

If the reader doubts, let him consider its practical results in any great emporiums of " best society." Marriage is there regarded as a luxury, too expensive for any but the sons of rich men, or fortunate young men. We once heard an eminent divine assert, and only half in sport, that the rate of living was advancing so incredibly, that weddings in his experience were perceptibly diminishing. The reasons might have been many and various. But we all acknowledge the fact. On the other hand, and about the same time, a lovely damsel (ah ! Clorinda !) whose father was not wealthy, who had no prospective means of support, who could do nothing but polka to perfection, who literally knew almost nothing, and who constantly shocked every fairly intelligent person by the glaring ignorance betrayed in her remarks, informed a fiend at one of the Saratoga balls, whither he had made haste to meet " the best society," that there were " not more than three good matches in society." *La Dame aux Camélias*, Marie Duplessis, was to our fancy a much more feminine, and admirable, and moral, and human person, than the adored Clorinda. And yet what she said was the legitimate result of the state of our fashionable society. It worships wealth, and the pomp which wealth can purchase, more than virtue, genius, or beauty. We may be told that it has always been so in every country, and that the fine society of all lands is as profuse and flashy as our own. We deny it, flatly. Neither English, nor French, nor Italian, nor German society, is so unspeakably barren as that which is technically called " society" here. In London, and Paris, and Vienna, and Rome, all the really eminent men and women help make up the mass of society. A party is not a mere ball, but it is a congress of the wit, beauty, and fame of the capital. It is worth while to dress, if you shall meet Macaulay, or Hallam, or

Guizot, or Thiers, or Landseer, or Delaroche— Mrs. Norton, the Misses Berry, Madame Recamier, and all the brilliant women and famous foreigners. But why should we desert the pleasant pages of those men, and the recorded gossip of those women, to be squeezed flat against a wall, while young Doughface pours oyster-gravy down our shirt-front, and Caroline Pettitoes wonders at " Mr. Dusseldorf's" industry ?

If intelligent people decline to go, you justly remark, it is their own fault. Yes, but if they stay away, it is very certainly their great gain. The elderly people are always neglected with us, and nothing surprises intelligent strangers more than the tyrannical supremacy of Young America. But we are not surprised at this neglect. How can we be, if we have our eyes open ? When Caroline Pettitoes retreats from the floor to the sofa, and instead of a " polker" figures at parties as a matron, do you suppose that " tough old Joes " like ourselves are going to desert the young Caroline upon the floor, for Madame Pettitoes upon the sofa ? If the pretty young Caroline, with youth, health, freshness, a fine, budding form, and wreathed in a semi-transparent haze of flounced and flowered gauze, is so vapid that we prefer to accost her with our eyes alone, and not with our tongues, is the same Caroline married into a Madame Pettitoes, and fanning herself upon a sofa— no longer particularly fresh, nor young, nor pretty, and no longer budding, but very fully blown— likely to be fascinating in conversation ? We cannot wonder that the whole connection of Pettitoes, when advanced to the matron state, is entirely neglected. Proper homage to age we can all pay at home, to our parents and grandparents. Proper respect for some persons is best preserved by avoiding their neighborhood.

ROMANCE OF THE DESERT.
FROM HOWADJI IN SYRIA.

THE simple landscape of the desert is the symbol of the Bedoueen's character ; and he has little knowledge of more than his eye beholds. In some of the interior provinces of China, there is no name for the ocean, and when, in the time of shekh Daheir, a party of Bedoueen came to Acre upon the sea, they asked what was that desert of water.

A Bedoueen, after a foray upon a caravan, discovered among his booty several bags of fine pearls. He thought them dourra, a kind of grain. But as they did not soften in boiling, he was about throwing them disdainfully away, when a Gaza trader offered him a red Tarboosh in exchange, which he delightedly accepted.

Without love of natural scenery, he listens forever to the fascinating romances of the poets : for beautiful expressions naturally clothe the simple and beautiful images he everywhere beholds. The palms, the fountains, the gazelles, the stars, and sun, and moon, the horse, and camel. these are the large illustration and suggestion of his poetry.

Sitting around the evening fire, and watching its flickering with moveless melancholy, his heart thrills at the prowess of El-Gundubah, although he shall never be a hero, and he rejoices when Kattalet-esh-Shugan says to Gundubah, "Come let us marry forthwith," although he shall never behold her beauty, nor tread the stately palaces.

He loves the moon which shows him the way over the desert that the sun would not let him take by day, and the moon looking into his eyes, sees her own melancholy there. In the pauses of the story by the fire, while the sympathetic spirits of the desert sigh in the rustling wind, he says to his fellow, "Also in all true poems there should be palm-trees and running water."

For him, in the lonely desert, the best genius of Arabia has carefully recorded upon parchment its romantic visions; for him Haroun El Rashid lived his romantic life; for him the angel spoke to Mohammed in the cave, and God received the Prophet into the seventh heaven.

Some early morning, a cry rings through the group of black square tents. He springs from his dreams of green gardens and flowing waters, and stands sternly against the hostile tribe which has surprised his own. The remorseless morning secretes in desert silence the clash of swords, the ring of musketry, the battle-cry. At sunset the black square tents are gone, the desolation of silence fills the air that was musical with the recited loves of Zul-Himmeh, and the light sand drifts in the evening wind over the corpse of a Bedoueen.

—So the grim genius of the desert touches every spot of romance and of life in you, as you traverse his realm and meditate his children. Yet warm and fascinating as is his breath, it does not warp your loyalty to your native West, and to the time in which you were born. Springing from your hard bed upon the desert, and with wild morning enthusiasm, pushing aside the door of your tent, and stepping out to stand among the stars, you hail the desert and hate the city, and, glancing toward the tent of the Armenian Khadra, you shout aloud to astonish Mac-Whirter,

"I will take some savage woman, she shall rear my dusky race."

But as the day draws forward, and you see the same forms and the same life that Abraham saw, and know that Joseph leading Mary into Egypt might pass you to-day, nor be aware of more than a single sunset since he passed before, then you feel that this germ, changeless at home, is only developed elsewhere, that the boundless desert freedom is only a resultless romance.

The sun sets and the camp is pitched. The shadows are grateful to your eye, as the dry air to your lungs.

But as you sit quietly in the tent-door, watching the Armenian camp and the camels, your cheek pales suddenly as you remember Abraham, and that "he sat in the tent-door in the heat of the day." Saving yourself, what of the scene is changed since then? The desert, the camels, the tents, the turbanned Arabs, they were what Abraham saw when "he lifted up his eyes, and looked, and lo! three men stood by him."

You are contemporary with the eldest history. Your companions are the dusky figures of vaguest tradition. The "long result of time" is not for you.

In that moment you have lost your birthright. You are Ishmael's brother. You have your morning's wish. A child of the desert, not for you are art, and poetry, and science, and the glowing roll of history shrivels away.

The dream passes as the day dies, and to the same stars which heard your morning shout of desert praise, you whisper as you close the tent-door at evening,

"Better fifty years of Europe, than a cycle of Cathay."

GONE TO PROTEST.
FROM TRUMPS.

THERE was an unnatural silence and order in the store of Boniface Newt, Son, & Co. The long linen covers were left upon the goods. The cases were closed. The boys lay listlessly and wonderingly about. The porter lay upon a bale reading a newspaper. There was a sombre regularity and repose, like that of a house in which a corpse lies, upon the morning of the funeral.

Boniface Newt sat in his office haggard and gray. His face, like his daughter Fanny's, had grown sharp, and almost fierce. The blinds were closed, and the room was darkened. His port-folio lay before him upon the desk, open. The paper was smooth and white, and the newly-mended pens lay carefully by the inkstand. But the merchant did not write. He had not written that day. His white, bony hand rested upon the port-folio, and the long fingers drummed upon it at intervals, while his eyes half-vacantly wandered out into the store and saw the long shrouds drawn over the goods. Occasionally a slight sigh of weariness escaped him. But he did not seem to care to distract his mind from its gloomy intentness; for the morning paper lay beside him unopened, although it was afternoon.

In the outer office the book-keeper was still at work. He looked from book to book, holding the leaves and letting them fall carefully—comparing, computing, writing in the huge volumes, and filing various papers away. Sometimes, while he yet held the leaves in his hands and the pen in his mouth, with the appearance of the utmost abstraction in his task, his eyes wandered in to the inner office, and dimly saw his employer sitting silent and listless at his desk. For many years he had been Boniface Newt's clerk; for many years he had been a still, faithful, hard-worked servant. He had two holidays, besides the Sundays—New Year's Day and the Fourth of July. The rest of the year he was in the office by nine in the morning, and did not leave before six at night. During the time he had been quietly writing in those great

red books he had married a wife and seen the roses
fade in her cheeks—he had had children grow up
around him—fill his evening home and his Sunday hours with light—marry, one after another,
until his home had become as it was before a
child was born to him, and then gradually grow
bright and musical again with the eyes and voices
of another generation. Glad to earn his little salary, which was only enough for decency of living,
free from envy and ambition, he was bound by a
kind of feudal tenure to his employer.

As he looked at the merchant and observed his
hopeless listlessness, he thought of his age, his
family, and of the frightful secrets hidden in the
huge books that were every night locked carefully
into the iron safe, as if they were written all over
with beautiful romances instead of terrible truths—
and the eyes of the patient plodder were so blurred
that he could not see, and turning his head that
no one might observe him, he winked until he
could see again.

A young man entered the store hastily. The
porter dropped the paper and sprang up; the boys
came expectantly forward. Even the book-keeper
stopped to watch the new-comer as he came rapidly toward the office. Only the head of the house
sat unconcernedly at his desk—his long, pale, bony
fingers drumming on the port-folio—his hard eyes
looking out at the messenger.

"This way," said the book-keeper, suddenly,
as he saw that he was going toward Mr. Newt's
room.

"I want Mr. Newt."

"Which one?"

"The young one, Mr. Abel Newt."

"He is not here."

"Where is he?"

"I don't know."

Before the book-keeper was aware the young
man had opened the door that communicated
with Mr. Newt's room. The haggard face under
the gray hair turned slowly toward the messenger.
There was something in the sitting figure that
made the youth lift his hand and remove his cap,
and say, in a low, respectful voice,

"Can you tell me, Sir, where to find Mr. Abel
Newt?"

The long, pale, bony fingers still listlessly
drummed. The hard eyes rested upon the ques-
tioner for a few moments; then, without any evidence of interest, the old man answered simply,
"No," and looked away as if he had forgotten the
stranger's presence.

"Here's a note for him from General Belch."

The gray head beckoned machanically toward
the other room, as if all business were to be transacted there; and the young man bowing again,
with a vague sense of awe, went in to the outer
office and handed the note to the book-keeper.

SARATOGA.
FROM LOTUS-EATING.

THE romance of a watering-place, like other romance, always seems past when you are there.

Here at Saratoga, when the last polka is polked,
and the last light in the ball-room is extinguished,
you saunter along the great piazza, with the "good
night" of Beauty yet trembling upon your lips,
and meet some old Habitué, or even a group of
them, smoking in lonely arm-chairs, and meditating the days departed.

The great court is dark and still. The waning
moon is rising beyond the trees, but does not yet
draw their shadows, moonlight-mosaics, upon the
lawn. There are no mysterious couples moving
in the garden, not a solitary foot-fall upon the
piazza. A few lanterns burn dimly about the
doors, and the light yet lingering in a lofty chamber reminds you that some form, whose grace this
evening has made memory a festival, is robing
itself for dreams.

*   *   *   *   *   *   *

And while the moon rides higher, and pales
from the yellow of her rising into a watery lustre,
you hear stories of blooming belles, who are
grandmothers now, and of brilliant beaux, bald
now and gouty. These midnight gossips are
very mournful. They will not suffer you to leave
those, whose farewells yet thrill your heart, in the
eternal morning of youth, but compel you to forecast their doom, to draw sad and strange outlines
upon the future—to paint pictures of age, wrink-
les, ochre-veined hands and mobcaps—until
your Saratoga episode of pleasure has sombred
into an Egyptian banquet, with your old, silently-
smoking, and meditative Habitué for the death's
head.

In fact, after a few such midnights, even the
morning sunshine cannot melt away this Egyptian
character from the old Habitués. As you cross
the court, after breakfast, to the bowling alley,
with a bevy so young and lovely, that age and
mobcaps seem only fantastic visions of dyspepsia,
and, of hearts that were never young, you will see
them sitting, a solemn reality of "black manhood,"
along the western piazza, leaning back in arm-
chairs, smoking perhaps, chatting of stocks possibly,—a little rounded in the shoulders, holding
canes which are no longer foppish switches, but
substantial and serious supports. They are the
sub-bass in the various-voiced song, the prosaic
notes to the pleasant lyric of Saratoga life.

They are not really thinking of stocks, nor are
they very conscious of the flavor of their cigars,
but they watch the scene as they would dream a
dream. As the sound of young voices pulses toward them on the morning air, as they watch the
flitting forms, the cool morning-dresses, the gush
of youth overflowing the sunny and shady paths
of the garden, they are old Habitués no longer;
they are those gentlemen, gallant and gay, dancing
in the warm light of bright eyes toward a future
gorgeous as a sunset, gossipping humorously or
seriously, according as the light of eyes is sunshine
or moonlight, and it is themselves as they were,
with their own parties, their own loves, jealousies
and scandals, moving briskly across the garden to
the bowling alley.

BAYARD TAYLOR.

[Born 1825.]

BAYARD TAYLOR, the eminent traveller, novelist, and poet, was born January 11th, 1825, in the village of Kennett Square, Chester County, Penna., of ancestors who formed part of the original emigration with Penn. Educated at the usual country schools, he became, at the age of seventeen, an apprentice in a printing office at the county borough of West Chester. His leisure time was spent in the acquisition of Latin and French, and writing occasional verses, which met with a favorable reception, as published in the New York Mirror, and Graham's Magazine, edited the one by Willis, and the other by Griswold. His success led him to collect his effusions, which were published in a volume entitled, Ximena and other Poems, in 1844. This gave him reputation sufficient to secure employment as a contributor to several leading newspapers, while on a tour of Europe he had projected. With the proceeds of his volume, one hundred dollars advanced by Chandler, of the U. S. Gazette, and Patterson, of the Saturday Evening Post, and forty dollars for some additional poems, he started on his first travels, continued at intervals, until he has visited every quarter of the globe, and become the greatest traveller, for his years, that has ever lived.

He spent two years in visiting England, Scotland, Germany, Switzerland, Italy, and France, at an expense of only five hundred dollars, travelling with a relative, and mostly on foot. On his return, in 1846, he reprinted his letters to the papers in "Views-a-foot, or Europe seen with Knapsack and Staff." The novelty of his mode of travelling, the youth of the narrator, and the unusual vigor and freshness of the style, with the quick perceptions of an intelligent American mind, combined to create an extraordinary demand for the volume, and established his reputation as a writer and a traveller.

He next edited a paper in Phœnixville, Pa., which proving unprofitable, he settled in New York in the latter part of 1847, as author, and wrote for the Literary World. In February, 1848, he became a permanent contributor to the Tribune, and shortly after published his Rhymes of Travel. In 1849, he became part proprietor, and one of the editors of the Tribune, and has been ever since connected with it. The same year he visited California, and returned by way of Mexico, reprinting his letters to the Tribune in Eldorado, a Path in the Track of Empire.

In the summer of 1851, he published his fifth volume, and third of poems, Book Romanees, Lyrics and Songs, and commenced a protracted Eastern tour. He arrived at Cairo in November by way of England, the Rhine, Vienna, and Trieste. Thence he went to Central Africa, passing through Egypt, Nubia, Ethiopia, and Soudân, to the White Nile, a journey of 4000 miles in the interior of Africa, and returned to Cairo in April, 1852. Thence he went north through Palestine and Asia Minor to Constantinople, where he arrived in July. After a month's stay, and visiting Malta, Sicily, and the Isles of the Mediterranean, he returned to England through Italy, Tyrol, and Germany. In October, 1852, he started from England, by the overland route, for Bombay, touching at Gibraltar, and spending a month in South Spain. He set out from Bombay January 4th, 1853, for a tour of 2200 miles in the interior of India, arriving at Calcutta February 22d. Thence he embarked for Hong-Kong, by way of Penang and Singapore, and arrived in China. He was attached to the American Legation at Shanghai for two months; upon the arrival of Com. Perry's squadron, he entered the naval service, to accompany it to the Loo-Choo Islands and Japan, which be explored; then returned to Canton, and thence took passage for New York, arriving December, 1853, after an absence of two years and four months, and 50,000 miles of travel. His graphic and entertaining history of this great journey, published in letters to the Tribune, was enlarged and published in three works: A Journey to Central Africa; The Lands of the Saracen; and, India, China and Japan.

687

In 1854, he published his Poems of the Orient, and in 1855 his Poems of Home and Travel.

In July, 1856, he started on a fourth journey, during which he visited Sweden, Lapland, Norway, Dalmatia, Greece, Crete, and Russia. In November, 1857, he published, in London and New York, Northern Travel, the journal of the above trip, and returned home in October, 1858. He next published Greece and Russia, in 1859, and in the same year a volume of accumulated material and sketches, entitled Home and Abroad, of which a second series was issued in 1862; and a similar volume, entitled Byeways of Europe, in 1868, which, with a volume of sketches of travel in the Gold Regions west of the Mississippi, completes his record of travel. His earlier volumes of travel, though published twenty-five years ago, are still called for, as indispensables in public and private libraries. Very few books, either of Travel or Fiction, thus retain their place so long, and continue in active demand, amidst all the competition of modern book-making, and the inference is not unreasonable that these volumes of adventure, in almost every corner of the earth, possess some lasting interest and vitality which makes them worthy of a permanent place in our literature. Two defects in most of Mr. Taylor's books of travel are: want of sufficient dates, that we may know *when* he was at the places mentioned; and of careful topography, that we may know exactly *where* to locate him.

In 1863, Mr. Taylor commenced a new vein, that of Fiction; his Novels were welcomed even more largely than the Travels. The first was Hannah Thurston, and, by many, thought to be his best: its quiet, but truthful pictures of real life seemed painted from the life with great vigor and freshness. This was followed, in 1865, by John Godfrey's Fortunes; some of the scenes of which were supposed to have had some foundation in the author's early fortunes. In 1866, appeared the Story of Kennett: a stirring tale of the early settlement of Chester County in Pennsylvania. Its ex-

quisite pictures of the rural landscape from the hand of an observant master, the stirring scenes of adventure in strong contrast with the lovely quiet of the rural life of the inhabitants of Kennett, and the knowledge of human nature displayed, all tend to stamp this novel one of rare power and skill. The latest of his Works of Fiction is Joseph and his Friend, published in November, 1870, reprinted from the Atlantic Monthly. His Tales will rank with those of Hawthorne, Longfellow, and Mrs. Stowe; they are delightful and refreshing reading, crowded with life-like characters, full of delicate and subtle sympathies, with ideas the most opposite to his own, and lighted up throughout with that playful humor which suggests always wisdom rather than mere fun; they are a great rest after the crowded artistic effects and the conventional interests of even the better kinds of English novels.

He has also published the Poet's Journal, and Picture of St. John, two volumes which met with a fair success. His poetical works have been collected in one volume, 32mo., and 16mo.

Successful as a traveller, an author, a poet and novelist, he has also been successful as a lecturer, having delivered popular lectures in every part of the Union.

The characteristics of Mr. Taylor's writings are, in his poems, ease of expression, with a careful selection of poetical capabilities, a full, animated style, with a growing attention to art and condensation. His prose is equable and clear, in the flowing style, the narrative of a genial, healthy observer of the many manners of the world which he has seen in the most remarkable portions of the four quarters.

In person he is above the ordinary height, manly and robust, with a quick resolute way of carrying out his plans of courage and independence; and with great energy and perseverance, he combines a happy natural temperament and benevolence. He has been twice married, the second time in Germany, and resides on a comfortable estate near Kennett, in Chester County, Pennsylvania

CHRISTMAS AND NEW YEAR IN GER-MANY.

FROM VIEWS A-FOOT.

WE have lately witnessed the most beautiful and interesting of all German festivals—Christmas. This is here peculiarly celebrated. About the commencement of December, the Christmarkt or fair, was opened in the Rœmerberg, and has continned to the present time. The booths, decorated with green boughs, were filled with toys of various kinds, among which during the first days the figure of St. Nicholas was conspicuous. There were bunches of wax candles to illuminate the Christmas tree, gingerbread with printed mottos in poetry, beautiful little earthenware, basket-work, and a wilderness of playthings. The 5th of December, being Nicholas evening, the booths were lighted up, and the square was filled with boys, running from one stand to another, all shouting and talking together in the most joyous confusion. Nurses were going around, carrying the smaller children in their arms, and parents bought presents decorated with sprigs of pine and carried them away. Some of the shops had beautiful toys, as for instance, a whole grocery store in miniature, with barrels, boxes and drawers, all filled with sweetmeats, a kitchen with a stove and all suitable utensils, which could really be used, and sets of dishes of the most diminutive patterns. All was a scene of activity and joyous feeling.

Many of the tables had bundles of rods with gilded bands, which were to be used that evening by the persons who represented St. Nicholas. In the family with whom we reside, one of our German friends dressed himself very comically, with a mask, fur robe and long tapering cap. He came in with a bunch of rods and a sack, and a broom for a sceptre. After we all had received our share of the beating, he threw the contents of his bag on the table, and while we were scrambling for the nuts and apples, gave us many smart raps over the finger. In many families the children are made to say, "I thank you, Herr Nicolaus," and the rods are hung up in the room till Christmas to keep them in good behaviour. This was only a forerunner of the Christ-kindchen's coming. The Nicolaus is the punishing spirit, the Christ-kindchen the rewarding one.

When this time was over, we all began preparing secretly our presents for Christmas. Every day there were consultations about the things which should be obtained. It was so arranged that all should interchange presents, but nobody must know beforehand what he would receive. What pleasure there was in all these secret purchases and preparations! Scarcely anything was thought or spoken of but Christmas, and every day the consultations became more numerous and secret. The trees were bought some time beforehand, but as we were to witness the festival for the first time, we were not allowed to see them prepared, in order that the effect might be as great as possible. The market in the Rœmerberg Square grew constantly larger and more brilliant. Every night

87

it was lit up with lamps and thronged with people. Quite a forest sprang up in the street before our door. The old stone house opposite, with the traces of so many centuries on its dark face, seemed to stand in the midst of a garden. It was a pleasure to go out every evening and see the children rushing to and fro, shouting and seeking out toys from the booths, and talking all the time of the Christmas that was so near. The poor people went by with their little presents hid under their cloaks, lest their children might see them; every heart was glad and every countenance wore a smile of secret pleasure.

Finally the day before Christmas arrived. The streets were so full I could scarce make my way through, and the sale of trees went on more rapidly than ever. These were commonly branches of pine or fir, set upright in a little miniature garden of moss. When the lamps were lighted at night, our street had the appearance of an illuminated garden. We were prohibited from entering the rooms up stairs in which the grand ceremony was to take place, being obliged to take our seats in those arranged for the guests, and wait with impatience the hour when Christ-kindchen should call. Several relations of the family came, and what was more agreeable, they brought with them five or six children. I was anxious to see how they would view the ceremony. Finally, in the middle of an interesting conversation, we heard the bell ringing up stairs. We all started up, and made for the door. I ran up the steps with the children at my heels, and at the top met a blaze of light coming from the open door, that dazzled me. In each room stood a great table, while the presents were arranged, amid flowers and wreaths. From the centre, rose the beautiful Christmas tree covered with wax tapers to the very top, which made it nearly as light as day, while every bough was hung with sweetmeats and gilded nuts. The children ran shouting around the table, hunting their presents, while the older persons had theirs pointed out to them. I had quite a little library of German authors as my share; and many of the others received quite valuable gifts.

But how beautiful was the heart-felt joy that shone on every countenance! As each one discovered he embraced the givers, and all was a scene of the purest feelings. It is a glorious feast, this Christmas time! What a chorus from happy hearts went up on that evening to Heaven! Full of poetry and feeling and glad associations, it is here anticipated with joy, and leaves a pleasant memory behind it. We may laugh at such simple festivals at home, and prefer to shake ourselves loose from every shackle that bears the rust of the Past, but we would certainly be happier if some of these beautiful old customs were better honored. They renew the bond of feeling between families and friends, and strengthen their kindly sympathy; even life-long friends require occasions of this kind to freshen the wreath that binds them together.

New Year's Eve is also favored with a peculiar celebration in Germany. Every body remains up and makes himself merry till midnight. The Christmas trees are again lighted, and while the tapers are burning down, the family play for articles which they have purchased and hung on the boughs. It is so arranged that each one shall win as much as he gives, which change of articles makes much amusement. One of the ladies rejoiced in the possession of a red silk handkerchief and a cake of soap, while a cup and saucer and a pair of scissors fell to my lot! As midnight drew near, it was louder in the streets, and companies of people, some of them singing in chorus, passed by on their way to the Zeil. Finally three-quarters struck, the windows were opened and every one waited anxiously for the clock to strike. At the first sound, such a cry arose as one may imagine, when thirty or forty thousand persons all set their lungs going at once. Every body in the house, in the street, over the whole city, shouted, "*Prosst Neu Jahr!*" In families, all the members embrace each other, with wishes of happiness for the new year. Then the windows are thrown open, and they cry to their neighbors or those passing by.

After we had exchanged congratulations, Dennet, B—— and I set out for the Zeil. The streets were full of people, shouting to one another and to those standing at the swinging windows. We failed not to cry, "*Prosst Neu Jahr!*" wherever we saw a damsel at the window, and the words came back to us more musically than we sent them. Along the Zeil the spectacle was most singular. The great wide street was filled with companies of men, marching up and down, while from the mass rang up one deafening, unending shout, that seemed to pierce the black sky above. The whole scene looked stranger and wilder from the flickering light of the swinging lamps, and I could not help thinking it must resemble a night in Paris during the French Revolution. We joined the crowd and used our lungs as well as any of them. For some time after we returned home, companies passed by, singing " with us 'tis ever so!" but at three o'clock all was again silent.

SAVED BY ROGER.
FROM THE STORY OF KENNETT.

THE black, dreary night seemed interminable. Gilbert could only guess, here and there, at a landmark, and was forced to rely more upon Roger's instinct of the road than upon the guidance of his senses. Towards midnight, as he judged, by the solitary crow of a cock, the rain almost entirely ceased. The wind began to blow, sharp and keen, and the hard vault of the sky set a little. He fancied that the hills on his right had fallen away, and that the horizon was suddenly depressed towards the north. Roger's feet began to splash in constantly deepening water, and presently a roar, distinct from that of the wind, filled the air.

It was the Brandywine. The stream had overflowed its broad meadow-bottoms, and was running high and fierce beyond its main channel. The turbid waters made a dim, dusky gleam around him; soon the fences disappeared, and the flood reached to his horse's belly. But he knew that the ford could be distinguished by the break in the fringe of timber; moreover, that the creek-bank was a little higher than the meadows behind it, and so far, at least, he might venture. The ford was not more than twenty yards across, and he could trust Roger to swim that distance.

The faithful animal pressed bravely on, but Gilbert soon noticed that he seemed at fault. The swift water had forced him out of the road, and he stopped, from time to time, as if anxious and uneasy. The timber could now be discerned, only a short distance in advance, and in a few minutes they would gain the bank.

What was that! A strange rustling, hissing sound, as of cattle trampling through dry reeds,—a sound which quivered and shook, even in the breath of the hurrying wind! Roger snorted, stood still, and trembled in every limb; and a sensation of awe and terror struck a chill through Gilbert's heart. The sound drew swiftly nearer, and became a wild, seething roar, filling the whole breadth of the valley.

"Great God!" cried Gilbert, " the dam!—the dam has given way!" He turned Roger's head, gave him the rein, struck, spurred, cheered, and shouted. The brave beast struggled through the impending flood, but the advance wave of the coming inundation already touched his side. He staggered; a line of churning foam bore down upon them, the terrible roar was all around and over them, and horse and rider were whirled away.

What happened during the first few seconds, Gilbert could never distinctly recall. Now they were whelmed in the water, now riding its careering tide, torn through the tops of brushwood, jostled by floating logs and timbers of the dambreast, but always, as it seemed, remorselessly held in the heart of the tumult and the ruin.

He saw, at last, that they had fallen behind the furious onset of the flood, but Roger was still swimming with it, desperately throwing up his head from time to time, and snorting the water from his nostrils. All his efforts to gain a foothold failed; his strength was nearly spent, and unless some help should come in a few minutes, it would come in vain. And in the darkness, and the rapidity with which they were borne along, how should help come?

All at once, Roger's course stopped. He became an obstacle to the flood, which pressed him against some other obstacle below, and rushed over horse and rider. Thrusting out his hand, Gilbert felt the rough bark of a tree. Leaning towards it and clasping the log in his arms, he drew himself from the saddle, while Roger, freed from his burden, struggled into the current and instantly disappeared.

As nearly as Gilbert could ascertain, several timbers, thrown over each other, had lodged, probably upon a rocky islet in the stream, the upper most one projecting slantingly out of the flood. It required all his strength to resist the current which sucked, and whirled, and tugged at his body, and to climb high enough to escape its force, without over-balancing his support. At last, though still half immersed, he found himself comparatively safe for a time, yet as far as ever from a final rescue.

He must await the dawn, and an eternity of endurance lay in those few hours. Meantime, perhaps, the creek would fall, for the rain had ceased, and there were outlines of moving cloud in the sky. It was the night which made his situation so terrible, by concealing the chances of escape. At first, he thought most of Roger. Was his brave horse drowned, or had he safely gained the bank below? Then, as the desperate moments went by, and the chill of exposure and the fatigue of exertion began to creep over him, his mind reverted, with a bitter sweetness, a mixture of bliss and agony, to the two beloved women to whom his life belonged,—the life which, alas! he could not now call his own, to give.

He tried to fix his thoughts on Death, to commend his soul to Divine Mercy; but every prayer shaped itself into an appeal that he might once more see the dear faces and hear the dear voices. In the great shadow of the fate which hung over him, the loss of his property became as dust in the balance, and his recent despair smote him with shame. He no longer fiercely protested against the injuries of fortune, but entreated pardon and pity for the sake of his love.

The clouds rolled into distincter masses, and the north-west wind still hunted them across the sky, until there came, first a tiny rift for a star, then a gap for a whole constellation, and finally a broad burst of moonlight. Gilbert now saw that the timber to which he clung was lodged nearly in the centre of the channel, as the water swept with equal force on either side of him. Beyond the banks there was a wooded hill on the left; on the right an overflowed meadow. He was too weak and benumbed to trust himself to the flood, but he imagined that it was beginning to subside, and therein lay his only hope.

Yet a new danger now assailed him, from the increasing cold. There was already a sting of frost, a breath of ice, in the wind. In another hour the sky was nearly swept bare of clouds, and he could note the lapse of the night by the sinking of the moon. But he was by this time hardly in a condition to note anything more. He had thrown himself, face downwards, on the top of the log, his arms mechanically clasping it, while his mind sank into a state of torpid, passive suffering, growing nearer to the dreamy indifference which precedes death. His cloak had been torn away in the first rush of the inundation, and the wet coat began to stiffen in the wind, from the ice gathering over it.

The moon was low in the west, and there was a pale glimmer of the coming dawn in the sky, when Gilbert Potter suddenly raised his head. Above the noise of the water and the whistle of the wind, he heard a familiar sound,—the shrill, sharp neigh of a horse. Lifting himself, with great exertion, to a sitting posture, he saw two men, on horseback, in the flooded meadow, a little below him. They stopped, seemed to consult, and presently drew nearer.

Gilbert tried to shout, but the muscles of his throat were stiff, and his lungs refused to act. The horse neighed again. This time there was no mistake; it was Roger that he heard! Voice came to him, and he cried aloud,—a hoarse, strange, unnatural cry.

The horsemen heard it, and rapidly pushed up the bank, until they reached a point directly opposite to him. The prospect of escape brought a thrill of life to his frame; he looked around and saw that the flood had indeed fallen.

"We have no rope," he heard one of the men say. "How shall we reach him?"

"There is no time to get one, now," the other answered. "My horse is stronger than yours. I'll go into the creek just below, where it's broader and not so deep, and work my way up to him."

"But one horse can't carry both."

"His will follow, be sure, when it sees me."

As the last speaker moved away, Gilbert saw a led horse plunging through the water, beside the other. It was a difficult and dangerous undertaking. The horseman and the loose horse entered the main stream below, where its divided channel met and broadened, but it was still above the saddle-girths, and very swift. Sometimes the animals plunged, losing their foothold; nevertheless, they gallantly breasted the current, and inch by inch worked their way to a point about six feet below Gilbert. It seemed impossible to approach nearer.

"Can you swim?" asked the man.

Gilbert shook his head. "Throw me the end of Roger's bridle!" he then cried.

The man unbuckled the bridle and threw it, keeping the end of the rein in his hand. Gilbert tried to grasp it, but his hands were too numb. He managed, however, to get one arm and his head through the opening, and relaxed his hold on the log.

A plunge, and the man had him by the collar. He felt himself lifted by a strong arm and laid across Roger's saddle. With his failing strength and stiff limbs, it was no slight task to get into place, and the return, though less laborious to the horses, was equally dangerous, because Gilbert was scarcely able to support himself without help.

"You're safe now," said the man, when they reached the bank, "but it's a downright mercy of God that you're alive!"

The other horseman joined them, and they rode slowly across the flooded meadow. They had both thrown their cloaks around Gilbert, and carefully steadied him in the saddle, one on each side. He was too much exhausted to ask how they had found him, or whither they were taking him,—too numb for curiosity, almost for gratitude.

"Here's your saviour!" said one of the men, patting Roger's shoulder.

THEODORE WINTHROP.

[Born 1828. Died 1861.]

THEODORE WINTHROP was descended on both sides from the most distinguished New England families ; by his father a direct descendant of John Winthrop, the first Governor of Connecticut, and by his mother, a descendant of Jonathan Edwards. He was born in New Haven, Sept. 22d, 1828. He entered Yale College, in his sixteenth year, and was a thorough student, carrying off the highest honors.

He went abroad for his health, storing his mind with the rich treasures of art and nature he saw. At Rome, he met Mr. W. H. Aspinwall, the founder of the Panama Railroad, became tutor to his children, and on the return of the party, accepted a desk in his office, which before long, he left for duties at Panama, thus becoming familiar with the Pacific coast in the early days of its settlement. Here he was prostrated by local fevers and the small-pox. As soon as able to leave for home, he was in the saddle for the long overland journey.

He returned to New York, was admitted to the bar, but his roving spirit induced him to join Lieut. Strain's famous expedition to the tropics. On his return, he settled on Staten Island, near his friend Geo. W. Curtis. In 1856, he made a vigorous electioneering tour in Pennsylvania, in the interest of the Fremont cause ; but ill health prevented him from the like exertion in the campaign of 1860. Spending the life of a dilettanté his ardent spirit chafed under inaction. His time was mostly spent in visiting studios, studying law, taking country rambles, riding fiery steeds, and such manly sports as his health would allow. His pen, however, was constantly busy writing sketches or novels.

His first published article was a sketch of Church's painting of "The Heart of the Andes," the progress of which he had watched to its completion. It was as brilliant and powerful as the painting it described. In 1860, he offered two of his novels for publication. They were accepted, with the warmest appreciation of their merits ; but were laid aside for issue until after the election which was absorbing public attention. His next sketch, Love and Skates, was sent to the Atlantic Monthly, and, though accepted, was laid aside for the same reason ; it had, however, created so favorable an impression upon the editor, that he was engaged, on his departure for the seat of war, to write a series of sketches ; the first of these, The March of the Seventh, one of the most stirring magazine articles ever written, was no sooner in print than the author's reputation was made.

Mr. Curtis has furnished an interesting record how the news of the fall of Sumter was received and talked over in his study. At the call of the proclamation, on the morrow, Winthrop obeyed the summons at once. His subsequent career is vividly before us in his sketches, animated as the music to which he marched, and a few fragments of private letters published by Mr. Curtis. He left the Seventh at Washington, to accompany Gen. Butler to Fortress Monroe as Secretary, with the rank of Major. He planned with his commanding officer, the attack on Bethel, and took part in the action. At a critical time on that disastrous morning of the 10th of June, 1861, he sprang upon a log to rally his men, in full sight of the enemy. A rebel shot pierced his heart, and he fell dead on his face. His remains were brought to New York, and the funeral service was read at the armory of the Seventh. The body was carried in funeral procession on the howitzer which he had helped to drag, only two months before, through the same Broadway. One of the earliest and most talented of those who fell in the war, his books excited immediate attention on their publication.

Cecil Dreeme was published soon after his death. It is a romance of life in the studios of the New York University, and a novel of its best society. Cecil is a woman disguised as a man, but perfectly pure, modest, and spirited. There is a shade of gravity, almost of sadness, a warning of impending evil, a submission of fate, which, in its subtle influence reminds us of Chas. Brockden Brown and of Hawthorne. The satirical points, though keen, are a little exaggerated.

John Brent soon followed; it is a narrative founded upon his saddle journey across the plains from California. The descriptions of prairie-life, of the mountain-passes, the wavy landscape, and of his matchless steed, are inimitable.

His other writings followed in rapid succession; Edwin Brothertoft, a novel; The Canoe and the Saddle, Adventures among the Northwestern Rivers and Forests, and the Isthmus of Panama; and Life in the Open Air, and other papers, including his sketch of the Heart of the Andes. These were all published without that revision, which, if the author had lived, he would have given. His writings have a charming freshness and vigor, with a background of dreamy sadness which is very attractive.

TO SAVE AND TO SLAY.
FROM JOHN BRENT.

[HUGH CLITHEROE, who has joined the Mormons, and his daughter Ellen, are journeying towards Salt Lake City. During the night their tent was entered by Murker and Larrap, two villians, the father gagged, and the daughter forcibly carried off. The Mormon elder, having tried in vain to gain the love of Ellen, who hates Mormonism for the baneful influence it has exerted over her poor, weak old father, refuses to assist in her rescue. John Brent, a lover of Ellen, with his friend Richard Wade, followed the caravan, trusting to dispel the illusion. The former, unable to give up all hopes of Ellen, hearing of the occurrence, immediately started with Wade, in pursuit. Just at that moment Armstrong, whose mother was murdered by Murker and Larrap, and who has followed them all the way from Bear River Crossing, rides up, and the three ride off "to save and to slay."]

WE galloped abreast,—Armstrong at the right. His weird, gaunt white held his own with the best of us. No whip, no spur, for that deathly creature. He went as if his master's purpose were stirring him through and through. That stern intent made his sinews steel, and put an agony of power into every stride. The man never stirred, save sometimes to put a hand to that bloody blanket bandage across his head and temple. He had told his story, he had spoken his errand, he breathed not a word; but with his lean, pallid face set hard, his gentle blue eyes scourged of their kindliness, and fixed upon those distant mountains where his vengeance lay, he rode on like a relentless fate.

Next in the line I galloped. O my glorious black! The great, killing pace seemed mere playful canter to him,—such as one might ride beside a timid girl, thrilling with her first free dash over a flowery common, or a golden beach between sea and shore. But from time to time he surged a little forward with his great shoulders, and gave a mighty writhe of his body, while his hind legs came lifting his flanks under me, and telling of the giant reserve of speed and power he kept easily controlled. Then his ear would go back, and his large brown eye, with its purple-black pupil, would look round at my bridle hand and then into my eye, saying as well as words could have said it, "This is mere sport, my friend and master. You do not know me. I have stuff in me that you do not dream. Say the word, and I can double this, treble it. Say the word! let me show you how I can spurn the earth." Then, with the lightest love pressure on the snaffle, I would say, "Not yet! not yet! Patience, my noble friend! Your time will come."

At the left rode Brent, our leader. He knew the region; he made the plan; he had the hope; his was the ruling passion,—stronger than brotherhood, than revenge. Love made him leader of that galloping three. His iron-gray went grandly, with white mane flapping the air like a signal-flag of reprieve. Eager hope and kindling purpose made the rider's face more beautiful than ever. He seemed to behold Sidney's motto written on the golden haze before him, "Viam aut inveniam aut faciam." I felt my heart grow great, when I looked at his calm features, and caught his assuring smile,—a gay smile but for the dark, fateful resolve beneath it. And when he launched some stirring word of cheer, and shook another ten of seconds out of the gray's mile, even Armstrong's countenance grew less deathly, as he turned to our leader in silent response. Brent looked a fit chieftain for such a wild charge over the desert waste, with his buckskin hunting-shirt and leggins with flaring fringes, his otter cap and eagle's plume, his bronzed face, with its close, brown beard, his elate head, and his seat like a centaur.

So we galloped three abreast, neck and neck, hoof with hoof, steadily quickening our pace over the sere width of desert. We must make the most of the levels. Rougher work, cruel obstacles were before. All the wild, triumphant music I had ever heard came and sang in my ears to the flinging cadence of the resonant feet, tramping on hollow arches of the volcanic rock, over great, vacant chasms underneath. Sweet and soft around us melted the hazy air of October, and its warm, flickering currents shook like a veil of gauzy gold, between us and the blue bloom of the mountains far away, but nearing now and lifting step by step.

On we galloped, the avenger, the friend, the lover, on our errand, to save and to slay.

* * * * * * *

We were ascending now all the time into subalpine regions. We crossed great sloping savannas, deep in dry, rustling grass, where a nation of cattle might pasture. We plunged through broad wastes of hot sand. We flung ourselves down and up the red sides of waterworn gullies. We took breakneck leaps across dry quebradas in the clay. We clattered across stony arroyos, longing thirstily for the gush of water tnat had flowed there not many months before.

The trail was everywhere plain. No prairie craft was needed to trace it. Here the chase had gone, but a few hours ago; here, across grassy slopes, trampling the grass as if a mower had passed that way; here, ploughing wearily through the sand; here, treading the red, crumbling clay; here, breaking down the side of a bank; here, leaving a sharp hoof-track in the dry mud of a fled torrent. Everywhere a straight path, pointing for that deepening gap in the Sierra, Luggernel Alley, the only gate of escape.

Brent's unerring judgment had divined the course aright. On he led, charging along the trail, as if he were trampling already on the carcasses of the pursued. On he led and we followed, drawing nearer, nearer to our goal.

Our horses suffered bitterly for water. Some five hours we had ridden without a pause. Not one drop or sign of water in all that arid waste. The torrents had poured along the dry watercourses too hastily to let the scanty alders and willows along their line treasure up any sap of growth. The wild-sage bushes had plainly never tasted fluid more plenteous than seldom dewdrops doled out on certain rare festal days, enough to keep their meagre foliage a dusty gray. No pleasant streamlet lurked anywhere under the long dry grass of the savannas. The arroyos were parched and hot as rifts in lava.

It became agonizing to listen to the panting and gasping of our horses. Their eyes grew staring and bloodshot. We suffered, ourselves, hardly less than they. It was cruel to press on. But we must hinder a crueller cruelty. Love against Time,—Vengeance against Time! We must not flinch for any weak humanity to the noble allies that struggled on with us, without one token of resistance.

Fulano suffered least. He turned his brave eye back, and beckoned me with his ear to listen, while he seemed to say: "See, this is my Endurance! I hold my Power ready still to show."

And he curved his proud neck, shook his mane like a banner, and galloped the grandest of all.

We came to a broad strip of sand, the dry bed of a mountain-torrent. The trail followed up this disappointing path. Heavy ploughing for the tired horses! How would they bear the rough work down the ravine yet to come?

Suddenly our leader pulled up and sprang from the saddle.

"Look!" he cried, "how those fellows spent their time, and saved ours. Thank Heaven for this! We shall save her, surely, now."

It was WATER! No need to go back to Pindar to know that it was "the Best."

They had dug a pit deep in the thirsty sand, and found a lurking river buried there. Nature never questioned what manner of men they were that sought. Murderers flying from vengeance and planning now another villain outrage,—still impartial nature did not change her laws for them.

Sunshine, air, water, life,—these boons of hers.— she gave them freely. That higher boon of death, if they were to receive, it must be from some other power, greater than the undiscriminating force of Nature.

We drank thankfully of this well by the wayside. No gentle beauty hereabouts to enchant us to delay. No grand old tree, the shelter and the landmark of the fountain, proclaiming an oasis near. Nothing but bare, hot sand. But the water was pure, cool, and bright. It had come underground from the Sierra, and still remembered its parent snows. We drank and were grateful, almost to the point of pity. Had we been but avengers, like Armstrong, my friend and I could wellnigh have felt mercy here, and turned back pardoning. But rescue was more imperative than vengeance. Our business tortured us, as with the fanged scourge of Tisiphone, while we dallied. We grudged these moments of refreshment. Before night fell down the west, and night was soon to be climbing up the east, we must overtake,—and then?

I wiped the dust and spume away from Fulano's nostrils and breathed him a moment. Then I let him drain deep, delicious draughts from the stirrup-cup. He whinnied thanks and undying fealty,—my noble comrade! He drank like a reveller. When I mounted again, he gave a jubilant curvet and bound. My weight was a feather to him. All those leagues of our hard, hot gallop were nothing.

The brown Sierra here was close at hand. Its glittering, icy summits, above the dark and sheeny walls, far above the black phalanxes of clambering pines, stooped forward and hung over us as we rode. We were now at the foot of the range, where it dipped suddenly down upon the plain. The gap, our goal all day, opened before us, grand and terrible. Some giant force had clutched the mountains, and riven them narrowly apart. The wild defile gaped, and then wound away and closed, lost between its mighty walls, a thousand feet high, and bearing two brother pyramids of purple cliffs aloft far above the snow line. A fearful portal into a scene of the thoes and agonies of earth! and my excited eyes seemed to read, gilded over its entrance, in the dead gold of that hazy October sunshine, words from Dante's inscription,—

"Per me si va tra la perduta gente;
    Lasciate ogni speranza voi, ch' entrate!"

"Here we are," said Brent, speaking hardly above his breath. "This is Luggernel Alley at last, thank God! In an hour, if the horses hold out, we shall be at the Springs: that is, if we can go through this breakneck gorge at the same pace. My horse began to flinch a little before the water. Perhaps that will set him up. How are yours?"

"Fulano asserts that he has not begun to show himself yet. I may have to carry you en croupe, before we are done."

Armstrong said nothing, but pointed impatiently down the defile. The gaunt white horse moved on quicker at this gesture. He seemed a tireless machine, not flesh and blood,—a being like his master, living and acting by the force of a purpose alone.

Our chief led the way into the cañon.

Yes, John Brent, you were right when you called Luggernel Alley a wonder of our continent.

I remember it now,—I only saw it then ;—for those strong scenes of nature assault the soul whether it will or no, fight in against affirmative or negative resistance, and bide their time to be admitted as dominant over the imagination. It seemed to me then that I was not noticing how grand the precipices, how stupendous the cleavages, how rich and gleaming the rock faces in Luggernel Alley. My business was not to stare about, but to look sharp and ride hard ; and I did it.

Yet now I can remember, distinct as if I beheld it, every stride of that pass ; and everywhere, as I recall foot after foot of that fierce chasm, I see three men with set faces,—one deathly pale and wearing a bloody turban,—all galloping steadily on, on an errand to save and to slay.

Terrible riding it was ! A pavement of slippery, sheeny rock ; great beds of loose stones ; barricades of mighty boulders, where a cliff had fallen an æon ago, before the days of the road-maker race ; crevices where an unwary foot might catch ; wide rifts where a shaky horse might fall, or a timid horseman drag him down. Terrible riding ! A pass where a calm traveller would go quietly picking his steps, thankful if each hour counted him a safe mile.

Terrible riding ! Madness to go as we went ! Horse and man, any moment either might shatter every limb. But man and horse neither can know what he can do, until he has dared and done. On we went, with the old frenzy growing tenser. Heart almost broken with eagerness.

No whipping or spurring. Our horses were a part of ourselves. While we could go, they would go. Since the water, they were full of leap again. Down in the shady Alley, too, evening had come before its time. Noon's packing of hot air had been dislodged by a mountain breeze drawing through. Horses and men were braced and cheered to their work ; and in such riding as that, the man and the horse must think together and move together,—eye and hand of the rider must choose and command, as bravely as the horse executes. The blue sky was overhead, the red sun upon the castellated walls a thousand feet above us, the purpling chasm opened before. It was late, these were the last moments. But we should save the lady yet.

"Yes," our hearts shouted to us, "we shall save her yet."

An arroyo, the channel of a dried torrent, followed the pass. It had made its way as water does, not straightway, but by that potent feminine method of passing under the frowning front of an obstacle, and leaving the dull rock staring there, while the wild creature it would have held is gliding away down the valley. This zigzag channel baffled us ; we must leap it without check wherever it crossed our path. Every second now was worth a century. Here was the sign of horses, passed but now. We could not choose ground. We must take our leaps on that cruel rock wherever they offered.

Poor Pumps !

He had carried his master so nobly ! There were so few miles to do ! He had chased so well ; he merited to be in at the death.

Brent lifted him at a leap across the arroyo. Poor Pumps !

His hind feet slipped on the time-smoothed rock. He fell short. He plunged down a dozen feet among the rough boulders of the torrent-bed. Brent was out of the saddle almost before he struck, raising him.

No, he would never rise again. Both his fore legs were broken at the knee. He rested there, kneeling on the rocks where he fell.

Brent groaned. The horse screamed horribly, horribly,—there is no more agonized sound,—and the scream went echoing high up the cliffs where the red sunlight rested.

It costs a loving master much to butcher his brave and trusty horse, the half of his knightly self; but it costs him more to hear him shriek in such misery. Brent drew his pistol to put poor Pumps out of pain.

Armstrong sprang down and caught his hand.

"Stop !" he said in his hoarse whisper.

He had hardly spoken, since we started. My nerves were so straitened, that this mere ghost of a sound rang through me like a death yell ; a grisly cry of merciless and exultant vengeance. I seemed to hear its echoes, rising up and swelling in a flood of thick uproar, until they burst over the summit of the pass and were wasted in the crannies of the towering mountain-flanks above.

"Stop !" whispered Armstrong. "No shooting ! They'll hear. The knife !"

He held out his knife to my friend.

Brent hesitated one heart-beat Could he stain his hand with his faithful servant's blood ?

Pumps screamed again.

Armstrong snatched the knife and drew it across the throat of the crippled horse.

Poor Pumps ! He sank and died without a moan. Noble martyr in the old, heroic cause !

I caught the knife from Armstrong. I cut the thong of my girth. The heavy California saddle, with its macheers and roll of blankets, fell to the ground. I cut off my spurs. They had never yet touched Fulano's flanks. He stood beside me quiet, but trembling to be off.

"Now Brent ! up behind me !" I whispered,— for the awe of death was upon us.

I mounted. Brent sprang up behind. I ride light for a tall man. Brent is the slightest body of an athlete I ever saw.

Fulano stood steady till we were firm in our seats.

Then he tore down the defile.

Here was that vast reserve of power ; here the tireless spirit ; here the hoof striking true as a thunderbolt, where the brave eye saw footing; here that writhing agony of speed; here the great promise fulfilled, the great heart thrilling to mine, the grand body living to the beating heart. Noble Fulano!

I rode with a snaffle. I left it hanging loose. I did not check or guide him. He saw all. He knew all. All was his doing.

We sat firm, clinging as we could, as we must. Fulano dashed along the resounding pass.

Armstrong pressed after,—the gaunt white horse struggled to emulate his leader. Presently we lost them behind the curves of the Alley. No other horse that ever lived could have held with the black in that headlong gallop to save.

Over the slippery rocks, over the sheeny pavement, plunging through the loose stones, staggering over the barricades, leaping the arroyo, down, up, on, always on,—on went the horse, we clinging as we might.

It seemed one beat of time, it seemed an eternity, when between the ring of the hoofs I heard Brent whisper in my ear.

" We are there."

The crags flung apart, right and left. I saw a sylvan glade. I saw the gleam of gushing water.

Fulano dashed on, uncontrollable!

There they were,—the Murderers.

Arrived but one moment!

The lady still bound to that pack-mule branded A. & A.

Murker just beginning to unsaddle.

Larrap not dismounted, in chase of the other animals as they strayed to graze.

The men heard the tramp and saw us, as we sprang into the glade.

Both my hands were at the bridle.

Brent, grasping my waist with one arm, was awkward with his pistol.

Murker saw us first. He snatched his six-shooter and fired.

Brent shook with a spasm. His pistol arm dropped.

Before the murderer could cock again, Fulano was upon him!

He was ridden down. He was beaten, trampled down upon the grass,—crushed, abolished.

We disentangled ourselves from the *mêlée*.

Where was the other?

The coward, without firing a shot, was spurring Armstrong's Flathead horse blindly up the cañon, whence we had issued.

We turned to Murker.

Fulano was up again, and stood there shuddering. But the man?

A hoof had battered in the top of his skull; blood was gushing from his mouth; his ribs were broken; all his body was a trodden, massacred carcass.

He breathed once, as we lifted him.

Then a tranquil, childlike look stole over his face,—that well-known look of the weary body, thankful that the turbulent soul has gone. Murker was dead.

Fulano, and not we, had been executioner. *Hi* was the stain of blood.

T. DE WITT TALMAGE

[Born 1832.]

THIS eloquent and popular Divine was born at Boundbrook, N. J., January 7th, 1832. He graduated at the New York University, and also at the New Brunswick Theological Seminary. His first charge was at Belleville, N. J., from which place he was called to Syracuse, N. Y. He remained there three years, meeting with remarkable success. At the end of that time he had attracted the attention of the congregation in Philadelphia formerly presided over by the Rev. Dr. Berg, and one of the strongest in that city, the Second Reformed Church. He accepted the flattering call made him, and here, in a wider field for the exercise of his peculiar talents, for seven years preached to a thronged church. During this time he delivered many popular lectures, always to crowded audiences, and never failed to claim their undivided and closest attention. He has stood before the principal Lyceums throughout the country, and commanded the highest compensation paid for such services.

From Philadelphia, after many and repeated calls, he removed to Brooklyn, L. I., and took charge of a church, which through many troubles had been reduced to an audience of fifty— though the building had capacity to hold thirteen hundred people. It soon became too small to hold the numerous applicants for seats; a vast Tabernacle was projected, and immediately built, capable of seating 3500 people; and even this is found incapable of holding the throngs applying for admission. It is intended to increase the capacity of the building to 5000, by the erection of galleries. The seats are free, the church being entirely supported by voluntary contributions of the members of the congregation.

Mr. Talmage's success as a preacher, as a popular lecturer, and as a writer, is owing to his peculiar style, and plain manner of speaking or writing. He expresses exactly what he means, and never fails to make his readers fully comprehend him. His illustrations are from incidents occuring in every-day life, something every one sees and understands. He has contributed to the popular journals of the country, and bids fair to become as well known in literature as in the pulpit.

From his book entitled, "Crumbs Swept Up," we extract the following, to show the general style of the author

~~~~~~~~~~

CHAMPS ELYSEES.

FROM CRUMBS SWEPT UP.

THE scarlet rose of battle is in full bloom. The white water-lily of fear trembles on the river of tears. The cannon hath retched fire and its lips have foamed blood. The pale horse of death stands drinking out of the Rhine, its four hoofs on the breast-bone of men who sleep their last sleep. The red clusters of human hearts are crushed in the wine-press just as the vineyards of Moselle and Hockheimer are ripening. Chassepot and mitrailleuse have answered the needle-gun ; and there is all along the lines the silence of those who will never speak again.

But Paris has for an interval, at least, recovered from her recent depression. Yesterday I stood at the foot of the Egyptian red-granite obelisk, dug out three thousand four hundred years ago, and from the top of which, at an elevation of seventy-two feet, the ages of the past look down upon the splendors of the present. On either side the obelisk is a fountain with six jets, each tossing into the bronze basin above ; a seventh fountain, at still greater elevation, overflowing and coming down to meet them. Ribbons of rainbow flung on the air : golden rays of sunlight interwoven with silver skeins of water, while the wind drives the loom. Tritons, nereids, genii, dolphins, and winged children disporting themselves, and floods clapping their hands.

From the foot of the obelisk, looking off to the south, is the Palace of the Legislature—its last touch of repairs having cost four million dollars—its gilded gates, and Corinthian columns, and statues of Justice, and Commerce, and Art, and Navigation—a building grand with Vernet's fresco, and Cortot's sculpture, and Delacroix's allegories of art, and the memory of Lamartine's eloquence ; within it the hard face of stone soft with gobelin tapestry, and arabesque, and the walls curtained with velvet of crimson and gleaming gold.

From the foot of the obelisk, glancing to the north, the church of the Madeleine comes into sight, its glories lifted up on the shoulders of fifty-two Corinthian columns, swinging against the dazed vision, its huge brazen doors, its walls breaking into innumerable fragments of beauty, each piece a sculptured wonder: a king, an apostle, an archangel, or a Christ. The three cupolas against the sky, great doxologies in stone. The whole building white, beautiful, stupendous—the frozen prayer of a nation.

From the foot of the obelisk, looking east through a long aisle of elms, chestnuts, and palms, is the palace of the Tuileries, confronting you with one thousand feet of façade, and tossed up at either side into imposing pavilions, and sweeping back into the most brilliant picture-galleries of all the world, where the French masters look upon the Flemish, and the black marble of the Pyrenees frowns upon the drifted snow of Italian statuary: a palace poising its pinnacles in the sun, and spreading out balustrades of braided granite. Its inside walls adorned with blaze of red velvet cooling down into damask overshot with green silk. Palace of wild and terrific memories, orgies of drunken kings, and display of coronation festivity. Frightful Catherine de Medicis looked out of those windows. There, Maria Antoinette gazed up toward heaven through the dark lattice of her own broken heart. Into those doors rushed the Revolutionary mobs. On that roof the Angel of Death alighted and flapped its black wings on its way to smite in a day one hundred thousand souls. Majestic, terrible, beautiful, horrible, sublime palace of the Tuileries. The brightness of a hundred *fête* days sparkle in its fountains! The gore of ten thousand butcheries redden the upholstery!

Standing at the foot of the obelisk, we have looked toward the north, and the south, and the east. There is but one way more to look. Stretching away to the west, beyond the sculptured horses that seem all a-quiver with life from nostril to fetlock, and rearing till you fear the groom will no longer be able to keep them from dashing off the pedestal, is the Champs Elysées, the great artery through which rolls the life of Parisian hilarity. It is, perhaps, the widest street in the world. You see two long lines of carriages, one flowing this way, the other that, filled with the merriment of the gayest city under the sun. There they go! viscounts and porters, cab-drivers of glazed hat taking passengers at two francs an hour, and coachman with rosetted hat, and lavender breeches, his coat-tails flung over the back of the high seat—a very constellation of brass buttons. Tramp, and rumble, and clatter! Two wheels, four wheels, one sorrel, two sorrels! Fast horse's mouth by twisted bit drawn tight into the chest, and slow horse's head hung out at long distance from the body, his feet too lazy to keep up. Crack! crack! go a hundred whips in the strong grasp of the charioteers, warning foot-passengers to clear the way. Click! click! go the swords of the mounted horse-guards as they dash past sashed, feathered, and epauletted.

On the broad pavements of this avenue all nations meet and mingle. This is a Chinese with hair in genuine pig-tail twist, and this a Turk with

trowsers enough for seven. Here, an Englishman built up solid from the foundation, buttressed with strength; the apotheosization of roast-beef and plum-pudding; you can tell by his looks that he never ate anything that disagreed with him. Here, an American so thin he fails to cast a shadow. There, a group of children playing blind-man's buff, and, yonder, men at foot-ball, with a circle of a hundred people surrounding them. Old harpers playing their harps. Boys fiddling. Women with fountains of soda-water strapped to their back, and six cups dangling at their side, and tinkling a tiny bell to let the people know where they may get refreshment. Here, a circle of fifteen hobby-horses poised on one pivot, where girls in white dresses, and boys in coat of many colors swing round the circle. Puff of a hundred segars. Peddler with a score of balloons to a string sending them up into the air, and willing for four sous to make any boy happy. Parrots holding up their ugliness by one claw, and swearing at passers-by in bad French. Canaries serenading the sunlight. Bagpipers with instruments in full screech. "Punch and Judy," the unending joke of European cities, which is simply two doll-babies beating each other.

Passing on, you come upon another circle of fountains, six in number—small but beautiful, infantile fountains, hardly born before they die, rocked in cradle of crystal, then buried in sarcophagus of pearl. The water rises only a short distance and bends over, like the heads of ripe grain, as though the water-gods had been reaping their harvest, and here had stacked their sheaves. And now we find toy-carriages drawn by four goats with bells, and children riding, a boy of four years drawing the rein, mountebanks tumbling on the grass, jugglers with rings that turn into serpents, and bottles that spit white rabbits, and tricks that make the auditor's hat, passed up, breed rats.

On your way through the street, you wander into grottos, where, over colored rocks, the water falls, now becoming blue as the sea, now green as a pond, and now, without miracle, it is turned into wine. There are maiden-hair trees, and Irish yews, and bamboo, and magnolias, and banks of azaleas, and hollies, and you go through a Red Sea of geraniums and dahlias dry-shod. You leave on either hand concert-castles, and party-colored booths, and kiosks inviting to repose, till you come to the foot of the Arc de Triomphe, from the foot of which radiate eleven great avenues, any one of which might well be a national pride, and all of them a-rumble with pomp and wealth, and the shock of quick and resonant laughter.

On opposite sides of the archway are two angels, leaning toward each other till their trumpets well-nigh touch, blowing the news of a hundred victories. Surely never before or since was hard stone ever twisted into such wreaths, or smoothed into such surfaces. Up and down frieze and spandrel are alti-rilievi with flags of granite that seem to quiver in the wind, and helmets that sit soft as velvet on warrior's brow; and there are lips of stone that look as if they might speak, and spears that look as if they might pierce, and wounds that look as if they might bleed, and eagles that look as if they might fly. Here stands an angel of war mighty enough to have been just hurled out of heaven. On one side of the Arch, Peace is celebrated by the sculptor with sheaves of plenty, and chaplets of honor, and palms of triumph. At a great height, Austerlitz is again enacted, and horse and horsemen and artillery and gunners stand out as though some horror of battle had chilled them all into stone.

By the time that you have mounted the steps, and stand at the top of the Arch, the evening lamps begin a running fire on all the streets. The trees swing lanterns, and the eleven avenues concentrating at the foot of the Arch pour their brightness to your feet a very chorus of fire. Your eye treads all the way back to the Tuileries on bubbles of flame, and stopping half-way the distance to read, in weird and bewitching contrivance of gaslight, an inscription with a harp of fire at the top and an arrow of fire at the bottom, the charmed words of every Frenchman,—CHAMPS ELYSEES !

OUR SPECTACLES.
FROM THE SAME.

A MAN never looks more dignified than when he takes a spectacle-case from his pocket, opens it, unfolds a lens, sets it astride his nose, and looks you in the eye. I have seen audiences overawed by such a demonstration, feeling that a man who could handle glasses in that way must be equal to anything. We have known a lady of plain face, who, by placing an adornment of this kind on the bridge of her nose, could give an irresistible look, and by one glance around the room would transfix and eat up the hearts of a dozen old bachelors.

There are men, who, though they never read a word of Latin or Greek, have, by such facial appendage, been made to look so classical, that the moment they gaze on you, you quiver as if you had been struck by Sophocles or Jupiter. We strongly suspect that a pair of glasses on a minister's nose would be worth to him about three hundred and seventy-six dollars and forty-two cents additional salary. Indeed, we have known men who had kept their parishes quiet by this spectacular power. If Deacon Jones criticized, or Mrs. Go-about gossiped, the dominie would get them in range, shove his glasses from the tip of his nose close up to his eyebrows, and concentre all the majesty of his nature into a look that consumed all opposition easier than the burning-glass of Archimedes devoured the Roman ships.

But nearly all, young and old, near-sighted, and far-sighted, look through spectacles. By reason of our prejudices, or education, or temperament, things are apt to come to us magnified, or lessened, or distorted. We all see things differently—not so much because our eyes are different, as because the medium through which we look is different.

Some of us wear blue spectacles, and consequently everything is blue. Taking our position at Trinity Church, and looking down Wall street, everything is gloomy and depressing in financials, and looking up Broadway, everything is horrible in the fashions of the day. All is wrong in churches, wrong in education, wrong in society. An undigested slice of corned-beef has covered up all the bright prospects of the world. A drop of vinegar has extinguished a star. We understand all the variations of a growl. What makes the sunshine so dull, the foliage so gloomy, men so heavy, and the world so dark ? *Blue* spectacles, my dear,

BLUE SPECTACLES !

An unwary young man comes to town. He buys elegant silk pocket-handkerchiefs on Chatham Street for twelve cents, and diamonds at the dollar-store. He supposes that when a play is advertised "for one night only," he will have but one opportunity of seeing it. He takes a greenback with an X on it, as sure sign that it is ten dollars, not knowing there are counterfeits. He takes five shares of silver-mining stock in the company for developing the resources of the moon. He supposes that every man that dresses well is a gentleman. He goes to see the lions, not knowing that any of them will bite ; and that when people go to see the lions, the lions sometimes come out to see them. He has an idea that fortunes lie thickly around, and all he will have to do is to stoop down and pick one up. Having been brought up where the greatest dissipation was a blacksmith-shop on a rainy day, and where the gold on the wheat is never counterfeit, and buckwheat-fields never issue false stock, and brooks are always " current," and ripe fall-pippins are a legal-tender, and blossoms are honest when they promise to pay, he was unprepared to resist the allurements of city life. A sharper has fleeced him, an evil companion has despoiled him, a policeman's "billy" has struck him on the head, or a prison's turnkey bids him a gruff " Good-night !"

What got him into all this trouble ? Can any moral optician inform us ? *Green* goggles, my dear,

GREEN GOGGLES !

Your neighbor's first great idea in life is a dollar ; the second idea is a dollar—making in all two dollars. The smaller ideas are cents. Friendship is with him a mere question of loss and gain. He will want your name on his note. Every time he shakes hands, he estimates the value of such a greeting. He is down on Fourth of Julys and Christmas Days, because on them you spend money instead of making it. He has reduced everything in life to vulgar fractions. He has been hunting all his life for the cow that had the golden calf. He has cut the Lord's Prayer on the back of a three-cent piece, his only regret that he has spoiled the piece.

CAXTON PRESS OF
SHERMAN & CO., PHILADELPHIA.

PHILADELPHIA, 822 CHESTNUT STREET.
September, 1870.

PORTER & COATES

PUBLISH THE FOLLOWING

LIST OF BOOKS.

☞ *The Books in this List, unless otherwise specified, are bound in Cloth.
All of our Publications mailed, postpaid, on receipt of price.*

SIR WALTER SCOTT.

WAVERLEY NOVELS. Complete in 23 vols. Illustrated. Toned
paper. Price per vol., *Globe Edition:* cloth, extra, $1.25; half calf,
gilt, $3.00. *Standard Library Edition:* cloth, extra, gilt tops, bev.
boards, $1.75; half calf, gilt, $3.50; half mor., gilt tops, $3.50.

Waverley.	Pirate.
Guy Mannering.	Fortunes of Nigel.
Antiquary.	Peveril of the Peak.
Rob Roy.	Quentin Durward.
Black Dwarf, and Old Mortality.	St. Ronan's Well.
Heart of Mid-Lothian.	Redgauntlet.
Bride of Lammermoor, and A Legend of	The Betrothed, and The Talisman.
Montrose.	Woodstock.
Ivanhoe.	Fair Maid of Perth.
Monastery.	Anne of Geierstein.
Abbot.	Count Robert of Paris, and Castle Dan-
Kenilworth.	gerous.

Chronicles of the Canongate.

This is the best edition for the library or for general use published. Its convenient size, the extreme legibility of the type, which is larger than is used in any other
edition, either English or American, its spirited illustrations, quality of the paper and
binding, and the general execution of the presswork, must commend it at once to
every one.

TALES OF A GRANDFATHER. Uniform with the "Waverley Novels."
Illustrated. 4 vols. Toned paper. Price per vol., *Globe Edition:*
cloth, extra, $1.25; half calf, gilt, $3.00. *Standard Library Edition:*
cloth, extra, gilt tops, bev. boards, $1.75; half morocco, gilt tops,
$3.50; half calf, gilt, $3.50.

The only edition containing the fourth series, "Tales from French History."

IVANHOE. A romance. Youth's Favorite Edition. Illustrated. Crown,
8vo., $1.50.

LADY OF THE LAKE. With twenty-five engravings on wood, from
designs by Birket Foster and John Gilbert. 16mo. Bev. boards,
$1.50; half calf, gilt, $3.00; full Turkey mor. antique, $4.00.

RUFUS W. GRISWOLD, D.D.

THE PROSE WRITERS OF AMERICA. With a Survey of the Intellectual History, Condition, and Prospects of the Country. New edition, thoroughly revised and completed to the present time, with a supplementary Essay on the Present Intellectual Condition and Prospects of the Country. By Prof. JOHN H. DILLINGHAM, A.M. With seven portraits on steel, and vignette title. Imperial 8vo. Cloth, extra, gilt tops, bevelled boards, $5.00; sheep, marbled edges, library style, $6.00; half calf, $7.50; full Turkey morocco, $10.00.

"We are glad to possess, in this form, portions of many authors whose entire works we should never own, and if we did should probably never find time to read. We confess our obligations to the author for the personal information concerning them which he has collected in the memoirs prefixed to their writings. These are written in a manner creditable to the research, ability, and kindness of the author."—*William Cullen Bryant.*

"An important and interesting contribution to our national literature. The range of authors is very wide; the biographical notices full and interesting. I am surprised that the author has been able to collect so many particulars in this way. The selections appear to me to be made with discrimination, and the criticisms show a sound taste and a correct appreciation of the qualities of the writers, as well as I can judge."—*William H. Prescott, the Historian.*

The present edition has been thoroughly revised, every page has been gone over, and notices of authors who have passed away since the previous editions were published, have been revised and continued to the period of their decease, and long and critical articles on the authors of the present day have been added, making the work complete in every respect to the present time. It should occupy a prominent place in the library of every cultivated American.

GEMS FROM THE AMERICAN POETS. With brief biographical notices. With a fine engraving on steel. 32mo., cloth, 60 cents; illuminated sides, 90 cents; Turkey mor., extra, $1.50.

FREDERICK H. HEDGE, D.D.

THE PROSE WRITERS OF GERMANY. With Introductions, Biographical Notices, and Translations. With six portraits on steel, and engraved title. Imperial 8vo. Cloth, extra, gilt top, bevelled boards, $5.00; sheep, marbled edges, library style, $6.00; half calf, gilt, $7.50; full Turkey morocco, $10.00.

"There is no book accessible to the English or American reader which can furnish so comprehensive and symmetrical a view of German literature to the uninitiated: and those already conversant with some of the German classics will find here valuable and edifying extracts from works to which very few in this country can gain access."—*Prof. A. P. Peabody, in North American Review.*

PROF. HENRY WADSWORTH LONGFELLOW.

THE POETS AND POETRY OF EUROPE. With Introductions, Biographical Notices, and Translations, from the Earliest Period to the Present Time. New edition, thoroughly revised and completed to the present time. With engravings on steel, and engraved title. Imperial 8vo. Cloth, extra, gilt tops, bev. boards, $6.00; sheep, marbled edges, library style, $7.00; half calf, gilt, $9.00; full Turkey morocco, $12.00.

"This valuable volume contains selections from about three hundred and sixty authors, translated from ten languages,—the Anglo-Saxon, Icelandic, Danish, Swedish, Dutch, German, French, Italian, Spanish, and Portuguese. Mr. Longfellow himself gives us translations from all of these languages but two. Among the other translators are Bowring, Felton, Herbert, Costello, Taylor, Jamieson, Brooks, Adamson, Thorpe, &c."—*Allibone' Dictionary of Authors,* vol. ii.

WILLIAM SHAKSPEARE.

COMPLETE WORKS. Dramatic and Poetical, with the "Epistle Dedicatorie," and the Address prefixed to the edition of 1623, a Sketch of the Life of the Poet, by ALEXANDER CHALMERS, A.M., and Glossarial and other Notes and References. Edited by GEORGE LONG DUYCKINK. With twelve full-page tinted Illustrations, designed by Nicholson, a superb portrait on steel, from the celebrated Droeshout picture, and beautiful engraved title, on steel. 976 pp. Imperial 8vo. Cloth, extra, gilt back, $3.75; sheep, library style, $4.50.

FINE EDITION OF THE ABOVE, on extra calendered paper, with the addition of a History of the Early Drama and Stage to the time of Shakspeare, a full and comprehensive Life, by J. PAYNE COLLIER, A.M., Shakspeare's Will, critical and historical Introductions to each play, and thirty-five full-page tinted engravings, from designs by Nicholson, a superb portrait on steel from the celebrated Droeshout picture, and beautiful engraved title on steel. Imperial 8vo. 1084 pages. Half calf, gilt, $8.75; full Turkey morocco, $10.00.

POEMS AND SONNETS. With a fine engraving on steel. 32mo. Cloth, 60 cts.; illuminated side, 90 cts.; Turkey morocco, $1.50.

THOMAS PERCY D.D., Bishop of Dromore.

RELIQUES OF ANCIENT ENGLISH POETRY: consisting of Old Heroic Ballads, Songs, and other pieces of the earlier poets, with some of later date, not included in any other edition. To which is now added a Supplement of many Curious Historical and Narrative Ballads, reprinted from rare copies, with a copious glossary and notes. New edition, uniform with the above. 558 pp. Imperial 8vo. Two steel plates. Fine cloth, bev. bds., gilt, $3.75; sheep, library style, $4.50; full Turkey morocco, $10.00.

"But, above all, I then first became acquainted with Bishop Percy's Reliques of Ancient Poetry. . . . I remember well the spot where I read these volumes for the first time. It was beneath a huge platanus tree, in the ruins of what had been intended for an old-fashioned arbor, in the *garden* I have mentioned. The summer day sped around so fast that, notwithstanding the sharp appetite of thirteen, I forgot the hour of dinner, was sought for with anxiety, and was still found entranced in my intellectual banquet. To read and to remember was in this instance the same thing, and henceforth I overwhelmed my schoolfellows, and all who would hearken to me, with tragical recitations from the ballads of Bishop Percy. The first time I could scrape a few shillings together, which were not common occurrences with me, I bought unto myself a copy of these beloved volumes, nor do I believe I ever read a book half so frequently, or with half the enthusiasm."—*Memoirs of his Early Life, by Sir Walter Scott, prefixed to Lockhart's Life of Scott.*

LORD BYRON.

COMPLETE WORKS. Prose and Poetry. With five engravings on steel. Imp. 8vo. Sheep, library style, $4.50; Turkey morocco, antique, $10.00.

"If the finest poetry be that which leaves the deepest impression on the minds of its readers—and this is not the worst test of its excellence—Lord Byron, we think, must be allowed to take precedence of all his distinguished contemporaries. 'Words that breathe, and thoughts that burn,' are not merely ornaments, but the common staple of his poetry; and he is not inspired or impressive only in some happy passages, but through the whole body and tissue of his composition."—*Lord Jeffrey, Edinburgh Review.*

THE MORAL AND BEAUTIFUL IN THE POEMS OF LORD BYRON. Edited by REV. WALTER COLTON. 32mo. Cloth, 60 cts.; illuminated side, 90 cts.; Turkey morocco, $1.50.

WILSON AND BONAPARTE.

AMERICAN ORNITHOLOGY; or, The Natural History of the Birds
of the United States. Illustrated with plates engraved and colored
from original drawings from nature. With a sketch of the life of the
author, by GEORGE ORD, F.R.S., &c., &c., with Bonaparte's continuation, containing the Natural History of Birds inhabiting the United
States, not given by Wilson. With figures drawn, engraved and
colored from nature, by Charles Lucien Bonaparte (Prince of Musignano). Complete in three volumes, imperial 8vo.; and a magnificent
folio volume of carefully colored plates, embracing nearly 400 figures
of birds, mostly life size. Elegantly bound in cloth, extra, bevelled
bds., gilt tops, uncut, $65.00; half Turkey morocco, marbled edges,
$75.00.

A new and magnificent edition of this world-renowned work, printed from new
stereotype plates, on the finest laid paper, and bound in the best manner. The plates
are printed from the original plates of Wilson and Bonaparte, engraved by Lawson,
"the first ornithological engraver of our age," and are carefully colored, after the
author's own copies. The superiority of this work for accuracy of description and
naturalness of drawing, has long been acknowledged. Daniel Webster speaks of it
in the highest terms, saying that of the salt water birds, mentioned in Wilson, "he
had shot every one, and compared them with his delineations and descriptions, and
IN EVERY CASE found them PERFECTLY ACCURATE TO NATURE." And the London
Quarterly Review characterized it as "an admirable work, unequalled by any publication in the old world, for accurate delineation and just description. A moment's
comparison of this work with any other on the same subject, will convince the most
skeptical of its great superiority. As a specimen of American bookmaking, it has
never been surpassed, and, at the low price it is now offered, should be in every public
and private library of any pretensions."

CERVANTES.

THE HISTORY AND ADVENTURES OF DON QUIXOTE DE LA
MANCHA. From the Spanish of Cervantes. With six full-page
illustrations, by Gustave Doré. Large 12mo, cloth, extra, $1.50.

CHARLES KNIGHT.

HALF HOURS WITH THE BEST AUTHORS. With short Biographical and Critical Notices. Elegantly printed on the finest
paper. With fine steel portraits. 6 vols., crown 8vo. cloth, bev.
boards, gilt tops, $9.00; half calf, gilt, $18.00; half morocco, gilt
tops, $18.00; or bound in 3 vols., thick crown 8vo., fine English
cloth, bev. boards, gilt tops, per set, $7.50; half calf, gilt, $12.00.

Selecting some choice passage of the best standard authors, of sufficient length to
occupy half an hour in its perusal, there is here food for thought for every day in the
year; so that if the purchaser will devote but one half hour each day to its appropriate selection, he will read through these six volumes in one year, and in such a
leisurely manner that the noblest thoughts of many of the greatest minds will be
firmly implanted in his mind forever. For every Sunday there is a suitable selection
from some of the most eminent writers in sacred literature. We venture to say, if
the editor's idea is carried out, the reader will possess more information and a better
knowledge of the English classics at the end of the year than he would by five years
of desultory reading. The variety of reading is so great that no one will ever tire of
these volumes. It is a library in itself.

5

A CHARMING WORK.

MOTHER GOOSE IN HER NEW DRESS. A Series of Charming
Sketches, beautifully chromo-lithographed. This book will create a
sensation. The distinguished authoress designed the original of this
work as a birth-day gift to her father, who occupies one of the highest
positions in the United States government, but several connoisseurs
happening to see it were so struck by its merits, that she was induced to have it published. Mother Goose never looked so charming as she does in her present dress. Cloth, extra, beautifully bound,
with linen guards, $3.75; full gilt, bev. boards, $4.50.

MISS JANE PORTER.

The two following are new stereotype editions, in large, clear type, with initial
letters, head and tail pieces, &c. The illustrations were designed expressly for this
edition, and engraved in the highest style of art.

THE SCOTTISH CHIEFS. Illustrated by F. O. C. DARLEY. Crown
8vo., 748 pp. Fine English cloth, gilt. Price, $1.50; half calf, gilt,
$3.50.

"Sir Walter Scott, in a conversation with King George IV, in the library at Carlton House, admitted that 'The Scottish Chiefs' suggested his 'Waverley Novels.'"—*Allibone's Dictionary of
Authors.*
"This is a new and by far the best edition of a national romance which has been as much read and
admired as almost any of Scott's or Dickens's novels. It is low-priced, well printed, and handsomely
bound. Thousands of readers will be glad to go over this stirring tale once more."—*Philadelphia
Press.*

ROBERT McCLURE, M.D., V.S.

THE AMERICAN GENTLEMAN'S STABLE GUIDE. Containing
a Familiar Description of the American Stable; the most approved
Method of Feeding, Grooming, and General Management of Horses;
together with Directions for the Care of Carriages, Harness, &c.
Expressly adapted for the owners of equipages and fine horses.
Cloth extra, illustrated. $1.50.

A handy manual, giving to the owner of a horse just the information of a practical
nature that he often feels the need of, and by an author who thoroughly understands
what he is writing about, and what is needed by every gentleman.

"Such a treatise has been needed for years, and we think this volume will supply the want. The
illustrations are very good and timely."—*Pittsburg Daily Gazette.*

JOHN J. THOMAS.

THE AMERICAN FRUIT CULTURIST. Containing Practical Di-
rections for the Propagation and Culture of Fruit Trees in the
Nursery, Orchard, and Gardens. With Descriptions of the Principal
American and Foreign Varieties cultivated in the United States.
Second edition. Illustrated with 480 accurate figures. Crown 8vo.
Cloth extra, bev. bds., gilt back. $3.00.

Unanimously pronounced the most *thorough, practical,* and *comprehensive* work
published. The engravings are not copies of old cuts from other books, but are
mainly original with the author.

MRS. ANNA JAMESON.

LIVES OF CELEBRATED FEMALE SOVEREIGNS AND ILLUS-
TRIOUS WOMEN. Edited by Mary E. Hewitt. With four Portraits on Steel. 16mo., beautifully printed on laid paper. Cloth,
extra, $1.50.

The celebrated Mrs. Jameson, who wields a powerful, ready, and pleasant pen, has
taken hold of some of the leading events in the brilliant lives of some of the most
world-noted women, and depicted them in very attractive colors. It is a lovely book
for young ladies, and will give them a taste for history.

J. H. WALSH, F.R.C.S. ("Stonehenge.")

THE HORSE IN THE STABLE AND THE FIELD; his Management in Health and Disease. From the last London edition, with
copious Notes and Additions, by ROBERT McCLURE, M.D., V.S., author of "Diseases in the American Stable, Field, and Farmyard,"
with an Essay on the American Trotting Horse, and suggestions on
the Breeding and Training of Trotters, by ELLWOOD HARVEY, M.D.
With 80 engravings, and full-page engravings from photographs
from life. Crown 8vo. Cloth, extra, bev. bds. $2.50.

"This Americanizing of 'Stonehenge' gives us the best piece of Horse Literature of the season.
Old horsemen need not be told who 'Stonehenge' is in the British Books, or that he is the highest
authority in turf and veterinary affairs. Add to these the labors of such American writers as Dr.
McClure and Dr. Harvey, with new portraits of some of our most popular living horses, and we have a
book that no American horseman can afford to be without."—*Ohio Farmer*, Cleveland. April 24, 1869.
"It sustains its claim to be the only work which has brought together in a single volume, and in
clear, concise, and comprehensive language, adequate information on the various subjects of which
it treats."—*Harper's Magazine*, July, 1869.

THADDEUS NORRIS.

AMERICAN FISH CULTURE. Giving all the details of Artificial
Breeding and Rearing of Trout, Salmon, Shad, and other Fishes.
12mo., illustrated. $1.75.

"'Norris's American Fish Culture,' published in this city by Porter & Coates, is passing around
the world as a standard. Mr. Norris's authority will be quoted beside the tributaries of the Ganges,
as already by those of the Hudson, the Humber, and the Thames. The English publishers of the
book are Sampson Low, Son & Co.; and a late number of the *Athenæum*, after an attentive review
of Mr. Norris's methods, concludes thus: 'Mr. Norris has rendered good service to the important
subject of fish culture by the present publication; and, although his book goes over ground (or water
rather) occupied to a great extent by English writers on fish culture, it contains several particulars
respecting this art as practised in the United States, which are valuable, and may be turned to profitable account by our pisciculturists.'"—*Philadelphia Evening Bulletin*.

THE AMERICAN ANGLER'S BOOK. Embracing the Natural History of Sporting Fish, and the Art of Taking Them. With Instructions in Fly Fishing, Fly Making, and Rod Making; and Directions
for Fish Breeding. To which is added Dies Piscatoriæ; describing
noted fishing-places, and the pleasure of solitary fly fishing. New
edition, with a supplement, containing a Description of Salmon
Rivers, Inland Trout Fishing, &c. Illustrated with eighty engravings. 8vo., cloth extra. $5.50.

"Mr. Norris has produced the best book on Angling that has been published in our time. If other
authors would follow Mr. Norris's example, and not write upon a subject until they had practically
mastered it, we should have fewer and better works. *His* volume will live. It is thoroughly instructive, good-tempered, and genial."—*Philadelphia Press*.

CECIL B. HARTLEY.

LIFE OF THE EMPRESS JOSEPHINE, Wife of Napoleon I. With a fine Portrait on Steel. 16mo. Printed on fine laid paper. Cloth, extra, $1.50.

" Her career and her character were alike remarkable; surrounded by the demoralizations of the French Court, she was a Roman matron in stern rectitude, with a pre-eminent fidelity to a sensitive conscience; and blended comprehensive genius with a warm heart and a noble personal presence. She was the peer of Napoleon, and in some respects his superior. Her executive force was less, but her foresight was greater. It is to her that the index finger of history points, as an example of female grandeur. Napoleon got a divorce from her because he wished his seed to inherit the French Crown. The son born of his Hapsburg marriage died crownless, while the grandson of Josephine now wears the purple of France—this is more than poetic justice. . . . . In the book before us, the story of her life is told in a simple, classic style, and possesses a fascination rarely met with in biography."—*Chicago Evening Journal.*

MARGARET HOSMER.

Author of " Cherry, the Missionary," " Grandma Merritt's Stories," " The Voyage of the White Falcon," &c , &c.

LITTLE ROSIE'S FIRST PLAY DAYS. Illustrated. 18mo., 160 pp., 75 cents.

LITTLE ROSIE'S CHRISTMAS TIMES. Illustrated. 18mo., 160 pp., 75 cents.

LITTLE ROSIE IN THE COUNTRY. Illustrated. 18mo., 160 pp., 75 cents.

" Very nice children's books, indeed, and we only wish that we had more space to say so, and more time to say it in. Any present-giving fathers, mothers, uncles, aunts, brothers, or sisters, who have a care for the little people, may safely order these for home consumption."—*The Hartford Churchman.*

" A charming series of stories for the younger class of readers, full of interesting incidents and good moral and religious instruction, brought down to the comprehension of a child in such a way as to produce a salutary impression. They are calculated also to teach parents how to keep children employed in what is pleasant and useful, thus superseding the necessity of imposing so many restraints to keep them from evil. This is apt to be the great fault in the management of children. They are given nothing innocent and useful with which to employ their active, restless minds, and then parents wonder that they need be always in mischief. Rosie's mother better comprehended the wants of a child, and forestalled temptations to evil by incentives to good."—*Springfield Daily Union.*

UNDER THE HOLLY; or, Christmas at Hopeton Grange. A Book for Girls. By Mrs. Hosmer and Miss ——. 12mo. Illustrated. Cloth, extra, $1.50.

" And this we can and do most confidently recommend to parents who are faithfully striving to provide only wholesome food for the intellectual appetite of their children. The tone of the book is pure and healthful, the style easy and graceful, and the incidents are such as to give pleasure without at all kindling the passion for exciting fiction, which is so rampant among the young people of our day."—*Maryland Church Record.*

" This is entitled, ' A Book for Girls,' but it would interest the youth of either sex. It is a succession of tales told at the Christmas season. We can recommend them all for their interest and moral. It is fo ' children of a larger growth,' not a mere story-book for the little ones."—*Philadelphia Daily Age.*

LENNY, THE ORPHAN; or, Trials and Triumphs. Illustrated by Faber. 16mo. Price, $1.25.

" A story book of an orphan boy, who is thrown loose upon the world by a conflagration, in which his mother and only surviving parent is burnt. The varieties of experience, both sorrowful and happy, through which the boy passes, are wrought up into a story of no little power, and yet are such as often occur in actual life. The religious teachings of the book are good, and penetrate the entire structure of the story. We recommend it cordially to a place in the Sunday-school library."—*Sunday School Times,* Philadelphia.

" The author of this book has written some of the best Sunday-school books which have recently been issued from the press of the American Sunday-School Union. The volume before us portrays the trials of a little boy, who loses his mother in early life, and is subjected to the intrigues of a designing person, from which he obtains a happy deliverance. The story is well planned and written, and its moral and religious lessons are good."—*Weekly Freedman,* New Brunswick, N. J.

REGINA MARIA ROCHE.

THE CHILDREN OF THE ABBEY. Illustrated by F. O. C. DARLEY. Uniform with "The Scottish Chiefs." Crown 8vo., 646 pp. Fine English cloth, gilt. Price, $1.50; half calf, gilt, $3.50.

"This classic is more neatly published in the new edition than we have ever seen it. It was long a standard, and had more favor than 'Thaddeus of Warsaw,' and it deserved better. It takes a new lease of existence now, and we almost envy those who read it for the first time."—*North American,* Philadelphia.

OLIVER BUNCE.

ROMANCE OF THE REVOLUTION. Being true Stories of the Thrilling Adventures, Romantic Incidents, Hair-breadth Escapes and Heroic Exploits of the Days of '76. Laid paper, with six illustrations. 16mo., cloth, extra, $1.50.

While the principal events of the history of our glorious Revolution are known to every intelligent American, much remains to be disclosed of the inner history of the war, and the motives and patriotism of the people. There were deeds of individual daring, heroism worthy of the proudest days of Greece and Rome, dashing and hazardous enterprises, and hardships bravely borne, performed by subalterns and private soldiers in the grand army of heroes, which should never be forgotten. To collect and preserve the sketches of these almost forgotten passages of the war, as they originally appeared in the newspapers and private letters of that stirring period, and the stories told by scarred veterans round the blazing hearthstone; these legends of the past; has been the object of this work, and the publishers are confident that none will rise from its perusal without acknowledging that "truth is stranger than fiction," and with a deeper feeling of reverence for the heroes of the days of '76.

JAMES HOGG, the Ettrick Shepherd.

THE MOUNTAIN BARD AND FOREST MINSTREL. Legendary Songs and Ballads. With two fine engravings on steel. 32mo., cloth, 60 cents; illuminated side, 90 cents; Turkey morocco, $1.50.

"He is a poet, in the highest acceptation of the name."—*Lord Jeffrey.*

PERCY BYSSHE SHELLEY.

POETICAL WORKS. With a fine engraving on steel. 32mo., cloth, 60 cents; illuminated side, 90 cents; Turkey morocco, $1.50.

ROBERT BLOOMFIELD.

THE FARMER'S BOY, and other Poems. Illustrated with a fine engraving on steel. 32mo., cloth, 60 cents; illuminated side, 90 cents; Turkey morocco, $1.50.

"Few compositions in the English language have been so generally admired as the Farmer's Boy. Those who agreed in but little else in literary matters, were unanimous in the commendation of the poetical powers displayed by the peasant and journeyman mechanic."—*Allibone's Dictionary of Authors.*

ROBERT BURNS.

POETICAL WORKS. With a fine engraving on steel. 32mo., cloth, 60 cents; illuminated side, 90 cents; Turkey morocco, $1.50.

"Burns is by far the greatest poet that ever sprang from the bosom of the people, and lived and died in an humble condition. Indeed, no country in the world but Scotland could have produced such a man; and he will be forever regarded as the glorious representative of the genius of his country. He was born a poet if ever man was."—*Prof. Wilson's Essay on Burns.*

WILLIAM DODD, LL.D.

THE BEAUTIES OF SHAKSPEARE. From the last London edition, with large additions, and the author's latest corrections. With two fine engravings on steel. Fine edition, on toned paper, with carmine border. Square 24mo. Cloth, gilt edges, $1.50; Turkey, $3.00; 32mo., cloth, 60 cents; illuminated side, 90 cents; Turkey morocco, $1.50.

This republication of a book so universally and deservedly popular as Dodd's Beauties, makes it peculiarly valuable as a gift book.

THOMAS HOOD.

POETICAL WORKS. With a fine engraving on steel. 32mo. Cloth, 60 cents; illuminated side, 90 cents; Turkey morocco, $1.50.

"Hood's verse, whether serious or comic,—whether serene, like a cloudless autumn evening, or sparkling with puns like a frosty January midnight with stars,—was ever pregnant with materials for thought. . . . . Like every author distinguished for true comic humor, there was a deep vein of melancholy pathos running through his mirth; and even when his sun shone brightly, its light seemed often reflected as if only over the rim of a cloud."—*D. M. Moir.*

THOMAS MOORE.

THE MORAL AND BEAUTIFUL FROM THE POEMS OF. Edited by Rev. WALTER COLTON, author of "Deck and Port," &c., &c. With a fine engraving on steel. 32mo. Cloth, 60 cents; illuminated sides, 90 cents; Turkey morocco, $1.50.

"The combinations of his wit are wonderful. Quick, subtle, and varied, ever suggesting new thoughts or images, or unexpected turns of expression—now drawing resources from classical literature or of the ancient fathers—now diving into the human heart, and now skimming the fields of fancy—the wit or imagination of Moore (for they are compounded together), is a true Ariel, 'a creature of the elements,' that is ever buoyant and full of life and spirit."—*Chambers's Eng. Lit.*

MISS H. B. McKEEVER.

Author of "The Flounced Robe, and What it Cost," "Edith's Ministry," "Woodcliffe," "Silver Threads," &c., &c.

"These stories have the merit of being entertaining, instructive, and really much superior to the common run of Juveniles. The Springfield *Republican*, which is competent authority, pronounces them the best and handsomest Juvenile Books of the season."—*Lyons Republican.*

"Miss McKeever always writes with point and meaning, and in a manner to gain and hold the attention."—*Sunday-School Times.*

ELEANOR'S THREE BIRTHDAYS. "Charity seeketh not her own." Illustrated. 16mo., 295 pp., $1.00.

MARY LESLIE'S TRIALS. "Is not easily provoked." Illustrated. 16mo., $1.00.

LUCY FORRESTER'S TRIUMPHS. "Thinketh no evil, believeth all things, hopeth all things." Illustrated. 16mo. Price, $1.00.

JEAN RODOLPHE WYSS.

THE SWISS FAMILY ROBINSON; or, the Adventures of a Father, Mother, and four Sons on a Desert Island. Two parts, complete in one volume. Illustrated. Large 12mo. Cloth, extra, price $1.50.

ADVENTURES IN CANADA; or, Life in the Woods. 16mo., illustrated. Cloth, $1.25.

This is not a mere work of fiction, but the true narrative of a bright boy who roughed it in the bush when Canada, the home of adventure and sporting, was much wilder than it is now. The boys, especially, will be charmed with the adventures with Indians, bears, and wolves, the raccoon hunts and duck shooting; while the older class of readers will be drawn to it by its charming description of the scenery and condition of what may, before long, become a part of the United States.

ANNE BOWMAN.

THE BEAR HUNTERS OF THE ROCKY MOUNTAINS. 16mo., illustrated. Cloth, extra, $1.25.

A story of trapper life in the Rocky Mountains. A better insight of real life in these uncivilized wilds is gained from books like this than from scores of the dry details of travellers.

R. M. BALLANTYNE.

New and beautiful editions of these world-renowned books, second only to those of Cooper and Marryat, and better than those of Mayne Reid, in the pictures presented to the reader of wild life among the Indians, the hairbreadth escapes and fierce delights of a hunter's life, and the perils of " Life on the Ocean Wave." Ballantyne's name is well known to every intelligent boy of spirit. Leading the reader into the jungles and forests of Africa, sweeping over the vast expanse of our Western prairies, "fast in the ice" of the Polar regions, or coasting the shores of sunny climes, he ever presents new and enchanting pictures of adventure or beauty to enchain the attention, absorb the interest, excite the feelings, and always at the same time instructing the reader.

THE GORILLA HUNTERS. A Tale of the Wilds of Africa. 16mo., illustrated, cloth, extra, $1.25.

"Thoroughly at home on subjects of adventure. Like all his stories for boys, thrilling in interest and abounding in incidents of every kind."—*The Quiver, London.*

THE DOG CRUSOE. A Tale of the Western Prairies. 16mo., illustrated, cloth, extra, $1.25.

"This is another of Mr. Ballantyne's excellent stories for the young. They are all well written, full of romantic incidents, and are of no doubtful moral tendency; on the contrary, they are invariably found to embody sentiments of true piety, manliness and virtue."—*Inverness Advertiser.*

GASCOYNE, THE SANDAL-WOOD TRADER. A Tale of the Pacific. 16mo., illustrated, cloth, extra, $1.25.

"Gascoyne will rivet the attention of every one, whether old or young, who peruses it."—*Edinburgh Courant.*

FREAKS ON THE FELLS; or, Three Months' Rustication. And why I did not become a Sailor. Illustrated, 16mo., cloth, extra, $1.25.

"Mr. Ballantyne's name on the title-page of a book, has for some years been a guarantee to buyers that the volume is cheap at its price."—*London Athenæum.*

THE WILD MAN OF THE WEST. A Tale of the Rocky Mountains. 16mo. Illustrated, cloth, extra, $1.25.

This is generally considered the best of Mr. Ballantyne's famous narratives of Indian warfare and border life. In this field he is second only to Cooper.

SHIFTING WINDS. A Story of the Sea. Cloth, extra, illustrated, $1.25.

R. M. BALLANTYNE—Second Series.

"Indulgent fathers and good uncles will look a long time before they will find books more interesting or instructive for boys than these. In the four volumes the author introduces his young readers to the wonders of the Arctic regions, the wild hunting-grounds of the Hudson's Bay Company, the rugged coast and midnight sun of Norway, and the exciting chase of the monsters of the deep on the pathless fields of the ocean. He is quite at home among the scenes he describes, and has the faculty of taking the boys along with him in his narrative, and making them feel at home in his company. His object is to give information and to inculcate sound principles of virtue, and he mingles enough of fancy with the fact and the moral lesson to make both more impressive and the more sure to be remembered. The boy who reads these volumes at the time when his mind is most susceptible to the stirring scenes of peril and adventure, will cultivate a taste for more complete and elaborate works of travel and discovery, in mature years."—*Rev. Daniel March, D.D.*

FIGHTING THE WHALES; or, Doings and Dangers on a Fishing Cruise. With four full-page illustrations. 18mo., illustrated, 75 cents.

AWAY IN THE WILDERNESS; or, Life Among the Red Indians and Fur-Traders of North America. 18mo., illustrated, cloth, extra, 75 cents.

It is one of the most delightful books this famed author has written. Whilst describing the exciting adventures of Indian life, he conveys new and attractive information about the far north portion of our continent.

Seldom, if ever, has there been a better description of life in the lands of the Hudson's Bay Company, than is found in this little work.

FAST IN THE ICE; or, Adventures in the Polar Regions. 18mo., illustrated. Cloth, extra, 75 cents.

"Is attractive and useful. There is no more practical way of communicating elementary information than that which has been adopted in this series. When we see contained in 144 small pages, as in 'Fast in the Ice,' such information as men of fair education should possess about icebergs, Northern lights, Esquimaux, musk-oxen, bears, walruses, &c., together with all the ordinary incidents of an Arctic voyage, woven into a clear connected narrative, we must admit that a good work has been done, and that the author deserves the gratitude of young people of all classes."—*London Athenæum.*

CHASING THE SUN; or, Rambles in Norway. 18mo., illustrated. Cloth, extra, 75 cents.

Describing a country almost new to us, the author tells of many strange natural curiosities, of the manners and customs of the people, and the curious modes of travel and conveyance.

DANIEL DE FOE.

THE LIFE AND ADVENTURES OF ROBINSON CRUSOE. Including a Memoir of the Author, and an Essay on his Writings. Large 12mo. Illustrated. Cloth, extra. Price, $1.50.

Carefully printed from new stereotype plates, with large, clear, open type, this is the best, as well as the cheapest, edition of this charming work published.

"Perhaps there exists no work, either of instruction or entertainment, in the English language, which has been more generally read and more universally admired, than 'The Life and Adventures of Robinson Crusoe.' It is difficult to say in what the charm consists, by which persons of all classes and denominations are thus fascinated; yet the majority of readers will recollect it as among the first works that awakened and interested their youthful attention, and feel, even in advanced life and in the maturity of their understanding, that there are still associated with Robinson Crusoe the sentiments peculiar to that period, when all is bright, which the experience of after-life tends only to darken and destroy."—*Sir Walter Scott.*

D. W. BELISLE.

THE AMERICAN FAMILY ROBINSON; or, The Adventures of a Family lost in the Great Desert of the West. 16mo., illustrated. Cloth, extra, $1.25.

FOSTER'S TRANSLATION.

THE THOUSAND AND ONE NIGHTS; or, The Arabian Nights' En
tertainment. A new edition. With eight full-page illustrations
Large 12mo., cloth, extra, $1.50.

"More widely diffused among the nations of the earth than any other product of the human mind.
While it is read or recited to crowds of eager listeners in the Arab coffee-houses of Asia and Africa,
it is just as eagerly perused on the banks of the Tagus, the Tiber, the Seine, the Thames, the Hudson, the Mississippi, and the Ganges. . . . . While there are children on earth to love, so long will
the 'Arabian Nights' be loved."—*Appleton's American Encyclopedia, article "Arabian Nights."*

GRIMM.

POPULAR GERMAN TALES AND HOUSEHOLD STORIES. Collected by the Brothers Grimm. With nearly 200 illustrations by
Edward H. Wehnert. Complete in one volume. New edition. Fine
English cloth, bev. bds., full gilt back, and side stamp, $2.50; half
calf, gilt, $4.50.

The stories in these volumes are world-renowned, and they will continue to be read
as they long have been in different languages, and to charm and delight, not only
the young, but many readers in mature life who love the recollections of childhood
and its innocent diversions.

COUNTESS DE SEGUR.

FRENCH FAIRY TALES. Translated by Mrs. Coleman and her daughters. With ten full-page illustrations by Gustave Doré and Jules
Didier. 16mo., price, $1.50.

The Countess de Segur, the authoress of this charming work, and the mother of
the wife of the French ambassador at Florence, the brilliant Baroness Malaret, is a
Russian lady, and a daughter of the heroic Prince Rostopchin, who ordered the
burning of Moscow when Napoleon captured that devoted city.

"Not many of the fairy stories written for children are so admirably contrived or so charmingly
written as these."—*Worcester Daily Spy.*

W. S. GILBERT.

THE BAB BALLADS; or, Much Sound and Little Sense. With 113
illustrations by the author. Square 12mo., cloth, bev. gilt edges,
$1.75.

These Ballads, first published in periodicals, rapidly achieved a whimsical popularity, which soon demanded their publication in a collected form. Much of this is
due to the series of inexpressibly funny drawings by the author, who is happy in
being artist enough to interpret his own humor in these admirable sketches: we pity
the man who cannot appreciate and enjoy them. The Ballads will rank with the
best of Thackeray, Bon Gaultier, or Ingoldsby. Let every one who in these dull
times has the blues, procure a copy as the cheapest remedy. While it is a nearly
perfect fac simile of the English copy, it is only half the price.

"Everybody likes, occasionally, a little sensible nonsense. 'Mother Goose' is enjoyed in childhood, and something similar, but more advanced, is needed to provoke a smile on a wearied face in
later years. This volume of comic poems answers such a purpose; some of them have a sly moral,
while others are simply amusing from their supreme absurdity. The mirth is aided by the author's
original cuts, which are quite in keeping with the poetry."—*Advance*, Chicago, the Great Religious
weekly.

C. M. METZ.

DRAWING-BOOK OF THE HUMAN FIGURE. With many Examples from the best Studies of the Old Masters, beautifully engraved in the first style of the art. Folio, half morocco, antique, $7.50.

H. B. STAUNTON.

THE AMERICAN CHESS PLAYER'S HANDBOOK. Teaching the Rudiments of the Game, and giving an analysis of all the recognized openings, amplified by appropriate games actually played by Morphy, Horwitz, Anderssen, Staunton, Paulson, Montgomery, Meek, and others. From the work of Staunton. Illustrated. 16mo., cloth, extra, bev. bds., $1.25.

"Among the great wants of students of this noble game of chess has been a handbook which should occupy a middle ground between the large and expensive work of Staunton and the ten cent guides with which the country is flooded. This want is happily supplied by the present volume. It is an abridgment of Staunton's work, and contains full accounts and descriptions of the common openings and defences, besides a large number of illustrative games and several endings and problems. It is a book which will be decidedly useful to all beginners in the game, and interesting to those who are already proficient in it."—*Peoria Transcript.*

"Will prove an invaluable guide for the admirers of the great and strategic game of chess. It should be in the hands of every chess-player."—*Galesburg Republican.*

"It is the best manual for the beginner with which we are acquainted,—exceedingly clear and intelligible."—*New Orleans Picayune.*

SARAH E. SCOTT.

EVERY-DAY COOKERY, FOR EVERY FAMILY. Containing nearly 1000 Receipts adapted to moderate incomes, and comprising the best and most economical methods of roasting, boiling, broiling, and stewing all kind of meat, fish, poultry, game, and vegetables; simple and inexpensive instructions for making pies, puddings, tarts, and all other pastry; how to pickle and preserve fruits and vegetables; suitable cookery for invalids and children; food in season, and how to choose it; the best ways to make domestic wines and syrups, and ample receipts for bread, cake, soups, gravies, sauces, desserts, jellies, brandied fruits, soaps, perfumes, &c., &c., and full directions for carving. Illustrated. 16mo., cloth. Price, $1.00.

MISS WETHERILL.

ROBINSON CRUSOE'S FARM YARD; or, Stories and Anecdotes of Animals, illustrating their Habits. By Miss Wetherill, author of "Wide, Wide World," "Queechy," "Ellen Montgomery's Book Shelf," &c. With eight full-page illustrations. Square 16mo., 228 pp., cloth, gilt, $1.00.

CONTENTS.—The Cow; The Horse; The Chamois; The Camel; The Reindeer; The Dog; The Monkey; The Polar Bear; The Buffalo; The Goat; The Wolf; The Beaver; The Squirrel; The Tiger; The Elephant; The Sheep; The Ermine; The Lion; The Seal; The Stag; The Hyena; The Hog; The Hare; The Cat.

MISCELLANEOUS.

THE LIBRARY; or, What Books to Read, and How to Buy Them. A few practical hints, by an old Bookbuyer. 16mo., paper cover, 10 cents per copy; $8.00 per hundred.

Everybody has felt the want of a reliable guide in selecting books for their library. In this little manual, the author has endeavored first, in a preliminary essay, to point out how to read books to the best advantage, and how to buy them; second, what books to buy, by giving lists of some fifteen hundred volumes of standard works, such as are *necessary* to every well-selected library; these are given with the number of volumes, the best and different editions, and the prices. It thus forms a complete and intelligent guide, as to what is best to buy first, such as every person of any pretensions to literary taste should possess.

THOUGHTS OF PEACE; or, Strong Hope and Consolation for the Bearer of the Cross. From the last London edition. Beautifully printed on tinted paper, with carmine border. Square 16mo. Fine English cloth, bevelled boards, red edges, $1.50.

"Remarkable as the assertion is, that very many of the best works are the product of the chastened and afflicted in society, it is nevertheless true that the world is greatly enriched by the presence of invalid gifted minds in all ages. This delightful little volume is the product of one who has felt the acuteness of disease, and it illustrates the experience of one who has long been an invalid. The scriptural texts, and poetic selections, evince a rich acquaintance with the Scriptures and the poets. The book is beautifully printed on toned paper, red line border, and richly bound. Many would prize it as a gift book."—*Pittsburg Gazette.*

"This is a reprint from the latest London edition, and is a beautiful little work, both in style of typography and binding, and in the sentiments judiciously selected and collated from the Sacred Scriptures and poets. It comprises three hundred and sixty-five of the most soul-comforting and inspiring texts of the Bible—one for each day of the year. Following each text is a short selection from some hymn, or sacred poem of corresponding sentiment. No better souvenir could be given to one having experienced some of life's sorrows—and who has not!—and who has learned to look for consolation to Holy Writ."—*Mauch Chunk Gazette.*

PAPA'S BOOK OF ANIMALS. Wild and Tame. Chiefly from the writings of Rev. J. G. WOOD and THOS. BINGLEY. With sixteen large and spirited drawings, by H. C. Bispham. Small 4to., fine English cloth, gilt, bev. bds. Price, $1.25.

SLOVENLY PETER; or, Cheerful Stories and Funny Pictures for Good Little Folks. With nearly two hundred engravings. Beautifully colored. Printed on heavy paper. Large 4to. Cloth, bevelled boards, extra, $1.75.

A new edition of this charming book, a standard among juveniles. Surely lessons of stern morality and humanity were never more pleasantly and effectually taught than in this book.

ROSE VALLEY LIBRARY. 6 vols. 32mo. Illustrated. In neat box. Per vol., 25 cents.

Robinson Crusoe.	Discontented Tom.
Eva Bruen.	Edith Locke.
Willie and Ned.	Ben Benson.

ALLADIN; or, The Wonderful Lamp. With fifteen large and beautiful illustrations, by F. O. C. Darley. Small 4to., fine English cloth, gilt, bev. bds., $1.50.

THE HAPPY CHILD'S PICTURES OF ANIMALS AND BIRDS. 4to. Illustrated with large colored pictures from drawings of animals and birds, by Harrison Wier. Fancy boards. Price, 45 cents.

MOTHER GOOSE'S COMPLETE EDITION OF HER RHYMES, CHIMES, AND MELODIES. 128 pp., profusely illustrated, colored, square 12mo. Fancy boards, 60 cents; cloth, gilt, 75 cts.

LETTER WRITER.

THE GENTLEMAN'S LETTER-WRITER. Bound in boards, cloth back. 139 pp. Price, 35 cents.

THE LADY'S LETTER-WRITER. Bound in boards, cloth back. 139 pp. Price, 35 cents.

THE COMPLETE LETTER-WRITER. For the use of Ladies and Gentlemen; containing both the above bound in one volume. 273 pp. Cloth, gilt. Price, 75 cents.

USEFUL HAND-BOOKS.

GOOD MANNERS. A Handbook of Etiquette and the Usages of Good Society. Elegantly printed, with red-line border. Square 24mo., cloth, illuminated side, bev. bds., gilt top, $1.50.

FLOWERS; Their Language, Poetry, and Sentiment. With choicest extracts from Poets, a complete Dictionary of the Language and Sentiment of every Flower, with lists of Bouquets for every month, Floral Dial, &c., &c. The most complete book on the subject issued. With beautiful colored plates of bouquets. Elegantly printed, with red-line border. Square 24mo, cloth, illuminated sides, bvd. bds., gilt top, $1.50.

THE ART OF PLEASING; or, the American Lady's and Gentleman's Book of Etiquette. The latest and best small book of Etiquette published; containing twice as much as any other book of this size. 32mo., cloth, extra, 40 cents; do., gilt edges, full gilt, illuminated sides, 50 cents.

FLORA'S POCKET DICTIONARY. A New Lexicon of the Language of Flowers, and of the Sentiment of Flowers. The most complete of this size ever published. Just ready. 32mo. Cloth, extra, 40 cents; do., gilt edges, with illuminated side, 50 cents.

THE GUIDE TO FORTUNE; A Collection of Receipts of Great value. Giving full, plain, and practical directions for the manufacturing, putting up, and selling of a great variety of useful and saleable articles needed and used in every store, workshop, household, or farm. Intended to furnish employment to those out of work, a saving of labor and money to every one, ways to make money fast, &c., &c. 16mo., 175 pp. Cloth, extra. Price, 75 cts.

Lightning Source UK Ltd.
Milton Keynes UK
UKHW011116281118
333023UK00008B/349/P